Praise for *The Last Empress*

"This is a triumph of both research and storytelling. Madame Chiang Kai-shek led an amazing life filled with fascinating people as she helped bring China into the modern age. This brilliant narrative provides a wonderful insight into why China is the way it is today."

—Walter Isaacson, author of *Einstein*

"Compelling . . . a must read."

—*Booklist*

"Fascinating. . . . Pakula's story of May-ling's conquest of America is extraordinary. . . . A glimmering cameo of an ambitious, over-indulged woman who—had she been born 50 years later—truly might have ruled the world."

—Julia Lovell, *The Guardian* (London)

"Hannah Pakula has done it again. . . . Impressive. . . . After reading this book, it is impossible not to conclude that . . . Madame Chiang Kai-shek deserves to occupy a permanent place among history's most illustrious women."

—Justin Liuba, *The Washington Times*

"This is rip-roaring true romance told with zip, clarity, and panache."

—Hilary Spurling, author of *Matisse the Master*

"It's a great story."

—*The Irish Times*

"Pakula's book presents a richly complex account of China in the twentieth century. . . . Meticulously researched and compellingly narrated, the book offers a wide array of anecdotes of Soong's life intermingled with important events in Chinese history."

—*Global Times*

"Hannah Pakula's recent book . . . can bring perspective and provide links between the opium wars of the 1800s and Secretary Clinton's forays today. China's history is difficult, but none is more fascinating. Mastering it can take years, but Pakula brings it together with grace and ability. It is a story everyone in power should know and understand. . . . [T]his is a door that has opened that will not be closed."

—Bernie Quigley, *The Hill's Pundits Blog*

"Pakula is supremely qualified to tell the story of one of the turbulent twentieth century's most paradoxical and charismatic women. Epic, cinematic. Let's hope Ang Lee buys the film rights."

—Steve Bennet, *San Antonio Express-News*

"Pakula's biography makes it clear that Madame Chiang lived one of the most extraordinary lives of the twentieth century."

—*The New Yorker*

"The quantity of detail . . . is incredible. Yet the high quality of the writing makes it all easy to absorb and understand. This is historical writing at its best. We owe Ms. Pakula a considerable debt of gratitude."

—James I. Lader, *The East Hampton Star*

ALSO BY HANNAH PAKULA

An Uncommon Woman: The Empress Frederick:
Daughter of Queen Victoria, Wife of the Crown Prince of Prussia,
Mother of Kaiser Wilhelm

The Last Romantic: A Biography of Queen Marie of Roumania

The
Last Empress

Madame Chiang Kai-shek and the
Birth of Modern China

Hannah Pakula

Simon & Schuster Paperbacks
New York   London   Toronto   Sydney

Simon & Schuster Paperbacks
1230 Avenue of the Americas
New York, NY 10020

First Simon & Schuster trade paperback edition November 2010

SIMON & SCHUSTER PAPERBACKS and colophon are
registered trademarks of Simon & Schuster, Inc.

For information about special discounts for bulk purchases,
please contact Simon & Schuster Special Sales at 1-866-506-1949
or business@simonandschuster.com.

The Simon & Schuster Speakers Bureau can bring authors to your live event.
For more information or to book an event, contact
the Simon & Schuster Speakers Bureau at 1-866-248-3049
or visit our website at www.simonspeakers.com.

Designed by Nancy Singer

Manufactured in the United States of America

3   5   7   9   10   8   6   4

The Library of Congress has cataloged the hardcover edition as follows:

Pakula, Hannah.
The last empress : Madame Chiang Kai-Shek and the birth of modern China /
Hannah Pakula. — 1st Simon & Schuster hardcover ed.
    p.   cm.
1. Chiang, May-ling Soong, 1897–2003.   2. Presidents' spouses—China—
Biography.   3. Presidents' spouses—Taiwan—Biography.   4. Chiang, Kai-shek,
1887–1975.   5. China—History—Republic, 1912–1949.
6. Taiwan—History—1945–   I. Title.
DS777.488.C515P35   2009
951.04'2092—dc22
[B]   2009017576

ISBN 978-1-4391-4893-8
ISBN 978-1-4391-4894-5 (pbk)
ISBN 978-1-4391-5423-6 (ebook)

The author wishes to thank the following institutions for access to material reprinted in this
book, and in some cases permission to reprint material from their collections:

Georgetown University Libraries Special Collections
Hoover Institution on War, Revolution and Peace
Academia Historica/Chiang Kai-shek Archive, Taipei, Taiwan
Franklin D. Roosevelt Presidential Library/Harry Hopkins Papers

continued on page 791

The
Last Empress

Madame Chiang Kai-shek and the
Birth of Modern China

Hannah Pakula

Simon & Schuster Paperbacks
New York London Toronto Sydney

Simon & Schuster Paperbacks
1230 Avenue of the Americas
New York, NY 10020

First Simon & Schuster trade paperback edition November 2010

For information about special discounts for bulk purchases,
please contact Simon & Schuster Special Sales at 1-866-506-1949
or business@simonandschuster.com.

The Simon & Schuster Speakers Bureau can bring authors to your live event.
For more information or to book an event, contact
the Simon & Schuster Speakers Bureau at 1-866-248-3049
or visit our website at www.simonspeakers.com.

Designed by Nancy Singer

Manufactured in the United States of America

3   5   7   9   10   8   6   4

The Library of Congress has cataloged the hardcover edition as follows:

Pakula, Hannah.
The last empress : Madame Chiang Kai-Shek and the birth of modern China /
Hannah Pakula. — 1st Simon & Schuster hardcover ed.
p.   cm.
1. Chiang, May-ling Soong, 1897–2003.   2. Presidents' spouses—China—
Biography.   3. Presidents' spouses—Taiwan—Biography.   4. Chiang, Kai-shek,
1887–1975.   5. China—History—Republic, 1912–1949.
6. Taiwan—History—1945–   I. Title.
DS777.488.C515P35   2009
951.04'2092—dc22
[B]   2009017576

ISBN 978-1-4391-4893-8
ISBN 978-1-4391-4894-5 (pbk)
ISBN 978-1-4391-5423-6 (ebook)

The author wishes to thank the following institutions for access to material reprinted in this
book, and in some cases permission to reprint material from their collections:

Georgetown University Libraries Special Collections
Hoover Institution on War, Revolution and Peace
Academia Historica/Chiang Kai-shek Archive, Taipei, Taiwan
Franklin D. Roosevelt Presidential Library/Harry Hopkins Papers

continued on page 791

To my friend Barbara Davis,
who has always been there

CONTENTS

RUSSIA

KAZAKHSTAN

KYRGYZSTAN

TAJIKISTAN

AFGHANISTAN

PAKISTAN

Tihwa•
(Di Hua or Urumqi)

SINKIANG
(XINJIANG)

GANSU

CHINGHAI
(QINGHAI)

TIBET

Mekong R.

Yangtze R.

NEPAL

Lhasa•
(Lasa)

BHUTAN

INDIA

BANGLADESH

YUNNA

0   200   400 miles

0   200   400   600 kilometers

Bay of
Bengal

MYANMAR
(BURMA)

THAILAND

AUTHOR'S NOTE

THERE ARE two systems of translating Chinese characters into the English language—Wade-Giles (developed in the mid-nineteenth century and used on Taiwan until 2009) and pinyin (a phonetic system developed by the Communists in the mid-twentieth century). Guided by what the reader is most likely to recognize and the time frame of the book, I have used Wade-Giles or common usage for names of people like Chiang Kai-shek and Sun Yat-sen. I have done the same for place names like Canton and Mongolia, occasionally falling back on postal map names, and, in the interest of simplicity, have left out quite a few dashes and apostrophes.

The pitfalls of transliterating Chinese into English are only surpassed by the difficulties of converting Chinese money into American dollars. Because of the constant fluctuation of currencies, their names, and their equivalents, most amounts cited in the book are footnoted on the page with their approximate value in U.S. dollars for that year and, in parenthesis, what those dollars would be worth in 2008.

LIST OF PRINCIPAL CHARACTERS

Acheson, Dean: U.S. secretary of state in the Truman administration.

Allen, Dr. Young J.: Head of the Southern Methodist Mission in Shanghai.

Alsop, Joseph: American journalist and syndicated columnist, related to the Roosevelts.

Arnold, H. H. ("Hap"): The only five-star general in both the U.S. Army and U.S. Air Force.

Belden, Jack: American journalist, one of the group that walked out of Burma with Stilwell.

Blucher, Vasily Konstantinovich: Known as Galen, he was the chief Russian adviser to Chiang Kai-shek at the military school of Whampoa.

Borodin, Mikhail (real name: Mikhail Markovich Gruzenberg): Russian member of the Comintern who organized Sun Yat-sen's government in the Communist style.

Brooke, Sir Alan (Lord Alanbrooke): Principal military adviser to Winston Churchill during World War II.

Burke, William B.: Charlie Soong's best friend at school in the United States and in China.

Caldwell, Oliver J.: An officer of the OSS.

Cantlie, Dr. James: A doctor and friend of Sun Yat-sen.

Carr, General Julian Shakespeare: The head of Bull-Durham Tobacco, he was Charlie Soong's benefactor in the United States.

Chang Ching-chiang ("Curio Chang"): Crippled art and antique dealer who befriended Chiang Kai-shek and probably paid for his second wedding.

Chang Tso-lin: Known as the Old Marshal, he was the warlord of Manchuria.

xii LIST OF PRINCIPAL CHARACTERS

Chang Tsung-chang: A warlord known as the Monster—huge, powerful, and none too bright.

Chen Cheng: A tough, decent Chinese general who became president of the Executive Yuan.

Chen, Jennie (Ch'en Chieh-ju): Chiang Kai-shek's second wife.

Chen Chi-mei: Supporter of Sun Yat-sen and patron of Chiang Kai-shek.

Chen, Eugene: Born in Trinidad, he was the brilliant editor of *The Shanghai Gazette*.

Chen Kuo-fu: The older of the two conservative Chen brothers, who controlled both Chiang's Kai-shek's schedule and Chinese thought.

Chen Li-fu: The younger of the Chen brothers, known together as the CC Clique.

Chennault, Anna: The first woman correspondent for China's Central News Agency and much younger wife of Claire Chennault. After his death, she became a figure in Republican circles of Washington.

Chennault, Claire Lee: Unofficial head of the Chinese air force, he competed with Stilwell for supplies and convinced the Chiangs that his Flying Tigers could win the war for them.

Chen Yi: Corrupt Chinese general named by Chiang as governor of Taiwan after World War II.

Chiang Ching-kuo: Chiang Kai-shek's only biological son, he was head of the Kuomintang and Taiwan after the death of his father.

Chiang Wei-kuo: Chiang Kai-shek's adopted son.

Chou En-lai: Second only to Mao Tse-tung in the Chinese Communist Party, he served as its first premier and foreign minister.

Chuikov, Vasilii I.: Chief Soviet military adviser to Chiang Kai-shek.

Chu Teh: The general who became commander-in-chief of the army of the CCP in China.

Cixi (Tzu-hsi): The dowager empress. The last powerful member of the Manchu dynasties, she ruled China from behind a yellow curtain.

Clark-Kerr, Archibald: English diplomat who served as ambassador to China from the late 1930s until 1942.

Cohen, Morris: Known as two-Gun Cohen, once a petty criminal in Canada, he served as bodyguard to the Suns and was devoted to them both.

Corcoran, Thomas G.: Known as Tommy the Cork by his friends and the first modern lobbyist by his detractors, he chartered China Defense Supplies for Tse-ven (T. V.) Soong.

Coward, Noel: English playwright, composer, and actor known for his highly sophisticated style and wit.

Cowles, Gardner, Jr. ("Mike"): Publisher of *Look* magazine and many newspapers, he accompanied Wendell Willkie on his world tour in 1942.

Currie, Lauchlin: Named White House economist in 1939, he was invited to China in 1941 and 1942 to help straighten out the country's finances. Attacked as a Communist after the war, he moved to Colombia.

Davies, John Paton, Jr.: Served in the State Department and as political consultant to General Joseph Stilwell. Won the Medal of Freedom, but was accused of being a communist by Senator McCarthy.

Deng Xiao-ping: A veteran of the Long March and survivor of the Cultural Revolution, he emerged as China's de facto leader after Mao's death. He spoke at both Chou En-lai's and Sun Ching-ling's funerals.

Dole, Robert J.: Former Republican senator from Kansas who ran for president in 1996. He was seriously wounded in World War II and won three medals for bravery.

Donald, William Henry: An Australian journalist who raised the Chiangs to the status of world icons and became May-ling's chief adviser.

Donovan, William: Known as Wild Bill, he was head of the OSS during World War II.

Dorn, Colonel Frank: Chief assistant to General Stilwell in China.

Dulles, John Foster: Named secretary of state by Eisenhower, he continued Truman's policy of neutralization of the Taiwan Strait.

Du Yueh-sen: "Big-eared Du" organized and controlled the opium market in Shanghai and in his later life was known as a philanthropist.

Fairbank, John K.: Reknowned academic and historian of China, who worked for the OSS and the Office of War Information in Chungking during World War II.

Falkenhausen, Alexander von: General who headed the German military mission to China.

Farmer, Rhodes: Australian journalist, whose story on Japanese atrocities earned him a place on their death list. He also edited Madame Chiang's first book—a collection of her articles.

Feng Yu-hsiang: "The Christian General," probably the most colorful of the Chinese warlords.

Gabrielson, Eric: Norwegian ship's captain who befriended Charlie Soong.

Galen: *See* Blucher.

Gandhi, Mohandas: Usually referred to as Mahatma ("Great Soul") Gandhi, he met the Chiangs on their trip to India and was not impressed with the generalissimo.

Gauss, Clarence E.: American ambassador to China during World War II (1941–44), whose warnings about the unreliability of the Chinese government were often ignored.

Gellhorn, Martha: Famous American journalist who met the Chiangs while reporting on World War II.

Gould, Randall: Old China hand who wrote for *The Nation* and later for *The Shanghai Post*.

Hakka General (real name: Chen Chiung-ming): A southern warlord who was trusted by Sun Yat-sen but not by Chiang Kai-shek.

Harriman, W. Averill: Democratic politician and diplomat who served as President Roosevelt's special envoy to Europe and ambassador to the Soviet Union during World War II.

Hart, Robert: Honest, beloved, and efficient head of Imperial Maritime Customs Service, which collected customs duties for the Chinese Government.

Hay, John: American diplomat responsible for the so-called Open Door Policy.

Ho Ying-chin: The highly corrupt general who controlled military affairs in China.

Hoover, J. Edgar: The first director of the Federal Bureau of Investigation.

Hopkins, Harry: Close friend and adviser to President Roosevelt, he was known as the Deputy President.

Hornbeck, Stanley K.: Chief of the U.S. State Department Division of Far Eastern Affairs from 1928 to 1937 and special adviser to the secretary of state during World War II.

Howard, Roy W.: Chairman of the board of Scripps-Howard News Service and friend of the Chiangs.

Hsiang, V. S.: Mow Pang-tsu's executive officer who helped uncover the corruption in the purchase of military equipment for China.

Hsu, General Chung-chih: Third in line to inherit the leadership of the Kuomintang until he deserted his post in the city of Waichow.

Hu Han-min: A conservative, he and his brother, Hu Yin, were second and third in line to inherit the leadership of the KMT.

Huang Jin-rong: Known as Pockmarked Huang; a major figure in Shanghai crime.

Hurley, Major General Patrick J.: Colorful character sent by President Roosevelt to China to bring the Nationalists and Communists together.

Hu Shih: A onetime pupil of Charlie Soong who became China's ambassador to the U.S. (1938–42).

Joffe, Adolf: He held secret meetings with Sun Yat-sen and signed an agreement of cooperation between Sun's government and the Chinese Communist Party.

Johnson, Nelson T.: U.S. minister, later ambassador, to China, 1929–41.

Judd, Walter: Doctor and medical missionary in China, he became a member of the House of Representatives from Minnesota. One of the idealistic members of the China Lobby.

Kerr, George H.: U.S. diplomat and influential commentator on Taiwan politics.

Kissanka: An anti-Chiang Russian agent sent to take Borodin's place in China.

Kohlberg, Alfred: A rich merchant active in the China Lobby and the search for Communists in high places.

Koo, Wellington: Famous Chinese diplomat who served as ambassador to the United States and Britain.

Kung, David: The elder of the two Kung boys, who accompanied Aunty May on her visit to the United States.

Kung, Louis: The younger Kung son, who acted as a "courier" for the China Lobby, went into the oil business, and married a movie star.

Kung Hsiang-hsi (H. H.): The seventy-fifth lineal descendant of Confucius, who married May-ling's elder sister Ai-ling and became China's minister of finance.

Kung, Jeanette: The younger of the two Kung girls. An obvious lesbian in a day when most women stayed in the closet, she accompanied her aunt to the United States dressed like a boy.

Kung, Rosamond: The elder of the two Kung girls, she helped her aunt in her (May-ling's) later years.

La Guardia, Fiorello: Mayor of New York from 1934 to 1945.

Lambert, Eleanor: The doyenne of fashion of her day and a friend of Madame Chiang.

Lattimore, Owen: China scholar sent to China to help Chiang Kai-shek with political problems.

Lee Teng-hui: The first democratically elected president of Taiwan, he was expelled from the KMT when he founded a new party.

Leonard, Royal: Pilot for Young Marshal Chang (Hsueh-liang), he ended up working for the Chinese air force.

Li Li-san: The de facto head of the CCP from 1928 to 1930, who clashed with Mao over communist theory.

Li Tsung-jen: Leader of the Warlords' Council, which Chiang defeated in the late 1920s, he became vice president in 1948 and took over when Chiang retired.

Lin Shiliang: A confidential assistant to H. H. Kung, involved in a smuggling scheme.

Lin Yutang: Chinese writer and philosopher.

Liu Chen-huan: Warlord of Kwansi province. In spite of his profiteering from opium and brothels in Canton, Sun Yat-sen dubbed him "Living Angel Liu" because he had been wounded fighting for the city.

Luce, Claire Boothe: Journalist, editor, playwright, and member of the House of Representatives, she traveled with her husband to China, where she met the Chiangs and became one of Madame's most enthusiastic admirers.

Luce, Henry: Publisher of *Time, Life,* and *Fortune* magazines, he was an unequivocal supporter of China and the Chiangs.

MacArthur, Douglas: Commander of the U.S. Army Forces in the Far East during World War II, he served as head of the United Nations Forces in the Korean War before being dismissed for not adhering to President Truman's policies.

McCarthy, Joseph: Senator from Wisconsin who claimed that the United States was riddled with Soviet spies and who hounded many unfortunate people out of government and the arts.

Magruder, John: Brigadier general who headed a U.S. military mission to China in 1941.

Mao Fu-mei: Chiang Kai-shek's first wife, to whom he was married at the age of fourteen.

Maring (real name Hendricus Sneevliet): Dutch Communist who convinced Sun Yat-sen to ally his revolutionary party with the Russians.

Marshall, General George C.: Sent to China to try to bring the Kuomintang and the Chinese Communist Party together.

McHugh, James M.: Naval attaché in the American Embassy and officer in charge of Far Eastern secret intelligence, he was a friend of Donald and the Chiangs.

McTyeire, Bishop Holland N.: Chancellor of Vanderbilt University, head of the Southern Methodist Mission in China.

Mills, Emma DeLong: May-ling's best friend at Wellesley. Their friendship continued on and off after college.

Morgenthau, Henry, Jr.: President Roosevelt's secretary of the Treasury. He did not trust the Chinese, but loaned them millions in accordance with Roosevelt's wishes.

Mountbatten, Lord Louis: Supreme Commander of the Southeast Asia Command, member of the English royal family.

Mow Pang-tsu: Former brother-in-law of Chiang Kai-shek who reported corruption in the purchase of military supplies for China.

New Shan-chow: May-ling's uncle, married to one of her mother's sisters and an old friend of her father.

Nehru, Jawaharlal: The first prime minister of India.

Oursler, Fulton: American writer, editor, and journalist, whose writing was based on Christian themes except for a series of detective novels, written under various pseudonyms.

Oursler, Grace: Fulton's wife and a friend of Madame Chiang, who helped her with her book about faith, *The Sure Victory.* Oursler started her career writing what were called "racy" novels under the pseudonym Dora Macy.

Pai Chung-hsi: An important general and close associate of Li Tsung-jen, who was named minister of defense after World War II and worked for Chiang Kai-shek in Taiwan.

Pearson, Drew: American journalist known for his muckraking column "Washington Merry-Go-Round."

Prohme, Rayna: Red-haired American Communist journalist who traveled to Moscow with Ching-ling.

Ricaud, Reverend T. Page: The man who converted Charlie Soong to Christianity.

von Seeckt, Hans: German general, author of Chiang Kai-shek's successful Fifth Extermination Campaign, which forced the Chinese Communists to go on their Long March.

Service, John Stewart: A "China hand" who served in the U.S. Embassy and warned that Chiang Kai-shek was not China.

Sills, Beverly: A highly successful operatic soprano who, after retiring from the stage in 1980, worked in opera management.

Simon, Paul: Member of the U.S. House of Representatives (1975–85) and senator from Illinois (1985–97), he supported Taiwan and disagreed with U.S. policy to isolate the island.

Snow, Edgar: American journalist, believed to have been the first to interview Mao Tse-tung.

Sokolsky, George: Columnist and radio broadcaster who started as a revolutionary and became an archconservative. A friend of Tse-ven (T. V.) Soong.

Somervell, Brehon B: Commander of the U.S. Army Service Forces in World War II, responsible for logistics.

Soong, Charlie Jones, né Han Chiao-shun, patriarch of the Soong clan.

Soong, Madame Ni Kwei-tseng: An aristocrat from an old Chinese family and matriarch of the Soong clan.

Soong, Ai-ling (Loving Mood): eldest of the Soong children and Madame Chiang's favorite sister, who married H. H. Kung.

Soong, Ching-ling (Happy Mood): second in line in the Soong family, a liberal who married Sun Yat-sen and supported the Communists.

Soong, Tse-an: Known as T.A. Youngest of the Soong family, he became a banker. His children often spent vacations with their Aunty May.

Soong, Tse-ven (Hardworking Son): Always referred to as T.V., Madame Chiang's older brother was a world-reknowned economist in his day.

Soong, Tsu-liang: Known as T.L.; fifth child in the Soong family who became a businessman.

Stilwell, General Joseph W.: Known as Vinegar Joe, he was sent to China in 1942 to reform the Chinese army. His contempt for appearances brought him into conflict with Chiang Kai-shek, for whom "face" was everything.

Stimson, Henry L.: U.S. secretary of war under President Roosevelt.

Stuart, John Leighton: Last of the U.S. ambassadors to China who dealt with the Kuomintang government on the mainland.

Sun Chuan-fang: A warlord with five provinces.

Sun Fo: Son of Sun Yat-sen, a changeable politician who served the KMT in several positions and took the remnants of the government to Canton as a last holdout against the CCP.

Sun Yat-sen: The George Washington of China, who succeeded in dethroning the last of the Chinese dynasties.

Tai Li: Head of Chiang Kai-shek's secret police.

Tang Shen-chih: The general left in charge of defending Nanking when the Japanese arrived.

Teng Ying-chao: The wife of Chou En-lai who served in various positions on the Central Committee of the CCP and fought for the rights of women and children.

Tong, Hollington: American-trained journalist and biographer of Chiang Kai-shek, who served as the KMT's publicity man during World War II and later as ambassador to the United States.

Utley, Freda: An English scholar, journalist, and author of a number of books, who supported the Communists until they arrested her Russian husband.

Vincent, John Carter: Director of the Bureau of Far-Eastern Affairs, he was hounded out of the State Department by the "absurd" charges of disloyalty by Joseph McCarthy.

Wallace, Henry A.: Vice president under Roosevelt from 1941 to 1945.

Wang Ching-wei: The top man in the Kuomintang after Sun Yat-sen, he was expected to succeed Sun.

Wavell, Archibald: A one-eyed Scottish general who did not get along with Chiang Kai-shek.

Wedemeyer, Albert C.: American general who analyzed German strategy during World War II and took Stilwell's place in China after he was dismissed.

Wen Bing-chung: May-ling's uncle, married to one of her mother's sisters and an old friend of her father.

White, Theodore H.: Major American journalist who covered China during World War II and wrote articles and books about the experience.

Willauer, Whiting: Lawyer who worked for T.V. Soong at China Defense Supplies and helped Claire Chennault start Civil Air Transport.

Willkie, Wendell: A corporate lawyer whom the Republicans ran against Roosevelt in 1940.

Winchell, Walter: Print and radio commentator, who broke precedent by talking about the private lives of celebrities.

Wu Kuo-chen (K. C. Wu): Liberal governor of Taiwan, whom Chiang Kai-shek failed to silence.

Xiang Ying: A Communist general assassinated either for gold or on the orders of Mao.

Yang Huang-kuan: Warlord who controlled the Army of Yunnan and profited from crime in next-door Canton.

Yang Hu-chen: Warlord of Shensi province and partner of the Young Marshal at Xian.

Yao Yi-cheng: Chiang Kai-shek's concubine, mother of his adopted son, Chiang Wei-kuo.

Yen Hsi-shan: A major warlord, known as the Model Governor of the Province of Shansi

Young, Arthur N.: Economic adviser to the U.S. State Department, the Chinese Government, and Central Bank of China (1929–47).

Youngman, William S. Jr.: President of China Defense Supplies from 1942 to 1945. A law partner of Thomas G. Corcoran and friend of T. V. Soong, he served from 1949 to 1968 as president of C. V. Starr, the insurance giant.

Yuan Shih-kai: Chief rival of Sun Yat-sen, he envisioned himself as the next Emperor of China.

The
Last Empress

FOREWORD

When China moves, she will move the world.
— NAPOLEON BONAPARTE

COLONEL FRANK DORN was nobody's fool. Chief aide and confidant of General Joseph Stilwell, commander of the U.S. Army in China, Dorn arrived in the Chinese wartime capital of Chungking in March 1942. Known as Pinky— "for his complexion, not his politics"—he was a big, handsome man of forty-one, a quality that endeared him to Madame Chiang, who was known to call on Dorn during periods of military crisis to vent her frustrations with the British, the Americans, and her husband, Chiang Kai-shek, head of the Chinese government.

In one of their conversations, May-ling complained to Dorn that she could not understand why he and other American officers called her *Ma*dame, with the accent on the first syllable, instead of M*adame,* as it is pronounced in France. After all, she fussed, it was common knowledge that this was the term for the head of a house of prostitution. Dorn replied that he and his fellow officers certainly had no intention of insulting her. As a matter of fact, he added, she was surely aware that the queen of England was always called "Madam" to indicate royalty. "You never saw a facial expression change so fast in your life!" the colonel commented when he recounted the incident, delighted with his own quickness of wit.

In trying to explain why a woman fathered by a Chinese peasant found it both soothing and appropriate to be compared to the queen of England, I have tried to take into account the special characteristics of May-ling's family, a clan that benefited from the disappearance of centuries-old societal structures and helped push China into the modern world. I have started my story with Madame's father, a man named Charlie Soong, whose life journey mirrored the upheavals taking place in his nation. In doing this,

I have hoped to put the reader in a position to understand the woman called Soong May-ling Chiang, how she came to be the way she was, and how she charmed the United States out of billions of dollars. More important, I have tried to show how she managed to influence if not change the history of the twentieth century.

PART ONE

1866–1900

1

CHARLIE SOONG, whose original name was Han Chiao-shun, was born in 1866 on the teardrop-shaped island of Hainan off the south coast of China. What was once known as a refuge for gangsters and is now a place for entrepreneurs was, in the middle of the nineteenth century, an undeveloped tropical expanse second in size only to the island of Taiwan, six-hundred-plus miles to the east. Charlie's father seems to have been a fairly well off trader from Wench'ang who owned boats that "go from Macow to Hanhigh about 6 days water"—i.e., west across the Gulf of Tonkin to modern-day Vietnam and east through the South China Sea to the Portuguese colony of Macao near Hong Kong. These trading boats were three-masted, oceangoing junks, known as "big-eyed chickens" for their red sails and the huge pairs of eyes painted on their bows, put there by the sailors who believed that these magic oculi could spot pirates lying in wait up ahead. Murder and robbery flourished in these waters, where pirates were particularly bloodthirsty, as were those who captured them. It was not uncommon for captors to cut the hearts and livers out of pirate corpses and eat them, and it was even said that in one case they ate the entire man so he could not be reembodied as a pirate.

When he was nine, Charlie and an older brother were taken to the island of Java (modern-day Indonesia) and apprenticed to an uncle. The younger boy was apparently not happy there. When a relative who owned a silk and tea shop in Boston appeared and offered to take him to the United States, he sailed off happily in the spring of 1878. Short and sturdy, he was twelve years old at the time.

There were not many Chinese living in Boston when Charlie, still known as Han Chiao-shun, arrived to work in his uncle's tea shop, but he soon made friends with two boys from wealthy Shanghai families, Wen Bing-chung and New Shan-chow. Wen and New, who had come to study the

progressive ways of the West, convinced Charlie that he too needed a Western education. But when Charlie asked his uncle if he could go to school, his
uncle said no. He had not brought Charlie halfway around the world to
study, but to work. After nearly a year in his uncle's shop, Charlie ran away.
He slipped down to Boston harbor and stowed away on a cutter, the *Albert
Gallatin*. He was not found until the ship was already out to sea.

The captain of the cutter, a Norwegian named Eric Gabrielson, was a
staunch, God-fearing Methodist, admired for his skill as a mariner. When
Charlie was discovered, he was brought before Gabrielson, who asked him
his name. "Chiao-shun," Charlie replied, giving his first name only.* Which
is how, at the age of fourteen (Charlie lied and said he was sixteen), Han
Chiao-shun became Charlie Soon, ship's boy of the *Albert Gallatin*, which
patrolled the waters between Portsmouth, New Hampshire, and Edgartown,
Massachusetts, "one of the roughest stretches of coast along the Atlantic."
The man who would become Madame Chiang Kai-shek's father was now
employed—and paid—by the Revenue Service of the U.S. Treasury Department, precursor of the U.S. Coast Guard. When Captain Gabrielson
was transferred to Wilmington, North Carolina, Charlie went along as his
mess boy.

A religious man, the captain had started to talk to the Chinese boy
about Christianity, and he decided to help Charlie get the education he
wanted as well. He arranged for his mess boy to be discharged from the service and introduced to several people in Wilmington, among them Colonel
Roger Moore, who ran a Bible class at the Fifth Street Southern Methodist
Church. In young Charlie Soon, the first "Celestial" (as the Chinese were
known in the United States) to appear in those parts, Moore seized his
chance to contribute to the great Methodist missionary movement of the
day: the exporting of Christianity to China. Nor did it take long for the
Reverend T. Page Ricaud, pastor of the church, to recognize opportunity
when he saw it, and he soon inculcated in the boy a fervent belief in Christ
the Savior. Ricaud explained to the eager teenager that he could be educated
in Western ways and Western religion, prepared as a missionary, and sent
home to China to save his people. On November 7, 1880, Charlie Soon
became an official convert and was baptized Charles Jones Soon—the name
Jones being chosen by Ricaud, who had to supply three names for converts.
A short announcement in the *Wilmington Star* informed the town's citizens
that a baptism was to take place during the morning service—"probably the
first Celestial that has ever submitted to the ordinance of baptism in North
Carolina."

---

* The Chinese always put their last names first.

To support himself, Charlie worked in a printing shop, where he acquired skills he used with great success in later life, and also sold rope hammocks, which he had learned to make on board ship. Meanwhile, his Wilmington friends looked around to see how they were going to help him go to school. Trinity College, the forerunner of Duke University, was then a Methodist institution in Randolph County, North Carolina, and Ricaud wrote to Trinity's president to ask if he would take his first Oriental student. Either he or Moore then contacted General Julian Shakespeare Carr of Durham, philanthropist and millionaire owner of Bull Durham tobacco, to ask if he would fund the boy's schooling. "Send him up, and we'll see that he gets an education," said Carr.

When Charlie arrived in Durham, he so impressed Carr with his intelligence and politeness that Carr took the boy into his own home, "not as a servant, but as a son." Although Charlie's cheerful nature delighted the five little Carr children, his Chinese face made the Carrs' white neighbors and black servants open their eyes in astonishment. But Charlie, who was used to people looking at him oddly, had learned how to ingratiate himself with Americans. It also helped to have one of the leading businessmen in town as his sponsor. Within a very short time, he was an accepted member of the tight little southern community. In June of 1881, Charlie sent a letter to the head of the Southern Methodist Mission in Shanghai, Dr. Young J. Allen:

Dear Sir:

I wish you to do me a favor. I been way from home about six years and I want my father to know where I am and what I doing, they living in South East China in Canton state called monshou County . . . my father name is "Hann Hong Jos'k" in Chinese. I hope you will be able to it out where they are. I was converted few months ago in Wilmington, North Carolina . . . so I am a great hurry to be educated so I can go back to China and tell them about our Saviour, please write to me when you get my letter, I ever so much thank you for it, good by.

> Yours respectfully,
> *Charlie Jones Soon*

With this, Charlie enclosed the following letter to his father:

Dear Father:

I will write this letter and let you know where I am. I left Brother in East India in 1878 and came to the United States and finely I had found

Christ our Saviour . . . now the Durham Sunday School and Trinity are helping me and I am a great hurry to be educated so I can go back to China and tell you about the kindness of the friends in Durham and the grace of God, he sent his begotton Son to died in this world for all sinners. I am a sinner but save by the grace of God. I remember when I was a little boy you took me to a great temple to worshipped the wooden Gods. Oh, Father that is no help from wooden Gods. If you do worships all your life time would not do a bit goods. in our old times they know nothing about Christ, but now I had found a Saviour he is comforted me where ever I go to. Please let your ears be open so you can hear what the spirit say and your eyes looks up so you may see the glory of God. Soon as you get my letter please answer me and I will be very glad to hear from you. give my loves to mother Brother and Sisters please and also to yourself. . . . Mr. and Mrs. Carr they are good Christian family. . . . Will good by Father, write to Trinity College, N.C. Yours Son . . .

Charlie Jones Soon

Charlie's father never got the letter. Dr. Allen said he couldn't find him. He probably didn't try very hard.

Three months later, Charlie Soon entered Trinity College along with twelve Cherokee Indians. Even after he left the Carr home, however, he remained under the influence of Julian Carr, addressing him as "Father Carr" and picking up a great deal of business sense from him. Charlie got along well with his fellow students and began to notice girls, particularly Ella Carr, the daughter of Professor Carr, a poor cousin of Julian who taught Greek and German at Trinity. But the adolescent attraction between Charlie and Ella caused deep concern among the worthy members of the Board of Missions of the Southern Methodist Church, who said that the boy must be shipped off immediately to Vanderbilt University in Nashville, Tennessee. Charlie didn't want to leave Trinity and his friends, but when he was told that he would meet people who could help him in his chosen path, that he would continue to receive Carr's financial support, and that he could return to the Carr home for his vacations, he agreed to go. Vanderbilt records show that in 1882 he entered the Biblical Department, where he studied for a certificate in theology.

Popular with most of his fellow students, Charlie was remembered by classmate Reverend John C. Orr with affection: "At first the boys paid little or no attention to Soon. He was more of a curiosity than anything else. He was just a Chinaman. But this soon changed. He fell into the classes of the writer, and they became . . . intimate friends. He had a fine mind, learned to use the English language with accuracy and fluency, and was usually bubbling over with wit and humor and good nature." Charlie's good humor was partly a veneer, painted on in order to maintain acceptance by his peers. A friend recalled his joining a group of fellow students who met on Sunday mornings in the chapel to pray and talk about their religious experiences: "One morning Soon (as we called him) got up and stood awhile before he said anything. Then his lips trembled and he said: 'I feel so little. I get so lonesome. So far from my people. So long among strangers. I feel just like I was a little chip floating down the Mississippi River. But I know that Jesus is my Friend, my Comforter, My Savior.' The tears were running down his cheeks, and before he could say anything more a dozen of the boys were around him, with their arms about him, and assuring him that they loved him as a brother. Soon broke up the meeting that morning." A short boy— one classmate describes him as "rather low of stature, probably about five-feet-four or six inches"—his closest friend at Vanderbilt was a six-foot-two, blue-eyed student of Irish descent who weighed more than two hundred pounds, named William B. Burke.

When Charlie announced he wanted to study medicine before going home to China, the chancellor of Vanderbilt, Bishop Holland N. McTyeire, who was also head of the Southern Methodist Mission in China, vetoed the idea, even though Carr had offered to pay for Charlie's further education. Claiming that there were "too many" medical missionaries in China already, McTyeire was clearly moved by other factors in rejecting Charlie's request. A little over a month after the young man's graduation, McTyeire sent the following letter to Dr. Allen in Shanghai:

My Dear Doctor Allen:

We expect to send Soon out to you this fall. . . . I trust you will put him, at once, to circuit work, walking if not riding. Soon wished to stay a year or two longer to study medicine to be equipped for higher usefulness, etc. And his generous patron, Mr. Julian Carr, was not unwilling to continue helping. But we thought better that the Chinaman that is in him should not all be worked out before he labors among the Chinese. Already he has "felt the easy chair"—and is not averse to the comforts of higher civilization. No fault of his. Let our young man, on whom we have bestowed labor, begin to labor. Throw him into the ranks: no side place. His desire to study medicine was met by the information that we have already as many doctors as the Mission needed, and one more. I have good hope that, with your judicious handling, our Soon may do well. It will greatly encourage similar work here if he does. The destinies of many are bound up in his case . . .

Yr. Bro. In Christ,
H. N. McTyeire

Meanwhile, Charlie continued to make and sell his hammocks. He also began to preach and hold revival meetings—an experience that improved his English. On May 28, 1885, he graduated from Vanderbilt, and seven months later joined Dr. W. H. Park, a medical missionary, on a transcontinental train bound for San Francisco, where they boarded a steamship for Yokohama and Shanghai. Charlie Soon, who had left China when he was nine and turned twenty the year he sailed back, had never before seen the Chinese mainland when his ship docked in Shanghai in January 1886.

꙳

ON HIS ARRIVAL, Charlie called on Dr. Allen, director of the activities of the six missionaries who composed the Southern Methodist Mission in China. An elitist, Allen had no use for oral evangelism among the Chinese peasants, who were often illiterate. To put it in his own words, Dr. Allen served God and the Methodist Church as missionary to "an empire ruled by an aristocracy of intelligence, to whom the sole appeal is through the printed page." The insignia on his home in the international section of Shanghai announced that his was an official residence, and except for members of the government, special scholars, and his servants, whom he dressed in immaculate white, no Chinese was ever invited to enter.

In a letter written just before Charlie's arrival, Allen had complained to his board about the new missionary and his salary: "He will be here in two days now and I have no information as to how the Board expects to treat him. . . . The boys and young men in our Anglo-Chinese College are far his superiors in that they are—the advanced ones—both English and <u>Chinese</u> scholars. . . . And Soon never will become a Chinese scholar, at best will only be a <u>denationalized</u> Chinaman, discontented and unhappy unless he is located and paid far beyond his deserts—and the consequence is I find none of our brotherin willing to take him."

The one who was not willing to take him on was Dr. Allen, who immediately packed Charlie off to live with his traveling companion, Dr. Park. He was there only a few weeks before being ordered to move in with an ignorant native preacher in order to learn the local Shanghai dialect. Before being given his first assignment, Charlie asked Dr. Allen if he might go to Hainan to visit his parents, whom he had not seen for ten years. Allen refused, saying he must wait over six months until the Chinese New Year, when the other missionaries would take their vacations. The refusal itself was not unreasonable, but the spirit in which it was delivered wounded Charlie's ego. Allen was not the only one who looked askance at the young Chinese convert. His countrymen regarded him as a "*denationalized* Chinaman," a native who did not speak their dialect and shared none of their customs. There was only one group in the mission that practiced the kind of populist evangelism Charlie had learned in America, and, like Charlie, resented Dr. Allen's dominion over their lives. The members of this group opened a mission in Japan not long after Charlie's arrival, but Charlie's application for a transfer was turned down. Instead, he was sent to a village outside Shanghai, where he was told to preach to a congregation of Chinese who had already been converted to Christianity and to teach their children—twelve unruly little peasant boys with not much interest in learning.

Among Charlie's charges was a boy named Hu Shih, who eventually graduated from Cornell University, became one of China's important philosophers, and served as China's ambassador to the United States. According to Dr. Hu, the boys in his class took special pleasure in taunting their English teachers. "One day," Hu recalled, "a short, stocky man, rather ugly, appeared on the teacher's platform. They immediately began to laugh at him and created such hullabaloo that I thought the teacher would leave the room for shame. Instead, Charles Soon waited for the hubbub to subside, then he opened his books and began to talk." Although Dr. Hu could no longer remember what Charlie said, he recalled that all the boys had grown quiet, realizing that they had someone who understood them because he had once been one of them. He said that Charlie Soon became the most popular teacher in the school, which, because of him, began to attract more students.

During the Chinese New Year, Charlie took a steamer to Hainan, arriving at the home of his parents without previous notice. Not too surprisingly, they did not recognize the man whom his father had left as a nine-year-old apprentice in Indonesia. During the family reunion Charlie learned that Dr. Allen had never bothered to forward the letter he had written his father from America.

Charlie Soon's second assignment was as a circuit preacher in Kunshan, an old walled city of about 300,000 inhabitants, where he lived in a little house by himself. Although he replaced his Western dress with native clothing, he was still shunned by the locals. One day, on a trip to Shanghai, he ran into New, his old friend from Boston. New thought that Charlie's lonely life would be helped by a wife. He suggested his eighteen-year-old sister-in-law, Ni Kwei-tseng, as an ideal mate for a Chinese man who had been educated in the West. Not only was she related to New, but she was also related to Wen, because the two friends had married the two older sisters in the Ni family.

The Nis were descendants of a famous scholar and government minister of the Ming Dynasty (1368–1644) who had converted to Christianity. Like upper-class Chinese girls, Kwei-tseng's feet had been bound when she was a toddler. Foot binding, which had existed for a thousand years among the upper classes, was the procedure by which the feet of female children were wrapped tightly in bandages in order to bend the toes into the sole and bring the sole and heel as close together as possible. The resulting tiny (as small as three inches), deformed appendages, termed "golden lilies" or "orchid hooks," were believed to increase a woman's attractiveness by forcing her to sway her hips in an erotic way, deter her from running away, and provide particular sexual delights to her husband. Chinese erotica and descriptions of famous courtesans always included detailed descriptions of these deformed feet. But Kwei-tseng had run a high fever each time the bindings were tightened. Deciding that marriage was not so important for their third daughter, the Nis had loosened the bindings and allowed Kwei-tseng's feet to grow normally into what upper-class Chinese referred to disdainfully as "big feet."

Kwei-tseng had also shown signs of high intelligence and curiosity, which encouraged her father to provide her with a tutor, who had taught her Chinese characters and classics from the age of five. At nine, she had been enrolled at a missionary school. From there she had gone on to high school, where she had developed a passion for religion, discovered mathematics, and learned to play the piano. Lacking the looks and graces of the traditional Chinese female, she was regarded as the inevitable spinster of the Ni family.

New and Wen arranged to take Charlie to church, where he could observe Miss Ni singing in the choir. She was small like Charlie, not particularly pretty but lively. Most of the traits that rendered Ni Kwei-tseng unmarriageable in Shanghai society made her attractive to Charlie Soon, but he still had to get the permission of her mother, who took her duties as a descendant of one of China's fine families very seriously. One of these was making sure that her children's marriages were arranged by a matchmaker. New offered himself, shuttling between the two parties, extolling their virtues and glossing over their failings. Although he was rather common-looking, Charlie Soon was deemed acceptable, and the two young people were married by a Southern Methodist missionary in the summer of 1887. It was a small wedding, but the reception was attended by important businessmen, military leaders, and people with connections at court. Kwei-tseng brought Charlie not only a substantial dowry but a bridge into a world he had never known. After the wedding, the young couple returned to Kunshan.

A few months later, Charlie's friend from Vanderbilt William Burke arrived in China to serve in the Southern Methodist mission. Welcomed enthusiastically—in sharp contrast to Charlie's grudging reception—Bill was invited to attend the Second Annual Conference of the China Mission of the Methodist Episcopal Church South in the city of Soochow, where he was greeted with great warmth by Dr. Allen. There were seven missionaries in all. One was Chinese. Bill met him as he entered the churchyard with Allen. Neither recognized the other until Allen introduced them:

"Brother Burke, I'd like you to meet Brother Soon, our first native conference member."

"Well, sakes alive, Charlie," Bill responded, grabbing hold of Charlie's hand and pumping it enthusiastically, "it's mighty good to see you again! It's been over two years!"

"I'm glad to see you too, Bill!" Charlie said. "I didn't know you with that beard."

"Well, I didn't know you in that Chinese getup of yours either." Charlie was wearing a long Chinese gown with a black skullcap. "Makes you look considerably older, I think."

The conference at Soochow gave the former classmates a chance to catch up on each other's lives. On the last day, the mission assignments were announced. Charlie was sent back to Kunshan, while Bill, a newcomer who spoke almost no Chinese, was assigned to open a new mission station in Shanghai. This was a particularly sensitive post, as during the previous year, a Presbyterian missionary who had been trying to sell religious tracts there was stoned, and a student mob had set fire to the property of the Catholic mission. The violence was China's answer to a wave of anti-Chinese barbarism swirling through the western United States, where rampaging gangs of unskilled white workers slashed, scalped, and hung by their pigtails Chinese laborers, whose willingness to work for lesser wages threatened their jobs.* The industrial boom following the American Civil War had brought in millions of immigrants, including Chinese contract laborers, many of whom helped build the transcontinental railroads. They were said to be excellent workers, "because, as a medical book of the era claimed, their poorly

---

* From this inhuman treatment came the saying "Not a Chinaman's chance." (Michael Schaller, *The United States and China in the Twentieth Century*, p. 20.)

developed nervous system made them immune to ordinary pain!" But with the completion of the railways, the American Congress, determining that the country no longer needed Chinese coolies to do its hard work, had passed laws to keep the Chinese out of the United States.

A few months after his arrival, Burke visited Soon in Kunshan. It was the fourth night of the New Year, the biggest festival of the Chinese calendar. Gongs rang and firecrackers exploded in the narrow, winding streets as they walked to Charlie's house. Soon informed Burke that this celebration was dedicated to the god of wealth, for whom there would be feasts the next day. Chinese traditionally paid their debts three times a year—on the Dragon Boat Festival, the Harvest Moon Festival, and the New Year, "the great day of reckoning." If a man was unable to pay his debts that day, he hid himself until the following morning, which was technically a holiday when monetary transactions were forbidden. On that day no one ever used a broom, lest he sweep away his good luck, and no water was ever poured on the ground in case the year's riches would be poured away with it. Employees invited to dinner by their boss would know they could keep their jobs for the following year. Those who did not receive invitations knew, in the Chinese way of saving face, that they were fired.

Charlie and his wife lived in the mission parsonage, a two-story row house. "Please enter my humble dwelling," Charlie said, mocking the typical Chinese greeting and leading Burke across a little court into a room that served the Soons as living and dining room. When Charlie's wife came in with cups of green tea, Bill was delighted to see that she walked easily like an American, not like a Chinese woman on golden lilies. "I think my mother was really happier than my father to stop binding my feet," Kwei-tseng told Bill when the subject came up. "She knew as much as anyone how painful it was." Charlie then told his friend the story of how his mother-in-law had once been forced to flee for her life, hobbling on her tiny feet over a distance of six miles from her home. On the way she had been forced to abandon the family pearls, which had been passed down from an ancestor, the daughter of the commander of the Imperial Forces. The gems, which made up a pearl-encrusted ceremonial coat and headdress, a gift from the emperor, were simply too heavy for her to carry that far.

Bill was delighted to see that Charlie appeared genuinely in love with his wife but distressed when his friend said that he thought he might "do more for my people if I were free of the mission." No matter how hard he worked, Charlie Soon was paid only $10.00 a month, the salary of a native preacher. "But please believe me, Bill," Charlie assured his friend. "If I do happen to leave the mission, it will never mean my giving up of preaching Christ and Him crucified. I will continue to work as much as I can for the mission always."

Soon thereafter, Charlie took a part-time job selling Bibles for the American Bible Society, a group that published and subsidized inexpensive editions of the Bible in many languages. Promoted to circuit preacher in the Shanghai district, he continued to work part-time as a salesman. His next appointment—as a "supply" preacher, who filled a vacancy but was not required to devote full time to his ministry—was made "at his own request," and in 1890, he left the Southern Methodist Mission altogether, explaining to his American friends that "I could not support myself, wife and children, with about fifteen dollars of United States money per month." What Charlie did not say then but told his family in later years was how humiliated he was by the white missionaries, who required that he stand before them to give his reports on his mission, while they all sat. Treated "more like a servant than a colleague," he finally quit working for the mission. His daughter Madame Chiang came to agree with him in later years about the racist prejudices of Americans toward Chinese. As she told one of her husband's American advisers, she had always felt that the subtext of the Americans was "Oh, yes, she is clever, of course, but after all she is only a Chinese."

Although he left the mission, Charlie continued his connection with the American Bible Society, which had been publishing Bibles for thirty years in literary "classical" Chinese, translated for the scholarly elite. It was not long before he took his knowledge of printing, gained in the United States, put it together with what he had learned at the Bible Society, and started publishing his own Bibles. Chinese labor was cheap, as were Chinese paper and cardboard bindings. But where Charlie got the capital to invest in presses is not known. One source guesses that he must have asked his old benefactor Julian Carr for backing; another assumes that the money was supplied by various Western missionary groups that needed Bibles for their converts. Wherever it came from, it was speedily repaid. Charlie's Sino-American Press was a success from the beginning—a fact attributed to its proprietor's acquired knowledge of Western business methods and inborn sense of baroque, Chinese courtesies.

To conduct his business, Charlie had calling cards printed, using the last name of Soong. It was not unusual for Chinese to change their names to reflect a new state of mind or a new life. To go with his advanced social status, Charlie chose the name of a dynasty (Song) that had ruled China from the tenth to the thirteenth century.* He added Western textbooks to his list and soon purchased an old warehouse in the French Concession for his presses. A few years later, he was approached by two brothers named Sun,

---

* Henry Luce's sister Elizabeth Luce Moore said that in later years, Charlie's children signed their names with the same character previously used by the royal dynasty (Moore, "China's Soong," *Fortune*, June 1933).

descendants of one of the richest families in China, who asked him to accompany them to the United States. Charlie, who understood Western commercial practices and spoke English, helped the Suns purchase a flour mill
from Allis-Chalmers, incorporate the company in Shanghai and negotiate
mill rights. Appointed corporate secretary of Fou Foong Mills, Ltd., Charlie
contributed to the success of the company, which grew to be one of the largest in the Orient. For this, he was given shares in Fou Foong and was well
compensated for the rest of his life.

While Charlie was moving up in business circles, Kwei-tseng was producing children. There were six in all, three girls and three boys. The first
four—three girls and a boy—were all born before 1900. The eldest, a girl
named Ai-ling (Loving Mood), was born in 1888; Charlie gave her the Christian name of Nancy in honor of Mrs. Julian Carr. Following Ai-ling into the
nursery two years later was Ching-ling (Happy Mood); her Christian name
was Rosamond, in honor of the daughter of Reverend Ricaud. Then in 1894
came the first son, Tse-ven (Hardworking Son), always referred to as T.V.
And in 1897, May-ling (Beautiful Mood), the third and last girl, who became
Madame Chiang Kai-shek, was born; her Christian name, seldom used, was
Olive. Two younger brothers, Tse-liang, known as T.L., and Tse-an, known as
T.A., were born a few years later.

Business success enabled Charlie to build a new home, located on the
outskirts of the city's International Settlement. Standing in the middle of
fields, surrounded by exotic trees, it was designed in a common Shanghai
style, half Chinese, half foreign. The first courtyard was surrounded by a
wall, erected to keep the Soong children from falling into a stream that ran
by. But the children soon learned to scale the wall and climb the trees, and
Charlie had to bribe the nearby villagers to allow them free rein of the neigh-
borhood. The house itself was divided into four large, airy rooms downstairs:
a Chinese parlor, a Western-style parlor with a piano, a dining room, and
Charlie's study. Behind these public spaces were smaller rooms with a bathroom and a staircase, both of which were highly unusual in Chinese homes
of the period. The staircase led to four bedrooms—one for the parents, one
for the girls, one for the boys, and one for guests. There were two bathrooms
with green-glazed bathtubs, painted on the outside with yellow dragons.
Another unusual feature was the use of Western-style beds with mattresses
instead of the decorative hard wood couches used by most Chinese. Neighbors who came to examine them stuck their fingers into the soft mattresses
and declared them unhealthy for children.

There was a second house in back of the family quarters. Situated behind
a small courtyard, it contained servants' quarters, storerooms, and the
kitchen. Since her husband could never really get used to Chinese cuisine,

Kwei-tseng had learned to prepare Western dishes for him on a stove in a pantry behind the dining room. It was in this pantry that her daughters also learned about American cooking. The main kitchen was the province of the family chef, a man who would not have tolerated girls in his workplace.

One of the interests the Soong parents shared was music. Madame Soong had studied piano, and her husband had a passion for singing. He was apparently blessed with a rather nice voice, as was Ai-ling, to whom he taught songs he had learned in the United States. As the eldest child in the family, Ai-ling was particularly close to her father. On her tenth birthday, he gave her a bicycle. They biked together regularly, and their outings included trips to Charlie's publishing office and the flour mill, where Ai-ling, wily beyond her years, stood silently, observing the workings of the business world.

Charlie was the parent who encouraged his children to learn, to dare, to believe in themselves. Taught by their father that they could do anything they wanted to do—hadn't he raised himself from peasant to entrepreneur?— they were kept in tow by their mother, who was less of a dreamer and more of a disciplinarian. Card playing was forbidden in the household. As was dancing. Pious and severe in her piety, Kwei-tseng spent hours in a room on the upper floor of their house that she kept solely for the purpose of prayer. These sessions often began before dawn. When one of her children asked for advice, she would inevitably answer, "I must ask God first." As Madame Chiang later recalled, "we could not hurry her. Asking God was not a matter of spending five minutes to ask him to bless her child and grant the request. It meant waiting upon God until she felt his leading."

Religion had made Charlie Soong's life. The Methodist Church had educated him and given him a place in the world. This was not necessarily the case with his third daughter. Required to live up to the behavior of her three older siblings, May-ling found daily prayers "tiresome" and "hated the long sermons" in church on Sunday. Family prayers were little better, and she often pled thirst in order to slip out of the room. "I used to think Faith, Belief, Immortality were more or less imaginary," she wrote in 1934. "I believed in the world seen, not the world unseen. I could not accept things just because they had always been accepted. In other words, a religion good enough for my fathers did not necessarily appeal to me."

2

The only thing Oriental about me is my face.
—SOONG MAY-LING

WHEN SHE was five years old, Ai-ling, the eldest of the Soong children, told her parents that she wanted to go to boarding school. A childish whim, it set high standards of independence for her two younger sisters, who were expected to venture bravely into unknown territory at a young age.

The Soong family attended Moore Methodist Church, a brick structure with a bell tower, where Sundays were spent listening to what May-ling called "tedious sermons and prayers." A pillar of the congregation, Charlie Soong was also head of the church Sunday school. Music for Sunday services was often provided by students from the expensive and fashionable McTyeire School, named for the bishop who had refused Charlie Soong's request to study medicine. Little Ai-ling, observing the special places accorded the McTyeire girls in church, decided that she wanted to go there—and as soon as possible. Although McTyeire was really for older girls, the principal, observing the child's determination, agreed to tutor her for two years. A few days later, dressed in a Scotch plaid jacket and green pants, Ai-ling climbed into a rickshaw with her father and set off for school, followed by a second rickshaw carrying a shiny new black trunk filled with her clothes. Not until her father had deposited her in the principal's study and left for home did the five-year-old break down in tears.

The Soongs' second daughter, Ching-ling, waited until seven before entering McTyeire, but May-ling started at five like Ai-ling, whom she adored and tried to emulate. Everyone liked May-ling, and classes were easy for her. Unlike the quieter and more thoughtful Ching-ling, she was determined to fit in. "Why do you ask Pastor Li questions?" May-ling demanded of her older sister during one of the school's weekly religious discussions. "Don't you believe?" Spoiled at home, she continued to get her way at school.

McTyeire was housed in two buildings with a passageway in between—a dark, unlit walk that frightened most of the younger girls. "Why can't you walk through there like May-ling?" the teachers asked her classmates. But May-ling, who put on a brave show, began to have nightmares at night, from which she would awaken in spasms of trembling. Standing by her bed, she would straighten her back and repeat her lessons for the day. She also broke out all over her body in little red bumps called wheals that itched and burned. She was finally sent home to study with a tutor. It must have been a dispiriting defeat for the anxiety-ridden five-year-old, unable to live up to the example of her older sister.

The youngest of a group of boys and girls who played together, May-ling, who was fat, was nicknamed "Little Lantern" by one of her uncles. Puffing along behind her older sisters and brother, dressed in flowered jackets tied around her ample middle, long trousers, and shoes embroidered to look like cats' heads (complete with whiskers and ears that stuck out), she was the baby whom all the other children tried to get rid of. She was particularly poor at hide-and-seek, anxious to be discovered when hiding and never able to find anyone when she was "it." One day the children told her that she could be "it" if she stood in the middle of the garden and didn't open her eyes until she had counted to one hundred. This was not easy for May-ling. She had learned to count to twenty, but after that, she jumped through the rest of the count, often by tens. When she finished in record time, one of the other children told her she must do it all over again. After she finished the second time, she looked around, but the others had disappeared, having gone off to play without her. It was Ai-ling who came back and told her that she too would one day be big enough to laugh at the older children, just as they now laughed at her.

If Ai-ling was an attentive older sister to May-ling, the combination of Ai-ling and Ching-ling scared off the younger McTyeire students, who thought them far too sophisticated to approach. The eldest Soong sister was, in fact, so mature that when she was fifteen, her parents decided to send her to school in the United States. It was fashionable in turn-of-the-century Shanghai for the sons of the very rich to be sent abroad, and Charlie Soong wanted the world to know that he had prospered. There was another reason as well: Charlie had never forgotten how his well-to-do brothers-in-law, Wen and New, had been schooled while he toiled in his uncle's shop. Neither Charlie's sons nor his daughters would ever have to struggle as he had for an education.

After consulting with his old classmate and friend William Burke, Charlie decided to send Ai-ling to Wesleyan College in Macon, Georgia, Burke's home. The president of the school, Judge Guerry, wrote Burke to say that he would be very interested in having a Chinese girl at Wesleyan; he had educated several American Indians in the past but never a Chinese. Wesleyan, or Wesleyan Female College as it was called then, was the earliest chartered women's college in the world.

In deciding to educate their daughters, the Soongs were in the forefront of the Chinese Reform Movement, putting them at odds with most other well-to-do families. When Charlie let it be known that his eldest daughter was going to America to school, the Shanghai community was shocked. How could a father be so foolish as to waste the money he would need to marry his daughter off in educating her? Not only was Charlie Soong endangering what would have been a handsome dowry, but no man in his right mind would want to take on a wife whose head had been filled with progressive ideas from the West. Ignoring the criticism, Charlie gave his eldest daughter a good-bye party and entrusted her to his old pal William Burke for the long journey to the United States.

Some years earlier, Burke had married Addie Gordon, and they were now the parents of four sons, whom they were taking back to the States on home leave. The previous winter Addie had suffered from typhoid fever, and it was thought that the three-week voyage in bracing ocean air would help her over the final stages of recuperation. Burke had booked passage on the Pacific Mail steamer *Korea,* leaving on May 28, 1904, and Charlie had arranged for Ai-ling to travel in the cabin next to the Burkes. (The *Korea* had only two classes of passengers: cabin and steerage.) Once he had purchased Ai-ling's ticket, Charlie paid a visit to the Portuguese Consulate, where he bought his daughter a Portuguese passport.

In an effort to stop the immigration of Chinese, Congress had passed an Exclusion Law in 1882, prohibiting Chinese laborers from entering the United States. Although students, teachers, merchants, and tourists were still accepted, the law nearly eliminated the number of immigrants; whereas forty thousand Chinese had entered the United States in 1881, by 1887 the number had plummeted to ten.* Under the 1882 Chinese Exclusion Law, extended as the Geary Act, Chinese living in America were required to carry a passport with their photo on it, which they could be required to produce at any time—a proviso that resulted in the frequent detention and harassment of highly respectable people. Legislation passed in 1904, the year Ai-ling traveled with the Burkes, extended this law indefinitely. With the Shanghai papers full of stories detailing humiliations and arrests, it is easy to see why Charlie, who carried a Portuguese passport stating that he had been born in the Portuguese colony of Macao, purchased the same protection for his daughter.

Charlie accompanied Ai-ling to the *Korea* on the day of her departure, boarded the ship with her, and remained for the three hours it took

---

* Figures on immigration obtained from *An Illustrated History of the Chinese in America* by Ruthanne Lum McCunn (San Francisco: Design Enterprises of San Francisco, 1979), p. 87.

for medical inspections to take place. When the gong sounded and he finally left her, they said their good-byes calmly and matter-of-factly. Ai-ling displayed no emotion at all until the ship let out a piercing blast of its whistle, at which point Burke noticed that she began to cry quietly to herself. The only Chinese girl in cabin (upper) class, Ai-ling attracted a certain amount of curiosity and attention. At fifteen, she looked older and more serious than her age. This may have been partly due to her at-tire. Dressed in Western-style dresses, designed and sewn by kindly mis-sionary ladies who had forgotten everything about fashion they had never known, she wore her hair in one long plait down her back, tied with black ribbons at the top and bottom. On the night before their arrival at Kobe, Japan, one of the ship's officers, trying to be nice, came over to ask her to dance.

"No, thank you, I cannot," she said.

"Well, there's no better time to learn. Come, I'll teach you," said the young officer.

"No, it is not right for me to dance."

"Why?"

"Because I am a Christian and Christians do not dance."

When the *Korea* docked at Kobe, Addie Burke was running a slight fever but was afraid that if she stayed in her cabin, the Japanese medical officers, famous for detaining ships, might think she was ill. A Chinese passenger had died the day before in steerage, and although the ship's doctor said that the death was due to pneumonia, the Japanese medic, alleging that it looked "like suspiciously plague," insisted that all the passengers be taken ashore and immersed in disinfectant while the ship was being fumigated, and that their clothes be treated for germs. Addie Burke returned from the station bathhouse with a high fever. Ten days later, when the *Korea* was finally re-leased from quarantine, she was desperately ill. Burke and the ship's doctor decided to take her off the ship and put her in the hospital in Yokohama. Not knowing how long she would be there, Burke took his children and their baggage as well; he left Ai-ling, who wanted to continue her trip, in the care of another Southern Methodist missionary named Anna Lanius, whom he had alerted to Ai-ling's plight before he disembarked. They arrived in San Francisco on the *Korea,* along with 7,000 tons of cargo, most of which was opium, expected to yield some $250,000 in duty; $2 million in gold that the Japanese, in the midst of the Russo-Japanese War, were sending to the United States for safekeeping; and the famous writer Jack London, who had been covering the war. On that day, Addie Burke died in Yokohama.

Ai-ling's new friend, Miss Lanius, described her as a "well-behaved young girl with a correct knowledge of English and a good vocabulary." When they docked and began unloading, Ai-ling, who was surprised to see "white men doing coolies' work," presented her passport for inspection in the lounge.

"Trying to get by on one of these things, are you?" the immigration officer said. "That's been tried by a lot of other Chinese, little sister. It won't work. You just stay here until we're ready to take you to the detention home."

"You cannot put me in a detention home," Ai-ling snapped back. "I am a cabin-class passenger, not from the steerage."

"You certainly won't put her in a detention home," added Anna Lanius. "I'm staying right here with her to see that you don't." One of the immigration officers agreed, referring to the detention house in question—a cell block on the waterfront—as "not fit for a self-respecting animal." Ai-ling, he said, should remain on the *Korea* until a ship could be found in which to send her back to China. The ladies were kept on board, confined to one small cabin, and fed steak, potatoes, and bread three times a day. Finally, on their third day of confinement, Lanius was allowed to go ashore and use a telephone. She called Dr. Reid, the missionary who had married Ai-ling's parents and was working in San Francisco at the time. He arrived the next day with a nurse, who took Lanius's place. Ai-ling remained in custody for another two weeks, transferred from one ship to another, until Reid finally reached Washington and arranged for her to enter the United States.*

Three days later, Burke arrived on another ship after burying Addie in Yokohama. When they reached Macon, there was quite a crowd at the railway station. Some were waiting to welcome Burke home; others came out of curiosity. Next morning, the *Macon Telegraph* reported the arrival of "the Chinese girl who was detained aboard ship at San Francisco while on her way to Wesleyan College," adding, "The girl is said to be quite a bright one." Judge Guerry, president of Wesleyan, who had once characterized the Chinese as an "immoral, degraded and worthless race," was quoted in the same article: "Of course she [Ai-ling] will not force herself or be forced upon any of the other young ladies as an associate. They will be free and conduct themselves as they see fit. I have no misgivings as to her kind and respectful

---

* A year later the teenager was in Washington visiting her Uncle Wen and was introduced to President Theodore Roosevelt. "America is very beautiful, and I am very happy here," she said, "but why do you call it a free country?" Explaining what had happened to her in San Francisco, she asked, "Why should a Chinese girl be kept out of a country if it is so free. We would never treat visitors to China like that." T.R. apologized for her treatment. (Emily Hahn, *The Soong Sisters*, p. 49.)

for medical inspections to take place. When the gong sounded and he finally left her, they said their good-byes calmly and matter-of-factly. Ai-ling displayed no emotion at all until the ship let out a piercing blast of its whistle, at which point Burke noticed that she began to cry quietly to herself. The only Chinese girl in cabin (upper) class, Ai-ling attracted a certain amount of curiosity and attention. At fifteen, she looked older and more serious than her age. This may have been partly due to her attire. Dressed in Western-style dresses, designed and sewn by kindly missionary ladies who had forgotten everything about fashion they had never known, she wore her hair in one long plait down her back, tied with black ribbons at the top and bottom. On the night before their arrival at Kobe, Japan, one of the ship's officers, trying to be nice, came over to ask her to dance.

"No, thank you, I cannot," she said.

"Well, there's no better time to learn. Come, I'll teach you," said the young officer.

"No, it is not right for me to dance."

"Why?"

"Because I am a Christian and Christians do not dance."

When the *Korea* docked at Kobe, Addie Burke was running a slight fever but was afraid that if she stayed in her cabin, the Japanese medical officers, famous for detaining ships, might think she was ill. A Chinese passenger had died the day before in steerage, and although the ship's doctor said that the death was due to pneumonia, the Japanese medic, alleging that it looked "like suspiciously plague," insisted that all the passengers be taken ashore and immersed in disinfectant while the ship was being fumigated, and that their clothes be treated for germs. Addie Burke returned from the station bathhouse with a high fever. Ten days later, when the *Korea* was finally released from quarantine, she was desperately ill. Burke and the ship's doctor decided to take her off the ship and put her in the hospital in Yokohama. Not knowing how long she would be there, Burke took his children and their baggage as well; he left Ai-ling, who wanted to continue her trip, in the care of another Southern Methodist missionary named Anna Lanius, whom he had alerted to Ai-ling's plight before he disembarked. They arrived in San Francisco on the *Korea,* along with 7,000 tons of cargo, most of which was opium, expected to yield some $250,000 in duty; $2 million in gold that the Japanese, in the midst of the Russo-Japanese War, were sending to the United States for safekeeping; and the famous writer Jack London, who had been covering the war. On that day, Addie Burke died in Yokohama.

When it came time for Ai-ling to return to China and Ching-ling was still at Wesleyan, May-ling was sent to live with the mother of one of Ai-ling's schoolmates so she could attend a regular eighth grade. Going to public school in Piedmont, Georgia, was an eye-opening experience for her, since many of her classmates were grown men and women who had worked for years to earn enough money to attend the higher grades of elementary school. "I suppose my contact with these people as a girl influenced my interest in the lot of those who were not born with a silver spoon in their mouths," Madame Chiang said many years later, "a contact which I may never have experienced otherwise."

In 1913, when Ching-ling graduated from Wesleyan, May-ling transferred to Wellesley College in Massachusetts to be near her brother T.V., who was attending Harvard. Considered "rather plain," she was sixteen years old at the time—short, chubby, round-faced, and childish in appearance, with a short haircut and bangs over her eyes that did nothing for her looks. Although she had to repeat her freshman year, the Soong family was extremely proud that she had been accepted at one of the finest girls' colleges.

At Wellesley, the Chinese teenager amused her professors and classmates with her "Scarlett O'Hara accent," or, as one teacher put it, "she spoke pure Georgia." Certainly, May-ling herself must have been in a state of culture shock when she arrived in the heart of New England from the depths of the old South. "Ah reckon Ah shan't stay aroun' much longer," she informed the freshman dean. But her English teacher, Miss Tuell, was impressed with her. "She wrote more cultured and idiomatic English than most of the girls in her class," the teacher said. "She didn't have to think first in Chinese and then translate, she thought in English. Things came easily to her." In spite of her quick mind, May-ling did not excel in her studies until late in her college career, when she attained the status of Durant Scholar, the college's highest academic distinction.

Perfectionistic and somewhat remote, May-ling started college life wearing navy skirts and middy blouses but grew progressively more Chinese during her four years at Wellesley, wearing traditional Chinese dress when she could and refusing to go out with any but Chinese boys. She kept a large scimitar hanging on the wall of her dormitory room, a weapon so terrifying that one freshman said she could never pass May-ling's door without starting to run. "She formed her own judgments, never accepting those of others," one old friend reminisced. "She was a most independent person, whose life might have gone in any direction." The young Chinese girl may have had her own ideas, but she still came from a country where women were considered inferior to men. When she was given a small part in a school treatment." One of the few southern colleges to remain open during the Civil War, Wesleyan, founded just sixteen years after Macon itself, could not help but mirror the prejudices of an insular, privileged student body. But none of this seems to have daunted Ai-ling. Hardly a pretty girl—short, inclined to be plump—she posed no visible threat to the daughters of respectable Macon families, who pronounced her "charming."

In 1907, when Ai-ling was a junior, the Soongs decided to send Ching-ling to join her at Wesleyan. May-ling announced to her parents that she wanted to go too. When they said she was too young, she reminded them of a promise they had given her during a recent illness, that if she would not fight the treatment, they would grant her anything she wanted. Ten years old at the time, she got her way. Escorted by an aunt and uncle, the two younger Soong girls started their American education with a year at a boarding school in Summit, New Jersey, arriving at Wesleyan in 1908. Ching-ling was old enough to pursue the regular curriculum and take care of herself when they got to the college, but Wesleyan was at a loss to know what to do with her little sister. May-ling was finally assigned to be tutored by the daughter of an English professor, who also took over the role of mothering the child. The ten-year-old apparently needed a lot of steadying. Plump, saucy, and smart, she was known for a certain degree of childish wit. Caught with makeup on her face in an era when cosmetics were a symbol of wickedness, she faced her accuser boldly:

"Why, May-ling, I believe your face is painted!" said one of the older girls.

"Yes," she answered, "China-painted!"

During May-ling's years in Macon, the presidency of Wesleyan passed from Judge Guerry to Dr. W. N. Ainsworth. Ainsworth had a young daughter about May-ling's age, and the two became friends. When May-ling and Eloise Ainsworth had an argument, Mrs. Ainsworth thought it was necessary to lecture May-ling, who became easily enraged, on the evils of fighting and the joys of forgiving:

"Aren't you ashamed," Eloise's mother asked, "to storm around like this?"

"Mrs. Ainsworth," May-ling replied, "I rather enjoy it!"

Queried after World War II, Dr. Ainsworth remembered May-ling "keeping up with everybody's business and a finger in everybody's pie." According to her history professor, she was "a vivacious child with a most un-usual mind." She was also willful. "She was a tempestuous student of music," said one of her teachers. "I do not wish to play this piece," she would announce before tossing it on top of the piano and replacing it with one she liked better.

3

[The] Great Within . . . had its own ways of life and its own standards. The corruption as well as the beauty of the past had crept into the very stones; the air itself was tainted with the virus of decay. This was no place for innocence; heredity and environment were in league against it.

—Bernard Llewellyn

THE DIFFERENCE between May-ling's education and graduation in 1917 and that of her father in 1885 is indicative of the seismic changes that had occurred in their country in the intervening thirty-two years. In 1885, the Chinese lived in a world ruled by an enigmatic figurehead of godlike status. By 1917, at the end of World War I, they were struggling to learn how to rule themselves. To grasp the magnitude of this progression, we should return for a brief summary of life in imperial China, which, in the late nineteenth and early twentieth centuries, was a society in flux, a volcano long dormant, about to erupt.

For some two thousand years, from 221 B.C. to 1912 A.D., the Chinese lived under the same form of government: an empire ruled by a monarch whose dictates were carried out (and frequently originated) by powerful courtiers and officials. It was a far-flung agricultural economy in which the local landlord skimmed the profits off the labor of the peasants, and the role of the tax collector was a ticket to prosperity. Since these two functions were frequently vested in the same person, a man who had to be able to read, write, and keep accounts in a language so difficult that many believe it was purposefully designed that way, only the sons of the rich could afford the education needed to perform the job. Which, according to one authority,* is why we find prosperity exemplified by "a civilized, sophisticated, and lavish court; families of great wealth and culture scattered over the country—and then, in the course of a few years, an appalling collapse into the wildest confusion marked by savage peasant rebellions. Out of these rebellions arose warriors and adventurers who seized power by the sword." Once a victorious warrior came to power, however, he had to establish his dynasty and find

---

* Owen Lattimore, to whom I am indebted for this explanation of the rise and fall of the dynasties.

27

people who could run his government for him. To do this, he needed the services of the educated class, the so-called mandarins. And so the dynastic roller coaster started all over again.

Rote and memorization were the essential elements of the education that produced mandarins. In a mandarin household, private tutors were engaged to teach the children to read Chinese characters, to produce beautiful calligraphy, and to memorize the classics of Chinese literature. From fifteen on, education was only for boys, who learned to write poetry and practiced the special technique required to compose the rigidly constructed "eight-legged" essays included in the national civil examinations required to enter the government bureaucracy. The enormous competitiveness of these examinations can be imagined when we consider that out of the approximately 2 million young men who sat for the first of three degrees, only about three hundred survived the final test. To qualify, the student had to compete first in his village, then in the capital city of his province. When and if he got to Peking, he remained for three days and nights writing essays on subjects selected and graded by famous scholars. There were four grades or degrees, the last three corresponding roughly to the bachelor's, master's, and doctoral degrees in the United States. This system lasted until 1905, when an imperial edict established an educational model patterned after that of the West.

The other group responsible for the perpetuation of the imperial system lived in the court itself, where dishonest attendants were the rule rather than the exception. They were the eunuchs—those desexed grotesques of harem life who had served in Chinese courts since at least 1,300 years before Christ. Dressed in long gray robes with navy coats and black trousers, palace eunuchs were the only outsiders trusted to inhabit what was essentially a female community. (The only other males in the palace were the emperor, the crown prince, and princes under fifteen years of ages.) There were many women for the eunuchs to connive with, watch over, and serve: the empress, the ladies of the court—three wives of the first rank, nine of the second, and twenty-seven of the third, fourth, and fifth ranks—plus the imperial concubines, who, in the nineteenth century, usually numbered somewhere between seventy and a hundred.

Although the original eunuchs had been unfortunate prisoners of war castrated by the victor, a man who underwent this operation in the nineteenth century did so voluntarily in pursuit of a place at court and the attendant riches. To do this, the would-be court attendant presented himself to a specialist, who performed the surgery in a hut just outside the western gate of the Imperial Palace. Seated on a warm, reclining couch and given opium while his sexual organs were washed three times in hot pepper water play, her brother T.V. came from Harvard to discuss it with the faculty member involved before she was allowed to appear on stage. "There always seemed to be some nice Chinese boy or other on the doorstep," said another housemate, who thought that May-ling worried about an arranged marriage being forced on her when she returned to China. According to biographer Laura Tyson Li, there was even a brief engagement to a Chinese boy at Harvard, but whatever plans she had were broken off before she went home.

It was popular in those days for Wellesley girls to keep what they called "confession books," autograph books that they traded back and forth, adding "confessions" to their names. "My one extravagance, clothes," May-ling wrote in hers; ". . . my favorite motto, don't eat candy—not one piece . . . my secret sorrow, being fat." According to Thomas A. DeLong, an heir to the estate of May-ling's best friend at Wellesley, Emma DeLong Mills, May-ling suffered from "occasional" bouts of "childlike vanity," and Emma could always tell when May-ling had been in her room because her hand mirror was not where it belonged.

May-ling and T.V. spent one summer in Burlington, where they attended summer school at the University of Vermont, and another summer on Martha's Vineyard. The story is told that she was visiting a friend's home, a place where it was necessary to take a bike to get the mail. One afternoon, May-ling disappeared and did not come back until close to dinnertime, when she appeared—messy, dirty, and exhausted. When someone asked where she had been, she said that she had thought it was her turn and had gone to get the mail.

"But you never knew how to ride a bicycle," her friend said.

"No, but I do now!" she answered.

MAY-LING OLIVE SOONG graduated from Wellesley as a member of the Class of 1917. She had majored in English and taken classes in American literature, English composition, philosophy, and Bible studies. Although none of her classmates would have predicted that she would become a twentieth-century icon, she had earned considerable respect for her sense of reality. Miss Tuell, the faculty resident in her dormitory, continued to admire May-ling:

> As things came easily to her, it would have been easy for her to lead an indolent life. . . . She always had a great loyalty to China. She recognized the problems before her when she would return, and I think she always was a little torn between two worlds so different. But she never considered not returning to her own country. She kept

up an awful thinking about everything. She was always questioning, asking the nature of ideas, rushing in one day to ask a definition of literature, the next day for a definition of religion. . . . She was a stickler for truth, and resented any discovery that she had ever been fed conventional misinformation . . . there was a fire about her and a genuineness, and always a possibility of interior force.

to numb them, the patient was asked, "will you regret it or not?"* If he showed any indecision, the operation was canceled. Otherwise, the surgeon ordered his attendants to hold down the man's waist and legs while he cut off the organs with a knife. The procedure cost about $84 and took a hundred days to heal. After a year's apprenticeship to a master, the new eunuch was qualified to work in the Imperial Palace. As to his *pao,* or "treasure," it was carefully preserved in a jar of fluid so that the owner could show the severed parts to the chief eunuch when it came time for him to advance in rank. Those who forgot to take home their *pao* or had it stolen while they lay unconscious had to pay as much as $700 to buy or rent someone else's. The *pao* was often sewed back on before burial so that the eunuch might be restored to his former masculinity in the next world.†

It says something about the power of eunuchs that a man was willing to subject himself to this ghastly procedure to gain access to the Imperial Palace. But the emperor, who was known as the Son of Heaven, could not, like the unknowable one he represented, reveal himself to ordinary people. Common citizens were not permitted to enter his sanctum, for they would then discover that he was a mere human being, and it was thought that he might lose control over the country. Hence the importance of the eunuchs—deformed, ill-smelling,‡ and eminently bribable. When sufficiently recompensed for their trouble, eunuchs were used to divert a weak monarch with unimaginable luxuries and erotic delights. If the future emperor was a baby or child, due to ascend the throne provided he survived the murderous schemes of his relatives, he was an open invitation to many and varied forms of corruption.

There were more than two thousand eunuchs in the Imperial Palace during the last half of the nineteenth century. Nicknamed "crows" because of their high voices, they were objects of derision outside the palace and the butt of imperial fury within. The emperor always had within reach a yellow satin bag of birch switches with which to punish them. If a eunuch tried to escape, he was beaten once and then a second time when the scabs from the first beating had started to form. A third attempt was punished with two

---

* If the candidate was a child, his parents answered for him.

† The Chinese feared dying without all of their body parts, which, they believe, would prevent their entering the next world. This is why the Chinese government put the heads of executed traitors or other criminals on posts above the city gates, out of reach of their families.

‡ The operation made it difficult to control urination.

months in the *cangue*, a wooden framework fastened about his neck and hands, used as a portable pillory.

Despite a law that specified decapitation as punishment for stealing, eunuchs were famous for pilfering, and some established homes of their own with the proceeds of their thievery. It is reported that when the last Chinese emperor finally abolished palace eunuchs in 1923, he had all the eunuchs brought together without warning and driven forcibly from the palace. Thereafter, they were permitted to return to collect their belongings, but only one or two at a time. The emperor knew that if he had given them notice, they would have stripped the palace bare.

⚜

ACCORDING TO CONFUCIUS, a good emperor was a benevolent being, a father who guided his people not by force but by example and moral inspiration. Not a pure philosopher and certainly no cleric—"As we do not understand life, how can we understand death?"—Confucius, who lived from 551 to 479 B.C., left his followers precepts in many other areas of life—an ideology for government, an ethic for society, an educational outline for scholars, and general rules of conduct for the family and the nation. Although he taught ethical philosophy and a moral code, his primary concern was the development of a proper method for governing the state.

Unlike Western political philosophies, which usually include civic duties, the Chinese model was "family-minded, and not social-minded." According to Chinese-American philosopher Lin Yutang, writing as late as 1934, "The word 'society' does not exist as an idea in Chinese thought, and in the Confucian social and political philosophy we see a direct transition from the family . . . to the state . . . as successive stages of human organization. . . . 'Public spirit' is a new term, and so is 'civic consciousness' and so is 'social service.' There weren't any such commodities in China."

Based on ancestor worship and filial piety, the Confucian system required everyone, from the Son of Heaven down to the peasant in the rice paddy, to discharge the duties appropriate to his station. There were, he said, only two main social classes in China: officials (including scholars) and all others. This was explained by Mencius (c.372–c.289 B.C.), probably the most famous follower of Confucius: "Without the gentleman there would be no one to rule the common people, and without the common people there would be no one to feed the gentleman." The common people were subdivided into three classes, the most important being farmers, followed by artisans, and, at the bottom, merchants.

Confucius was the greatest influence on Chinese education and political ideology for well over two thousand years, setting a standard that formed the basis of many of the country's laws. He taught that a ruler motivated by wealth and power rather than altruism toward his subjects is no longer able to exercise authority and will eventually lose the "Mandate of Heaven" to rule. Certainly the Manchu Dynasty, the last Chinese ruling house, might well have retained the throne for a longer time had it not been for a fatal combination of weakness and rigidity, which, when confronted by the ambitions of the Western powers, spawned an entirely new and different type of rebellion. As befits the mood of the late nineteenth and twentieth centuries, this upheaval was revolutionary rather than dynastic.

❦

AT THE TIME Charlie Soong returned to China, the Manchu or Ch'ing ("pure") Dynasty, which originated in Manchuria, had been in power for approximately 250 years, during which it had doubled the size and tripled the population of the Empire.* To show their subjection to the Manchus, Chinese men were required to shave the front of their heads and braid the back into long queues like those of Manchurian tribesmen. Some of these queues hung down as far as the bearer's knees.

Like rulers of previous dynasties, Manchu emperors lived in Peking in splendid isolation within the thirty-five-foot-high scarlet walls of the Forbidden City. An enclave of palaces, temples, and pavilions set on terraces with twenty-foot-high double doors, yellow-tiled roofs, and balustrades carved in white marble, it was surrounded by gardens with ancient cypresses, pagodas, statues, and goldfish ponds. Also known as the Great Within, the Forbidden City was situated in the heart of the Imperial City. Nothing in Peking was allowed to be built higher than its walls for fear of offending the *feng shui,* the spirits of wind and water, who, like Chinese emperors, were easily displeased. Imperial edicts were lowered over a particular section of the wall in a gilded box shaped like a phoenix. These edicts were received by government officials who waited below on their knees.

No one was allowed to enter the Forbidden City without permission, and only Manchu officials were privileged to inhabit the Imperial City, which surrounded it. Protected by a moat and a wall wide enough to accommodate a man on horseback, the Imperial City was only a part of what was called the Tartar City, the northern two thirds of Peking; in the Tartar City, the houses were painted gray and other dull colors so as not to outshine the yellows, reds, and purples of the Forbidden and Imperial Cities. The southern third of Peking, which was inhabited by native Chinese during the reign

---

* By adding Tibet, Outer Mongolia, Turkistan, Dzungaria, and Nepal, thus increasing the number of inhabitants from 150 million to 450 million.

of the Manchus, was known as the Chinese City. All of these areas—the Forbidden City, the Imperial City, the Tartar City, the Chinese City, and the entire city of Peking—were, at one time or another, walled enclosures, guarded by the famous Great Wall of China, situated less than one hundred miles to the north. Forty feet high, fifty feet thick, and nearly two thousand miles long, this once-impassable bulwark is said to be the only man-made structure visible today from outer space.

It would never have occurred to a Chinese—whether peasant, mandarin, minister, or prince—to question this sort of physical separation from and intellectual servility to the sovereign. Taught that the emperor ruled by the Mandate of Heaven, his subjects knew that as long as there was harmony in the land, not too many uprisings or natural disasters, this mandate rested securely with the head of state. But when the country degenerated into chaos and rebellion, they believed that their emperor had fallen from Heaven's favor and another would take his place.

❦

IT IS A truism of Chinese history that no matter what dynasty conquered China or where it originated, it was eventually subsumed into the Chinese way of life. This belief in the inevitable assimilation of onetime enemies, along with an intense pride in their ancient culture, gave the Chinese a sense of superiority and an attitude of condescension toward the West. Up until 1898, the Chinese government did not even have a permanent Ministry of Foreign Affairs, since it did not believe in conducting relations with other countries. China, according to its inhabitants, was the Middle Kingdom, the only true civilization. Its emperor ruled from the top of the pyramid of monarchs, while all other monarchs, from the tsar of Russia to the emperor of Japan, were considered his "younger brothers" and were ranged beneath. Outsiders—commonly referred to as "foreign devils," "big-nosed hairy ones,"* or more politely, "barbarians"—were not welcome, and, as history eventually proved, the Chinese were remarkably foresighted in this regard.

Nevertheless, the British East India Company had conducted a lively trade with China during the eighteenth century, exchanging large amounts of silver for luxuries like Chinese silk, tea, and porcelains. Looking for a product to make up the balance of trade, the company began to transport opium from India, making cultivation of the poppy "compulsory" on their Indian lands. People living on the southeastern coast of China, where the

---

* There was an ancient Chinese belief that since the Chinese themselves had little body hair, the hairier the person, the more uncivilized he was bound to be.

drug was imported, soon became addicted, and by the end of the century, opium made up half of all British cargo transported from India. In spite of imperial decrees prohibiting its use, imports continued to grow, spurred by dishonest customs officials and porters willing to carry the drug into the interior for a price. By the 1830s, consumption had reached something like 20,000 chests, or more than 2,500,000 pounds, of opium.*

Up until this time, the Chinese had been able to keep foreign traders under firm control, and any commerce with the outside world was carefully regulated and heavily taxed for the benefit of the imperial court. Merchants had always been regarded as inferiors and their pursuit of profit, ignoble. Those who came to establish trade relations were required to execute three genuflections and nine prostrations before being allowed to approach the emperor, since it was beneath the Son of Heaven's dignity to engage in conversation or diplomacy. Westerners sent to China also looked funny: "They had ugly noses and coarse manners and wore ridiculous clothes with constricting sleeves and trousers, tight collars and coats that had tails down the back but failed to close in front . . . not the garments of reasonable men."

When Lord Napier went to Canton in 1834, empowered by the British Parliament to negotiate "for the purpose of protecting and promoting . . . trade," the governor of Canton refused to even accept a letter from him. "There has never been such a thing as outside barbarians sending a letter," the governor bristled. ". . . It is contrary to everything of dignity and decorum. The barbarians of this nation [Great Britain] . . . have, beyond their trade, not any public business; and the commissioned officers of the Celestial Empire never take cognizance of the trivial affairs of trade. . . . The some hundreds of thousands of commercial duties yearly coming from the said nation concern not the Celestial Empire to the extent of a hair or a feather's down. The possession or absence of them is utterly unworthy of one careful thought."

Brave words, but China soon found itself threatened by bankruptcy due to a huge outflow of silver, as well as the social problems of a nation where one in every ten citizens was said to use opium. Even the appointment of an opium suppression commissioner, who placed offending British merchants under house arrest and burned twenty thousand chests of opium, did not improve the situation. As a matter of fact, it only riled up the culprits, as did a letter sent by the commissioner to Queen Victoria, noting that since importing opium into Britain was illegal, "even less should you let it be passed on to the harm of other countries. . . . Let us ask, 'where is your conscience?' "

---

* This is according to foreign records, as, for obvious reasons, Chinese records no longer went through customs offices.

Prodded by the merchants who were realizing a 60 percent profit on the contraband, the British government registered its objections to the commissioner's actions, claiming that Chinese courts had no jurisdiction over Her Majesty's subjects, that the seizure of their property was illegal, and that China owed the merchants reparations.

When a Chinese man was killed by a group of British soldiers in Hong Kong and the British refused to turn the guilty men over for punishment, Chinese warships set sail for Hong Kong, where the British navy was stationed. The British, who had been looking for an excuse to legalize their presence in China, fired the opening shot in what came to be called the Opium Wars. They bombarded Canton, occupied Hong Kong, invaded the North, and within three years brought China to her knees. The Treaty of Nanking, which ended the First Opium War in 1842, ceded the island of Hong Kong to Britain, required the Chinese to pay $21 million indemnity, and opened the so-called treaty ports of Shanghai, Canton, Amoy, Foochow, and Ningpo to foreign trade. In a treaty port, foreigners could do business under their own laws, and if they committed crimes, they were subject not to Chinese law, which mandated death by decapitation or strangulation for trafficking in opium, but to the friendlier laws of their own countries.

A Second Opium War, started fourteen years later and lasting until 1860, was equally devastating to China. To guarantee ratification of the Treaty of Tientsin, which was to end this war, the British and French anchored warships off the northern Chinese coast, requesting permission to sail inland toward the capital of Peking. The court countered with a proposal that foreign delegations be sent overland, a request the British chose to regard as another provocation. They sent Lord Elgin, the man whose father had conveyed the Elgin marbles from Athens to the British Museum, as their representative to the imperial court and, a few months later, joined the French in attacking the mainland. They also dispatched a small group of representatives to Peking to negotiate safe passage back for Lord Elgin. In the middle of September, word arrived that their men had been ambushed and confined in iron collars and shackles. Furious, Elgin ordered a retaliatory attack on the Chinese capital.

Hearing that the British were on their way, the emperor hastily decamped, leaving his brother Prince Kung in charge, along with twenty eunuchs to guard the priceless treasures of the Dragon Throne. The French, who arrived in Peking first, scattered the eunuchs with a few shots over their heads before entering the Son of Heaven's summer home—60,000 acres of palaces, gardens, goldfish ponds, and tranquil groves dedicated to pleasuring the senses. "The walls, the ceilings, the dressing tables, the chairs, the footstools are all in gold, studded with gems," one French nobleman wrote in his diary. But by the time the British arrived the next day, many of these price-less artifacts had been looted or smashed. "Alas! Such a scene of desolation," said Elgin. "There was not a room I saw in which half the things had not been taken away or broken into pieces."

When word of the destruction reached Prince Kung, he released two of his hostages from their shackles. They immediately headed off to the Sum-mer Palace to join in the looting. Six days later, two more hostages arrived—packed in boxes filled with quicklime. One could be identified only by his boots. At the sight of these men, Elgin, known as the "Big Barbarian," set fire to the Summer Palace.

This precipitate destruction was followed by less impulsive but more economically debilitating retaliation, i.e., the terms enforced by the victori-ous Westerners on the Chinese at the end of the Second Opium War. More treaty ports were opened, and—far more devastating—the importation of opium was legalized. From the denizens of the Imperial Palace to the poor-est of coolies, opium was the preferred method of escape from a society that was ceasing to function both politically and economically. In 1895, an Aus-tralian journalist put it this way: "Edicts are still issued against the use of opium. They are drawn up by Chinese philanthropists over a quiet pipe of opium, signed by opium-smoking officials, whose revenues are derived from the poppy, and posted near fields of poppy by the opium-smoking magis-trates who own them."

If the Chinese were complicit in their own destruction, the English were masters of hypocrisy: "A pipe of opium is to the Chinese workman what a glass of beer is to the English labourer, a climatic necessity," said one British consul. And from Jardine, Matheson & Co., a chief importer of the drug, came this statement: "The use of opium is not a curse but a comfort to the hard-working Chinese; to many scores of thousands it has been productive of healthful sustention and enjoyment." This writer could find only one trader, a Scotsman, who admitted any personal concern in spreading the ad-diction. Sales had been so brisk, the gentleman confided to his diary, that he had had "no time to read my bible."

❦

FROM THE MOMENT Shanghai was designated a treaty port, it became the pre-ferred home of foreign traders. The name "Shanghai" means "up from the sea," which is a fair indication that "as recently as 2,000 years ago," much of Shanghai was still under water. Considered a young city by Chinese stan-dards, it had started as a small fishing village, blossoming into a full-fledged town and commercial port divided into two unequal parts by the waters of the Whangpoo River, In the sixteenth century, residents built a twenty-seven-foot-high wall to protect themselves from Japanese pirates. Within the wall, dark alleys overhung with long poles draped in drying laundry led off both sides of the major roads, while streets where workers in the same trade tended to congregate acquired such names as Pickled Melon Street, Jade Alley, and Jiang Family Medicine Lane. During the seventeenth century, "mud men" were employed to clean out the huge silt deposits that often clogged the river in order to keep it navigable, and by the early eighteenth century, Shanghai had begun to serve overseas as well as domestic trade. After the end of the First Opium War, the city gave 140 acres of muddy shoreline to the British, who employed local coolies to drive piles deep into the swampy muck—underpinnings for their future homes away from home. American traders moved into an area next to the British, while the French took possession of a large piece of land located between the British and the Chinese, and the famous International Settlement was born. Paved avenues, neoclassical mansions surrounded by walls, and large brick industrial buildings known as *hong*s composed the dignified outposts of empire along the famous Bund.

It did not take long for the privileged residents of the International Settlement to learn to overlook the problems of their neighbors living in the Chinese city to the south. Their attitude was exemplified by the laconic words of a reporter for the English weekly paper, the *North-China Herald*, when a secret society called the Small Swords entered the old Chinese walled area of Shanghai in 1853: "The Small Sword Society men attacked the city early this morning. . . . We suspect it will end in the S.S. men taking possession . . . and organizing a government of their own. . . . Foreigners need be under no apprehension." Beyond indifference there was greed, and the foreigners soon discovered they could make fortunes erecting cheap housing that could be rented out to the Chinese rich enough to take refuge from the Small Swords in the International Settlement. In answer to the British consul, who criticized his countrymen's eagerness to profit from the tragedy of their fellow citizens, one taipan* (manager of a trading firm) expressed the point of view of many: "It is my business to make a fortune with the least possible loss of time. In two or three years at farthest, I hope to realize a fortune, and get away; and what can it matter to me, if all Shanghai disappear afterwards. . . . We are money-making practical men. Our business is to make money, as much and as fast as we can."

Money was only part of the recompense for a taipan or griffin, the as-

---

* *Taipan* means "great manager" or "big boss." (Ernest O. Hauser, *Shanghai: City for Sale*, p. 18.)

sistant to a taipan.* The rest was a way of life far more luxurious than anything these men could have afforded back home. "Philistines to the core," as one chronicler describes them, the residents of the International Settlement and the French Concession took advantage of quantities of cheap servants along with inexpensive food and wines to indulge in a modicum of work and a maximum of pleasure. In the afternoons they paraded in the park, conveyed by sedan chairs borne by Chinese bearers dressed in the colors of their consulates or their business firms. Even the poorest among them had a Chinese "boy" to lay out his clothes and keep his liquor cabinet well stocked. For those with families, there were armies of chefs, amahs, gardeners, porters, laundresses, table boys, houseboys, and stable boys. Even in their offices, the taipans and griffins had native managers who allowed their employers plenty of time for long lunches and billiards at the Shanghai Club. These native managers—called compradores—were never allowed to forget their inferior position. A compradore's office was in the basement of the hong, and he was not allowed to use the front door.

Although sports were the foreigners' chief form of amusement—cricket, tennis, riding, and hunting were favorites—it was said that you could always spot a taipan by "his florid complexion and wide girth." No wonder. According to one doctor, "they begin dinner with rich soup and a glass of sherry; then they partake of one or two side dishes, with champagne; then some beef, mutton, or fowls and bacon, with more champagne, or beer; then rice and curry and ham; afterwards game; then pudding, pasty, jelly, custard, or blanc-mange, and more champagne; then cheese and salad, and bread and butter, and a glass of port wine; then in many cases oranges, figs, raisins, and walnuts are eaten with two or three glasses of claret or some other wine; and this awful repast is finished at last with a cup of strong coffee and cigars!"

Shanghai did, however, offer certain inconveniences. As late as 1917, Europeans had to protect themselves with netting from the swarms of mosquitoes bred in the swampy land, and their servants walked around the house spraying the ankles of the family and guests with a kerosene solution. As the city grew and prospered, the canals and ponds were filled and the open municipal drains were sprayed with an oil solution that nearly eliminated the pests.

Since the ratio of European men to European women never fell below ten to one and there were laws prohibiting British griffins from marrying until after they had been in China for five years, many European men took

---

* "Griffin" was actually the name for the semiwild Mongolian horses sent to Shanghai for auction.

Chinese mistresses. This commingling of the races, along with drinking, dancing, and card playing, appalled the only other important group of Westerners in China—the missionaries. Protestant missionaries, who had begun arriving at the beginning of the 1830s, were, by the 1880s, a well-established fact of Chinese life. Called "the biggest evangelical army in Christendom," the missionaries had set themselves the dual task of converting the heathen and criticizing the ungodly ways of their more prosperous countrymen.

It was into this multilayered, bifurcated society that Charlie Soong had been sent by the Southern Methodist Mission. As we have seen, however, the father of the Soong family refused to be satisfied with what one historian called the "abstemious ways and threadbare clothing" of his fellow missionaries.

4

*I have often thought that I am the most clever woman that ever lived, and others can-
not compare with me. . . . Although I have heard much about Queen Victoria . . .
I don't think her life was half so interesting and eventful as mine. . . . She had . . .
really nothing to say about the policy of the country. Now look at me. I have
400,000,000 people dependent on my judgment.*

—THE DOWAGER EMPRESS OF CHINA

THE AVERAGE Westerner stakes his honor on truth, or what he believes to be
the reality lying beneath the surface. Honor for the Chinese, however, re-
sides in appearances or "face"—how matters are perceived by others. On
either scale—actuality or appearance—the West emerged the winner of the
Opium Wars, humiliating the inhabitants of the Middle Kingdom. The unfortunate emperor who ruled China during this period was a young man
named Hsien-feng. Twenty at the time of his accession in 1851, he was well
meaning but lacked conviction, competence, and enough money to deal
with the problems confronting him. He died in Jehol less than a year after
the British entered Peking, a victim of alcohol and other dissipations.

What one chronicler calls Hsien's "most lasting contribution" to the history of China was to father a child with the concubine Cixi (Tz'u-hsi), a descendant of a poor branch of the Manchurian clan that had produced a wife
for the founder of the Ch'ing Dynasty. Cixi was endowed with what must
have been considered an unfeminine amount of curiosity and managed to
teach herself the basics of reading and writing. When she was eighteen, her
father was discharged from his banner* for deserting his post in the face of
marauders, but the captain of the banner still included the names of Cixi
and her sister when assembling a list of possible concubines "to bring the
harem of the young Emperor Hsien-feng up to full strength." Dressed in the
best silks and jewels their families owned or could borrow, Cixi, her sister,
and fifty-eight other girls joined a procession to be carried into the Imperial
City sitting cross-legged on yellow satin sedan chairs, hidden in curtained
conveyances from thousands of curious onlookers. Upon arrival, they were
ushered into the Department of the Imperial Household to be inspected for

---

* A division of the Manchu army.

defects and diseases by the staff of the emperor's stepmother, who checked under their makeup for signs of smallpox and goiter, common ailments of the day. Cixi was then told to lie on a couch so that a midwife could examine her for virginity and *yin*, her ability to arouse sexually and be aroused. This, it was believed, could be told by looking at her hair, eyes, breasts, and vagina. It was the test most feared by the candidates. The story—possibly apocryphal—is told that Cixi went into the room wearing a pair of valuable jade bracelets. "When her turn came . . . she went into a theatrical tantrum and indignantly refused to be pawed over. As she did . . . she deftly slipped off the costly bracelets, and unseen by the eunuchs, dropped them into the eagerly waiting hand of the midwife. The elder nodded her head; and [Cixi] was able to stand in line with the other selected maidens." True or not, the story is indicative of the corruption that pervaded the Imperial Palace.

Selected as one of twenty-eight concubines out of the sixty candidates brought to the palace, Cixi was assigned the position of concubine of the fifth (lowest) rank. This did not mean that she would necessarily ever even meet the emperor. Once accepted into his household, however, she would be forced to remain in the Forbidden City for the rest of her life, whether or not she was ever called to the emperor's bed. Meanwhile, as one writer put it, she "tried, just as keenly as any pretty shop-girl in a Los Angeles drugstore, to attract the attention of the man who could make her a star." Even if selected, she would be put there only to arouse him in preparation for the appearance of a consort or concubine of higher rank. Nevertheless, for the rest of her life she would live in an apartment of her own, where she would be waited on by two eunuchs and two maidservants and supplied with court robes, shoes, and jewels. As payment for his daughter, Cixi's worthless father received one or two horses with elegant saddles and bridles, gold, silver, silks, and a tea set.

It took a long time for Hsien-feng to notice Cixi. Meanwhile, she took advantage of her new surroundings by improving her calligraphy and studying the classics, the history of the Ch'ing Dynasty, and the objets d'art in the palace. Her interest and perception did not go unnoticed, and within three years, she was raised in rank to imperial concubine, a grade that carried with it the right to be addressed as "Lady" and to be served by twice the number of maids and eunuchs. That same year, the chief eunuch turned over the jade tablet on which the emperor wrote his choice of companion for the night and read her name. As tradition dictated, the eunuch went to her apartment to inform her of the honor, undressed her, wrapped her in scarlet, and carried her on his back to Hsien-feng's bed, where he laid her naked. Tradition also required that she crawl on her hands and knees from the foot of the bed to the emperor, who waited behind crepe curtains on three yellow brocade mattresses covered by silk sheets and a yellow satin coverlet. In spite of the fact that the entire procedure was observed by eunuchs posted around the room, their coupling was successful. Too successful. According to the rules of the imperial court, the emperor was supposed to ejaculate only seven times a year—three times in the spring, twice each in summer and fall—and on those days only an important concubine, a consort, or the empress was allowed to share his bed. Nevertheless, at dawn the chief eunuch recorded the date of sexual relations and carried Cixi, just impregnated by the emperor's seed, back to her apartment. Nine months later, she gave birth to a son—the emperor's first male child—and was raised to concubine, second rank.

Cixi soon gained extraordinary influence over Hsien-feng, whose problems with a depleted treasury and ongoing incursions from the West had seemingly overwhelmed him. During the five years following the birth of her son, she became a major figure in the court, eventually convincing Hsien-feng to name their son, age six at the time of his father's death, as his successor. After Hsien-feng's death, Cixi allied herself with his nondescript widowed empress, who had no sons, and Prince Kong, Hsien-feng's energetic younger brother, who convinced his other brothers to name Cixi and the emperor's widow coregents and himself prince adviser to the empresses. (As women, they had to hide themselves behind a yellow curtain in back of the miniature Dragon Throne built for the child emperor, although strategically placed mirrors allowed them to see everything taking place in front of the curtain.) The widowed empress, who could not read or write, was content to let others manage affairs of state, but Cixi kept a hand in everything concerning the court and the empire. To exhibit her newfound status, she wore yellow satin robes, an elaborate headdress, triple jadeite earrings, a 108-bead court necklace, and "a transparent cape of 3,500 pearls the size of canary bird eggs," from which were hung forty drops of imperial green jade. She is said to have floated a foreign loan for "naval construction," which she used to build a fabulous pleasure boat in her lily pond, and had a private theater built over the water "to soften the voices of the actors."

If Cixi was concerned with the luxurious trappings of her status, Prince Kong was a born reformer. Under his influence, a Ministry of Foreign Affairs and an Institute for Foreign Languages were established. Westerners were given the job of collecting customs duties for the Imperial Maritime Customs Service, thus avoiding the traditional "squeeze" (skimming off the top) by the collectors. The new service was run by an extraordinary Englishman, Robert Hart, called "the most influential Westerner in China" and known by both Prince Kong and Cixi as "Our Hart."

Prince Kong also believed that it was wiser to cooperate with the Westerners, seemingly an immovable force, than to fight them. He advocated strengthening the Chinese army and arranged for the international community to help him subdue the Taiping Rebellion, a fourteen-year-long revolt against the Manchus in the middle of the nineteenth century that eventually cost 20 million people their lives. Led by a village schoolteacher who believed he was Jesus's younger brother and a coal worker who conceived the idea of digging tunnels to undermine the walls of cities they wanted to conquer, the Taipings attracted hundreds of thousands of adherents, who helped them butcher their enemies—Manchus, opium addicts, and prostitutes. They were eventually suppressed by a combination of two fighting forces—one Chinese and the other, known as the Ever-Victorious Army, sponsored and financed by the West and led by the well-known Charles G. "Chinese" Gordon.

While Prince Kong dealt with the outside world, Cixi faced problems within the court. Her son* reacted against his mother's domination by turning to the palace servants, who were only too happy to indulge his tastes for rampant luxury and homosexuality. Said to be "always fooling around with eunuchs," he was married off at sixteen but died three years later of syphilis, smallpox, or regicide. When his pregnant empress committed suicide by swallowing gold dust two months after his death, palace gossip pointed to Cixi. These suspicions were increased when that lady, now known as the dowager empress, designated her four-year-old nephew, the son of her sister and Hsien-feng's brother, heir to the throne. This child, who took the name Kuang-hsu (Guangxu) when he became emperor, lived from 1871 to 1908. A slight boy with large, sad eyes and a chronic lung condition, he was intelligent, well educated, and, like Prince Kong, aware of China's need for reform and modernization.

As can be seen, it had taken quite a few years for the accumulating forces of history to gather sufficient momentum to overtake China. During the middle and later years of the nineteenth century, the Manchus were temporarily bolstered by their defeat of the Taipings, but as the century drew to a close, a conflict with Japan over Korea escalated into a war, which was won by the Japanese in 1895. Previously in a tributary relationship with China, Korea was given autonomy after the war, and China was forced to sign a treaty in which it gave up Taiwan, the Pescadore Islands, part of Manchuria, and four treaty ports to Japan. Along with these territorial losses, there was general unease in the countryside, based on the harsh living conditions of the peasants as compared with the privileges of the foreigners, both traders

---

* T'ung-chih (1856–1875).

and missionaries. These and other issues helped to bring on another rebellion, started by the Boxers in 1898.

The Boxers, or Righteous and Harmonious Fists* began as a mystical, antidynastic society, but rallied behind the dowager empress when she welcomed them as a ready-made army to rid China of the hated foreigners and a ready-made cause to divert public discontent from the court. The Boxers, who attacked both Chinese and foreign Christians, also declared war on the treaty powers in June 1900, killing two hundred Americans and Europeans and laying siege to the legation quarter in Peking, where nearly five hundred foreigners and three thousand Chinese Christians had taken sanctuary. Two months later, a long-awaited international force descended on China, looting and killing everything and everyone in its path and routing the Boxers. The imperial court, having bet on the wrong side, was forced to flee the capital.

After their victory, the treaty powers imposed even harsher terms on the Chinese than they had after the Opium Wars: an indemnity of 200 million ounces of silver, punishment of the officials who had supported the Boxers, and the right to billet troops between Peking and the sea. Russia used the opportunity to occupy Manchuria, building a naval base at Port Arthur, where it remained until its defeat by Japan in the Russo-Japanese War of 1904–1905, while Britain, France, and Germany established naval bases elsewhere. The victorious treaty powers also demanded long-term leases of Chinese territory to develop mines and railways and arranged to loan the Chinese money to build the railroads at enormous rates of interest. In September of 1898, the American secretary of state, John Hay, sent notes to Britain, France, and Russia, recommending that each nation refrain from interfering with the other nations' "spheres of influence" and avoid levying excessive tariffs on the others' goods. Known as the Open-Door Policy, it kept peace among thieves under the guise of protecting China. These and other degradations of the dynasty forced the Manchu court to take stock of itself and embark on a period of reform and reorganization, called "self-strengthening," aimed at improving both function and image.

Two types of Chinese reformers had already appeared on the scene by the end of the nineteenth century. First, there were those who wanted to return China to its original glory by helping the Manchus rebuild their defeated army and regenerate national life morally and economically. The most famous example of this type of reformer was Kang You-wei, the oldest surviving son in a well-to-do family, who grew up believing that he "stood, towering and lofty, above the common people" and that he had been en-

---

* Their physical training reminded observers of the art of boxing.

dowed by Heaven "with the intelligence and ability to save them." He drafted a long "memorial"—a written document in which citizens were allowed to recommend policy changes to the emperor or an appropriate surrogate—which he sent to the twenty-eight-year-old Emperor Guangxu and the sixty-year-old dowager empress, advocating reform in six areas of national life: taxes on the rich, a countrywide network of railroads, Western-style mechanization of industry, domestic exploitation of mineral resources, unification and stabilization of currency, and a national postal system.

The emperor was impressed by Kang's memorial. But Kang ran into trouble with the emperor's aunt, the dowager empress. As a young woman, she had been embarrassed by her father's cowardice, and, once having won a place at court, had thrown herself into upholding tradition and orthodoxy as exemplified by her new (imperial) family. Now old—a "painted, brocaded despot amid her eunuchs"—she had become an archconservative. As soon as the emperor began to promulgate reforms based on Kang's suggestions, she sent troops to Peking to arrest Guangxu. Confined to an island on the grounds of the palace, "relegated to the nothingness of harem life," Guangxu and his progressive ideas were suppressed. Warned of the clampdown by friends, Kang fled. In his place, the soldiers took his younger brother along with four other young reformers and beheaded them for treason.*

The next reformer to come on the scene, however, was not so easy to silence. Sun Yat-sen, who would one day be known as the Father of China, unseated the Manchus and changed the Chinese Empire into a republic, and he did this with the help of Charlie Soong.

---

* According to one author, they were "barbarously executed by being cut in half at the waist." (Israel Epstein, *From Opium War to Liberation*, p. 36.)

PART TWO

❧

1894–1927

5

China cannot borrow our learning, our science, and our material forms of industry without importing with them the virus of political rebellion.

— THE NEW YORK TIMES, 1881

AT THE age of twelve, Sun Yat-sen, who had been born into a poor family, was sent to a prosperous older brother who lived in Hawaii. Enrolled in the very British Bishop's School, obliged to speak English, and required to attend daily prayers, the boy was subjected to "every reasonable persuasion" to convert to Christianity. When he announced at the age of sixteen that he wanted to be baptized, his brother sent him back to China.

After being ousted from his village for breaking wooden idols in the temple, Sun went to Hong Kong, where he managed to get himself baptized and studied at the Diocesan School of the Church of England. He attended Queen's College for two years, during which his family married him off to a village girl, possibly to counteract the ill effects of his professed Christianity. She moved into his family's home, but since Sun continued his studies for eight years more, they rarely saw each other. In 1886, his older brother summoned him back to Hawaii and tried to force him to give up Christianity. Sun refused. Stranded and penniless, he finally raised enough money from fellow Christians to return to China. Coincidentally, it was the same year that Charlie Soong arrived in Shanghai, but while Charlie was struggling with missionary prejudice, Sun got the chance that Charlie had longed for— to study medicine—and he graduated from the new College of Medicine for Chinese in Hong Kong in 1892. From there he went to Macao to practice surgery. James Cantlie, the English doctor who established the College of Medicine, said that Sun "performed important operations, requiring skill, coolness of judgement, and dexterity." But due to the enforcement of a law requiring medical practitioners to hold Portuguese diplomas, he did not stay long in Macao.

In 1894, Sun returned to Canton, where he became involved in the reform movement and was introduced by an old friend, Lu Hao-dong, to Charlie Soong. Sun told Charlie that he was writing a memorial that he intended to send to the grand secretary to the emperor, a patron of the College of Medicine. He showed Charlie the memorial, in which he spelled out his qualifications for joining the bureaucracy: his degree in English medicine, his studies abroad, his interest in laws "for reforming the people," and his belief in Western "methods of achieving a prosperous country and a powerful army."

"What China needs is a man like George Washington or Abraham Lincoln, not written memorials," Charlie told Sun.

"You're right," Sun answered. "But who could be the Washington or Lincoln of China?" "You," Charlie answered. Educated by the British, Sun knew little more than the name of Abraham Lincoln until Charlie recited for him the end of the Gettysburg Address: "government of the people, by the people, and for the people." Before the evening was over, Charlie had invited Sun to visit his publishing house, where Sun discovered that his own book, *The Uses of Agriculture*, was being printed. "I wrote this book!" he told Charlie.

"But I thought it was an article from a book by Cheng Kuan-ying.* How could you have written it?"

"I wrote it," Sun repeated, going through the pages one sentence at a time. "There are some changes, but it has been edited for the better," he said, explaining that he had shown the article to Zheng and that Zheng had revised it and included it in his book.

"Zheng should have given you credit," Charlie said.

"I don't mind," said Sun, who was clearly happy to see his article in print.

"In that case, why don't you show Zheng the memorial you're planning on sending to Li? Maybe he can give you some good ideas."

The next day, on their way to see Zheng, Sun and Charlie ran into Wang Tao, a well-known journalist and Western scholar. Charlie introduced Sun to Wang, who looked at his article and agreed to edit it. Charlie disagreed with Sun's contention that agriculture and commerce could revitalize China. Only industry and the development of machinery, Charlie contended, would modernize their country. His arguments convinced Sun, who added the importance of these areas of growth to his memorial. But after Wang returned the edited version, Sun tore it in two. "It's no use," he said, contemplating the effect of his recommendations on the powers in Peking. "It would be like asking a tiger to give away his hide."†

---

* Referred to as Zheng Guanying (Cheng Kuan-ying) in the original. He was a Cantonese compradore and reformer.

† I.e., it would be futile to ask the mandarins to stop skimming profits off the peasants' land.

5

🙼

Charlie encouraged Sun to submit it anyway, and Sun agreed to try. But the doctor's timing proved to be unfortunate. The emperor's secretary was too involved with the deteriorating situation between China and Japan* to pay attention to the memorial. In any case, Sun told Charlie, "Reform can't start until the Ch'ing Dynasty is overthrown. There's no reason to support the Manchus, only to overthrow them." Charlie cautioned Sun against premature revolution. He claimed that only the Western powers could determine the outcome of an uprising, particularly in Shanghai, and suggested that Sun go west to determine what position they would take.

"Just give me 100 people and I'll go after the yamen† now," Sun responded.

In spite of such blatant impracticality, Charlie admired his friend's courage. He took a sword off the wall of his home, which he had meant to give one of his children, and offered it to Sun.

"I'll be back to accept this sword when I overthrow the Ch'ing Dynasty," Sun responded.

"I'll support you," Charlie promised. ". . . I'm a minister and can't fight as a soldier, but I'll support you behind the lines. You will need enormous sums of money. Let me raise that money for you."

At Charlie's instigation, the three of them—Charlie Soong, Sun Yat-sen, and Lu Hao-dong—took an oath on the Bible to drive out the Manchus, establish a republican government, and revitalize China. From then on, Charlie Soong's publishing house served as a meeting place for revolutionaries. Although they gave their group a name, the "Revive China Society," they decided not to set up an organization until they numbered more than ten.

Over the next few months, Charlie Soong and Sun Yat-sen became extremely close friends, and Charlie began publishing revolutionary material for Sun in his publishing house, safely located in the international section of Shanghai, outside the jurisdiction of the Ch'ing police. Sun also became an intimate of the Soong family, spending most of his time at their home when he was in Shanghai. The two men certainly had a great deal in common. Born within a year or so of each other, both were poor boys who had left China at a young age. Converted to Christianity, they had served or wanted to serve in the ministry. Both had been educated at least partly in the West and spoke fluent English. And they were both keenly aware that China was no longer the center of the world, that unless it did something to bring

---

* The Sino-Japanese War had broken out in August 1894.

† *Yamen:* provincial governor's office and residence.

itself up to date, the Celestial Empire was at risk of being dismembered by other nations. Both Sun Yat-sen and Charlie Soong were convinced that the ruling Manchus had failed the Chinese and lost the Mandate of Heaven.

At the end of 1894, Sun returned to Hawaii, where he tried to enroll people in the Revive China Society, but his efforts yielded minimal results. In six months he was able to attract only 120 members at an initiation fee of $5.00 each and raised a mere $700 more by selling "revolutionary bonds," to be redeemed when the Manchus were no longer in power. As China expert Jonathan Spence put it, $1,300 "seems an absurdly tiny base from which to launch a rebellion." While in Hawaii, however, Sun received a letter from Charlie, telling him that China was losing the war against Japan and that things were going very badly for the Manchus. The time, according to Soong, was ripe for revolution, and Sun should come home at once. On the strength of Charlie's letter, Sun headed back to China.

The first attempt that Sun and his fellow rebels made at overthrowing the Manchus was in the city of Canton, where they opened an office in the guise of an agricultural association, while secretly purchasing pistols, rifles, and dynamite in Hong Kong. Unfortunately, one of the arms shipments was discovered at customs, and their headquarters were raided. More than seventy men were arrested, and three were executed. Execution for rebels was not always a quick beheading; the Chinese, who made an art out of torture, had developed several long, carefully drawn-out ways of killing, one of which involved fastening the victim to a cross and peeling off strips of his skin. He was left hanging there until death released him.

Sun managed to escape this ghastly fate. With the government offering a reward of 10,000 taels* for his capture, he fled to Kobe, Japan. Fortunately for Charlie, his name was not connected by the police with the uprising. But from then on, he lived with the knowledge that he and his family might have to leave Shanghai at a moment's notice.

In Kobe, Sun cut off his queue, let the hair on his head grow, cultivated a mustache, and bought a Japanese suit. But since the Manchu government was known for punishing not only criminals but their families, Sun's widowed mother, his wife, and their three young children fled to Hawaii. Sun followed them there and prepared to assume the life of a traveling revolutionary in disguise. Before he left Honolulu, however, he ran into an old friend.

"The vehicle in which I was driving was stopped by a man, apparently a Japanese, looking very trim in European dress and with a moustache of respectable dimensions, who proffered his hand, raised his hat, and smiled

---

* 1,000 silver dollars.

affably," wrote James Cantlie, ". . . and it was some time before we recognized it was Sun minus his cue [queue] and Chinese dress. A cordial greeting ensued and a visit to us in London was arranged."

Sun traveled to Europe via the United States. Starting in San Francisco, he enjoyed what he called "a sort of triumphal journey through America"— a triumph mitigated by reports that the Chinese minister in Washington was trying to have him kidnapped and returned to China. "I well knew the fate that would befall me—" he said, "first having my ankles crushed in a vice and broken by a hammer, my eyelids cut off, and finally, be chopped to small fragments, so that none could claim my mortal remains. For the old Chinese code does not err on the side of mercy to political agitators."

In September of 1896, Sun sailed for England, where he spent most of his time in the library of Dr. Cantlie's London home reading books on politics, diplomacy, and military matters. The Cantlie house was on Portland Place, as was the Chinese Legation. The Chinese government had asked the British to extradite Sun as a political criminal, but the British, having no extradition treaty with China, had refused. One Sunday morning on his way to church, Sun was stopped by a Chinese gentleman who started a conversation with him and led him into the Chinese Legation. He was cordially welcomed and shown around, but on the third floor a door was closed and locked behind him. He was told that he would be detained until the legation received money from Peking to send him back to China. Meanwhile, he was kept prisoner on the third floor.

"While I was in the Chinese Legation in London, I prayed constantly," he wrote a friend. "For six or seven days I prayed without ceasing." At the end of the seventh day, Sun convinced one of the legation's English servants that the emperor of China wanted to kill him because he was a Christian "striving to secure good government for China." That day he managed to get a note addressed to Dr. Cantlie to the servant, who gave it to his wife, who herself wrote a letter. At 11:30 that evening, the doorbell rang at Dr. Cantlie's house. When he answered, there was no one there, but a note had been pushed under the door: "There is a friend of yours imprisoned in the Chinese Legation here since last Sunday; they intend sending him out to China. . . . It is very sad for the poor young man, and unless something is done at once he will be taken away and no one will know it. I dare not sign my name, but this is the truth, so believe what I say. Whatever you do must be done at once, or it will be too late."

The doctor went to the head of the local police and from there to Scotland Yard. "Scotland Yard said it was none of their business, and that I had done my duty when I reported the matter to them, and that I ought to go home and keep quiet. . . . It was not until I got in touch with a member of the clerical staff at the Foreign Office . . . that the matter was taken up and dealt with." Even then, the "matter" bogged down in government red tape. Only when a reporter from *The Globe* got wind of the story and interviewed Cantlie did the Chinese admit that they were holding Sun prisoner. By that time, Sun's case had also progressed through channels to the prime minister, who said that the legation had infringed upon British law. The following Friday, Sun was turned over to men from the Foreign Office and moved in with the Cantlies. The day after his release, the money for shipping him home arrived at the Chinese Legation.

The publicity surrounding Sun's kidnapping gave him wide name recognition in the English-speaking world, as did the substantial price on his head. But he himself spent the next two years wandering around Europe with little money, passing his days in great libraries, studying the books of famous revolutionaries. It was during this time, we are told, that he formulated his Three Principles of the People Doctrine, which established the foundation for his future thinking and writing. Basing his work on the words of Lincoln that Charlie Soong had quoted to him, the former doctor evolved his tripartite doctrine of Nationalism ("government of the people"), Democracy ("by the people"), and Socialism ("for the people"). Unlike previous would-be revolutionaries, he tried to explain these principles in words simple enough for any Chinese to understand. Called by one author "the most famous formula in modern China," Sun's Three Principles—national union, political power, and economic entitlement—would be achieved in a three-stage Chinese revolution: first, military conquest; second, political tutelage in self-government; and third, constitutional government.

In the spring of 1898, Sun returned to Shanghai, where he lived in the Soong house, disguised by his beard and Western suit. Recognized by a group of revolutionaries at a meeting one day, he immediately left for Japan, where the law protected him from extradition. "The five years between 1895 and 1900," he later wrote, "constituted the most difficult period of my entire revolutionary career." After an aborted second attempt at revolution in 1900, however, Sun began to notice a change in the attitude of the Chinese: "After my first failure, the entire country regarded me either as a bandit or as a rebel. . . . After the failure in 1900, not only the people stopped cursing me, but the progressive elements expressed sympathy with me. . . . The prestige of the Manchu government was altogether lost, and the poverty of the country had increased. As the sense of patriotism was gradually aroused throughout the country, the revolutionary movement in China became more and more popular."

There were actually ten failed attempts at revolution. Sun took part personally in some of these uprisings, but as the Chinese government convinced other Asian nations to banish him, he spent more and more time traveling in Europe and the United States, gathering overseas Chinese adherents to his cause and raising money for arms. On these trips he carried a minimum of luggage and lived in fourth-rate hotels. When a reporter offered to walk him home one night, citing the £100,000 price on his head, he refused: "If they had killed me some years ago," he said, "it would have been a pity for the cause; I was indispensable then. Now my life does not matter. . . . There are plenty of Chinamen to take my place."

In 1905, another coup, this one in the province of Hunan, failed, and its two leaders fled to Japan. Sun met them there, and the three agreed to call a joint meeting of dissident Chinese in Tokyo, the refuge of choice for revolutionaries on the run from the Manchus. Out of the meeting came a new organization, called the Revolutionary Alliance, with Sun Yat-sen as president. "As soon as the Revolutionary Alliance was formed, in which the best of the younger generation of China was represented," Sun wrote, "I realized that the success of the great revolutionary work might come in my lifetime. . . . In less than a year after the Revolutionary Alliance was formed, its membership had increased to over ten thousand and its branches were established in all provinces. Henceforth the progress of the revolutionary movement was so rapid that it was beyond anyone's expectations."

It is one of the ironies of history that when the revolution against the Manchus finally succeeded—on the eleventh try—Sun Yat-sen was not in China but in Denver, Colorado, in the middle of his third overseas tour in search of money. One morning he woke up to astonishing headlines: "Wuchang* occupied by revolutionists." The body of the story explained that a group of Chinese army officers had been planning a rebellion when one of their homemade bombs accidentally detonated, bringing the police to their headquarters. With their barracks surrounded and the city gates closed to prevent their escape, soldiers from the artillery and engineering corps, who were secretly friendly to the rebels, mutinied and burned the yamen of the governor-general. He fled, and by the next day, four battalions of renegade soldiers had taken control of the city. With Sun out of the country, they decided to ask Colonel Li Yuan-hung of the Chinese army to act as their temporary leader. After being pulled out from under a bed where he had hidden, assuming the soldiers had come to his house to kill him, Li issued a proclamation announcing the overthrow of the Ch'ing Dynasty, and on October 12, 1911, the revolutionaries put a republican government into place. Their astonishing success was followed by the secession of one province after another—thirteen within the first month—declaring themselves no longer subjects of the Manchus.

---

* Wuchang is in the province of Hupei in central China.

❦

FROM COLORADO, Sun headed to the East Coast, traveling in his usual low-key manner, avoiding publicity. Passing through Saint Louis, he saw another newspaper, which said that the revolution had broken out under his orders and, if it was successful, he would be the first president of the republic. Realizing the importance of foreign support for the infant Chinese Republic, he headed for Washington to see the secretary of state. The secretary refused to see him. When he got to London, he received an official invitation* to return to China to assume the presidency of the republic. "Yes," he said, "for the time being, if no-one else can be found better in the meantime." As in the United States, however, he was unsuccessful in interesting the British government in providing financial support for his cause. In Marseilles he boarded a boat bound for China, having by now, according to one report, been around the world three times.

When Sun reached Singapore on Christmas Eve 1911, there was a crowd gathered to welcome him, and for the first time in sixteen years, he did not have to assume an alias to land in Hong Kong. One week later, on New Year's Day 1912, he was inaugurated president at Nanking. Charlie Soong was there with daughter Ching-ling to congratulate him and hear him issue a proclamation announcing the new Chinese Republic. Meanwhile, however, the government in Peking continued to function as it had before the revolution, and a new National Assembly, created six years earlier by imperial edict, had named Yuan Shih-kai, a military leader and one of the most ambitious men in the imperial government, China's premier.

It was clear that the North and South were locked in stalemate. The North did not want Sun Yat-sen as its president. Not only was he from the South, but his revolutionary credentials sat poorly with the monarchists remaining in Peking, and he had no practical experience in governing. It looked as if China could be headed for civil war until on January 15, two weeks after he had taken office, Sun wired Yuan to offer him the presidency. His offer was dependent on three conditions: abdication of the child emperor; Yuan's agreement to break with the Manchus; and Yuan's acceptance of the republic.

A month later, Sun tendered his resignation as president in favor of Yuan, whom he called "a good and talented man" and "a most loyal servant of the State," going so far as to assert that the "abdication of the . . . Emperor and the union of the North and South" were "largely due" to Yuan's efforts. On

---

* In one of the nicer ironies of history, the wire was misdelivered to the Chinese Legation, the same place where Sun had been held prisoner.

February 14, 1913, Yuan was elected president of the fledgling Chinese Republic. The next day, in accordance with an old rite of ancestral worship—the practice of informing the dead about current events—Sun led a procession to the Ming Tombs outside Nanking, where he formally addressed the founder of the Ming Dynasty (1368–1644), castigating the Manchus* in lively prose and informing the former emperor of the success of the revolution.

It was not until six weeks later, however, that Sun was actually able to turn the presidency over to Yuan. The delay was caused by a disagreement over the seat of government. Yuan wanted to remain in Peking; the revolutionaries pressed him to move to Nanking, the seat of their government. After a major riot in Peking, which some people suspected was instigated by Yuan to prove that he was needed in the North, the southerners gave in and the capital was located in Peking.

Sun himself, however, remained a figure of reverence throughout China. Wherever he went, he was treated with enormous affection and asked to address the large crowds gathered in his honor. An effective orator, he could keep an audience enthralled for as long as three and four hours. The high point of his popularity came in August 1913, when he visited Peking at the invitation of Yuan. Housed like an honored guest of state, Sun spent many hours in conference with Yuan, whom he had never before met. Yuan not only treated Sun well but appeared to agree with all of the little doctor's republican ideas and ideals, so much so that Sun emerged from their conferences pledging "to devote my best and every effort to aid him in the great and noble work he has undertaken."

Sun's rosy outlook was at least partially colored by the fact that during their time together, President Yuan had given him carte blanche to pursue a $3 billion, ten-year plan that Sun had devised to construct 75,000 miles of railways around the country. Yuan appointed Sun director for construction of all railways in China and gave him a monthly stipend of 30,000 Chinese dollars, along with a train with sleeping cars, two dining cars, and the dowager empress's reception car with its gold-embroidered blue velvet rug and yellow silk curtains.† One is tempted to think that Yuan, who was having problems creating a workable constitutional government out of the detritus of some two thousand years of monarchy, figured that this was a good way to keep the figurehead of republicanism happy, occupied, and out of his way.

This sort of reasoning would never have occurred to Sun, who headed

---

* The Manchus had gained the throne by overthrowing the Ming Dynasty.

† 3 billion Chinese = $3.04 billion U.S. in 1913 ($68.1 billion today); $30,000 Chinese = $30,416 U.S. in 1913 ($682,150 today).

for northern China with a large group of aides, both male and female, and camp followers. Among these was May-ling's eldest sister, Ai-ling, who had graduated from Wesleyan in 1909 at the age of twenty-one and was serving as Sun's private secretary. She was not the only member of the Soong family on Sun's railway committee. At Sun's insistence, her father had been made treasurer of the railway development group. Up until this time, Sun's relationship with Charlie and his family had always been hidden from the public; now, for the first time, the Soongs were openly identified with the famous revolutionary.

Oddly enough, it was just about this time of public association that their private relationship nearly ended. The first person to perceive the danger was an Australian journalist, William Henry Donald, a China expert who had been traveling with Sun and advising him. Many years later, Donald confided to another friend that he could never write his memoirs because he would "have to debunk Sun Yat-sen. Sun was not only an impractical visionary," Donald said, "but the worst of it was that the old boy could not keep his hands off women." One day on the train, Donald and Sun were in consultation. As usual, Ai-ling was there taking notes. As soon as she left, Sun informed Donald that he wanted to marry her.

"Ai-ling's Charlie Soong's daughter," Donald said. "Charlie has been your best friend. Without him, you'd have been in the soup many a time. And as for Ai-ling and the rest of the children, you've been their uncle. They've been almost like your children."

"I know it, I know it," Sun replied. "But I want to marry her just the same." He asked Donald to accompany him to the Soong home that evening, where he planned to discuss the marriage with Charlie. Charlie reacted, as predicted by Donald, with fury, when Sun told Charlie what he wanted.

> The color drained from his [Charlie's] cheeks, and he looked haggardly at the man by whose side he had stood for nearly twenty years. After a while, he said:
>
> "Yat-sen, I am a Christian man. All the time, I thought you were, too. I did not bring up my children to live in the sort of looseness you propose.* I will not accustom myself to people who trifle with marriage. We are a Christian family and, Lord willing, we will go on that way. I want you to go, and I never want you to come back. My door is closed to you forever."

That was, however, not the end of Sun's attempt to marry one of the daughters of Charlie Soong.

---

* Sun was, of course, already married to his village wife and the father of three children.

6

For the Chinese it is not only honourable, but also admirable for a girl to worship the hero of a great cause and to want to marry him.

—JUNG CHANG

IF SUN Yat-sen's uncommon ability to believe what he wanted to believe had enabled him to pursue his revolution to the brink of success, it is obvious that it often blinded him in both personal and political relationships. This was nowhere more clear than in his dealings with his successor as president of the new Chinese Republic, Yuan Shih-kai.

Fifty-two years old when he became president, Yuan had started his life in the military, modernizing and building up the North China Army before entering the civil administration. There, his "upward mobility," which China scholar John Fairbank termed "phenomenal," had propelled him into a number of important posts before he was ousted by the Manchus. Known as a can-do operator with a knack for organization, Yuan was always "the shortest man in any group." He was also overweight and preferred the comfort of Western shirts to mandarin collars, which cut into his fat little neck. A wily gentleman of the mandarin class, he was a skillful manipulator of situations and men.

But even an experienced leader like Yuan could not change the Chinese political psyche overnight. In spite of the success of the revolution, there remained a wide gulf between the upper class and the peasants. The former—educated, wealthy, used to centuries of privilege—expected to run the country while the latter farmed the land, hauled heavy equipment, and carried their betters around in sedan chairs. The highest goal of a civilized Chinese society was then—and still is—not compromise worked out through differing points of view representing divergent interests but harmony achieved through unquestioning acceptance of authority. The so-called loyal opposition that existed in Western parliamentary systems was, to the Chinese mind—and to Yuan—a contradiction in terms.*

One of the people determined to change this was a young follower of

---

* See John Fairbank for an explanation of "several stumbling blocks inherited from imperial Confucianism" (*The Great Chinese Revolution*, p. 171).

57

Sun Yat-sen named Sung Chiao-jen. Having drafted the first constitution for the republic, Sung set himself the task of making multiparty parliamentary government into a reality, organizing a merger between Sun's Revolutionary Alliance and four small political factions to form the famous (some would say infamous) Kuomintang (KMT), the Nationalist Party of China. In elections held in February of 1913, the KMT had roundly defeated the other parties, winning a majority of seats in the National Assembly. This, of course, meant that the prime minister would be chosen from within its ranks, i.e., Sung himself. A week later, a triumphant Sung, age thirty, was at the Shanghai Station preparing to board the train for Peking. Before he could leave, he was gunned down by an assassin.

Along with democratic activists like Sung, Yuan had inherited an economic problem endemic to fledgling governments: the inability to raise the funds necessary to jump-start the engine of a new administration. It will be remembered that the first thing Sun Yat-sen did upon hearing of the success of the revolution was to go to Washington and London, where he tried unsuccessfully to secure loans for the new Chinese Republic. While in London, Sun also contacted the head of the International Banking Consortium, which had been handling loans to the Imperial Chinese government, in an effort to reroute the money into the coffers of the revolutionaries; not surprisingly, his request was refused. But as soon as Sun resigned in favor of Yuan, negotiations began with the consortium for a huge "reorganization loan," which the consortium advanced for the immediate needs of the republic. As Fairbank put it, "The imperialist powers knew how their bread was buttered in China. They could work with Yuan. He would not rock the boat or mobilize Boxer-type risings against foreign privilege."

China's credit line with the West had originally been established through the customs service, run by Britisher Robert Hart. This arrangement had worked nicely until the Boxer Rebellion, when the Chinese government ran out of money. The consortium then announced that China's national salt tax would be sufficient security for further loans—but only as long as these taxes were collected, like customs service duties, by foreigners. Sun Yat-sen and his cohorts in the Kuomintang spoke out against accepting these terms. His position was strengthened when President Woodrow Wilson announced the withdrawal of the United States from the consortium on the grounds that conditions like these cast aspersions on Chinese independence.

Embarrassed by the terms of the loan and ever-increasing proof that he had ordered the murder of Sung, Yuan now faced charges by the Kuomintang that the money was a personal loan, made to Yuan himself. When the money disappeared without contributing to the promised "reorganization" of the new government, rebellion again broke out in the South. It was quickly suppressed by Yuan, who also dismissed three provincial governors, all members of the KMT. At that point, Sun sent Yuan a wire demanding his resignation and offering peace in the South in return. Yuan refused; Nanking declared its independence; and the KMT organized a "punitive expedition" against Yuan. Yuan fired Sun from his post as director of railway development, charging that the funds he had been given to build railways had been used to pay for what was now being called the "second revolution." When Yuan sent his northern army to repress the southern revolutionaries, Sun once again fled to Japan.

Two months later, on October 10,* the anniversary of the revolution, Yuan held a magnificent inauguration for himself, attended by the diplomatic corps, whose appearance signified the formal recognition of the fledgling republic. Less than a month later, he formally outlawed the Kuomintang, unseated more than three hundred KMT members of Parliament, and arrested eight others. One enterprising KMT leader, the vice president of the Senate, escaped the gunmen surrounding his house by disguising himself as an old woman and pretending to be led by his servants to his carriage.

At the beginning of 1914, the year World War I broke out, Yuan declared himself president for life and, as the war progressed, made moves toward becoming emperor. In preparation for his new royal position, Yuan is said to have held a dress rehearsal for the ceremony, at which he had intended to invest his favorite ladies with royal rank until two of them got into a clawing catfight, leaving their elaborate gowns in shreds. Yuan had even chosen an imperial name for himself and set the date for his enthronement. This was, according to Jonathan Spence, the result of unbridled personal ambition coupled with a sincere conviction that as a monarchy, China would be in a better position to continue to attract foreign loans.†

Certainly, the first and most disastrous effect of the European war on China was the drying up of funds from the members of the consortium, now engaged in their own expensive battles for survival. The Japanese government stepped quickly into the vacuum, trading loans for concessions, and by May of 1915 felt sufficiently entrenched to issue—under threat of attack—what came to be known as the Twenty-one Demands. These included the extension of Japanese rights in Manchuria and Mongolia; the takeover by Japan of German concessions in the province of Shantung; joint operation with China of her largest iron and steel company; and an obligation on China's part to employ Japanese advisers in the political, financial, and mil-

---

* Known by the Chinese as the "Double Tenth."

† See Jonathan Spence, *The Gate of Heavenly Peace*, p. 97.

itary spheres—a provision that would have given the Japanese partial control, among other things, of the Chinese police. Although Yuan was able to eschew this last provision, he had to accept the others. The following year, in an effort to unseat Yuan and destabilize China, the Japanese persuaded the group that administered China's salt tax to withhold the monies left after they had deducted payments for loans and indemnities, thus starving Yuan of the wherewithal to control his civil and military administrations. Forced to abandon his imperial ambitions in March of 1916, Yuan died three months later, a defeated man. His death opened the way for Sun Yat-sen to return to China.

❦

FROM 1913 TO 1916, Sun had been living in exile in Japan, slipping into China occasionally to further his republican aims. Although many of his fellow revolutionaries had deserted him for Yuan, others had followed him, either by choice or necessity. Among those who felt it was healthier to leave China was Charlie Soong, who closed the Soong house on Avenue Joffre in the French Concession, gathered the members of his family then living with him,* took the household servants, and left for Kobe under an assumed name. The family later moved to Tokyo and finally settled in Yokohama in a house overlooking Tokyo Bay, where they lived for nearly two years.

Among the emigrants was the Soong's second daughter, Ching-ling, who had graduated from Wesleyan and arrived in China in time to accompany her father and Sun on one of their last railway trips. Back in 1911, when Charlie Soong had sent his middle daughter the flag of the new Chinese Republic with its twelve-pointed white sun, her roommates reported that she had climbed on a chair, pulled the old yellow-and-blue imperial dragon flag off the wall, and stomped on it. The following year, she wrote an article about the Chinese Revolution for the college magazine entitled "The Greatest Event of the Twentieth Century"; in it she described "the emancipation of four hundred million souls" from the Manchu Dynasty as "a most glorious achievement . . . the greatest event since Waterloo." A passionate patriot and idealist, Charlie's second daughter had been invited by her father to accompany the party when he realized that he could no longer trust Sun with his eldest daughter, Ai-ling. In any case, Ai-ling, now in her midtwenties, was a practical, business-oriented young woman, less interested in romance than in money and position. And it did not take long after the family arrived in Japan for her to find the man of her dreams.

In Tokyo, Charlie was introduced to a young man named Kung Hsiang-

---

* May-ling and T.V. were still in the United States in college.

hsi, known as H. H. Kung, who was working with the Chinese YMCA. Kung was a member of an old family from Shansi, a province in the interior of China, southwest of Peking. Generations of successful bankers and store operators had made the Kungs very rich. Or, as one journalist phrased it, "They owned chain stores in North China, Mongolia, and Canton before Woolworth and Walgreen bore surnames—centuries before." Sickly as a child, H. H. Kung had been taken to a number of Chinese doctors before landing in a mission hospital. There he had been operated on by a doctor who had not only restored him to health but converted him to Christianity.

During the Boxer Rebellion, Kung had tried but failed to help a family of missionaries escape from the marauders. After it was over, he sailed for the United States with letters from them to their families explaining their fate. Once he had fulfilled his promise and delivered the letters, he enrolled in Oberlin College, from which he graduated, going on to get a master's degree in economics at Yale. A budding revolutionary, Kung returned to China, where he served as commander of the Revolutionary Forces in Shansi. Asked to be governor of the province, he refused in favor of starting a school, explaining, "You can't carry out a revolution overnight. The military turn-over, yes; that can be done all at once. But where are you going to get the men for the government afterwards? It needs training to govern a country, and education is the first and most important step in a revolution." The death of his young wife of tuberculosis and the rise of Yuan convinced him that he too ought to leave China, which is how he happened to be in Tokyo at the same time as the Soongs. When Kung told Charlie that he had met Ai-ling at a party in New York, Charlie invited him home for dinner.

An unprepossessing, chubby young man with round glasses on his nose, whose life had been far more interesting than his looks would indicate, Kung was delighted to see Ai-ling again, and she saw in him the family, the money, and the future power she was seeking. On her return to China from the United States, she had realized that she would have to adjust to the inferior position of her sex and fulfill her ambitions through a husband. Kung, called by one reporter "the Greatest Living Aristocrat," was, in fact, the seventy-fifth-generation direct descendant of Confucius (Kung Fu-tzu). When he announced this to the Soongs, Ching-ling started referring to him as "The Sage." A rich man into the bargain, Kung was an ideal choice for the "intel-ligent, suave, utterly charming, most devastatingly shrewd" eldest daughter of the Soongs. But, according to her fiancé, "This was really love!" They married in September 1914. It was an excellent match from the standpoints of all concerned.

A year after their marriage, the Kungs were able to visit his family home of Taiku. At the time, there were no roads to the family seat. Kung and

Ai-ling traveled as far as they could by train; he rode horseback the rest of the way, while she was carried in a sedan chair by sixteen bearers. Having prepared herself for the worst of primitive conditions, Ai-ling was thrilled to find that her husband's family home was a veritable palace and that there were five hundred people in her new household. As in all great Chinese families, the Kung family home would have been a series of courts, each surrounded by rooms opening onto galleries and terraces sheltered by wide eaves. Some of the larger courts held gardens with walks, fish ponds, fountains, and flowering trees.

Kung had started his school—called Oberlin in China after his American alma mater—with nine male students. When one of the professors wrote at the last minute to say he could not come, Ai-ling agreed to substitute for him. It was a brave thing to do, since women were still considered chattel in the provinces and all of her students were men, most of them older than she. Although Ai-ling convinced her husband that Oberlin in China could play a role in his future political career by using American dollars to train young men as his followers, none of the graduates ever became powerful players on the political scene.

Ai-ling had another idea, however, that did help Kung's political image. When Yuan announced that he would become the next emperor of China, she apparently outlined an essay for her husband to write and sign, which he did, presenting a written argument against Yuan's imperial ambitions. The essay, published both in China and abroad, marked Kung as a political thinker. During their time in the north, Ai-ling also encouraged her husband's efforts to establish relationships with local warlords so that he could become a bridge between the North and the South, where all of Dr. Sun's revolutionary contacts and power were concentrated.

BEFORE HER MARRIAGE, Ai-ling—called by one of the Luces a "perennial fixer"—had suggested that Ching-ling take over her job as secretary to Sun Yat-sen. Whether or not she knew what she was doing, it was nearly inevitable that the young and idealistic Ching-ling, enamored of the revolution, would also fall for its creator. As she wrote May-ling in November 1914, "I can help China and I can also help Dr. Sun. He needs me." Sun taught Ching-ling to decode secret letters and write in invisible ink, both tools of the political underground. He also taught her to be precise, punctual, and spot government spies.

It is reasonably clear that during their initial time together, Sun was going through something of an emotional breakdown. His defeat by Yuan had severely undermined his belief in himself. His damaged ego got the upper hand; he lost his remarkable selflessness and belief in his fellow men; and, for the first time in his life, he gave in to bitterness. Ousted from the ruling group, he became petty, angry, and resentful. He blamed the consortium for his defeat by Yuan: "Not our own people, not our own mistakes, drove us from China, but foreign money power, deliberately employed for the breakup of our country," he claimed. "The foreign bankers of the five Power group held the balance of power between the North and the South for three years. When we were in power they starved us of the credit, except on the most humiliating terms. . . . Last year's personal loan. . . . to Yuan Shih-kai . . . simply put a club in the hands of the North with which they straightway smashed our cause. That huge bribe and that alone, is the reason why we are here today."

Just as it is easy to see how Ching-ling's love for Sun's ideals slipped over into infatuation with the man himself, it is not hard to imagine her appeal for Sun. His marriage had been one of convenience, and he had spent a minimum of time with the uneducated woman his family had chosen for him when he was still in school.* Moreover, his attempt to marry Ai-ling had been rebuffed in such a way as to wound his pride. Now, nearing fifty, he was thrown into daily contact with a pretty, well-educated girl, barely twenty years old, bursting with worshipful love both for his cause and for himself. Where else could a man who had been dropped from the heights of glory find such delicious solace?

There are many variations in the story of the wedding and marriage of Sun Yat-sen and Ching-ling. Taken all together, it seems to be as follows:

Ching-ling went to her parents while they were living in Japan to announce that she wanted to marry Sun. They were horrified. Not only was there nearly thirty years' difference in their ages, but both the Soongs and the Suns were Christians, who believed, unlike the Chinese, in strict monogamy. But even if they had been unconverted Chinese, the union would have had to be proposed by the elders, not the principals, and it would have been necessary to get the permission of both families for the man to take a second wife.

Marriages in China had nothing to do with love or infatuation. The joining of men and women was a contract between two families for the benefit of both, and the children who followed were there to add continuity to the

* Sun's wife had made only a brief visit to Japan. While there, she and their daughter, Annie, had been hurt in a car accident. Returning to Shanghai, where she was hounded by Yuan's police in their efforts to find her husband, Mrs. Sun took Annie and fled to Sun's brother's home in Macao (he had moved from Hawaii), where the girl subsequently died.

power of the family and tend its ancestors' graves. The mere *idea* of a child choosing his or her own mate was anathema to the traditional Chinese way of life, and, although Charlie Soong had raised his daughters to be thoughtful, educated women, there were certain lines that could not be crossed. In China, the welfare and reputation of the family superseded those of its members, and, as one author put it, "the bigger and more powerful the Chinese family, the more its individual member was its well-beloved prisoner." At the core of this belief was the concept of filial piety. Like the emperor in his palace, the father in his home was the ultimate authority, not to be crossed or even disturbed with unpleasant truths.*

It is therefore not surprising that as soon as Charlie Soong felt it was safe, he took his family back to Shanghai and, after Ching-ling refused to marry a younger, more appropriate man, locked her in her room. But Ching-ling would not have been Charlie's daughter had she given up. Without her parents' knowledge she sent Sun a note asking if she should return to Japan. When the answer came back that he needed her, she escaped from the Soong house.

"I didn't fall in love," Ching-ling told journalist Edgar Snow. "It was a hero-worship from afar. It was a romantic girl's idea when I ran away to work for him—but a good one. I wanted to help save China and Dr. Sun was the one man who could do it, so I wanted to help him. On my way home from Wesleyan College I went to see him, in exile in Tokyo, and volunteered my services. He soon sent me word in Shanghai that he needed me in Japan. My parents would never consent and tried to lock me up. I climbed out of the window and escaped with the help of my amah." She left immediately for Japan—a daring move and a sin against the Methodist religion and the moral integrity of the Soong family. She arrived on October 24, 1915. In the meantime, Dr. Sun, realizing that he was exposing Ching-ling to calumny by getting her back to Japan under questionable circumstances, arranged for a "divorce" from Mrs. Sun.

"I had no knowledge that he had gone through a divorce proceeding and that he intended to marry me until I arrived," Ching-ling told Snow. "When he explained his fear that I would otherwise be called his concubine and that the scandal would harm the revolution, I agreed. I never regretted it." They were married the day after her arrival, October 25, 1915, at the house of a prominent Japanese lawyer. No family attended the ceremony or the reception.

---

* An extreme example of this is the story of a sixty-odd-year-old man who romped on the floor, pretending to be a toddler, so his parents would not realize that they had grown old and soon would die.

News of the marriage did not appear until three months later—first in the Japanese press, then overseas. What Snow called Sun's "rather vague divorce," undertaken to blunt criticism, seems to have failed to do so. Chinese Christians refused to accept Ching-ling as Sun's legitimate wife, and after their marriage, Sun was no longer asked to speak in missions and churches. His name was dropped from missionary journals as a good example of a Chinese Christian.

Needless to say, the reaction within the Soong family was far worse than that of the Christian community at large. Ching-ling's mother, a fastidious practitioner of the Methodist faith, was appalled; her father simply tried to take her home. "My mother wept and my father who was ill with liver disease pleaded. . . . Although full of pity for my parents—I cried bitterly also—I refused to leave my husband," she explained to one biographer. "My father came to Japan and bitterly attacked Dr. Sun," she told Edgar Snow. "He tried to annul the marriage on grounds that I was under age and lacked my parents' consent. When he failed he broke all relations with Dr. Sun and disowned me!"

The marriage caused a rift in the Soong family, although it did not last very long. According to one Chinese writer, it was Ai-ling who kept up contact with her sister and eventually patched matters up with her parents. Ever practical, Ai-ling said that it was only a matter of time until Sun would come back into power and the connection would be good for the Soongs. It took some time, but eventually love (on their part) and reason (on Ai-ling's) won out, and the family accepted the situation. The parents sent the newlyweds a suite of Chinese furniture, and Ching-ling's mother sent the couple a traditional silk wedding quilt embroidered with one hundred baby boys. In typical Chinese fashion, the Soongs kept their disapproval within the confines of the family, and the only time Charlie seems to have unburdened himself outside his home was to his old friend William Burke. "Bill," he told Burke, "I was never so hurt in my life. My own daughter and my best friend."

7

❧

The [Chinese] matrimonial system is the same as a tea set. Who in the world would think of having only one teacup for one teapot?

—ANONYMOUS

THROUGHOUT THE drama surrounding Ching-ling's marriage to Sun, May-ling and T.V. were still in college, and they did not return to China until nearly two years later. "Just think," Ching-ling wrote Ai-ling from Sun's headquarters in Canton, "little Mayling will graduate this June and return to China in July. . . . She is a popular lassie and enjoys her college life immensely."

So much so that after her train left Grand Central Station, the new graduate wrote her best friend, Emma Mills, that she "broke down completely." She was not cheered by the "deadly" train journey across Canada, 'which made her "nervous and headachey," and she did not like the Canadians. The women were dowdy, and everyone seemed "so damnably ignorant and narrow-minded." At one stop, they saw a train of coolie laborers. "If one of them should die," May-ling wrote Emma, "the family gets $150.00! Such is the price of life to them. If ever I have any influence, I shall see to it that no coolies are being shipped out, for China needs all her own men to develop the mines."

The highlight of the trip west was apparently a stay in the Hotel Vancouver. She and Brother, as she referred to T.V., had decided to splurge during their travels, and they reveled in the luxury of the hotel. "The tips [*sic*] to the waiter at each meal," she wrote Emma, "is more than a month's allowance for me at college!" May-ling rationalized their extravagance by saying that once they got home, they would no longer be able to be "as irresponsible as we are now."

Given her determination to have a good time, it is not surprising that there was the inevitable shipboard romance on the long sea journey to China. "I lost my head over a man whose father is Dutch and mother is French," she wrote her friend three weeks after she returned home. The man, an architect on his way to Sumatra, asked May-ling to marry him and came to see her in Shanghai; her family, who would never have allowed her to marry a foreigner, was "greatly wrought up" by his appearance, and she ended up "having a rather uncomfortable time." Once home, she was also courted by someone she referred to as "H.K.," who often came from Peking with a friend to see her. "I like them, but that's all," she wrote Emma. Another suitor—despite his wife and family—was Eugene Chen, the editor of *The Shanghai Gazette*, who had been born in Trinidad. "He is very clever, and brilliant, but horribly egoistic and vain. . . . He is coming to call on me this week, and I hope I won't be rude," she wrote, adding the information that she had been attending "a great many dinners, and teas, & other affairs" since her return. A month later, she said that there had been only one evening when she was neither entertaining at home nor attending a dinner somewhere else.

As soon as she moved back, May-ling was put in charge of the family house, a large home that she described as "one of the loveliest in Shanghai." Her duties included managing twelve household servants—seven men and five women. "Let me tell you it is no joke!" she wrote Emma. Four stories high, the house had sixteen large rooms plus kitchen and baths, verandas and sleeping porches. Located on Avenue Joffre, the longest street in Shanghai, it was very far from the center of town, which made it more fashionable but also less convenient, at some distance from the shopping district, theaters, and restaurants. The servants' quarters in their home, she noted, were better than the students' rooms at college.

May-ling's mother did not like living so far away from her charities and board meetings and had suggested that the family move back into their old home in the Hongkew section of Shanghai, where they had lived before May-ling was born. Since the area was getting crowded and the prices were the highest in Shanghai, May-ling advised selling it. Her mother, she wrote her friend, was "shocked and grieved at my callousness towards our old home," and May-ling did not bring the subject up again. For a while, the family considered buying a new home with all the modern conveniences, one that Charlie Soong thought would increase in value. "With the house in Honkew, & one on Ave Joffre, and . . . [the new one] . . . we have pretty good land securities," May-ling wrote her friend, "not to mention our land on the Bund which is valuable." As to transportation: "We have a lovely carriage and two coachmen, but horses are such bother. One can only use them just so much. Next week we are going to get an automobile for running around town, and let Mother keep the carriage for her private use."

The Soongs eventually decided not to move, and May-ling and T.V. were given four large rooms for themselves on the fourth floor of the family home. "We . . . enjoy our freedom greatly," she wrote Emma, adding that since T.V. was away working during the days, she had the space all to herself. "There is a servant up here whose only duty is to keep these rooms in order, and answer my bells. . . . I have dismissed my maid. I have found that I simply did not need her, as Mother's maid does all my mending and picks up my clothes for me, and it grated on me to have my maid around when I could execute my own orders in less time than it took for me to explain to her what I wanted done. You see, all the years in democratic America have their effect on me. I am quite contented with this one servant who attends to brother's and my wants. He polishes our shoes, dusts, sweeps and make[s] up the beds, etc., and is of infinitely less trouble than my maid who used to quarrel with him all the time."

Along with running the house, May-ling had also taken over much of the responsibility for her two younger brothers, both of whom had flunked school the previous year. The family, she wrote, was "furious. The poor kids have two tutors (one English & a Chinese) to come every day. . . . The fact that the two kids flunked enhances the value of my Demarest Scholarship [an academic award from Wellesley] in the eyes of the family. They think I am a wonder. . . . I have complete control over the boys, as mother is so disgusted that she handed them over to me bodily. They are hard to manage because they are deucedly clever and lazy at the same time. I have whipped the younger one several times, & they both are afraid of me. You don't know what a good disciplinarian I can be!"

Among the things May-ling had loved in the United States were milk shakes and ice cream sodas, and when she returned to Shanghai, she weighed between 127 and 130 pounds. Her mother immediately put her on a diet and kept her on it until she was down to 100 pounds, a weight she proudly maintained into old age.

A more difficult adjustment was learning to be part of her family and her country. "Two letters from you just came!" she wrote Emma. "They were like an oasis to a stranger lost in the desert! Now do not think from this that I am unhappy or dissatisfied with my home life. Far from that. Only . . . I haven't quite found exactly where I am. Your good advice to lose myself in the lives of my people here is well timed, for you know I am a very independent soul, who for ten years has lived only according to her own will. It is hard, therefore, to remember that I must think of others. And I am afraid too that I am not so patient as I should be."

Her impatience could also be traced to the young man known as H.K., who kept returning to Shanghai. "He has been here quite often," she wrote Emma in the middle of August. "I fear, however that I care nothing for him. . . . Of course with him it is as it used to be." Two months later, H.K. gave a dinner for May-ling, during which a friend of his also decided he liked her.

She was furious because H.K. apparently told his rival that he and May-ling were engaged: "he always acts as though I belong to him . . . and . . . I have no opportunity to deny it." She also claimed that she was "rather indifferent" when it came to men in general. "At dinners, I meet mostly prominent men who are already married," she wrote Emma. ". . . Mother and Father object to my seeing men very much as they don't want me to get married for the next three years. As I myself am quite contented at home, I do not want to marry either,—especially as I told you, that I met 'my fate' on the boat. Since I cannot marry someone I really care for, I shall not marry for anything else except fame & money. I know you think I am mercenary, but after all, Dada* dear, now all men are alike to me. I know I sound world-weary, but isn't it just my luck though not to meet him until on my way home! The way the family scorns him because he is a foreigner would make you think that he is a Barbarian!"

Eager to find work—something to keep her "busy & interested"— May-ling complained to Emma that she was not contributing to either the welfare of her family or her own intellect. Nor was she permitted to go places unchaperoned. "And the curious fact is that I am not resentful in the least. I am just passively acquiescing. You cannot believe this of the little vehement spitfire, can you? . . . I just feel my mental powers getting more and more dulled every day."

On October 10, May-ling and her brothers asked their mother to give the servants the day off, and the family visited the largest marketplace in the city, where, as she wrote Emma, "we <u>actually</u> bought our vegetables etc. from the stands. We even prevailed on Father and Mother to go with us, and we all wore the oldest clothes we had. You can well imagine what my aristocratic mother thought of the whole business." The Shanghai marketplace, "a large tent-like structure covering some five acres," had a cement floor, a blackened brick roof, and stalls rented by the farmers. After their excursion, the family gathered in the kitchen and cooked their favorite dishes. May-ling made fudge, the only thing she knew how to prepare. After lunch, the children wanted to go to the horse races, but, "as Dad & Mother are looked upon as 'The Pillars' of the Church," they went for a ride instead. "When we returned the servants had prepared dinner which we all ate with zest. After dinner, we found out that some of the ungrateful wretches of servants had again gone out to the theatres without permission. Dad was furious; so he

---

* According to Thomas DeLong, Emma chose the nickname "Dada" as indicative of her nonconformist attitude represented by the Nihilist movement, which spread from a European protest against World War I into the realms of art and literature. Since May-ling was two and a half years younger than her friend, she signed her letters "Daughter." (Thomas DeLong, *Madame Chiang Kai-shek and Miss Emma Mills*, p. 16.)

ordered all the doors to be locked. The poor knaves therefore had to spend the cold night out in the stable! I guess they won't steal out again!"

Like overprivileged young women all over the world, May-ling had returned home from college to a life of social fun and charitable good works. But she also seemed to seek out activities that made it clear she was not bound by convention. An atypical young member of the monied class, she rather enjoyed shocking Shanghai society with her American ways and ideas. Her first job—teaching Sunday school—was hardly unusual for a girl of her station, although she was the only female teaching a class of boys and her favorite student called her "Sir." Her next job was more fun: "Like your honorable lazy self," she wrote another friend in October 1917, "I am not doing anything at home except amusing myself. . . . I can go to movies free of charge. How do you suppose I work it? Simply because I am a member of the Film Censorship Committee of China." With Emma, she was honest about her qualifications for the post: "Fancy a young, pure, and unsophisticated being . . . censoring what should be instructive for the public. Bah!" Like many others before her, May-ling also volunteered at the YWCA, where she promoted organizations of Chinese women. But she was clearly not satisfied. "I think I wish that I were doing something real: something towards a career," she wrote Emma after four months at home. "The life I am leading now will end in marriage only . . . even at college, I never worked unless I had to or thought I had to. And I am not changed in that respect now. If I had a profession I could force myself to work, and work hard. . . . Even now I can feel that my 2 married sisters are putting their heads together for me to make a "grande alliance.' . . . I object to being parceled off in this manner. But I grant that their logic is irrefutable. They say, 'Now is the time for you to make the biggest match of the season.' . . . I have marriage drummed to me morning, noon and night."

About this time, May-ling's face began to break out—probably a new manifestation of the nervous attacks of her childhood and the neurodermatitis that would plague her throughout her life. Although she called it acne, it must have been something else, because she talked about the terrible pain caused by steaming and massage and the injections given her to cure it. Abiding by her mother's wishes, she did not go out, except at night and only with a veil. Soon, however, she decided to go ahead with her life "as though nothing is the matter. . . . I have found that the closer I stick at home, the more uncertain my temper becomes," she wrote Emma.

She also began to think in terms of politics and the country, reporting to her friend that there was "so much misery . . . everywhere! Sometimes when I look at the dirty, ragged swarming humanity in our slums, I feel the sense of utter futility in hoping for a great and a new China, and the sense of my smallness. Dada, you cannot conceive how useless one feels in such surroundings; the percentage of poor here is greater than any you could conceive of in America." After the *Peking Gazette* was suppressed and the cabinet fell, she wrote, "Chinese politics are impossible, one never knows what next is going to happen, and one never knows when one's head is going to be the next to be chopped off."

The Shanghai Municipal Council asked her to join the Child Labor Commission, on which no Chinese had ever before served. For a girl who had lived in a refined stratum of American society for ten years, the experience of investigating working conditions in Shanghai's factories was quite a shock. In the economic boom that followed the end of World War I, conditions in these plants were, according to one chronicler of the city, "as abysmal as any in the world." Contractors searched the countryside for areas of drought or flood, bought all the girls in a village "for a song," put them into rooms converted from cheap tenements into factories, and kept them at their machines for as many as fourteen hours a day, seven days a week. Only one holiday, Chinese New Year, was observed.

"I . . . spent much time in visiting various factories in Shanghai and was repelled at the long hours . . . and poor working conditions of women and children in the so-called International (but mainly run by the British) Settlement of Shanghai," May-ling said many years later. "The sanitation was appalling, and little babies were lying in the aisle as their mother worked on the machines."

The "factories" in which these unfortunate women worked were dimly lit and stifling. Few had windows. Women and children as young as six were kept, as one writer put it, "wards of the subcontractor." For working 364 days a year, he gave them "food which is poor, clothing which is meager, and shelter which is crowded. He charges them for these services, which must be worked off before they leave his employ." For the average worker, a twelve-hour working day was a dream, as was the right to sit down during working hours. After a few years of unbearable working conditions and inadequate nutrition, industrial workers were often ill and unemployable. Tuberculosis was common.

One of the worst places to work was a silk factory, or filature. "In the silk factories," May-ling reported, "the women's hands were purplish-red and often blistered by having to work with hot vapor issuing forth from open vats." Since the slightest breath of air might disturb the threads, no ventilation was allowed to mitigate the putrid air that rose from the dead cocoons lying in heaps on the floor, and the odor in these factories was said to be unbearable. Whereas women actually spun the silk, children were employed to stir the cocoons in vats of boiling water in order to loosen the threads. The children's eyes were universally red, according to one visitor, and their arms were covered with burns from scalding. "Women and children grow very skillful in keeping their hands out of the water, yet they are loose-skinned and par-boiled, for fingers must of necessity be continually dipped in," said another visitor. "Then, too, the Chinese women overseers, passing constantly up and down the lines, occasionally punish a child's inefficiency, or supposed laziness, by thrusting the little hand into the bubbling cauldron."

Because of the cheap construction of the plants, fires were frequent. In one appalling calamity, a hundred women died in a fire that engulfed a silk filature because the owner had locked them in from the outside. Like others of his kind, this man kept his female employees virtual prisoners. Even when they were not kept under lock and key, the difficulty of negotiating narrow staircases, cluttered with filth and trash, turned these factories into firetraps.

❦

IN 1917, THE year May-ling returned to Shanghai, the position of women in China, even under the best circumstances, was still an unenviable one. A poem from the *Book of Odes,* called "the richest and most authentic source of material for . . . the social life of ancient China before the 8th Century B.C.," describes how the earliest Chinese felt about women:

> *When a son is born*
> *Let him sleep in the bed,*
> *Clothe him with fine dress,*
> *And give him jades to play with.*
> *How lordly his cry is!*
> *May he grow up to wear crimson*
> *And be the lord of the clan and the tribe!*

> *When a daughter is born*
> *Let her sleep on the ground,*
> *Wrap her in common wrappings,*
> *And give her broken tiles for her playthings.*
> *May she have no faults, nor merits of her own;*
> *May she well attend to food and wine,*
> *And bring no discredit to her parents!*

Even after two thousand years of civilization, the Chinese family remained a strict patriarchy, and the Chinese woman was expected to obey three generations of men—first her father, then the husband chosen for her by her family, and finally, if she survived her husband, her firstborn son. Reduced to the position of an unpaid, often mistreated servant, an intelligent woman was often worse off than her illiterate sister. "The woman with no talents," Confucius had said, "is the one who has merit," It should come as no surprise that Confucius's own marriage, as well as those of his son and grandson, all ended in divorce.*

Whereas marriage gave many Western brides a taste of freedom, it made life worse for a Chinese girl, who was expected to serve her mother-in-law and her husband's family for the rest of her life. On the eve of her marriage, one bride was given the following advice by her father: "Tomorow you will belong to the Yen [her future husband's name] family. Fom now on, this is no longer your home and you are not to contact us without permission from your husband. Your duty will be to please him and your in-laws. Bear them many sons. Sublimate your own desires. Become the willing piss-pot and spittoon of the Yens and we will be proud of you."

An account by another young woman who married the boy her family chose for her in 1920, three years after May-ling returned home, gives us an idea of what this sort of life was like, even under the best of circumstances. May Tan belonged to an old mandarin family with ties to the West. The bride's father served as China's minister to the Court of St. James's, her uncle was the minister of justice, and her mother-in-law came from the same family as the dowager empress. But enlightenment stopped at the gates of the family compound.

"Being a bride in a large old-fashioned family was no easy task . . ." Ms. Tan said:

> In following the established traditions, I had to present tea three times a day to my husband's father and mother. There were many men and maid servants, but I had to do these presentations personally. . . . I had my meals with my sisters-in-law. . . . Men and women were seated separately. On Sundays or holidays when my husband had his meals at home, he would sit with the men folks. I could not eat with him at the same table, or sit in the same room. Day in and day out, I would have my sisters-in-law as my companions, and we usually played Mahjong in the afternoons to pass the time away. The evenings I spent with my mother-in-law. I could not leave her

---

* See Kristopher Kowal, "The Sage We Love to Hate," *Free China Review* (Taipei), August 1999, pp. 48–53.

presence without first asking permission and then bowing low in obeisance . . .

In October I found myself pregnant. Realizing that once my condition was known I would never be allowed to go out again, I kept it entirely to myself. But, when November came I began feeling rather queer and thought I had better inform my mother-in-law. . . . Mother-in-law immediately . . . ordered the servants to remove my husband's bed and belongings to the library in the outer compound. According to what she said, this would make the baby bright! As a result I had less chance of seeing my husband and sometimes I would not see him for the whole day. . . .

In December everybody was busy buying Christmas and New Year presents. . . . I had a private rickshaw pulled by a strong coolie . . . [and] decided to go out shopping. . . . The roads were covered with snow and ice. . . . The coolie stepped on slippery ice and fell down. . . . Mother-in-law was very angry. . . . Miscarriage occurred. . . . This event further angered the mother-in-law. During the Christmas and New Year season . . . I . . . stayed in bed. . . . My only consolation was that after returning from the office, my husband would drop in and chat with me for a while. . . . In the holidays, he went out playing golf with his friends and in the evenings went dancing with his girl friends at the Grand Hotel.

One cannot imagine any of the Soong girls, particularly May-ling, submitting to this sort of life. Nor would her parents have wanted this for her. She had not been given a Western education in order to spend her afternoons at the mah-jongg table. Like her sisters, once she was out of college, May-ling had to invent herself.

8

There is a Chinese saying that "bandits and soldiers are breath from the same nostrils." . . . The bandit had no official position; he killed and stole and fled. The warlord had military rank; he killed and stole and stayed.

—James E. Sheridan

ALONG WITH marital customs and good works, there was a great deal for May-ling to absorb when she returned to China after ten years in the States. Unlike America, where she had done her bit for the war effort by knitting socks for soldiers, her own country had remained determinedly neutral or, as one writer put it, "engaged in guarding and perpetuating her traditional impotency." Although it had become apparent that China must at some point declare for one side or the other, it was not until December 1916, when President Wilson sent out an initial offer of peace, that the Chinese woke up and realized that in order to be taken seriously as a world power and gain entry to a future peace conference, they had to take sides in the conflict.

At this point, their immediate concern was the province of Shantung, where the Japanese had taken over two hundred square miles of German territory early in the war. Unaware that Japan had signed secret agreements with the European Entente to support their claim on Chinese territory when the war was over, China, believing it would be accorded equal treatment at the peace table, cast its lot with the Allies in August 1917, when the United States invited it to join other nations in breaking off diplomatic relations with the Germans to protest their submarine warfare. This declaration served another purpose as well: by severing their ties with the Germans, the Chinese could legally stop paying the indemnity they owed Germany from the Boxer Rebellion and use the money to fill their depleted treasury.

Unfortunately, China's decision to enter the war came at a time of confusion within the country itself. After the death of Yuan his "well-meaning but powerless" vice president had stepped up to the presidency, restored the constitution of 1912, recalled Parliament, and dissolved Yuan's North Chinese Army. But without a strong leader in Peking, Yuan's generals, who had been occupying various provinces around the country, began to use these areas as personal bases, guarded by their own armies.

China was now entering the Warlord Era, a period of a dozen or so years during which provincial strongmen were able to defy or ignore the central government while battling with one another. Thus, China was divided up during the late teens and twenties by these warlords (tuchuns), who fought over territory, preferably lands with a large populace from which to collect taxes (opium was the most remunerative crop), and a seaport to receive shipments of arms. A typical warlord not only fought against but bargained with other warlords, whom he might then support against the central government. Warlords were sometimes financed by foreign nations, who played them off against each other in the hope of finding one strong enough to take over the country and lease out its rich, untapped resources. Unlike other nations, Japan always supported more than one warlord, since the Japanese wanted to keep China divided and ripe for conquest.

The warlords themselves were quite a colorful bunch. Perhaps the most famous was the "Christian General," Feng Yu-hsiang, who became a soldier at eleven and rose to be a brigade commander in the North China Army. Six feet, four inches tall, 240 pounds, "shaped like a pyramid, with a melon-sized head" Feng dressed like an oversize coolie with a huge straw hat tied under his chin. Converted to Christianity in 1913, he married a secretary from the YMCA and from then on baptized his troops with a hose and marched them into battle singing "Onward, Christian Soldiers." His soldiers were noticably neater and cleaner than those of other warlords. (After examining their rifles, he often checked their fingernails.) They were not only trained in practical matters like road building, tree planting, and carpentry but given instruction in reading and writing and required to learn two new Chinese characters before being given their dinner. As Feng gained power, however, he discovered that he needed a constant supply of money to support his army, and he quickly learned the art of looting the countryside. He also betrayed (his choice of word) his superior, Marshal Wu Pei-fu, and by 1924 had conquered Peking, which he held on to for two years—until Wu and another warlord joined forces and threw him out.

This was pretty typical of the warlords, who took great pleasure in double-crossing each other. One of the most interesting, known as the Old Marshal, was Chang Tso-lin, a small tyrant with delicate hands, a paunch, and a large mustache grown to hide a harelip that had been badly sewn together. Thought by some to be "the greatest warlord of them all," Chang had started out as the uneducated leader of a band of Manchurian brigands, then joined the Chinese army. In 1913, he was named military governor of one of the Manchurian provinces; five years later, he controlled all of Manchuria. Chang was the man who had joined Feng for the purpose of conquering Peking. Chang wore a black satin skullcap that sported a gigantic pearl—reputedly the biggest in the world—and harbored imperial ambitions. Once established in the capital, he began to hold court on a thronelike chair with a stuffed tiger on either side, worship in the sections of the Forbidden City set aside for the emperor, and insist that streets be closed and shop windows shuttered when he went out into the city. He even started making his own imperial porcelain. He had five wives, loved gambling, and was fond of opium. Manchuria was the part of China where the Japanese were strongest, and Old Marshal Chang considered himself an honest man, since he bargained with other warlords over territory but refused to deal with the Japanese. Because of this, he eventually lost his life.

Marshal Wu, the man whom Feng betrayed, was the very opposite of Feng, a highly learned scholar-soldier, fine-boned and thin with an aquiline nose that gave him the appearance of a mandarin. Like Feng, Wu had only one wife. Red-headed with pale brown eyes, his coloring was strangely un-Chinese, but he was, in fact, a Chinese gentleman from his cultivated speech to his Confucian core. He was said to have fought a battle in the rain, which was not considered a proper thing to do; when the battle was over, he contacted the general of the beaten force and offered to give up his gains and fight the battle a second time when the sun came out. Unlike many other warlords, Wu paid his soldiers their entire salary on a regular basis, a practice that earned their loyalty and the gratitude of the local peasants, from whom they were not forced to steal their food. He was a modest man and cared little for money, indulging himself in only two areas: he had a custom-made bulletproof French touring car upholstered in brown leather, and he kept on his payroll a private spittoon bearer, who followed him wherever he went. Another warlord, Sun Chuan-fang, was less aggressive than his peers. He issued a Three Love Principle in 1926: love of country, love of the people, and love of the enemy. When Sun lost his territory to the KMT, he retired from war and took up Buddhism. He was killed in the middle of a Buddhist ceremony by the daughter of a man who had been executed by Sun's soldiers two years earlier.

Then there was General Yen Hsi-shan, the so-called "model governor" of Shansi province, the inland province that was home to the Kungs. According to historian John Gunther, Yen was so suspicious that when he was getting a shave, he had one of his soldiers hold a gun to the head of the barber, just in case someone had bribed the man to cut his throat. Yen also built his railroads on another gauge from other warlords' to stop would-be invaders. There was also Chang Tsung-chang, who was said to have "the physique of an elephant, the brain of a pig and the temperament of a tiger." He was called "Three Things Not Known"—how much money he had, how many soldiers, and how many concubines.* Another name was "Old Eighty-six,"

---

* It was said that the ladies represented twenty-six different nationalities, each with her own washbowl emblazoned with her national flag.

since it was said that it would take a pile of eighty-six silver dollars to make up the length of his penis (nine inches in repose).

The warlords moved their armies on the rivers, railways, and roads of China, plundering the countryside as they traveled. "Pockmarked, syphilitic soldiers, often wolfish with hunger, often looting for sustenance, marched back and forth over the map of China, establishing chaos as the normal state of civil affairs" was journalist Theodore White's description of the Warlord Era. On their way to battle, the soldiers were followed by coolies bearing coffins—visible reassurance that if killed, their bodies would be properly buried and not just left to rot on the battlefield.

During the Warlord Era, Fairbank tells us that the Chinese suffered mainly from the deterioration of the infrastructure, as there was no one to see to the irrigation and drainage that fed an agricultural economy, no one responsible for repairing the dikes, the roads, or the rolling stock. Except in a few isolated cases, the warlords were too busy fighting and extending their territory to pay attention to the floods and famines that inevitably resulted from this lack of repairs, while their inferiors, officials who received no salaries beyond what they could squeeze out of the peasants, had even less reason to keep things up.

❦

AMONG THOSE WHO had wanted to retain China's neutrality during World War I was May-ling's new brother-in-law, Sun Yat-sen, who had returned to China from Japan in April of 1916. It was not a comfortable homecoming. "We stayed in disguise in Shanghai, in the garret of a French newspaperman's house," said Ching-ling. "We never went out in the daytime, only by night, and even then, we were heavily disguised." Throughout this period of political turmoil, Sun continued to look for support wherever he could get it. "He spoke conservatively to those whose help he needed," Ching-ling told Edgar Snow, "and his books were edited so as not to divide his followers. 'We have to be very careful how we go at things,' he was always warning me. 'Do it the Chinese way—roundabout—never directly at the goal.' "

The Suns moved to Canton in the summer of 1916 so that he could establish his government in south China. Although no foreign power would recognize the new government, the appearance of the recently married couple caused quite a stir. According to one of her biographers, Ching-ling was the first Chinese woman to appear in public with her husband and was often the only woman present at political gatherings. Reserved by nature and training, she now had to learn to deal with people she did not know. "You know how I dread publicity," she wrote a friend in America. "But since my marriage I have had to participate in many affairs which I'd otherwise escape."

Important Warlords
and Their Territories, 1926

Ching-ling's life in the limelight did not last long, as her husband's tenure, first as generalissimo, and then as president of the South China government, was brief. In April 1918, Sun was demoted by more blatantly ambitious men from head of the government to one of a directorate of eight. Disgusted with the party he had brought to power, he left Canton in May and traveled to Japan, once again in search of money. But the Japanese would not even allow him to enter Tokyo. At the end of May, Sun and Ching-ling retired to their home at 29 Rue Molière in the French Concession in Shanghai.

A tranquil setting for a life of the mind, their gray stone house, purchased with funds from overseas Chinese, had a covered porch looking out over a lovely garden with large stones* and a two-story birdhouse. It is here that Sun was able to devote himself to writing and compiling books out of his earlier articles, with which Ching-ling helped him. Clearly the home of a reader and thinker, it was simply furnished, notable primarily for the wooden bookcases lining the walls, not only in Sun's study but in the halls as well. It was said that there were more than five thousand volumes in all, including many on history—everything from the Monroe Doctrine to a book by Theodore Roosevelt on World War I. Elegant but simple, the home served its owner—who mortgaged it a number of times—as a peaceful retreat. According to Sun's bodyguard, the "most important member of the staff was Mme. Sun herself. She never interfered during his office hours, but it was she alone who made his life possible by keeping him cheerful and happy no matter what went on."

❦

WHEN NEWS FROM the peace conference at Versailles reached Asia in the spring of 1919, the Chinese were furious to discover that their government in Peking had promised to return the territory ceded by Germany to Japan during the war to the Japanese. On May 4, three thousand students in Peking demonstrated against the government, and some of them broke into the home of one of the officials responsible. The police were called, and thirty-two students were imprisoned. Others organized themselves in an effort to arouse sympathy for their incarcerated comrades, to demand the resignation of the offending officials, and to keep the government from signing the Treaty of Versailles. This demonstration, its aftermath, and the resulting upheavals in Chinese society became known in history as the May Fourth Incident.

News of the May 4 demonstration reached Shanghai the next day. During that afternoon, the chamber of commerce, institutes of learning, and

---

* Stones were considered an essential element in Chinese gardens, where they represented mountains.

various guilds sent wires to Peking demanding that the government dismiss three of its important officials and release the students who had been taken into custody. The students of Shanghai also went on strike, and two days later its citizens started a boycott of Japanese goods. On May 26, a much larger strike took place, and Shanghai became the center of student activity as their peers from Peking, Tientsin, and Nanking converged on the city. On June 5, the merchants, shop owners, and clerks of Shanghai joined the striking students, and by noon the walkout had encompassed the entire city, including the foreign (British, American, and French) concessions. As workers from various trades became involved, it was estimated that around one hundred factories were affected by the strike, and by the time it ended, on June 12, Shanghai's beggars, thieves, singsong girls,* and gangsters had joined their fellow citizens in supporting the students. Two weeks later, the Chinese delegation left Paris without signing the Treaty of Versailles.

May-ling had an interesting reaction to the strikes and general sense of fury in the city, which she wisely confined to letters sent to Emma Mills. It is clear from her comments that her American education had not been wasted.

"Several papers in the city have called me up to ask for my opinion on this boycott question," she wrote Emma on June 5,

> but I am refusing to be interviewed, for whatever I say will be twisted around. To tell you the truth, I feel that this boycott movement is effective only in so far as it leads to a constructive program. You may be sure that Japan will hold everything regarding this movement against the Chinese, and when the day comes they will make us pay if they can. And if we are not ready to face them . . . we will get the worst of it. Therefore while I approve of this boycott movement, in that it shows to the world . . . the oneness of our eighteen provinces, I feel that boycotting is after all a passive state. I would suggest that in every school . . . the students should be taught contemporary history. . . . It is really discouraging when one thinks of the amount of history the students study, but not one jot of it is about China since the Revolution. Our oriental mind seems to be steeped in the glories and conquests of the past, and if something is not done to change this, we shall be a second Korea.
>
> If I had the means I would open an industrial school for the children of the streets. They should be taught trades such as mat weaving etc. The Japanese get all our trade in making mats etc. and

---

* "Singsong" was a Western name for the highest class of Chinese prostitutes, versed in the arts of singing and storytelling.

really if the children were taught, they would be able to do as well as the products sent from Japan, and the products could be sold infinitely cheaper. The children too should have two or three hours a day of instruction in Chinese and arithmetic so that in time they would be able to read the newspapers in the colloquial tongue and thus be informed of the state of affairs in the country. . . . The Japanese however have such a hold on our market that they could easily cripple any one who dares to finance the movement. . . .

Mother has just returned from down town. . . . She said that many of the students were running wildly away from the policemen who have orders from the Government to arrest them. It is thought that because the Japs have bribed certain officials in Peking. . . . [They] have promised to do away [with] the boycott. . . . My heart bleeds for the poor students, and I hope those who are so rotten, so damn greedy and inhuman as to sell their country will Go to Hell. It is bad enough to hate men of another nation, but to feel perfectly helpless with rage against the very men who by all laws of decency and humanity should be patriotic is Hell. . . . The Japanese are not afraid of our Government, for they know that it is weak and largely composed of self interested men; they are tho [sic] afraid of the Chinese people, for in spite of what they say about our lack of patriotic feeling, they know only too well that when roused we are a terrible people to deal with. They have had a taste of what length we might be driven to as evinced in the fact that a few days ago several Japanese settlements were destroyed by fire.

"Shanghai," she continued ten days later,

is under the authority of the Municipal Council. The men who composed this Council are all foreigners, and of course as there is a Japanese on it, he would be against the good of the community etc. As a result the Council forbade the students to have parade[s] or put up posters . . . the students behaved in a remarkably sane manner. They moved their headquarters to the Chinese City . . . they wrote pamphlets for the benefit of the foreign population telling them that the movement was not anti-foreign in its aim. . . . They regretted that the foreigners were inconvenienced in the general closing of the shops etc. but as that was the only and most effective method to bring pressures upon the Peking Government, we Chinese had to resort to it. . . . Before this movement, the Japanese behaved with the most remarkable hauteur and superiority. You ought to see the way they slink around the corners now. They would make you think of a cur with his tail between his legs. . . . The Japanese Government is so terrified that they have sent four gun-boats to Shanghai.

❧

UNDER CIRCUMSTANCES such as May-ling described, it is hardly surprising that Chinese students and intellectuals began looking for answers other than traditional Confucianism. The teens and twenties were times of great cultural and intellectual ferment in China, particularly among the young. In 1915, Ch'en Tu-hsiu, the son of a rich family who had studied in France and Japan, founded a magazine, *New Youth,* which denounced Confucianism and the old traditions in favor of the new gods of Science and Democracy. Chinese thought, he claimed, was a thousand years behind that of the West, and China was doomed to end up like Babylon unless the entire social structure of the country was changed. In another area of reform, Charlie Soong's former student Hu Shih began a movement aimed at supplanting the old classical Chinese language with the vernacular. This, he claimed, was the appropriate medium for all forms of written communication, including scientific, and by 1930, this simplified language was being taught in elementary schools.

It is hardly surprising that one of the most compelling waves of thought gaining ground among young Chinese intellectuals was Marxism. After October 1917, many students looked north to Russia, where revolution had also swept away the monarchy, to find solutions to the problems that followed their own upheaval. One morning in July 1921, a secret meeting was held in a girls' school on Joyful Undertaking Street in the Chinese quarter of Shanghai. It was attended by a twenty-eight-year-old schoolteacher from Hunan province:

> At 106 Rue Watz he paused, then slipped in quickly through the carved portals. . . . There were perhaps a dozen men in the room. . . . Two were not Chinese: a representative of the Trade Unions International . . . and another Soviet agent. . . . The gathering was clandestine, and none of those present was to remember the details very well. But the twenty-eight-year-old delegate, and the resolves he took home with him to Hunan, were presently to change the world. The man was Mao Zedong, and the meeting was the opening congress of the Chinese Communist Party."*

---

* According to the recent biography of Mao by Jung Chang and Jon Halliday, a representative of the Comintern had established the Chinese Chinese Party the previous year,

The meeting lasted four days. During that time the delegates lived in the nearby Bo Wen Girls' School, whose students were on holiday. They ate meals cooked by the school janitor and remained undisturbed—until the fourth day, when a stranger appeared at the door asking for an address that was only a few houses away. The delegates, realizing that he must be a spy, got out just before the police arrived. They moved to a lake eighty miles south of the city and hired a pleasure boat, on which they finished their meeting.

One of the men at this meeting was an agent for the Comintern, a tall Dutchman with a mustache who used the name Maring.* Although the Kremlin, anxious to encourage revolution to the south, was willing to make use of any warlord who seemed agreeable, Maring decided to ally the new Chinese Communist Party (CCP) with Sun Yat-sen. Shortly after the Congress ended, Maring went to Shanghai to see the leader of the Kuomintang. He was the first of many emissaries sent by Moscow to make friends with the little doctor.

Sun, who had sent Lenin a note of congratulations after the revolution of 1917, was both embarrassed and encouraged by repeated offers of Russian friendship and advice. Still resentful of the Western nations that had refused to bankroll the Kuomintang, he allowed himself to be convinced that an alliance between Russia and the KMT was possible and would help his cause. For his part, he hoped to absorb the fledgling Chinese Communist Party into the KMT. The Russians, of course, had other intentions. A Chinese nation, freed from its bonds with the imperialistic nations of the West, might stand as a bulwark against them. Moreover, as Stalin later spelled out in a speech to three thousand Communist functionaries, "At present, we need the Right," he declared, explaining that the KMT had "connections with the rich merchants and can raise money from them. So they have to be utilized to the end, squeezed out like a lemon, and then flung away."

Sun, who could never be brought to question the motives or examine the aims of contributors to his cause, was confused about the failure of his republic. He had always thought that the hard part would be overthrowing the Manchus, not establishing a workable government. "When the period of destruction closed," he said, "revolutionary reconstruction seemed an easy thing to me." Although Sun had helped destroy the mandarins, it had not occurred to him that he needed to replace the men who had performed

and Mao was not counted among the eight founders. The new party was 94 percent funded by the Russians.

* His real name was Hendricus Sneevliet, but he used more than a dozen aliases.

many of the functions of Chinese society. Most peasants had no comprehension of the role of a citizen in a representative form of government, and there had been no effort to train them or, in fact, even to teach them to read. Moreover, the leaders of the Kuomintang, having allied themselves with one military man or another over the years, had never paid any attention to building up an army of their own. Realizing the need for military control, Sun had himself elected not president but generalissimo of the southern government. As his chief of staff he appointed one of his disciples, a thirty-six-year-old whom he sent to Moscow in the summer of 1923 to study Russian military organization.

The man whom Sun sent to Moscow was Chiang Kai-shek, who would one day become China's leader and the husband of May-ling Soong.

9

[B]efore he [Chiang Kai-shek] was forty, there was "no doubt" in his mind that he was China's son of destiny.

—PINCHON LOH

CHIANG KAI-SHEK came from the village of Chikow in the province of Chekiang, located on the seacoast south of Shanghai. For hundreds of years, his ancestors* had lived in and around this village, which lies in a secluded valley among purple mountains. Waterfalls and streams cascaded down the hills around the town, and nearby terraces were planted with rice and tea. Surrounded by huge forests of bamboo prized for their height, width, and the straightness of their trunks, Chikow had only one street, divided into Upper, Middle, and Lower. The Chiang family lived above their salt store, a whitewashed building at number 51 Upper Street, where Kai-shek† was born on October 31, 1887.

Chiang's paternal grandfather was a great influence on the boy. "In my grandfather's time," Chiang Kai-shek wrote, "he established himself by commerce and became very wealthy in the salt business. He had a kindly disposition. In dealing with others he was always generous. But in bringing up his children and grandchildren he was very strict. He never wore silk and was a vegetarian. He was devoted to the study of Buddhism. . . . As a boy I was more often unwell than not. My grandfather always treated and nursed me. He was constantly by my bedside. If the malady was serious he would keep watch over me, never going to bed himself at night. . . . Nearly all my ailments were healed by the medical skill of my grandfather."

If Chiang was sickly, he was also difficult and full of mischief. At three he apparently stuck a pair of chopsticks down his throat to see how far they would go. They got stuck, and when they were removed, there was some

---

* Some said the Chiangs were descended from the third son of the duke of Chou, a contemporary of Confucius. A highly unlikely connection, it was an ancestry that, according to at least one of his biographers, Chiang Kai-shek "went to much trouble" to prove. (Brian Crozier, *The Man Who Lost China*, p. 31.)

† Kai-shek, which means "Upright Stone" or "Firm Rock," was actually named Jui-yuan by his grandfather but became known as Kai-shek.

question as to whether he had damaged his vocal cords. At six, he was playing with one of the mammoth jars placed under the eaves of Chinese houses
to catch and store rainwater. Trying to get hold of a piece of ice, he fell into
the water and barely got out before freezing to death.

To keep him busy and out of trouble, his mother started his lessons at
the age of four or five. She tried, he said, "to teach and persuade me to
study," and when that failed, she had "to use the birch repeatedly in order
not to spoil me." He was, however, a natural leader among the neighboring
children. As their self-appointed general, he led them in war games or told
stories from a platform, "his manner haughty, his gait lordly, and his ges-
tures extremely free." According to one of his tutors, "At play, he would regard the classroom as his stage and all his schoolmates as his toys: he could
be wild and ungovernable. But when he was at his desk, reading or holding
his pen trying to think, then even a hundred voices around him could not
distract him from his concentration. His periods of quietude and outburst
sometimes occurred within a few minutes of each other: one would think he
had two different personalities."

We know very little about Chiang's father, who died when the boy was
nine, two years after his beloved grandfather. Chiang, who was not fond of
him, adored his mother, his father's third wife, who had been married at
twenty-two to a man twenty years her senior. A devoted Buddhist, she ran a
large household, which included a stepbrother and stepsister by Chiang's
father's first wife and Mrs. Chiang's own six children, two of whom died in
childhood. According to Chiang, his mother "endured thirty-six years of
hardship" and "swallowed much bitterness" from the time of her marriage in
1886 to her death in 1921. This was due to the fact that she was left the
female head of the house, unprotected from the local authorities after the
men in the family died. He himself, he said, was "frequently discriminated
against . . . because of my humble origin."

"It will be remembered that the then Manchu regime was in its most
corrupt state," Chiang wrote in later years. "The degenerated gentry and corrupt officials had made it a habit to abuse and maltreat the people. My family, solitary and without influence, became at once the target of such insults
and maltreatment. From time to time usurious taxes and unjust public service were forced upon us and once we were publicly insulted before the
court. To our regret and sorrow none of our relatives and kinsmen was stirred
from his apathy. Indeed the miserable condition of my family at that time is
beyond description. It was entirely due to my mother and her kindness and
perseverance that the family was saved from utter ruin." When one of the
citizens of Chikow failed to pay his rice tax and fled the district, the local
authorities, knowing there was no adult male in the Chiang household, ar-

rested young Chiang, took him to court, and threatened to throw him in jail if he or his family did not pay the fine owned by the missing citizen. It was apparently an enormous humiliation for both the boy and his mother, one that he often mentioned in later years as "the first spark that kindled my revolutionary fire."

In spite of this, Chiang was not his mother's favorite. That role was held by the youngest boy, who was, as Chiang put it, "endowed with extremely good looks, which none of the others of us had." With his older brother the head of the family and his younger brother the favorite, there seems to have been no special role left for Chiang. His sense of being left out was reinforced by a traveling fortune-teller who told him—in front of the entire village—that his cranium was different from everyone else's and that he was an "exceptionally strange child."

Before he was nine, Chiang had read and memorized the four Confucian Classics, which, we must assume, he understood no better than any other Chinese boy of his age. After that came the Confucian Canons.* Having completed the usual classical education by the age of fifteen, Chiang tried out for the civil examinations, which would have qualified him to enter the bureaucracy. "He went to the examination to satisfy his curiosity," said his tutor, "and was disgusted by the cruel and humiliating regulations of the examination hall. He severely disparaged the Manchu court for the contempt with which the young scholars were treated and for the despicable habits of decadence and pedantry it encouraged, and was greatly pleased when he learned, not long afterward, of Yuan Shih-kai's memorial to establish a new educational system in place of the civil service examination." According to the author of the book from which this is quoted, "We may assume that Chiang failed in the examination."

The year before, when he was fourteen, Chiang had been married by his mother to an illiterate local girl, Mao Fu-mei. Nineteen at the time of their marriage, Fu-mei was a heavyset girl with a pleasant disposition. The marriage was never a success, although Fu-mei claimed that they were happy for the first two months, until her mother-in-law began to berate her for joining Chiang in the long daily walks through the mountains that he adored.

She blamed me bitterly for being a disturbing influence on her son and accused me of aiding and abetting him in his idleness. She even said I was leading him astray: "You are a shameless hussy to gallivant

* The Classics: *The Great Learning, The Middle Way, The Analects,* and the *Sayings* of Confucius's pupil Mencius. The Canons: *The Book of Odes, The Book of Ancient History, The Book of Changes, The Spring and Autumn Chronicles,* and *The Book of Rites.*

all over the mountains and monasteries with a man. . . . It ill becomes a young married woman like you, and it must stop." . . . But
trouble did not end there. Things became intolerable whenever Kai-
shek and I talked or laughed in the house. Our mere conversation
irked Mama Huang terribly, and she cursed me for talking. In order
not to cause any more unpleasantness, therefore, I kept quiet and
seldom spoke. . . . The strain gradually caused a split between Kai-
shek and me.

Having managed to destroy the relationship between her son and his
wife, Chiang's mother was apparently no worse than Chiang himself, who,
Fu-mei confided to friends, beat her. As their son later recalled, he also
dragged her down the stairs by her hair.

After failing the civil service examinations, Chiang attended the Phoenix
Mountain School near his home, then transferred to a school in Ningpo to
study under a professor who gave him special assignments and pushed him
toward an exacting Confucianism that preached self-discipline and self-
denial. He brought the boy into contact with *The Art of War,* by Sun Tzu,*
who explained his theories of divide and conquer and the use of intelligence
agents. A teacher at Chiang's next school, the Dragon River Middle School,
described the young man at the age of eighteen: "Chiang Kai-shek was an
early riser, and, after his matutinal ablutions, it was his custom to stand erect
on the veranda in front of his bedroom for half an hour. During this time
his lips were compressed, his features were set in determination, and he
stood with arms firmly folded." The teacher, Hollington Tong, who later
worked for Chiang and wrote his authorized (i.e., highly laudatory) two-
volume biography, said that the future leader of China made a "deep impression" on him. It was during his years at the Dragon River Middle School
that Chiang underwent a typical teenage rebellion, cutting off his queue and
sending it home to declare his independence from the Manchus and his village. When he was nineteen, he asked his mother for travel costs and left for
Japan to prepare himself for a career in the military.

Japan, the most up-to-date militarily of the Asian nations, had just
emerged the proud victor over Russia in the Russo-Japanese War (1904–
1905). Upon his arrival in Japan, Chiang discovered that he needed the endorsement of what was called the Chinese Board of War in Peking to enroll
in a Japanese military academy. He returned home and entered a competi-

---

* This book, along with *Record of the Warring States,* which enumerates the arts of playing
rivals off against one another and the judicious use of bribes, became Chiang's two favorite books and the sources of his method of governing.

tion to qualify as one of fourteen merit students (as distinguished from forty-six others nominated by the government) from his home province. Deemed ineligible since he had not taken the school's course in the Japanese language, he petitioned the head of the school, saying that he had studied the language while he was in Japan; he was then allowed to take the exam, passed, and was sent to the Shimbu Gakkô School in Tokyo for three years' training. It was during these years that Chiang, given only one or two small bowls of rice per day with "tiny portions of fish and a small dish of daikon [radish]," developed the spartan appetite for which he was later known. He graduated in 1910, the year before the Chinese Revolution, and was assigned to a field artillery regiment in the Japanese army for a final year of training.

It is interesting to note that Chiang Kai-shek, who was often said to have impressed his Chinese superiors, had little or no effect on his Japanese ones. He was not popular with the other students, and the general who commanded the 13th Division of the Japanese army, to which Chiang belonged, had difficulty remembering much about him. All he could say was that he had once invited Chiang to tea, that the young man had arrived immaculately dressed, "like a smart filmstar," and was extremely courteous, leaving a written commentary—four Chinese characters meaning "Never neglect Master's instructions." From this, the general drew the erroneous conclusion that Chiang's later successes were due to loyalty and gratitude.

It was during his years in Japan that Chiang became involved in the Chinese revolutionary movement. This came about through his association with Chen Chi-mei, a member of Sun Yat-sen's inner circle. Regarded by many as the most gifted of Sun's early followers, Chen, a former military governor of Shanghai with a huge price on his head, had fled to Japan with Sun after Yuan's victory over the KMT. An unlikely-looking revolutionary with round glasses and ears that stuck out from his head, Chen came from the same province as Chiang and was nine years his senior. "More manipulative, more of an organizer and less of an idealist" than Sun, he was said by his detractors to be "ruthless and unscrupulous" and "a none too savory item of the Shanghai underworld." Under Chen's influence, Chiang began leading a group of young men in secret Sunday meetings "to deliberate and make plans for important matters of the revolution." In spite of his high voice and plebeian accent, Chiang used his unusual gifts as a speaker who "never failed to make his listeners' hair stand on end." If his early experience with the civil service examination had left him disgusted with the Manchus, his new friend and newly discovered political cause supplied an alternative to the reigning dynasty and the Western powers, both of which he felt had exploited his native land. The revolution also gave him a ready outlet for his seething anger.

During his summer vacations Chiang worked at the secret revolutionary headquarters in the French Concession in Shanghai. It looked as if Chiang's mother was destined to have no grandchildren—until one summer when she took matters in her own hands. Having heard from a fortune-teller that Fu-mei would give birth to a boy who would become an official of high rank, she took her daughter-in-law to Shanghai, where she threatened to kill herself unless Chiang fulfilled his conjugal duties. Chiang and Fu-mei's only child, a son, was born in April of 1910. He was named Ching-kuo and registered in the Chiang family records at his grandmother's request as the son of Kai-shek's younger brother, deceased at four but still their mother's favorite.

In 1911, the year of the revolution, Chiang returned to Shanghai, where Chen put him in charge of a brigade of 3,000 men, "recruited from the riff-raff of Shanghai." After whipping them into shape, Chiang led another hundred men in the "liberation" of Hangchow in his home province. He then "abandoned himself" to dissipations readily available in Shanghai, disappearing from headquarters for months at a time into the brothels on the Kiangsi Road (the red-light district), contracting venereal disease several times and apparently becoming sterile. He rationalized his excesses in a letter written over a decade later: "Everybody says that I am given to lust, but they do not know that this is a thing of last resort, in a state of utter depression." In 1912, he met Yao Yi-cheng, a maid in a Shanghai brothel, who became his concubine and stayed with him for the next eight years.

An upper-class woman of the day describes Shanghai's prostitutes as

big and sturdy, yet their extravagantly bound feet were the size of a four-year-old child's. . . . Their coiffures were fearfully complicated, hair coiled at the neck, generous bangs, and sideburns which reached almost to the chin and which were lacquered to the cheeks. During their occasional daytime outings they drove around in victorias dressed in brightly brocaded jackets and trousers, their faces half concealed by the dark glasses which were the high fashion of the moment. But in the evening the sing-song girls were magically transformed into exotic creatures from the Arabian Nights . . . carried to their various rendezvous on the shoulder of huge, half-naked coolies. The coolie draped a towel over one shoulder and held the sing-song girl firmly on her perch, with an arm around her waist and one hand grasping both pathetic little feet. He moved with a swift practised rhythm, his sweat-streaked face glistening in the dim light of the street lamps; the girl, with her arm around his neck, swaying slightly to his stride.

Along with uncontrolled lust, Chiang began to exhibit a "fiery, uncom-promising temper which weighed very tryingly on his friends." This unat-tractive trait, which caused his voice, high-pitched at the best of times, to soar to a near falsetto, was noted by one of his most sympathetic biogra-phers, who also noted his "obdurate" nature. "Not infrequently," the writer said, "he would fly into storms of temper before which few human beings could stand. No-one could endure him, and by degrees he became more and more disagreeable to his associates." Sent to see a hospitalized rival of Chen's, Chiang argued with him, lost his temper, and shot him in his hospi-tal bed. Probably because of this incident, he returned to Japan, where he spent some months writing for a magazine, *Military Voice*. Whereas his early articles spoke of world harmony, he came to believe that China needed a huge army, requiring an expenditure of between half and two thirds of the national income.

Returning to China, Chiang joined the abortive Second Revolution against Yuan in 1913. The next year he was sent on a mission to Manchuria to investigate the local Kuomintang agent's report that the time was ripe for an uprising. Chiang, who reported just the opposite, spoiled the plans of the agent, who had been hoping to raise funds ostensibly for the revolution but really for himself. In 1916, Chiang led a group of soldiers in capturing a fortress lying between Shanghai and Nanking, only to find that on the fifth day his men had deserted and left him alone. What one biographer calls his "sense of persecution and alienation" was heightened by this experience, along with the untimely death of his close friend and mentor, Chen Chi-mei, which occurred around the same time.

It will be remembered that Yuan Shih-kai, the Chinese prime minister with monarchical ambitions, had died in the spring of 1916. But before his death, which he must have expected, he had his agents assassinate his old enemy Chen, using a ruse based on the Kuomintang's lack of funds. Offered some money for the cause by a fellow member of the KMT who said he knew where to apply for help, Chen was gunned down on his way to the "meeting" with the supposed benefactor. Chiang Kai-shek, who appeared at the funeral in white mourning robes, was devastated. "Alas!" he cried. "From now on, where can be found a man who knows me so well and loves me so deeply as you did?" Fearing he would be Yuan's next victim, Chiang hid out in a brothel and then moved in with one of Chen's nephews. Later on, he would claim that it was Chen's death that had pushed him "into a life of debauchery."

Before Chen was killed, he had introduced Chiang to a Shanghai mer-chant known by foreigners as Curio Chang,* a crippled dealer who had

---

* His real name was Chang Ching-chiang.

grown enormously rich selling Chinese curios in Paris and who now befriended Chiang. Curio Chang was from Chiang and Chen's home province, had given a great deal of money to Sun Yat-sen for his revolution, and was said by one knowledgeable journalist to be "the brains in the Sun Yat-sen movement. He had the intelligence and the Western orientation. Sun had tremendous respect for him." Others, however, called Curio Chang "one of the most sinister characters in the Revolutionary Movement," due to his close ties with the Shanghai underworld, most of whom belonged to the powerful secret society known as the Green Gang. Shanghai was, in the words of author Han Suyin,* "a fabulous gangster city . . . unparalleled by any other metropolis. Beside it the Chicago of Al Capone was a staid, almost pious, provincial town." Through Curio Chang, Chiang met other members of the Green Gang. A "kingmaker by instinct," Curio Chang, like Chen before him, apparently realized that Chiang Kai-shek had the makings of a leader.

After Chen's death Chiang apparently suffered some sort of breakdown, and his mother came to Shanghai to take care of him. Wanted by Yuan's police, he was probably helped to avoid arrest by members of the Green Gang. In 1917, he was appointed military counselor to Sun and spent the next three or four years with the 2nd Detachment of the Cantonese army under the command of a man known as the Hakka General.† Chiang did not trust the Hakka General and warned Sun to be wary of him. Prevented from choosing his own officers or disciplining his soldiers, Chiang recommended that his detachment be disbanded and spent most of a year on home leave (which he took to include Shanghai and Tokyo) and eventually resigned from the detachment. This was the first instance of an oft-repeated maneuver in which Chiang would resign from a post when things were going badly in order to prove that he was irreplacable. He learned that this usually led to an improvement in the circumstances of his job and an increase in his power. As it would in the future, the scheme worked. Both Sun and the Hakka General begged Chiang to return and reorganize the Kwantung army. Chiang hesitated until the Kwangsi Clique, a group from Kwangsi province that opposed Sun, assassinated another of his friends, Chu Ta-fu. His change of heart may also have been due to the following letter, which he received from Sun:

> The sudden tragic death of Chu Ta-fu is a loss to me comparable to that of my right or left hand. When I look upon the members of our

---

* Han Suyin's most famous book was *A Many-Splendored Thing*, later made into a movie. Born of a Chinese father and Belgian mother, she was a doctor before becoming a well-known writer.

† His name was Ch'en Chiung-ming.

party I find very few who are experts in war and also loyal. Only you, my Elder Brother,* are with us, you whose courage and sincerity are equal to those of Chu Ta-fu, and your knowledge of war is even better than his. But you have a very fiery temper and your hatred of mediocrity is excessive. And so it often leads to quarrelling and difficulty in cooperating. As you are shouldering the great and terrible responsibility of our party, you should sacrifice your high ideals a little and try to compromise. This is merely for the sake of our party and has nothing to do with your personal principles.

Returning to his post, Chiang was furious when he learned that the Hakka General had not finished off the Kwangsi Clique according to the plan Chiang had drawn up. But when he went to Shanghai to complain about this to Sun, the leader gave him no satisfaction. Thoroughly disgusted with both men, Chiang used the death of his mother in June of 1921 as the excuse he needed to absent himself from a frustrating situation. He returned to Chikow, where he stayed on and off until her funeral in November.

The following month, on December 5, 1921, Chiang married again, this time a girl of his own choosing. Her name was Chen Chieh-ju, known as Jennie Chen. Chiang had first met her in 1919. She was tall and thin, the opposite of his village wife. In Jennie's version of their courtship, she was not particularly interested in him and avoided him for some time, particularly after he tricked her into going to a hotel and tried to force himself on her. (He was thirty-two at the time; she was thirteen.)

But Chiang persisted, and Jennie's mother, concerned about her daughter's future, engaged a professional investigator to look into his past. The report stated that Chiang lived in Shanghai, was essentially unemployed, and already had a village wife and a concubine. But shortly after the death of Jennie's father in the fall of 1921, Jennie's mother received a visit from Curio Chang, Chiang's dealer friend and Jennie's godfather, who assured her that Chiang's first wife, Fu-mei, had "become a devout Buddhist and renounced the world" and that his concubine Yao was currently living in Soochow and "had recently accepted a settlement of $5,000 to relinquish any and all claims on Kai-shek." After this, Jennie's mother gave Chiang permission to marry her daughter. The wedding was celebrated in a civil ceremony at the Great Eastern Hotel in Shanghai. Around fifty relatives and friends were present at the feast presided over (and probably paid for) by Curio Chang. During their honeymoon, Jennie discovered that Chiang had

---

* Addressing someone as "Elder Brother" was a customary honorific and had nothing to do with age or relationship.

disobeyed his doctor and married her before completing a series of treatments for venereal disease. He gave her gonorrhea, a disease that left them both unable to have children,* and in repentance he swore never to drink alcohol again.

Meanwhile, Chiang's concerns about the Hakka General had been proven right. When Sun arrived in Canton, he found that the Hakka General had expropriated for himself a long list of impressive titles, including minister of war and governor of the province of Kwangtung, leaving Sun, the founder of the revolution, with nothing but the title of minister of the interior. To counter this, Sun had himself elected provisional president of China by a rump Parliament, called together for that purpose. But the Hakka General was no longer willing to subordinate himself to Sun. Commander of a huge army, in charge of all the arms and provisions Sun needed for his troops, the Hakka General was in effect the warlord of southern China, and the Peking government, always willing to side with whoever was on top, supported him over the revolutionary Sun. Sun's scheme of having himself named president had failed. Whatever he called himself, the foreign embassies in Peking refused to recognize him or turn the customs duties over to him. Taking advantage of the situation, the Hakka General sent troops to attack Sun's headquarters in Canton. Chiang, who was not there at the time, claimed that the Hakka General had offered his soldiers a bonus of $200,000 and three days' free looting if they managed to kill Sun. Sun's staff finally convinced him to flee.

"About two o'clock on the morning of June 16th Dr. Sun roused me . . . telling me to hurry and dress, that we were in danger and must escape," Ching-ling wrote in the only description she ever gave of the perils of being Sun Yat-sen's wife. ". . . I thought it would be inconvenient for him to have a woman along with him, and urged him to leave me behind for the time being. . . . At last he saw the sense of my argument, but he would not go even then until he had left all fifty of our bodyguard to protect the house. Then he departed alone.

Half an hour after he had gone . . . rifle shots rang out. . . . The enemy fired downhill at us from two sides, shouting, 'Kill Sun Wen

---

* Chiang already had two sons: Chiang Ching-kuo by Fu-mei, and Chiang Wei-kuo, an adopted child, the son of a friend (Tai Chi-tao) and Yao, the concubine they are said to have shared when he lived in Japan. Chiang always claimed he had adopted Wei-kuo to spare his friend embarrassment, but there were many people who thought he was Chiang's own child. In 1996, however, Wei-kuo announced that he was, in fact, the son of the friend, born out of wedlock in 1916.

[Sun Yat-sen]! Kill Sun Wen!' Pitch darkness covered them completely. . . . As day broke our men began to reply to the fire. . . . My bath was smashed to bits. One-third of our handful of troops had been wiped out, but the remaining men resisted with more determination than ever. . . . By eight o'clock our store of ammunition was running low. . . . Our Captain advised me to leave . . . promising . . . to stay there in order to halt any possible pursuit. . . . Later, all of the fifty were reported killed. Four of us . . . taking with us only the most necessary supplies . . . crawled along . . . to make our escape. . . . Twice bullets brushed past my temple without injuring me. From eight in the morning till four that afternoon we were literally buried in a hell of constant gunfire. . . . Once the entire ceiling of a room I had left only a few minutes before collapsed. . . . Our iron gates were soon smashed and we were confronted by the bloodthirsty bayonets and revolvers of the soldiers. . . . I succeeded in making an escape, wearing Colonel Bow's hat and Dr. Sun's raincoat. . . . I was absolutely exhausted, and begged the guards to shoot me. Instead they dragged me forward, one on each side supporting me. . . . Corpses lay about everywhere. . . . Their chests were caved in, their arms slashed, their legs severed. . . . Again our way was cut off by a group of the mob. . . . The whisper ran through our party that we should lie flat in the street, pretending to be dead. In this way we were left unmolested; then we arose and continued our journey. . . . Half an hour later . . . we came to a small farmhouse. The owner tried to drive us out, fearing the consequences of sheltering us; his attempt was forestalled, however, by a timely swoon on my part.

I woke up to find the guards washing me with cold water, and fanning me. One of them went out to see what he could . . . when suddenly there came a tattoo of rifle shots. The guard indoors rushed to shut the door; he told me that the other one had been struck by a bullet, and was probably dead by this time. When the firing subsided I disguised myself as an old countrywoman, and with the guard in the guise of a pedlar we left the cottage. I picked up a basket and a few vegetables on the way, and carried them with me. At last we reached the house of a friend which had already been searched that morning. To go on was absolutely impossible, so we spent the night there. Shelling never ceased the entire night, and our relief was enormous when we heard cannon shots at last from the gunboats. Dr. Sun, then, was safe. . . . Next morning . . . another friend, a foundry worker, arranged for a small motor-boat for me. . . . The river was thronged with boats full of booty, both girls and goods. . . . It was reported that two women unfortunate enough to answer to my description had been thrown into jail. That same afternoon I left Canton; the house in which I had stayed the night was searched again. At last, that night, I succeeded in meeting Dr. Sun on board ship, after a life-and-death struggle.

Sun had boarded a gunboat anchored at Whampoa, where he was joined by Chiang and Chiang's new wife, Jennie. This proof of Chiang's loyalty to Sun had a profound effect on their future relationship, and the trio remained on the boat for fifty-six days. When news arrived that the Hakka General had beaten Sun's forces, they convinced the captain of a British warship to escort them to Hong Kong, where they were joined by Ching-ling. A week or so later, Ching-ling wired May-ling for $500 to secure passage on a boat back to Shanghai. "Small, slight, very pale, and altogether the loneliest thing I have ever seen" was how one of May-ling's friends described Ching-ling when she arrived at the Suns' home on Rue Molière.

In an attempt to disclaim personal responsibility for turning on his former leader, the Hakka General sent news releases to papers all over China declaring that Sun's policy was "pro-Russian and Bolshevik." The general claimed that his soldiers had found "important papers in his [Sun's] locked iron safe at his Presidential Palace" giving "documentary proof of a far-reaching plan to communize China as a first step to usurping the legal Peking government." Sun, who had retreated to Shanghai once again, issued his own statement, declaring that the treachery of the Hakka General was worse than that of even his "bitterest foe." Disgusted and discouraged, Chiang settled down for a time into a job he had held on and off since 1917, trading stocks in Curio Chang's brokerage firm. Successful at first, he was finally ruined by a tendency toward inordinate speculation and a crash in the market, after which he returned to military life.

Fortunately, not everyone believed the propaganda released by the Hakka General, and a certain amount of sympathy for Sun swept over the country. On October 13, 1922, part of Sun's army, which had remained loyal to their leader and to their general, a man named Hsu Chung-chih, captured Fuchow, a former treaty port and the capital city of Fukien province. Sun immediately rewarded General Hsu by making him commander in chief of his forces with Chiang as his chief of staff, a position that held little appeal for Chiang. Joined by other soldiers, Sun's supporters reached Canton in the middle of December, and the Hakka General went into hiding. By February of 1923, conditions in Canton were calm enough for Sun to make a triumphal return. He wired Chiang to "come quickly," but as usual, Chiang procrastinated. Heading off for Shanghai instead, he explained that he was having eye trouble—illness being an acceptable alternative to saying no, a breach of manners in China.

"What rubbish you talk!" Sun wrote Chiang. "Since I could not go . . . I entrusted you with the responsibility of punishing the traitors. How could you so hurriedly think of giving it up like that? . . . To ensure success, it always depends upon your fortitude and persistence, your disregard of jealousy and hard work. . . . Don't you, my Elder Brother, remember the days when we were in the gunboat? All day long we could only sleep and eat, hoping to hear good news. . . . Whatever difficulties you meet, whatever hardships you suffer, do stay in the Army as long as I am struggling here." To sweeten the invitation, Sun allowed Chiang to resign as chief of staff to General Hsu and reappointed him as his own chief of staff: "The need for your assistance here is urgent," he wired. "Anxiously request your immediate arrival. Do not delay. Your appointment as chief-of-staff has been announced."

Chiang left Shanghai three months later, arriving in Canton in time to help deal successfully with two traitorous generals: his old enemy, the Hakka General, and a new would-be warlord. Whether he felt insufficiently rewarded for these efforts, he resigned again "in anger" two months later and left Canton. "If I return to Kwangtung [Canton's province] I will not be able to control my despicable habit of violence," he claimed. Not possessing "the natural gifts to be a staff officer," Chiang said of himself that he might be better in a position that permitted him "to act summarily without interference from anyone." He asked to be assigned to an investigative mission to Russia, since "in my opinion there is nothing to which I can contribute" at home.

Chiang left China for Russia in the middle of August 1923. The nature of his mission was laid out by Sun in a letter to the Russian ambassador in Peking: "Some weeks ago I sent identical letters to Comrade Lenin, Tchitcherin [Chicherin], and Trotsky introducing General Chiang Kai-shek, who is my Chief of Staff and confidential agent. I have dispatched him to Moscow to discuss ways and means whereby our friends there can assist me in my work in this country. . . . General Chiang is fully empowered to act on my behalf."

Chiang Kai-shek was thirty-six years old when he traveled to Russia for Sun Yat-sen. It was a trip that would turn out to be highly significant for him personally, as well as for the country he would one day lead.

10

Psychologically, all the Soongs are Americans.

—George E. Sokolsky

While her future husband was working his way up the political ladder, May-ling was coming to terms with a life of ease that seemed to be leading nowhere. Headstrong and pampered, the youngest Soong sister would occasionally join other wealthy young women for an afternoon of mah-jongg but could not bring herself to observe traditional protocol. She inevitably got bored before everyone else and instead of waiting until the polite moment to depart, which depended on the score, she would simply jump up and leave. She was apparently no different in the evening. "Miss Soong was serious minded even in those care-free days," said one of the young party-goers, "and I remember that she made no move to join our silly group which laughed and joked throughout the evening. I was very much aware of her vibrant, beautifully modulated voice and her faultlessly proportioned feet."

Like many young woman in the process of figuring out who they are, May-ling started with her appearance. Just as she had gradually become more and more Chinese-looking in America, she now took plenty of time giving up her Western attire. Meanwhile, she caused a great deal of comment by appearing in clothes nipped in at the waist (Chinese women always wore straight dresses), hats of all descriptions (Chinese women never wore them), jodhpurs for horseback riding, and tennis clothes.

Once back in China, May-ling realized that she was not as familiar as she should have been with her own culture and, in an attempt to make up for her years abroad, engaged an old-fashioned scholar to fill in the gaps in her education. She studied with him for years, learning to recite the Chinese classics, chanting and moving her body back and forth in the traditional manner. At the same time, she enjoyed life in Shanghai, which was exceedingly pleasant for the rich after the end of the First World War. As one American phrased it, "When she went back at nineteen it was to lead the life of a Newport set in Shanghai." Businesses were thriving. Everyone with money had cars and chauffeurs, entertained lavishly with parties that lasted not hours but days and featured elaborate entertainment by troupes of famous actors. "The streets are crowded with hungry, sullen, half-starved peo-

99

ple and among them roll the sedans and limousines of the wealthy Chinese, spending fabulous sums on pleasure, food and clothes, wholly senseless to the others," wrote author Pearl Buck in disgust. If May-ling was not insensitive to others, she was still full of youthful energy, vivacious, and a popular guest at both Chinese and foreign parties. She was also smart enough to ration her appearances and seemed in no hurry to find a husband. She kept busy learning Chinese and working for her charities, but also attended the races at the Kiangwan International Race Club and helped plan fashion shows.

The story is told that when she came home, May-ling asked her father to buy a mansion on Seymour Road in place of the old family house on Avenue Joffre. "Don't send your children abroad," Charlie laughed to a friend. "Nothing's good enough for them when they come back. 'Father, why can't we have a bigger house? Father, why don't we have a modern bathroom?' Take my advice; keep your children at home!" It is hard to know whether Charlie really disapproved of his daughter's request or if he was showing off his ability to provide anything for his children that they wanted. And, as it turned out, May-ling moved into the home she wanted—after her father's death in 1918.

Charlie, who had been suffering for some time from the cancer that eventually killed him, had the good fortune to see and entertain his old benefactor, General Julian Carr, while he was still well enough to enjoy a visit. In 1917, the American Trade Commission asked Carr to go on a fact-finding tour of the Orient to assess business opportunities, and he arrived for a five-day visit to Shanghai in March of 1917. While he was there, Charlie escorted him on sightseeing trips and to meetings with educators and missionaries. On March 31, May-ling's father gave Carr "a great reception attended by a great crowd," and when the visitor left a week later, there were three mammoth porcelain vases, carefully packed and placed in the hold of the ship—gifts from Charlie "in appreciation for all kindnesses."

A year later, in the middle of March, May-ling wrote Emma that her father had "become very thin, and the doctors tell us to expect the worst at any time." Although she admitted that it was hard for her to appear "cheerful" and control her "hot temper" in the face of Charlie's growing irritability, May-ling gave him nightly massages with olive oil. The family moved him to a hospital, but a week later, when the doctors told Madame Soong that her husband had only a 20 percent chance of recovering, she moved him back home. "Mother says she does not believe in doctors, & that no one could cure him but God. Hence she refuses to let him be sweated to throw off the poison," May-ling wrote Emma Mills. ". . . I am almost going crazy with the tension and mother's refusal to follow the doctors' directions. At the hospital, he was forced to drink water; here at home he hasn't drunken [*sic*] any water at all. With two babies in the house* under three years old, it is impossible to keep the house quiet. . . . The doctors say that the poison has gone to Father's brain. He sleeps most of the time, and his face is swollen."

Charlie Soong's wife, two of his sons, and all three daughters were with him when he died on May 3, 1918. One writer† hints at foul play, suggesting that since none of his immediate family mentioned his illness to friends and the customarily long eulogies were absent from the funeral, Charlie's fatal cancer might well have been a "grand euphemism" for some sort of sinister plot. This seems to be nothing more than an ill-considered charge by someone who disliked the Soongs. Like many of his countrymen, Charlie was known for his reticence in discussing matters he felt should be kept within the confines of the family (a trait the family retains to this day), and certainly his failing health would have fallen into this category.

During her father's last illness, May-ling came down with influenza. "I took to bed with the world looking like winter, and came down to see that it has blossomed into bewitching spring," she wrote Emma three weeks later, "a soft, delicate mass of apple blossoms, cherry blossoms, tender willow shoots, silky magnolia buds and nodding daffodils." Asking forgiveness for the general listlessness of her letter, she told her friend that she felt "even too weak to lose my temper—a fact which did not by any means escape my sharp-eyed maid."

After Charlie's death, May-ling's mother moved into one of their other houses for a while and, in the middle of the summer, took her two younger boys away for a short time. May-ling and T.V., who loved to give parties, were left alone at the home on Avenue Joffre. "We certainly did have a good time," she wrote Emma, "giving dinners and card parties. Then we went out for long midnight rides. . . . We had our cousins come up, and so had a regular house-party. I am afraid though the servants did not enjoy themselves as much as we did, for we kept them hopping busy doing one thing after another. For instance one day we had them make ice-cream three times during the day. And as the rain comes off and on during the day, they had to put up and put down the tennis net and lines constantly." Not surprisingly, two weeks later May-ling found herself "wrestling with cooks—we've had six cooks in ten days!" Still, she found time to write an article on "Women's Colleges in America," which was picked up by *The Shanghai Ga-*

---

* Ai-ling's children.

† Sterling Seagrave in *The Soong Dynasty.*

zette. Her success led her to think about writing articles about needed social reforms in Shanghai. "I wish you were here to help me sort out the essentials from the rest of my thoughts," she wrote Emma. ". . . I am starting a course in Macauley for my sole benefit. I want to get the swing and rhythm of analytical writing."

Part society belle, part would-be reformer, May-ling moved with her mother and brothers into the house she had fallen in love with before Charlie's death. Huge solid iron doors and a thickly woven bamboo wall still suround the property, making it impossible for passersby to catch even a glimpse of the big yellow, green-roofed home or the beautiful garden planned around a giant magnolia tree. Built like a European country house with plenty of balconies and porches, May-ling's new home boasted an attached two-car garage and was, in the words of one observer, "really a rich man's house."

"The inside is beautifully finished in teakwood with carved doors, double flooring, and a wonderful tiled conservatory, and a tiled kitchen!" May-ling wrote Emma before the move.

> Downstairs, there is a medium sized hall, a lavatory, a smoking room, a large dining room with <u>panelled</u> ceiling carved, the butler's pantry and the kitchen. On the second floor are three bedrooms, a large living room, a large square hall and a wonderfully spacious bathroom. There are also two large closets for clothes—and closets in Shanghai are so rare. On the third floor is the roof garden where we are going to spend our afternoons . . . by the house is a green house where I and the gardener are going to cultivate roses for the flower shows. We are going to build the garage three stories high, as the second floor is for the servants' quarters, and the third floor for a trunk room. . . .

This house on Ave. Joffre is too large for our needs," she continued, ". . . and we think of Father every time we turn around. . . . It looks spacious and elegant, but not cosy or "homey." With both my sisters away, and their servants and children gone, Mother and I should feel lost in this big house all by ourselves . . . and we need a horde of servants about this place. At the other house we shall be quite comfortable with a cook, a boy, a coolie, a chauffeur, a gardener and the two amahs for Mother and myself. Father left everything in order, and as Mother knew all about his affairs, we have had no trouble. Speculations by people outside as to whether Father died a millionaire or only mediumly well off would be amusing at any other time. As for the past seven years, Father has been "a gentleman of leisure," no one outside the family knows how he stands regarding property. . . . He has been such a wonderful Father to us! And we love him even though he is no longer with us.

Unlike other well-to-do Chinese, including her eldest and youngest daughters, Mrs. Soong did not succumb to the money fever that infected Shanghai society during and after World War I. As Western industrialists returned home to take part in the war, the Chinese compradores, who had learned Western business techniques, now applied them to replenishing the stores of European goods diminished by the war, investing in everything from cement plants to textile concerns and starting their own banks. Sensing opportunity, Chinese who had been living overseas came home to work, opening the first two department stores in the city—concrete "towers" set firmly into the Shanghai mud. Getting and spending became the newest way of life, "one that was brash, flashy, and unapologetically luxury-loving." Even Wallis Simpson, who danced around the fountain of the Majestic Hotel on the famous Bubbling Well Road—one of the places where foreigners first mixed with the newly rich Chinese—found the life highly seductive: "the moonlight, the perfume of jasmine, not to mention the Shangri-la illusion of the courtyard, made me feel that I had really entered the Celestial Kingdom," sighed the twentieth-century icon of the upward social scramble.

A former Shanghai correspondent for the London *Times*, J. O. P. Bland, marveled at the scene. "The evidence of Shanghai's wealth . . . abounds on every side," he wrote in an article for London's *National Review*.

The ease with which money has been made, by both merchants and mandarins, is reflected in the monstrous cost of living and in a degree of luxury in some respects unequaled either in New York or Buenos Aires. I have seen something of the stupendous wealth of both these cities during and since the war. I have walked their streets and dwelt in their hotels. . . . But in the matter of mellow creature comforts of savoury fleshpots deftly served, no Croesus of America, North or South, can ever hope to attain to the comfortable heights and depths that Shanghai takes for granted. And neither Fifth Avenue nor the Calle Florida is in the habit of treating the dollar with quite the same splendid insouciance as Shanghai's Nanking Road.

Shanghai, according to John Fairbank, "came to represent both the best and the worst aspects of China's modernization." This was due primarily to two factors—its geographical location and its colonial-derived city government. City services had evolved under the Shanghai Municipal Council, a ruling body started by the foreign residents in the middle of the nineteenth century, to which Chinese were not invited until 1921. The port was run by the Imperial Maritime Customs Service, which collected taxes from foreign ships under the direction of a British inspector general, a successor to the famous Englishman Robert Hart. The Chinese government whose authority was confined to areas outside the International Settlement, was not a body that Chinese residents could look to for help or services. For that, they had to turn to the Green Gang, a secret society that worked with the foreign police—especially those in the French Concession—in what Fairbank called a "marriage of convenience."

One of the major political purposes of secret societies before 1911 had been the overthrow of the Manchus. Once that was accomplished, their political functions were taken over by the parties: the Kuomintang and eventually the Communists. In societal and economic matters, however, the secret societies remained active, representing the poorest members of urban society and the overtaxed peasants in the provinces, offering spiritual support and a sense of belonging. The three most important secret societies in China were the Green Gang, centered in Shanghai; the Red Gang, which had started as an organization for sailors stopping off in port and operated in southern China; and the Society of Elder Brothers, strong in Szechuan and the Northwest. They were known as the Triad. There were also quite a number of smaller secret organizations and, in the words of one agent of the U.S. Office of Strategic Services (OSS), forerunner of the CIA, "Some were benevolent and some were sinister." As Shanghai emerged as the most important industrial center in China, it had attracted—along with armies of unskilled workers—petty smugglers, bandits, and police from the provinces who had come to the city to make their fortunes. Unlike some other societies, the Green Gang had embraced these criminals and organized their activities to a degree the Sicilian and American Mafias might well have envied. By the beginning of the twentieth century, it had become the most important secret society in the city—and the most dangerous.

The Green Gang was elaborately intertwined with the successful business establishments in Shanghai, since it controlled the many and varied forms of vice in which the new industrialists indulged themselves. A highly visible force, it was headed by Huang Jin-rong, known behind his back as "Pockmarked Huang." Aside from the pits left by a bad case of smallpox, Huang was not bad-looking as a young man; his nose was square, his eyes piercing, his head bald or shaved. But by the time he reached middle age, he gave off what one writer called a "sinister aura. . . . This was the face of a man . . . accustomed to the vicious deployment of power."

Huang's father had owned a teahouse next to the French Concession

where Huang started his work life as a waiter. There he met the petty criminals who lived under and around a nearby bridge, along with two neighbor-
hood bosses—an expert in martial arts and a dark-skinned enforcer known as
"Black-skin lord"—to whom the local merchants paid protection money.
With the help of these two, Huang organized the local riffraff into a gang.
When he was twenty-four, his father arranged for him to join the police
force in the French Concession; using his contacts in the world of petty
crime, he became invaluable to the force and moved up quickly to the rank
of detective. It was said that Huang could find a piece of jewelry stolen anywhere in the concession within twenty-four hours, merely by speaking to
one of the local gangsters. When members of the French police returned to
Europe to serve in the armed forces of World War I, Pockmarked Huang
became chief superintendant of the force. According to one of Chiang's
biographers,* Huang carried around a tiny gold-plated gun that folded up
and could be hidden in the palm of his hand.

The second most powerful criminal in Shanghai was Du Yueh-sen, or
"Big-Eared Du." Aside from his famously large ears, Du's face was narrow
with searching eyes, a drooping left eyelid, and sensuous mouth. He had
been born in a small town across the river from Shanghai to a family so poor
that he had attended school for a total of only five months. Orphaned at a
young age, he was sent to live with an uncle who treated him so badly that
he ran away. In Shanghai, Du got himself apprenticed to a fruit seller who
worked near the waterfront of the French Concession. There he came into
contact with the lowest-rung members of the Green Gang, which he joined
at the age of sixteen. He also met runners who worked for Pockmarked
Huang. Hanging around Huang's home, he managed to impress Huang's
wife, the former madam of a brothel, and then meet Huang himself. An addicted gambler and gifted criminal, Du was soon managing one of Huang's
gambling houses, and he was often seen in Shanghai's cabarets with three or
four girls in furs and diamonds. A writer from the West described the scene:
"A carload of advance bodyguards came and 'cased' the cabaret from kitchen
to cloak-rooms, then took up stations to wait for the boss. Du himself always
travelled in a large, bullet-proof sedan. . . . Behind the leader's limousine a
second carload of bodyguards travelled. Du never got out until these had
surrounded him. Then, with one at each elbow, he ventured to cross the
footpath and enter the cabaret. . . . Inside, while he and his party sat at a
front table, guards sat beside and behind, guns in plain view!"

Huang's main source of income was opium. Before the turn of the cen-

---

* Jonathan Fenby, who wrote that it can now be seen in the Shanghai Museum of
Public Security.

tury, the Chinese had begun planting their own poppy fields, and in 1908, the British agreed to restrict their exports of opium from India. To "protect and dispose of 'existing stocks,'" the Westerners employed a private police force—an arrangement that lasted until the end of World War I, when the Chinese bought out Western holdings. Suddenly, the opium business was thrown open to every gangster and petty criminal in the city. Members of the Green Gang competed with lesser bandits to steal shipments of opium while they were still in the harbor, the train station, or en route within the city from one building to another.

At this point Big-Eared Du hit upon a solution to the dangerous and unprofitable chaos: he convinced Pockmarked Huang to allow him to organize a new concern under Huang's leadership and unify all the factions by arranging for them to share the take. The new organization was called the Black Stuff Company. Under this system, opium hongs were charged $3,000 to $10,000 a month,* yielding $180,000† to the authorities and heaven knows how much to the Green Gang. In addition, Du established the Opium Pipe Company, which earned $.30 per day per pipe, collected by Du's men every afternoon. (Those who attempted to cheat were charged $50 a pipe.) This part of the operation alone earned the Green Gang some $100,000 a month.‡ The selling and use of opium were so open in the French Concession, carefully protected by Huang, that dealers put their names and addresses on packages of the drug.

Under Du's sponsorship, opium in varying grades was available to rich and poor alike. The former took their opium lying on silken couches with servants standing by to fill their pipes, while the latter had to beg or steal a few grains of the bitter, sticky, yellowish brown substance. Opium dens, frequented by those who fell on the social scale somewhere between the wealthy and their servants, were divided into cubicles, each of which was outfitted with a low table holding the necessary paraphernalia. The raw opium was twisted around a pin and cooked over a lamp until it hardened, then placed in the bowl of the pipe, which was inhaled next to the heating lamp. It took only a few minutes to complete a pipe, and some smokers would have six or more before declaring themselves satisfied. It also took practice to learn to smoke opium. "Imagine that you are a child that sucks its mother's breast" was the advice given one British writer when he started.

A member of the Anti-Opium Information Bureau in Geneva met Big-

---

* $10,000 Chinese = $12,400 U.S. in 1920 ($133,220 today).

† $180,000 Chinese = $223,200 U.S. in 1920 ($2,398,000 today).

‡ $100,000 Chinese = $124,000 U.S. in 1920 ($1,332,200 today).

Eared Du in Shanghai and left a devastating picture of the opium king at home:

> a gaunt, shoulderless figure with long, aimlessly swinging arms, clad in a soiled, spotted blue cotton gown; flat feet shod in untidy old slippers; a long, egg-shaped head, short-cropped hair, receding forehead, no chin, huge, batlike ears, cold, cruel lips uncovering big, yellow, decayed teeth, the sickly complexion of an addict. . . . He came shuffling along, listlessly turning his head right and left to look whether anyone was following him. We were presented. I had never seen such eyes before. Eyes so dark that they seemed to have no pupils, blurred and dull—dead, impenetrable eyes. . . . A huge, bony hand with two-inches-long brown, opium-stained claws.

Appearances aside, Du was very rich. Unlike most other gangsters, he used much of his wealth to support supplicants—from scholars and politicians to widows and orphans. Beggars lined up on the street when they knew he would be in their part of town, and his following grew enormous. Moreover, Du never tried to replace Huang, the man who had given him his big chance. He was, according to one journalist who knew him, "an amazing character because he was also an honest businessman . . . and a great patriot during the Sino-Japanese War." With riches came power—and respectability. It was said that Big-Eared Du held positions on more directorates of banks and businesses than any other man in the city, and his name eventually appeared in Shanghai's *Who's Who* as a "well-known public welfare worker." By that time, he had become president of two banks, a member of the French Municipal Council, head of the Chinese Red Cross, and, ironically, a member of the board of the Opium Suppression Bureau. More important, Du had by then befriended Chiang Kai-shek, the man who would capitalize most successfully on the symbiotic relationship between the world of crime and that of Shanghai society.

11

If we want to know how developed a nation is, we have to look at the status of women in that nation. . . . Unfortunately, a large number of Chinese women . . . live a life similar to that of hundreds of years ago.

—MADAME CHIANG KAI-SHEK

IN 1918, May-ling, who had supervised the the family's move to the new house on Seymour Road, ended up with little blisters all over her body, diagnosed as paint poison* but probably what she later called urticaria (hives) and what the doctors termed neurodermititis. "Mother said it was because I refused to go to Revival meetings with her that it was a case of Retribution," she wrote Emma. "Well, anyway I was and [am] miserable for it itches and swells. If you ever had a bad case of ivy poison you would have an idea of one tenth of the agony I am now undergoing."

The Soong sisters never underestimated the discomfort of their physical ailments, and May-ling was probably the most dramatic of the three. As sometimes happened when she was bedridden (which was frequently), she took the opportunity to evaluate her life. "I felt and feel that I am going to pieces, so to speak, through lack of mental exercise," she wrote her friend.

> I have tried writing; but gads! I have not succeeded in turning out anything worth a penny. . . . I am supposed to have an active mind, and yet since I have returned home, I am surrounded with every deadening force possible. . . . What about the various committees I belong to? . . . They are superficial and the members meet more to observe each other's clothes than to discuss means of improvement. . . . But I am going to tell you a secret. I am going to get connected with some <u>active</u> social work, active in the sense of hard, real, live, amount-to-something, worthwhile work, some work that will make me damnably uncomfortable physically, work that would make me too tired to care what kind of bed I shall be sleeping on. And a work that is not going to have any frills.

---

* Her brother's room had been painted three months before.

Added to this letter was a P.S.: "I've committed myself. I have just made an appointment by phone with one of the secretaries of the Y.W.C.A. to find me a <u>hard</u> job without pay."

Meanwhile, she took a pleasure trip to the North with brother T.V., sister Ai-ling and Ai-ling's husband, H. H. Kung. Their first stop was Tientsin, the major port of northern China, where, as she wrote Emma, they had

> a whopping good time . . . Sister has so many friends here that we are motored . . . dined, and treated every minute of our waking hours. We never get to bed before 1:30 A.M. We have Mr. Kung, my sister, the two children, three servants, an uncle, my brother and I here all in the hotel. We have a wing all to ourselves. . . . The rickshaw coolies here are far better dressed than those in Shanghai, and here I have not seen a single beggar whereas Shanghai is full of them. . . . As my sister never gets up before 11, and as I am always up by seven, I take the children out quite a bit. We go to the bund to watch the ships come in; it's lots of fun.

From Tientsin, the family moved on to the capital. "The streets are on the whole narrow and bumpy with dust ten inches thick," she wrote two weeks later,

> & when it rains, the mud is over a foot thick, and squashy! Except in the Legation Quarter, the streets are very winding and narrow. Mule carts are in great evidence; on the whole, belonging to the Manchus. The Manchu women still effect [*sic*] their ridiculously unsightly and tall head-dress, & their faces are clownish with powder and paint an inch thick. . . . In Peking, you will find China as it was before it came under foreign influence. . . . Palaces sometimes have over a hundred rooms, each of which in one direction or another open to one or more courts. On the whole, the palaces are of one story high, but beautifully finished with brilliant tiles and carvings. Some of our friends live in these palaces. . . . We were invited to the President's Reception. My brother-in-law Mr. Kung was ordered by the President to his office. He wanted to consult Mr. Kung on matters of state. We were too busy to attend the Reception as we were buying rugs. Fancy that, can you?

Somerset Maugham, who visited China the following year, was also captivated by shopping in Peking, and Sir Osbert Sitwell, who arrived in the 1930s, was fascinated by Peking's pigeons, which had whistles attached to their tails and created various melodies as they circled overhead. "In former years," according to Sitwell's Chinese source,* some of the pigeons had been taught to steal. They flew to the Imperial Granaries, where they swallowed as much rice as they could, and returned home to be "dosed with alum and water and made literally to disgorge their booty. After being washed, the rice would then be sold."

Returning to Shanghai, May-ling volunteered two mornings a week at the YWCA doing office work. She was also put on the committee for the financial campaign and enjoyed it tremendously, developing a skill that would serve her well—some might say too well—in the future: "I go to the managers of the Banks personally and look them in the eye, and literally the money rolls in!" she wrote Emma.

I never say the same thing to two men; I first size them up to see which of my arguments would more likely appeal to him, and then I strike while the iron is hot! For instance, one man might be interested in the development of Social Service, another would like a more "commercial" argument. . . . In each case, however I tell them then that I am a volunteer worker and that I get nothing for my service except the satisfaction of knowing that I am trying to work for the betterment of China, and that because they cannot give their service, I am now giving them the privilege of giving financial support. I find that my being a volunteer worker, they are most impressed with that fact. I am liking the job! The men are very polite and seem interested. They are mostly foreigners. I thank they are impressed with the fact that Chinese are interested in Chinese! . . .

I always take one of the old maid secretaries along for chaperone, but I do all the talking because as I told you the appeal coming from a Chinese girl is more effective than from a foreigner. . . . I always put on my best clothes . . . when I go to the offices, for to my mind nothing gives one more confidence than the feeling that she has on a becoming hat, plenty of powder to keep the shine off the nose, and sumptuous furs. And then too, to be well dressed means that a larger contribution will be assured, for the men would be ashamed to give any sum too small to buy my shoes with at least! And then again, I never ask for money as charity. I always give the men the privilege of contributing to something which would in time benefit them, for a better China socially means a greater China commercially. I am enjoying my work very much and as I have the motor

---

* Tun Li-ch'en, *Annual Customs and Festivals in Peking,* p. 21.

at my disposal, I do not have to exert myself unnecessarily and can reserve my strength for the interviews.

Back in the social life of upper-class Shanghai, May-ling began to think again about marriage, recommending it for her friend Emma and adding that she herself believed that "women lose interest in life, at least they feel a distinct lack, as though they have been cheated out of life, if they do not marry. . . . And then too, really what has one to look forward to if one does not have children?"

In attempting to help her friend, who was currently going through an emotional crisis, May-ling was also trying—sometimes rationally, sometimes not—to sort out her own ideas about life, love, and responsibility: "you are not sure which is the correct path to take if there is such a thing as a correct path," she wrote Emma. "I have had something very like the experience you are having, only in my case I was sure what I wanted only the gods did not see fit to give it to me. . . . I have noticed that the most successful men are usually not the ones with great powers as geniuses but the ones who had such ultimate faith in their own selves that invariably they hypnotise others to that belief as well."

Realizing that she had been under a strain since Ai-ling and her children had taken up residence in the family home, May-ling wrote Emma that her "idea of paradise is a place where as few people as possible ever step in there, and those few people would have to be quite careful to disappear occasionally so that I could be by myself . . . one type of person . . . that I would rule out of my Utopia . . . is the sort that . . . is always right, the sort that is always giving other people advice." Six weeks later, in the summer of 1919, Ai-ling moved her family to a house nearby. "I am going to regain freedom and have a little privacy of the mind," May-ling wrote. ". . . I have been getting my own things in order as things were rather in a chaos when they were here. . . . I think it is absolutely essential that one should have a sense of privacy, a feeling impossible when there are too many around."

It was clear that their correspondence served both young women as a sounding board for their frustrations, discoveries, and evolving ideas—some touching, some humorous. In July, May-ling received a letter from Emma about a sexual encounter that had clearly disturbed her. "I think . . . you may just consider that incident as a beastly unpleasant one . . . that . . . awakened in you the knowledge of brutal passion . . . which we in our college days knew absolutely nothing about," May-ling wrote back.

> . . . I think the best way for you to become normal in your attitude towards men would be to ignore the question of sex entirely. Of

course, that is difficult, for almost without exception when a man becomes interested in a girl, he becomes sentimental. . . . Love is partly sexual in its composition, and there is nothing disgusting about it if you consider it in conjunction with the other elements which make up love in the real sense. For instance, physical love is like certain parts of Bach's or Beethoven's works which if considered by themselves are discords but which if combined with the parts the authors meant to have them considered, they become harmonious and beautiful. In all probability, the man who looked at you so disgustingly was only attracted to you by your physical attractions, and a man who is that sort is certainly a beast, a brute and an animal. . . . But, Dada, not all men are like that. . . . Do not begin to think that you are disgusted with love, for you aren't. You are only disgusted with a certain element [in] it, an attitude quite natural to all pure-minded girls who are what you are.

May-ling was also having problems where men were concerned—but of a different sort. "The town of Shanghai is at present full of rumors about my being engaged," she wrote Emma, adding that her friends were

not sure which one it is but they are sure it is somebody. What makes the situation so funny is that none of the men are either denying or acknowledging the rumors. I am quite put out, for Mother of course thinks that I must have done something or another to have justified the rumors. The result is she has made me stop seeing any of my men friends for the last month, and because she told me not to let any one call, I believe that I am almost willing to be engaged out of revenge, a perfectly childish attitude, I quite realize. She is quite worried about me because for the last months I seem to have taken a craze to be gadding about all over town. The truth is, I am dreadfully bored, outrageously so. I have even had teas unchaperoned a couple of times, just because . . . I feel so wretchedly oppressed. And the funny part is I do not care a snap about any of the men.

She was nonetheless flattered when an old beau resurfaced in her life, although her mother disapproved of him because he was divorced:

He is different in that he is a man now instead of a headstrong jealous boy . . . but to tell you the truth I am bored, horribly and unspeakably so. I have begged Mother to let me leave home and do

something. Volunteer work is not real work. . . . I have a position
offered to me on a newspaper, but I need not tell you that if I were
to take it, the family would be so furious that I shall never be able
to live thru the fuss, especially as the Celestials can not get into
their nutty domes that a girl can be decent morally if she works with
men. . . . Damn it all, I think that if I had my way, I could amount
to something.

Another ego boost came in the form of an extremely wealthy man fifteen years her senior. Dangling before her an opportunity to improve the
education and social development of the "many hundreds of labourers in
his factories," he asked May-ling to marry him in spite of the fact that she
told him she did not love him. There was also a married man, whom she
"had the misfortune to care about . . . more than words can tell" but whom
she refused since "neither one of us would do what is not honorable."

With sister Ai-ling giving birth to a new baby and sending her other
children to live in the family home with May-ling and her mother, brother
T.V. heading for America on business, T.L. off to college in the United States,
and T.A. at boarding school, May-ling wrote Emma that "all my fine plans
of getting a position and really amounting to something worth while will
have to be put off again. Well," she added, "that comes of being the youngest daughter." She was pleased at being elected vice president of the American College Women's Club of Shanghai. She was also secretary of the
McTyeire Sorority, and, although sister Ai-ling was the president, it was May-
ling who was pictured in *The Shanghai Gazette* in connection with the school's
building campaign. At the time she was doing "a great deal of writing" for
the *Gazette*—mostly old Chinese stories translated into idiomatic English in
which she tried to keep what she called "the original flavor without making
a chop-suey out of the whole." She turned down a number of offers to teach
school but, when asked to give a series of lectures on philosophy, was tempted
to try to write them, although she refused to take herself or her qualifications
too seriously. "Sometimes I wake up in the middle of the night to laugh at
myself," she wrote Emma, "because it seems ludicrous for me to lecture on
Philosophy, I who am a veritable scatter-brain."

May-ling had always been a big reader and was particularly excited when
a large box of schoolbooks reached her in the spring of 1919, almost two
years after it was sent from Wellesley. A few months later, she wrote Emma
that H. G. Wells's *Outline of History* put her in an "ecstatic mood," while the
works of Guy de Maupassant disgusted her. Since her return, she had asked
Emma to subscribe for her to *The Nation, The Saturday Evening Post, Ladies'
Home Journal, Women's Home Companion, Harper's, Scribner's, House Beautiful,*

The New Republic, and *The Atlantic,* which she had read in freshman English at Wellesley and which, she said, she had "become so accustomed to having . . . by my side that I invariably keep a copy near to fill in spare moments between engagements." She also returned to her Chinese lessons. This time, she worked with a "terribly strict" scholar, T.V.'s Chinese secretary, who not only was conversant with the new terms brought into the language by China's contacts with Japan and the West but expected her to memorize long passages in the old-fashioned way. She studied with him for three hours every morning and after some months wrote Emma, who wanted to be a writer, that "I am planning on a time when I shall have sufficient grasp on [*sic*] the language to translate beautiful quaint & colorful Chinese gems into English Fiction for you to work on. Won't it be fun for you . . . to collaborate in turning out versions of . . . our Chinese literature? I could translate the essence and spirit of the masterpieces, and you could shape them into form! How would works of 'Mills & Soong' strike you!"

Age twenty-three and still living at home with her mother and brothers, May-ling longed to run her own life. In the winter of 1920, she admitted that she had been "as irritable as an uncovered electric wire . . . very unsociable and snappy, and contrary." Three weeks later she said that she was better, "especially after I made my family understand that a part of my time belongs to me exclusively and cannot be tampered with by anyone else." By breaking dates "right and left" that had been made without consulting her, she said that she thought "the family finally understood that I was all in physically and stopped expecting me to be merry sunshine under all circumstances."

One day she went too far. "As you know," she wrote,

> my mother is very conservative and never lets me dance altho she thinks that I should go to the dances my friends gave [*sic*]. If you remember, I like dancing and enjoyed it very much while I was at college. And so one day when I went to a dance and the men began asking for dances, out of recklessness, I danced and later I went home and told Mother about it. Well, I wish you had been here. . . . You would think that I was the most disgraceful creature on the face of the earth because I had danced, and that the only thing that I could do to show my repentance and to wipe out this stain of disgrace from the Soong name would be to sit in sack cloth and ashes the rest of [my] natural life and to turn my eyes away in pious disgust at all others who ask me to dance with them. Mercy, it was some scene, old dear.

It would seem from the following that Madame Soong did not put the same pressure on her sons as on her daughters—or that T.V., unlike his sister, did not feel he had to report his transgressions to his mother. George Sokolsky, a Communist turned right-wing journalist, who was in Shanghai at the time and knew the whole family quite well, wrote that "he [T.V.] and I and the lady who was to become my first wife . . . arranged the first dance at which Chinese and foreigners danced with each other—and it was a deed to be talked about! Mrs. Soong, the mother, disapproved of dancing, as she disapproved of all the vices enumerated by Southern Methodist preachers. Hers was a Spartan code, and the children were expected to live by it."

At the next dance to which May-ling was invited, her mother tried to make her promise not to dance. "I had decided not to dance anyway," May-ling wrote Emma, "but when she tried to make me promise, I became very much provoked and told her that I certainly intended to dance and to dance a lot too. She was so upset though about it that finally I weakened and promised her that as long as I bear the name of Soong I shall not dance in CHINA. Please notice the last word, for if ever I get back to America, I am going to kick my heels off."

A few months later, May-ling started talking about going back to America to study medicine—a calling that had attracted her father as well—but her mother vetoed the idea. After having her tonsils removed, however, she wrote Emma about "a thing which I have learned since I have been home. That is this: friends are very nice, but remember when you actually really get to a hard fix, the family is the one that will stand by you." Ailments and illnesses were always hard on May-ling—far more than circumstances warranted. "I have been desperate and most miserably ill these past two weeks," she wrote. ". . . The doctors found the tonsils terribly infected, and they have come to the conclusion that bad tonsils have been the cause of the breakouts on my face. Did you know that I am of an exceedingly nervous temperament? Well, it seems that I am; although I never knew it. The operation went hard with me, as I was on the verge of a nervous break-down. I am still resting, and not taking an active part in anything socially or in my social service work. I am well on the road to being pampered to death by the family."

After an extended recuperation May-ling traveled to Canton to visit sister Ching-ling and Ching-ling's husband, Sun Yat-sen. Having bested the local warlords and abolished the military government, Sun was currently establishing his revolutionary government in opposition to the government in Peking, and Ching-ling had apparently asked May-ling to come help her for a month or so. After explaining to Emma that Canton was "not nearly so foreignized as Shanghai," May-ling wrote that the Suns' mountain house looked down on

soldiers' barracks, my brother-in-law's soldiers. I think 5,000 of them are stationed below. We can hear bugle calls all day long, and can see them practising and drilling on the marching grounds. . . . In going to town, we are obliged to pass all the barracks and the Government House where many many people are patiently waiting to get an interview with Dr. Sun. . . . From the Gov't house to our house is a private covered passage something like an elevated bridge. . . . At either end are guards, whom one can only pass if he has a pass from Doctor Sun! This passageway is only used by us, and by our callers.

Living with Ching-ling, who had thrown herself into her husband's crusade, made May-ling feel more useless than ever. "I think you are about the only one among my friends and family that I can face to review my thoughts, and to confess that the last four years have been absolutely barren of results so far as accomplishing anything worth while," she wrote Emma in April 1921.

. . . If I really had something in me, I could have overcome all the obstacles, swept them aside, left the comfortable homeside, and gone into the interior and done some work "on my own," away from people who know my family—and particularly away from Shanghai where because of my family, anything I choose to do in the way of Social Service has the approval of the public. . . . I am well and favorably known as being public-spirited and with some claim to executive ability. . . . I am also known as being "intellectual" and "brainy," rather proud but pleasant . . . a good sport but somewhat apart from the "common herd" because of my family position . . . I dress very well, and in foreign clothes, ride around in a motor and does [sic] not have to teach to get my living. . . . Oh, Dada, what is the matter with me? I have had moments when I feel that the one way to solve my problems is by a life of self-abnegation, to become either a Catholic nun, to renounce all . . . and to live a life of . . . selflessness. At moments, too, I have had the temptation of getting married, and be done with the whole thing, and then just drift along and keep myself from thinking. . . . You know, of course, that no men really view life as we women do. If they have not already had liaisons, they will eventually have them. I have seen so many instances of this in men whom I thought were absolutely reliable. . . . Especially is this true in China, where the standard of morality is so different from that of America.

Nevertheless, a month later, May-ling, who said she was "literally dragged" home from the South by her brother, sent a letter of introduction to Emma for "a very good friend of mine, a Mr. B____.* I want to tell you a secret," she continued.

> I like him tremendously, and he does me too. I only met him the night before I sailed from Hongkong at a friend's house, and altho we were on board ship together only three days, we became very good friends. The day we arrived in Shanghai was his birthday; and so in spite of the fact that I had been away from home three weeks, I spent the day with him as the boat sailed that afternoon. We had a beautiful time together and I am glad I was so rash for once in my life. Needless to say, the family was furious with me. . . . They were also furious because he is a foreigner. . . . Since he left Saturday afternoon, I have received two wireless messages from him saying how much he misses me. The family tried to keep the wireless away from me, but did not succeed . . . you know our family is so conservative and puffed up with family pride over keeping "pure" the family blood that they would rather see me dead than marry a foreigner. Ordinarily I would too—but—Now I am thinking seriously of accepting another man. I like him; he is one of the most brilliant younger men, has excellent family, morals, educated etc. But I am still debating the question. You know lots of time, one may [be] reasonably convinced and yet not emotionally convinced about a certain course of action as being advisable. . . . But do not tell anyone, please, because I have to work this out myself. In the meanwhile when Mr. B comes to call, be awfully nice to him; but do not let on that I have told you anything at all.

In the summer, when the heat always got her down, May-ling hit another low. "I know friends, relatives & acquaintances all envy me," she wrote Emma,

> because they say I seem to have everything good in life, everything worth having! . . . I do seem to have the richest life of any one of my friends or acquaintances. Then why . . . am I such an ingrate, and feel so tired of life? . . . I have tried "Social Service," "self-improvement," "butterflying," in fact all the possible ways which seemed to promise a richer, fuller life. And I have failed!! Now I am trying something new, new at least for me. . . .
>   You know Dada, I am not a religious person. I am too darned

---

* Identified by DeLong as Mr. Birnie.

independent and pert to be meek or humble or submissive. As you probably know too, my sister Mrs. Kung was even <u>more</u> independent than I. She is very much keener than I, a really brilliant woman, and very social—always has been <u>the</u> leading Social light up to two or three years ago, she even denied the existence of a God, and whenever religion was mentioned in her presence, she either shunned the topic or else plainly said that it was all old women's nonsense etc. But now she is very religious, and she told me that the reason why she is so changed is because she has seen the error of her former manner and attitude towards God. She told me she has gone through periods of agony far worse than any I have been through, and that because of her misery and sufferings she turned to God—and now she has found solace in life and faith in living. I wish you could know her, for she is undoubtably [sic] the most brilliant miss in the family, and is unusually keen & quick witted, vivacious, quick and energetic. She is not the sort I would consider at all fanatical, and yet she is deeply religious, and now prays to God to help the solution of her problems. More than this, she has found <u>peace</u>, such peace as she has never known . . .

She told me that the only way for me to conquer this lassitude of mine is to become religious, and to really commune with God. You know, she has been telling me this for a long time now up to the present. I used to get furious just because her words irritated me, and used to tell her to keep still. But now I am trying her advice, and so far I cannot say <u>how</u> it will work out. I will say this, though, since I tried her advice, I feel a great deal happier, as though I no longer am carrying a heavy burden alone when I pray. Now, I am in a receptive mood, so to speak. I cannot explain this to you; but I wish you were here for Mrs. Kung to talk to you. You know becoming more religious has not changed her outward mode of living, because she is just as gay, and goes out to parties etc. just as much as before, but somehow or another, there is a difference in her. She is great deal less critical, more thoughtful, and not so intolerant of the shortcomings of others.

In having closer communion with God, the essential feature is faith that this Supreme Being is <u>close</u> to you all the time. Such external forms as Church worship & the Bible etc. are good only in so far as they help you in getting closer to God. The essential character though is this belief in the all-powerful love of God. . . . I wish you would try yourself. I have found that the best way to get into close communion with God is to select a hymn, the meaning of which is exactly what you desire, then read or sing the words till the idea permeates through your consciousness, and you really feel that your mind is ready for communion with God; then pray, as you would talk to your father or with a very close friend. Of course every one has a different way of praying; but to me, this is really the way . . . I can most strongly feel the presence of God.

You will likely think I have gone crazy, but really, Dada, I have tried and tried everything else. Probably you think I have been "goody-goody," but no! I am even this very minute sitting on the verandah outside my room writing you and smoking a good cigarette, and enjoying its flavor.

❦

ON JANUARY 26, 1922, Emma received a letter from May-ling telling her about a newspaper job she had found for her friend in Shanghai. Emma had trained to become an army nurse but had left Walter Reed General Hospital, discouraged by bad working conditions and cockroaches. After unsuccessful attempts to land a job as a reporter in Washington, she had gone to Chicago and San Francisco, where she had finally settled for a course in secretarial skills. "Of course I'll go," Emma wrote in her diary. "Perhaps within a month." Two months later to the day, she arrived in China. May-ling met her at the boat, and Emma discovered that although she had originally been invited to live with the Soongs, May-ling had made arrangements for a room in a boardinghouse—a change the hostess explained as a chance for her friend to really experience life in China. The next day Emma was interviewed at *The Shanghai Gazette*. She got the job and stayed in China for three years—first in Shanghai, where she worked for the *Gazette,* and then in Peking, where she taught English at the North China Language School. During her first months in Shanghai, she saw May-ling almost every day.

DeLong tells us that Emma thought May-ling seemed nervous when she arrived, unable to sit still and jumping in conversation from one subject to another. Apparently, however, "she never faltered as a consummate hostess and eager guide," taking her friend with her to lunches, teas, dinners, and dances, at which the other guests did all the "latest steps, including cheek to cheek dancing." Emma was clearly surprised about May-ling's attitude toward servants, both her own and others'. One day she turned a wastebasket over on the head of her number one houseboy and, when the boy at Emma's boardinghouse failed to do her laundry on time, demanded his name and address, thus frightening him into working harder. Moreover, according to DeLong, "May-ling rarely hesitated to ask Emma to do special tasks" like shopping, banking, delivering messages, and handling orders from overseas.

"They call these creatures private secretaries and pay them a salary!" Emma wrote in her journal. Then the *Gazette* let Emma go, and when May-ling asked for the reason, she was told that her friend "hadn't the faculty for nosing out news."

Emma also spent time with Ai-ling and Ching-ling, both currently in Shanghai. Before she left the city, she was actually spending more time with Ching-ling than with May-ling—a situation that may have had to do with Ching-ling's neediness at the time (she and Sun had just fled from Canton) or, more likely, a cooling of interest on the part of May-ling, who was going through a period of religious intensity. In August, Emma wrote her mother,

> Mayling has acquired a cast-iron, cut and dried classification of the world. The people who are interesting and have a good time are "fast," and one must have nothing whatever to do with them; the people one may associate with are mostly missionaries and YWCA workers—and boring. She really has grown fearfully narrow-minded and straight-laced. And when it is a question of Chinese people, dreadfully snobbish. All of which I tell her in no uncertain terms but without the slightest effect. She wanted me to vacation with one of her YW friends, a very nice, but fearfully colorless middle-aged English woman, but I rebelled. Would infinitely rather go off by myself.

It is clear that May-ling's girlish admiration for her friend lessened in the early months of Emma's sojourn in China, as did what DeLong called May-ling's "magnetic pull" over Emma, and their friendship nearly ended. Emma moved to Peking, where she taught English, complaining that she rarely heard from May-ling, who was also late forwarding her mail and packages. It was not until the summer of 1923 that May-ling, on a visit north with the Kungs, asked Emma for tea and the two seemed to get back on a better footing. But May-ling's letters became "comparatively infrequent and inconsequential"—so much so that Emma, who had treasured and saved the earlier ones, now threw many of them away. Whatever the pleasures of their relationship in the early or later years, only six months after arriving in China, Emma had left both Shanghai and May-ling.

12

We are the poorest and weakest state in the world, occupying the lowest position in international affairs; the rest of mankind is the carving knife and the serving dish, while we are the fish and the meat.

—SUN YAT-SEN

IN 1922, the year Emma Mills arrived in China and the year before Chiang Kai-shek left on his mission to Russia, Lenin had sent one of his most accomplished diplomats, Adolf Joffe,* to Peking with instructions to establish diplomatic ties for the new Soviet government with the Chinese Ministry of Foreign Affairs. But the Chinese government, under heavy pressure from the Great Powers, refused to recognize the Communists. Unable to fulfill his commission in the North, Joffe turned south—to Sun Yat-sen and the Kuomintang.

Sun was embarrassed by the association, but he had as few choices of allies as the Soviets did. He conducted his meetings with Joffe in secret, confiding his dream of a great Northern Expedition—a campaign in which a revolutionary army would overcome the warlords and bring all of China under the umbrella of the KMT. To accomplish this, he told Joffe, he needed financial aid and military advisers. In January of 1923, Sun and Joffe signed an agreement and issued a joint manifesto designed to assuage those who said that Sun was selling out to the Communists. "Dr. Sun Yat-sen holds that the communistic order, or even the Soviet system, cannot actually be introduced into China because there do not exist the conditions for the successful establishment of either communism or Sovietism" read the opening paragraph. "This view is entirely shared by Mr. Joffe, who is further of the opinion that China's paramount and most pressing problem is to achieve national unification and to attain full national independence; and regarding this great task he assured Dr. Sun Yat-sen that China has the warmest sympathy of the Russian people and can count on the support of Russia."

---

* Joffe was head of the delegation that had signed the armistice at Brest-Litovsk that took Russia out of World War I. A friend of Leon Trotsky, with whom he founded the newspaper *Pravda*, Joffe eventually committed suicide in protest against the policies of Stalin.

Six months later, Sun rationalized his actions to a reporter from *The New York Times*:

> The real trouble is that China is not an independent country. She is
> the victim of foreign countries. . . . The foreign nations have pur-
> sued the disastrous policy of endowing a corrupt and inefficient
> clique in Peking and insisting upon the fiction of calling it a Govern-
> ment. . . . The Peking Government could not stand twenty-four
> hours without the backing it receives from foreign Governments. . . .
> The foreign countries have blindly and persistently declined to
> recognize the Southern Government. . . . The revenue . . . goes to
> Peking, and a considerable proportion of it is used to fight us. . . .
> We have lost hope of help from America, England, France or any
> other of the great powers. The only country that shows any signs of
> helping us in the South is the Soviet Government of Russia.

The month after Sun issued this statement, in August 1923, Chiang Kai-shek led a four-man delegation to Russia. He had met earlier with Maring, who supplied two of his traveling companions, both members of the Chinese Communist Party. Arriving in Moscow, Chiang was amazed by what he called "the European atmosphere" of the city. "Everything looks so different from Asia," he wrote Jennie. He met Georgi Chicherin, the people's commissar for foreign affairs, the chairman of the Supreme Soviet, and Trotsky, with whom he was impressed. "Mr. Trotsky is an important man in Russia," he wrote Jennie. Chiang's greatest regret was that Lenin was very ill* and unable to see anyone.

Chiang studied what he was shown of the Soviet system, but his comments on the political scene were vague—an uncomfortable distillation of Soviet propaganda and his own observations. When he looked into military matters, however, he was on solid ground and more specific in his analyses. "I found that in the 144th Regiment of Infantry . . . the commanding officer is in charge only of military matters. Political and spiritual training and lectures on general knowledge etc. are done entirely by the Party representatives. . . . The system works very well." Chiang learned another lesson from the Russian military—one that many Chinese and his allies wished he had not taken quite so much to heart: the Soviet army was primarily a defensive force, and Chiang's later refusals to follow defensive successes with offensive forays may well date back to this time. He also attended official banquets, receptions, theatrical performances, and mass meetings, one of which had

---

* He was in fact already in the coma that would end in his death.

over 220,000 people in attendance. "For my reading," he wrote his wife, "I have bought Karl Marx's *Das Kapital*. I find the first half of this work very heavy-going, but the second half is both profound and entrancing."

Chiang arrived home on December 15. He was angry when he heard that while he was away, the Russians had sent another emissary to China, a man currently serving as Sun's primary counselor. "Our leader has caused me to lose face," Chiang told Jennie. "How could he accept Borodin [the counselor] . . . while I was away in Russia? At least he should have cabled me for my advice or waited for my return to consult me. It is not ethical! Now I'll let him wait for my report. I'll let him wait, wait, and wait."

Mikhail Borodin, Sun's new adviser, was already well on his way to becoming an influential figure in China. Born Mikhail Markovich Gruzenberg in Yanovichi, Russia (now Belarus), a tiny village in the Jewish Pale, he had grown up in Latvia, where he belonged to the General Jewish Workers' Union before joining the Bolsheviks and becoming one of fewer than a hundred followers of Lenin. Lenin sent him to Switzerland, where he remained until "Bloody Sunday," January 22, 1905, the day the tsar's troops fired on a demonstration of workers in front of the Winter Palace. That was the day when, as Lenin's wife put it, "The realization came over everyone . . . that the revolution had begun."

One of the first Bolsheviks to return to Russia, Borodin was arrested in 1905 and exiled. He went to the United States, attended Valparaiso University* in northwest Indiana, and founded a school for emigrés in Chicago. Returning to Russia after the revolution of 1917, he worked as an agent of the Comintern (Communist International) in Scandinavia, Mexico, Spain, Turkey, and Great Britain. Although his native language was Yiddish, by this point in his life Borodin had cut himself off from both the language and his Jewish heritage, identifying himself only as a Russian from Saint Petersburg.† He was sent to China in 1923 and, according to the right-wing journalist George Sokolsky, "No foreigner had ever so thoroughly succeeded in influencing Chinese thought and action." Glib, charming, and eminently adaptable, Borodin spoke English and could therefore communicate with Sun; he also had great organizational skills and was a skillful proselytizer for the Communist cause. He soon realized that Sun was an extremely effective public speaker. "He made it all up on the spur of the moment," said Ching-

---

* Second only to Harvard in size during the first decade of the twentieth century, Valparaiso University counted Walter Bedell Smith, Lowell Thomas, and a member of the Court of International Justice at the Hague among its graduates.

† Later in his life, he told an American reporter that he had taken the name of Borodin in honor of the great Russian composer.

ling. "It all depended on the political situation and the audience. I would be nervous as a cat, sitting next to him on the platform and wondering what was coming next." Sun was also an excellent conveyor of political philosophy, and, from the time Borodin began to advise him, he started issuing manifestoes in which he simplified and clarified the political principles of his party in a style accessible to those with a limited reading knowledge of Chinese. Borodin also set up a new Department of Propaganda in order to distribute posters, pamphlets, newspapers, flags, and the writings of Dr. Sun.

❧

"YOU CANNOT TRUST a Communist," Chiang told Jennie when he came home from Russia. The forty-page report on his mission that he prepared for Sun after his return echoed and reechoed this theme. "From my observations, the Russian Party lacks sincerity," he wrote. ". . . The sole aim of the Russian Party is to make the Chinese Communist Party its legitimate heir. . . . I feel that they wish to make Manchuria, Mongolia, Sinkiang, and Tibet a part of their own Soviet Union. As to China Proper, they wish ultimately to Sovietize it, too."

Sun did not reply to Chiang's account of his mission. Nor did he send a letter acknowledging its receipt. After what Jennie Chiang called "an interminable period of nervous waiting," Chiang wrote Sun again:

I have spent half a year of my time, and more than 10,000 dollars on the Russian mission. . . . But as to my report of this trip and as to what I saw and heard, you have not given it even the slightest attention. Apparently you feel that I have completely failed on the mission. Or perhaps you no longer have faith in me. In either case, I feel an intense slight and that my reputation has plunged to the ground! I feel, however, that my conduct in Russia was impeccable. . . . Once, when they tried to force me to join the Communist Party, I refused by saying that I had to obtain Dr. Sun's permission first. For this I was jeered and ridiculed as being too loyal to an individual and not loyal to the state; that I was fostering an idolatrous cult by revering an individual!

Three days later Chiang received a wire from Sun:

To My Brother Kai-shek,

On your shoulders you have an extremely heavy responsibility from your trip. Please come immediately to Canton to make a report personally on all matters and to prepare detailed plans for cooperation with the Soviets. I wish to know what your proposals are. Whatever you suggest will be respected.

But as usual when he was miffed, Chiang took plenty of time getting to Canton. Once there, he tried to explain to Sun that the Russian Communists were no less dangerous than the old Western imperialists. But as usual, Sun did not listen to what he did not wish to hear.

Meanwhile, Borodin had discovered just how insecure Sun Yat-sen's position in Canton really was. Driven out of the city by the Hakka General the previous year, Sun had been allowed to take back the title of generalissimo by two other warlords: General Yang of the Army of Yunnan and General Liu of the Army of Kwangsi, both provinces lying west of Canton's province of Kwangtung. Yang and Liu, who had done this primarily as a cover for their criminal activities, had taken over Canton in order to profit from its opium dens and brothels. In spite of this, Sun always referred to the Kwangsi general as "Living Angel Liu" because Liu had suffered wounds in his stomach and shoulder during the fight for the city. Having divided Canton up into individual fiefdoms, Yang and Liu were planning to leave with the illegal taxes and protection money they had collected. Sun had to deal with their forces, which numbered around 40,000, with a personal bodyguard of fewer than 200 men. And, as usual, the Kuomintang was facing a serious shortage of funds.

At a meeting of the executive committee of the KMT, Borodin recommended that its members go out and find volunteers to defend the city. When 540 men answered the call and the Hakka General's army began to retreat, Sun, who had refused to follow Borodin's advice in other matters, acquiesced to Borodin's suggestion of an all-China Kuomintang Congress, which opened on January 20, 1924, with three ceremonial bows to the KMT flag and one to a picture of Sun Yat-sen. Members of the Chinese Communist Party (CCP) had been ordered to join the KMT. Although they made up less than 15 percent of the delegates present, it was clear that the KMT and its new manifesto—reorganization of the party, establishment of a new relationship between the KMT and the CCP, and a definition of terms for cooperation between Moscow and Canton—had fallen under their influence. Aware of how this looked to non-Communists, Li Ta-chao, the first member of the Chinese Communist Party to join the KMT, issued a statement saying that he and the other members of the CCP had joined the KMT "because we have something to contribute to it . . . certainly not because of any intention to take advantage of the situation to propagate Communism in the name of Kuomintang."

On the sixth day of the congress, news arrived that Lenin had died in

Moscow. Before the meeting adjourned for a three-day period of mourning, Sun delivered a speech to the delegates in which he addressed the soul of Lenin, saying that he wished "to proceed along the path pointed out by you.... You are dead ... but in the memory of oppressed peoples you will live forever, great man." When the congress reassembled, it established a permanent Central Executive Committee for the Kuomintang, most of whose members, along with the chairmen of nine new departments, were chosen by Sun and Borodin, the latter managing to insert a disproportionate percentage (20 to 25 percent) of Chinese Communists into key positions. Among these were Li Ta-chao, the author of the disingenuous speech to the Congress, and Mao Tse-tung.

Having arrived in Canton only a few days before the congress, Chiang realized that he was now an insignificant player in both the party and the congress. Appointed chairman of the preparatory committee for a proposed military academy to be established on Whampoa Island downriver from Canton, he sloughed the work off on someone else. Named commandant-designate of the same academy, he declined and left in a huff for his old home in Chikow. "The military academy has been opened for you to take charge of," Sun wrote Chiang shortly after he left. "Preparations are afoot, and we shall find means of raising funds. From considerable distances some hundreds of military officers and cadets have come already, mostly because they admire the choice of the superintendant of the school. You should not disppoint them. I urge you to come without delay."

But it was May before Chiang returned to Canton to take over the new academy, which opened on June 16, 1924, with five hundred students. Sun presided over the opening ceremonies. "Because of the lack of a revolutionary army, the Republic has been mismanaged by warlords and bureaucrats," he told the assembled group. "... With the establishment of this school a new hope is born. . . . This school is the basis of the Revolutionary Army of which you students form the nucleus."

Chiang Kai-shek also spoke to the students, but in an entirely different vein: "You must memorize, step by step, your duties so that there is no way for you to forget them. First is discipline. Your leader's orders must be obeyed unconditionally. . . . Secondly, whatever your individual task, you must do your utmost to complete it to the best of your ability. . . . Thirdly, you must regard death as glorious. It is an honor to give one's life for one's country. So, do not be afraid to die. Only cowards are afraid of death. The ancients had a saying. 'One must regard death as going home.' "

The academy was located in a newly renovated, two-story building on Whampoa, an island in the Pearl River fourteen miles from Canton, where Chiang and Jennie were given a three-room apartment. According to Jennie, her husband rose promptly at five every morning. After his usual half hour of meditation, he headed for the barracks at the back of the main building where the cadets were lodged, admonishing those who were not up and about. He was, in the words of his wife, "a very exacting commander." He demanded exemplary behavior—no gambling, no whoring—and cadets learned to fear his penetrating gaze, "which seemed to pierce through as if from an inner head behind a mask." Those who were caught with their tunics partly unbuttoned or shoes unlaced were reprimanded in his blasting, high-pitched voice or sent to the brig. In one instance, when a cadet was giving a patriotic reading before an audience of three thousand people, he forgot a line and reached into his pants pocket to retrieve his speech. "Stop!" Chiang shouted. "You should know better than to put a folded paper in your trouser pocket where it would get crumpled! It should be placed in your shirt pocket! Remember that, you blockhead!"

"The audience," according to Jennie, "sat agog and exchanged glances with one another. Meanwhile the orator turned red for having been so publicly ridiculed." According to Jennie, Chiang himself was "sensitive to criticism and quick to anger. He seldom praised anyone. . . . And he only cultivated those friendships that might be useful to him in furthering his aims. Once that usefulness was outlived, however, most of the friendships, regardless of how close they had been, died a natural death."

"Each Sunday morning for four uninterrupted hours he [Chiang] would lecture to the three thousand cadets, drawn up in ranks before him on the drill grounds," according to Han Suyin, who eventually married one of those cadets. "Bareheaded under the intense sun of Nanking, Marshal Chiang expounded; rigid at attention the cadets listened. Though he talked of history, of politics, of military tactics, the emphasis of his teaching was ethical . . . more important than learning and technique was the development of character. He used the term *tso jen*—'to be man'—defining all the pride and dignity inherent in the word. No one who heard him could ever forget."

Funded largely by the Russians, Whampoa employed about fifty Soviet military instructors who had been sent to China along with guns, ammunition, and various other kinds of military equipment. The chief Russian military adviser was a red-haired, neatly mustached man who called himself Galen but was really the Russian general named Vasily Konstantinovich Blücher, who had joined the Bolsheviks in 1916 and risen to a high position in the civil war that followed their revolution. Unlike the other Russian instructors, Galen got along well with Chiang.

The six-month course at the new academy was patterned after the military schools Chiang had visited in Russia, which included large doses of Communist indoctrination. Along with drilling and instructions in warfare,

the Chinese cadets studied military and political science and the history of
the KMT. "The aim of the academy was not only to train good soldiers but
also to cultivate staunch supporters of the Kuomintang," said Jennie.
". . . Most of the academy's planning was done by Kai-shek. . . . He made a
draft of the curriculum, decided on the length of the course, set salaries for
teachers and officers as well as the pay and rations for the cadets, and selected a board of examiners. He knew exactly what he wanted and was very
thorough in his planning, telling me time and again: 'Once I have decided
on my plans, I don't want anything changed.' "

Intransigence aside, it should be noted that one of Chiang's problems
was a basic ideological division within the KMT, a schism that was bound to
be reflected in its military academy. On the left were the political commissar
of the academy; Wang Ching-wei, Chiang's longtime rival and the current
head of the KMT's Propaganda Department, soon to be succeeded by Mao
Tse-tung; and Chou En-lai, Deputy Director of the Political Department;
Chou, who described himself as "an intellectual with a feudalistic family
background," had returned from France after founding a French branch of
the Chinese Communist Party. Opposing this stellar trio was Hu Han-min,
a conservative who hated the Left and was loathed by them. Chiang's position in the middle of these factions was an ambivalent one. Few people knew
about his trip to Russia and his subsequent disillusionment with the Soviets, and the fact that he now worked hand in hand with Russian military
advisers did nothing to change his reputation as a supporter of the Communists.

Neither of the two warlords whose private armies were occupying Canton at the time was kindly disposed toward Chiang's academy, which was in
the process of creating the kind of soldier who, they realized, would eventually make trouble for them. Outside the citadel of Whampoa, in the city
of Canton itself, matters were in serious disorder. At the end of 1923, Sun,
who was still being refused permission to keep the Canton customs surplus
for his government, had announced that he would seize the money by force.
In response, an international flotilla, led by the British, steamed into the
harbor. In May of 1924, just about the time that Chiang arrived, the Cantonese merchants, responding to Sun's proposal to levy taxes on them, were
threatening to strike. A few weeks later, word reached Sun that these merchants had raised an army of 9,000 men and that a Norwegian ship carrying
9,000 rifles for their use was heading for Canton. At this point, Sun turned
to Chiang for help.

First Chiang countered the machinations of the wily General Yang, who
had suggested to Sun that he give the merchants their rifles in exchange for
a fine of $1 million, which he, of course, would collect for the little doctor.

After warning Sun not to pursue this, Chiang declared martial law and sent armed cadets to board the Norwegian ship and bring the rifles to Whampoa. Meanwhile, the British consul general threatened to bombard Canton if Chiang fired on the merchants. In a state of high alarm, Sun wrote an open letter to his followers:

> Kwangtung [Canton's province] is now a place of death, the causes of which are three . . . (1) the pressure of the British . . . (2) a possible counteroffensive by our enemy Ch'en [the Hakka general] . . . (3) the waywardness of so-called friendly armies [of the two warlords, Yang and Liu] in Canton. . . . With these worries, we cannot stay here a moment longer . . . the best outlet is the Northern Expedition. . . . We will use battlefields as the training school for the cadets; this will yield wonderful results. Comrades of our party, you must not hesitate, but heed my call!

Sun escaped with his guards, a small air force, and all available soldiers to a base in northern Kwangtung province, while Chiang, who refused to follow him, was left to face the armies of the warlords and the angry Cantonese merchants. He wrote Sun to ask for reinforcements. On October 9, 1924, Sun wired back, saying that he was "concentrating on the Northern Expedition only. Since you feel there is danger in Canton, I hope you will leave Whampoa and come at once with all the arms and ammunition. Also, bring the cadets. We will gamble everything on the Northern Expedition. Act immediately, as soon as this telegram reaches you. You must not be reluctant to leave. I will never go back to relieve Canton. So do decide instantly and hesitate no more."

"I have determined to defend this isolated island until death," Chiang wrote back, "so I still await your early return with your army to relieve us. We will never give up our base, without which our party will lose its foundation forever. . . . If you return, our army can launch a counteroffensive . . . we can wipe out all opposition and make Canton a safe and solid base for our revolution. I will not go even a step from here, and I earnestly entreat you to return soon."

Before Sun left, the Cantonese merchants had begun haggling with him over the release of their rifles, offering Sun a "loan" of $200,000 in exchange. Sun had agreed and told Chiang to turn the arms over to the merchants. Furious, Chiang did as he was ordered. The next day was the Double Tenth (October 10), the anniversary of China's independence from the Manchus. The celebration ended in tragedy when the merchants turned their newly acquired rifles on Chiang's soldiers, several of whom were killed. Sun, who finally realized that Chiang had been right about defending the KMT's authority in Canton, sent reinforcements from his base in the north of the province. With these additional men, Chiang was able to rout the merchants in two days and restore order in the city. According to the *North-China Daily News*, Chiang was now known as the "Protector of Canton." According to his wife, success had made him arrogant.

Although Sun's advisers urged him not to go north, he left on November 12, 1924, taking an entourage that included his colorful bodyguard known as Two-Gun [Morris] Cohen,* a petty crook and self-promoter from Canada whose best trait was his unswerving devotion to Sun and Ching-ling. Before leaving for the North, Sun, Ching-ling, and their oddly assorted retinue stopped at Whampoa Island and spent the night at the Military Academy. While Jennie entertained Ching-ling, Chiang led the cadets in a formal review before Sun. Before he left, Sun told Chiang that he was going to Peking and was "not sure" he would return. The truth was that Sun, who was not feeling well, must have guessed that he did not have long to live and wanted to start his long-dreamed-of Northern Expedition while he still could. He arrived in Kobe at the end of November. The high point of his Japanese visit was a speech in which he appealed for racial solidarity against the West and reminded his audience of Japan's victory over the Russians in 1905. Ching-ling also delivered a speech, on the emancipation of women. The Japanese government, which ignored the Suns' presence in the country, did not invite them to Tokyo.

Sun was in considerable pain by the time he sailed for Tientsin. Arriving on December 4, he was confined to bed two days later. On the last day of the year he finally got to Peking, where he was taken to the Grand Hotel de Pékin and then moved to the Peking Union Medical College Hospital, considered the best hospital in China. He was operated on by the head of surgery on January 26 and diagnosed with incurable cancer of the liver.

Two weeks earlier, Emma Mills, who was still in Peking but leaving for home the following month, received a letter from May-ling, enclosing a let-

---

* According to a visitor to Sun's home on the Rue Molière in Shanghai, the bull-faced Cohen "always sat on a bench in the front hall and carried a large revolver in his hip pocket, which caused the seat of his trousers to sag grotesquely." Whereas this might lead one to think that Cohen bought a second gun to even out his appearance, it seems he acquired the name "Two-Gun" only after a wound in his left arm made him realize that if "it had been my right arm and I carried my gun that side, I'd not have been able to use it . . . [so] I got me a second gun, another Smith and Wesson revolver, and I packed it handy to my left hand. I practiced drawing and soon found that I was pretty well ambidextrous—one gun came out about as quick as the other." (Daniel S. Levy, *Two-Gun Cohen*, pp. 120–25.)

ter for Ching-ling and asking her to deliver it in person. Emma ended up by joining Ching-ling for dinner in the Sun suite: "The doctor [Sun] is getting better she [Ching-ling] thinks, but the general opinion around town is that he is not going to survive," Emma wrote home. ". . . I haven't seen him, of course. They have two nurses on the job, and all the doctors. . . . There is hope of Mayling coming up some time, but not till after I go, I am afraid."

By the time Emma left for the United States in February, Sun was much worse. After the Western doctors gave up on him, it was decided to try old Chinese remedies. Since it was not considered ethical to practice herbal medicine in a Western-type hospital, Sun was moved to the home of Wellington Koo, a famous diplomat and former minister of foreign affairs. Koo's home in Peking, sprawling over ten acres of gardens and comprising an eastern and western palace, had once been the home of a singsong girl, mistress of the father-in-law of the last Ming emperor.

During his last illness, Sun was attended by his devoted Ching-ling, his grown son and daughter (without their mother), and various members of his political entourage, including Borodin. Also present were May-ling and Ai-ling, who had taken the train up from Shanghai. There was no food, nothing to drink, and no heat on the train. Even the water was frozen. "We felt thirsty, hungry and cold," May-ling wrote the son of one of the KMT leaders many years later. "Before we left Shanghai, we knew that trip would be full of hazards, and it was hard to estimate when we would reach Peking. However, we went out of love for the premier, and it was our way of giving material and spiritual support to our elder* sister."

Along with the relatives gathered at Sun's bedside were old friends and KMT associates, who, under the direction of Borodin, decided to use the iconization of Lenin as the pattern to be followed for Sun. To keep him in the public eye, the leader of the party was encouraged during his final illness to sign messages to his followers, along with a highly publicized will, drafted by Wang Ching-wei and read to him for his approval. According to Sun's brother-in-law H. H. Kung, "one day when we thought Dr. Sun was strong enough, some of us gathered before his bed to read him the will. Madame Sun . . . broke into the room and began to weep. This interrupted the reading. But we had to have Dr. Sun's signature. Later, Dr. Sun became too weak to write, so we asked Madame Sun to support his hand in signing the will." This scene occurred on March 11, 1925, and Sun died the next day.

After his death, Sun Yat-sen became what he had not been able to achieve in life—the glorification of "Revolutionary Saint." Boy children were named for him, as were streets, hospitals, colleges, even racehorses. Pictures of him

---

* Ching-ling was May-ling's older sister but Ai-ling's younger sister.

hung everywhere—in fine homes and peasant huts, offices and factories. His image was reproduced on huge posters and plastered on city walls. Even his last will and testament became the basis for a quasi-religious ceremony conducted in barracks, factories, and union halls, where celebrants would gather bareheaded, bow three times to his picture, and stand in total silence for the reading of the document. "No one whispers or even dares to cough as the oft-repeated words of the dead leader are pronounced," said a journalist who observed one of these ceremonies. After the reading, there was always a three-minute silence set aside for "self-examination and revelation," for "consideration of the doctrine," and for "self-determination of fitness for participation in the work of the Kuomintang." As one observer put it, "Sun Yat-sen, as it turned out, was worth more to Chiang Kai-shek and the Kuomintang dead than alive."

13

If I control the army, I will have the power to control the country. It is my road to leadership.

—CHIANG KAI-SHEK

THE STRUGGLE for the top position in the Kuomintang broke out immediately after the death of Dr. Sun. Among the contenders—but way down the list—was Chiang Kai-shek. In spite of the fact that the Whampoa Military Academy was a major player in the politics of south China, Chiang, according to his wife, "stood at the bottom of the ladder" of power—number seven among the remaining leaders of the KMT.

There were three men at the top. The first was Wang Ching-wei. A "humbler of female hearts" married to an heiress, Wang had been with the leader in the hospital and at his deathbed, where he had taken down—some say composed—Sun's will. Called "brilliant and erratic" by one source, indecisive by others, Wang, who had tried to assassinate the prince regent in 1910 and been sentenced to life imprisonment, had been released only after the success of the revolution in 1911. At the age of forty-two, Wang was the youngest of the likely contenders. Number two was the former editor of a revolutionary newspaper, Hu Han-min, who represented the right wing of the party. He and his brother Hu Yin were old associates of Sun. Another contender, listed by Chiang's wife, Jennie, as number four in order of importance, was Liao Chung-kai, a friend of Chiang's. An extreme leftist, small, thin, and "dapper to the point of being a dandy," Liao was in charge of the finances of the KMT.*

While Sun was heading north to Peking, Chiang had been doing his best, as he wrote the leader, to "make Canton a safe and solid base for our revolution." His major objective—and personal obsession—was the elimination of his old enemy, the Hakka General, now in the stronghold of Waichow, a city ninety miles from Canton. When the first class of 2,000 cadets graduated from the academy, Chiang, who had never before had his own army to command, stormed the town of Tamshui, the Hakka General's

---

* Number five was Liu Chen-huan ("Living Angel Liu"); number six was Wu Chih-hui, an educator, known as one of the Four Elder Statesmen of the Kuomintang.

first line of defense, twenty miles south of Waichow. Aided by troops from
Canton, Yunnan, and Kwangsi, Chiang and his men occupied Tamshui after
a day and a half of fighting. "The defeat of the enemy at Tamshui was due to
your brave attack," Chiang told his soldiers. "With but 2,000 revolutionary
cadets we have defeated 6,000 soldiers . . . [and] . . . taken prisoner more
than 2,000 officers and men. . . . I have telegraphed this report to our leader
Dr. Sun in Peking, who will certainly be cheered by the news. . . . I congratulate you on your bravery!"

The bastion of Waichow, however, was not so easy. Waichow's city walls
were protected with four lines of barricades—a row of barbed-wire loops on
the outside, a wooden expanse riddled with nails protruding three inches
above the flooring inside the barbed wire, rows of sawhorses with more
barbed wire, and finally, the wall itself, which was covered with electrically
charged netting fifteen feet high. As Chiang's soldiers ran or crawled through
this torturous jungle, they were easy targets for enemy sharpshooters. Once
they managed to cut through the first barrier of barbed wire, those who survived had to get across the wooden expanse, where their feet stuck on the
nails. As they fell under a barrage of bullets, another wave of soldiers climbed
over their bodies to reach the third barrier, while more soldiers advanced
with dried straw to set fire to the electrically charged netting. With the netting breached, the attackers blasted the wall with dynamite. As the city fell
to Chiang and his men, the Hakka General and his officers escaped on their
gunboats, which were waiting at anchor in Waichow Bay.

Chiang occupied Waichow, reorganized the soldiers who had surrendered, and returned to Whampoa, leaving General Hsu Chung-chi in command of the city. Hsu was number three in seniority in the Kuomintang,
currently serving as commander of the Kuomintang army—a position that
gave him nominal command of the soldiers Chiang had led to victory. As
commander of the town of Waichow, he was installed in a "most aristocratic" mansion with a green-tiled roof, red lacquer columns, and many servants. But Hsu, who liked the bright lights and diversions of the big city,
soon grew restless. After a month of monotonous splendor, he handed the
seal of office over to his friend Lieutenant General Hoong Lok and headed
for Canton. Hsu, who did not consult with anyone about this move, apparently did not know that Hoong Lok was a cousin of the Hakka General's
chief assistant. Within forty-eight hours of Hsu's departure, Hoong Lok had
opened the city gates to the Hakka General, who moved back in with his
soldiers and set about repairing the city's fortifications.

When the news of what had happened reached Chiang, he became
"almost hysterical" with fury. As Chiang's superior, however, Hsu had to
be handled with extreme caution. "What happened is unfortunate," Chiang

told Hsu. "It means that a large number of my cadets and soldiers have died in vain. However, I will lead another expedition to recapture the city. For me to accomplish this, however, you must furnish me with some of your troops."

"Certainly! I'll be glad to arrange that," said Hsu, who was understandably chastened.

"But the discipline of your whole Cantonese army, from top to bottom, is deplorable," Chiang contended.

"What do you suggest be done?"

"Let me reorganize your army for you. Will you grant me permission to do that?"

"I will agree to whatever you suggest."

"To make a success of it, however, I must have a period of one year and a free hand to do a thorough job."

"What do you mean?" Hsu asked.

"I cannot reorganize your army while you are here in Canton," said Chiang. "That you can well understand. It will take me a year to do a good job, and you during that period must go to Shanghai for a holiday. When your army is fully reorganized, I will invite you to come back and resume command."

"Marvelous," said Hsu, for whom the idea of a year in Shanghai was a blinding inducement.

The following week, Hsu transferred the command of the Cantonese army, 100,000 strong, to Chiang. Two of Hsu's generals, however, refused to take orders from their new commander, warning Hsu, "You have fallen into a trap! You may as well say good-bye to the army, for it will not be returned to you even after thirty years!" Two days later, the two generals accepted an invitation to a banquet in a private dining room in one of the best restaurants in Canton. While they were eating and drinking, an officer with a warrant for their arrest walked in, followed by a phalanx of soldiers who drove the two generals to the Eastern Parade Grounds and shot them.

✶

Sun's trip north had coincided with an attempt by the Chinese Communist Party to take over the KMT in Canton, starting with trade unions, student associations, and workers' guilds. According to the *North-China Herald*, "one could not walk a block without seeing Lenin's head peering out at him from the wall of some building or other." Two specific events, called "incidents" by the British and "massacres" by the Chinese, boosted the Communist cause. The first occurred on May 30, when police from the International Settlement fired on a Communist-inspired demonstration of cotton mill workers in Shanghai, killing some of them. Borodin was ecstatic: "We did not make May 30th. It was made for us." The effect was redoubled a few weeks later when a French gunboat, joined by British machine guns, bombarded demonstrators in Canton who had gathered to protest the killings.

Meanwhile, faced with the necessity of another assault on Waichow, Chiang had approached Generals Yang and Liu to ask for soldiers from their armies but had received no response. Realizing that the Communists were the only people who could help him oust the Hakka General, Chiang did what all warlords did—he made alliances where he could, even going to the extent of putting on a red tie every morning. One of the Communists whom Chiang proposed for membership in the Kuomintang during this period was Chou En-lai, who, because of his wit and scholarship, was able to write petitions for the party. Chiang recommended Chou for head of the Political Department attached to the First Army.

Chiang's subsequent capture of Waichow nearly coincided with Sun's death in Peking, and although he and all his officers wore the appropriate black armbands, he was so busy reorganizing the administration of the city that he had little time to grieve. His inborn sense of entitlement fed on triumph, and he started issuing "imperious commands . . . far beyond his own domain. . . . He took it for granted that he was the genuine heir to Dr. Sun's revolutionary work," said his wife. "Everyone understood that all followers of Dr. Sun would now move up a step in the invisible rankings within the Kuomintang. Wang Ching-wei and Hu Han-min were by seniority the logical ones to take the leader's place. . . . But the fever of leadership entered Kai-shek's veins, so he forged ahead to achieve his ambition."

Jennie was not the only one to comment on her husband's aspirations. According to an article in the *North-China Herald*, Chiang's "every move has been actuated by the desire for self-aggrandizement." To further these plans, he began by removing Generals Yang and Liu. Liu, it will be remembered, had been wounded driving the Hakka General and his army from Canton in early 1923 and had ever since been known as "Living Angel Liu," a fact that Jennie says she brought to her husband's attention. "The past is past," Chiang replied. "Liu Chen-huan has outlived his usefulness. He must be eliminated along with the others. . . . He has collected taxes from the Canton citizens for over a year and has been amply repaid for whatever services he rendered."

Two days before he was due to march his troops back into Canton, triumphant from their victory over the Hakka General, Chiang arranged for all the railway and public transportation workers to go on strike. Unable to position their soldiers around the city to face Chiang's army, Generals Yang and Liu fled. On June 12, less than three months after Sun's death, Chiang assumed sole responsibility for the security of Canton. He had now moved up from number seven to number four in the hierarchy of the Kuomintang. Eight days later, when the Central Executive Committe of the KMT met to reorganize itself in light of the changes in Canton, Chiang asked the members to elect him to the committee. They could not refuse. Given the title Defense Commander of Canton, which essentially made him head of the army, now called the National Revolutionary Army, he also served on the new National Military Council, headed by Wang Ching-wei.

Throughout this period after Sun's death, there were major upheavals in both the left and right wings of the Kuomintang. Chiang's old friend Liao Chung-kai, number four in the list of party seniority, was assassinated, presumably for his leftist politics. The assassin was believed to be Hu Yin, brother of the rightist Hu Han-min, listed as number two. While Hu's brother was imprisoned, Hu himself was told to go abroad on a tour of "inspection" of Russia. With Liao dead and both Hu brothers out of the way, Chiang now moved up to number two. Meanwhile, other disgruntled right wingers left Canton for Peking, where they gathered before Sun's coffin and issued a resolution for the expulsion of all Communists from the KMT, the dismissal of Borodin, and the transfer of KMT headquarters from Canton to Shanghai.

It is no wonder they were concerned. At the Second National Congress of the Kuomintang, which took place in January 1926, more than a third of the delegates from the party were members of the Chinese Communist Party (CCP), among them Mao Tse-tung, Wang Ching-wei's former assistant who now ran the Propaganda Department and edited the party's journal. At the congress, Wang delivered the political report, and Chiang, the military one. According to Chiang, the treatment of ordinary Chinese soldiers had improved. Their pay had been raised from $9 to $11 a month, and officers received between $160 and $500. He proposed that average soldiers be given several dollars more a month and that they be paid in silver dollars instead of the discounted currency they were now receiving.* This would be important, he said, for the success of the Northern Expedition, which he planned to undertake in about six months. At this second annual meeting of the KMT, Chiang was elected to the Central Executive Committee. Ching-ling, who had been met by "an enormous crowd" when she arrived in Canton and was subsequently elected to the Presidium of the congress, attended the meeting with sister May-ling.

---

* In a plan he submitted a few days later to the Military Council, Chiang recommended that soldiers be provided with winter clothes, health and medical supplies, better living quarters, and entertainment for their hours off duty. He also proposed a shorter period of service.

"Dearest Dada," May-ling wrote Emma, reverting to the familiar mode of their early correspondence,

> I came here [to Canton] some two weeks ago with Mrs. Sun as she had to attend the Second Congress of the Kuomintang. . . . We are visiting my brother T.V. who is Minister of Finance here. Since he came into office four months ago, he has increased the Government Revenue from $1,700,000 to $4,200,000 per month every month without increasing taxation on necessities. Even all the Hongkong papers which jeered at him four months ago when he announced his intention to stabilize finances now say that he has accomplished the seemingly impossible. People call him the official who is honest and who has the last word to say in the Canton Government. . . . Canton is so clean and peaceful, and very different from what the newspapers paint it to be.

Between January and September of 1926, May-ling made two trips to Canton. Chiang mentions her for the first time in his diary on January 17, at the graduation ceremony at Whampoa, noting only that "Madame Sun [Ching-ling] and her sister also were there." But the fact that Chiang asked T.V. to accompany the army on their northward surge, appointed H. H. Kung in his place as acting minister of finance in Canton, and took the Kungs' eldest son, David, along as the army's mascot indicates that there was now a connection between him and the Soong family.

The following month, in February of 1926, Borodin left Canton for Peking to discuss the future of communism in China with a secret commission composed of members of the Central Committee of the Communist Party of the USSR, sent by Stalin from Moscow. Their assignment: to assess the possibilities of a Communist takeover in China. In his place, Borodin left a man named Kissanka in charge of the Soviet Military Mission. Although Borodin had approved Chiang's plan to start the Northern Expedition, Kissanka contended that the expedition was bound to fail. Chiang believed that Kissanka was also the author of a smear campaign against him—a conviction strengthened when handbills attacking the expedition and Chiang himself began to appear around Canton. Then an incident occurred that only increased his suspicions.

No one seems to know exactly what happened on March 20, 1926, but a highly detailed and colorful story is told by Chiang's wife Jennie, who did not hesitate to cast herself in the role of her husband's savior. Although Jennie is left out of Chiang's own version, which he wrote thirty years later, the basic elements of Chiang's and Jennie's stories are similar—with one notable difference: Jennie implicates Wang and his wife in the plot, and Chiang does not. Other chroniclers have seized on different elements of this tale of political skullduggery, which came to be known as the "Incident of the Gunboat *Chung Shan.*"

Chiang's new duties required that he live part of the time in Canton, where he and Jennie rented a small house with a telephone so that he could keep track of matters at the academy in Whampoa. In the gunboat story as related by Jennie, Becky Wang, the wife of Wang Ching-wei, called the Chiang house on the afternoon of March 18 and asked to speak to Chiang, who was not home. Becky asked Jennie which jetty Chiang would take that evening for Whampoa, where he had a meeting, so that her husband, Wang, could go with him. After Becky's fifth call, Jennie began to get suspicious, and when Chiang got home, she advised him not to leave the house. On Chiang's insistence that he had an important meeting at Whampoa at 7:00 P.M., Jennie called the academy and put her husband on the phone. He was told by the dean of the school that there was a gunboat* waiting outside, sent down from Canton for fueling.

Chiang stayed home that night. The following morning he learned that the acting director of the Naval Forces Bureau, a Communist named Li, had received an order to send the gunboat to Whampoa, where it would be loaded with enough coal for a long voyage. (Jennie said that Wang had issued the order; Chiang said it was Li's commandant, i.e., Chiang himself, thereby concluding that Li had forged his name.) Chiang was to have been taken on board when he arrived at the academy and sent as a prisoner to Russia, thus leaving the field open for the Communists to take over the Kuomintang. Chiang took quick advantage of his position as defense commander of Canton to declare martial law, imprison or place under supervision twenty-five members of the Chinese Communist Party, including Li and Chou En-lai, and put China's Soviet advisers under house arrest. He issued these orders at three in the morning on March 20, 1926. In retaliation, the Communists called for a strike against what they called his "reign of terror." Chiang had the leaders arrested and ordered some one hundred courts-martial.

Next day, there was a meeting of the Central Political Committee with Wang as chairman. The committee endorsed Chiang's action. Either during or after the meeting, Wang asked to be removed from his political responsibilities and allowed to go to the hospital for treatment of his diabetes. He remained there for six weeks, after which he left secretly for France. Chiang,

---

* The *Chung Shan,* coincidentally the same gunboat on which Sun and Chiang had taken refuge in 1922.

who had overstepped his authority, offered to submit himself to discipline by the Central Political Committee, but the committee turned down his offer. With Wang out of the picture, Chiang Kai-shek was now the sole head of the party and the government.

Chiang's coup had taken the Russians by surprise, and a representative of the Soviet Consulate was sent to inquire if Chiang's actions had been directed against the plotters or the Soviets. Chiang assured him that it was only the former, adding, however, that he wished Borodin would return to Canton. The consular officer requested Kissanka's recall, and Borodin returned six weeks later. Meanwhile, a raid on Russian premises in Peking had disclosed links between the Soviets and the CCP. After two weeks of conferences between Chiang and Borodin, the Central Executive Committee of the KMT passed eight regulations concerning Communist members of the Kuomintang. These included a requirement that the CCP submit a complete list of its members with dual membership in the KMT; a ruling that members of the CCP were no longer eligible to head departments in the KMT;* and a prohibition against members of the KMT joining the CCP. "Though these measures are harsh," Chiang told Borodin, "a large party must prevent itself from being ruined by allowing a smaller one to undermine it from inside."

Another result of Chiang's coup was the establishment of a secret service. After the assassination of Liao the previous year and two attempts on his own life, Chiang had started compiling files on possible enemies from either the Right or Left and assigning a secret force to keep them under surveillance. The new group was organized by the two sons of his first mentor, Chen Chi-mei, whom Chiang called his "nephews." Members of Chiang's secret service, according to Jennie, were "told to forget all other duties except fealty to their boss and to be ever ready to arrest, kill, torture, or mutilate any suspect or culprit that fell into their hands." For this, they were compensated with a yearly bonus and a promised pension after ten years' service.

With the Communists temporarily under control, Chiang was ready to set about making preparations for the great Northern Expedition. In early April, he presented detailed plans to the KMT. Two months later, he was named commander in chief of the Northern Punitive Expedition and, as the Chinese had a habit of doing, given more titles, i.e., chairman of the Central Executive Committee and of the Military Council, thus becoming head of both the party and the army. On July 1, Chiang issued mobilization orders,

---

* Along with other important members of the CCP, Mao Tse-tung was removed from his position as head of the Propaganda Department, although he remained head of the Peasant Movement Training Institute.

and on July 9, in an elaborate ceremony, the soldiers of the National Revolutionary Army took an oath of loyalty and approved a manifesto specifying that "the purpose of the military campaign is to build an independent nation on the basis of the Three People's Principles and to protect the interests of the nation and of the people." They also called on other Chinese soldiers to join them in their fight for national revolution. During the ceremony, Dr. Sun Fo, Sun Yat-sen's son, held a portrait of his father beneath the blue flag of the republic.

▼

WHEN CHIANG STARTED out on the Northern Expedition, there were three major warlords standing in his way: Chang Tso-lin of Manchuria, Wu Pei-fu of Central China, and Sun Chuan-fang, who controlled the five southeastern provinces, including Chiang's home province of Chekiang. Called the Old Marshal to distinguish him from his son, Chang had recently marched down from Manchuria, which he controlled, and taken over Peking. He had an army of about 300,000 men. Wu Pei-fu will be remembered as the scholar warlord with his personal spittoon bearer. His army also consisted of about 300,000 soldiers. Once a date had been set for Chiang's Northern Expedition, Marshal Chang and General Wu, formerly at loggerheads with each other, decided to cooperate to defeat the National Revolutionary Army coming up from the south. The third warlord, Sun Chuan-fang, had about 200,000 men in his army. Taken together, the major armies opposed to Chiang counted some 800,000 soldiers.

But before he could even leave on his great mission, Chiang had to cope with the general strike in Canton, sending some of his soldiers to reinforce the police and secret service in order to keep track of Communist agitators. In addition to the unrest, the Canton Chamber of Commerce, which represented the city's merchants, balked at meeting its obligation of collecting 500,000 Chinese dollars* to finance the Northern Expedition. Chiang made it clear to the local businessmen, whose coffers had already been picked clean by Generals Yang and Liu, that it was in their best interest to fund the expansion of the revolution. While Chiang was settling these problems and before he was free to join his soldiers, the National Revolutionary Army made its way north through the (friendly) southern half of the province of Hunan to the (unfriendly) northern half. Accompanying the army was General Galen (Blücher). This was in mid-July of 1926, "a momentous year," according to May-ling, "in the surge and sweep of revolutionary modern China." By the end of the month, when Chiang joined his men, his army

---

* $500,000 Chinese = $380,000 U.S. in 1926 ($4,622,300 today).

had captured the city of Changsha in the province of Hunan and grown from 85,000 to 100,000, including political commissars styled after those in the Soviet army.

Unlike the armies of the warlords, Chiang's men had been and continued to be indoctrinated with reasons for sacrifice. But just in case the lessons failed to take hold, Chiang introduced harsh penalties for cowardice on the field of battle. If a company of soldiers retreated, their commander was to be shot on the spot; if the commander of an army corps stood his ground and was killed, his divisional commanders were shot if *they* then retreated; and if a divisional commander died under similar circumstances, those below him in rank were shot for falling back. The punishment for any soldier caught stealing was death.

Draconian though these measures were, they were an attempt by Chiang to set the National Revolutionary Army apart in the minds of the people from the armies of the warlords. Soldiering was not an admired profession in China, and the average Chinese soldier of the day had no motivation to keep him from switching from one army to another. Moreover, Chinese soldiers were forced to live off the land they conquered. During the Warlord Era, an invading army would enter a town, call a meeting of the members of the Chamber of Commerce, and demand that the local merchants provide two or three months' pay for the army's soldiers. The warlord would commandeer a large number of private houses for billeting his troops, and if the houses were not vacated immediately, the army packed up the contents and kept them. The inhabitants of the town were also expected to provide transportation and local laborers for the invaders.

But when Chiang's troops entered a town, the accompanying propagandists held public meetings at which arguments for the national revolution were interspersed with entertainment. They also passed out posters. "We paid as much attention to posters as to rifles," Borodin said. As to the soldiers themselves, Chiang's men slept in temples or other empty public buildings. Moreover, everything Chiang's soldiers needed on the march was paid for with the money requisitioned from the Cantonese government. "I expect to win the war 30 per cent by fighting and 70 per cent by propaganda," Chiang asserted. Realizing that they did not need to flee, as they had been accustomed to doing with warlord armies on the march, the locals worked as guides and carriers for Chiang's soldiers and sold them water and food, all the while being indoctrinated with revolutionary propaganda.

Two days after catching up with his army in Changsha, Chiang issued a proclamation to the nation—a statement that indicates how much he had already learned from Borodin: "The revolutionary army is about to wage a decisive campaign against the followers of Wu Pei-fu. . . . It is a struggle between the people and the militarists, between the revolutionaries and the re-actionaries, between the Three Principles of the People and imperialism. . . . As a revolutionary I am fighting for the people. The object of the expedition is . . . to give birth to a unified government . . . and . . . to lay the foundation for liberty and independence."

With these high-sounding motives and his new rules of warfare, it is not surprising that Chiang's brown-clad soldiers moved north with dizzying speed. Nothing seemed to stop them, even an epidemic of cholera. Both the army and its commander gained credence from their march, and Chiang Kai-shek quickly assumed the aura of an unbeatable leader. According to *Fortune* magazine, "he conquered China, and it does not dull his glory that he won by an astuteness less military than human and political." And from *The New York Times:* "China has a new strong man, a new conquering general . . . he is master of half of China. In all the long centuries of Chinese history there is no parallel for this amazing series of sudden victories." Like Sun Yat-sen, Chiang dressed simply in a plain cotton uniform with straw sandals; he nei-ther drank alcohol* nor smoked. Moreover, he kept discipline among his soldiers. Within eight months of the death of Sun Yat-sen, it looked as if the Chinese nation had found another hero.

---

* His self-imposed penance for infecting Jennie with venereal disease.

14

*General Chiang . . . wishes to gain supreme control of the political administration as
well as the army.*

— NORTH-CHINA HERALD, 1926

BY SEPTEMBER of 1926, Chiang and his army had reached the Yangtze River,
some five hundred miles north of their base in Canton. In spite of the fact
that 15,000 men had died or been disabled in battle, the National Revolutionary Army had tripled in size to 220,000. Many of the additions were
mercenaries, men who had not yet been indoctrinated with the Three Principles of Dr. Sun but who had been lured by defeat or bribery over to the
revolutionary forces.

"Very soon our army will arrive at Wuchang and Hankow," Chiang announced. "I hope the people will give it all assistance, and simultaneously
arise and try to save the country." As might be surmised from this rather
tentative statement, the prospect of conquering the triple-city enclave of
Wuhan (Wuchang, Hankow, and Hanyang), the next major landmark on
he road to Peking, was causing the general of the National Revolutionary
Army some trepidation. Known as "the Chicago of China," Wuhan was a
metropolis—a port and railway hub where 170,000 workers toiled in mostly
foreign-owned factories, making them prime candidates for the kind of radi-
calism that the Russian and Chinese Communist Parties were trying to fo-
ment within the army and the country. To avoid getting bogged down in
strikes and demonstrations, Chiang sent part of his army under the leadership of General T'ang, a warlord from Hunan, to Wuhan, while he himself
took the best of his soldiers into the province of Kiangsi.

For the first time the Northern Expedition ran into trouble—not only at
Wuhan, where one general told of having to rein in his horse so as not to
trample the dead soldiers littering the ground at the front, but at Nanchang,
a one-industry (enamelware) town in the northern part of Kiangsi. Dating
back to the middle ages, Nanchang, capital of the province, was a maze of
dirty, winding lanes, potholes, and stagnant pools of water, surrounded by a
wall twenty-two miles long that, Chiang claimed, had not been scaled in the
previous nine hundred years of the city's history. Continually repulsed in his
own efforts to breach the wall, Chiang was finally enabled to take the city
when General T'ang sent more men, equipment, and money from Wuhan.

An enclave of retired landowners, Nanchang, according to Jennie, who followed her husband, was "very conservative, proud and wealthy. The people," she observed, "still looked with suspicion upon any innovations. . . . Western influence had not yet penetrated."

But Chiang's decision to split his army had been a serious mistake, resulting in a division of authority between two camps, the other one directed by Soviet advisers who were primarily interested in fomenting a Communist revolution. During the march north, the headquarters of the Kuomintang had remained in Canton with Borodin at the helm, angling to take back some of the authority he had been forced to cede to Chiang after his trip to Russia. Toward that end, the Soviet adviser spearheaded a party conference aimed at attracting discontented peasants, encouraging workers' strikes, and convincing Wang Ching-wei to return to China.

Partly to keep an eye on these maneuvers, Chiang proposed that the offices of the KMT be moved north to Wuhan and that the members of the government stop to see him in Nanchang on their way. Among the group that headed for Wuhan with Borodin were Chiang's future brother-in-law T.V. Soong; his future sister-in-law Sun Ching-ling; her stepson Sun Fo, called by Han Suyin "a morose nonentity"; and Eugene Chen, the KMT's foreign minister. Chen, who wore gold-rimmed glasses and white spats, had received his legal training in England, served as private secretary to Dr. Sun at the time of his death, and worked as Borodin's "mouthpiece" in Canton. Mostly Chinese and partly West Indian, Chen was described by American journalist Vincent Sheean as "a small, clever, venomous, faintly reptilian man, adroit and slippery in the movements of his mind . . . with a kind of lethal elegance in appearance, voice and gesture." Those who admired Chen spoke of his brilliant mind and the clever jabs of his pen. According to a journalist on *The New York Times,* Chen threw political polemics around "as if they were confetti at a carnival."

The trip north had been an uncomfortable and precarious one, involving daily rainstorms, muddy roads, and sedan chair bearers who had to be hired from local opium dens every morning because their predecessors had run away during the night. Although the Chinese members of the group were perfectly willing to be carried, Borodin and other Russians, insisting that this mode of transport was not appropriate for members of the Communist Party, stowed their luggage in the palaquins and rode on donkeys or walked. Before reaching Nanchang, they were met by Chiang, who had prepared a welcoming ceremony and subsequent feast. This was followed by a conference at the Fairy Glen Hotel* in the resort of Kuling, a mountain re-

---

* The only other hotel in the resort, called the Journey's End Inn, placed Bibles and books of French pornography in its guest rooms. (Jonathan Fenby, *Chiang Kai-shek,* p. 254.)

treat for the wealthy. To get up the steep twelve-mile-long path, guests had to be carried in sedan chairs—assistance that we assume even Borodin did not refuse. In spite of the lovely setting, the meetings did nothing to heal the rift developing between the left and right wings of the KMT.

When Borodin & Co. finally arrived in Wuhan in early December of 1926, they found a city in revolutionary chaos. Forty-eight hours after General T'ang's entry into the tri-city complex, more than 60,000 workers had gone on strike. A week later, fifty-two factories closed down. Schools were set up to teach techniques of striking; street meetings followed by boisterous parades were a daily occurrence; and the main avenues were filled with pickets flaunting the red star or the hammer and sickle, greeting each other with raised and clenched fists. Importers no longer dared bring in their goods, and exports remained in the warehouses or on the wharves of the Hankow Bund. Trade, the lifeblood of the city, had been cut "to a trickle."

Treated like a hero and welcomed by the occupying forces of General T'ang, Borodin was taken to shore on a small motorboat decorated with flags and bunting. It must be noted, however, that as the boat drew close to land, a British cruiser turned and deliberately sideswiped it, thus issuing a warning that the Great Powers might react if matters got any more out of hand. Which they did a month later, when a crowd, inflamed by anti-imperialistic diatribes, gathered in a square near the British Concession in Hankow* to taunt the British marines guarding the Hong Kong and Shanghai Bank. The marines fired on the demonstrators, wounding several. The next morning a furious mob attacked the British Concession, smashing windows, destroying automobiles, surrounding the British Consulate, and yelling "Beat the foreigner!" and "Kill the Englishmen!" Outnumbered by the mob, the English abandoned the British Concession and escaped to their gunboats, anchored along the Bund—the first time that the British had given up any Chinese territory in sixty-six years. When KMT leaders got to the scene, they calmed the crowd and arranged for the release of British subjects who had been taken prisoner. Borodin was ecstatic. "The situation is strengthened," he wired triumphantly to Chiang in Nanchang, "the masses believe us. The taking of the concession . . . demands the presence of the national government in Wuhan; the leaders must be at the head of the people at the time of the movement." A second telegram also urged Chiang to come to Wuhan. Chiang, who arrived during the second week of January 1927 and quickly realized that Borodin and General T'ang were now his enemies, demanded that Borodin dispense with the services of Tang. Once back in his own headquarters in Nanchang, he let it be known that Borodin must leave China if he, Chiang, was to make any accommodation with the radical camp.

---

* The largest city in the three-city complex of Wuhan.

Chiang was not the only person appalled by the government in Wuhan. May-ling, who spent three months in the winter of 1926–1927 with her mother and Ai-ling visiting sister Ching-ling and brother T.V., reported that "the divergencies between our National policy and the policy of The Third International" had "developed into gaping chasms due to the pervasive excesses of Communist Cadres." Wuhan, she said, had become the unhappy scene of "indiscriminate arrests, public lashings, illegal searches and seizures, kangaroo courts and executions. The chaos," she concluded, was "purposely accelerated and exacerbated by the Communists . . . to subvert the Kuomintang."

During her three-month visit to Wuhan, May-ling engaged Borodin in long conversations, during which he expounded at length on his views on revolution and communism. These exchanges took place in brother T.V.'s apartment in the Central Bank building in Hankow, where May-ling and Ai-ling were staying. They were "outwardly congenial," although, as May-ling put it, "We three and Borodin were poles apart basically in thinking." Many years later she would describe him as "undoubtedly the most competent of the competents" and "one of the most persuasive and fascinating Bolshevik propagandists ever sent out from Moscow to spread the revolution abroad."

There was nothing particularly unusual in what Borodin said: "he kept on asseverating* and re-asseverating Lenin's preachment that the true revolutionaries are those who are willing to resort to all sorts of strategems [sic], illegal methods, artifices, evasion and subterfuges," May-ling wrote years later, adding the obvious conclusion that "the Communist end justifies the Communist means." An ardent Christian, May-ling was probably shocked when Borodin told her that the Communists "must find ways and means to either deal with, neutralize or expose Judeo-Christian thought as a phony, a bogus belief designed to make people resign to their fates." The Judeo-Christian tradition, Borodin said, was politically "dangerous" precisely because of its enormous power in the Western world and because it permeated "the two great imperialist anti-Communist citadels . . . the British Empire and the United States of America."

Nonetheless, Borodin, who received wired instructions every other day from Moscow, clearly fascinated May-ling, as he fascinated others:

As I recollect, even now I can see Mr. Borodin in my mind's eye . . . pacing to and fro in my brother T.V.'s apartment living-room . . . with his inveterate cigarette dangling between his index and middle

---

* "To asseverate" means "to declare." By 1927, when May-ling wrote this, she had begun to use long and/or uncommon words that she thought would impress people.

finger of his left hand. . . . In person he was of a tall,* commanding
presence with a leonine head, with a shock of neatly coifed, long,
slightly wavy dark brown mane that came down to the nape of his
neck, with an unexaggerated but ample moustache. . . . He was rather
heavy-set with strong regular features. . . . Speaking in a resonantly
deep, clear, unhurried baritone voice of mid-America intonation
without a trace of Russian accent, he lowered still more his voice
into a slow basso profundo when emphasizing the importance of a
certain point he was making. He was a man who gave the impression
of great control and personal magnetism. . . . He was capable, able,
shrewd if entirely cynical. . . . He could see cruelty, injustice and
degradation committed with detached coolness. He acted out his
misguided role as the instrument of The Third International with
aplomb and with dedication.

What May-ling may or may not have been aware of were Borodin's feelings for her. According to Emily Hahn, who interviewed all three sisters, one
day a "delighted" servant brought a scrap of paper taken from Borodin's
bedroom to another one of the Soongs. On it the Comintern operative had
written over and over, "Mayling darling. Darling Mayling." Her sisters, of
course, could not resist teasing her about this.

❦

UNWILLING TO WORK with Borodin or his Soviet sponsors, Chiang declared
war on the Communists. In January and February of 1927, he contacted his
friends, high and low, in Shanghai. As the leader of the eminently successful
National Revolutionary Army and longtime associate of Dr. Sun, Chiang
expected and received support from the Great Powers and their Shanghai
bankers, as well as anti-Communists and less radical revolutionaries. Frightened that the Kuomintang would be absorbed into the Communist Party,
capitalists of all stripes, both foreign and Chinese, contributed to an initial
short-term loan of 3 million Chinese dollars,† followed by an additional
7 million.‡

In February, Chiang began to make his move toward Shanghai, the largest and wealthiest city in China and the center of Western industry, finance,
and trade. Shanghai's citizens, particularly its 70,000 foreigners, were in a

---

* Borodin was five feet, ten inches tall.

† $3,000,000 Chinese = $2,070,000 U.S. in 1927 ($25,658,000 today).

‡ $7,000,000 Chinese = $4,830,000 U.S. in 1927 ($59,868,000 today).

state of near panic at rumors of the expected assault. Unable to count on the police, who were either underpaid or owned by the Green Gang, women and children from the foreign concessions crowded onto outgoing ships, as 40,000 soldiers from a dozen nations around the world arrived in the port. Members of the so-called Shanghai Volunteer Corps dug trenches and put up sandbags and barbed-wire barricades on the borders between the Chinese city, where bare, low-wattage bulbs lit the dark alleys at night, and the foreign concessions, where residents continued to wine and dine in brightly lit splendor.

According to *The Manchester Guardian,* the members of Shanghai's foreign community suffered from a willful inability to understand why they were not loved and appreciated by the Chinese, on whose backs they had built their fortunes. "These people . . . look round on their magnificent buildings and are surprised that China is not grateful to them for these gifts, forgetting that the money to build them came out of China." This sentiment was echoed by Sheean: "The coolie population . . . was easy prey for manufacturers who wished to make the modest profit of a thousand per cent. . . . I never met anybody in Shanghai who revealed the slightest feeling of shame . . . in thus taking advantage of human misery. . . . On the contrary . . . Shanghai saw itself as the benefactor of all China, and was horrified at the rising Chinese demand for better conditions of life and a recognized share in the spoils."

Chiang called for a general strike in Shanghai, and more than 100,000 of the city's workers obeyed him. To discourage the strikers, one assistant to Shanghai's chief warlord, Sun Ch'uan-fang, had his chauffeur drive his headsman from one demonstration to another; stopping every so often so the headsman could get out and behead any worker with a red hat, a red muffler, a red notebook, or even a red pen. This bit of butchery infuriated the demonstrators, and three days later, there were 350,000 men on the picket lines. Believing that Chiang's troops would enter the city momentarily and support them, the revolutionaries turned their strike into an armed uprising. The armies that still controlled Shanghai retaliated, executing more than a hundred strikers and placing their heads on stakes, on platters, or in bamboo cages that were hung on telephone poles in the busiest streets in the Chinese sector of the city. When it rained, the black hair on the bodiless heads dripped on the pedestrians below.

While Shanghai's revolutionary workers lost their lives, Chiang, unwilling to share the glory of conquering Shanghai with the Communist-inspired rabble, kept putting off his assault. With Chiang's army now only twenty miles away and supposedly due to enter Shanghai between March 20 and March 22, plans went forward for a great demonstration to take place at noon on March 21. When the army failed to appear, the workers struck anyway—some say there were as many as 800,000 of them—and followed their strike with an armed uprising. By that evening they had taken over six of the seven sectors of the city, and by the twenty-second, Shanghai, the great urban symbol of imperialism in China, had fallen to the Chinese Communist Party and its sympathizers.

But no one heard about the fall of Shanghai until the next day, March 23, when Chiang's National Revolutionary Army entered the city and claimed the honor of conquest for itself. And since everyone had been expecting the army, no one challenged its claim. Even in Moscow, the fall of Shanghai was triumphantly celebrated—in headlines, hymns, parades, and demonstrations—as a great victory for Chiang Kai-shek.

Chiang, however, had not been anywhere near Shanghai. He was on the road to Nanking, 160 miles to the west. The city of Nanking, lying between the Yangtze River on the west and the Purple Mountain on the east, had served as the ancient capital of China from the third to sixth centuries and periodically from the fourteenth century on. A center of political, literary, and artistic life, Nanking was a city of old Ming temples and tombs, museums and palaces, the site of the treaty that had ended the Opium Wars in 1842, and the setting for Sun Yat-sen's inauguration in 1911. On the day after the National Revolutionary Army moved into Shanghai, forces commanded by Chiang took over Nanking, shooting, looting, killing foreigners, and setting fire to their homes. Six people were killed, including five Westerners and the vice president of Nanking University. In an effort to exculpate himself, Chiang wrote about it many years later: "On March 24, 1927, following the entry of Revolutionary Forces into Nanking some soldiers suddenly broke loose and began attacking European and American residences, including those of members of foreign consular staffs and missionaries. This resulted in the loss of several lives. . . . Communists in the armed forces had created this incident in the hope of provoking a direct clash between the foreign powers and the Revolutionary Forces." Perhaps. But according to James McHugh of the U.S. Embassy, one of the generals involved in the killings and destruction in Nanking was later named by Chiang to head the Chinese air force and then promoted to chief of the general staff.

At the time, however, the West wanted to believe Chiang Kai-shek. Up until this point, it had associated him with the more radical revolutionaries. Now, according to the American secretary of state, he was "apparently a leader of the Moderates." Even President Calvin Coolidge made excuses for Chiang, explaining that it was difficult to protect the lives and property of foreigners in the midst of battle and that Chiang would "no doubt . . . make adequate settlement for any wrongs we have suffered." The word was pretty much the same at home. Although the Shanghai *North-China Herald* called for expiation of the "Nanking outrage," it added, "We do not think that anyone holds General Chiang to blame.... On the contrary, most people agree that it was a plot of the Hankow Communists to embroil him with foreigners."

Whatever the real story behind the marauding, it took Chiang only two days after the disaster at Nanking to move on to Shanghai, where he got busy bribing local warlords and urging moderate members of the KMT to join him. Even before his arrival, he had begun a major assault on the Communists. Soviet advisers were arrested and deported, while the Chinese Communists, according to one journalist, were treated with "a little more cruelty than was necessary"—witness the head of the Chinese Communist Party, a former professor at Peking University, whom Chiang had put in a cage and beaten. In early April, Chiang declared a new government and the next day invoked martial law, forbidding all meetings, demonstrations, and strikes. As historian Barbara Tuchman put it, "The revolution was turned from Red to right. Chiang's coup was both turning point and point of no return."

Some say that Chiang extorted $3 million* from the business community to finance his fight against the Shanghai Communists, while others insist that the money was freely given by the Federation of Commercial and Industrial Bodies, a group that included every important banking, commercial, and industrial group in the city. Frightened by the Communists in their midst, these business leaders "frantically sought to ally themselves with a more moderate wing of the Kuomintang." Apparently Chiang also made an arrangement with Big-Eared Du and Pockmarked Huang—a deal that involved exchanging their assistance for a guarantee to protect the Green Gang's opium monopoly. Sterling Fessenden, the American head of the International Settlement, told the story this way:

> In late March the French chief of police phoned me. I went to the address he gave me. I was surprised it was a Chinese residence, with armed guards at the front gate ... the large entrance hall was lined with stacks of rifles and sub-machine guns ... the French official entered with Du Yuseng [Big-Eared Du].... We got down to business immediately. Du ... was willing to move against the Reds, but had two conditions; first he wanted the French to supply him with at least five thousand rifles and ample ammunition, then turning to

---

* $3,000,000 Chinese = $2,070,000 U.S. in 1927 ($25,658,000 today).

me he demanded permission to move his military trucks through the International Settlement, something which the Settlement authorities had never granted to any Chinese force.

With Pockmarked Huang still serving as chief of the French Concession detective force, the French contribution to the crackdown was important, as were the efforts by both the British and Japanese. As one author put it, "And so foreign Shanghai and the forces of the underworld, joining hands, were ready to ambush the left."

On April 11, Chiang Kai-shek, who managed to be far enough away to avoid being implicated, ordered a planned purge of the radicals of Shanghai. At 4:00 A.M. on the twelfth, a shotgun went off in the French Concession, followed by the whistle of a gunboat, giving the signal for 1,500 members of the Green Gang, joined by specific units of the National Revolutionary Army, to attack the Communists at twenty-four places around the city. "Simultaneously," *The China Press* reported, "the machine guns broke loose in a steady roll." Members of the Green Gang traveled in trucks and armored cars supplied by the British, and in eight hours, the battle was over. There were no trials. Some five hundred workers were forced into local prisons before being shot or, in one particularly gruesome scene, taken to the railroad station and "fed alive into the fireboxes of locomotives." Hundreds or thousands* of radicals were arrested. Among those who escaped was Chou En-lai, who left for Wuhan with a substantial price on his head. The Chinese Communist Party ceased to exist in Shanghai, and within a few days, it was destroyed in several other cities, including Nanking and Canton, home of the revolution. In Canton, it was said that every woman with bobbed hair was taken out and shot. In Hankow a young woman was disemboweled for saying that Chiang Kai-shek did not represent the Kuomintang or the principles of Dr. Sun. "Her intestines were taken out and wrapped around her body while she was still alive," reported Sheean. And in a paradigm of Chinese understatement, even Chiang's personal secretary admitted that "many innocent people were killed."

This assault on the Left was repeated throughout China. Executions were popular entertainment in the countryside, where the victim, hands bound, was kicked down on his knees, so the executioner could more easily sever his head from his body. When the blood spurted forth, women and children ran up to immerse strings of copper coins in it. These homemade necklaces were hung around the children's necks to keep the evil spirits at bay.

In Peking, the Great Powers, prevented from using their own troops for

---

* Estimates range between 800 and 8,000.

fear of inciting a diplomatic incident, conspired with the government to send the police and specific units of warlord Marshal Chang Tso-lin's army to invade the Soviet Embassy. The Old Marshal, who had been executing as many members of the CCP as he could get his hands on, had driven others into taking refuge in the Russian Embassy, located in the safety of the Legation Quarter. When he attacked the embassy, both the Russians and the Chinese began burning their files, but the firemen assigned to the legations extinguished the fire and saved most of the incriminating papers. Some eighty Russians and Chinese were arrested during the attack, and twenty members of the CCP were imprisoned and strangled by Marshal Chang's soldiers. Strangulation was a terrible death in China, where an able practitioner, using his bare hands, could make the agony last as long as fifteen minutes, while the victim, in full view of his enemies, lost control of his bladder, his sphincter, and his last shred of human dignity.

Wang Ching-wei, whom the government at Wuhan had called back as an alternative to Chiang, had arrived in Shanghai on the April 1, ten days before Chiang's purge. Chiang, who played the situation with Wang with noteworthy sangfroid, had written his old enemy urging him to return, addressing Wang as his "beloved friend and teacher" and offering to "share power" with him. "I, your younger brother," Chiang wrote, "am not educated and have no manners, so have offended you. . . . You, my Elder Brother, left everything behind without casting a look at me, your younger brother, and the result has been that I have gone through all these difficulties single-handed." After a week in Shanghai, which included consultations with Chiang, Wang left for Wuhan, where he announced that he had come as the successor to Dr. Sun and that conciliation between the two factions of the Kuomintang was possible if the Wuhan camp joined Chiang in trying to unite the country. But Wang, who still bore a grudge against Chiang, joined enthusiastically in the anti-Chiang rhetoric, the current lingua franca of Wuhan, which one authority dubbed "the new Jerusalem on the Yangtze."

Foreign advisers had been sent by Moscow to Wuhan to stir up the workers, who made outrageous demands on their employers: salaries to be paid two or three years in advance; fifteen months' salary for twelve months' labor; a four-week paid vacation every year plus two weeks off for Chinese New Year, three days for the Western New Year, and one day for all revolutionary holidays. For a death or a marriage in the family, the worker was to be given a six-month bonus, and a worker let go without cause was to receive three years' salary. With exactions like these, it is not surprising that two thirds of the foreign population left Wuhan, along with many well-off Chinese. Most English, Americans, and Japanese who remained lived on board ships because the city was so dangerous.

Borodin remained a local celebrity. As his biographer explained, it was in the "self-interest" of reporters looking for headlines "to build Borodin into a figure of Herculean proportions. . . . In their columns . . . he never worked less than eighteen hours a day for the revolutionary cause. Still he found time to ride horseback, to read and play chess, at which he was 'unbeatable.' He was interested in art, literature, history. He read everything that came his way. . . . A philosopher, a man of remarkable physique, with a booming voice and an iron will, he was a magnet toward whom all eyes were drawn."

Even Stalin, who had made the Soviet relationship with Chiang an issue in his struggle over power with Trotsky, finally conceded to Borodin in the matter of Chiang Kai-shek. Up until this time, Stalin, contending that the Soviet Union should concentrate its limited resources on internal development while supporting nationalist movements fighting imperialism, had tied Borodin's hands, not allowing him to launch his missiles against Chiang. Now, denouncing Chiang as an "ally of the Imperialists and an enemy of the labour movement and the Communist International," he gave Borodin the go-ahead to pursue an all-out anti-Chiang campaign. Propaganda was Borodin's speciality, and handbills reading "The Revolution Will Never Succeed Without First Striking Down Chiang Kai-shek!" appeared all over the Wuhan area. There was more. The regime at Wuhan, under the leadership of Wang, passed a resolution expelling Chiang Kai-shek from the Kuomintang. Listing twelve "crimes" he had committed—including "massacre of the people and oppression of the Party"—it offered a reward of 250,000 taels* for him alive or 100,000 dead.†

Back in Nanchang, Chiang was informed by telegram that the party had taken away all his power and that he should "await orders." Chiang reacted, according to Jennie, by behaving "like a madman," smashing anything he got hold of and, when he couldn't find his revolver, breaking up the furniture. An emissary arrived from Wuhan with two letters for him. The first was from his old commander, General Hsu, the man who had allowed the town of Waichow to fall back into the hands of the Hakka General; Hsu said that he hoped Chiang would "do what is right and . . . confess his mistakes." The second was an open letter from Wang, in which he urged his comrades in the party to "rise up in arms and wipe away this rebel [Chiang] before it is too late! Only in this way," Wang declared, "can we save our country from annihilation and save the people from servitude to the imperialists."

---

* 250,000 taels = $172,500 U.S. in 1927 ($2,138,150 today).

† 100,000 taels = $69,000 U.S. in 1927 ($855,200 today).

But while Wuhan indulged itself in condemnations of and threats to Chiang, foreign banks in the tri-city area closed, banks in Shanghai refused to accept Wuhan currency, and Ichon, a center of the opium trade and a major source of Wuhan's income, was captured by forces allied to Chiang. On April 21, 1927, the largest British ship in the area, a 9,750-ton cruiser appropriately named *Vindictive*, joined a line of thirty-five foreign warships that stretched a mile and a half along the Bund at Hankow, blocking commerce and threatening the Wuhan government. The following week another group of ships arrived from Shanghai, bringing the number of foreign warships up to forty-two. Wuhan could and did make a great deal of noise, but for all its bravado, there was "no rice, no oil, no coal, and no money." The economy of the tri-city area and therefore its validity collapsed under the weight of the freewheeling Communist regime.

"Business men are rallying to the support of General Chiang as their only hope against Bolshevism," a reporter observed in *The North-China Herald*. ". . . Moscow thunders denunciations against the 'traitor.' Chiang has burnt his boats."

15

Our only fault at Wuhan was that we did not get rid of the Communists sooner.
—WANG CHING-WEI

HAVING VOTED Chiang out of the party, the Wuhan regime sent its army north to conquer Peking. Seventy thousand soldiers left from the train station, where such left-wing luminaries as Wang Ching-wei, Sun Ching-ling, Sun Fo, and Eugene Chen gathered to wish them well. Large crowds, collected to demonstrate, obediently shouted, "Down with Chiang-Kai-shek! Down with northern militarists! Down with imperialism!" Preceding the soldiers was another train of twelve cars filled with adorable young girls in blue uniforms, so-called propaganda cadres, sent out to spread the Communist word and "pacify the countryside."

But the troops that started out with such fanfare did not do well in the field. Many of the soldiers defected to Chiang; 20,000 were killed; and within six weeks 9,000 wounded had arrived back in Wuhan. As they continued to be brought in at the staggering rate of 500 men a day, Ching-ling arranged a series of money-raising benefits to pay for their care in the emergency hospitals that sprang up in the tri-city area.

By this time, Sun's widow, called by Chou En-lai "the jewel of the nation," had become a Communist Party icon. "Mme. Sun was 'China's Joan of Arc'; she was the leader of a Chinese 'woman's battalion'; she was this, that and the other thing, depending on the fantasies of the headline writers. The notion that she had actually led troops in battle was so widespread that even in China some of the foreigners believed it," wrote Vincent Sheean, who was about to meet her for the first time. ". . . Although I had sense enough not to believe most of the stories . . . they must have made, collectively, an impression; for I had certainly expected to meet something formidable." Sheean was not expecting what he saw:

> The door at the end of the darkened reception room on the second floor of the Ministry of Finance opened, and in came a small, shy Chinese lady in a black silk dress. . . . When she spoke her voice almost made me jump; it was so soft, so gentle, so unexpectedly sweet . . . here I was face to face with a childlike figure of the most

enchanting delicacy. . . . You had to know her for a good while before you realized the power of the spirit beneath that exquisite,
tremulous envelope. . . . She had a dignity so natural and certain
that it deserved the name of stateliness. . . . She also possessed moral
courage to a rare degree. . . . Her loyalty to the name of Sun Yat-sen,
to the duty she felt she owed it, was able to withstand trials without
end. These qualities—dignity, loyalty, moral courage—gave her character an underlying strength that could, at times, overcome the impressions of fragility and shyness created by her physical appearance
and endow her figure with the sternest aspect of heroism.

Edgar Snow, who met Ching-ling a few years later, agreed. "Like Sheean,"
he said, "I found the contrast between her appearance and her destiny star-
tling. . . . She was a modest and naturally self-effacing person. It required
great moral and physical courage for her to resist the pressures put upon
her to compromise with her own conception of the role assigned to her by
history."

Ching-ling's brother T.V. had not been endowed with the same single-
minded convictions as his sister, and while the government at Wuhan was
struggling to supersede Chiang, he was groping his way through a political
crisis of his own. Four years younger than Ching-ling and three years older
than May-ling, T.V. was the third child and first son in the Soong family.
Having earned a master's degree in economics at Harvard and a doctorate at
Columbia, he had returned with May-ling to Shanghai, where he went to
work for a major industrial conglomerate, promptly setting the company
accounts and financial affairs in order. Since T.V.'s English was so good, the
head of the company, Sheng Hsuan-huai,* asked him to tutor his daughter.
When the two fell in love and asked permission to marry, Sheng objected on
social and economic grounds—the Soong family was not yet considered on
a par with the Shengs—and transferred T.V. out of Shanghai.

He went south to Canton, where the financial situation was chaotic and
where his older sister Ching-ling suggested he help her husband, Dr. Sun,
solve the ever-troubling financial and banking problems of the KMT. Dominated by foreign banks, the city ran on foreign currency, since Chinese
money had not yet been standardized. The first thing that Sun Yat-sen asked
T.V. to do was organize a bank in Canton that would serve as the central
bank of the southern (KMT) government and issue its currency. T.V. tried to
introduce Western concepts into the new bank, advising the government not

---

* There are several stories, possibly apocryphal, told about T.V. and the Shengs. See the
endnotes to this chapter for a few of them.

to use it merely as a storehouse of money to be drawn from whenever the need arose. He failed. Nevertheless, the central bank was opened with great ceremony in August 1924, and T.V. was named its president.

In July of 1925, four months after the death of Sun, Chiang Kai-shek established his Kuomintang government in Canton and appointed T.V. finance minister. During the workers' strikes, T.V. voiced the dilemma of a liberal financier faced with revolution: "On the one hand, I should protect the businessmen, but on the other I should be responsible not to destroy the workers. I must pursue profits for the business community, but I cannot let down the patriotism of the workers." When the left wing of the government moved to Wuhan, T.V. was one of its core members. Chiang objected to moving the government's money to Wuhan. Without money, the Wuhan faction could not function, and it asked T.V. to talk to Chiang. Chiang was delighted to confer with his brother-in-law, who was known as the best money man in China, and he invited T.V. to come into his wing of the government as minister of finance. In spite of both "persuasion and threats," T.V., who still held that position in Wuhan, refused. Angry but determined to avoid direct confrontation, Chiang closed the central bank of the southern government, making it clear that T.V. could accomplish nothing if he did not join his faction of the party. He sent spies to watch Ching-ling's house in the French Concession in Shanghai, to which T.V. retreated when he could no longer stand the pressure at the Kungs' or his mother's home.

If Chiang was determined to have T.V. in his government, so were his rivals. "Hankow [i.e., Wuhan] needed T.V. badly," said Vincent Sheean. "The ability of that young man to inspire confidence, to make the books balance, to coax money out of hiding places, was an ability nobody at Hankow possessed. . . . In Hankow the financial situation was beginning to be desperate." When Sheean left Wuhan to report from Shanghai, Ching-ling gave him a letter to take to her brother saying that "she wished he would return to his post in Hankow."

"When I went to see him [T.V.] in Shanghai," Sheean reported, "he seemed ready to fall in with the plan." T.V., the journalist noted, had become extremely nervous. Aware that the Sun house was being watched, he was afraid to leave the French Concession for fear of being nabbed by Chiang's soldiers. According to Sheean, T.V.'s alternatives, if he were caught by Chiang, were to join the Finance Ministry or go to prison. "He was, in fact, in a rare state of funk, and the suggestion I brought from Hankow seemed to offer him a way out of all his troubles." Although T.V. agreed to return to Wuhan and asked Sheean to book a ticket for him under a false name, by the next day, he had changed his mind. "In the interim," said Sheean, "he had talked to his mother, his sister, his brother-in-law [H. H. Kung], and they were a fundamentally reactionary family. 'There's no point in my going to Hankow,' he said, worried and nervous. 'You see the truth is that I'm not a social revolutionary. I don't like revolution, and I don't believe in it. How can I balance a budget or keep a currency going if the labour policy frightens every merchant or factory owner into shutting up shop? . . . Look at what they've done with my bank notes, my beautiful bank notes. . . . They've been inflated out of existence. . . . Nothing can be done if they keep on encouraging strikes and mass meetings.' "

T.V.'s hesitation also had to do with the fact that during one of the many demonstrations in Wuhan, his car had been mobbed and a window smashed by an angry crowd, leaving him with a residual terror of mass behavior. "How can I be sure that I will be safe if I return to Wuhan? Maybe the mob will pull me out of the Finance Ministry and tear me into pieces. . . . I'm not popular, mind you. I've never been popular. The mob doesn't like me. They would have killed me last winter, if the soldiers hadn't come in time." T.V. continued to seesaw back and forth for a week, and on the day Sheean was to collect him for the trip back to Wuhan, he "happened to be in one of his pro-Hankow states of mind." The journalist went to pick him up at midnight, but by the time he got to the Sun home on Rue Molière, he had changed his mind again. " 'I can't go,' he said the moment he came down the stairs.' " He then went to see his mother, May-ling, Ai-ling, and H. H. Kung. "After some hours of argument T.V. came out of the recesses of the Kung house and spoke—dejectedly, gloomily. 'It's all settled,' he said, 'I'm not going. Tell my sister [Ching-ling] I shall write to her. I'm sorry you were troubled for nothing.' I have never seen him since," Sheean concluded, "and the events of that night were to give my final impression of Soong Tse-vung . . . as . . . the honest Liberal at sea between opposing shores."

This is a fair assessment of T. V. Soong at the time. Before the split in the KMT became irreparable, T.V. had sold bonds to Chinese businessmen to raise funds for Chiang's government. But the day after Wuhan put a price on his head, Chiang announced the establishment of his rival government in the city of Nanking and began to issue his own government bonds. But the bankers and businessmen, aware of the rift between Chiang's government and Wuhan, wanted guarantees that their loans would be repaid, and they asked to have T. V. Soong, whom they trusted, cosign them as finance minister. When T.V. made it known that he would not cosign the loans, Chiang appointed another minister of finance and closed T.V.'s office. Eventually, Chiang was able to force his future brother-in-law into his own camp.

If Chiang refused to take no for an answer from T.V., he also hesitated at nothing to get "loans" from the business community in Shanghai. According to the correspondent of *The New York Times*, "The plight of the Chinese merchant in and about Shanghai is pitiable. At the mercy of General Chiang Kai-shek's dictatorship, the merchants do not know what the next day will bring, confiscation, compulsory loans, exile, or possible execution." This was written in early May 1927, and matters got worse after that. In the middle of the month, the son of a rich indigo merchant was seized as a counter-revolutionary and released only after his father donated 200,000 Chinese dollars* to the Nationalists. The cotton and flour king of Shanghai was arrested on grounds of corruption, and the order to seize his mills was withdrawn—but only after a donation of 250,000 Chinese dollars† was obtained. And the three-year-old son of the director of the Sincere Company Department Store was kidnapped, requiring a donation of 500,000 Chinese dollars‡ to the KMT coffers for his release. Strong-arm tactics quickly engulfed Shanghai's bankers and merchants in what the American consul called "a veritable reign of terror among the money classes." An Australian who happened on the scene noted with some irony, "Millionaires were arrested as 'Communists'!"

Another way of extricating funds for the government was through an anti-Japanese boycott, begun in June 1927. At the end of May, Japanese troops were sent to Shantung province to guard Japanese interests against the soldiers of the Northern Expedition. This led to anti-Japanese demonstrations in various cities around China and the boycott of Japanese goods. Using this as an excuse, government inspectors ransacked Chinese shops for Japanese products, levied fines, and blackmailed their owners. Merchants in the protected International Settlement were treated to the sight of large cages placed along settlement boundaries with signs threatening to fill them with those who violated the boycott. Although Chiang's KMT agents could not operate legally in these foreign-controlled areas, his alliance with members of the Green Gang gave them access, particularly in the French Concession, where Pockmarked Huang was still chief detective of the police force.

❦

MEANWHILE, THE RADICAL contingent in Wuhan, left relatively defenseless with its army in the north, had begun to hear rumors of imminent attacks by the forces of Chiang. By the middle of May, it had been confirmed that Chiang's allies were less than a hundred miles away and that a general whom Wuhan considered its man had gone over to the other side. On May 16,

---

* $200,000 Chinese = $138,000 U.S. in 1927 ($1,710,400 today).

† $500,000 Chinese = $172,500 U.S. in 1927 ($2,138,000 today).

‡ $500,000 Chinese = 345,000 U.S. in 1927 ($4,276,000 today).

Moscow ordered the Communists to be ready to leave Hankow—a flight facilitated by the arrival of a special courier with a check for $150,000* in gold. When he received his instructions, Borodin ordered his secretaries to burn his papers. A few days later the government called for the removal of all the anti-Chiang posters plastered on the walls of the tri-city area. Bad news for the radicals came on May 22 with the fall of Changsha, capital of the province of Hunan, to the supporters of Chiang. Changsha, where the teaching of the classics had been outlawed and magistrates had been replaced by citizens' councils, was the center of what even Wuhan radicals referred to as "left infantilism." Word from Moscow that "the mass of the poor peasants is the reliable basis of the revolutionary Wuhan government" did not help bolster the confidence of those who wondered if it was already too late to escape the vengeance of the counterrevolution. "The Communists propose to us to go together with the masses," said Wang Ching-wei at a meeting of the Wuhan Military Council. "But where are the masses? Where are the highly praised forces of the Shanghai workers or the Kwangtung or Hunan peasants? There are no such forces. . . . To go with the masses means to go against the army. No, we had better go without the masses but together with the army."

In any case, with the exception of Ching-ling—called by Borodin "the only man in the whole left wing of the Kuomintang"—the leadership in Wuhan was not a particularly staunch group. Certainly Wang Ching-wei had not proved to be much of a leader. He was, as left-wing journalist Harold Isaacs put it, "indecisive in all things except his readiness to retreat before stronger personalities." Isaacs, a friend of Trotsky and author of a classic history, *The Tragedy of the Chinese Revolution,* had even less regard for Dr. Sun's son, Sun Fo. Sun Fo, in Isaac's words, was "a squirmy politican who changed his views and allegiances so often that even his own colleagues, hardly noted for their steadfastness, contemptuously called him 'Sun Wu-k'ung' after the mythical monkey who covered 10,000 miles in a single leap."

Outside KMT headquarters, things were no better. Ordinary citizens gathered at the central bank to change their paper money into silver but found the doors locked and bolted. "The area around the Central Bank got to looking like a mob scene from 'Ben Hur,' " wrote one American reporter. "Day after day, the hungry and the poor collected there. They howled for silver and copper, they shrieked and threw their bodies against the bronze doors." The well-to-do, of course, had other options. "Open carriages, jewels of black lacquer and crammed with people of fashion, went clattering over the cobblestones in the general direction of the French Concession," the

---

* 150,000 Chinese = $103,000 U.S. in 1927 ($1,282,800 today).

reporter continued. "The French would as usual give refuge to the rich Chinese, at a price."

The coup de grâce for the Wuhan leaders arrived in the form of a wire from Stalin, ordering, among other things, the arming of twenty thousand members of the Chinese Communist Party, the creation of a 50,000-man army from the peasants of Hunan and Hupeh, and the seizure of the KMT Central Executive Committee by the radicals. Borodin, no fool he, realized that Stalin had sent impossible instructions in order to avoid taking the blame for the failure of his China policy.

With their political position, their finances, and their army all collapsing, the radicals' last hope of wresting the KMT from Chiang was the Christian warlord Feng, who commanded an army of 200,000 soldiers. Feng had recently returned to China after a period of "instruction and contemplation" in Moscow. By the previous August (1926), Moscow had invested some 6 million rubles in Feng—in guns, cannons, planes, and ammunition, along with the usual quota of military and political advisers. Since then, the Russians had continued to pour millions more into his coffers. Or, as Borodin's biographer put it, "Moscow thought it had bought Feng in spite of considerable evidence to the contrary."

The evidence was pretty clear. General Feng had never permitted the Chinese Communist Party to operate in areas under his control and had always suppressed its strikes. More recently, he had ordered the removal of anti-Chiang posters and stopped demonstrations against him. Ignoring these obvious signals, the Wuhan government set up a meeting with Feng for Wang Ching-wei, Madame Sun, and Sun Fo. The Christian General was late, arriving on a freight train, to which he had switched, having traveled from the front on a luxurious coach appropriate to a rich warlord. A man who clearly understood appearance versus reality, it didn't take him long to figure out that Moscow's government in China was broke and on the way out. Nevertheless, its representatives offered him three provinces—Honan, Shensi, and Kansu. In exchange, Feng demanded that members of the Chinese Communist Party be removed from the Wuhan government and that Borodin be sent back to Moscow. Convinced that they had made a deal, the delegates arrived back in Wuhan to a jubilant demonstration complete with fireworks. Wang announced that the trip had been successful and that "Feng Yu-hsiang supported Wuhan."

A week later Feng met with Chiang Kai-shek, and by the end of two days, Feng, a typical warlord looking for the best deal, had decided to join forces with him. For this he was promised $2 million a month and control of the province of Honan. Toward that end, Feng sent Wang a wire suggesting that Borodin return to Moscow and that members of the Wuhan government who wished to join the Nanking national government should do so. The others, he added, ought to take this opportunity to visit foreign lands. But with the exception of Ching-ling and her friend General Teng Yen-ta, a man with the "courage of his convictions that lifted him a long notch above his fellows," Wuhan had already decided to go with the winner.

On July 15, 1927, the Chinese Communists were officially thrown out of the KMT, and soldiers friendly to Chiang began to take over parts of the tri-city area. No one of note appeared on the street without a bodyguard, and summary executions became "commonplace" on both sides. An unsuccessful attempt was made on the life of Galen, who left for Shanghai to say good-bye to Chiang. After this, the Russian general purchased trucks and cars for his escape through northern China and from there across the rocky steppes and desolate deserts of Inner Mongolia to Russia. As *The North-China Herald* put it, "Having achieved fame almost equal to that of the 'Mysterious Borodin,' he [Galen] goes—like Borodin—unheralded and unsung . . . a successful military leader, a failure by the turn of Chinese political events."

Borodin himself, with a price of $30,000* on his head, hid in T.V.'s apartment until he could safely and secretly get out of the tri-city area. Concerned about his safety, T.V. accompanied him to the city of Lushan until plans for his escape could be finalized. Lushan, a summer resort in the mountains, had been founded by the English in the nineteenth century. An oasis of villas surrounded by pines, bamboo, and waterfalls, it could be reached only by palanquins and bearers, who negotiated the three-hour trip up narrow mountain trails, planting little sticks below the boulders to propitiate the spirits holding up the mountainside and crossing bridges that swayed back and forth in the wind. After a week or so, word reached Lushan that Feng had been bribed enough to guarantee Borodin safe conduct through his territory. Accompanied by a retinue of thirty people, five cars, and five trucks, Borodin left Wuhan on July 27 for the two-month overland trip through the desert.

Ching-ling still refused to switch sides or flee. On July 14, she issued a statement condemning Chiang Kai-shek and his nationalist government:

> [A]ll revolutions must be . . . based upon fundamental changes in society, otherwise it is not a revolution, but merely a change of government. . . . Dr. Sun . . . was determined that the lot of the Chinese peasant should not continue to be so wretched. . . . Yet today . . . men . . . who profess to follow his banner . . . think in terms of "rev-

---

* $30,000 Chinese = $28,750 U.S. in 1927 ($356,360 today).

olution" that would virtually disregard the sufferings of those millions of povery-stricken peasants of China. Dr. Sun's policies are
clear. If certain leaders of the party do not carry them out consis-
tently then they are no longer Dr. Sun's true followers, and the party
is no longer a revolutionary party, but merely a tool in the hands of
this or that militarist.

Before this was published—and immediately suppressed—Ching-ling
left for Shanghai, where she returned to her old home on Rue Molière. From
there, she continued to denounce Chiang Kai-shek's government—a practice that for anyone else would have led, according to Sheean, to "a certain
and terrible death." It is said that a frustrated member of the KMT called on
her one day. "If you were anyone but Madame Sun, we would cut your head
off," he said sullenly. "If you were the revolutionists you pretend to be," she
smiled back, "you'd cut it off anyway!" Continally pressured by her family
to join the pro-Chiang faction and unable to prevent the use of her husband's
name to invoke a blessing on the counterrevolution taking place around her,
she passed ten days of frustration before deciding to visit Moscow. She arranged to meet an American friend, a woman named Rayna Prohme, and
leave in secret at 3:00 A.M. one night. Joined by Eugene Chen and two of his
daughters, they were met in Vladivostok by a special train sent by the Soviets, which took them to Moscow. "I think she is more confused than anything else," Ching-ling's friend commented on Sun's widow. "I haven't yet
been able to determine what the revolution really means to her, if it is blind
loyalty to her husband, or some active driving force in herself. If the latter,
there will be much to overcome, an instinctive withdrawal from contacts, an
almost pathological distaste for anything that is not scrupulously clean, both
in things and people, and an impulse to be surrounded always by nice
things."

Under any circumstances, however, this was, in the words of one of
Ching-ling's biographers,* "the worst possible time" for Ching-ling to visit
the Soviet Union. About to break with Trotsky, Stalin had "misread the situation in China badly, and was on the lookout for scapegoats . . . anyone who
had been in China, or was connected with the Chinese Revolution." Borodin, who arrived shortly after Ching-ling, was "muzzled and shunted into a
minor post," while Joffe, the Soviet emissary to China, committed suicide.
With her income from China cut off, unwilling to accept help, Ching-ling,
according to Sheean, was "now the loneliest of exiles." Isolated except for a
few Chinese friends, she and Eugene Chen went to see Stalin, who urged

---

* Sung Chang.

them to go home and cooperate with Chiang. She did not take his advice. After six months in Russia, she went to Brussels for a meeting of the League to Struggle against Imperialism and Colonial Oppression and then moved on to Berlin. It was May of 1929 before she returned home.

While the diehards were trying to cope in Russia, the other radicals, with the exception of Ching-ling's friend General Teng, had made a quick accommodation with Chiang. In spite of this, the rivalry between the two factions continued its angry course. There was only one solution to the problem insofar as Chiang was concerned, and it was his old response to a new situation. He, Chiang Kai-shek, head of the army and the government, announced that since he was the cause of this hostility, he would resign and go home, rest, and study politics, economics, and military tactics. As was his custom, he dressed the part, shedding his uniform for the long robes of a scholar.

Of all Chiang's resignations, this was the most carefully thought out, the most disingenuous, and possibly the most politically savvy. With his previous record of making himself unavailable to prove his worth, it would be foolish to believe that he meant what he said. Four days after his resignation, the *North-China Herald* reported that the morale of the National Revolutionary Army had collapsed, and local papers were reporting that the Nanking government was "at a standstill." Chiang knew he was well on his way to achieving the pinnacle of his desires. He was head of the army and de facto leader of the party, and he had just bested the faction, backed by the entire USSR, that wanted him out, dead or alive. He intended to pursue the Northern Expedition, but before he could do this, he needed a united party behind him. He assumed that the radical element of the KMT would learn to appreciate him in his absence. Or at least it would realize that it could get nowhere without him.

In addition to military and political factors, Chiang had a specific personal plan in mind. This break in his campaign would give him time to bring it to a fruition.

PART THREE

❧

1928–1936

16

By education and training she [Madame Chiang] is equipped as no other women in modern politics to take her place in the affairs of state.

—T. CHRISTOPHER JESPERSON

IT IS an accepted fact that May-ling's marriage to Chiang Kai-shek was arranged by her sister Ai-ling, but when the deputy secretary of an important women's committee told Madame Chiang that she admired Ai-ling for conceiving the idea, Madame, who was seldom averse to juggling history, not only disagreed but, according to her personal assistant, told an entirely different story:

"Pardon me, my dear lady," she said tapping her fingers impatiently on the table in front of her,

> I can scarcely believe that you would accept such a fabrication. How could this have been so? Among my brothers and sisters, Ching-ling is the most obstinate, I am somewhere in the middle, and Ai-ling is the gentlest. Never, neither as girl nor woman did Ai-ling impose her opinion on others. Although she introduced Ching-ling to Dr. Sun, she knew her sister had adored him since she was a young child. As to my marriage to Chiang Kai-shek, Ai-ling neither suggested it nor persuaded me to marry him. However, when my mother disapproved of the idea, Ai-ling and T.V. tried to help me convince her that it would be all right. My marriage with Chiang Kai-shek was totally my idea. It was I who persuaded my mother, my elder brother and my eldest sister to accept Chiang and got them to support me. . . . Ever since I was a young girl I have adored heroes. Many was the time I heard Sun Yat-sen praise Chiang Kai-shek's talent. I met Chiang for the first time in Dr. Sun's home in 1923.* I was attracted by his shining eyes. . . . I lost my heart to him. We spoke in Shang-

---

* According to Chiang, they were introduced for the first time in December of 1922 at a party given by T.V. in the Suns' residence in Shanghai. He said he was "deeply attracted by her elegant appearance and delightful conversation." (Chen Jin-jin, "Stories of Love," *A Study of Modern Chinese Women*, Vol. 2., pp. 275–88.)

hai dialect, and we exchanged addresses and telephone numbers. Later, I invited him to my mother's birthday party.

Aside from the fact that May-ling would never, ever have invited an unknown man to her mother's birthday party, this story of love at first sight is at best an exaggeration. She probably did meet Chiang at the Suns' home on Rue Molière around that time, but Chiang—described some years into their marriage as "a small, ascetic-faced man . . . who might have passed for an Episcopalian minister or a Y.M.C.A. secretary"—was not yet endowed with the charisma of a national hero. Only one of several assistants to Sun Yat-sen, he was in Russia from August until the end of 1923, and there is no record of May-ling visiting Canton, where he was stationed.

According to Emily Hahn, who interviewed the sisters in the 1940s, Chiang—never one to be bothered by other attachments when desire and power were involved—asked Dr. Sun at some point if he thought he could have a future with the youngest Soong daughter: "Do you think Miss Soong could be persuaded to accept me?" At which point Sun made the mistake of asking his wife, Ching-ling, who said that "she would rather see her little sister <u>dead</u>" than married to a man with at least one other wife—an interesting objection considering the background of her own marriage. With the usual Chinese refusal to deliver bad news, Sun simply told Chiang, "Wait a while"—advice he reiterated the two other times that Chiang brought up the subject over the next couple of years.

There is another story floating in the fogs of historical gossip that Chiang had also asked for the hand of Ching-ling. According to Edgar Snow, Ching-ling told him that shortly after Sun's death in 1925, Chiang had proposed to her through a middleman. "She thought it was politics, not love," said Snow, "and declined." This would certainly confirm the theory that what Chiang Kai-shek wanted was not a wife but a political and financial asset—the usual Chinese criterion for picking a spouse. According to the independent newspaper *Ta Kung Pao:*

> Chiang's remarriage was a calculated political move. He hoped to win over Madame Sun Yat-sen (Soong Ching-ling) and T. V. Soong by becoming their brother-in-law. At that point, Chiang also began to contemplate the need to seek support from the West. With May-ling as his wife, he would have the "mouth and ears" to deal with Westerners. Besides, he thought very highly of T.V. as a financial expert. But it would be unfair to say that Chiang did not fall for May-ling. Chiang obviously considered himself a hero. And in Chinese history, heroes tended to fall for beauties. For political consid-

erations, Chiang would have done anything. To have a new wife would seem a logical move for Chiang to make in those circumstances.

May-ling and Chiang did meet in Canton in 1926, when May-ling was visiting the Suns. She may well have been attracted, and so, obviously, was he, judging from his diary. In the first entry, dated the end of January, he only mentions that she attended graduation services at Whampoa Military Academy, but by the second, dated the end of June, he reports going to visit her, and at the end of July he laments the fact that "May-ling will be going back to Shanghai. I do not want her to leave." During the first half of that year, Chiang himself was very busy—evading the Communist plot to spirit him off to Russia (the incident of the gunboat), pulling off his coup against the Communists, making plans for the Northern Expedition, and mobilizing his soldiers. By the end of July, he was ready to leave Canton for the big drive north, and it seems clear that they could not have seen each other again until the winter and spring of 1926–1927, when May-ling spent three months in Wuhan. From her comments on the local Chinese Communists and "the divergences" between them and "our National policy," it seems likely that they spent time together when he went there in January of 1927 to deal with Borodin and the Communist faction of the KMT.

Chiang first mentions her name on March 21, 1927, by which time she must have left Wuhan. "I missed Sister May-ling very much today," reads the entry in his diary; and two months later, "I can't help thinking about May-ling." According to the person who wrote an introduction to this section of his diary, they had already started corresponding with each other.

Whatever the state of their relationship, it was not too long after Chiang and Jennie moved into their new house in Canton that they received an invitation to dine at the home of the Kungs in Canton. According to Jennie, Chiang was terrifically excited: "An invitation! I never, never expected it," he told her, pacing back and forth. "And now, at last, after all this time, you and I have a chance to dine with this great personage. It is really too wonderful to be true." Chiang then explained to his wife that she must "realize how very important" it was to him "to get closer to the Soong family. You know that I wasn't able to get as close to our leader [Sun] all those years as I had wished, so this is a chance to get closer to his relatives. . . . You know just as well as I do [that] Canton is full of military experts, but by a stroke of pure luck I was made head of the academy. I have position, but I lack prestige. So my strategy is to cultivate the friendship of his nearest relatives. I want the names of Sun, Soong and Chiang to be linked tightly together. . . . We are on the threshold of great achievement. You know how much this means to me. You must not refuse to go to the dinner."

Because Chiang himself could not get away from his duties at the military academy until late that day, Jennie did as he asked and arrived alone at the Kungs' at the appointed hour. The other guests were May-ling, Eugene Chen, and Ho Hsiang-ning, the widow of Chiang's friend Liao Chung-k'ai. According to Jennie, the hostess and her sister, dressed in bright silk gowns, "looked as if they had stepped out of a Shanghai fashion book." Chiang's wife, who had been given a tour of the house and was returning to the living room, overheard the two sisters gossiping about her. Suddenly, her white crepe de chine dress, white kid shoes, and beaded white handbag seemed less than perfect for the evening. "She's only a middle-class housewife!" Jennie overheard Ai-ling saying to May-ling. "How can she ever qualify to be the wife of a budding leader? Something must be done about it."

Quizzed for two hours about Chiang, his village wife, his ex-concubine, and his famous temper, Jennie was seemingly still unaware that this little dinner, which had "seemed to be just an ordinary get-together," was the "beginning of a long-range intrigue" to separate her from her husband. But by the time Chiang himself arrived, "thrilled beyond words to be a guest of Mme. Kung," Jennie had begun to notice little things—like her hostess's constant praise of her younger sister. "No one," according to Ai-ling, "was as clever as May-ling Soong." Still, Jennie claimed that she was surprised the next day when Ho warned her to stay away from Ai-ling: "We have known her for at least four years," Ho said, ". . . she used to ignore Kai-shek as if he were a common soldier. She never did have any respect for him. In fact, I remember distinctly, when Dr. Sun introduced us, she rudely turned her head the other way. It embarrassed Dr. Sun terribly. . . . Today the situation is different. Kai-shek is the most important personage in Canton and is an attractive prize to be ensnared. You must remember that she still has an unmarried sister."

Then one day, "out of the blue," a letter arrived for Chiang from May-ling. Jennie was stunned. Caught, Chiang showed her the letter:

Dear Big Brother,

For a few months I have not been near you to receive your profitable instruction. In your busy military life you have wired inviting me to accompany my sister and family to visit Wuhan [Hankow] to see our Nationalist Party's new achievement. For this I am grateful. But the day before yesterday I left Canton for Shanghai to see my mother. Big sister is still in Canton and may shortly return to Shanghai. When I have time

I shall certainly accompany her to visit the Yangtze cities. I am now taking advantage of Yung-chih's [H. H. Kung's] departure for Hankow to write you these few lines to ask after your well-being.

May-ling

By way of explanation, Chiang said that May-ling's note was in answer to a telegram he had sent to thank her for her congratulations, presumably on his successful military campaign. "I invited her to Hankow," he told Jennie. ". . . It shows how important it is to hold high position. Once you are up, people flock to you." Chiang also explained to his wife that "the subtle way" and the best way to get T. V. Soong to leave Wuhan and join Chiang's faction of the KMT was through Ai-ling Kung. Having forewarned his wife, Chiang invited Ai-ling to a meeting. According to Jennie, their conference proceeded as follows: "Mme. Kung came posthaste, sailing on the Central Bank of China's cruiser. On arrival, she did not disembark but stayed on board and sent for Kai-shek." Although Jennie thought that Ai-ling "did not come ashore because . . . she had reasons for avoiding me," it is clear that, in the Chinese way, Ai-ling was also putting herself in the stronger position of the two. And whereas Chiang told Jennie that they "spent twenty-four hours discussing the political situation," their conversation obviously ranged way beyond politics.

"Mme. Kung" Jennie said, "was a formidable negotiator."

She was the most able of the Soong sisters, a hardheaded female . . . shrewd, cunning, and ambitious. Kai-shek knew that her passionate interest was money, for she speculated on the exchange market and took a fierce joy in business manipulations and enterprises. . . . After the twenty-four-hour meeting . . . she returned directly to Hankow. Kai-shek came home to tell me in great detail what had transpired. He said: "I have not kept any secrets from you and I don't want to begin now, especially now when I need your help." Mme. Kung said this to me:

"You are a rising star. Will you allow your star to set as quickly as it has risen? Will you allow the Communists . . . to throw you out? . . . In fighting alone for the Nationalist cause, you do not have enough personality, although I must say you have the spirit. But spirit is not everything. This gigantic task of liberating and reconstructing China . . . needs great influence, money, personality, and prestige. As it is, you have none of these. . . . I will make a bargain with you. . . . I will not only convince my brother T.V.

to leave the Hankow government as you wish, but will go one better. He and I will rally the leading bankers of Shanghai to back you with the necessary funds so that you can buy the ammunition you need to carry on the expedition. In return, you will agree to marry my sister May-ling. And you will also agree that as soon as the Nanking government is established, you will name my husband, H. H. Kung, Prime Minister and my brother T.V. your Minister of Finance."

Another version of their conversation, quoted in a recent biography of H. H. Kung, outlines this exchange somewhat differently. When Chiang asked Ai-ling to help him convince T.V. to break with the government at Wuhan and join him, she answered with another question: "Do you have any other requests?"

"I think this one matter is very important, and it is enough to ask," Chiang replied.

"Then what is the quid pro quo?"

Somewhat surprised, Chiang replied that he would work for the goals of the KMT and that if he achieved the unification of China, it would be thanks to her help. He added that if Madame Kung had any personal desires, he would do everything to help her achieve them after he succeeded in destroying the rival government at Wuhan. Ai-ling then got down to business.

"Brother Kai," she said, "you are the future star of the country, but if you think in such a simple way and offer empty promises, you will fall as soon as you rise. You should know that Borodin plans to take over your powers and give them to General Galen. Your soldiers will be beaten sooner or later. . . . The people on your side are mostly incapable cowards seeking self-advancement. You cannot succeed if you rely on them."

"So I hope Madame can help me," Chiang said.

"Yes, both I and my husband have made many efforts."

"Mr. Kung is a great man, and I'm grateful to him," Chiang said. "He does things for the party without asking to be paid for them. I have great admiration for him."

"Kung is a banker. He looks for profits. He hasn't asked for payment because he did not want to mention it at the present time, but this does not mean that he doesn't care about money. I care about it. I am completely different from my husband. I only work with others under fair conditions. So we must clearly set out the quid pro quos. Listen to me. I will beg T.V. to leave the government at Wuhan. Moreover, I will call on the leading bankers of Shanghai to give you the money to buy ammunition. But in return you must promise first to take my sister May-ling as your proper and permanent wife, and you must legally get rid of your three former wives."

"Certainly," Chiang replied. "The marriage with Mao Fu-mei was arranged by my family, and I have no love for her. I left her ten years ago. As to Yao Yi-cheng, she was sent to Soochow to live."

"I mean Ch'en Chieh-ju [Jennie], who is living with you now. You will have to get rid of her. I have information that she is a Soviet spy. She will spoil everything if she stays with you."

"To call Ch'en Chieh-ju a Soviet spy is a malicious lie. I met her when she was thirteen years old, and she married me at sixteen. She has been constantly at my side ever since. I know what kind of person she is. She is not a Soviet spy."

"If you don't want to see her die," Ai-ling responded angrily, "you must send her abroad."

"All right, I promise I will."

"Secondly, once this government is established, you must appoint Mr. Kung as president."

"But, according to resolutions passed by the Kuomintang, the title of president can apply only to Dr. Sun. No one else is allowed to use it. You must know this."

"You can always change the name."

"I'm afraid that Mr. Kung is not qualified to assume this position, and such an appointment will be fought by the party."

"He . . . became a follower of Dr. Sun before you. . . . If you are reluctant to appoint him president, then you must take the position yourself," Ai-ling said as she stood up, indicating an end to the conversation.

"Madame, please sit down," said Chiang. "Mr. Kung has not been in the government a long time, but I know that he is very capable of fulfilling such a position."

"Thirdly," she added, "T.V. should be the financial minister in your government. No matter what other changes occur, his official rank cannot be lower than that of a minister."

"Certainly. T.V. will enhance the prestige of our government."

"How will you guarantee to make good on these promises?" Ai-ling asked.

"I don't think I need to sign a contract, do you? I swear with my good name and my life."

"The conditions we have discussed should not be put down in writing. We should keep them in mind and carry them out one by one," she said.

"Please trust me," said Chiang. "If I do not keep my word, you can punish me in any way you choose, including killing me."

"I will, but I certainly do not want it to come to that."

When Chiang got home, he told Jennie that he was "desperate." Ai-ling, he said, "struck a very hard bargain, but what she says is true . . . her offer is the only way for me to achieve my plans to unite China. I now ask you to help me. I beg you not to say no. After all, true love is measured by the size of the sacrifice one is willing to make!"

When Jennie asked Chiang what he wanted her to do, he asked her to "step aside for five years" so that he could marry May-ling "and get the necessary help to carry on the expedition without the support of Hankow! It's only a political marriage!" he told her. He then offered his wife a trip abroad "to study in America for five years. . . . By the time you return, the Nanking government will have become a reality and we can resume our life together. Our love will be the same. I swear to that. You know I love no other woman but you."

It was clear to Chiang's second wife that matters had already "reached a point of no return," and she returned home to her mother in Shanghai. When Jennie finished repeating her promise to her husband to "step aside so that he could realize his dream," she reported that her mother embraced her and wept. "Oh, my dear daughter, you are such a good wife. Chinese history will one day record your sacrifice for our country!"

Allowing for Jennie's habit of giving herself full marks for selflessness, it is obvious that the idea of a marriage between Chiang and May-ling was anything but an ultimatum from Ai-ling. One can easily imagine the general and the lady sitting on the deck of the carrier, concocting a plan to rid Chiang of his current wife. What they both knew was that it would be easier for Jennie to believe this story than the truth. Jennie was no longer what Chiang wanted, and he certainly did not need Ai-ling to convince him of this.

What Chiang did not tell Jennie, of course, was that he had already started seeing May-ling and that she had begun to be mentioned frequently in his diary, often disguised as "third brother":

May 4:   "I telegraphed May-ling today."
May 11:   "I sent my photo as a gift to May-ling."
May 18:   "At 7:00 I reached Shanghai and then went to visit May-ling right away."
May 30:   "I was thinking about May-ling the whole day."
June 7:   "I woke up at 6:00 A.M. and wrote to third brother."
June 11: "I went to visit third brother at 3:00 P.M."
June 12: "I talked to third brother until midnight."
June 14: "I sent a letter to third brother."
June 25: "I received third brother's letter and then replied to her right away."

IT WAS JUST two months after these last entries, on August 13, 1927, that Chiang announced his "retirement," mentioned at the end of the last chapter. Twelve days earlier, he had paid an unannounced call on Jennie at her mother's home in Shanghai. "He came into the house alone," Jennie reported, "leaving his bodyguards . . . standing in the courtyard." Chiang brought Jennie three tickets on the SS *President Jackson*—one for her and two for friends. The ship was due to sail for the United States in a few weeks' time. When she refused to accept them, he "pleaded nervously" with her: "Your departure for the United States is one of the demands of Ai-ling Kung. I know it is a great deal to ask of you, Chieh-ju, but it is entirely for the unification of China that I dare call upon your patriotism to help the country. As long as you remain in Shanghai, the deal is off. Don't you understand my problem?"

Jennie's mother came into the room, and Chiang explained that he wanted his wife "to go abroad for five years."

"When you say five years, are you telling the truth or are you merely saying it to deceive my daughter?" the mother asked.

"I swear to it!" he answered. "When I say five years, I mean five years!"

"Very well, then, let us hear you swear it before the Buddha!" said Jennie's mother as she picked up three joss sticks and a pair of candles and lit them before the family altar. "Without hesitation," Jennie reported, "Kai-shek stepped over to the shrine, stood at attention before the image, and swore, 'I promise to resume my marital relationship with Chieh-ju as husband and wife within five years from today. Should I break my promise and fail to take her back, may the Great Buddha smite me and my Nanking government. And if within ten or twenty years I do not do my duty toward her, then may Buddha topple my government and banish me from China forever.' "*

Jennie Chiang left Shanghai on August 19, 1927. When the boat reached Kobe, she was handed a newspaper announcing that "Mme. Chiang Kai-shek, wife of the former commander-in-chief of the Nanking Nationalists, sailed for the United States today. . . . Friends said that she expected to make a tour of the United States before reaching New York." But by the time she had crossed the Pacific to San Francisco, the story had changed: "General Chiang Kai-shek, former Nationalist commander in chief, is quoted as declaring in a recent interview . . . that the woman who arrived at San Francisco aboard the liner *President Jackson* from China early this month is not his wife. He asserted that the report that she is his wife is 'the work of political

---

* Chiang's government fell to the Communists twenty-two years later, at which time he was forced to leave the Chinese mainland.

enemies' seeking to so embarrass him. He added that he does not know the 'Mme. Chiang Kai-shek' mentioned in the dispatches." And by the time that Jennie got to New York, the story had expanded to include May-ling. According to *The New York Times*:

Political enemies are blamed by Chiang Kai-shek for what he denounces as false reports concerning the young woman now in the United States who is said to be his wife. The retired Nationalist leader returned to Shanghai . . . with Cupid, not Mars, as his patron deity. As previously announced, he hopes to wed Miss May-ling Soong and is on his way to Kobe, Japan, to see her mother and request parental sanction of the proposed marriage. . . . "The reports concerning my first wife and this young woman who recently went to America," he said, "were circulated widely in order to discredit not only me but my proposed marriage to Miss Soong. . . . I divorced, in 1921, my first wife.* Since then I have set free two concubines. I was surprised to learn that one of them went to America as my wife."

After issuing the statement announcing his retirement, Chiang had left Nanking and returned to his home in the mountains of Chekiang. He chose as his retreat a Buddhist monastery 3,000 feet above his old village of Chikow, where he remained for a little over a month. From there, he apparently wrote May-ling a suitably touching letter, later reprinted in a newspaper in Tientsin:

I am no longer interested in political activities. But thinking about the people I admire in this life, you, my lady, are the only one. . . . Now that I have retreated to the mountain and wilderness, I find myself abandoned by the whole world, full of despair. Recalling the hundred battles fought on the front and my own type of heroism, I cannot but feel that the so-called achievement is just an illusion or a dream. And you, my lady, your talent, beauty and virtue are not things I can ever forget. The only question is: what does my lady think of this retired soldier who has been abandoned by the whole world?

* According to members of their household, Chiang did not divorce his village wife until he was preparing to marry May-ling, when he gave the divorce papers to her family.

Shortly thereafter Chiang returned to Shanghai. On September 23, he had a long talk with May-ling, confiding to his diary, "We love each other and had a wonderful day. I think this is the happiest hour of my life." The next day May-ling accepted his proposal of marriage, and two days later they became officially engaged. On September 28, he sailed for Japan. He wired her twice that night from the ship: "I'm not sure whether I can fall asleep tonight or not. How about you?" He also called her from Nagasaki; "It does not matter whether it is morning or night, you are the only thing on my mind. I cannot work or sleep. All I do is think about you."

Before leaving China, Chiang gave an interview to George Sokolsky, saying he had come to Shanghai "to arrange, if possible, for my marriage with Miss Soong May-ling." When asked about the lady who had left for America, he dodged the question and lied:

> Foreigners perhaps do not understand all the intricacies of the Chinese family system. That lady has been divorced in accordance with Chinese customs. I am at present married to no one and am free to marry in accordance with the most monogamous practices. Miss Soong would not consent to a marriage in any other circumstances and I should not dare ask a lady of her character to marry me in any other circumstances. Please make it clear that this marriage is in no way a political marriage. It is accidental that we are all so prominent in politics. . . . I have been courting Miss Soong these many years without a thought of the political bearing of such a marriage.

Ten days after her arrival in New York, Jennie went to the Chinese Consulate to collect her mail and was turned away by a very cold and what must have been a very frightened vice consul acting on "instructions from Nanking." Realizing that she had become "an outcast," the young woman tried to commit suicide by jumping into the Hudson River but was stopped by an old gentleman who walked her back to her apartment and extracted a promise from her not to try again.*

---

* In 1931 Jennie sent Chiang a letter, asking for permission to return to China and for $10,000 in travel expenses. "I got mad and lost my temper and tore it into pieces," he wrote. "I thought this showed my sincerity and loyalty. The letter might have been sent deliberately to destroy our marriage. I better ignore it and not allow myself to get trapped by such a dirty trick." May-ling, who caught Chiang reading the letter, was so angry that she left Nanking, where they were then living, for Shanghai. (See Wang Xiaohua, et al, *The Six-Dimensional Puzzle of Chiang Kai-shek*, Taipei: Xianzhi Chubanshe, 1995, p. 77.) In 1933 Jennie did return to China, where she apparently lived on money Chiang gave her along with what she earned as a language teacher. In need of money more than thirty

▼

AFTER ARRIVING IN Japan, Chiang had some difficulty getting to see the mother of his proposed bride. The Soongs had rented a house in Kobe, but when May-ling's mother heard that Chiang was on his way to see her, she got sick and left with Ai-ling for the other side of the island. Once there, it was apparently Ai-ling who convinced Madame Soong that she should hear him out.

Chiang knew that Madame Soong disapproved of him as a mate for her youngest daughter. In the first place, he was already married. In the second, he was a soldier. In China, soldiers ranked very low on the social scale—certainly below the Soongs, who had long risen above mere mercantile status, and far, far below that of May-ling's mother, who was descended from Chinese aristocracy. Moreover, Chiang was not a Christian. No one followed her religion with more devotion than the mother of the Soong family, and this was his greatest drawback in the eyes of Madame Soong.

There was nothing May-ling's mother could do about Chiang's profession. He was a soldier—and the most successful one in the country. As to his previous entanglements, Chiang brought a document proving that he had divorced his village wife, and he had already lumped Jennie with the concubine he had paid off some years earlier, refusing to admit that they had ever been married. That left the biggest drawback, the problem of religion. Ma-

---

years later, she wrote the story of her marriage to Chiang in English with the help of James Zee-min Lee, a former English tutor to the Chiangs. After arranging for the book to be published by Doubleday, her literary agent, Lawrence Hill, was informed that he would be sued by two major New York law firms if he allowed publication to proceed. To further assure his cooperation, he was beaten up twice. Doubleday subsequently withdrew its offer. Lee and his brother, who lived in New York, then offered the book to Chiang's son's lawyer to be destroyed. Jennie gave the lawyer two (out of three probable) copies of the manuscript, for which she was paid $170,000. Twenty years later, Professor Lloyd Eastman, a China scholar at the University of Illinois, found what was probably a third copy, kept by her agent, in the archives at the Hoover Institute at Stanford, and the book was finally published in 1992. For these cloak-and-dagger details, see Ch'en Chieh-ju, *Chiang Kai-shek's Secret Past*, edited with an introduction by Eastman, pp. xi–xxviii. Meanwhile, according to the FBI, Jennie had apparently tried to blackmail Chiang for $1,000,000 to keep her from publishing her story; in response, he gave her an allowance of $500 every three months. The FBI also reported that the U.S. State Department "attempted to suppress publication of the book because the CHIANG government is friendly to the United States and such a book could have a deleterious effect on the relations between the two countries." (FBI files, #62-71649-64 to 77. Materials furnished to the author by the Department of Justice in response to a Freedom of Information Act inquiry.) Jennie died in 1971.

dame Soong asked him if he would become a Christian. He didn't say yes and he didn't say no. He said that he would read the Christian Bible and decide. She was impressed with his straightforwardness, decided that she liked him, and said she would accept him as a son-in-law.

Chiang saw her on October 3. "I reached Kobe at 8:00 A.M." he wrote in his diary. ". . . I took a car with T.V. to visit Madame Soong. She has recovered from illness, and she has generally agreed to our marriage. But she does not wish third brother [May-ling] to come here, because she is worried that third brother and I will stay in Japan and marry right away. I was feeling rather disappointed, and therefore wired third brother to ask her to fly to Japan as soon as possible." May-ling refused, and Chiang returned to China.

The would-be groom announced his and May-ling's engagement to the gaggle of journalists gathered on the dock to meet him when he returned to Shanghai. In his diary he noted, "At 1:30 P.M. the steamer reached Shanghai, and most of my close friends came to greet me. I heard that third sister* was ill, so I went to see her right away. She looked emaciated and weak, and I believe it was because of too much stress and worry. . . . After dinner third sister and I had a long and good chat. I had mixed feelings of grief and joy."

♈

IN SPITE OF a telegram from Ching-ling urging her not to marry "that bluebeard," May-ling and Chiang were married on December 1, 1927. There were two ceremonies: a private Christian service conducted at the bride's home on Seymour Road by the general secretary of the YMCA† and a public ceremony at the Majestic Hotel, attended by 1,300 family, friends, members of the diplomatic corps, the commander in chief of the American Pacific Fleet, Big-Eared Du, and everyone else who could get an invitation. It was the social event of the season, as indicated by the crowds of people outside the hotel on Bubbling Well Road, trying to get a look at the principals and their guests. Unlike the Christian rite, this was a traditional Chinese wedding—a civil ceremony made up primarily of formal bows between the bride and groom. The only non-Chinese elements were May-ling's white satin gown and lace veil (Chinese brides wore pink or red) and the playing of "Here

---

* I.e., May-ling.

† A clause in the Discipline of the Methodist Church prohibited ministers from conducting marriages of divorced persons, if in fact anyone believed that Chiang Kai-shek was legally divorced.

Comes the Bride." T.V., recently married himself, gave his sister away. May-ling and Chiang bowed three times to a life-size portrait of Sun Yat-sen, which had been placed over a platform in the middle of the ballroom and draped with the flags of the Chinese Republic and the Kuomintang. The marriage certificate was read to the assembly and sealed. May-ling and Chiang then bowed to each other, to the official witnesses, and to their guests.

According to *The Shanghai Star,* "Throughout Chinese history, the marriages of the prominent, famous or notorious were often marriages of convenience—by marrying they formed alliances that would benefit each other. So it was with Chiang Kai-shek and Soong Mei-ling." *The Shanghai Times* was less blunt and more descriptive: "It was a brilliant affair and the outstanding Chinese marriage ceremony of recent years. It unites on the one hand the former all-powerful leader of the Nanking armies, and on the other the family of Dr. T. V. Soong, brother of the bride, in addition to the family of the late Dr. Sun, founder of the Kuomintang. . . . Contrary to the Christian custom, the bride was not embraced or kissed by the bridegroom, minister or others. The ceremony itself was brief and simple." The wedding even hit the front page of *The New York Times,* which noted that Chiang and Kung had both worn cutaway coats, giving the celebration a "foreign atmosphere, as far as outward appearances were concerned."

The journalist covering the occasion for the *North-China Herald* chose to describe the bride and her attendants:

> The bride looked very charming in a beautiful gown of silver and white georgette, draped slightly at one side and caught with a spray of orange blossom. She wore also a little wreath of orange buds over her veil of beautiful rare lace made long and flowing to form a second train to that of white charmeuse embroidered in silver which fell from her shoulders. She wore silver shoes and stockings and carried a bouquet of palest pink carnations and fern fronds tied with white and silver ribbons. She was followed by four bridesmaids . . . wearing peach charmeuse. . . . After the bridesmaids followed little flower girls . . . dressed in ribbed peach taffeta and carrying little baskets laden with flower petals, and the train was ended by two small pages . . . in black velvet suits with white satin vests.

As for the groom, he made the following entry in his diary on the day of his wedding: "In the morning I wrote a love composition for my beloved wife. At 1:00 P.M. I went to H. H. Kung's house to dress up. At 3:00 P.M. I went to Soong's house for a religious service, and at 4:00 P.M. to the Dahua

Assembly Hall for the official wedding ceremony. When I saw my beloved wife slowly walking in just like a floating cloud in the glow of evening, I experienced such an unprecedented feeling of love that I hardly knew where I was. After the wedding ceremony we went for a ride. In the evening we held a banquet at the Soong home. At 9:00 P.M. we went back to our bridal chamber in our new house." The following three sentences were deleted. "Today I stayed at home," he wrote the next day, "holding my beloved wife and chatting together. At that moment I realized that nothing can compare with the happiness of being newly married."

Their honeymoon lasted only a week or so before the government called Chiang back to resume his position as head of the National Revolutionary Army. Shuttling between the capital in Nanking and Shanghai, the Chiangs lived in a rental house until T.V. purchased a home for them in the French Concession in Shanghai as May-ling's dowry. Chiang dubbed it Ai Lu, the Avenue of Love, which May-ling inscribed on a huge rock. A large home on the Route Garnier, built in the French style with outside walls pebbled in black, white, and yellow, it reminded Chiang of Sun Yat-sen's home, which, as Sun's successor, he considered entirely appropriate—so much so that, according to one of May-ling's biographers,* he sent a statement about his marriage to a Shanghai newspaper, portraying their union as a milestone in the road toward reform and May-ling as the more determined partner. "When I first saw Miss Soong," Chiang wrote, "I felt she was my ideal wife, and she vowed that if she could not win Chiang Kai-shek as her husband, she would rather die a spinster. . . . Our wedding is more than a celebration of our happiness in marriage; it is a symbol of the reconstruction of Chinese society."

---

* Laura Tyson Li.

17

Subordination and deference to male leadership was the lot of most women in late-nineteenth and early-twentieth century China, regardless of their station in society.

—THOMAS L. KENNEDY

THERE ARE several stories told about the early days of the Chiang marriage. They may well be apocryphal, but all are grounded in reality. The first concerns a marital fight that occurred a few weeks after the wedding. According to Chiang's diary, the newlyweds had spent Christmas Eve, which Chiang called "the most cheerful day of the past ten years of my life," at her mother's home. Five days later, however, came this entry: "I have been extremely unhappy and lonely since third sister left, because she was puffed up, and also because I was not sufficiently aware of my rudeness, which was generated by her stubbornness and hot temper.... That very night...I could not wait to go see her. She felt that her illness had been caused by a lack of personal freedom. She advised me to improve my temper, which I promised her I would."

May-ling's stated determination to remain an individual, not just an adjunct to her husband, seems a likely cause for a flare-up between an ultra-traditional Confucian and an atypical Chinese bride. A month later, she wrote Emma that she did "not think that marriage should erase or absorb one's individuality. For this reason I want to be myself, and not as the General's wife. I have been May-ling Soong all these years, and I believe I stand for something, and I intend to continue to develop my individuality, and to keep my identity. Naturally my husband does not agree with me. He wants me to be identified as his wife; but I say nothing, and I am going to stand for something myself.... I... want to be recognized as a factor because I am I and not because I happen to be his wife."

The second story revolves around an entry in Chiang's diary saying that May-ling suffered a miscarriage on August, 25, 1928, eight months after their marriage. Chiang was very worried about her, writing that "her pain and suffering was in the extreme, so much so that it could not be described." But with no corroboration of the pregnancy from a doctor* or anyone in the

---

* According to DeLong, the doctors told May-ling that she was not pregnant. (Thomas A. DeLong, *Madame Chiang Kai-shek and Miss Emma Mills*, p. 80.)

family, with Chiang's history of venereal disease, and with May-ling's penchant for illnesses—real and imagined, gynecological and otherwise—it is hard to believe the incident was anything other than wishful thinking. Moreover, Chiang's second wife, Jennie, claimed that Chiang's doctor had told him after their marriage that he was sterile—something he would never have admitted to May-ling, who might not have married him had she known.

As it happened, the so-called miscarriage was blamed on May-ling's fright over an attempt to assassinate Chiang—a story that ties into May-ling's belief in spiritual experiences, occasions when she "believed that she received guidance from Almighty God . . . sometimes while she was awake and sometimes in dreams." As she told the story to a friend,* she had left her husband in Nanking and flown down to Shanghai, where her mother was in a sanitorium. She took a room next door, and a few days later, when Chiang came to Shanghai, he took the room next to hers. The night Chiang arrived, May-ling dreamed that she was walking in the hallway outside her door but could still see herself inside all dressed in white. A man with an evil face stood outside her room and was about to open the door to attack her when (now inside the room) she locked the door. Nevertheless, she could still see him. He raised his hands, in each of which he held a revolver. She screamed, and her screams roused Chiang, who came into her room and woke her.

The next morning Madame Soong told her daughter and son-in-law to go home. That night May-ling had a second dream. She was standing with her mother in the garden at the rear of their home, holding a bag of flour and sprinkling a circle of white dust on the grass. In the middle of the circle, the form of a woman dressed in white arose; although the form resembled the goddess of mercy, her face was evil. "I know everything and will tell you anything," she said. Catching her mother's glance of warning, May-ling demanded to know if the apparition was God or the Devil, at which point the figure melted away screaming and May-ling screamed along with her. When she awoke, she heard Chiang groaning in his sleep. He woke up, they chatted for a moment, and, stepping out of their room, he clapped his hands to call for his guard. Two men instead of one appeared. He thought it strange but said nothing.

The following night May-ling dreamed that there were two men creeping toward the bedroom door, intent on murder. She screamed and woke up but found Chiang's bed empty. She ran into the corridor, where she found her husband with a group of police officers. They had rung the bell at 4:00 A.M. and had arrived just in time to prevent the assassination of both husband and wife. Two men, now in handcuffs—two of Chiang's trusted

---

* Fulton Oursler, an American writer known primarily for his books on Christian themes.

guards—had come to the house to murder them. They had been trying to kill the couple for three nights. The first night they had been about to reach Chiang's door in the hospital when May-ling's screams had woken him. The second night they had come to the bedroom door, had been frightened off by the generalissimo's groan, but had answered his call for his guard. On the third night one of the guards had worn a hat and raincoat over his uniform and arrived in a taxi to join the other conspirator, but the taxi driver had been suspicious and called his garage, which had notified the police. May-ling believed that the Almighty, through her strange dreams, had saved the lives of her husband and herself.

The third story about the newlyweds was not life-changing, although it might have been. A month or so after their wedding, the Chiangs arrived in Shanghai. May-ling had evidently persuaded Chiang that since he was the most important man in China, he need not, unlike other government officials, pay the usual protection money to Big-Eared Du. Two hours after their arrival, Chiang went out on business. A limousine arrived to take May-ling "to her sister." Chiang's wife left the house with her maid but never arrived at Ai-ling's home.

When Chiang came back several hours later and found her gone, he was very frightened. Knowing, however, that "propriety would not permit of personal inquiry" he called his brother-in-law T.V. T.V. telephoned Big-Eared Du, who informed him that Madame Chiang was "safe and in perfect health; that she had been found motoring alone with only a maid accompanying her through the streets of Shanghai, a very imprudent thing to do; that she had been escorted to a comfortable villa, and surrounded with the respect due a lady in her elevated position, but that, notwithstanding all this, she showed signs of displeasure and refused to take any nourishment, solid or liquid." Du, as the story goes, "deplored the fact that the Generalissimo had found no time to arrange for suitable protection for himself and Madame— a very dangerous omission in a big city like Shanghai." He suggested that T.V. come to his house, where he could "arrange jointly with him the customary formalities required to assure the safety of his charming sister, and would he then escort her back to her husband, who was probably full of anxiety?"

T.V. hurried over to pay Du his protection money. Only then was he allowed to take May-ling back to Chiang.

❧

CHIANG'S "RETIREMENT" FROM office, which had culminated in his marriage to May-ling, did not, as we have seen, last very long. It was only a little over three months, from mid-August to December, before the members of the

Kuomintang realized that whatever his faults and misdeeds, he was the only man strong enough to hold the party together. On December 3, 1927, just two days after his wedding, the Central Executive Committee of the KMT nominated Chiang in absentia as supreme head of China's military forces.

In the first week of 1928, Chiang took a train to Nanking, where he was to resume his former position as commander in chief of the National Revolutionary Army. During the trip north, there were two separate attempts to derail the train, both of which were discovered barely in time to save his life. Promising to resign at the end of the military campaign, he assumed the position of a temporary military commander who would serve until the meeting of the next KMT Congress, due to take place the following August. It was hoped and assumed that by this time, the Northern Expedition would be successfully completed and his military services would no longer be needed.

On January 14, Chiang announced that he had agreed to resume leadership of the KMT "in face of persistent demands from the various Party organs and all ranks of the Army and repeated requests from the government and the people for me to emerge from my retirement in order to help shoulder the heavy responsibility . . . etc., etc." Apologizing for having "not yet fulfilled my duty" and promising to "make amends for my evasion of duty last year" by tendering his resignation as soon as the Northern Expedition was completed, Chiang noted that since he had left the government, the authority of the KMT had "broken down and the political atmosphere is charged with uncertainty." It was a typical Chiang statement—an apology where none was appropriate and an attempt to appear indispensable, which, at the moment, he seemed to be.

May-ling, who was ill, remained in Shanghai. But when Chiang let her know how much he missed her, she came to Nanking, arriving the day after he reassumed control of the party. "She is not yet recovered, and I felt bad when I saw how weak she was. I shouldn't have 'obliged' her to come," he wrote in his diary. This, however, did not prevent him from calling her again in the middle of February to register his loneliness. May-ling said that she was still sick and could not travel. Having confided to his diary how "extremely unhappy" he was, Chiang wrote that he remained "in a bad mood" until he got word that she would, in fact, join him again in Nanking. She arrived on February 21. "I had a rest today," he wrote. "I spent the whole day with May-ling, and I was so happy. I have not been so happy for a long time."

Shortly after his reinstatement, Chiang met with General Feng to draw up plans for the resumption of the Northern Expedition. Chiang was to lead the First Army; Feng was slotted to lead the Second; the Third Army was to go to General Yen Hsi-shan, the governor of the province of Shansi; and a

Fourth Army, kept in reserve, was to be put under General Li Tsung-jen, an old comrade of Chiang's who later became acting president of the Republic. The Nationalist Army would be fighting an army led by the son of the Old Marshal, Young Marshal Chang Hsueh-liang, along with six other generals. The offensive was to start in three months time, at the beginning of April. Having made these plans, Chiang returned to Shanghai.

No one understood the lure of Shanghai better than Chiang Kai-shek. Even the rather prudish American general Joseph W. Stillwell, who would one day play a large role in the life of the Chiangs, agreed with him about the dangers of the city. "This town would ruin anybody in no time," Stillwell had commented when he first visited in 1922. "The babes that twitch around the hotels need attention so badly that it is hard not to give it to them." Reviewing the troops, Chiang issued a stern warning to the officers to keep their soldiers out of trouble—as regarded both "babes" and politics. A few days later, when he discovered that about fifty of them had taken part in antiforeign riots started by the Communists the year before, he had them all executed on the spot. These extreme measures were aimed not only at increasing military discipline but at the Western powers, whom Chiang could not afford to antagonize at the beginning of his drive north, since he planned to ask them to stop supporting the warlords with money and armaments. "During past years China's civil warfare has continued without cessation because the militarists have received much support from the imperialists," he claimed, echoing Sun's complaints. "Arms and ammunition have been imported into this country in a steady stream. Huge sums of money have been secretly lent to our enemies. . . . The militarists . . . oppose the power of the Revolution and thus prolong civil war in this most unhappy country."

Chiang needed additional funds to support the National Revolutionary Army during the Northern Expedition. Putting pressure on the bankers and businessmen of Shanghai, he and T.V., who was once again serving as finance minister, raised some $15 million.* "We are throwing money and men into the fight with almost heart-breaking extravagance," said T.V., "because we want to make this a fight to the finish." But, according to *The North-China Herald,* "One may well suspect that Mr. Soong is sick of the part he has had to play for the past few months as a machine to extract money from the business community without any control over the spending of it. And certainly the business world is equally weary of it." In retrospect, however, Parks Coble, an expert on the subject, would probably disagree, contending that "Soong replaced coercion with persuasion and in the process effected a genuine alliance between the bankers and the regime."

---

* $15,000,000 Chinese = $10,650,000 U.S. in 1928 ($133,857,000 today).

WHILE HER HUSBAND was juggling his various duties, May-ling was getting used to a very different life from the one she had known. Although her surroundings had always been, as she herself put it, "easy and comfortable," she did the unexpected by moving to Nanking, headquarters of the National Revolutionary Army and the KMT. The only one of the official wives to follow their husbands—the rest stayed in Shanghai—May-ling was the token woman at dinners and receptions given by civil and military leaders. "I think the officials themselves were . . . very conscious of me . . . but later on I forgot about myself . . . and they also began to regard me not as a woman but as one of themselves." She also traveled with her husband. "Up to the time I was married I never really lived in the interior under circumstances and in [an] environment so pure[ly] Chinese as I did after my marriage when I accompanied the Generalissimo on all his campaigns and lived in any thatched hut, railroad station or whatever quarters we could find."

"Nanking," she said, "was then nothing but a little village with one so-called broad street. . . . Even then the street was so narrow that if two motor cars were coming in opposite directions one of them had to back off on a side street until the other passed. The houses were all very primitive, cold and uncomfortable." May-ling's assessment of the city is seconded by James M. McHugh, the assistant naval attaché at the U.S. Embassy, a man who later became head of Far East secret intelligence. "There was no city water or sewage system," McHugh said. "The fastidious Minister of Portugal . . . complained that the only way he could get a bath in Nanking was to use bottled mineral water."

From Shanghai's steam-heated splendor to chilly government housing, May-ling seems to have reveled in the discomfort of her current life. Taking on the role of the leader's wife, she developed an adjunct of what had been known at the Whampoa Military Academy as the Officers' Moral Endeavor Association, originally a club at which young officers were given a political education. May-ling established a meeting place in Nanking as a sort of Chinese canteen—a place where officers who had nothing to do after work could go to relax, listen to music, learn to draw, and, at the same time, help the party by making posters for propaganda. They were, however, not allowed to drink or smoke there. To run it, May-ling brought in J. L. Huang, a worker from the YMCA.

"It was just a little low shack at first, in the middle of a lot of other shacks," Huang said. "Near by was the Y.M.C.A. building, a fine new house. I admit it was a temptation to stay with the 'Y' . . . but . . . I agreed to take it on . . . A lot of the cadets were prejudiced against us, feeling that the O.M.E.A. was a new method of foreign propaganda and a hidden way of forcing them to become Christian even if they didn't want to. They used to throw things at me when I was out walking in the streets. . . . But little by little they began to like coming up and using the place. Now all the officers belong."

The soldiers were not wrong; the OMEA was definitely a new form of propaganda—not foreign but homegrown, an attempt to carry the revolution into the hearts and minds of the officers. In seeking out a wife with money and power behind her, Chiang had found a woman with ideas and energy as well.

✦

ON MARCH 31, having completed his arrangements for the Northern Expedition, Chiang wrote his new wife, "I see you in my dreams, and I feel so bad when I find you are not in my bed when I wake up. Oh, soldiers cannot enjoy the happiness of family. How pitiful they are!" The final phase of the Northern Expedition started on April 7, 1928. A week later, he wired, "I miss you so much. Our current battle is expected to be a success, but there will probably be a very large number of wounded soldiers. Another thousand came in today. There are not enough sheets or gowns in the hospital. It is a terribly shocking scene. Please send medicine as soon as possible, and please try to hire as many good doctors as you can."

By the end of April, Chiang and his soldiers had reached Tsinan, the capital of Shantung province, where they ran into trouble. Ever since the peace treaty of Versailles, which China had refused to sign, the Japanese had continued to pursue their commercial interests in Shantung. They had even invoked the treaty as an excuse to send a large number of Japanese troops into the capital. Since the city had already been evacuated, there was no need for Chiang or his soldiers to enter, and he gave his officers orders to stay out—instructions that were either misunderstood or ignored. Because of this, Chiang found his men facing the Japanese in a clash he had tried to avoid. What followed can only be called an atrocity.

The first thing the Japanese did was to surround the office of the Chinese diplomatic official who represented the Ministry of Foreign Affairs in Nanking; they cut off his nose and his ears, as well as those of the sixteen members of his staff, and then murdered the official, his wife, and all the others. When Chiang sent his foreign minister to negotiate with them, they arrested him on the spot and forced him to sign a statement in which the *Chinese* took the blame for starting what came to be known as the "Tsinan Incident." For several days, the Japanese continued to refuse to parley with Chiang, while at the same time bombarding the city. Hallett Abend, an American reporter, followed the Japanese soldiers into Tsinan.

"The streets . . . were entirely deserted," he wrote. "No Chinese were to be seen—that is, no live Chinese. . . . On the sidewalks, in the doorways, and often in the middle of the thoroughfares, lay Chinese dead, in uniforms and civilian clothes, of all ages and both sexes. Most of the corpses were already bloated and discolored. And there were many dead horses, their legs sticking up stiffly at grotesque and pathetic angles. . . . Nearly all the shops had been broken open, and showed the disorder left by hasty looters." Abend wandered around the city until after dinner. "At the hotel there was no water, and no light—not even a candle . . . so I went to bed, but not to sleep. Never before had I seen death from violence in the mass. As a newspaper reporter . . . I had often arrived with the police. . . . Morgues had become commonplace to me. But Tsinan, on that hot May afternoon, had shown me wholesale massacre in new and shocking forms. . . . I had been surprised at myself, and rather proud, because during the afternoon I had not felt squeamish about the revolting sights I had seen. But lying there . . . I suddenly was seized by a violent attack of retching."

The Japan Times claimed that China's reponse to Japanese "efforts at conciliation and moderation" was "to loot Japanese homes and barbarously to murder defenceless Japanese." Chiang responded, saying that the "malice and oppression" of the Japanese troops was "beyond description," and wired the Government Council, "In a true Revolutionary spirit I cannot bow to such bullying. I propose to expose such Japanese deliberate brutality to the world so as to hasten our own awakening and enlist more support to others and then proceed with the Expedition." But Chiang, worried about endangering the entire Northern Expedition, ordered his men to evacuate Tsinan and shifted the thrust of his march west to Honan.

Early in May, an obviously concerned May-ling wired Chiang, "I just heard that a Red Cross doctor who practices Western medicine was imprisoned in Hsuchou and thrown into boiling oil. This kind of story will certainly take a huge toll on our ability to help the wounded. Please investigate and deal with this immediately. Moreover, please try your best to protect Red Cross doctors from now on. . . . I will try to get together some famous doctors to save our soldiers. . . . I plan to go with you next time to manage hospital affairs." To which Chiang replied that the imprisonment and death of the doctor were "absolutely a rumor." He then asked his wife to speak to T.V., who, he had heard, was planning to resign his role in funding the Northern Expedition.* "Please persuade him to change his mind, so that I

---

* The same situation occurred two years later. When T.V. refused to commit himself to finding the money, May-ling told him that she would sell her house, the one he had given the Chiangs as her dowry. "If we cannot get money for the army, we will be beaten," she said. "Kai-shek will sacrifice himself on the front lines, and I will die with him." (Chen Jin-jin, "Stories of Love," *A Study of Modern Chinese Women*, Vol. 2., pages 275–88.)

have nothing else to worry about besides military matters." He also wanted her to join him but worried that "she may get sick because of the bad conditions and her weakness." Nevertheless, he asked her to come, which she did in the middle of May. She arrived at the Hsuchou railway station, and he picked her up. "We haven't been together for forty-six days," he wrote in his diary that night. "How happy I am with today's reunion!"

Although the Tsinan Incident had delayed Chiang's northward advance by a week, he had, by the end of May, overcome two of the three warlords who had stood between him and Peking. "Please send disinfection liquid enough for 50,000 people," Chiang wired May-ling after she returned to Nanking. And on the same day came a second requisition: "Please buy 10,000 cans of meat, bamboo shoots and sugar, and send them as soon as possible to the front lines along with 10,000 towels and liquid medicine. Please be quick," he added as he set out to conquer the only warlord left in his path, the Manchurian Old Marshal Chang Tso-lin.

For hundreds of years, Manchuria—the land beyond the Great Wall—had been considered part of China, and ever since the collapse of the Manchus, Old Marshal Chang Tso-lin, who was supported by Japan, had controlled it. Called by Snow the "uncrowned Emperor of Manchuria," Chang had begun his life as a bandit—"ruthless, uncompromising, and faithless"—gradually extending his conquests to over 350,000 square miles, an area larger than France and Germany combined. Manchuria is fertile land, rich in waterpower, coal deposits, and iron ore. On June 3, the Old Marshal, who was occupying the capital of Peking at the time, sent out a circular telegram announcing that he and his army were withdrawing from Peking to the Manchurian capital of Mukden. This may have been due to latent patriotism—he always said that he was happy to be financed by the Japanese but refused to deal with them—or the fact that the National Revolutionary Army had already triumphed over two other warlords and he foresaw defeat for himself. Whatever his reasoning, in publicly announcing his plans Chang signed his own death warrant.

The Japanese, particularly a group of lesser officers, had wanted for some time to dispose of Old Marshal Chang. (It was said that from 1915 to 1928, some three thousand men had been employed to assassinate him.) His removal, the Japanese thought, would expedite their control of Manchuria, and in any case, they assumed he would prefer working with Chiang Kai-shek than with them. Acting without permission from their superiors, the officers planted a mine on the tracks of Chang's twenty-car private train that was taking him and his possessions home. It went off at 5:30 A.M. while the train was running at full speed. Although it could never be traced to the Japanese officers, the assassination occurred within an area controlled by the Japanese and was set off by a detonator whose wires led past the Japanese guards. Moreover, the Japanese must have had a spy on the train itself, since the Old Marshal was not in his private blue car but the one next to it when the bomb, timed to blow up that particular car, exploded.* He died four hours later in a Japanese hospital.

Old Marshal Chang died a very rich man. The Manchurian branch of an American bank had devoted itself exclusively to managing his private investments, even though he was known to keep a great deal of his fortune in gold, and he seems to have left a legacy of around 50 million Chinese dollars,† mostly to his son. Young Marshal Chang hid the fact of his father's death—everyone knew about the explosion but not its outcome—for a full week while he gathered his forces and weighed his options. The Japanese offered him a deal similar to the one they had given his father, informing him that his father was in their debt. "I know nothing of my father's debts," the Young Marshal answered. "I only know my responsibility to preserve our territorial integrity. . . . If the debts are real, you must ask the National Government to pay them. I am a Chinese. I love China, as the Japanese love Japan. I believe that Chinese should not fight Chinese." Many years later, when he was an old man, the Young Marshal elaborated on this theme: "I would have been the Emperor of Northeast China if I had cooperated with the Japanese," he said, explaining that his father had died because he had refused to be Japan's figurehead. ". . . You had to be the puppet of the Japanese if you wanted to be the Emperor of Northeast China."

Raised and educated like a prince of a royal family, thirty-year-old Young Marshal Chang Hsueh-liang was an unusual combination of political savvy and physical infirmity. His frame was slight, his cheeks hollow, and, in spite of his twinkling eyes and what Snow called "an air of determination about the set of his shoulders," his body shook convulsively whenever he needed an opium fix. He had become addicted in the summer of 1926 while leading his father's soldiers in the fight against Feng. At the time he had fallen ill with the flu but refused to leave his men while they were fighting. His father had always smoked opium and when the son was advised that opium was his only alternative to entering a hospital, he put opium in a jade pipe and became addicted.

Chang had met May-ling at a party in 1925. A year younger than she, he

---

* The fact that the Japanese party in power failed to force the army to punish the assassins brought about the political intervention of the emperor and the fall of the government in question—one of the few times this ever happened in Japan.

† $50,000,000 Chinese = $35,500,000 U.S. in 1928 ($446,191,000 today).

was crazy about her and said that he would have done everything possible to marry her if he had not already been attached. Two years after she married Chiang Kai-shek, he joined the couple for dinner at the Peking Hotel. "How do you know each other?" Chiang Kai-shek asked when he saw them in close conversation. "We became good friends several years ago," the Young Marshal answered, clearly pleased to have known May-ling before her husband. He said that Chiang didn't kill him on the spot because May-ling guaranteed that he was a gentleman. The Young Marshal said that May-ling was responsible for his conversion to Christianity and that she later convinced him to divorce his first wife and marry another woman. He also claimed that it was their friendship that saved his life later, when he came into conflict with Chiang Kai-shek.

Meanwhile, following on the heels of his Third Army, Chiang Kai-shek made a triumphal entry into Peking in early July, well within the timetable set earlier that year. All the warlords had been overcome, and almost all of China, except for certain remote areas, had been brought under the umbrella of the KMT. Peking, which means "Northern Capital," was renamed Peiping, which means "Northern Peace," since Chiang planned to establish his capital in Nanking. The walls of Peiping, previously a "glorious red," were painted blue.

From his capital at Mukden, the Young Marshal sent emissaries to negotiate with Chiang, but they were unable to come to a satisfactory settlement. Chiang then sent a team of his own to Manchuria; it included a journalist known for his skill in the Young Marshal's favorite pastimes of dancing, drinking, and golf. After weeks spent at these occupations, the journalist reported back to Chiang that Young Marshal Chang had agreed to support the National Revolutionary Army in exchange for being allowed to keep his own troops in Manchuria. During their negotiations, Chiang had offered Chang the title of deputy commander in chief of the National Revolutionary Army, which the Young Marshal accepted, raising the Nationalist flag over his headquarters in Mukden. As one member of the diplomatic community put it, "Thirty-year-old Chang Hsueh-liang, the Young Marshal, heir to a lusty army and a fabulous fortune, became uncrowned king of Manchuria."

In spite of Chiang's concerns that May-ling could not "stand the muggy weather" in Peiping, the first thing he did after his formal entry into the capital was return to Nanking to get her, and she joined him in a pilgrimage to the grave of Sun Yat-sen, holding her parasol over him as they walked away. Two days later, flanked by his three commanding generals, Chiang stood with uncovered and bowed head before the coffin. General Feng described Chiang's behavior: "When he prayed before the altar of Tsangli, he wept so bitterly that he could not even hold up his head . . . at last, like

Northern Expedition, 1926–1928

someone who goes up to a filial son and begs him to stop weeping after a parent's death, I went up to him and begged him to cease. But it was a long time before he stopped weeping." Chiang then read out a speech, aimed at those who remained rather than the leader who had died. In it, he spoke of adhering to Sun's Three Principles and putting an end to "widespread heresies"—a reference to both the Communists and those he considered troublemakers within his own party. He spoke of reconstructing the city of Nanking as the national capital and announced that the army must now be reduced in size.

While the Chiangs were still in Peiping, the wives of the staff of the Medical College who had graduated from Wellesley invited members of the foreign community to a reception honoring the new Madame Chiang Kai-shek. Both May-ling and Chiang stood in the receiving line. "She was charm itself," said McHugh, ". . . beautiful, vivacious, gracious and speaking flaw-less English. She wore a gaily printed Chinese cheongsam with the skirt slit to the knee, displaying a very shapely leg. And she was wearing lipstick, too—new in those days. She was lovely looking, and she knew it!" The American naval attaché was not as impressed with Chiang, who stood next to his wife grunting "How how"* as the guests were introduced. The best thing about the general, said McHugh, who had never met either of them before, was that "he looked you squarely in the eye and his gaze was compel-ling. His eyes, dark and small, were exceptionally bright and piercing, but he smiled pleasantly when he greeted you. You felt he was genuinely friendly. It was plainly evident that he was in love with his wife. He glanced at her from time to time with obvious pride and affection, and occasionally furtively held her hand."

This happy picture was disturbed, however, by what McHugh called an "ugly rumor" spread around Peiping before the departure of the Chiangs. It seems that someone had recently rifled the tomb of the dowager empress, stealing pieces of jade and other objets d'art. The gossips said that they had been taken by T. V. Soong as a gift for his mother, Madame Soong, in Shang-hai. "The public justification for the charade," according to McHugh, "was that Soong's mother, through the marriage of her daughter to China's new head of government, had thereby attained equal status with the old empress, and, since objets d'art were state property, Mrs. Soong was entitled to pos-sess them." It was a nasty story, carefully calculated to cast dark shadows on the newly powerful Chiangs and May-ling's family, the Soongs.

---

* Short for "Hao pu hao?" or "How are you?"

18

Wherever she [Madame Chiang] went, whatever she saw strengthened her desire to clean it up. . . . The more she saw of her country the more energetic she became.

—EMILY HAHN

WHILE CHIANG was celebrating his victory, the so-called "widespread heresies" to which he had referred in his memorial speech were being enacted some two thousand miles to the south. Back in September 1927, while he was busy pursuing his marriage to May-ling, members of the Chinese Communist Party under Mao Tse-tung had begun a series of rebellions in the province of Hunan, known as the Autumn Harvest Uprising. "In September we had succeeded in organizing widespread uprisings," Mao said, ". . . recruits drawn from the peasantry, the miners, and insurrectionist troops which revolted against the Wuhan government when it surrendered to Chiang Kai-shek." What Mao did not say was that he and his peasant army had been roundly defeated by the Nationalists and he himself had lost face.

One of the places chosen for rebellion was the city of Changsha, but Mao, realizing that such an attack was doomed to failure, had canceled the order. For this, he was stripped of his positions in the Chinese Communist Party. But due to the poor communication system in China, Mao did not get word of his demotions until the following spring. Meanwhile, he had marched his men to the Ridge of Wells, a mountain range between the provinces of Hunan and Kiangsi, where he was joined by the future commander of the Communist armies, Chu Teh, with several thousand soldiers. The amalgamated army was called "The Fourth Red Army of the Chinese Workers' and Peasants' Army"—a name carefully chosen to convince the Nationalists that the Communists were stronger than they really were. It was here with these men, according to Crozier, that Mao "created the political instrument for his future conquest of all China." He did this by integrating the soldiers and peasants, who were then encouraged to round up and kill local landlords.

A second Communist uprising erupted in Canton on December 11, just ten days after the Chiangs' marriage. The radicals disarmed the police and issued orders, per instructions from Stalin, for the confiscation of land, redistribution of wealth, cancellation of debts, and nationalization of industry. Chiang's government launched a counterattack the next day, and thousands of Communists were summarily executed. Turning against the demonstrators, the citizens of Canton were also responsible for killing hundreds of innocents. According to the U.S. vice consul, "One picked one's way carefully around the corpses, skirted pools of blood, dodged overhanging electric wires, stepped over scattered bricks and passed trucks into which the police were directing coolies to throw the bodies of the executed. Some of the victims in the truck were still quivering." During the crackdown, papers were found in the Russian Consulate and various commercial establishments that proved that the buildings had been used as centers for espionage. When Chiang returned to service, he closed the consulate and broke off diplomatic relations with the Soviets.

The following summer, Chiang's army again attacked the Communists, now embedded at the Ridge of Wells. This time, however, the Nationalists only lost around 1,000 soldiers, through either capture or desertion; on July 22, an entire Nationalist regiment defected to the Communists, joined with local peasants, and styled itself the Fifth Red Army. Six months later, Mao and his followers moved east to a much larger base on the border of the provinces of Kiangsi and Fukien. Mao, who believed that the power in China lay with the peasants, had not yet overcome his failures of the previous autumn and had been superseded in party politics by Li Li-san. Li, an intellectual who followed the Marxist-Leninist theory that rebellions must be started with workers in urban centers, ordered Mao to seize Wuhan and other big cities. Although the Reds were able to occupy Changsha briefly during the summer of 1930, they were driven out after ten days. As to Wuhan, they could not even get near it. Having failed, Li was ousted from the Politburo and sent to Moscow in disgrace,* while Mao, who had been proved right, was elected president of the Chinese Soviet Republic, which was proclaimed on November 27, 1931. Chou En-lai, whose expertise in military affairs had previously earned him a place in the Politburo of the CCP, was named vice chairman under Mao.

❦

THE OTHER PROPONENTS of what Chiang called heresy were men within the party itself. As soon as the Northern Expedition was completed, the members of the KMT began quarreling among themselves—conservatives

---

* Li stayed in Moscow for a number of years, survived Stalin's purges, and returned to his home after the Communist victory. After recanting his "youthful errors," he rose to become minister of labor in 1958 but was pushed to suicide during the Cultural Revolution. (Crozier, *The Man Who Lost China*, pp. 143–44.)

versus liberals, pro-Chiang versus anti-Chiang. At a meeting of the Central Executive Committee of the party in the summer of 1928, Chiang had tendered his promised resignation but was immediately asked to resume his duties. Two months later he was named chairman of a new State Council, a group of eighteen that included General Feng as minister of war and Young Marshal Chang. Chiang alone, however, had the power to receive foreign envoys. The president of China in all but name, he was now the acting head of his country, writing in his diary that "within two years of our marriage, the Northern Expedition was completed, and the northwestern rebels had retreated. . . . Half of these achievements were due to the assistance of my wife."

It is strange that the party was willing to turn over so much power to Chiang, for he had begun to exhibit in public the traits that up until now seem to have disturbed only his intimates. He was, in the words of one colleague who dared not write under his own name, "arrogant and conceited, uninhibitedly practising dictatorship," and it is not surprising that other leaders found it difficult to accept his conviction that he was the legitimate inheritor of the mild-mannered, trusting Dr. Sun. By the time the party meeting closed in the middle of August, the rightists had walked out in disgust, and there was no quorum to continue work.

At the end of 1928, Chiang undertook a tour of inspection, returning to Nanking in a state of frustration with local officials of the party. "I have often observed that many . . . do not seem to know what they are supposed to do. . . . Our office hours are short—only six hours a day. . . . But yet I have often observed that many staff members just sit at their desks and gaze into space, others read newspapers and still others, sleep." In line with a new work ethic and moral crackdown, Chiang ordered the brothels and opium dens of Pengpu, a city west of Nanking, to be closed and told the magistrates of Anking, a city southwest of the new capital, to get busy building roads, opening schools, and ridding themselves of local bandits.

But these were minor problems when compared with the need for reducing the size of the National Revolutionary Army, which currently numbered more than 2 million men and cost the nation around $300 million* a year. Since the entire annual revenue of the country was in the vicinity of $400 million,† this was far more, Finance Minister T. V. Soong said, than China could afford. Soong called for a reduction of military expenditures along with specific plans for demobilization, but cutting the army back to 715,000

---

* 300,000,000 Chinese = $213,000,000 U.S. in 1928 ($2,670,000,000 today).

† 400,000,000 Chinese = $284,000,000 U.S. in 1928 ($3,570,000,000 today).

men—the number suggested as sufficient for China's current needs—was more easily proposed than accomplished.

The Chinese army, unlike those of many other nations, was not a collection of draftees happy to return home but a group of mercenaries for whom fighting was the only way of life and subsistence they knew. Chinese armies were traditionally composed of men recruited from areas of famine. In the service of the government or the warlords, they could get food, clothing, and a place to sleep and, if their employer was rich or generous, an occasional sum of money. Even if these soldiers had been willing to give this up, the warlords had no intention of turning over the source of their power to a central authority. Chiang's official biographer, Hollington Tong, explained the situation: "After the Northern Expedition . . . the area of which the National Government actually ruled comprised only a few provinces. . . . China was still broken up into regional spheres of influence, almost feudal states, and the situation was potent with danger." Or, as another writer put it, "The Northern Expedition did not eliminate the warlords; it simply brought them into the Kuomintang." Moreover, many of the warlords refused to remit to the central government the taxes collected in their provinces.

Although they had no intention of reducing the forces under their personal control, in true Chinese fashion the warlords agreed with Chiang that this was a necessary step and had signed a statement to that effect in July 1928. Six months later, a Disbandment Commission met at Nanking. Explaining how Japan had become a rich and powerful nation, Chiang contrasted the Japanese samurai—noblemen who had overthrown Japan's military government and immediately handed their lands and troops to the Mikado—to the Chinese warlords, who continued to fight among themselves and ignore the central government. "The Japanese militarists are loved by their own people but the Chinese militarists are hated by the Chinese. Which would you prefer?" he asked the members of the commission.

It was a good parable, and by the end of the month, the Disbandment Commission had divided the country into six areas, agreed that the armed forces would be cut to 65 divisions of 11,000 men each, and set a figure of no more than 41 percent of the national revenue for their upkeep. But, in fact, nothing of the sort was done. What followed the conference was not demobilization but civil war. Although it would appear that Chiang and his party had succeeded in unifying China, it seems that no sooner was he able to quell one rebellion than one or two others broke out in its place.

The first group to turn on the central government was a coalition of three warlords from the southern province of Kwangsi who called themselves the Warlords' Council, established themselves in the tri-city area of Wuhan, and collected taxes from the rich provinces of Hunan and Hupeh.

When General Lu Ti-ping, who had been loyally remitting the revenues from his area directly to the central government, refused to reroute the money through the Warlords' Council, it threw him out of office. Chiang's initial response was to issue an edict prohibiting branch councils from hiring or firing officials without approval from Nanking. This insipid reaction was followed by the appearance of soldiers sent by the Warlords' Council to fight General Lu, who quickly retreated.

The rebellion of the three warlords had coincided with preparations for the Third National Congress of the KMT, due to take place in Nanking in March 1928. Shortly before the congress convened, Wang Ching-wei sent a wire denouncing Chiang's government and encouraging other Leftists to refuse to serve as delegates. Very little could be accomplished at the congress anyway, since the members were obsessed with the revolt of the Warlords' Council and urged Chiang to take military action. His only move for the moment was against one of the Kwangsi generals, Li Chen-shen, who, having received a safe conduct to attend the congress, was arrested as soon as he arrived in Nanking.

Although it took some time for Chiang to decide to fight the Warlords' Council, he eventually defeated it. Some ascribed his victory to better disciplined and equipped troops, while others claimed that Chiang had successfully bribed a large number of soldiers to switch sides. In exchange for acceptance of his authority, he appointed two of the warlords to government offices, naming General Li Tsung-jen pacification commissioner for Kwangsi and giving General Pai Chung-hsi a place on the Standing Committee of the National Military Council.* Chiang emerged from his victory with increased prestige, and—even more to the point—his government could now collect taxes from twenty-two of the twenty-three provinces (not counting autonomous regions and municipalities) of China.

As usual, it all came down to money, and the problem of taxation continued to plague Chiang as it had other Chinese leaders. According to one historian, nothing had changed since the days of the Manchus:

> At every turn the peasant is dominated by the landowner; police, judicial, education systems are all built upon the landlord class, and the taxation system is also run by tax-collectors who are the agent of the landlord-officials. Poor peasants failing to meet their obligations are imprisoned and even tortured by the landlord-official; peasants owning small farms cannot secure credit from the banks,

---

* Both Generals Li and Pai ended up fighting for China and Chiang Kai-shek during World War II, when they were known as "the Two."

run by landlord-usurers. . . . The rate of interest on loans is around thirty-six percent per annum, but when money is tight (as in time of drought, flood, poor crops), reaches sixty per cent . . . the few landowner-official-usurer-militarist families who are *also* the provincial authorities . . . thus exercise a complete monopoly over all so-called public funds, derived from taxes, which become their private treasury. . . .

The land-tax, supposed to be assessed only once a year, was sometimes collected two or three times. . . . On top of that were extra taxes to be paid by the tenant-farmer: tax for release from . . . forced labour . . . release from military service . . . local grain transport; upkeep of roads and dykes, patrol of highways (by the landlord's privately recruited retainer armies) . . . support of schools . . . the schoolmaster being one of the landlord's cousins. There was a bandit eradication tax, pacification tax, door and window tax, roof tax. . . . Here are some of the forty-four taxes payable until 1949, in the one province of Kansu: kettle tax, stocking tax, bedding tax, wheat bran tax, water-mill tax, copper tax, flour-shop tax, extraordinary tax, hog tax, penalty tax, wealthy house tax, "purification of countryside" tax, army mule tax, kindling wood tax, skin overcoat tax, miscellaneous expenses tax, temporary expenses tax, soldier enlistment tax, circulation (of money) tax, hemp shoe tax, troop movement tax, soldier reward tax. After Chiang Kai-shek came to power, none of these taxes was repealed; on the contrary they were increased, both in number and in amount. There was even inaugurated in certain areas a "happy tax," for the purpose of promoting happiness on the day taxes were paid.

It must also be remembered that ever since the end of the First Opium War in 1842, China's customs had been under the control of the West, which had earmarked them for repayment of past loans. In fact, all taxes on salt, railroads, and internal transportation were used to repay foreigners, who had to be reimbursed before China ever saw any of her own money. Thus, according to Han Suyin, "the enormous profits benefitting from China's cheap labour remitted back to the West."

It was not until May 1930 that Chiang's Nationalist government finally succeeded in regaining tariff autonomy and was able to pass a surtax of 2.5 percent over and above the 5 percent tariff fixed by the West in the previous century. T.V. made this into a new source of government revenue and used it to issue bonds. According to Coble, it was the "wizardry of Soong" that "kept Nanjing [Nanking] financially afloat until the outbreak of the Sino-

Japanese War in 1937." But from 1928, when the Kuomintang took over the country, to 1943, the tax burden on the peasantry, who made up 85 percent of the population, increased by nearly 40 percent. And like the mandarins of old, certain members of Chiang's extended family were said to be skimming what they could off the top, or, as Hallett Abend of *The New York Times* put it, the Chiangs and their relations were now referred to as "the royal family." According to one American who served on a financial commission in China in 1929 and worked with the Lend-Lease Administration in 1943–1944, "Although we didn't have proof at the time, I think we rather sensed the way in which his wife's relations were simply looting the country."

Under circumstances like these, it is hardly surprising that as each new faction arose, complaining about Chiang, his relatives, and the KMT, it gained enough of a following to cause the central government a great deal of trouble. The next challenge came from the Christian General, Feng.

After the successful outcome of the Northern Expedition, Chiang had tried to pacify Feng by giving him the post of minister of war. As such, Feng cut quite a figure in Nanking. He received visitors only between 5:00 and 7:00 A.M., rode around the capital in a truck, and continued to sport the uniform of an ordinary soldier with cotton shoes and his trademark straw hat. A rich man who ate well and traveled in great luxury when no one was looking, Feng believed in appearances, delivering lectures on the virtues of simple living to his conspicuously consuming peers. Openly disapproving of almost everything in Nanking, he finally resigned his post, retired to his fiefdom in the North, and began his rebellion by intriguing with the Warlords' Council, which he planned to join. He first tried to gain control of the province of Shantung, which Japan had finally ceded back to China, but, unfortunately for him, the Kwangsi generals started their campaign before the Japanese evacuated the area, and he was afraid to delay his move any longer. As a prologue to entering the fray, Feng took on the benevolent title of "Commander in Chief of the Northwestern Army to Protect the Party and Save the Country."

Busy directing the fight against the Warlords' Council in the South, Chiang was not prepared to take on a second war in the North. To keep Feng on hold, he began an exchange of "unbelievably long" telegrams with the Christian General, designed to forestall military action. Throughout this exchange, neither man ever admitted that he was making active preparations for war against the other. The main subject of their correspondence was a disagreement over the allegiance of Feng's soldiers: Chiang said that all commanders must submit to the central authority, while Feng believed that his troops belonged exclusively to him.

Chiang even invited Feng to Nanking, explaining that he was planning to go to Peiping to accompany the body of Sun Yat-sen back from the old capital for a state burial in the new one.

> Before I leave for Peiping I fervently hope you will come to Nanking to take charge of the Government; otherwise you must come to the Capital for the state funeral . . . you are suspected by the nation of having stored up arms and war materials to hold the North-west in defiance of the Government . . . you are, in addition, suspected of refusing to come to the Capital because you had made a previous alliance with Kwangsi [the Warlords' Council] and were planning to attack Wuhan. . . . All such rumours, it is quite needless to say, are not worth listening to. . . . Therefore we can only hope that, as you are loyal to the Government, you will not remain in the North-west. Your presence here will quash all rumours and the nation will be certain of peace.

To which Feng replied that considering what had happened to General Lu (the Kwangsi leader who was arrested on his arrival in Nanking), he had no intention of coming to the capital and that, in any case, he was too ill to travel. He also demanded to know why Kuomintang soldiers were massing along his borders.

After a few more similar exchanges, Feng was formally dismissed from the KMT and the State Council issued a mandate against him. Chiang sent off one last wire, listing Feng's crimes against the state and suggesting that he go abroad. "There are but two courses open to you: either you obey or you revolt. If you awaken to the realities with your customary alertness and resolutely pull yourself out of your present evil environment, your mistakes will not affect your future. . . . if you wish to go abroad, I shall speak on your behalf to the Government so that you may go under full protection."

At this point Chiang could afford to issue an ultimatum to Feng, for he had successfully outwitted the Christian General's scheme to take over the province of Shantung. The Japanese had agreed to leave the province within two months after signing an agreement to do so, but just as they were about to withdraw, Chiang had asked them to delay so that government troops, rather than Feng's, could move in. Chiang then offered an "enormous" bribe to one of Feng's trusted commanders, General Han, who defected to the Nationalists with about 100,000 (one third) of Feng's most experienced soldiers. Chiang also bribed another of Feng's men, General Shih, a man who had changed sides so often that he was dubbed "Triple-crosser Shih."

But while Han and Shih were switching their allegiance to the central government, Feng managed to make an alliance with the other important warlord in the north, the wily General Yen who had led the Third Army in the Northern Expedition. This new alignment, Chiang realized, changed "the entire political situation in northern China" to the disadvantage of the Nationalist government. Emissaries of all three men met in June 1929 and reached an agreement whereby Chiang would cancel his threats to arrest Feng; the government would pay Feng's soldiers their salaries in arrears with a first payment of $3 million;* Feng's troops would be kept together; and Feng's trip would be postponed. It was, as we have seen, a typical bribe for an atypical warlord.

❦

AT THE SAME time that Chiang was trying to pacify the warlords, May-ling was helping convert Nanking, a city of a quarter-million inhabitants, into an appropriate capital for a new era. Lying in the shadow of the Purple Mountain on the southern bank of the Yangtze River, Nanking was once encircled by the longest city wall in the world, something over twenty miles in length. Built of bricks, each one of which was stamped with the name of the brick maker and the overseer for that section, the Nanking wall, much of which still stands, dates back some six hundred years to the Ming Dynasty and was the first city wall to be contoured to the rise and fall of the land rather than laid out in a precise square. Nanking, the site of the treaty that ended the First Opium War in 1842, had also served as the capital of the Taipings. It was now, almost a hundred years later, the official home of the Nationalist government.

Starting with the streets—narrow paths of cobblestone, smelling of night soil—the Chiangs tried to turn venerable antiquities into buildings suitable to modern life without offending those eager to accuse them of desecrating tradition. They envisioned the old Chinese architecture—sloping roofs, colorful tiles, interior courtyards, and painted ceilings—cleaned and made comfortable with the addition of electricity.† It must have been May-ling's idea to hire an American architect to work out an appropriate style for the new buildings, but Chiang seems to have enjoyed the process immensely. While the Ministry of Foreign Affairs was under construction, he and May-ling visited the site daily, and it is said that they strolled around the area arm

---

* 3,000,000 Chinese = $1,920,000 U.S. in 1929 ($24,132,000 today).

† Up until that point, Chinese homes were usually heated by raised brick sleeping platforms called *kangs*.

in arm—a distinctly un-Chinese display of marital intimacy.* But the true measure of their success came during the summer of 1928, when Great Britain recognized the new national government and the British ambassador presented his credentials to Chiang in Nanking. Diplomats from eleven other countries—ambassadors and ministers who had thus far refused to leave "the luxury and heedless spending of Peking's officials circles"—eventually and "with reluctant feet," followed. By transferring their diplomats to Nanking, these nations tacitly recognized the right of Chiang's government to exist and, more important, to collect taxes.

With the diplomats stationed in Nanking, May-ling's role became essential to the government. Chiang did not speak English when he married her, and he was never able to learn. She apparently tried to teach him, and one day he decided to try out his English during a meeting with the new British ambassador, Sir Miles Lampson, "Good morning, Lampson," he said. "Kiss me, Lampson," he added.

After that, Chiang gave up, and May-ling was left to do his translations, acting as both secretary and interpreter with the foreign community. Up until this point in her life, she had filled her days with activities considered appropriate to an educated Chinese woman. As one journalist put it, "The institution of 'First Lady' is virtually nonexistent in China, where woman's prime role is that of wife, mother and mother-in-law." Now she acquired work that was difficult enough to keep her mind occupied and an infinitely larger stage on which to perform. It would be fascinating to know how accurately she translated the messages to and from her husband, whose famous intransigence and abrupt temper must surely have been showing up by now. This author is convinced that May-ling rarely translated anything that he said or was said to him without changing and/or softening both the words and their meaning.

While helping to bring Nanking up to date, May-ling also established two Schools for the Children of the Heroes of the Revolution just outside the city. "These children, I thought, would be the most valuable material if they were molded right," she explained in a total abandonment of logic, "as they all had revolutionary blood in their veins." The children entered school at the age of six and stayed until eighteen. "What I have learned about the training of students," she said later,

has come mostly through observation of how students should not be taught . . . book knowledge alone was emphasized and no at-

---

* To quote the wife of China's most famous diplomat, Wellington Koo, "A public show of affection . . . is considered in the worst possible taste." (Koo, *Hui Lan-koo*, p. 56.)

tempt was made to point out the necessity of assimilating learning with practical living or to prepare the students for their future by teaching them how to live as citizens of a community. In the Schools for the Children of the Revolution, my children were taught to . . . reason out why such and such a thing should be done in a certain way. In so far as possible, I tried to get away from the idea of regimentation by emphasis upon the necessity of developing initiative . . . in self-discipline. Also, I organized rural service clubs in the schools so that the students could help the farmers in the community, and, at the same time, put into practice the theory of learning by doing.

In a letter to a Wellesley classmate written in August 1928, May-ling proudly reported that her students raised "some very good watermelons and had a good showing in bees and silkworms."

Called by one of her assistants "the last word in modern college architecture, airy, spacious, well-furnished," May-ling's schools had classrooms, playgrounds, a gymnasium, dormitories, a covered court for bad weather, and a swimming pool. Determined to make these model schools for the nation, May-ling located them in the most beautiful part of the area, at the foot of the Purple Mountain. "The children who are privileged to study in the Institute," she said, "will certainly enjoy the esthetic influence of nature, which, coupled with the guidance of their teachers, will tend favorably to the development of their talents and characters."

In choosing teachers for her schools, May-ling caused surprise and resentment by rejecting a number of candidates recommended by the KMT, explaining that she was "opposed to mixing up education with politics." The teachers, she declared, were to be judged solely on their qualifications for the job. Along with book work, there was training in agriculture and dairy farming for the boys, sewing, embroidery, and weaving for the girls. "Hygiene, discipline and physical training were unequaled anywhere else," said the assistant, Ilona Ralf Sues, who also noted that only healthy children were enrolled and that students were not allowed to go home except for the funeral of an elder relative.

But Sues worried about "unmistakable resemblances to Mussolini's Fascist Youth, and to the Hitler Jugend—severing the children from their families and grouping them round one leader. On the other hand," she speculated, "charity was not a part of Fascist or Nazi doctrine. Madame might consider it a Christian virtue; but . . . charity is neither a Chinese virtue nor a Chinese vice, it is essentially un-Chinese . . . poor relatives can come to the house of the better-off members of the family, eat there, live there, and get help . . .

those who have no family . . . are given the same hospitality by strangers who are natives of their province. . . . It is not charity but the deep-rooted feeling of common decency, so common that no Chinese would ever think of playing it up as a virtue."

⚘

THE CHIANGS THEMSELVES had started life in their new capital in a small red-brick and gray cement house in the midst of the barracks of the Huangpu Military Academy, a large campus enclosed by a high wall where several thousand officers were always in training. The only women permitted inside the walls were Madame, her personal maid, and a nurse. A visiting female reporter recalled having to sign her name for the sentries with a Chinese brush in a guest book kept in the guardhouse before being escorted to May-ling's door. Chiang's wife, who had recently given up Western clothes, wore a wine-colored gown of leaf-patterned cut velvet with real pearl buttons for the interview. She had a diamond-and-platinum wedding band with a circle of jade on the fourth finger of her left hand and on the third finger of her right, a large jade and diamond ring. "As she sat before a window," the reporter wrote in the New York *Sun,* "I could see the bright yellow light piercing the long carved pendants of her transparent, priceless jade earrings." But a male reporter, initially impressed by the Chiangs' "rather modest" home, told Madame Chiang that "she had an opportunity to be a modern-day Joan of Arc," providing she "take off those rubies and those emeralds . . . and . . . get out in the fields. You've got to take off that silk and put on padded clothes. That's the only way you're going to save China." Madame's response? She got up from her chair and walked to the door of the room. "Mr. Rounds," she said à la Marie Antoinette, "will you have another piece of cake?"

The Madame was not fond of her residence in the military compound, and in 1931, the Chiangs built a weekend home outside the city. It featured a large conference room with appropriate wall maps on the second floor and a meeting room on the third (family) floor for religious worship. This floor also contained the Chiangs' bedroom, which opened onto his study and their bathrooms. Symbols of temporal success found on these upper floors included two huge carved wooden dragons playing with a jade ball—a symbol of power—and more than one thousand phoenixes—symbols of renewed life—on the roof and carved on the white marble railings of a large second-floor terrace. Designed in the Chinese style with an elaborate roof of shaped green tiles supported by several rows of flat, multicolored (yellow, red, blue, and green) decorative tiles, the house still bears indisputable signs of newly acquired power. Perhaps the most notable of these are the green tile sculptures on the four corners of the roof: the head of a bull, a lion, a sea-horse, and a man riding a hen—the latter meant to call to mind the Chinese proverb "If a man becomes a god, his hen goes to Heaven." It can be no coincidence that these same symbols appear on the roofs of various pavil-ions of the Forbidden City, the home of the emperors of China.

19

He [Chiang Kai-shek] read the Bible every day and frowned on sin with the intensity of one who has sampled it and found it less rewarding than piety.

—THEODORE WHITE AND ANNALEE JACOBY

ONE FACTOR that had delayed a military clash between Chiang and Feng was the official state funeral of Dr. Sun Yat-sen, which took place on June 1, 1929. Located high on the slope of the Purple Mountain and three years in the planning and building, Sun's tomb became the most prominent landmark outside the city of Nanking. Ching-ling, who was in Berlin at the time, had agreed to attend the ceremony but insisted that her presence not be misinterpreted, as had happened a few years earlier when left-wing American journalist Agnes Smedley visited the site with one of Chiang's closest aides, Colonel Huang. When they came to a small house under construction, Huang explained to Smedley that it was "being built for Madame Sun Yat-sen" and that "she will live here near the tomb."

"Do you think Madame Sun will live here?" Smedley asked.

"Oh, certainly! She is a member of the Central Committee of the party!"

"I thought she was in exile," Smedley said, at which point Huang's "manner and voice became offensively sarcastic" as he asked her if Ching-ling was still in Moscow and inquired as to the whereabouts of Borodin.

Having been misrepresented by Chiang before, Ching-ling was taking no chances this time. "I am proceeding to China for the purpose of attending to the removal of the remains of Dr. Sun Yat-sen to the Purple Mountain where he desired to be buried," she announced. "In order to avoid any possible misunderstanding . . . my attendance at the burial is not to be interpreted as in any sense implying a modification or reversal of my decision to abstain from any direct or indirect work of the Kuomintang so long as its leadership is opposed to the fundamental policies of Dr. Sun."

Two weeks before the ceremony, a train painted gold, white, and blue, bearing Sun Yat-sen's coffin, arrived in Nanking. Embalmed in what one observer called "the life-like, decay-proof manner that the Russians had employed for Lenin's body" and dressed in a blue satin gown with a black silk jacket, the body had been placed in a new coffin covered with glass. In the train were Chiang Kai-shek, standing at attention beside the coffin, and Ching-ling, busy avoiding her brother-in-law. When the train arrived in Nanking, Sun's body was taken to the headquarters of the KMT, where Chiang put a wreath on the coffin, which lay in state until the ceremony.

The funeral cortege, led by four armored cars, left the center of Nanking at 4:00 A.M. Traveling with the body were Chiang, May-ling, Sun Fo, and Ching-ling, who was dressed in black rather than the usual white for mourning and observed to be crying.* It took six hours for the procession to cover the ten-mile route, which was lined with thousands of spectators, soldiers, government workers, representatives of provincial governments, and students, held back by a "thin line" of police with fingers firmly on the triggers of their Mausers.

Set across the lotus marshes from Nanking above the ruins of an old Ming temple, the mausoleum faces south and commands a glorious view. Passing through a triple archway along a long, pine-bordered walk, the visitor comes to a gate bearing the inscription "The world belongs to the people." At this point in the pilgrimage, he or she begins to climb one mile of white stone steps—392 stairs with ten platforms—leading to another three arches, flanked by two Western-style bronze lions and two oversized urns for the burning of incense. On the way up there is a pagodalike pavilion, which holds a statue of Sun under a bright red ceiling emblazoned with the flag of the Kuomintang. The walls of the pavilions are white granite, and the roofs are tile, glazed in a luminous shade of blue. Still ascending, the pilgrim finally reaches the last pavilion, where a large, deep white marble circle has been cut into the floor. At the bottom of the circle is the sarcophagus holding the body of Dr. Sun.

Working in relays of sixteen men at a time, the casket bearers for the ceremony marched to the beat of a foreman who marked time by banging on a hollow bamboo pole. According to the reporter for *The North-China Herald*, "the men showed signs of strain"—so much so that "several of the mourners bent their weight to the ropes they held and assisted in dragging the massive structure upwards." Located at different points on the steps were bands—all playing the same dirge, but not in unison and at different speeds.

Although May-ling and the rest of the Soongs were present at the dedication, Ching-ling refused to mount the steps with them, forming a procession of one. She also issued several more statements making it "abundantly

---

* It is often said that Ching-ling refused to attend the ceremonies. There are, however, photographs showing her in the family funeral procession, albeit keeping her distance from the others.

clear that she had no intention of lending her name and reputation to the government or party" of her brother-in-law.

❦

THIS GRAND STATE burial, with which "Chiang sanctified his capital," served only as an interlude between battles. A few months later, Wang Ching-wei sent out a circular wire saying that Chiang was treating China as if it belonged exclusively to him and that he had placed his friends and relatives in all the important positions. Chief spokesman for yet another faction of the KMT, the Reorganizationists, Wang announced that the time had come to "raise arms to wipe away this rebel," thus leaving room for Wang himself to be installed in Chiang's place. Toward this end, two of Wang's supporters started separate military campaigns against Chiang, but both were beaten. Seeing his chance, Feng jumped into the fray but was also defeated. All in all, during 1929, Chiang managed to put down four separate rebellions.

Although 1930 dawned in an atmosphere of comparative peace, foreigners in China began to anticipate what they snidely referred to as the "annual spring revolts"—the outbreaks of the Chinese warlords as they tried to increase their power. The first challenge came in February from General Yen of Shanxi, the foxy governor-warlord who had recently teamed up with Feng. Yen suddenly disarmed all the government troops in his area and seized Nanking's local assets, while Feng (now minus 100,000 soldiers) was reduced to serving as Yen's deputy commander. The year, which had started semi-auspiciously, degenerated into six months of horrendous warfare in which it was estimated that 150,000 of Yen's troops were killed or wounded, while 30,000 government soldiers lost their lives and double that number were injured. After Chiang's final victory, Feng was forcibly retired from all his positions, while Yen, now "one of Chiang's stable of tamed warlords," was allowed to return to run the province of Shanxi.

Civil war continued throughout 1930. During the summer, Wang had himself inaugurated as head of a State Council, meant to take the place of the council headed by Chiang Kai-shek. The date for Wang's investiture had been planned around the lucky number nine, the Chinese character that also means "long-lasting." It was to take place at 9:00 A.M. on the ninth day of the ninth month in the nineteenth year of the Chinese Republic. Both Wang and Chiang had sent lobbyists to Mukden to gain the allegiance of the Young Marshal, who announced his support of Chiang, allowing Nationalist soldiers to take over what was now called Peiping without a fight and negating Wang's new government. In the words of one of Chiang's biographers, Robert Payne, 1930 turned out to be "a year of shame, of vast expenditure of effort and human lives, with nothing gained. The spectacle of the Chinese destroying themselves was vastly amusing to the Japanese Imperial General Staff."

When he was not fending off rebellious warlords, Chiang was worrying about the Communists. In October 1930, he addressed a meeting at the Central Party Headquarters of the KMT:

It is highly deplorable that in almost all the places to which I have of late repaired, Party members have left extremely unfavourable impressions in the minds of the people . . . all are stigmatized for the most reprehensible practices, such as corruption, bribery and scrambling for power. The Manchus were overthrown because they constituted a special caste. But now, we who staged the Revolution . . . have ourselves come to be regarded by the people as a privileged caste. They are now cherishing toward us the same hatred and repugnance with which they looked upon the Manchus. . . . Unless we quickly correct our faults, the Party will meet with rapid downfall. . . . It is all of us Party members who are responsible for the virulence of the Communist menace in the country . . . if we carry out proper duties with vigour, the Communists will never be able to disturb the country.

❦

THROUGHOUT HIS BATTLES with warlords and Communists, May-ling continued to help Chiang. "My wife is very happy to see that I put national affairs before everything else," he wrote. ". . . She is concerned with my safety. I know that she is always thinking about me. I believe that she understands me." Chiang worried about May-ling's frequent illnesses and even broke an appointment with an important KMT statesman to stay home with her one day in the spring of 1931. "The deeper the worries, the deeper our love seems to be," he confided to his diary that day. And in August three years later, when he himself was sick, she remained with him. "I felt so exhausted after the injection," he wrote. "My wife was sick too, but she seemed to forget her illness in order to take care of me. When I saw her tired face, it was very painful."

It is clear from both her words and actions that May-ling had finally found the raison d'être for which she had been searching in the responsibilities that her marriage to Chiang implied. She was almost touchingly proud of her recently discovered abilities to withstand hardship, find useful work, and immerse herself in a cause. Like her elder sister, Ching-ling, she too had found a man to love, follow, and serve—albeit at the other end of the political spectrum.

At the same time that Chiang Kai-shek was giving his wife a cause to work for, she was indoctrinating him with the Methodist faith of her family. Acting on his promise to her mother to read the Bible in order to decide if he could embrace Christianity, May-ling began inviting missionaries to their home shortly after their wedding; she also got out her old textbooks from a Wellesley Bible class and began daily 6:30 A.M. sessions of devotional readings and discussions with her husband. By February of 1930, Chiang was clearly feeling pressure to convert: "Rev. Jing Chiang-chuan came to Nanking from Shanghai," he wrote in his diary on February 21. "My mother-in-law and my wife were both urging me to be baptized. As I am still not very clear about the true spirit of Christianity, Rev. Jiang persuaded me by explaining that one could only truly understand Christianity after being baptized. I then asked for three months to study Christianity."

During that summer, May-ling remained at the front with Chiang, and in the fall he expressed a desire to be accepted into the Methodist Church. There were many who thought his conversion had more to do with political convenience than belief, but Chiang claimed that it had occurred one day on a battlefield when he was worried about being cut off from his soldiers. He had prayed to the Christian God, promising that he would convert if he were saved from the danger. A sudden storm had conveniently stopped the enemy from advancing and given his reinforcements time to arrive for the battle.

The baptism was performed by the pastor of the Young Allen Memorial Church, one of the ministers who had refused to perform the Chiang marriage. When he asked the general whether he sincerely wanted to become a Christian, Chiang, replied, "I feel the need of a God such as Jesus Christ." The minister then sprinkled water on his head and admitted him to the Church. All three of Madame Soong's sons-in-law, it was noted, now belonged to the Christian Church. May-ling said that she stood by her husband's side throughout the ceremony, repeating the relevant answers and thus rededicating herself as well.

Only relatives and a few intimate friends were present for the ceremony, which took place at May-ling's mother's home. Afterward, the Chiangs received officials at T.V.'s home and the next day left for Chiang's birthplace for a visit to the tombs of his ancestors and a ten-day rest. The conversion had been kept secret and, according to an article in the *St. Louis Post-Dispatch*, "startled all Shanghai and Nanking." Another American paper said that Chiang had "embraced the Christian faith against the wish of the majority of his people," that his baptism was "a direct blow at everything that was sacred and traditional in China," and that it was "purely political." Still others, claiming that he was looking for American support in the inevitable fight against Japan, cited the current political bon mot: "There's Methodism in his madness." It would seem that the only people truly rejoicing were the missionaries, those evangelists of Western religion for whom this important conversion was a sign that their work had not been in vain. Certainly, the Chiangs were, as author Karen Leong observed, "not shy about publicizing their cooperation with various mission organizations." Their dedication, according to Leong, had a point: "Soong [May-ling] perceived that Christianity and nationalism could coexist to their mutual benefit in improving China's international status."

Whatever the motivation for Chiang's conversion, he remained a Confucian in the depths of his soul. He believed in the Mandate of Heaven and continued to apply a rigorous if unenlightened examination to personal morality. His code was a simplistic one, and the application of a Christian veneer did not seem to deepen in him any comprehension of self. Nonetheless, after 1930, the year of his conversion, he considered himself a Christian, and in 1938 amended the law that had forbidden the compulsory teaching of religion in Christian schools in China—a decision that May-ling described as "the greatest testimony in the history of China of our appreciation of the value of the real, vital contributions that Christianity has made to the spiritual well-being and the livelihood of our people."

Chiang's adoption of Christianity was not received favorably by the Chinese, who blamed it on politics and his Methodist wife. May-ling claimed that it was not she but her mother who had brought it about and who died ten months after his baptism, in July of 1931. With her mother, May-ling wrote some years later,

> religion was not a one-way traffic. She often emphasized to me that we should not ask God to do anything if the request hurts someone else. I can see her now, quite ill, a few months before her death. She had an unusually active mind and was vitally concerned about the country. At that time, the Japanese were beginning their aggressive program against China, and, one day while talking to her, a thought which I considered quite bright occurred to me: "Mother, you are so powerful in prayer, why don't you pray to God to destroy Japan in an earthquake so that she can no longer harm China?"
>
> She turned her face away from me, and then replied: "Don't ask me to pray to God to do anything that is unworthy even of you, a mortal. 'Vengeance is mine,' saith the Lord. It certainly isn't yours."

May-ling was apparently with her mother when she died. "We Chinese believed that in times of crisis for their children, a parent might choose to die in the place of their child; and I just knew that if such a thing were possible, Mother would have done it for my brother," May-ling later told a young member of the family. "Of course, there is no way to know if that is what really happened, but Mother did, in fact, die at that moment."

May-ling could often believe what she wanted to be true—even when it was not. "SHOTS FIRED AT MINISTER" read a headline in *The New York Times* of July 23, 1931: "Three men attempted to assassinate T. V. Soong, Finance Minister, on his arrival here at 7 o'clock this morning from Nanking." The attempt to assassinate T.V. had indeed taken place early that morning, but it was four hours later that Madame Soong died. In any case, July 23, 1931, was a terrible day for the Soongs. Instead of rushing off his train with the crowd anxious to get into the city, T.V., dressed in what another newspaper described as "foreign garb" with a white helmet, was easily spotted as he made his way through Shanghai's North Station, followed by his young secretary and bodyguards. Suddenly voices were heard yelling "Down with the Soong Dynasty!" At the same time, shots were fired from all four corners of the station, and two bombs were detonated. T.V. removed his helmet and stepped behind a pillar while pulling out his revolver. His bodyguards were of little use, but a member of the railway police told him to throw down his hat and follow him to the safety of a boardroom upstairs in the station. Seeing T.V. escaping, the would-be assassins ran after him; failing to catch him, they left the station unapprehended. T.V. himself, according to an account in the papers, "was remarkably composed and able to give an account of every little detail" of the attack before leaving for his mother's home.

Known as "The Mother-in-Law of the Country" and eulogized by the *North-China Herald* as "one of the most remarkable women in modern China," Madame Soong had been ill for some time before she died. Three days after her death, a wire arrived from Chiang: "Oh, my heart is aching," he wrote his wife. ". . . I have lost another good mother. . . . You, my love,* and your elder sisters must be heart-broken, but please take care of yourselves." Ching-ling had to come from Germany for the funeral, which was not held until more than three weeks later.

Led by a Sikh trooper, twelve motorcycles, 180 troopers, 200 sailors and marines, and a naval band, a hundred cars lined up for the funeral cortege. The three Soong sisters sat in one car, while their three brothers occupied an

---

* The endearment is highly unusual in their correspondence. Chiang always signed his cables to his wife "Brother Kai."

armored Buick. T.V. was protected by six bodyguards, guns drawn, while Chiang Kai-shek, accompanied by H. H. Kung, was surrounded by twenty-five graduates of Whampoa, twelve on each side of the car in which he was driven. The procession led to the International Cemetery, where Madame Soong was buried.

May-ling seems to have been going through a religious crisis at the time of her husband's conversion—a fact that explains her repetition of his vows—and the death of her mother. She characterized the early years of her married life as falling into three phases. "First," she said, "there was a tremendous enthusiasm and patriotism—a passionate desire to do something for my country." But even in her dedication, she said, she realized that "something was lacking. There was no staying power. I was depending on self." During the second phase, she described herself as being "plunged into dark despair. A terrible depression settled on me—spiritual despair, bleakness, desolation. At the time of my mother's death, the blackness was greatest. A foreign foe was on our soil in the north. A discontented political faction in the south. Famine in the northwest. Floods . . . And my beloved mother taken from me. . . . As long as Mother lived I had a feeling that whatever I did, or failed to do, Mother would pray me through," May-ling explained.

> Though she insisted that she was not our intercessor, that we must pray ourselves, yet I know for a certainty that many of her long hours of prayer were spent interceding for us. . . . I realized that spiritually I was failing my husband. . . . I began to see that what I was doing to help, for the sake of the country, was only a substitute for what he needed. . . . Out of . . . the feeling of human inadequacy, I was driven back to my mother's God. I knew there was a power greater than myself. . . . But Mother was no longer there to do my interceding for me. It seemed to be up to me to help the General spiritually, and in helping him I grew spiritually myself. Thus I entered into the third period where I wanted to do, not my will, but God's.

❦

IT IS SURELY no coincidence that May-ling's personal crisis came at a time when her husband's political stature was at a low ebb. During the summer and fall of 1931, when Chiang and the Kuomintang appeared to have reached the nadir of popularity and efficacy, a thirty-year-old member of the party, Liu Chien-chun, wrote an essay in which he declared that the KMT "seems to have dissipated the hopes of the masses! Not only has it become remote from the masses, but in many places it is simply hated by the masses!" The blame, he said, rested with the party itself, which had ceased to be a revolutionary organization, and the members, who had stopped working for China or its people. According to Liu, the problems did not lie simply in the corruption of its functionaries. "We firmly believe that the turmoil of the party, the impotence of the party, the decadence of the party, are problems not of individuals, but problems of poor methods, an imperfect system, and of insubstantial content." To solve these problems Liu advocated "preserving the old shell of the party, but in addition organizing within the party a corps devoted to the common people of the nation that will give substance . . . and create the party's soul."

This corps was formally and secretly founded by Chiang in the spring of 1932. Calling together a group of young army officers to form an elite organization like the one Liu suggested, Chiang said that he would serve as the permanent head and that graduates of Whampoa should take positions of leadership. Named the Blue Shirts by the Japanese, who tried to equate it with Mussolini's Black Shirts, the group adopted many of the tenets of fascism, currently in vogue in Italy and Germany. In explaining this phenomenon, Eastman refers to "the depths of desperation and humiliation" felt by thinking Chinese in the 1930s as a result of the failure of the republic to engage the common people. He also explains the attitude of the intellectual elite towards Fascism:

"To many Chinese in the 1930s, fascism did not appear as a pernicious or retrogressive doctrine. On the contrary, it appeared to be at the very forefront of historical progress. Parliamentary government had been attempted in China since 1912, and with obviously tragic consequences. And, throughout the world, democracy and laissez-faireism were being rejected in favor of one-man or one-party dictatorships. To the Blue Shirts . . . it seemed idiotic to reject a system that had proven to be effective in Italy and Germany in favor of a governmental system that had manifestly outlived its historical utility." According to Chiang Kai-shek, "In the last several decades we have in vain become drunk with democracy and the advocacy of free thought. And what has been the result? We have fallen into a chaotic and irretrievable situation."

Moreover, ever since 1928, when Chiang broke off diplomatic relations with the Soviets and replaced Russian military advisers with officers from Germany, Chinese officers had been, in Eastman's words, "richly exposed" to the fascistic principles the Germans carried east with them. Lieutenant Colonel Hermann Kriebel, who took over as head of the German Military Mission in China in 1929, had marched in the front of the Beer Hall Putsch of 1923 with Hitler and had, in fact, shared a cell with the Führer during their subsequent imprisonment. It was not unusual for Chinese officers to go abroad to study. Just as Chiang himself had gone to Japan in 1906 for military training, by 1930 the majority were going to Germany. In 1932, Chiang sent two officers to study the Nazi organization and consult with high-ranking Nazi leaders. Shortly thereafter, he spoke to a meeting of the Blue Shirts: "What China needs today is not an ism that discusses what kind of ideal future China will have, but a method that will save China at the present moment. . . . Fascism is a stimulant for a declining society. . . . Can fascism save China? We answer: yes. Fascism is what China now most needs. . . . At the present stage of China's critical situation, fascism is a wonderful medicine exactly suited to China, and the only spirit that can save it."

The Blue Shirts lasted about six years. At their height—at the end of 1935—they probably numbered no more than 10,000. Although the group never succeeded in its original aim of inserting a "soul" into the Kuomintang, its members dominated political training within the army and controlled many of Chiang's security organizations: the military police, the Public Security Office, and the Department of Special Services (i.e., secret police). This last entity was run by a Blue Shirt named Tai Li, a onetime student at Whampoa who began his career by gathering information about the Communists in his class. Although he never completed the course at Whampoa, Tai was given special dispensation and became chief of China's secret police. "Cold, hard, crafty and brutal," he was a slender, good-looking man with ramrod posture and small, beautiful hands who came to be known as "the Himmler of Nationalist China." He built a spy organization that, by the end of World War II, numbered 40,000 to 50,000 men.

Two of the major tenets of the Blue Shirts were (1) exaltation of the nation, implying as it did, subjugation of the individual, and (2) blind obedience to the leader. This last, of course, was enormously attractive to Chiang, particularly when an editorial in a distinguished Blue Shirt publication concluded that China needed "the establishment of a central idol" as "the important condition of a unified Kuomintang and the first step toward resurrecting China. *We must not disguise that we demand China's Mussolini, demand China's Hitler, demand China's Stalin!* said the author." After all his fights with rebellious factions of the KMT, Chiang certainly agreed. "The most important point of fascism is absolute trust in a sagely, able leader," he said. ". . . I believe that, unless everyone has absolute trust in one man, we cannot reconstruct the nation and we cannot complete the revolution." Although Chiang denied publicly that he aspired to be that person, he was the man whose portrait the would-be Blue Shirter faced when he vowed to obey the leader and keep the secrets of the group on penalty of death.

In sponsoring the creation of the Blue Shirts, Chiang was apparently trying to seize on a philosophical movement strong enough to counter both the rebels within the party and the Communists without. Unable to develop an administration that answered the needs of the Chinese people or give the people themselves a sense of national responsibility, Chiang reverted to the kind of militarism he had discovered when he was a student—an unquestioning, self-abnegating, blind obedience to authority. The irony is, of course, that the Blue Shirts, while they lasted, were not all that different from the Communists whom Chiang had sworn to destroy—those dedicated followers of Mao who were working just as hard to lure ordinary Chinese to the other end of the political spectrum.

But even the Blue Shirts, called by historian Lloyd Eastman "one of the most influential and feared political movements in China," were powerless to help their leader when it came to fighting the Japanese, greedy for more land, more natural resources, and supreme power in Asia.

20

It is becoming increasingly evident that the plans of Japanese militarists in the Far East are more or less limitless.

—ROY HOWARD

EVERYONE WHO should have known was aware that Japan had been preparing to invade China for quite some time. Edgar Snow, who had arrived in the country only in 1928 and was on his first assignment writing tourist pamphlets, told readers of the *China Weekly Review* that the Japanese were anxious to provoke an incident that they could escalate into war. A brief review of recent Japanese history explains why.

From the time the Chinese began to fight incursions from the west, Japan, observing the defeats and humiliation of its neighbor, had decided to pursue a different course. By 1853, the year Commodore Perry arrived in Japan, China had already been forced to cede Hong Kong to Great Britain, open five treaty ports, and pay a huge indemnity—all as a result of the First Opium War, the second not yet having even begun. It was clear to Japan that with its feudal society crumbling, it would be wise to comply with Occidental demands and open itself to trade with the West.

During the period of the Meiji emperor (1868–1912), the remnants of the old Japanese feudalism and military rule gave way to a strong, centralized government patterned on those of the Western nations. Great changes took place in the fields of education, science, and art, and, in an effort to speed up its industrial revolution, Japan moved its peasants into factories like those of Victorian England. By the end of the century, after engaging China in a war from which it emerged victorious, Japan was able to extract large enough indemnities to fund the next stage of its industrial development. Another big victory—this one over the Russian navy in 1905—whetted the Japanese appetite for domination over Asia. But to accomplish this, the small island nation needed huge supplies of men and raw materials, all of which were tantalizingly available in China. Meanwhile, the West continued "gorging on China's inexhaustible capacity for producing wealth for others." As early as 1898, one Japanese statesman had already begun to worry. "The vampires are feasting," he noted, "we may be too late."

In the mid-1920s, the Great Depression that would devastate the Western world started earlier in Japan, and the military rose to prominence. In April of 1927, Japanese hawks forced out the moderates, and the militaristic Baron Giichi Tanaka took over as Japanese prime minister. One of Tanaka's early acts was to send the emperor a memorial* urging Japan's colonization of Asia. "In order to conquer China," the baron wrote, "we must first conquer Manchuria and Mongolia." After that, he said, Japan could set about taking over the rest of the continent. "The way to gain actual rights in Manchuria and Mongolia is to use the region as a base and under the pretence of trade and commerce penetrate the rest of China. . . . Armed by the rights already secured we shall seize the resources all over the country. Having China's entire resources at our disposal we shall proceed to conquer India, the Archipelago, Asia Minor, Central Asia and even Europe."

❦

IT CERTAINLY LOOKED as if the fall of 1931 was an excellent time for the Japanese to make their move. It had been a terrible year for the Chinese. Aside from the usual uprisings, there were disastrous spring floods over the valley of the Yangtze River. Whole villages had been swept away, something like 2 million people had drowned, and 50 million peasants had lost their farms. At one point, the streets of Hankow itself were under water. The flood, which lasted for two months, was followed by famine, cholera, and dysentery. The effects of the disaster were felt as far as Shanghai, whose factory workers and rickshaw drivers were normally recruited from the flooded areas, and Peiping, where one writer described her horror at finding dead babies on the sidewalks, wrapped in newspapers like parcels.† The Western powers, who might have helped the Chinese with military and/or economic aid, were now totally occupied coping with the Great Depression.

Like the murder of the Old Marshal, the conquest of Manchuria was masterminded by lesser Japanese military officers, none with a rank above colonel. To do this, they had to invent reasons for invading their neighbors.

---

* Although most of today's scholars believe that the Tanaka Memorial was a forgery, Crozier points out that the question is irrelevant since the Japanese ended up trying to do exactly what the memorial proposed.

† The following comment about the flood in the *North-China Herald* must have been inserted by a clever critic of Chiang Kai-shek: "It is related that the first Ming emperor, who founded his capital at Nanking, placed all his friends in high offices and thereby aroused the indignation of the gods. The consequence was that the gods placed a terrible curse on the Kompo [flood] district, vowing that it should be forever an area of famine and drought. The curse has been broken with grim reality." ("Notes and Comments: The Yangchow Floods," *The North-China Herald*, September 1, 1931.)

Pointing to an explosion on the South Manchurian Railway, they said that Manchuria was in a state of lawlessness, and when the Chinese arrested and executed four Japanese spies caught in an off-limits area of Manchuria, they claimed malfeasance. These were only excuses, as the plans for the Japanese invasion had been in the works for some time. But the conspiring officers had not dared inform Tokyo of their intentions. Once the government leaders heard what was happening, they tried to stop it but were unable to do so. Or, as Australian journalist William Henry Donald put it, "The military party of Japan found it vitally necessary to reassert their dominance . . . and they had to seek an outside adventure in order to secure the backing of the nation as against the non-military party then in power."

Donald (he was always known by his last name), a former reporter for the *Sydney Daily Telegraph,* the *New York Herald,* and the *China Mail,* was described by W. H. Auden as a "red-faced, serious man, with an Australian accent and a large, sensible nose," while Mrs. Theodore Roosevelt called him "as influential a white man in Chinese affairs as there is in China or elsewhere." Donald spoke no Chinese but adored China and its people. He had served as an adviser to Sun Yat-sen, for whom he had composed the manifesto proclaiming the new republic in 1911, and those who knew him found him smart and completely trustworthy. An "adamant nondrinker," he hated Chinese cuisine and, on being invited to a presidential banquet, took along a loaf of bread to eat. In response to a request by the Chiangs, he had established a Bureau of Economic Information that provided foreigners with statistics, books, and a journal (the *Chinese Economic Monthly*) about China. After several years and four attempts to resign, Donald, who was disgusted with the leaders of the Nationalist government—he dubbed them "Nationalusts"—had moved to Mukden, the capital of Manchuria, as chief adviser to Young Marshal Chang.

The Japanese attacked Mukden on September 18, 1931. Crozier dates the most significant of Chiang Kai-shek's mistakes to September 11, one week earlier, when Chiang told the Young Marshal, whose vast territories were on the line, to avoid direct confrontation with Japan. It was at this point that Chiang revealed his military priorities: to subdue interior rebellions first and engage outside forces only after the country was united. According to the Young Marshal, neither he nor Chiang had a choice. "There was no way we could win," he said many years later. ". . . The quality of the Chinese army could not compare with the Japanese. . . . 'Non-resistance' . . . was the only feasible policy.' " Payne agreed: "To declare war against the Japanese at this time was to invite a general massacre. China was in no position to make any effective resistance."

Instead of fighting the Japanese, Chiang appealed to the League of Nations. "Little did he realize," quipped his most admiring biographer, Hollington Tong, "that the League of Nations was about as good as Westminster Abbey—merely a resting-place for great statesmen." The League did select a commission of inquiry, but it did not arrive in China until the spring of 1932, some six months after the invasion. Headed by Lord Lytton, the members of the group were enthusiastically welcomed when they arrived in Shanghai. "Everyone, peasants, coolies, shopkeepers, even the autocratic northern military commanders, shared an almost mystical faith in the power of the League of Nations," observed the wife of the minister of foreign affairs. "They were firmly convinced that . . . the Japanese would be swiftly ejected." After two weeks in Shanghai, the commission, accompanied by Fox Movietone News, proceeded to Nanking and two weeks later arrived in Peiping, "smothered in flags" in its honor. Even the schools in the former capital had been closed so that the children could be "trotted out in squads . . . given flags and told to wave them energetically."

The commission eventually reached Manchuria, where it was dogged by Japanese spies, who trailed after the delegates and parked themselves in the lobbies of their hotels. One day, the wife of the secretary-general of the group returned unexpectedly to her hotel bedroom, where she found a man, clearly a Japanese spy, going through her bureau drawers. She asked him what he was doing.

"I'm just tidying up your room, Madame!"

"Oh, in that case you might as well clean up the whole room, the floor hasn't been scrubbed in ages!" she replied, settling down into a comfortable chair to watch the man get down on his knees and refusing to let him go until he had scoured the entire floor.

The Lytton Commission eventually issued a report condemning Japan in favor of China. Adopted by the League of Nations in February 1933, it evoked a self-righteous response from the Japanese, who resigned from the League. This did not help China or its leader, who did not seem to grasp the fact that he was being presented with an excellent opportunity to unite the country against a common enemy—a political ploy recommended at the time by at least one newspaper and used by countless politicians and statesmen since the beginnings of history. Instead, Chiang allowed inflamed anti-Japanese sentiments to fester and erupt, while he continued to fight the Communists and issue useless appeals to rebellious elements of the KMT.

The nation's student population, "almost insane with anger and frustration," expressed the country's outrage. Seventy thousand schoolboys descended on Nanking to demand that Chiang declare war on Japan, and by the end of November 1931, two months after the invasion, 12,000 students were camped in front of government buildings in the capital, demanding to see him. Chiang let them wait in the winter cold for twenty-four hours before telling them in his furious falsetto that their demands were unreasonable and they should go home. When still more students arrived from Hankow—tougher and better organized than the first group—Chiang told them that they were tools of the enemies of the government. Then a third group, this one from Peiping, arrived and attacked both the Ministry of Foreign Affairs and the headquarters of the KMT, while other students destroyed the printing plant and offices of the *Central Daily News*. At that point, Chiang Kai-shek called on the local garrison of soldiers, which drove the students out of Nanking. He then did what he often did at moments of political crisis: he resigned. This time, however, it was under pressure.

Chiang and May-ling flew to his old home in Chikow. It is said that Chiang seemed to welcome the escape from responsibility; he probably also enjoyed showing the beauties of his native province to his new wife, something he had done with Jennie some years earlier. Their country idyll did not last long, and on January 2, an emergency meeting, held in Nanking, resulted in a request to Chiang to return as head of the government. In spite of (or perhaps because of) anxious telegrams from members of the government, Chiang took his time returning to the capital. As *Time* magazine put it, "With a smile that was childlike and bland Chiang Kai-shek arrived in Nanking last week. A thousand chastened members of the Kuomintang party assembled to welcome him. Only six weeks ago these same men forced him to resign . . . and his opponents shouted to the winds that they were heartily glad to be rid of him."

Wang Ching-wei met Chiang near his old village home and traveled with him to the capital, where Wang assumed the presidency of the Executive Yuan. But by the time the government had put itself together again and returned to operational status, Japan had started moving men and arms into the Japanese section of the International Settlement in Shanghai. Japan was determined to compel China to rescind a boycott of Japanese goods, effected during the last two months of 1931, that had reduced their imports by five sixths. Shanghai was the center of the boycott movement, and, as the Japanese press had announced at the beginning of the year, "The coming war will be a struggle for the domination of the world; the conflict in Manchuria was merely the curtain raiser."

In the middle of January, five Buddhist monks from Japan were attacked by a group of Chinese as they were leaving the International Settlement in Shanghai, and one was killed. As a result, a group of Japanese residents rioted, leaving one Chinese policeman and one Japanese dead. According to Chiang's most recent biographer, Jonathan Fenby, the incident was planned by the Japanese; the Japanese military attaché in Shanghai had hired the

Chinese (a group of thugs) and paid them $20,000* to attack the monks. Nevertheless, the Japanese government demanded apologies, reimbursement for all hospital bills, and the disbanding of all anti-Japanese groups. On the evening of January 24, the Japanese navy sailed into Shanghai, claiming that it was "extremely anxious about the situation in the Chapei [a district of Shanghai], where Japanese nationals resided in great numbers." Their Japanese consul general said that they would take action if the mayor of Shanghai did not respond to their demands by the morning of January 28. The following report, issued by the League of Nations, describes what happened on the night of January 27.

> Japanese marines and armed civilians . . . advanced along the North Szechuan Road . . . dropping parties at the entrance of alley ways as they went along, and at midnight, at a given signal, all those parties advanced . . . in the direction of the railway . . . Japanese were harassed by a Chinese armoured train which issued from the station. . . . It subsequently took refuge in the station, which was also strongly defended by Chinese troops. Thereupon the Japanese . . . bombed the station and destroyed the train with airplanes. Other buildings . . . were also set on fire by incendiary bombs. . . . The Mayor of Greater Shanghai . . . lodged a protest against the Japanese action with the Consular authorities. The Japanese authorities contended that their action was not connected with the demands they had made and which had been accepted, but was based on the necessity of protecting the Japanese population living in a part of the area they decided to occupy.

In other words, some 70,000 Japanese soldiers had landed at Shanghai, attacked the Chinese garrison there, and destroyed Chapei, the area they claimed they were worried about protecting. In so doing, they bombed an encampment of 8,000 Chinese refugees established by the International Flood Relief Commission. Edgar Snow, who was in Shanghai at the time, was appalled by the destruction:

> It was dark midnight, January 28, 1932. Suddenly Japanese rifle and machine-run fire laced Jukong Road up which I hurried from the Shanghai North Station. . . . The street emptied like a drain; iron shutters closed as if clams lived inside, and the last light disappeared. . . . Outrage piled on outrage: cases of banditry, kidnapping, homicide and brutality. Obviously certain Chinese had been marked

---

* $20,000 Chinese = $6,800 U.S. in 1932 ($107,180 today).

well in advance; these were leading merchants or businessmen who had declined to trade with Japanese. Some were abducted, not to be heard of again; their families were attacked and wiped out completely. I saw a helpless old Chinese woman dragged from her home and kicked in the face.

During the battle, more than 600,000 people were forced to abandon their homes, and an estimated nine hundred factories and shops were closed or destroyed. Three divisions of the Chinese Nineteenth Route Army fought furiously but, lacking supplies and reinforcements,* were finally forced to retreat. Nevertheless, their three commanders became heroes, compared by the Chinese to George Washington and Lord Nelson, and one of them (T'sai T'ing-k'ai) was immortalized as a brand name for cigarettes. In spite of the fact that $40 million was contributed to the war effort by local and overseas Chinese, China was defeated within a month and on May 5, signed an agreement with Japan, establishing a demilitarized zone around the International Settlement and ending the boycott of Japanese goods. Feelings were running so high that the unfortunate man who had to sign the agreement was beaten up by a mob of students.

In February 1932, the Japanese announced the occupation of the three eastern provinces of Manchuria. Putting them together with the province of Jehol, overrun the following year, they created a new country they called Manchukuo, naming Pu-yi, the last emperor of the Ch'ing dynasty, now in his late twenties, as regent. (Two years later, they made him their puppet emperor.) The governor of Jehol, a onetime bandit named Tang Yu-lin, had refused to fight. He commanded a tenth-rate army of 20,000, stole artifacts from the days of the Manchus, and had an opium factory on the grounds of his palace. When Donald and the Young Marshal arrived in the capital of Jehol, they discovered that Tang had loaded several hundred trucks with his personal belongings and dispatched them to safety. Moreover, the only soldiers they could find were guarding his opium factory.

✦

IN THE SPRING of 1933, the month after the creation of Manchukuo, Chiang, who needed someone to blame for China's failure to retain Jehol, met Young

---

* Chiang Kai-shek's detractors say that he could have sent in the necessary reinforcements but sent only 15,000 poorly trained soldiers, who were of little use. A more sympathetic theory suggests that Chiang was trying to withstand the Japanese without actually declaring war, which would have led to massive invasions of the country. (See Sterling Seagrave, *The Soong Dynasty*, pp. 306–7.)

Marshal Chang in a town south of Peiping and told him that he had to sacrifice himself by taking responsibility for the loss. After several long conferences with Donald, Chang handed over his army, planes, and war material
to Chiang, directing his soldiers to "obey Generalissimo Chiang's orders and
support the government unanimously." In doing this, Donald told his biographer, the Young Marshal "spoke with a patriotism that was rare" in the
world of warlords. The reasons he gave for his resignation—among them
the failure to inspire confidence in his troops and direct the campaign
properly—sound as if they were dictated by Chiang Kai-shek himself. But
the Young Marshal got no thanks for his selflessness from Chiang. When he
tried to arrange a press conference in Shanghai, he arrived to find that many
journalists had boycotted it, since they had to be frisked before entering, and
someone had posted a sign on the door saying "Do you remember that you
have lost Manchuria? And now, through you, Jehol is lost to China." De-
prived of the chance to explain his sacrifice, the Young Marshal did what
most warlords did when they were in trouble. He left China to travel abroad,
and Donald went with him.*

Two months later, Japan forced China to sign the Tangku Agreement,
which took its name from the "ramshackle village" of Tangku, said to be
"one of the most unattractive seaports of China." This odd choice of venue
and a superfluity of armed Chinese soldiers were, according to Hallett Abend
of *The New York Times*, "inspired by the terror of the Chinese delegates, who
fear assassination by their enraged countrymen." The terms of the treaty—so
humbling that it was kept secret from the Chinese people—included the
establishment of a boundary line just ten miles north of Peiping, beyond
which no Chinese troops were allowed to be garrisoned; the use of Japanese
planes to inspect the enforced retreat of the Chinese troops; and the establishment of a no-combat zone south of the line. Abend described what he
called "one of the most humilating spectacles I ever witnessed"—the signing
of the Tangku Agreement:

> It was a day of muggy, oppressive heat. On a siding at the Tangku
> station stood a long train. . . . At each end of the train were two ar-
> mored cars, and between them a long string of Wagons-Lits com-
> partment coaches. . . . Presently from the curtained coaches there

---

* Before they left the country, Chang and his two wives were put into rehab in Shanghai
by a doctor friend of Donald, emerging sometime later free of their dependence on
opium. According to the head of his bodyguard, Chang's secretaries, servants, and two
attendant doctors had been keeping him on the drug, deriving a tidy profit from his ad-
diction. It is not surprising that they "disappeared" the day after he entered the clinic.

descended nearly a score of high Chinese officials. No automobiles or carriages had been provided. They had to walk down the narrow, dusty . . . street which had no sidewalks. At the gate of the Japanese Consulate they were brusquely challenged by the Japanese sentries, and were then kept standing in the broiling sun for nearly ten minutes. At last they were admitted, and were received by a group of Japanese officials, all of whom had been selected with studious care from ranks below those of the Chinese delegates. A paper was produced and signed. . . . Then the Japanese served champagne. . . . And then the Chinese, having virtually signed North China over to the Japanese, trudged through the dust back to their special train.

Keeping the terms of the agreement from the people was not easy, and the Chinese government punished newspapers that mentioned it and students who spoke out against it. But Chiang himself was still obsessed with the Communists and the KMT rebels. "Internal security," he insisted as the Chinese were forced to withdraw behind the Great Wall, "must precede foreign aggression."

🌱

JUDGING FROM CHIANG's telegrams to her, May-ling was ill throughout the late winter of 1932 and spring of 1933. "What is the result of your exam?" he wired on January 8. And two months later: "It has been one month since you had your operation.* Do you feel well? Has the incision healed?" While she was laid up, May-ling must have heard a great deal of political gossip, because the next day her husband wired again: "Shanghai is full of important information as well as rumors. If you stay there too long after your illness is cured, you will hear many unfortunate things. If you can move now, why don't you leave the hospital as soon as possible and come north to help me?"

We do not know when or even if May-ling managed to get to Shanghai. What we do know is that the Chiangs were together to celebrate their sixth anniversary on December 1, 1933, and spent Christmas Day of that year traveling from his old home in Chekiang south to Fukien. It was a long trip—more than three hundred miles—two hours by plane and eight hours in a heavily armored car, described by May-ling as "very powerful but so weighty that the brakes were not much use." They traveled on a road that had just been cut through the mountains: "we were on such a high and nar-

---

* The author was unable to discover what this particular operation was supposed to cure.

row strip of plateau that the least swerve would have sent us dashing like atoms over the precipice. . . . Curiously enough, it was not until I had time to retrospect [*sic*] that I began to realize how dangerous the trip had been, especially when my husband began to reproach himself for submitting me to such hazards."

On New Year's Eve the couple took a walk in the mountains of Fukien, where they found a tree of white plum blossoms in full flower—a good omen, since the five petals of the winter plum stand for joy, good luck, longevity, prosperity, and peace. "He carefully plucked a few branches," Mayling wrote in a letter to one of her professors at Wellesley, "and when we returned home and lit the evening candles, he presented them to me in a little bamboo basket. A real New Year gift! I think from this perhaps you will understand why I am so willing to share life with him. He has the courage of a soldier and the sensitiveness of a poet!"

21

❦

The Kuomintang had become a symbol of pessimism, stagnation and repression.
                                                            —EDGAR SNOW, 1935

LIKE THE late-nineteenth-century Emperor Guangxu,* who encapsulated his proposed reforms in the slogan "Self-strengthening," Chinese leaders often wrap their political and economic drives in neat bundles with soul-stirring titles. Thus, in February of 1934, Chiang Kai-shek delivered a major speech in which he introduced a campaign to solve China's current problems, called the New Life Movement. Based on an unlikely mélange of Confucianism and Methodism, the New Life Movement dictated four basic principles that Chiang commanded the Chinese to follow: *li, yi, lien,* and *ch'ih* (propriety, loyalty, integrity, and honor). "Cultivate these high qualities in your daily living," he ordered. "Show your indomitable courage, and carry on the task for which your comrades in the trenches are fighting and dying." The reasoning behind these four concepts, augmented by ninety-five rules for daily behavior, was explained in an essay on the New Life Movement, said to have been composed by Chiang and translated by May-ling. The explanation, however, sounds far more Western than Chinese:

> The struggle of China to emerge from the Revolution . . . has been hampered by the unpreparedness of the people for the responsibilities of public life. . . . For hundreds of years the people of China were discouraged from interesting themselves in the affairs of government and were taught, even with the executioner's sword, that the administration of the country was the exclusive concern of the official class. The people consequently . . . ceased to have any interest in government . . . confining themselves to seeking the welfare of the family and the clan, and knowing nothing, and caring nothing, about the responsibilities of citizenship. . . . In forced conditions such as these, the habits of the great population of China developed along lines quite contrary to those characterising the peoples of other countries, with the result that when the political window

---

* The nephew of the dowager empress, 1871–1908.

opened they were, in a sense, blinded by the light that suddenly and unexpectedly poured in upon them. They found themselves without understanding of political life, bewildered owing to lack of universal education. . . . The aim of the New Life Movement is, therefore, the social regeneration of China. . . . These four virtues [*li, yi, lien,* and *ch'ih*] were highly respected by the Chinese people in the past, and they are vitally necessary now, if the rejuvenation of the nation is to be effected.

Chiang said that the immediate inspiration for the New Life Movement came one day when he was driving through Nanchang and saw a schoolboy acting "in an unbecoming manner" on the street. Although he did not specify what the boy was doing, he said he realized that sloppy and unclean personal habits were having a bad effect on the people. A week after he announced the inception of the New Life Movement, a torchlight parade through the streets of Nanchang featured banners painted with edifying commandments such as "Don't spit";* "Avoid wine, women and gambling"; "Kill flies and rats"; and "Politeness and obedience smooth the way." In a speech held before a large crowd in 1934, Chiang scolded his people for spitting, smoking, and, above all, "hosing urine around the streets in public."

"If we are to have a new life that accords with Li-yi-lien-ch'ih," said Chiang, "then we must start by not spitting heedlessly." "If we are to restore the nation and gain revenge for our humiliations, then we need not talk about guns and cannon, but must first talk about washing our faces in cold water." There is something quaint in Chiang's apparent belief that heavy doses of cleanliness and courtesy would cure the complex political and economic ailments of China. If his theories sound like those of the eighteen-year-old provincial student who willed himself to stand at rigid attention for half an hour every morning and the "very exacting commander" who railed at cadets for unbuttoned tunics, the similarities are not coincidental.

The New Life Movement was, in fact, a *folie à deux*—a naive program conceived by husband and wife to fight the centuries of poverty-enforced squalor and insularity of the Chinese masses in order to bring them up to twentieth-century standards of personal hygiene and civic duty. What was dangerous about the movement, however, was less its naiveté than its close connection to fascism. "In fascism the organization, the spirit, and the

---

* Spitting was a time-honored custom in China, and not just among the working class. Spittoons were placed by the chairs of Chinese leaders at banquets and ceremonies, and Deng Xiaoping was famous for his aim. There was an attempt to stop this during the 2003 SARS epidemic, when citizens were fined if they were caught spitting in public.

activities must all be militarized," Chiang had said at one point, adding later, "What is the New Life Movement that I now propose? Stated simply, it is to thoroughly militarize the lives of the citizens of the entire nation." To do this, Chiang called on the Blue Shirts, who became the leaders of the movement and promoted its tenets. Military salutes and even goose-stepping were required. In adopting these outward manifestations of Western fascism, the New Life Movement was also declaring war on Western-style appearances and amusements.

"Priggery and hypocrisy, it seemed, were flavored unpleasantly with police bullying," observed one visitor from the West. "A specimen frock, showing the correct length of sleeve for a chaste woman, had been exhibited in Peking. A young English traveler had been reprimanded in the streets of Sian for smoking a pipe out of doors. Some people even had had their teeth compulsorily scrubbed. Mixed walking, it was rumored, was forbidden in the cities of the interior."

The rules became more and more absurd: "Holding that the permanent wave and curled hair not only do not add to the beauty of women but also are detrimental to their health," the *Peiping Chronicle* noted in January of 1935, "General Chiang Kai-shek has instructed his provisional headquarters at Nanchang to draft an order forbidding Chinese women throughout the country to wave or curl their hair. In addition the Generalissimo is considering the issue of an order to all service men in the country, forbidding them to marry women who do not dress their hair properly." And indeed, after due consideration, Chiang issued orders that "in the future no military men are permitted to wed girls with bobbed hair." Then there were the edicts on marriage ceremonies: "All wedding gifts and dowries of brides must be of Chinese native goods, the banquets given on the wedding day shall not exceed $4* for each table; wedding gifts shall not exceed the value of more than a dollar;† neither bands nor firecrackers shall be used at weddings and guests at wedding parties must leave the bridal couple alone before 12 o'clock midnight."

The reforms piled up. Coolies were told to carry out their jobs fully clothed or tie a towel around their shoulder so as not to show their upper bodies; those who could not afford a towel could be thrown in jail. It was strongly suggested that waiters in restaurants and hotels be required to wear uniforms, and anyone appearing on the street in civilian clothes or uniform must have "each and every button fastened." The Chinese were no longer

---

* $4.00 Chinese = $1.44 U.S. in 1935 ($22.50 today).

† $1.00 Chinese = $.38 U.S. in 1935 ($5.63 today).

allowed to dance—a throwback to Mme. Soong's strict Methodism—and
fanatics were known to burst into dance halls and theaters, where they
poured acid on the unfortunates dressed in Western-type clothes. Movies,
although permitted, were circumscribed as to content, and directors were
told that their films should be 70 percent education and only 30 percent
entertainment. Smoking, even by foreigners, was frowned on, and zealous
guards were known to stop people smoking cigarettes in the street. May-ling,
like many others, continued the habit in private. Lighting up one day under
a "No smoking" sign, she shocked an American journalist by saying that the
ban was only for the masses.

But movies and dancing were neither as seductive nor as habit-forming
as opium, and Chiang soon extended the New Life Movement into a campaign to rid China of its national vice, even though the drug was transported
with help from his army and police force, which were also involved in selling
it. Government officials were told to stop winking at the opium traffic and
given three years to break themselves of the habit. Institutions were opened
where opium addicts could go for a cure. Those who failed to do so were
told that they would be executed, as would manufacturers and sellers of the
drug, and, as was fairly typical of Chiang, he proved his point by having an
offending policeman in Peiping killed. The following year, he assumed the
title of inspector general for opium suppression—a blatant cover-up for his
own activities. It was his public stance, however, that was noted by the
"stunned" Anti-Opium Information Bureau at the League of Nations in Geneva. According to an official there, "China loomed large as the biggest
victim of her own opium and Japanese-imposed narcotics. . . . Everybody
knew that Japan was systematically poisoning China—as a matter of national policy and to prepare the ground for an all-out conquest." Like the
New Life Movement itself, however, the attempt to rid China of its opium
habit was not successful, and Chiang "added a revenue-yielding opium monopoly to his radical Suppression Plan."

It soon became clear that individual moral regeneration was not going
to be embraced by the inhabitants of a country that desperately needed
large-scale political reform. In spite of May-ling's statement that the New
Life Movement was "welcomed by our people as water is craved by the famishing," the Chinese were either too poor to pay attention or too rich to
want to change. To get around an ordinance that a group in a restaurant was
to order no more dishes than half the number of diners around the table,
restaurants began to use larger plates that could accommodate two dishes at
once. To fool the food inspectors, liquor and wine arrived at the table in
teapots.

It was not until the Second World War, when the New Life Movement developed offshoots such as the Wounded Soldiers League, that it began to make any significant contribution to the country. Meanwhile, as the American minister, Nelson T. Johnson,* noted, "It is doubtful whether the personalities interested in the movement are sufficiently pure themselves to give the movement much prestige."

✼

IT SEEMS PROBABLE that the New Life Movement was another attempt on the part of the Chiangs, conscious or unconscious, to develop an ethos with which to battle the Communist ideology that was steadily gaining adherents throughout the country. Ever since the uprisings at the end of the 1920s, Chiang had been trying to eliminate the Chinese Communist Party in what he called his "bandit suppression campaign." The choice of terminology was unfortunate. To quote a leading Chinese journalist:

> In the early 1930s, he [Chiang Kai-shek] equated the Communists with bandits, hoping to impress ordinary people that Mao Tse-tung and Chu-teh [general, later commander in chief of the Communist army] were mere criminals. He banned Communist propaganda and literature, but it would have been better if he had let them circulate openly so that the people could see for themselves that the Communists meant to overthrow the whole society and were far more dangerous than ordinary bandits. The Chinese people have been the victims of banditry for many generations. They tended to underestimate the menace of the Communists because they knew that bandits can always be bought or vanquished. Fighting bandits has never been taken very seriously by Chinese soldiers. When they were told to fight Communist bandits, they were psychologically unprepared to face a far tougher job.

Although Chiang's soldiers had managed to chase the Communists out of Hupei, Honan, and Anhwei, they were not successful in the southeastern province of Kiangsi, where Mao had taken refuge with his troops. A few months before his venture into moral reformation, Chiang had also embarked on what he hoped would be the final campaign of the national government to exterminate the Chinese Communist Party. This was to be the fifth in a series of attempts, each more ambitious than its predecessor. The first of these so-called extermination campaigns had taken place in late 1930 and employed 100,000 soldiers; the second, launched in May 1931, required

---

* His rank was raised to ambassador in 1935.

twice as many men; the third, begun immediately after the second, put 300,000 soldiers into the battle; and the fourth, which took place in April 1933 after almost a two-year hiatus, lasted six months and required the services of 250,000 men. None had succeeded. In each case, the Communists had managed to kill off whole divisions of the KMT, refurbish their armament supplies, entice or compel members of the enemy to join them, and increase their territory.

In one memorable instance of generosity, noted by the normally anti-Chiang journalist Edgar Snow, Chiang Kai-shek actually released one of the Communist commanders. The young man, Chen Ken, had saved Chiang's life in the early days in Canton, when he served as his aide. Chen, who later joined the Communists, was captured in 1933 by Chiang, who offered him a division of the Nationalist army to command; when Chen refused, the generalissimo put him in prison, hoping that he would change his mind. When he realized that this would never happen, Chiang freed Chen to return to the Red Army.

For the fifth extermination campaign, begun during October of 1933, Chiang called up more than 900,000 soldiers, 400,000 of whom he sent into battle immediately, armed with heavy artillery and protected by 400 planes. Mao and his cohorts, who numbered about 180,000 soldiers plus 200,000 partisans and Red Guards, possessed fewer than 100,000 rifles. The plan of attack had been largely developed by Hans von Seeckt, the German general known for successfully preserving the core and spirit of the German army despite the heavy restrictions imposed on Germany after World War I.* Seeckt's plan called for Chiang to blockade the Communists and cut off both their access to supplies and their means of escape. To do this, hundreds of miles of new military roads, dotted with thousands of small fortifications, were built in a giant circle around Mao and his followers—a "Great Wall," as Snow described it, ". . . which gradually moved inward." Using tanks and armored cars, protected by heavy bombardment from land and air, Chiang's forces advanced around the Communist camp. Moving toward the center, the Nationalists continued to build new forts, and "the concrete vice was gradually tightened." Described by the commander of the Communist army as "the tactics of drying the pond and then getting the fish," it was extremely successful.

Seeckt met May-ling when he was working with her husband, and, whatever the prejudices that often afflicted those with a "von" before their names, he was impressed, calling her Chiang's "best collaborator" and referring to her as the Marschallin (feminine for Marschal). "The most striking thing

---

* The Treaty of Versailles limited the German army to 100,000 men and did not allow it to employ a general staff.

is her complete confidence of social form, through which she becomes a lady," he wrote in his diary. "I have met very few women of such complete tactfulness. She is completely aware of her and/or her husband's position, but that does not lead her to the least superiority or arrogance. Her household . . . is run extraordinarily well but simply. She dresses in attractive Chinese style with subtle taste. Little jewelry, but the individual pieces [are] suitable and valuable. She is very interested in politics, but politics to them means military affairs. She is surprisingly well informed and despite my dislike for women who talk about politics and military matters I rapidly abandoned my original reservation." Seeckt concluded his notes on May-ling with the following self-relevatory observation: "Being a lady is more important than race. That is nothing new for me, but the recognition is so timeless that it can be from Confucius."

The fifth extermination campaign started in the fall of 1933 and lasted nearly a year. In early October of 1934, Mao, Chou En-lai, General Chu, and other CCP leaders decided that in order to save themselves and their cause, they had to abandon their stronghold in Kiangsi. "Go north where our comrades have already carved out a base against the Japanese," Chou counseled, arguing against "one last-ditch battle," which, he said, would only permit Chiang's soldiers to complete their siege and require the Communists to regroup their men. According to one of Chou's biographers, this was "the first time" that Chou found himself . . . in agreement with Mao," and it "marked the beginning of the Chou-Mao collaboration." Two weeks later, the Communists started out on their famous 6,000-mile, 368-day Long March, leaving behind thousands of Red soldiers to fight a rearguard action and enable the majority to get away. Around 90,000 men and 35 women plus pack animals loaded with machinery parts, rifles, and ammunition headed out under cover of darkness, first to the south and west, then north. And if they noticed a plane dipping down every so often to ascertain their position and their miseries, it was Chiang Kai-shek, who had told his pilot to follow, so he could watch his enemy in defeat.*

According to one survivor,

> we ourselves did not know, at the beginning, that we were actually on the Long March, and that it was going to be such a big thing. All

---

* In their recent biography of Mao, Jung Chang and Jon Halliday contend that Chiang Kai-shek deliberately allowed the Chinese Communists to escape. They may be right—this author has not seen the relevant archives—but from everything we know about Chiang and his extermination campaigns, it is highly unlikely that he would not have disposed of the CCP if he could have done so. Chang and Halliday also claim that Mao did not walk like the others but was carried on a litter while he read.

we knew is that we were getting out of the bases; we were surrounded and being choked, a million men against us, tanks, aeroplanes . . . defeat after defeat. . . . In that September of 1934 when we began to get away we broke through one cordon of encirclement, then a second, then a third, and we marched through the late autumn and early winter, westward, always westward, with the rain soaking us to the skin, and the wind in our faces, and we headed towards Szechuan province. . . . But we had so much equipment with us; trains of stores, and even bedding and furniture, all sorts of things; and this slowed us down. We were . . . very visible, a long slow caravan. Every day we were attacked, front and back and both sides by Kuomintang armies and by local warlords' armies; we fought them and defeated them, and went on, but every time many of us died, and then we got to Tsunyi* and it was January of 1935 . . . by that time most of us wanted Mao Tsetung to lead us. . . . The first thing that Comrade Mao made us do was to throw away all the useless things we carried with us; all of them we threw away and travelled light and swift and clean. Thus we survived the hard, long journey . . . and we were not disheartened. And we trusted Mao Tse-tung.

They traveled, according to Mao, "across the longest and deepest and most dangerous rivers of China, across some of its highest and most hazardous mountain passes, through the country of fierce aborigines, through the empty grassland, through cold and through intense heat, through wind and snow and rainstorm." In their immensely long and circuitous journey, they crossed twenty-four rivers, eighteen mountain ranges—five of which were permanently snowcapped—and twelve provinces before arriving in Yenan in the central province of Shensi, some 450 miles southwest of Peiping. The countryside was barren and rough and the roads were terrible, but Yenan was less accessible to Nationalist soldiers than their previous home.

They had walked for a full year, and by the time it was safe to stop, their numbers had dwindled to about 20,000 men plus wives, children, and dependents. Chou En-lai, who had become seriously ill during the trip, arrived on a stretcher. These survivors joined 10,000 fellow Communist guerrillas already established in the area. It was, as history has noted, a heroic trek. And if the Long March has lost some of its luster since 1935, it is not because of the lack of courage of its participants but rather the excessive burden of propaganda with which it has been weighed down in the intervening

---

* In southwest China on the road to Szechuan.

years. Although the Communists were forced out of Kiangsi to escape destruction by Chiang's army, the reason subsequently given for their flight is not that the CCP was running for its life but that it was going north in order to fight the Japanese.

❦

WHILE MAO AND his followers were on the Long March, Chiang and Mayling, accompanied by Young Marshal Chang and Donald, his adviser, were starting out on a very different kind of journey. After a year spent curing his opium addiction, the Young Marshal, accompanied by two wives, several children, and a suite of servants, bodyguards, and secretaries, traveled to Italy. When he first arrived there, he was impressed by the efficiency of Benito Mussolini's government, but by the time he got back to China, he seems to have changed his attitude: "Oh, it [Italy] was all right," he reported, "macaroni on every table, Mussolini on every wall."

From Rome, Chang and his retinue left on a motor tour of Europe. In Britain he met Prime Minister Ramsay MacDonald and rented a house in Brighton, where he hosted black-tie poker games that lasted all night and well into the next day. He rode horseback and played golf, although without opium he was becoming as round as his father. Throughout the trip, Donald coached his charge on European politics. It was already November and the party was in Copenhagen when Chang received a wire from his office: "REVOLT HAS BROKEN OUT IN FUKIEN STOP THERE IS A MOVEMENT UNDER WAY TO GET US TO JOIN FACTIONS AGAINST CHIANG KAI-SHEK STOP COME BACK AT ONCE."

Donald left immediately. He told the Young Marshal to stay in Europe and he would let him know what was going on. When Donald got to Nanking, he went to see T.V., who told him that he had resigned as minister of finance. The leader, according to his brother-in-law, understood nothing about money and insisted upon spending an excessive amount of the national budget on the military. It was obvious to Donald that Chiang Kai-shek was in trouble, that the anti-Chiang faction was gaining strength over the pro-Chiang, and that the person who held the balance of power was the Young Marshal. He called a press conference: "The return of the Young Marshal to China is desired by his officers," Donald announced. "But, in view of conditions now prevailing in this country, it is difficult to say when he will return. I have a strong feeling that he may go to Soviet Russia." His announcement had the desired effect, and by the next day, representatives of the KMT were waiting to speak to Donald about how important it was that the Young Marshal—previously sacrificed by Chiang Kai-shek to public opinion—rejoin the Nationalist government.

Young Marshal Chang arrived home in China on January 8, 1934. After picking up two hundred bodyguards, he and Donald went to Nanking, where they saw Chiang. According to Donald's biographer, "the meeting between the granite-faced, solemn Chiang and the ambitious, effervescent young man got off to a fiery start." It ended when the Young Marshal told Chiang that Europe "doesn't think much of either you or China," and Chiang suggested that since he and May-ling were on their way to Hangchow, perhaps the Young Marshal and Donald would like to join them there. During one famous dinner, Donald and Chang told the Chiangs what was wrong with China. Donald, who, it will be remembered, had quit working with the government in disgust, was known for his bluntness.

"You people sit in your yamens, and your horizon is your window sill," he said.

> You are ignorant because no one dares to correct you. You might lose face, and what's more, someone might lose his head. . . . This country is ridden with graft. It's full of swindlers who will steal anything from American Red Cross funds to a . . . rake-off on every government or private transaction . . . opium is flooding the country. It flows up and down the Yangtze right past your front door. Thousands die of it every month. Thousands, yes millions, die because there is no flood control . . . because China, a nation of farmers, is really a poor farmer. There is no protection against disease, and epidemics sweep like the wind across the land. Millions more die . . . because you cannot stop killing yourselves in civil war. Where are your schools? Where are your fine highways . . . the network of railways . . . the industries, the steel, the hydroelectric power . . . your [engineers] . . . your skilled administrators. . . . There is . . . the obeseness of wealth on one hand—the hog wallow of poverty on the other. The ricksha man and the wharf coolie are worse off than the horse and camel in many another land.

When Donald had finished, the Young Marshal continued, assailing Chiang for his apathy in the face of corruption and inefficiency in government. By the time the two men had finished voicing their criticisms, it was nearly midnight. Dinner had started at 7:00 P.M. As Donald escorted May-ling out of the room, she told him, "You were wonderful. We needed that." As they walked through the lobby of the restaurant, she asked, "Why don't you come to work for us? We need a brain like yours." When Donald answered that he did not work for women because they "can't take it," she disagreed. "If I couldn't I wouldn't have dared translate everything you said."

"That's right," added the Young Marshal. "She even put in your god-dams."

"I'm going to write you some letters." Donald laughed as he told May-ling, "If you can get the generalissimo to act on them, then some day I might be working with you."

Within several weeks, Donald had set up an office in Hankow, the Central China Economic Investigation Bureau. Free to investigate anything he pleased, he wrote a letter in which he railed at "rotten officialdom," which he characterized as "squeeze, corruption, militarism, overtaxation." The customs police needed strengthening, he said, since smuggled goods were being protected by the Japanese. Japanese coal, mined in "so-called Manchukuo," was cheaper than Chinese coal. "Every energy of the rulers of China," he said, "should be bent to the one object of manufacturing all those things that Japan exports to this country." In the same letter, he campaigned to wipe out the union bosses, who siphoned off 60 percent of a laborer's meager wages, and urged the Chinese to forget about face, since it kept people from ever telling the truth about a situation. "The whole civil service (if it can be called that) of China," he complained, "is crammed with dead wood, eating up small salaries amounting to millions, because face would not allow the sacking of the worthless."

Whenever and wherever they could, the Japanese were certainly waging an economic war. There was a special "smugglers' freight car" attached to Chinese trains for the use of Japanese and Koreans who wanted to evade Chinese customs duties. According to *Time* magazine, "One can buy Japanese goods openly in China today at prices less than the Chinese duty which should have been collected on them." While Chinese customs guards were no longer permitted to carry weapons, the "smugglers swagger about with pistols in their belts."

In October of 1934, Donald joined the Chiangs and the Young Marshal on what began as a three-day trip to open a new military academy in the province of Honan but was expanded on the spur of the moment to include a visit to Sian, farther west in the province of Shensi. The city of Sian dates back more than four thousand years. It was said to have been the center of civilization (not unlike China itself), and any progress made in the outer world had seeped out—above, under, or through its walls. These walls were the thickest of any in China; their gates resembled long tunnels; and a gate key was so large that it took two men to wield it. Christopher Isherwood, who visited Sian a few years later, said that in going through the city walls he felt that he was entering a huge prison. "And here, at the gate, were the gaolers, surly and unsmiling—typical soldiers of the sullen north-west."

The Chiangs had a different reaction to Sian, where they were met with "a tremendous ovation from both citizens and soldiers." They had planned to spend only a few hours in the city but ended up staying for three days, during which May-ling convinced the local women to establish a clinic to cure female opium addicts. From Sian the quartet flew to Lanchow in Kansu province, located on the swiftly flowing Yellow River and noted for its huge water wheels—some more than a hundred feet in diameter—placed near the banks to provide local irrigation. The four travelers—Chiang, May-ling, the Young Marshal, and Donald—walked the streets of the city, engaging the locals in conversation, learning their views on politics, and urging local missionaries to get behind the New Life Movement. Donald said he began to "sense a change" in Chiang. "His face was more relaxed and, if only infinitesimally, more animated. Hitherto, this far western territory had been something of a menace to him—the breeder of rebellions and mutinies. Now he found that he could walk about without fear, almost an idolized figure."

As their plane prepared to take off from Lanchow, May-ling and Donald talked Chiang into stopping in Ninghsia, a small province situated between the Gobi and Ordos deserts, populated by Muslims. This was the first time the inhabitants of Ninghsia had ever seen high government officials. Returning to Sian, the travelers headed out by train into provinces in the south and west. At this point, the Young Marshal left them to return north, while the three others flew to Peiping for medical checkups. From Peiping they flew to Kalgan, south of Mongolia proper, where they met the Mongolian Prince Teh, a lineal descendant of Genghis Khan. The inhabitants of Kalgan gathered in great crowds to see them, as did the residents of the neighboring provinces. Altogether, it was a five-thousand-mile odyssey—ten provinces in five weeks—that ended in the three southwestern provinces of Yunnan, Kweichow, and Szechuan. These areas, still run by warlords, were currently under attack by the Communists on their Long March from Kiangsi. In Szechuan, Chiang nearly ran into Mao.

At this point in the Long March, the bulk of Mao's forces, disguised in National Army uniforms, had managed to ferry their men across the Yangtze River into the province, subsequently destroying the boats captured from Chiang's army. Hoping that his army could stop the Communists at a deep gorge spanned by a famous iron-chain suspension bridge, Chiang and May-ling flew to Szechuan, where he organized the defenses and gave orders for a counterattack. When the Communists arrived at the bridge, they discovered that half of the floorboards had been removed and there was a machine-gun nest lying in wait for them at the northern end of the span. Volunteers started to cross anyway—barefoot, swinging from chain to chain toward the middle. Three were shot and fell into the swirling waters below. Finally one man made it to the center, where he succeeded in crawling up on the bridge floor and hurling a grenade into the machine-gun nest. He was followed by others, running full speed over the planks, which had been set on fire, until they all reached the other side. As a result, Chiang lost his last chance to cut off the Communists on the run.*

In spite of the Communists' escape, Chiang's ventures into the hinterlands did a great deal for his prestige. "He has flown to almost every province of China," May-ling wrote after their return. ". . . He has been enabled . . . to meet officials of remote regions in their own *yamen* . . . and give them assurances of Nanking's close interest in them and their worries. At the same time, he has been able to acquire a working knowledge of the topography and characteristics of the country such as no high official has ever been able to do before, and this . . . has provided him with unprecedented equipment for the performance of those duties which fall to his lot. . . . What the airplane has done for the Generalissimo in his official work is truly wonderful."

If the trip served to energize Chiang, it also added to the prestige of his wife. Even the crotchety U.S. minister (soon to be ambassador) Clarence E. Gauss wrote his predecessor, Nelson Johnson, saying he had heard that Madame Chiang had become "a tremendous factor" in China. "She sits alongside the Generalissimo and tells him what to do and he does it. She issues instructions and they are obeyed. Many reports are addressed to her; others are addressed to her and the Generalissimo. She has developed tremendous influence." Foreign visitors were also impressed—witness the report of Sven Hedin, a Swedish explorer who met May-ling on the trip: "She is intelligent, clever, gifted, and stands at the peak of Chinese as well as occidental culture. . . . No doubt Madame CKS is the most remarkable woman of our time. . . . Long after the thunder of war has been silenced she will remain a blessed mother among her people, and her name will be mentioned with reverence and admiration."

It was on this trip that Donald began to help Chiang's wife with the vast number of papers she now handled for her husband. According to his biographer, Donald would find Madame Chiang "in an unending blizzard of paper work. . . . She would look up, chewing the frayed end of a pencil, and he would laugh, scoop up an armful and go to work." When the trio returned to Nanking, Donald moved into a bungalow located just outside the

---

* I have included here the classic story of crossing the bridge, but it must be noted that Chang and Halliday claim that the legend of heroism was "a complete invention" and that there were "no Nationalist troops at the bridge when the Reds arrived." (Chang and Halliday, *Mao: The Unknown Story*, p. 159.)

east gate of their residence, where he occupied a chair at a large desk across from Madame. Seated before his typewriter while May-ling sat in front of hers, he was able to help her wade through the stacks of documents that came to the generalissimo. "Missimo," he had told her while they were still on their tour, "you think like a man."

22

THREATENED BY Communists, greedy warlords, and voracious Japanese, Chiang was also facing a personal problem involving his only son, Ching-kuo. Born in 1910, Chiang Ching-kuo had grown up in a quiet home atmosphere with his mother and grandmother, both of whom doted on him. An obedient child, small for his age, he was ten years old before his father, who must have realized that this was the only child he would ever sire, sent his old tutor to study the boy's potential. In his very first letter to his son, he wrote that the tutor had reported that he was "not brilliant but like[d] to study very much," an assessment that, Chiang said, he was "somewhat comforted in learning." He arranged for a teacher to instruct Ching-kuo in the classics and the Four Books before sending him to the Phoenix Mountain Academy. Chiang supplemented the boy's education with self-relevatory rules for proper behavior: "in talking and walking your manner must be serious"; "never conduct yourself with levity . . . don't be frivolous."

During the previous year Chiang's concubine, Yao Yi-cheng, had arrived at the family home with Chiang's adopted son, Wei-kuo. It will be remembered that Chiang had agreed to adopt the boy, since his real father already had a family. But, knowing Chiang's reputation with women, many people still maintained that Chiang Wei-kuo was Chiang's biological son. In any case, Yao, who had apparently had what was euphemistically referred to as "good emotional relations" with both Chiang and his friend, moved into the Chiang family home with her child. Chiang's first wife, Fu-mei, resented Mama Yao and put her and her son in a room in back of the house normally used for wood and hay. The place was full of fleas, which tormented Wei-kuo—so much so that an uncle eventually moved Yao and Wei-kuo to his own house.

It was during the lengthy Confucian rituals surrounding the death of Chiang Kai-shek's mother in 1921 that Chiang had paid more attention to his sons, noting that "Ching-kuo is teachable and Wei-kuo is lovable." At the end of that same year, Chiang had married Jennie and brought Ching-kuo to Shanghai to continue his studies. Always nervous in the presence of his father, Ching-kuo was not a good-looking boy but an extremely courteous one. He was required to write a letter to his father every Sunday, reporting on his studies and the books he had read. When Chiang did not have time to answer the letters, he simply sent along more reading assignments, recommending that his son read each of the classical works "more than one hundred times." Concerned with his own inelegant brushwork, Chiang berated Ching-kuo: "Your calligraphy has not yet improved. You should copy one to two hundred characters every other day." He also insisted on Ching-kuo's studying English, remarking from experience that "those who don't speak English are like being mute."

In 1925, the year of the great wave of Communist demonstrations around the city, Ching-kuo entered high school in Shanghai. Having decided that the Communists were the only people who could help him eliminate the Hakka General, Chiang was then known in the West as "the Red General," and Ching-kuo was selected by his fellow students to lead them in four "mass uprisings." When Sun Yat-sen University in Moscow asked China's revolutionary government to send it some Chinese students, Chiang included Ching-kuo in the group.* Chiang Kai-shek was Stalin's current darling. Whenever Ching-kuo went to the movies in Moscow, he saw newsreels of his father, and when he read Russian newspapers, they were full of admiration for Chiang. According to Ching-kuo's biographer Jay Taylor, "Every Chinese student at Sun Yat-sen University knew that the youngest one among them was the son of the famous General Chiang." An ardent revolutionary, Ching-kuo wrote an article that so impressed the university staff when it appeared on the university bulletin board ("the Red Wall") that they made the fifteen-year-old editor of "the Wall."

Two years later, when Chiang turned on the Communists, Ching-kuo denounced his father from the stage of Sun Yat-sen University. "Chiang Kai-shek," he told his fellow students, "was my father and a revolutionary friend. He has now become my enemy. . . . Down with Chiang Kai-shek. Down with the traitor!" Ordered home along with the other Chinese students in Moscow, Ching-kuo sent a message, dictated by the head of the Chinese Communist Party delegation in Moscow, in which he refused to obey. He began an affair with the Christian General Feng's daughter, considered one of the prettiest girls in the school. Short, broad-featured, and muscular with a husky voice, Ching-kuo was a natural leader, and the Feng girl wrote him letters in which she expressed love and wonder that he could care for her. According to Taylor, Chiang's son had started on "a long and varied roman-

---

* Taylor says that attending the school was his own, not his father's, idea.

tic career," pursuing women who were his peers rather than the singsong girls who had attracted his father.

Selected as one of the top five students to be trained in advanced studies at the Military and Political Institute in Leningrad, the top academy of the Red Army, Ching-kuo excelled in his work and graduated in 1930 with the highest grades in his class. His file described him as "very talented . . . the best student at the academy." Although he expressed a desire to return to China after graduation, he was sent as an apprentice to the Dynamo Electrical Plant in Moscow, a manual job in which he could "learn about the life of the proletariat." He attended engineering school at night and, by suggesting certain technical improvements at the plant, more than doubled his meager salary. But he made the mistake of criticizing Wang Ming, the Chinese Communist leader who had written his original letter of refusal to return to China, and the Comintern tried to send him to a mining plant in Siberia—a fate he avoided by pleading his poor health (he was a diabetic).

After the Japanese seized Manchuria, Ching-kuo was summoned to a meeting with Stalin, apparently to discuss the situation of China and Russia vis-à-vis Japan. Taylor assumes that Stalin asked Chiang's son whether he thought there was a possibility of their two countries forming a united front against Japan, because shortly thereafter, his aunt Ching-ling visited Chiang Kai-shek—clearly at Moscow's instigation—to propose exchanging the former head of the Chinese Communist Party, currently imprisoned in Shanghai, for Ching-kuo.

Moscow's timing was excellent. An entry in Chiang's diary for November 1931 noted, "I miss Ching-kuo very much. I am bad because I am not taking good care of him. I am sorry about that." Although May-ling urged her husband to accept the Russian proposition, he refused. "I have been unable to see my son since he went to Russia," he wrote in his diary. ". . . Alas! I am neither loyal to the nation and the Party nor filial to my mother or kind to my children. I feel ashamed. . . . I would rather let Ching-kuo be exiled or killed in Soviet Russia than exchange a criminal for him. God decides whether you will have an heir. . . . It is not worth it to sacrifice the interest of the country for the sake of my son." A month later, Chiang was obviously still struggling to come to terms with his decision. "A person will be remembered because he has moral integrity and achievements but not because he has an heir. Many of the heroes, martyrs and officials . . . in the history of China did not have children, but their spirit and achievements will always be remembered."

When Stalin was informed that Chiang would not exchange his son for the imprisoned head of the CCP, he retaliated by sending Ching-kuo to a collective farm on the outskirts of Moscow. The peasants on the farm started by mocking the young man who "knows how to enjoy his bread without knowing how to plow," but within ten days, Ching-kuo had proved that he too could till the soil. They then selected him as their representative to conduct negotiations for loans, taxes, and the purchase of farming tools, and within a few months Ching-kuo was named chairman of the collective. Ordered back to Moscow, he was told by Wang Ming that he must be separated from other Chinese exiles, and he was sent to work in a factory in the city of Sverdlovsk in the Urals, then for nine months to the Siberian Gulag. In the fall of 1934, he was summoned to the office of the chief of the Urals branch of the NKVD and told that the Chinese government had requested his return. The chief wanted him to write to the Ministry of Foreign Affairs in Moscow saying that he would not go. Ching-kuo refused. In the middle of December, Chiang Kai-shek made the following entry in his diary: "When I was told that Ching-kuo was reluctant to come back from Russia, I knew that was invented by our Russian enemy. I took that calmly. I thought that I had made progress because I dismissed this family problem with a smile."

In March of 1935 Ching-kuo married a good-looking eighteen-year-old blond from Belarus named Faina. A quiet girl with apparently no connections to the Communist Party, she gave birth at the end of the year to their first child, a boy weighing only 3½ lbs. Ching-kuo named him Ai-lian (Love of Virtue). During the first three months of the baby's life, the infant's parents took turns at night feeding him every hour with an eyedropper.

In 1936, Chiang again asked Ching-kuo to come home. This time, the refusal was accompanied by a devastating letter addressed to his mother. In the version of the letter printed in *Pravda* and subsequently in *Time* magazine, Ching-kuo called his father "the enemy of the whole people and therefore the implacable enemy of his son." Saying that he was "ashamed of such a father," he reminded his mother of what she had suffered when she was living with Chiang: "Don't you remember, Mother, how he dragged you by the hair from the second floor? Whom did you implore on your knees not to throw you out of the house? Who drove my grandmother to the grave by beatings and insults? Wasn't it he? That was all done by the man who now babbles of filial affection and family morals."

But according to Ching-kuo, he did not write this letter. It had been written by the same Wang Ming who had dictated the boy's response to his father several years before. Ching-kuo refused to sign the letter drafted by Wang, substituted one of his own, and complained to the head of the NKVD, who instructed Wang to destroy the first letter. But Wang ignored the orders, sending out his own version.

In November of 1936, Ching-kuo applied for membership in the Communist Party of the Soviet Union. According to Taylor, "the implication was clear—he [Ching-kuo] felt that he was likely to spend the rest of his life in the USSR." A few weeks after he submitted his application, however, China's new ambassador to the Soviet Union arrived in Moscow with the information, given him secretly by May-ling, that her husband "wished very much that his son, Ching-kuo, would return to China." One of the first things the ambassador did on arrival was inquire as to Ching-kuo's whereabouts. Although the deputy commissar for foreign affairs told him that it would be difficult to find out, he would do his best. Shortly after this, however, a bizarre event—one that hit the headlines of newspapers all over the world—made it possible for Ching-kuo to return home.

❦

FOR THE CHIANGS, 1936 had started out like most years. Kai-shek was in the field, while May-ling moved between Shanghai and Nanking. In April, she wired her husband that she would accompany Ching-ling, who had to go to the hospital for an appendectomy. Three days later, she reported that Ching-ling was fine after her operation except for a fever but that sister Ai-ling had been in bed for three weeks and that she herself, "tired because of my low blood pressure," was planning on a "good rest." In any case, she added, "don't worry about us." But May-ling must have written that she was ill again, because two weeks later, Chiang wired, "If you are still not recovered when I get to Nanking, I will change my plans and come to you later in Shanghai."

Summer brought more of the same:

Chiang to May-ling:	Have you recovered from your sickness? I miss you very much.
May-ling to Chiang:	I slept very well last night, so I'm in good spirits this morning. According to division commander [Doctor?] Fang, the inner measles have not cleared up. Considering my weakness, it would be wrong to "attack" them again, and we have decided to adopt a more "peaceful" method of curing them. When I become stronger, I will receive strict therapy.

Toward the end of October, five days before Chiang's fiftieth birthday,* May-ling sent another ill-health report: "The result of my examination is

---

* The Chinese believe that a baby is one year old when he or she is born.

that there is a canker on the mouth of my stomach. The doctor says I must take care of myself. . . . Brother H. H. Kung is suffering not only from heart disease, but from schistosome [parasites] in his liver. Yesterday he was running a fever." The news alarmed Chiang: "How are you feeling now? Did the doctor tell you how it can be cured? How about Brother Kung? Has his temperature gone down to normal? I care about you two very much." Two days later, however, May-ling wrote that "October 31 is your birthday. I plan to come to wherever you are to spend the whole day with you. Please send the plane to Shanghai right now. The doctor said that I could only be away for a very short period of time, so I will come back to Shanghai after your birthday to continue my therapy." In response to what he called this "touching telegram" Chiang sent his plane to pick her up. And on October 31, 1936, the month before his son applied to become a member of the Russian Communist Party, Chiang Kai-shek celebrated his fiftieth birthday.

He had chosen to spend the day at the army base in Loyang, where he and May-ling were joined for a celebratory lunch by the Young Marshal. May-ling personally served slices of birthday cake to the locals, their wives, and their children, and her husband gave a typical self-deprecating tribute to his mother in his birthday speech: "Now that the trees by her grave have grown tall and thick, I cannot but realize how little I have accomplished and how I have failed to live up to the hopes that she had placed in me." He also spoke about his New Life dreams for China: "We should not imitate the superficialities of the West," he said, "nor plagiarize the Doctrine of Might of the Imperialistic nations. . . . My hope lies in the revival of our old national traits." Along with his speech, there was an hourlong parade in honor of the occasion, for which May-ling wore a Western-style fur coat against the cold.

In other parts of China, the celebrations were noisier and more jubilant. A fund honoring Chiang's half-century mark had raised enough money to buy a hundred American airplanes, and in Nanking, some 200,000 citizens gathered at the airport to watch them fly over, dipping their wings before a huge likeness of Chiang. The salute was repeated three times, and each time the people in the enormous crowd bowed their heads.

May-ling returned to Shanghai after her husband's birthday. "My situation is getting better," she wired on November 29, "but it still aches when I lift my arms. Now we are using electrotherapeutics and I take medicine at noon and in the evening. I also have a slight fever. I will remember to take care of myself. Please don't worry too much about me. I heard that your legs are giving you trouble. I think you may have caught cold. I will send clothes and medicine. Please try the ointment." All of which elicited a return wire the next day in which her husband said he was "very worried," about her.

"I got your telegram this morning," May-ling wired back. "Thank you very much. I prayed for you at 6:00 A.M. this morning—for your progress, for the victory of the revolution, and for achieving the goal of national survival." Chiang replied with thanks, saying how grateful he was for the clothes and medications, inquiring about her health, and saying, as usual, that he missed her.

⚘

ALONG WITH HEALTH bulletins, November 1936 brought Chiang word of the defection of an entire regiment of the National Army to the Communists along with the destruction of one calvary and two infantry brigades, sent to fight the CCP. On December 7, he flew to Sian in order to force the Young Marshal to join his sixth extermination campaign, which had been planned for some time.

During the previous year, Stalin had suggested establishing a united front with China against Japan, but Chiang had not been interested, ordering Young Marshal Chang to attack Mao and the others who had survived the Long March and recently arrived in Yenan. Although he was not particularly optimistic about his prospects and still hated the Japanese for killing his father, the Young Marshal did as he was instructed and attacked the Communists. But when the Japanese seized more land around Peiping and student riots broke out, it began to occur to him that the time had come to join the Communists against Japan. Moreover, the CCP was attracting many of his soldiers, who defected—willingly or otherwise*—to their ranks. Faced with a dwindling army, Chang had met secretly with officials of the Chinese Communist Party in February 1936.

In his most recent encounter with the generalissimo, the Young Marshal had refused to attack the armies of the CCP because, as he explained to Donald, when he and his soldiers started out to fight the Chinese Communists, "he found that their Red propaganda among his troops was much more damaging than their bullets." It seems that when Chang's troops "got within yelling distance" of the soldiers of the CCP, their leaders would call out to ask why they were fighting their own countrymen instead of the Japanese. They also taunted the government soldiers with the corruption of their generals and officers: "Why do you Chinese fight us, who are Chinese, to help a lot of worthless officers make money to ride about in motor cars, to get concubines, to gamble and to live a life of luxury?" As Chang put it to Donald, "it was difficult to combat these arguments, for they were abso-

---

* According to Young Marshal Chang, the Communists were known for their ghastly methods of torture if the soldiers did not comply.

lutely right." According to Donald, the government had already spent more than $300 million to stamp out the Chinese Communists, "to say nothing of the loss of life and property"—all without success.

When Chiang arrived at Lintung, a famous hot-springs resort at the base of the mountains a few miles outside Sian, he called his commanders to a meeting to finalize plans for the sixth extermination campaign, letting it be known that if Young Marshal Chang did not attend or chose to disobey his orders, he would be relieved of his command. He also invited Chang and General Yang Hu-cheng to dinner. Yang was a "bull-necked, loudmouthed" warlord, who commanded an army of former bandits and thought of the province as his personal fiefdom. He had a reputation for stubborness, earned during an eight-month seige of Sian when he had refused to surrender "until every cow, every horse, every cat, and every dog" had been eaten. Commander of the Seventeenth Route Army, Yang refused to go to Chiang's dinner, and Young Marshal Chang seemed noticeably ill at ease during the meal. Since his recent refusal to do Chiang's bidding, the Young Marshal and Chiang had been on extremely cool terms, and during dinner they argued about a petition that Chang had passed on from some students asking for permission to have a parade. Chiang scolded the Young Marshal, saying that he was a double-dealer, representing both the government and the students. He then said that if the students proceeded with their plans, he would call out soldiers with machine guns to shoot them down. "How can you use machine guns on students instead of the Japanese?" Chang said he had wanted to blurt out, but had forcibly controlled himself. Only his face, which turned red at the effort to keep silent, betrayed his fury.

The idea of gunning down Chinese students instead of the invading Japanese was, according to the Young Marshal, the straw that finally broke his back, leading him to join Yang and order his soldiers to take extreme action in order to force Chiang to listen to reason.

23

❦

Chinese politics are remote, obscure, and picturesque only on occasion. The remoteness and obscurity are a convenient excuse for preoccupation with the picturesque.

—James M. Bertram

SOMETIME DURING the night after the argument between Chiang Kai-shek and Young Marshal Chang, the Blue Shirts who had accompanied Chiang to Sian were arrested, most of his personal staff was imprisoned, and fifty planes and their pilots were taken over by rebel soldiers.

At 5:30 the next morning, December 12, 1936, Chiang, who had just risen to do his ablutions, heard gunfire outside. "I sent one of my bodyguards to see what was the matter," he wrote,* "but as he did not come back to report I sent two others out and then heard guns firing again which then continued incessantly." A dozen or so truckloads of soldiers had surrounded the building where Chiang was staying. His personal bodyguards managed to hold the soldiers off just long enough for him to escape.†

Chiang and two of his men scaled a wall outside. It was, he said,

only about ten feet high and not difficult to get over. But just outside the wall there was a deep moat, the bottom of which was about thirty feet below the top of the wall. As it was still dark, I missed my footing and fell into the moat. I felt a bad pain and was unable to rise. About three minutes later I managed to stand up and walked with difficulty . . . [to] . . . a small temple, where some of my bodyguards were on duty. They helped me to climb the mountain. . . . After about half an hour we reached the mountain top. . . . Presently gun firing was heard on all sides. Bullets whizzed by quite close to my body. Some of the bodyguards were hit and dropped dead. I than realized that I was surrounded. . . . So I decided not to take

---

* The majority of the following quotes are taken from a book that was written after the incident, giving both Chiang Kai-shek and May-ling time and opportunity to edit their stories and present themselves in the best light.

† It is said that Chiang was dressed only in his nightshirt and was without his false teeth. The first is unlikely; the second is apparently true.

shelter, but to go back to my Headquarters. . . . I walked down the mountain as quickly as I could. Halfway down the mountain I fell into a cave which was overgrown with thorny shrubs. . . . Twice I struggled to my feet but fell down again. I was compelled to remain there. . . . As the day gradually dawned, I could see . . . that the Lishan Mountain was surrounded by a large number of troops. Then I heard the detonation of machine-guns and hand grenades near my Headquarters. I knew that my faithful bodyguards . . . continued their resistance. . . . It was about nine o'clock after which time no more firing could be heard.

By this time, most of Chiang's soldiers, hugely outnumbered, had been either killed or wounded.

The rebels sought for me. Twice they passed the cave in which I took cover, but failed to discover me. About twenty or thirty feet from my refuge I heard someone hotly arguing with the rebels. It was Chian Hsiao-chung's [Young Marshal Chang's] voice. The rebels made a more thorough search. I heard one of the mutinous soldiers about the cave saying, "Here is a man in civilian dress; probably he is the Generalissimo." Another soldier said: "Let us first fire a shot." Still another said: "Don't do that." I then raised my voice and said: "I am the Generalissimo. Don't be disrespectful. If you regard me as your prisoner, kill me, but don't subject me to indignities." The mutineers said: "We don't dare." They fired three shots into the air and shouted: "The Generalissimo is here!"

Chiang said that one of the Young Marshal's battalion commanders knelt before him "with tears in his eyes" and asked him to go down the mountain. When they got to Chiang's headquarters, the ground was littered with dead bodies. The battalion commander asked Chiang to get into a car that would take him to Sian, where the Young Marshal was waiting for him. Chiang admitted that he was very surprised to be driven to the headquarters of General Yang, whom he trusted. When the Young Marshal appeared a half hour later, he was "very respectful," but, according to Chiang, "I did not return his courtesies." When Chiang asked him if he had known in advance of the revolt, the Young Marshal answered "in the negative."

Chiang: If you have no previous knowledge of the affair,
               you should see that I return immediately to

Nanking or Loyang. Then it may not be difficult to settle this affair.

Chang: I did not know anything of the actual developments, but I wish to lay my views before Your Excellency, the Generalissimo.

Chiang: Do you still call me the Generalissimo? If you still recognize me as your superior, you should send me to Loyang; otherwise you are a rebel. Since I am in the hands of a rebel you had better shoot me dead. There is nothing else to say.

Chang: If Your Excellency accepts my suggestions, I shall obey your orders.

Chiang: Which are you, my subordinate or my enemy? If my subordinate, you should obey my orders. If you are my enemy you should kill me without delay. You should choose either of these two steps, but say nothing more for I will not listen to you.

When Chang tried to explain that he wanted to talk about policy, Chiang became even angrier, refusing to discuss such matters with anyone of lower rank. For Chiang, there was only right or wrong, loyalty to China or disloyalty to the leader. To quote Edgar Snow, "Chiang's concept of loyalty" was "the classical one of old China—not as a bond between equals, but as a somewhat feudal code between inferior and superior: son to father, subject to ruler, soldier to general, general to Heaven." When the Young Marshal asked him why he was so obstinate, he retorted:

What do you mean by "obstinate"? I am your superior, and you are a rebel. According to military discipline and the law of the land, you, as a rebel, deserve not only reprimand but also punishment. My head may be cut off, my body may be mutilated, but I must preserve the honour of the Chinese race, and must uphold law and order. I am now in the hands of you rebels. If I allow the honour of the 400,000,000 people whom I represent to be degraded by accepting any demands in order to save my own life, we should lose our national existence. . . . If you are a brave man, kill me; if not, confess your sins and let me go. . . . Why don't you kill me now?

After this, Chiang closed his eyes and refused to talk. Food was brought to his room, but he refused to eat. The next day, he ate nothing and again refused to speak to Young Marshal Chang, although the latter came to see him four times. When the governor of the province of Shensi, who had been detained along with Chiang, advised him "to be more lenient to Chang," he replied, "I used to have high hopes of Chang. On former occasions he treated me as if I were his father. I could speak harsh words to him without hurting his feelings. In ordinary circumstances Chang could say anything to me, but today I will listen to his words only when he does not present any demands or conditions to me. . . . He should awake from his dream of a Sino-Russian Alliance. . . . He should realize that if he commits such folly . . . [he] will lose the respect of the whole world."

Later, Chiang, mindful of his place in history, wrote in his diary, "The courageous life as taught by the late Dr. Sun should be followed by us all. Unless we do, this calamity will certainly overtake us. Jesus Christ was tempted by Satan and withstood him for forty days. He fought against evil influences more strongly than I do today. I am now, however, fighting . . . with ever-increasing moral strength. I must maintain the same spirit which led Jesus Christ to the Cross, and I must be ready to meet any death."

On the third day of Chiang's captivity, Young Marshal Chang came to see him again, "standing behind the door, with tears in his eyes," according to Chiang, "as if he regretted very much what he had done." Chiang still refused to engage in conversation with him. The Young Marshal came back later in the day and asked Chiang to move, explaining that the guards in his current residence were not his (Chang's) soldiers. He himself had only four hundred bodyguards inside the city and six thousand outside, and he could not take full responsibility for Chiang's safety under these conditions.

By now, Donald had arrived from Nanking and had given the Young Marshal a section of Chiang's diary that May-ling had told him to take along. When Chiang again refused to move, the Young Marshal told him that they had read his (Chiang's) diary and discovered that he had intended to fight the Japanese as soon as he was able to crush the Communists. "Your loyalty to the revolutionary cause and your determination to bear the responsibility for saving the country far exceed anything we could have imagined," the Young Marshal said. ". . . If I had known one-tenth of what is recorded in your diary, I would certainly not have done this rash act. . . . Now that I realize your qualities of leadership I feel it would be disloyal to the country if I did not do my best to protect you. . . . If you are unwilling to walk out yourself I will carry you out on my back." But when Young Marshal Chang said that he wanted to send him back to Nanking secretly, Chiang refused, saying that he would return to the capital "openly and in a dignified manner or not at all." According to Chiang, the Young Marshal left him reluctantly, again in tears. Earlier that day, Donald had spoken with the younger man. "I cursed him," Donald wrote an American correspondent; "went and saw the Generalissimo and ... cursed all and sundry for giving me so much trouble." Donald had brought Chiang a letter from May-ling saying that she too was coming to Sian. Only when Donald suggested that Chiang move closer to the home of the Young Marshal did he finally agree.

Later that day, Chiang asked the Young Marshal if he and his fellow rebels would send him back to Nanking, since he had now complied with the projected move. The Young Marshal said that they had laid out eight conditions for his release, including reorganization of the government, cessation of civil wars, pardon of political offenders, release of those arrested during the Shanghai crackdown, and freedom of political dissent. Chiang rejected them all, saying that he had decided to sacrifice his life rather than sign anything under duress. When the Young Marshal tried to argue, the older man said that he had not "learned the great principles of revolution.... If I should try to save my life today and forget the welfare of the nation ... my character as a military man will be destroyed, and the nation will be in a precarious position. This means that the nation will perish when I live. On the other hand, if I stand firm and would rather sacrifice my life than compromise my principles, I shall be able to maintain my integrity till death, and my spirit will live forever. Then multitudes of others will follow me, and bear the duties of office according to this spirit of sacrifice. Then, though I die, the nation will live." Chiang Kai-shek, as Donald wrote an American friend, "was quite content to be a martyr. In fact I think he was very disappointed when he did not succeed in that respect."

Donald was not wrong, and during the generalissimo's captivity he wrote a new will, asking May-ling to "regard my two sons as your own children." Then he addressed his sons: "Chiang-kuo and Wei-kuo, I was born for the revolution and I will die for revolution.... Soong May-ling is my only wife. If you regard me as your father, Madame Soong May-ling should be your only mother. When I die, you two must obey your mother."

The following evening, Young Marshal Chang explained to Chiang that General Yang had "long wanted to rebel, and that although he himself had been repeatedly instigated to participate, he hesitated to do so." That was until their last meeting, when Chiang berated him for supporting the Chinese students. It was at that point that Chang had decided to join forces with Yang.

"I was only twenty eight years old when I controlled one-third of China," Chang wrote some fifty years later.

I launched the Sian Incident without any thought for myself.... There was nothing I wanted because I already had both power and fortune. . . . Did I ask Mr. Chiang for money? Did I ask Mr. Chiang for territory? I did not. I sacrificed myself. Why did I sacrifice myself? The first reason is that the civil war had to be stopped. Both the CCP and we are Chinese. Why were we fighting the CCP? It was a political problem, which could have been resolved by negotiation. I stood for negotiation. I told Chiang that he could not exterminate the CCP. When he asked for the reason, I answered that the CCP had won the support of the people which we had lost. . . . He believed that we should stabilize the domestic situation before resisting foreign aggression, while I said that we should resist the foreign aggression first. There was no other conflict between us.

During the next four days of Chiang Kai-shek's captivity, there was a great deal of back-and-forthing about the possibility of releasing him. Meanwhile, he confided to his diary that he was suffering from pain "so acute that I can hardly sit up." On December 20, T.V. arrived to negotiate his release. "I gathered the impression that the Generalissimo's life was in the greatest danger," he later wrote, adding that one man had told him that "if war once broke out on a large scale the committee had decided to hand the Generalissimo to the communists for safe keeping. This was no empty threat."

Representing the Communist camp was Chou En-lai, Chiang's Kai-shek's old underling and associate from Whampoa, who was considered by all, friends and enemies, not only a military authority but a superb diplomat. "I met with Chou En-lai," the Young Marshal said, recalling those days many years later. "I admire Chou most of all among the men in contemporary Chinese history. I realized that he understood me completely when we met for the very first time. He admired me a lot . . . we felt like old friends at our first meeting." Chou apparently paid the Young Marshal the ultimate compliment, telling him, "We in the CCP can give up all these things [the bones of contention between the two sides] if you can be the leader. We hope that you can be the leader. We prefer you as the leader."

Meanwhile, T.V. saw Chiang alone: "He [Chiang] was much moved and wept bitterly. I comforted him and told him that instead of being humiliated the whole world was concerned and sympathise[d] with him." T.V. had brought a letter from May-ling. "Should T.V. fail to return to Nanking within three days," she wrote her husband, "I will come . . . to live and die with you." Chiang's eyes, he admitted, "got wet." Nevertheless, he asked T.V. not to allow her to come to Sian. The next day T.V. flew back to Nanking and returned with May-ling.

THE NEWS OF Chiang's capture had been given to his wife by her brother-in-law, H. H. Kung, currently serving as minister of finance and vice premier. "There has been a mutiny," Kung told her, "and there's no news of the Generalissimo." May-ling, who was in Shanghai consulting a doctor, immediately left for Nanking. Kung then approached his sister-in-law Ching-ling to ask for her signature on a document denouncing the Young Marshal. "What Chang Hsueh-liang [the Young Marshal] did was right," she retorted. "I would have done the same thing if I had been in his place. *Only I would have gone further!*" According to Edgar Snow, who interviewed Ching-ling some months later, Chang had met earlier with Ching-ling, who had urged him to take action, saying, "You must do something to wipe out your disgrace [the loss of Manchuria]."

With Chiang in captivity, Kung, who was in Shanghai at the time, was now acting head of the government. "I was the one who had to shoulder the responsibility. . . . I saw it was absolutely essential that I go to Nanking immediately . . . many of my colleagues were strong for military action. They wanted to bomb the whole city [Sian] . . . I could not help but feel that the solution of the problem was not to use military force, but that by personal appeal . . . things could be settled peacefully." In spite of Kung, the trigger-happy generals in the capital sent bombers and troops to Sian. Chiang agreed to ask the central government to postpone its assault for three days. "It was obvious," Donald said, "that a gang in Nanking wanted to take advantage of the situation to secure the reins of Government, thinking that the Generalissimo would never return to Nanking because, if he was not killed by the so-called rebels he would be killed as a result of bombardment which they had ordered." It was said that General Ho Chien, a KMT commander, and others wanted Wang Ching-wei to form a more pro-Japanese administration, and Chou En-lai told T.V., in the course of their negotiations, that "important functionaries at Nanking are giving banquets to take over control expecting that the Generalissimo would never return."

In spite of the fact that May-ling realized that she was "regarded as a woman who could not be expected to be reasonable in such a situation," she held a series of "stormy conferences" with members of the government, lobbying for calm instead of what she called "an unhealthy obsession on the part of leading military officers who asserted that they felt it their inexorable duty to mobilize the military machine forthwith and launch an immediate punitive expedition to attack Sian." Once again, Donald, who wrote a friend that May-ling "had a devil of a scrap" with the military, summed up the situation: "the Gissimo was in less danger from the Sian people than he was from the gang at Nanking who tried to use his detention as an excuse to put him out of business and get the seats of the mighty."

Added to the warlike generals, led by Chiang's trusted General Ho, were the rumormongers. Some spread a story that the Young Marshal was demanding a huge ransom in exchange for Chiang; others—inspired by a Japanese news agency—insisted that Chiang was already dead and if by some miracle he was still alive, he would never be allowed to leave Sian. But Donald called May-ling from Loyang to assure her that her husband was being well treated, that he was "still furious and resentful," but that he had spoken with the Young Marshal, who had admitted his mistakes. "I feel sorry for Chang Hsueh-liang [the Young Marshal]," said his old friend May-ling more than once during the crisis. The Young Marshal, knowing that May-ling was the only person who could reason with her husband, had, in fact, wired her to come to Sian.

Before May-ling could leave, the head of Chiang Kai-shek's secret police, Tai Li, arrived in Sian, claiming that he was "wracked with remorse for his inability to forestall this crisis." Armed with two revolvers, saying that he would "share life or death" with Chiang, he fell to his knees the moment he was ushered into Chiang's room. He then walked over to the generalissimo's bed, took hold of Chiang's legs, and, weeping "bitterly," reproached himself for having failed in his duty to his chief. "Tai Li's dramatic behavior may have been contrived," said his biographer, "but . . . his presence in Sian was crucial" in the eventual outcome of the situation. It also raised his value in the eyes of May-ling, who arrived the next day.

By the time she left for Sian, however, the disaster scenarios had gotten to her, and Chiang's wife admitted feeling "anxious and apprehensive." T.V. and Donald, whom Chiang had "repeatedly asked . . . not to leave him," had returned to Nanking to make the trip with her. Before landing, she gave Donald her revolver and made him promise "that if troops got out of control and seized me he should without hesitation shoot me." A good actress, the May-ling who landed in Sian managed to appear calm and at ease. When the Young Marshal, "looking very tired, very embarrassed, and somewhat ashamed," came on board the plane to escort her off, she greeted him as usual and asked him not to let his soldiers mess up her bags by searching them. When General Yang appeared, she shook hands with him as if she were "arriving on a casual visit." Yang too, she said, was "obviously very nervous and just as obviously very relieved at my calm attitude." Even with her husband—or perhaps more with him—she wrote that she "felt it advisable to remove whatever tension I could from the situation."

"I was so surprised to see her," Chiang wrote, "that I felt as if I were in a dream. . . . I was very much moved, and almost wanted to cry." He said that he had been reading the Old Testament that morning and had come across the passage in Jeremiah that said, "Jehovah will now do a new thing, and that is, He will make a woman protect a man." Taking no chances, however, Chiang warned May-ling not to do anything or agree to anything on his behalf that would compromise his principles.

"My husband was in bed," she wrote later, "suffering from a wrenched back. He looked wan and ill. . . . As I saw him lying there injured and help-less, the shadow of his former self, with his hands, legs, and feet cut by brambles and bruised by the rocks he clambered over when scrambling about the mountain, I felt surge through me an uncontrollable wave of resentment against those responsible for his plight." In a more practical vein, May-ling had brought her husband a spare set of false teeth, which she gave him to put in his mouth, while those accompanying her looked the other way.

She then sent for the Young Marshal, with whom she spoke quietly about the situation. She told him that whatever he and his cohorts thought, the people of the nation were not with them, "he had made a bad mess of things," and the big question now was, how did he plan to extricate himself? "If you had asked me," she said, "I could have told you that you could not get the Generalissimo to do anything by using force."

The Young Marshal explained that they had done this "for the good of the country" but that Chiang would not even talk to them. "Please, you try to make the generalissimo less angry," he begged her, adding, "I know I have done wrong, and I am not trying to justify myself or this action. The motive was good and it would never have happened if you had been here with the generalissimo as you usually are. I tried again and again to speak to the gen-eralissimo, but each time he shut me up and scolded me violently."

"The generalissimo only scolds people of whom he has hopes," she told him. "If he thinks people are useless he just dismisses them—he won't take the trouble to scold them."

"You know I have always had great faith in you," Chang said, "and my associates all admire you. When they went through the generalissimo's pa-pers . . . they found two letters from you . . . which caused them to hold you in even greater respect. They saw by those letters that you were heart and soul with the people, and therefore they know, as I know, that you can adjust this situation so far as the generalissimo is concerned so that he can quickly leave Sian." Chang then explained that he himself was perfectly willing to release Chiang "immediately," but he had to get the consent of the other kidnappers. "Well, then you had better go and talk to them," she said. ". . . I will wait up for your reply." But the Young Marshal did not return until after 2:00 A.M. "Yang and his men are not willing to release the generalissimo," he told her. "They say that since T.V. and Madame are friendly towards me, my head would be safe, but what about theirs? They now blame me for getting them into this affair, and say that since none of our conditions are granted they would be in a worse fix then ever if they now released the generalissimo."

During the following days, "days of increasing anxiety," according to May-ling, T.V. was kept "incessantly occupied with conferences with this group of officers or that. He seemed to be involved in a perpetual motion contest of defeating one set of 'final' arguments and requirements to be immediately confronted with a dozen others just as 'final' and just as impracticable." Her husband, May-ling said, "was not of so much help just then; he was so tired of the shilly-shallying, the impossible arguments . . . that he did not care whether he left Sian or not. 'I'll refuse to go,' he exploded at one time, 'if this kind of thing continues.'

"Christmas Eve was filled with beliefs and dashed hopes. I told Hanching [Young Marshal Chang] that he should get the Generalissimo out on Christmas Day; that the truce was up on that day, and if an attack were launched we would surely be killed, and he with us. . . . He explained that he had practically no troops in the city, and that Yang's soldiers held the gates." When the Young Marshal suggested that May-ling and Donald fly to Loyang while he disguised Chiang and smuggled him out of the city, May-ling refused. "He will not be disguised, and if he cannot go openly by airplane then I will stay with him, and if he is to die because of attacks on the city by the government forces then I will die with him." T.V. and the Young Marshal thought she "was just as obstinate as the generalissimo" and behind her back made arrangements to get her out if the worst were to happen.

By this time, the entire incident had been reduced to a question of "saving heads." That evening the Young Marshal had a fight with General Yang. "You started the coup and without securing anything you are allowing the generalissimo to go," Yang said. "He will surely cut off our heads." In response, May-ling assured the rebel leaders that "if they really repented their heads would be safe. . . . They knew the Generalissimo was magnanimous, and they would have to depend upon his magnanimity." The person who finally convinced the Young Marshal, according to Tai Li's biographer, was the head of the Secret Service: "According to foreign intelligence reports at the time," he wrote, "no one other than Tai Li could have convinced the 'Young Marshal' that he would enjoy the protection of the Nationalist secret service once they were both back."

But the real source of Chiang's deliverance was not Tai Li but a telegram, which had suddenly arrived from Stalin for Ching-ling with instructions to forward it to Mao. The wire said that the Chinese Communists must use their influence to see that Chiang was released. Otherwise, "they would be denounced by Moscow as 'bandits' and repudiated before the world." After he read it, Mao "flew into a rage . . . swore and stamped his feet. Until then they had planned to give Chiang a public trial and to organize a Northwest anti-Japanese government."*

"In reality," May-ling said, "all the political reforms the Sian leaders espoused, had long been in the mind of the Generalissimo himself, as they themselves saw from his diary and private papers. True to his nature, however, he kept what was in his mind to himself, and was, perhaps, too intolerant of others when they endeavoured to express views to him, especially if those others (as in this case) were subordinates who, he thought, were not performing their duties according to orders. Being a rigid disciplinarian he resented any departure from fundamental military requirements by officers. 'Theirs but to do and die, theirs not to reason why' was what he expected."

At 10:30 on Christmas morning, the Young Marshal told the Chiangs that their plane was ready, "but nothing is settled." T.V. then went to see General Yang, who, after a conversation with Chou En-lai, agreed to go along with the Young Marshal's plan to send Chiang back to Nanking. Before he left, however, Chiang insisted on seeing both the Young Marshal and General Yang and giving them (from his bed) what he called "a long and sincere talk," a version of which he later included in his diary. He told them that their coup d'état had had a grave effect on "the continuity of Chinese history of five thousand years and the life and death of the Chinese nation" but that their decision to return him to Nanking was "an indication of the high moral and cultural standard of the Chinese people." He said that since they had acknowledged their error, they were "entitled to remain as [his] subordinates" and that he would urge the Nanking government to treat them with leniency. He then reiterated the importance of the nation over the individual.

After the lecture, Chiang got up, dressed, and went to the airfield with May-ling and the Young Marshal—"the first time on record," according to May-ling, "that any high officer responsible for mutinous conduct had shown eagerness to proceed to the Capital to be tried for his misdeeds."

---

* Many Chinese Communists, including Chou En-lai, agreed with Mao and felt that if they had been able to keep Chiang in Sian a bit longer, they could have made some headway in bringing the two sides together. But, according to Snow, "There is little doubt that Stalin was interested in saving Chiang Kai-shek out of fear that the Kuomintang generals, without Chiang, would in rage turn and join the Japanese in an anti-Russian pact." (Edgar Snow, *Random Notes on Red China*, p. 4.)

When they got to the airport, there were four lines of the Young Marshal's soldiers, bayonets fixed, guns ready to shoot. The Young Marshal climbed into the copilot's seat next to his pilot. The others sat or lay down in the back of what was known as Chang's "Flying Palace"—a silver twin-engine monoplane lined in red plush, with upholstered chairs, sofas, a writing desk, a radio, and a refrigerator.

Chiang had urged the Young Marshal not to accompany him back to Nanking, but Chang insisted, telling his subordinates that his presence would show that he was sorry and would help the leader regain his reputation after Sian. "A true man is always responsible for what he has done. I don't care about my punishment. Let him do as he likes, I will never regret it," he confided to a fellow Manchurian. He later told an interviewer that he had been prepared for death when he accompanied Chiang back to the capital.

"Are you ready to go?" May-ling asked Chang's pilot, Royal Leonard.

"Yes."

"Okay," she said. "Get out of here! Let's get going!"

Leonard, who was instructed to go to Loyang, said that from time to time, he "looked back into the cabin" to observe his passengers. "Madame," he said, "was looking out of a window, a faint smile of happiness on her face. Donald was chuckling to himself. T. V. Soong occasionally looked at some papers but spent most of the time resting, with his eyes closed. The Generalissimo [who was lying down] continued to sleep. When we arrived at Loyang just at dark the Young Marshal asked me to circle once or twice to let them know we were landing."

"Nobody send message we come?" the pilot asked in pidgin.

"No. Not many people in Sian know we leave. No want anyone to know we come," the Young Marshal replied.

When the soldiers and students who had gathered on the airfield after the warning saw May-ling step out of the door of the plane, they saluted, and two officers came forward to help her alight. When the Young Marshal followed her out, the soldiers pointed their guns at him and asked if they should kill him. "No! Let him alone!" she said, putting her arm around him. He, in turn, put an arm around her. When Chiang Kai-shek was carried off the plane, the soldiers threw their hats in the air and began to cheer. Apparently, some even had tears in their eyes as they helped him into his automobile.

The next morning the Chiangs returned to Nanking, where they were welcomed with great enthusiasm. When the news of his release reached Peiping, the entire city is said to have "erupted with joy. Firecrackers were set off everywhere and the streets were packed with cheering crowds. Many people gave parties to celebrate the occasion."

The story of what had occurred during those two and a half weeks in December 1936 came to be known in Chinese history as the Sian Incident. It reverberated throughout the country and sent shock waves around the world. It also made Chiang Kai-shek (however briefly) into the icon he aspired to be and May-ling into a universal symbol of the fearless and devoted wife.

PART FOUR

1937–1942

24

Recent events in China constitute not only a warning but a final signal that the white man's burden soon will be taken over by a very willing Japan. The reign of the white race in the Far East is coming to an end.

—Dr. Sven Hedin, Swedish explorer in Asia, 1937

In spite of May-ling's assurances of her husband's generosity and promises given him by Tai Li and T.V.,* Young Marshal Chang, who returned to Nanking with the Chiangs to stand trial, was court-martialed and sentenced to ten years in prison, followed by five years' deprivation of his civil rights. The harshness of his sentence probably had to do with the fact that the man who "unquestionably saved the Generalissimo's life" told the court that "with the exception of the Generalissimo he despised the whole Nanking bunch and would, when he got out, even if single-handed, agitate against them." Although his sentence was reduced the next day to house arrest and military surveillance, Chiang's generals retaliated by keeping pressure on the generalissimo to prolong his detention. Once the strongest warlord in the North, the Young Marshal became, according to one of Chiang's biographers, "the perpetual prisoner of the Generalissimo, traveling about like a parcel in the retinue of his captor, never permitted to speak for publication or to explain himself." Royal Leonard says that he tried to see his employer every day for three weeks after his return to Nanking but was refused admittance. According to him, there were twenty-five guards around H. H. Kung's house, where the Young Marshal was being detained.

While some contend that Chiang never forgave the younger man, Kung claimed that Chiang "pleaded with the government" to treat Chang "leniently." The Young Marshal himself said that Chiang "always found me the best place to stay anywhere I went" and took care of him when he was ill, sending a doctor from the government hospital. "He really cared about me all along," Chang said. "Of course, political problems have nothing to do with personal emotion." It must be noted, however, that the Young Marshal also said that "the longer Soong May-ling lives, the longer I will live," ac-

---

* Crozier says that according to an eyewitness, T.V. "personally guaranteed that Chang would not be punished in Nanking." (Crozier, *The Man Who Lost China*, p. 188.)

knowledging the fact that it was probably her influence as much as or more than Chiang's generosity that kept him alive after Sian. Asked at the end of his life if he thought that the generalissimo had been a success or failure, Chang said, "I think he was a failure. . . . He was too conservative and too stubborn. The truth is he wanted to be an emperor. He believed that what he said was right and should be considered right."

In 1974, thirty-eight years after the event, the Young Marshal finally released his memoirs, in which he claimed that Chiang's kidnapping had been the result of a "Communist plot." He said he had met Chou En-lai before the actual incident to discuss the terms under which the CCP would agree to cooperate with Nationalist troops in fighting the Japanese. Chou had promised him that the Communist troops would be disbanded as soon as the war with Japan was over and that all the CCP wanted was to be "allowed to function as a legitimate political party. . . . I felt elated in the belief that the country will march toward the goal of fighting the Japanese against a backdrop of internal harmony. Now I know how foolish and naive I was." The Young Marshal explained that he had written the memoirs in 1940 for Chiang Kai-shek, who apparently released them in order to expose "the treachery of the Chinese Communists."

Time magazine, which reported the Sian incident over a period of three weeks in excessive detail, most of it wrong, fastened on Donald as the most newsworthy of the exotic cast of characters. According to *Time*, Donald had owned "perhaps the most sumptuous home in Peking, certainly the most artistic summer residence in a magnificent abandoned temple. His collection of Chinese antiques, historical paraphernalia for opium smoking, French wines, Scotch whiskeys, and Cuban cigars was astounding for a man who himself never took a puff or a drop." Moreover, Donald had "perhaps killed more ladies (in the complimentary, Edwardian sense of 'lady-killing') than any other man in China's swift, hard, cheap, international Shanghai-Peiping set."

"I never read such balderdash," Donald wrote a friend who sent him the article. "I wonder how they happen to get hold of such material, and who gets paid for writing it. I could give them a much better tale at half the price and twice as accurate."

All the other participants except General Yang* came out of the Sian

---

* Yang, a member of the Sian Military Commission of the Anti-Japanese Allied Army, which demanded the release of the Young Marshal, traveled to Europe and the United States as its "special military investigator"; when he returned in 1938, he was arrested by Chiang's government. His wife went on a hunger strike in protest and died. Eight years later, his eldest son wired T.V., "My father . . . has been imprisoned since he returned. . . .

Incident very well. Chiang emerged with his principles intact and his popularity noticeably increased. During his captivity, he had told the governor of Shensi—in one of his sanctimonious inversions of logic—that the coup had been (Chiang's) fault because "I trusted others too much and neglected to take necessary precautions. For this reason," he said, "a great injury has been done to the country. After my return to Nanking I shall tender my resignation again and ask the Central Government to punish me." True to his word, he did just that: "I sincerely hope that the Central Executive Committee will censure me for my negligence to duty," he told them. "I further request the Central Executive Committee immediately to appoint some other competent man to take over my duties, so that I may retire from active service and await disciplinary punishment. In that case the discipline of the State will be upheld and my conscience may be set at ease."

Chiang knew that this resignation and one that followed would not be accepted, and on January 2, 1937, he and May-ling traveled to Chikow, where he could recuperate from his injuries in the serenity of old surroundings. Since his first wife was in his old house, the Chiangs took up residence in his favorite home, a former Buddhist temple in the mountains. Their quarters, which were upstairs in the low, two-story structure, consisted of three large rooms—a living room, dining room, and bedroom, furnished with a large soft bed for May-ling and a narrow bed, "hard as a monk's pallet," for Chiang, who had also had himself fitted with a back brace. He interrupted his hiatus only once, when he flew to Nanking to repeat his resignation to a combined meeting of the Central Executive and Supervisory Committees of the Kuomintang. As expected, this time it was refused as well. He was also given an additional leave of two months.

The Chinese Communist Party also emerged from the Sian Incident with tangible gains, although Mao, only marginally less hypocritical than Chiang, issued a statement calling on Chiang to reverse his "wrong policy" of the previous decade and "remember that he owes his safe departure from Sian to the mediation of the Communist Party" along with the generals involved. Changes in the status of the CCP came about in several stages, starting in February 1937, when the Communists sent a wire to Nanking, promising to discontinue their efforts to overthrow the central government, to abolish the Soviet government in China, to subsume the Red Army into

---

I hope you can help him regain his freedom." But T.V. told his secretary not to reply. In 1949, Chiang Kai-shek had Yang executed before the Communists, who would have released him, came into power. (Boorman, *Biographical Dictionary of Republican China*, vol. 4, p. 7, and Si Jiu-yue, "Diary of T.V. Soong Concerning the Xian Incident," *International Herald Tribune*, June 22, 2004.)

the National Revolutionary Army, and to carry out Sun's Three Principles of the People. In return the CCP asked the KMT to stop the civil war, guarantee freedom of speech, release political prisoners, improve living conditions, convene a multiparty conference of national salvation, and complete preparations to fight the Japanese.

Neither the government nor Chiang Kai-shek, currently on sick leave, would agree to these points, but open fighting between the Kuomintang and the Communists stopped, as did Chiang's Communist extermination campaigns. During the spring of 1937, negotiations between Chou En-lai and a representative from the KMT resulted in restoration of communications between the KMT and the CCP, lifting of the economic blockade of the Red-controlled areas, the release of some political prisoners, and an end to the kidnapping and torture of Communists by the Blue Shirts, who now turned their attention to Japanese spies. Chiang also placed the Red districts within the "national defense area." In return the CCP said it would stop seizing landlords' farms, although it refused to return lands already confiscated, and would stop issuing antigovernment and anti-Kuomintang propaganda—promises it did not honor.

With the CCP and the KMT agreeing to cooperate against a common enemy, the way was finally open for Stalin to send Chiang's son Ching-kuo back home, and in April of 1937, the stocky, unpretentious twenty-eight-year-old arrived with his Russian wife and family. "Welcome, my son!" Chiang Kai-shek is reported to have said. "And now you must meet your new mother."

"That is not my mother," Ching-kuo replied, saying that he wished to go see his real mother. Although May-ling tried to build a relationship with him, he continued to refer to her as Madame Chiang for several years. Chiang's other son, Wei-kuo, had come home earlier and been placed under the supervision of May-ling. Since she could not manage him, he had been sent to Germany for military training but had emerged in London during the coronation festivities of King George VI, insisting that the Chinese delegation get him invited to all the good parties.

During his twelve years in the Soviet Union, Ching-kuo had been thoroughly indoctrinated with an ideology at the opposite end of the political spectrum from that of his father. Hence, Chiang embarked on a course of retraining his son, who, for his part, seemed to accept his new education with good grace. "With a view to the fact that I went abroad as a young boy and stayed in a foreign country too long," Ching-kuo explained, "Father feared that I lacked deep understanding of China's moral philosophy and national spirit. . . . Apart from studying the Three Principles of the People and books of a similar nature, I was also instructed by my father to read classics and history books extensively, as well as Chinese philosophers. More than that, Father repeatedly asked me to re-read what I had read before, memorising many classical pieces by heart." Beyond reading and memorizing, Chiang insisted that Ching-kuo put his reactions and comments on paper so that he could correct them.

The major result of the Sian Incident, however, was the decision of Japan to get on with its plans to conquer China, since the ongoing unification of the Chinese would only make them harder to subdue. What the Japanese now needed was an incident that they could escalate into open hostilities. Meantime, they planted several signposts on the road to war. In early May of 1937, three divisions of the Japanese army arrived in China. Ten days later the Japanese minister of war issued a public complaint about the fact that the Chinese were acting in an overconfident manner that was insulting to the Japanese. On May 24, the Japanese foreign minister said that if Japan's honor were slighted by the Chinese, Japan would have no alternative but to declare war. And on July 7, 1937, Japan manufactured an incident that it could blow up into a casus belli.

On that evening Japanese soldiers knocked on the gates of the small walled garrison town of Wanping, fifteen miles southeast of Peiping. Wanping is near the Marco Polo Bridge, a huge structure dating back to the thirteenth century (hence its name), resting on thirty arches and embellished by 108 stone lions. The Japanese complained that they could not find one of their soldiers. When the Chinese garrison commander replied that he had no information about the man, Japanese soldiers entered the town, roaring through the streets on motorcycles, searching for the missing soldier, knocking on doors, and threatening the residents. It was 2:30 A.M. before they found him—asleep in a brothel.

Within a week Japan had moved 20,000 troops into the area, and on July 10, it attacked Wanping, meanwhile spreading a story that the townspeople had kidnapped and killed its soldier. A week later, Chiang said that the Chinese "seek peace, but . . . not . . . at any cost. We do not want war, but we may be forced to defend ourselves." Chiang's peace terms, sent to the Japanese government, included guarantees of Chinese territorial integrity and freedom of movement for Chinese troops in the area of the capital. The commander of the Japanese forces in north China replied that he could not tolerate Chinese troops in Peiping, and he therefore intended "to chastise the Chinese for their outrageous behavior."

The Japanese also attacked other garrison towns. A Chinese counter-attack in the coastal city of Tientsin led to a four-hour bombardment of the city in which the major target was Nankai University. The Japanese told the press that this was necessary, since the school was the home of "anti-Japanese elements." Attacks on educational institutions had become standard Japanese procedure, undertaken in order to keep students, traditionally the front line of national pride, from organizing demonstrations, distributing pamphlets, and agitating against the invader. After the bombing, the Japanese occupied both Tientsin and Peiping. On the road to the Temple of Heaven in the capital, they ambushed a large group of Chinese soldiers, leaving some five hundred to six hundred bodies and body parts scattered on the ground. The remaining citizens of one village said that the invaders had offered to let the soldiers go if they gave up their arms, but when they did so, the Japanese had slaughtered them with machine guns and grenades. The old capital of Peiping fell about a month after the original incursion, and within four days, all Chinese soldiers had been removed from the area.

Peiping under the control of what one American general called the "arrogant little bastards" was apparently an irritation to the soul. Japanese planes buzzed the U.S. Embassy at 150 feet just "to show us what they think of us." As reported by the Americans still remaining in the legation quarter of the city—most had been told to leave by the U.S. government—the Japanese swaggered around the streets, striking the Chinese out of their way with the butts of their rifles and calling press conferences in which they delivered statements about Japan's "divine mission" as the leader of Asia. The Japanese also floated balloons over the capital, announcing the capture of other Chinese cities along with the astonishing information that "The Japanese army preserves the peace of East Asia."

A week before the fall of Peiping, May-ling addressed a group of delegates from various Chinese women's organizations. Her speech, delivered in the Nationalist capital of Nanking, was supposed to be a call for courage in the face of war, but in the light of her husband's disinclination to fight, it sounded more like an apologia. "We Chinese women are not one whit less patriotic or less courageous or less capable of physical endurance than our sisters of other lands," she said, urging the women to "remember always that a final national victory, no matter how belated it may be in coming, will erase forever the 'humiliation days' that have for so long crowded our calendar and will remove the sorrow that for years past has bent our head and bowed our hearts."

It is at this point in the story that no less an authority than Barbara Tuchman claims that Chiang Kai-shek, officially named generalissimo by an emergency resolution of the Kuomintang in August of 1937, purposefully drew Japan into a battle over Shanghai. He did this supposedly to build up Chinese resistance to the aggressors by luring them into the heart of China, but Tuchman believed that his actions were "more likely" aimed at engaging "foreign intervention. From first to last," she maintained, "Chiang Kai-shek had one purpose: to destroy the Communists and wait for foreign help to defeat the Japanese. He believed battle at Shanghai, the international city with its large foreign investments, would lead to mediation and possibly even intervention by Britain and the United States and other powers."

Shanghai was certainly the biggest, richest, and most exciting city in the country. The fifth largest port on the globe, it received 51 percent of China's foreign imports and sent out 30 percent of its exports. "Hong Kong's views might be more magnificent, Peking's monuments more ancient, Yokohama's climate more salubrious, and Singapore less expensive," said one chronicler of the city, ". . . but ask any Orient-bound traveler his prime destination and the answer would invariably be 'Shanghai!' "

Shanghai was also China *in extremis*—"the glitter and wealth of the upper crust, and the grinding poverty of the lower classes." Between the British Consulate, a fortress guarded by black-bearded Sikhs at one end of the Bund, and the Shanghai Club with its stone facade and pillared doorway at the other, the international community lived "like royalty," erecting signs in so-called public parks that said "No Dogs and Chinese Allowed."* Foreign banks, foreign firms, foreign hotels, and all the other symbols of the lavish colonial life occupied land that cost more than the best locations on Fifth Avenue or the Champs-Élysées. Reproducing many styles of Western architecture with no particular regard for consistency, these buildings seemed to have incorporated every available historical embellishment from the cupola to the clock tower. One of the most impressive was the mammoth Hong Kong and Shanghai Bank. With its huge white dome and octagonal marble entry, it was guarded on the outside by two life-size bronze male lions, which were supposed to roar if ever a local virgin passed by. There was also the old Shanghai Club, said to have the longest bar in the world and some of the most potent drinks.

Alongside the old colonial establishments were the homes and businesses of the newly rich Chinese, whom no one could outdo in architectural extravagance. Although they each owned other homes in the city, the members of the Soong family (with the exception of Ching-ling) had established a good-sized compound on Dongping Road in the French Concession. On the corner was T.V.'s French château with elaborate iron railings, a large lawn, and decorative gardens. Next to it was the guardhouse for the Chiang residence—a two-story gray stone house with red trim and a high iron grating. Not a particularly welcoming building, the Chiang home looked out on very beautiful gardens, as did the Kung house next door, a more

---

* Some say that there were actually two signs: "No Dogs Allowed" and "Only for Foreigners." (Stella Dong, *Shanghai: The Rise and Fall of a Decadent City*, p. 198.)

cheerful-looking establishment with white balustrades and lots of ornamental ironwork.

While the rich Chinese and the colonials lived like kings, life among the poor still counted for very little. During 1937, 20,000 Chinese died of hunger and cold on the streets of the International Settlement (the only place anyone kept count). Immigrants from the countryside still labored under appalling working conditions, while coolies in straw sandals and pants held up with string did the lifting and hauling performed elsewhere by animals or machines. According to one authority, only 2 percent of Chinese citizens had attended high school.

Tuchman said that Chiang Kai-shek sent his best troops from Nanking down to Chapei, the Chinese industrial section of Shanghai north of the International Settlement, home of factories, cheap cabarets, brothels, and opium dens. In doing this, she said, he was deliberately challenging the enemy at a site where "any fighting would be likely to produce an incident involving foreigners or foreign property." According to her, the "Japanese had . . . filled the river with their warships whose menacing naval guns were intended not to fire but to overawe. . . . But the challenge of the Chinese advance on Shanghai provoked . . . the Japanese [who] suddenly found themselves thrown back under ardent attack. From then on a battle of suspense and tragedy was fought out under the eyes of the foreign bystanders." Or, as Han Suyin put it, the foreigners in Shanghai watched "with detachment the bombardment and burning of Chapei across the Soochow Creek" and held "roof parties at night for the thrill of seeing the fire sweeping through densely populated streets of the Native City."

"Under incessant bombing," Tuchman said, ". . . the Chinese held their lines for three desperate months. . . . At a terrible cost in casualties, greater than any since Verdun and the Somme, they [the Chinese] were kept in position . . . after that position was hopeless. Chiang Kai-shek had no other military plan at Shanghai than that of the death stand, but he was playing for world opinion. . . . The last few days of the defense . . . wrecked the army. . . . Sixty percent of the force was lost including 10 percent of the entire trained officer corps." Aside from soldiers, another author* estimates that 450,000 citizens were killed.

According to Tuchman, the fight for Shanghai did succed in making the world "China-conscious. . . . Journalists flocking to the drama and richly nourished twice daily at Chinese Government press conferences reported tales of heroism, blood and suffering. China was seen as fighting democracy's battle and personified by the steadfast Generalissimo and his marvel-

---

* Emily Hahn, *Chiang Kai-shek*, p. 217.

ously attractive, American-educated wife." But in the words of one American reporter seriously wounded in the bombing of Shanghai, "Americans speak of our 'great sister republic' across the Pacific . . . without realizing that there is not an iota of democracy in all this great land. . . . China is governed by super-dictator Chiang Kai-shek. . . . Chiang Kai-shek and Mme. Chiang are the Chinese government. . . . Chiang is extremely Oriental in both thought and action and . . . has developed a marked preference for conservatism and compromise. Madame Chiang . . . has supplied that quality of daring which the Generalissimo has seemed to lack. . . . She is easily the world's most powerful woman."

Although May-ling spoke to the women of Great Britain and the United States about the "wholesale slaughter of non-combatants . . . which can go on unchecked when an aggressive nation [i.e., Japan] decides not to declare war," warning them that the same type of warfare "might be started in their country at any time," Tuchman said that "the primary object of American policy in the months after the Marco Polo Bridge was to keep out of conflict with Japan." Mindful of old Delano family connections with the China trade, President Franklin D. Roosevelt constantly tried to think up ways to stop the Japanese, but American public opinion was at that time totally iso-lationist. After a speech in which the president suggested a "quarantine" of the nations that were fomenting "international anarchy," one of the rightist members of Congress suggested he be impeached. "It's a terrible thing to look over your shoulder when you are trying to lead," Roosevelt told a friend, "—and find no one there."

In the middle of the battle over Shanghai, May-ling, Donald, and an aide-de-camp were on their way to the city, planning to visit wounded sol-diers en route, when their open-topped car hit something in the road, blow-ing out one of the rear tires and veering out of control. The car careened off the road and turned over. The aide was not hurt. Donald was thrown out and saw May-ling being hurled over his head. He found her in a ditch nearly twenty feet away. She was unconscious, and her face was covered with mud. He picked her up, and as he carried her toward a farmhouse, she began to show signs of life. In his relief, he parodied the Chinese custom of shouting loudly to frighten the devils that come to claim the lives of the dying. "Oh, she flies through the air with the greatest of ease," he sang lustily, "this dar-ing young girl who fights Japanese." He took her to the farmhouse to wash her face. When she came out, she was still weak and pale but insisted on continuing their journey. Many hours later, when they arrived in Shanghai, the doctor found that she had broken a rib and confined her to the house for a week.

Since the Japanese did not yet feel strong enough to engage the armies of England, France, or the United States, most of the battle for Shanghai took place in the Chinese quarters of the city, and thousands of Chinese refugees tried to escape into the relative safety of the International Settlement via the Garden Bridge,* the only entrance left open. "How the families stick together!" commented an American, also trying to get away from the fighting. "That ancient grandmother with the bound feet and face as old as the bark of a tree was assuredly being pushed along in the wheelbarrow by her youngest son. The smallest grandchildren . . . were rocking along in baskets swinging at the ends of carrying poles slung over the gray-haired eldest son's shoulders. Two generations of sons and daughters of this family were . . . on the run with everything they possessed. . . . My feet were slipping . . . on blood and flesh," he continued. "Half a dozen times I knew I was walking on the bodies of children or old people sucked under by the torrent, trampled flat by countless feet."

At the beginning of 1937, there had been around 250,000 people living in the International Settlement; after the Japanese invasion, there were possibly ten times that number. Not everyone could be accommodated in the warehouses and theaters turned into temporary shelters, and many were forced to sleep on the streets. "For endless miles, the city's sidewalks became the bedroom of a million refugees," said the man forced to climb over corpses at the Garden Bridge, while veteran correspondents decried the "filth, disease, hunger and madness." According to *Time,* among the refugees one baby was born every minute, one person died every three minutes, and twelve mothers died in childbirth every hour.

The International Settlement also came in for a share of mayhem or, as one cool Englishman put it, "bodies and bits." In trying to sink a Japanese ship, Chinese bombers accidentally dropped a bomb in front of the pink-and-gray-marble Cathay Hotel, another through the roof of the Palace Hotel next door, and two more at the intersection of Avenue Édouard VII and Thibet Road, where many of the refugees had gone to get handouts of rice and tea. More than 1,700 people were killed in these incidents of friendly fire, and over 1,400 were injured. It was, according to one author, "the worst civilian carnage in a single day anywhere in the world up to that moment."

On September 12, May-ling spoke on the radio to the American people, apologizing for the inadvertent killing of foreigners and moving on to a plea for help:

You can see by what Japan is now doing in China that she is sinister, ruthless, well armed, well organized and acting on a preconceived

* A bridge over Soochow Creek from Hongkew to the Bund.

plan. For years she has been preparing for this venal attempt to conquer China even if she has to annihilate the Chinese to do so. Curiously no other nation seems to care to stop it. . . . It was to avert such a catastrophe that the Great Powers signed the Nine-Power Treaty,* which was specially created to safeguard China from invasion by Japan. They signed the Kellogg Peace Pact† to prevent war, and they organized the League of Nations to make doubly certain that aggressive nations would be quickly prevented from inflicting unjustified harm upon their weaker fellows. But strange to say all these treaties appear to have crumbled to dust. . . .

The militarists of Japan have already shown the world their contempt for any codes of international honor. . . . Look at the square miles of bloodstained debris heaped with dead. Look at the fleeing thousands of Chinese and foreigners, screaming, panic-stricken, running for their lives . . . from the horrors of Shanghai. . . . Thousands of them a few days ago were crowded on the South Station to get into a train when Japanese bombers came overhead, dropped bombs upon them and blew three hundred of them to ghastly fragments. . . . No soldier was anywhere near the station, and there was no justification for the terrible massacre. . . . Perhaps you can hear over the radio the noise of the cannonade, but hidden from your hearing (though I hope ringing in your hearts) are the cries of the dying, the pain of the masses of wounded, and the tumult of the crashing buildings. And from your sight is hidden the suffering and starvation of the great army of wandering, terrified, innocent homeless ones; the falling tears of the mothers and the smoke and the flames of their burning houses.

If the pictures drawn by the generalissimo's wife were dramatic, so was her sign-off. "Good-bye, everybody," she said as the conclusion to her speech.

By the end of the battle for Shanghai, the entire district of Chapei, for-

---

* Signed in 1922, the Nine-Power Treaty (the United States, Great Britain, France, Italy, Belgium, the Netherlands, China, Japan, and Portugal) guaranteed the territorial integrity and administrative independence of China, along with equal opportunity for the other nations doing business there. Since the treaty did not promise to defend that integrity, it was, in effect, a moral sop to the conscience of the West.

† The Kellogg-Briand Pact, signed in 1928 by the ninth assembly of the League of Nations, renounced wars of aggression but, like the Nine-Power Treaty, made no provision for sanctions.

merly housing some 1 million citizens, had been set on fire—a wall of flames that extended for six miles. This was done by the Chinese themselves in accordance with Chiang's directive to leave nothing behind that the Japanese could use. By this point in the conflict, close to 350,000 Chinese had left the city, and some 5,000 British and Americans had done the same. Shanghai's trade had been diverted to other Chinese ports, and its silver had been sent to Hong Kong, where many rich Chinese moved during the Japanese occupation. Those who remained were required to bow to the Japanese sentries who stood at the Garden Bridge. If their bows were not sufficiently low, they risked being kicked, beaten, or thrown into the river. Even the trams that ran on the bridge had to stop while their Chinese passengers descended and paid obeisance to the conquerors.

"In this city—conquered, yet unoccupied by its conquerors—the mechanism of the old life is still ticking, but seems doomed to stop, like a watch dropped in the desert," wrote Christopher Isherwood when he visited Shanghai the following year. "In this city the gulf between society's two halves is too grossly wide for any bridge . . . we ourselves, though we wear out our shoes walking the slums . . . belong, unescapably, to the other world. . . . In our world, there are the garden-parties and the nightclubs, the hot baths and the cocktails, the singsong girls and the Ambassador's cook. In our world, European business men write to the local newspapers, complaining that the Chinese are cruel to pigs, and saying that the refugees should be turned out of the Settlement because they are beginning to smell."

25

One thing which makes Chiang's position unique among world leaders is the influence and power exercised by his wife. . . . Madame Chiang has been at times a decisive personality, perhaps second to none but her husband.

—EDGAR SNOW

AFTER THEY conquered Shanghai, the Japanese moved up the Yangtze River. The roads were jammed with refugees fleeing before the enemy and soldiers ordered to withdraw from the broken city. Razing everything on their way— cities, villages, and farming communities—enemy soldiers arrived in Soochow, famous for its silk industry and the main defense enclave between Shanghai and Nanking. In order to gain access to the city, the advance Japanese guards put on hoods to disguise their nationality. Once inside the walls, they plundered and burned and dragged off hundreds of women for enforced prostitution.

In September, the Japanese took Paoting, a city on the railway line between the old capital of Peiping and Hankow. Again they attacked centers of learning, burning all the schoolbooks along with the library and the laboratory equipment of the medical college in a bonfire that lasted a full week. By this point in the invasion, brutality and savagery had taken hold of the invaders. In an orgy of murder, pillage and rape, some 30,000 Japanese soldiers ravaged the city and its inhabitants. "A self-defeating ferocity accompanied them like a hyena of conquest," said Tuchman, "growing more ravenous by what it fed on."

A week earlier, May-ling had made a special broadcast for the United States in which she again criticized the Western nations for their silence in the face of Japanese aggression. "Japan is acting on a preconceived plan to conquer China," she said. "Curiously, no other nation seems to care. . . . All treaties and structures to outlaw war and to regularize the conduct of war appear to have crumbled, and we have a reversion to the day of savages."

Five days later, the generalissimo gave a press conference for foreign journalists. "He looked fit and smiling," according to one reporter.

> . . . He sat behind a mahogany Chinese desk in a corner of the room, facing the visitors, who gathered round his desk in a semicircle. Ma-

dame Chiang Kai-shek, in a serious black dress and plain black pumps, sat on her husband's right, slightly in front of him and interpreted for the Generalissimo. . . . Both of them expressed gratitude for the visit of foreign corespondents to Nanking despite the Japanese bombings, and especially for the sympathy shown and the accurate reports published in the world press concerning China's struggle against Japanese aggression. Commenting on America's attitude, the Generalissimo declared that China was fighting not only for her own existence, but to uphold the principles of the Nine-Power Treaty and the Covenant of the League of Nations. Therefore, he contended, it was up to all the signatories of these instruments to support China's struggle.

Not only the interpretation but the message and wording clearly originated with the generalissimo's wife.

Before its ground troops reached Nanking, Japan sent bombers, and on October 12, May-ling wrote an article describing what it was like to observe a Japanese air raid of the capital.

The alarm sounded fifteen minutes ago . . . and I came outside as I always do . . . 2:42 p.m. . . . Three heavy Japanese bombers come through a blue cleft between the piles of cumulus. . . . Three more follow. Anti-aircraft guns put clusters of black smoke puffs around the first three. Now they are bobbing up about the second three. Here come three more—so there are nine altogether. High above the clouds I hear pursuit planes. . . . The sound of machine gun fire is now high above me and, above the clouds, the pilots are fighting. The nine bombers proceed in steady progress across the city. . . . 2:46 p.m. Great spouts of flame; columns of smoke and dust ascend. They have dropped several bombs. Then they scatter. . . . 2:50 p.m. There is a dogfight in the north-west. . . . The combatants are sweeping in and out of the clouds. . . . 2:56 p.m. . . . High in the air, a little to the west there is a dogfight. Another is going on over the city, in full view of all who can see. A Chinese Hawk is chasing a Japanese monoplane. They are looping and turning and diving—and zooming up again. . . . The Japanese plane seems to stall in mid-air. He is hit. The Hawk sweeps round to attack again. The Japanese pauses awhile, then goes into a headlong dive; flames stream out; the doomed machine is heading for a thickly populated part of the city. . . . Orange flame with a long comet tail of smoke, cleaves through the sky. The Hawk flies in circles, watching his enemy crash.

. . . 3:20 p.m. There is now no sound in the skies. The raid lasted about 40 minutes. So I shall go, as usual, and inspect the damage and find out the score of gains and losses. . . . People are in the streets as if nothing unusual had occurred.

Three years earlier, the generalissimo's wife had taken on the title of secretary-general of the Chinese air force. "Aviation," according to Claire Lee Chennault, the American pilot who created the group known as the American Volunteer Group (AVG) or "Flying Tigers,"* was "strictly an Occidental export to the Orient." While the Japanese learned to fly from the French, the Chinese looked primarily to the Russians, Americans, and Italians to supply them with aircraft and instruct them in their use.

Colonel Claire Chennault was a highly controversial figure who engendered love or hate in nearly everyone he met. Handsome in a craggy, bulldog way, he impressed Winston Churchill, who met him at one of the summits during the war. "My God, that face," the prime minister muttered. "Thank God, he's on our side." Chennault had learned to fly during World War I, although he was not sent into combat, and he had remained in the army after the war as a flying instructor with a reputation as a superb tactician. In 1934, Chennault supervised the Flying Trapeze Army Air Show, "the most spectacular air troupe ever organized in the history of military and civil aviation," according to Royal Leonard, the Young Marshal's former pilot, who worked later for the Chiangs. Three years after the air show Chennault was retired from the air force. The official reason was that he was deaf, but most observers believe it was because he had written a book on strategy in which he advocated developing all kinds of aircraft, especially fighter escorts, in opposition to the "bomber generals" in Washington, who believed that waves of bombers sent on the attack could protect themselves. Shortly after being retired, Chennault received a wire from Lieutenant Colonel Lucius Roy Holbrook II, of the U.S. Army Air Corps, asking him to come to China for three months to make a confidential appraisal of the Chinese air force for Madame Chiang Kai-shek.

May-ling's brother T.V. had organized the first Chinese air force, arranging for an American mission to establish flying schools patterned after those

---

* According to Chennault, the nickname "Flying Tigers" was first used by American newspapers looking for encouraging stories in "an Allied world rocked by a series of shattering defeats." The group's first insignia—a shark tooth design on the nose of its planes—was replaced by the picture of a winged tiger flying through a large V for Victory, designed by an artist at the Walt Disney Studio. (Claire Lee Chennault, *Way of a Fighter*, pp. 135–36.)

in the United States. Some twenty Army Air Corps reserve officers set up
schools in Hangchow in 1932, but two years later the United States refused
to help the generalissimo put down a rebellion in Fukien province, where
the rebels had withdrawn inside an old walled town. It was clear that nothing
but airpower could be used to force them out. A "half-dozen rickety crates"
from the Nationalist government finally broke enough holes in the ancient
walls to allow the infantry to get through and rout the insurgents. It was not
until then that Chiang Kai-shek saw the need for a Chinese air force.

Irritated by the U.S. refusal to help subdue the rebels, the Chinese turned
to the Italians, who sent forty pilots, along with a hundred engineers and
mechanics, to Asia—the former to teach flying, the latter to set up a factory
to assemble Italian planes. By the time Chennault arrived in June of 1937,
the Italians "were in complete control of the Chinese Air Force and had
cornered the Chinese aviation market. Italian military pilots swaggered
around Nanking in full uniform," said Chennault, who had written "peasant" as his occupation on his passport. "General Scaroni [head of the Italian
mission] roared through the streets in a big black limousine, his uniform
dripping medals and gold braid. The elaborate ceremony and flowery courtesy of the Italians impressed the Chinese more than the brusque efficiency
of Americans. It was an excellent deal for the Italians. The mission cost them
nothing, since its expenses were paid out of Italy's share of the Boxer indemnity. Chinese orders for Italian military planes soared to many, many millions of dollars and helped finance expansion of Italy's aircraft industry,
which was already preparing for war." Not only was the mission an economic
windfall for Italy, but, Chennault claimed, the Italians used their position in
Asia to help the Japanese. "In contrast to the German military mission, then
in China, the Italians did all they could to sabotage China," he wrote, offering as "final evidence of the Italians' sabotage" their recommendation that
the Chinese stop buying combat planes just two months before the Japanese
invaded Shanghai. "It was no coincidence that Mussolini later became the
first official to suggest that China accept Japan's peace terms or that Wang
Ching Wei* . . . use the Italian embassy in Hankow to maintain communications with the Japanese."

Not only was the mission an economic and strategic windfall for Italy,
but, according to Chennault, the Italians did little to help the Chinese air
force, since they graduated everyone, competent or not, from pilot school,
while the Americans had given licenses only to those who deserved them.
"However," Chennault explained, "the Generalissimo was pleased with the
Italian method," since those who trained as pilots were from a socially supe-

---

* Chiang Kai-shek's old rival.

rior stratum of society, and if they did not succeed in graduating, there were the inevitable protests from important families. "The Italian method solved this social problem," Chennault said, "and all but wrecked the air force." Chennault also blamed the Italians for the habit of not removing a plane from the official roster even after it had been wrecked and scrapped for parts—a practice resulting in a roster of 500 planes, of which only 91 could fly.

"I reckon you and I will get along all right in building up your air force," Chennault told May-ling when they first met. "I reckon so, Colonel," she drawled in her best Georgia accent. But Chennault had barely started his assessment of the Chinese air force when the Japanese attacked the Marco Polo Bridge in early July 1937. He immediately volunteered his services to the generalissimo, who sent him to Nanchang to train fighter pilots. "Combat training at Nanchang was a nightmare I will never forget," said Chennault. Aside from a few American-born flyers from Canton and some pilots who had been trained by the American mission, the rest of the trainees, who had learned to fly from the Italians, were, in Chennault's words, "a menace to navigation."

The Chiangs were spending part of the summer of 1937 in Kuling, the resort in the mountains above Nanking, when they summoned Chennault and General P. T. Mow,* the acting chief of the Chinese air force at Nanchang, for a meeting. According to one of the Americans stationed with Chennault, Mow was "a crackerjack pilot, a likeable fellow, and . . . very capable of running the Air Force, while the 'figurehead' chief, General Chow Chin-jou, the trusted man of Chiang Kai-shek . . . took a back seat." When the gentlemen arrived, Chiang spoke first to General Mow:

"How many first-line planes are ready to fight?" he asked.

"Ninety-one, Your Excellency," said the nervous general.

At that point, according to Chennault, Chiang turned "turkey red" and began pacing up and down the porch of the house—"loosing long strings of sibilant Chinese that seemed to hiss, coil, and strike like a snake." Madame Chiang stopped translating for Chennault, as Mow, standing at attention, turned pale.

"The Generalissimo has threatened to execute him," Madame whispered to the American. "The Aero Commission records show we should have five hundred first-line planes ready to fight."

---

* General Mow was a former brother-in-law of Chiang Kai-shek, having been married to Chiang's first wife's sister. The marriage was terminated sometime before the early 1950s—whether by death or divorce is unknown.

As Chiang began to simmer down, he asked Chennault how many planes his survey showed.

"General Mow's figures are correct," said Chennault.

"Go on," Madame urged the American, "tell him all of the truth."

With May-ling translating, Chennault told the generalissimo what was wrong with the Chinese air force.

The next time Chennault was called before the generalissimo, it was early August and Chiang was back in the capital of Nanking, which was preparing for war. Street vendors were selling gas masks while government workers covered the roofs of important buildings with gray paint. Chiang was under tremendous public pressure, primarily from students and the press, to end his policy of withdrawal and entrapment. "Stand and fight," the newspapers demanded; "an end to compromise."

Chennault claimed that he and Donald were "the only foreigners present" at several meetings that took place between the Chinese warlords and the generalissimo in the Nanking Military Academy. Pushed by the warlords, Chiang announced that China would fight the aggressor, even if it was inadequately prepared. He sent the air force north to Kaifeng, a major railway junction on the Yellow River and the only natural barrier left between the Japanese in Peiping and the Chinese in Nanking. Madame Chiang, who had heard that the Japanese were preparing to occupy Shanghai—they would begin their attack on August 13—summoned Chennault. She was, he said, "greatly agitated."

"You must go to Shanghai immediately and warn American officials to evacuate their nationals and protect their property before it is too late," she told him.

Chennault, who had sent his luggage on to Kaifeng, pointed to his only clothes, the khaki shorts and green polo shirt he was wearing. May-ling, he said, "threw a handful of money" at him. "Buy new clothes," she said. "But get to Shanghai as fast as you can."

He got there a few hours after the last Japanese citizens had left the International Settlement, bought a white summer suit (standard wear for foreigners in Shanghai), and went directly to the U.S. Consulate. But the official he saw didn't believe him. He moved on to the China National Aviation Corps offices and repeated the warning. The men there, he said, were "highly amused"; they gave him permission to recruit pilots from their roster if, in fact, there was a war, "but of course there would be no war." He found the same attitude wherever he went in Shanghai.* Even the next day, which

---

* The only person who believed Chennault was the Swedish minister, who later sent him a silver pocket flask in thanks.

turned out to be the day before the invasion, no one seemed concerned by the Japanese warships that had already begun arriving in the Whangpoo River.

On the evening of the assault on Shanghai, there was a "big war council meeting" in Nanking, and the next day May-ling asked Chennault to take over the Chinese air force. His efforts eventually led to what he referred to as "Black Saturday," the day Chinese bombs, aimed at a Japanese warship, hit the International Settlement. Absolving himself of responsibility for a disaster that seriously damaged China's image in the world, Chennault explained that the weather over Shanghai that day was "bad for high-level bombing" and that Chinese bomber pilots had been trained to bomb from an altitude of 7,500 feet. "Rather than turn back . . . the Chinese pilots went on down below the overcast to make their bomb runs at 1,500 feet in a shallow dive that boosted their air speed above their accustomed bomb run. They violated orders to avoid the International Settlement and failed to adjust their bomb sights for the new speed and altitude. As a result their bombs fell short of the *Idzumo* [the warship that was their target] and smack into the middle of the International Settlement."*

By the time, the Japanese got to Nanking, however, Chennault had had a chance to work with the Chinese pilots. On one particular day, fifty-two Japanese bombers came roaring over, according to Royal Leonard, "in right and stately formation like a Gilbert and Sullivan chorus." The Japanese were perfectly predictable, and from past performances, Chennault knew that they would maintain a constant speed of 160 mph. and a constant altitude of around 11,000 feet. The Chinese "in their obsolete Hawk-35s and P-26s, went up like monkeys on an invisible rope," Leonard continued. "Up in the sky they waited. The Japanese bombers thundered toward their goal. . . . The Chinese pilots swarmed over them like bees. They got under the bellies of the bombers, behind their tails, and let go bursts of machine-gun fire. It was an old Flying Trapeze stunt." The same sequence of events took place on the next two days. At the end of the third day, the Japanese squadron limped home. Forty-four planes had been shot down. The Chinese under Chennault had lost only five planes and no pilots, and he had vindicated his theories about the invincibility of bombers.

"We love Chennault, we called him Leather Face," recalled one Chinese pilot. ". . . He looked after us, was concerned for us. He said to the KMT: 'How come you give my flying students only two buns, a bowl of rice and

---

* The *Idzumo* was later bombed successfully but reappeared in three days in perfect condition, leading Chennault to believe that the Japanese had sent its sister ship back to the Whangpoo to save face.

some salt vegetable. Their health will weaken if they keep on eating that diet. No, you have to give them some meat.' The KMT was very corrupt, they squeezed your money. But immediately there was a change and we were given meat. Chennault was good to us."

Known as the civilian adviser to the secretary of the Commission for Aeronautical Affairs, Chennault, who never held an official position with the Chinese government, was the virtual commander of the Chinese air force as well as its adviser on ground tactics. For this, he was paid handsomely by Chiang Kai-shek. In addition, Madame Chiang—whom he called a "princess"—gave him his own plane, a $55,000 so-called Hawk Special,* and a Packard limousine, which she had used in the past. Even when directing combat operations for the Chinese air force, the American never issued orders, only "suggested" what was to be done. These suggestions often came with an endorsement from the generalissimo, requesting that they be followed "without fail." It was only later, Chennault said, he learned "that 'without fail' on the G-mo's orders meant that the penalty for failure was a firing squad."

Chennault was "greatly disturbed" in 1941 when he was informed that, due to jealousy in the ranks, his messages to Chiang were no longer to be sent via May-ling but directly to the generalissimo himself. "Your assistance and support are essential," he wrote her. ". . . I hope you will remember that I undertook my present duties relying on you to serve as liaison between me and the Generalissimo. As I have so often told you, past experience has shown that when you do not serve in this capacity, interested persons take the opportunity to persuade the Generalissimo to issue unacceptable orders and otherwise make it very difficult for me to work for you and China."

The only disinterested and trustworthy person close to Chiang, May-ling continued to be informed of all casualties and deaths among the airmen and delivered the speeches when pilots were singled out for outstanding achievements. One of the best Chinese pilots was an American-born man named Art Chen. One day Chen took on three Japanese planes in a dogfight but ran out of ammunition after shooting the first one down. So he rammed the second one, wrecking it, and then bailed out of his own plane near the wreckage. He examined what was left of the plane, found one machine gun

---

* According to the columnist Joseph Alsop, who worked for Chennault but swore he checked the story with the Chinese, Chennault used his American Hawk-75 monoplane to shoot down more than forty Japanese planes "at a bounty of $500 per plane. As Mme Chiang and the generalissimo grew more pleased with the results," Alsop added, ". . . the ante was raised to $1000 per enemy plane destroyed." (Joseph Alsop with Adam Platt, *I've Seen the Best of It,* p. 166.)

in good condition, took it, and walked the eight miles back to base, carrying the gun on his shoulder. There he ran into Chennault. Before Chennault had a chance to say a word, he held out the gun. "Sir," he said, "can I have another airplane for my machine gun?"

While serving as nominal head of the Chinese air force, May-ling often risked her life and her emotional well-being by going out to the airfield, a major Japanese target, to encourage the Chinese pilots. "It was strong medicine even for a man—the grim and hopeless manner as they went off to face ever lengthening odds, the long nerve-racking waiting, and the return of bloody, burned, and battle-glazed survivors," Chennault said. "It always unnerved her, but she stuck it out, seeing that hot tea was ready and listening to their stories of the fighting." May-ling managed to remain calm and consoling until the day four pilots were killed and five out of eleven planes returning from a mission were wrecked in trying to land. On that day she turned to Chennault and "burst into tears. 'What can we do. . . . We buy them the best planes money can buy, spend so much time and money training them, and they are killing themselves before my eyes.' "

Her concern and her knowledge of airplanes endeared her to the pilots. One of the Americans described a particularly bad day:

> We got out there to survey the damage, but before we got out of the auto we see Madame Chiang out walking around the airplane that had been severely damaged. She had beaten us to the airport . . . she was a mighty brave woman. She was taking chances all the time during the war, as if she was one of the soldiers herself. After an air raid she seemed to hasten to the airport to count the boys when they came back in, and she insisted on there being coffee for them and was trying to do what she could to make it as easy as possible for these brave boys that really were fighting against odds and without replacements.

The generalissimo's wife also talked another American into working for the Chinese air force. After the bombing of the International Settlement, she called Royal Leonard and asked him to come see her. "I was called to the Generalissimo's headquarters at Nanking, on a small country estate outside the city," Leonard wrote in his memoirs. "Madame Chiang Kai-shek met me in the living room. With her serious face and shining dark hair, dressed in brown slacks, she looked like a schoolgirl, but her attitude was all business. I knew that she was head of the air force. . . . I also knew that there was a great deal of jealousy among the air-corps generals because she held that post. They did not care to take orders from a woman. The records show, however, that during the time when Madame was in charge of Chinese aviation the corps was at a pitch of efficiency that has since been unequaled."

"I want you to take charge of all Chinese bombardment," she told Leonard.

"I am a pursuit pilot," he answered. "I don't know anything about bombardment."

"That doesn't matter," she told him. "You are a good flyer and you have a good head. We need your judgment. You can be trusted. That is what we want." Leonard said he would try.

May-ling resigned from her position with the air force in 1938, giving as her excuse the injuries she had suffered in the car accident on the road from Shanghai to Nanking. The real reason, however, was the discovery of corruption in the purchase of planes and aviation equipment—a scandal involving an agent named A. L. Patterson, a Chinese general, and her sister Ai-ling. According to the memorandum of a conversation between the American ambassador, Nelson T. Johnson, and a member of his staff, "Wing Commander Garnet Malley . . . was satisfied that Patterson had doubled, and in some cases trebled, the price of American aircraft sold to the Chinese Government over the list prices in the United States. This was done . . . to provide a larger 'squeeze' to Chinese officials handling the orders. Patterson . . . had even gone so far as to have special catalogues printed in China showing the adjusted prices and purporting to be the American catalogues. Malley said that Madam Chiang had asked him to suggest means of stopping the 'squeeze.' " In one instance Patterson "had sold to the Aviation Commission one hundred if not two hundred radio sets; not only was the price . . . four times the right price, but the sets themselves were quite unsuitable for use on Chinese military planes, since it was impossible . . . to alter the wave length."

According to this memo:

General Tzau had been mentioned for some time as the agent of Mrs. H. H. Kung in collecting 'squeeze' on the purchase of airplanes. I inquired . . . how it was that Mrs. Chiang Kai-shek, Mrs. Kung's sister, could take any action which would, if carried to its conclusion, expose Mrs. Kung's alleged part in these transactions. He [Malley] said that Mrs. Chiang Kai-shek had given orders to sift the matter to the bottom and that the bribery in connection with air plane purchases had been the subject of a struggle between the two sisters for some time. Commander Malley did not seem to think that Dr. H. H. Kung had any part in these corrupt practices nor even that he was cognizant of what was taking place.

Purchases made for the Chinese air force apparently passed through an entity called the Central Trust, a Chinese organization that, biographer Laura Tyson Li tells us, was under the influence of Madame Kung and that refused to give orders to any company not represented by Patterson. Mayling's efforts to clean up the corruption were stopped by Chiang, who worried that this would have "gutted" the air force. According to Li, "He—and no doubt Mayling too—was reluctant to bring to light a scandal that would embarrass him and cast a pall over foreign aid that the country desperately needed as it struggled to resist the Japanese invasion." Heeding the advice of Donald, May-ling "abruptly" resigned, taking the Chinese air force officers "completely by surprise and very crestfallen."

In any case, by October of that year, fewer than twelve out of the ninety-one planes that had begun the fight with Japan were left, and many of China's best pilots were dead. When Chiang's government put out an official call for help to all the Great Powers, only Russia responded, sending four fighter and two bomber squadrons, complete with pilots, ground crews, and supplies. The Russians—"a sour and surly lot" according to one observer—were hoping that the Chinese would keep the Japanese occupied, hence too busy to attack the Soviet Union.* Later on, they sent another three hundred combat planes and a quantity of anti-aircraft artillery, although they complained that much of what they had sent was "misused," "cracked up by inexperienced personnel," or "disappeared" into squeeze. The total credit given China by Russia, according to Crozier, was $350 million, which the Chinese partially paid for in tungsten, wool, and tea.

Along with war materials, Stalin sent Chiang some advice on achieving national unity: "Tell the Generalissimo that if he wants to do away with any manifestation of disloyalty on the part of his people while the fight continues, he should arrange to shoot at least 4,500,000 persons. Otherwise," Stalin said, "I fear that he will not be able to bring the war of resistance to a successful conclusion."

---

* This, of course, was before the Hitler-Stalin pact in August 1939. The situation changed back again in June 1941, when Hitler attacked the USSR, and the Chinese became popular with the Russians once again.

26

The morning papers report that the hostilities in China must continue because China refuses to show "sincerity." Henceforth I shall always hate that word because it will always remind me of the Japanese connotation of it: if I hit you and you hit back, you are obviously insincere.

—JOSEPH C. GREW, U.S. AMBASSADOR TO JAPAN, 1937

HAVING SENT his best troops to fight the Japanese in Shanghai, Chiang had to decide whether to try to defend Nanking or abandon it—an issue he threw open to a meeting with some of his top military men. Only one general recommended fighting it out with the Japanese. That was Tang Sheng-chih, who argued that by defending Nanking, the Chinese could slow down the Japanese army, thus giving the rest of their troops a chance to rest and regroup. It was a valid idea, but none of the generals present was willing to take on the job of leading the doomed. "Either I stay or you stay," Chiang said, pointing to Tang—at which point Tang was forced, in the presence of his peers, to volunteer. He then held a press conference in which he promised to fight to the death for the capital. Reporters gave him an enthusiastic round of applause, although some noticed that, having just recovered from a major illness, he seemed "dazed if not doped," and, according to Iris Chang,* was sweating "profusely."

Having sent his government out of Nanking, the generalissimo called for 50,000 Chinese soldiers to move in and prepare the capital for invasion. The troops fortified the city walls, placed machine guns on the battlements, sandbagged the gates, and closed all but one to traffic. They burned a battle zone a mile wide around the perimeter of the city walls, causing untold misery to those who lived there. Meanwhile, the Chiangs had two hundred boxes packed with artworks and artifacts from the Palace Museum and put on a boat to be sent to a safe place.† In light of all this preparation, one would have thought that the Chinese could have put up more of a fight for

---

* The author of *The Rape of Nanking.*

† After the Japanese overran Manchuria in the early 1930s, T.V. had arranged to have these major works of art moved from Peiping to Nanking to protect them not only from the Japanese but from local officials, who would have sold them to antiques dealers.

the city. But, according to Iris Chang, the officials who left the city took with them most of the communications equipment, so that one part of the army could not talk to another. Moreover, the Chinese air force decamped with the officials, making it impossible for Tang to get any information on the location of Japanese guns. Worse, many of the soldiers brought in to defend Nanking were not seasoned fighters but new conscripts or men exhausted from recent battles.

With all the odds against him, Tang tried to arrange a truce with the Japanese, but the terms were rejected by the generalissimo, who ordered Tang to go to the dock, where he would be picked up and taken to safety. The only escape route from Nanking was its harbor—a frantic melee of screaming, pushing citizens and soldiers, all attempting to cross the Yangtze River to the place where junks waited to take them away. Once the boats were filled, some tried to escape by clinging to pieces of wood or swimming. Many drowned in the attempt. Those who remained were left to fend for themselves.

✲

WHEN THEY ARRIVED in Nanking, the Japanese demanded that the city be surrendered intact, dropping leaflets that said that in order to "protect innocent civilians and cultural relics in the city," the Chinese must give up without a fight. In return for compliance, they promised to be "kind and generous to non-combatants and to Chinese troops who entertained no enmity to Japan," but to those who put up a fight, they would be "harsh and relentless." When the Chinese tried to mount a pathetic defense, the Japanese field commander, an uncle of the emperor, gave his soldiers leave to mutilate, rape, and murder anyone they found. Orders were given to take no prisoners, and what came to be known in the history of holocausts as the Rape of Nanking began.

There were only some 50,000 Japanese soldiers to deal with about 500,000 Chinese civilians and 90,000 Chinese soldiers in the capital. This meant that the Japanese had to deceive those they planned to kill into believing that they would be treated according to international rules of warfare. Posters were put up bearing the message "Trust our Japanese army—they will protect and feed you," but Chinese soldiers who gave up their arms were herded into outlying districts, divided into small groups, and beheaded or shot. With so many bodies, there was a problem of disposal. One Japanese general complained how hard it was to find ditches large enough to take 7,000 or 8,000 corpses. It was difficult to get enough fuel to cremate the vast numbers of bodies, and many were simply thrown into the muddy waters of the Yangtze.

With most of the soldiers gone, the citizens of Nanking were left to face the enemy on their own. Under the pretext of searching for soldiers, the Japanese soldiers moved from house to house and store to store, demanding that the doors be opened to welcome the victors and then gunning down the residents and shopkeepers. After looting, they often burned the premises. Even Japanese journalists were shocked by the results of these forays: "On Hsiakwan wharves," one wrote,

> there was the dark silhouette of a mountain made of dead bodies. About fifty to one hundred people were toiling there, dragging bodies from the mountain of corpses and throwing them into the Yangtze River. The bodies dripped blood, some of them still alive, and moaning weakly, their limbs twitching. . . . On the pier was a field of glistening mud under the moon's dim light. Wow! That's all blood! After a while, the coolies had done their job of dragging corpses and the soldiers lined them up along the river. Rat-tat-tat machine-gun fire could be heard. The coolies fell backward into the river and were swallowed by the raging currents. . . . A Japanese officer at the scene estimated that 20,000 people had been executed.

There was a great deal of sadism as well. Some Chinese citizens were nailed to wooden boards to be run over by tanks, crucified on trees or electrical posts, stripped of long pieces of skin, or had their eyes put out and noses and ears cut off before being killed. Other prisoners were tied together, thrown into pits, doused with gasoline, and set on fire. In one lethal game, the Chinese were driven to the top stories of buildings, the stairs were removed, and the buildings were incinerated. Still others were buried up to their waist and ripped apart by German shepherd dogs. There were medical experiments carried on in a secret location where scientists fed or injected prisoners with germs, poisons, and various lethal gases, killing about ten people a week.

Photographic evidence of the invaders' inhumanity eventually made its way to the West. It came from snapshots taken by the Japanese themselves and given to Japanese photography shops in the International Settlement of Shanghai to develop. Risking their lives, a few Chinese employees made extra prints, which they sent to the Chinese Ministry of Information in Hankow, where the government had fled. These prints were given to an Australian journalist, Rhodes Farmer, who had them reproduced and sent, along with a covering story, to *Look* magazine. The pictures, declared spurious by the Japanese, were published around the world, while Farmer's name was added to Japan's death list. He wrote that he had other "pictures that the world will never see: Japanese soldiers in the act of raping Chinese women,

Japanese soldiers tearing the clothes off young girls, and Japanese soldiers revoltingly examining the bodies of Chinese women. In one picture of a mass beheading, Japanese camera-fiends have climbed a tree to get better pictures."

The worst suffering was endured by the women of Nanking. In the words of one Japanese soldier, "No matter how young or old, they all could not escape the fate of being raped. We sent out coal trucks . . . to seize a lot of women. And then each of them was allocated 15 to 20 soldiers for sexual intercourse and abuse." According to another soldier, "It would be all right if we only raped them, I shouldn't say all right. But we always stabbed and killed them. Because dead bodies don't talk. . . . Perhaps when we were raping her, we looked at her as a woman, but when we killed her, we just thought of her as something like a pig." Iris Chang said that many of the Japanese soldiers believed that raping a virgin would make them more powerful on the battlefield, while some were even known to have the pubic hair of the girls they raped made into amulets to guard them against injury. According to a European observer, "There were girls under the age of 8 and women over the age of 70 who were raped and then, in the most brutal way possible, knocked down and beat up. . . . I saw the victims with my own eyes."

As word of the unspeakable treatment of women drifted out of Nanking, there was, according to Iris Chang, a "massive outcry" from the nations of the West. In response—and in one of the strangest quirks of this or any other war—the Japanese established their infamous comfort houses. "By luring, purchasing, or kidnapping between eighty thousand and two hundred thousand women," Chang said, ". . . the Japanese military hoped to reduce the incidence of random rape of local women (thereby diminishing the opportunity for international criticism), to contain sexually transmitted diseases through the use of condoms, and to reward soldiers for fighting on the battlefront for long stretches of time."

One Japanese doctor who took part as a soldier in the Rape of Nanking and who tried to atone for the rest of his life had this to say: "Few know that soldiers impaled babies on bayonets and tossed them still alive into pots of boiling water. They gang-raped women from the ages of twelve to eighty and then killed them when they could no longer satisfy sexual requirements. I beheaded people, starved them to death, burned them, and buried them alive, over two hundred in all. It is terrible that I could turn into an animal and do these things."

It is estimated that somewhere in the range of 200,000 (some say closer to 300,000) Chinese were butchered in the first six weeks of the massacre. Some survivors made it into the Safety Zone, an area set up by about twenty Europeans and Americans who risked their lives to save their Chinese neighbors. Among these, the most notable were John Rabe, the leader of the Nazi Party in Nanking, "a splendid man" with "a tremendous heart"; Dr. Robert Wilson, the son of missionaries, who ruined his own health in attempting to care for the battered and broken Chinese; and Wilhemina Vautrin, an educator who took it upon herself to save as many women and girls as she could from rape and death. On December 18, 1937, Wilson wrote his family, "Today marks the sixth day of the modern Dante's Inferno, written in huge letters with blood and rape. Murder by the wholesale and rape by the thousands of cases. There seems to be no stop to the ferocity, lust and atavism of the brutes."

WHILE THE CITIZENS of Nanking were undergoing these horrors, May-ling and Chiang were in Hankow, where they had fled just two days before the arrival of the Japanese army. Japanese planes tried to shoot them down, and they were saved only because the American plane in which they flew outdistanced its pursuers.

From December 1937 until October 1938, Chiang ruled China from the city of Hankow. Of all the foreign concessions that had once existed in the old treaty port, only the French Concession was left, although other consulates, warehouses, offices, and banks with their European facades still rose along the north shore of the reddish brown Yangtze, and spectators often gathered around the gates of the British Consulate to watch the consul general in his garden practicing his putting. Along with what Christopher Isherwood and W. H. Auden called "a good lending-library," there remained an American drugstore, a YMCA, and a red-light street in the temporary capital. According to the English visitors, the clothing stores, cafés, and restaurants were all run by White Russian immigrants—"a fat, defeated tribe who lead a melancholy indoor life of gossip, mah-jongg, drink, and bridge. . . . Their clocks," according to Auden, "stopped in 1917. It has been tea-time ever since."

The Chiangs lived across the river in the Chinese city of Wuchang in an old military headquarters with a stone gateway and a large dugout in the front yard. Auden and Isherwood were taken by Donald to have tea there with the generalissimo's wife. "She is a small, round-faced lady," Isherwood later wrote,

> exquisitely dressed, vivacious rather than pretty, and possessed of an almost terrifying charm and poise. Obviously she knows just how to deal with any conceivable type of visitor. She can become at will the cultivated, westernized woman with a knowledge of literature and

art; the technical expert, discussing aeroplane-engines and machine-guns; the inspector of hospitals; the president of a mothers' union; or the simple, affectionate, clinging Chinese wife. She could be terrible, she could be gracious, she could be businesslike, she could be ruthless. . . . Strangely enough, I have never heard anybody comment on her perfume. It is the most delicious either of us has ever smelt.

After the interview, Isherwood concluded that "Madame . . . for all her artificiality, is certainly a great heroic figure."

Although they accepted May-ling's artifice, Isherwood and Auden, like most foreign writers and reporters, were disgusted with the daily briefings held in the offices of Hollington Tong, Chiang's chief of publicity. "Every Japanese advance is a Chinese strategic withdrawal," Isherwood complained. "Towns pass into Japanese hands in the most tactful manner possible—they simply cease to be mentioned."* The news was read aloud by Mr. Li, a gentleman who, according to Isherwood, bore a strong resemblance to "the most optimistic of Walt Disney's Three Little Pigs."

✿

IN JANUARY 1937, Emma Mills received a formal Christmas card from the Chiangs—a typical head of state greeting with a photograph of one of their homes. "My last letter from May-ling had been nearly ten years ago," Emma recalled ruefully, "and several of mine since had gone unanswered." Nonetheless, urged to get a group of Wellesley women together to hear about the situation in China, Emma invited a dozen or so of her classmates to a luncheon, at which they helped compose a letter to May-ling. The following month, Emma got a letter back to be circulated to the ladies, thanking them for the message and outlining China's position:

Our national existence is at stake. . . . The rest of the world is slowly realizing that China is fighting not only her own battle but their battle as well. . . . The [boycott] movement is spreading in all parts of the world, and the more people adhere to it and refuse to buy, sell, and transport Japanese goods, the more chance there will be for this bloody war to terminate at an early date. . . . Pray for us—yes, but, at the same time, do what you can to carry on the boycott

* The same was apparently true of the Japanese, who, according to Donald, "never report losses" and "always have victories." (Hoover Archives: Stanley K. Hornbeck papers, copy of letter from W. H. Donald to H. J. Timperley, February 28, 1939, Box 150.)

movement. I shall not tell you about the horrible atrocities we have
been witnessing in our country for the past three months. . . . I
have seen them with my own eyes, those terribly mangled bodies.
I have heard the children call their dead parents, after the bombing
of hundreds of refugees at the South Station at Shanghai. My shoes
were blood-smeared when I walked through there. . . . Help us stop
this war.

The above crossed a letter May-ling received from Emma, offering to
keep the generalissimo's wife up to date on American public opinion as it
related to China. It was a letter that had obviously been hard for Emma to
write—she confided to her diary that she had spent "all evening" doing it—
and, given the care with which the words were chosen, it is clear that she still
felt estranged from her old friend. "You should remember me well enough
to be assured of my personal loyalty to and deep felt sympathy with you,"
Emma wrote May-ling. "What you may not realize, is that my interest in
China has continued and even grown with the years. . . . American sympathy is entirely with China," she wrote but then was forced to add, "Americans are by no means ready yet for any large scale boycott. Rightly or wrongly,
the majority seem to feel that it would be a first step inevitably leading to
war." Informing May-ling that she had started a campaign among members
of their old Wellesley class to raise funds for civilian relief, Emma finished
by saying "If there is anything at all that I can do for you, or that you think
I might do for China's cause, surely you know you can count on me."

Once May-ling gave her the go-ahead, Emma's efforts to raise interest in
and money for China became a full-time job. By this point in her life Emma
had finished everything she needed except a thesis for a M.A. in Chinese
studies. She was unmarried; her social life, she said, was "very sketchy," since
she lived with her eighty-nine-year-old grandmother and, as she put it, "one
can't do much in her house." As to May-ling, her letters and requests see-
sawed between an occasional exchange of confidences that recalled their
former intimacy and the sort of formalized political writing that the wife of
a head of state might direct to someone whom she knew she could trust to
understand her country's needs. May-ling now used the salutation "Dear
Emma" in place of "Dear" or "Dearest Dada," and her sign-offs vary from
"With love, May-ling Soong Chiang" to the oddly formal "Yours very sincerely, Madame Chiang Kai-shek."*

---

* As she became more famous, May-ling worried about the openness of her earlier letters to her friend. "I seem to recollect seeing somewhere that you had promised the
Mayling Soong Foundation the letters I have written to you," she added at the end of a

The Soong family in July of 1917, at home in Shanghai.

This is the first picture of all eight members of the family (May-ling and T.V. had just returned from college in the United States). Front row: T.A.; second row from left: Ai-ling, T.V., and Ching-ling; third row: Charlie and Ni Kwei-tseng; standing in back: T.L. and May-ling.

2

Charlie Soong, father, at the age of forty-nine. Taken at the time of his voluntary exile to Japan, following Sun Yat-sen. Tokyo, April 1915.

3

Ni Kwei-tseng, mother. Undated.

4

May-ling (front row, center) at Wesleyan, age fifteen. She came to the United States when she was ten.

5

May-ling, T.V., and Ching-ling in Boston in 1913. May-ling was sixteen, T.V. was nineteen, and Ching-ling, who graduated from Wesleyan that year, was twenty.

7

May-ling at Wellesley. Taken from a group shot of the Tau Zeta Epsilon Society (the Arts Society) and dated 1916–1917.

6

Emma Mills.
    She was May-ling's closest friend at college.

The Dowager Empress. Named Tzu Hsi (known as Cixi), she rose from being a concubine of the fifth rank to the most powerful person in China. Note the nails on her fourth and fifth fingers.

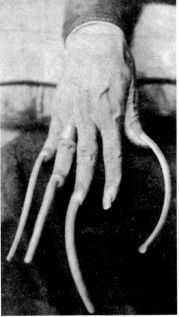

A hand of a member of the leisure class. Ludicrously long nails were a sure indication of the privileged, idle life of an upper-class Chinese.

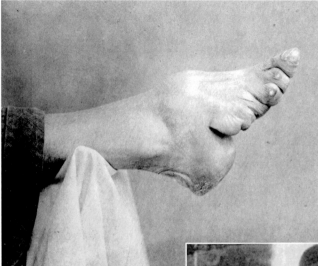

A deformed foot. The result of footbinding, this is a typical "golden lily," probably somewhere between three and five inches long. Note the resulting callouses on the heel and toes.

11

A castrated man. There were as many as 3,000 men who voluntarily gave up their sexual organs to prosper in the Chinese Court.

The three Soong sisters.

As young women, they were usually photographed with Ai-ling, the eldest, seated in front of Ching-ling (on the left) and May-ling (on the right).

The Soong sisters with Chiang Kai-shek. Due to Ching-ling's dislike of her brother-in-law, she usually kept her distance from him. This photograph must date from World War II, when she joined forces with her sisters in a common cause. May-ling is on the left, then Ai-ling, Chiang, and Ching-ling.

The sisters walking through the rubble of war. Ai-ling is holding on to Ching-ling; May-ling, who did more of this than her sisters, is following.

Ai-ling and husband H. H. Kung, a seventy-fifth-generation descendant of Confucius.

Ching-ling and husband Sun Yat-sen, known as the George Washington of China.

T. V. Soong and wife Laura, an elegant socialite.

May-ling and husband Chiang Kai-shek, the man who united China.

19

Mao Fu-mei. Chiang's first
wife, his mother's choice.

20

Yao Yi-cheng. Chiang's
concubine, mother of
Chiang Wei-kuo.

21

Ch'en Chieh-ju. Chiang's
second wife, his own
choice, known as Jennie.

Soong May-ling and Chiang Kai-shek's wedding portrait, December 1, 1929.

23

Huang Jin-rong. Known (behind his back) as "Pockmarked Huang," he headed the police force in the French Concession and controlled crime in Shanghai from the inside out.

24

Du Yueh-sen. "Big-eared Du" was an orphan who made good, organizing the opium trade and adding philanthropy to his accomplishments.

25

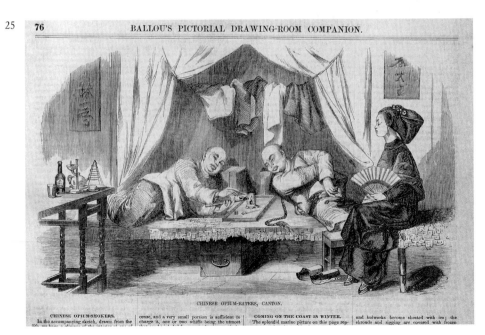

An Opium Den, complete with paraphernalia and a female attendant.

Warlords

Feng Yu-hsiang.
The Christian general.

Wu Pu-fei.
A scholar and philosopher.

Chang Tso-lin.
The lord of Manchuria.

Yen Hsi-shan.
The "model governor" of
Shansi Province.

Sun Chuan-fang.
He controlled five
provinces.

Chang Tsung-ch'ang.
Known as "The Monster,"
he was 6 foot, 6 inches tall.

Mao Tse-tung was already known as one of the founders of the Chinese Communist Party in 1924, at the age of thirty-one.

Chou En-lai studied in Paris, where he recruited and organized young revolutionaries. After his return to China, he never appeared in a suit and tie.

Mao in Wuhan in 1927, the year
when revolutionary chaos was
followed by the retreat of the
Communist Party faithful back
to Russia.

Chou in 1924, dean of the Political
Department of Whampoa Military Academy.

Mao on the march against the Kuomintang.

Chou on horseback. He was deputy chairman of the Red Army Military Council.

❦

CHRISTMAS OF 1937 brought the Chiangs a visit from the German ambassador with overtures of peace from Japan. Giving the note to May-ling, the ambassador said, "I am instructed to hand you this without comment." "I should think so," she answered, changing the subject immediately. According to Donald, who was present, nothing further was said about the so-called peace terms, which, the Japanese admitted, "were those of a victor." The Italians then tried to make a peace deal with T.V. by suggesting that he overturn the Chinese government. "That, of course," said Donald, "was laughed at."

During the winter of 1937–1938, the Chinese reached a new low point. One of China's most enthusiastic and idealistic boosters admitted that Hankow was "filled with men and women who take no apparent interest in the war," while the American ambassador, Nelson T. Johnson, was even more blunt. According to Johnson, the general attitude of the current inhabitants of Hankow was "Let us fight to the last drop of coolie blood" while "in the midst of it all the Soong family carries on its intrigues which sometimes disgust me completely."

In that regard, Barbara Tuchman told a story about May-ling, who invited a group of journalists, who had just returned from a visit to the Communists in Yenan, to tea. When the reporters spoke enthusiastically about the integrity and sense of sacrifice of the members of the Chinese Communist Party, Madame walked over to a window, saying that she could not believe what they were telling her. After a few minutes of silence, she turned back to the group. "If what you tell me about them is true," she said, "then I can only say they have never known *real* power."

The Australian journalist Rhodes Farmer gave a different picture of May-ling as she paid an incognito visit to the city of Hsuchow,* which the Japanese were bombing regularly twice a day. Described by the matron as "a beautifully dressed Chinese woman [who] had asked to see the hospital . . . [she] talked cheerfully with every wounded soldier and civilian but did not reveal her identity. As she was leaving," Farmer later wrote, "the puzzled missionary asked for the name of her visitor."

"I am Madame Chiang Kai-shek; I am visiting the front with my husband . . ."

---

letter in 1953. "Now, my dear girl, put a codicil in your will that those letters are first to be turned over to me to be censored, for I do not know what nonsense I might have written in years gone by which was meant for your eyes only."

* In the eastern province of Kiangsu.

"You know," the matron told the journalist, "my hair just about stood on end with surprise. I could scarcely believe Madame Chiang would come to such a dangerous spot. I told her she was foolish to make such trips, but she just smiled back at me and said she felt far safer when she was sharing her husband's perils. That was my first glimpse of her. I think she must be a very fine woman."

Another journalist, Freda Utley, interviewed Madame Chiang about this time. Raised as an atheist in an intellectual English family, Utley had joined the Communist Party, married a Russian who had been purged, and then fled the Soviet Union. Two years later, she spoke with the generalissimo's wife:

> After an hour's talk . . . the alarm sounded. She [Madame Chiang] continued to talk as if nothing had happened. . . . When the bombs seemed to be falling close she took me down to their dug-out, and there in the tense atmosphere of an airraid I had a more intimate and revealing talk with her than in any other interview. She is a very lovely woman and can be as simple and unaffected and friendly as an American. Her wide dark eyes become particularly beautiful when she is under some emotional stress. . . . Although I was to see her again in the role of gracious queen receiving those favoured to enter her presence, I never forgot the two and a half hours I had spent with her that morning when she became an intelligent Western educated woman tackling a sea of troubles with patience and understanding and without illusions. . . . When I said that the general impression was that the Communists were the least corrupt and best element in China, she exclaimed: 'Incorrupt, yes; but that's because they haven't got power yet.' There is certainly much truth in this remark, and Madame Chiang is obviously, unlike her sister Madame Sun Yat-sen, a political realist. Nevertheless, in conversation with her one felt an emotional bitterness . . . towards the Communists and an unwillingness to recognize their merits. Her hatred of those who not only fought against Chiang Kai-shek so long, but who to-day still challenge her own religious and social concepts, obscures her political judgement, which in other respects is so penetrating. On the other hand, her Christian beliefs, which are most sincerely held, blind her to the shortcomings of those who share them, or appear to share them.

In her first letter to Emma of 1938, May-ling wrote about the Japanese slaughter of refugees and complained that "the democratic powers were so afraid of Japan" that they had even stopped supplies on their way to China: "America turned airplanes off a ship at San Diego, which we bought and paid for before hostilities broke out. . . . America is virtually assisting Japan to defeat China." A few months later, she changed her tune, writing that the Chinese understood the situation in the United States and "the motives which prompt the Government to refrain from antagonizing Japan. We know they fear Japan, and that they fear war just as much." But, she added, it was hard for the Chinese to understand why the Allies did not try to penalize Japan for "inhumanities which would bring the blush of shame to the cheeks of the barbaric tribes who disgraced even the Dark Ages. What they knew about inhumanities was nothing in comparison to the refined methods of slaughter, robbery, and torture, displayed by the Japanese."

At the end of April, the G-mo's wife wrote Emma that she had just returned from the front.

> I visited just as many base hospitals as I had time at each stop, and also managed to arrange the placing of two thousand war orphans with four Catholic missions. Those kids will be well looked after, as the Sisters pour out all their love onto their charges. Do I hear you say, "vicarious motherhood"? Perhaps. Anyway I inspected some of their institutions incog and saw enough to convince myself that I am doing a wise thing by having some of the children at least under the sisters. . . . We are also placing as many as possible in other mission institutions. . . . The money that you promise to send me shall be used for the children's work. You would like that, won't you? Later I shall send you pictures of all of your orphans and they will know that you and your friends are taking care of them.

Meanwhile, Madame Chiang sent Chinese cups and saucers, packages of green tea, and silver spoons ("to show that a spoon may be licked but China can't") to her Wellesley class and the class of 1938, which had made her an honorary member. "You are doing so many things for me that you might as well do some more," she wrote, asking Emma to distribute the gifts.

"I've sometimes said that I knew Mayling Soong well, but don't know Mme. Chiang at all," Emma wrote back in an obvious reference to Mayling's previous stiffness, "but after reading the second letter, I guess maybe they're the same person, after all. Yes, of course I'll look after all the gifts. . . . You shouldn't have gone to so much trouble for us, with so much else on your mind." In distributing May-ling's gifts, Emma said that she herself had "shone a good deal by reflected glory, which had its amusing aspects," among them being invited to have dinner with Mildred McAfee, the president of Wellesley College. McAfee, who was criticized for favoring China over Japan in the current conflict, was reported to have countered, "After all we can't help it if we have no Japanese alumna of similar prominence!"

In the middle of June 1938, the generalissimo's wife had a series of three articles printed in *The New York Times*. Warning readers that "my views are unpalatable—sometimes unprintable," she launched into a sarcastic condemnation of the other nations in the League for leaving China "frigidly alone . . . to fight as best we can . . . for the principles which the democracies espouse" and the "studied neutrality of the democracies that enables Japan . . . to continue killing our people, violating our women and making a wilderness of all of our territory that she has been able to penetrate." The second article, no less judgmental than the first, referred to "a crippled and, apparently, a useless League of Nations," while the third detailed Japan's attempt to control the Chinese population with opium as "a surcease from their mental and physical tortures."

Emma's reaction to May-ling's articles was guarded. "They are certainly frank, and any earlier would not, I think, have had a sympathetic reaction. Now we are in the mood for them." The managing editor of the *Times* was not so sanguine. "I quite agree with the *New York Times* managing editor when he says that I am 'writing too much,'" May-ling wrote Emma. "He is right. . . . That last set of articles for the *Times* was really not written for publication. . . . Sometime ago I had concluded that I would write no more for the newspapers, and also would refrain from writing to individuals, since so many rush the letters into print.* No one realizes better than I do how tired people can become of repetition of arguments."

Nevertheless, during her winter in Hankow, May-ling asked Hollington Tong to copy her speeches, newpaper articles, broadcasts, and letters for Rhodes Farmer to edit into a book. Farmer, given six weeks to accomplish the job, said it was "the strangest and most difficult assignment of my varied life as a newspaperman," since the Chinese typesetters knew no English and all the type had to be set by hand, even though there was enough for only forty pages at a time. During the process, Farmer lost his unalloyed admiration for the generalissimo's wife: "Several times the 10,000 copies of those forty pages were completed and then Madame—She Who Must Be Obeyed—decided upon alterations. . . . Madame . . . was extremely proud of her first book. But when . . . she saw me she was Madame the Martinet. What about that printing error on such and such a page, and the line of her poetry that had been misplaced?"

---

* Which may or may not have happened in this case.

Although she did not allow the book to be sold in the United States or Britain, May-ling sent more than three hundred autographed copies to Wellesley, saying that it would be "of interest because some of the imperfections are due to the unusual difficulties we are undergoing in Hankow owing to war conditions." She asked Emma to distribute the books, enclosing a check for $100.00 for packing and postage.

I am terrifically busy going to the country to inspect the work our war service teams are doing to mobilize the women in the rear. No joke these trips. Mud—squishy, mushy, sticky goo—over the ankles as we tramp through muddy roads to reach our destination; bumps from the springless rickshas, and standing for hours in the drizzling rain. You will be surprised to know that I have developed to be quite a stump speaker. Next you know I shall become an inveterate soap-box orator. . . . When this war is over I think my hair will turn white, but there is one comfort: I am working so hard I am not in danger of ever becoming a nice, fat, soft, sofa cushion or having a derriere.

27

❦

The rest of the world is bound to catch fire from the Asiatic blaze. A great war is inevitably coming and China has only to hold out until that happens.

—T.V. SOONG, 1937

As THE JAPANESE cut a bloody path through China, May-ling assumed the voice of the victim, crying out for help to the rest of the world. Forty years old in 1937, at the height of her beauty and confidence, the generalissimo's wife had wisely enlisted Donald as her adviser. According to James McHugh, "There is little doubt that Donald deserves the lion's share of the credit for the rise of the Chiangs" to their position of "international prominence . . . as liberal leaders." As a former journalist, Donald knew how to present them to the international press, particularly those in the countries whose help China needed to survive. He was, McHugh said, "bound by a blind faith and devotion" to May-ling and a firm belief in her ability to bridge the gap between East and West. To accomplish what we today would call the media blitz surrounding Chiang and his wife, Donald hired a team of assistants. Their job was "to build about the tiny frame of Madame Chiang the sparkle, the words, the voice to command the compassion, the dollars and the moral support of democratic people everywhere."

On August 16, 1937, three days after the Japanese attacked Shanghai, the lead article in *Life* magazine—"Mei-ling ('Beautiful Mood') Helps Her Husband Rule China"—featured a three-quarter-page picture of the generalissimo's wife, asserting that she was "probably the most powerful woman in the world." The author credited her with giving foreign correspondents a free hand in dispensing the political news from China (untrue) and noted that she was "not only China's censor" (also untrue) but secretary-general of China's air force and a prime mover in the Chinese Red Cross. The article included pictures of May-ling at Wesleyan, May-ling at Wellesley, and May-ling with the "crude, brash warlord named Chiang Kai-shek," who, after his marriage to her, had miraculously graduated to adjectives like "matured" and "gentle." The author of the piece* referred to Chiang and May-ling as "China's George and Martha Washington."

---

* No author is given, so we must assume it was written under the direction of Henry Luce, a noted admirer of and apologist for the Chiangs.

This was just one of "innumerable" articles on May-ling that appeared in 1937 in magazines and newspapers all over the United States. *The Boston Herald* and *The New York Times Magazine*, as well as papers in Charlotte and Cincinnati, carried enthusiastic pieces in which reporters described the physical and mental attributes of Madame Chiang. "The greatest man in Asia is a woman," wrote Fulton Oursler, editor of *Liberty* magazine, who called May-ling "the real brains and boss of the Chinese government" after interviewing her in Nanking. "A fabulous woman: a legend of fearlessness, beauty, and wisdom hard to believe," Oursler gushed, adding that although he had met "many of the great persons" of his time, he had "never met any one else who affected me quite as did Madame Chiang Kai-shek." This feeling was no doubt encouraged by Donald, who escorted him to his interview, letting him know that he was "very fortunate to be having tea with Madame." The generalissimo's wife, he told Oursler, was "on the verge of a nervous collapse. Madame now sees almost no one. But she defies her doctors!"

Donald's publicity campaign also had a decided effect on the Russians, who collected and collated materials on May-ling throughout the 1930s and '40s. Their information came from the CCP, the NKVD, miscellaneous journalists, the Comintern Executive Committee, and anywhere else they could gather tidbits. There is even an article in a confidential file, entitled "The Person Chiang Kai-shek Trusts," by Chou En-lai; in it Chou rightly contended that May-ling was far more democratic than her husband. In another file she was characterized as "an active woman with a will of steel." Still another called her "very aggressive and arrogant," stating that luxury was as important to her as it was to her sister Ai-ling and arguing that she used a "mixture of authoritarianism, selfishness, fake liberalism and charitable activities to conceal her reactionary politics." Most of the Soviet files, however, simply stressed her effect on the diplomatic stage, internal Chinese affairs, and her husband.

"Almond-Eyed Cleopatra Is 'Power Behind Power' in War-Time China" read an article in the *Cincinnati Times-Star*, published in the spring of 1938. The author, a female journalist known for her own beauty and wit, had first interviewed Madame Chiang in 1928, the year after her marriage, and reported that the generalissimo's wife had grown more dignified and sure of herself in the intervening ten years. Lady Grace Drummond-Hay wrote that the reason Madame's "name and fame is vastly greater throughout the world than it is in China" was that for the Chinese, "there is no greater reproach to a woman, whatever her rank, position or wealth, than that she is childless." She also claimed that Madame sought no "glory for herself" but "turns it all over to her husband," characterized by the author as "medieval-minded" and "no military genius." Whatever glory the generalissimo's wife might or might not have sought, she was still living in a country inhabited predominantly by tillers of the earth, men and women who did not think beyond the farm, the neighbors, or the village. One Chinese peasant, asked what he thought of Madame Chiang, answered, "Well, he's got to have a wife, doesn't he?"

When friends and enemies were not collecting information on and writing about May-ling, she herself was producing dozens of articles and speeches. Some of these were directed to the Chinese, especially women, outlining their obligations during wartime, but most of her exhortations were aimed at the Western democracies. In these, she detailed the horrors of war and the unfairness of the Allies—particularly the United States—which continued to supply the Japanese with gas and oil to fuel their bombers.

At the same time that he was promoting Madame Chiang and her message, Donald was conducting his own private campaign aimed at friends and acquaintances. In answer to a letter from Theodore Roosevelt, Jr.,* Donald blamed the fact that Americans did not understand the situation in China on Japanese propaganda. "It is advisable," he wrote, "to discount Japanese reports by fifty percent, if not more." The Japanese "seem to think that their success will be assured if they can only make people in the outside world believe that . . . [they] are really super-men," whereas "the Chinese have successfully exploded the myth of their invincibility." Japan's only chance to win the war, Donald claimed, would be if the democratic nations of the world "refuse to help China secure the equipment and munitions which will be required by her to continue her defence." To which T.R. Jr. sent a discouraging response: "Our people are sympathetic but only willing to help to the point that this can be done without embroiling themselves . . . the United States has no intention of being drawn into war unless it be necessary to defend her own shores. . . . Mme. Chiang still continues to be the figure in China that has caught the American people's imagination. A visit by her to this country would, of course, have an excellent effect, but I don't believe the effect produced would counterbalance what she is doing for China by being with her people now."

Seven months later, Donald wrote Roosevelt another letter—this one covering thirty-nine single-spaced typewritten pages. In it he described the Chinese people's ability to face disaster with the inborn knowledge that what

---

* Theodore Roosevelt, Jr., the eldest son of the former president, was a Republican who had served as assistant secretary of the navy, governor of Puerto Rico, and governor-general of the Philippines before his Democratic cousin Franklin Delano Roosevelt was elected president. Joking that he was FDR's "fifth cousin, about to be removed," which is exactly what happened, he served in both world wars and won the Medal of Honor. At the time of this correspondence with Donald, he was vice president of the publishing firm Doubleday and Company.

is down will inevitably rise and vice versa—a life-enhancing virtue often envied by Westerners, along with the sense of humor that usually accompanies it. T.R. Jr. was so impressed that he sent copies to Arthur Sulzberger, publisher of *The New York Times,* as well as editors at the Associated Press, *The New York Herald Tribune,* and other major outlets. The letter read:

> Since I last wrote innumerable cities in China have gone up in smoke and dust, and veritable rivers of blood have flown on various fronts . . . the Japanese have, with vicious ferocity, desolated vast areas of China, have massacred hundred of thousands of innocent Chinese, have demolished their homes and their businesses . . . have been guilty of unparalleled rape and rapine, and have, with calculated remorselessness, set about the demoralization as well as the impoverishment of survivors by destroying or removing means of livelihood and setting loose a deluge of opium and narcotics upon the land . . . "military establishments" is the terminology understood in Japan . . . to indicate the homes of the population. . . . Most of these towns had nothing to do with the war, contained no military objectives, and had nothing at all with which to defend themselves. . . . What becomes of the people of all the bombed areas? Thousands of them are blown to fragments, of course, and those who die . . . are fortunate in the sudden death that overtakes them, for there are continual thousands being maimed and who live with their terrible wounds, while millions more are made destitute. . . . They take what they can on their backs, or on barrows, or any wheeled vehicles that they can use. . . . People in flight fill the highways, and they crowd the mountain trails, climbing like ants . . . hoping to achieve immunity from raiders and find safety from the tortures of war. . . . The remarkable and outstanding feature of this great migration is the fortitude of the sufferers in their adversity. They live or they die, as the case may be, but they do not complain. The philosophy which they exhibit in the midst of crushing calamity approaches the sublime. . . . It is this inherent faculty for enduring desperate suffering, this power of recuperation, that makes it impossible for Japan to subjugate or conquer China. Natural calamities . . . have bred in the blood and bone of the Chinese race these powers of survival that enable them quickly to subdue and overcome the effects of appalling catastrophes.

Japan's soldiers apparently fared little better than those they were sent to destroy. One member of the Red Cross observed that the Japanese

put only a few soldiers in a field hospital near Hankow and that they were
only slightly wounded. The same observer noticed a large burial ground
nearby. "There wasn't a shadow of doubt that the Japanese were doing
away with their badly wounded men," he said. "Crippled men back in Japan
would have spoiled the picture of easy conquest the High Command was
painting."

During 1937 and 1938, the generalissimo's wife turned out more than a
hundred articles, speeches, press dispatches, and statements, not counting
interviews and letters, written to be circulated into monied or powerful
hands. No occasion was allowed to be lost, especially gatherings of women,
missionaries, any group that might listen to her complaints, respond to her
calls for help or bow (in the case of the Chinese) before her demands for
sacrifice. It was an impressive output—an opportunity for May-ling to use
her love of writing to produce something more essential than the Chinese
tales she had once dreamed of creating with Emma.

Although the bulk of her pronouncements were self-generated, every
so often she wrote in response to a request, like the speech broadcast to
a convention of YWCA delegates in Columbus, Ohio. Not surprisingly,
she could not resist the impulse to compare and contrast: "To the delegates
of the Fifteenth National Convention of the Young Women's Christian Association . . . the women of war-torn China send greetings. Because my
country is at war and because so many thousands of my fellow women have
met a fate worse than death, it seems almost unreal that several thousand
American women should be able to hold a convention in peaceful surroundings to discuss such subjects as leadership, religion, and democracy."

Two weeks earlier Emma had written May-ling that Americans had
become more interested in and informed about the war. "The Panay* did
more . . . and Hitler's seizure of Austria has shocked the most indifferent
into some thought on the matter. . . . Importers have cut the prices on Japanese dinner ware to such an extent on account of the boycott, domestic
manufacturers are worried. So many lisle hose are being made, there's a
shortage of thread. . . . Boys at the University of Washington have declared

---

* The USS Panay was sunk by the Japanese on December 12, 1937, as it was taking members of the U.S. government out of the Nanking war zone. It was attacked by a large
contingent of bombers, which continued to fire on the men who had escaped in life-
boats, even strafing the reeds on the riverbanks for survivors. There was no question that
the attack was a deliberate attempt by the Japanese military to provoke the United States
into war, since the U.S. Embassy had informed Japan of the Panay's departure in
advance. Nevertheless, the United States accepted the Japanese government's formal
apology—it claimed that American flags had been mistaken for Chinese ones—and offer
of reparations.

a 'boycott' on girls who wear silk stockings. Student groups are beginning a campaign to prevent American participation at the Olympics scheduled for Tokyo in 1940." By the end of the year, Emma could report that both du Pont and the Celanese Corporation had announced that they were building plants to produce an artificial fiber that would have all the attributes of real silk for the manufacture of ladies' stockings. "It will be a year before large scale production begins," Emma said, "but the Japanese are already reported worried."

In May, Emma told May-ling that what was needed to galvanize the American public into contributing money were concrete examples and human interest stories. "Not atrocity material . . . not bare statistics . . . but definite accounts of what is being done to meet the huge refugee problem, particularly by the Chinese themselves . . . eyewitness accounts and specific needs are much more appealing than general." As to May-ling's campaign for war orphans, the agency hired to help raise money for China told Emma that it would "prefer pictures of individual children, with names on the back, to be given to prominent adopters when the time comes and reproduced in the newspapers. Glossy prints at least 4x4 inches are best for that, or the negatives themselves."

Later in the year, Emma wrote to complain about the publicity releases issued by the Chinese government. They were, she said, "too long and too frequent . . . most of the stories should be cut to about a half or a third . . . and certain types of stories are not really useful to us here. . . . One letter I have says, 'We don't want . . . student essays . . . or general speeches or general denunciations. . . . What exactly are conditions under Japanese occupation? . . . Specific details about dismantling of Chinese factories, about impressment of coolies, about burning of villages, specific name, place, etc. What is life like under Japanese occupation?' "

THE YEAR 1938 turned out to be almost as bad for the Chiangs as 1937, although it started with *Time* naming them "Man and Wife of the Year," putting them on the cover of the magazine, and stating that "Through 1937, the Chinese have been led—not without glory—by one supreme leader and his remarkable wife. . . . No woman in the West holds so great a position as Mme. Chiang Kai-shek holds in China." Lovely words from Mr. Luce, echoed by the *Missionary Review of the World*, which declared some months later that "China has now the most enlightened, patriotic and able rulers in her history." Unfortunately for the Chiangs, this much-lauded leadership did not translate into more than a few victories for the Chinese army. Having captured the coastal city of Tsingtao in early January, the Japanese advanced south through the province of Shansi, reaching the Yellow River in early March. They now controlled about one seventh of China's approximately 4 million square miles of territory and were still on the march.

In the spring of 1938, there was a sudden reversal of mood in Hankow when word came through that the Chinese had scored a big victory over the Japanese at a town in the province of Shantung, lying on the enemy's road to the interior. The battle, which lasted for seventeen days, cost the Japanese 16,000 casualties plus 200 military vehicles. The victory had been achieved by pursuing a plan developed by Chiang's German advisers, which involved bringing up reinforcements from the rear and cutting the Japanese infantry off from its source of supplies. But Chiang refused to follow up the victory by advancing or pursuing the enemy. The head of the German Military Mission in China, General Alexander von Falkenhausen, was said to be "tearing his hair" in frustration. "I tell the Generalissimo to advance, to attack, to exploit his success. But nothing is done. Soon the Japanese will have 8 or 10 divisions before Hsuchow. Then it will be too late."

General Falkenhausen was right. The Japanese broke through the Chinese defenses, and Hsuchow fell at the end of May. Meanwhile, another Japanese army was advancing from the north, putting the entire region between the Yellow and Yangtze Rivers in danger. Chiang ordered one of his generals to blow up the dikes on the Yellow River behind the Japanese vanguard. The locals were apparently not warned, and 2 million people were rendered homeless, eleven cities and four thousand villages flooded, and the farms in three provinces ruined. This massive destruction held the Japanese back for about three months.

Meanwhile, moving westward from the coast, the Japanese army continued its advance, occupying the old walled city of Kaifeng in the province of Honan, capital of seven former dynasties, along with the capital of the province of Anhwei and the port city of Amoy. Four months later, in October of 1938, the Japanese occupied Canton, China's last outlet to the sea. Some 3,000 Cantonese had already lost their lives in five months of bombing, and 860,000 residents, terrified that the Japanese would repeat the barbarity they had exhibited in Nanking, had fled the city. But one wartime visitor noted that when the government offered a reward to anyone who could bring down an enemy plane, "anti-aircraft defence . . . became a local sport, like duck-shooting. When the planes came over, everybody blazed away—even the farmers."

Chiang had made little provision for the defense of Canton, relying instead on the presumption that the British, across the bay in Hong Kong, would never allow the city to fall. But Britain could elicit no promise that the United States would help if it ended up in a war against Japan, and Canton fell on October 21. Donald, who had been ill and away for the past four months, arrived in Hankow two days later. He saw an ambulance, which had been purchased with funds from the United States, stop in front of a bank in which one of the high government officials had big interests. A crowd had gathered to watch the ambulance take away a part of the official's huge fortune, and Donald could hear people murmuring that this was proof that Hankow was about to be taken over by the Japanese.

"When I got into Hankow I found it completely changed," he wrote Theodore Roosevelt, Jr.

> The evacuation of thousands of people, the crowding of thousands more into the ex–foreign concessions, and the daily raids by Japanese bombers, made the erstwhile clean bund look like a back alley of a poverty-stricken town. Refugees were camped there, men, women and children, their belongings scattered higgledy-piggledy everywhere. . . . Canton's collapse meant withdrawal from Hankow, and late on the night of October 24, we flew out, "we" being the Generalissimo and Mme. Chiang and myself. At 2 o'clock the next morning we landed in Hunan province, and then began a tour of all the fronts which lasted until December 9, when we got to Chungking.*

If the Chinese were ever going to fight the Japanese or even sustain themselves in their new wartime home in Chungking, their resistance and sustenance depended on heavy industry, which was now far more important than the production of pricey consumer goods such as tea and silk in which the country had traditionally excelled. Although China had produced only 100,000 tons of steel before the war, whatever equipment there was had to be removed from the cities. In Shanghai the Chinese packed machinery from the factories into rowboats, covered it with branches and leaves, and sent it up the Yangtze, hiding the boats in the reeds along the river at the first sound and/or sight of Japanese bombers overhead. In what Crozier called "a staggering achievement of primitive muscle power and equipment," whole factories were moved to the province of Szechuan, home of the wartime capital, where munitions plants were set up deep in caves. By the end of the migration, some $3,448,275 in equipment had been transported. "We moved whatever we could of our factories," May-ling said. "We moved our arsenals and all available machinery. We even marched our Jersey and Guernsey cows from Nanking. We used every conveyance imaginable: trucks, rickshas, wheelbarrows, litters, palanquins, sedan-chairs, carts, and the human back."

---

* China's capital for the remainder of the war.

By the end of 1938, the Japanese had stopped advancing, the Chinese army was cut off from access to the sea, and there were 1 million Japanese soldiers in China. Chiang's government, which had moved to Chungking, was now isolated except for supplies shipped from Russia overland through Central Asia and the illegal traffic in smuggling and bribery carried on with the Japanese. Although there had been and still were many critics of the generalissimo's strategy of baiting the enemy and then withdrawing, the Japanese themselves seemed to have recognized its efficacy. According to Masanori Ito, a military historian,

> the great headache for the Japanese army was the Chinese army's strategy of "retreating instead of advancing." . . . China's territory was "wide and deep," and the Chinese troops moved very fast. The weary Japanese forces had no way of catching up with them, especially since the supply lines were often cut. Therefore no devastating blow had ever been dealt on the main force of the Chinese army. . . . As far as the Japanese army was concerned, this was a defeat. From the angle of the Chinese army, this was certainly not a victory; but on the other hand, it was not a defeat either. . . . When the Pacific War broke out, the Japanese army had already paid the huge sacrifice of 1,150,000 lives, including the victims of war illness.

On December 22, 1938, the Japanese premier gave a speech in which he offered peace and said that China was ready for a "rebirth," providing it would agree to recognize Manchukuo, sign a mutual anti-Communist pact with Inner Mongolia, cooperate economically with the Japanese in northern China, abolish foreign concessions and consular jurisdiction, and refrain from asking for reparations. In return for China's agreeing to these terms, the Japanese promised to withdraw their armed forces within two years. Four days later, Chiang Kai-shek delivered his refusal: "We must understand that the rebirth of China is taken by the Japanese to mean destruction of an independent China and creation of an enslaved China. The so-called new order is to be created after China has been reduced to a slave nation and linked up with made-in-Japan Manchukuo."

One of the more intriguing sidelines to this abortive exchange was the position of Wang Ching-wei, who had urged Chiang to accept the peace terms. Wang's wife had left China in early December 1938 with their family, a quantity of luggage, and some furniture, and on December 20, two days before the premier's speech, Wang and his entourage had left as well. They were headed, they said, for Kunming, a city in the western province of Yunnan, but they actually flew to Hanoi in French Indo-China. According to Crozier, it was impossible at that time to fly out of Chungking without permission of the Military Bureau of Investigation and Statistics and, in the case of high officials, that of Chiang Kai-shek himself. Under these circumstances, one can only conclude that the generalissimo knew his deputy was dealing with the Japanese and was not displeased to get rid of the untrustworthy Wang once and for all.

W

EARLIER THAT YEAR, an extraordinary congress in Hankow had modified the Chinese constitution in order to elect Chiang Kai-shek *Tsung-ts'ai* (leader) of the Kuomintang. According to Crozier, the "position gave him virtually unlimited power to dictate to the Executive Yuan, bully the Legislative Yuan, and by-pass the Judicial Yuan," but in the words of Edgar Snow, it was "merely recognizing with a title the dictatorial authority which he has long exercised over the party, the government and the army." In his role as virtual dictator, Chiang divided his office staff into three areas: military, political, and administrative. Although he was regarded as very tight when it came to paying his subordinates, anyone who went to work for him was referred to as a "phoenix" for his sudden rise in social status. Chiang himself, however, relied primarily on three men—Chen Li-fu, Ho Ying-chin, and H. H. Kung*—each of whom had a clique of supporters in back of him. He manipulated them in ways that forced them to compete with one another for power, thus recalling the traditional politics of warlordism. It was an ineffectual system at best, and James McHugh said that Madame Chiang and Donald wore "themselves out trying to get Chiang to take drastic action against the inefficiency" around him.

The most famous and important of the factions was the CC Clique, run by the two Chen brothers, nephews of Chen Chi-mei, the man who had befriended Chiang Kai-shek when he was young and whose death had caused Chiang to suffer a near emotional breakdown. The Chens came from a family of landowners. Chen Kuo-fu, eight years older than his brother, was a sickly man, subject to bouts of tuberculosis, who had served as governor of the east coast province of Kiangsu, where he had made great strides in education, public health, and conservation. In 1939, after the government was moved from Hankow to Chungking, he took over the department that selected its personnel, thus wielding influence "that could hardly be matched by any other official in the wartime capital."

---

* Although H. H. Kung is said by Crozier to have been the head of a third clique, he belonged to the Soong family, and his relationship with and influence on the generalissimo will be discussed in a later chapter.

Chen Kuo-fu's younger brother, Chen Li-fu, had earned his B.S. and M.S. at the University of Pittsburgh before giving up a promising career in engineering to work as a revolutionary. Li-fu believed that China must learn about science and technology from the West, but at the same time he clung to an unwavering belief in the old Confucian values. Starting as Chiang Kai-shek's confidential secretary in 1926, he moved in with Chiang, ate his meals there, and noticed, then remarked on Chiang's "bad temper. . . . 'If anyone lost his temper with me, I would resign at once,' " he told his employer. Chiang promised to hold his tongue, and the younger man remained with the generalissimo throughout the Northern Expedition. In 1928, he became director of the investigative division of the Kuomintang, responsible for ferreting out Communists from the party, the military, and the government. One American ambassador to China said that although Li-fu had an "obsession about the Communists . . . he has advanced social ideas. He is personally honest, he lives very simply, and he never has indulged in graft or squeeze."

Known as narrow conservatives and great supporters of Chiang, the Chen brothers—aristocratic, inflexible, and incorruptible—formed the center of the CC Clique, which was highly influential in KMT affairs. They arranged all the generalissimo's appointments and set up his daily schedule. As White put it, "Two silent and mysterious brothers . . . practically control the thought of the nation through a combination of patronage, secret police, espionage and administrative authority."

The head of the military clique was General Ho Ying-chin, a thickset man with a round face who served as the generalissimo's war minister from 1930 to 1944. Called by Edgar Snow "one of the worst degenerates in China," General Ho "came to symbolise the gross corruption and inefficiency" of the Chinese army under Chiang. A general in the bandit suppression campaign, Ho was the top military commander during the abduction crisis, and it was he who had suggested bombing Sian—a plan ultimately prevented by May-ling, T.V., Donald, and H. H. Kung. An angry man, unused to the niceties of diplomacy, General Ho gave a banquet shortly after the outbreak of World War II to honor the ambassadors of China's new allies. "Let us drink to the day when every damned foreigner has been run out of China," he said, raising his cup of rice wine. An embarrassed secretary was forced to explain to the group that "The minister is drinking to the defeat of the Japanese."

28

Madame Kung is the practical one of the three [sisters], Madame Sun the extreme idealist, Madame Chiang is both, and in this sense, the greatest of them all.

—PEARL BUCK

THE CHIANGS arrived in their wartime capital of Chungking in October 1938. Theodore White, then a fledgling journalist, followed six months later. "The runway was a sandbar paved with stone," he wrote, "and on both sides of the sandbar the river rushed by. . . . The airstrip was usable only from winter through spring . . . in summer and early fall, swollen with the melting snows of Tibet, the river flooded the airport." The airport buildings, made of straw matting on bamboo poles, were taken down one at a time as the river rose.

Located 400 miles behind Japanese lines and 1,400 miles from the ocean, the city itself lay 600 feet above the runway, perched on a rocky plateau beyond the cliffs and surrounded by what was left of a five-hundred-year-old wall. It was reached by steep steps zigzagging up the mountain from the river, a climb usually negotiated by Chinese coolies carrying their betters in sedan chairs. "Every drop of water," according to journalist Sheean, had to be "carried up the towering hills on human shoulders; every object we use has been borne painfully at some time or other up from the life-giving river."

Chungking is located in the southeast of the province of Szechuan. Known in May-ling's day as "the Heavenly-endowed province," it is blessed with some of the richest land in China. The area harvested four crops annually, but its semitropical climate guaranteed that winters were wet and chilly, summers hot and humid. "Shanghai," according to May-ling, "was a summer resort compared to the damp, oppressive atmosphere of this place." The old city of Chungking had been built at the confluence of the Yangtze and Chialing Rivers. Terraced rice paddies rose on both sides of the rivers, while the peasants planted vegetables near the riverbanks, hoping to harvest them before the annual floods. White was amazed by the abundance of flowers and said that there were more flower stalls within the walls of Chungking than in the entire city of his native Boston.

If Szechuan was the richest province in China, the richest residents were the ex-warlords turned landowners and the merchants who dealt in its produce. "The city," according to White, "repaid the countryside by returning all its bowel movements; collectors emptied the thunder boxes of every home each morning, and padded barefoot down the alley stairs to the river-side, two buckets of liquid mush jiggling from their bamboo staves, until they reached what foreigners delicately styled the 'honey barges.'" Sewage ran in the gutters of Chungking, and its alleys were narrow—so narrow that White said a man walking with an open umbrella caught drippings from eaves on both sides of the street at the same time. According to another American, there was "no escape from the stink that attacked our nostrils at every turn." Even worse were the Chungking rats, "numerous . . . large and . . . ferocious." They were particularly active at night, when sleepers "were woken by rats pulling their hair. Even in the hotels there were rats nesting in the bathrooms. Cats were imported to deal with the situation, but the cats fled with fright!"

There had been no wheeled vehicles in Chungking before 1928; by 1939, even after the government set up its wartime headquarters, sedan chairs out-numbered rickshaws. Although the Kuomintang changed the names of streets to patriotic inanities such as Road of the People's Republic and Road of the People's Livelihood, White said that when he received an invitation to go somewhere, he had to translate the name for his rickshaw puller back to the Cliff of the Merciful Buddha, the Slope of Seven Stars, or White El-ephant Street. The generalissimo, of course, traveled in a procession of black cars, and the citizens of Chungking soon learned to take their umbrellas from over their heads and hold them down to protect their feet and ankles from the filth sprayed out by the cars in his cavalcade.

Once a town of 300,000 people, the arrival of the Nationalist govern-ment nearly doubled Chungking's population to 550,000.* In an attempt to use wartime exigencies to revive the New Life Movement, the generalissimo banned opium in the city immediately upon arrival. Two months later, he closed the local brothels, where businessmen were accustomed to dining and slipping out between courses to relax in steaming tubs, to be washed, massaged, and otherwise serviced by local prostitutes. Spitting in the streets—one of Chiang's pet peeves—was also forbidden.†

Upon its arrival, the government took over all the hotels, office build-ings, and schools. The four most important banks were moved from Shang-

---

* By the end of the war, it would reach around 800,000.

† Chiang's spitting obsession was finally vindicated during the SARS epidemic of 2002–2003 when spitting was prohibited on pain of being fined. Elizabeth Rosenthal, "SARS Forces Beijing to Fight an Old but Unsanitary Habit," *The New York Times*, May 28, 2003.

hai, as was Fudan University. But the government employees and students who came in 1938 were used to the trappings of modern life like electricity and flush toilets. It was, White said, "as if the ablest and most devoted executives of New York, Boston and Washington had been driven from home to set up resistance to an enemy from the hills of Appalachia."

What bothered White most, however, was the Americanization of senior Chinese officials, most of whom had been educated in the United States and, in his view, had little or no understanding of their own people. The exception, of course, was Chiang himself, who spoke no English, controlled the army, made deals with the warlords, and never allowed a capable man to rise too far lest he become a rival for power. He and May-ling lived in a two-story, ten-room house surrounded by a stone wall. Two heavily armed soldiers guarded their driveway, and the grounds were patrolled by soldiers, personal guards, and plainclothesmen. Invited guests entered the premises, passed under a gigantic rubber tree, and climbed a series of steps interwoven with roots into a beautiful garden, terraced in the Chinese style, with bamboo and azaleas. Except for the dining room, the rooms were small. It was, in the words of Chiang's personal physician, "not a very luxurious frame house," but it had been given to them by General Chen Cheng, second in command to Chiang himself, and had come completely furnished. The living room, according to one guest, was "a solemn Victorian room . . . simple and gray," the furniture placed "in neat rigidity" with lace doilies on the backs of the chairs. "If I only had my own silverware and linen, I would be completely happy here," May-ling told a reporter, pointing out two silver frames with colored photographs of her husband as practically the only things in the house that she could call her own. Later on, an autographed picture of President Roosevelt was added to a table in the living room facing a photograph of Chiang. The generalissimo's explanation to visitors for this peculiar arrangement was that these were pictures of two friends.*

Chiang's doctor tells us that husband and wife shared a bedroom—two beds side by side, covered with a huge mosquito curtain. Adjoining the bedroom was a large room divided into two offices—one for him and one for her. The G-mo, who rose between 5:00 and 6:00 A.M., still did his exercises before breakfast, when May-ling, who got up at 6:30, joined him. From 7:00

---

* This was wishful exaggeration, as witness the following memo from White House economist Lauchlin Currie to Roosevelt's secretary, Missy LeHand: "You might also pass along to the president an intimation from T. V. Soong that nothing would be more appreciated by Chiang than an autographed photograph of the President." (FDR Library: Franklin D. Roosevelt's Personal File, File 7308, General Chiang Kai-shek, Memorandum, January 23, 1941.)

to 7:30 they read a short passage from the Bible in Chinese, discussed it, and knelt to say prayers. Chiang was healthy, except for his ill-fitting false teeth, which gave him canker sores. He neither drank nor smoked and disapproved of those who did; the only person besides May-ling who was allowed to smoke in his presence was H. H. Kung. After a spartan breakfast and a visit from his doctors, Chiang read reports from the front and sent instructions to his commanders in the field. On Monday mornings he held a meeting for ministers and department chairmen. The gathering began with the assembled gentlemen bowing three times to a portrait of Sun, after which Chiang read the doctor's will. The third part of the program consisted of a lecture on whatever subject the G-mo chose. In spite of the fact that it could run as long as two hours, his audience, forbidden to wear coats even on the coldest winter days, had to stand at attention during the entire procedure. Only when he had finished speaking would he "grunt" the Chinese words for "That's all" and leave the room.

The Chiangs usually lunched alone or with Donald and a friend from the U.S. Embassy, James McHugh,* who spoke fluent Chinese. "With the Generalissimo and his wife lunch was strictly a family occasion," said McHugh. ". . . I was acceptable to Chiang Kai-shek for one main reason—I was a pipeline to the American Government." Guests were more often invited for dinner, which was served at 7:30. Meals were never fancy, and Chiang amused himself by offering important people what he called his New Life dinner, which cost 40 cents (Chinese) per person.† Liquor was barred from the house, and the inevitable toasts were drunk with tea. Sir Stafford Cripps, the British Labour Party leader and future chancellor of the Exchequer, who visited Chungking in early 1940, was impressed with the atmosphere, pronouncing the Chiangs "perfect dears, so kind and simple and natural." Like most Westerners, he was particularly affected by May-ling, whom he found "extraordinarily intelligent and superbly kind to every-

---

* McHugh, who was in charge of Far East secret intelligence, lived in a house across the Yangtze with the American ambassador, Nelson T. Johnson. "Fat and cheery," Johnson allowed his naval attaché to serve as his contact with Chiang "because it was an arduous trip across the river . . . in a sampan . . . which navigated the river crabwise in the strong current and ended up about half a mile down river from where you started across. Then one had to retrace one's steps to the point where the stairs, 367 of them, climbed to the heights on which Chungking was located." (Cornell University Library, Division of Rare and Manuscript Collections, James M. McHugh papers, letter, McHugh to Donald, March 6, 1940, and draft for book, foreword, 7, Box 13, Folder 4, no. 2770.)

† 40 cents Chinese = 2.4 cents U.S. in 1940 (37 cents today).

one and full of courage and initiative often in the most difficult circumstances."

After lunch, the generalissimo read the newspapers, including the local
Communist publication, underlining words and phrases as he went along.
After an afternoon of work, he usually called for his tea and then took a
walk, sometimes with his wife, peering around corners and into dark places,
looking for something wrong. One journalist found him in the middle of a
road haranguing a policeman for the way he was handling traffic. In another
instance, he returned from a drive through town only to dash to the phone
to call the mayor of Chungking. "I just saw a beggar on the corner of Rice
Flour and Pottery streets. Looks like he has leprosy or something. Why don't
you take care of your city?"

It was a different story, however, when someone wanted to sound him
out on a particular subject or obtain an interview. It had never been easy to
get to see the generalissimo, and the older he got, the harder it became. "His
niggardly, grudging use of the spoken word is the despair of visiting journalists who may be granted an audience of ten or 15 minutes with the great
man," White wrote in 1942. "They usually spend two or three minutes outlining long involved questions to which Chiang listens in quiet patience.
When the question is over and translated Chiang usually murmurs softly,
'yes' or 'no' or 'very difficult.' " Even Donald, who was virtually part of the
Chiang family, had trouble conversing with Chiang, who was comfortable
only when giving orders and/or expounding on his limited point of view.

While the generalissimo rested comfortably on old principles, May-ling
was out doing various kinds of war work or making flying visits to Changsha
or Nanchang. For diversion, he practiced his calligraphy while she read or
listened to music and news reports on the radio. Although May-ling had
been asked to visit the United States, she had thus far refused all invitations.
According to a friend, she was simply too energized to give up her war work.
Tillman Durdin of *The New York Times* used the phrase "intense nervous energy" to describe Madame Chiang when he interviewed her. There is, he
wrote, "very little repose in her. She leans forward in her chair and speaks
rapidly and in a low tone. Her manner is a combination of American direct-
ness and the self-effacing modesty of the Chinese woman, with a touch
of . . . restlessness."

May-ling's working day also started early. "Take that up with Madame"
was often the advice given to people with problems to solve, since even
government officials often had to wait weeks to get an appointment with
Chiang. A troubleshooter for her husband, May-ling spent hours over her
correspondence, often working until midnight. According to James McHugh,
she did "the work of several men daily, organizing and directing relief work

of all kinds and constantly spurring on those around her to action. She and Donald have worn themselves out trying to get Chiang to take drastic action against the inefficiency which surrounds him." Weekends were spent in a home in the mountains. Chiang, who had always lived and dined simply— ostentatiously so—was angry when someone told him that this home, called the "Eagle's Nest" because of its location, bore the same name as Hitler's in Berchtesgaden. He replied that Hitler's house had cost a fortune, whereas his could have belonged to a prewar, high-level bank clerk. Not exactly. Set high on a hill, the Chiang's country house was a well-designed one-story structure with a lovely veranda overlooking a garden of ferns, irises, and lilies. It was part of a compound built by a very rich businessman in 1925. Chiang's of- fice was in a separate two-story building, where he also had a bedroom. Like everyone else in Chungking who could afford it, the Chiangs had their own tunnel-shaped bomb shelter, which was reached via the garden.

Chiang and May-ling were an odd combination—basically an attraction of opposites. "He was a man I learned first to respect and admire, then to pity, then to despise," said White. Described by a former Oxford professor as a "slim, rather stooping, monkish figure," Chiang greeted visitors "with the Chinese inclination, hands clasped together" and responded to their remarks with "a courteous grunt." At this point in his life he seemed to many to remain static—in both body and mind, with no new thoughts and few signs of age aside from the flecks of gray in his hair and his false teeth. "There were no wrinkles, no sagging muscles," said Payne, who described Chiang's life as "a calm, sedentary, unexciting existence . . . little was de- manded of him except that he assume the role of symbolic ruler."

As specific in her own way as Chiang was in his, May-ling was rightly called the most important of Chiang's advisers. She was certainly the one who best understood the foreign devils. She told him when and how to re- spond to his allies and enemies, explaining the workings of their minds and governments to her husband, who understood little beyond his own bor- ders. Writing in 1938, Edgar Snow said that "few Chinese except Chiang's own staff have access to him without Madame's approval" and told of the time he "had the misfortune to incur her displeasure over a brief sketch I wrote about the generalissimo. The repercussions of this episode lasted more than three years, and were an amazing revelation of the thoroughness with which she follows everything written about him."

John Carter Vincent, who served in the U.S. Embassy, disliked Madame. "I feel, and others confirm my feeling," he wrote, "that . . . she is a hard, shallow, and selfish woman—she certainly looks it, but she can turn on the charm to melt the heart of the most hard boiled foreigner . . . not so with her own countrymen. They dont [sic] trust her—but the Generalissimo does and that is what counts." White, who called May-ling "the chief liberalizing element in Chiang Kai-shek's life," did not like her much better than Vincent did, but her looks impressed him, her influence on her husband pleased him, and her artifice amused him. "She is a beautiful piece of woman," White wrote in 1940, "her figure is probably the best in Chungking and she has . . . the prettiest legs I ever have seen . . . she looks in the flesh far more attractive than in photographs. . . . She is personally brave, physically courageous. . . . By education and training she is equipped as no other woman in modern world politics to take her place in the affairs of state. . . . She is . . . sure of self, imperious. 'The Madame has expressed her will,' I have heard one of the lesser members of her entourage say (Madame Chiang Kai-shek is usually called 'Madame'), 'we cannot ask her again.'" By the 1970s, White had refined his feelings about her: "A beautiful, tart and brittle woman, more American than Chinese, and mistress of every level of the American language from the verses of the hymnal to the most sophisticated bitchery. Madame Chiang, always stunning in her silk gowns, could be as coy and kittenish as a college coed, or as commanding and petty as a dormitory house mother. She swished briskly into any room like a queen."

There is little question that May-ling, her sisters, brothers, and their spouses conducted themselves much like the Chinese dynasties that had preceded them, making important decisions for the country and making sure that those decisions were financially beneficial to their family. Like the Manchus and their predecessors for centuries past, who believed that the best of what belonged to China automatically belonged to them, the Soongs apparently saw little or nothing wrong in skimming the family cream off the country's milk. Wisely, they tried to keep their money and treasures out of sight. During the war, however, it became impossible to keep their jealousies and quarrels from seeping through the walls of their various homes and estates nestled comfortably in the hills in and around Chungking.

THE PERSON WHO originally broke through the solidarity of the family corporation was Ching-ling—first when she married Sun Yat-sen and later when she took up the Communist banner. Considered the family beauty, she was described by writer Pearl Buck as "a great lady . . . slender but not thin," blessed with "exquisite skin, large, frank, fine eyes, a lovely profile" and "shining black hair." Up until the Japanese invasions, Ching-ling had stayed apart—at least publicly—from the rest of the Soongs. The difference in politics or economic circumstances, however, does not seem to have lessened her relationship with her sisters. Randall Gould, a correspondent for *The Nation*, described a scene he observed in the early 1930s: "I was waiting in

Dr. Sun's house in Rue Molière . . . suddenly the door opened and in trooped the three sisters . . . laughing and chattering like schoolgirls. This was at a period when Madame Sun was being watched by plainclothes agents of the Nanking regime . . . it was a time when the sound of her typewriter clacking away by night was reported to the Government as 'a secret radio set communication with Moscow.' Yet here was Madame Sun bringing home . . . the wives of two of the highest officials of the National Government against which she had set her face."

It was about this time that Ching-ling started working with a friend (some say lover), General Teng Yen-ta, to establish an alternative to the Nationalists and the Communists, neither of whom she trusted. After Teng was arrested, tortured, and executed,* Ching-ling issued a statement condemning her brother-in-law and his government. But when the young journalist Harold Isaacs came to a "parting of ways" with the Communists and went to say good-bye to her, she told him "to be careful. I thought she meant to be careful of Kuomintang thuggery. But no, she said, she meant our Communist friends. I looked at her incredulously. 'Yes,' she repeated, 'be careful. You don't really know these people. They are capable of anything.'"

Nevertheless, to quote Edgar Snow, Ching-ling "embraced all revolutionaries as her own, and through her personal intervention saved many lives." She was, however, unable to save Teng or six young leftist writers led by Lu Hsun. Lu Hsun was, according to Snow, "China's greatest contemporary writer" and definitely not a Communist. Even so, he and his five followers were forced to dig a large pit, bound by their hands and feet, thrown into the muck, and buried alive. "That," Ching-ling said, "is our Christian Generalissimo—burying our best young people alive. Evidently in his Bible studies he has not yet reached the Corinthians."†

For minimally more fortunate prisoners, there was Zhazidong Prison, a small building, once a coal pit, lying about an hour out of Chungking. With sixteen cells for men and two for women, it still has emblazoned on its walls the four virtues of the New Life Movement and other exhortations commanding those who have strayed to change their ways. To encourage this, there remain the vestiges of a torture room with one huge chair, a device for hanging, a brazier for heating, and various tools like mallets and hooks.

As a sister-in-law of Chiang, Ching-ling always remained untouchable,

---

* She was not able to save him. Chiang allowed her to beg for his life, waiting until she had finished her plea before telling her he was already dead.

† The author assumes that Ching-ling means the quotation from I Corinthians, 13:13: "And now abideth faith, hope, charity, these three; but the greatest of these is charity."

although she continued to issue statements against her brother-in-law's government. She moved to a small flat in Hong Kong and in 1938 founded the China Defense League, a relief organization that became the major outside supply source for the areas under Communist control. "Among the things she sent us were materials and directions for making penicillin—at that time new in the world," said a grateful American doctor. According to her biographer Jung Chang, Ching-ling sold the jewelry left to her by her mother to pay for her relief work. "Luxury to her was criminal in a poor country at war like China," said Chang. "In this she set herself off decisively from the insensitive extravagance of her sister Mme. Chiang." It was not until Pearl Harbor that Ching-ling rejoined the family, began to be seen and photographed with her sisters, and, although she never changed her opinion of Chiang Kai-shek, even allowed herself to appear occasionally in pictures with him as well.

AI-LING, THE ELDEST and most powerful of the Soong siblings—even Chiang hesitated to cross her—did her part for the war effort, but in the manner of a grande dame. Ever since 1932, when a Red Cross worker had told her that there were not enough hospital beds for soldiers wounded in the defense of Shanghai, she had worked to fill the need, turning the Lido Cabaret into a modern hospital with three hundred beds. When soldiers were released from treatment, Ai-ling gave them clothes, food, and money. She also established a hospital for children on the border of the International Settlement, and it was said that she started both these institutions mostly with her own money.

Although Ai-ling insisted that she "devoted her time exclusively to her family and to welfare work," according to Edgar Snow, her "chief interests" were "finance, commerce and jewelry. It is through Madame Kung that most of the family's wealth has been amassed." Three years later, Snow saw no reason to change his mind. "Though few dispute the greatness of Mme. Chiang and Mme. Sun, there is less agreement as to the eldest sister, Soong Ai-ling . . . Perhaps she has been less sympathetically regarded because of her immense wealth, amassed especially since her husband, Dr. H. H. Kung, became the generalissimo's finance minister. Yet nobody knows the exact extent of this wealth, nor how much of it is held only in proxy for other members of the family."

While one social contemporary* remembered Ai-ling as "very bossy" and "very stubborn," there were those who found her fascinating. "To her

---

* Interviewed at the age of 101.

must go the leadership of this clan," said George Sokolsky, who contended that she was "the most brilliant of all" the Soongs. "Less strikingly pretty than her youngest sister, Soong Ai-ling was equally impressive," wrote Edgar Ansel Mowrer, a British journalist who visited China in the late thirties. "There was about her anything but tall figure, something so authoritative, so personally powerful, so penetratingly keen, that one would have been struck with her anywhere. Here was authority, conscious of itself, conscious of power, but withal wonderfully good-natured, resourceful, helpful in need. . . . I suspected a mind that forgot nothing and forgave little, but that knew how to repay affection richly." Whether one admired or disliked Ai-ling, she and her husband were clearly the favorite topic of gossip in Chungking, about which it was said that "90 percent is untrue but ten percent is even worse than the gossip."

Chiang's political adviser Owen Lattimore was "amazed by the almost universal dislike for Madame Kung," which he blamed on the fact that everyone "believed that she controlled one particular bank, through which she bought American dollars just before each new steep decline in the value of the Chinese dollar." After attending a family Christmas dinner, Lattimore gave his opinion of all three. "Madame Kung," he said, "had an extremely shrewd but unscrupulous pecuniary mind. Madame Chiang was interested in power and influence and had a talent for intrigue. Madame Sun was the least clever . . . but a woman of complete integrity and simple honesty." Others simply repeated the well-known saying that Ai-ling loved money, May-ling loved power, and Ching-ling loved China.

During the war, Ai-ling maintained a fine home in what journalist Sheen called "purse-proud and contented Hong Kong"—an elegant refuge that May-ling, pleading ill health and claiming that her doctor "had told her she would acquire cancer if she did not rest," visited fairly often. She was there in March of 1939 when Chiang wired, "When will the dentist cure your illness? I hope you can return to Chungking as soon as possible." To which she replied, "The problem with my teeth is still not cured, so I don't know when I can come back to Chungking. I am so sorry. I will be back as soon as the dentist finishes with me." Chiang was not happy. "I read your telegram," he wired back. "I hope you can get back soon. There is a lot of work waiting for you to do, and all of it is urgent."

May-ling returned to Chungking but was back in Hong Kong a year later for an operation on her sinuses, which, she complained, were aggravated by the climate of Chungking. "I am feeling very uncomfortable," she wired Chiang in February 1940. "Things were even worse yesterday. I vomited six times, and my heartbeat was too slow. I'm a little better today. I think I will be okay." Her husband was, as usual, lonely and concerned. "How do you feel now?" he wired. "I am so worried about you. It would be better for you to go to the hospital and have a thorough rest there." Four days later, she answered that she was "much better now. I don't like the British hospital here and I prefer to convalesce at home. Please don't worry about me."

At some point after May-ling's recuperation, the three sisters attended a party in the ballroom of a hotel. "My sisters have persuaded me to come out to dinner," she informed their biographer Emily Hahn. "We are going to dine at the Hong Kong Hotel tonight, and I thought that it would be worth seeing us all together." It was, as Hahn put it, "a bombshell: Word went around quickly and in a few moments the dance floor looked something like the crowd at Wimbledon as couples danced past the long table, their heads turning as if they had owls' necks, staring as hard as British courtesy allowed. . . . I'll believe two of them are there,' protested a newspaperman, but I won't believe that's Madame Sun. She would never, never be with the other two—and in this outpost of Empire!"

The war correspondent Martha Gellhorn met the Kungs in Chungking in 1941. H.H. had taken what Gellhorn called an "avuncular shine" to her, presenting her with a large box of chocolates, from which he had already eaten his favorites, and a red satin Chinese dress, embroidered in yellow and purple flowers that her traveling companion* said looked like the "latest model they were wearing in the Chungking whorehouses." Dr. Kung gave a dinner for her, seating her to his right and placing in her bowl "choise morsels . . . sea slugs, bits of black rubber with creepers, thousand-year-old eggs, oily black outside with blood-red yolks." It was Ai-ling, however, who bothered Gellhorn. "She reminded me of stout rich vulgar matrons in Miami Beach hotels," the journalist wrote. "The CNAC pilots were down on her for demanding that they offload passengers to make room for her trunks, whenever she flew to Hongkong. She was good at clothes. I remember her dress as one of the most beautiful I have ever seen. It was the classical Chinese model . . . of black velvet. The . . . buttons that close these gowns from collar to knee are usually made of silk braid, hers were button-size diamonds. She said she had ruby and emerald buttons too."

Gellhorn also wrote about Chiang and May-ling, who invited the Hemingways to lunch in an "intimate foursome," so that Chiang could hear news of the Canton front, where the journalists had just been. "Their house was modest" Gellhorn wrote, ". . . furnished by Grand Rapids including doilies

---

* Referred to by Gellhorn in her book as "U.C.," standing for "Unwilling Companion," it was Ernest Hemingway, who had married Gellhorn the year before and was covering the trip for *PM*, a new liberal newspaper. (See endnote for what happened to Hemingway's report.)

but clean and thug-free. Display in Chungking was useless. Madame Chiang did not stint herself when abroad. . . . Madame Chiang, still a beauty and a famous vamp, was charming to U.C. and civil to me." During lunch Chiang apparently delivered his usual vitriol on the CCP four separate times. "With thirty-five years' hindsight, I see that the Chiangs were pumping propaganda into us, as effective as pouring water in sand," Gellhorn wrote later.

> We had no idea of what was really going on in China, nor that the Generalissimo and Madame Chiang, to whom power was all, feared the Chinese Communists not the Japanese. They were not fools. The Japanese would disappear some day. . . . The true threat to the Chiangs' power lay in the people of China and therefore in the Communists. . . . I didn't need political expertise to decide, in a few hours, that these two stony rulers could care nothing for the miserable hordes of their people and in turn their people had no reason to love them. . . . I asked Madame Chiang why they didn't take care of the lepers, why force the poor creatures to roam the streets begging. She blew up. The Chinese were humane and civilized unlike Westerners; they would never lock lepers away out of contact with other mortals. 'China had a great culture when your ancestors were living in trees and painting themselves blue.' . . . I was furious and sulked. To appease me, Madame Chiang gave me a peasant's straw hat which I thought pretty and a brooch of jade set in silver filigree which I thought tacky. . . . U.C. behaved with decorum until we had done our bowing and scraping and departed. Then he said, laughing like a hyena, 'I guess that'll teach you to take on the Empress of China.

Gellhorn must have been in a bad mood during that lunch, because her description of May-ling when she and Hemingway went back the next day, is of a woman "who can charm the birds off the trees, and she knows exactly what appeals to each kind of bird. . . . She is as beautifully constructed as the newest and brightest movie star and she has lovely legs. Her face is oval, with cream-colored skin, a round chin and a smooth throat. . . . Every pose of her hands, her head or her body is pretty to see. She is so delightful to look at, and her low voice, speaking English with a charming, somewhat slurred accent, is so entrancing, that you forget you are talking to the second ruler of China."

Gellhorn's change of attitude clearly brought out a different side of Madame as well: "We have been married fourteen years," May-ling told her. "We get on very well, two people with such tempers. When we married, everybody said it would not last. And he takes care of me. Sometimes I get so overworked I cannot think. I am like a fly stuck in flypaper. Then my husband says, 'Now you go over to the south bank to the country,* and stay there a few days.' He just picks me up and sends me off."

When Gellhorn told May-ling that she and Hemingway had met Ai-ling, May-ling said that her sister was

> an angel. She has the most heart of us all. . . . And people say terrible things about her. They say of my sister that she speculates. . . . You know how that lying story started? Dr. Kung was in Europe at the coronation. The government bonds were falling in the market. My husband talked with us about it. We must prevent this decline. So my sister said she would buy them, as a private individual, to support the market. But she was really buying for the government.† Afterward, the real speculators, who had tried to force the bond down, and had been caught, accused my sister of speculating. . . . People are wickedly unjust. Stories start and no one checks them and they are repeated. I get so angry when I hear bad things about Dr. Kung. No man in China would have stayed at the job so long, and worked so hard, or given such wholehearted co-operation. He has sacrificed his health and his family; he has let his own affairs go. He gets nothing for himself except endless work. . . . And then people talk about him. I would fight back. But they are nobler than I am.

❧

IT WAS MAY-LING, however, who was now the most important member of the Soong family—the first lady of the land, in locus empress, wielding, as Pearl Buck put it, "an influence which it is impossible to overestimate." Along with her duties as the wife of the generalissimo, she established a Women's Advisory Committee of the New Life Movement, an umbrella group with nine departments, including one to deal with refugee children. There were thousands of these orphans (or warphans, as May-ling liked to call them) after the Japanese bombardments of Shanghai and Nanking. With forty-nine orphanages under her direction, May-ling arranged to house, feed, and clothe some 25,000 youngsters and set up a program of "adoption," whereby

---

* The south bank of the river was where most of the foreign embassies, along with the Standard Oil and American Petroleum compounds, were located. This area, cooled by a breeze in the summer, was relatively safe from the incessant bombing by the Japanese.

† Not true (see next chapter).

anyone anywhere in the world could pledge $20.00 a year to cover the basic costs for one child. Like similar programs today, the benefactor received a photo of the orphan and a yearly report on his or her progress. May-ling had strong opinions about these institutions, which reflected her American upbringing. The children's food was served in individual bowls, rather than the one central dish into which everyone was used to plunging his or her chopsticks, sharing not only food but germs. Dishes were washed carefully after meals and rinsed three times. Even the floors of her orphanages, traditional repositories of spit and dust, were kept spotlessly clean. This was quite an innovation when we consider that in 1935 one out of every two Chinese died before the age of thirty and that three quarters of these deaths could have been prevented with adequate methods of sanitation.

The generalissimo's wife also used the exigencies of war to improve the position of women in China. And like the wives of other wartime heads of state around the world, she was photographed visiting orphanages, distributing gifts to wounded soldiers, dabbing a wound, admiring a portable X-ray machine, holding an outdoor clinic, and tramping through the mud in the countryside.

But behind the facade of a family united for the defense of the country, there were hidden factions, particularly a rivalry between T. V. Soong and H. H. Kung. In this situation, Kung was invariably backed up by his wife and May-ling, who was not always on good terms with brother T.V. Since the competition between the brothers-in-law had a serious impact on the economy of China, it seems like a good idea to stop our story at this point and examine the history of these two men vis-à-vis Chiang Kai-shek and the Kuomintang.

29

[T]here has been no crisis, international or domestic, in the past 20 years that T.V. hasn't been summoned to handle sooner or later.

——Vanya Oakes, Magazine Digest, 1945

Kung, described by White as "a round man with a soft face draped with pendulous flabby chins," was "undoubtedly more Chinese than Soong." Kung's ancestral ties were certainly more impressive than those of Charlie Soong's eldest son, but they had also left Kung with certain vestigial impediments. He was, like his ancestors in the Middle Kingdom, "basically anti-foreign" and, like Chiang Kai-shek, ever willing to put up with second-rate subordinates. The consummate gentleman, easily swayed, and overly concerned with "face," Kung's "one great desire was to be loved, and those who knew him well found him so lovable that they called him Daddy."

A tall man of imposing bearing, T.V. was quicker, far more intelligent, and less tactful than Kung. He did not appear to care about personal popularity—a tendency that led to periodic fallings-out with the G-mo as well as others: "in a country where compromise is an art, he refuses to compromise, and among people who assiduously practice circumlocution, he talks straight from the shoulder," said one American journalist, who described the men who worked for T.V. as "direct, young, and energetic. As a correspondent . . . I found that if I wanted facts, not platitudes, the person to look for was a T.V. man."

Owen Lattimore, a China scholar appointed in 1941 by Roosevelt as political adviser to Chiang, preferred Kung's style to T.V.'s substance. Lattimore's dislike for May-ling's brother can be traced to his first formal call on T.V. in Washington. Burly, with a Boston accent, T.V. "was sitting behind a big desk, behaving like his idea of an American big boss. . . . He was brisk and brief. No oriental courtesies here. . . . He congratulated me on my nomination* . . . he had not been consulted. His manner was as distant as it could be without being rude. . . . T.V. Soong wanted to give

---

* Lattimore was being sent to China as Roosevelt's personal representative to Chiang Kai-shek.

the impression that he was not only Chiang's brother-in-law, but his confidential man in the United States, and anything important should go through him."

K. C. Wu, who served as T.V.'s vice minister and later as governor of Taiwan, said that what appeared as arrogance in T.V. was actually deficiency in his native culture and speech, plus an inability to make small talk. T.V. had what Wu called "a brilliant mind. Very sharp. If you say half a sentence he knows the rest already." Wu added that "T.V. had a very low opinion of H. H. Kung's intelligence"—a judgment echoed by McHugh, who added that T.V. was unable to "conceal his contempt . . . toward Kung." He pointed out the rift in the Soong family between May-ling, Ai-ling, and T.L. on one side versus T.V., Ching-ling, and T.A. on the other. But the intense competition between T.V. and Kung was due largely to Kung's wife, Ai-ling, whose political ambitions for her husband and financial ambitions for her family seemed to many observers to be well nigh insatiable. According to T.V.'s good friend, journalist Joe Alsop, "Mme. Kung called the tune and her husband danced."

In the early days when Dr. Sun was alive, however, Ai-ling had helped T.V. find a job in the government. Starting in the position of Dr. Sun's English secretary, he had quickly graduated to manager of the salt audit office of Kwangsi and Kwangtung provinces. He reorganized the collection of salt duties, which became a valuable source of revenue for the revolution, and was promoted to president of the Central (revolutionary) Bank. In 1925, he was named minister of finance and minister of commerce for Sun, laying the foundation for his later title, the "King of Finance" in China. Kung, on the other hand, did not go into the government until after Sun's death, when his wife secured a position for him on the Central Political Committee of the Kuomintang. She also arranged for him to take over the post of finance minister for the province of Kwangtung from T.V.

Thus, after the establishment of Chiang's government in Nanking, T.V. was in a far more powerful position than Kung. In spite of the fact that both Kungs had voluntarily supported Chiang against the Communist faction in Wuhan, whereas T.V. had to be forced into eventual compliance, T.V. was immediately made minister of finance, and Kung was rewarded only later with the lesser position of minister of industry, commerce, and labor. T.V., who was in his thirties at the time, changed government policy toward the businessmen of Shanghai—reducing the element of financial coercion imposed earlier by Chiang, substituting a policy of collaboration, and creating a market for government bonds that he offered to Shanghai bankers at huge discounts. Although he proved that he was the only man capable of dealing with China's financial problems, he is reputed to have made a number of enemies along the way, men who were anxious to destroy his reputation.*

At the end of 1931, shortly after Japan invaded Manchuria, Chiang Kai-shek submitted one of his periodic resignations, and among the members of his cabinet who resigned with him were his brothers-in-law, T. V. Soong and H. H. Kung. When Chiang returned to his post at the end of January 1932, T.V. was quickly reinstated as minister of finance, president of the Central Bank, and commissioner of the Economic Committee. But by the time Chiang returned, his old rival Wang Ching-wei had assumed the presidency of the Executive Yuan, and Kung's position as minister of industry, commerce, and labor had been taken over by a supporter of Wang. In this situation, Kung and his wife did what Chinese officials often did in similar circumstances—they took a trip to Europe and the United States. They stayed away for nearly a year, returning just about the time that T.V. had begun to quarrel with Chiang over the huge amounts of money the generalissimo demanded from his finance minister to fund his campaigns against the Communists. Chiang and T.V. had never gotten along very well anyway, due partly to the influence of Donald. James McHugh, who often lunched with the three of them, reported that Donald "lost no opportunity to stress both to Madame Chiang and the Generalissimo that Soong was ambitious, unscrupulous, selfish and domineering." Moreover, T.V. had now started to question Chiang's policy of ridding China of Communists before attacking the Japanese. The month after Kung returned from his travels, T.V. resigned as president of the Central Bank, which acted as the public treasury, and Kung took his place. Although the usual Chinese excuse of illness was the official explanation, T.V. called a press conference. "I have one remark to make, and only one," he announced. "I am in perfect health." The first man ever to balance the Chinese national budget, T.V. then took off for the World Economic Conference in London and from there traveled to the United States. His arrival was preceeded by the publication of a flattering profile in *Fortune* magazine written by Elizabeth Moore, Henry Luce's sister.

Luce, the right-wing publisher of *Fortune* and *Time* magazines,† had visited China the previous spring and interviewed T.V. at the time. "He refused to see anyone—except the Editor of *Time* and *Fortune*,‡ to both of which he subscribes," the publisher boasted in his sister's article about Soong's ability

---

* See endnotes for stories on this.

† *Life* magazine was not started until 1936.

‡ This is not true. T.V. had given an interview to Karl H. von Wiegand that appeared in May 1932 in the *New York American*.

to raise money and, at the same time, retain his credibility with the bankers and merchants of Shanghai. The piece praised Soong for abolishing the *likin*, a tax levied by individual cities that had delayed shipments and cost merchants a fortune in bribes over and above the normal squeeze. Hailed by the Luces as a financial genius, T.V. arrived in the United States in 1933 to great acclaim. While there, he arranged for a $50 million wheat and cotton loan to China. He was not, however, able to interest the big Western banks in helping China develop its industries, since the bankers were too afraid of provoking war with the Japanese. Before leaving China, T.V. had tried to do away with the preferential treatment accorded Japan in China's tariff schedule, and the Japanese had retaliated by trying to force him out of the Chinese government. While he was away, they wired both Chiang and Wang to say that he must be removed from office.

T.V. returned to China at the end of August 1933. He discovered that while he was abroad, Kung had issued new bonds to pay for Chiang's war against the Chinese Communists. Soong was infuriated. In October, after a fight with the generalissimo, he resigned his positions as minister of finance and deputy general of the Executive Yuan. "Being minister of finance is no different from being Chiang Kai-shek's dog," he said. "From now on, I am going to be a man, not a dog."

There were as many other explanations for the fight between Chiang and T.V. as there were people to speculate about it. K. C. Wu, who was close to the Soongs, claimed that Ai-ling had "engineered the ousting" so her husband could take his place. Emily Hahn, who interviewed the Soong sisters in the 1940s, claimed that T.V. was involved with a friend of Ai-ling; he resented her trying to break it up and, as Hahn phrased it, "he who quarrels with Madame Kung quarrels with Madame Chiang." Hahn also said that because of this, May-ling did not try to smooth things over with Chiang, as she usually did, but simply allowed, perhaps even encouraged, her brother to withdraw. Li* goes further, saying that May-ling, acting under the aegis of Ai-ling, flew to Shanghai to get T.V.'s resignation. Most people thought the G-mo and his brother-in-law split over the issue of Japan, but T.V.'s friend George Sokolsky said that T.V. had criticized Chiang openly during his visit to the United States and had even "suggested" to the London bankers that "their interests lay in supporting him and in opposing Chiang."

"T. V. Soong is a curiously complex personality," Sokolsky said. "Brilliant, hard-working, single in his ambitions, he might have been one of the great men of this earth." But according to Sokolsky,

---

* The author of *Madame Chiang Kai-shek, China's Eternal First Lady.*

Soong's major weakness has undoubtedly been his jealousy of his brother-in-law, Chiang Kai-shek. Often, in conversations with me, Soong was sharply critical of Chiang's policies and methods.... Soong hoped for an end to military dictatorship and for civilian government. Such a government would place him in control. So long as the armies dominated China, Chiang must be supreme. It is utterly absurd to suggest that Chiang and T.V. split on the Japanese policy of the Nanking Government.... It was not Japan that split these two men; it was jealousy.... To me, knowing with intimacy his every fault, he remains the most attractive personality in China.

Once again, T.V. refused to give the usual Chinese excuse of illness for his departure from government: "I wanted to resign because I was unequal to my task [of raising funds for the military]," he said. After leaving the government, T.V. organized the China Development Finance Corporation, a semiprivate group created to facilitate industrialization through a consortium of banks for privately funded enterprises from which the new company profited. The corporation arranged financing for government railways, acquired control over state-run projects that it privatized and helped private firms that needed financing.

After T.V. resigned, Kung took over his brother-in-law's official positions—a move that delighted Ai-ling and pleased Chiang, since Kung, who was far more cooperative and self-effacing than Soong, served the generalissimo as "a willing and subservient cashier." Indeed, at his inauguration as minister of finance, Kung promised to support Chiang by raising the funds for the fight against the Communists, saying that a balanced budget was a good thing but the suppression of the Chinese Communists was more important. The British were not so sanguine about Kung, and Cyril Rogers, the quiet-spoken representative of the Bank of England in China, believed he was incompetent. "If I were to record his conversations with me about banking and play it back, nobody would ever take Chiang's government seriously again," he said. The *North-China Herald* was a tad more subtle, commenting that Kung's "new shoes are a size larger than those which he comfortably and usually fills." During 1934, when China tried to get loans from abroad, the British still insisted on conducting their negotiations with T.V. rather than Kung.

Kung's detractors were proven right. To raise the required funds for the military, he sold government bonds at high interest rates to the Shanghai bankers, who bought them only because they were a better investment than the farming and industrial sectors of China, currently in a depression, and by early 1935, a little over a year after he took over the Ministry of Finance,

China was facing a major financial crisis. Kung then turned to the Central Bank of China to buy up the government bonds, but with all its resources it was not able to finance China's deficits by itself. As the crisis deepened, the second and third most powerful banks in the country, the Bank of China* and the Bank of Communications, stopped cooperating with the government, and the president of the Bank of China began to divest the bank of government bonds. After meeting with Chiang and T.V., Kung announced that since the banks were doing nothing to help industry and business during the current depression, the government would take them over. A year and a half after T.V. left the government, Kung asked him to resume his old position as president of the Bank of China. The outgoing president claimed that he was being intimidated by the secret police and had been warned by Big-Eared Du not to raise any objections "for the sake of my health."

One of the consequences of bringing T. V. Soong back into the fold was the addition of another point of view on foreign affairs. Kung, in deference to Chiang, had never strayed from the policy of repressing the CCP and letting the West take on the Japanese. T.V., as we have seen, felt differently. In 1935, he told Hallett Abend of *The New York Times,* "This is the time for fighting [Japan]. If we do not resist now, our chance may be lost for good . . . the Japanese appreciate nothing but force. . . . This aggression will continue until we have to fight."

After his banking takeovers, Kung attacked the silver problem. During the last half of 1931, England, Germany, Japan, and Canada had gone off the gold standard, and in March 1933, the United States had followed suit. This sent silver prices soaring, pushing China, whose currency was based on silver and whose products had become less competitive on the world market, further into depression. On November 3, 1935, Kung announced the *fa-pi* (legal tender) reform, saying that from November 4 on, China was off the silver standard and the only legal currency would be the banknotes of the three government banks.

In January 1936, a fourth government bank, the Farmers' Bank of China,† was also given the power to issue bank notes. The Farmers' Bank was reputed to be controlled by Chiang Kai-shek, who used it to fund his military campaigns. According to one authority, the Farmers' Bank "apparently had been very free in issuing banknotes, supplying funds when Chiang needed them. It allowed no audits of its reserve funds . . . [and] . . . may have been a conduit for opium revenues." Under the direction of Kung, the Farmers' Bank, the Central Bank, the Bank of China, and the Bank of Com-

---

* The oldest bank in China, founded in 1912 after the fall of the Manchus.

† Sometimes referred to as the "Opium Farmers' Bank."

munications, with their monopoly on the power of issuing banknotes, became known as the "four banks."

Having taken control of the banking sector, Kung was able to follow his policy of deficit financing and its inevitable corollary, printing money on demand, which led to a quick recovery from the depression and catastrophic wartime inflation. A pair of shoes that had sold for $80 in 1939 cost between $900 and $1,200 in 1943. When General H. H. "Hap" Arnold arrived in Chungking that same year, a package of cigarettes cost $120.00, a tangerine, $20.00, and a gallon of gasoline, $180.00 Chinese.* The American general registered surprise at seeing piles of paper left on the ground at the airport in Kunming. "What is all that?" he asked one of the crew.

"That is Chinese money, General."

"How much?"

"Why, I don't know. Maybe two, three, four million Chinese dollars."

"What are you going to do with it?"

"We are taking it in our airplane to Chungking."

"Isn't anyone responsible for it?"

"Yes, we are responsible for taking it in there."

"Does anyone have to sign up for it?"

"No sir."

"Had it been a pack of cigarettes or a jeep," Arnold said, "it would have disappeared hours before."

Kung's takeover of the four banks also led to claims that the various branches of the Soong family turned these banks into bases for their private financial empires. Chiang Kai-shek certainly regarded the Farmers' Bank as his own private source of money, liberally funded by his government's involvement in the sale and transport of opium. T.V. used the assets of the Bank of China to organize a number of public/private corporations that invested in everything from automobiles to tobacco, while Kung used the Central Bank as a base for insurance and industrial investments. Not everyone profited in the same way. According to Crozier, "There has been an unfortunate tendency to link his [T.V.'s] name with Kung as another reprehensible KMT type, but the two men were very different. T. V. Soong had made a great fortune, but unlike his brother-in-law, he had made it by dynamic, entrepreneurial capitalism, creating wealth for China and jobs for ten

---

* In 1939, a Chinese dollar was worth $.30 U.S.; by 1943 it was down to $.05. The pair of shoes that would have cost $24.00 U.S. in 1939 cost between $45 and $60 U.S. in 1943. (In today's dollars that would be somewhere between $560 and $746 U.S.) The price for a pack of cigarettes was $6.00 U.S. ($75 today); a tangerine $1.00 U.S. ($12.45 today); and a gallon of gas $8.00 U.S. ($100 today). These figures come from Crozier, *The Man Who Lost China*, p. 244.

of thousands." At one point, T.V. even lured the eminent French banker Jean Monnet to China to help him reorganize China's finances and railroads. "While it was easy for me to deal with T. V. Soong, whose culture was European," Monnet said, "I never stopped learning the art of negotiating with traditional Chinese businessmen. It took me a long time to understand that in China, one should not ask for a reply but guess it."

There were many complaints of illegitimate manipulation in the Ministry of Finance under Kung, which was "widely considered to be a venal and corrupt organization." One critic charged that Ai-ling was the prime speculator on the various exchanges, and it was generally believed that she used advance information gleaned from her husband to make her investments. With what Snow called "a mixture of contempt and admiration," Ching-ling spoke to him about her sister's activities: "She's very clever, Ai-ling. She never gambles. She buys and sells only when she gets advance information from confederates in the ministry of finance about changes in government fiscal policy." Dr. K. C. Wu agreed: "She is the shrewdest, most capable and absolutely unscrupulous character I have ever known." In one instance, Ai-ling caused the downfall of a minister of industry, Wu Ting-chang. In the course of trying to curb speculation on the Cotton Goods Exchange, Minister Wu ordered an investigation and issued a report that named Madame Kung as one of the "influential persons" responsible for an attempt to manipulate transactions on the exchange. The report was sent to Chiang, who immediately dismissed the minister. According to one member of the government, "Madame Kung had already made a trip and seen Chiang Kaishek. When [Minister] Wu called upon Chiang he was ready to give a full report, but the first thing Chiang said to him was, 'I know now everything about this case; it is needless for you to make any report.' "

Dr. K. C. Wu (as distinguished from Minister Wu) offered an interesting explanation of why Ai-ling was permitted to do what she did: "I think the argument which Madame Kung advanced was that all the money that had been made had been made as a reserve for Chiang in order to bolster him in power or to prepare for any emergency situation when he might have to go into retirement. Of course, between the sums which she reported to Chiang she had made on his behalf, and the sums which she had actually made, there could be much difference." Queried as to whether Kung's reputation for not being "too bright" was accurate, Wu replied, "That's why he was useful."

Big-Eared Du also benefited from the government's new currency policy. Although known by now as "one of the outstanding business and banking leaders in Shanghai," he remained king of the underworld. On being questioned about putting Du on the Currency Reserve Board, Kung explained that Du was "undoubtedly a speculator; he was also leader of the gangsters, but one hundred thousand men in Shanghai obeyed his orders; he could create a disturbance at any moment." A story went around Shanghai soon after the currency reform that Ai-ling had given Du inside information on the government's position on foreign exchange. Du made some speculative purchases but having assumed that Ai-ling would not have told him the truth, lost 50,000 pounds. He insisted to Kung that the Central Bank make up his loss. Kung refused. "That evening," according to Sir Frederick Leith-Ross, Chief Economic Adviser to the British government, "a No. 1 style coffin was deposited on Dr. Kung's doorstep by half a dozen funeral attendants." The next day, Du got his money back from the bank.

Athough most authorities feel that the Kungs profited hugely from his position as minister of finance, it is impossible for this author to determine the extent of their honesty or dishonesty without a paper trail. According to James McHugh, writing in 1938, "specific proof of corrupt activities is almost impossible to obtain in China due primarily to the endless chain of underlings who always come in for their share of the spoils and none of whom would dare to squeal." Moreover, the stories told by current Chinese historians remain subject to question, since they write at the pleasure of a Communist government. What is known is that Kung was born into a wealthy family and had multiplied his personal fortune by acting as an agent for Standard Oil and selling pig iron to the United States during World War I. When he joined the government, however, Ai-ling is said to have taken over their personal finances, apparently depositing money in banks in the United States, Switzerland, and France. This is not something that Ai-ling could have done by herself, since it was forbidden by law to move public monies. It has therefore been surmised that as finance minister, Kung managed to change public funds into private in order to avoid the restrictions. The Kungs dealt mostly in commercial ventures until the 1930s, when Ai-ling began speculating in the stock market, reputedly using inside information to determine her investments. Author Parks Coble summed it up this way: "The protection of family gave the Soongs power, but power, of course, can corrupt. . . . Particularly notorious were Soong Ai-ling, her son David Kung,*

---

* The Kung offspring apparently considered themselves above the law. According to McHugh, writing in 1938, their "undisciplined and over-bearing activities . . . continue to arouse widespread dissatisfaction and criticism both from within and without the Government." (Cornell University Library, Division of Rare and Manuscript Collections, James M. McHugh Papers, "Strictly Confidential, Present Political Situation in China," Report September 14, 1938.) The story is told that one of the sons, who was driving very fast on a crowded street, "felt himself too important to be stopped by a traffic light" and "when the policeman insisted upon arresting him, fired at him with the small pistol he carried, hitting the policeman's thumb. The incident," according to author Pearl Buck, "might have caused serious trouble except for Madame Kung's swift

and the younger Soong brothers.* Rumors circulated that they had made large sums speculating in currency and commodities using inside information supplied by H. H. Kung, then minister of finance. How deserving this reputation is still needs an impartial assessment. Yet there is no question that their status as family members permitted much unfettered activity."

During the early years of the war, when Kung was serving as minister of finance, head of the Executive Yuan, and president of the Central Bank, he established an official secretariat in his residence, thus affording Ai-ling the opportunity of keeping abreast of financial plans. Referred to by the mild-mannered Rogers as a "modern Borgia," she is also said to have made money through the Yu Hua Bank, which was allowed to sell government bonds. Private banks were normally not allowed to do this, but the head of the Yu Hua Bank was Kung himself, who was also finance minister at the time. In its capacity of selling government bonds, a bank received 2 yuan as a handling charge for every 100 yuan in bonds. When the Yu Hua Bank was founded, it had a capitalization of 50,000 yuan.† In the 1920s, it was worth 200,000 yuan,‡ in the 1930s, 2 million yuan,§ and, by the last years of World War II, 1 billion yuan.¶ Nor was Kung apparently above the traditional Chinese squeeze. A story is told that Big-Eared Du, who was trying to transport crude opium out of Szechuan, could not get the necessary papers until the Finance Ministry received a check for 5,000,000 yuan made out to H. H. Kung.

It was Ai-ling's financial manipulations that were, according to Donald's biographer, at least partially responsible for the Australian journalist's departure from China in 1941. Donald, who usually defended the Kungs, dismissing the rumors about them and claiming that if he was ever presented with proof of financial wrongdoing, he would "go away from China on his boat as he has long wanted to do," apparently had a change of heart. One afternoon he received a call from an American acquaintance, the president of a

---

balm of gifts and apologies." (WCA: Pearl S. Buck, "The Sister 'Dictators': Behind the Chinese Dragon," scrapbook of items by or about Madame Chiang Kai-shek, collected by Hetty S. Wheeler (1935–1940), unidentified magazine, September 1937.)

* This is the only instance this author ever found in which T. A. and T. L. Soong are accused of sharing their eldest sister's penchant for speculation.

† 50,000 yuan = $33,500 U.S. in 1914 ($744,340 today).

‡ 200,000 yuan = $168,000 U.S. in 1925 ($2,063,370 today).

§ 2,000,000 yuan = $720,000 U.S. in 1935 ($11,290,000 today).

¶ 1,000,000,000 yuan = $50,000,000 U.S. in 1945 ($598,064,000 today).

Chinese university. "Someone has to tell the Soongs and the Chiangs to put a stop to this nonsense," the man said. "Some of their official family are making money hand over fist in the exchange market. Lord, haven't they any sense of decency!"

Donald walked over to the Chiangs', took May-ling's arm, and led her out into the garden (i.e., away from listening devices), where he told her that she "would have to order a halt to such ostentatious and vulgar display of wealth while the nation tumbled all about them, while the cries of the hungry and the suffering mounted." As an example, he mentioned her sister Ai-ling. May-ling turned on him in fury: "Donald, you may criticize the government or anything in China, but there are some persons even you cannot criticize!"

Although the Australian continued to work for the Chiangs, he began to rethink his career. Not only had he long resented Chiang's continued detention of the Young Marshal, but "the Chinese Government had failed to adopt the uncompromising anti-Axis policy" that he had recommended, and he did not want "to continue as adviser to Chiang Kai-shek under these conditions." This issue came to a head a year or so after his conversation with May-ling, when the speeches he had been writing for the G-mo became "more and more pungently anti-Hitler." One day he received a speech back from Chiang with a note saying "I'm not at war with Germany." To which Donald retorted (doubtless to himself), "I am." He got up from his desk, walked over to see May-ling, said good-bye, and that night caught a plane for Hong Kong.

❦

IN THE SUMMER of 1937, four years after T.V. had been replaced by Kung, Chiang sent representatives to Hong Kong, where T.V. was living in a house on Repulse Bay, to ask him to come back and assume responsibility for financing the war. In response, T.V. turned to his friends who were in the room and suggested they all go out for a game of tennis. "Let's leave the affairs of state to others," he said. "We are clearly not needed." Chiang then sent May-ling to talk to her brother, but T.V. did not return until war broke out in Shanghai shortly thereafter. Three years later, the generalissimo asked T.V. to go to Washington as his personal representative to President Roosevelt. It was a brilliant move. According to the journalist Ernest O. Hauser, T.V.

> engaged a suite at the Shoreham, shaved and bathed and took a taxi
> to the White House to see his old friend, the President of the U.S.
> After a chat with the President, Soong called on Hull, Morgenthau
> and [Secretary of Commerce] Jesse Jones. He explained that he

wanted money in vast amounts, but that he did not propose to beg
for it. Told that it might be a good idea to contact a few Congressmen ("a little lobbying" wouldn't hurt), T. V. Soong snorted. He had
come to Washington with a business proposition and the President,
Congress and Mr. Jesse Jones could take it or leave it. The President, Congress and Mr. Jones took it. . . . They knew a bargain when
they saw it. . . . For $100,000,000 China promised to keep 1,125,000
Japanese troops pinned in the field; to keep Japan's formidable fleet
blockading the China shores; to retard the aggressor's march in the
direction of immediate U.S. interests . . . this $100,000,000 loan
gave China a new lease on life. It ensured Chiang Kai-shek's ability
to carry on for at least six months more in full control of the monetary, if not the military, aspects of his war.

And even if the story was not as simple as Hauser claims, it was still an
enormous coup for T.V., whose work in Washington on behalf of his country
proved invaluable.

Meanwhile, H. H. Kung was sent abroad by Chiang. His stated mission
was to represent China at the coronation of King George VI of England, but
he was also looking for armaments and financial aid from the West. In the
words of James McHugh, Kung "assumed the role of an international beggar, grabbing at every small credit he could get . . . in order to be able to
flourish such credits before the Generalissimo to strengthen his own political position." Kung traveled with his wife,* two of his children, and at least
thirty secretaries and assistants. While in Europe, Kung spent two hours with
Hitler: "Hitler spoke against communism and the Communists. He said, 'I
understand that people in China think the Soviet Union is their friend. But
from our talk I understand that you, Herr Doktor, realize the danger of
Communist doctrines.' " While Hitler railed against the Russians, Kung tried
"to convince him of my view on the danger of Japan." The Germans had
apparently planned to invite the brother of the Japanese emperor to speak at
a Nazi Party convention.

But after my talk with Hitler, the plans were changed. . . . I was
able to make Hitler understand that Japan wanted to dominate the
world. . . . Japan and Germany were already allies through the Anti-
Comintern Pact of 1936. They were getting closer and closer, but

---

* The fact that Ai-ling joined her husband on this trip effectively negates the story May-
ling told Martha Gellhorn about her sister's effort to save the price of the government
bonds and support the Chinese stock market at the same time.

I was able to make Hitler think twice before getting too close with Japan. . . . Hitler was against England. He said that England was only a second-class power; she was getting weaker and weaker. He said that France was rotten. . . . He had only contempt for France. . . . But he had a good word to say of Italy. . . . Italy was Germany's friend. What were my impressions of Hitler? I thought he was a little unbalanced . . . his eyes gave me that sort of funny feeling. He had a strange look.

Kung also met with Mussolini in Italy. "I thought Mussolini was doing great things for Italy" he wrote later, ". . . we got along well. I thought he would be a good ally for our Government." His wife was not so easily impressed. She made an appointment with Il Duce, and, according to a friend,

went to keep it, equipped and prepared to exercise the charm to which so many had succumbed. She experienced the customary technique, which so many of us have known. She was first kept for a considerable time in a waiting room: and did not appreciate it. At last she was shown into a vast room, at the far end of which the great man was writing furiously with a carefully studied industry and indifference. She looked across the large intervening space, skilfully designed to break the spirit of the visitor by making him wonder, as he walked across it, whether his trousers were properly creased or, if the visitor was a woman, whatever may be the equivalent anxiety about feminine apparel. She noticed the indifference and preoccupation—and again, did not appreciate it. She waited, in silent dignity, at the entrance. At last Mussolini looked up, saw the gracious figure in the distance and made a beckoning gesture but no more. She smiled, and with Chinese grace bowed slightly with clasped hands—and stayed where she was. Mussolini returned to his writing, expecting her to be walking across the room in the meantime. After a minute he looked, saw that she had not moved, and beckoned more impatiently; she bowed once more with clasped hands—and again waited. So the little drama continued, the impatience of the dictator increasing, the smiling dignity of his visitor still unruffled—till at last he rose, walked across the room and escorted her to her chair by his desk.

From Europe the Kungs moved on to the United States. While they were there, Ai-ling paid a visit to a former teacher in Georgia or, as an imaginative reporter for the *Shanghai Spectator,* put it, "A royal daughter of China . . . who is able to trace her Chinese ancestry back more than 2,400 years . . . was Atlanta's guest last week." The *Spectator* continued its mythical meanderings in the royal vein: "Following her graduation [from Wesleyan] she [Ai-ling] was presented at the Court of St. James's in London, and was the toast of half a dozen courts on the European continent. . . . All the sophistication of Western culture is combined with the subtle charm of the Orient, the age-old heritage of aristocratic birth and breeding, in this young Chinese woman. . . . Perfectly costumed in the latest Chinese style . . . she wore for dinner a fragile dark blue silk lace posed over the softest white Chinese silk. . . . 'Our gowns are always so plain that one must wear jewels,' she explained with characteristic modesty."

Meanwhile, Kung met with Roosevelt and Hull. He told them that the Japanese government was "controlled by the young militarist clique who were determined to make war on China and conquer the world. That meant that America was going to be involved. . . . Roosevelt agreed with me," he said. "Roosevelt was really a good friend of mine." Although Kung was apt to think that anyone who agreed with him was a "good friend," his faith in Roosevelt's friendship was bolstered by Roosevelt's chief adviser and troubleshooter, Harry Hopkins, who told him that the president had "one hundred percent confidence" in him.

Before leaving England, Kung had cabled Secretary of the Treasury Henry Morgenthau, Jr., to ask if the U.S. Treasury would buy the 50 million ounces of silver that China had in New York. Kung had tried but failed to get a loan in London and needed foreign money to back China's currency reforms. When he arrived in the United States, Morgenthau refused, so Kung, as he put it, "appealed to Roosevelt. . . . I think Morgenthau was trying to hold me up. He thought our price for silver was too high. He wanted it to go down so that he could get a bargain. After Roosevelt told him to buy more silver from me, Morthenthau and I arrived at an agreement." What Roosevelt really told Morgenthau was that he wanted to treat Chiang "real nice" since the generalissimo's government was trying to put its economic house in order. When he gave Kung the good news, Kung complimented the Americans for preserving a "strong China," which, he said, would lead to peace and stability in the Far East. One of Kung's associates then explained that what his superior really meant to say was that Morgenthau was a great statesman.

While Kung was in the United States, he received an honorary degree from Yale in acknowledgment of the fine work he had done in the fields of education and finance.

30

❦

The Japanese are a disease of the skin, the Communists a disease of the blood-stream.
—CHIANG KAI-SHEK

ONE OF THE major factors in the economic manipulations of both Kung and Soong was Chiang Kai-shek's constant demand for money to fight China's Communists. The generalissimo's bandit suppression campaigns had always been expensive, and he relied on two sources to fund them: his finance minister and his squeeze on the drug trade. The story of how Chiang managed to channel the proceeds of the opium market into his war against the CCP, while at the same time issuing self-righteous edicts against the use of drugs, is the tale of a successful politician with one hand on the Bible and the other in the till.

"Millions have been raised out of opium for military operations and civil propaganda," complained the Peking-based secretary of the International Anti-Opium Association in 1928, the year Chiang established himself as head of the KMT. It was this sort of censure from the West, where Chiang was looking for aid, which must have encouraged him to make an outward show of outlawing the drug, and in August of 1928 he established the National Opium Suppression Bureau. "The national government will not attempt to get one cent from the opium tax," he told its members. "It would not be worthy of your confidence if it should be found to make an opium tax one of its chief sources of income."

Chiang's promises meant nothing. Profiting from the drug trade was an old warlord game, and although General Feng spoke out against drugs and prohibited their use by his soldiers, he is said to have received as much as $20 million in opium revenues in a single year. As it was with the Christian General, so it was with Chiang. The Opium Suppression Bureau was, "in effect a licensing agency," Sokolsky explained. "That is, you paid your money, you got a receipt, and the receipt meant that you could carry the goods, because it had already been 'punished,' a Chinese doctrine. So, the Opium Suppression Bureau collected the money and the money went to feed the soldiers."

During the year after Chiang's promise not to profit from opium taxes, the provinces of Hupei, Shansi, and Kwangsi raised some $17 million in what was euphemistically termed "opium prohibition revenue." In 1930,

130,000 pounds of opium were imported into Shanghai from Persia and India, while the provinces of Yunnan and Szechuan sent hundreds of tons more down China's "opium highway," the Yangtze River, guarded by soldiers from Chiang's army. Three years into the Chiang regime, China was producing seven eighths of the world's narcotics. That year and the year after, the Nationalist government organized an opium monopoly in order to force out competitors, but the press raised such an outcry that it had to abandon its plans. In both instances, T.V. and Wang Ching-wei, then president of the Executive Yuan, supported Chiang. Even the influential British journalist H. G. W. Woodhead backed the idea, saying that it was the only way to surmount China's economic troubles. According to *Time* magazine of April 27, 1931, "Finance Minister T. V. Soong cheerfully declared last week that China will soon have 'a new and realistic opium policy . . . a 'realistic' opium policy, according to Minister Soong, cannot be one of prohibition. . . . If shrewd Minister Soong does harness opium to his Treasury chariot, he may find a way to balance the Chinese budget for some time to come."

Up until this time, Big-Eared Du and his Green Gang had controlled the opium trade in Shanghai. After the gang's help in suppressing the Communists in the city, Chiang had named both Du and Pockmarked Huang "honorary advisers" to the Chinese army, titles that carried with them the rank of major general. In what one writer terms "more substantive concessions," the generalissimo turned his opium rights in Shanghai over to one of Du's companies and arranged for members of the police and the Chinese navy to help guard the Green Gang's opium, whether in transit or in storage.

But Du reaped more than money. When he arranged a grand opening of an ancestral temple in Kaochiao village where he was born, 80,000 visitors showed up to pay their respects. Aside from $600,000 worth of gifts, Du received presentation scrolls singing his praises from the mayor of Shanghai, Wang Ching-wei, and Chiang Kai-shek himself. After the celebration, Du located his largest morphine factory in Kaochiao. An American diplomat, curious about how and why Chiang always met with Du in Shanghai, had it explained by a Chinese official this way: "whenever General Chiang went to Shanghai the first thing he did was to send Du his card . . . the present relationship between the two men involved merely an arrangement whereby Du and his gangster colleagues were to keep the Communists and other lawless elements in order, in return for freedom of action with respect to what can best be described by the American slang term 'rackets' connected with gambling, the opium traffic, and vice." To satisfy Du's ongoing desire for status, Chiang named him chief Communist suppression agent for Shanghai. Nevertheless, when their opium monopoly fell through and the leaders of the Green Gang demanded a refund—they had paid the government 6 million yuan in start-up money—T.V. offered them payment in government bonds, which he (and unfortunately Du) knew were worthless. It is hardly surprising that on July 23, 1931, the day of Madame Soong's death, the attempt was made on T.V.'s life,* after which we can assume that the refund owed to Big-Eared Du was promptly paid in cash.

Up until 1933, Du's organization had operated out of the French Concession in Shanghai, and of the $6 million per month it yielded in opium revenues, the French Concession police netted some $150,000. This cozy relationship came to a sudden halt, however, when a French naval officer arrived in Shanghai to investigate the corruption. In spite of Du's messengers, whom he sent off to Paris loaded with bribes, and members of the Chinese government anxious to stop the investigation, the French remained determined to clean up the graft. After a big dinner given by a new, incorruptible consul general and an old police captain who had once double-crossed Du, several officials died in agony from poisoned food. The French assumed that the culprit was Du, and he was forced to take his opium trade out of the French Concession and conduct his business from the Chinese district of Shanghai.

The move did not hurt Du's business for long. He rebuilt his organization and continued to protect his turf by dispensing huge bribes. His men operated ten morphine factories in the vicinity of the city for which they paid the Nationalists $400,000† a month in protection money. In late 1932, Du requested official sanction for his opium monopoly in the city. For this he offered a monthly payment of $3 million to the Ministry of Finance, and the deal was made. When T.V. took over the Finance Ministry from Kung, he put the Hankow Special Tax Bureau, the central point of the operation, under the jurisdiction of Chiang's headquarters, and the next month, the government put Chiang in charge of opium suppression. By the beginning of May 1933, Chiang had his opium business—officially called opium "suppression"—up and running. By the end of the year, the Hankow Special Tax Bureau had collected well over $16 million‡ in opium taxes, and one expert estimated that all the opium tax bureaus under the Nationalists netted around $30 million§ a month.¶

---

* See chapter 19.

† $400,000 Chinese = $118,000 U.S. in 1932–1933 ($1,960,000 today).

‡ $16,000,000 Chinese = $4,720,000 U.S. in 1932–1933 ($78,412,800 today).

§ $30,000,000 Chinese = $8,850,000 U.S. in 1932–1933 ($147,024,000 today).

¶ These figures as well as most of the above information come from Jonathan Marshall, "Opium and the Politics of Gangsterism in Nationalist China, 1927–1945," *The Bulletin of Concerned Asian Scholars*, July–September 1976, p. 21.

Not surprisingly, there were many Chinese intellectuals and Western observers who decried Chiang's use of opium to fund his government. But according to the American consul in Hankow, "Inasmuch as the Nanking Government has for several years been piling up a mounting deficit by reason of Chiang's tremendous military expenditure, it is not believed that the latter is prepared to cut off a lucrative source of revenue such as he has in the opium monopoly merely for the promotion of the common good."

"In the central provinces of China, especially in Hubei and Hunan, nearly every government organization has come to depend on opium revenue for maintenance," said one authority, citing figures from a particular locality in which one picul (approximately 140 pounds) of opium cost $400.* To this basic cost, officials added $320 in ordinary taxes, $32 for Communist suppression, $3.20 for the national government, $1.50 for the local Chamber of Commerce, $2.50 for Special Goods (opium) Association fees, $2.50 for a local girls' school, and $7.00 for protection fees. To this total, the monopoly authorities then added $920, increasing the original cost of the opium by more than 400 percent, to $1,688.70.†

What angered the West was the fact that the Nanking government continued to blame foreign governments for China's dependence on opium. To quote H. G. W. Woodhead, "It is rather curious to read in the newspapers on the same morning a report from one Chinese news agency stating that altogether 204 opium traffickers have been executed in China during the current year; from another that at present there are about 3,000,000 opium and drug addicts in the country; and from a correspondent in Poseh [Kwangsi] a description of the arrival in that city of a caravan carrying 1,800,000 ounces of opium, which was stored in the offices of the Opium Suppression Bureau until it had paid the required taxes." There was a story, reported by the *North-China Daily News,* of a customs officer in Kiukiang who was arrested for smuggling opium, when, in fact, his real crime was "being over-zealous in seeking out smuggled consignments." Or, as the *North-China Herald* put it, "The scandal is so deep that it must be stirred up very gingerly."

In 1935, Chiang abolished the Opium Suppression Bureau and declared himself opium suppression superintendent. But he soon ran into competition from the Japanese, who had turned the areas of north China under their control into "one vast poppy field," from which they refined opium derivatives and other narcotics. On January 1, 1937, the generalissimo promulgated strict laws making the use of these narcotics illegal. Ac-

---

* $400 Chinese = $104 U.S. in 1933 ($1,727 today).

† $1,688.70 Chinese = $439 U.S. in 1933 ($7,293 today).

cording to Inspector Papp of the Shanghai Municipal Police, "the Chinese Government had a monopoly in the opium trade in China while Japanese subjects were dominant in the narcotic drug traffic. Therefore, the concerted efforts taken by China to eradicate the narcotic drug traffic and habit principally affected Japanese subjects . . . meanwhile, fearing extreme punishment if apprehended trafficking or consuming narcotic drugs, Chinese subjects were tending to turn from narcotic drugs to opium with the result that opium consumption is being increased and Government revenues thereby benefitted."

It would be instructive to know just how much Madame Chiang knew about her husband's involvement in the opium trade. Like him, she may well have been able to keep the contents of her mind carefully compartmentalized. This sort of mental gymnastics was exemplified in her statement about Big-Eared Du, who, after attending prayer meetings at the Kung's, was baptized in 1936. Madame Chiang is said to have told an American bishop that "Du Yueh-sheng is becoming a real Christian because ever since he was baptized there has been a marked decrease in kidnapping cases in Shanghai."

In 1939, Madame Chiang published a series of ten articles entitled "Resurgam," meaning "I shall rise again." Printed in a special supplement to the Chungking *Central Daily News,* these articles were notable for two things: first, May-ling's view of the history of China and where its people had gone wrong, and second, an inescapable contrast between what the G-mo's wife recommended as appropriate conduct for a good citizen and the behavior of the members of her own family. "It is the duty of each of us to clear our national records of the old stigma of dishonesty and corruption," she wrote in the second installment. ". . . Only a traitor . . . would . . . divert to his own pockets directly or indirectly, funds intended for national purposes or for the pursuance of our resistance." In the seventh and eighth installments, she outlined what she considered the "Seven Deadly Sins" to be expunged from Chinese life. "1. Self-seeking, i.e., the "squeeze"; 2. The concept of "Face"; 3. "Cliquism"; 4. Defeatism; 5. Inaccuracy; 6. Lack of self-discipline; and 7. Evasion of responsibility. Long ago they combined to retard our emergence as a first-class world Power," she declared, "and they now delay our victory in this war." These articles were incorporated in a book of essays and speeches entitled *China Shall Rise Again,* published in 1940. In it, the generalissimo's wife claimed that "China was strangled to death by an economic noose fashioned by Japan out of British appeasement, American profiteering and French fear."

During 1939, May-ling also kept up a lively correspondence with Emma Mills, alternating as before between the voice of a loving, if complaining, friend and that of a wary politician. Emma had been urging her old friend to come to the United States—a visit she and others thought would help China's cause—but Madame demurred. "I have thought much about it," she wrote Emma in the middle of January after a two-month tour of the various fronts. "I am convinced that I would not be able to stand the mental and physical strain. . . . I work from daylight to dark, and I have no reserve left . . . it seems to me I would offend all whom I could not see and would consequently do more harm than good. . . . If I had the physical strength I might risk it, but . . . I would be a nervous wreck after the first day." In her next letter, she remarked that she was "glad . . . you told me of the opinion expressed by one of your friends that he was darned tired of reading about the Chiangs. You can tell him I feel exactly the same way, and that the continual requests from abroad for messages, etc., have worn me to a frazzle." When Emma offered to come to China two years later, May-ling discouraged her, citing air raids, poor living conditions, constant strain, and lack of social life. As a sop to her friend's ego, she had the Chinese government award her its Medal for Distinguished Service.

Emma, who had been named executive vice president of the American Bureau for Medical Aid to China, informed May-ling that China was "almost non-existent in the daily papers—always a short column somewhere, but in an inconspicuous place. . . . We go on with money raising efforts, but don't get enormous returns." She herself, however, had been noticed by the U.S. intelligence service (then the OSS) and approached by a man who said he was sent by the State Department to find "some way to get to" Madame Chiang "without going through official Chinese channels." But in a letter to May-ling, she explained that she "wasn't cut out for intelligence work."

In November, May-ling took another trip to the front—two thousand miles by airplane, car, sedan chair, sampan, and pony—"an assortment of conveyances, all of which were threatened each day by Japanese bombing planes. Several times I had to dodge into ditches and hide in holes to avoid being seen by the Japanese machine-gunners who consider it sport to mow down people on the highways." During that month, she wrote Emma to say that she realized that it would be "difficult to help our relief funds now that war has broken out in Europe. . . . So far we have not had any particular repercussions. . . . It may interfere with our supplies of munitions, but we trust that the large-scale counter-offensive which is being planned for when a propitious time arrives will not be interfered with." To which Emma replied wisely, "It comes down to the fact that Europe is after all much nearer to us all, most of us are second or third generation overseas Europeans."

About this time the Japanese sent planes to bomb Chiang Kai-shek's home province of Chekiang and specifically his family home in the town of Chikow. One of the bombs exploded in the courtyard, killing his first wife (Ching-kuo's mother), Fu-mei. The three-foot-high monument Chiang Ching-kuo erected over her grave bore the inscription, "It takes blood to wash out blood." Four years later, the Japanese commander in charge of the area swept the graves of both Chiang Kai-shek's mother and first wife and sent photographs of this to Chiang and his son, who were not impressed with the gesture.

❦

By 1939, the Sino-Japanese War had reached more or less of an impasse. There were a million Japanese soldiers holding what they considered the most strategic points in China, including all the ports and big cities, while 4 million Chinese troops were fanned out over crucial spots in the interior. It is generally agreed that once Chiang Kai-shek withdrew his government behind the mountains in Chungking, he did very little either to fight the Japanese or to help the Chinese in the occupied territories—even after enemy planes dropped fleas carrying plague germs over Chekiang and later tried to infect the population there with anthrax, plague, typhoid, and cholera. While the peasants starved, the petty provincial officials, at the mercy of Japaneses soldiers and Chinese bandits, were vulnerable to kidnapping and even torture until they told the intruders where to look for money or goods. "In some districts," according to the *North-China Herald,* "it has been customary to roast the victims in big kettles, without water, until the flesh falls from the bone." At this point in the conflict, however, the generalissimo was concerned primarily with the actions of two old enemies: his former rival Wang Ching-wei and the Chinese Communists.

Having been out of the political picture for some time and believing that China could never hold out against Japan, Wang, it will be remembered, had left the country with his wife and family for Hanoi. Expelled from the KMT on January 1, 1939, he waited only seventeen days before sending a wire to Chiang urging him to "make a bold decision to end a futile war and to negotiate an honorable peace with Japan." In referring to Wang's twelve-point agreement with the Japanese as "the most abject and shameless document in 4,000 years' Chinese history," the *South China Morning Post* joined other papers attacking him as an "arch traitor," a "Japanese tool," and "a piece of rotten meat." Later that month, Chiang sent a man to Hanoi to assassinate Wang, but he failed. In March, a group of Nationalist secret agents entered Wang's house early one morning and fired dozens of shots, missing Wang himself but killing his secretary. If there had ever been a chance of Wang's rethinking the situation and turning back to his native China, these attempts at assassination sealed his newfound loyalty to Japan. He was inaugurated as the head of a puppet government in Nanking in a solemn ceremony in March 1940. His defection, according to Luce's *Fortune* magazine, was a "godsend" to the enemy. "Here was one of the flaming characters of the Chinese revolution . . . one of the outstanding figures in the Chinese Government. Suave, handsome, a brilliant speaker, highly emotional . . . here was a man of unquestioned standing and ability in China, a focus about which all the elements of compromise in Chinese society could gather." Adopting the old Kuomintang slogans, Wang raised the KMT flag, which now flew over both his Japanese-backed administration in Nanking and Chiang's government in Chungking. To conscript an army, Wang gave captured Chinese soldiers the choice of serving or being shot. In September 1941, just three months before Pearl Harbor, 30,000 of these soldiers manged to kill their Japanese officers and returned to serve under the generalissimo.

CHIANG'S OTHER OBSESSION, the Communists, were still busy increasing their bases of operations. After the Sian Incident, the Chinese Communist Party gained 200 seats of the People's Political Council in Chungking, a group established by Chiang to make policy during the war. Chou En-lai was named deputy minister of the Military Council, and he floated the old idea of allowing members of the CCP to also belong to the Kuomintang. Although Chiang rejected Chou's plan, it was later found that a number of Communists were, in fact, in key positions in the KMT. One of these men served as an important executive of the Central Bank, and, according to Brian Crozier, "enjoyed H. H. Kung's unreserved trust." For a while at least, the Communists had decided to praise their new ally, Chiang Kai-shek, and a "horde of leftist writers" descended on Chungking from various countries to spread the current Communist word.

After Sian—and the resulting absorption of Chinese Communist soldiers into the Nationalist army under Chiang—the Shensi Red Army of 20,000 soldiers had joined the Eighth Route Army of the Nationalist forces. During that same winter of 1937, the government had authorized the creation of another Communist army, the New Fourth Army, built around the soldiers that Mao had left behind three years earlier when he had set out on the Long March. When the Japanese conquered the lower Yangtze Valley, the New Fourth was ordered by Chiang to reorganize itself as part of the Nationalist army. Supposed to fight the Japanese, these two armies set out, under orders from Mao, to enlarge Communist control over whatever areas they could and, in the process, dispose of any Nationalist forces they met on the way. They did this by announcing that the Nationalist soldiers they wanted to eliminate were collaborating with the Japanese, thus killing off all the Chinese soldiers who would not enter their ranks. These encounters were brutal, and the Communists often buried recalcitrant Nationalists alive. In this way, the Eighth Route Army increased from 45,000 men in 1937 to 400,000 in 1940, while the New Fourth Army grew from 15,000 to 100,000. Not only did the CCP win adherents—by fair means or foul—but it propagandized its expansion of territory as hard-won victories over the Japanese. According to White, however, "during the significant campaigns, it was the weary soldiers of the Central Government who took the shock, gnawed at the enemy, and died."

In January of 1941, the fiction of cooperation between the Nationalist and Communist troops was pretty well dissolved over what came to be called the New Fourth Army Incident. At that time the New Fourth Army, led jointly by a Communist general, Xiang Ying, and a non-Communist general, Yeh Ting, was positioned south of the Yangtze River, not far from Shanghai. A few months earlier, Chiang's chief of staff had ordered the army to cross the river, move north, and take up a new position in the Japanese-occupied province of Anhwei. Although the leaders protested, the greater part of the soldiers were ferried over the river, leaving behind a detachment from headquarters of somewhere between 2,500 and 5,000 people*— commanders, staff, some combat troops, hospital workers, wounded soldiers, teachers, and students. But the local commander of the KMT said that the remaining group must be moved as well. The Communists complained that the route laid out would take them straight into the midst of the Japanese and asked Chou En-lai to take this up with Chiang. The generalissimo approved the change of route and invited Chou to Christmas dinner, where they drank to peace.† Suddenly, Communist headquarters heard that the New Fourth Army was trapped in a narrow valley, surrounded by KMT soldiers who had been hidden in the hills and who had opened fire on them; many were killed, and their commander, General Yeh, was taken captive. When Chou rushed back to tell Chiang what was happening, he was not able to see him but was assured that everything was fine and that the soldiers of the KMT were being told not to interrupt the Communists' march.

---

* Crozier says there were about 2,500; the figure of 5,000 comes from White and Jacoby. As with everything in the New Fourth Army Incident, there are few consistencies in the story.

† It is said that during dinner Chou told Chiang that his Nationalist government was undemocratic. "You mean you call *me* undemocratic?" Chiang retorted. (White, *In Search of History*, p. 114.)

Clearly someone was lying. It could well have been the Communists. According to Chang and Halliday, Mao had purposefully changed the route of General Xiang's soldiers but had not notified Chiang, since he wanted to get rid of his old enemy, General Xiang. Moreover, Mao wanted to put the Nationalist army in a position where it would have to shoot at the CCP troops, who were not where they were supposed to be, thus forcing Stalin, who had instructed Mao to fight the National Army only if attacked, to support his (Mao's) attempt to draw Chiang into open war. Or the lies may have come from Chiang, who denied that his soldiers had attacked the Reds, claiming that the Communists had fired on Nationalists first. Whatever the facts, the city of Chungking "buzzed with rumors of an open breach, of an all-out civil war." As the rumors quieted down, word came that the headquarters of the New Fourth Army had been destroyed and several thousand people, along with its commander, had been killed. Added to this was a report that the KMT had treated its CCP captives "with Japanese ruthlessness." This was confirmed years later by a university professor, a man who was not a Communist, who told White he had been captured with the group. He said that the KMT soldiers had raped their women captives and that the entire group was force-marched four hundred miles to a concentration camp. On the way, they were made to carry the baggage of the government soldiers, who beat some of them and shot others. Only three hundred people emerged from the journey alive.

But the Communists themselves were acting under false pretenses, as witness a secret directive containing Mao's instructions to the Eighth Route Army: "The Sino-Japanese War affords our party an excellent opportunity for expansion. Our fixed policy should be 70 percent expansion, 20 percent dealing with the Kuomintang, and 10 percent resisting Japan. There are three stages in carrying out this fixed policy: The first is a compromising stage, in which self-sacrifice should be made to show our outward obedience to the Central Government . . . but in reality this will serve as camouflage for the . . . development of our party."

The story of the New Fourth Army Incident varied according to the politics of the teller, but correspondents on the scene and historians agree that it marked the end of the united front against Japan. Negotiations between the two Chinas stopped, and Chiang cut off all supplies to the Communist armies. Writing a report home from Chungking in March 1941, White noted, "The communists have expanded and flourished during this war as never before. . . . Fighting between Chinese and Japanese in China has almost ceased. The Japanese are too wise to use their armies to seal Chinese unity."

Although White prefaced the above with a warning that the information he transmitted was "as complete an account of opinion and interpretation as I am permitted to send out," there was an unexpected consequence to the New Fourth Army Incident set in motion by Edgar Snow. Snow knew that the KMT massacre of the New Fourth Army soldiers would never have gotten by the censors in Chungking, so he filed his story through Hong Kong. The report caused a furor in newspapers in the West. According to Snow, his "dispatches had so interested Washington that negotiation for a new Chinese loan was suspended" and "Mr. Morgenthau had gone so far as to intimate that Chungking could expect no further financial aid from the United States in the event of any renewal of civil war." Naturally, the Chungking government denied everything, and Snow—not for the first time—lost his press privileges. But in the face of other correspondents' complaints about the suppression of their stories, Chungking was forced to temporarily lift its usual controls over reports filed by foreign journalists.

According to Crozier, the New Fourth Army Incident also strengthened Mao's position. Mao had never liked the policy of cooperation with the KMT but had been forced to adhere to it, partly because of pressure from Moscow and partly because of the Japanese invasion. "Now," Crozier said, "the united front was seen to be irrelevant as well as unpractical." And indeed, early in the following year, Mao called for a meeting of about a thousand members of the CCP, supposedly for a Seventh Congress of the Party. But there was no congress. Instead, Mao instigated a purge, and it is said that during 1942 and 1943, some 40,000 to 80,000 party members were expelled or executed. From that time on until his victory over Chiang in the Chinese Civil War, "Mao Tse-tung's power was never again seriously challenged."

31

The Japanese ... seemed to have an obsession in regard to Chungking; it was as though the continued existence of life upon that rocky spur between the rivers was an insult to their might.

—HAN SUYIN, 1940

IN EARLY May of 1939, seven months after the arrival of the Chinese government in its wartime capital of Chungking, the thick, sulfurous fog that hung over the city throughout the winter lifted, and the Japanese began the first of a series of horrific bombing raids. These assaults, which often lasted eight to nine hours, were designed not only to inflict physical damage but to break the spirit of the city's inhabitants. The first bombers caused five thousand casualties, since there were no anti-aircraft guns to ward off the planes and no shelters in which people could take cover. Chungking, according to one writer, "resembled nothing so much as a charred, overturned anthill," with terrified citizens running out of their flaming homes with no place to seek safety.

"The bombing was the worst exhibition of cold-blooded mass murder that the Japanese have so far been able to perpetrate," May-ling wrote Emma,

> ... they dropped both demolition and incendiary bombs. ... On this sixth day after the last bombing, lines of coffins still stand in front of every heap of wreckage—big ornate coffins for the affluent, wooden boxes for the less fortunate. But the bombs have reduced rich and poor, wise and stupid, to one common level—pieces of burnt flesh which are extracted from the smouldering piles with tongs. ... I went to see what was being done in rescue work after the bombings. The areas affected were raging infernos. ... Most of the houses which climb the hillsides are made of timber, perched on long poles. They burned like tinder. ... Chungking is a city of houses packed tightly together on a long, high tongue of land, girt with cliffs. Houses climb the slopes to the cliffs. They are reached by narrow stone passages, and each house has but one door. There is no escape through the back when incendiary bombs set the front ablaze. ... Fathers, mothers watched their children burnt alive.

Other children saw their parents struggling to fight across the flames only to disappear in the ruins of falling beams and pillers. The cries and shrieks of the dying and the wounded resounded in the night, muffled only by the incessant roar of the ever-hungry fire . . . the stench is increasing and living in the vicinity is impossible.

The Australian journalist Rhodes Farmer described one of the worst scenes, which took place in the legation quarter:

The door of the German Embassy was open. . . . I walked in. . . . One of the girl secretaries was having hysterics. . . . "Take a look over the wall. They screamed all night and nearly drove us crazy." . . .

The embassy had been built on top of the ancient city wall. I thought I was inured to horror, but when I looked down I nearly overbalanced with nausea. Thirty feet below me were several hundred Chinese. Some were roasted black but others had been so slowly overcome by the blasts of heat that their clothing was not even scorched. . . . This little community had lived within a pocket formed by the city wall. The fire had blocked their escape and then the wind-driven flames had forced them back against the wall . . . in nearly every case the top joints of their fingers were just bone. They had ripped the flesh away in their frantic efforts to climb the thirty-foot barrier of smooth stones. . . . I raged back to the Germans and asked why they hadn't thrown some ropes or sheets over to the trapped people. One of the Germans said: "The embassy was in danger. There were too many of them. Besides, they were only coolies."

The bombing raids lasted through the summer of 1939, and it was not until 1940 that dugouts and shelters were carved into the mountains.* Meanwhile, the citizens of Chungking were forewarned about oncoming raids by paper lanterns strung high on the city's gallows. Along with homes and businesses, the Soviet and British embassies were bombed, as were United Press and TASS (the Soviet news agency), both of which moved underground, as did the vital factories. "Do what you can," May-ling wrote Emma, "to make

---

* Even these did not always help. On June 5, 1941, too many people crowded into a tunnel in the center of town. The shelter was packed full, people panicked, and many of Chungking's ordinary citizens suffocated. After what came to be called the Great Tunnel Disaster, shelters were built with more than one opening.

your people realize that this death and havoc come to us with the help of American gasoline and oil, and materials for bombs."

Han Suyin observed Chiang Kai-shek during one of these raids: "Other generals converse in low tones or look over papers. The Generalissimo sits erect and stiff on a hard wooden chair, his arms folded, his back six inches from the back of the chair. He is resting. He is never seen to relax, to slouch or cross his legs; not a muscle moves. Overhead, bombs crash. Others in the shelter start, glance upward. They open their mouths and some stop their ears. Not Chiang Kai-shek. His face wears an expression of curbed annoyance, as though he was trying not to listen to a boring speech. Staring straight before him, he sits motionless—resting." For May-ling, bomb shelters were a new form of torture. She complained to T.V. that being "obliged to sit for hours in a dark and damp underground enclosure is an ordeal. The humidity there . . . is very high. I am covered with water blisters which itch like Job's old sores!"

During that winter May-ling visited hospitals at the front, which, she said, had "improved by at least sixty to seventy percent" from the year before. Doctors and nurses were kinder to patients; delousing equipment had been installed in some hospitals, while others had rigged up makeshift showers, using five-gallon cans with strings attached. Food, however, was still a big problem. Only $.25 (Chinese)* a day had been alloted to each soldier, and this included his ration of rice. As a supplement, some of the hospital superintendents, aided by patients, had begun to grow vegetables. Milk was exceedingly rare, but some hospitals made their own, using soybeans and old-fashioned stone grinders. The G-mo's wife brought gifts worth $2.00 (Chinese),† a towel, a bar of soap, and a bowl of well-cooked meat.

In the spring, May-ling took her sisters on a series of inspection trips, and in April they made a joint broadcast from Chungking to New York, a carefully orchestrated appeal to the West. Ching-ling gave the introduction, informing "Friends of Democracy" that the "struggle of the Chinese people against the aggression of Japanese militarism" was almost three years old and that the Chinese were "continuing their fight with determination" in spite of the fact that "Japan, with her superior military power, boasted she would bring [them] to their knees within three months." Ching-ling then introduced Ai-ling, who spoke witheringly of the "puppet show" government set up by the Japanese, claiming that it "represents nothing in China but the dregs of a political cesspool." It remained for May-ling to make "a direct

---

* 25 cents Chinese = 1.2 cents U.S. in 1941 (17 cents today).

† $2.00 Chines = 10 cents U.S. in 1941 ($1.46 today).

appeal to all liberty loving people to see that China is promptly given the justice . . . she has earned for almost three long years unparalleled in blood-shed and suffering." The generalissimo's wife asked "that a stop be put to one of two things: either Congressmen . . . should stop expressing horror at aggression, or they should stop encouraging aggression by permitting gaso-line, oil, and other war materials to be sent to Japan."* Emma wrote May-ling that she had been "told that there has been some criticism" of this last remark. "It suggests an attempt to put pressure on our sacrosanct lawmak-ers," she explained.

During the early months of 1940, the Nazis, who had already taken over Czechoslovakia and Poland, invaded Denmark, France Belgium, Luxem-bourg, and the Netherlands, all of which surrendered by the end of June. "Society people dash to the rescue of France at the drop of a hat," Emma wrote May-ling, "a little less eagerly to the rescue of England. . . . China is an old story, now, and your average citizen just doesn't think of it from one month's end to the next. The big industrialists who are making money in China and should give big gifts there, are also making money in Japan and are afraid of reprisals."

Nevertheless, in 1940, the U.S. government put an embargo on scrap iron and steel destined to be exported to a number of countries, Japan in-cluded, and Roosevelt froze Japanese assets in the United States. Chiang believed that if Japan attacked the United States, China would benefit from more U.S. aid, but he was afraid that it might be the wrong China, i.e., that of the Communists. His fears were not unfounded. One of Roosevelt's rep-resentatives told the generalissimo that the president thought that the Chi-nese Communist Party seemed more like socialists to him, and that the Nationalists and Communists ought to try to work together.

It was during the summer of 1940, White says, that "the spirit of the Chinese reached one of its all-war lows." The Japanese had captured Ichang, a port on the Yangtze River, which put their bombers only 300 miles from Chungking, and in May they began intensifying their bombing of the war-time capital, making it, according to Chang and Halliday, "the most heavily bombed city in the world" up to that time. "We have had so many raids the past month," May-ling wrote Emma on June 16, "and all the objectives have been of a non-military nature. . . . Last week, our house in Chungking was bombed, but with their usual inaccuracy the Japs merely made some bomb-holes in the yard. The house still stands sans panes, and looks like a blind man staring through sightless eyes. Many of my friends lost their homes and possessions during the last few raids. Some of them even in dug-outs had

---

* The United States was still supplying Japan with two-thirds of its war materials.

their clothes blown off. . . . I have distributed a few necessities in various friends' houses so that when worse comes to worst, I won't have to walk around the streets of Chungking clothed in fig-leaves!"

With France under the jackboot of Hitler and Britain suffering from the withdrawal at Dunkirk, the Japanese felt free to issue demands—first, that the French close the railroad from Hanoi into China and second, that the British close the Burma Road, running from Lashio, India, in the west to Kunming, China, in the east. The Burma Road, which was, as one American engineer put it, "scratched out of the mountains with fingernails," had been completed in 1938. It covered a distance of only 360 miles but, according to *Fortune* magazine, meandered "through 726 miles of the foulest driving country in the world, twisting and contorting through some of the deepest gashes on the wrinkled face of the earth." The only qualification the British were able to wring from the Japanese was that the closing of the Burma Road—now China's last link to the world—would last for only three months, a period of time that would give Japan and China an opportunity to reach a peace settlement.

It was during this interval that smuggling, called by White "an unbelievable phenomenon of piracy, bribery, racketeering, [and] corruption," reached its height. The smugglers were concentrated in three cities: Hong Kong, Shanghai, and Tientsin. Hong Kong was the point of departure for what came to be known as the "human railway"—thousands of men carrying small pieces of American trucks dismantled for that purpose, along with medical supplies, textiles, and gasoline. Waiting at the receiving end were agents of the Chinese government, prepared to pay the original cost of the goods, the expenses of the carriers, and reimbursement for goods lost en route due to enemy attacks. Another route, via Macao, served the middle class and was used by officials, journalists, and missionaries. There was also the coastal route, "dangerous but extraordinarily profitable." For 34,000 Hong Kong dollars* paid to agents of the Japanese navy, a smuggler was given the right to take one tug with as many barges as it could tow up the coastline out of Hong Kong over a period of one month. On board the tug was a Japanese agent to deal with Japanese warships encountered on the way.

But the real center for contraband was Shanghai. According to White, "The great smugglers rings with depots on the islands off the coast, with firm and fixed connections with the Japanese army and navy, with headquarters in Shanghai's swank and not-so-swank hotels bargained in millions." According to White, these rings were composed of Japanese merchants, ex-

---

* $34,000 Hong Kong = $10,438 U.S. in 1938 ($159,500 today).

Chinese pirates, Chinese merchants, Korean intermediaries, White Russians, and Japanese Special Service (army and navy) agents.

All these routes eventually met "like the meshed strands of a spider's web" in Chungking—where prices soared to ten times the value of the item, covering "the loss along the coast, the cost of the bribe, the cost of transport, the risk of confiscation within China and the time during which the capital is invested and is unretrievable" (usually about six months). This was not, as Westerners might have thought, a one-way business; goods were "not all coming in to China; probably an equal amount of the trade was outgoing." Moreover, it was a terribly risky way to make a living. Smugglers were often killed—shot if they were lucky or, if not, "exposed to fierce German police dogs" trained to "tear them to pieces." The smuggling trade flourished during 1940, accounting for probably three or four times the amount of goods that reached China through legitimate channels, and it did not subside until the end of that year, when the Japanese cracked down on both the Chinese and their own soldiers.

❦

DURING THE SUMMER of 1940, the generalissimo called a meeting of his councillors to discuss the last set of Japanese terms, offered during the closing of the Burma Road. "When I started 15 years ago," he said, "I had only 2,000 cadets. . . . America was against me, and France, and England, and Japan . . . the Communists were more powerful than they are today. And I had no money. And I marched north. . . . I united the country. Today I have 3,000,000 men and half of China and the friendship of America and England. Let them come. . . . In five years I will . . . conquer all China again."

Brave words, but Chiang's most recent biographer, Jonathan Fenby, claims that Chiang sent a member of the Secret Service—a man who looked strikingly like May-ling's younger brother T. L. Soong—to Hong Kong, where he was introduced as T.L. and pursued secret peace talks with the Japanese. The negotiators, who met at night, got as far as planning a meeting between Chiang, Wang Ching-wei, and the Japanese chief of staff in China, but negotiations collapsed over Manchukuo, which the Japanese insisted that the Chinese recognize. Chiang, who knew he would be called a traitor if he conceded on Manchukuo, also knew that these secret maneuvers could always be used to threaten Washington. Fenby says that this meeting was the basis of at least one U.S. loan to China, secretly arranged by T.V.

Chiang subsequently rejected the Japanese peace terms; there were no more peace talks; and on October 12, 1940, three months after they had closed it, the British reopened the Burma Road. Two weeks earlier, Japan had officially joined the Axis. Convinced more than ever that Japan and the

United States would soon be at war, Chiang announced in November that China was allying itself with Britain and the United States. Having received a $25 million loan from the United States in September, China was quickly rewarded with another $50 million. This was in 1940, the year Wendell Willkie ran for president against Roosevelt, who was up for an unheard-of third term. "Both parties," Emma informed May-ling, "have come out against our participation in the European war."

Early in 1941, Chiang Kai-shek issued an invitation to White House economist Lauchlin Currie to come to Chungking at China's expense to survey its problems of inflation and foreign exchange. A Washington gossip columnist reported that the hidden reason for the Currie mission was to check out rumors that U.S. loans, sent to aid China's war effort, had "stuck to the fingers of some Far East lovers of the democratic way of life," while Currie's biographer contends that the Chinese used the visit to show the world that the United States backed the Nationalist government. Others say it was arranged in order to establish a "direct channel of communication between Chiang and Roosevelt," thus bypassing the State Department, "which neither leader trusted."

Whatever the reason for his trip, Currie arrived in Chungking with a verbal message from Roosevelt to Chiang, expressing the president's fervent hope that war between the KMT and the CCP would not interfere with the united Chinese fight against the Japanese. Currie told Chiang that the Chinese Communists were receiving "a very favorable and sympathetic press in the United States" and that the best way to counteract this was for the KMT to follow a "policy of removing grievances rather than attempting to suppress or ignore disaffection." But the generalissimo, he reported on his return, "has little faith in the ability of the people to govern themselves."

While he was in Chungking, Currie saw Chou En-lai, who complained that there were "many incompetent and pro-Japanese elements" in the national government and that Kung was "a very bad influence." He said that Chiang's position was not as strong as before but that there was no one who could take his place. Currie found the greatest resentment of government policy among university students, professors, and young government workers. "I got virtually nothing from an interview at which there were two Chinese present," he reported. "I got very much more when I had one at a time . . . when they finally ventured on certain criticisms they would draw their chairs close to mine and their voices would fall to a whisper."

Economically, Currie said, the situation had already "reached a dangerous state," and he recommended one "absolutely indispensable" step: reformation of the land tax. There were, he reported, some 200 million acres of land yielding about $600 million to local governments, whereas they could be yielding some $2 billion to the central government. Transferring the land tax to the central government and making sure it was collected by an "honest, patriotic and efficient administration" would not only "cut the ground out from under the Communists" but please the peasants, provide the government with revenue it desperately needed, and put the onus squarely on the landlords, who had heretofore managed to avoid taxes because they controlled the tax collectors. "I did not," Currie reported to Roosevelt, "meet one person whom I considered competent in the whole Ministry of Finance." In his private notes, Currie jotted down his opinion of Kung, the current minister of finance: "too long on job—older, cynical, weary . . . not trusted— ugly stories widely believed." Kung's sole virtue, Currie noted, was that of being "loyal and accommodating." In spite of the fact that Kung gave Currie what one columnist called "4 coolie-loads of presents" during his stay in Chungking, Currie told Roosevelt that he was "convinced that the budgetary reforms necessary . . . will not be carried through by the present Minister of Finance. A change for the better here is absolutely essential."

At one point in his visit, Currie spent a weekend with the Chiangs in their country home. Having returned to Chungking from Hong Kong a few weeks after Currie's arrival, May-ling was preoccupied with her health. She was, Currie thought, "quite neurotic—dates her physical ills back to the death of [her] mother." She "talks of gland deficiencies," he said.

But along with her usual hypochondria, there was a family problem. May-ling had received a letter from Ai-ling suggesting that T.V. be named ambassador to the United States. What worried the Kungs was the knowledge that when T.V. returned to China, he would be more powerful than his brother-in-law—hence the attempt to keep him on the other side of the ocean. Having failed to influence Chiang thus far, Ai-ling wrote May-ling to say that T.V. was the best candidate for the office of ambassador, as he got along very well with Americans. When May-ling forwarded Ai-ling's letter to her husband in Chungking, one of T.V.'s trusted associates got hold of it and warned him, causing a deepening of the rift between the two factions of the family.

IN OCTOBER OF 1940, the Chinese had asked the United States for five hundred planes to be flown by Americans in the service of China, along with a large loan to finance them. This request was the brainchild of Colonel Claire Chennault, who had floated the idea that American planes could "carry the war into Japan proper" while at the same time harassing the Japanese navy on the sea-lanes. According to Chiang, who presented the request, the fulfillment of this proposal would also prevent Japan from bombing the recently opened Burma Road. Both Chennault and T. V. Soong had lobbied Washington for this ready-made air force, and T.V. told Treasury Secretary Henry Morgenthau that just sending five hundred planes over Japan once "would have a very decided effect on the Japanese population." When Morgenthau asked him about retaliatory bombings, T.V. was philosophical: "They're doing it anyway. . . . This would give us the chance to hit back."

T.V. was China's most successful solicitor of loans and equipment. From his impressive oak-paneled office in Washington, D.C., the man known as "the Morgan of China" was able to keep an eye on the beneficiaries of U.S. aid and try to make sure that China got her share. An article in a Canadian newsweekly called T.V. "one of the six most important men" in Washington as well as "a realist who knows that a foreign minister who can supply guns, tanks and planes need not worry about foreign relations." Barbara Tuchman put it more succinctly. "T.V.," she said, "was the most unembarrassed and untiring lobbyist of his time."

But according to Morgenthau, asking for five hundred planes was "like asking for 500 stars." It was certainly in the interest of the United States for China to keep Japan occupied, thus giving the United States more time to arm, but the Americans were not producing enough war material to go around. "It is of the utmost importance," said the editors of *Fortune* magazine, ". . . that the U.S. strengthen China with everything that can be spared from the Battle of the Atlantic." The story of how the Chinese got the leftovers was told by Thomas Corcoran, one of Roosevelt's close assistants:

> Early in the winter [of 1941] Lauchlin Currie, Roosevelt's aide for the Far East, called on me. . . . The President wanted to help Chiang, he said, to bolster his beleaguered government. If Chungking fell, China fell . . . if China remained an active adversary, Japan would continue to be distracted from her broader ambitions. . . . Acting for the President, Currie then suggested that as a private individual I . . . charter a Delaware corporation to be known as China Defense Supplies. In fact it would be the entire Lend Lease operation for China. This civilian company, supported entirely with government funds, was in one respect a simple conduit behind a facade of utmost respectability. Frederick Delano, the President's elderly uncle, was a co-chairman of the board. The other was T. V. Soong. . . . This was an unorthodox operation . . . what we were doing was dubious according to the letter of the law. . . . Though legally a private corporation, CDS didn't operate in a normally competitive market. Its sole customer was the government of China; its only source of income the Treasury Department. . . . CDS had cash enough for whatever

costs it had to cover. . . . The problem was to locate and acquire the goods we wanted to buy. . . . The logistics were horrible and the "leakage" exhorbitant, but we delivered some goods.

All that could be scraped together at that time were a hundred P-40 fighter planes that had been destined for Britain. "The British didn't want these planes now that something faster was about to be available. The P-40's were big, heavy and out-of-date as last year's hemline." The Chinese took them.

One hundred American pilots, attracted by salaries of $750 a month and bonuses of $500 for every Japanese plane shot down, were recruited from the army, navy, and marine air forces and, in April 1941, released by a secret Executive Order to serve as mercenaries in the pay of China. One hundred ten pilots and 150 mechanics and support personnel left San Francisco two months later, traveling on a Dutch merchant ship and carrying passports that identified them as "actors, farmers and other fictions." The Japanese threatened that their ship would never reach Rangoon, but it did—with no interference on the way. The reason they landed in Rangoon was that the Chinese, after all their lobbying for planes and pilots, had not bothered to prepare an airfield for them.

But it was the passage of the Lend-Lease Act* on March 11, 1941, that had, according to Tuchman, "opened the faucet of real aid to China." Thereafter, China's demands increased rapidly. "The business generated by Lend-Lease through China Defense Supplies was even more lucrative than most military procurement operations," Tuchman claimed. "It made the fortunes of the Americans involved in the group and added to Soong's, which through his previous tenure as Minister of Finance and chairman of the Bank of China was already considerable."†

❦

A MONTH AFTER the passage of Lend-Lease, the Soviets signed a five-year neutrality pact with Japan. According to General Vasilii Chuikov, the chief

---

* The Lend-Lease Act was Roosevelt's solution to the fact that Great Britain had run through $6.5 billion in credits for arms, food, and raw materials from the United States two months earlier. Under Lend-Lease, "any country whose defense the president deems vital to the defense of the United States" became eligible for defense material through lease, sale, transfer, or exchange.

† Michael Schaller agrees: "Many of those who joined Soong's effort made fortunes in the lucrative sales to China financed by American credits." (Michael Schaller, *The United States and China in the Twentieth Century*, p. 55.)

Soviet military adviser to Chiang Kai-shek at the time,* both Chiang and Madame had been "doing everything possible to bring us into open war with Japan." It was the generalissimo's wife, according to Chuikov, who "took an active part in troublemaking," provided "misinformation" to the Soviets, and "frequently made the point that the greatest support the Soviet Union could render China would be to declare war on Japan." He also blamed the Madame for articles that appeared in Chinese newspapers expressing China's appreciation for weapons received from the Soviet Union while reproaching the West—pieces he claimed had been written "to provoke the Japanese: to show them that the Soviet Union was more dangerous than America or Britain."

The Soviet-Japanese neutrality agreement was a stunning blow to the Chiangs. Ever since the Japanese invasion of China, Stalin had been sending military supplies to China to use against Japan. Suddenly, in total disregard of the Sino-Soviet Nonaggression Pact of 1937, he reversed his position, essentially granting Japan carte blanche to do whatever it wanted in China, since it no longer had anything to fear from its Russian neighbor. The Chiangs reacted to the bad news by urging T.V. to have "a frank heart-to-heart talk with the President." There was, obviously, nowhere left for China to look for help besides the United States—a fact the G-mo drove home in a flattering speech delivered at a farewell dinner to U.S. Ambassador Nelson T. Johnson in May. Later that month, while outlining Hitler's plan for world domination, President Roosevelt stated that it "would be near its accomplishment today, were it not for two factors: One is the epic resistance of Britain. . . . The other is the magnificent defense of China." Chiang's rapid response to Roosevelt's unwarranted praise was prompted by a wire from T.V., whom Chiang had recently named China's foreign minister. T.V. not only recommended that the generalissimo telegraph the president but also supplied the text. The fact that T.V. told Chiang the contents of the president's speech a week before Roosevelt delivered it attests to the efficacy of his Washington connections.

During May 1941, Henry and Clare Boothe Luce paid a thirteen-day visit to China. The son of missionaries, born in Tientsin in 1914, Luce was primed to be impressed with the country and the Chiangs. As one of his writers and old friends put it, "The trouble with Harry is that he's torn between wanting to be a Chinese missionary like his parents and a Chinese warlord like Chiang Kai-shek." An ardent political reactionary, Luce had already taken on the Chinese Nationalist cause, spearheading a new organization called United China Relief, which would raise $7 million for aid to China. The Luces stayed with the Kungs in Chungking and had tea with the

---

* Chuikov later gained renown as the commander of the famous defense of Stalingrad.

Chiangs, affording Henry Luce an opportunity to declare Chiang Kai-shek "the greatest ruler Asia has seen since Emperor Kang Hsi 250 years ago." Having heard that Madame's pantry had been destroyed by a bomb, the guests brought a huge supply of cigarettes, which they presented to the Chiangs along with a portfolio of photographs of their host, his wife, and leaders of the KMT. "An hour later we left," Luce wrote, "knowing that we had made the acquaintance of two people, a man and a woman, who, out of all the millions now living, will be remembered for centuries and centuries." In August, May-ling wrote Mrs. Luce to thank her "so much for what you and Mr. Luce have done to help China since your return to America. Since you left," she added, "I have been having malaria and lately dengue fever."

Four months after their trip, Luce devoted most of *Fortune* magazine to China. "The time has come for Americans to awake to the realization that further appeasement in the Pacific will be just as fatal as appeasement was in Europe," the magazine announced. The message was timely. The month after the Luces' visit, on June 22, 1941, Hitler had invaded Russia without warning. Stalin asked the Chinese Communists to go to battle against the Japanese in northern China, thus enabling the Soviets to concentrate on defending European Russia, but Mao refused.

During the second week in August, President Roosevelt and Prime Minister Churchill held a meeting on board the warships *Augusta* and *Prince of Wales* off the coast of Newfoundland. Resentful that he had not been invited to this or an earlier meeting of what was known as the ABDA (American-British-Dutch-Australian) talks on cooperation in the Far East, Chiang had asked for a political adviser, who, he hoped, would improve his standing in and access to the White House. After consultations with Lauchlin Currie, the president chose Owen Lattimore, a former journalist and academician described by one American admiral as "the greatest authority in America on China and Manchuria." Before leaving the United States, Lattimore met with the Soviet ambassador. "I suppose you know what kind of a son of a bitch you'll be working for?" the Russian asked him. Ignoring this, the adviser-to-be told a group in San Francisco, "Among the handful of great world leaders, Generalissimo Chiang Kai-shek is conspicuous for the fact that he is not only a great leader, but a leader who has steadily grown in strength and stature in the last four years, a growth commensurate with that of the country itself." Lattimore, who had arrived in Chungking in the middle of July, was able to consult with the generalissimo without an interpreter. Both Chiang and May-ling warmed up to him immediately. A month later, at the time of the Atlantic Conference, he reported to Washington that the Chinese were worried that they would not be given "equal status and fair treatment" after the war.

On August 23, 1941, in spite of the fact that anti-Russian discussions were still taking place between the Japanese and the Germans, the Germans and Russians signed the Nazi-Soviet Nonaggression Pact, leaving the Japanese out in the cold. Shortly thereafter, Chiang's forces managed to drive the Japanese out of the province of Kwangsi in the south. Although some thought that this victory should signal the beginning of an aggressive fight against Japan, Chiang withdrew. As Crozier put it, "He [Chiang] had no plans for victory, only for survival, for outsitting the enemy. In time, he had guessed, the Americans would be drawn into the war; then he would be rewarded for tying up a million or so Japanese soldiers. . . . In these circumstances, why should Chiang exert himself militarily and fritter away the strength he would need for the forthcoming confrontation with the Communists?"

During July, the United States had sent a military mission to China, headed by Brigadier General John Magruder. If U.S. largesse camouflaged self-interest, it became clear to Magruder and his team that Chiang Kai-shek had no intention of using what he received for the purposes it was intended. The group's artillery expert returned from a tour of inspection to report that China's requests for men and arms were not "for the purpose of pressing the war against Japan, but . . . to make the central government safe against insurrection" once Japan had been forced out of China. This home truth was repeated by the naval attaché in Chungking, who was surprised by the belief, currently widespread throughout the United States, that China could actually be counted on to fight the Japanese—a misconception carefully fostered by May-ling and the magazines owned by Henry Luce.

Another representative of the U.S. government, a transport expert named Daniel Arnstein, was sent by Roosevelt's chief troubleshooter, Harry Hopkins, to find out why "not a god damn thing was moving over the Burma Road." What Arnstein found was an "impossible situation" created by incompetence, inefficiency, and the inevitable corruption—a situation Chiang Kai-shek had been told about nearly two years earlier but had done nothing to alleviate. Hundreds of trucks were stranded for want of grease, and there was a lively market in black-market parts. At Kunming, the point at which the road started in China, truck drivers had to pass through eight different customs checkpoints before receiving permission to go ahead. At one point on the border, Arnstein found 250 trucks whose drivers had been waiting anywhere from twenty-four hours to two weeks to get clearance. In addition, there were fifteen more checkpoints on the road where provincial officials took tolls, passing the squeeze on to various government ministries. Because of this, goods shipped under Lend-Lease had piled up on the docks of Rangoon and at the terminus of the connecting railroad, and it was estimated that it would take eight months to move the backlog.

v

SUDDENLY, ON December 7, 1941, Japan attacked the U.S. Navy at Pearl Harbor, sinking 5 battleships and 3 cruisers, and destroying 177 planes. More than 2,000 American sailors were killed, over 1,200 injured, and nearly 900 men were missing. Japan also attacked the British in Hong Kong and Malaya. The next day both the United States and Britain declared war on Japan. China, which had waited for the United States' declaration, followed suit. No longer alone, Chiang sent the following wire to President Roosevelt: "To our new common battle we offer all we are and all we have, to stand with you until the Pacific and the world are freed from the curse of brute force and endless perfidy." The wire was clearly written by May-ling.

32

If you want a decent war, first thing you do is get rid of your allies.
—Major General Fox Conner

In contrast to the rest of the Allied world, the reaction to the bombing of Pearl Harbor was greeted in Chungking with jubilation. "Kuomintang officials went about congratulating each other as if a great victory had been won," wrote Han Suyin.

> From their standpoint it was a victory, what they had waited for, America at war with Japan.* At last, at last. . . . Now China's strategic importance would grow even more. American money and equipment would flow in; half a billion dollars, one billion dollars. . . . Now Lend-Lease would increase from a mere 1.5 per cent (England got 95 per cent). America's navy had been partly destroyed . . . that Japan had knocked out the Great White Fleet, made the Whampoa officers almost delirious with pleasure, both because Japan had delivered a big blow to a White Power . . . and because the telling criticisms of Chinese chaos, inefficiency, and defeat, could now be shrugged off with a triumphant "And what about you?"

Both of May-ling's sisters were in Hong Kong when the Japanese struck Pearl Harbor. Although Two-Gun Cohen tried to get Ching-ling to leave the British colony immediately, she refused on the grounds that "if there is fighting here," she might be needed to help the refugees. After the Japanese attacked the city, he tried again, explaining that she must realize that "she was a sort of national heroine" and if she stayed, many people would be killed trying to save her life. This time she agreed to leave "as soon as a plane was available." Although the British did not surrender Hong Kong to the Japa-

---

* In his memoir, Marshal Chuikov posited a disturbing possibility: "I have also thought that Chiang Kaishek and Dai [Tai] Li were intentionally withholding intelligence in their possession from the Western powers so as not to put any impediments in the way of the expected Japanese strike, whether against the Soviet Union in the north or against Britain and the United States in the south." (V. Chuikov, *Mission to China*, pp. 156–57.)

nese for seventeen days, T.V. was very worried about her. "Where is Second Sister?" he wired May-ling on December 8. "Please reply as soon as possible." This cable was followed by a second one, sent the same day: "Hong Kong is in danger. Can you try to rescue Second Sister by plane at night? Looking forward to your answer."

Ching-ling did manage to leave Hong Kong before Britain surrendered it to Japan. "I would not have been able to get out so quickly if it were not for the fact that Sister E. [Ai-ling] happened to be in HK," she wrote T.V. a month later. ". . . We escaped on the very last plane, after waiting from 12 P.M. to 5 A.M. the next day . . . at the airport, expecting every minute to be killed by shells or bombs, as firing was going on furiously around us. Six damaged planes and two craters at the airport reminded us of the risk we were taking. There was no ferry service between Kowloon and HK. Only people provided with special military passes could get on the boats. So it was not until the evening of the 8th that I managed to go over to HK during the blackout with the help of P. N. Chung of the Central Bank, who risked his life to rescue me."

Following the sisters' escape, a nasty story about Ai-ling circulated around Chungking. It seems that a special plane had been sent to take her and her entourage, which included her sister, to safety. As she was boarding the plane, Ai-ling insisted that her favorite dog, a dachshund, go with her. The pilot replied that the plane was already overweight. In response, Ai-ling told one of her security guards to stay behind, and the poor man was captured and killed. Since it is unlikely that such a small dog would have added enough weight to jeopardize the plane, the pilot must have disliked Madame Kung enough to try to blacken her reputation. A more damning version of this same story, however, was told by Joseph Alsop,* who claimed that Ai-ling's dog—a "large, well-fed" animal—had taken his place on the same flight, thus leaving him in Hong Kong, where he was interned in a Japanese prison camp. A third variation, related by an American living in Shanghai, claimed that Ai-ling, a "tough, grasping" woman, had loaded one of the last planes out of Hong Kong with her furniture, leaving her servants behind. Whatever the truth or falseness of these stories, when they got to Chungking, the sisters were, as Ching-ling put it, "welcomed . . . by . . . a libelous editorial accusing us of bringing tons of baggage, seven milk-fed foreign poodles and a retinue of servants. The truth was there were 23 persons on our plane, so you may well imagine how much luggage each could bring

---

* Alsop, a socially prominent journalist and great-nephew of Theodore Roosevelt, had joined the U.S. Navy and arranged to get himself assigned to Chennault's Flying Tigers. He was on a supply mission for Chennault at the time.

along. I wanted to answer the editorial, which was cunningly written, giving
no names but directed at us, but was told to hold a dignified silence. Meantime rumours fly thick and fast. Sister E [Ai-ling] said that she has been accused of so many things that she doesn't care about correcting rumours now.
I could not even bring along my documents and other priceless articles, let
alone my dogs and clothing."

On her arrival in Chungking, Ching-ling moved into Ai-ling's large
home—a former palace built in the 1930s for a general with four concubines
and comprising four separate buildings. Ching-ling remained there until
early 1943, when T.V. arranged for her to have a government house. An ordinary two-story home, it had a small garden with a sewer running through
it, crossed by a wooden bridge. It also had its own bomb shelter. Chungking
bomb shelters were divided into grades—for peasants, townspeople, officials, and so on—but Ching-ling invited all her neighbors, regardless of social status, to share hers. She and her two sisters also had a private telephone
line connected to their homes, which they used to speak to each other
throughout the war years in Chungking.

The day after the Japanese attack on Pearl Harbor, Chiang Kai-shek sent
identical wires to Roosevelt, Churchill, and Stalin, proposing that the Allies
in Asia hold a conference to coordinate their efforts. Stalin declined on
the grounds that Russia was not ready to take part in a war in the Pacific.
The other two accepted, and on December 23, Chiang offered them a plan
whereby the Allies would use air attacks to isolate the Japanese, after which
the Chinese army could finish them off. He was clearly thrilled when
Roosevelt wired him to suggest that he was the appropriate leader for the
undertaking, and he answered the president with an extra dollop of Confucian humility: "If it were simply a question of my own capacities and military qualifications I could not accept this supreme command with its
attendant duties and responsibilities. However I do not hesitate to accept it
at your suggestion. . . . I shall spare myself nothing to second your efforts
and to serve the common good." The generalissimo asked that the United
States "control priorities and supplies," thus preventing the British from
preempting the war materials that had been collecting in Burma.

Chiang had previously offered to send Chinese forces to Hong Kong to
help Britain defend its colony. The British declined his offer, but nonetheless he had sent a good-sized force to attack the Japanese from the mainland.
When the British withdrew on December 18, Chiang's soldiers were left to
be killed by the enemy. For this and other reasons, the Chinese neither liked
nor trusted the British. Britain had been the first imperial power established
in China; it had allowed the Japanese to force it to close the Burma Road,
however temporarily; and above all, the British treated the Chinese like an

inferior race. "This meeting in Chungking," Tuchman said, ". . . was almost as calamitious as Pearl Harbor. It brought to the surface . . . the hostility between two of the three major Allies." In spite of their mutual animosity, China and Britain were both interested in defending Burma—China because it wanted the Lend-Lease supplies that were there, Britain because Burma was the last barrier separating the Japanese from India. Nevertheless, the British, convinced that China had never renounced some "vague traditional claims" to Burma, did not want Chinese troops operating there.

The British representative to Chiang's meeting in Chungking was General Archibald Wavell, a one-eyed veteran of the First World War, a Scotsman "of formidable silences" who argued that Burma, currently under threat of Japanese attack, must be top priority. But when Chiang, who had told the British military attaché that he would send up to 80,000 Chinese troops to Burma, was informed by Wavell that the British could use only one Chinese division and that it must be provisioned from China, the generalissimo was infuriated. Moreover, they disagreed over Lend-Lease. A huge supply of munitions had been collecting in warehouses and stranded trucks—material the Chinese were loath to hand over to the British. To settle the problem, U.S. Lend-Lease officers impounded everything in question. Chiang, still seething at Wavell's offer to use only one Chinese division, offered to send Wavell twenty machine guns to defend Burma, refused to meet with the British ambassador, and threatened to stop cooperating with Britain altogether.

When word of the contretemps between Chiang and Wavell reached Washington, the Americans became considerably alarmed. Roosevelt had always worried that the Chinese would give up fighting and allow the Japanese free rein in Asia; U.S. Army Chief of Staff George C. Marshall contended that it was necessary to build up China's "faith and confidence in British-American joint purposes in the Far East"; and Secretary of War Henry Stimson offered the opinion that Wavell had been "rather peremptory and tactless and had acted in an old-fashioned British way toward China." The Americans believed that the days of empire were over and China's allies had better start treating the country and its generalissimo as equals. But Churchill, who had declared that he had not become prime minister to preside over the dismemberment of the British Empire, did not agree, saying that while in Washington, he had "found the extraordinary significance of China in American minds . . . strangely out of proportion. I was conscious of a standard of values which accorded China almost equal fighting power with the British Empire." Or, as White and Jacoby put it rather more bluntly, "The British were fighting two separate wars. In Europe they stood with all honor for the freedom of humanity and the destruction of the Nazi slave system; in Asia, for the status quo, for the Empire, for colonialism."

On January 1, 1942, Chief of Staff Marshall, called General Joseph W. Stilwell in to discuss the British-Chinese problem and to say that he was looking for an American officer of high rank to send to Chungking to smooth things out. Stilwell suggested Lieutenant General Hugh A. Drum, the pretentious commander of the First Army. "The G-mo's a stuffed shirt; let's send him the biggest stuffed shirt we have," Stilwell said. Magruder, who had led the U.S. Military Mission to China, was not high-ranking enough and was already disillusioned with the Chinese. The only other alternative was Stilwell himself, who had served in China in a lesser capacity three times before. "Me? No, thank you. They remember me as a small-fry colonel that they kicked around. They saw me on foot in the mud, consorting with coolies, riding soldier trains. Drum will be ponderous and take time through interpreters; he will decide slowly and insist on his dignity. Drum by all means." But on January 14, Stilwell was invited to Secretary of War Stimson's home, where he was told that Drum had arrived in Washington with an entourage of forty to fifty staff officers and had turned down the assignment in China as unworthy of a man of his importance and experience.* Now, Stimson told Stilwell, "the finger of destiny is pointing at you." Stimson laid out Stilwell's duties: the "entire disposition" of Lend-Lease in the Far East; command of U.S. air operations in China; and command of one or two of Chiang's armies, which the generalissimo, according to T.V., had agreed to turn over to an American adviser. This was something Chiang had previously refused to do, but T.V. had promised that his brother-in-law would give Stilwell "executive control" of the Chinese troops in Burma. Marshall added that Stilwell was to "arm, equip and train the Chinese forces" to enable them to fight the Japanese.

❦

IF THERE WERE ever two men ill suited to work with each other, they were Chiang Kai-shek and Joseph Stilwell. It was not that they weren't more alike than either would have admitted, even to himself. Physically, both were slight of build,† agile, and devoted to keeping their bodies in condition.

---

* It was later said that Drum was not the fool pictured by Stilwell but demanded "some clarification of the War Department's muddy thinking" about China and was, in fact, "a general of prescience, who deserves more than the shabby treatment he received." (Hanson W. Baldwin, "The Place of Vinegar Joe in History," *The New York Times*, April 12, 1953.)

† In 1962, when Chiang was seventy-five, May-ling wrote T.V. that her husband's weight was up to 130 pounds, "the heaviest he has been at any time in his life." (Hoover Archives: T. V. Soong files, Madame Chiang Kai-shek to T. V. Soong, Box 63, Folder 33, December 10, 1962.)

Temperamentally, both were quick to anger and unable to forgive. And both men subscribed to noble but all-consuming codes of behavior that brooked no deviation and made few concessions to on-the-ground realities. In other words, here were two ideologues from incompatible ideologies expected to work together.

Stilwell came from an old Yankee family that had immigrated to the United States in 1638. He had entered the military on a fluke: as a high schooler, he had stolen some ice cream at a dance, and his father, deciding that the boy needed discipline, sent him to West Point. A summer in Guatemala had left him with deep compassion for the underclass and hatred for the officials who kept the peasants illiterate. The inability to read and write, Stilwell said, "suits very well the purpose of the Government which takes him from his farm at any time and puts him in the army for an indefinite period, not caring whether or not his family starves." Stilwell's background, as it turned out, was perfect preparation for China.

During World War I, Stilwell had served in France as an intelligence officer, for which he received the Distinguished Service Medal. Following a year spent studying Chinese, he had set out with his wife and family for China in the summer of 1920. After six months in Peking, the International Famine Relief Committee borrowed him from the army to work on a road building project in Shansi, the interior province that was home to the Kung family. In the course of directing some six thousand men, Stilwell met a number of local farmers, who worked on the road to earn extra money. He was shocked by the hardship of their lives, commenting that "the daily struggle even to reach his fields would appall a white man." At the end of a four-year tour of duty in China, the Stilwells were sent back to the States, but he returned to Tientsin as battalion commander of the 15th Infantry in 1926, at the time that Chiang Kai-shek took over the KMT and headed north with his army to unify the nation. The American major admired the generalissimo's "determination and energy" but said that his march was "more in the nature of a parade than a campaign." He noted that the troops Chiang would have come up against had simply "oozed out of town" before the G-mo and his soldiers arrived.

Back in the United States in 1929, Stilwell was assigned to head the Tactical Section at Fort Benning, Georgia, where he earned his nickname, "Vinegar Joe." Famously impatient with incompetence, he had been particularly acidic about the performance of his students one day and, when he returned to the barracks, found a caricature of himself rising from a vinegar bottle with three Xs on the label. It had been drawn by a young officer who had pinned it on the bulletin board, much to the amusement of everyone in the barracks—including Stilwell himself, who asked permission to keep it.

Six years later, in July 1935, Stilwell was sent back to China as military attaché to the U.S. Embassy in Peiping.* Now a colonel, he arrived the day after Chiang's government was forced by the Japanese to withdraw its soldiers from the old capital, and there was a sense of growing frustration with Chiang's inability or refusal to fight the Japanese. Ambassador Johnson, who complained that "the Government at Nanking has been reduced to a jelly," still held to his conviction that there was no alternative to the generalissimo, who was the only person who could keep China unified.

The problem for any American working in China in those days was how to keep it going without direct interference. Every time the West made a loan or provided aid, the Japanese threatened to go to war. This was fine with the higher-ups in the Chinese Communist Party, who knew that if Chiang were forced to go to war against Japan, he would not be able to continue to fight them. But Chiang simply sat back and waited for help from America, although he had assured Ambassador Johnson that his policy was to "continue" actively fighting Japan—a leap over reality if there ever was one. Part of Stilwell's new job as military attaché was to see just how much of this "armed resistance" there really was, and he made two trips to southern China to investigate. He was not impressed. "No evidence of planned defense against further Japanese encroachment," he reported. "No troop increase or even thought of it. No drilling or maneuvering." But Stilwell agreed with Johnson on the subject of Chiang: "Unfortunately for China, there is no other influential leader in sight . . . who can take his place and carry on with anything like the prestige he has gained."

Stilwell liked Madame Chiang, whom he met in 1938 in Hankow. He thought she was "very charming, highly intelligent and sincere," and, in spite of the fact that she "pushed out a lot of propaganda about the way the government is looking out for the common people," he believed that "she is alright and doing a good job." After their initial meeting, he sent her flowers.

Posted back to the United States in May 1939, Stilwell was promoted to brigadier general by his friend General George C. Marshall, who was about to assume the post of Roosevelt's army chief of staff. But, as Tuchman points out, the U.S. Army itself currently ranked a pathetic number nineteen in the armed forces of the world, behind Portugal and just ahead of Bulgaria. In the belief that the United States was still protected by the oceans, Congress had repeatedly cut military appropriations, reducing the United States to what Marshall called "the status of a third rate power."

Ranked first in merit of the U.S. Army's nine corps commanders, Stilwell was named commanding general of U.S. Army Forces in the China-Burma-

---

* The foreign legations had not yet been transferred to the new capital of Nanking.

India (CBI) theater in the last week of January 1942. The title made him chief of staff to the supreme commander of the Chinese theater, i.e., Chiang Kai-shek, and supervisor of Lend-Lease in the area. In assuming his new role, he was doubtless unaware of two letters sent out by T.V. at the time. The first, addressed to Assistant Secretary of War John McCloy, noted that the American officer chosen as commanding general of the U.S. Army Forces in China "need not be an expert on the Far East"; in other words, the less the American knew about China, the better he would get along with the G-mo. The second went directly to the secretary of war, Henry L. Stimson: "I take it for granted that both as Chief of the Generalissimo's Joint Staff and as American Commander, the American officer selected for the post will be subject to the command of the Generalissimo."

Before leaving for China, Stilwell asked to meet with the president so that he might carry a personal message from Roosevelt to Chiang Kai-shek. "Tell him we are in this thing for keeps," Roosevelt said, "and we intend to keep at it until China gets back ALL her lost territory."

Clarence Gauss, the ambassador to China, a thin-lipped, nearsighted worrywart, had warned Roosevelt and Congress that loans with no restrictions could be ill used by "the retrogressive, self-seeking and, I fear, fickle elements" at the top of the Kuomintang. But they had ignored him, passing China's request for an unrestricted loan of $500 million by voice vote in the House of Representatives and unanimously in the Senate. In spite of those who had dealt with the G-mo on his home ground, he was still known in the United States as "a military technician of surpassing skill" and "the shrewdest politician in China."

❦

BY EARLY FEBRUARY 1942—a month before Stilwell arrived in Asia—it had become apparent that Rangoon would soon be lost to Japan. The British had sent two Indian brigades back to Burma from the Middle East to reinforce their own troops. According to Tuchman, these men had been trained for desert warfare against the Germans, "rather than for service in their own area where they might become contaminated by dangerous ideas of Asian nationalism." The combined British and Indian troops, withdrawn to a position before the Sittang River, didn't have a prayer of success; as Tuchman put it, "an inferior force with its back to a river is in a classic position from which not to fight." On February 23, the Japanese clobbered the British-Indian brigades.

To counteract the now-probable fall of Rangoon and subsequent isolation of Chungking, T.V. had recommended to President Roosevelt an air route between northeast India and Kunming in Yunnan (the province of

China bordering Burma), neglecting to mention that between these two points lay the Himalaya Mountains, "probably the most hazardous flight route in the world." Another possibility was a road from Ledo in northeast India across the mountains, forests, and rivers of northern Burma to connect with the Burma Road. Chiang Kai-shek said it could be built in five months, but, according to the U.S. Military Mission to China, it would take two and a half years. Both of these projects had been approved before Stilwell got to China.

It took Stilwell and his staff twelve days to fly from Miami to Chungking. Before they arrived, Singapore had fallen and 80,000 soldiers— English, Australians, and Indians—were in Japanese prison camps. Rangoon, which the British evacuated on March 7, was rapidly descending into a state of lawlessness. There was little support among the Burmese for the British, who had refused to offer Burma independence or even dominion status after the war, and, conversely, a great deal of admiration for the Japanese, who were showing the Westerners something about war. The Burmese premier explained it this way: "We Asiatics," he said, "have had a bad time since Vasco da Gama rounded the Cape."

This was the general feeling throughout the Far Eastern colonies. Chiang and May-ling had visited India just before Stilwell's arrival. Encouraged by both Indian and British leaders, Chiang had been led to believe that he was in a position to convince the British to accede to some of the Indians' demands and, at the same time, rally their support for the Allies at a moment when their regard for the British was at a particularly low ebb. According to Crozier, the personal, unstated purpose of the generalissimo's trip was to establish himself as the great leader of Asia in the coming postwar world. Ambassador Gauss thought that the visit might prove useful but added that matters were really "too delicate for Chiang's knowledge and temperament." It was a secret trip, and for five days after their arrival, the Chiangs' presence in the country was not even announced.

No sooner had they arrived, however, than they ran into a problem of official protocol. Chinese tradition required that Chiang go to Wardha near Bombay to visit Mahatma Gandhi, while Indian protocol demanded that Gandhi meet his visitor in New Delhi, where the Chiangs were staying in a villa on the grounds of the Viceroy's Palace. The English ambassador to China, Sir Archibald Clark-Kerr, brought May-ling a letter from the viceroy (the marquess of Linlithgow), explaining that he would be subjected to "grave political embarassment" if the Chiangs traveled to Wardha to meet Gandhi. At the same time, Churchill cabled Chiang asking him not to go against the wishes of the viceroy; such a trip, he said, "might impede the desire we have for rallying all India to the war effort against Japan" and "might well have the unintended effect of emphasising communal differences at a moment when unity is imperative." This was a legitimate concern for the British. If the Japanese were able to convince 390 million Indians that to fight for Britain would be, as White put it, "like a fish fighting for the frying pan," Asia would soon fall to the Axis powers. If, on the other hand, Chiang could help convince the Indians that both they and the Chinese would be better off defeating Japan, his trip might be a boon to the British.

Once it was clear that the Chiangs were in the country and cooperating with the British, the viceroy gave them a celebratory dinner in his huge sandstone palace with its eighteen-foot windows, lovely terraces, and gardens. "It was white tie and tails and beyond doubt one of the biggest things that has been given in New Delhi in a long, long time," said Thomas M. Wilson, an American diplomat.

> Certainly nothing on this scale has been done since the war. . . . There were eighty-five who sat down to the table. I was grabbed . . . and marched over to Madame Chiang Kai-shek. . . . [Her] first question was, "Mr. Wilson, what good do you think is going to come from this visit of ours?" She seemed very serious in putting the question. I told her . . . "I don't even know what the purpose of the visit is or what you expect to achieve." Weighing her words very carefully Madame Chiang started telling me . . . that in fact it had been hoped something would be achieved in the way of greater effort on the part of India in aid given to China.

In between the pomp and circumstance, the Chiangs looked at border fortifications, met with British officials, and saw Jawaharlal Nehru, whose Self-Rule Party believed that India must be guaranteed independence as payment for an out-and-out war effort. Nehru had visited the Chiangs three years earlier, and, according to Li, May-ling had started corresponding with him—"bubbly letters . . . [that] had the air of a schoolgirl crush." He now joined the Chiangs after it was finally determined that they should meet Gandhi in Calcutta. The old mahatma was not easy for Chiang to convince. He said that the generalissimo's treatment at the hands of the Allies argued against his demands to support them in the war effort. "They will never voluntarily treat us Indians as equals," Gandhi told Chiang, "why, they do not even admit your country to their talks." This argument hit home with Chiang, currently suffering because he had not been allowed to join the Munitions Control Board in Washington, the entity that doled out military supplies. He promptly sent T.V. a letter to be shown to Roosevelt, quoting Gandhi and adding "If we are thus treated during the stress of war, what becomes of our position at the peace conference?" Nevertheless, on the last day of their visit, May-ling broadcast a message from her husband to the Indian people, calling on them to support the Allied struggle against the Axis nations but adding the wish that the Indians would be given the right to run their own country.

According to the viceroy, the Chiangs' visit was fairly successful, even though the generalissimo "quite failed to understand the complexity of Indian politics." He called May-ling a "very clever and competent little lady . . . clearly invaluable to him. When they are on a big job, she starts with the family trousers firmly fixed on her limbs, but by the final stage of any venture the generalissimo is invariably discovered to have transferred the pants to his own person. The process is well worth watching." Gandhi's reaction, as expressed in a letter to one of his supporters, was just as cynical: "He [Chiang] came and went without creating any impression, but fun was had by all. I would not say that I learned anything, and there was nothing that we could teach him. All that he had to say was this: Be as it may, help the British. They are better than others and will now become still better."

On their way home, May-ling wrote Nehru, "We shall leave nothing undone in assisting you to gain freedom and independence. Our hearts are drawn to you, and . . . the bond of affection between you and us has been strengthened by our visit. . . . When you are discouraged and weary . . . remember that you are not alone in your struggle, for at all times we are with you in spirit." But May-ling did not stop with personal expressions of support; her public comments on India aroused Churchill's ire, earning for her brother T.V. "a cool reception" when he visited London the following year.

"The time has passed when we can determine a man's status or his nation by the color of his skin or the shape of his eyes," May-ling said in a radio address to Wellesley alumnae shortly after her return to China. She also wrote two articles, indicating that her experience in India had raised her awareness of the attitude of the white man toward other races. In the first, published in *The New York Times* in April 1942, Madame Chiang rebuked the Western world for two hundred years of profiteering off China and "the superiority complex" that, she claimed, was "a cardinal point in the creed of the Western world in its dealing with all things Chinese." In the second, which appeared in May 1942, in *The Atlantic Monthly*, the G-mo's wife was more explicit, referring to "the exploitation of our country by the West in the past and the hard-dying illusion that the best way to win our hearts was to kick us in the ribs. Such asinine stupidities must never be repeated as much for your own sake as for ours."

A necessarily anonymous letter to the editor was published in *The Atlantic* two months later, objecting to the choice of May-ling as the voice of China: "Madame Chiang's charges of foreign exploitation of China are largely camouflage to hide the exploitation of the country by the present regime. . . . Tell our friends in America to stop praising the present Chinese Government." Along with detractors, however, there were always the Chiang supporters. In an article published in *The Atlanta Constitution,* Clare Boothe Luce claimed that Madame Chiang "is the nearest thing to a Joan of Arc . . . and a Florence Nightingale that this decade has produced." And while they were still in Delhi, the generalissimo had received word that His Majesty's government had made him an honorary knight of the Bath, Military Division, in honor of "outstanding achievement in the Allied cause." A cable had also arrived from President Roosevelt, announcing a loan of $500,000.* "The gallant resistance of the Chinese armies against the ruthless invader of your country," the president wired, "has called for the highest praise from the American and all other freedom-loving peoples." Such blatant hyperbole prompted a gracious response, written by his wife for the generalissimo: "Your far-sightedness in this world's greatest crisis is deservedly the envy of all real statesmen."

❦

ON HIS WAY to China, Stilwell stopped in India and flew on to Lashio, the junction of the railway and highway systems in Burma northeast of the capital of Mandalay. There, he ran into Chiang and May-ling. Lashio was the site of the Chinese General Staff, and the G-mo had come to give his orders for the campaign in Burma. In his entourage was Hollington Tong, the vice minister of information, who had graduated from the Columbia School of Journalism. Although Holly Tong was said to be trusted by a number of foreign journalists—"one of the Generalissimo's keenest instruments, as faithful as a dog and as clean as a dog's tooth"—Stilwell couldn't stand him, referring to him as "oily and false."

After Lashio, Stilwell left for Chungking, stopping overnight at Kunming, where he met Claire Chennault. Both men had originally been told that Chennault would be the ranking commander of the air force in China, but Chennault had been pushed down the ladder of command by the appointment of Stilwell. "Had a long talk with him and got him calmed down," Stilwell said. "He agreed to induction [of the American Volunteer Group] into the American Air Force† and said he'd be glad to serve under me. That's a big relief."

After a bumpy two-hour flight—"Chinese passengers all puking"—the

---

* Equivalent to $6,604,000 today.

† The AVG was dissolved on July 4, 1942. Some of the pilots remained, forming part of a new China Air Task Force, which became the Fourteenth Air Force in March 1943.

American general arrived at Chungking. Ignoring Chinese protocol, he insisted on climbing up the 365 steps from the landing strip on the Yangtze River to his assigned residence. Stilwell moved in with a staff of eight, including Colonel (later Brigadier General) Frank Dorn, his aide and closest associate. A modern concrete home originally built by T.V. for himself and taken over by the government, the residence had three stories, a roof terrace, a pool, and a view of the river. It came complete with a staff of twenty-nine—including seven gatesmen, two gardeners, four houseboys, one cook, two kitchen boys, three general servants, and four men to haul water to the tanks on the roof. The servants had been supplied by Tai Li, head of the Chinese Secret Service, and at least once during his residence there, Stilwell found agents going through the papers in his desk. The comfort of his quarters, it would seem, had little to do with the hazards of his assignment. To defend the Burma Road, Stilwell would have to find a modus vivendi among the British, Chinese, and U.S. governments. To succeed in everything else, he would have to serve three conflicting authorities: China's generalissimo, the commanding British officer in the region, and last, but most important, the U.S. government.

While he was in China, Stilwell kept what he called "The Black Book," in which he jotted down his thoughts and reactions. "I'm a worrier," he wrote before arriving in China. "I'm always imagining dangers, & experiencing them mentally. Many never occur, but those that do I'm mentally prepared for, so maybe it pays." Unfortunately, there was no amount of intelligent worry that could have prepared this American general to deal with the job before him.

PART FIVE

1942–1943

33

*Among the Old Hundred Names, as the common Chinese people often called them-
selves, to become a Soldier was the worst fate that could overtake a man, equivalent
to being sold into prostitution for a woman.*

—OLIVER J. CALDWELL

STILWELL'S FIRST official meeting with the Chiangs took place the day after
his arrival in Chungking. He told the generalissimo that he thought Burma
could be saved if his soldiers would go on the offensive, and Chiang promised that they would set up a joint staff meeting the next day. "It was a relief
to find that the G-mo contemplates command in Burma for me," Stilwell
wrote in his diary. ". . . He seems willing to fight, and is fed up with the British retreat and lethargy. . . . Madame made some caustic remarks about the
British, and their broken promises. She kept after me after the conference to
talk about Chennault. Worried for fear he would be pushed aside." Buoyed
by the meeting, Stilwell wrote that Chungking wasn't "half bad when the
sun shines," except for the inflation, which was "fantastic." Under Kung,
prices had taken off on a dizzying upward spiral. As one observer put it, referring to the author of the inflation, "No-one ever saw a fat Chinese below
the rank of Minister of Finance."

While he waited for the promised word from Chiang, Stilwell made
plans for the Chinese army's campaign in Burma, not realizing that the generalissimo never ordered his troops to take the offensive. According to Tuchman, the Nationalist army was supposed to number 3 million men broken
into three hundred divisions, but the fighting ability of these divisions varied
greatly, since the G-mo gave the best arms, equipment, and uniforms only to
the ones he liked best. While a favored division might be supplied with regu-
lation tan uniforms and chartreuse leggings, another might have only boots
and leg wrappings, while still others had to march in straw sandals and sleep
five men under one blanket. Those who could get together the enormous
sum of $100 Chinese dollars* could bribe their way out of military service.
The others were marched to camp for three weeks' basic training, tied together with rope around their necks to prevent escape, and given nothing

---

* $100 Chinese = $5.00 U.S. in 1943 ($62.23 today).

more than old rice and pickled vegetables to eat en route. Death by starvation on the road was not infrequent. There were also epidemics of typhus, smallpox, dysentery, beriberi, and something called "relapsing fever" borne by lice. When a soldier dropped out of his column to relieve himself, he was accompanied by an officer with pistol at the ready, just in case the man tried to get away. Saving lives was not a priority among commanders, or as one of them put it, "The one thing we have plenty of in China is men."

Chinese divisions were usually short of ordinary foot soldiers, since payment came through the commanding general, who could pocket what was left over after paying the men under him their salaries of $16 to 18 Chinese dollars* per diem. Thus, while the commander of a division might show a roster of 10,000 men, for whom he received money and supplies, he might have as few as 5,000 to 7,000 bodies to feed. Corruption was rampant among both commanders and officers, and, according to White and Jacoby, the man who was "probably responsible, more than any other man except Chiang Kai-shek," for this state of affairs was General Ho. "Payrolls were padded; rice rolls were padded; the abuse became so flagrant that a general's graft was finally recognized as his right." Stilwell's chief aide, Frank Dorn, was appalled: "Chinese higher commanders and staff officers are stupid, self-seeking, irresponsible and incompetent. Leadership in any sense of the word does not exist. The supply system is so mismanaged and irresponsible as to be beyond description." Dorn found small-arms ammunition, hoarded by the officers for as long as eight years, "so incrusted with filth and corrosion as to be useless, while warehouses nearby are stocked with tens of millions of new American ammunition [sic]." Worse, White and Jacoby reported that "Chinese officers treated their soldiers like animals." They could be beaten, even killed, "at a commander's whim"; less lethal punishments included flogging until the bones showed and cutting off ears.

The fear of bearing bad tidings prevented the generalissimo from being told the truth about the appalling conditions that existed in his army. As late as the summer of 1944, Chiang was driving along a country road when he saw an army officer leading recruits roped together and prodded by soldiers with bayonets. The G-mo was so angered that he beat the officer until one of his bodyguards rescued the man. Clued in to what it was like for these poor conscripts, Chiang called in the general in charge, beat him, and had him executed the next year.†

---

* $16 Chinese = $.80 U.S. ($9.96 today); $18.00 Chinese = $.90 U.S. ($11.20 today.)

† Chiang's temper was not always used against the deserving. Watching a movie in his home one evening and vastly annoyed by a particular scene, he stalked out of the room and ordered that the projectionist be thrashed.

After waiting three days for Chiang's plan for a Burma offensive, Stilwell received an invitation to dine at the Chiangs' home. He was the guest of honor; the other guests were clearly frightened; and everyone could see the boots of the Secret Service men peeking out from under red curtains. "They told me to stay after dinner 'for a few moments,' " he wrote in his diary. The few moments turned into two hours, during which the generalissimo, echoed by what Stilwell called "a stooge staff general," lectured Stilwell on the situation in Burma. " 'If the British run away,' Chiang contended, 'the Japs will get to Mandalay and crucify us.' I showed him the solution, but stooge jumped in and made a long harangue about how right Chiang Kai-shek was. I let them rant." When May-ling asked Stilwell what he thought, he said that he "preferred the G-mo's first plan . . . ATTACK." Two days later, at a second conference with Chiang, Stilwell tried to explain why Burma was more important to China than it was to Britain. All Britain wanted was to protect India, he explained. "If China should lose Burma, the communication line between her and the world is cut."

But Chiang wanted Stilwell to go to Burma to ascertain whether the British would fight, whether they would give China the gas they had promised but not yet delivered, and whether they were expecting the Burmese people to hold Mandalay for them, in which case China would not send troops. "What a directive," Stilwell wrote in his diary. "What a mess. How they hate the Limeys. And what a sucker I am. Well, at least, Chiang K'ai-shek is sticking to one part of the agreement. Never before has a foreigner been allowed any control over Chinese troops."

The Chinese soldiers who had been promised to Stilwell were mostly elsewhere when he arrived in Burma, except for the 200th Division. The Japanese had almost encircled the 200th but in so doing had left themselves open to counterattack, and Stilwell wanted to bring two divisions of Chiang's well-equipped Fifth Army down from the North to rescue them. His plan depended on the ability (or desire) of the British to hold the front and the quickness of the Chinese in moving south. The British had little idea of what they were supposed to do, while the Chinese were averse to any concentration of soldiers needed for an offensive, since they thought in terms not of what they could do but rather what they were risking in terms of arms and material.

Stilwell established his headquarters at Maymyo, a hill station about 3,000 feet high, the summer capital of Burma, surrounded by pine groves, grasslands, and a lake. When he introduced himself to the governor-general as the commander of the Chinese armies in Burma, the gentleman expressed some surprise, particularly when General Tu, commander of the Fifth Army, introduced himself under the same title. "Ah, Your Excellency," said Tu, "the American General only thinks that he is commanding. In fact, he is doing no such thing. You see, we Chinese think that the only way to keep the Americans in the war is to give them a few commands on paper. They will not do much harm as long as we do the work."

In the middle of March, Stilwell flew back to Chungking to try to convince Chiang to move his troops. "We had a battle," Stilwell wrote in his diary, "and every point he set up I knocked down." The next day, buoyed up by four Chinese generals who thought he was right and May-ling, who told him to "keep it up," he saw Chiang again. "Stubborn bugger. But he gave in a bit. . . . In a month, if nothing happens, maybe we can take the offensive." The generalissimo's brain, it seems, was riveted on the capital city of Mandalay, which lay two hundred miles behind the Allied line of defense and was militarily insignificant.

Before Chiang could change his mind, Stilwell flew back to Burma. Although General Tu had agreed to send two divisions to back up the 200th, his soldiers had been sent to Burma with no rations, rail transportation, or fuel for their trucks—all of which had been supplied by the British. Moreover, a raid by two hundred Japanese bombers caught both British and American planes by surprise. The former retreated to India without bothering to inform their commanding general, and the American pilots, unable to keep even a few planes in the air, left as well. That night Stilwell wrote Stimson to say that it had taken too long to get Chiang to agree to move his armies and that the delay had "fatally compromised any chance we might have had here in Burma."

During the following week, Stilwell made "a frantic effort" to bring one Chinese division down from the North in order to break through the Japanese troops threatening to encircle the 200th Division. After four days of "mysterious" railway delays, Stilwell ordered the troops to take the offensive—not once but twice. Nothing happened. All Stilwell's orders went to General Tu, then to a second man, and finally to another Chinese general with a secret radio set connected to the generalissimo in Chungking, who decided if and when they should be obeyed. Moreover, every plane that arrived from Chungking held a box with letters from May-ling containing warnings and tactical advice from her husband. When Stilwell ordered 150 trucks, he got 50, since the chief of supply, who had 700 trucks at his disposal, was using them to take military supplies to private warehouses in China. By the last two days in March, Stilwell realized that no matter what he did, there would be no offensive. "The pusillanimous bastards," he wrote in his diary before leaving for Chungking to have it out with the G-mo once again.

"Through stupidity, fear, and the defensive attitude we have lost a great chance to slap the Japs back," Stilwell wrote in his diary on April 1. ". . . The basic reason is Chiang K'ai-shek's meddling. . . . Had he not stopped the 22nd Division when I ordered it in, we would have had plenty of force to cut off the Japs . . . Had he not gone behind my back to Tu and Lin Wei [Stilwell's chief of staff], they might have obeyed my orders. . . . He curses the British for falling back, and does the same thing himself. . . . His constant interferences . . . have the effect of completely nullifying my little authority. . . . The army and division commanders are vitally interested in doing what they think he wants them to do. Why should they obey me?"

When Stilwell went to see the generalissimo, Madame was with him. The American general said he "threw the raw meat on the floor. . . . Pulled no punches and said I'd have to be relieved." Chiang offered to "investigate" and promised that "if the divisional commander disobeyed, I'll shoot him." The G-mo's reaction was seemingly one of concern, and he agreed to replace Stilwell's chief of staff. "Chiang Kai-shek and Madame are worried," Stilwell wrote, although he was not fooled by either of them: "I have to tell Chiang K'ai-shek with a straight face that his subordinates are not carrying out his orders, when in all probability they are doing just what he tells them."

While he was in Chungking, Stilwell had a chance to observe May-ling, whom he called "Madamissima" in his diary:

A clever brainy woman. Sees the Western viewpoint. (By this I mean she can appreciate the mental reactions of a foreigner to the twisting, indirect and undercover methods of Chinese politics and warmaking.) Direct, forceful, energetic, loves power, eats up publicity and flattery, pretty weak on her history. No concession to the Western viewpoint in all China's foreign relations. The Chinese were always right; the foreigners were always wrong. Writes entertainingly but superficially, with plenty of sarcasm for Western failings but without mention of any of China's little faults. Can turn on charm at will. And knows it. Great influence on Chiang K'ai-shek mostly along the right lines, too. A great help on several occasions.

Both May-ling and Chiang were with Stilwell when he returned to Burma in early April. After a welcome by the Burma Rifles playing bagpipes, the generalissimo called a meeting with General Tu and Stilwell's new chief of staff, at which May-ling was present. He told them that Stilwell was "the boss," that they were to obey his orders "without question," and that he had "full power to promote, relieve, and punish any officer in the Chinese Expeditionary Force." It seemed to Stilwell that Chiang "has come around to my contention: i.e., it is necessary to fight where we are." May-ling spoke up to say that "this is just what I've been telling them from the beginning, and if they'd done as I said, we'd have been better off." She left Stilwell a jar of marmalade and a letter saying "We are back of you. . . . I am at the other end of the line. . . . You have a man's job ahead of you but you are a man—and shall I add—what a man!"

There were many journalists in Chungking taking pictures of Stilwell and the Chiangs arm in arm. "Before I have a chance to get my feet on the ground, a flood of crap is released, to justify which I would have to be in Rangoon within a week," Stilwell complained to his diary. "What a sucker I'll look like if the Japs run me out of Burma." Clare Boothe Luce was there, writing a cover story for *Life* magazine that was published a couple of months later. She wanted to know if Stilwell's talks with the generalissimo had been a success. "Yep, yep, yep, yep. The Gissimo handed it to everybody including his own generals straight. . . . So did I. And Madame translated it all straight too. Without pulling a punch. Yep. Everybody took it right out of the spoon."

Chiang told Stilwell that his authority would be confirmed in the form of a seal with his official title to stamp documents to make them valid. But when the seal arrived a week later, it bore the title of chief of staff of the Allied Armies instead of the promised commander in chief of the Burma Expeditionary Force—a switch that made Stilwell, in the eyes of the Chinese soldiers, an adviser rather than their commanding officer.

During the Chiangs' flight back to China, the Japanese sent eighteen planes to try to do away with them. Many years later, May-ling described their trip to a reporter:

> When we were ready to take off, there was no escort, so we had to fly back without. Just as we were airborne, we received the message "thirty-seven Japanese planes on your tail."* There were only five parachutes, so the crew gave one to the president, one to me and the other three to high ranking generals. My maid began to cry and I told her not to worry. I said parachutes were made to carry 250 pounds and the two of us together didn't weigh that much. If we had to jump, I said, we would put our arms around each other and both float down with the same chute. She stopped crying and said, "Madame, if I die, I won't be missed, but you are needed by our people. I would not think of risking your life to save mine." We were able to fly into some clouds and elude the enemy planes, but I have never forgotten that. The maid . . . is with me still. She is getting on in years and is sometimes crochety, but I am never cross with her as I

---

* The number of enemy planes varies with the raconteur.

am always mindful of that day in Burma and her many years of faithful service to me.

Perhaps there were clouds and perhaps not. In any case, Li reports that shortly after this touching scene, fifteen fighter planes arrived from Kunming to escort the Chiangs to safety.

On his return to Burma, Stilwell discovered that Chiang had already sent a division to defend Mandalay. But the Chinese could not bring down the Japanese planes which bombed the fabled city with its many towers, killing four hundred people, destroying the railway station, the hospital, and "acres of streets." When Stilwell got there five days later, the Burmese capital was still burning, the police and most of the citizens had fled, and the British were struggling to bury their dead. Chiang and May-ling, who arrived the same day, took the occasion to lash out at them. "In all my life of long military experience," Chiang wrote Roosevelt, "I have seen nothing to compare with the deplorable unprepared state, confusion and degradation of the war area in Burma." As if to prove the point, the compound in which the Chiangs were staying was bombed as well.

"The Generalissimo and I returned yesterday from the Burma front," May-ling cabled Lauchlin Currie on April 12. "The situation there is unspeakably dangerous with complete disorganization of both front and rear, collapse of civil administration, breakdown of communications, and population panicky. . . . British seem hopeless and helpless, while Burmese people are antagonistic and the country side is honeycombed with Fifth Columnists. . . . Generalissimo told [Field Marshal Harold] Alexander if such conditions obtained in China, heads would have been chopped off." The next day in another cable clearly written by his wife, Chiang sent the same information to President Roosevelt, detailing the "complete absence of fighting spirit . . . among the civilian defense personnel, the public servants and the masses alike," along with the "intolerable stench from the corpses . . . and from the carcasses of animals which had not been removed." As usual, the disasters had been brought about not by the Chinese but by the failures of their allies.

The Chiangs were not entirely wrong. Stilwell radioed Marshall that he believed the British had long since written off Burma, that they had plenty of troops they "could have . . . marched in long ago had they meant business." But he thought that they preferred to sacrifice Burma rather than owe anything to the Chinese or promise Burmese nationalists a change in status after the war. As Tuchman put it, "They intended to regain it at the peace table in any event and wanted it free of any commitments as to future form of government."

Five days later, the Japanese broke through the Allied front. The Chinese soldiers were not where they were supposed to be and could not get there, since the trucks that should have been available were being used to transport goods to China. When the head of the British forces asked the Chinese general what had happened to the field guns he had seen the previous day, the general said he had moved them to safety.

"Then you mean that they will take no part in the battle?"

"Exactly."

"But then what use are they?"

"General, the Fifth Army is our best army because it is the only one which has any field guns, and I cannot afford to risk those guns. If I lose them the Fifth Army will no longer be our best."

With the Japanese threatening to envelop the Allies on all sides, there was nothing to do but try to get the Allied troops out of Burma before they were trapped. On May 1, Stilwell woke up to find that his Chinese chief of staff had commandeered a locomotive with seventeen cars and run his train into another, blocking the railway for two days. "Unfortunately," Stilwell said, "he was not killed." The order for the British to evacuate came through the next day. While their commander left by car, his soldiers set off on a six-day march. They beat the Japanese but were forced to abandon tanks and guns on the way. Of those who left, only 12,000 got back to India, while 13,500 were killed or left by the wayside.

On May 6, May-ling cabled Currie that the "responsibility for the Burma debacle rests on the British. . . . It is claimed that the British destroyed 300,000 gallons of gasoline . . . although previously they had informed the Chinese that they regretted their inability to supply any more gasoline. . . . The outcome of the Burma campaign has resulted in an intensification of anti-British sentiment in Chungking." Although she assured Currie that "Chiang Kai-shek thinks very highly of Stilwell" and that this "regard is shared by other Chinese officers," the defeat of the Allied forces resulted in a major split between the generalissimo, who worshiped appearances, and Stilwell, who took devilish pleasure in ignoring them.

When the pilots of the DC C-47 sent by General Hap Arnold to evacuate the American commander informed Stilwell that they had come to get him, he refused to go with them, even after being told that enemy troops had been sighted a mere twenty miles away. Stilwell's "sole idea," according to Tuchman, "was to go out with the Chinese troops. This was his duty as commander which, for him, allowed no deviation." According to Dorn, Stilwell was "physically courageous. . . . He possessed the *quality of mind**

---

* Dorn's italics.

that enabled him to encounter danger with firmness and without fear. At times he was actually foolhardy."

After sending part of his staff on the planes, Stilwell started to walk out of Burma with about a hundred people, including American soldiers, two doctors,* Burmese nurses, Chinese guards, an ambulance unit of British Quakers, cooks, porters, British officers and civilians, an American missionary, and American journalist Jack Belden, plus an odd collection of miscellaneous vehicles. Stilwell chose a little-traveled and difficult route in order to avoid the multitudes of other refugees, mostly Indians and Chinese, running away. It was a shortage of food that, Tuchman said, "made fellow refugees as great a danger as the enemy." The road they were on soon gave out, and all their vehicles except jeeps had to be left behind, including their radio truck and radio. Before abandoning the radio, Stilwell sent out his last message to the U.S. War Department. It was typical of him not to admit the desperateness of their plight: "We are armed have food and map and are now on foot. . . . No occasion for worry. . . . Believe this is probably our last message for a while. Cheerio." He then had the radio axed and all the codes and copies burned.

What Stilwell did not do was inform the generalissimo of his plans. Chiang had specified that in case of defeat, the Chinese soldiers should be withdrawn to northern Burma and from there to China. Stilwell had thus countermanded the G-mo's orders by heading for India, ignoring the Chinese tradition that "when cornered, Chinese troops will not degrade themselves by seeking shelter in a foreign country."

On the morning after they abandoned their vehicles, Stilwell addressed his odd company of travelers. He told them that they were embarking on a trip of some 140 miles that would take them across a river and through a mountain pass 7,000 feet high. They had to make fourteen miles per day (1) in order to get there before the summer monsoons and (2) so that their food would last. They would be allowed one five-minute rest every hour. Their food had to be pooled and all personal baggage discarded except for what each person could carry along with his weapons and ammunition. If anyone was unwilling to abide by his orders, he could leave now and be given a week's food rations. No one left. "By the time we get out of here," he told them, "many of you will hate my guts but I'll tell you one thing: you'll all get out."

Blazing heat—just before the monsoon is the hottest time in Burma— malaria, dysentery, ants, insects, leeches, and bearers who disappeared—all

---

* One of whom was Lieutenant Colonel Gordon Seagrave, the famous "Burma Surgeon."

these slowed the group and forced Stilwell to extend the rest period to ten minutes per hour. Two officers collapsed from sunstroke and had to be hoisted onto the backs of mules. The group's box of medicines was stolen. While they were rafting down the Uyu River—Stilwell had sent messengers ahead to order the rafts—they heard an airplane, which they recognized as British. It opened its bomb doors and let out sacks of food and medicine, but before the travelers could beach their rafts, natives appeared from the jungle to help themselves to the first of the drops.

On May 14, as the group struggled to climb 3,000 feet up the mountains, they were met by a British district official, who brought a supply of pigs for dinner and word that more food, ponies, whiskey, cigarettes, a doctor, and porters were on the road in back of him. When Stilwell asked the man how he had figured out which of the four possible routes they were on, he said that he had called Delhi to "find out what kind of man you were. Delhi said you were very intelligent. This is the only trail it makes common sense to take so I figured you would be on it." After five more days of hard climbing, they started down the mountains, racing against the monsoon. On May 20, they reached Imphal, the capital of India's easternmost state of Manipur—"the only group," Tuchman tells us, "military or civilian, to reach India without loss of life."

Stilwell's subsequent report to the War Department was so damning vis-à-vis the British and Chinese that all copies of it were destroyed. The British, he contended, had never planned to hold Burma and had deliberately let it go in order to weaken China. He also lashed out at the Chinese for their "stupid gutless command" and the "interference by CKS." But the Chinese blamed Stilwell for getting out of Burma on foot. "No doubt it was a titanic march," commented Corcoran from the safety of Washington. "But in Chinese eyes it was craven and undignified. He might have lost the battle, and they could almost forgive him that, but to disregard the safe exit by plane—which was a high commander's prerogative—was incomprehensibly undignified."* Foreign correspondent Eric Severeid had a more generous reaction. Stilwell, he said, had "an exalted concept of true soldiering and an impossible ideal of what a true soldier should be."

The defeat in Burma meant that much of the Chinese army's small supply of heavy weaponry was lost and all possible routes to bring in more men and weapons were now in the hands of the Japanese. But in typical fashion, Chinese reports on the retreat from Burma talked about Japanese columns being "completely wiped out" or "annihilated." The Chinese, they said, were

---

* Stilwell later apologized to the generalissimo via Madame Chiang for having left Burma without her husband's permission.

"closing in on Mandalay from east and west with the object of recapture"—a bit of fantasy upped by the AP correspondent in Chungking to a "smashing defeat" of the enemy. The UP correspondent was no more accurate, reporting that the Japanese were "fleeing in disorder." American editors then translated this information into headlines like INVADING JAP FORCE CRUSHED BY STILWELL! and STILWELL'S CHINA TROOPS TRAP JAPS, INVASION ARMY IN FULL RETREAT, ENEMY CUT OFF.

Greeted by a crowd of journalists when he got to his hotel in Delhi, Stilwell agreed to hold a press conference and answer questions about the campaign. "I claim we got a hell of a beating," he told the reporters. "We got run out of Burma and it is humiliating as hell."

34

Chiang thought of himself as a soldier, but his true genius lay in politics; he had no equal in the ancient art of hog-trading. . . . If his soldiers starved, that was the price of keeping the loyalty of dubious generals, who profited from their death. If he sent into battle soldiers who were doomed before they heard gunfire, that was one way of reducing the forces of a commander who might have challenged him.

—THEODORE WHITE AND ANNALEE JACOBY

BY THE time Stilwell got out of Burma, he and Chiang Kai-shek had settled even more firmly into their chosen acerbities. "Suspicious, secretive, and intolerant" was the way a Stilwell aide described the American general at this point in his life. "Stilwell's devotion to . . . what he considered to be his duty was intense, as was his hatred of his enemies. . . . Disagreement with those he did not respect as men brought out his negative qualities."

"Obstinate, pig-headed, ignorant, intolerant, arbitrary, unreasonable, illogical, ungrateful, grasping" make up just one list of adjectives that Stilwell applied to Chiang in "The Black Book." "He [Chiang] wants to be a moral potentate, a religious leader, a philosopher. But he has no education! . . . No one tells him the truth—no one. . . . He will not listen to anything unpleasant, so nobody tells him anything but pleasant things. . . . He flies into a rage if anyone argues against him." "Peanut" was Stilwell's favorite nickname for Chiang. He was also known to refer to the generalissimo as "a lily-livered Chink" and a "slant-eyed snake." According to one author, "The fact that the descriptions were not wholly inaccurate did not lessen the nature of his offense."

But Stilwell failed to take into account one of the basic tenets of Chiang's Confucianism. According to John Leighton Stuart, the United States' last ambassador to Chiang's government on the mainland, "Among a people to whom good manners are a part of morality, the tact and courtesy with which advice is given are of primary importance. Mencius commends the starving beggar who refused a crust of bread insultingly offered." Moreover, on a practical level, Stilwell's reforms would have undermined Chiang's position. "They would cut out the heart of Chiang's power structure," historian Michael Schaller explained. "No longer would he alone be able to control the contentious KMT factions through selecting commanders and distributing aid to those personally loyal. . . . [He] would become extraneous and expendable. Understandably, the Generalissimo did everything possible to prevent this."

In spite of the fact that he must have been aware of Stilwell's contempt for him, Chiang continued to assume a surface cordiality toward the American general, while at the same time making every effort to bypass him on the issue of Lend-Lease. Chiang warned Washington that the only thing that would prevent a "total collapse of Chinese resistance" was a major influx of armaments, which China was unable to get through regular channels, i.e., Stilwell. May-ling wrote to advise Lauchlin Currie, currently head of the Lend-Lease Administration, that for the "first time" since the war began, her husband was showing signs of pessimism. This bit of information was followed by a letter from Chiang to Roosevelt—drafted by T.V. in Washington— asking him to send Harry Hopkins to China because the situation was "crucial." The next word out of Asia was that defeatism was rampant within the walls of Chungking, that reactionaries were "making headway with anti-war propaganda," and that there were plenty of Chinese ready to make peace with Japan. All of this added up to a carefully orchestrated campaign geared to convince the United States that the generalissimo could not hold the line against Japan unless he received a great deal more military hardware.

To underscore her husband's campaign, May-ling wrote an article for *The New York Times Magazine* in which she divided the relationship between East and West into three stages: first, the historical exploitation of China, a policy that had left the Chinese scornful of the "power-worshipping" West; second, the invasion of China by Japan, during which the West had acted like "spectators at a college football game cheering from the safety of the stand while taking no personal risk in the game themselves"; and third, the early years of World War II, during which the West had "felt the shattering impact of Japan's might," to which it had bowed, while, according to Madame Chiang, there had been "no instance of Chinese troops surrendering to the enemy" in the past five years!

This was followed by a longer piece in *The Atlantic Monthly* outlining a plan for China, geared to appeal to Americans and calling for specific reforms: "no exploitation of any section of society by any other section or even by the state itself"; giving private capital "its rightful place" in order to further the initiative of the individual; and "progressive taxation," including an income tax. Claiming that "China is the Columbus of democracy," May-ling harked back to 2400 B.C. when "Chinese emperors succeeded each other by their subjects' wish instead of hereditary right. Over a thousand years before Confucius, an articulate political platform proclaimed, "The people's views are heaven's voice." Moreover, in the fourth century before Christ,

Mencius "enunciated the theory that the people rank first, the state second, the ruler last." As if this were not democracy enough for anyone, Madame Chiang declared that she was "opposed to any system which permanently gives absolute power to a single party"—adding, however, the crippling qualification that "freedom of thought and action should be given to minorities as long as the activities of such groups are not incompatible with the interests and security of the state."

Along with articles, the generalissimo's wife cabled multiple requests for planes and armaments to Lauchlin Currie, and it says something unattractive about Currie that he used this opportunity to boost his personal prestige with the Chiangs. In answer to one of May-ling's wires, he wrote to say that he had immediately taken it to the president and that it was "a pity that Stilwell was out of touch with the War Department for so long while he was getting out of Burma. The Chief of Staff very naturally and very properly is inclined to place most reliance upon the word and recommendations of his man on the spot. What TV and I can do is to bring support for those recommendations, but it is more difficult to secure action in the absence of such recommendations."

So the G-mo's wife called a meeting of the military brass—Stilwell, Chennault, Brigadier General Clayton L. Bissell of the U.S. Army Air Corps, and three Chinese generals—"to rough out a plan for the 500 airplane program." She asked Stilwell and Chennault to list their requirements, requested information on replacement parts, and insisted that an airfield currently under construction near Kunming be finished in two months' time. She asked Stilwell to write a recommendation based on their discussion and requested a copy of his proposal. If Currie couldn't get her what she wanted without Stilwell, she would supply a written request from the general himself.

But planes were not Stilwell's priority. As stubborn in his own way as Chiang was in his, he had become even more determined to reform the Chinese army and to recover his damaged pride by reconquering Burma. His plan was to train two Chinese armies, one in India and the other in the province of Yunnan, for the assault. The first group would be known as the X Force, the second as the Y. These forces would attack the Japanese from east and west while the British sent ships to southern Burma. In this way, the X and Y Forces would open the Burma Road while the Brits kept the enemy busy in the South.

To follow through on his plan, Stilwell needed Chiang's cooperation but for some inexplicable reason decided that he must first tell him everything that was wrong with his army. He sent the generalissimo a memo. "I told him the whole truth," Stilwell wrote his wife, "and it was like kicking an old lady in the stomach. However, as far as I can find out, no one else dares . . .

so it's up to me all the more." Stilwell outlined a program for the reform of the Chinese army, which included disbanding and merging divisions in order "to bring all units up to full strength" and a "rigid purge of inefficient high commanders." Stilwell left his memo with May-ling, who looked at it before giving it to her husband. "Why, that's what the German advisers told him!" she said.

During the discussion of Stilwell's recommendations, Madame Chiang, in Stilwell's words, "jumped up and . . . sat by me and said the G-mo had to consider 'certain influences' etc." This was, in fact, quite true, and it was well understood by Stilwell. In order to keep the country together, Chiang had allowed various warlords to assume the position of commanders in the army, and if they didn't like his orders or were offered better terms, they were perfectly capable of defecting to the Japanese or the Communists.

Moreover, an alternative to painful reform had already been presented to the generalissimo and his wife by Chennault, the "supremely confident" head of the Chinese air force, who got along beautifully with the Chiangs and made his solution to China's problems sound absurdly easy. At the time, Chennault was operating the Air Transport Command (ATC) with only twenty-five planes, but he told the Chiangs that if he could get five hundred combat planes plus one hundred transports to bring in the necessary supplies, he would be able to cut through Japan's sea-lanes, neutralize its air force, and make way for the Chinese land forces to take action. Claiming that his flyers had "borne [the] brunt in [the] defense of Rangoon, Burma and Yunnan," Chennault made requests that necessitated increasing the amount and speeding the progress of war material over the Hump—the 550-mile "Skyway to Hell," which took off from the northern part of the Indian province of Assam and landed in the southwestern Chinese province of Yunnan. After the fall of Rangoon in March 1942, "flying the Hump" was the only way for supplies to reach China. The perilous journey required unarmed cargo carriers to weave through or fly over 15,000-foot peaks through air currents strong enough to break up their planes. According to one account, "The five-hour 1,130 kilometer route was considered suicide by the pilots, with freak winds, monsoons, unpredictable turbulence, and the most treacherous landscape on earth."

Conquering the Hump was only the central part of the problem. The supplies had to be shipped first from the United States to western India—a distance of 12,000 miles—then another 1,500 miles over Indian railways to Calcutta, and finally over a narrow-gauge railway to airfields in Assam. This railway, originally built to ship tea, was, in Tuchman's words, "a bottleneck that drove men to despair." Not only did it change rail beds three times, but shipments had to be unloaded and reloaded to cross an unbridged river by barge. Strikes due to labor conditions, sabotage by anti-British Indians, shortages from agreed-upon estimates, and the rigidity of the Indian railway managers tied up traffic for years until finally, in early 1944, the line was militarized and taken over by the Americans.

The Chinese side of the Hump was no better. Incoming fuel for planes and supplies had to be hauled over land and rivers several hundred miles past their landing place in Kunming to Chennault's air bases, a trip that could take as long as eight weeks. In July of 1942, Chennault's ATC became part of the U.S. Tenth Air Force, which was based in India. The incorporation did not improve its efficiency. The ATC burned one gallon of gas for every gallon it delivered to China, and eighteen tons of supplies were required for the ATC to drop a single ton of bombs on the Japanese.

With everything from gasoline and cigarettes to spark plugs and soap in such short supply, it is not surprising that intense competition developed among the users. Chennault wanted the bulk of the supplies for his airmen, while Stilwell wanted them for his ground troops. At the same time, both England and Russia were pressuring the United States for more planes and equipment. But T.V. chose to believe that Stilwell wasn't pushing hard enough on behalf of China, and he took great pleasure in saying so. In a series of secret cables to Chiang sent in June and July 1942, he did everything he could to undermine Stilwell's standing with the generalissimo. He apparently convinced Chiang that there was plenty of war material available, that Stilwell had the power to get it, and that the reason China was not first on the receiving end of American largesse was that Stilwell refused to ask for it. According to a wire Stilwell received from T.V., the U.S. War Department was reacting much too slowly to the generalissimo's requests "in the absence of supporting telegram from you." In order to encourage his cooperation in procurement, Chiang called a meeting to discuss Stilwell's plan of training troops in India to go back into Burma. With May-ling pushing each of Stilwell's points on her husband, he agreed to most of Stilwell's recommendations.

Earlier on, however, the United States had promised to send 100 transport planes—a number that was cut first to 75 and then to 57. Now Stilwell had to tell Chiang that under these conditions, the 5,000 tons a month of war material that China expected would be cut to less than one tenth. The generalissimo was convinced that this shortfall was Stilwell's fault for not sufficiently impressing Washington with China's need, while May-ling believed that he was insufficiently powerful at home. "We're going to see that you are made a <u>full general</u>,"* she told him, thinking he would be pleased. "The hell they are," he wrote in his diary.

But the reason for the cuts had nothing to do with China. On June 21,

---

* He was ranked lieutenant general until 1944.

the Germans had captured the coastal city of Tobruk in Libya, raising the possibility of a German breakthrough in the Middle East. To meet the emergency, bombers from the Indian-based U.S. Tenth Air Force, along with their transports and crews, were ordered to proceed immediately to Egypt. A group of B-24 bombers already on its way to China was told to stop at Khartoum to help the British, and, as usual, Stilwell was the bearer of the bad tidings. The Chiangs—both of them—exploded. May-ling said that every time the British got into trouble, it was the Chinese who suffered, "and such being the case there is no need for China to continue in the war." Chiang complained that less than 10 percent of the material promised him by Roosevelt was being delivered; this, he claimed, amounted to "disobedience" of the president's orders. "As chief of staff to me," Chiang told Stilwell, "you are responsible for seeing to it that the promised material is forthcoming." This was followed by an ultimatum delivered by May-ling: "The Generalissimo wants a yes or no answer whether the Allies consider this theater necessary and will support it."

Three days later, Chiang issued what was called "The Three Demands," to be fulfilled within two to three months' time: (1) three American divisions to rebuild communications to China through Burma; (2) 500 combat planes; (3) delivery of 5,000 tons of war material a month. If these "minimum requirements" were not met, Chiang threatened, there would be a "liquidation" of the Chinese theater and a "readjustment" of China's position. Stilwell agreed to forward Chiang's terms to Washington but refused to include his personal recommendation—an addition that May-ling demanded. This, Stilwell said, would constitute his sending an ultimatum to his own government. "Madame," he reported, "got hot . . . and started to bawl me out." Stilwell took the occasion to inform May-ling that among his other, more exalted titles, he was also "a U.S. Army officer sworn to uphold the interests of the U.S. . . . If she doesn't get the point," he concluded, "she's dumber than I think she is."

Chiang's threat to make "other arrangements" for China if he did not receive his designated quota of supplies was followed by purposeful rumors in appropriate places that an envoy from Japan and representatives from the puppet government in Nanking had arrived in Chungking to arrange peace terms with the Nationalist government. Ambassador Gauss agreed with Stilwell that the story was a "bluff" and so informed Washington. But Roosevelt, who did not want to take too many chances, wrote Chiang a conciliatory letter promising that as soon as there were sufficient armaments to go around, China would get them.

Chiang followed his "Three Demands" with a scheme to divest Stilwell of his control over Lend-Lease, since, as he wrote Roosevelt, Stilwell's responsibilities to two governments were in conflict. Unlike other nations on

Lend-Lease, which could use U.S. aid where and how they wanted, China was required to list its specific needs by project and give the list to Stilwell—a procedure that had been devised by the Russians, who wanted to keep Chiang from using U.S. war materials to fight the Chinese Communists. The numbers were not in China's favor. During 1942, the Lend-Lease Administration allocated 77 percent of available goods to Britain, 17.7 percent to Russia, and only 2 percent to China, of which, according to one member of the House of Representatives, less than one fourth ever even reached the Chinese.*

Aware that Lend-Lease was Stilwell's ultimate power over the generalissimo, Chief of Staff George C. Marshall drafted a reply for the president to send Chiang in which he said that it was "not practical for all of General Stilwell's duties to be subject to orders from you," adding that any successors to Stilwell would face precisely the same problem. This letter broke the old Chinese convention of never saying no directly. Because of this, T.V. decided to take matters into his own hands; when it came across his desk, he changed the wording both as to what the president had said and how he had said it. He then forwarded his revised copy to Chiang. Meanwhile, Marshall had sent a copy of the original to Stilwell. After a few weeks of international misunderstandings, T.V.'s alteration was discovered. Chiang was insulted by the original letter and threatened once again to make a separate peace, while T.V. was called to the White House and informed that Stilwell's status was not to be changed. Undeterred, T.V. continued to alter the content and wording of letters from Washington to Chungking until Roosevelt ordered that all communications from the president to the generalissimo be delivered by an official of the United States.

On July 20, 1942, Lauchlin Currie returned to Chungking. There is a school of historical thought, headed by Tuchman, that believes Currie was bamboozled by Chiang Kai-shek, "captivated" by May-ling, and, therefore, easily convinced that the Chinese "thought just as we did." This view can now be disproved by the recent release of Currie's papers, including his heretofore classified report to Roosevelt on this trip to China. Currie's notes indicate that whatever his personal failings—and there were many—he understood Chiang, his wife, their party, and the causes of the most important misunderstandings between China and the United States.

Acting on the advice of T.V., the Chinese had asked the president to send Harry Hopkins to Chungking instead of Currie. Realizing that this was a matter of "prestige" and that Hopkins "did not know China," Roosevelt decided to send Currie instead. T.V. was furious, going so far as to ask Currie

---

* Figures from *China Monthly* 4, no. 4 (March 1943), p. 14 (Wellesley College Archive).

to "stall" his trip and "see if we couldn't get Hopkins after all." Currie refused to stall; T.V. couldn't get Hopkins; and Currie spent twelve days in Chungking in the summer of 1942, emerging with a comprehensive and perceptive forty-three-page report on the situation he found there.

While he was in Chungking, May-ling told Currie that T.V.'s stockbroker had been instructed to attribute his personal transactions to their sister Ai-ling. At one point, Currie said that Madame was positively "vitriolic" on the subject of T.V. and then suddenly blurted out, "He is my brother and I love him!" In a subsequent meeting with Madame and the G-mo, Currie talked about the misunderstandings in Washington caused by T.V.'s refusal to cooperate with the U.S. War Department in procuring war material for China. Instead of following normal procedures, Currie complained, T.V. tried to route China's requests via the White House and, in so doing, put Roosevelt in embarassing situations.*

In his report to the president, Currie blamed the deterioration in relations between China and the United States on "the prior existence in both countries of illusions regarding the other." Americans in China, he said, became disillusioned "when they discovered the degree of waste, inefficiency and corruption that pervades Chinese affairs," while the Chinese, comparing their share of Lend-Lease to that of other countries, felt that "the Americans think far more of their fellow white allies than of their yellow allies." Currie laid much of the blame for these misunderstandings on T.V.'s reluctance to forward the unvarnished truth from Washington. As an example, he cited the fact that T.V. had led Chiang to believe that Stilwell's position would be advisory, while the United States considered Stilwell's mandate multifunctional with the explicit power to command. The relationship between the two men, Currie said, was "the most difficult problem I had to deal with in Chungking," and due to the clash of personalities, Currie recommended that Stilwell be replaced. He also advised that in "dealing with the Generalissimo, great care should be exercised not to wound his pride . . . the old Chinese forms really do matter to him, and it would pay large dividends for us to . . . make a point of consulting him on any of the moves we proposed in the Far East."

On his return to the United States, Currie told one Chinese reporter that "Gen. Chiang has no intention" of engaging in an "effective war against

---

* What really bothered Currie was a wire he discovered from T.V. to an associate on the subject of Currie himself: "Please confidentially advise all CDS [China Defense Supplies] department chiefs to have as little to do with him [Currie] as possible as War Department, Lend-Lease, American Embassy and Stilwell do not have any regard for him." (Hoover Archives: T. V. Soong papers, Box 11, T.V., wire to Dr. Rajchman, November 11, 1925.)

Japan at any time" but that he "only wanted to get enough war materials from America to keep himself in power." Currie's analysis of the Chinese situation was followed by that of Stilwell's aide Colonel Dorn, who wrote the War Department a few weeks later that "all aid to China must have a string which demands action from them." Otherwise, "the present regime will do nothing but hoard the material in order to perpetuate itself after the war. . . . They expect an upheaval or revolution of some sort. In fact, T. V. Soong . . . expressed the opinion that the present regime would be out of a job six months after the war. He ought to know."

❦

STILWELL, WHO WAS still determined to lead a Chinese army back into Burma, had meanwhile managed to get the loan of Ramgarh, a former Indian prisoner-of-war camp west of Calcutta, in which to train the men. Britain agreed to house, feed, and pay the troops as payment for U.S. Lend-Lease, while the Americans supplied the equipment and personnel.* The program, aimed at reentering Burma in February of 1943, started in August with 8,000 to 9,000 men, and over a period of two years, 53,000 men were put through the training camp.

A large proportion of the first group, those who had survived the first Burma campaign and walked to India, had to be hospitalized on arrival. Starving, dressed in rags, riddled with malaria and dysentery, their flesh was rotted by sores caused by infected leeches that had attached themselves to the men in the jungles. They were given shots against cholera, typhoid, and smallpox, fed three meals a day, and on average gained around twenty-one pounds. In spite of a promise to send the rest of the trainees in good condition, the next groups to arrive were rejected by the American medical officers on an average of four out of ten, due to disease and underweight. The Chinese had packed thirty-five to forty men into cargo planes, some of which lacked doors, to send them to India. Chinese General Lo Cho-ying had had an even better idea: "Put 50 in a plane naked. It's only three hours!" On the theory that it was ridiculous to waste uniforms if the men were to be given new ones in India, the soldiers were put into the planes wearing nothing but undershorts and carrying paper bags for airsickness. After several died

---

* Currie was furious that Stilwell did not give him credit for this arrangement. As he wrote John Paton Davies, Jr., Stilwell's political adviser, "Seeing as how it was my bright idea, concocted mainly to save lend-lease to China, cleared by me with the Generalissimo and Ho Ying-chin [General Ho], and cleared again by me back here. . . . I think the General might have given me a little credit. In fact he is pretty deeply in my debt for having patched things up and having got this new project started." (Hoover Archives: Lauchlin Currie papers, Box 1, Currie to Davies, November 26, 1942.)

of the cold en route, the Americans at the receiving end asked that quilted cotton jackets be left on the planes to protect the men from the freezing air, but the Chinese thought them unnecessary. Only the crew were given oxygen masks.

Once the men were inoculated and properly fed, they were issued uniforms, helmets, and boots, and put into training. Although Stilwell welcomed the recruits in their own language, their training was based on demonstration, since the rest of the American officers spoke no Chinese. "They are the greatest mimics in the world and are learning very, very fast," said one of the generals. American officers working in tandem with Chinese officers, however, led to distinct clashes. One point of contention was the harsh discipline imposed by the Chinese. A man could be shot for using a grenade to catch fish or beaten to the bone for losing his blanket. One American general was appalled to see his Chinese counterpart throw a paper listing the number of soldiers who had died on their way to the camp into the wastebasket, while carefully accounting for lists of supplies. The biggest disagreements, however, arose over the issue of the traditional Chinese squeeze, since the enlisted men's pay no longer went through the hands of their superiors but was distributed directly to them. General Lo, the Chinese general who had suggested sending the men to India naked, left Ramgarh when it became clear that he could no longer net the 100,000 rupees* a month he was accustomed to keeping for himself.

Every so often Stilwell had to fly to Delhi for meetings and what he termed "poisonous paper work." He was disgusted, as only he could be, by the magnificence of both American and British headquarters, where, it was said, the "gleam of brass hats . . . lit the way for airplanes to land in a fog." On August 30, he wrote his wife that he had "now arrived at the pinnacle of social success," having been invited to lunch by the antediluvian marquess of Linlithgow, a six-foot, six-inch Scotsman who served as His Majesty's viceroy in India. The Viceroy's Palace, which Tuchman called "the architectural apotheosis of the British Empire," required a staff of three hundred Indian servants, all of whom wore white robes. Stilwell, who had never been fond of the British, thought it the apotheosis of pretension.

Returning from India to Chungking, Stilwell showed Chiang photographs of the training camp at Ramgarh. With the help of his wife, Chiang was playing both ends against the middle—encouraging Stilwell because he was still in control of Lend-Lease and at the same time actively supporting a bid by Chennault to take over Stilwell's position. Chennault did not believe in ground campaigns. He pointed with pride at the past successes of his Flying Tigers and sent a personal letter to President Roosevelt claiming that if

---

* 100,000 Indian rupees = $19,400 U.S. in 1943 ($365,890 today).

he were given 105 modern fighter planes, 30 medium bombers, and 12 heavy bombers, he could "accomplish the downfall of Japan . . . probably within six months, within one year at the outside."* As a follow-up to Chennault's letter, Chiang increased his campaign for Stilwell's recall, relying on James McHugh,† who could be counted on to pass information he had gleaned in the Chiang home on to the U.S. government. After lunch with the Chiangs, McHugh sent off a letter to Frank Knox, secretary of the navy, in which he said that Stilwell's plan to recapture Burma was, in fact, purely a matter of regaining personal pride and not the best way to conduct the war. The secretary of the navy showed the letter to Secretary of War Stimson, who passed it on to Chief of Staff Marshall, who said that McHugh, then on his way back to the United States, should never again be allowed to serve in China.

Both Stimson and Marshall believed that getting back into Burma was a necessity—not as a replacement for airpower over the Hump but as a much-needed alternative—and members of the State Department were furious at Chennault for bypassing proper channels and trying to appeal directly to the president. Marshall reprimanded T.V., who was on his way home to China, informing him that the U.S. military was completely committed to Stilwell and his plan. When Currie later informed the chief of staff that relations between Chiang and Stilwell had improved, Marshall replied that "he took a good deal of the credit for this himself because of his bawling out of Soong. He thought that Soong would never forgive him . . . but that the action was necessary and salutary."

T.V. returned to Chungking, convinced by Stimson and Marshall that it was better to cooperate with Stilwell than to oppose him, and in a general about-face, Chiang offered Stilwell five Chinese divisions, which, at Mayling's suggestion, he was allowed to choose for himself. But when the British said that they did not have enough naval resources to support a landing at Rangoon, Chiang pulled out of the operation. "If the navy is unable to control the Burma seas," he wrote Roosevelt in early January 1943, just five weeks before Stilwell was due to take his newly trained Chinese soldiers back into Burma, the Burma campaign would have to be postponed.

---

* As Tuchman points out, it eventually took nine army air forces, ninety naval carriers, 14,847 combat planes, and two atom bombs to do this.

† It will be remembered that McHugh was a friend and frequent guest whom the Chiangs had met through Donald, as well as the officer in charge of Far East secret intelligence.

35

One makes a tour such as Mr. W[illkie]'s to make the maximum ephemeral impression on the press, newsreels, and radio, or to make a few close friends and contacts, or to gain as much information as possible. Mr. W. seems to be doing the first of these.

—JOHN FAIRBANK

THREE MONTHS before Chiang canceled Stilwell's march back into Burma, Wendell Willkie arrived in China as part of a fact-finding goodwill tour of the world. Described by a friend as "a great hulk of a man, with attractively shaggy hair, a booming voice . . . charm, vitality, and . . . charisma," he was called by one historian "the most memorable defeated candidate for the Presidency since William Jennings Bryan." Willkie came bearing a letter from Clare Boothe Luce to Madame Chiang, introducing him as "a dear friend of my husband and mine, and a new but great friend of China. . . . You are bound to hit it off magnificently," she added, suggesting that May-ling not lose the opportunity to discuss her ideas on the Sino-American situation, India, and the United Nations with their visitor. The letter had obviously caused Mrs. Luce some concern, as the initial draft is a mass of insertions, cross-outs, and penciled-in phrases.

Willkie's advocacy of a "one world" philosophy made him an ideal international envoy for the man who had defeated him, Franklin Delano Roosevelt, while his appearance in China was seized on as a great opportunity to impress a man who might well become the next president of the United States. Meanwhile he could help get planes and armaments for China. To that end, Chiang had ordered Chungking's worst hovels razed and local beggars put outside the city limits. On his arrival in Chungking, Willkie was assigned one of T.V.'s residences, described by his traveling companion, publisher Gardner "Mike" Cowles, as "a magnificent modern home . . . with all sorts of luxurious trappings, as well as dozens of perfect servants to attend to our needs." Ambassador Clarence Gauss had wanted Willkie and his party to stay in the U.S. Embassy across the Yangtze, where he could have some influence on their activities during their six-day sojourn in Chungking, but the Chiangs had taken over, and Gauss was annoyed. Stilwell was mildly amused. "Willkie arrives this afternoon and he has a full schedule for his visit," he wrote in his diary. "He has to go to lunch, tea, and dinner every day he is here. They are going to drag him around to see schools and factories and girl scouts and sewing circles and arsenals and keep him well insulated from pollution by Americans. The idea is to get him so exhausted and keep him so torpid with food and drink that his faculties will be dulled and he'll be stuffed with the right doctrines." The Chiang plan worked wonderfully. Willkie was, in the words of one writer, "quite carried away by the warmth and splendour of Chinese hospitality, Mme. Chiang's insidious charm, and the Generalissimo's air of scholarly wisdom."

As further guarantee against contamination, Chiang had assigned two escorts to meet Willkie the moment he set foot in China. This was at the small, "incredibly muddy" town of Tihwa, capital of Sinkiang, a province east of Afghanistan, north of Tibet, and twice the size of France. To greet his visitor, Chiang had sent Hollington Tong, his English-speaking, American-educated publicity man, along with the commander of the northwestern war zone. Willkie, who spent several days in Tihwa, did not arrive in Chungking until late in the afternoon of October 2. His plane, delayed by Japanese aircraft along the way, was finally spotted in the sky by Ambassador Gauss, H. H. Kung, and several other high officials along with their wives, who had dressed up for the occasion and were carrying "fat bouquets" of flowers. They marched down the runway toward the plane in a tight little group, followed by a uniformed army band playing "America the Beautiful." Suddenly, the plane turned around and headed for them. "There were squeals and a great dropping of bouquets and band instruments as the greeters scattered," an eyewitness reported. "Of course the plane turned again and came to rest," and by the time Willkie got out, the welcoming party had managed to pull itself together.

"Before we reached the middle of the city, the crowds stood packed from curb to store front," Willkie wrote,

> . . . they packed eleven miles of road over which our cars slowly moved on our way to the guesthouse in which we were to stay. . . . On all the hills of Chungking . . . they stood and smiled and cheered and waved little paper American and Chinese flags. Any man who has run for President of the United States is used to crowds. But not to this one. . . . The paper flags waved by the people were all of the same size, suggesting that the . . . Mayor of Chungking . . . had had a hand in planning this demonstration. It was perfectly clear that not all these people, many of whom were barefoot or dressed in rags, had any clear idea of who I was or why I was there. . . . But in spite of all my efforts to discount it, this scene moved me profoundly.

There was nothing synthetic or fake about the faces I looked at. They were seeing, in me, a representative of America and a tangible hope of friendship and help. . . . It was a mass demonstration of good will.

Journalist Graham Peck had a different reaction:

The school children had been marched out en masse and had been told who Willkie was, for they hallooed and waved with enthusiasm. Some of the better-dressed adults, probably newspaper readers, cheered and waved too. But many welcomers were the very poor, the kind who were hired as substitutes for annoying . . . duties, while others were cripples and old men and bound-footed women, the useless non-working people sent out by their own families. With resigned expressionless faces they stood silently by the road in their mean clothes, boredly holding up their Kuomintang and American flags in one hand, while they scratched themselves or picked their noses with the other. At intervals behind them, police were posted to see that they did not escape until all the cars had passed.

As predicted by Stilwell, there were daily activities, nightly banquets, and five long conferences with the generalissimo, all geared to dazzle the American with the efficiency and worthiness of Chiang's government. A chorus of ten-year-old war orphans appeared at a tea given in Willkie's honor two days after his arrival. "These orphaned children symbolize what Mme. Chiang Kai-shek is doing in order to bring about a world where children can grow up and live decent respectable lives," Willkie said. To which Madame responded with a smile, describing their visitor as "the embodiment of warmth and spontaneity, the vibrant, dynamic symbol of a free world society of free nations."

Treated to a military review the day after his arrival in Sinkiang, Willkie had been struck by the apparent health, neatness, and training of the soldiers. During his stay in Chungking, he was taken to the largest military academy in China, where he watched several thousand cadets cut through barbed wire, drive across a mine field, and swim a river with their rifles held above their heads. For this maneuver, the American visitor was attended by a Chinese graduate of West Point, who never left his side. In his book *One World*, Willkie wrote about his impressions of the Chinese army as a whole: "Military China is united; its leaders are trained and able generals; its new armies are tough, fighting organizations of men who know both what they are fighting for and how to fight for it, even though they markedly lack any quantity of modern fighting equipment. In China . . . this is truly a people's war. Even the sons of those of high estate enlist as privates in the army, an unthinkable act in China a generation ago, when service in the army was for hired and ignorant mercenaries."

Willkie's impression of the Chinese army was ludicrously off the mark, and it is not too difficult to guess that the source of his information, particularly the last and most outrageous assertion, was Hollington Tong, the master propagandist. The charade continued when Willkie said that he wanted to visit the Chinese front. "At first," Willkie wrote, "it seemed impossible. It was only later that I learned that the Generalissimo's solicitude for my safety . . . had had to be overcome, and that 'Holly' had required time to accomplish this."

The Chinese flew Willkie to Sian, the scene of Chiang's kidnapping, and from there drove some distance outside the city, where they climbed up a mountain by the light of Chinese lanterns until they reached a military academy. They continued their journey—"incongruously enough," according to Willkie—in "luxurious sleeping cars" on the railroad. At dawn they transferred to handcars, then walked as they approached the Yellow River and the 1,200-yard-wide so-called Japanese front. From their side, Willkie reported, they could "look down the muzzles of Japanese guns pointed at us and see the Japanese soldiers in their own encampments." They were met there by Captain Chiang Wei-kuo, Chiang's second son.

"Captain Chiang, who speaks perfect English," Willkie wrote, "showed us in a long day the reasons why the Japanese had been unable to push across the river here, where there is a gap in the mountains, the traditional invasion route of south China. We saw artillery and infantry and armored cars and fortresses built into the hills so deep that Japanese would have to blast them out." Willkie was also treated to a review of the 208th Division, which he described as "well trained, well uniformed, and equipped with good, modern weapons." He was asked to speak to some 9,000 Chinese soldiers: "It seemed to me that not one man wavered in his attention until I had finished, although I was speaking in English. When what I said had been translated, they cheered so loudly that the Japanese must have heard them and wondered what the excitement was all about."

Back in their train for dinner, Willkie claimed that Chiang's son "demonstrated conclusively . . . that the front I had just seen was more than a showplace. He walked into the dining car with his arms full of Japanese cavalry swords, as presents for my party, and excellent French wine. Both had been captured by raiding parties which crossed the river at night, struck swiftly behind the Japanese lines, and returned with booty like this and more important trophies, including prisoners and military plans. Sometimes, Captain Chiang told me, such raiding parties stay for weeks inside the enemy lines, cutting communications and organizing sabotage, before returning to their own headquarters on the west bank of the river." But according to Tuchman, journalists stationed in China had been treated to quite a few similar tours of "cold battlefields" and were used to being shown quantities of Japanese helmets, guns, and other military equipment. "To test the theory that the material was transferred from one place to another for their benefit," one enterprising journalist reported that he had scratched his initials on a helmet, which he later found on another tour in another location.

Unlike Willkie, his traveling companion, Mike Cowles, had his suspicions about the whole show. He found that there was "an unreal quality to the war that one would never find on the battlefields of Western Europe," as well as "very active commercial trading going on between the Japanese and the Chinese across the Yellow River." Cowles said that the Americans thought that some of the shooting they heard as they left one area on their way to another was "staged," and he concluded that "the front may have been relatively dormant." Nevertheless, according to *The New York Times*, the Japanese twice tried to kill Willkie—once when they machine-gunned a railway carriage and a second time when he and his party were riding a handcar.

Willkie was always inclined to give the Chinese the benefit of the doubt, particularly Chiang Kai-shek himself. "Only a truly great man could present such an humble outward appearance and yet remain great," he commented after a day or two in Chungking. "I can write no account of China without setting down my own conclusion that the generalissimo, both as a man and as a leader, is bigger even than his legendary reputation." Willkie found Chiang "strangely quiet" and "soft-spoken," so much so that when the G-mo was out of uniform and in Chinese dress, he gave the impression of being a scholar "rather than a political leader." He heard that Chiang spent time each day reading the Bible and praying and believed that this habit gave him "a reflective manner, a quiet poise, and an occasional appearance of thinking out loud. He is undoubtedly sincere, and his dignity and personal imperturbability have something almost severe in quality."

Willkie was also struck by Chiang's "unbreakable" ties to the Soong family. "I could not document this," he wrote, "but no one can stay in Chungking even for a short time without realizing that the young republic . . . has already developed a sort of 'old-school tie' of its own which automatically keeps some men in high position." Mike Cowles looked at the situation from a historical point of view. "Before the Communist takeover," he wrote in his autobiography, "family dynasties ruled China for many centuries. Few, though, have left a greater mark on recent Chinese history—for better or for worse, depending on which history book you read—than the Soong family. . . . I met all three sisters during our visit, but it was Madame Chiang who most fascinated me—and Wendell."

One evening, the generalissimo gave a reception for the Americans. At a certain point during the party, Willkie whispered to Cowles that he and May-ling would be disappearing in a few minutes and that Cowles was to cover for him. "I stationed myself alongside the Generalissimo and unleashed a flurry of questions about China every time I felt his attention wandering," said Cowles. After about an hour, Chiang clapped his hands to summon his aides and left the party, indicating that everyone who wanted to could now leave. Cowles returned to the Soong guesthouse, poured himself a scotch from a bottle that May-ling had sent over,* and by nine o'clock had begun to worry about where the couple had gone. Not long after dinner, Chiang Kai-shek "stormed in, visibly furious," accompanied by three bodyguards, each with his own tommy gun. He gave Cowles a stiff little bow. "Where's Willkie?" he asked.

"I have absolutely no idea. He's not here in the house," Cowles answered, then asked Chiang if he would like some tea, knowing that to refuse an invitation to tea in China was a social offense. The generalissimo called impatiently for the tea, which the two men gulped down in silence. "Where's Willkie?" he demanded again.

"I assure you, Generalissimo, he is not here and I do not know where he could be."

Trailed by Cowles and the bodyguards, Chiang searched the house, opening closets and even looking under beds. Without another word, he left. Cowles, who had "visions of Wendell in front of a firing squad," said he was "really scared."

Around four in the morning "a very buoyant" Willkie came back, "cocky as a young college student after a successful night with a girl." After giving Cowles "a play by play account of what had happened between him and the Madame," adding that "there was never anything like this before" and that it "was the only time . . . he had ever been in love," he told his companion that he had invited May-ling to go back to Washington with them.

"Wendell, you're just a goddam fool!" Cowles said, enumerating all the reasons why this was impossible. Agreeing with Willkie that "Madame Chiang was one of the most beautiful, intelligent, and sexy women either one of us had ever met" and that he "could understand the tremendous attraction" between the two of them, he told his friend that there was already too much gossip about them among the reporters in Chungking, that pre-

---

* A rarity in Chungking at the time since one bottle of scotch cost $100 at the American PX.

sumably Willkie wanted a second chance to run for president, and that Willkie's wife and son would probably meet them at the airport when they returned home.

Cowles was not wrong about the gossip. According to John Paton Davies, Jr., Stilwell's political consultant, "There is little doubt that Little Sister [Madame Chiang] has accomplished one of her easiest conquests. Presiding at a relief organization tea, with the cloak of an air marshal thrown over her shoulders, she admitted with disarming feminine frailty that Mr. W. was a very 'disturbing influence,' a confession which visibly gratified the President's Personal Representative."

When Cowles came down for breakfast at eight the next morning, he found Willkie already at the table. "Mike," he said, "you're going to see the Madame and tell her that she cannot fly back to Washington with us."

"Where will I find her?"

"Sheepishly," Willkie described the location of an apartment on the top floor of the Women's and Children's Hospital, May-ling's pet charity. It turned out that this was where she had taken him the night before. Cowles arrived around eleven in the morning and was ushered into May-ling's sitting room. "I told her bluntly she could not fly back to Washington with Mr. Willkie," he said.

"Who says I can't?" May-ling asked.

"I do," he said, explaining that it would be "unwise politically" for Willkie. "Before I knew what was happening," he added, "she reached up and scratched her long fingernails down both my cheeks so deeply that I had marks for about a week."

The next Willkie event was a dinner party given by H. H. Kung on the lawn of his house, at which Wendell was seated between May-ling and Ching-ling. The American visitor had requested that Chou En-lai, whom he had met with twice, be invited—the first time that Chou had ever been entertained by any member of the Soong family. When dinner was over, May-ling led Willkie into the house to see sister Ai-ling, who, she said, was suffering from "neuralgia in her arm and couldn't come outdoors for the party." Madame Kung, her arm in a sling, greeted them. "The three of us talked and had such a good time we forgot about the hour and the people outdoors." Finally, at about 11:00 P.M., Kung came in, "gently scolded Madame and me for our failure to return to the party," and sat down to talk. "Finally, just before we were to leave, Madame Chiang said to Dr. and Mme. Kung, 'Last night at dinner Mr. Willkie suggested that I should go to America on a good-will tour.' The Kungs looked at me as if questioning. I said, 'That is correct, and I know I am right in asking her.' "

"Mr. Willkie, do you really mean that and, if so, why?" Kung asked.

Willkie asked May-ling to leave the room while he explained. "Someone from this section with brains and persuasiveness and moral force must help educate us about China and India and their peoples. Madame would be the perfect ambassador. . . . She would find herself not only beloved but immensely effective. We would listen to her as to no one else. With wit and charm, a generous and understanding heart, a gracious and beautiful manner and appearance, and a burning conviction, she is just what we need as a visitor."

The day Willkie left China, Cowles told Washington columnist Drew Pearson, the car stopped on the way to the airport so that Wendell could say good-bye to May-ling. Willkie went into the house, and his party waited outside for an hour and twenty minutes. When he finally emerged, he had May-ling with him, and she joined them on the trip to the airport. Just as he was about to board the plane, so the story goes, May-ling "jumped into his arms. Willkie picked her up and gave her a terrific soul kiss."

❦

IT CERTAINLY DID not take May-ling long to follow Willkie back to the United States. She had been vacillating about a trip to consult doctors about her health, and a letter written by Eleanor Roosevelt a month earlier indicates that an invitation from Washington was already lying on her desk. Although there had been some previous discussion at the White House about inviting the generalissimo's wife, it was not until Pearl Harbor that Roosevelt's advisers suggested that such a visit might not only help give the appearance of a united front in the Pacific theater but also counter Japanese attempts to suggest that the war was about the white versus the yellow race. Eleanor's letter outlined the benefits that a visit to the United States would confer. "I have discussed the matter [of a visit] with my husband," the first lady wrote Madame Chiang, "and we both feel that a visit with us at the White House would not only enable us to get to know you better and to secure a better appreciation of China's problems, but would also, in large measure, serve the ends of publicity. . . . We could, of course, send a comfortable plane for you."

Six week after Willkie's departure from China, on November 27, May-ling arrived in Florida, via a special stratoliner provided by the U.S. War Department.* She left for New York the same day and was met at the airport

---

* According to Jonathan Fenby, Chiang was worried that May-ling might have stomach cancer and wanted her to take tests not offered in China. He therefore had her carried onto the plane, and she was accompanied on her journey by two nurses. According to Li, her severe abdominal pain was caused by an intestinal parasite.

by Harry Hopkins. He drove with her to the Harkness Pavilion of New York Presbyterian Hospital, where she had taken a suite under a false name, reserving the rest of the rooms on the twelfth floor for her staff. Harry Hopkins and T. V. Soong were friends, and their daughters attended the same school. This may have been one of the reasons Madame had sent word to Roosevelt that she was "most anxious" to see Hopkins "before she talks business with anyone else." A better reason was that Hopkins was directing Lend-Lease at the time. On the way to the hospital, she told Hopkins that she wanted it made clear to Roosevelt that she had only come to the United States for medical treatment, then launched into complaints about Stilwell, who "does not understand the Chinese people and . . . made a tragic mistake in forcing Chiang Kai-shek to put one of his best divisions in Burma where it was later lost." She followed this "more forcibly than I had heard anyone express it before her belief" in the importance of defeating Japan before Germany. "I did not argue this point unduly with her," Hopkins added, "beyond saying that I thought such a strategy was unfeasible."

Owen Lattimore, Chiang's political adviser, who had traveled on the same plane with May-ling, was deeply offended by her when they arrived in New York. According to Lattimore, the generalissimo's wife "still seemed to consider me a part of the household" until the moment their plane landed. "When Madame Chiang was received at the foot of the gangway by Harry Hopkins," Lattimore said, "she immediately turned her back on me, and from that moment on cut me dead."

Eleanor Roosevelt came to the hospital at ten the following morning. May-ling told her she had come to America for her health, not to make any demands on the U.S. government. The first lady said that Madame Chiang was much admired in the United States, and the president looked forward to being able to discuss postwar problems with her. When Eleanor asked about May-ling's attitude toward Britain, May-ling wisely demurred, asking what the president thought. Mrs. Roosevelt outlined FDR's opinions, which led them into a conversation about India, on which the ladies discovered that they were in agreement. After nearly an hour's visit, Eleanor left, promising to return the following week. According to a cable May-ling sent home, Eleanor Roosevelt was "so moved that she came up to kiss my cheek. She said she wished to be my personal friend." During her second visit they discussed the importance of women in the postwar world. "She expressed her admiration for me, several times during our talk," May-ling wrote Chiang, "which made me blush a lot."

Eleanor Roosevelt wrote about these visits in her autobiography, saying that Madame Chiang seemed to be "highly nervous and to be suffering a great deal; she could hardly bear to have anything touch any part of her body." The first lady said that "Madame Chiang seemed so small and delicate as she lay in her hospital bed that I had a desire to help her and take care of her as if she had been my own daughter." The president's wife was also grateful to May-ling, who had arranged for her son James, just operated on for a gastric ulcer, to be fed the right food on a visit to China. On a few occasions Mrs. Roosevelt took people to the hospital to meet Madame. "I felt she would tire of seeing only me," Mrs. Roosevelt explained, "and many people were anxious to meet her."

There was enormous curiosity about Madame Chiang on the part of the press and the public, and DeLong tells us that while in the hospital, the G-mo's wife received up to a thousand letters a day. One of these was from Frances Gunther, a writer and journalist like her well-known ex-husband, John. The two women had met in China, and May-ling invited Frances to come see her in the hospital. A careful note taker, Gunther described Madame in her corner room in the Harkness Pavilion with plenty of flowers, her bed up, resting against embroidered pillow slips, lying under a pale green Chinese silk bedspread embroidered in coral. Her face "perfectly made up," May-ling was wearing a pink velvet bed jacket with coral earrings. She was smiling, although Gunther was aware of "an aftermath of recoiling horror still in her eyes."

May-ling also received a letter from Emma—a

> brief note to welcome you, and to tell you that I stand ready to be of any service to you in any way at all. . . . You have been rumored so many times to be on your way here, or even already here, but in seclusion somewhere that it hardly seems possible yet that you are actually now actually this side of the Pacific. I do hope that the medical aspects of your visit will be speedily taken care of, and that you . . . get some of the rest that you must so badly need. . . . Of course I am anxious to see you—it is so many years ago that you saw me off on that station platform in Peking—but I fully realize all the demands there will be on your time, once your health is taken care of, and that you are here, perforce, largely as an official personage, with all the limitations that implies.

It was not until two months later, in fact, that May-ling invited Emma to lunch with her at the hospital.

On the day before Christmas, Harry Hopkins flew back to New York to see May-ling, who asked him about Russia's postwar expectations. Hopkins told her that Russia was planning to set up regimes in the Baltic countries—Lithuania, Latvia, and Estonia—and wanted certain priorities in the Balkan nations as well. But, he said, neither Roosevelt nor the British were too worried about the ambitions of the Soviet Union, that the president felt sure he could find a way to deal with Stalin and that circumstances in Russia would prevent the Soviets from communizing the rest of the world. "Thinking over the talk with Hopkins," May-ling later wired Chiang, "I came to the conclusion that Britain, America and Russia will focus on their own postwar interests without paying attention to China. I think that we can obtain an important position in the peace talks if the right preparations are made." In this cable she said that she was "alone here without funds. Thus it is necessary to ask Eldest Sister [Ai-ling] to come to America to lend me a hand. You better urge her to set off as soon as possible."

There was another talk with Hopkins ten days later, reported by May-ling to her husband. Hopkins had asked May-ling if there had been any fighting in China, and she replied that, due to a lack of planes, no major counterattack had been started. She wired Chiang that there was seldom any news about the war in China in American papers and that Hopkins had said there ought to be more. He suggested that he could help if he was kept informed from time to time of what was really happening, that such news releases would be far more valuable than the propaganda currently being given out by the Chinese News Agency, and that bona fide information would make it possible for China's supporters to avoid the kind of falsified news that inevitably led to ridicule.

May-ling began a seventh secret wire to her husband on a note of concern: "Roosevelt has arrived in Africa [for the Casablanca Conference, the first summit of World War II]. Stalin has also been invited . . . and I'm not sure whether there are any important representatives from our side. . . . Given the warm invitation to Russia by the American government, it is clear that Russia cannot be bullied."* She suggested that since neither Russia nor China had been represented at the conference, China might try to come to some kind of "concrete understanding" with Stalin in order to improve the position of both in the international arena. The G-mo's wife went on to say that she had been telling Americans that China's "great sacrifice" was being made not just for the Chinese but for the peace and happiness of "people all over the world." As a result, she reported, there were now a few commentators speaking and writing with admiration of China's "pure and lofty goal." But, she said, there were still many people hostile to China.

Known by the State Department code name Snow White, guarded day and night in the hospital by members of the U.S. Secret Service and agents

---

* Stalin had refused an invitation to participate because the Red Army was engaged in serious fighting against the Germans at the time.

of the FBI, May-ling was also tended to daily by a hairdresser and a beauti-
cian. She was kept up to date on Chinese business, receiving on January 12
a copy of a wire from her husband to Roosevelt, appealing for a $500 mil-
lion loan. During her stay she was taken from the hospital in a limousine for
several drives around New York and to see a dentist. She certainly must have
seen Willkie, who sent her more than one bouquet of flowers. On December
11, he wrote a letter to May-ling's private secretary offering to see to anything Madame needed, saying that he "would naturally like to see her very
much" but "would not intrude" and would "await her command."

May-ling was supposedly in the hospital to get treatment for the injury
she had suffered when she had been thrown out of a car six years earlier on
the road between Nanking and Shanghai. In a letter to Chiang Kai-shek, her
doctors said that although "no organic disease of a serious nature has been
found," she was treated for painful abdominal spasms and for sinus trouble
brought on by an earlier operation. Her wisdom teeth were also extracted.
But even an extended time in the hospital and a week's further rest at the
president's family home in Hyde Park did not, apparently, give her back her
health, for she was said to be "on the verge of collapse more than once" during her subsequent tour of the United States. "She should have been an invalid with no cares," according to Eleanor Roosevelt, "but she felt that she
had work to do, that she must see important people in our government and
in the armed services who could be helpful to China, and that she must
fulfill official obligations."

Concerned about her guest, Mrs. Roosevelt met with one of Madame's
doctors, Dana Atchley, and was "very favorably impressed by him." He and
Madame's primary physician, Robert Loeb, told Mrs. Roosevelt in late January that Madame Chiang's "progress" had been "quite satisfactory." Nevertheless, Dr. Loeb wrote T.V. in February, "As you know we did not consider
your sister cured upon discharge from the hospital. . . . Madame is suffering
from the strain of years." Along with medications, May-ling's doctors said
that she should remain in bed until 10:30 every morning and rest at least
one hour every afternoon and one day every week. She was to limit her
American speeches to five, make no more than one official dinner engagement every month, attend no more than one large reception a month, and
limit difficult conferences to one a day.

But, of course, that was not why she had come to the United States.

36

If the Generalissimo could take the Japs as Madame took Congress, the War in the Pacific would be over in the bat of an eyelash.

—FRANK MCNAUGHTON

THE OFFICIAL part of Madame Chiang's tour of the United States did not begin until February 17, 1943, when she arrived at the train station in Washington, D.C., accompanied by her niece and nephew, Jeanette and David Kung, along with an entourage of twenty-five, including nurses, secretaries, and four reporters. David, currently a student at Harvard, did not cause as much immediate comment as eighteen-year-old Jeanette, whose "Chinese boy's robe and boyish haircut"* were tactfully dubbed "interesting-looking" by the reporter for *The Christian Science Monitor.* The party was met by Mrs. Roosevelt, Madame T. V. Soong, the Chinese ambassador, his wife, and a large contingent from the Chinese Embassy. For her initial appearance in the nation's capital, May-ling wore a mink coat, a black dress trimmed in red, and a black sequined scarf. Escorted into a reception room, she emerged arm in arm with Eleanor Roosevelt, who took her to meet the president, who was waiting in an official White House car outside the station.

Warned about May-ling's legendary charm, Roosevelt had determined not to be "vamped" (one of his favorite words) by her. Usually he sat on a sofa with his guest of honor next to him, but for their initial discussion in the Oval Office, he had a card table placed between them, explaining to his daughter, Anna, that he didn't want her "too close." Madame lived up to his fears, inviting him and others at the top of the administration to return to China with her. During one tête-à-tête, Roosevelt asked her about Wendell Willkie's visit to China. She replied that China had liked having him there.

"What do you really think of Wendell Willkie?" he continued. An ardent gossip, the president was probably aware of the stories about their affair.

"Oh, he is very charming," May-ling answered.

---

* Her appearance caused the president to address Jeanette as "my boy," while the White House servants, thinking she was her brother, unpacked her suitcases in his room. (Tuchman, p. 448, and Li, p. 198.)

"Ah, yes, but what did you *really* think?" Roosevelt asked again.

"Well, Mr. President, he is an adolescent, after all."

"Well, Madame Chiang, so you think Wendell Willkie is an adolescent—what do you think I am?"

"Ah, Mr. President," she replied, "you are sophisticated."

In spite of her attempts to charm him, May-ling was not successful in getting the president to commit to sending large amounts of war material to China. According to a Chinese reporter, she was noticably unhappy: "some of the servants . . . sensed and noticed her disappointment, and the others misunderstood her for being unpolite and snobish [*sic*]. Of course, Madame Chiang was alone at the White House, and Mrs. Roosevelt was away and President Roosevelt did not come in to see her very often, and only says a few words of greeting to her whenever he happened to see her."

Observers also noted that, for whatever reasons, personal or political, May-ling avoided joint conferences and close contact with T.V. during her visit to the United States. T.V., who had been in China, returned to Washington twelve days after her arrival, setting off speculation that he had come to help her get more aid for China. This supposition was confirmed when he declared in a press conference that he certainly approved of his sister's requests for arms and planes. "If I said she was satisfied with what we have received from Lend-Lease," he said at a dinner at the home of Secretary of State Edward Stettinius, "I would not be telling the truth."

If May-ling's legendary appeal failed with the president, it succeeded brilliantly with Congress. Her best-remembered and most dramatic appearances took place the day after her arrival, when she addressed the Senate and the House of Representatives. The first private citizen and only the second woman* invited to do so, she had dressed carefully in a black cheongsam with sequin trim and jade jewelry. Led down the green-carpeted center aisle of the Senate to take a seat on the dais next to Vice President Henry Wallace, she made quite a sensation. She told the senators that she had not planned to give a speech, was not "a very good extemporaneous speaker, in fact, no speaker at all," but had *just* been asked by Wallace to address the House. Having sufficiently disarmed her audience, she told a story about one of General James Doolittle's pilots† returning from a bombing mission over Tokyo who bailed out in the interior of China. When he landed and saw

---

* Queen Wilhelmina of the Netherlands was the first.

† The pilots in the first American bombing of Tokyo, commanded by James H. "Jimmy" Doolittle, were successful in dropping their bombs on the Japanese capital but crash-landed or had to parachute out of their planes on their way to the airfield in the province of Chekiang.

Chinese running toward him, he waved and yelled out the only Chinese word he knew—"Mei-kuo," which means both "America" and "beautiful country." The Chinese, she reported, laughed and "greeted him like a long lost brother. . . . He . . . told me that he thought he had come home when he saw our people; and that was the first time he had ever been to China."

After explaining that she herself had been educated in the United States and felt that she too had come home, she told another story about a young monk who went to a Buddhist temple, where he sat cross-legged day after day with his hands clasped in prayer, reciting "Amita-Buddha! Amita-Buddha!" Having noticed the father prior of the temple, who sat all day with a brick, rubbing it against a stone, he finally got up enough courage to ask the father what he was doing. "I am trying to make a mirror out of this brick."

"But it is impossible to make a mirror out of a brick, Father Prior."

"Yes," the old man replied, "it is just as impossible for you to acquire grace by doing nothing except 'Amita-Buddha' all day long, day in and day out."

"So, my friends," she continued, "I feel that it is necessary for us not only to have ideals and to proclaim that we have them, it is necessary that we act to implement them. And so to you, gentlemen of the Senate, and to you, ladies and gentlemen in the galleries, I say that without the active help of all of us our leaders cannot implement these ideas. It is up to you and to me to take to heart the lesson of 'Rub-the-Mirror' pavilion. I thank you," she said, concluding her "extemporaneous" speech, for which she was given a standing ovation.

Madame Chiang's reception, according to Eleanor Roosevelt, who had accompanied her in the car from the White House and listened from the Senate gallery, "marked the recognition of a woman who through her own personality and her own service, has achieved a place in the world, not merely as a wife . . . but as a representative of her people. . . . When I saw her coming down the aisle, she seemed overshadowed by the men around her. I could not help a great feeling of pride in her achievements as a woman, but when she spoke it was no longer as a woman that one thought of her. She was a person, a great person, receiving the recognition due her as an individual valiantly fighting in the forefront of the world's battle."

The first of Madame Chiang's American speeches—"extemporaneous" or preplanned—was a fitting prelude to the triumphs that were to follow. Speaking in slow, deliberate tones, not unlike the aristocratic cadences of Franklin Roosevelt and Winston Churchill, May-ling had a lovely voice, one that demanded both attention and respect. Moreover, she usually managed to pick the right parable or war story and deliver it with perfect timing. Her effects, which must have been carefully studied, sounded spontaneous. If one analyzes her speeches for style and content, it is clear that she spoke better than she wrote. As was obvious in her next speech—to the House of Representatives—she was far too smart to be caught trying to cater to her audience. She was a dignified public speaker and, according to Tuchman, "aroused a greater outpouring of admiration and welcome than anyone since Lindbergh flew the Atlantic."

A few minutes later, accompanied by Speaker of the House Sam Rayburn and other distinguished escorts, she entered the House and walked to the speaker's rostrum. "A little, slim figure in Chinese dress, she made a dramatic entrance as she walked down the aisle, surrounded by tall men. She knew it, for she had a keen sense of the dramatic," commented Mrs. Roosevelt. "She wore a long, tight-fitting black gown, the skirt slit almost to the knee, which was, of course, as revealing of American orientalising fancies as of the garment that it praised," said John Gittings of *The Manchester Guardian*. When Speaker of the House Sam Rayburn introduced her, the official book of her visit says, that "the chamber fairly shook with applause."

A few days earlier, Chiang had sent his wife a list of five points* that she should emphasize during this all-important speech. "I have received all the wires you sent me," she cabled him. ". . . I really admire and appreciate your thoughts. The speeches . . . will be made according to your indication, focusing on such principles as preserving our nation's dignity, announcing the contributions of our nation to the whole world and clarifying China's traditional friendship with America." But unlike Chiang's wooden pronouncements, in this, her formal address to the House of Representatives, May-ling managed to touch the important bases and appear idealistic at the same time. She spoke of a world in which "modern science has so annihilated distance that what affects one people must of necessity affect all other peoples." Stretching the truth, she recalled 160 years of "traditional friendship between our two great peoples . . . which has never been marred by misunderstandings." Looking ahead, she added in one of her more baroque phrases that the Chinese "have faith, that, at the writing of peace, America and our gallant Allies will not be obtunded by the mirage of contingent reasons of expediency." She also appealed to the concept of America as the worldwide refuge for immigrants: "I met . . . first generation Germans, Italians, French-

---

* The traditional friendship of China and the United States; gratitude for American support of China in the Sino-Japanese conflict; the danger of Japanese ambitions; the emancipation of mankind; and the fact that China and the United States were the gigantic pillars of peace in the Pacific. In two subsequent wires, Chiang added that along with these, his wife should mention Washington, Lincoln, Jesus, Confucius, and Sun Yat-sen.

men, Poles, Czechoslovakians and other nationals. . . . But there they were all Americans . . . united by the same high purpose."

Her dominant theme was an appeal to national pride: "You, as representatives of the American people, have before you the glorious opportunity of carrying on the pioneer work of your ancestors. . . . Their brawn and thews braved undauntedly almost unbelievable hardships to open up a new continent. . . . You have today . . . the immeasurably greater opportunity to implement these same ideals and to help bring about the liberation of man's spirit in every part of the world." From there she finally segued into her real message: "The prevailing opinion seems to consider the defeat of the Japanese as of relative unimportance and that Hitler is our first concern. . . . Let us not forget that Japan in her occupied areas today has greater resources at her command than Germany. . . . Let us not forget that during the first four and a half years of total aggression, China has borne Japan's sadistic fury unaided and alone."

According to the official record of May-ling's visit, "a veritable storm of cheering and handclapping" followed the end of her address, which was carried live on radio. "Goddam it," said one congressman, "I never saw anything like it. Mme. Chiang had me on the verge of bursting into tears." It was a brilliant presentation, carefully thought out, engagingly presented. If the Chinese are known for face, the substitution of the correct appearance for the reality, the hint for the demand, the effects of Madame Chiang's two appearances before Congress have probably seldom been equaled.

One of the best descriptions of her came from Allene Talmey of *Vogue* magazine: "There is a communicable greatness about Madame Chiang, a tight-rope tension, a living control. Standing beside ripened politicians on platforms, she looked like a steel sword, thinned, beautiful, purposeful. . . . Her mind sees the target, figures the attack, and dives."

There were many other comments on the lady's looks. "In just a few short minutes, Mme. Chiang had Congress in the palm of her hand," noted one lady reporter. "Petite as an ivory figurine, Mme. Chiang stands barely five feet tall in her high-heeled American slippers. . . . Her poise is perfect, and she used to good advantage her small, expressive hands. Her movement, like her mind, is quick and graceful." Less enthused were the journalist for *The Des Moines Register,* who remarked on Madame's "tight-fitting" dress, and a patronizing reporter from Missoula, who dubbed her a "lovely oriental person." Nevertheless, she had used her small size and feminine wiles to great advantage—appealing, if ever so subtly, to those big, mostly male American congressmen who could help her and her country, and she had done it in a language and mind-set with which she, who had grown up in the United States, was fully conversant.

There were numerous commentaries on Madame Chiang's use of esoteric historical references and unusual words. "Mrs. Chiang Puzzles Newsmen with 'Gobineau' and 'Obtunded,'" read one headline. Turning to
Webster's the reporter discovered that to "obtund" means to "dull," "blunt,"
or "quell." In discussing Japan after Pearl Harbor, Madame had said that
"the world began to think that the Japanese were Nietzschean supermen,
superior in intellect and physical prowess—a belief which the Gobineaus
and the Houston Chamberlains and their apt pupils, the Nazi racists,
had propounded about the Nordics." This sentence sent reporters running
to their encyclopedias to identify Count Joseph Arthur de Gobineau, a
nineteenth-century French diplomat who claimed that only the white race is
capable of creating a culture, and Houston Stewart Chamberlain, who had
written a book about the Germans as the master race.

Of the many favorable reports published throughout the country, the
editorial in the *New York Herald Tribune* was typical: "The extraordinary ovation which greeted Mme. Chiang in the House of Representatives at her
entrance and for sentence after sentence of her moving speech—was, after
all, a personal tribute to a great individual. The gallantry of her long journey
in war time, her wisdom, her dignity, her loveliness have won admiration
throughout America. . . . It will be noted that with characteristic dignity
Mme. Chiang complained of nothing and asked for nothing—except a better world and a safer future for all of us."

Among the multitudes looking for that "better world" were May-
ling's countrymen who wanted to immigrate to the United States. She had
no sooner finished her speech than the Democratic representative from
Manhattan introduced a bill to repeal the Chinese exclusion laws. "We welcome you also, as a daughter is welcomed by her foster-mother, to the land
where you received an American education," he gushed. ". . . I take this aus-
picious occasion, in your gracious presence, as an indication of my un-
bounded admiration of a nation's courage which has amazed the world, to
introduce this day a bill to grant to the Chinese rights of entry to the United
States and rights of citizenship." The bill was passed before the end of the
year.

But as far as May-ling was concerned, the cheering and compliments
were secondary to the comments by many senators and congressmen that
the United States must immediately try to furnish as much aid to China as
possible. "There can be little denying that China has thus far been the poor
relation at the United Nations table," said *The New Republic.* According to
Clare Boothe Luce, currently a Republican representative from Connecticut, Madame Chiang was "too proud to beg us for what is China's right and
too gracious to reproach us for what we have failed to do." Her references to
American soldiers stuck on isolated islands in the Pacific were, in the words

of Luce, a "brilliant parable," reminding Congress of China's lonely fight and long wait for armaments.

This message was brought home with more clarity at a joint press conference at the White House the next day—an appearance throughout which Madame sat on the edge of President Roosevelt's large swivel chair at his desk between the president, lounging in an oversized armchair with his cigarette holder in hand, and his wife, sitting ramrod straight but with a gentle hand on the visitor's arm. "It was high state drama played by real characters," Washington journalist Raymond Clapper wrote. "Someday they may put Helen Hayes* in the part, but she will never do it better than Madame Chiang acted it in real life. It was the delicate, feminine, shrewd, quick First Lady of the East against the Great Master himself." To prove his point, Clapper reported that when the president began the conference, he asked the reporters not to "put any catch questions to Madame," and May-ling returned the favor by playing "up to the President as a big strong man who could work miracles. Madame Chiang, tiny, with feet dangling from the high-seated Roosevelt chair, was working smoothly while toying with her compact to coax a promise from the president for China. Roosevelt, a master of press conference technique, was trying with equal smoothness not to melt overmuch under Madame's technique." When a reporter said that he had heard criticism that China was not making use of its vast manpower in the war effort, May-ling replied rather crisply that China's soldiers were fighting "to the extent of the munitions available for them. When more munitions are sent to China," she said, "more men will fight." President Roosevelt explained that the United States would send more war material "as soon as the Lord will let us." Flashing a ready-made smile at the chief executive, May-ling reminded him in front of 172 eager journalists that "the Lord helps those who help themselves."

❦

THE REMAINDER OF Madame Chiang's visit to Washington was filled with the usual VIP duties: laying a wreath at the Tomb of the Unknown Soldier, a journey to Mount Vernon, a gala reception held by the Chinese at the Shoreham hotel, and a presidential tea. But her presence in the capital soon began to wear thin, particularly on the chief players. In spite of the fact that she was a guest in the Roosevelt White House, Dr. Wellington Koo, the premier Chinese diplomat of the world,† noted in his diary that the G-mo's wife did

---

* A famous American actress of the day.

† Koo had been ambassador to France (1936–1941) and was currently serving as ambassador to the Court of St. James's. In 1945, he was named China's chief delegate

not hesitate to entertain a parade of Republican politicians: "Joe Kennedy,*
Mr. J. Farley, Wendell Willkie had seen her several times. . . . They are all
opposed to the Pres. politically. . . . The Pres. had been evidently uneasy and
Mrs. R. had suggested that it might be more comfortable for her to live in
Hyde Park." In another breach of etiquette, Madame told Koo that she had
taken pains *not* to show her speeches to her hosts, in spite of the fact that
"they intimated their wish to go over them before delivery." Worse, she
had neglected to mention the president in them. The more Roosevelt saw
of May-ling, the less he trusted her, finding her quite different from the image she presented to the world, and although his wife seemed to like their
guest at first, her attitude changed once their guest was released from the
hospital.

It is not difficult to trace the pro-China line in the American press that
had led the first lady, no fool where people were concerned, to react to Madame Chiang with such openhearted acceptance. No less a personage than
her husband's rival for president of the United States, Wendell Willkie, had
just returned from China with a report that "the wife of China's Generalissimo is the only international celebrity whose personal attractiveness far
exceeds her advance notices." Beyond the political types there were popular
columnists like Bob Considine, who wrote in the summer of 1942 that "five
years ago" Madame Chiang's husband "was prepared to give China constitutional democracy as the final step in uniting its countless millions"—a
fanciful invention that could only have led another (unnamed) reporter to
claim, "Today unconquered China has the framework of democracy" as well
as "a modern civil service." And if Clare Boothe Luce could write that "Madame Chiang Kai-shek is the greatest living woman," Washington hostess
Elsa Maxwell felt free to say that Madame Chiang was "one of the greatest
women in the world," who "will go down in history as the mother of modern China."

But, according to Eleanor Roosevelt,

I saw another side of Madame Chiang while she was in the White
House, and I was much amused by the reactions of the men with

---

to the United Nations and served as ambassador to the United States from 1946 to
1956.

* Kennedy was not a Republican but had been against the United States entering the
war. He had incurred the wrath of the British when, as U.S. ambassador to the Court of
St. James's, he argued for the appeasement of Hitler. Resigning under pressure in 1940,
he had tried to reinstate himself after Pearl Harbor by wiring Roosevelt, "Name the
battlefront—I'm yours to command," but he was never again offered an important post
by the president. (James MacGregor Burns, *Roosevelt: The Soldier of Freedom*, p. 211.)

whom she talked. They found her charming, intelligent, and fascinating, but they were all a little afraid of her, because she could be a coolheaded statesman when she was fighting for something she deemed necessary to China and to her husband's regime; the little velvet hand and the low, gentle voice disguised a determination that could be as hard as steel. A certain casualness about cruelty emerged sometimes in her conversations with the men, though never with me. I had painted for Franklin such a sweet, gentle, and pathetic figure that, as he came to recognize the other side of the lady, it gave him keen pleasure to tease me about my lack of perception. I remember an incident at a dinner party . . . which gave him particular entertainment. John L. Lewis was acting up at the time and Franklin turned to Madame Chiang and asked: "What would you do in China with a labor leader like John Lewis?" She never said a word, but the beautiful, small hand came up and slid across her throat. . . . Franklin looked across at me to make sure I had seen. . . . He enjoyed being able to say to me afterwards: "Well, how about your gentle and sweet character?"

It was May-ling's imperious behavior, however, that distressed the White House staff. Although her room at the White House was equipped with bells and telephones, when she needed something, she went to her doorway and clapped her hands to summon the White House servants. This was the custom in her home in China when calling coolies but considered very bad form in the White House. It was not only May-ling who expected royal treatment but her niece and nephew as well, and Jeanette apparently made a scene complaining about the poor service at the White House. The Kung children, according to Eleanor Roosevelt, gave "the impression that they felt we . . . thought all Chinese were laundrymen and looked down on them, and they were anxious to dispel that idea. It seemed at times that they had chips on their shoulders." Not everyone was so generous. Referring to Madame's nephew and niece as the "Kung brats," the Chinese minister claimed that they "seriously damaged China's prestige among the elite American circles." In that regard, one old-time journalist told how the famous Dr. Wellington Koo "was kept waiting three days before David Kung let him into the Presence."

Koo was an experienced diplomat, long inured to the peculiarities of the powerful. This was, however, not necessarily the case with the White House staff. One day the president's secretary, Grace Tully, ran into Wilson Searles, one of the White House ushers on the second floor, where the guest quarters were located. When Tully heard "an imperative clapping of hands from Madame's room," she was amazed.

"Wilson, what goes on here?" she asked.

"This goes on all day," he answered. "That Chinese crowd has run us ragged. They think they're in China calling the coolies."

"What do you do?" the secretary asked.

"I keep going, but in the opposite direction."

More than two years later, Eleanor Roosevelt said that Madame could "talk beautifully about democracy, but she does not know how to live democracy." Treasury Secretary Morgenthau told his staff that Roosevelt was "just crazy to get her out of the country." This, according to Tuchman, had less to do with Roosevelt's personal annoyance than with his concern that her private persona might garner enough publicity to spoil her image and his China policy. According to one observer, "of all the notables who visited the Roosevelts during their 12-year tenure, Madame posed the most problems." Another complained that "Madame regarded virtually everybody below Cabinet rank as coolies." Having moved from college directly into a home where, at the age of twenty, she was put in charge of twelve servants, Mayling had no idea how Americans lived inside their homes. "How do you manage when you go so many places alone?" she asked Mrs. Roosevelt. "Who packs for you? Who buys your tickets? What do you do about telegrams? How can you do it alone?"

Roosevelt did, in fact, ask Dr. Walter Judd, a congressman from Minnesota who had spent ten years working in China, to come to the Oval Office to speak with him about Madame Chiang, who had been treating the outspoken American press, to which she was not accustomed, rather badly. "Well," the president said to Judd, "the Chinese certainly have lots of problems, and not the least of them is their prima donna."

"Do you mean Madame Chiang Kai-shek?" Judd asked.

The president said "yes," noting that May-ling's "prima donnaishness" was making it harder to help her country. It might be a good idea, he told Judd, if she were to return to China soon. Judd replied that, as a physician, he could understand the lady's condition, given the extended physical and emotional strain of the war years in China followed by the "greatest acclaim ever accorded to a woman in this generation." Roosevelt said he understood this as well, but it would still be better if she could be convinced to leave the United States before she did any further damage.

As Judd left the White House, he was waylaid by newsmen, who wanted to know about his conversation with the president. Although he denied that they had discussed Madame Chiang, one reporter asked about the resentment caused by her high-handedness with the press, while another queried him on the ongoing criticism of the Chinese reception at the Shoreham, where "more champagne flowed" than he had seen "in 10 years in Washington." Judd said that in China, when things were bad, people kept face by celebrating, even when it was beyond their means, and in that sense, although overdone, the grandeur was a symbol of how the Chinese were trying to uphold their self-respect among the nations of the world. A clever explanation, it did not stop journalists from pointing out the enormous gulf between May-ling's pleas for help for her starving countrymen and the costly receptions that she had attended and would continue to attend on the rest of her tour of the United States.

It was also during her stay at the White House that the well-known story was circulated about her insistence on having her silk bedsheets changed every time she used them. What the story did not include was the fact that the Soongs had a familial skin problem related to the wheals that had dogged May-ling as a child and the outbreaks that followed. Whatever the source of the ailment—some say nerves, others urticaria (hives), still others an allergy to cotton—it afflicted several members of the Soong family* and was probably the reason for Madame Chiang's constant changing of linen.

Before leaving Washington, May-ling joined Eleanor Roosevelt at the first lady's weekly press conference with women reporters. According to one journalist, it was the first time that Mrs. Roosevelt had ever remained silent from the beginning to the end of the Washington ritual. Dressed in black silk embossed in satin with high-heeled black sandals piped in gold, Madame Chiang stressed China's need for armaments and gave her views on the position of women in the world. Asked by one of the reporters if she believed in equal rights for women, she said that since men expected women to bear half the burdens of the world, they ought to give them equal privileges. "I have never known brains to have any sex," she said.

In spite of the adverse reactions of those in and around the White House, the comments on May-ling's appearances in Washington were close to reverential. "Madame Chiang Kai-shek has made a deeper impression upon the American consciousness than any public figure since the appearance of Franklin Roosevelt," said Eliot Janeway, the economist dubbed "Calamity Janeway" for his gloomy forecasts on the stock market. Writing in *Fortune* magazine, Janeway seems to have been blinded by Madame's charisma or

---

* In 1973, sister Ching-ling complained to a friend that she had been "a victim of neurodermatitis for over 5 months" with "itching and insomnia"; five years later, she wrote that the bright klieg lights at a party congress had "caused my old skin trouble to return, while my body and face are covered with red itchy patches. Naturally insomnia follows." Moreover, one of May-ling's younger brothers was apparently known as "the Frog." (The quotes are from Israel Epstein, *Woman in World History*, p. 589; Sylvia Wu, *Memories of Madame Sun*, p. 11; and interviews with family friends.)

overly influenced by Luce. According to him, Madame Chiang had "appeared before the country with no ulterior motives, either ideological or political. She came to offer us a way—a way that would benefit us as much as the Chinese—a deal in which Chinese manpower would use American equipment." She was, he said, "the most effective ambassador ever to represent a foreign power in the U.S."

37

FROM WASHINGTON, Madame Chiang took the train to New York, arriving at Pennsylvania Station, where she was greeted by Mayor Fiorello La Guardia, the Chinese consul general, and her brother T.L. The crowd, which had gathered outside the station long before her train was due, broke out in cheers as she left for the Waldorf-Astoria, where she had reserved the entire forty-second floor of the Waldorf Towers for herself and her suite. In spite of the fact that her doctors had wired the consul and written members of her family emphasizing "the need for continued rest and the avoidance of all unnecessary overactivity in the form of social engagements and functions of state," May-ling's program in New York was just as demanding as the one in Washington. After a short rest, she was taken to the first of several events planned for the day—an official reception at City Hall, where she met a few hundred important people. At one point she seemed not to feel well and appeared on the verge of fainting but, after being checked by a nurse, continued with the program. The first to speak was the mayor, who apologized for the history of the West's incursions into China: "Few of the great nations are entirely guiltless," La Guardia said, "but let us make up for the past by assuring the independence of China fully and completely for the future."

Madame Chiang responded with a two-thousand-year-old story taken from Chinese history at the time of the building of the Great Wall. It seems that in the province of Kwangsi, there were two rivers that were continually overflowing, drowning local farmers and destroying their crops. The emperor sent a high official to build dikes to prevent further floods, but he failed and paid for the failure with his life. The emperor then sent another man, who suffered the same fate as the first. The third man the emperor sent succeeded and was given many honors. Madame said that when she and the generalissimo visited the site, they found three graves. When she asked why, she was told that the third official had declined his honors and killed himself because he said he could not profit from the failure of others. "In other words, he disdained to benefit himself by the price others had paid with their lives. I feel," she said, "that the American people have the same high-mindedness."

Madame's most important appearance in New York came on the evening of the second day, when she addressed 17,000 people at Madison Square Garden. A prizefight had originally been scheduled that evening, but the fight was preempted by the generalissimo's wife. According to radio's most influential commentator, Walter Winchell, "she was more important than any boxing match. . . . More important? She's the best scrapper the Garden ever had." Among the dignitaries present were Willkie, Governor Thomas E. Dewey of New York, and the governors of Connecticut, Maine, Massachusetts, New Hampshire, Pennsylvania, Rhode Island, and Vermont, plus the consular representatives of twenty-five countries. T.V. was there with his wife, as were John D. Rockefeller, sponsor of the event, the chairmen of the boards of J. P. Morgan and the Chase National Bank, and the president of Columbia University. For this evening, Madame wore another black dress, this one with gold trim, along with black gloves and what one reporter inadequately described as "green" (obviously jade) earrings. According to *Time* magazine, she looked "more like next month's *Vogue* than the avenging angel of 422,000,000 people."

Led on stage by an honor guard of Flying Tigers, she and the other guests were treated to the sight of Chinese girls marching down the aisles with lighted Chinese lanterns, color guards from the army, navy, marine corps, and coast guard, and a rendering of a Chinese marching song, sung by opera star Lawrence Tibbett. Governor Dewey spoke first: "In these days of swift conquest, we have just seen one on our shores. Nothing could be swifter or more complete or more gratifying to all of us than the conquest of America by Mme. Chiang." Dewey's introduction was followed by tributes from the other governors present and an overview of the problems in the CBI [China-Burma-India] theater presented by H. H. "Hap" Arnold, chief of the U.S. Army Air Force. Willkie then introduced the honoree. As might have been expected, it was a gallant tribute. "I am delighted to reciprocate an introduction to an American audience for Madame Chiang, for she introduced me to several Chinese audiences in Chungking several months ago," he said, smiling broadly at her. "I have met a good many war leaders and it is not inappropriate for me to say that she is the most fascinating of them all, and also the most beloved of her people. We speak of her wit and charm, and her beauty, but you miss the point of her if you think of her only as an angel—although she is one, an avenging angel. It was China which first understood the true nature of this war. And Madame Chiang is one of the two driving forces behind that great nation. She is a leader of 450,000,000 people. . . . I hope no American thinks of our friendship for China in terms of patronage, for the time will come when China's friendship for America will be as important as America's friendship for China."

Willkie escorted May-ling from her seat to the speaker's rostrum. Her speech was a long one, including a homily on Christian charity—"no matter what we have undergone and suffered, we must try to forgive those who injured us and remember only the lessons gained thereby"—and her thanks for all the "contributions large and small [that] have poured in."* She ended with a sentence that must have pleased Willkie: "The goal of our common struggle at the conclusion of this war should be to shape the future so that this whole world must be thought of as one great State common to gods and men." May-ling's effect on her audience was remarkable. It was reported that a large stained-glass window bearing her likeness was installed the following year in St. John's Church in Massena, New York; pictured among the flowers of China, Madame Chiang is holding a scroll bearing the message from her speech, "We must try to forgive." Even her doctor, Robert F. Loeb, sent a note to tell her that her speech was "incomparable. I would never have believed an audience of seventeen thousand capable of such intense interest and sincere appreciation," he wrote, adding, however, that his patient's "task in Washington is now completed, and the remainder of your activities in this country is of less importance to the future than is the restoration of your health."

During her third day in New York, May-ling addressed a gathering of more than three thousand Chinese Americans at Carnegie Hall. Her speech, in good Chinese tradition, lasted over an hour. On the evening of the fourth day, the Chinese consul gave a huge reception for her at the Waldorf. May-ling did not make her appearance until shortly after 6:30, and three ladies who had arrived at the stated time of 5:00 P.M. fainted and had to be revived. Gowned in black velvet trimmed with scarlet sequins, she was, according to the pastor of the First Presbyterian Church in Passaic, New Jersey, "the most effective woman speaker" he had ever heard. "The two greatest diplomats in the world today," he declared, "are Winston Churchill and Mme. Chiang

---

* Shortly after her Madison Square Garden speech, Henry Luce said that over $300,000 had already come in for China and $1 million more was on the way. Luce had, by this time, managed to merge eight different groups appealing for various kinds of aid to China (war orphans, medicine, Christian colleges, etc.) into something called United China Relief and had put Willkie, Paul Hoffman (president of Studebaker, later head of the Ford Foundation, delegate to the United Nations, and managing director of the U.N. Special Fund), David O. Selznick, and himself on the board of directors.

Kai-shek." But, according to notes made by Chiang's former adviser Lauchlin Currie, the reception itself "turned very sour," since the honoree stayed
for only a few minutes and many of the guests did not even see her, let alone
have a chance to meet her.

May-ling's early departure may have had to do with her health. In early
March, Dr. Loeb sent David Kung

> a schedule which in our judgment represents the maximum load
> compatible with Madame's continued improvement. Since Ma-
> dame's departure from the hospital her activities have been far in
> excess of the recommended schedule. . . . Madame is growing pro-
> gressively more tense and nervous, and is having again to increase
> the sedatives necessary to obtain her much-needed sleep . . . the
> health of Madame . . . must not be jeopardized at any cost, and I
> can only appeal to you . . . to see that Madame's activity is sharply,
> radically, and consistently curtailed for the remainder of her stay in
> this country. If the present pace is continued, serious collapse is, in
> my own opinion, certain.

Nevertheless, Madame held a press conference the next day in her suite
at the Waldorf. As in Washington, she kept the reporters at bay, dealing with
them with far more formality than they were accustomed to and maintaining an invisible wall beyond which they dared not venture. "In her queenly
way," said a journalist from Buffalo, "Mme. Chiang masters the press without offending them." Certainly, she managed to dazzle some of the most
sophisticated among them. According to one reporter from Shanghai, "It
seemed that the goggle-eyed scriveners were much more interested in watching her than in getting the news. At one point when she was talking about
her 'warphans,' this correspondent glanced over the shoulder of one of New
York's roughest, toughest police reporters, Jimmy Bishop of the *New York
News*. With a stubby pencil . . . Bishop was tracing the words, 'Her hands
speak as eloquently as her dulcet voice. Her skin is blush-olive. Her eyes are
onyx laughter. Her hair is a sweep of jet black. Hers is an ageless beauty.' "
As if this weren't enough, the Chinese reporter sneaked a look at a colleague
from *The New York Times*, who was writing "Her eyes are limpid pools of
midnight inkiness. Her teeth are visual symphonies of oral architecture. Her
hands are lotus fronds swaying in a summer breeze." Fortunately, these meanderings were edited out of the printed stories.

By now there was no question that May-ling had a near-hypnotic effect
on men. According to one of Willkie's biographers,* Wendell spent a lot of

---

* Steve Neal, author of *Dark Horse*.

time with her when she was at the the Waldorf. In that regard, Mike Cowles wrote about an interesting scene that took place in her suite: "One morning I received a call at my OWI* office in Washington from the Chinese Ambassador. The Madame wanted me to come to a black-tie dinner that evening in her Waldorf Towers apartment. I was expected at eight-thirty. It was most inconvenient for me to dash up to New York and, besides, I had to get an appropriate permit during the war to fly on a commercial airline. But I did make it to New York, decked myself out in black tie, and showed up at the Waldorf on time." Cowles was met in the lobby by May-ling's majordomo and taken up to her floor. The door to her suite, he noticed, was opened by the same butler who had served Willkie and him in Chungking. "Madame begs your pardon, Mr. Cowles," he said. "She's going to be a few minutes late. I recall that you prefer Scotch and water." A Chinese waiter appeared with Cowles's, drink on a silver tray. Eventually, so did Madame. When she suggested they go right into dinner, he realized that this was not a party but a tête-à-tête. There were four servants standing in the dining room, one at each corner of the room. May-ling smiled at her guest. "Don't be nervous about the servants, Mike," she said. "None of them understands English. We can speak freely." In spite of this, she did not come to the point of the dinner until they had both finished eating.

Her marriage to Chiang, she told Cowles, had been a marriage of convenience arranged by her mother. They scarcely knew each other when they married. On their wedding night, he told her that he did not believe in sexual relations unless it was to produce children, and since he already had one son and did not want any more, they would not sleep together. "I wasn't sure that I believed all this," Cowles wrote, "but I kept listening." The above tale was apparently "only a warmup" for what followed. "It was time now," he said, "for serious business."

"She was convinced," according to Cowles, "that Willkie could be nominated again for the presidency in 1944. It was my duty, she told me, to give up whatever I was doing and devote myself exclusively to getting him the 1944 Republican nomination. I was to spend whatever amount of money I thought was necessary. She would reimburse me for all expenditures. . . . 'You know, Mike,' " she told him, " 'if Wendell could be elected, then he and I would rule the world. I would rule the Orient and Wendell would rule the Western world.' And," Cowles added, "she stressed the word *rule*."

It is fascinating to speculate on how May-ling planned to manipulate Willkie and the United States once he got the presidency she thought she could buy for him. The story of her marriage being arranged by her mother is a clear falsification, not only of the stories related by others but of the one

---

* Cowles was domestic director of the Office of War Information during World War II.

she herself told. It also stretches the imagination to think that Chiang, a man with an enormous sexual appetite, would have denied himself the pleasure of sex with his highly attractive wife. The rest of the story was too far-fetched, even for Cowles. "It was a totally mad proposal, of course," he later wrote. "But I was so mesmerized by clearly one of the most formidable women of the time that this evening I would not have dismissed anything she said."

Another story was told by Eleanor Lambert, the woman who raised recognition of American fashion to the level of the French. Lambert often saw the G-mo's wife when she came to New York. "She had a perfect figure when I first met her . . . she had a white cheongsam. Every button, every frog was fastened with a diamond the size of my little finger . . . but it wasn't showy. It was just there. You could see that they were diamonds if you were up close. That was it."

In 1959, Lambert's husband, publisher Seymour Berkson, died suddenly of a heart attack. Lambert said that May-ling, who was visiting in New York at the time, called on her, attended the funeral, and invited her to dinner at her apartment about two weeks later.

> We were just alone and she had prepared (she always had and still has a wonderful Chinese chef) . . . a divine dinner just for the two of us. Then she took me into the sitting room, sat me down, and she proceeded to give me a sermon. She got up, and it was really an evangelist sermon. It was like a Baptist harangue . . . she told me that I must, I must realize that this was God's will, that I must not fight it because God had further plans for Seymour's life after death. . . . And then she went on to tell me, 'Don't think I don't know what you're going through, because I too had a deep love for someone that I was thinking of giving up everything for.' . . . She said she was willing to divorce the general, do anything, etc . . . It was Willkie.*

❧

THE NEXT STOP on Madame Chiang's tour was Wellesley College. During the previous year, the school had awarded her an honorary LLD and established a fund in her name. There was, however, some confusion about the donations, since the college planned to use them to "cultivate an interest in China on the Wellesley College campus," while Madame Chiang expected them to be sent directly to her. The money was eventually put aside to pay for scholarships, and later that year, Madame Chiang sent the fund a gift of $25,000.

---

* Willkie had died in 1944.

Madame and her party arrived at Boston's South Station, where, in spite of a snowstorm, five thousand people were waiting to greet her. Traveling in an armored car with Secret Service men lent by President Roosevelt, she made a hurried trip through Boston's Chinatown before heading out to Wellesley, where a battery of photographers was waiting for her. Later that day she joined eighty members of her class for tea. Unlike May-ling, who had progressed from pudgy to svelte, many of her classmates had put on weight and settled into stout middle age—a fact Madame didn't hesitate to mention to one or two of them. In the style of the day, many had arrived wearing large, unattractive hats, which May-ling asked them to take off so she could see their faces. Their reactions to her must have added to a vanity already well nourished by the press: "It was hard to believe that this slender, graceful person . . . was the same chunky little Chinese girl with the round chubby face and sometimes frizzed pompadour of our freshman year," commented a classmate from Pittsburgh. "She looked at least 15 years younger than most of us did." And according to another, "She seemed so young and fresh and vivacious, and the rest of us seemed so fortyish."

The one time during her tour that May-ling seemed to be overcome with genuine emotion occurred at the beginning of the speech she gave at the college. As she started speaking, she teared up and gripped the sides of the rostrum. According to an observer, "Students, Faculty, Friends, they all held their breath, as Madam Chiang set her teeth hard into her lip ('I bit it as hard as I could,' she said later that afternoon. 'It still hurts!')." After a little more than a minute, two applications of smelling salts, and a glass of water supplied by one of the nurses who had accompanied her, she gained control and was able to speak. "Strong emotions often tend to render one inarticulate," she said. "It is not easy for me . . . to express my feelings today. . . . During the years of absence from Wellesley I have often thought and wished for the moment when I would be able to return."

After her speech, there were the usual comments about Madame's esoteric vocabulary. In an article called "Mme. Chiang Stumps Even Her Teacher," the reporter for *The Christian Science Monitor* listed indehiscence (a botanical term for the state of being closed at maturity), maunder (to move slowly and uncertainly), and cenote (a sinkhole) among a list of eight difficult words she had used, saying that even Wellesley professors had to consult their dictionaries. There were also endless articles about the fact that during a walking tour of the campus, Madame wore slacks—a departure from college rules that encouraged Wellesley to change its clothing regulations.

After her visit to Wellesley, Madame Chiang spoke at Symphony Hall in Boston, then returned to New York, where she spent some days in seclusion before setting off for the West. During her several stays at the Waldorf, the

Secret Service men assigned to her were informed by her nephew when she was planning to go out so that they could clear the hall between her suite and the elevator and between the elevator and the hotel exit. More often than not, however, she did not appear until several hours later. When the head of the Secret Service asked her to try to stick more closely to the time indicated, she insisted that he be removed. Apparently, her young niece and nephew were just as arrogant in their behavior as their aunt.

There was the usual crowd of onlookers waiting outside Union Station in Chicago when Madame arrived there on March 19, the usual gathering of officials to greet her, and the usual refurbished suite at the best hotel in the city. Once again, an excess of security had been provided—seventy policemen, four policewomen, and a quantity of Secret Service. There was the usual reception, for which she wore black velvet trimmed with red sequins, matched by earrings, rings, and brooch of rubies and diamonds. As before, she emphasized China's need for more airpower at her press conference, accepted more money for China relief, and gave another address in favor of cooperation among the nations. Responding to a recent speech by Churchill, in which he had suggested that Britain, the United States, and Russia should be in charge of the postwar world, she wrote Chiang that she had not only set in motion action by Roosevelt to counteract Churchill but had been promised that there would be speeches in the Senate and House as well, saying that China should be among the four postwar powers. And as usual, she made a superb impression. Carl Sandburg, Chicago's famous poet, commented on her "perfection at chiseling syllables. She is a marvel at timing her pauses and making each word count," he said. ". . . Yet she doesn't know how she does it any more than Ty Cobb knew which one of his eleven ways of sliding to second he was using."

On March 25, the train containing Madame's private Pullman car, previously used by President Roosevelt, arrived at the Oakland station across the bay from San Francisco. Transferring to a U.S. Navy yacht escorted by two Coast Guard cutters and a fireboat spewing water displays, Madame Chiang and a large reception committee arrived at a San Francisco pier, where they were met by an honor guard of soldiers, sailors, marines, the city's municipal band, and Chinese children waving flags. From the Embarcadero, the party proceeded up Grant Avenue, the main street of the Chinese quarter of the city, where kites were flying, streamers were blowing in the breeze, and most of the inhabitants of the largest Chinese colony in the Western Hemisphere had gathered to greet her. When she reached the Palace Hotel, she retired with her youngest brother, T.A., until it was time to go to her first public event, which took place at City Hall and included more Chinese children, marching bands, and military units, along with flowered floats. During a press conference the following day, she answered a question about postwar trade between the United States and China by saying that the possibilities "are so great that man's imagination can hardly encompass them. We have great need of your engineering and technical skill and of your manufactured products. In return, we have raw materials and we are a market of 450,000,000 people."

While in San Francisco, May-ling invited General Stilwell's wife and daughters to tea. "Mme. Chiang saw my husband before she left China," said Mrs. Stilwell afterward, "and she says he's in fine shape. It will be the greatest thing for General Stilwell's morale when he hears about this," she added in what one might guess was purposeful (or inadvertent) sarcasm. There was the usual banquet for more than a thousand people and the usual speech at the Civic Auditorium. It is not surprising that Lauchlin Currie found fault with Madame's excessive rhetoric. The man who had once admired her way with words took exception to the following sentence: "The present Nazi and Shintoistic indoctrinations of mendacity and deceit I attribute to the disjunctive reasoning of warped minds and they cannot endure; for only the truth and the conviction of the truth of human postulates can withstand the onslaughts of time and violence."

But as in other cities, reporters fell all over themselves trying to describe her. "Who is this woman of the ivory satin skin, the perfect English tinged with a slight Southern accent, the soul of an unconquerable nation in her piercing eyes?" asked one woman reporter. An editorial writer for the *San Francisco Chronicle* was even more carried away: "Madame Chiang's visit to San Francisco marks a turning point that perhaps is of the most profound importance in our entire record of civilization . . . she is the symbol of a China where, for the first time since history was put into written records, there is a practically united people. Moreover, she is the symbol of women's power and achievement, for she, more than any other single human factor, performed the miracle of unity."

But another old friend and adviser, Owen Lattimore, now director of Pacific Operations and head of the Office of War Information in San Francisco, was hurt and infuriated by her. Having just sent her a collection of recordings of all of her speeches and broadcasts in the United States, he was surprised and distressed not to have been invited to a reception "for chosen important Americans." According to Lattimore, he spoke to her public relations aide, saying "in a rather mild way, that I thought it was a mistake from the Chinese point of view not to invite to this reception the man who had been the personal adviser to the Generalissimo, because people might misinterpret it as a sign of a disagreement or trouble within his regime." The PR man agreed and invited Lattimore to the reception. But when his turn came to file past Madame and shake hands, "she did not say a word to me, nor did she put her hand out. She looked at the next person coming up, acting as if I were not even there. I do not think that the cold attitude of Madame Chiang was because she was angry with me. . . . She thought that I was no longer useful and dropped me."

May-ling's last stop on her official tour of the United States was Los Angeles, where the celebrations had been taken over by Hollywood—the studio executives behind the scenes and the stars whose appearances they ordered up for various events. These included a reception held for what the *Los Angeles Times* called "the elite . . . the ultra-elite, and . . . a small group of about 12 . . . who constituted the ultra of the ultra." This event took place in the Ambassador Hotel, where Madame Chiang was staying. With her astute sense of the hierarchical—political, financial, and social—it probably came as no surprise to her that the heads of the studios—"the ultra of the ultra"— were the people chosen to meet her privately in her suite. But the highlight of her stop in Los Angeles was a superproduction at the Hollywood Bowl. It was, according to the official book of her visit, "one of the most stirring and gorgeously staged events of Mme. Chiang's entire tour." In another book, it was more accurately described as "overdetermined historical display."

The shell of the Bowl had been painted bright blue, and an enormous stage had been erected, along with special boxes for the most important dignitaries. A trumpet blast, which announced the program, was followed by a welcome to the audience of thirty thousand by the mayor of Los Angeles. Spencer Tracy then introduced a parade of famous female stars led by Mary Pickford. The audience applauded for each one: Joan Bennett, Ingrid Bergman, Ida Lupino, Ginger Rogers, Irene Dunne, Deanna Durbin, Marlene Dietrich, Kay Francis, Judy Garland, Janet Gaynor, Rita Hayworth, Dorothy Lamour, Rosalind Russell, Norma Shearer, Barbara Stanwyck, Shirley Temple, Lana Turner, and Loretta Young. After a drumroll, a detachment of infantry came onstage, followed by a large contingent of marines, sailors, and cadets from the Army Air Corps—all with their appropriate anthems. Last came the merchant marines, who stood at attention along with their compatriots while the Los Angeles Philharmonic "reinforced by several bands," played a marching song from the Chinese army. After the servicemen presented arms, Madame finally appeared, riding into the amphitheater in an open Rolls-Royce with eight Chinese cadets walking alongside. The audience stood while she was handed out of the car and led to a box, where she sat just in front of the stars. As she took her seat, Mary Pickford, wearing an enormous flowered hat, came over, bowed, and presented her with a bouquet of American Beauty roses.

An invocation by a Methodist bishop, followed by "The Star-Spangled

Banner" and the Chinese national anthem, led into an elaborate pageant called "China, a Symphonic Narrative"—an enactment of Chinese history with five hundred Chinese extras, narrated by Walter Huston. "A woman has swept the cobwebs from this nation's past," he announced as a huge flag crossed the stage with the carriers hidden behind it. After the flag came actors dressed as Chinese peasants, their bodies doubled over to indicate hardship, their faces hidden by coolie straw hats. They were followed by nubile Chinese girls bearing flowers. "Soon the nation will celebrate its harvest" was the announcement interrupted by booming guns, which sent the actors fleeing into the wings. "China which was never bred for war. . . . People of China, take heart, do not despair. . . . The China of tomorrow speaks through a valiant woman's voice. . . . The China that gives us our great and gallant guest."

If Madame Chiang was amazed by this overwrought and graceless rendering of Chinese history, she gave no sign of it. Speaking slowly and deliberately, she wove her usual spell over the audience, demanding respect with her voice—never too high nor too low—and her message. She was the only person that this writer has ever heard utter the words "Yes, alas!" and not sound like a fool.* If anything, the blatant artificiality of what preceded her speech only made her appear more genuine and dignified. "We were simply bowled over by Madame, who was way ahead of her press agentry," said David O. Selznick, adding that he was disappointed that people did not seem to have paid enough attention to the "symphonic narrative" and "march" created for the occasion—compositions he called "the first important serious music to come out of the war."

❧

THE HOLLYWOOD BOWL was Madame Chiang's last public appearance in the country, although she did not return to China until three months later. T.V., who had originally disapproved of her trip, thought she had overstayed her welcome and told her so more than once. His concerns were borne out when she returned to New York in April and began commenting on the situation in India, causing the infuriated viceroy to lodge a protest and request a promise that Madame Chiang would issue no more "mischievous statements."

In early May, Chiang cabled May-ling to come home. In spite of this, she traveled to her old school in Georgia and paid an official visit to Canada before returning to the East Coast. She enjoyed her trip to Canada, where she addressed Parliament, throwing in a few words like "ochlocracy" (mob

---

* I am indebted to the Wellesley Archive for showing me a tape of this event.

rule) and "immane" (monstrously cruel). According to DeLong, Madame believed Canada gave her "a bigger welcome than [it] would have her nemesis Churchill." When Emma told her that she had missed the broadcast of her speech there, May-ling read it aloud to her friend herself. "How do you think it compares with the other talks?" she asked. "Which one did you like best?"

She had asked Emma to meet her at Bear Mountain State Park in the Hudson Valley, fifty miles north of Manhattan. When Emma arrived, May-ling told her that she had seen Willkie the day before, and since it was raining they had played gin rummy at $10 a game, the winnings to be given to war orphans. Willkie kept winning. "I tried everything to distract him," May-ling said, "teased him about kissing the ballerina in Moscow, and kissing Chinese babies, but to no avail. After he had won seven games straight, I threw the cards in his face and quit." That morning she had received a wire from him: "The gospel according to Hoyle* prescribes that angels don't throw cards and the[y] should pay their debts." There were other communications as well. In one letter sent to "My dear May" and signed "Affectionately yours," Willkie said he "would never forget the delightful chats we had together while you were in the United States and also your little lectures."

Joseph Kennedy had three long visits with Madame Chiang at the Waldorf before she returned to China. "She strikes me as a most interesting and attractive woman," he wrote in his diary.

> There are definitely two facets to her personality, one is the statesman, the manager of the airplane business, assistant to the Generalissimo. . . . The other definite side of her character is a charming female. She smiles. She appeared to be horrified when I told her she had sex appeal and immediately asked if I meant like Gypsy Rose Lee. I said not exactly that, but if she wanted another word, charm. I said I thought that it helped her to sell herself to the American public, but she said that women like her as well as men and I said her charm did that for the women, but her appeal helps her with the men. She always appeared to be horrified but I secretly thought she rather liked it.
>
> On my first visit she read me two of her stories that she had written when she was 19, one rather a staid one and one rather a naughty one. . . . She reads beautifully and on my last visit she read me her two broadcasts. . . . She told me she writes all her own speeches and

---

* Li explains that *The Gospel According to Hoyle* is a book of card tricks with Christian messages used by evangelists.

does all her own research. . . . She told me she had been approached
here by a syndicate for three articles a week and she asked me how
much I thought she had been offered. I said possibly $10,000 a week
and she said a million and a half dollars. This sounds almost incredible, but . . . it may not be unlikely because of the international force
of her personality and her ability.

At the end of June, May-ling's old friend and "official shopper," Mrs.
C. T. Feng, went home to California—a sure indication that Madame herself
was about to return to China. Wife of the Chinese consul general in San
Francisco, Feng had been in attendance on May-ling for close to three
months, purchasing silk and woolen fabrics and shopping for items of clothing, shoes, and furs at Saks Fifth Avenue and Bergdorf Goodman.* One
woman, who was young at the time, with a body similar to May-ling's still
recalls trying on fur coats at Bergdorf to be sent to Madame's hotel.

By the time May-ling left the United States, an amount of $800,000 to
$900,000† had apparently been deposited in her account, representing the
total of several different transfers, most of them made in May before she left.
In each case, she had endorsed the checks and turned them over to David
Kung for deposit to his personal account. There is no way of knowing where
the money came from, but some say it was given to Kung to open an office
in New York to deal with his aunt's correspondence and some shipping business of his own. David, who complained that he was exhausted from the
strain of his aunt's visit, had asked an American girl from the Chinese News
Service, who had been assigned to May-ling's staff, to be his secretary, but
she had refused because, as she put it, "I hate his guts and so does everyone
else." Queried about David's sister, Jeanette, who had apparently made
unwarranted advances to her, the secretary labeled her an "insufferable
pig." This attitude was echoed—although more politely—by the ever-obliging
publicity man, Hollington Tong, who had been blamed for the many confu-
sions arising from contradictory orders given by the two young Kungs. Having been "insulted by the Kungs, pushed around and brushed off," he had
evidently become "so fed up with the entire show" that he was considering
resigning from government service.

There was also "a deep-seated resentment" among members of the em-

---

* It was said by the Chinese in New York and Washington that she had bought forty
pairs of shoes and spent $45,000 on furs. $45,000 U.S. in 1943 = $533,333 today.

† $945,000 U.S. in 1943 = $11,200,000 today. (See Hoover Archives: Lauchlin Currie
papers, Box 3, Folder Madame Chiang Kai-shek, LC notes of May 24, May 26, and June
10, 1943.)

bassy staff about Madame Chiang's "lack of consideration for them." They complained that they were kept on twenty-four-hour-a-day duty, although they often had nothing to do but sit outside her suite just in case she wanted them. In conversations with American friends, they criticized "the lavish entertainment," the "heavy expenses" incurred at a time when the Chinese at home were starving, as well as "the stupidity and bungling by David Kung." They believed that Madame's lengthy visit had "reduced the good will gained upon her arrival and the early days of her visit," pointing out that most high government officials from other countries stayed in the United States no more than ten days. She had remained for eight months.

38

There is no more entangling alliance than aid to indigent friends.

—BARBARA TUCHMAN

FROM NOVEMBER 1942 until July 1943, while Madame Chiang was traveling through the United States garnering sympathy, money, and armaments for China, her husband's government in Chungking was beginning to show increasing signs of interior rot. "The consensus of most American officials and correspondents working in China," Tuchman said, "was that the Kuomintang was incompetent, corrupt, oppressive, unrepresentative, riddled by internal weakness and unlikely to last." Pearl Buck,* in an effort to gray down the rosy pictures being painted in America by the generalissimo's wife, wrote Eleanor Roosevelt that the Chinese people would rebel against their government as soon as they recovered from the war.

There was certainly a vast disconnect between the China that Americans were hearing about from the Madame and the reality of the situation in the Middle Kingdom. Journalists posted to Chungking were required to obtain credentials from the Chinese War Department and, to do so, had to sign agreements promising to run their stories by the censors before sending them home—a practice that inevitably led to reportorial inhibition and self-censorship. "Probably never before," Tuchman said, "had the people of one country viewed the government of another under misapprehension so complete."

A more specific and personal form of censorship plagued Theodore White, who traveled to the province of Honan, north of the Yangtze River, to report on the famine of 1942–1943, one of the worst in Chinese history. It is estimated that some 2 million to 3 million people died of starvation and disease, and an equal number fled the province. In his original story for *Time,* White wrote about the "stupidity and inefficiency" of the relief efforts as well as the unconscionable practice by local officials of continuing to collect taxes from starving peasants. The government in Chungking, he said, preserved its "bland equanimity" in the face of this human disaster, since all

---

* Raised in China, Buck was the first woman to win the Pulitzer Prize for Fiction with her novel about Chinese peasants and the land, *The Good Earth.*

it cared about was the money. Only too aware of the ongoing tragedy, it failed to act until too late and then sent wads of paper money instead of food to citizens reduced to cannibalism.

It should come as no surprise, considering that Madame's picture had appeared on the cover of *Time* just three weeks earlier, that statements to this effect were cut out of White's article when it was published in the magazine. But some of the more arresting phrases did survive Luce's blue pencil, those having to do with "dogs eating human bodies by the road" and "peasants seeking dead human flesh under the cover of darkness." There was also a description of a banquet given for White and a fellow reporter by the Honan tax collectors—"one of the finest and most sickening banquets" the journalist said he had ever attended. It consisted of "sliced lotus, peppered chicken, beef, and water chestnut . . . spring rolls, hot wheat buns, rice, bean curd, and fish . . . two soups and three cakes with sugar frosting." After she read *Time*'s coverage of the famine, May-ling asked her friend Henry Luce to fire White. He refused.

When White returned to Chungking, he asked Ching-ling to help him get an interview with Chiang Kai-shek. To do this, May-ling's sister told the generalissimo that "the matter involved the lives of many millions." She then gave some advice to the journalist before the meeting: "May I suggest that you report conditions as frankly and fearlessly as you did to me. If heads must come off, don't be squeamish about it . . . otherwise there would be no change in the situation."

White met Chiang in his office, where the G-mo stood "erect and slim, taut, holding out a stiff hand of greeting." He listened to White, as the reporter put it, "with visible distaste because his meddling sister-in-law insisted he had to." White told him about the people who were dying, about the taxes they were being forced to pay, and about the extortion in the province. Chiang replied that the peasants were not being taxed: "he had ordered that taxes be remitted in distress areas." White quoted what he had heard from the peasants. Chiang turned to one of his aides. "They see a foreigner and tell him anything," he said.

It soon became clear to White that Chiang had no idea what was happening outside Chungking. To bring him down to earth, White tried to tell him about the cannibalism, but he answered that this was impossible. White told him he had seen dogs eating dead people at the side of the road.

That was also impossible, according to Chiang. White, who had asked a colleague to accompany him, told his friend to bring in photographs of what they had seen. The pictures showed dogs standing by "dug-out corpses." According to White, "The Generalissimo's knee began to jiggle slightly . . . as he asked where this picture had been taken. We told him. . . . He asked for names of officials; he wanted more names; he wanted us to make a full report to him, leaving out no names . . . he said that he had <u>told</u> the army to share its grain with the people. Then he thanked us; told me that I was a better investigator than 'any of the investigators I have sent on my own.' . . . Heads, I know, did roll . . . lives were saved—and saved by the power of the American press." There was, however, only one mention of the famine in the Chinese press. Published in *Ta Kung Pao,* which White called "the greatest paper in China," the report included a "powerful" description of the suffering peasants but skirted the corruption and inefficiency of the local officials. Nevertheless, it was shut down by the government for three days after the article appeared.

The efficiency with which the Chungking government silenced the offending paper was equaled only by its speed in printing a book written by Chiang and published in March 1943. He had started writing it in November, as soon as May-ling left for the United States, and after four months, it appeared. Entitled *China's Destiny,* the generalissimo's book looked back with nostalgia to the days of Confucius and blamed the foreign powers for all of China's ills: opium, gangsterism, warlords, prostitution, and the chaos following the revolution. *China's Destiny* was, among other things, a particularly ungrateful response to treaties, signed just two months before, in which the United States and Britain had voluntarily given up their old territorial privileges in Shanghai and Peiping.

Starting with a picture of a China that had never existed—a country where battles were fought only "to help the weak and support the fallen" in a country that "benefits other people by extending her blessings and asking nothing in return"—the generalissimo's opus was hailed in Chungking as the most important book since Sun Yat-sen's *Three Principles of the People.* It was supposed to have sold 500,000 copies before it was pulled from circulation for what was euphemistically termed "revision." When an English translation was finally issued, an undertaking that gave those involved "chills and fever," many of the most offensive parts had been cut. Still, no less an authority than China expert John Fairbank declared himself "appalled" by Chiang's work. "I never saw a more pernicious use of history for political purposes," he said. ". . . The book is a tract unworthy of a statesman." Another American said that Hollington Tong's office had pleaded "with the Embassy to use its influence to keep any dissemination of the contents from the American public," and the edition available in the United States was reduced to a four-page summary. We must assume that if May-ling had been in Chungking at the time, she might have been able to stop Chiang from publishing *China's Destiny*—or, at a minimum, soften its xenophobia.

Since Chiang had not been invited to the Casablanca summit and

Roosevelt needed his approval for reviving the ground campaign to recon-
quer Burma, now labeled ANAKIM, the president sent a high-level group of
military brass, including General Hap Arnold of the U.S. Air Force, General
Brehon B. Somervell, chief of the Army Service Forces, and Sir John Dill,
the British representative of the Combined Chiefs of Staff, to see him in
January 1943. They started their tour at British headquarters in Delhi, where,
in Arnold's words, Wavell's "plan" for the Burma campaign consisted of
"several pages of well written paragraphs, telling why the mission could not
be accomplished." Their visit to China was at least as disillusioning. Formerly an admirer of Chennault's Flying Tigers, Arnold was "astonished" that
Chennault himself "was not realistic about the logistics of his operations."
After several meetings with Stilwell, Chennault, and the G-mo, Arnold reported that Chiang "would not listen to logic or reason," that he refused to
accept a promise of 5,000 tons of equipment per month to be delivered over
the Hump, and that both he and Chennault "glossed over" necessities like
fuel and airfield maintenance. Chiang had, in fact, recently come up with
new demands: 10,000 tons a month over the Hump, autonomy of command for Chennault, and five hundred combat planes for China within a
period of nine months. "Tell your President," he told Arnold, "that unless I
get these three things I cannot fight this war and he cannot count on me to
have our Army participate in the campaigns." After he returned to the States,
Arnold wrote Stilwell a letter. "Dear Joe," it began, "You have one S.O.B.
of a job."

Arnold left Chungking convinced that Chiang Kai-shek "brushed too
many important things aside" and was conspicuously lacking in "a global
outlook. His only thought was: 'Aid to China! Aid to China!' " He said that
"Dill agreed with him in his estimate of Chiang, but suggested that perhaps
the absence of Madame Chiang Kai-shek had had an effect; perhaps her influence on the Generalissimo would have made a difference." In the end, it
was Dill the Britisher who convinced Chiang to join Operation ANAKIM—
a commitment the generalissimo repeated in a letter to Roosevelt along with
a rundown of his demands.

While Chiang hesitated, Chennault's public relations man, columnist
Joseph Alsop, tried to undercut Stilwell's Burma campaign in what Fairbank
called the journalist's "poison pen style." Alsop, who believed in reporters as
advocates, never hesitated to use his family connection to the Roosevelts
to bombard the White House with his ideas. Well aware of this, T. V. Soong
and Claire Chennault had wooed him assiduously, and Alsop had gone to
work for Chennault's American Volunteer Group in October 1941, doing
everything from public relations to procurement of supplies. As one old
China hand put it, "Alsop was Chennault's hatchet man." Caught by the

Japanese in Hong Kong at the time of Pearl Harbor, Alsop had spent seven months in a prison camp followed by a period of recuperation in the United States. During his incarceration, it was T.V. who had kept his family informed about him, and when Alsop returned to Chungking, T.V. introduced him around the city as "a cousin of President Roosevelt." For his part, Alsop advised T.V.—thirty wires in three months—to get more supplies for Chennault, and he warned the White House of an "apocalypse in Asia" unless the U.S. government arranged for the material to be sent. He contended that Stilwell's ground campaign was "grandiose" and "dangerous" and that by pursuing it, the United States was passing up a "brilliant and easy opportunity in the air." At one point Alsop even tried to convince Roosevelt that Stilwell wanted a Communist victory in China. Alsop was not the only Chennault supporter. During the previous summer, Henry Luce had put Chennault on the cover of *Life* magazine, along with an article by journalist Jack Belden, who called Chennault "the one genius that war on the Asiatic mainland has yet produced."

❦

ONE OF THE reasons that May-ling had not left the United States in early May, when her husband asked her to come home, was that she had wanted to be around for the next summit between Roosevelt and Churchill, which took place in Washington from May 11 to May 27, 1943. Code-named TRIDENT, it was the second big meeting of the year (Casablanca being the first) and the largest of the strategy-setting conferences held so far during World War II. Returning to New York just as Churchill arrived in Washington, Madame Chiang contacted him immediately, sending word that she would be delighted to receive him at her suite in the Waldorf. To save Churchill the extra trip and to improve the strained relations between England and China, Roosevelt invited her to lunch at the White House—an invitation that both Chiang and T.V. urged her to accept. "Churchill is really physically unable to come to New York," T.V. wrote her, "and the President's idea of giving a luncheon for you both is an excellent way out. I saw the President today and he again inquired if you will attend; after all we must remember that we are all in this country as his guests." Complimenting his sister on "the part you have played . . . in moulding Chinese relations with the Western world," he reminded her that "it is most important that we keep on friendly relations with the British and you could make a real contribution now."

But the G-mo's wife declined to go to Washington and suggested Hyde Park as a compromise, Churchill responded that he was too busy in Washington to come to New York, and everyone blamed the Madame for being temperamental. Her nephew David Kung, who carried diplomatic papers in spite of the fact that he was neither tactful nor schooled in diplomacy, told Ambassador Koo that "as a Lady, Mme Chiang should be called on by Churchill, and as a statesman, she could meet him only half way," i.e., at Hyde Park. During the negotiations, she herself was quoted by Koo as saying that "Great Britain must realize that China of today is no longer the China of yesterday and she should not accept the same old, paternal patronizing attitude toward her." Whatever May-ling was trying to prove, the Roosevelts' invitation was refused "with some hauteur," leaving the president "somewhat vexed." However, according to Churchill, "in the regretted absence of Madame Chiang Kai-shek, the president and I lunched alone in his room and made the best of things."

If May-ling thought it was beneath her dignity to go to Washington to lunch with the British prime minister, she wanted to be in the center of things when the war material was passed out, and, much to Roosevelt's annoyance, she moved back into the White House for the duration of TRIDENT. T.V. was also in the capital and, as China's foreign minister, emphasized Chiang's need for planes and supplies. When asked to explain China's attitude to the assembled leaders, T.V. said that the generalissimo would not go along with the Burma campaign unless the British agreed to try to recapture Rangoon; he also said that the Chinese would make a separate peace with Japan if the necessary armaments were not forthcoming. Roosevelt reacted as T.V. had hoped, saying that the Allies must not be "responsible for the collapse of China."

Meanwhile, back in China, the G-mo was feeling left out. According to an American officer at the embassy, "In conversation with one of the officials who is very close to Generalissimo Chiang Kai-shek, he said he failed to understand the reason why no effort had been made to arrange a meeting between Generalissimo Chiang and President Roosevelt. . . . He admitted that Chiang could have asked for such a conference but that he refrained from doing so on account of 'face,' which is still the predominating force in the Chinese political and social world." Chiang's distress had doubtless been exacerbated by a wire from T.V. stating that it was "on record that in the British and American council held last Friday, General Stilwell criticized Generalissimo Chiang openly for being hesitant in making decisions, and having no definite views on military strategy."

It was clear from the start of TRIDENT that Roosevelt and Churchill disagreed on China. There was also a split within the American camp itself, with Marshall supporting Stilwell and Harry Hopkins on the side of Chennault. As Marshall tried to explain to the president, Chennault had been "for many years a paid employee of the Chinese Government and hence under the undue influence of the G-mo." Chiang had asked Roosevelt to call Chennault back to Washington for talks that would not include Stil-well, but Marshall had countered with a request to the president to bring both men home to the States to fight it out: "To call in Chennault and ig-nore Stilwell, which is the probable purpose of the Generalissimo's propo-sal, would . . . necessitate Stilwell's relief, and Chennault's appointment to command of ground and air, which so far as I am concerned would be a grave mistake." *The New York Times,* reacting to the anti-Stilwell campaign leaking out of the White House, welcomed the general's return. "We hope he gets what he wants," it said in an editorial praising Stilwell for "his un-equaled fitness for his post. . . . He makes no blunders," the paper claimed. "He commits no offenses against etiquette," it added hopefully, and then, in a burst of specious improvisation, "from the Generalissimo down, they all like him."

Up until that point, Stilwell had been allotting three eighths of the Lend-Lease supplies to Chennault's air force and five eighths to the ground forces and everything else—a division of goods to which the generalissimo ob-jected. Claiming he could wipe out Japan's air superiority if given the where-withal, Chennault was asking for nearly all the material coming over the Hump, while Stilwell argued that an air assault uncoordinated with a ground offensive would only spur the Japanese to bomb the airfields in China, which the Chinese army was obviously incapable of defending. But Stilwell faltered when it came to presenting his case before the president at the White House. Although he had prepared a "cogent and forceful brief," once in the Oval Office, he hunched himself over his papers and became, if not sullen to the point of rudeness, totally inarticulate, so much so that Roosevelt thought he might be ill. For some unfathomable reason, Stilwell seemed to feel that he could not and should not lower himself to state the obvious to the president of the United States, who, he knew, did not particularly like him. After Stilwell's miserable presentation, Roosevelt ordered that Chen-nault's requests must have first priority. The president, according to Stilwell, based his decision on a "total misapprehension of the character, intentions, authority and ability of Chiang Kai-shek," and wrote in his private "Black Book" that "The Madame put it over FDR like a tent. He's a sucker for a skirt."

During the course of the TRIDENT conference, Roosevelt asked both Stilwell and Chennault what they thought of the inscrutable Chinese leader. "He's a vacillating tricky undependable old scoundrel who never keeps his word," Stilwell replied. "Sir," Chennault countered, "I think the Generalis-simo is one of the two or three greatest military and political leaders in the world today. He has never broken a commitment or promise made to me."

Since neither Roosevelt nor Churchill was anxious to put any effort into

Operation ANAKIM, it was temporarily shelved, and those in attendance at
TRIDENT agreed to try to get 7,000 tons of gas and munitions over the
Hump for July, building up to 10,000 by September. Chennault was to be
given the first 4,700 tons each month, with the next 2,000 destined for everything else—making it practically impossible for Stilwell to mount his ground
campaign.

Another factor in Stilwell's defeat might be traced to a cable sent by T.V.
to Chiang two weeks before the meeting in the Oval Office, in which T.V.
said that "Sister [May-ling] will be arriving at Washington D.C. on Monday.
I will ask her to join me in lobbying the President." The Soong team was
obviously convincing, because Hopkins congratulated T.V., as did Alsop,
who wrote saying that "against overwhelming odds . . . you have succeeded
in obtaining infinitely more for China and Chennault than the most optimistic of us could have hoped when we started the fight." T.V. also bragged
to the G-mo that "when Stilwell returns to China, his stance may not be as
arrogant as before. If any misunderstanding occurs in the future, the Generalissimo might feel comfortable to telegraph [the president] and ask to
replace Stilwell at any time."

T.V. did not stop there. In a conversation with Stanley Hornbeck, the
chief of the Division of Far Eastern Affairs of the State Department, he
claimed that "the Chinese find it very difficult to work with General Stilwell"
and that they "feel that . . . an officer needs to have personal, political and
diplomatic assets in addition to his qualifications as a soldier." Just as scath-
ing is a memorandum in T.V.'s files, dated August 1943, enumerating
Stilwell's "bad or questionable" decisions, most of which involve his not
procuring enough planes for China and concluding with the following assessment: "General Stilwell is a fine man. He does not smoke, drink, or
chew. He would make a typical highly-regarded Boy Scout leader in any
country . . . there can be no doubt that General Stilwell is completely unfit-
ted to be a major military leader in China." A month later, T.V. wired Chiang,
"It is my opinion that General Stilwell must be recalled at any cost," and
again, shortly thereafter, "General Stilwell should be replaced immediately."

T.V.'s friend Joe Alsop told the story of the TRIDENT decision from an
entirely different perspective. According to Alsop, from the very beginning
of the conference, May-ling had been trying "to persuade Hopkins, and
through Hopkins the president, to communicate with her instead of with
her brother [T.V.], the Foreign Minister." Alsop was apparently at the office
of China Defense Supplies when Madame burst in and "cried triumphantly,
'I have won for China! I have got the generalissimo everything he wants!'"
T.V. asked her to come into his office, where they remained for an hour, and
when May-ling finally emerged, Alsop, who had manufactured some excuse

to stay around to watch the fireworks, wrote that "the thunder clouds accompanying her were all but visible" as she walked away. Madame, according to Alsop, had been sold a bill of goods by Roosevelt, and it subsequently took some skillful maneuvering on T.V.'s part to get Chiang to cable the president that his wife "had no right to negotiate on his behalf" and to kindly return to his original request for "an increase in supply over the Hump as well as an additional 80 fighter planes and 40 bombers to operate under Chennault's command."

Later, after they had all returned to China, Alsop claimed that May-ling invited him to tea for the express purpose of getting him to back up her claim to her husband that it was she, not T.V., who had been responsible for Roosevelt's largesse: "you must remember, Mr. Alsop, how I saved the day for China when the conference [TRIDENT] was going the other way. You remember how I got the generalissimo everything he wanted?" she inquired in what Alsop characterized as "sweetly stern" tones. Alsop panicked. "I cannot," he said, "recall feeling so trapped socially on any other occasion in my life. Fortunately, I remembered one of my mother's . . . contemporaries," a lady whom he claimed to have heard "converse at great length without using a single word. Her method was to intone 'Mmmmm mmmmm' emphatically or soothingly or with horror . . . but always noncommittally. So I borrowed this device. . . . I do not think that Mme. Chiang ever forgave me, and I myself came away with a deep conviction that Mme. Chiang would do in her brother T. V. Soong whenever the opportunity arose." Alsop, who always sided with T.V. in the Soong family feud, did not like his youngest sister: "I finally came to the conclusion that Mme. Chiang was one of the most coldhearted and self-centered women I have known," he said. "At base, she always struck me as artificial. I often had the impression that I was being purposely charmed, the purpose being to make later use of me."

In spite of his inability or unwillingness to try to convince the president of the necessity of ground support for the air forces, Stilwell had managed to present his point of view to a number of senators, congressmen, members of Roosevelt's cabinet, and several leading journalists while he was in Washington. Churchill asked him to come to the British Embassy to, as he put it, "get acquainted," and since Stilwell felt he was speaking to someone who wanted to hear what he had to say, he spoke well and impressed the British prime minister. Churchill not only agreed with him on the lethargy and defeatism prevalent at British military headquarters in India but later said that he had "great respect and liking for General Stilwell."

Returning to China, Stilwell still faced the difficulties of getting deliveries over the Hump up to 10,000 tons a month. One of the big problems was morale. Not only were the C-46 planes "full of bugs," but the men knew that

the Chinese were reselling on the black market much of the material the
Americans were risking their lives to transport. American soldiers called the
U.S. government "Uncle Chump from over the Hump" and referred to
Chiang Kai-shek as "Chancre Jack." According to one veteran of the war,
"The planes were being seriously overloaded with blackmarket material to be
sold on the streets of Kunming. The result was that we had an inordinately
high number of crashes as time went on, and sulfanilamide [an early antibi-
otic] could be bought on the streets of Kunming while Chinese troops in the
field were dying of infection." According to Tuchman, there was apparently
nothing "from medicine to half-ton trucks [that was] not for sale on the
black markets of Kunming," and this sort of thievery "could hardly have
been accomplished without American connivance. . . . Smuggling of gold,
sulfa drugs, foreign currency, cigarets, gems and PX supplies was carried on
by American Air Force, Army, Red Cross and civilian personnel for an estimated take of over $4,000,000 by the end of 1944."

Kunming, capital of the southwestern province of Yunnan, had become
the home of Chennault's AVG after the loss of the Burma Road. Called by
White a "medieval cesspool," it was an even more primitive city than Chungking before the war—a major center of the opium trade, where rich families
bought female slaves for their households and prostitutes were kept confined
in a street cut off at each end by chains, called Slit Alley. Now it was riddled
with black marketeers who dealt in goods stolen by the Chinese and Americans. "Some of the Chinese here are planning to co-operate with a few Americans in the Volunteer Group with the hope that they could utilise the
American Volunteer Group trucks to smuggle goods into China from Burma
and sell them here at market price," Chennault was informed by his secretary
in December 1941. Meanwhile, everything from raspberry jam to liquor,
cigarettes, and toilet articles vanished from the depot where supplies were
kept for the use of the AVG.

Kunming was also a town of bordellos. Since the Japanese, Prussians,
and French all "had whorehouses for their troops," Chennault decided that
the Americans needed one too. As he explained to White, "That whore-
house of mine, that's worrying me. . . . The boys have got to get it, and they
might as well get it clean as get it dirty." With only eighty planes at his
disposal, half of which were too often grounded because their crews were
hospitalized with venereal infections,* the commander of the American Volunteer Group sent a U.S. plane with a medical team to India, where they
recruited twelve young women, who were inspected by the medics, found to

---

* A report as of April 1942 lists fourteen men in the AVG with various forms of venereal
disease, causing a loss of seventy-six days of work.

be free of disease, and brought back to Kunming. Stilwell got wind of what was going on and ordered the establishment closed. "Officers pimping," he wrote in his diary. "Hauling whores in our planes. Sent for Chennault. He knew." Stilwell also recorded his version of the facts in his "Black Book" under a section titled "Chenault's whore-house," noting that on June 24, 1943, he had received a wire from Dorn saying that a Captain Reed was in India, "selecting tarts for 14th A.F. house in K.M. [Kunming]. Capt. Howard brought in 13 on transport plane to-day. . . . Questioned Chennault. . . . Admitted he knew that Chinese were setting up house for e.m. [enlisted men]. . . . Denied that any officer was concerned. . . . Dorn told Glenn to investigate & ship women back. . . . Undoubtably [sic] Chennault knew officers were concerned. He probably sent Reed down to pick the damsels. He probably authorized the transportation. He probably lies to me about it.— Radioed G.C.M. [George C. Marshall]."

Despite his feud with Chennault, Stilwell managed to increase tonnage over the Hump from 3,000 tons in May to an amazing 13,000 in November. The gain was accomplished at the expense of the construction of a road from Ledo in northeast India to connect with the Burma Road in China—a project started just before Stilwell's appointment—from which manpower and equipment had to be diverted to work on the airfields. But by the middle of the summer of 1943, it was obvious that no matter what was done, the capacity of the road and the Hump together would never suffice to provide enough fuel and supplies for both the troops on the ground and Chennault's air transport. It was therefore decided to build a pipeline from Calcutta to Kunming. It would be "the longest pipeline through the worst territory in the world" and was referred to as "Pipe Dream" by those given the task of building it.

There was one problem, however, that amused Stilwell, who was far from the most forgiving man on the planet. It was Chennault, who, now that his demands had been fulfilled, suddenly started "screaming for help" because, in his words, "The Japs are going to run us out of China!" Stilwell laughed, noting in his diary that six months earlier, Chennault had sworn that "he was going to run them out." The reason for Chennault's panic was that his attacks on Japanese merchant shipping had incited Japan into bombing Chinese air bases—exactly what Stilwell had always predicted would happen.

39

My Chinese friends sometimes asked, "Why do you Americans work with a man like Tai Li?"

—OLIVER J. CALDWELL, OSS OFFICER

MADAME CHIANG did not return from America to China until the summer of 1943, when she had what the local newspapers optimistically called "a joyful reunion with her husband." Although she came home in the same style as she had left—courtesy the U.S. Army Air Forces—it had taken more than a dozen letters from Harry Hopkins at the White House, the chief of the Air Staff of the War Department, and the commander of the U.S. Army Air Forces to arrange her trip and the transport of her luggage with her nephew David Kung. "The President wants her to have a DC-4 take her all the way back to China," Hopkins wrote General Arnold. "It will be necessary to have two bunks prepared in the plane. . . . I know this is an awful headache but I am afraid it has to be done."

With all the preparation—arranging to have the same TWA crew as had flown her from China to the United States, making sure the berths were surrounded by drapes and so on—the flight home turned out to be a precarious one. The plane hit bad weather over India, headed for Calcutta, and, in trying to find the Gaya airport northwest of the city, got in touch with the enemy instead. "We thought we were going to land at Gaya, but the pilots suddenly discovered that we were over Japanese-occupied territory in Burma," Madame later explained. Asked if she had been informed of the danger, she answered that she "was feeling so sick at that moment that I did not care where we landed." According to one of her American pilots, "The weather was rough as the devil and she was in a pretty bad way. She didn't say a word the entire trip." From India, the plane proceeded over the mountains at an altitude of 24,000 feet to Chungking, and during the last leg of the flight, the passengers had to use oxygen masks. It took seven days and five nights to get her home, and she arrived in Chungking complaining of being "weary and airsick."

"The generalissimo had flown to Chengtu to meet me," Madame Chiang said, "as he did not know we were going to land in Chungking. I was so sick on arrival that I did not mind not being met." Her niece Jeanette felt differently. There were only two American attendants at the airfield when they arrived. "Where the hell is everybody?" she asked as she helped Aunty May into the Americans' station wagon, pulling one of the men (a mechanic) out by his arm and taking the wheel herself. She then put her aunt, who was by this time in tears, into the car and drove away. In true Chinese fashion, Madame's arrival, complete with welcoming husband and appropriate fanfare, was later reenacted for the newsreel cameras.

❦

IN SPITE OF the fact that she was still pale from her ordeal at a news conference held six days later in the darkened drawing room of her home, May-ling had managed to be at Chiang's side two or three days earlier, dressed in a chic sleeveless print dress, for a ceremony at which he received the American Legion of Merit. "Peanut was half an hour late," complained Stilwell, who was furious at having to bestow the award, which Roosevelt thought would make up for a lack of supplies. ". . . He was ill at ease during the performance. I read the Chinese citation & made my speech in Chinese." Stilwell later wrote his wife, "When I grabbed his coat and pinned it on, he jumped as if he was afraid I was going to stab him." Stilwell also had a few choice words for May-ling: "Mme. present & full of herself & what she's going to get out of the President. Said he had promised two divisions." Stilwell was annoyed that the crew of May-ling's plane had arrived at the ceremony with Chinese decorations around their necks, bestowed in appreciation for their performance on her trip home. "What a gag. They get decorated, but nobody in our headquarters has been except E* . . . for being in a plane crash."

Another jaundiced reaction to May-ling's homecoming came from sister Ching-ling: "M.L. looks so Fifth Avenue and behaves so '400' that we have found she has undergone a great physical change," Ching-ling wrote a friend in New York.

> . . . She seems very adaptable and takes on the colors of her surroundings easily, in that way she is remarkably like Clare Boothe. Whatever one may say, she has given widest publicity to China's cause and as she herself remarked to a gathering of admiring throng, "I have shown the Americans that China is not made up entirely of coolies and laundrymen!" I suppose China must be grateful for that. The crew of her plane related what a lot of trunks she brought in, and the amount of tinned food, etc. But I haven't seen a single

---

* An unidentified flyer.

can of baked beans or . . . pair of shoes. I am told that she has no room for them so my shoes will be brought on "the next plane." Hooray! . . . after the war, I suppose. Seriously the immediate result of her trip was the decision by the Gissimo to start an anti-CP [Communist Party] campaign in America.

Ching-ling's pique may well have been based on the fact that she too had received several invitations to visit the United States but had not been allowed to go abroad. She believed that this was a result of a report she had written, published in the British Labour Party magazine, *Reynold's Weekly,* and sent to various people in the States, complaining about Chiang's blockade of Communist troops in Yennan and calling for its removal. She had subsequently endured visits from three KMT leaders who had criticized her for "washing China's dirty linen in the foreign press." According to U.S. diplomat John Service, she knew that her family was "very annoyed" with her, but, as she put it, "All they can do is to keep me from traveling." Service, who served as second secretary at the U.S. Embassy, described Ching-ling's life in Chungking as being "outside the pale. People," he said, "were able to get in and see her, but they had to be willing to be in the doghouse."

Although she sided with the Communists, Ching-ling seldom hesitated to allow her sisters to provide her with luxuries from the capitalist world. The Soong sisters were all addicted to lovely things, and it was Ai-ling who usually provided them for the other two. "I'm always thinking about whether you have all the things you need for your comfortable and happy life. . . . Please . . . ask for anything you might need," Ai-ling wrote Ching-ling a few years later. And again:

I wonder if you have received the black coat I bought for you not long ago. I gave May-ling a long overcoat (made of silk). . . . The one I gave you is suitable to wear in the spring. . . . I asked Wang Z to send you several amethysts including a pair of earrings, three buttons and a ring. In addition there is a beautiful black coat with a fur lining, material for four dresses, and a black handbag. . . . H.H. has something for you as well, maybe two pairs of gold earrings. Please send me the prescription for your eyes by the Russian doctor. . . . If you need money, please ask. Have you got the liquid for hair-growing and the eyebrow pencil. Be sure to tell me.

May-ling had returned in an American military plane, but her baggage had to be transferred to other planes in Assam to lighten the load over the

Hump. According to author Graham Peck, who was working for the Office of War Information in China at the time:

> This [transfer] was done in a rather remote part of the field, and the GI's who were doing it happened to drop one crate. It split open and its contents rolled out . . . it was full of cosmetics, lingerie, and fancy groceries with which Madame Chiang planned to see herself through the rest of the war. The GI's were furious, for this was one of the times when the Hump transport was in a bad state, with many American fliers losing their lives to get war supplies to China. The soldiers dropped and broke all the other crates they transhipped. When they had kicked every fur coat and trick clock around in the dust as thoroughly as time would permit they threw the mess into the waiting planes.

❦

Two DAYS AFTER receiving the Legion of Merit, Chiang agreed to take part in the ground campaign to reenter Burma. "After a year of constant struggle, we have finally nailed him down," Stilwell wrote triumphantly in his diary. ". . . What corruption, intrigue, obstruction, delay, double-crossing hate, jealousy and skulduggery we have had to wade through." But according to Tuchman, even Stilwell had finally begun to take cognizance of what always held Chiang back. As he wrote Marshall, looking at the situation from the generalissimo's point of view, "it would be risky to have an efficient trained ground force come under the command of a possible rival."

In the middle of August 1943, Roosevelt and Churchill met at Quebec, where they set D-Day for May 1, 1944, and reorganized the Southeast Asia Command (SEAC). T.V., who had been lobbying for China to be named one of the four Great Powers and included in the Munitions Assignment Board, came to the conference in order to determine the status of his requests. The Americans and British, who were having enough trouble agreeing with each other, refused T.V. on the ground that adding China would have meant including the Soviet Union, which was not possible since the Soviets were not yet at war with Japan; they also knew that the countries of Western Europe were unlikely to accept decisions made by China; and, finally, they did not trust the Chinese government to keep a secret.

The day before the conference ended, Roosevelt and Churchill invited T.V. to lunch. Before they sat down, the president spoke to T.V. "in a confidential manner" about his difficulties with the prime minister. After his arrival, Churchill informed T.V. that the British government had appointed Lord Louis Mountbatten, a member of the royal family, as the new commander in chief in the Far East. T.V., whom Churchill had introduced to Mountbatten in London, wired Chiang that "he is indeed an able man . . . young and energetic" and "has long admired Your Excellency." Before he left the lunch, T.V. was warned not to mention Mountbatten's appointment in his dispatches back home.

There had been a series of "bad leaks" during recent months in Chungking, one of which was a highly important dispatch from the American chargé d'affaires to Washington that wound up in Chinese hands. That fact plus T.V. Soong's boast—"No conference takes place regarding which I do not have accurate and complete information"—had worried Lauchlin Currie enough to send a warning note to the White House. Moreover, the Americans had learned that the Japanese had broken the Chinese code, but the British refused to pass this information along to T.V., lest he radio it to Chiang Kaishek. Marshall finally called T.V. in to swear him to secrecy—with upraised hand—before telling him that the Chinese code had been broken and that if he radioed this information to Chungking, he would be finished.

One of the theories behind the American concern about sharing information with the Chinese was a strong suspicion that the head of the Chinese Secret Service, Tai Li, was exchanging intelligence with the Japanese and their puppet government in Nanking. The Office of Strategic Services (OSS) was of two minds about Tai Li. One side, under the command of a naval captain named Milton Miles, worked with Tai's secret police in an organization called the Sino-American Cooperation Organization (SACO), arming and training Chinese soldiers. The other side, those who did not trust the head of the Chinese Secret Service, told stories like the one about two OSS officers who were teaching the art of guerrilla warfare to their Chinese counterparts near the Yellow River. Although SACO rules prohibited the Americans from engaging actively in combat, their Chinese students got so excited that they blew up enough of a bridge to delay a Japanese assault for three months. Not only were the Americans recalled by Tai Li, who was in charge of SACO, and reprimanded for usurping authority, but the Chinese group was forcefully disbanded. As one member of the OSS put it, "The only logical conclusion was that Tai Li did not want either his own men or the Americans . . . to fight the Japanese." By late summer 1943, the OSS had proof that Tai Li was withholding important information from Miles, and William "Wild Bill" Donovan, head of the OSS, arrived in Chungking to dissolve SACO. T.V. gave a dinner for Donovan at which, according to eyewitnesses, most of the men drank far too much:

Only Donovan and Tai Li drank little or nothing and remained cool and collected. The two great spymasters competed in charm, each smiling and urbane, each so very agreeable.... Then ... Donovan bluntly informed Tai Li that if the OSS could not perform its mission in cooperation with him, the OSS would operate separately.

"If OSS tries to operate outside SACO," said the smiling Tai Li, "I will kill your agents."

"For every one of our agents you kill," said Donovan, "we will kill one of your generals."

"You can't talk to me like that," said Tai Li.

"I am talking to you like that," said Donovan evenly.

The OSS chief smiled but a chill that even the most besotted diner soon recognized settled over the room. The party broke up.

Donovan then severed U.S. ties with Tai Li's Secret Service.

One of the most powerful men in China, Tai Li also directed the Smuggling Prevention Office, a government operation under the Ministry of Finance that employed 60,000 men. Like Chiang's Opium Suppression Commission, Tai Li's Smuggling Prevention Office was a cover for major squeeze. May-ling became involuntarily involved with it through something that came to be called the Lin Shiliang Case.

Lin Shiliang was a confidential assistant to H. H. Kung, whom he had met under the auspices of Big-Eared Du. Lin was employed by the Trust Bureau of the Central Bank, and his job was to purchase military goods abroad and arrange to have them brought into China through Hong Kong. Kung's eldest son, David, who was manager of the Trust Bureau in Hong Kong, also used Lin Shiliang to "manage" the transportation of goods over the Burma Road after its completion.

The Lin Shiliang Case involved a group of speculators and war profiteers who commissioned Lin's assistant to transport tires and other valuable goods over the Burma Road to Chungking—a hugely profitable deal in which some of the Kung offspring (David Kung, his sisters, and brother-in-law) were to receive a share of the profits. The shipment was divided into several parts, two of which were seized by agents of Tai Li's Smuggling Prevention Office. When Tai Li called Chiang to report the case, the G-mo, who thought that Lin Shiliang had been using Kung's name to conduct the illegal operation, ordered Lin arrested and sentenced to ten years in prison. When it was discovered that Lin had been spending a great deal of money—personal and public—on drinking, gambling, and women, Chiang ordered him executed by firing squad. But Lin refused to take the rap for Kung's children. He said that the smuggling scheme had been the brainchild of David Kung, who then appealed to his Auntie May. She took the problem to her husband, who decided in favor of his relations, partly because the case had brought the feuding Soongs and Kungs together. Chiang then proceeded with the execution of Lin Shiliang, but he also removed Tai Li from his place as head of the Smuggling Prevention Office. The Americans, who understood nothing about the case, thought that Tai Li's removal was due to the Gestapo tactics of his Secret Service.

❦

DURING THE SUMMER of 1943, what Tuchman calls "the first honest statement" of China's deficiencies began to appear in the American press. A story written by *The New York Times* military correspondent Hanson Baldwin was published in *Reader's Digest* in August. In the article, entitled "Too Much Wishful Thinking About China," Baldwin said that the American people had been oversold on the ability of China to win the war against Japan by a combination of "missionaries, war relief drives, able ambassadors and the movies." According to him, China "has as yet no real army . . . most of her troops are poorly led and incapable of effectively utilizing modern arms. . . . They require intensive and protracted training, and capable leaders bound together by a common loyalty to a common cause. Today there are few such leaders; too many of them are still old war lords, in new clothing, for whom war is a means for personal aggrandizement and enrichment."

A fairly recent book by Paul Fussell—historian, literary critic, and soldier in World War II—labels Chinese public relations during the war as "The Great China Hoax" and confirms its effectiveness. According to Fussell, "Lin Yutang became a vendor of the highest wisdom" and "Mme. Chiang's loveliness and desirability were obvious to all. . . . Wendell Willkie's immensely popular book *One World* published in 1943, helped to solidify the myth of a high-minded, powerful, united 'democratic,' almost Christian, Western-world-loving China."

But perhaps the most informative piece, entitled "Our Distorted View of China," appeared in *The New York Times Magazine* several months after Mayling's return home. Tracing the history of America's unrealistic love affair with China ("it was a democracy pure and Jeffersonian") through the disillusionment of Americans sent to Asia ("China is a Fascist dictatorship. China is vilely corrupt"), author Nathaniel Peffer argued that "every country must be judged by its own standards" and outlined the major reason behind Chinese corruption: "A good deal of what is withheld from public funds by private officials in China is what would be considered elsewhere legitimate compensation for public service." But as for their military, "judged by modern western armies, the Chinese Army is a comic opera chorus."

In that regard, Madame Chiang invited Stilwell to a meeting at her home with sister Ai-ling and herself, the first of several meetings in which the sisters began to manipulate Stilwell under the rubric of concern over the dreadful state of the Chinese army. "Summoned to audience . . . with May & Sis," Stilwell noted in his "Black Book" on September 13, 1943. ". . . Apparently T.V. has told them they had better get behind me & co-operate, as result of G.C.M.'s [General Marshall's] prodding. Alarmed about state of preparations, & hot to do something about it. Gave them the lowdown on conditions in the army, & they were appalled. Told them about blocks & delays & who was responsible. . . . May craves action. . . . Sis said she didn't know how I had the patience to carry on. We signed an offensive & defensive alliance. Whatever the cause, they mean business now & maybe we can get somewhere."

Meanwhile, claiming that the appointment of Mountbatten as head of SEAC made Stilwell unnecessary, T.V. had submitted a plan to Roosevelt to replace him with a Chinese, who would control American Transport Command and all other military units in China. He also asked that China be made part of the Munitions Board in order to have a say in Lend-Lease. In doing this, Tuchman says, T.V. was trying to gain a position of strength for himself and "lead China in Chiang's place."

But, according to George Sokolsky, an ultraconservative journalist and "close associate" of T.V., May-ling's brother, unlike her husband, was no politician. Sokolsky said that T.V. had "over the years striven to build a machine, yet inevitably . . . quarreled with supporter after supporter." T.V., he said, had "always wanted to be head of his family. . . . He resented Chiang and felt that if Chiang hadn't been brought in he would have become unquestionably the head of the civilian side of China's government." Whatever his current aims, T.V. was now fighting for the ultimate power within the family—a phenomenon Tuchman compared to "the same, grim infighting of a reigning family that led to murdered heirs and poisoned nephews in the days of the dynasties."

Thwarted by Marshall in his efforts to oust Stilwell, T.V. had recently returned to China, saying that he had obtained a promise from Roosevelt to send Stilwell home. With this story in hand, he got Chiang to demand Stilwell's recall. But when Mountbatten arrived in Chungking—he brought May-ling a Cartier vanity set with her initials in diamonds—and was told of the generalissimo's demand, he announced that he could not carry out the plans for using Chinese soldiers if the one man who had commanded them for two years was to be removed.

Meanwhile, May-ling and Ai-ling continued to confer with Stilwell. "Lunch & conference with May," he wrote on September 18. "She craves action, wishes she'd been a man, & abominates Ho Y. C. [General Ho] & his gang . . . he had apparently laughed her off because she's a woman & she was

furious. 'Why in God's name that God-damn old fool doesn't do something, I don't know. They are like a lot of ostriches with their heads in the
sand & their bottoms sticking out. How I would like to take a big club and
go after them!' "

They met again two days later, this time with Ai-ling.

May & Ella . . . had been working on the Peanut. . . . May made a
speech today at the People's Political Council meeting & bawled out
critics of people who were doing their stuff. "Don't criticize till you
<u>know</u> mistakes are being made. Don't criticize out of jealousy."
Looking directly at Ho. She enjoyed it. They both say that Ho must
go, but I don't see how they are going to do it. . . . May & Ella have
sworn in as fellow conspirators, & are talking very frankly. They are
convinced that I mean business and they will play ball. And all the
time the Peanut sits on his golden throne & lets us struggle. He's
afraid to take action—that's the only explanation.

Three days passed, and Stilwell was still trying to figure out what lay
behind May-ling and Ai-ling's sudden friendship. "I get more and more the
idea that these two intelligent dames have (1) been told by T. V. Soong to get
behind the U.S. effort, & that (2) the family, less Peanut, realizes the gravity
of the situation . . . the Peanut is even more whimsical & flighty than even I
had thought. May keeps letting it out that he is very hard to handle, that you
have to catch him at the proper moment, that he forms opinions on little
evidence, that 'they' are telling him all sorts of stuff about me." "They" were
disgruntled Chinese generals and members of the KMT, who claimed that
Stilwell was "haughty" and "anti-Chinese" and was behind a plan to push
Chiang out and make T.V. the head of the civilian government so that he,
Stilwell, could fully control the military.

On September 28, Stilwell met again with the sisters. "May let out that
she has a hell of a life with the Peanut," he wrote in his diary; "no one else
will tell him the truth so she is constantly at him with the disagreeable news.
It can't be easy to live with the crabbed little bastard and see everything
balled up."

According to her secretary/stenographer, Pearl Chen, May-ling was, in
fact, extremely frustrated with her husband during this period. Gossiping
with an American informant a week or so later, Chen asserted that "Mme.
Chiang isn't in love with the Generalissimo. In fact, she doesn't care a darn
for him except insofar as it helps her position. Of course she takes pride in
his achievements and her role in building him up from a common soldier
into a national leader. And I'm sure she regards him as a 'great man,' too, but

she doesn't love him. The one person who is closest to her is her sister, Mme. H. H. Kung. They are intimate friends as well as sisters. That's why Mme. Chiang brought that Lesbian, Jeanette Kung . . . along with her from China and appointed David Kung . . . as her Secretary-General on the American tour."

On October 16, Stilwell was told by the chief of the Army Service Forces, General Somervell, "The G-mo says I must be relieved." The next evening, May-ling asked him to come over.

Ella was there. They are a pair of fighters, all right, & Ella said there was still a chance to pull the fat out of the fire. I was noncommittal & calm & told them I did not want to stay where I was not wanted. They talked "China" and duty, etc., and asked me to be big enough to stick it out. Ella said if we put this over my position would be much stronger than before. ("Your star is rising"). . . . What they wanted was for me to see Peanut & tell him I had only one aim,—the good of China, that if I had made mistakes it was from misunderstanding & not intent & that I was ready to co-operate fully. I hesitated a long time, but they made it so strong that I finally said O.K., & May said we'd go right now. Went over and put on the act, the Peanut doing his best to appear conciliatory. . . . Now, why was Ella so sure it would come out O.K.? This P.M. she had attacked the Peanut & he had turned his back & left the room. A hell of an insult but she just waited and he came back. Both she and May went to bat for me. Maybe they got him half-turned around as they claimed, ready for me to complete the act. And maybe the Peanut realized finally what a stink would be raised & decided to reverse himself. . . . But it is suspicious that Ella was so sure that it would come out all right, if I made the advances. As if the thing had been arranged . . . May said everybody expected her to divorce the Peanut within a year after their marriage. Both May & Ella reiterated that they had put [i.e., bet] the family jewels on me, and would continue to back me up.

Another four days passed before Stilwell finally discovered that the driving force behind his unaccomplished removal was T.V., who had twice wired Chiang from Washington that he must be recalled. "He [T.V.] had it all set up with the G-mo, when May & Ella heard of it," Stilwell wrote. "At once there was a hell of a fight. Ella finally told me yesterday that I didn't know the half of it but ultimately would. Said she had to choose between 'her own flesh and blood' (T.V.) and the good of China. Gave me a lot of slop on their size-up of me. Regrets we did not get together a year ago. . . . Says my position is greatly improved & that no further attacks will be made,—positive about this, so I suppose T.V. got a good swat."

Needless to say, the sisters never told Stilwell that their campaign was based on the split in the Song family. According to Alsop, who worked in an annex of Soong's house and saw him when he came home, there was "a tremendous family fight which went on for about two days in the Generalissimo's villa up on the hill. I can recall Dr. Soong coming back from these sessions in a state of complete exhaustion. Madame Kung and Madame Chiang* . . . maintained . . . that American aid for China depended on General Stilwell. . . . The ladies said, 'If you throw the American hero out of command in China, you will become very unpopular with the United States and you won't get any airplanes or any guns, or anything else."

Having failed in his machinations and caused Chiang to lose face, T.V. underwent what John Service called a "dramatic eclipse" vis-à-vis Chiang. According to Stilwell, "there was a fight there and he [T.V.] was told [by Chiang Kai-shek] to be sick and go home." What Stilwell did not realize was that the fight had been about him. Many years later, T.V. told his nephew Leo Soong that he had returned from Washington to inform Chiang that he had finally "secured the unqualified support and understanding of the U.S. Administration" for Stilwell's removal. He met with the G-mo over breakfast, but when he gave him the good news, Chiang said that he had recently seen Stilwell (the meeting arranged by the sisters), who had "pledged that he would be much more cooperative in the future." Hence, Chiang wanted to give him "another chance." T.V. was infuriated. "Are you the chief of an African tribe that you should change your mind so capriciously?" he asked. Chiang became so angry that he slammed his fist on the table, upsetting and breaking dishes. In the opinion of Leo Soong, "Dr. Soong had over stepped the boundaries of normal argumentation or discourse and crossed over into personal insult which failed to respect the office of Chief of State." As punishment for his insubordination, T.V. was forced to stay in seclusion in his home in Chungking—his every move monitored by Chiang's goons—and to remain there while Chiang and May-ling attended the Cairo Conference the following month. On their return, Chiang received the following letter of apology. Dated December 23, 1943, it remains a masterpiece of Chinese *mea culpa*:

"In the past two months," T.V. wrote,

---

* Referred to by Alsop as "these ruthlessly self-centered women." (Alsop with Platt, *I've Seen the Best of It: Memoirs*, p. 223.)

I have isolated myself and undergone deep introspection. My faults and recalcitrances are numerous, and there is no limit of my pain and regret. Although officially our relationship is like a subordinate to a superior, affectionately we are just like one's own flesh and blood.... After the outbreak of the War of Resistance ... the only thing I kept in my mind was to immerse myself in work and, under your guidance, devote my tiny strength to winning the final victory. However, I am a foolish and naive person, and my behavior is always fraught with sharpness and foolhardiness. When it comes to looking at the general situation, I was careless and uncomprehending. What is worse, I have been spoiled by your over-protection and over-affection for me, so that whenever I tried to argue for my position, I was bigoted in my opinions and so tactless that it hurt. These are my ... mistakes, and I must rely on Your Excellency's teaching and inspiration to correct my stubbornness and dullness.... After you admonished me and I repented, I realized how generous you are in giving me the chance to improve myself. Now ... waiting to be punished, I dare not indulge in wishful thinking or improper expectations.... I will only follow Your Excellency's order. I bend down and beg Your Excellency to examine my honest sincerity, and give me instructions ... my loyalty to you will be shining eternally like the blue sky and the white sun.... I anxiously and fearfully submit this letter for Your Excellency's close examination. I respectfully kowtow to Your Excellency and wish you well.

The letter, which must have cost the writer a piece of his soul, led to an attempt at reconciliation, which failed when T.V. criticized the manner in which economic matters were currently being handled in the country, implying that he was the only one competent to run China's finances. He remained out of power until the following June, some nine months later. Even then, although he resumed his job as foreign minister and was named president of the Executive Yuan, he complained about his sister. "Madame Chiang recently told Mrs. Hemingway [writer Martha Gellhorn], who told Mrs. Roosevelt, that the members of the Finance Ministry had not been doing their best under Kung because they were left over from his (T.V.'s) administration.... The people around the Generalissimo are very jealous of me. They would do anything to destroy me. Under these circumstances, how can I work and have the President believe in me?"

Meanwhile, May-ling had started addressing Stilwell as "Uncle Joe."

PART SIX

❦

1943–1945

40

What a gag the Big Four will put on: <u>STALIN</u>, the COMMUNIST, really ap-
proaching the <u>democrat</u>, with <u>capitalistic</u> tinges. <u>ROOSEVELT</u> the <u>DEMOCRAT</u>,
backing Imperialist Britain. <u>CHURCHILL</u> the <u>IMPERIALIST</u>, giving lip ser-
vice to the Atlantic Charter. <u>CHIANG</u> <u>KAI-SHEK</u> the <u>FASCIST</u>, posing as a
democrat.

—GENERAL JOSEPH STILWELL, 1943

THE GENERALISSIMO's first summit meeting with Roosevelt and Churchill, which took place in Cairo during the last week of November 1943, was, according to Crozier, "the climax of Chiang Kai-shek's wartime career in international eyes." With her husband now on a level with the U.S. and British heads of state, Madame Chiang, fully aware of his inadequacies, had insisted that Stilwell accompany them to Egypt in order, as she phrased it, "to put China right with the powers." Fortunately for Chiang, there had been the reconciliation with Stilwell before the conference, carefully engineered by May-ling and her eldest sister.

The protocol for the Cairo meeting had not been easy to establish. Since Russia was not at war with Japan, it was impossible to have one meeting to include all four leaders, and it was decided that Roosevelt and Churchill would meet Chiang in Cairo—the generalissimo insisted on being first—and then move on to confer in Tehran with Stalin, who demanded that "there should be absolutely excluded the participation of the representatives of any other power." One of the purposes of the summit, the largest so far in the war, was to determine how much effort and money should be spent in China to prepare for the oncoming fight with the Japanese. Roosevelt had insisted on inviting Chiang over Churchill's objections. He wanted not only "to keep China in the war tying up the Japanese soldiers" but to lay the groundwork for rapprochements between China and Russia and the two competing political factions in China itself—the KMT and the CCP—thus getting a jump on postwar issues. The president, according to Fairbank, "had a most unrealistic sentimentality about China." This was probably due in large part to growing up in a home surrounded by Chinese artifacts collected over the years by his mother's family, the Delanos. It was, Fairbank said, as if Roosevelt's "trading ancestors had given him possession. He [Roosevelt] tried to dispose of the insoluble China problem by saying that it should take the place of Japan in the East Asian power scene. Meantime he was willing to throw money at the problem in the typical American fashion and hope it would go away."

The other participants in the Cairo Conference were naturally curious about Chiang Kai-shek, who at one point held more than eighty official government positions simultaneously. His arrival at the airport had been kept secret for reasons of security, however, and he was hurt that neither of the other two leaders was there to greet him. For this and other reasons, Roosevelt made an effort to confer at length with him before the sessions got started. The president also insisted that the generalissimo be present at the first meeting of the conference, making it impossible for the British to influence the U.S. position in prior consultations about China. This irritated Churchill, who felt that the attention of the delegates to the conference was "sadly distracted by the Chinese story, which was lengthy, complicated, and minor" but wound up occupying "first instead of last place in Cairo." Nor was the prime minister impressed by the generalissimo. Nevertheless, he had what he called "a very pleasant conversation with Madame Chiang Kai-shek, and found her a most remarkable and charming personality":

Churchill:	You think I'm a terrible old man, don't you?
Mme. Chiang:	I really don't know. You believe in colonialism and I don't.
Churchill (after a long long conversation):	Now tell me what do you think of me?
Mme. Chiang:	I think your bark is worse than your bite.

This was the first time that Roosevelt, Churchill, Hopkins, Marshall, et al. had had to deal with Chiang Kai-shek in person and come to grips with what Stilwell's political adviser, John Paton Davies, Jr., gently referred to as the G-mo's "capriciousness." In an attempt to cover for her husband's lack of knowledge, May-ling, the first woman to attend a conference of the Allied war leaders, insisted on being present at all meetings to translate what he said, explaining that she needed to convey "the full meaning of the thoughts the Generalissimo wishes to express." In spite of this and her efforts to camouflage his ignorance and shifting attitudes, Mountbatten wrote in his diary that Roosevelt, Churchill, and their chiefs of staff were "driven absolutely mad" by Chiang's constant reversals.

Just before the first session of the conference, Stilwell, who had been asked by the Chiangs to make the presentation for China, received a message from the generalissimo saying that he would attend the meeting himself. This was followed by several other messages with Chiang waffling back and forth as to his intentions. Finally, surrounded by his generals, Chiang deigned to appear. "Terrible performance," Stilwell wrote in his diary that evening. "They couldn't ask a question. Brooke* was insulting. I helped them out. They were asked about Yoke [the Y Force of Chinese soldiers, which was supposed to enter Burma from the east] and I had to reply. Brooke fired questions and I batted them back." When Mountbatten presented his views for the Chinese to comment on, Stilwell advised Chiang to stall answering until the next day. In an ill-considered attempt to distract the gentlemen from her husband's poor performance, May-ling, who was wearing a black satin sheath dotted with yellow chrysanthemums, continually arranged and rearranged her feet in order to give glimpses of what Brooke called "the most shapely of legs" via the long slits in her skirt. "This caused a rustle amongst those attending the conference," he wrote, "and I even thought I heard a suppressed neigh come from a group of some of the younger members!"

In his diary, General Brooke wrote that Chiang reminded him "of a cross between a pine marten and a ferret. . . . A shrewd, foxy sort of face. Evidently with no grasp of war in its larger aspects but determined to get the best of the bargains." May-ling, he noted on the first day of the conference, was "a queer character in which sex and politics seemed to predominate, both being used indiscriminately individually or unitedly to achieve her ends." Unlike most men, Brooke did not find her attractive: "Not good looking, with a flat Mongolian face with high cheek bones and a flat, turned up nose with two long circular nostrils looking like two dark holes leading into her head. Jet black hair and sallow complexion. If not good looking she had certainly made the best of herself and was well turned out. . . . Tapered fingers playing with a long cigarette holder in which she smoked continuous cigarettes."

A dozen years later, the English general still remembered the day he met the Chiangs:

This very Chinese day has remained rooted in my memory. I have never known whether Madame Chiang gatecrashed into the

---

* General Alan Francis Brooke (later Viscount Alanbrooke), chief of the Imperial General Staff and principal military adviser to Churchill.

morning's meeting or whether she was actually invited. It makes little difference, for I feel certain she would have turned up whether she was invited or not. She was the only woman amongst a very large gathering of men, and was determined to bring into action all the charms nature had blessed her with . . . she certainly had a good figure which she knew how to display at its best. Also gifted with great charm and gracefulness, every small movement of hers arrested and pleased the eye. . . . The trouble that lay behind all this was that we were left wondering whether we were dealing with Chiang or with Madame. Whenever he [Chiang] was addressed his Chinese General sitting on his right interpreted for him, but as soon as he had finished Madame said "Excuse me gentlemen. I do not think that the interpreter has conveyed the full meaning to the Generalissimo!" Similarly, whenever Chiang spoke his General duly interpreted the statement, but Madame rose to say in the most perfect English, "Excuse me, Gentlemen, but the General has failed to convey to you the full meaning of the thoughts that the Generalissimo wishes to express. If you will allow me I shall put before you his real thoughts." You were left wondering as to whom you were dealing with. I certainly felt that she was the leading spirit of the two and I would not trust her very far. As for Chiang, I think the description I gave of him fits him very well: a shrewd but small man. He was certainly very successful in leading the Americans down the garden path. . . . I often wonder how Marshall failed to realize what a broken reed Chiang was.

Brooke seems to have disapproved of almost all the Americans at the conference. Stilwell, he said, "was nothing more than a hopeless crank with no vision and Chennault a very gallant airman with a limited brain."

On the day before the conference, Churchill's doctor, Lord Moran, was called in to see Madame Chiang in a "well-guarded villa" near Mena House Hotel, where most of the other conferees were staying. He was greeted downstairs by a middle-aged Chinese doctor, who looked both "intelligent and apprehensive"—so much so that, as Moran put it, "I am not sure that his expectation of life was as good as that of his patient." He filled Moran in on May-ling's medical history and explained that she was currently suffering from "nettle-rash," for which over the years she had received every kind of treatment and advice. (She was also complaining about her eyes and her stomach at the time.) The English doctor was then led by the nervous physician upstairs, where he found May-ling in bed. "She is no longer young," he wrote later, "but there is about her an air of distinction; there is still left a certain cadaverous charm." May-ling complained that the rash was keeping her awake at night. After he had finished examining her, she asked what was the matter with her.

"Nothing," he answered.

"Nothing?" she asked with a slight smile. "I shall soon get well, you think?"

"Madame," he replied, "you will only get better when the strain of your life is relaxed."

"I have seen many doctors in the States," she said, scrutinizing the Englishman; "they have all told me stories saying that if I did something I should soon get well. You are about the first honest doctor I have seen." With that, she rang for a servant, who appeared immediately and whom she sent out of the room. After a few minutes, the servant returned with a package, which May-ling presented to the doctor with her thanks. It held an "exquisitely carved" ivory tablet. With the appearance of the gift, Moran, as he phrased it, "saw that the audience had come to an end."

Roosevelt and Hopkins met privately with the Chiangs at least four times during the conference. Although no minutes were kept, we know that the generalissimo asked the president for a loan of $1 billion and that Hopkins thought the Chiangs were in many respects "childish." Although the U.S. State Department had sent a Chinese-speaking diplomat to translate during the discussions, he was quickly dispatched back to Washington so that May-ling could continue to reinterpret what was said to and by her husband.

The evening after the G-mo's first abysmal performance, Stilwell went to the Chiangs' villa to help him formulate his questions and answers for the next day, and he returned the next morning to prepare May-ling for lunch with Chief of Staff Marshall. It may have been at this lunch that the general remarked that he hoped "we will all be able to get together on this matter." At this point one of the general's biographers says that Madame Chiang "leaned forward, put a slim hand on Marshall's knee, looking directly into his eyes, and said, 'General, you and I can get together anytime.' " According to this biographer, his subject "was a sucker for beautiful and intelligent women, and Madame Chiang could do no wrong from that time on." The same was not true, however, of the general vis-à-vis the generalissimo. The next day, Chiang repeated his back-and-forthing, eventually deciding to attend the session but then refusing to agree to use his Y Force in the assault on Burma. At the same time, one of his top generals continued to demand American planes, pilots, and war material, saying that China had its "rights" in the matter. Marshall was infuriated. "Now let me get this straight," he said to the offending general. "You are talking about your 'rights' in this matter.

I thought these were *American* planes, and *American* personnel, and *American* material. I don't understand what you mean by saying that we can or can't do thus and so."

To counter Chiang's intransigence, Roosevelt sent Mountbatten. Although the ever-charming Lord Louis explained that there were simply no extra planes available, Chiang continued to demand 535 transports. "The President will refuse me nothing," he told the head of SEAC. "Anything I ask, he will do." Even if that many planes could be found, Mountbatten responded, there was no way the Allies could meet Chiang's demands and, at the same time, mount an air assault on Mandalay before the monsoon. After this, there was apparently a long dialogue in Chinese between husband and wife. Finally, May-ling turned to Mountbatten. "Believe it or not," she told him, "he does not know about the monsoon"—the annual deluge that Tuchman called "the governing fact of life and of war in Southeast Asia." China had no real monsoons. Therefore, Chiang Kai-shek, generalissimo of the Middle Kingdom, knew nothing about them.

On November 25, Thanksgiving Day for the Americans, Roosevelt announced that Chiang had finally agreed to send troops for the invasion of Burma. But by 9:30 that evening, the G-mo had reneged. The following morning, Roosevelt asked Mountbatten, Stilwell, Arnold, Chennault, and three other generals to go see him. Although Chiang continued to insist on his 10,000 tons of supplies a month, he agreed to join the Burma campaign—until the next day, when he changed his mind again. As he was leaving to return to China, he instructed Stilwell to protest in his name and continue to demand an air assault on Mandalay along with 10,000 tons of supplies monthly over the Hump for China.

During the conference the leaders agreed on a four-point program vis-à-vis China and Japan: (1) The Japanese must agree to return to China all the islands it had seized since the beginning of World War I; (2) Manchuria, Formosa, and the Pescadores (21 islands lying between the mainland and Taiwan) were to be ceded back to China; (3) Japan would "be expelled from all other territories which she has taken by violence and greed"; (4) Korea was to become independent; and (5) the allies would "continue to perservere in the . . . operations necessary to procure the unconditional surrender of Japan." In other words, Japan's territory was to be reduced from 3 million square miles to about 146,000 and its population from 500 million people (including Chinese) to 75 million.

On departing from Cairo, Chiang left a note for Roosevelt, handwritten by May-ling: "My dear Mr. President: . . . the Generalissimo wishes me to tell you again how much he appreciates what you have done and are doing for China. When he said goodby to you this afternoon, he could not find words adequately expressive to convey his emotions and feelings, nor to thank you sufficiently for your friendship. He felt, too, wistfulness at saying a farewell, although he feels that only a short time will lapse before his next meeting with you. Meanwhile he hopes that you will consider him as a friend whom you can trust." The letter contained a postscript from Madame Chiang herself: "I do hope 'Uncle Joe' [i.e., Stalin] came up to expectations, did he?" Two days later, Chiang wrote in his diary that his "wife's support" was the greatest factor in their success. "Otherwise, we could not have achieved so much."

Meanwhile, Roosevelt and Churchill left for Tehran, where they met Stalin, who told them that the Chinese army suffered from "poor leadership" but agreed to join the war on Japan after Germany was defeated. One reason, according to a prominent Chinese diplomat, was that the USSR could not continue to receive Lend-Lease unless it remained in the war. The official Cairo Statement was issued on December 1, while Roosevelt and Churchill were still in Tehran. It was a triumph for Chiang Kai-shek, since it called for the unconditional surrender by Japan plus the return of all territories that she had taken from China. But the conference at Tehran radically altered the plans for Burma, since Stalin insisted that a giant cross–English Channel invasion take place in the spring of 1944—an assault that would require the landing craft that the United States and Britain had planned to use for the amphibious invasion of Burma. Churchill, who had never wanted to send British troops to the Bay of Bengal anyway, used this as an excuse to cancel the British assault on Burma. Having previously dismissed the Chinese as "four hundred and twenty five million pigtails," the prime minister argued for three days with the president before convincing him to abandon the Burma operation for the time being. When Chiang arrived home, he was informed of the change in plans.

Five days later, Stilwell, who needed to know what to tell the generalissimo, met with Roosevelt, Hopkins, and John Paton Davies, Jr. He described the meeting in his diary:

Roosevelt: Well, Joe, what do you think of the bad news?

Stilwell: I haven't heard yet how bad it is.

Roosevelt: We're at an impasse. I've been stubborn as a mule
                 for four days but we can't get anywhere, and it
                 won't do for a conference to end that way. The
                 British just won't do the [Burma] operation, and
                 I can't get them to agree to it.

Stilwell:	I am interested to know how this affects our policy in China.
Roosevelt:	Well, now, we've been friends with China for a gr-e-e-at many years. . . . You know I have a China history. My grandfather went out there . . . in 1829. . . . He did what was every American's ambition in those days—he made a million dollars, and when he came back he put it into western railroads. And in eight years he lost every dollar. Ha! Ha! Ha! Then in 1856 he went out again and stayed there all through the Civil War, and made another million. This time he put it into coal mines, and they didn't pay a dividend until two years after he died. Ha! Ha! Ha!

According to Davies, this "lore of Cathay appeared to be the most vivid part of his [Roosevelt's] knowledge of China." The president then told stories about financial negotiations with Kung, while Hopkins asked questions about China's economy, but "at no point did either give the general [Stilwell] a coherent statement of what they wanted him to do" now that the British had canceled their part in the assault on Burma. Stilwell finally said, "I take it that it is our policy to build China up."

Roosevelt: "Yes. Yes. Build her up. After this war there will be a great need of our help. They will want loans. Madame Chiang and the G-mo wanted to get a loan now of a billion dollars, but I told them it would be difficult to get Congress to agree to it. . . . How long do you think Chiang can last?"

Roosevelt, who had already cabled the news about Burma to Chiang, asked if the G-mo would agree to accept an "altered plan" or would postpone the assault until the following November. In spite of Stilwell's warning to May-ling not to let her husband try to blackmail the United States, Chiang, according to Stilwell, had come back with a "squeeze play": "O.K. if you give me a billion dollars and double the air force." Stilwell, who wrote that this "brief experience with international politics" had confirmed him in his "preference for driving a garbage truck," felt that May-ling had done the best she could with her husband. "She realizes the implication and it drives her nuts. . . . I can see she is pretty low & hasn't much hope of changing the little bastard over." The next day, he met with both sisters. "They're close to nervous prostration," he wrote. "Can't sleep. May said she prayed with him

[Chiang] last night. Told me she'd done 'everything except murder him.' Ella says when he's tired he takes refuge in being 'noble.' "

CHIANG'S CONTINUING DEMAND for money was based on more than just pique at having the plans for the Burma campaign changed behind his back. Throughout the two previous years (1942 and 1943) the U.S. Treasury, according to Fairbank, had "denied the Chinese nothing that the loan agreement permitted them to request, though the temptations to refuse were inherent in the persistent inefficacy of Chinese financial policy, which failed to pursue the most practicable courses to stem inflation." The loan agreement in question was a request from the generalissimo, submitted just twenty-three days after Pearl Harbor, for $500 million. The money, Chiang said, was necessary to boost the morale of the Chinese people after the Japanese attack. The G-mo had refused to say what the money would be used for and had put on "an elaborate act of claiming that to make any accounting for it would be so very, very humiliating to a proud Chinese that he would rather commit suicide, etc., etc."

Concerned by both the corruption and inefficiency of Chiang's government, Treasury Secretary Henry Morgenthau had hesitated to give China the money, even after meeting with T.V., who "went through a long rigamarole, trying . . . to justify" the loan. "The President and the State Department want me to make a loan to China," Morgenthau had told his staff in mid-January 1942, ". . . but . . . I would like to do this thing in the way that we could sort of kind of feed it out to them if they keep fighting, but I would hate to put $300,000 million on the line and say, 'Here, boys, that is yours.' " But the loan, according to Chiang, should require "no security or other pre-arranged terms as to its use and as regards means of repayment." Morgenthau complained to Secretary of War Stimson, "The attitude that they're taking . . . is—really . . . a hold up." Maxim Litvinov, the Soviet ambassador to the United States, was more succinct. "This," he said "is nothing but blackmail."

In the end, Morgenthau did what the president wanted, telling T.V. to pass the word to Chiang that he was going to Capitol Hill to get congressional approval for the loan. "This proposal is a war measure," Morgenthau testified in early February 1942. "The effective continuance of the Chinese military effort—so invaluable in our fight against the Axis Powers—depends largely upon the strength of the economic structure of Free China. . . . The Chinese financial and monetary system should be made as strong as possible."

Four days later, Roosevelt wired Chiang, "The unusual speed and unanimity with which this measure was acted upon by the Congress and the enthusiastic support which it received throughout the United States testified to the whole-hearted respect and admiration which the Government and people of this country have for China. . . . It is my hope and belief that use which will be made of the funds . . . will contribute substantially toward facilitating the efforts of the Chinese Government and people to meet the economic and financial burdens which have been thrust upon them by an armed invasion." Or, as John Morton Blum* pointed out, the president managed to "put into idealistic cadence the high price of Chinese friendship." Two months later, Finance Minister Kung asked that $200 million be deposited to the Chinese account at the New York Federal Reserve Bank to be drawn on to back the sale of securities to the Chinese public. But according to Blum, Kung and his ministry "made a fiasco of its sales of the dollar-backed securities, which were traded . . . to the considerable personal advantage of members of the Soong and Kung families."

In the months before the Cairo Conference, the United States had spent nearly $20 million† a month on military and civilian projects in China, and Morgenthau announced that it could not afford to continue these expenditures at the present rate of exchange. The legal rate of exchange at the time was around 120 yuan to the dollar, but the black market went up as high as 600 to 1. Kung suggested a ratio of 40 to 1. According to Blum, "There was little reasonable about Kung, who held that it was impossible to keep secret any special price he gave the United States," and a few months later, Morgenthau came to the conclusion that the Nationalist Party could not tolerate the "grafting family at the head of the Government" much longer.

After his return from the meeting at Tehran in December of 1943, Roosevelt had told Morgenthau about Chiang's request for the loan of $1 billion. Everyone, including Roosevelt himself, agreed that there was no need for China to be given more money, particularly as it still had unused funds in the United States left over from the previous loan of $500 million. A big problem for the United States had surfaced in the army, however, which was behind schedule in constructing airfields in China and needed local currency to pay the Chinese laborers and buy food. At the official rate of exchange, the cost of building an airfield was $40 million, while the cost of a bamboo latrine was figured at $10,000 and up. At this point, Washington received a discouraging report from Chungking: "The United States Government has not committed itself to pay for these . . . bases at the offi-

---

* A historian and editor of the Morgenthau diaries.

† Equivalent to $249,000,000 today.

cial exchange rate and China is, therefore, holding up the work on them. . . .
Progress is being made . . . on only four of the seven bases which China
promised to construct. . . . The war effort in this theater will seriously be
impeded by the delay."

"Nothing could be more conducive to lowering the prestige of China in
the United States . . . than the knowledge that China was not cooperating
fully . . . in the building of these airbases," Morgenthau cabled the generalissimo. "I firmly believe that I speak in the best interests of China when I
recommend that immediate action be taken for the construction of the remaining bases . . . leaving for future determination the final question of the
U.S. currency equivalent." In answer to this, Chiang sent Roosevelt "a very
tough cable" arguing that China needed the $1 billion loan to pay for help-
ing the American forces, and if the Treasury disagreed, the United States
would have to pay its own expenses in China at the official rate of exchange.
If neither of these alternatives was acceptable, then China "would have . . .
no means at its disposal to meet the requirements of United States forces in
China and consequently the American Army in China would have to depend upon itself to execute any and all of its projects."

But there was increasing resentment in the U.S. government, according
to Ambassador Gauss, because Chinese officials had been accumulating
"large reserves of U.S. dollars out of our expenditures for the war effort."
According to Morgenthau, "They [the Chinese] are just a bunch of crooks,
and I won't go up [to the Hill] and ask for one nickle." The secretary of war
had the same reaction as the secretary of the Treasury. "China has been riding us pretty hard with the aid of Madame Chiang Kai-shek's influence over
the President," Stimson noted in his diary. ". . . I do not fear that the Chinese are going to drop out of the war now that we are so close and I think
that their present demands show a good deal of the Chinese bargaining." As
if to substantiate this opinion, Kung told Ambassador Gauss that it would
break China's "economic backbone" to alter the official rate of exchange.
The man who had caused China's runaway inflation now blamed it on the
growing expenditures of the U.S. Army and claimed that China had repaid
its previous $500 million loan with all the assistance it had given to the
Americans in China. The Japanese, he told the U.S. ambassador, had recently made "some very good offers."

In the end, Lucius Clay, the youngest brigadier general in the U.S. Army,
a man known for producing order out of chaos, came up with a solution. It
was based on the United States' placing a stipulated amount of dollars in a
China account, out of which the Chinese could then advance yuan to the
U.S. Army. The United States would set the rate of exchange for a period of
three months at somewhere between 100 and 200 to 1. The amount of yuan

paid out would remain secret, but the Chinese would be allowed to publi-
cize the contribution of American dollars in order to stabilize the value of
their currency. Accounts would be settled after the war was over.

Construction of the airfields proceeded in typical Chinese fashion.
Some 450,000 peasants were brought in from local districts, each district
supplying its quota of men, women, and children along with tools and a
three-month supply of food. The people walked from their districts to the
work sites, bringing what they needed in wheelbarrows. They cleaned off the
topsoil, carried it away in wicker baskets on shoulder poles, and flattened
what was underneath by pulling enormous rollers back and forth by hand.
They then gathered stones from the riverbeds and hauled them to the site to
make a cobblestone base. They covered this with layers of soil mixed with
mud slurry alternating with layers of rock that had been crushed by the
women and girls working with hammers. Over this they put back the topsoil they had taken off. The work was directed by foremen representing each
village. In ninety days all the fields—four with 9,000-foot runways—were
completed.

"I should like to take this opportunity to congratulate you . . . upon having faced and passed an important military crisis," Morgenthau wrote the
president in early June 1944. "General Somervell informs me that the United
States installations in China are now practically completed . . . despite the
financial problems which arose to disturb the cordial relations of this government with the Chinese government."

❦

OVER AND ABOVE specific monetary loans to China were the aid programs
started by the United Nations Relief and Rehabilitation Administration
(UNRRA) in 1943. Fifty-two countries eventually participated in this effort,
contributing 2 percent of their national incomes for a total of nearly $4 bil-
lion. These monies were spent on distributing food and medicine, restoring
public services, and supplying aid to agricultural and industrial sectors.
China was the chief beneficiary of UNRRA,* receiving goods and services
valued at over half a billion dollars, of which $470 million came from the
United States. But whereas European countries receiving aid yielded control
of all supplies until they arrived at the recipient's door, the Chinese government maintained that no one knew how to operate in China except the
Chinese and that the "dignity of the Chinese people" would not allow others to distribute the goods and services. Therefore, UNRRA could operate in
China only as an adviser, while the Chinese would assume title to all sup-

---

* The others were Czechoslovakia, Greece, Italy, Poland, the Ukrainian SSR, and Yugo-
slavia.

plies the moment they were put on a dock anywhere in the country. It was, according to George H. Kerr, a naval officer and later vice consul in Formosa,

> a gigantic blackmail scheme. . . . The American public was not told that Madame Chiang's family dominated the warehousing and shipping interests of China . . . and most of the principal warehousing facilities along the docks at every important riverport and anchorage in the country. These were the docks at which the UNRRA relief supplies would be unloaded and the warehouses into which they would be carried. UNRRA would be billed for both storage and transport.
>
> Through the Executive Yuan (T. V. Soong, President) the Chinese Government created an organization known as the "Chinese National Relief and Rehabilitation Administration" or CNRRA . . . which was authorized to take possession of relief supplies and to carry through a rehabilitation program for which UNRRA specialists would make recommendations, but in which they would exercise no authority. Insistence upon Chinese supremacy in the administration of relief was prompted in some degree by national pride and considerations of face. . . . Chiang wanted credit to accrue to the Nationalist Party Government; Kung and Soong wanted funds and materials to pass through the family's banks and warehouses. Hardly less astonishing . . . were the arrangements which the Chinese devised to increase the value of the international gifts. Although a half-billion dollars' worth of goods and services were being *donated* to China, the [Chinese] Government complained that it could not afford to distribute relief goods. . . . UNRRA had to agree that CNRRA could sell relief goods 'at a moderate rate' to generate funds with which to pay for distribution. In subsequent accounting to UNRRA, China charged off $190,000,000 as "administrative costs," and an enormous percentage of relief goods disappeared into private channels once they had passed through those yawning warehouse doors.

Or, to quote journalist Randall Gould on what he called the "outrageous" UNRRA fiasco: "Its amateur Lady Bountiful start-off . . . conclusively demonstrated to our friends and allies in Nanking that we were a bunch of gullible suckers who would never exact real self-help performance in any field and who would stop at nothing in their eager enthusiasm to give China their shirts."

41

❦

The manners of the Kuomintang in public were perfect; its only faults were that its leadership was corrupt, its secret police merciless, its promises lies, and its daily diet the blood and tears of the people of China.
                                    —THEODORE WHITE AND ANNALEE JACOBY

RATHER THAN improving with the elevation of China to the status of one of the four Great Powers, morale in the Middle Kingdom continued to degenerate during the last half of 1943 and the first half of 1944. So much so that while Chiang Kai-shek was in Cairo, a group of young officers tried to remove him along with the pillars of his government: Chief of Staff General Ho; head of the Secret Service, Tai Li; Minister of Finance H. H. Kung; and those ultraconservative arbiters of the nation's thought, the Chen brothers. Known as the Young Generals' Plot, the attempted coup involved something like six hundred men, angered by the corruption and inefficiency of their superiors. Tai Li got wind of the scheme, which was thwarted. Unfortunately, the event did not inspire Chiang to institute any reforms and ended with the execution of sixteen good young generals.

Another attempt to remove Chiang took place in the spring of 1944, when an OSS officer named Oliver J. Caldwell was contacted by a sixty-year-old Presbyterian minister who introduced himself as Mr. Chen, vice president of the Society of Elder Brothers, of which the Christian General Feng was president and Chiang Kai-shek, honorary president. According to Chen, the Elder Brothers was one of the most important secret societies in China, boasting 600,000 members drawn from provincial elders and community leaders. They had helped Sun Yat-sen fight the Manchus and, after the revolution, had morphed into what the OSS man called "a philanthropic organization with political overtones." Chen asked Caldwell to inform President Roosevelt that the Elder Brothers could no longer back the generalissimo, and if the United States continued to support him, the Chinese Communists would take over the country. The society proposed to substitute a moderate government under the presidency of General Li Tsung-jen, currently vice president. Li, who commanded the strongest army in China, had agreed to take part in a peaceful coup. Caldwell forwarded Chen's proposal to Washington, where OSS chief William Donovan took it to the president, who put it before his cabinet. Although it generated quite a bit of support in the cabinet, it finally lost in a poll of the members taken by Roosevelt.

But the most intriguing of the plots to dispense with Chiang Kai-shek was related by Colonel Dorn, Stilwell's chief of staff, who was in Kunming preparing the Y Force for Burma while Stilwell was at the Cairo Conference. Shortly after his return to China, Stilwell went to see Dorn. When the two men were alone, he told Dorn that he had been "shocked by a verbal order he had received at Cairo." Hesitating, seemingly "unwilling to continue," the general finally "shrugged his shoulders, sighed, and said: 'Well, an order is an order. I have no choice but to pass this one on. You ready for a shocker?' "

Dorn: I think I can take it . . . whatever it is.

Stilwell: Well, here goes then. I have been directed to prepare
               a plan for the assassination of Chiang Kai-
               shek. . . . The order did not say to kill him. . . . It
               said to *prepare a plan*. And that means a *plan* only.
               One that can never point the finger of guilt at the
               U.S. Government or at any American, you included.

Dorn: That's a big order.

Stilwell: I know damned well it is. Think it over carefully.
               And remember: absolutely nothing in writing, ever.
               I don't need to tell you this whole business has to
               be super hush-hush. If anything leaked out while
               the war is still going on, we'd be in one hell of a
               mess.

Dorn: But why me?

Stilwell: I've thought it over ever since I left Cairo. I decided
               on you for two reasons: you understand the Chi-
               nese setup about as well as anyone, and you know
               what can *not* be done in China, which in this case
               is just about as important as knowing what *can* be
               done.

Dorn: If I dream up a workable plan, will I have to carry
               it out?

Stilwell: We'll cross that bridge when we come to it. But I
                 can tell you this: if you ever are directed to carry
                 out any such plan, it better by a damn sight suc-
                 ceed. The order for its execution will come to
                 me from above, and I will transmit it to you person-
                 ally. . . . Until I receive such an order, which I doubt
                 will ever come, I will do nothing. And neither will
                 you, except make the plan. . . . I doubt very much if
                 anything ever comes of this. The Big Boy's fed up
                 with Chiang and his tantrums, and said so. In fact
                 he told me in that Olympian manner of his: "If you
                 can't get along with Chiang and can't replace him,
                 get rid of him once and for all. You know what I
                 mean. Put in someone you can manage."

Stilwell himself was clearly not in favor of the scheme, confiding in
Dorn that "no matter how big a pain in the neck the Peanut can be, or how
impatient we may feel, or how mad we get, *this* is not the solution for the
China problem."

Dorn: Sometimes I've almost felt like murdering the old
                 bastard myself.

Stilwell: Sure, I know. So have I. So have a lot of his gener-
                 als. And I suppose Mei-ling has, too. She doesn't
                 have too easy a time with the old boy. But still, the
                 United States doesn't go in for this sort of thing.

Dorn: May I ask, sir, who directed that this plan be made?

Stilwell: Sure. You may ask all you want. But I'm not answer-
                 ing your question. . . . It comes from the very top.
                 Draw your own conclusions. Next time I pass
                 through Kunming, let me know what you've
                 cooked up. . . . I leave for Chungking in the morn-
                 ing to iron out a few of the usual hassles. But know-
                 ing what's in the wind, I'm going to feel damned
                 queasy when I sit down with him over a cup of tea.

With the help of two of Dorn's most trustworthy officers, "dozens of
ideas"—shooting, poison, bombing, a palace revolution—were considered

and discarded until one of the men suggested taking Chiang on a trip to inspect the Ramgarh Training Center in India, arranging for the plane to crash on the way, and fixing his and Madame's parachutes so they would not open properly. As to the pilot, he would not know "one damned thing" until the plane was over the Hump, when he would be given "sealed top secret orders." Stilwell agreed to the plan, which, fortunately for those involved, was never ordered to be carried out. "Nor," according to Dorn, "did General Stilwell ever mention the matter again."

❦

NEFARIOUS PLOTS NOTWITHSTANDING, there was little question that Chiang Kai-shek was in serious trouble. What there was left of a Chinese middle class, once the backbone of the KMT, had been impoverished by the war, and the extreme right wing of the party had taken over. With inflation out of control, taxes delivered to the government reduced by two thirds (due to the same graft in politics that characterized the military), warlordism back on the rise, and the G-mo unwilling to take any action beyond hoarding arms and preparing for civil war against the CCP, the country was in no way equal to fighting off the Japanese, who started a new offensive in April 1944. To prepare for their march south, the enemy had cleaned out the province of Hunan, site of the recent famine, at the end of 1943. After they bombed the city of Changteh, on which they had previously dropped fleas infected with bubonic plague, only thirty of its ten thousand buildings were left. This destruction was preceded by a "propaganda blitz" in which pamphlets were distributed claiming that it was not Japan that was the enemy of China but "the white-faced demons." Japanese soldiers were instructed to stop mistreating local Chinese and taught to sing a marching song the words of which proclaimed their kindness to fellow Asians.

Code-named ICHIGO, the Japanese spring assault, the second phase of which coincided with the D-Day landings in Normandy, started with 60,000 soldiers moving down from the Yellow River, cutting easily through any Chinese defenses in their path. Facing the enemy in the province of Honan* were thirty-four Chinese divisions, reputedly some of China's best. But the Chinese soldiers were poorly led, and their ammunition supply was low. Moreover, one of their commanders, Tang En-po, was away at the time of the attack. Known as one of China's worst generals, Tang not only kept his units purposefully under strength in order to pocket the extra cash but traded with the Japanese. Once attacked, the Chinese soldiers simply turned and ran, leaving the province to enemy pillage and local peasants turned looters.

---

* As distinguished from Hunan, which is to the south, Honan is in the north.

At Loyang, the capital of Honan, there were seven to eight hundred military trucks, only about a hundred of which were used to send reinforcements to the front, since the rest had been commandered by army officers to remove their personal belongings to safety. At another headquarters, the staff was killed off when the Japanese found them playing basketball.

To compensate for the lack of supplies, the Chinese soldiers began to expropriate the peasants' oxen. Since Honan is a wheat-producing area where the peasant's most valuable assets were the oxen that dragged his plow, the farmers revolted. After years of "merciless military extortion," they turned on the army with bird guns and pitchforks. Starting with individual soldiers, they graduated to entire companies, and by the end of the uprising, it was estimated that 50,000 Chinese soldiers had been disarmed by their own countrymen. It took the Japanese less than three weeks to overcome those who had not fled and take over the railroad.

With that much of the railway secured, the enemy headed down toward Changsha, capital of the province of Hunan and key to 500 miles of railway tracks leading to the airfields located in Kweilin and Liuchow in the coastal province of Kwangsi. General Hsueh Yueh, a "peppery Cantonese" who loved being called the Tiger of Changsha, ruled over this area and commanded about 200,000 soldiers. White and a reporter from Reuters joined one of his Chinese armies on the march—the only one that took a stand against the enemy. "As far as we could see ahead into the hills and beyond were marching men," White said.

> They crawled on foot over every footpath through the rice paddies; they snaked along over every ditch and broken bridge in parallel rivulets of sweating humanity. One man in three had a rifle. . . . There was not a single motor, not a truck . . . not a piece of artillery. . . . The men . . . were wiry and brown but thin; their guns were old, their yellow-and-brown uniforms threadbare. Each carried two grenades tucked in his belt. . . . Their feet were broken and puffed above their straw sandals; their heads were covered with birds' nests of leaves woven together to give shade from the sun and supposedly to supply camouflage. The sweat rolled from them; dust rose about them. . . . [The army] . . . had two French seventy-fives, from the First World War. . . . It had 200 shells . . . it expended them as a miser counts out gold coins. . . . The Chinese mortars whistled fitfully over the crest where the Japanese were dug in. . . . All that flesh and blood could do the Chinese soldiers were doing. They were walking up hills and dying in the sun, but they had no support, no guns, no directions. They were doomed.

Although unable to dislodge the enemy soldiers from their position, General Hsueh and his soldiers managed to hold out for forty days. One by one, Chungking sent other armies to break through the Japanese lines, but the soldiers were tired, malnourished, and directed by telephone calls from Chiang, hundreds of miles away. The G-mo never ordered a concentrated action of all the troops available, and, as in past campaigns, new units were sent in only to replace the wounded. General Hsueh, who had successfully countered three Japanese assaults in the past, fell victim to inadequate arms for his soldiers, since Chiang did not trust him and refused to send more. When the Japanese resumed the offensive, they overcame the Chinese in less than a week and headed south to take over the airfields built by the peasants and paid for by the United States. By the summer of 1944, Chennault's pilots had managed to destroy one fifth of Japan's transport ships but were unable to stop enemy advances on the ground. Having assured Chiang that all he needed to rout the Japanese was a sufficiency of planes and supplies over the Hump, Chennault found that he had painted himself into a cloudy corner and was reduced to complaining that his supplies were still "hopelessly inadequate."

"Over in China things look very black," Stilwell wrote his wife from Burma. "It would be a pleasure to go to Washington and scream, 'I told you so,' but I think they get the point. This was my thesis in May last year, but I was all alone and the air boys were so sure they could run the Japs out of China with planes that I was put in the garbage pail. They have had their way. . . . If this crisis were just sufficient to get rid of the Peanut, without entirely wrecking the ship, it would be worth it. But that's too much to hope."

※

By the spring and summer of 1944, even the Luce publications were forced to admit that all was not well in the Middle Kingdom. According to the April 24 issue of *Time* magazine, "the nation of Sun Yat-sen has faltered on its path toward democracy, gone off into some darkly undemocratic byways. The man who said so was none other than Founder Sun Yat-sen's stocky and genial son, Dr. Sun Fo, liberal president of China's Legislative Yuan. . . . [The KMT] regards itself as 'the sovereign power in the state, entitled to the enjoyment of a special position,' though it directly represents only an 'infinitesimal portion' (less than 1%) of China's 450,000,000 people." A week later, *Life* magazine published an article by White in which he blamed American misconceptions about China on several things, among them the recent visit to the United States of Madame Chiang. "Perhaps nothing attests more eloquently the genius of this brilliant woman," said White, "than the skill with which she has clothed all China in the radiant glamor of her personality."

Madame Chiang, in fact, seemed to be the only bright spot in an otherwise dismal Chinese landscape. *The Four Queens,* a propaganda book published in England that spring, named her the Queen of Clubs, one of the four most important woman in the world, a woman who epitomized "power, fame and ability."* Recognized as Chiang's "alter ego, able to speak for him and to act as his representative abroad," she was, according to the author of the book and Diana Lary, a China scholar who wrote an article based on it, the first person to defy the traditional role of women in China and who, in doing so, had risen above the wives of the other Allied leaders. She was, Lary said, "in a class of her own, intelligent, active, committed and beautiful, a combination of talents which no other wife approached."

But while China's first lady earned herself a place in this pantheon of women, her country, according to White, was currently suffering from three disastrous problems. The first was the blockade, which was causing life-threatening shortages of food, transportation, and armaments. The second was runaway inflation. By 1944, prices were five hundred times higher than they had been before the war, and planes were still hauling in quantities of banknotes, printed in the United States, which the government was issuing at the rate of 5 million Chinese dollars every month. "There are no real sources of revenue left in the country," White wrote, explaining that China had been reduced to financing the war with paper currency since there was no industry left in the country to produce revenue. The gap between official salaries and the staggering rate of inflation had led to unprecedented—even for China—corruption and extortion. "You get your money where and how you can" was White's cynical but realistic assessment of the situation. The third problem, according to White, was the political deadlock between the Communists and the Kuomintang, described by him as a "corrupt political clique that combines some of the worst features of Tammany Hall and the Spanish Inquisition." But the American journalist still pled for America's understanding and help. "To keep the permanent friendship of this great nation almost any price is small," declared White.

In June of 1944, President Roosevelt sent Vice President Henry Wallace to China to try to make peace between Chiang and the CCP and to arrange for a military mission to visit Yenan, the area held by the Communists. Ac-

---

* The others were Eleanor Roosevelt (Queen of Diamonds) for her enterprise and energy; Queen Wilhelmina of the Netherlands (Queen of Spades) for the tragedy of her country; and Queen Elizabeth of England (Queen of Hearts) for her support of her husband and country's war efforts.

companying Wallace were Owen Lattimore and John Carter Vincent, one of
the best known of the China Hands.* "The Generalissimo asks questions
and the Madame translates my replies," Wallace wrote about his initial meeting with the G-mo. ". . . 'How—how—how' all the time. He has an almost
feminine charm." Wallace met with Ambassador Gauss, who gave him a
rundown on the family: "Gauss says T.V. Soong is O.K. . . . says Madame
Kung and Madame Chiang through stooges used the U.S. advance of
$100,000,000† as a medium of speculation. . . . Kung may or may not have
been in on it. The Generalissimo found out. . . . Kung took the stooges with
him to the U.S., and it will be a long time before they venture back."

During a second meeting with Wallace, Chiang "launched forth into a
lengthy complaint against the Chinese Communists," who, he said, had
managed to sway American public opinion by claiming that they were not
really revolutionaries but agrarian democrats. Members of the CCP were not
independent, the generalissimo told Wallace, but were under the orders of
the Third International. Chiang's "case against the Communists," according
to Wallace, ". . . was full of bitter feeling and poor logic. I like the Gimo, but
fear his lack of vision will doom him. . . . I was very sad after the second
conversation. I told both Madame and T.V. so. They passed it on."

Chiang also complained to Wallace about Stilwell. Wallace was apparently struck by Chiang's recital of his problems with the American general,
suggesting that Roosevelt send a replacement to China, perhaps Albert
Wedemeyer, a man who could combine political and military authority.
Stilwell, he said, had lost Chiang's confidence. It must be noted, however,
that Stilwell was fighting in Burma during Wallace's sojourn in China, and
the vice president did not go to Burma to speak directly with him. Moreover, his negative attitude toward the American general was "given every
nourishment" by Chennault, who hosted Wallace in Kunming and assigned
Alsop as his "air aide." Like others who had preceded him into the unreality

---

* The China Hands were a group of Foreign Service officers stationed in the U.S. Embassy in China, called by journalist and commentator Eric Sevareid "the ablest group of
young diplomats I have ever seen in a single American mission abroad." (E. J. Kahn, Jr.,
The China Hands, jacket copy.)

† This was part of the $500 million credit the U.S. Treasury had deposited in China's
account. According to John Morton Blum, who edited Wallace's diaries, "Though American officials in Chungking suspected that members of the Soong family had used some
of that deposit for their personal gain, those suspicions were never proved. Incontestably
Kung and others did use American aid unwisely." (Henry A. Wallace, *The Price of Vision*,
pp. 349–50.) (Note: This is the only time that this author found a direct reference to
Madame Chiang being involved in speculation.)

of Chungking, Wallace was fooled into believing that "with the right man to do the job it should be possible to induce the Generalissimo to reform his regime."

During the Wallace mission, Lattimore met privately with Madame Chiang. She told him that she was planning to go abroad because of illness and wanted Wallace "to comment on her ill-health to the Generalissimo"—a request that made Lattimore wonder whether Chiang was refusing to let her go. "She even pulled down her stockings to show that she was really sick. That part, at least, was convincing, for she did have some sort of skin disease." The G-mo's wife had been complaining for some time about "painful maladies"—her ever-returning skin ailment and something she referred to as "nervous eye strain," which, she said, had made it necessary to dilate her pupils during the Cairo Conference. During their conversation, May-ling kept hinting at the question of a check for $1,000, which David Kung had delivered to Lattimore as a gift from her husband after Lattimore left China in 1942. Lattimore had refused the money, and the G-mo's wife said she had never received the letter he wrote explaining why he had done so. During their conversation, he explained to her why such a gift would not be considered proper in the United States.

The American government did not give up trying to get the KMT and the CCP to cooperate. In the middle of June, Ambassador Gauss was sent to talk to Chiang and to explain that the generalissimo should try to come to some agreement with the Chinese Communists whereby their soldiers could join the fight against the Japanese. Not only was the United States anxious for help—the CCP apparently trained dedicated soldiers—but it wanted to avoid the chaos of a civil war at the end of World War II. The Americans had convinced themselves that the CCP was not out to dominate China but only to find a political modus vivendi with Chiang. This theory was underlined by the fact that Stalin had assured Ambassador Averell Harriman that the "Chinese Communists are not real Communists, but ersatz or 'margarine' Communists.* Nevertheless," Stalin added, "they are real patriots and they want to fight Japan." But Chiang continued to refuse to comply with American requests to cooperate with them.

In July, the U.S. Joint Chiefs of Staff sent President Roosevelt a memorandum detailing the situation in China, which, they said, was "deteriorating at an alarming rate." Not only were the Chinese ground forces "impotent," but "Chennault's air alone can do little more than slightly delay the Japanese advance." In this situation, "the military power and resources remaining to China must be entrusted to one individual. . . . That man is General

---

* At another time Stalin spoke of the members of the CCP as "radish Communists," i.e., red on the outside but white on the inside. (Herbert Feis, *The China Tangle*, p. 141.)

Stilwell." They recommended promoting Stilwell to full general—a matter of face for the Chinese—and convincing Chiang to place him in command of China's armed forces. Two days later, Roosevelt sent the generalissimo a message saying that "drastic measures must be taken immediately," among them naming Stilwell to head the Chinese forces. Although the president said he was "fully aware of your feelings regarding General Stilwell. . . . I know of no other man who has the ability, the force, and the determination to offset the disaster which now threatens China . . . the future of all Asia is at stake."

❦

WHILE WALLACE, LATTIMORE, and Gauss were dealing with Chiang, Stilwell had returned to the task of opening a land route to China through northern Burma. The plan was two-pronged: he himself would lead the X Force on a drive to the city of Myitkyina in northern Burma. Once he accomplished this, the Y Force, based in Yunnan, would move west to link up with the X Force, thus clearing a road into China and ending the blockade. All this had to be accomplished before the monsoon.

In the battlefield from December 1943 until June 1944, emerging only twice for quick forays to Delhi and Chungking, Stilwell had taken 30,000 raw troops, removed all possibility of retreat, abandoned his own supply lines except airdrops, and led them 200 miles through the swampy jungle and over 6,000-foot-high mountains. His personal presence at the front impressed the Chinese officers, although it did not make them a great deal more aggressive. To urge the Chinese pilots to fly in their airdrops of food and supplies despite less-than-perfect weather, Stilwell made them change places with the men on the battlefield. "After the air boys learned what it was like down there," said one transportation officer, "they flew in every day, flew when you thought no one could, when clouds were on the tree tops." Before the advent of Stilwell, Chinese soldiers had always said they were not afraid of death but were terrified of being left on the field (which they always had been) to die of their wounds. To encourage the ordinary conscripts, Stilwell insisted that the wounded be carried to field hospitals* and, if necessary, to a larger hospital at Ledo in India, where he had harassed the powers into building an airfield. In the middle of March, he himself flew to Ledo to visit the wounded.

---

* One nurse described the primitive conditions of the wards—raised straw pallets for the patients with rats and cockroaches running around underneath—plus the uncaring attitude of the staff, men and women "who had been associated with the Chinese Army for a long time . . . [and] . . . were squeezed dry of compassion." (LaVonne Teleshaw Camp, *Lingering Fever*, p. 41.)

But even as Stilwell struggled to clear a path for a supply line into China, Chiang was refusing to send the Y Force, equipped by the Americans, to help him. Using the generalissimo's refusal as his excuse, Mountbatten tried to take the British out of the assault force as well. He proposed that Stilwell stop trying to fight through northern Burma, substituting a new plan to go by sea and to include Hong Kong within the SEAC territories. Stilwell referred to Mountbatten as "a limey mountebank . . . sometimes as dumb as that thick-headed cousin of his, the King," but Tuchman offered an explanation for Lord Louis's position: "The British intended to reach Hong Kong by sea before the Chinese were able to reach it by land." Not surprisingly, Churchill backed Mountbatten. Chennault and his buddies also continued to oppose the Burma campaign. Alsop wrote Hopkins that Stilwell was "arrogantly courting disaster," forcing his way through a "trackless, foodless, mountainous waste," trying, in Alsop's words, to "breath life into the Burma campaign's corpse. . . . In my opinion he has no more chance of doing so than of flying over the moon."

"It takes a long time to even locate the Japs," Stilwell wrote his wife in January, "and a lot more to dig them out. We are in tiger and elephant country, although I haven't seen any yet. Some of the men have and I've seen droppings and tracks. When an elephant leaves his card in the trail, it takes a pole vaulter to climb over it. I expect to see Tarzan any day now. The jungle is full of his long swinging vines." In spite of the wild terrain and the snakes that got into his tent, Stilwell remained pleased with his soldiers. "Good work by Chinese: aggressive attack, good fire control, quick action. They are full of beans and tickled to death at beating the Japs." As was Stilwell, whose faith in the Chinese soldiers had finally begun to pay off.

Britain would probably have succeeded in pulling out of the Burma campaign, had the Japanese not launched a surprise attack on the Imphal Plain in India, destroying the road to the city of Imphal and leaving it isolated except by air. The situation for the British was critical. If they were forced to pull back, the province of Assam in northern India would be separated from Calcutta, and the air bases for the Hump, located in Assam, would be cut off. Many years later, Tuchman pointed out the irony of the situation. "By provoking the Japanese offensive," she said, "Stilwell's march had succeeded, if not in the way he planned. . . . The battle was to be decisive though not of Britain's choice, and Mountbatten . . . would emerge after the war as Earl Mountbatten of Burma."

At the moment of crisis, however, Mountbatten emerged not with a new title but from the hospital. A man who, according to a member of his own PR staff, "took an intense interest in everything to do with publicity, especially his own," the head of SEAC had gone into the jungle to mend fences with Stilwell and get a jump on him in the public relations war, which the

American seemed to be winning. Mountbatten arrived, escorted by sixteen fighters. "We had four fighters working on the battle," noted Stilwell acidly, offering the additional comment that Lord Louis "didn't like the smell of the corpses" he encountered on the battlefield. But while conferring with Stilwell, Mountbatten had managed to get a bamboo splinter in his eye and had had to be hospitalized. When he came out of the hospital, he was asked the inevitable question by Stilwell's deputy in Delhi: "How was it possible that three Japanese divisions could come through the mountains in suffi- cient strength to endanger Imphal when the British staff had been claiming for two years that to send an expedition in the opposite direction through the same country was impossible?" Beyond embarrassment, there was a need for reinforcements, and Mountbatten, who had thus far scorned Chinese troops, turned to Churchill and Roosevelt to ask Chiang personally for the Y Force. Chiang remained obdurate.

On April 3, Roosevelt radioed the generalissimo, "A shell of a division opposes you. . . . To take advantage of just such an opportunity we have dur- ing the past year been equipping and training your Yoke [Y] forces. If they are not to be used in the common cause our most strenuous and extensive efforts to fly in equipment and furnish instructional personnel have not been justified." Underscoring presidential disgust, Marshall assured Stilwell that if the Y Force did not move, Lend-Lease to China would be at an end. Stilwell wrote his chief of staff in Chungking, "I agree fully with George [Marshall]. If the Gmo won't fight, in spite of all his promises and all our efforts, I can see no reason for our wasting another ton. I recommend diver- sion . . . of all tonnage being delivered to any Chinese agency." To save Chiang's face, Stilwell's man in Chungking told General Ho (rather than the G-mo directly) that if the Y Force did not move, the Hump tonnage for the current month would be diverted elsewhere. Within two days, Ho was in- structed to order the Y Force to proceed. The decision to move the soldiers, Ho informed Marshall, "was made on initiative of Chinese without influ- ence of outside pressure."

Stilwell now advanced toward Myitkyina and, with the help of an Amer- ican group called Merrill's Marauders, seized the Myitkyina airstrip. Out of fear that he might fail, Stilwell had not told Mountbatten that he was con- tinuing his march into Burma, and it was, Tuchman reported, "brutally em- barrassing for the Supreme Allied Commander to wake up and discover a component of his* forces in Myitkyina when he had not known the expedi- tion was on its way." He was furious at Stilwell and thoroughly discomfited by an inquiry from Churchill, who wanted to know how "the Americans by a brilliant feat of arms have landed us in Myitkyina." But the English, rarely

---

* Mountbatten was the commander of SEAC and Stilwell's superior.

at a loss for the right thing to do, came up with an Order of the Day, sent to Stilwell in Mountbatten's name: "By the boldness of your leadership, backed by the courage and endurance of your American and Chinese troops, you have taken the enemy completely by surprise and achieved a most outstanding success by seizing the Myitkyina airfield." It was an historic victory and, according to White, "the only offensive combat victory won by Chinese troops against the Japanese in eight years."

Although everyone expected that control of the Myitkyina airport would lead easily and quickly to taking the city, the Japanese rushed in reinforcements—some 5,000 soldiers within two weeks—and Stilwell was forced to order in American convalescent soldiers to maintain an Allied presence in the area. In the middle of the crisis, Stilwell received a request from Mountbatten for transportation for Noel Coward and his troupe to the Ledo front. Out of either pique or the realization that Coward was not the right entertainer for Chinese and American troops, Stilwell refused. "I consider this a slam in the face," Mountbatten wrote back. Coward got his transportation, but, not surprisingly, his first performance fell "completely flat." At the second performance, given for the soldiers at the Ledo General Hospital, the audience was instructed "to show expressions of approval," which they apparently did. "If any more piano players start this way," Stilwell told his man in Delhi, "you know what to do with the piano."

"Summoned" from the Burma battlefields to Chungking in early June, Stilwell was prevailed upon to get Chennault his 10,000 tons by taking 1,500 away from other forces, providing the War Department agreed. But Marshall balked, saying that Chennault's air war had not justified the requisitions taken from other theaters of warfare. "It has been bleeding us white in transport airplanes" was his comment. "Instructions understood," Stilwell replied, "and exactly what I had hoped for."

❦

IN THE MIDDLE of September, on the day after the Japanese broke through the last effective defenses guarding the area around the airport in Kweilin, Stilwell and Chennault flew south to survey the situation. To keep the enemy from using their facilities, Stilwell ordered the Chinese commander to destroy all the American airstrips and installations except one. On the last night in Kweilin, 550 barracks and shacks were blown up. Harold Isaacs, the local *Newsweek* correspondent, described the scene for the readers of *CBI Roundup:*

A corporal, who comes from New Jersey, aimed along the thin beam of a lieutenant's searchlight and fired at the bottom of a gasoline drum through the open door. In great, hungry, licking sheets, flames split the darkness, raced along the floor, up walls and through the roof. The destruction of the American air base at Kweilin had begun. . . . Roaring yellow blazes produced bizarre lighting effects against the high, craggy fantastically misshapen limestone masses which jut in the most improbable contours from the earth's floor in Kwangsi, looking like a mad surface of Mars or the moon viewed through a powerful lens. . . . The 14 Air Force was pulling away from Kweilin which was waiting, stripped and unpeopled, for the will of the enemy.

A week later the Japanese reached a point just twenty-five miles from Kweilin and, after a reorganization period of five weeks, resumed the offensive, slicing easily through the leftovers of the Chinese army. By the middle of November, both Kweilin and Liuchow were in enemy hands, and the only active Allied soldiers remaining in the area were fifteen members of the OSS, sent in to destroy everything that might help the Japanese. Under the command of Major Frank Gleason, they went about systematically razing the countryside. With no money to pay for help, Gleason engaged Chinese coolies, whom he paid for their services by allowing them to loot the towns they passed through before the enemy got there.

When the OSS team got to the town of Tushan, Gleason heard that there was a lot of ammunition buried in the hills. He investigated and found three huge ammunition dumps, each with twenty to thirty warehouses about two hundred feet long. There were mortars, thousands of mortar shells, fifty new pieces of artillery, and vast supplies of ammunition—in all some 50,000 tons of supplies, hoarded by the Chinese military. Nearby, their troops, starved for arms, had been forced to abandon their positions. Gleason also found twenty tons of dynamite, which he used to blow up the dumps and their contents.

Having accomplished their mission of opening a route through China from Hankow to the Indo-Chinese border, the Japanese dug in for the winter. "Thus in December 1944," White said, "the invasion of China by Japan reached its high-water mark and receded. For the government and its armies 1944 had been a year of unmitigated disaster. Almost half a million Chinese soldiers had been lost, the entire coast was cut off from the Central Government, eight provinces and a population of more than 100,000,000 men had been ripped from the direct control of Chungking. The Kuomintang could explain its defeats in convincing terms of poverty and weakness. . . . But it could not explain why another Chinese army, that of the Communists, was moving from success to success in North China."

42

❧

It would of course have been undiplomatic to go into the nature of the military effort Chiang Kai-shek had made since 1938. It was practically zero.

—GENERAL JOSEPH STILWELL

IN SEPTEMBER 1944, President Roosevelt sent another troubleshooter, Patrick J. Hurley, to China with instructions to "try to keep the Chinese Nationalists in the war, tying up Japanese who would otherwise be killing Americans." Chiang liked Hurley, a rich Oklahoman who assured him that the U.S. government stood solidly behind him. Hurley also told Chiang that the aid China wanted would be forthcoming as soon as the generalissimo agreed to allow Stilwell to take over as commander-in-chief of the Chinese army and use Communist soldiers against Japan—solutions devoutly sought by Roosevelt and the brass in Washington. But, as Senator Judd put it, "There is no head of any government . . . that will make somebody else officially Commander-in-Chief of his own troops in his own country," and although Chiang seemed to agree, he did not follow through.

What the G-mo wanted was the right to control Lend-Lease. Stilwell and Hurley met with T.V., recently restored to Chiang's favor, and, according to Stilwell's diary for the day, "T.V. says we must remember the 'dignity' of a great nation, which would be 'affronted' if I [i.e., Stilwell] controlled the distribution." To which Hurley responded, "Remember, Dr. Soong, that is *our* property. We made it and we own it, and we can give it to whom we please." Much to Stilwell's delight, Hurley added that "there were 130 million Americans whose dignity also entered the case, as well as the 'dignity' of their children and their children's children, who would have to pay the bill."

On September 13, Stilwell received a visit from two representatives of Mao Tse-tung, who told him that Communist troops would fight under him but not under "a Chinese commander designated by CKS." Although Stilwell said he would go to Yenan to discuss it, the mere fact that he might consider using Communist soldiers to help fight the Japanese (along with the fact that the Chinese Communists clearly admired Stilwell's military judgment more than his own) drove Chiang crazy. The G-mo had probably heard that Chou En-lai had told John Service of the U.S. Embassy, half in jest, that he himself would have led the Communist troops in a campaign to retake Burma and "*I* would obey General Stilwell's orders."

In the meantime, the situation in Burma had changed. After bitter battles, the Y Force was now on its way over 11,000-foot mountains and the Salween River gorges toward the city of Lungling, currently occupied by the Japanese. An Allied occupation of Lungling was necessary to open the Burma Road, but the Y Force ran into trouble on the outskirts of the city. It desperately needed reinforcements to continue its advance, and Hurley told Chiang that he must send in more men. But the G-mo refused, saying that he wanted to bring back the soldiers who were already there to defend the front in east China. Chiang was afraid that if the Chinese lost the battle at Lungling, the Japanese would move on to Kunming and then to Chungking, and he was ready to sacrifice Stilwell's campaign, which was about to open up the Burma Road, to his fears. The situation was urgent, and the Japanese, numbering somewhere between 5,000 and 7,000 men, had decided to fight to the death. Chiang was finally convinced to give the orders that allowed the Y Force to proceed.

But Stilwell had wired Marshall concerning Chiang's threat to withdraw the Y Force and use it elsewhere. His telegram arrived in the middle of the second Quebec Conference, a summit between Roosevelt and Churchill held in September 1944, at which they laid out the strategy for defeating Japan. Marshall gave Roosevelt, Churchill, and the other members of the conference the essence of Stilwell's message: that is, Chiang's refusal to take part in breaking the blockade of China or his threat to do so. Marshall also seems to have brought along a draft of a reply, which became a six-hundred-word telegram written by his staff and signed by Roosevelt. The message, according to Tuchman, "adopted the tone of a headmaster to a sullen and incorrigible schoolboy." It explained that "the only thing you [Chiang] can do to prevent the Jap from achieving his objectives in China is to reinforce your Salween armies immediately and press their offensive, while at once placing General Stilwell in unrestricted command of all your forces. It appears plainly evident to all of us here that all your and our efforts to save China are to be lost by further delays." If Chiang failed to do this, he "must . . . be prepared to accept the consequences and assume the personal responsibility."

Instructed to deliver the wire in person, Stilwell arrived at the Chiang home during a dinner meeting that included Hurley, General Ho, and T.V. He showed Hurley the message before giving it to Chiang, and Hurley told him to soften the phrasing—exactly what May-ling, who was away, had always done when translating for her husband. Hurley even offered to deliver the crux of the message himself. Stilwell refused. It was, White says,

"the harshest document . . . delivered to Chiang in three years of alliance."
Chiang's knees apparently shook when it was read to him, and afterward,
according to White, his "wrath was incandescent."* Referring to the letter as
"the greatest humiliation I have been subjected to in my life," Chiang told
Hurley that the "Chinese were tired of the insults which Stilwell has seen fit
to heap upon them" and that the American general must be removed from
China. Hurley, Chiang, and T.V. wrote a letter to Roosevelt recommending
that Stilwell be recalled. Hurley showed it to Stilwell, who said it was like
"cutting my throat with a dull knife." When it looked as if Roosevelt might
not follow his advice, Hurley sent two more messages reiterating his position. "Thus," as historian Michael Schaller put it, "a man completely ignorant of actual conditions in China took it upon himself to insure that the
United States would sustain Chiang against all challenges."

It is interesting to contemplate what might have happened if May-ling
had been in Chungking at the time. During the war, "in accordance with
usual Army procedure," messages from the president to Chiang Kai-shek
were routinely delivered to May-ling, who gave them to her husband and
translated them for him. But while Madame was away, messages were re-
routed to Stilwell. Had she been at dinner, she would have been handed the
letter to translate and would have softened it considerably. Had she even
been in Chungking, friends who spoke of her "immense influence" over the
generalissimo believed that she would have been able to calm him down.
But Hurley was blindly supportive of Chiang, and T.V. had been trying to
get rid of Stilwell for years.

H. H. Kung, who was in the United States, suddenly entered the picture.
He saw Harry Hopkins at a dinner party and asked what Roosevelt was planning to do about Stilwell. Whatever Hopkins said, Kung, ever anxious to
please and never too bright, understood him to say that if the generalissimo
insisted, Roosevelt would remove Stilwell. Kung could not wait to cable
the good news to Chungking. On receipt of the cable, the G-mo met with
the top leaders of the KMT and told them that Stilwell "must go," that if the
United States insisted on keeping him in China, he would refuse U.S. aid
and retreat into the mountains with his loyal soldiers. T.V. confirmed that
"on this point [the] Generalissimo will not and cannot yield." By the time
Hopkins wired back that he had been misquoted,† Chiang had committed

---

* According to Alsop, Chiang "burst into convulsive and stormy sobbing" after everyone except T.V. had left the room. (Alsop with Platt, *I've Seen the Best of It: Memoirs*,
p. 241.)

† He had actually told Kung that the president would take no action on Stilwell without
consulting Marshall.

himself. Roosevelt tried to effect a compromise, but the generalissimo, who would have lost face with the party leaders, refused to consider it.

The day after Chiang's meeting, Stilwell wired Marshall that "the situation now has reached a deadlock and the real reason is not that the generalissimo objects to me but rather that he desires to avoid any further voluntary military effort. . . . It is possible that if a way could be indicated . . . by which he could recover from the results of his premature announcement to the central executive committee . . . the problem can still be solved." To accomplish this, Stilwell recommended setting up a joint Sino-American Military Committee, which would make policy and "give the generalissimo a boost in prestige" by allowing him "to win his point with regard to me personally to the extent that I would not be anything but a field commander executing orders. . . . As field commander I could ensure that orders were obeyed and that the plans and policies, which would be largely created by the . . . committee, were actually executed and that the maximum military effort was made." Stilwell finished his wire by stating, "If I considered that my removal would be the solution I would be the first to suggest it."

Two weeks later, Stilwell and Chiang were informed that the American general would be relieved of his command, that he should leave immediately for the United States, and that there would be no other American commander in chief for the Chinese army. In addition, Chiang was advised that the CBI theater no longer existed but had been split into a China theater and an India-Burma theater. American troops in China would be under the command of General Albert C. Wedemeyer. Forty-eight years old, tall and tactful, Wedemeyer was known as a superb strategist. "THE AX FALLS." Stilwell wrote. ". . . Hurley feels very badly. Told me he had lost me the command. Sees his mistakes now—too late."

Secretary of War Stimson thought Stilwell's removal was unwarranted and unfair. "Stilwell has been the one successful element of the three forces that have been supposed to operate in Burma," he said. ". . . This campaign in all the difficulties of the monsoon has been a triumphant vindication of Stilwell's courage and sagacity. He has been pecked at from both sides, carped at by the British from India, and hamstrung at every moment by Chiang Kai-shek." Nevertheless, the recall went through.

The head cheerleader on the other side was Joseph Alsop, whose attacks on Stilwell came thick and fast, mostly after the general's death in 1946. Alsop, who referred to Vinegar Joe as "the pro-Chinese-Communist Gen. Joseph W. Stilwell," claimed in an article in *The Saturday Evening Post* that "Stilwell's dismissal interrupted a program that would have brought the Chinese communists to power." According to Alsop, Stilwell "warmly admired the communists" and had "intrigued" with the "incompetent and reaction-

ary Minister of War, General Ho." As to Chiang, who, Alsop admitted, preferred "pliant bad lots to independent-minded good men," he was, in Alsop's
words, "one of the great men of our time," and "those who deny his greatness are fools or worse."

Before leaving China, Stilwell wrote a "very decent" letter to Chennault
and another to the head of the CCP army in Yenan, saying that he was sorry
not to have been able to fight the Japanese with "you and the excellent
troops you have developed." He visited Ching-ling, who cried and told him
she wished she could go to the United States and tell Roosevelt the truth. He
later wrote that she was "the most sympatica of the three women [sisters],
and probably the deepest." Stilwell also went to see Ambassador Gauss, who
resigned his post shortly thereafter, and then called on the generalissimo,
who offered him the highest Chinese decoration, the Special Cordon of the
Blue Sky and White Sun. Stilwell refused to accept it.

On October 20, 1944, Joseph Stilwell left China secretly. Along with
General Hurley, who had recommended his removal to Roosevelt, and General Ho, the only other person at the airport to say good-bye was T. V. Soong,
who had been trying for two and a half years to get him recalled. His trip to
the United States was kept under wraps. His victories had made him a hero
at home, and the Democrats worried that his dismissal might prompt
Republican charges of improper action. He arrived in Washington only
days before the presidential election. His arrival, like his departure from
China, was kept secret, and he was hustled out of the nation's capital so as
not to embarrass Roosevelt, who won his fourth term as president shortly
thereafter.

Nevertheless, there was wide speculation about him in the press. An
editorial in the *New York Herald Tribune* called the president's explanation
that Stilwell's recall was merely a personality clash "nonsense" and declared
both countries at fault. The Chinese were responsible for corruption in the
military and the failure to come to terms with the CCP, but the Roosevelt
administration had also made mistakes, mainly in its choice of representatives. Stilwell was, in the words of the *Tribune,* "a superb commander" but
"the right man in the wrong job," while Gauss, who was "disliked by Chinese officials, to whom 'courtesy and suavity' were so important," was another. "The most adroit general and the most skillful ambassador would
have had no easy time in such a situation," the editorial concluded, but
"General Stilwell and Ambassador Gauss, able as they were, did not have the
required qualities."

During that same month, Chiang Kai-shek found himself rid of another
enemy when word came of the death of Wang Ching-wei. Suffering from his
old complaint of diabetes along with the wounds he had suffered in Chiang's

attempts on his life, Wang, who had served for four years as head of the puppet government in Nanking, was taken to a hospital in Japan, where he died in November of 1944. His remains were put in a tomb in Nanking, which was later destroyed by the Nationalists, presumably under Chiang's orders.

❦

THE REASON THAT Madame Chiang was not in Chungking to translate the unfortunate wire that led to Stilwell's dismissal was that she was in the United States, to which she had retreated in the middle of the summer of 1944. Complaining of nervous exhaustion and skin disease, she was also trying to put an end to a private drama that had been raging in the Chiang household since before her return from the United States the year before. Toward the end of that earlier trip, rumors had begun circulating that her husband was living with another woman, and on her arrival in Chungking, she was met by a story that during her absence her husband had been having an affair with a Miss Chen, variously identified as the G-mo's second wife who had returned to China, a young nurse, or a girl from the province of Chekiang. Whoever she was, the affair was obviously payback for May-ling's romance with Wendell Willkie. Madame did not stay in her own home for long but moved in with the Kungs, then apparently went to Hong Kong. Rumors of impending divorce began to make the rounds.

John Fairbank interviewed May-ling two months after her return. Her mission to the United States, he said, had been "lushly reported" in Chungking. He was not as bowled over by her as his fellow Americans:

Chungking, Sept. 16, 1943

My small hour with the great lady: I have just come back from an hour's talk [with Madame Chiang], with a number of mixed impressions. . . . The sum is that she is trying so hard to be a great lady. Conversation too cosmic to be real. An actress, with a lot of admirable qualities, great charm, quick intuition, intelligence, but underneath, emotions that are unhappy . . . bitterness about something. . . . Usually the beautiful but sad expression and the well-modulated tones with pauses for effect, upper lip pulled down in a strained way; but occasionally a real laugh, with a round relaxed face and higher-pitched voice, which seemed natural and at ease and made all the rest seem forced and tragic. . . . She was tired and her head shook a bit as old men's do. I get the impression that she was unhappy about many things.

Eight months later, in May of 1944, the U.S. Embassy's John Service addressed the rumors directly:

Chungking is literally seething with stories of the domestic troubles of the Chiang household. Almost everyone has new details and versions to add to the now, generally accepted story that the Generalissimo has taken a mistress and as a result his relations with the Madame are—to say the least—strained. There is so much smoke, it would seem that there must be some fire. Normally such gossip about the private lives of government leaders would not be considered as within the scope of political reporting. This is hardly the case, however, in China where the person concerned is a dictator and where the relationship between him and his wife's family is so all-important. . . . If the Madame . . . should openly break with her husband, the dynasty would be split and the effects both in China and abroad might be serious. . . . The stories generally agree that the Generalissimo (whose sexual life was not particularly monogamous) . . . took up with his present attachment while the Madame was in the United States. . . . The prevalence and belief of these stories, and the humorous elaborations which are passed around, are at least indications of the unpopularity of the Madame (it is generally regarded by Chinese as a joke at her expense) and the decline in respect for both her and the Generalissimo. . . . Typical of these anecdotal stories are: The Madame now refers to the Generalissimo only as "That Man." The Madame complains that the Generalissimo now only puts his teeth in when he is going to see "that woman." The Madame went into the Generalissimo's bedroom one day, found a pair of high-heeled shoes under the bed, threw them out of the window and hit a guard on the head. . . . The Generalissimo at one time did not receive callers for four days because he had been bruised on the side of the head with a flower vase in a spat with the Madame. . . .

All these stories may be nothing more than malicious gossip. But a number of surface indications might be interpreted as indicating at least serious tension between the Generalissimo and the Madame. The Madame . . . has avoided social life and public appearances. She has been rarely seen with the Generalissimo, and when together, they have seemed to observers to be very cool. The Madame is not well: her complaint, a skin irritation, is regarded medically as being a result of nervous strain. She avoids photographers. And people who have seen her at close range have remarked . . . that she seems irritable. . . . If the situation as reported is true, it has undoubtedly been a great strain on the Madame—because of her pride as a woman, her puritanical Methodism . . . and her knowledge of the effect it will have on her prestige. Nonetheless, most observers believe that the stakes of power are so important to the Soong family that they . . . will do everything to prevent an open break and that she will swallow her pride and put up with the situation. Critics of the Generalissimo regard it all as evidence of the hollowness of his Christian and New Life moralizing, and another indication that he is after all not far from being an old-fashioned "warlord."

Everyone had a different story to tell. According to the London *Daily Mail*, the generalissimo and the Madame had split, and she was thinking of making her home in Florida. Another paper reported that Chiang Kai-shek's first wife, Ching-kuo's mother (who was dead and whom Chiang had never much liked anyway), had moved into his house. Even the Communists got into the act, predicting that Madame would soon sue the G-mo for divorce. When May-ling told Chiang that she had decided to join sister Ai-ling in a trip to Brazil "on the advice of [her] doctors," he invited sixty people—members of his cabinet, major officials, a handful of journalists, and the odd missionary—to a seated tea party in the garden, in the middle of which he stood up and gave a highly emotional, forty-five-minute speech, claiming that, ugly rumors to the contrary, he had remained true to his wife and his Christianity: "On the departure of my wife for Brazil on account of her health, I decided to give this farewell party for her. You are all my friends and I think the time has come to speak very frankly about a subject. I feel it is most important to do this for the good of the country. Perhaps my Chinese friends here think that I should not speak so frankly. But it is necessary."

"In leading my fellow countrymen," he said, "I rely not on power or position, but on my character and integrity. As a member of the revolutionary party, I must abide by revolutionary discipline. As a Christian, I must obey the commandments. Had I violated the discipline and the commandments either in public or private moral conduct, I should have been a rebel against Christ, against our late father Sun Yat-sen, and against the millions of my countrymen who have given their lives to our cause. Any one of them should impeach or punish me in accordance with discipline and the commandments."

Chiang's strange speech struck one foreign guest at the party as "very impressive, and in a cockeyed way convincing. There he stood, talking in the most logical way, saying in effect that if he were guilty of such conduct he was unworthy to be the leader of China. But he <u>was</u> the leader of

China. Therefore he could not be guilty of such conduct. Oddly enough, I was convinced."

Although May-ling answered publicly—first in Chinese, then in English—that she had never for a second doubted her husband, it would be interesting to know why Chiang felt obliged to make such a point of his supposed fidelity. He must have thought that it was the way to get public opinion back on his side in the deteriorating political situation in which he now found himself. According to one account, it was May-ling who told him he must deal with the stories swirling around them. "Even during a month of disastrous military defeat," according to White and Jacoby, "this garden confessional got top billing in Chungking conversation for days." According to the reporters, "semiofficial transcripts of the Generalissimo's denial could be obtained from the government on request."

This must have seemed an excellent time for the generalissimo wife to take a sabbatical. Even in the United States, the press, which always gushed sympathy and admiration for her, had taken a second look at her stylish clothes and serious furs. "First Lady of China Too Chic" declared *The Boston Post* in July 1944. "When it was announced that Madame Chiang would make her personal appearances in America, the public expected to feast their eyes upon the sad-smiling lady whose photograph they knew in scenes of rubble among China's war-stricken orphans ... the illusion somehow was broken when they saw her in her priceless sable coat and muff, adorned with diamonds and jade worth a king's ransom."

Suffering from bad publicity and nerves, a "pale and listless" May-ling left China for Brazil on July 1, 1944, with a party of ten: Ai-ling; Ai-ling's daughter Jeanette; Ai-ling's son Louis; Louis's wife; plus Madame's personal maid, Ai-ling's personal maid, two other maids, a secretary, and a cook. They departed secretly, in order to avoid an attack by the Japanese. At the beginning of the trip, Madame took up residence in a house on the tiny island of Brocoio off the coast of Rio de Janeiro, living quietly under the care of doctors, seldom going even as far as Rio.* On July 20, Chiang wired, "I haven't heard from you yet. I miss you very much. Did you receive my wire of the

---

* According to Seagrave, while May-ling rested, sister Ai-ling "wheeled and dealed" with their host, Getúlio Vargas, the dictatorial president of Brazil, a man who was said to have brought the more ruthless, if superficial, elements of European fascism to Latin America. Kung's wife, Seagrave wrote, "transferred sums of money" and bought properties in industrial São Paolo. He also contends that the Kungs and Soongs had been investing in South America for some time. (Sterling Seagrave, *The Soong Dynasty*, p. 413.) According to a member of the British Information Service, the purpose of Ai-ling's visit was "to inspect her investments in that hemisphere," which were "said to be very large." (National Archives: RG 226, Entry 210, Box 401, July 26, 1944.)

13th? Have you recovered from your illness?" In August, she heard from Emma: "I have been so distressed that you have had to leave Chungking again, although not very surprised after what you wrote about yourself. . . . I do hope . . . you have been left more in peace than you were up here [i.e., during May-ling's last trip to New York]."

Only in her journal did Emma write about what really concerned her: "Mayling is strongly under the influence of Mrs. Kung. I wish she had almost anyone else with her in Rio. And the weird Jeannette and rather gross young nephew are along as well. . . . H. H. Kung's adherents are taking charge of the Bank of China, and he has succeeded in liquidating China Defense Supplies . . . a newly returned American army officer said Kung was taking 10 to 20% of the total national income of China."

In the middle of August, May-ling cabled T.V. that she was "not supposed to stay [in Brazil] too long because of the humidity," and on September 6, 1944, the Chinese party flew from Rio to the United States. They arrived in style on the presidential plane known as the "Sacred Cow," a C-54 fitted out with a stateroom and an elevator for Roosevelt.* Once more, May-ling took over a floor in the Harkness Pavilion of Presbyterian Hospital. Her illness was described as nervous exhaustion, for which her doctors prescribed the usual rest. A month later, she moved to River Oaks, a seventeen-room mansion Louis Kung leased for her in the Riverdale section of the West Bronx, although she continued to return to the hospital for treatments. When Willkie died in early October, she was not told, because "physicians fear that excitement might hinder her recovery."

Just before May-ling and Ai-ling left for Brazil, H. H. Kung had left China for Washington. The war years had not been easy for Kung. He had spent most of his time alone, rattling around his huge Chungking home while his family retreated to Hong Kong or the United States. He suffered from malaria as well as a condition of the spleen that made his life a misery. His son David had been named a director of the Central Trust, but, according to White, David's "conduct was outrageous." Kung's daughter, Jeanette, was not much better. Returning from the United States to China with Auntie May on an American military plane that arrived over the Hump with barely enough fuel to get back, the young woman insisted that the American ground crew drain the tanks so she herself could have the gas.

It was said that Kung had left China to attend the three-week-long U.N. Monetary and Financial Conference held at Bretton Woods in New Hampshire, the postwar conference that established the International Monetary

* The 5,300-mile trip down to Rio and back to the United States made aviation history— the first time any airplane had flown more than 5,000 miles in one day.

Fund. But a U.S. State Department dispatch indicates that Chiang, aware of the "bad odor surrounding Dr. Kung and members of his family," had exiled Kung to the United States—a conclusion Kung went to great lengths to deny in his "Reminiscences," which he dictated in 1948. A shining example of Chinese "face," Kung was annoyed when Treasury Secretary Morgenthau was late getting to the airport to greet him, and nothing about his arrival appeared in the papers until he himself held a press conference. According to the reporter for *The Washington Post*, the "indifferent reception" was "intolerable" to Kung, who immediately set up a branch of the Chinese News Service in the United States.

The day after her arrival in New York, May-ling called Emma, saying she was "suffering the tortures of the damned" and asked her friend to come to the hospital the next evening for dinner. During the next day, which brought torrential rains and hurricane warnings, Emma called to beg off, but after receiving a call from May-ling's secretary, Miss Garvey—"Madame has had a wretched day and been looking forward so much to your coming"—she went. During a steak dinner served in her hospital suite, May-ling talked about love and the rumors about her marriage to Chiang. "She admitted she had never been in love herself, but spoke of her husband in a natural, easy manner," Emma wrote in her journal. "Once again she said she could be completely herself with me." From love they passed on to looks, and May-ling told Emma that "more than anything, I always wanted perfect beauty—more than brains or money."

"Who has such 'perfect beauty'?" Emma asked, disregarding May-ling's lack of concern for money as "nonsense."

"Mrs. Luce. But she's losing it now," May-ling answered, launching into her version of her last conversation with Joe Kennedy, who had told her that she had more sex appeal "than any woman I've ever met."

"You really mean charm," May-ling said she had answered.

"No, Clare Luce has charm but doesn't stir me in the least," Kennedy claimed. "What did you think has been the cause of all the enthusiasm about you? Why, sex appeal, of course." Eventually, in May-ling's version of the story—which differed considerably from Kennedy's—she had managed to get rid of him, refused his subsequent efforts to see her, and did not answer his wire saying good-bye.

If Joe Kennedy found May-ling attractive, her husband was clearly suffering from her absence. "Are you feeling better now?" he wired at the end of November. "It's a pity that I cannot take care of you myself. Tomorrow is our seventeenth wedding anniversary. We will not be able to spend the great day together at home as we had promised each other. The only thing that I can do is pray in my heart every morning and evening, hoping that my beloved wife will recover and that we can live together soon again." By the time May-ling's birthday rolled around in March, Chiang seems to have calmed down a bit: "Your birthday is coming up soon," he wired. "It is a pity that we cannot be together to toast you. I sincerely hope that God will help you recover and return to our homeland as soon as possible."

May-ling saw a lot of Emma during her stay in New York, mostly in the spring, after her health improved. The two old friends went to the movies, the circus, and the Bronx Zoo. When May-ling's energy returned, she even got one of her Secret Service men to teach her to drive, and she drove Emma around Manhattan, up to Hyde Park to see Eleanor Roosevelt, and to the state prison for women in Westchester to study conditions there. She was also wont to call her friend at all hours of the day and night, asking her to come to Riverdale and edit articles she was writing. Nine years later, Emma remembered being frustrated by May-ling's passion for esoteric language. "How she loves long words. . . . I longed to simplify some of those tortured phrases." At one point May-ling handed Emma a check for $1,000. "I'll be so far away soon and some day you may need money in a hurry," she said when Emma protested. "I worry you live alone, and what you would do in case of sudden illness or accident."

Frank Dorn, Stilwell's former aide, who had been recalled to the United States shortly after Stilwell himself, was currently serving as a brigadier general in charge of the Armed Forces Information School in Pennsylvania. He was there during the time that May-ling was in Riverdale. Although he tried to see her, he was told by Ai-ling that she was suffering from "a chronic nervous condition and mental depression which had destroyed her digestive system," that she had "eruptions . . . over her entire body," and that it might be three to six months before she could stand the "excitement or nervous upset" of seeing anyone. After what Dorn called "some mutual conversation sparring" between them, Ai-ling told Dorn that she wanted to ask him a strictly confidential question: Was the story she had heard that Stilwell was "definitely a Communist sympathizer (politically) and that he had attempted to aid them to power" true?

Dorn answered that Stilwell was "not interested in politics or parties as such; he looked on the Chinese Communists as another possible source of military manpower just as he considered any other groups of able-bodied men in China . . . his attitude was that they were all Chinese (rather than members of parties—in the same sense that we are all American, whether Republicans or Democrats); and that he, like everyone else, hoped that the two groups could come together for the good of China." He must have convinced Ai-ling, because she wound up saying that Stilwell's "deep and sincere feeling for China and her people and soldiers was above all politics."

Moreover, she claimed that she had been "shocked" at his recall and hoped to be instrumental in bringing him back. She also stressed the confidentiality of her conversation with Dorn three or four times. As for May-ling, she kept silent on the subject of Stilwell's dismissal for many years but then attacked him in a commentary about the book of his successor, General Wedemeyer, *On War and Peace.* When it was published in the 1980s, she compared Stilwell to Wedemeyer who, she said, "changed discord into harmony . . . following the arrogant divisiveness and cantankerous friction . . . left by the know-it-all . . . Stilwell cabal."

May-ling was often at her worst when she was with Ai-ling. During her year in the United States, Ai-ling's daughter Rosamonde became engaged and was due to marry in New York. According to Fenby, May-ling ordered her niece's trousseau to be sewn by the Women's Work Department she had set up in China to make clothes for soldiers. The clothes and linens were to be flown to the United States, but the plane crash-landed and a newspaper got hold of the story. The article said that the work that had gone into making the trousseau could have clothed a regiment of men; the cost of flying Rosamonde's trousseau would have fed many thousands of starving refugees; and the price of the wedding would have endowed a Chinese university.

There were many stories flying around Chungking of May-ling's "antics" in the United States, mostly aimed at her love of expensive trappings. United Press claimed that many Chinese high in KMT circles were predicting "with lightly concealed pleasure" that Madame Chiang would never return to her position of power if the elder statesmen had anything to do with it. They were critical of Madame's Western ideas, Western manners, and what they called her " 'extravagant' use of jewelry, nail polish and other items of personal adornment." She was, they told Chiang, "setting a bad example for the Chinese people who were being urged to lead a life of austerity during China's war of resistance." Shortly after May-ling's departure for Brazil, a reporter asked a high government official, "When could the madame be expected to return to China if as reported she planned to visit the United States and possibly England?" The official waited a moment before answering, then "replied, with obvious satisfaction: 'Young man, I don't believe you or I will live to see Madame Chiang return to China.' "

43

⚜

History is the folding of miscalculations.

—Barbara Tuchman

On November 7, 1944, the day Roosevelt was reelected to his fourth term in office, Brigadier General Patrick J. Hurley, bristling with "overbearing self-confidence," flew from Chungking to Yenan to effect a rapprochement between the Chinese Communist Party and the Kuomintang. Hurley, the fourth in a parade of what China Hand John Davies called "a preposterous series of plenipotentiaries to China," had already failed in his other two assignments—the first being to solve the Chiang-Stilwell problem and the second to establish U.S. control over the Chinese army. Nonetheless, he approached this, his most difficult task, with a cheerful bravado resulting from naiveté and a lack of information about the aims of the parties on both sides.

Hurley was a tall, good-looking man with straight posture and a bristling white mustache. An orphan born in Oklahoma, he had been a coal miner, cowboy, soldier (he had fought in World War I), lawyer, millionaire, and secretary of war for President Hoover. He had served every president since Theodore Roosevelt except Warren Harding and was pulling strings to succeed Gauss as U.S. ambassador to China.* Regarded as an experienced troubleshooter, he was social and gregarious. He was also given to doing war dances in the middle of embassy parties and letting out war whoops of the Choctaw Indians, whose language he had learned early in life.

Hurley was sixty-one when Roosevelt sent him to China. Never much of an intellectual—he pronounced Mao Tse-tung "Moose Dung" and called Chiang "Mr. Shek"—he was having trouble with his eyes and used the junior officers in the U.S. Embassy to read to him what they considered essential papers and dispatches. Most of these men spoke Chinese and had had experience in the country, which Hurley himself had not. "He works almost entirely alone and without advice from Embassy personnel," noted Frank

---

* Hurley outmaneuvered Lauchlin Currie, who was also campaigning for the assignment. (Hoover Archives: Lauchlin Currie papers, LC, "Memorandum for the President: Re: Ambassador to China," November 13, 1942.)

Dorn, "and being unfamiliar with the ramifications of Chinese wheels within wheels, has made some peculiar mistakes." State Department officer John S. Service had predicted that Hurley's appointment would be a "disaster," and it came as no surprise that Hurley and his diplomatic associates in Chungking were constantly at odds. While they referred to the famous six adjectives describing the generalissimo's government—"inept, incompetent, inefficient, un-Democratic, corrupt, and reactionary"—Hurley blindly supported his new best friend, Chiang Kai-shek, not even allowing reports critical of the G-mo to go out from the embassy. Roosevelt's new emissary branded those who disagreed with him as Communists, and several men were recalled from Chungking on his say-so. (As one wag put it, they were "Hurleyed out of China.") Within three months of the Oklahoman's arrival in Chungking, he had become, according to White and Jacoby, "an island of outraged dignity in the American community," a man who "saw in the differing opinions of other Americans a constant plotting to undermine him." Hurley seems not to have realized, as White put it, "that the Kuomintang was not China but one Chinese party, with a party dictatorship and a party army." With this lack of knowledge and perspective, Hurley set out from Chungking for Yenan to make peace between the leaders of the KMT and the CCP.

❧

BY THE TIME Hurley arrived in Yenan, the Chinese Communists, who had started with only 35,000 square miles at the end of the Long March in 1937, had gained control over a region of 155,000 square miles with a population of 54 million souls and an army of 475,000 men.* They had, according to White and Jacoby, "exploded rather than expanded," inhabiting an area containing the largest concentration of Japanese soldiers and industry in China apart from Manchuria. By moving in behind Japanese lines, the CCP had also been able to establish enclaves in northern Kiangsu and Hupei, in the south near Canton, and on the island of Hainan. Since the Communists offered the locals a reduction in taxes and a political organization free from KMT-style corruption, they had won the support of the peasants in their areas, who now lived better than they had ever lived before.

To quarantine the Communists, Chiang Kai-shek kept twenty of his best divisions (300,000 soldiers) tied up blocking 50,000 soldiers of the CCP. According to the KMT, the Communist troops were in league with the Japanese; according to the CCP, theirs were the only troops fighting the common

---

* Statistics from Tuchman, *Stilwell and the American Experience in China, 1911–45,* p. 589. White and Jacoby's figures differ; they estimate twice as many inhabitants and twice as many soldiers. (White and Jacoby, *Thunder out of China,* p. 199.)

enemy. Neither claim was true. The Nationalist soldiers bore the brunt of the conflict in spite of poor leadership, lack of food, and a paucity of arms. The CCP was in a position to choose its battles; its soldiers were better fed; and more care was taken of the wounded.

Communist soldiers obtained their arms by attacking small groups of Japanese soldiers and taking their weapons. They fought in bands of 300 to 400 men, connected by telephone or radio to their headquarters in Yenan. These bands could be called up quickly and put together for an assault of anywhere from 15,000 to 20,000 men, then sent back home. Guerrillas were also called out to attack the enemy's long, extended columns of soldiers, and from 1942 on, mine warfare, which the Communists taught the peasants, was raised "almost to the level of an indigenous national sport." As White and Jacoby put it, "no Chinese group other than the Communists ever dared to arm the people, for that meant enabling peasants to rectify their own grievances. The Communists, serene in the consciousness of popular support, could arm hundreds of thousands and know that the arms would not be turned against them." Like Chiang, however, the CCP did not hesitate to enrich itself through the sale of narcotics, although the use of opium was banned within Yenan.

The American and foreign press had started asking the G-mo's permission to visit the Communists in Yenan in 1943. Chiang had agreed to let them go but kept putting off their trip. He eventually allowed three reporters from New York, London, and Sydney to leave in May of 1944 and a second group, consisting of Theodore White, Harold Isaacs, and Brooks Atkinson, to follow in September. A master dissembler, Mao told the first group, "The Chinese Communist Party has never wavered from its policy of supporting Generalissimo Chiang Kai-shek, the policy of continuing the cooperation between the Kuomintang and the Communist Party and the entire people, and the policy of defeating Japanese imperialism and struggle for the building of a free democratic China." Atkinson, reporting for *The New York Times*, said that the soldiers of the Communist Eighth Route Army were "among the best-clothed and best fed this writer has seen anywhere in China."

Due, no doubt, to the journalists' enthusiastic reports on military and agricultural progress in Yenan, the military mission sought by Washington continued to be politely put off. Early in 1944, the president had formally asked Chiang to allow military observers to travel "immediately" to Shansi and Shensi (both Communist-held areas), and Chiang had agreed to "facilitate" their trip but specified that the Americans could enter only those areas under Kuomintang control. The mission—code-named DIXIE*—was ready to go in March, but the G-mo continued to delay. Roosevelt, who repeated

---

* As in rebels and "Is it true what they say about Dixie?"

his request in April and May, had instructed Wallace to "insist" that the military mission be allowed to proceed, whereupon Chiang finally gave in.

One of the journalists who traveled with the mission described their arrival: "The Yenan people . . . were mighty glad. Within two months the door to their blockaded, forbidden areas had opened for the second time. And with all due respect to us, these [military] guests obviously carried more weight than the representatives of the world's most important newspapers." Men like John Service, who accompanied the military mission, were impressed by the youth and vigor, both physical and intellectual, of their hosts. "They are cordial and friendly—but not demonstratively anxious to make a good impression," said Service, who also noted their "sincerity, loyalty and determination." A Chinese journalist was more perceptive: "if you ask the same question of twenty or thirty people, from intellectuals to workers, their replies are always more or less the same . . . [although] . . . they unanimously and firmly deny the Party had any direct control over their thoughts." John Davies, who described Mao as "big and plump with a round, bland, almost feminine face," had been clued in by Ching-ling before he left. She told him that the Communists were "playing a waiting game. . . . The longer they wait the stronger they become." Because of this, Davies took the long view, as did Brigadier General Dorn. "The Communists feel that their growing strength among the people of China will win them the entire country after the war, and that they are safe in biding their time. It is certain that the acute dissatisfaction among all classes indicates a break-up of the present Chinese Government at some time in the not too distant future."

❧

NOVEMBER 7, 1944, was a cold, gray day in northern China, and Brigadier General Hurley, his uniformed chest blazing with medals and ribbons, seemed a particularly bright spot as he stepped off his plane onto the otherwise bleak airstrip that served the home of the CCP. The Communist leaders, notified only after his arrival, climbed into the beaten-up ambulance that Mao used for transportation* and dashed out to the airport, running across the landing field to greet him. After saying hello, Hurley let out one of his famous war whoops and climbed into the ambulance. It was apparently a jolly ride as the big American bounced along with the leaders of the CCP, sharing the ups and downs of the deeply rutted road. When they passed a shepherd boy, Mao said that he himself had once worked as a shep-

---

* Fenby tells us that the ambulance had been given to the CCP by the New York Chinese Laundrymen's National Salvation Association and still bore the name of its donor on its side.

herd, and Hurley countered with stories of his life as a cowboy. When Mao commented on the Yen River, which rose in the winter and dried up in the summer, Hurley talked about similar rivers in Oklahoma, where you could recognize schools of fish only by the amount of dust they raised. Colonel David Barrett, the head of the U.S. Military Mission, translated Hurley's comments and jokes into flawless Chinese, and by the time the ambulance arrived at Yenan, everyone seemed happy. That evening the Communists gave a banquet for their American visitor.

The negotiations, which opened the next day, did not go as well as the preliminaries. Up to this point, Hurley had been his usual undoubting self. "Don't worry," he had told Service, "I'll bring these two sides together. . . . That's what I'm here for. . . . I've had experience with this sort of thing." But Hurley had not had enough experience with the generalissimo and had come to Yenan "convinced that Chiang Kai-shek personally is anxious for a settlement." Toward that end, he brought a proposal from Chungking that offered to legalize the Communist Party, share some of the supplies the KMT received from Lend-Lease, and allot the CCP one seat on China's Supreme National Defense Council; in return, the generalissimo demanded that the Communists place their army and the people in their subject areas under his command. Chiang's plan infuriated Mao, who used the opportunity to rail against the Kuomintang. In response, Hurley claimed that Mao was only repeating the propaganda of China's enemies. Mao answered that he was expressing what most of China's friends knew. Hurley responded with a defense of the KMT, and the day ended with nothing accomplished.

That evening and the next day, Hurley drafted what he believed to be a solution to the problem. He proposed a coalition government, which would include the CCP, an integration of the Communist armies under the control of the central government, and a bill of rights including freedom of speech and assembly. "An impressive document," according to White, it was "an excellent outline for unity—and an even better outline of how little Hurley understood his friend Chiang Kai-shek." The Communists were delighted. Although Hurley pointed out that he could not speak for Chiang, he told them that this document represented his views, and, as a token of good faith, he signed one copy for them and one for the Americans. Mao signed as well, and Chou En-lai was delegated to fly back to Chungking to discuss the proposal with Chiang.

While Chou waited to see Chiang—the G-mo was said to be ill when he arrived—he negotiated some of the finer points of the Hurley document with T. V. Soong and Wang Shih-chieh, a former educator and future minister of foreign affairs. T.V.'s reaction when Hurley first showed him his proposal was not encouraging. "You have been sold a bill of goods by the

Communists," he told the Oklahoman. "The National Government will never grant what the Communists have requested." And indeed, when the final paper was presented to Chiang, he said he would have nothing to do with it. He refused to accept any solution that challenged his authority, saying that it was a sacred trust from Sun Yat-sen and a responsibility he was not free to share. Or, as Service put it, Chiang Kai-shek was "an extremely adroit political manipulator and a stubborn, shrewd bargainer . . . he . . . listens to his own instrument of force rather than reason." Chou, who saw Chiang only once during his stay, was apparently treated with such contempt that he swore he would never return to Chungking.

For their part, the leaders of the CCP were unwilling to accept any scheme that left China under the exclusive control of Chiang Kai-shek. They had other solutions in mind. "The Chinese Communists are so strong between the Great Wall and the Yangtze that they can now look forward to the post-war control of at least North China," John Davies wrote. "They may also continue to hold not only those parts of the Yangtze Valley they now dominate but also new areas in Central and South China. . . . The Communists have survived . . . and they have grown. . . . The reason for this phenomenal vitality and strength is simple and fundamental. It is mass support."

Hurley still managed to persuade the two sides to go back to the bargaining table. He assured the Communists that Chiang was promising more concessions if they would agree to abide by the authority of the KMT. But it had become clear to Mao and his men that the generalissimo would continue to refuse any coalition in which his power might be challenged. Nevertheless, since neither side wanted to be accused of obstinacy, they agreed to a future conference "to take steps to draft a constitution to pass control of the National Government to the people and to abolish the one party rule of the Kuomintang."

Writing his report on the situation, Hurley managed to regard the negotiations in the most optimistic, if not delusionary, light. "I pause to observe that in this dreary controversial chapter two fundamental facts are emerging: (one) the Communists are not in fact Communists, they are striving for democratic principles; and (two) the one party, one man personal Government of the Kuomintang is not in fact Fascist. It is striving for democratic principles. Both the Communists and the Kuomintang have a long way to go, but, if we know the way, if we are clear minded, tolerant and patient, we can be helpful."

But Hurley, according to Dorn, was looked on as a "buffoon" and "something of a clown"; the Communists even derided him out loud. Both the CCP and the KMT resented what Dorn called the Oklahoman's "bland assumption that he could settle their difficulties by charm, by kidding, by so-called frank talks, and by empty promises." For Dorn, there was only the thinnest hope for Hurley's success. "It is not impossible," he said, "that the common resentment against Hurley may tend—tend only—to throw the two parties together for the purpose of ridding themselves of his 'negotiations.'"

❦

UNKNOWN TO HURLEY at the time, Roosevelt, who was on his way to the Yalta Conference, was planning to come to an agreement with Stalin about China. The president's intentions were made clear in a memo that circulated in the State Department a few weeks before he left for the Crimea. "We must," the memo read, "have the support of the Soviet Union to defeat Germany. We sorely need the Soviet Union in the war against Japan when the war in Europe is over. The importance of these two things can be reckoned in terms of American lives."

Although the United States and Great Britain knew they could defeat Japan without Soviet help, they feared the body count both on the Asiatic mainland and in an invasion of the Japanese home islands. The Americans were already having tough fights on other islands in the Pacific, a situation that left General Douglas MacArthur, who was to command the invasion of Japan proper, anxious to "secure the commitment of the Russians to active and vigorous prosecution of a campaign against the Japanese . . . [so] as to pin down a very large part of the Japanese army." According to MacArthur, "the help of the Chinese would be negligible."

The Yalta Conference, which included Roosevelt, Churchill, and Stalin, took place from February 4 to 11, 1945. The most urgent business had to do with the end of the war in Europe, and most of the official meetings centered around that part of the world. The Far East was left to the end, although Stalin had given notice that he was planning to raise the question of the conditions under which the Soviet Union would enter the war against Japan. As payment, he wanted the Kurile Islands, the southern half of the oil-producing island of Sakhalin, and a warm-water port (Roosevelt had previously suggested Dairen). On the afternoon of the fifth day of the conference, Stalin added the proviso that the USSR needed to share control over the railways and ports in Manchuria. "It was clear," Roosevelt said, "that if these conditions were not met, it would be difficult for him . . . to explain to the Soviet people why Russia was entering the war against Japan . . . they would not understand why Russia would enter a war against a country with which they had no great trouble." The president, understandably skeptical of Stalin's concern about Russian public opinion, said that he had not yet discussed these points with Chiang Kai-shek because anything that was told to the Chinese was known throughout the diplomatic world within twenty-four hours.

The summary of the conference did not include the agreement made by the president that the Russians would enter the war in the Pacific, nor did Roosevelt mention it in his report to Congress after his return. The Yalta Conference, he said, had "concerned itself only with the European war and the political problems of Europe—and not with the Pacific war." This and other provisions were kept secret so that Japan would not close the port of Vladivostok, which the Japanese might well have done had they known, and it avoided what would certainly have been lengthy debates in Congress. Moreover, it put off any immediate, angry reaction from Chiang Kai-shek.

During their meeting, Roosevelt and Stalin also discussed the current situation in China. Stalin said that Chiang needed new leadership around him and that he couldn't understand why the G-mo did not bring the best people in the KMT into his government. There is nothing to indicate whether or not the American president and the Soviet premier talked about what they would do if Chiang, who had not been invited to Yalta, refused to go along with the decisions made there, but Roosevelt promised Stalin that he would discuss the pertinent matters with the generalissimo. As it happened, most of the important decisions made during that week remained secret until the end of the war, and the complete text of the agreements was not disclosed until 1947. Apart from demanding the unconditional defeat of Germany and its subsequent division into four zones of occupation, plans for war crimes trials, and a decision to invite China and France to join them in sponsoring the founding conference of the United Nations, Russia secretly agreed to enter the war against Japan within three months of the defeat of Germany. In other secret accords, the USSR was to gain back the Kurile Islands and the southern half of Sakhalin Island, taken over by Japan after the Russo-Japanese War of 1904–1905; the port of Dairen was to be internationalized; Port Arthur was to be restored to its pre-1905 status as a Russian naval base; and the Manchurian railways were to be put under joint Chinese-Soviet administration.

"It should be remembered that at this time the atomic bomb was anything but an assured reality," according to the State Department White Paper,* published four years later; "the potentialities of the Japanese . . . Army in Manchuria seemed large; and the price in American lives in the military campaign up the island ladder to the Japanese home islands was assuming ghastly proportions. Obviously military necessity dictated that Rus-

---

* The book, *United States Relations with China*, published by the State Department in 1949, was known as the "White Paper."

sia enter the war . . . in order to contain Japanese forces in Manchuria and prevent their transfer to the Japanese home islands. . . . It was, however, unfortunate that China was not previously consulted. President Roosevelt and Marshal Stalin, however, based this reticence on the already well-known and growing danger of 'leaks' to the Japanese from Chinese sources. . . . Here again military exigency was the governing consideration. At no point did President Roosevelt consider that he was compromising vital Chinese interests."

Roosevelt left the Yalta Conference in a state of exhaustion. He had arrived looking tired, although his mind seemed as active as always. Harry Hopkins, who was ill, attended no meetings or dinners but sent comments from his bed and stayed behind to rest when the others left. Roosevelt, who said that he had three kings waiting for him in the Middle East, remained an extra day for a last meeting and lunch with Churchill and Stalin. Final agreements were signed at the lunch table with the papers scattered among the plates. It was a sad trip home, during which General Edwin M. "Pa" Watson, the president's military aide, died.

❦

A FEW DAYS after the Yalta Conference, Hurley, who thought he had figured out a way to bring the KMT and the CCP together, left for Washington in a buoyant mood. "The generalissimo and I have not only become friends," he told the press, "but I may say we have achieved a degree of comradeship. The recent government changes* are largely responsible for the fact that the Chinese Government, the US command, and this Embassy are now working as one team."

Before he left China, the conference to write the charter establishing the United Nations was announced for April in San Francisco. In that regard, Hurley had received two letters from Chou saying that the Chinese Communists should be included in the Chinese delegation to the San Francisco Conference. As a means of fostering unity, Hurley suggested that Roosevelt recommend this to Chiang, and, somewhat surprisingly, Chiang agreed. He included one member of the Communist Party, one person from each of two other parties, and three people with no political connections in the del-

---

* Prompted by the dismissal of Stilwell, Gauss had resigned as ambassador to China, and Hurley had taken over his position. Upon being named ambassador, the Oklahoman had had the ambassadorial residence redecorated and bought a new Cadillac, which, according to John Service via Drew Pearson, was "shipped over the Hump by airplane during the height of the war when the Chinese were desperately hard up for supplies." (*Drew Pearson: Diaries, 1949–1959,* ed. Tyler Abell, p. 181.)

egation, which was under the chairmanship of T. V. Soong. Chiang himself
had decided not to go. "If CKS goes to San Francisco for the conference of
April 25," Dorn wrote, "it will be necessary for him and Mme. Chiang to
resume the fiction of their happy married life, for the benefit of the American press and public." T.V. was certainly more comfortable working in the
United States and the English language than anyone else whom Chiang
could have appointed, and his opening statement at the First Plenary Session of the San Francisco Conference began with a graceful tribute to President Roosevelt.

In going to Washington, Hurley had left behind in Chungking a substantial group of Foreign Service officers who strongly disagreed with the
new ambassador's policy of unconditional support for Chiang Kai-shek.
These men believed that the U.S. government should also be working with
the CCP with or without Chiang's consent. Shortly after Hurley and Wedemeyer, who accompanied him, arrived home, a group from the embassy in
Chungking sent a wire to Washington expressing these views. Their attitude
can be summed up in a memo John Service had written four or five months
earlier:

> Our dealings with Chiang Kai-shek apparently continue on the basis
> of the unrealistic assumption that he is China and that he is neces-
> sary to our cause. . . . The Kuomintang Government is in crisis. . . .
> The prestige of the party was never lower, and Chiang is losing the
> respect he once enjoyed as a leader. In the present circumstances,
> the Kuomintang is dependent on American support for survival. But
> we are in no way dependent on the Kuomintang. . . . We need not
> fear the collapse of the Kuomintang Government. . . . Finally, we
> need feel no ties of gratitude to Chiang.

Although the State Department argued that the seriousness of the situation had made it necessary, Hurley felt that the mere act of sending the
telegram was disloyalty on the part of the diplomatic and military officers,
several of whom were subsequently dismissed or posted elsewhere.* Longtime targets of the China Lobby, who were later denounced by Senator Joseph McCarthy, these men were reduced in rank and sent as far as possible
from China, thus creating a dangerous vacuum in the State Department of
officers with knowledge of and experience in China. Meanwhile, President
Roosevelt supported his new ambassador, and the position that the United
States could not help the Chinese Communist Party without the approval of
Chiang Kai-shek remained U.S. policy.

---

* See endnotes for a résumé of what happened to Service, Davies, and Vincent.

44

Has China really been sold out at Yalta?

—CHIANG KAI-SHEK, 1945

ALBERT COADY Wedemeyer had arrived in Chungking in October 1944, the month in which Stilwell was recalled, and taken over the latter's positions as commanding general of the U.S. forces in China and Chiang Kai-shek's chief of staff. Wedemeyer had drawn up the first war plan for the United States in 1941, traveled with Marshall to all the great conferences of World War II, and served in the Combined Anglo-American Southeast Asia Command as deputy chief of staff to Mountbatten. Given the job of turning the Chinese army into a decent fighting force, he was assigned Major General Gilbert X. "Buck" Cheeves to handle military supplies. Cheeves a "hardboiled, shrewd, driving, don't-ever-tell-me-why-you-can't-do-it" commander, had been brought in from India. He is said to have insisted that transport crews always leave the hoods of their vehicles lifted up, his theory being that "an engine left open to constant casual inspection will be kept in tiptop shape by the men responsible for it."

To handle the soldiers, Wedemeyer had set up the China Training and Combat Command under Stilwell's trusted comrade Brigadier General Dorn. Like Stilwell, who called Wedemeyer "the world's most pompous prick," Dorn found Wedemeyer "sententious" and complained that he was "not a soldier" but "a paper and a theory man." If Dorn was upset with his new commanding general, Chennault was furious that Wedemeyer had appointed Stilwell's man Dorn to a position of responsibility and sent Wedemeyer a long letter concerning his old bête noir:

> General Stilwell from the first did not trouble to conceal his antipathy to me. . . . So far as I was ever able to observe, General Stilwell's dealings with the Chinese leaders were chiefly marked by arrogance, self-righteousness and open contempt. . . . With the Generalissimo . . . and the other Chinese leaders . . . he either bullied or he threatened, seeming to know no means of securing cooperation except to assert that American supplies would be withheld if the Generalissimo did not accede to his demands. . . . These are the facts of deep military and political significance. The nature of General

Stilwell's relations with the Chinese leaders poisoned Sino-American relations for three years; rendered impossible truly effective Sino-American military cooperation, and was perhaps the basic cause for the disheartening course of events in this area until you assumed command.

Chennault wrote Wedemeyer two more letters, urging the new commander to put aside any "misapprehension or misinformation" he might have about Joe Alsop, who was indeed a trustworthy fellow. Wedemeyer forwarded Chennault's letters to Marshall with the comment that Chennault "has been built up as a great leader. I believe that he is an outstanding fighter pilot, but it is my conviction that he is not a man of fine character."

For his part, in keeping with the necessity to improve relations between China and the United States after the nastiness over Stilwell's removal, Chiang Kai-shek made a few changes in his hierarchy. But, according to left-wing journalist Harold Isaacs, "In the American military establishment there is a great process of weeding out and reorganization in progress. In the Chinese top establishment there is a great deal of talk about weeding out and reorganizing."

As Wedemeyer wrote Marshall:

The Chinese have no conception of organization, logistics or modern warfare. The Generalissimo is striving to conduct the war from Chungking. The management of affairs of State in itself would require a Disraeli, Churchill and Machiavelli all combined in one. The Gissimo will not decentralize power to subordinates . . . it is amusing and also tragic to note that many highranking Chinese officials are asking me to facilitate their evacuation to America by air. One very highranking Chinese general stated that he wanted to take forty outstanding Chinese army and naval officers to Europe . . . to study the European battlefields. . . . Another Chinese general asked me for permission to send ten Chinese officers to America to study strategy. . . . Self-sacrifice and patriotism are unknown quantities among the educated and privileged classes. . . .

The Chinese soldiers are starving by the hundreds . . . due to graft and inefficiency . . . the Chinese march an outfit from A to B and make no provision for bivouacs, food, and so forth along the route. . . . The Generalissimo often asks me to move by air 50,000 men from A. to B, and after . . . we make appropriate arrangements . . . he will order a change. . . . Neither he nor his advisors really understand supply and movement problems. . . . I have already indicated to the Generalissimo that here in Chungking we must issue broad policies and directives to responsible commanders in the field and that we definitely must not tell them how to carry them out. . . . I emphasized that it is wrong to direct operations from Chungking. Although he has agreed . . . he violates his agreement almost daily. . . . I receive continual reports of the inefficiency of General Ho. Apparently he is a suave self-seeking individual, very rich and dissolute. For political reasons the Generalissimo does not desire to remove him from a position of responsibility in the war effort.

Chiang did finally relieve General Ho of his position as head of the War Ministry but allowed him to retain his post as chief of staff and named him commander in chief of the Chinese armies in the Southwest. Chen Li-fu was removed as minister of education but left in a position where he could continue to function as "one of Chiang's trusted hatchetmen specializing in 'youth control.' " And Kung, who was "advised to continue his long course of recuperation in the US," was replaced by one of his faithful acolytes.

Associated in the public mind with graft in high places, illegal speculation, and war profiteering, the Kungs had judiciously withdrawn from the scene, basing themselves in New York. Nevertheless, Chiang, who was still afraid to offend Ai-ling, had made sure that T.V. arranged for a plane to take them to the States.* From there, Ai-ling contacted her younger brother T.A., asking him to wire T.V. to inquire about Kung's reputation in the press and political circles of Chungking. She received the following wire back in March of 1945: "Elder sister asked for a consensus of opinion on Brother Yong [H. H. Kung]. She mentioned this the last time I saw her. I must not have made myself clear, because now she has asked again. I will be more direct. It is my observation that the public's attitude towards Brother Yong has not changed for the better."

---

* Jeanette Kung also seems to have considered herself an official personage; witness a letter sent to T.V. by Wedemeyer, who had received a request from Madame Chiang "to transport the Kung sisters to the States." The general wrote: "when I indicated that I was unable to do so, Madame Chiang requested that I give the Kung sisters first priority on Air Transport Command. I informed Madame Chiang that at present time there are several thousands of Americans awaiting return. . . . If I were to give the Kung sisters, who insofar as I can learn contributed in no way to the war effort, I would be personally subject to severe criticism and rightly. . . . Later on it may be possible to transport civilians . . . provided they pay for same. Also commercial airways will be open and available." (Hoover Archives: Wedemeyer papers, Box 83, Folder 7, Albert C. Wedemeyer to T. V. Soong, November 12, 1945.)

The overall situation in China was improving, however, and the condition and morale of the Chinese troops had begun to change. Although Wedemeyer apparently enjoyed "frequent and direct contact with Chiang Kai-shek"—it was said that the general had a telephone in his office with a line directly into the G-mo's bedroom—his opinion of Chiang was not much different from that of his predecessor. In the summer of 1945, ten months after his arrival, he wrote Marshall that Chiang had "many intricate problems and frankly I have determined that he is not equipped either mentally or in training and experience to cope with most of them." Nonetheless, Wedemeyer managed to deal with the G-mo and wrote about him without the personal rancor exhibited by Stilwell. The person he obviously admired—and kept up a serious correspondence with long after he left China—was May-ling.

It was clear by now that T.V. had been returned to power at the expense of Kung and that the entire Kung family had become a liability to Chiang and his government. In December of 1944, Chiang named T.V. deputy president (i.e., premier) of the Executive Yuan, of which Chiang himself was president. In at least this one instance, the G-mo had finally opted for efficiency over adulation. T. A. Soong, who was apparently the family peacemaker, advised the Kungs, "We are all one family and should cooperate and help each other. The Generalissimo is lucky to have brother [T.V.] to deal with everything. We should support T.V., particularly if there is gossip. Although he is now Deputy President of the Executive Yuan, everything—big and small—is run by Chiang himself. I'm sure this is something of which you yourselves are well aware."

But Soong's new status only pointed up his lack of popularity. Harold Isaacs called the new premier "an ambitious, power-hungry, unprincipled politician. His propensity for playing his hand a little too independently in the often bitter struggle for power within the Kuomintang caliphate is what has kept him out of the front rank for long periods of time. The present tangled situation offers him a fresh opportunity. He represents no policy. He represents T. V. Soong." From the conservative side of the political spectrum, George Sokolsky wrote about T.V. with more understanding: "Madame Kung picked Chiang Kai-shek. T.V. has always wanted to be head of his family. . . . He resented Chiang and felt that if Chiang hadn't been brought in he would have become . . . head of the civilian side of China's government."

OUTSIDE THE COUNTRY, there was good news of Japanese defeats in the northern Philippines. American planes were now dropping bombs on Japan's home islands; Japanese troops had made no further progress in southern and southeastern China; transport over the Hump had reached more than 46,000 tons a month; and on January 26, 1945, three months after Stilwell's departure, the Ledo Road was linked with the old Burma Road, which led to Kunming. In the ensuing celebration, Stilwell's picture was displayed along with those of Chiang Kai-shek and Roosevelt. "We have broken the siege of China," Chiang announced when the first convoy drove into Kunming. "Let us name this road after General Joseph Stilwell, in memory of his distinctive contribution and of the signal part which the Allied and Chinese forces under his direction played in the Burma campaign and in the building of the road." "I wonder who put him up to that?" Stilwell asked.

Still doggedly determined to bring about a rapprochement between the KMT and the CCP, Hurley traveled back to Chungking via London and Moscow. He arrived in London convinced that some of the British thought a divided China might be better than a united one, since this would enable Britain to keep Hong Kong and its other possessions in the Far East. Churchill, who referred to the position of the United States vis-à-vis China as "the great American illusion," nevertheless agreed to support the U.S. policy of unification of China, and Hurley left for Moscow feeling that he had achieved what he set out to do.

On April 12, 1945, Franklin D. Roosevelt died, and Harry S. Truman was sworn in as the thirty-third president of the United States. Three days later, Hurley met with Stalin, who assured him that he would help bring about unification of military forces to China. Hurley then asked about informing Chiang of the agreements at Yalta, explaining that Roosevelt had told him to keep them secret until Stalin authorized him to tell the G-mo and that Truman had said he would follow the policy laid out by his predecessor. Stalin said he would be ready—politically and militarily—in two to three months' time, and Hurley said he would check with him before informing Chiang. Stalin assured Hurley that he would not discuss any of this with T.V., who was due to arrive in Moscow in May.

Hurley's subsequent report to Washington sparkled with unwarranted optimism and self-satisfaction. "Stalin agreed unqualifiedly to America's policy in China as outlined to him during the conversation," he said. Averell Harriman, currently the U.S. ambassador to the USSR, did not agree. He flew back to Washington and told Truman and the State Department that Hurley was far too trusting of Stalin and that the Soviet government would probably support the Chinese Communists. George Kennan, left in charge of the embassy in Moscow during Harriman's trip home, predicted that the Soviet Union would not rest until it controlled Manchuria, Mongolia, and north China. And Mao gave a speech on April 24 in which he said forthrightly that "our future, our ultimate program is to push China forward to Socialism and Communism." But Hurley, his head in clouds of wishful thinking, continued throughout the spring and into the summer to believe he could bring the KMT and CCP together.

By the summer of 1945, Wedemeyer had accomplished many of the reforms that Stilwell had tried to effect before he was replaced. About five hundred American officers and the same number of enlisted men were serving in and with the Chinese army, whose soldiers were being paid in cash and given sufficient arms. The Tenth Air Force had been transferred from India and combined with the Fourteenth, and both were under new command. In April and May, the Japanese had made their last serious assault in western Hunan, but they had been driven back by a combination of the now stalwart Chinese soldiers and American planes. Two months later Chiang gave a press conference, his first since 1941, in which he made it clear how pleased he was to have Hurley and Wedemeyer in China. "It is the first time in [the] entire Chinese-American history," he told reporters, "that action and cooperation have been so satisfactory."

The economic situation, however, had not improved, and the food supply remained sadly reduced due to the Japanese conquest of the rice-producing areas. Once more, Soong went to Washington to ask for increased shipments of gold to retard inflation. At first, Morgenthau refused, remarking that "the impression has arisen in the United States that the two hundred million of U.S. dollar certificates and bonds and the gold sold in China have gone into relatively few hands with resultant large individual profits and have failed to be of real assistance to the Chinese economy." But when Soong reminded the secretary of the treasury that on July 27, 1943, the United States had agreed "that two hundred million be made available from the credit on the books of the Treasury in the name of the Government of the Republic of China for the purchase of gold," Morgenthau felt he must honor the earlier commitment. The advance did little good for the country as a whole, and the Chinese dollar continued to depreciate.

❦

ON APRIL 30, 1945, three weeks after Roosevelt succumbed to cerebral hemorrhage, Hitler committed suicide. One week later, German resistance to the Allies collapsed. Even before that, early in April, the Soviets had told the Japanese that their neutrality pact had "lost its meaning" and would be allowed to lapse. Ignoring the terms of the pact, which stated that it was to remain in effect for a year after such notice had been given, the Russian armies were already moving to the Far East, supplied by American equipment. When news of this transfer of men and arms reached Chungking,

Ambassador Hurley thought it was high time he get Stalin's okay to give the generalissimo an account of what had been agreed upon at Yalta. But when Hurley asked Washington's permission to go ahead, he was asked to hold off.

There were two reasons for the delay. In the first place, the U.S. government had noticed a definite change in the attitude of the Soviets, who were now openly leaning toward the Chinese Communists. More important, but utterly secret, were recent reports on the atom bomb, which were proving very hopeful and meant that America might not need immediate help from the Soviet army. Meanwhile, Hopkins, sent to speak with Stalin, had managed to get the date of August 8 for Russia's entry into the Pacific war, provided China accepted the terms of the Yalta Agreement. They had also decided that T. V. Soong was to be called to Moscow to be informed of the Yalta accord, while at the same time Hurley told Chiang in Chungking. Stalin said that the Soviet Union had no territorial claims on China, that if Russian troops entered Manchuria, he would ask Chiang to take over the civil administration and that the generalissimo might set up his government in any area liberated by the Soviets. Both Hopkins and Harriman, who attended the meetings, thought that Stalin was genuine in his offer to work with the United States in China.

T.V. was then advised that Truman wished to speak with him in Washington and that Stalin wanted to see him in Moscow before the first of July. In their meeting, Truman informed him in general terms about the agreement at Yalta without giving him the exact phrasing. Soong went home to Chungking, where Hurley was anxiously awaiting the day he could officially tell Chiang. The G-mo, who had already been informed by the Chinese ambassador to Washington, "clearly indicated his chagrin and disappointment"; he asked that the United States and Britain cosign any agreement between China and the Soviet Union, that Port Arthur be designated a joint naval base for all four great powers, and that the transfer of the islands to the Soviets be subject to further discussion by the same four powers. Hurley was instructed to tell Chiang that these conditions were unlikely to be accepted.

Soong then left for Moscow, where it became only too apparent that Stalin's attitude toward China had undergone a radical change. Russia now wanted total control over Manchuria, the establishment of a military zone including the ports of Dairen and Port Arthur, the independence of Outer Mongolia, and ownership of the Manchurian railways. Meanwhile, Chiang had sent T.V. a list of maximum concessions he was prepared to give the Russians: in return for Stalin's guarantee to withdraw aid from the CCP and give China full sovereignty in Manchuria, Chiang would grant rights for the

Soviet navy to share the use of Port Arthur, accept the establishment of Dairen as a free port under Chinese administration, and join in creating a combined Sino-Soviet company to manage the Manchurian railroads. The two sides were so far apart that Ambassador Harriman could only advise Soong to try to adjourn their meeting on as friendly terms as possible. While Soong was contemplating how to make a decent exit, the Russians suddenly reduced their demands and Stalin declared "categorically" that he would support the KMT and that all military forces in China must be controlled by the Chinese government. This left open the question of control over the ports and railways of Manchuria—provisions that Soong said he could not move on without Chiang.

When Soong left Moscow, Stalin was still insisting that Dairen be specified as a Soviet military zone and that the Manchurian railways be under Soviet control. Soong told Harriman, who was leaving for the Potsdam Conference, that he hoped President Truman could solve the Manchurian problems. Returning to Chungking, he threw up his hands and told Hurley, "I am a broken man. I am personally ill from strain and overwork." Later he predicted that the "proposed agreement will be destructive politically to the man responsible for it."

A conference of the Big Three—Truman, Churchill, and Stalin—was scheduled to take place in Potsdam from July 17 to August 2, 1945. As the group was gathering on the sixteenth, the first atomic bomb was set off at Alamogordo Army Air Field in New Mexico. It was noted that one of the principal participants, Stalin, was not as surprised or impressed as he might have been, and it was discovered only later that the Soviet intelligence service had warned him about the bomb at least a month earlier. The Potsdam Declaration, sent to Chiang Kai-shek for approval and issued on July 26, called for the unconditional surrender of Japan—a demand the Japanese ignored in favor of trying to get the Soviets to negotiate less drastic peace terms. The Soviets refused, and discussions continued as to when they would enter the war, although Stalin said he would not order his troops to march until he had an agreement with China.

Meanwhile, Soong had reported his conversation with Stalin to Chiang, who sent a message saying that he hoped the Russian leader would realize that China had made an enormous effort to fulfill Soviet desires but that he could not make any concessions beyond what the Chinese people could understand and accept. A copy of this communication sent to Truman elicited the suggestion that if Chiang and Stalin continued to differ on the interpretation of the Yalta Agreement, Soong should return to Moscow for further negotiations. Soong, who did not want to go, arranged for Wang Shih-chieh, formerly minister of education and a high-ranking member of the KMT, to be appointed foreign minister in his place and then agreed to accompany him. Harriman was instructed to tell Stalin that the U.S. government thought that Soong had met the provisions of the Yalta Agreement.

On August 14, 1945, a Treaty of Friendship and Alliance between the USSR and China was finally signed, the result of a week of negotiations between Soong, Wang, and Stalin with Ambassador Harriman backing up the Chinese. Stalin had worn T.V. down to the point where, in return for a promise that the Russians would not exercise military authority in the city of Dairen, its port, or the connecting railroad, the Chinese would agree to put Dairen within the Soviet military zone. T.V. even gave in a bit regarding management of the Manchurian railways. In return, Stalin promised to support the Chinese national government. But when Wang asked for a more specific pledge on this, Stalin replied, "What do you want me to do? To fight against Mao?" Stalin also told Soong that the Chinese government should come to a quick agreement or the Communists would move into Manchuria. (Soviet soldiers were already on their way.) Harriman later said that he had "repeatedly urged" T.V. not to give in to Stalin's demands; that he himself had talked to Stalin and Molotov and "insisted" that the Soviet position was not justified; and that the United States would consider that any concessions that went beyond the Yalta Agreement "would be made because Soong believed they would be of value in obtaining Soviet support in other directions." But, Harriman said, "in spite of the position I took, Soong gave in on several points in order to achieve his objectives."

On the same day that the treaty between China and the USSR was signed, Japan surrendered. On August 6, the United States had dropped its first atomic bomb on Hiroshima. On August 8, the Soviets entered the war against Japan. The next day, the Americans dropped the bomb on Nagasaki, and five days later, on August 14, 1945, at 7:00 P.M., President Truman announced the Japanese surrender. Three hours later, Madame Chiang, "looking somewhat worn," was on the air, broadcasting from her temporary home in Riverdale. "Now that complete victory has come to us," she said, "our thoughts should turn first to the rendering of thanks to our creator and the sobering task of formulating a truly Christian peace. Unless we implement and maintain in action the professed ideals for which we of the United Nations entered this war, all the bloodshed and sacrifice of our loved ones will be of no avail." Her husband, she added, "has been trying to get me back as soon as possible." Although she claimed that her poor health did not permit her to go back immediately, she said she would return to China "soon."

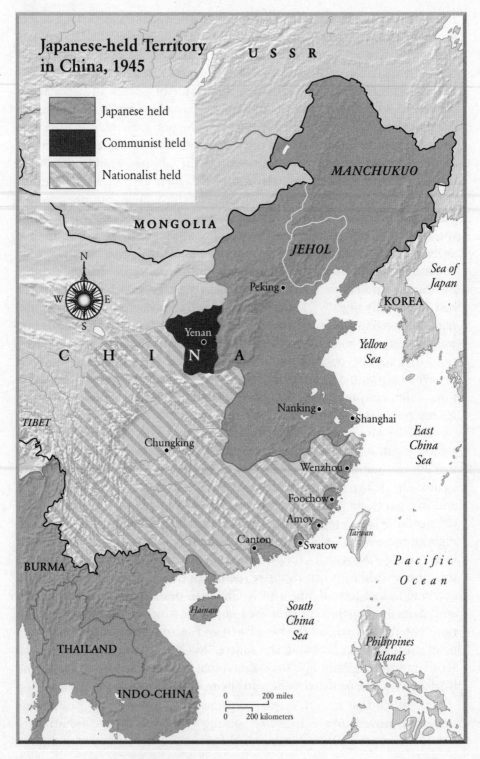

Japanese-held Territory in China, 1945

Japanese held
Communist held
Nationalist held

U S S R

MANCHUKUO

MONGOLIA

JEHOL

Peking

KOREA

Sea of Japan

N
W   E
S

Yenan

C H I N A

Yellow Sea

TIBET

Nanking

Shanghai

East China Sea

Chungking

Wenzhou

Foochow

Amoy

Taiwan

Canton

Swatow

BURMA

Pacific Ocean

Hainan

South China Sea

Philippines Islands

THAILAND

INDO-CHINA

0   200 miles
0   200 kilometers

45

Manchuria has been a tensely significant piece of contested—and contesting territory. Its principal natural resource—and enticement—was its whereabouts.

— JOHN PATON DAVIES, JR.

THE SUDDEN end of the war in the Pacific, which caused rejoicing among leaders in Europe and America, signaled further troubles for the Chiangs. Fifteen days after the end of the war in Asia, May-ling arrived in China from the United States, and reports that the Chiangs had separated—they had not seen each other for fourteen months—were duly attacked as "false, vicious and poorly thought-out propaganda." On August 29, 1945, the day of her departure from Washington, Madame had paid a formal call on President Truman and then hosted a luncheon at the Chinese Embassy, attended by General Marshall, now Truman's chief of staff, with whom she spoke at length. Returning home after a year abroad, she found her country in chaos.

The crux of the Chinese problem, according to John Robinson Beal, a former journalist and *Time* magazine correspondent, was "a largely illiterate peasant mass scarcely a generation removed from life under despotic imperial rule . . . undergoing all the stresses inherent in leaping virtually overnight from the oxcart to the airplane." Beal's presence in China was due to a suggestion by Marshall that the Chiang government hire an experienced person to advise it on how its actions were playing in the United States. Chiang, however, remained unwilling or unable to enact reforms to help his people bridge the transition to the twentieth century.

During the war, much of the fertile land and most of the industrial areas of China had been occupied by the Japanese. The declaration of peace revealed a shortage of livestock, fertilizer, and farm tools; there was no trade with the outside world; 90 percent of the railways were inoperable; much of the rolling stock, along with many bridges and tunnels, had been destroyed; river shipping, on which the country had always depended, was little better; and the roads were ruined. During the six days preceding the official end of the war, it was estimated that about 700,000 Russian soldiers had moved into Manchuria, looting the factories and industries of the northern province and stripping the area of at least a billion dollars in assets.* According to the first foreign businessman to follow them there, they had destroyed about 80 percent of the city of Mukden, bringing in their soldiers who had taken Berlin and turning them loose "for three days of rape and pillage. Later they relieved these troops with two convict divisions from the salt mines of Siberia," who "stole everything in sight, broke up bathtubs and toilets with hammers, pulled electric light wiring out of the plaster, built fires on the floor and either burned down the house or at least a big hole in the floor, and in general behaved completely like savages."

More than a million Japanese soldiers had been left stranded in China proper and another million in Manchuria—all waiting to be repatriated. Close to a million Chinese puppet troops who had served the government of Wang Ching-wei were also scattered around the country, 600,000 or so in China proper and another 350,000 in Manchuria. White and Jacoby point out what they called "one of the scandals of the war," i.e., an "intimacy," as they put it, that had developed between certain elements in the Chungking government and the puppet collaborators in Nanking and Peking. They claim that messengers had traveled back and forth during the war "making alliances across the battle lines"—a situation that the KMT denied in public but justified in private by saying that it hoped that at the end of the war the puppets would shift sides from the enemy to the Nationalist government instead of the CCP. The bet was a good one, and the 500,000 to 1 million soldiers formerly under Japanese control garrisoning cities and railways in Communist-held territories raised the banner of the Kuomintang—at least temporarily.

Chiang still needed U.S. assistance to move his troops into the areas of contention, particularly Manchuria and the coastal cities of eastern China. The United States came to his rescue with over 50,000 marines stationed at railways, ports, and airports, plus naval and air forces sent to ferry soldiers from southern to northern China. But when the Chinese veterans of Stilwell's victory in Burma were flown in to take possession of the capital of Nanking, they met a sorry welcome. White and Jacoby ascribe this lack of enthusiasm partly to the fact that Nanking's citizens feared the Nationalist soldiers as much as those of the puppet government. What everyone seems to have overlooked at the time was the ghastly experience of Chinese citizens during the rape of Nanking, a period in which the average person was left unprotected by both his army and his government.

Shanghai was a different story. There the troops were properly welcomed by cheering crowds, banners, and a brass band, along with the inevitable movie cameras. The inhabitants of Shanghai, who had largely remained

---

* Estimates vary between 1 and 2 billion.

loyal to the KMT, put up huge portraits of Chiang Kai-shek—albeit a younger Chiang since the pictures dated from prewar days—around which they wove garlands of flowers and crepe paper. The city, White and Jacoby said, "was obsessed with the spirit of holiday . . . parades of jubilation formed like froth in every street; people cheered all men marching in government uniform." The Communists of Shanghai, instructed by Yenan not to provoke trouble, simply melted away and moved up north. Mao and his followers had decided, according to the journalists, "to trade Shanghai for the much richer prize of Manchuria."

One of Chiang's immediate problems was to reestablish his government in the cities and towns before the Communists, whose forces were closer and more mobile, could take them over. Along with its regular army, the CCP relied on a large number of guerrillas and local defense troops surrounding the cities and railways of northern China. On August 9, 1945, five days before the official end of the war, Mao had announced what he called a "nation-wide counter-offensive" against the Japanese. On the next day the commanding general of the Chinese Communist forces, General Chu Teh, declared that *any* Chinese army in the liberated areas could demand that Japanese and Japanese puppet troops give up their arms; he then ordered all Communist soldiers to advance against the Japanese wherever they found them. "Our troops," Chu said, "have the right to enter and occupy any city, town and communication center occupied by the enemy or the puppets . . . to maintain order, and appoint a commissioner to look after the administrative affairs of the locality. Those who oppose or obstruct such actions will be treated as traitors."

Denouncing Chu's action as "abrupt and illegal," Chiang Kai-shek issued an order forbidding the Communist soldiers from taking independent action against the Japanese. This was quickly countered by a broadcast from Yenan calling Chiang a "Fascist chieftain." Wedemeyer, to whom Chiang appealed for help, sent Chu's pronouncement to Washington. The State Department responded by suggesting to General MacArthur that when he talked to the Japanese, he should make it clear that the clause in the Potsdam Declaration that dealt with their repatriation applied only to those who surrendered to the government of Chiang Kai-shek. A note was also sent to General Chu, informing him that the United States, Britain, and the Soviet Union had agreed that Chiang, who was the Allied commander in chief in the China theater, was the person entitled to receive the surrender of the Japanese troops, and the U.S. government hoped that the CCP would cooperate with him.

Meanwhile, Ambassador Hurley, who still clung to the idea that he could bring about a rapprochement between the CCP and the KMT, had been urging Chiang to invite Mao to come to Chungking for a meeting. An invitation was sent off on August 16, two days after the official Japanese surrender: "We have many international and internal problems awaiting settlement," Chiang wrote Mao. ". . . Please do not delay coming here." But Mao was nervous about his safety, and it was not until Hurley said he would fly to Yenan, bring Mao back to Chungking, and be responsible for his life and those of other Communist leaders while they were in the wartime capital that Mao accepted the invitation. It had been eighteen years since Chiang Kai-shek and Mao Tse-tung had seen each other. Their talks began on August 28 and lasted seven weeks. Throughout their meetings, Chiang continued to insist that the Communist forces be disbursed and incorporated into the Nationalist army. Whereas Mao agreed to their formal induction into Chiang's army, he said that they must remain in their old units under their existing officers. Moreover, Chiang refused to allow the CCP to administer the provinces* where, for the past five years, the Communists had been defending the people against the Japanese and collecting their taxes.

During the negotiations, Hurley, who was anxious to return to the United States for medical treatment and diplomatic consultations, told Mao that he had to leave for Washington. Mao asked him to stay in Chungking in order to see him safely back to Yenan. Hurley turned to Chiang, who said he would vouch for Mao's safety, but Mao still insisted on a written guarantee from Hurley himself that he would be safe until his return to Yenan. Hurley left on September 22, as did Wedemeyer.

Before leaving Chungking, Hurley sent off another of his unrealistic reports to Washington: "The spirit shown by the negotiators is good, the rapprochement between the two leading parties of China seems to be progressing, and the discussion and rumors of civil war recede as the conference continues." Hurley was absolutely wrong, a fact that Walter S. Robertson, the man left in charge of the U.S. Embassy during the ambassador's absence, tried to impress on the State Department. "We are of the opinion," Robertson said, "that the two sides are far apart on the basic question of political control of the liberated areas now dominated by the Communists." But the powers in Washington listened to Hurley and made his report the basis for the job of General Marshall, the next American unfortunate enough to be sent to find a solution to the Chinese puzzle.

On October 11, the day Mao flew back to Yenan, he and Chiang issued a joint communiqué on their meeting. Since almost no progress had been made during their conference, it was a bland statement, studded with meaningless phrases about "peace, democracy, solidarity, and unity" that "should

---

* Hopei, Shantung, Chahar, Jehol, and northern Shansi.

form the basis" of China's future. Although they said that "cooperation should be perpetuated and resolute measures taken to avert internal strife," neither man offered a route toward this admirable end.

The inability of either Chiang or Mao to make headway toward settling their differences was an embarassment for Hurley, a failure underlined by an editorial in the *New York Herald Tribune* accusing him not only of creating American policy in China but of suppressing information that did not conform to his personal views. Hurley, said the editors, "has become so nearly omnipotent that he ought to be added to the pantheon of the Far East. Won't one of the minor gods of Asia please step down so that Mr. Hurley can take his place?" Whatever his motivation—humiliation or hubris—Hurley offered President Truman his resignation several times during October and November of 1945, but each time was persuaded to stay in his post.

Although he finally consented to return to China right after a speech he was scheduled to give before the national press, during that afternoon Congressman Hugh DeLacy from Washington told the House of Representatives that "Ambassador Hurley's reversals of the Roosevelt-Gauss policy in China have made the present civil war unavoidable." Reading the speech, Hurley convinced himself that certain statements made by DeLacy showed that his (Hurley's) secret reports to the State Department had fallen into the hands of the Communists. His final letter of resignation, which, according to one authority, "so twirls about that it is hard to locate its center," charged that "a considerable section of our State Department is endeavoring to support Communism generally as well as specifically in China." Hurley's resignation not only angered Truman but speeded up the appointment of General George C. Marshall, the president's recently retired chief of staff, to mediate between the warring parties.

❦

EVEN THOUGH WEDEMEYER had warned Chiang against it before he left for Washington, the generalissimo decided to occupy Manchuria, which was his right under the treaty with the Soviets. Russian soldiers, who had swarmed into Manchuria from the north and west, had been joined by a large force of Chinese Communists, who immediately set up defenses and established administrations in small northern towns; a second Russian army, crossing into southern Manchuria, provided another Chinese Communist force with railway transport, thus allowing it to set up similar arrangements in the south. To observers, it was clear that the Russians had timed their withdrawals from these areas in order to allow the CCP to take over before Chiang's forces could get there. "If we have Manchuria," Mao said, "our victory will be guaranteed."

Moreover, when American ships tried to land Chinese soldiers at the Manchurian port of Dairen, the Soviets refused to let them disembark on the grounds that Dairen was a commercial port and could not be used by the military. (This was said in spite of the fact that the post-Yalta Agreement between T.V. and Stalin had guaranteed that the Soviets would not exercise military authority in Darien or its port—a right reserved for the Chinese.) After a two-week standoff, General George E. Stratemeyer, temporarily in charge while Wedemeyer was in Washington, decided that the American ships could not wait indefinitely in the waters outside Dairen. The commander of the Soviet forces in Manchuria proposed three other Manchurian ports: Artung, Yingkow, and Hulutao. Chiang decided to try Hulutao, but the Chinese Communists refused to allow his soldiers to land there, and the Russians said that they could not "guarantee" a safe debarkation. The ships then headed off to Yingkow, but the Chinese Communists, already on the spot, refused to let them off there either. When asked for an explanation, the Russian commander said he was not responsible for the whereabouts of the Chinese Communists, who had come up from the south; he could not, he said, interfere in the internal affairs of China.

A similar incident occurred at Chefoo, a port on the northern coast of the province of Shantung. The cruiser USS *Louisville* and several destroyers were about to steam off to land a detachment of American marines when Yenan got wind of their plan. General Chu announced that if American forces disembarked at Chefoo, the Communist Eighth Route Army would not understand, since there were no Japanese nearby and they were in control of the area. Such a move would lead the Communists to believe that the United States was interfering with internal Chinese matters. Three days later, General Chu sent word to U.S. military headquarters that if the landing took place without a previous agreement with the CCP and there was trouble, the responsibility would lie with the Americans. He also broadcast this message on the radio. Although the American ships were already in the harbor at Chefoo, their commanders recommended that the landing be aborted. Nevertheless, some of the U.S. ships remained in the area to see what was going on. According to them, there was a great deal of traffic between the Chinese Communists in Chefoo and the Russians in Dairen as well as between the members of the CCP in Chefoo and those in Hulutao and Yingkow.

Meanwhile, Chiang clung desperately to old self-defeating resentments, and his attempts to rehabilitate Manchuria, occupied by the Japanese during the war, exemplify his shortsightedness. There was what one author called "general agreement" among Manchurians that the Young Marshal was the only leader who could still generate sufficient support for the Nationalists in the area. But Chiang, still angry with Chang for the Sian Incident, refused even to discuss releasing him for duty. Instead he divided the three Manchurian provinces into nine separate areas and appointed nine nonentities—none of whom had ever been contaminated by associating with the Manchurian house of Chang—to govern them. He also named the former governor of the southern province of Kiangsi to head the Manchurian government and chose his son Chiang Ching-kuo as special commissioner for foreign affairs in charge of dealing with the Russians.

Chiang's attitude toward the Young Marshal was typical of his animosity toward anyone who had worked for or been forced to work with the Japanese, even those innocents who had been left behind to survive under enemy occupation. The Chinese people, who thought that the end of the war signaled freedom, were sadly disillusioned by what one American called the "Chinese carpetbaggers" sent to take over by the Nationalist government. "Today there is no such thing as a modest percentage of squeeze," observed one American; ". . . everyone is out to get just as much as he can."

We've been expecting the central government,
We've been longing for the central government.
But once they come, they are worse than the plague.

ran a ditty that gained popularity among the Chinese people. And with good reason. Officials sent to the provinces from Chungking behaved, according to Crozier, like "locusts. Everything was for confiscation: gold, houses, cars, women. On their lips, the word 'Chungking' meant 'Open, Sesame,' giving them rights without limit. Collaborators were rounded up and thrown into gaol, but only after bribes in cash or kind had been extorted from them as a guarantee of freedom from arrest."

✲

IN SPITE OF his feelings toward T. V. Soong, Chiang, who always called on him when the government was in trouble, had done so again in 1944. Described by an Oxford professor of political science Sir Arthur Salter as "one of the most notable figures in both national and international politics," T.V. was looked upon as an economist of celebrity status in the higher reaches of Washington but not so well regarded at home. According to Howard Boorman,* he was "often criticized in China because of family relationships. Although he often was on less-than-cordial terms with Chiang Kai-shek and H. H. Kung, he nevertheless was invariably associated with them

---

* Editor of the comprehensive four-volume *Biographical Dictionary of Republican China.*

as a target of public censure." But even more important than questions of family probity were issues of incompetence, and it was T.V. who had to tackle the inflation his brother-in-law Kung had left behind when Chiang removed him as finance minister in 1944.

As the person primarily responsible for dealing with runaway prices, T.V. became more and more discouraged throughout the year following the declaration of peace. At the end of the war, China's reserves in gold and dollars had stood at U.S. $900 million, but by December 1946, they had dropped to about half that amount. Interest on bank loans was running 15 to 28 percent a *month*. UNRRA had shipped most of $658 million worth of food, clothing, and capital equipment; the American Export-Import Bank had issued credits of nearly $83 million; and the Canadians had sent credits of another $60 million. But, as Crozier put it, "many of the supplies and much of the cash went into the private stores or bank accounts of Kuomintang officials or ministers." According to Arthur Young, financial adviser to the Chinese government, the balance of trade for 1946 was "unfavourable," with officially recorded imports amounting to $605 million while exports added up to only $161 million. "If the large unrecorded amount of illicit trade were added," Young wrote, "the result would probably be even more unfavourable."

James McHugh, Donald's old friend who was head of Far East intelligence, tells a typical story about UNRRA, which tried to hire him. It seems that by the summer of 1946, only about 50,000 tons of supplies had been moved out of the Shanghai warehouses, which were stacked up with 250,000 tons of goodies provided by the United Nations. Someone made a deal with the U.S. Navy to move the cargo up the Yangtze and to other ports free of charge except for the fees to be paid to the pilots of the boats. The Chinese demurred, saying that they would lose face by allowing the U.S. Navy to move their supplies. The navy then sent them a bill for $250,000 instead of the original $15,000 it would have charged. Clearly, someone (or someones) pocketed the difference.

In the summer of 1946, Ching-ling issued a statement protesting the presence of American soldiers in China as a detriment to peace, asked the American people to review their policy of loans given only to Chiang, and called for a coalition government. In an article entitled "Madame Sun—China's 'Conscience,'" published in *The New York Times Magazine*, reporter Henry R. Lieberman explained that Ching-ling was not herself a Communist*—"a left-wing Democrat yes, but not a Communist . . . she believes that

---

* This was true. The CCP felt she would be more valuable as an independent voice and did not induct her until just before her death, so it could advertise her allegiance to posterity.

sweeping land reforms and a coalition Government with Communists and other parties participating are the answers to China's present ills." At the same time as the article about Ching-ling appeared in the *Times,* an assessment of the current American attitude toward China arrived for May-ling from Emma. "I have heard various tried and trusted friends of China of late express considerable pessimism," she wrote. "The feeling is that if the present government would institute some real measure of reform, the ground would pretty much be cut from under the feet of the opposing side. They suggest that new blood is needed among the leaders. Also, they feel no confidence whatever in the outcome of large scale fighting. . . . I pass this on for what it is worth, but I think it is a fair boiling down of a fairly widespread point of view, from people who have long terms of service in the country, some of whom are very recently returned. Some Chinese even share it."*

From Washington, Wedemeyer sent his friend T.V. a letter along the same lines, recommending that the Chinese government concentrate its effort and resources south of the Great Wall. Learning from the Communist example, Wedemeyer stressed the point that

> we should concentrate on one area where we should build roads, railroads, improve internal waterways, create airlines, inaugurate social and tax reforms, minimize corruption in government, facilitate existing and create new industries. Nothing, T.V., that we might do would be more effective against the spread of communism . . . than the successful execution of the above program. I am certain that the vast majority of the Chinese people do not accept communistic ideologies. However, at the present time it is difficult for them to choose because they experience terrible living conditions, corruption in government and continued chaos.

Wedemeyer also suggested that rich Chinese follow the example of many American families [who had] amassed great fortunes . . . that would have jeopardized the economic stability of this country, had . . . [they] . . . not expended large sums on public institutions such as hospitals, libraries, schools, educational foundations, scientific research, public recreational facilities, all of which contributed to the well-being and contentment of large masses of people in the country. . . . My suggestion . . . is that you organize

---

* Four years later Emma was even more embarrassed when she had to inform May-ling that one of the Chinese charities she (Emma) was helping had been closed due to "our funds over there . . . being manipulated." (Wellesley Archive: Emma DeLong Mills papers, Emma Mills to Madame Chiang, April 11, 1950.)

such philanthropies among the wealthiest families of China." Wedemeyer, who said he had "investigated holdings and deposits here" (i.e., in the United States), offered to share "information that would indicate most of the Chinese families who have amassed great fortunes and who would be in a position to cooperate."

But at the end of December of 1946, T.V. told Chiang's PR man, John Beal:

> I would to God that Chang Chun [head of the Political Science Clique of the Nationalist Army] could become Prime Minister. I have done it for two years and it has worn me out. . . . There is no one who wants my job now. There is no one who is willing to do the things that are necessary, because they are unpopular. And if China collapses, it will be my responsibility. . . . I'm almost afraid to talk to Marshall any more because he will think I want to borrow money. I don't want to borrow money. This isn't like America, where you can say, "All right, let the Republicans run the country for a while." The alternative here is Communism. If China collapses, the Communists will take over.

PART SEVEN

1945–1949

46

He [Marshall] never says die and maybe he will wear the Chinese down instead of their doing him in.

— KATHERINE (MRS. GEORGE C.) MARSHALL, 1946

IN LATE December 1945, George Marshall arrived in China as President Truman's personal representative. His instructions were to help create a unified China that could resist Stalin's attempt to take over Manchuria by offering enough weapons to persuade the KMT and the CCP to unite to resist the Russians. The U.S. government had clearly failed to take into account the realities of the situation, as witness a memo issued in November 1945 in which Truman affirmed America's "continued support of Generalissimo Chiang Kai-shek and the Central Government of China," while warning that "Americans must not participate in clashes between Chinese Forces" and "Americans must not be employed to facilitate Central Government operations against dissident groups within China [i.e., Communists]." Somehow, in some way, Marshall was supposed to help Chiang resist the CCP, reestablish America's credentials as an impartial mediator between what White and Jacoby called "a vigorous, dynamic, cocksure Communist Party and a decadent, unprincipled, corrupt governing party," and "persuade the two to discuss once more a subject they had been discussing for eight years without the slightest approach to solution." It was a thoroughly unrealistic approach to what we today would call nation building, and diplomatic historian Herbert Feis explained it this way: "We had realized that it was essential to create a powerful military force to win the war. But we had not learned that it was no less essential to maintain an adequate military force in order to secure a satisfactory peace. . . . Blithely we thought that the world—even the Communist part of it—would be responsive to our pleas and our dollars."

Marshall had not seen either Chiang or May-ling since Cairo, and his relationship with the former was improved by his "renewed encounter" with the latter. As one of his biographers put it, "To everyone else she was a high-powered female of fearsome personality, compared by some Americans to the Dragon Lady in 'Terry and the Pirates,'* but in Marshall's presence she

---

* A well-known comic strip of the time, created by Milton Caniff.

seemed to melt into an adoring deb . . . she went out of her way to make him feel welcome, sending him gifts of candy, urging him to go out and 'get some color in your cheeks.' " May-ling also lavished gifts and affection on Marshall's wife, Katherine, to whom, she said, she could talk in the same way she spoke to her own sisters.

While Marshall was settling in to his new assignment, Chiang's son Ching-kuo made a secret trip to Moscow to confer with Stalin about whether the Russians would allow the KMT to take over their holdings as they moved out of Manchuria. He met twice with the Russian leader and was briefed by Vyacheslav Molotov, Stalin's famous commissar of foreign affairs, who dubbed him a "very mediocre" young man. Stalin complained to Ching-kuo about the presence of U.S. troops in China. If the United States withdrew its soldiers, he said, he would help China build up heavy industry in Manchuria* and tell the CCP that it must support the Kuomintang. Molotov thought that by sending his son, Chiang was really trying to arrange a visit for himself, and Stalin suggested that the G-mo meet him in Moscow or somewhere on the border between their two countries. But Molotov was wrong in both his estimate of Ching-kuo and the reason for his visit. Chiang was worried about being put into a position where he would be pushed into agreeing to the coalition government that both the United States and the Soviets seemed to be trying to force on him, and he was afraid that if he refused, he might drive an angry Stalin into stronger support of the CCP. He ignored Marshall's advice to meet with Stalin and declined the invitation.

The major stumbling block on the road to securing an accord between the Kuomintang and the Communists was the latter's insistence that any settlement must be preceded by an agreement that did away with the one-party dictatorship of the KMT and gave the CCP power commensurate with the fact that it now dominated nearly a third of the country. But Chiang continued to demand obedience from the Communists—in both the military and administrative spheres—before he would even discuss political questions. In spite of this, on January 10, 1946, Marshall actually succeeded in getting two agreements between the KMT and the CCP—one political and one military. Having managed to bring the KMT, the Communists, the Democratic League, and several minor parties together, he convinced them to agree to a program whereby the dictatorship of the KMT would be abolished and an interim government composed of all parties would be put in its place. Plans were even discussed for a National Assembly to meet for the

---

* It will be remembered that the Russians had already removed everything the Japanese had built in the way of factories and equipment.

purpose of writing a new constitution. On the military side, the KMT and CCP agreed to a cease-fire on January 13 and the incorporation of Communist units into a new national army. Everyone from Wedemeyer—he had incurred Marshall's wrath by telling him that there was not "the remotest chance" that he could make peace between the KMT and the CCP—to the U.S. State Department was amazed at Marshall's success. His press attaché explained how the American general had dealt with the ever-stubborn generalissimo: "Inasmuch as you can not hope to obtain military victory over your opponents without massive American aid—which is 'utterly out of the question'; and since, on the other hand, your opponents, the Communists, ARE in a position to obtain covert Soviet aid sufficient to overthrow you by force of arms, it follows that 'the only hope of maintaining a sovereign China' lies in a political settlement. . . . You must accordingly make the concessions necessary to achieve such a political settlement."

After the agreements were made, Marshall left for the United States and Chiang sent May-ling on a brief visit to Manchuria to deliver a "special message of friendship" to the Russians. Pointing out that there were no two nations in the world with a longer common boundary than China and Russia, Madame Chiang told the guests at a celebratory banquet, "It is therefore my conviction that the future must hold for China and Soviet Russia common aspirations of live and let live, a policy which will benefit not only our two peoples but also those in every other part of the world."

But three days after Marshall's triumphant departure from China, when KMT officials, armed with gold pens and decorated scrolls, gathered to sign the agreements, Chou En-lai arrived with bad news. He was sorry to report that his instructions had changed and he could not sign for the CCP. Moreover, even while the peace talks were in progress, the Chinese Communists had continued to dispatch troops to widen the areas under their control. Taking advantage of the cease-fire, they had built up their strength in Manchuria, sending more than 130,000 soldiers into the area, all of whom disembarked at Soviet-controlled ports. They also continued their propaganda war, issuing regular news dispatches from their headquarters. Since theirs was the only source of news—the talks were supposed to be secret and Nationalist journalists were afraid to incur Chiang's wrath—they won plenty of hearts and minds to their cause. In addition, the Communists apparently had a spy system that was "just about a hundred per cent perfect."

The Kuomintang did not behave much better than the Communists. The CC Clique encouraged anti-Communist demonstrations in order to sabotage the peace negotiations and tried to break up communications between Chou En-lai, head of the Communist delegation, and the other leaders of the CCP in Yenan. (Marshall was so disgusted that he gave Chou a

radio to use for communicating with his home base and sent his own plane
to take Chou from Chungking to Nanking.) The reactionaries "ran a steam-
roller" over those who wished to abide by the agreements with the Communist Party, insisting that Chiang be given dictatorial powers and cutting
CCP and other party participation to minor representation in any new government. In response, the Communists attacked the Manchurian railways
and seized the Manchurian capital of Changchun.

Marshall, who had flown to America, returned in late April to renewed
fighting and once again brought the clout of the United States to bear. He
urged the Communists to leave Changchun, which they did, turning the
Manchurian capital over to Nationalist troops nearly without bloodshed.
Chiang flew north, and Nationalist soldiers pressed on toward the city of
Harbin, north of Changchun. His pride assauged, the G-mo agreed to negotiate another truce with the CCP, which lasted from the middle of May until
the end of June 1946. During the hiatus, the capital of Nationalist China was
officially moved from Chungking back to Nanking.

But on his return from Manchuria, Chiang also closed down 776 papers
and periodicals in Peiping, a forewarning of the suppression and cruelties
that would follow throughout that summer. All the liberals whom Tai Li's
Secret Service could entrap were imprisoned, killed, or otherwise silenced.
In Shanghai, intellectuals and even so-called "thinkers" were registered by
the police and given identification cards of various colors.

For their part, some Chinese officials, believing that Marshall had come
to China to clean up the corruption in Chiang's government and frantic at
the idea of not satisfying "their greedy appetite for bribes," launched an
attack on Marshall and his wife. Hence, the following letter from Marshall
to Dwight D. Eisenhower, then chief of staff, in June of 1946:

> I gave Mrs. Marshall your message of concern regarding her reported
> illness. The facts are these, amusing and a commentary on the viru-
> lence of the present propaganda warfare: she merely made a week-
> end trip to Shanghai with Madame Chiang, but some of the diehard
> Government political boys, in their assaults on me, to weaken my
> influence and clear the way for a war of extermination [against the
> Communists], which they are incapable of carrying through without
> our assistance, built up a press attack that Katherine and I had fallen
> out and she had left Nanking in a huff. Then I had gone to Shanghai
> to bring her back, but she immediately went into the hospital. They
> left her there, I returning empty-handed. She was never sick, never
> saw a hospital, and returned here with me and Madame Chiang. The
> part which greatly amused us but outraged Katherine was a descrip-

tion: "Mrs. Marshall, though over 60, still demands her diversions. Throughout the war, General Marshall had to take her to the movies and other diversions. Since he came to China, he has been too busy, so she left him, etc., etc."

The ingenuity and power of the right-wing forces did not go unnoticed. In August of 1946, President Truman wrote Chiang that he had been following the situation "closely," noting that there

exists in the United States an increasing body of opinion which holds that our entire policy toward China must be reexamined in the light of . . . the increasing tendency to suppress freedom of the press as well as the expression of liberal views. . . . There is a growing feeling . . . that the aspirations of the Chinese people are being thwarted by militarists and a small group of political reactionaries, who, failing to comprehend the liberal trend of the times, are obstructing the advancement of the general good of the nation. . . . Unless convincing proof is shortly forthcoming that genuine progress is being made toward a peaceful settlement of China's internal problems, it must be expected that American opinion will not continue in its generous attitude towards your nation.

To counteract the bad publicity, Beal wanted Chiang to hold a press conference. Knowing that "it was a case of getting her [May-ling] to persuade her husband," he went to see her. "I began immediately with a lecture on what a lousy press China was getting. . . . She agreed. . . . 'I know what you want me to do,' she said. 'You want me to be there (at the Gimo's meeting with the press) and interpret. I did that during the war, and I'm tired of it, and I'm not going to do it any more. . . . That's what a minister of information is for.' " According to Beal, May-ling objected to Chiang's giving a press conference in any case, saying that "he was President of all China, above politics, and to hold a public press conference would put him on a level with Chou En-lai." Beal suggested that he be replaced by one of the Chinese negotiators; May-ling agreed and suggested that the press be brought in for "tea and an off-the-record chat" afterward with her husband. She also told Beal that the *Encyclopaedia Britannica* had asked her to write 5,500 words on the history of China from 1937 to 1946 and asked him to read it for her when she was finished. Her attitude toward both her role in her husband's pronouncements and her newfound celebrity seems to indicate a shift in the balance of their marriage. The Madame had clearly become less the worried wife and attentive translator and had moved farther on toward a very un-Chinese feminine independence.

❦

DURING THAT YEAR, May-ling also dealt with the hospitalization and death of her old friend and adviser W. H. Donald, who had left China in early 1941. While on an island-hopping vacation with a young woman, the Australian journalist had continued to receive letters from May-ling asking him to return. He finally decided to go back, but while on a freighter bound for China, word came that Pearl Harbor had been bombed. The ship's captain headed for Manila, where Donald was interned by the Japanese. Dubbing him "the evil spirit of China," Japan had put a hefty price on his head. "Time and again Japanese searched the camp records for my name. I always was known as W. H. Donald. I registered on the internees' list truthfully as William H. Donald. That confused the Japanese. But what fooled them most was my recorded age—nearly 70. See that, they would shrug their shoulders and say, 'That's not the same man. We're looking for a much younger man.' . . . Internees held my identity in strictest confidence. That is something for which I shall ever be grateful."

Released in early 1945, Donald traveled to the United States, and by fall of that year, the war was over. Since he was not feeling well, he returned to one of his favorite spots, Tahiti, where he was diagnosed with lung disease. Advised by a French doctor to get to an American hospital, he contacted May-ling, who sent a plane to pick him up and fly him to the naval hospital in Pearl Harbor. While in bed, he worked on his memoirs with his future biographer for an hour every other day until he became too ill to continue. "One day, I found him morose," the biographer related, "and in a way so subtle that I was not aware of it until I returned home, he let me know that he had been waiting in vain for weeks to hear from Madame Chiang. In all his talks with me, his abiding admiration and affection for the M'issimo were evident. It seemed plain he felt that she, who had used so much of his strength, now might supply some for him. I wired her, not omitting a sting."

A week later Hollington Tong arrived in Hawaii to say that permission had been granted by the Navy doctors to fly Donald back to China, which was what he had said he wanted. "I guess I have enough of those people in me," he said, "to want to go home to die." A special navy plane, complete with berth and attendant nurses, arrived on March 14, 1946, to carry the old journalist to Shanghai, where he lived for seven months longer. May-ling decorated his hospital room with a handsome rug, a large easy chair, bright curtains, and embroideries and made sure that he always had fresh flowers.

When she was in Shanghai she visited him every day, and whether she was there or not, she sent a member of her staff to see if he needed anything.

The Kungs had been very nice to Donald, and on the day he died, he asked to see H. H., to whom he gave his Masonic ring. He had also asked to see May-ling and, when she did not appear on time, kept inquiring "Do you think she could be hurt?" "Is the weather fine for flying?" "I thought I heard her voice outside." When she finally arrived, she read him the Twenty-third and Ninety-first Psalms and later went home to rest. When his pulse became weak, she was called back to the hospital. He kissed her hand and told her to take care of herself. According to someone who was there at the moment of death, he just slipped away with no pain. For his funeral the chapel was hung with white satin scrolls bearing the Chinese characters for "China's Best Friend" and "Australia produced this man; can there ever be another so fine." Madame had him buried in the Soong family plot.

❧

THUS FAR, THE Russians had done little to help the Chinese Communists get arms and ammunition. Suddenly, in the summer of 1946, Stalin produced 1,226 guns, 369 tanks, 300,000 rifles, 4,836 machine guns, and 2,300 vehicles* for the CCP, all of which had been taken from the Japanese. He also arranged for 100,000 troops from North Korea to be incorporated into the Chinese Communist army. These moves, although they did not bear fruit immediately—the Chinese soldiers had to be trained to use modern equipment—would soon give the Communist army an advantage over that of the Nationalists.

In June of 1946, Marshall asked Hu Lin, an important journalist and editor, to visit him at his residence in Nanking and give his frank opinion on the prospects for peace. The journalist made eight points, the most important of which were the following:

1. The Americans were wrong in believing that the Chinese Communists were merely "land reformers." To drive home his point, Hu quoted an old Chinese proverb: "The crows are black all over the world."
2. There was no basis for a coalition government with the KMT and the CCP. It would be like setting up a "United Republic of Germany and France."
3. A temporary peace, even a cease-fire, would require international supervision.

---

* Figures from Crozier, *The Man Who Lost China*, p. 291.

Present at the briefing was John Leighton Stuart, former president of Yenching University, who would be named U.S. ambassador to China within the month.*

Although Marshall listened politely to Hu, he apparently did not hear what he was being told. Moreover, from the time that Marshall returned to China, his relationship with the generalissimo had begun to deteriorate. (Marshall told Beal that the "only thing that kept him on reasonable terms with Chiang was the great shine the Gimo has taken to Mrs. Marshall, who has introduced him to the game of Chinese checkers.") Chiang wanted Marshall to guarantee that the Communists would observe the January cease-fire, and if he did not do this, Chiang said, the Nationalists must go ahead and occupy Manchuria. He proceeded to Mukden to direct his armies and in July ordered them to take the offensive. By the middle of September, they had gained control over the largest railway network in north China, trapping the Communist soldiers in the mountains of Shantung and Shansi. He then set out to capture the Mongolian city of Kalgan, currently serving as the capital of the CCP.

Unable to hold Kalgan militarily, the Communists returned to diplomacy, and on September 30, Chou wrote Marshall that if "the Kuomintang Government does not instantly cease its military operations against Kalgan and the vicinity areas, the Chinese Communist Party feels itself forced to presume that the Government . . . has ultimately abandoned its pronounced policy of peaceful settlement."

"The more I hear and see of this situation out here, the more I am inclined to think that we should pull out completely and let this civil war take place," said James McHugh. "It would unseat Chiang and T.V. and all of the other crooked politicians, all of whom are growing rich now on all that we have given China . . . there is a hopeless stalemate between the KMT and the Commies which can never be resolved except by civil war. And there will never be any reform in the Central Govt until it is forced by civil war. . . . Corruption is rampant. . . . Everyone knows about it; the Chinese all admit it; and the foreigners all fume at it. Yet Washington goes right on blandly overlooking it and pouring more and more of our own patrimony into the hopper."

McHugh was not the only observer to come to that conclusion. Mar-

---

* Marshall had originally chosen Wedemeyer, who very much wanted the job. But Wedemeyer's pessimistic attitude toward Marshall's mission, an ill-considered letter he sent Marshall to that effect, his obvious bias toward the Chiang government, and an honest appraisal of the situation in China before the Senate Foreign Affairs Committee lost him the appointment. Stuart was named to the post in July of 1946.

shall told Chiang that if the Nationalist army did not halt its Kalgan offensive, he would leave China and the U.S. government would declare an embargo on all military equipment going to the KMT. In response to this ultimatum, the G-mo delivered "a long speech in which he quoted the Bible and indulged in generalities but did not budge an inch." It was not until Chiang learned that Marshall had already radioed Washington about cutting off U.S. aid that he actually backed down and agreed to a ten-day truce on Kalgan. "His old foot went round and round and almost hit the ceiling," Marshall said, referring to Chiang's habit of jiggling his foot when he was upset. To save face, Chiang sent May-ling to speak with Marshall. She came over at 9:00 P.M. with a statement from her husband about the truce that, Marshall told her, was "terrible." May-ling gave the American general permission to change it. "Finally," Marshall reported, "I cut out a page and a half of the Gimo's generalities—just cut it right out." After four meetings with his advisers the next day, Chiang accepted the edited version. "The Madame sold it," said Marshall. Marshall told Beal that Chiang always insisted that May-ling be there for his conversations with the G-mo, "even when she was sick, or tired, or tried to beg off." He said that during a discussion of Chiang's "lack of understanding of Western democracy," she had told Marshall that "in all her years with him [Chiang] she felt she had made only a 'two per cent impression' on him."

In agreeing to the Kalgan truce, Chiang demanded certain minor conditions having to do with delegates to the upcoming National Assembly, and it was probably sometime on October 10, Chinese Independence Day, that the Communists released a statement officially refusing Chiang's terms. In retaliation, the Nationalist army took Kalgan, and Marshall immediately carried out his threat to stop all aid to the Nationalist government. The edict was neither made public nor communicated to Chiang, who did not discover what had happened until a month later, when a request for deliveries of military equipment was turned down.

Without American equipment and no longer in a position to take the offensive, Chiang said he was ready for a rapprochement, but by then the Chinese Communists had lost interest and motivation (if, in fact, they had ever had any). Instead of a truce, they now demanded that the Nationalist armies pull back to positions held on January 13 in China and June 7 in Manchuria. Moreover, both the Communists and the Democratic League refused to attend the National Assembly, which met on November 16, 1946, to pass the first Chinese Constitution.

For that event, the hall was hung with red, while blue and white banners bearing Sun's portrait served as the backdrop for the stage. After a kowtow to their dead leader, the delegates were sworn in en masse. "The abstention of the Communists and other minority representatives," one observer noted, "left many vacant seats on the floor." Chiang delivered a twenty-minute opening speech "in a detached sort of way," after which the meeting was adjourned. The day before the Assembly, Chiang had apparently spoken for more than an hour to the delegates from the KMT, urging its members to treat the minorities with consideration, and during a subsequent session, it was decided to keep seats open on the presidium in case the Communists decided to join. But while Chiang was issuing his final statement to the Assembly—a speech involving a cease-fire "except to defend against attack" and negotiations with the Communists for unconditional cessation of hostilities—his armies were trying to capture the port of Chefoo. "He must have known about it," Marshall said in disgust. "It made a mockery of the statement. . . . The Communists did it in June . . . but this time it was the Nationalists. Every time there is a gesture for peace the army makes an attack that nullifies it."

Chiang and Marshall met two weeks later. Marshall complained that Chiang not only had damaged his attempts at mediation with his military actions but had contributed to China's financial collapse by designating 80 to 90 percent of its budget for the military. In doing this, the generalissimo had impoverished the Chinese and left them ripe for the spread of communism. Chiang argued that the Communists had never intended to join a coalition and that their sole purpose had been to disrupt the government. Both were right.

The Assembly minus the Communists and other minority parties that had refused to attend,* passed the new constitution on Christmas Day, 1946. "It is unfortunate that the Communists did not see fit to participate in the Assembly," Marshall said, "since the constitution that has been adopted seems to include every major point that they wanted." Two weeks later, on January 7, 1947, the American general, having failed to do the impossible, returned to the United States to be named secretary of state by President Truman. Ambassador Stuart described the last exchange between Chiang and the general as "one of dramatic intensity," in which the G-mo "pled with great earnestness" for Marshall to stay and act as his supreme adviser, "offering to give him all the power which he himself possessed and promising to co-operate with him to the utmost." Marshall, Stuart said, was "deeply moved," but was, of course, not at liberty to explain why he had to leave.

One correspondent describes Marshall's departure on a "very cold

---

* The Communists had delayed the Assembly, originally scheduled for May 1, by refusing to name their delegates, leading one to believe that they never had any intention of going.

morning" under "a slight snowfall. . . . His private plane . . . was waiting on the runway. . . . And there this pathetic little group stood, all waiting for him to bring about the final breach. Madame Chiang was there in a very handsome heavy beaver coat. The Generalissimo was there, Ambassador Stuart, T. V. Soong." Chiang followed Marshall into the plane to say good-bye. When he had emerged and the plane had taken off, "the Madame turned to her brother, T. V. Soong, and said, 'Shall we have a cup of coffee?' That was the end of the Marshall mission."

Marshall's last report—released an hour after his departure—blamed the failure of his mission on the reactionary members of the KMT, who were "interested in the preservation of their own feudal control of China" and the Communists, who, while issuing "vicious" propaganda, "do not hesitate at the most drastic measures to gain their end . . . without any regard to the immediate suffering of the people involved." William Bullitt, a former ambassador to the USSR and France, summed it up this way: "Never," he said, "was a distinguished soldier sent on a more hopeless and unwise political mission."

47

Chiang stood for a moment within reach of statesmanship. His assent to the Communists' terms would have brought peace. Dissent meant bloodshed—and Chiang dissented.

—THEODORE WHITE AND ANNALEE JACOBY

ON MARCH 12, 1947, President Truman gave a speech before Congress, spelling out what came to be called the Truman Doctrine. The president started by announcing that immediate military and economic assistance would be given to Greece to fight the Communist revolutionaries who were seemingly about to take over the government. Truman's largesse was based on a new direction in foreign policy, which was to "support free peoples who are resisting attempted subjugation by armed minorities or by outside pressure," i.e., Communists. Sure that China qualified for the same assistance, Chiang sent his troops back on the offensive and dispensed with the financial services of T. V. Soong.

T.V. had arrived from Shanghai for a meeting of the Executive Yuan in Nanking in what the correspondent for *Time* referred to as "a howling gale of antipathy and criticism," a storm set in motion by a Chinese historian who had denounced T.V.'s economic policies, his "haughty and taciturn" personality, and his ignorance of his homeland: "As for his knowledge of Chinese culture, even after chemists analyzed it down to the smallest fraction, one can hardly find any trace of it." Shortly after arriving in Nanking, T.V. walked into a meeting of the Legislative Yuan, took a seat in the center of a long curved table facing the other members, and read his resignation slowly and calmly. "Three times during the course of the last year I submitted my resignation. . . . The Generalissimo has finally granted my request." Complaining that neither the government nor the people had shown self-restraint regarding their currency and that the only recourse had been to print more, he described the current economic crisis as "the cumulative result of heavily unbalanced budgets carried through eight years of war and one year of illusory peace accentuated to some degree by speculative activities." After a few minutes of heckling, he rose, answered the hecklers, and prepared to leave. "I have made my report," he said. "I had better go."

There is an intriguing note in T.V.'s handwriting dating from this period.

The person for whom it was intended is not named, but in thinking about what he wanted to say, T.V. had jotted down several points: "Because of my experience always felt sorry for Marshall . . . Sorry for Chiang also because he was fumbling about democratic instruments which he did not know how to handle." T.V. also referred to his brother-in-law as a "bad administrator," adding "what I was trying to do. . . . make effective use of American aid & build up economy & keep fighting inflation so that gov could have demo-cratic institutions. With running away inflation no gov't let alone demo-cratic gov't could exist. . . . With Chiang force counts not money but I [Chiang] am the state."

T.V. left the government just in time. Shortly after Truman's speech, Undersecretary of State Dean Acheson told the House Foreign Affairs Com-mittee that "the Chinese government is not in a position at the present time that the Greek government is in. It is not approaching collapse. It is not threatened by defeat by the Communists." Ergo, there would be no help for the Chinese. The Communists reacted to this statement with renewed offensives in Manchuria, Jehol, and Shensi. Alarmed by these developments, the United States temporarily lifted the embargo on military equipment, and the KMT was able to purchase enough ammunition to stop the Com-munist thrust, but not enough to go on the offensive. On May 1, 1947, Mao renamed his soldiers the People's Liberation Army, and by June it had taken over the initiative in Manchuria. In early July, Chiang ordered a general mobilization.

On July 9, Truman and Marshall sent General Wedemeyer back to China to assess the situation. The Wedemeyer mission was the president's answer to political pressure from several fronts, primarily the members of Congress, who were "accusing the Administration of pursuing a negative policy in China." The KMT was pleased with Truman's choice of investigator, since Wedemeyer hated the Communists. Directed "to appraise the political, eco-nomic, psychological and military situations," Wedemeyer traveled from Mongolia to Taiwan. When he returned to Nanking, Chiang asked him to prepare a speech for officials of the government and the military. Both Chiang and Ambassador Stuart urged him to speak frankly, which he did, reporting that on his tour he had "found evidence of maladministration, cor-ruption and lethargy." But Wedemeyer's honesty got him in trouble. In try-ing to "jolt the Nationalist leaders into taking action which would convince America that they were worth supporting," he had placed himself in opposi-tion to U.S. policy, eventually ending his own career in the military.*

---

* Sometime after Wedemeyer left the military, May-ling wrote to say that she and her husband wanted him to know "that we are thinking of you. . . . We heard of your retire-

◆

AT THE BEGINNING of January 1948, the Nationalists numbered nearly twice as many men under arms (1,250,000) as the Communists (700,000)—a fact that may have encouraged Chiang Kai-shek to try to hold on to Manchuria, rather than negotiate while, as one writer put it, "he still had something to negotiate with." The generalissimo was irrational on the subject of Manchuria.

It was there, at the capital city of Mukden, that the Japanese had launched their war on China in 1931, and he apparently felt that if he gave it up, he would lose the Mandate of Heaven. What Chiang failed to realize was that insofar as the Chinese and particularly the Manchurians were concerned, he had already lost it. Stubborn as always, Chiang moved to Peiping in order to direct the northern campaign. His military strategy—concentrating his troops in widely separated towns—necessitated the use of the railways, which, by this time, had nearly all been captured or destroyed by the Communists.

In February, Marshall, now secretary of state, informed an executive session of the Foreign Affairs and Foreign Relations Committees that he had warned the G-mo that "the odds were too heavy" against the KMT, and therefore the United States should supply no more military aid. He said that he had tried to convince Chiang of this, but that there was "constant insistence on the part of the Generalissimo and his high military and political group that the only way the issue could be settled was by force." Beyond military weakness, Marshall said, there was "conspicuous ineptitude and widespread corruption among the higher leaders" which had resulted in the "consequent low morale of the Chinese Government armies." He said that in order to keep the KMT going, the United States "would have to be prepared virtually to take over the Chinese Government and administer its economic, military and governmental affairs." Such a course of action, Marshall contended, would "most probably degenerate" into a "dissipation of U.S. resources [that] would inevitably play into the hands of the Russians." The Chinese Communists, he said, "have succeeded to a considerable extent in identifying their movement with the popular demand for change in present conditions"; on the other hand, there had been no sign that the current

---

ment from the army with mixed emotions. We realize how wearing and frustrating the past few years have been for you . . . now that you are out of the Army, we do hope and pray that you will find surcease of inner turmoil from an impossible situation. . . . What a true and tried friend you are!" (Hoover Archives: Albert C. Wedemeyer papers, Box 31, Folder 5, Madame Chiang Kai-shek to Wedemeyer, July 27, 1951.)

38

Mao and Chou in 1945 in
Yenan, the Communist base,
photographed ten years after the
Long March.

39

Mikhail Borodin and his wife,
Fanya. A smart and effective
member of the Comintern,
Borodin succeeded in
organizing Sun's government
along Soviet lines and
infiltrating it with a number
of his fellow Communists.

40

Mao with General Chu Teh (left),
later commander in chief of the
Chinese Communist Army.

41

Wang Ching-wei. Rich, handsome, and expected to succeed Sun Yat-sen as head of the KMT, he advocated collaboration with the Communists, but ended up as a puppet of the Japanese.

42

Chang Hsueh-liang. Known as the "Young Marshal," he inherited Manchuria before he turned thirty.

43

Ho Ying-chin.
  Chiang's chief of staff and the personification of corruption.

44

Hollington Tong.
  Chiang's PR man who wrote a biography of him.

45

Chen Kuo-fu.
  The older brother of the CC Clique. Rigid and uncorruptible, the Chen brothers controlled Chiang's schedule and served as the nation's thought police.

46

Chen Li-fu.
  The younger brother, a devoted conservative and anticommunist.

Chiang and May-ling greeted by officials at the Nanking airport on their return from his kidnapping in Sian, December 26, 1936.

Chiang and May-ling safe at home and smiling.

Japanese using live Chinese for bayonet practice.

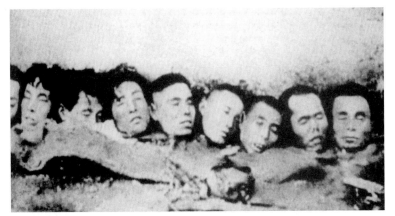

Severed heads of victims.

Madame with Chiang and General Joseph W. Stilwell. This picture was taken before the two men learned to despise each other.

52

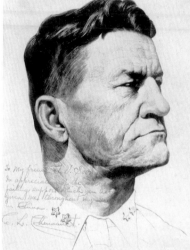

Claire Chennault. His solution to the war in China was simple: more U.S. planes and supplies. The Chiangs loved him.

53

T. V. Soong, General Albert C. Wedemeyer, Chiang Kai-shek, and General Patrick J. Hurley. Wedemeyer became a lifelong friend, and Hurley became ambassador to China for a brief period.

54

William H. Donald. He and his publicity team built the Chiangs into world icons.

55

Owen Lattimore. Political advisor to the generalissimo. He was accused later by Senator Joseph McCarthy of spying for the Soviet Union, but the charges against him were dismissed.

56

57

Lauchlin Currie. Economic advisor to the Chinese government.

General George C. Marshall. President Truman sent him to China to do the impossible—unite the Kuomintang and the Chinese Communists.

58

Madame Chiang welcoming Wendell Willkie to Chungking. Chiang was pleased with him at first.

59

Willkie greeting Madame in New York, March 1943.

60

Madame Chiang
and President
Roosevelt. He came
to the train station
to meet her,
February 1943.

Madame Chiang and
Eleanor Roosevelt
photographed on the
White House lawn.

61

62

WOMEN WELDER

MADAME CHIANG

CHINESE-AMERICAN FRIENDSHIP

REG·MANNING

Cartoon published during her
visit to the United States.

63

Madame addressing the House of Representatives.

64

The Hollywood Bowl just before Madame's arrival.

65

Madame speaking.

Nationalist Conscripts. The men were roped together so they could not escape.

The Cairo Conference, November 1943: Chiang, Roosevelt, Churchill, and Madame. Madame did the translating, talking, and interpreting.

Chiang speaking to the National Assembly in October of 1948, warning the Kuomintang of the danger of the situation with the Communists. The portrait behind him is of Sun Yat-sen.

Chou and Mao at their victory celebration one year later (October 1949).

Mao reviewing tanks on the outskirts of Peking, March 1949.

Red Army soldiers sleeping on the streets of Shanghai, so as not to disturb its citizens, who probably compared them favorably to the marauding troops of the Kuomintang.

Chiang's favorite residence on Taiwan. It was converted into his mausoleum after his death, and is known as the Cihu Presidential Burial Place.

Chiang, Madame, and Chiang's son Ching-kuo, c. 1955.

Chiang Kai-shek's family at his coffin. Left to right, Chiang Hsiao-wu, a grandson; Taiwan Premier Chiang Ching-kuo; Madame Chiang; and General Chiang Wei-kuo, Chiang's adopted son.

Madame Chiang and Senator Robert Dole. Senators Dole and Paul Simon invited her to Washington to celebrate the fiftieth anniversary of the end of World War II.

Madame Chiang in 1997, a classic Chinese portrait. She was 100 according to Western calculation, 101 according to the Chinese.

Chinese government "could satisfy this popular demand or create conditions which would satisfy the mass of Chinese people." It was at this point, according to Crozier, that the China Lobby "rallied to the Generalissimo's defence."

THE HISTORY OF the lobby goes back to June 1940, when T. V. Soong arrived in Washington with instructions to get financial and military help for his brother-in-law's government. He set about making friends with influential types like Harry Hopkins, Henry Morgenthau, Joseph Alsop, and Henry Luce. But, according to Ross Y. Koen, whose book *The China Lobby in American Politics* was originally banned by the U.S. government under pressure from Taipei and the lobby, T.V. had "achieved only a modicum of success between 1940 and V-J Day in securing financial aid for China."

He had first teamed up with a Polish doctor named Ludwig "Lulu" Rajchman, a former head of the Health Secretariat at the League of Nations who knew his way around the diplomatic world. A "clever and charming" man, according to *Reporter* magazine, Rajchman was disparaged by a confidential source in the FBI files as "a Polish Jew [who] should be watched." After the passage of the Lend-Lease Act in March 1941, Rajchman advised T.V. to set up China Defense Supplies, an entity that would represent China in dealing with Lend-Lease. Roosevelt suggested that Soong hire William S. Youngman, Jr., as head of the agency. Formerly a general counsel for the Federal Power Commission, Youngman helped Soong staff China Defense Supplies with "influential Americans and a few persuasive Chinese." The agency's counsel was Roosevelt's close friend and adviser Thomas G. Corcoran, who described China Defense Supplies as "an unorthodox operation . . . dubious according to the letter of the law." Chinese requests for Lend-Lease arrived with endorsements from Hopkins or Currie, were "expedited" by the China Defense team, and put through the system by high-placed friends of Corcoran or Rajchman.

In 1942, in response to Roosevelt's concern about the deteriorating relationship between the United States and China, Lauchlin Currie blamed T.V., claiming that relations between China Defense Supplies and the U.S. Army were "very bad" due to the peremptory way Chiang's brother-in-law was handling Lend-Lease. An example of T.V.'s high-handedness can be seen in the case of Leland Stowe, a Pulitzer Prize–winning journalist who wrote for the *Chicago Daily News* syndicate from hot spots around the world. In a series of articles, only two of which ever made it into print, Stowe documented one of the major reasons that China was short of armaments: "Because the Burma road has for years been dominated by racketeers and war profiteers, ten thousand Chinese soldiers have gone without rifles, hand grenades or munitions." T.V., whom Chiang had designated foreign minister during the fateful month of December 1941, protested to the White House, and the rest of Stowe's articles were killed.

As we have seen, the bill granting $500 million in credits to China with no strings attached had passed Congress in February 1942. According to *Reporter* magazine, which devoted two issues to the China Lobby in the spring of 1952, around $220 million of the half billion dollars was used, per Kung's request, to buy gold in the United States, supposedly to stabilize the ever-shrinking Chinese dollar. But much of this money was apparently put up for sale in China "under circumstances that allowed insiders to make big killings in a single evening." *Reporter* alleged that Ai-ling Kung "would buy Chinese dollars on the Shanghai exchange just before new credits to the fund were publicly announced, then sell when the announcement sent the currency up temporarily—thereby, of course, helping to send it back down."

Another $200 million of the loan, *Reporter* claimed, had been set aside to redeem U.S. bonds and savings certificates issued by the Chinese government. Although the bonds were not redeemed as promised, those in the know were able to sell their holdings before the redemption clause was publicly rescinded. These same people, who knew in advance that the savings certificates would, unlike the bonds, be redeemed, quickly bought up the certificates. *Reporter* said that T.V. had invested $5 million in these securities "as a patriotic duty," while the Kungs invested some $70 million.

The story is also told that one day in 1945, H. H. Kung's luggage was opened during a flight over the Hump into China, and it was discovered that he was carrying $1 million in cash. He informed the pilots, who were not permitted to carry this kind of cargo, that not only was the money insured in the United States but he had another $9 million* waiting in New York to be sent to China, thus intimating that the $1 million did not mean much to him. Nevertheless, he compromised with the crew; they allowed him to take his cash into China, providing he did not try to have the rest of it flown over the Hump.

The Allied victory over the Japanese in the summer of 1945, a sudden development that might well have ended or at least slowed down the China Lobby, only altered its composition. After the war there were, according to *Reporter,* three distinct groups of lobbyists: the realists, who feared a Communist victory in China; the opportunists, who looked to enrich themselves through loans and gifts to the national government; and the evangelists,

---

* Approximately $104 million in today's dollars.

who were themselves incorruptible and believed that Chiang's government could be reformed.

Typical of this last group was Dr. Walter Judd from Minnesota. Judd, who had started working as a medical missionary in China in 1925, had run for Congress in 1942, where he helped see that the bill repealing the Chinese Exclusion Act was passed in 1943. Called by *Reporter* a "selfless, altogether dedicated man who had seen China suffer and had suffered with it," Judd was typical of the idealistic members of the China Lobby.

Alfred Kohlberg was a different breed of lobbyist. A "mild-mannered, unassuming little man," Kohlberg was less than five feet, five inches tall, with a soft face and bald head. Perhaps the most famous of the nongovernmental figures connected with the Lobby, Kohlberg owned a business—he was known as "the handkerchief king"—an enterprise that brought in around $1 million a year until its owner ran afoul of the Federal Trade Commission for selling Chinese-decorated lace handkerchiefs under European names such as "Valenciennes" and "Cluny Venise." Like Hurley and later Joseph McCarthy, Kohlberg never stopped trying to ferret out Reds in high places, particularly the U.S. State Department.

Another important member of the China Lobby was William C. Bullitt, former U.S. ambassador to the Soviet Union and France. Bullitt wrote an article for *Life* magazine in 1947, in which he claimed that Roosevelt, Stalin, and Churchill had signed "secretly, behind the back of China, an agreement by which vital rights of China in her province of Manchuria [called by Bullitt 'the finest piece of territory in Asia'] were sacrificed to Soviet imperialism." According to Bullitt, an ardent believer in superlatives, "No more unnecessary, disgraceful and potentially disastrous document has ever been signed by a President of the United States."

A major recipient of help from the Chinese Lobby was Claire Chennault, who started a commercial airline with Whiting Willauer, a former official of China Defense Supplies. The initial capital came from a $2 million U.S. loan; operating capital was provided by private Chinese and American investors. CAT, as it was known, flew everything from seeds, medicine, farm equipment, and banknotes to herds of cows and sheep into the interior and brought back tung oil, hog bristles, cotton, wool, tobacco, silk, and tea. According to *Reporter,* Chennault and Willauer "were able to exchange their Chinese dollar profits for U.S. dollars at the fixed rate of exchange," and CNRRA (the Chinese equivalent of UNRRA) arranged top priority for all CAT airlifts at the open-market rate, which was "many times the legal rate."

In spite of these and other less profitable efforts, at the beginning of 1948 there were still 10 million Chinese on the verge of starvation, while

officials of the KMT officials continued to rob the people. One historian*
told a story about the magistrate of Hsiaoshan county, who announced that
the county would sell coupons to buy rice from outside the area to make up
for shortages within. The magistrate then had all the rice transferred from
the granaries to the stores of the local rice merchants. First the money taken
in from the sales of the coupons was divided among the conspirators—
county officials and big rice merchants. Then, when the public brought
in their coupons to exchange them for rice and found none in the granaries,
they were forced to go to the merchants, who grossly overpriced it. When
the story came out, the magistrate fled. Later, some of the conspirators were
caught, but not until the Communists took over the area.

Politically, militarily, and financially, Chiang's government was obviously falling apart. According to eminent Chinese history professor Lloyd
Eastman, "the fabric of rural society was becoming unraveled; industrial
production was faltering; the transportation system was in a state of continual disrepair (largely owing to Communist sabotage); and inflation was daily
eroding the value of the *fa-pi*, the national currency." In spite of this, the
Chinese National Assembly reelected Chiang president at the end of March
1948. Reflecting their growing disillusionment with the generalissimo, however, its members chose General Li Tsung-jen, a former Kwangsi warlord, as
vice president. This was, as a member of the U.S. Embassy staff put it, "a
disastrous blow" that "seriously undermined the position of the Generalissimo," who had promised the position to Sun Yat-sen's son, Sun Fo.

Twenty years earlier, Chiang had fought and beaten General Li, who,
along with his partner General Pai (they were known as "The Two"), had
made up the strength of the rebel Kwangsi Clique in the early days of
Chiang's republic. Having proved his authority over Li, Chiang had designated him pacification commissioner for the province of Kwangsi, and under the direction of Li and Pai, Kwangsi had developed local industry,
sponsored education, and become relatively crime-free. After the end of
World War II, Chiang appointed Li director of his (Chiang's) presidential
headquarters in Peiping and, as the situation in Manchuria deteriorated,
tried to persuade him to take over the Manchurian campaign. But Li refused,
hanging on to his Peiping office until 1948, when he announced that he
would run for vice president. In beating out Sun Fo, Li not only caused
Chiang to lose face—the gravest sin in the eyes of the G-mo—but put him
on notice that he could no longer ignore calls for government reform. "The
Generalissimo," according to Roger Lapham of the Economic Cooperation
Authority (ECA), "was urged to welcome the elected Vice President, take

---

* R. Keith Schoppa from Loyola College in Maryland.

him into his confidence, and with him work to bring all elements of the KMT together, thus strengthening the central government. The president refused this good advice, kept the vice president and the progressive elements of the KMT at arms' length, and went his own sweet obstinate way to rule China as he saw fit."

Military news from Manchuria during the spring of 1948 was no better than the political situation at home. "Poorly fed, poorly paid, poorly clothed . . . often short of ammunition," ordinary Chinese soldiers were "easy prey for the clever and impassioned propaganda of the Communists." Moreover, Chiang's forces were apparently riddled with moles, among whom was the commander of over half a million of the G-mo's best troops. Forced to evacuate Kirin in central Manchuria in March, the Nationalist army moved south to Changchun, where food supplies had been cut off by the Communists* and starvation was setting in. Mukden, south of Changchun, was also in danger. The head of the Joint U.S. Military Advisory Group urged Chiang to abandon Mukden, but he rejected the idea and continued to look to the United States for aid, refusing to admit that Nationalist defeats were due not to a lack of war material but to the defection of his troops to the Communists. As Lapham phrased it, Chiang was still "a stubborn, obstinate man, who refused to delegate authority, who relied on incompetent favorites for many of his subordinates, and who put on the shelf competent military men who could have helped him."

One Chinese tried to explain Chiang's attitude to Lapham: "You must understand that the Generalissimo looks upon himself as the father of a huge family . . . in the family, the sons took precedence. . . . Chiang Kai-shek regarded his Whampoa schoolmates as his sons. If a son was a black sheep or utterly incompetent, he had, nevertheless, to be taken care of. . . . That explained why the Generalissimo had kept so many incompetent generals in authority. His first loyalty was to his Whampoa 'sons'; and he could count on their loyalty to him in return—the son's duty to the father, whether the father be right or wrong." But, as we have seen, that loyalty was, to say the least, questionable.

According to Eastman, it was during the summer of 1948 that "the economic situation worsened, and the nation seemed to be plunging toward utter collapse. . . . Rice riots . . . spread rapidly across the country. Prices of other goods rose so fast that shopkeepers changed price tags several times a day." Although economists like T. V. Soong had warned against simplistic

---

* According to Chang and Halliday, Mao was selling all the food Manchuria could produce in return for arms and goodwill, thus condemning hundreds of thousands of Manchurians to death by starvation in 1948. (Chang and Halliday, *Mao*, p. 310.)

solutions and advocated reducing military expenditures to balance the budget, on August 19, 1948. the generalissimo established a new currency called the gold yuan, convertible to the U.S. dollar at 4 to 1. The Chinese were required to turn in their paper money along with all their gold, silver, and foreign currency, against which they would be given new gold yuan notes. To effect the transition, called "Beating the Tiger," the G-mo appointed economic supervisors in major coastal cities, only one of whom took his job seriously. This was Chiang's son Ching-kuo, dubbed by the English press "the general-in-charge of economic war in Shanghai."

A general needs an army, and Ching-kuo ordered a force known as the Sixth Suppression and Reconstruction Brigade to come to the city, designating different squads to watch everyone from the Shanghai police to the garrison commander. Notices were posted saying that informants who denounced noncompliers would be given anonymity plus 30 percent of the value of the confiscated gold and currency. These noncompliers were subjected to trials, fines, and prison, while corrupt officials could be (and were) sentenced to death. Shanghai, "the nation's financial, commercial, and industrial center, where hoarding and speculation had become a way of life among the most wealthy and influential entrepreneurs," was suddenly subject to unexpected, unforgiving, and relentless reform that stopped at nothing and nobody. Although Big-Eared Du invited Ching-kuo to dinner on his arrival in the city, Chiang's son sent his regrets, then arrested Du's son for speculating, hoarding, and making illegal stock transactions. Du himself left for Hong Kong, and shortly thereafter, his son made a "substantial payment" to the government, closed his company, and joined his father.

"For over four weeks," the Italian ambassador said, "Shanghai was practically terror-stricken into good behaviour." After the first month of housecleaning, three thousand lawbreakers had been arrested; the wholesale index had risen by only 6 percent; and prices had stabilized far more than anyone expected. Even the most cynical citizens were impressed. On September 11, the *North-China Daily News* announced that "The experience of the past three weeks . . . has aroused a very considerable amount of hope." The next day Ching-kuo delivered a speech reflecting his early Communist training: "Stabilizing prices is only technical work," he declared; "our objective is to put an end to the unequal distribution of wealth. To be more specific, we should prevent the rich from getting richer while the poor are becoming poorer."

The very rich, of course, included his stepmother and her family. Mayling received a telephone call from Shanghai informing her that Ching-kuo had confiscated large quantities of goods, apparently on their way to the black market, from the Yangtze Development Corporation, which had been started by David Kung. Madame was further informed that Ching-kuo had charged the corporation with economic crimes, had already arrested some of its employees, and was planning to arrest David, its general manager. The G-mo told her to deal with the situation, and she took off by special plane for Shanghai. When she arrived, she met with the two young men, admonishing them that they were "brothers" and had "no reason to fight each other." While Madame, according to the U.S. Embassy, threatened to leave China if "her favorite nephew"* was attacked, David apparently intimated that if Ching-kuo did not drop the charges against him, he would tell things that would embarrass the Chiang family and the KMT government. Along with this threat, however, he agreed to pay the government a huge settlement—$6 million† was the sum reported—before leaving for Hong Kong and New York.

But what had originally looked like a triumph for Ching-kuo ended in economic disaster. In an effort to reduce the deficit, the government raised taxes on tobacco, liquor, tin foil, and joss paper, allowing merchants to adjust their prices accordingly. When the price of cigarettes suddenly shot up by 100 to 120 percent, the public, assuming that similar taxes and prices on more essential items would follow, went on a giant shopping spree, cleaning out the stocks of goods in the city within three weeks. The poor were hardest hit: there was no food to buy; medicine was unavailable; and there was no powdered milk for infants or coffins for the dead. In late October, the government's top administrators—minus the G-mo, who was elsewhere on military inspections—met in Nanking to oppose the emergency measures. They assigned the blame to Chiang Ching-kuo and revoked the price controls. Citizens stopped turning in their currency, and the gold yuan became worthless. But by then, the rich had fled to Hong Kong or Taiwan and Ching-kuo had resigned, issuing the following *mea culpa,* reminiscent of similar statements by his father: "After [the] past seventy days of my work I feel that I have failed to accomplish the duties which I should have accomplished. Not only did I not consummate my plan and mission but in certain respects I have rather deepened the sufferings of the people. . . . Today aside from petitioning . . . for punishment so as to clarify my responsibility I wish to take this opportunity of offering my deepest apology to citizens of Shanghai."

* The next day the embassy added the information that the "David Kung Stock Exchange scandal" was "further complicated" by reports that the brokerage firm that had performed the transaction was connected with Du Vee-pin, the eldest son of Big-eared Du. (National Archives: microfilm file 184, roll 58, September 3, 1948.)

† $6,000,000 Chinese = $1,500,000 U.S. in 1948 ($13,411,000 today).

A LITTLE OVER a month before this financial debacle, Chiang Kai-shek, finally admitting that the Nationalists could no longer hold Mukden, had ordered the commander of the area, General Wei Li-huang, to evacuate his soldiers from the city. Wei procrastinated for ten days—with the result that his army was overcome by the Communists. The general escaped by air, was court-martialed, and eventually joined the CCP. Other commanders began to change sides as well. The capital of Chungchun was evacuated, and Mukden fell at the beginning of November. According to a report from the CIA, "The orderly and efficient Communist take-over of Mukden . . . favorably impressed diplomatic officials there and . . . won the Communists wholehearted support from the populace."

A week later, the generalissimo, whose foray into Manchuria had cost his country seven armies and more than 400,000 men,* sent a "direct and urgent appeal" to President Truman. Saying that the Communist soldiers were "within striking distance" of Shanghai and Nanking, Chiang asked for "speedy and increased military assistance" along with "a firm statement of American policy in support of the cause for which my Government is fighting. Such a statement," Chiang contended, "would serve to bolster up the morale of the armed forces and the civilian population and would strengthen the Government's position." But, according to a memorandum prepared by the Joint Chiefs of Staff for the secretary of defense, "There is now obviously grave doubt as to whether the arrival in China of any further military equipment for the Chinese national Government will buy any time at all. It might, in fact, have the opposite result in that such equipment might pass into the hands of victorious Communist forces."

By now, morale was disastrously low in the Nationalist army, whose regular soldiers felt little loyalty toward the government that had dragooned them. The Communists also made it easy for Nationalist soldiers to defect, incorporating them into their army and often sending them home to their own provinces, where they would be more effective in fighting the government. Hu Lin, the journalist who had once tried to explain Communist goals to General Marshall, said that the fall of Manchuria was due to Chiang's refusal to release the Young Marshal, his arbitrary divisions of the area, his choice of southerners as northern governors, and the disbanding of 300,000 Chinese soldiers from Wang's puppet regime.† In sum, Chiang had made the Manchurians feel that they had merely gone from one occupation (the

---

* These figures come from Seymour Topping. *Journey Between Two Chinas*, p. 14.

† These men, it will be remembered, had originally declared for Chiang but later joined the Communists.

Japanese) to another (the by now famously corrupt officials of the Kuomintang). Even that bulwark of Chiang champions *Time* magazine wondered what the generalissimo would do next, noting that the "Communists were overrunning China like lava," and in the big cities, "the prestige of Generalissimo Chiang Kai-shek had sunk lower than the Yangtze." According to *Shanghai Post* journalist Randall Gould, Chiang "couldn't be elected dog-catcher even in his native village."

It was at this point that May-ling decided to go to the United States to beg for more aid. Although her husband was "quite dubious about the adventure," she called Ambassador Stuart on Thanksgiving Day 1948 to ask him to come to see her "at once," explaining that she had just been talking long distance with Marshall about a visit to the States. "I was sorely tempted to advise her against making a trip which was almost certain to prove fruitless," the ambassador said, "but I confined myself to assisting her in the practical arrangements." In the United States, publisher and friend Roy Howard saw an announcement of her intended visit and warned the Chinese News Service that since her success or failure in the United States would depend largely on the ability of those handling her public relations, he hoped that "this task . . . will not be trusted to the unskilled hands of the young gentleman [David Kung] who balled things up so badly for her and for the cause of American good will on her last visit to the U.S." And Wellington Koo thought May-ling had embarked on this trip "on what he considered to be a girlish whim," placing him, as Chinese ambassador to the United States, "in a very embarrassing position." Nevertheless, on November 28, 1948, the generalissimo's wife and her party left China. Two days later, the American staff began to evacuate the U.S. Embassy in the KMT's capital city of Nanking.

48

They wanted me to send in about five million Americans to rescue him [Chiang], but I wouldn't do it . . . he was as corrupt as they come. I wasn't going to waste one single American life to save him. . . . They hooted and hollered and carried on and said I was soft on Communism. . . . But . . . I never changed my mind about Chiang and his gang. Every damn one of them ought to be in jail, and I'd like to live to see the day they are.

—Harry S. Truman

MAY-LING, WHO had asked the United States to send a plane for her, arrived in Washington bearing what one chronicler called "demands of a magnitude to match the scale of her country's disasters"—i.e., $3 billion over three years in economic and military aid. In exchange, she was prepared to offer the United States military bases on Formosa. Her trip was, in the words of columnist Drew Pearson, "a frantic, hopeless mission to woo back the Chinese supply line," and she was forced to wait nine days before being invited to tea with the president, who referred privately to her husband as "Cash My-check." "She came to the United States for some more handouts," Truman said. ". . . I wouldn't let her stay at the White House like Roosevelt did. I don't think she liked it very much, but I didn't care one way or the other about what she liked and what she didn't like."

In his biography of the postwar president, composed of conversations with his subject, Merle Miller quoted the following: "I discovered after some time," Truman told Miller, "that Chiang Kai-shek and the Madame and their families, the Soong family and the Kungs, were all thieves, every last one of them, the Madame and him included. And they stole seven hundred and fifty million dollars out of the thirty-five billion that we sent to Chiang. They stole it, and it's invested in real estate down in São Paolo and some right here in New York [this conversation was held in Manhattan]. And that's the money that was used and is still being used for the so-called China Lobby. I don't like that. I don't like that at all. And I don't want anything to do with people like that."

The week after May-ling's arrival, Secretary of the Interior Harold Ickes noted her presence in the country and said that there had been "a change in feeling toward her husband and the precious gang of corruptionists surrounding him, who have made a tragic mockery of both American and Chinese hopes for a free and democratic China." If Madame Chiang "should persist in her belief that the sentiment of the American people can still be swung back to the pouring out of more billions of tax money in the wake of the more than three billions that have gone already down the sink of Chiang's graft-smeared and bloody-handed regime," Ickes told the press, he would offer the lady a famous quote from Omar Khayyam:

The Moving Finger writes; and having writ,
Moves on; nor all your piety nor wit
Shall lure it back to cancel half a line,
Nor all your tears wash out a word of it.

Aware of her recent bad publicity, May-ling had brought one instead of the many fur coats that had engendered criticism on her previous trip to the United States, and she traveled with only two suitcases and a cosmetic case. "Her traveling costume was a dark brown silk gown, ankle length," said one reporter. "Her nutria coat, with out-moded tuxedo collar, turned-back cuffs and padded shoulders showed wear." Hearing that General Marshall was in Walter Reed Army Hospital, where he had had a kidney removed, she immediately went to see him. He told her that he was not feeling well enough to discuss "official affairs," but promised to "arrange another meeting as soon as he felt better." Marshall's wife, Katherine, who was at the hospital, invited May-ling to come stay at Dodona Manor, the Marshalls' farmhouse in Leesburg, Virginia. The two ladies spent the next few days working in the kitchen garden, and Katherine told May-ling that when her husband was a boy, he had been nicknamed Flicker for the lock of hair on his forehead. Before leaving Washington, May-ling sent Marshall a letter, written in the form of a military report and headed:

TOP SECRET, FOR YOUR EYES ONLY
REPORT FOR GENERAL FLICKER.

A diary of the heavy work she had been doing while Marshall was "lolling in silken sheets" in the hospital, May-ling described her "back-breaking efforts" in "planting giant-caliber daffodils of the Holland type," "raking leaves to keep off enemy frost" and, afterward in the kitchen, "peeling spuds, boiling bully beef," and inventing a "wonderful new salad," full of garlic, that "tastes like mud—but [was] sure to faze the enemy in close contact in combat." The report ended:

Repeated requests to Deputy Commander [Katherine Marshall] for payment have fallen on deaf ears, who countercharges that since billeting in
the present bivouac the undersigned has browner cheeks, better color,
and there is a noticeable increase in girth. Any claims of a financial nature are therefore invalid and illegal.... Undersigned calls upon high
heavens to witness this un-Chinalike treatment.... I am awaiting
prompt and immediate Congressional attention ... due to one who is
on the soil of the Pilgrim Mothers—down with slave labor.

Respectfully submitted,
Mei-ling Soong.

Marshall, who, according to his biographer, "roared with laughter,"
promised never to show the letter to anyone else, lest he ruin Madame's
reputation as the Dragon Empress of China. Nonetheless, he proved no
more receptive to her request than the president.

Unfortunately for Chiang's wife, less than three weeks before her arrival
in the United States, General David Barr of the Joint U.S. Military Advisory
Group in China had reported that "no battle has been lost ... due to lack of
ammunition or equipment. Their [the Chinese] military debacles in my
opinion can all be attributed to the world's worst leadership and many other
morale destroying factors that lead to a complete loss of will to fight." Shortly
after meeting Madame Chiang for tea at the White House, the president sent
Paul G. Hoffman, head of the Economic Cooperation Authority, to Shanghai; when Hoffman returned, he also advised Truman against loaning the
Chinese any more money.

Calling Madame Chiang "an unpredictable mixture of a Chinese lady
tyrant and an American girl sophomore from Wellesley," Edgar A. Mowrer,
a columnist for the *St. Louis Star-Times,* cast her appearance in the United
States as an oblique, utterly Chinese way of saying that the generalissimo
was prepared to consider reforming the Kuomintang and the country. Nevertheless, the United States canceled its reconstruction aid program for
China, signaling the failure of May-ling's mission.

"I hope my beloved wife can come back soon," Chiang cabled ten days
after her arrival. A week later, he sent her a message to be given to Truman.
In it he claimed that he was being "pressed" by members of his government
"to make peace with the Communists through Russia," since "it has been
proved hopeless to expect any further American support. Please ask for definite reply from highest source if any support moral or material forthcoming
from American Government as otherwise I will step aside to make way for
negotiation so as to prevent useless suffering of the people in the fight against

communistic world domination." The G-mo concluded his message by assuring the president that he was "thinking not only of our 450 million people but also of the principles of world freedom." A standard piece of self-righteous cant, it could not have done much to improve Truman's opinion of the generalissimo, if, in fact, it ever reached the president's desk

Most people assumed that Madame Chiang, having failed to get U.S. support, would turn around and go home, but she had another plan, involving settling down in the United States and strengthening the China Lobby, which she apparently believed to be at least partially responsible for the abrupt end to the country's generosity.* Claiming that her husband "urgently needs assurance . . . that Americans understand that he is fighting Soviet communism in China just as the Americans are fighting Soviet communism in Berlin," she radically reduced her requests to "an expression by the United States that it is backing Chiang in spirit." Such a statement, she said, would be "more valuable at this time than military and financial aid."

On December 20, she wired Chiang that she would "try my best and spare no efforts working for you and for our nation in this difficult situation," warning that the "conditions in our nation and the statements of our high-level officers will exert a great influence on the U.S. government and General Marshall and will also impact my work in America. Please pay attention to this." May-ling was clearly worried about stories she was hearing, and the next day she sent two more cables home. In the first, she wrote that

> according to the Associated Press in Nanking . . . you have transferred the peace negotiations [with the Communists] over to members of your new government. . . . If they decide to make peace, you will have to accept it . . . and retire from the scene. According to information from a high-ranking officer of another government, the new government has made up its mind to make peace with the Communists. . . . These stories are very bad for us. If they are not true, please correct them. Please also wire me about the domestic situation, military picture, and your future plans, so that I can use this information in my conversation with Marshall.

In the second wire, she explained that Marshall's condition still prohibited her from discussing serious issues with him, that even President Truman was not allowed to see him, and that therefore, there had been no decision taken on Truman's new China policy. Chiang cabled back that the rumor of

---

* See endnotes for the results of Truman's investigation into the China Lobby.

his retirement and "peace-making with the Communists" had come from the U.S. Embassy in Taiwan, for which he blamed Ambassador Stuart, Stuart's secretary, and the Communists.

Whoever was responsible, the story of Chiang's retirement was still out there a week later, and, according to May-ling's next cable to her husband, "having a very bad effect. I had to explain the truth, and I found it very difficult to counter the rumors. . . . If you still want to retire, I will suspend my work in the U.S. Please tell me what you have decided to do as soon as possible so that I can make my plans." And the next day:

I spoke with leaders in the U.S. Congress, all of whom thought that you should persist and wait for assistance. If necessary you can move the government to Guangzhou [Canton]. Aid from America will come sooner or later. . . . I insist that you not give up. As long as you can sustain your position anywhere on the mainland, the assistance from America will finally arrive. As to the rumor spread by the Associated Press that the U.S. government wouldn't help China unless you resign, I discussed it with all the media and corrected it yesterday. I am trying to get the U.S. to send VIP officers to China, and the White House is now considering my request.

On January 1, 1949, Madame Chiang issued a gloomy New Year's message through the Chinese Embassy, predicting that "the year 1949, for my country, will probably be as tortured, as bitter as the year 1948 has been." But in fact, it was far worse. With Manchuria gone, the next area to fall was northern China. During the previous summer, American aid officials, disgusted with Chiang, had started separate negotiations with General Fu Tso-yi, one of the best of the Nationalist generals, currently in charge of defending the Peiping-Tientsin area. Three of Fu's armies were insufficiently armed, and the fourth had no equipment at all. The Americans offered to supply Fu with $16 million worth of armaments to enable his soldiers to defend north China and eventually open a corridor to the Nationalists marooned in Manchuria. But the first shipment of arms came late and was missing essential parts. Tientsin fell on January 14, 1949, leaving Peiping open to the Communists. To avoid the destruction of China's historical and cultural heritage, Fu turned the old capital over to the Communists on January 21. The Communist army gained twenty-five divisions; Fu was later given a position in the Communist government; and Peiping again became Peking, although the Nationalists refused to use the name.

At this point Chiang had already lost 400,000 soldiers trying to defend the city of Hsuchow, a market town and railway junction 175 miles north of

Nanking. Hsuchow was the key to a decisive encounter between the KMT and the CCP, known as the Battle of Hwai-hai, which lasted for nearly three months and was fought on a huge plain reaching into four different provinces. The villagers, under Communist control for many months, had dispensed with their landlords through trials and less savory methods, and local farms had been redistributed. Each adult member of a household was now the proud owner of about a third of an acre of land. Armed by the Communists, they had been organized into militias and trained in what was euphemistically termed "self-defense."

Although both sides in the battle started out with around 600,000 soldiers, the Nationalists, with more ground equipment and control of the skies, still lost the seminal battle in what Crozier called "one of the greatest military defeats in modern history." According to journalist Seymour Topping, this defeat was directly attributable to Chiang, who bypassed his best strategist and took the wrong position, assigning command of the forces to Generals Liu Chih and Tu Yu-ming, "two notorious incompetents." Liu had apparently never won a battle, while Tu tried to escape from the battlefield disguised as a prisoner of his own bodyguards, dressed to look like Communists. Moreover, one of Chiang's assistants was a spy, who kept the other side informed of his plans. During the fighting, the G-mo followed his usual method of telephoning orders to his commanders without being aware of developments on the ground. His soldiers, underfed and underpaid, willingly gave their arms to the Communists in exchange for food. Deng Xiaoping, then forty-five years old, had mobilized the local peasants to furnish logistical support for the Communist troops, who never hesitated to force the civilians to march ahead of them into battle. The Nationalist defeat was the final blow to Chiang's government, since it opened up the route to Nanking and Shanghai.

Under pressure from various KMT officials to negotiate for peace with the CCP and/or resign, Chiang Kai-shek called a dinner meeting of forty leading members of the government. "I did not want to quit, but you members of the Kuomintang wanted me to resign," he announced in furious high tones. "I intend to leave, not because of the Communists, but because of certain sections of the Kuomintang." As soon as he finished excoriating the party leaders, Chiang released a statement saying that he was willing to negotiate for peace with the Communists, but only on his own terms—the ones they had always rejected and he knew they would never accept. After meeting with the G-mo, a peace group under Vice President Li began a campaign on city walls and in the press: "Unless President Chiang retires, the Communists will not talk peace" read one notice; "Unless President Chiang retires, there is no hope of American aid" read another.

The day Tientsin fell, the Communist radio issued a statement from Mao calling Chiang "China's number one criminal" and accusing him of selling out "the national interest wholesale to the U.S. government." Having already published a list of forty-three "war criminals," headed by Chiang, May-ling, and T. V. Soong, Mao broadcast eight conditions for peace, including punishment for these so-called criminals, reform of land ownership, and the formation of a democratic coalition government to take over the powers of the KMT. Three days later, Chiang cabled May-ling that if the Kuomintang should "decide to sue for peace with the Communists, I will have to retire from my current post, for I am not going to compromise before the Communists." It took the peace proponents only five days to decide that, however harsh the terms, they had no choice but to accept them, and the Executive Yuan issued a statement saying that it was ready "to cease-fire simultaneously with the Communists, and both sides [were to] send representatives to start peace negotiations."

On January 21, Chiang turned over the presidency to Vice President Li, claiming that he was sacrificing himself in order to end the war and his people's torment. As usual, his explanation had nothing to do with the real reasons for his withdrawal and everything to do with saving face: "My earnest prayers will have been answered if the Communist Party . . . orders a cease-fire and agrees to open peace talks with the government. Thus the people will be spared their intense sufferings, the spiritual and material resources of the nation preserved, and its territorial integrity and political sovereignty maintained. Thus, also, the continuity of the nation's history, culture and social order will be perpetuated and the people's livelihood and freedom safeguarded." Reporters who came to the Kungs' Tudor mansion in Riverdale to get Madame Chiang's comments on her husband's resignation were told, "She has no statement to make and she will answer no questions."

In resigning, Chiang had left Li literally without resources. In the first place, there was no money to use for bargaining with the Communists, since the generalissimo had ordered the governor of the Central Bank to transfer the government's entire gold reserve to the island of Taiwan. This operation took place late one February night after Nationalist soldiers had cordoned off the Bund. A British journalist who just happened to be looking out the window of his office on the fifth floor of a building near the bank was stunned: "I could hardly believe what I saw," he said, describing a "file of coolies padding out of the bank," balancing 500,000 ounces of gold bullion in wrapped packages at the end of their bamboo poles and chanting the traditional "Heigh-ho" of the dockyards. The bullion was then loaded on a waiting ship, which left for Taiwan. When he discovered this, Li forbade the transfer of any more assets to Taiwan. His order came just as the bank was about to send a large quantity of diamonds and other precious stones that the KMT had confiscated during the war—gems that eventually wound up in Communist hands. Chiang had also sent 300,000 of his best soldiers, twenty-six gunboats of the Chinese navy, and the entire Chinese air force to Taiwan. Although 900,000 soldiers remained on the mainland, only 120,000 of these belonged to Li's old partner General Pai and thus could be relied on by the acting president. Chiang had taken away everything from General Li except the ability to make peace, honorably or dishonorably, with the Communists.

Li named a committee of five men to negotiate with the CCP, and on January 24 he announced the end of martial law, the release of political prisoners, and the disbanding of Chiang's secret police. He tried to release Young Marshal Chang from detention, only to find that the generalissimo had already sent him to Taiwan. On January 27, Li wired Mao his agreement to the eight-point Communist proposal for peace, but Sun Fo repudiated the agreement and left for Canton with the tag end of the Nationalist government. Meanwhile, Chiang had taken Ching-kuo with him to his old home in the province of Chekiang.

During the previous week, May-ling had wired Ching-kuo, "Your father is planning to return to his home, and I am extremely worried about his safety and the condition of his health. Only if your father's security is guaranteed can we continue to work for our country. Although we have not received any assistance recently, I have been promoting our work with many people." A week later she cabled Chiang about the mood in America: "The U.S. authorities are much more worried about China since you retired . . . so I hope that you can return to the political arena, but, of course, you will need domestic support to kill the rumor that the Chinese oppose your reign. . . . It is said that Li Tsung-jen [Vice President Li] and Huang* have sent men to the U.S. to spread nasty rumors about you. . . . A group of senators will put forward the idea of assisting China and will campaign among military leaders. So we urgently need money to promote our position. I heard that our government deposited two million U.S. dollars. . . . Can you wire ten or twenty thousand now?"† Shortly thereafter, she cabled again to see if her husband, now that he had resigned, would travel with her. "There is magnificent progress in both industry and the military in Europe and the

---

* Probably Huang Shao-hung, an associate of Li.

† $2,000,000 in 1949 would be the equivalent of $18,054,000 today. $10,000 would be worth $90,270, and $20,000 would be worth $180,540.

United States. I think that Brother Kai might take this opportunity to visit these countries and widen your horizons. Sister [i.e., May-ling] will meet you anywhere you want to go, and we can travel together." But Chiang, who knew nothing and cared less about the world outside China, was not interested, cabling back that he hoped she would return soon and that they could "talk about everything."

Two weeks earlier, the G-mo's wife had wired Ching-kuo that she was "not anxious to return, nor would it be helpful at this time. This is a difficult period, and my stay in the U.S. will help our party and our nation." Shortly thereafter, she cabled that she was ill, apologized for her delay in returning, and promised to do her best to offset the bad publicity her husband was receiving in the United States. Although she was eager to help Chiang and China, it seems reasonable to assume that May-ling was currently more concerned about the politics of the situation than in playing the attentive wife. According to Li, she received three cables from Chiang in early March, begging her to return, but she sent her nephew Louis Kung instead. As before, she pleaded illness: "I have been away from you for about three months," she wrote on March 5, 1949, "and I miss you very much. Although I am still in the U.S., my heart is already back home. My doctor told me that my health was much better after the treatment I received, and my weight is up. It looks like the treatment will be finished at the end of this month, and my doctor says that it is important to continue. As far as my work goes . . . both democrat and republican senators believe that the U.S. needs to help China. The only problem there is that peace talks with the CCP are taking place. But I think that if we continue to fight the CCP, the U.S. will come to our aid sooner or later." The following month she again put off her trip because "close friends" were coming to visit her from Washington. As it turned out, May-ling remained in the United States for over a year, not returning to her husband until January of 1950. By then, their life, location, and circumstances had completely changed.

49

*The Communists are inheriting the ant heap. Now they are faced with the ancient,
unanswered question which has faced all China's rulers: how are the ants to be fed?*

—STEWART ALSOP, 1949

SINCE SHE was in New York, May-ling made her usual stop at the Harkness
Pavilion of Columbia Presbyterian Hospital. She engaged a private room
as far as possible from the nurses' station but had twenty-four-hour-a-day
security. She was, according to one physician who attended her, not very ill.
"In my view," he said, "there was a lot of feigning of discomfort." While in
the hospital she underwent an elective gynecological procedure. "She was a
very unpleasant person," according to this doctor, who compared her unfa-
vorably to other important world figures who had been patients there. "The
nurses had a hard time with her. She was very demanding."*

While May-ling tended to her illnesses, real and imagined, and Chiang
settled down to a peaceful life in the country, funded on loans from the
Farmers' Bank and punctuated by news of events on the mainland, Mao was
making Li's life a misery. The peace talks began in the newly renamed Peking
on April 1. The Communist negotiators, led by Chou En-lai, arrived with
twenty-four nonnegotiable provisions to be added to Mao's original eight;
taken together, they amounted to total surrender. A few days after their
arrival, Mao announced to the delegation and the world that in case of a
World War III, the Chinese Communists would join Russia in fighting the
United States. Unable to trust the head of the Nationalist delegation, Li
turned to two other members of his peace team. But one used his time in
Peking to angle for a position in the new CCP government, while the other,
who had been working secretly for the Communists for years, kept Chou
En-lai up to date on the latest maneuvering by the delegation for the KMT.
The entire Nationalist delegation not only capitulated to the Communists
but joined them, remaining in the capital with the victors.

---

* It is interesting to note that Madame Chiang's records have been removed from the
hospital data center. This is not only highly unusual; it would have been illegal in
the state of New York unless Madame herself signed a letter of authorization for their
removal.

In the middle of April, Chou gave the other side an ultimatum: the Nationalists had five days to accept Mao's terms or Communist troops would cross the Yangtze River. On April 17, Li wired Chiang, asking him to take back the presidency. The G-mo responded by suggesting a conference in Hangchow with Li, General Ho, and others. "What attitude do you think we should adopt?" Li asked Chiang after explaining the Communists' ultimatum. "I am prepared to send someone to Peiping to negotiate the terms."

"There is no point in doing this," said Chiang. "The Communists agreed to peace negotiations, but only because they had not yet deployed their forces to cross the river. Now that their preparations are complete, there is no room for negotiations. Besides, the first item of the peace terms puts all the blame on our party, writing off the party's glorious history of sixty years. This is totally unacceptable!" Prepared with an alternative, Chiang produced the draft of a telegram that, he said, "can be signed jointly by ourselves—by you as the acting President, and by me as Director-General of the KMT." The draft stated that (1) peace negotiations with the CCP had broken down and (2) the Nationalist Government was moving to Canton, where Sun Fo had taken his stand, and would continue to resist. Li agreed to sign and then withdrew to Kweilin in the south for a two-week rest.

Meanwhile, the ultimatum expired, the Communists crossed the Yangtze River with practically no resistance, and Li ordered the evacuation of Nanking. Unlike previous occupiers, the Communists neither looted nor raped the citizens of the city, nor did they touch foreigners. Nevertheless, the occupation of Nanking by the Communists changed the attitude of the diplomatic corps, which, up until this point, had clung to the belief that the Chinese Communists were agrarian reformers who would compromise with the Kuomintang. Now the embassies moved to Canton—all except U.S. Ambassador Stuart, who stayed in Nanking for four more months, thinking he could persuade the CCP to set up diplomatic relations with the United States. Soon after he left, Mao wrote an essay titled "Farewell Leighton Stuart"* in which he called Stuart the "symbol of the complete defeat of the U.S. policy of aggression."

On April 25, Chiang left for Shanghai, where he spent eleven days in what Stewart Alsop† called "the thick, heavy atmosphere of a frightened

---

* Stuart, who had been born in China, died in Washington, D.C. In his will he had written that he wanted his remains moved to China. This was accomplished—"after years of negotiations about the political implications of such a burial"—in 2008, forty-six years after his death. (David Barboza, "John Leighton Stuart, China Expert, Is Buried There at Last," *The New York Times*, November 20, 2008.)

† Joseph Alsop's brother, who often collaborated with him on columns.

city." Chinese-American journalist Stella Dong was more specific: "Chiang Kai-shek's henchmen made Shanghai's last weeks under Nationalist rule a nightmare of disorder and brutality," she wrote, and she was right. Martial law was declared; businesses and homes were requisitioned for the billeting of Nationalist soldiers, who "lost no opportunity to rob and loot" the premises of their hosts. "But worst of all was the wave of political terror" as Communists and anyone else who could be blamed for the Nationalist loss were executed without benefit of trial on street corners and other public places. One American was appalled by "the street execution of half a dozen captive students. Bound and kneeling, they had their brains blown out by Chiang's warriors before a great crowd of people . . . while shouting gendarmes beat back the crowd with long bamboo whips, their customary weapon."

While Chiang was still in Shanghai, acting president Li wrote President Truman stating that America's generosity in "moral and material assistance" had been "rendered fruitless by the lack of sincerity on the part of both the then Government and the Chinese Communists. . . . It is regrettable that, owing to the failure of our then Government to make judicious use of this aid and to bring about appropriate political, economic and military reforms, your assistance has not produced the desired effect. To this failure is attributable the present predicament in which our country finds itself."

Chiang, the master of sanctimony, left Shanghai about three weeks before it fell to the Communists. He flew to Canton, where he told the Central Executive Committee of the KMT that he was "ashamed to be back in Canton in the present circumstances of retreat and failure. I cannot but admit that I must share a great part of the defeat," he added before delivering an irrelevant and hypocritical swipe at his surroundings: "I am appalled at the existence of gambling and opium smuggling in Canton under the very nose of the government." Although he told his audience that he was "ready to perish with the city," he left five days after his arrival to look for another place in which to make a last stand.

From America May-ling wired her husband that the "CCP in the United States is putting a lot of propaganda out against you. Most of our American friends suggest that we establish a propaganda organization to attack them back." And two days later: "The foreign powers are all disappointed in us. I have been busy contacting everyone and telling them our side of the story according to your orders. I hope that what I am doing is helpful." To which Chiang responded, "Please remember the following three points. (1) The United Kingdom will try hard to persuade the United States to recognize the government of the CCP in order to guarantee their position in Hong Kong. So you should remind the U.S. government not to betray their war-time ally China. . . . (2) You should tell them that if I do not take the leadership and continue the anti-CCP campaigns, China will be split into four or five parts. . . . The Americans must know that the only power that insists on fighting the Communists is the one under my leadership. . . . (3) You should recommend that the nations of the Pacific form an anti-Communist alliance, and I should be named as the only Chinese leader in the organization."

Although Madame, subjected to stories of imminent defeat of the Nationalists in the American press, tried to get her husband to hold a full-scale press conference—even going to the extent of wiring likely questions and appropriate answers—she was not successful. He did, however, grant an interview to two American journalists, one from Scripps Howard and the other from the International News Service. Following his wife's directives, Chiang made several points: "If communism is not checked in China, it will spread over the whole of Asia. Should that occur, another world war would be inevitable." All the Chinese asked of the United States at the moment was "moral support," he stated, claiming that the "erroneous impression that the present situation" was "beyond repair" had been "created by Communist propaganda in disseminating defeatism." Not only the ideas but the language clearly came from May-ling.

In the middle of September, May-ling cabled her stepson that she had heard the Communists planned to assassinate Chiang Kai-shek. "I'm so worried," she wrote, ". . . please reply as soon as possible." Having succeeded in getting Chiang to talk to the press during the summer, May-ling tried to get him to resume his position as head of the government in the fall. "You are blamed for interfering with political affairs," she wrote in October, "so it would be better for you to return to the political stage as soon as possible. It is your duty to assume your responsibilities and lead the anti-Communist campaign."

❦

WHEN SHE WAS not cabling advice to Chiang, May-ling spent quite a lot of her time in the United States with Emma, enjoying lunches, dinners, and outings with old Wellesley friends. Explaining that there were "too many people and interruptions here in Riverdale [where she was living with the Kungs]," she used Emma's apartment whenever she needed to concentrate on her writing. One weekend, she stayed in her friend's home along with her secretary-companion, Dorothy Garvey. "These stocks [i.e., flowers] are here to greet you & as an expression of the lovely week-end appreciation of your two perfect guests to a perfect hostess," May-ling scrawled on a large sheet of paper. "The leaves are broken, but not our memories! We've dusted and cleaned everything in sight. Heavens aren't we good?" And in another note:

"You should never leave the dish spray on the stone. The heat will melt the rubber. Also shake it well after using, other wise the water collects in the compartment for the detergent. Signed, The Neat Housemother." According to DeLong, Emma discovered that May-ling had replaced her window drapes and bedspread.

The reason for May-ling's working into the early morning hours and her extended stay in the United States was explained in a cable she had sent Chiang back in January. "Since I first arrived in the U.S. . . . the attitude of the American Administration has changed," she reported. "They have now adopted a policy of wait and see instead of abandoning China. . . . Now our American friends and our friends in the Congress have suggested to me that we establish an organization that will make good connections for us here and implement effective propaganda which will help me gain support in seeking American aid."

The Madame had, in fact, already started holding weekly meetings with important Chinese living in America, men who were qualified by position or economic clout to help pressure the U.S. government into reviving its support for the KMT. In its series on the China Lobby, *Reporter* magazine divided them geographically into men of wealth operating out of New York and those in official positions based in the nation's capital. What they had in common was Madame herself, who took on the responsibility of developing an overall "strategy to mesh the Nationalist cause with the interests of the most effective among the power-hungry American politicians." According to one author, these human targets belonged to the Republican Party, the military establishment, and the Christian missions—all of whom had good reasons to back the Lobby. The Republicans took on the fight against the Communists as a moral cause; the military men were concerned about a future conflict with the USSR; and the churchmen embraced it as a struggle against the Antichrist in Asia.

Chief among the group of important New Yorkers was H. H. Kung, who had been sent away from China in the summer of 1944, and T.V., who did not leave until May of 1949 and moved into the Kung home along with May-ling. T.V. set about making new friends to add to his wartime roster, even lowering himself to consort with Alfred Kohlberg, who was not his usual style. From his former days in Washington, he had a number of friends in Congress: Styles Bridges of New Hampshire, Karl Mundt of South Dakota, and William Knowland from California in the Senate; Walter Judd of Minnesota and Richard Nixon from California in the House—all men who had seemingly bought into the pro-Nationalist propaganda. But, according to informants quoted in FBI files, T.V. was even more "concern[ed] with speculation than with politics . . . speculating with 'foreign funds' . . . imported . . . from Hong Kong" and converting his profits back into bonds sold on the Hong Kong market, thus avoiding U.S. income taxes.*

One objective of the China Lobby, according to *Reporter,* was to remove Dean Acheson, who had succeeded Marshall as secretary of state in 1949. Acheson had done nothing detrimental to the Lobby, but the members of the group had misread his intentions and informed Chiang that the United States would continue to supply China with unlimited military aid. Since the lobbyists were wrong and needed a scapegoat, they settled on the new secretary of state, who, they said, was surrounded by Communists and fellow travelers in the State Department. Having gone this far down the slippery slope of accusation, it was an easy step to blaming the U.S. State Department for the CCP's victories in China.

"The persistent hope of these merry gentlemen," said Luce's biographer,† referring to the China Lobby, "was that America would go to war against Russia and Mao so that the Chiang people could ride comfortably back to power on the thermonuclear wings of World War III." To back this up, the author cited a Chinese cable that read, "Our hope of a world war so as to rehabilitate our country is unpalatable to the [American] people." He also described a formal dinner held at the Chinese Embassy, attended by Senators McCarthy, Bridges, and Knowland, all of whom rose and joined in a shouted toast: "Back to the mainland!"

According to *Reporter,* however, money was "the most important and fascinating of the many fascinating characters in the China Lobby—a character capable of endless disguises." During Madame Chiang's sojourn in the United States, she arranged for more than $1 million‡ to be placed under the control of an entity called the National Resources Commission and dispensed to members of the Lobby. The National Resources Commission, which was meant to concern itself with the industrialization of Nationalist China, tended to veer off quite regularly into other areas. In 1948, it had hired William J. Goodwin, a man with prewar connections to men like Ger-

---

* It may or may not be a coincidence that, according to those same files, *Ta Kung Pao*, a Hong Kong newspaper, reported in September 1949 that over a three-month period an estimated $500 million had been taken out of China's bureaucratic capital and that T. V. Soong and H. H. Kung had "nearly completed their removals and had placed their money in the United States, Thailand and a small amount in Indonesia." (FBI files, WFO 97-766, June 19, 1953, p. 12. Material furnished to the author by the Department of Justice in response to Freedom of Information inquiry.)

† W. A. Swanberg.

‡ The equivalent of $9,027,000 today.

ald L. K. Smith, who had been quoted in 1941 declaring his admiration for Hitler and Mussolini. Goodwin's work was aided and abetted by the Luce magazines and the Calvinist *Reader's Digest*. Goodwin had been put on an annual salary of $30,000* to handle public relations for the commission. He gave dinners for congressmen, estimating at one point that he had entertained something like a hundred senators and representatives a year, converting at least half of them into supporting aid for China. He also claimed that he "helped materially" to lay the groundwork for McCarthy's attacks on the State Department, which started in February of 1950.

The National Resources Commission apparently became involved in the case of the United Tanker Corporation, a company that had begun by chartering vessels to Soviet agencies for oil shipments. According to the *Congressional Quarterly*, a firm set up by the commission called the China Trading and Industrial Development Company, a "subsidiary" of the Nationalist government, had invested $2.5 million in United Tanker. During the Korean War, according to *Reporter*, "the C.T.I.D. itself . . . chartered ships to handle twenty-six cargoes to Red China." Which led *Reporter* to the conclusion that the "same Nationalist government agency that was supplying funds to . . . attack Americans for the slightest contact with the Communist elements was itself carrying on a very profitable trade with Red China."†

As for the Bank of China, allegedly controlled by Kung, its New York branch hired a public relations firm, Allied Syndicates, founded by a man named David B. Charnay. Paid an annual retainer of $60,000, the firm was supposed to help prevent the United States from recognizing the Chinese Communist government and keep it from freezing the assets of the bank held in the United States, estimated to be "between one and three hundred million" dollars. Wedemeyer placed the amounts much higher: "Privately held foreign exchange assets [of the Chinese] are at least $600 million, and may total $1500 million."‡ During 1949, the year that Madame Chiang was in the United States, a great deal of Nationalist money was said to have been

---

* Luce's biographer W. A. Swanberg says that Goodwin's salary was only $25,000 and was eventually taken over by the Chinese News Service.

† In the investigation into the China Lobby, noted in chapter 47, it is said that the Yangtze Trading Company, of which Louis Kung was a director, "was denied the privilege of using export licenses by the Department of Commerce because of alleged shipments of tin to Communist China." (Truman Library: James S. Lanigan to Theodore Tannenwald, Jr., Memorandum Re: China Lobby, October 9, 1951.)

‡ $100,000,000 in 1949 would be the equivalent of $902,737,000 today, $300,000,000 would be worth $2,708,211,000 today, and $1,500,000,000 would be worth $13,541,000,000 today.

stashed away in private, numbered accounts in case the worst should befall the Nationalist government.

A sidebar to the story of the China Lobby involves May-ling's nephew Louis Kung. Known as "the Major" or "the little fellow," the Kungs' second son had served as technical adviser to the office of the Chinese air force in Washington until he was appointed to the Chinese delegation to the United Nations. Meanwhile, according to *Reporter,* Kung worked primarily as "a courier or paymaster" for the Lobby. Said to be "a very good friend" of Charnay, he was apparently in and out of the offices of Allied Syndicates a great deal, particularly during the congressional campaign of 1950, when the Lobby had helped elect Nixon in his run against Helen Gahagan Douglas in California. Personally, Kung was known to spend money freely, "usually in the form of bills of a hundred dollars or larger," and had homes in both New York and Washington. In 1955, Louis Kung went into the oil business in Texas, apparently made a lot of money and moved to Houston, where, according to an article about him in *Texas Monthly,* he lived "in the style of a Texas oil millionaire." He married a movie actress, Debra Paget, had a son by her, and built a fabulous compound at a cost of $18 million. Located outside the city, Kung's home consisted of a combined office-residence surrounded by an electric fence with an underground bomb shelter. Larger than Hitler's bunker, it could accommodate a thousand people. Outside were two pagodas with typical Chinese blue tile roofs and concealed gun ports. After the death of the G-mo, Auntie May paid him and his wife a lengthy visit.

❦

BACK IN CHINA, Chiang and his right-wing supporters in the KMT continued to follow what the CIA explained as "the line that China is the outpost of the Third World War, and the Chinese civil war is not merely the suppression of an internal revolt but a national war against the forces of Soviet Communism." The Legislative Yuan went even further, claiming that the United States was "largely responsible for China's plight" because of the agreements made at Yalta, U.S. efforts to mediate between the KMT and CCP, and insufficient supplies of money and armaments. Therefore, U.S. military aid to the Nationalists was "an obligation."

The Nationalists offered Wedemeyer $5 million for his services as an adviser, but he refused, explaining that he "could get by financially," and if the Chinese government had "such a large sum of money, private or public," he suggested using it "for the welfare of the people in order to enhance the force against the Communists." It was said that the idea of hiring Wedemeyer came from T.V., who, along with Ambassador Koo, was frantically searching for a way to counteract the information in a book formally titled

United States Relations with China but known as the "White Paper," which came out during the summer of 1949, while Madame Chiang was in the United States.* A 1,054-page tome issued by the State Department, the White Paper attempted to explain why the United States would not be responsible when China fell to the Communists. In doing this, it effectively countered Madame's requests for more money by detailing how the generalissimo's government had wasted $3 billion in U.S. aid between the end of World War II and the middle of 1948, and it explained the success of the Communists in terms of the incompetence and unpopularity of Chiang and his regime. In a prepared statement after the release of the document, Secretary of State Acheson said that the KMT "has been unable to rally its people and has been driven out of extensive and important portions of the country, despite very extensive assistance from the United States and advice from eminent American representatives which subsequent events proved to be sound," thus contradicting the China Lobby, which claimed that Chiang Kai-shek was "more the victim of State Department 'subversives' than of his own weaknesses." According to Truman, the conclusion was obvious: "We picked a bad horse," he said.

❦

ON OCTOBER 1, 1949, Mao proclaimed the new Republic of China at a celebration in Peking† attended by Ching-ling. May-ling's older sister had originally refused the invitation, saying that Peking was a sad place for her since the death of Dr. Sun, but her biographer Chang Jung explains that "the Chinese would never accept an invitation [the] first time out of almost ritualistic politeness," and that Ching-ling was "readily convinced" to change her mind by Madame Chou En-lai, who delivered a second invitation by hand. Met at the train station by Mao, Chou, Madame Chou, and other

---

* Immediately after the publication of the White Paper, Marshall invited May-ling to his estate in the Adirondack Mountains, where she spent ten days on a "purely social" visit—a kindly invitation that was attacked in a cable from the Chinese military attaché to the G-mo, claiming that "all our American friends" regarded Marshall's invitation as "an insidious and malicious gesture." (Charles Wertenbacker, "The Ubiquitous Major," *Reporter*, April 15, 1952, p. 21.)

† After establishing the PRC, the Communists not only changed the name of the capital, currently called Peiping ("Northern Peace"), back to Peking ("Northern Capital") but adopted a different method of spelling in the Latin alphabet, which resulted in the capital being called Beijing. This was used along with Peking until sometime in the 1980s, when the Chinese began to enforce the use of the official name, i.e., Beijing, on government documents, flights, etc. It is now common usage. It should be noted, however, that all three names and spellings (Peking, Peiping, and Beijing) are only approximations of Chinese sounds and spellings.

high officials, Ching-ling stood on the platform at Tiananmen Square with them for the inauguration. "It was a solemn, awe-inspiring ceremony," she said. ". . . Today, Sun Yat-sen's efforts at last bore fruit."

The day after the inauguration, the Soviet Union recognized Mao's new Republic of China, and the day after that, the Nationalist government broke off diplomatic relations with Moscow. On October 4, Chiang flew to Taiwan. He did not stay long, and in the middle of November returned to Chungking—the newest temporary capital of his government. What he found there did not please him.

General Li had left the day before, claiming that an old abdominal disorder had resurfaced. After ordering the release of some thousand Communists and Communist sympathizers, Li wrote Chiang saying he needed a checkup and maybe an operation. "Meanwhile," he said, "I shall sound out the attitude of the U.S. Government towards China. In view of the grave situation, I shall come back in a short time to take up my responsibilities." The acting president had left for Hong Kong on November 20, 1949. The generalissimo sent a delegation of four men to convince him to return with a doctor and any medical equipment he needed. But Li did not return. The Central Executive Committee of the KMT sent the delegation back for a second time, but Li said he was on his way to the United States, where he would request financial support for the government and would return to China in one month's time. He left on December 5 and did not return to China until 1965, fifteen years later, when he was said to be suffering from cancer and wanted to come home to die. His return to Peking, according to FBI files at the time, "could be regarded as [a] propaganda coup for communists and Chinese communist authorities lost no time in quoting his denunciation of the United States. . . . Li is a rank opportunist, and it is believed he will disappear from sight after his 'defection' has been milked by the Chinese communists."

In the middle of December of 1949, Madame cabled Chiang some disturbing news from the United States: "Our embassies in North America, South America, and Canada are owed months of back pay, and the Communists are using bribes to get close to the embassy staffs. . . . We must pay their salaries. We should have paid them before and avoided this situation."

This last piece of advice was sent to Taiwan. Although Chiang had told his wife early in the year that neither he nor his government would ever give up, another series of defections had finally convinced him that he could not set up a base on the mainland. On December 8, 1949, the Executive Yuan had voted in an emergency session to move the capital of Nationalist China to the island, and two days later, Chiang himself left for Taiwan.

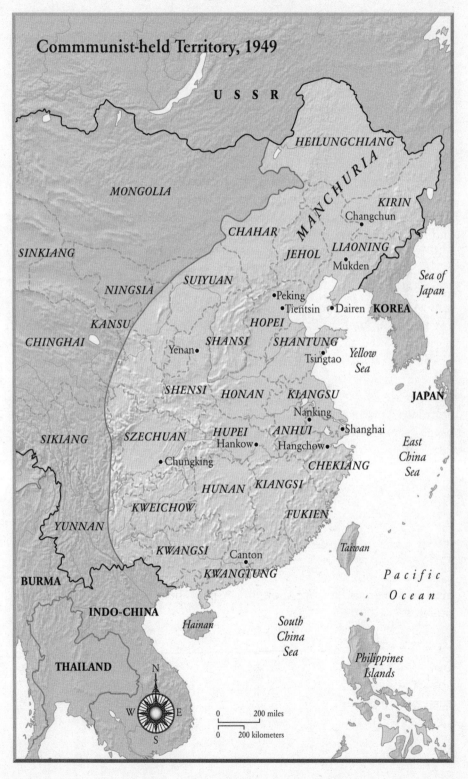

Commmunist-held Territory, 1949

U S S R

MONGOLIA

HEILUNGCHIANG

SINKIANG

CHAHAR

KIRIN
•Changchun

JEHOL

LIAONING
•Mukden

NINGSIA

SUIYUAN

•Peking
•Tientsin   •Dairen   **KOREA**

KANSU

HOPEI

Sea of
Japan

CHINGHAI

SHANSI   SHANTUNG
Yenan•   Yellow
          Tsingtao   Sea

SHENSI   HONAN   KIANGSU

JAPAN

Nanking•

SIKIANG

SZECHUAN   HUPEI   ANHUI
              Hankow• Hangchow• •Shanghai

East
China
Sea

•Chungking   CHEKIANG

HUNAN   KIANGSI

KWEICHOW

FUKIEN

YUNNAN

KWANGSI   •Canton

Taiwan

Pacific
Ocean

BURMA

KWANGTUNG

INDO-CHINA

Hainan

South
China
Sea

Philippines
Islands

THAILAND

N
W   E
S

0   200 miles

0   200 kilometers

PART EIGHT

1949–1975

50

Taiwan became part of unified China nearly 200 years before Sicily became part of unified modern Italy. Taiwan came under China's direct administration system about 200 years before Hawaii achieved statehood in America.

—RICHARD CHU

AN OLD Chinese tale says that the island of Taiwan was built by a fire-breathing dragon piling up gigantic rocks in the sea. More likely, it came about as the result of two earthquakes: the first, burying the East Asian coast in the ocean, and the second, throwing up enough rocks and soil to create a landmass shaped like a tobacco leaf, twice the size of New Jersey. Originally populated by headhunting aborigines, it got its name from Portuguese sailors on their way to Japan. They called it "Ilha Formosa," beautiful island.

The Dutch invaded Taiwan in 1624 but didn't last long. They were followed by Chinese loyal to the Ming Dynasty, who fought forty-five bloody rebellions against the Manchus. Even though Formosa was considered "one of the most dangerous and unhealthy spots in the Orient," its tiny population prospered and by 1893 had grown to over two and a half million. Like their countrymen, the Taiwanese suffered from the ubiquitous Chinese squeeze. According to one Canadian missionary, "From the highest to the lowest, every Chinese official in Formosa has an 'itching palm,' and the exercise of official functions is always corrupted by money bribes. . . . In the matter of bribing and boodling, the Chinese official in Formosa could give points to the most accomplished office-seekers and money-grabbers in Washington or Ottawa."

In 1885, Taiwan was declared a province in its own right with its own governor, who transferred the island's capital to Taipei, built a power station and a railroad (the second in all of China), and started a limited postal system. But the Sino-Japanese War of 1894–1895, which had started as a fight over Korea, ended with China's being forced to cede Taiwan to Japan. To quote a Japanese historian of the day, "The white people have long believed that it has been the white man's burden to cultivate the uncivilized territories and bring to them the benefits of civilization. The Japanese people now have risen in the Far East and want to participate with the white people in this great mission."

The Japanese, who began their takeover with a savage repression of revolts, established peace within four years. Although two thirds of the island
was mountainous and less than one third of the rest was arable, Taiwan became a model of agricultural and industrial prosperity with a far higher standard of living than the mainland. The island produced sizable amounts of
copper, aluminum, and gold, and its citizens acquired radios, bicycles, and
watches sent by Japan in exchange for rice and sugar. In spite of a strict quota
on Chinese immigrants, Taiwan's population doubled between 1895 and
1945. This was undoubtedly due to Japanese standards of hygiene and public health—areas in which the Chinese had always been deficient. The
350,000 or so Japanese residents of the island also took care not to fraternize
socially with their Chinese subjects.

During World War II, Japan used Taiwan as a base of operations, and the
island suffered from U.S. bombing raids. In September 1945, Japan was
forced to give Taiwan back to China, and Chiang Kai-shek sent troops to
take over the government. According to George H. Kerr, a navy man who
had taught in Taiwan before the war and was made vice consul afterward, the
island was "rich, orderly and modernized" when the Chinese arrived. "It is
difficult," he said, "to convey . . . the atmosphere of great expectation which
enveloped the island" when the Chinese replaced the Japanese. Delighted
citizens were quickly disillusioned, however, when they discovered that their
own countrymen were rapacious, corrupt, and at least as "brutal and insensitive" as their predecessors. According to the Taiwanese, "We think of the
Japanese as dogs and the Chinese as pigs. A dog eats, but he protects. A pig
just eats."

The dishonesty prevalent among Chinese officials was encouraged by
General Chen Yi, whom Chiang appointed governor of the island in 1945.
A native of Chiang Kai-shek's home province of Chekiang, Chen Yi—short,
fat, jowly, and beady-eyed—considered himself above the law. He had previously served for eight years as governor of the province of Fukien, where it
was said that he had managed to hide a thriving trade carried on between his
powerful patrons and the Japanese enemy. In his new role, Chen appointed
commissioners of finance, transport, industry, etc., who staffed their departments with relatives and friends. Kerr tells us that the police chief of
one city listed more that forty relatives on his payroll, while a "prominent
Commissioner was alleged to have a concubine on the Department payroll,
listed as a 'technical specialist.' " These officials and their appointees expropriated the best houses for themselves, taking over 90 percent of the
important industries and replacing the Taiwanese workers with their own
people, regardless of competence or experience. They and their cronies
confiscated approximately $1 billion worth of nonmilitary properties and

$2 billion worth of military supplies, most of which disappeared into the black market. Within a year and a half of their arrival, the economy of the island had collapsed.

While Chinese officials hoarded rice and smuggled it to the mainland, raising the price of food by 700 percent during the year after the war, deterioration in sewage disposal, house-to-house disinfection services, and other health measures led to epidemics of cholera and bubonic plague. When something called the "Peace Preservation Corps" expropriated Taipei's garbage trucks to haul stolen goods to the waterfront, gigantic piles of trash collected in parks, alleyways, and side streets, and the population of rats on the island "multiplied fantastically." Attempts to rehabilitate public water systems failed, due to widespread theft of plumbing fixtures, faucets, pipes and fire hydrants. The director of public health tried to stop the free distribution of antimalaria tablets in order to put his own pharmaceutical company into the quinine business. His successor finally distributed 45 million Atabrine tablets that had been lying in warehouses for more than a year while the government collected storage fees, which were eventually charged to the U.N. Relief and Rehabilitation Administration. "The range and variety of fraud and speculation," said Kerr, "was limitless, extending into every sector of island life."

In October of 1946, the generalissimo and Madame had paid a visit to the island, purportedly to celebrate the first anniversary of Japan's surrender but really to avoid a meeting General Marshall had set up for Chiang with Chou En-lai. The couple made their triumphal entry into Taipei, where a holiday had been declared, but the citizens, who had been "marched into place" hours before, mostly kept silent when the Chiangs passed. Shown only what officialdom wanted him to see, Chiang praised the unscrupulous Chen, and moderate Taiwanese, who had been hoping that conditions would improve "if the Generalissimo only knew the truth," were devastated. Four months later, a group of young Formosans delivered a petition to the U.S. Consulate, addressed to Secretary of State Marshall, begging the United Nations to take the island under its protection. "Our fine island, Beautiful Formosa," it read, was being "trampled away by Chinese maladministration."

On the evening of February 27, 1947, a Taiwanese woman with two small children who was selling black-market cigarettes from a portable stand was pistol-whipped to death by agents from the Monopoly Bureau for not paying her taxes. The next day, a protest march over the killing encountered more agents from the same bureau abusing two children also selling cigarettes. The angry crowd beat the agents to death and sacked the storerooms at a Monopoly Bureau branch office. Meanwhile, at least four members of a silent crowd of islanders who had gathered in protest before the governor's gate were gunned down by heavily armed Nationalist soldiers. The Taiwanese organized a "committee for the settlement of the February 28th Incident," which they presented to Chen, along with demands for various kinds of reform. Although he promised to organize a committee composed of "representatives from the people of all walks of life," Chen ordered in reinforcements from the mainland, and trucks filled with government soldiers and machine guns drove through the streets killing pedestrians and looting at will. Along with some ten thousand ordinary Taiwanese, certain educators, doctors, politicians, publishers, and businessmen had been targeted for systematic elimination. "We saw students tied together, being driven to the execution grounds," said Kerr. ". . . One foreigner counted more than thirty young bodies—in student uniforms—lying along the roadside . . . they had had their noses and ears slit or hacked off, and many had been castrated." Thus, according to *The Wilson Quarterly*, "a whole generation of Taiwanese leaders was lost."

A month later, the Central Executive Committee of the Kuomintang adopted a resolution censuring Chen Yi and demanding that he be dismissed. On March 28, he bowed to the pressure and offered his resignation. To save his face, Chiang allowed Chen to remain in Taipei for six weeks— plenty of time to kill off old enemies and fill his suitcases with money. Five days before his departure, his government decreed a Day of Thanksgiving for which all schoolchildren had to contribute money to thank the Nationalist army for the protection they had been given during the protests. Each primary school child was assessed five yen,* and middle school students had to contribute twice that amount. Even after dismissing Chen from the governorship of Taiwan, however, the generalissimo appointed him governor of their old province of Chekiang, and it was not until Chiang learned that Chen had been dealing with an old Communist associate that he had him arrested. Chen Yi was eventually executed—not for stealing and mass murder but for double-crossing Chiang.

On April 22, 1947, Chiang Kai-shek, who had originally offered a public defense of Chen Yi, was given a full report on the massacres by Ambassador Stuart. Stuart recommended that T.V. take over the governorship, but Mayling's brother refused to move to Taiwan, and Chiang replaced Chen with a former ambassador to Washington. A year and a half later, the new governor was abruptly dismissed by the G-mo and replaced by Chen Cheng, the general who had given his house in Chungking to the Chiangs. Called by Crozier "one of the great men of modern China," Chen Cheng was tough, loyal, and popular with Americans.

---

* 5 yen = 0.13¢ in 1947 (1.34¢ today).

By the time Chen Cheng took over, refugees from the mainland were arriving in droves (one estimate puts the number at 5,000 per day). Rich immigrants sent what Kerr describes as "entire shiploads of personal property, industrial raw materials, dismantled factories and foodstuffs" across the strait, while the poor just managed to get themselves to the island, landing at junk harbors, river mouths, and beaches. To handle the influx, General Chen brought in Ching-kuo to deal with security issues, and, according to Kerr, "1949 is remembered on Formosa as a year of terror." It is estimated that Chen and Ching-kuo arrested some 10,000 people—some interrogated, some imprisoned, some executed. As a correspondent from the *London Daily News* reported, "The Formosans are probably the only Orientals who wouldn't be sorry to see the Japanese back."

On December 10, 1949, Chiang Kai-shek retreated to the island with his loyalists, machinery, and hardware salvaged from dismantled factories on the mainland and the huge collection of art treasures, originally from Peking, that had been packed up a dozen years before and hidden in caves around Chungking during the war. Eleven days after his arrival, General Chen was moved over to the position of president of the Executive Yuan (i.e., premier), and Chiang appointed Dr. Wu Kuo-chen, known in America as K. C. Wu, governor of Taiwan—the third governor in as many years. A liberal, a man of integrity, and an experienced administrator, Wu had attended college in the United States (Grinnell and Princeton) and had served as mayor of Chungking, vice minister of foreign affairs, and mayor of Shanghai. According to one observer, Chiang's choice of Wu was indicative of his desperation. Chiang's state of mind could not have been helped by President Truman's announcement on January 5, 1950, that the U.S. government was not interested in establishing military bases on the island, that it did not intend to get involved in the civil war in China, and that it would "not provide military aid or advice to Chinese Forces on Formosa."

Three days after Truman's discouraging statement, Madame Chiang left the United States for Taiwan.

FIVE OR SIX years after the event, the generalissimo's wife wrote about why she had decided to "return to share the fate of my husband and my people on Formosa," in spite of the fact that both friends and family had tried to "dissuade" her:

> In those dark days, I kept on praying. . . . Over and over again I would ask my sister, Madame Kung, "How can God allow anything so wicked to happen? How can He allow the Communists to overrun the mainland? Doesn't He know they are His enemies?"

She would reply, "Keep on praying and be patient. I am certain He will open a way." "Then one morning at dawn, unaware whether I was asleep or awake, I heard a Voice—an ethereal Voice saying distinctly: *"All is right."* Fully awakened by the words, I immediately rose and went to my sister's room. . . . Before I could speak, she sat up and said: "What has happened? Your face looks radiant." I told her that I had heard God speak to me. This was not the first time in my life that I heard The Voice, for I had other experiences when I was somehow aware of His Presence. . . . Fortunately my sister understood what I meant. When I announced that I was going home by the first available plane, she helped me to pack. No longer did she protest.

During her sojourn in the States, the G-mo's wife had given no speeches and had refused to meet with reporters. Her silence made her fifteen-minute farewell address, broadcast over NBC, even more dramatic. She delivered it at noon on January 8, 1950, from the living room of the Kung home on Riverside Drive. She was, she said, returning "to my people on the island of Formosa, the fortress of our hopes, the citadel of our battle against an alien power which is ravaging our country." For more than twenty years, she said, her husband had "led his people in the fight against Communism. . . . Chiang Kai-shek, of all the world's statesmen, was first to perceive the treachery of the communist. . . . A few years ago he was exalted for the courage and tenacity of the fight he waged. Now he is pilloried. Times have changed, but the man has not changed. My husband remains resolute." Nationalist China, according to Chiang's wife, now stood "abandoned and alone," shouldering "the only rifle in the defense of liberty." She was, she said, too proud to ask the American people for any more help. "When a nation, like a man, does an act of justice," she said, "it must be of his conscience and not by request or demand."

Having discovered that the United States would not provide her with transportation home—Washington had billed the Chinese government for her trip from China in a U.S. navy transport plane—the Madame arrived in San Francisco looking "tired and pale after a rough and stormy cross-country flight aboard a Trans World airliner." After a stopover in San Francisco, she boarded a Pan American Stratocruiser for Hawaii, where she rested at the Royal Hawaiian Hotel before taking a tour of Honolulu. She and her party then left for Guam, Manila, and Taiwan. After more than a year's separation, she and Chiang greeted each other with what one reporter called "a brief handclasp."

The Chiangs had not lived together for some time, but May-ling moved into her husband's residence in Shilin, a village just outside Taipei.* Built in the Western style seven years earlier, the residence was adjacent to a park and hidden from the main road. It was a modest two-story granite house that lent itself to a far quieter life than any they had shared on the mainland—the sort of pseudo-simplicity that Chiang relished and May-ling put up with for the sake of appearances. Moreover, they were now in a political situation that left little room for personal animosity or extracurricular activities. The first couple eventually built a chapel on the grounds, which May-ling encouraged their friends and visitors to attend with them.

In summers the Chiangs moved up to Grass Mountain Château, a villa built by the Taiwan Sugar Corporation to house the Japanese crown prince while on a visit to the island. Fairly high up in the mountains, their summer retreat was only a twenty-minute drive from the center of Taipei.† The best thing about it was apparently the view; built on the side of a hill, it looked out beyond a narrow strip of garden many miles to the south and the west. Inside the front door, the visitor entered what one reporter referred to as "a strange room," nearly twenty by thirty feet. The expanse was broken up by four square stone columns; standing in the central space was a dining table seating eighteen along with some overstuffed, slipcovered chairs. The walls—gray below, pale green above—were accented by a soft blue band around setbacks containing indirect lighting fixtures. Tables with potted plants—azaleas and orchids—were placed around the room, each plant carrying a tag with its Latin name. Beyond the great room were four small ones: his study, her study, a small conference room, and a private dining room. There were four cubicles, originally for servants, now shared by secretaries and aides, and one bathroom.

The move to Taiwan had not changed Chiang's favorite kind of workday. Rising at daybreak, he finished exercising and dressing by 7:00 A.M., while May-ling, according to the family doctor, often stayed in bed until 11:00 A.M. "Chiang and Madame Chiang," he said, "had entirely different lifestyles. He went to bed at nine or ten and got up at six, while Madame never went to sleep before one or two in the morning. . . . Both of them moved quietly in order not to disturb the other." Chiang breakfasted on rice, pickled vegetables, and cold water and read his reports until noon. With General Li still absent in the United States, the generalissimo had taken over

---

* This was after a four-month hiatus at Grass Mountain, since the house in Shilin was not ready when she arrived.

† The house, which was turned into a museum, was burned down in April of 2007. Gasoline stains in several places led experts to suspect arson, and as of this writing, there is an ongoing investigation to determine the source of the fire.

his responsibilities, and the two or three aides with whom he had started his exile soon increased to around twenty. They prepared folders containing information they thought he should have and deposited them on his desk at precisely 9:00 A.M. Around 11:00, officials began arriving for conferences. Some stayed for a simple lunch, which Madame attended if she was interested in the subject or the people.

The afternoon schedule, a virtual repetition of the morning, started for Chiang with a short nap and proceeded to the reading of newspapers, dispatches and more conferences. He usually took a fast walk with his wife or an aide at 4:30, which was followed by tea and more work until 7:00 P.M., prayers, and dinner. When she returned, May-ling ordered one foreign meal each day "because," she explained, "he eats too fast." Non-Chinese meals, served one course at a time, forced the G-mo to slow down, and according to his wife, who was interviewed the month after her arrival, "his health is much improved." Evenings were spent working or watching movies, and the generalissimo's day ended with a hot sulfur-spring bath and a daily entry in his diary.

May-ling's return, however, made a significant difference in Chiang's mode of life. Whether it was the fact that she had been in the United States for more than a year, subject to the slurs cast on her husband, or whether she realized just how aloof and distant he kept himself vis-à-vis the islanders, she set him firmly on a course of consultation and reform almost from the moment she arrived. A week after her return, *The New York Times* noted that "Mme. Chiang Kai-shek appealed today to the United States to send military and technical advisers to Formosa to aid the Nationalists' fight against communism," adding that she had emphasized that the Taiwanese were not asking for armed troops. "I know the American people do not want to go to war. Nobody wants American troops here. China does not want American soldiers. . . . We have enough manpower." Having "made that clear," May-ling told American reporters at a press conference, "Your Government says it is fighting communism. So are we. So why don't they send somebody to help us do it? . . . a United States military mission could give needed help in technical advice such as communications, transportation and radio development. . . . It should not be necessary to have to ask someone who is a real friend for help. If they are your friends that would be unnecessary."

May-ling then tackled reform. On January 22, United Press reported that "Mme. Chiang Kai-shek ordered an immediate investigation of army payrolls today after hearing that soldiers wounded in battle were not being paid." The article went on to explain that after touring two military hospitals and speaking with some four hundred men, May-ling discovered that they were no longer receiving their pay. One soldier, blinded in battle, said that he had received no money for two months. The G-mo's wife took the number of his unit and told an aide to investigate. "I'll see that you get paid," she promised him. But in spite of her efforts, there was notable unrest among Taiwanese conscripts, as well as hunger strikes. The government ordered an investigation into charges of bad food, clothing, housing, and sanitation, but at the same time did not hesitate to arrest some of the demonstrators.

Ten days later Madame visited the island of Quemoy, where Chiang had stationed Nationalist troops. "Quemoy" means "Golden Gate," according to a reporter from *The New York Times*, who could not resist noting that it would be a "golden gate for the Communist invasion of Formosa." May-ling flew there with cigarettes, food, and New Testaments to "offer aid and encouragement" to the soldiers. She arrived in one of two planes, the second of which carried sixteen newsmen. The islanders asked for more and better food, modern communications equipment, and books to read. The generalissimo, she told them, was "acutely conscious" of their supply problems and worried about them, so much so that he was having trouble sleeping. She said that her stay in the United States had been "the most painful experience of her life" because it was being said everywhere that the Nationalist soldiers would not fight. "You have fought. You have fought superlatively well," she told them. As expected, her question "Will you fight again?" was met with a roaring "Yes!"

Moreover, according to a *New York Times* journalist based in Hong Kong, it seemed "pretty well established that . . . more frequent and effective Nationalist air raids on coastal cities didn't coincide accidentally with Mme. Chiang Kai-shek's return from the United States." These raids, which started in March of 1950, partially crippled "every important city" by bombing its utilities, while the Nationalist navy choked off a good bit of trade by blocking the sea-lanes near Shanghai.

Nevertheless, the arrival of their former leader and his wife had not thrilled the Taiwanese, who expected nothing from them and would have preferred being left alone rather than thrown into the center of conflict. The generalissimo still seemed distant to the man on the street, and wherever he went, he was accompanied by a fleet of black Cadillac limousines with guards posted on the roads. The number of these guards increased during his first few years in Taiwan, "not so much because the danger of assassination . . . increased," according to Hahn, "as because most of the guards who served him on the mainland now have sons and nephews who need jobs."

At this point, the population of Taiwan ranged between 10 and 11 million people. The G-mo's military strength added up to around 800,000 well-trained soldiers, not quite 1,000 tanks, around 600 airplanes (some obsolete), and about 70 ships. Officials at the Pentagon predicted that Chiang and his followers would not last on the island for more than a year. But having learned his lesson in Manchuria, Chiang soon gave up all his other territory except the Pescadores and the islands of Quemoy and Matsu off the coast of Fukien. Four months after his withdrawal to Taiwan, Chiang ordered an evacuation of his troops from the island of Hainan as well.

On March 1, 1950, six weeks after May-ling's return, Chiang formally reassumed the leadership of the national government. Having replaced the last governor of the island with the American-educated K. C. Wu, Chiang named George Yeh, another graduate of an American college (Amherst) his new foreign minister. Five of the top posts under Chiang were now held by men educated in the United States. The Madame was said to be her husband's chief adviser on matters of diplomacy and Taiwan's relationship with the United States, and she strongly supported men with this kind of background.

The following month May-ling established what she called the Chinese Women's Anti-Aggression League. Eventually known simply as the Women's League, the group was, according to Hahn, "a volunteer organization, but there are few wives of Nationalist officials who would dare not volunteer." Originally organized to help Nationalist soldiers by building housing for them and their families, the league enlisted wives of local business leaders, who prevailed upon their husbands to donate what was needed. In setting up her group, the G-mo's wife succeeded in establishing an organization that far outlasted its original purpose, eventually becoming a major factor in many areas of charitable work on the island.

In her current position as executive secretary of the American Bureau for Medical Aid to China, Emma Mills visited Taiwan in April of 1950 for a two-week inspection tour of medical and health care facilities on the island. While she was there, she spent time with May-ling, who was "very tired" and "going around in circles." May-ling asked her old friend to stay on for an extra week to help.

Mills, who had once trained as a nurse, was clearly pleased with what she found on the island. "When I left Peking 26 years ago," she said on her return, "there was to all intents and purposes no Chinese medical profesion. . . . The Chinese soldier was a scarecrow, the camps a mess. This time . . . everything was neat and orderly. . . . The soldiers seemed to be in good physical condition, their uniforms fitted and they walked with their heads up and seemed to have a pride in their profession."

Meanwhile, Premier Chen had started a "land rent reduction programme," in which absentee landowners were required to sell their property to the state, which then sold it back to the landowners' tenants with ten-year mortgages repayable in installments of 25 percent crop yield.* Landlords who lived on their farms were permitted to keep only two hectares of irrigated land or four of dry land. They were compensated in cash, land bonds, or stocks in publicly owned industry, thus transferring their financial base from agriculture to industry. The program was completed in two years, and by that time, nearly 80 percent of the arable land was owned by the tillers themselves. As one historian put it, "No blood was shed, in striking contrast to the land reform programme initiated in June 1950 by the Communist regime, which involved the physical liquidation of the landed gentry as a class."

Governor Wu worked at liberalizing the administration, a daunting task pitting him against Chiang's son Ching-kuo, who, in spite of his folksy appearance—he usually wore a baseball cap and turtleneck jacket—had launched what Kerr called a "policy of terror," sprinkling secret police and security agents throughout the government. Their unannounced house searches and brutal interrogations, aimed at ferreting out Communist agents who had entered Taiwan with the Nationalist loyalists, naturally frightened the locals. But Ching-kuo's biographer Jay Taylor explains that "the Gimo and his son were now focusing every possible resource" on preparing for a mass invasion from the mainland and that the "secret police thus began to concentrate almost entirely on uncovering CCP agents who had come to Taiwan during the chaotic influx of the previous year. In the first half of 1950 the security network broke 300 alleged Communist spy cases, involving more than 3,000 people." Taylor says that CIA reports "indicated that Mao's intelligence units were in fact concentrating heavily on infiltrating the Nationalist military," and as examples of CCP plants, he cites the vice minister of national defense and the chief of army supply services. As in most dictatorial states, Taiwan soon became riddled with informers.†

For Communists who escaped prison and execution, Ching-kuo set up a reeducation school on Green Island off the east coast of Taiwan. With no fixed terms, the "students" were freed as their minds were cleansed and their thinking reformed—a process "often encouraged by torture." Ching-kuo, who claimed that 95 percent were eventually repatriated to Taiwan, was asked what happened to the others. "Oh, we don't hurt them," he answered. "We give them a boat, food supplies and a radio, and send them back to the Chinese mainland. After three or four days, we start sending radio messages

---

* Tenants had previously paid their landlords 50 to 70 percent.

† One authority estimates that as late as 1969 there were nearly 250,000 full- or part-time informers out of a population of something over 11 million people on the island.

to them asking: 'When are you going to report?' And the Communists take care of them."

On March 1, 1950, the day Chiang Kai-shek reassumed his leadership of the government, the Communist commander-in-chief, General Chu Teh, had told members of the Taiwan Liberation League in Peking that the "elimination of the Chiang Kai-shek regime from Taiwan has become the most pressing task of the whole country." Chu said that he and the other Communist leaders were putting together a great army for the invasion. Certainly, there would have been nothing that Chiang could have done to survive a major assault. Fortunately for him, however, Mao's outspoken hostility to the United States, plus the advent of the Korean War, combined to save his regime.

51

Even Chiang Kai-shek is opposed to the so-called two Chinas, and he is also opposed to the one China and an independent entity of Taiwan . . . on this question we share a common point of view. There can be only one China. That is a fact, and a way can be found.

—CHOU EN-LAI, 1971

As IT had during World War II, Chiang's security still depended on the Americans, who, after years of supporting him, his family, and his government, had finally become disillusioned. Moreover, the day after Truman announced that the United States would steer clear of involvement in Taiwanese affairs, the British, worried about Hong Kong and anxious to restart trade with the mainland, recognized the Chinese Communist government—a move that led the generalissimo's wife to brand them "moral weaklings" for "forsaking us." But Crozier tells us that "the Americans were in a mood" to do the same thing, and according to James Chace,* Secretary of State Dean Acheson wanted to drop Chiang, recognize Communist China, and wean it "away from a Soviet alliance." Fortunately for the G-mo, the Chinese Communists had made some major blunders that forstalled the secretary's plan.

Not only had Mao issued a statement in July of 1949 saying that China would look with friendly eyes on the Soviet Union, but during the occupation of Nanking, ten or twelve soldiers from the People's Liberation Army had barged into the home of U.S. Ambassador Stuart. It was a little before 6:30 A.M., and Stuart was still in bed (he was reportedly ill at the time). "I shouted at them, asking what they were doing, and they withdrew, one or two muttering angrily," he related. "I jumped out of bed to see what it was all about, when the whole group . . . returned, and the spokesman quite politely explained that they were only looking around for fun and meant no harm . . . finding me none too cordial [he] led the others out."

According to Stuart, "the incident had a very simple explanation": these were "country boys," who knew nothing about diplomatic immunity, roaming the capital. "They had been dosed with unassimilated notions as shown

---

* The author of the first complete biography of Dean Acheson.

in the comment one of them made to a servant to the effect that all of this belonged to the people of China anyhow.... But the State Department took it very seriously and instructed me to make an emphatic protest both in Peiping and in Nanking." Word later reached Stuart that Communist officials in both cities were "mortified"—a comment "borne out by the lack of any reference to it in their publicity which as a rule unscrupulously denounces the other side as the best defense." Nevertheless, the CCP never bothered to apologize for the diplomatic gaffe. Worse, on January 13, 1950, Chinese Communists took over the American consular office in the capital and, in another incident on the same day, arrested the American consul general in Mukden, Angus Ward, jailing him for four weeks on specious charges. Word of these events set off a wave of concern in the United States, and the day after Ward was arrested, the State Department recalled 135 consular officers and their families from Peking, Tientsin, Nanking, Shanghai, and Tsingtao.

News like this cheered the China Lobby, and, urged on by his fellow lobbyists, Senator Knowland convinced Acheson of the need for continued economic aid to Taiwan—a program that was nearly derailed by an article in the *New York Journal-American* questioning "whether the American taxpayer should dig deeper into his pockets when high-ranking Nationalists, who have escaped from China and now are in the United States, could help the cause themselves. It is reported in reliable quarters that T. V. Soong and H. H. Kung, wealthy former Chinese finance ministers . . . have more than a billion dollars on deposit in this country . . . in various banks on the East and West coasts, either in the form of cash or gilt-edged securities."

If so, where was the money? Truman had asked the FBI for information about Soong's and Kung's holdings almost exactly a year earlier, and Director Hoover had sent out a memo to be given "preferred and expeditious attention . . . to immediately determine extent of domestic bank accounts of captioned individuals as well as industries, corporations or enterprises under their control. . . . Every possible lead to secure the information should be pursued." Inquiries had been sent out to banks in New York, Chicago, Los Angeles, San Francisco, Boston, Washington, D.C., Philadelphia, even Seattle and New Orleans—with no results—and Senator Knowland had read letters into the *Congressional Record* from both Soong and Kung, giving their permission to allow an investigation into their holdings in the United States, thus killing the story. Still, as May-ling had discovered on her last trip to the United States, Truman did not intend to continue his predecessor's support of the Chiang regime. This came about only when North Korea crossed the Thirty-eighth Parallel to invade South Korea, thus starting a war that Joseph Lelyveld of *The New York Times* called "the biggest piece of luck Chiang Kai-shek . . . had in his 30-year losing streak."

❦

POSTWAR ATTEMPTS TO establish a unified government in Korea, which had been placed under U.S. and Soviet occupation during the Potsdam Conference in 1945, had failed, and the country was still divided into the agricultural South, occupied by American troops, and the industrial North, occupied by the USSR, when the North Korean army, trained and equipped for battle by the Russians, invaded the South on June 25, 1950. Two days later, Truman ordered the U.S. military to help the South Koreans. Taiwan, he said, should remain neutral during the conflict, and he ordered the Seventh Fleet to patrol the Taiwan Strait, thus preventing the generalissimo from launching operations against the mainland and vice versa. This saved Chiang from 15,000 Communist troops readying themselves on the opposite shore to invade his island—an assault that had so worried the G-mo's family that Ching-kuo had already made provisional asylum arrangements for his father in the Philippines.

Three days after Truman named him commander in chief of the U.N. forces in Korea, General MacArthur took it upon himself to fly to Taipei to demonstrate the importance of Taiwan in the war. As *Time* put it, neither the president, the State Department, nor the Pentagon knew anything about the trip until "they looked in their newspapers and read of diplomatic gallantries between MacArthur and Mme. Chiang [he kissed her hand in greeting] and fervid comrades-in-arms exchanges between MacArthur and the Generalissimo." (In a "historic blunder," MacArthur had first grabbed hold of Premier Chen Cheng, whom he kissed on both cheeks, saying "I have been waiting all my life for this moment," while Chiang Kai-shek, clearly miffed by not being recognized, looked on.) While MacArthur was there, the G-mo, prompted by his foreign minister, George Yeh, proposed sending 33,000 Chinese soldiers to augment the U.N. force, and, although MacArthur advised his government to accept Chiang's offer, it was refused.* Washington did, however, recommend that the United States resume military aid to the Nationalists on the grounds that Taiwan was now strategically important and its defenses must be improved. But Truman, who was "most anxious that Chiang Kai-shek not become involved with us," sent Harriman to warn MacArthur to keep his distance from the G-mo in future and not get the United States into a war with mainland China.

After MacArthur's visit to Taiwan, Marshall received a "chatty private missive" from May-ling, one paragraph of which, disturbed the recipient:

---

* Chiang had originally objected to Yeh's idea and followed his recommendation only after the foreign minister assured him that the United States would never accept his offer.

The Generalissimo . . . told General MacArthur that from various quarters, including the guerrillas, there have come requests and suggestions that I head the guerrilla movement on the mainland. He asked the General what he thought of the matter. The General replied that as far as the effectiveness of the work is concerned, he thought it would be fine. The person heading the movement should be someone the enemy would not suspect and certainly I would be the last one the enemy would suspect. But [General MacArthur] thought that the sacrifice on my part would be tremendous because whoever heads the movement would be fraught with danger and subject to torture and death if caught. . . . His last words as we left the car at the [air]field to me were: "I would not like to see you in such danger."

Marshall clearly agreed, and the matter was dropped.

Unless May-ling and Chiang were trying to signal desperation or fervor for their cause in some roundabout Chinese way, the fact that either of them would have entertained such an idea and spoken of it to MacArthur says something very strange about their relationship at this time. The summer of 1950 was a hard one anyway for the G-mo's wife. "I know you are ever so busy, but when I get your letters you and Mrs. Marshall do not seem so far away," she wrote the general with atypical melancholy. "This island feels very isolated sometimes, and of all my friends in America, you two are among the very few who have any idea of what my life in China is like."

About this time, *U.S. News & World Report* interviewed Chiang Kai-shek by radio, asking him what he thought American policy in the Far East should be. His answer was no surprise: "The most pressing task today is to find the means to prevent the conflagration started by the Communists in Korea from spreading to the other parts of Asia. . . . American co-operation in the air and naval defense of Taiwan should no longer carry with it the condition that free China should refrain from all military operations against the mainland." Published in the same issue was an interview with Stanley K. Hornbeck, former chief of the Far Eastern Division of the State Department, who said that the "Chinese Nationalists are the only people who are in any position today to put up any substantial resistance to the Chinese Communists."

Thus, during the first two years of the Korean War, the U.S. Office of Policy Coordination (OPC), successor to the OSS of World War II, ran all of its covert operations out of Taiwan. Having acquired Chennault's bankrupt CAT airline for just under a million dollars in 1949, the United States had air transport for its clandestine operations, flying 15,000 support missions and overflights of the mainland. As the Korean War heated up, Taiwan became the base where the United States collected its intelligence and from which some six hundred agents waged secret warfare against the Communists. In return, the United States provided the Nationalists with "a cornucopia of money, arms, equipment, and training." Although Ching-kuo supervised Taiwan's intelligence operations, including those run in tandem with the Americans, it was Madame Chiang who dealt with the high-level agents of the OPC/CIA, reporting on matters of intelligence and covert action directly to her husband.

But May-ling, who was usually more realistic than Chiang, had lost her political perspective since her arrival on the island: "I have faith that before the end of the year, we shall be back on the mainland," she wrote Emma in January 1951.

> . . . Evidently the American public is getting educated, and from recent signs I would say that the State Department, too, is learning its lesson. Some two years ago when I came to America, I warned your people that what was happening to mainland China then would have repercussions on practically every individual American, and now the enormous taxes, if nothing else, imposed for defense and for carrying on the war in Korea, should be sufficient proof of my observations and prognostications. I remember, too, I pointed out that when Russia starts to make the Asia mainland a base for her nefarious activities, Formosa would be invaluable as a spring-board to launch an anti-Communist offensive. Now, again, I assert that the only effective resistance against Russia and the Chinese Communists in Asia, lies in Formosa, for what other country besides Free China has millions of guerrillas on the mainland and 600,000 troops just "rarin" to spring at the throat of the Red Beast?

If May-ling harbored grandiose dreams, so did MacArthur, and it did not take him more than a few months after the onset of the Korean War to run afoul of President Truman. In early April of 1951, a member of the House of Representatives read a letter from the general in which he said that the United States should stop confining itself to limited engagements and pursue an all-out war. "If we lose the war to communism in Asia," he declared, "the fall of Europe is inevitable." He also asked the Joint Chiefs of Staff for permission to drop atomic bombs on Chinese military installations in Manchuria. In response, Truman, who feared that any aggravation of the limited war might lead to World War III, dismissed MacArthur in favor of General Matthew Ridgway, ending the G-mo's plan of piggybacking his return to the mainland on MacArthur and the U.S. Army.

There were, however, some compensations. The next month, Assistant Secretary of State Dean Rusk declared that Chiang "more authentically represents the views of the great body of the people of China" than the Communists. Five months later a U.S. mutual security appropriation of $535,250,000 in military aid and $237,500,000 in economic support for Asia and the Pacific area was passed, much of which was sent to Taiwan.

▼

DURING THE PREVIOUS month, the peace treaty ending World War II with Japan had finally been signed in San Francisco by forty-eight countries,* but it was not until the end of April 1953 that the Nationalists and Japanese came to an agreement under which the latter renounced title to Taiwan and the Pescadores Islands, thus officially ending the world war. In discussing the settlements with an interviewer a decade later, Madame stressed her husband's magnanimity: "our government did not ask for any damages from the Japanese . . . regardless of the losses to lives and property of our people . . . the President wanted to emphasize to our people that we should not take an attitude of revenge . . . we had every right—moral right and legal right—to ask for war damages, but we did not."

As for the Korean War, a cease-fire, called in the summer of 1951, was followed by what one historian called "interminable truce negotiations" eventually leading to an armistice in July 1953. The war had been a big issue in the presidential campaign of 1952, and the China Lobby was pleased when Dwight D. Eisenhower won the election. The new president announced that the U.S. Seventh Fleet would continue to protect Taiwan from an invasion from the mainland and canceled the injunction against the Nationalists launching an attack on the Communists. But Chiang, knowing that he could not capture the mainland alone, settled back to wait, as he had in World War II, until others had reason to wage war for him. He also agreed not to attack the mainland without consultation with and agreement from Washington. He was particularly pleased when the United Nations insisted that prisoners of war must be allowed to decide for themselves where they would go after the Korean War armistice, and 72 percent of the 14,000 Chinese prisoners chose Taiwan over the Communist mainland.

▼

IT WAS DURING this period that May-ling, who needed an outlet for her nervous energy and creativity, discovered painting. "An astounding thing has

---

* The final session of the peace conference was boycotted by the Soviet Union and other Communist countries.

happened; you simply won't believe it," she wrote Emma in the fall of 1951. "I have been learning Chinese painting the past five months and all the artists and connoisseurs of Chinese painting say that I have the possibilities of a great artist. Some even say, perhaps the greatest living artist. . . . I myself believe that what the Chinese authorities tell me is true because, curiously enough, it is no effort to me at all to paint. . . . I must confess that at first I did not believe them. . . . Painting is the most absorbing occupation I have known in my life. When I am at work, I forget everything in the world, and I wish that I could spend all my time in doing nothing but painting and painting."

May-ling employed two master artists, who were picked up in her private car and brought to her residence to teach her her craft. Chiang had laughed at her when she started—"If you were any good at painting, you would have discovered it before. . . . You'll never be any good at it at your age"—but, as she became more proficient, he allowed her to hang her paintings when visitors came, so that they would admire her work. In what Hahn called "a time-honoured face-saving formula," he also changed his tune: "I thought you could do it, but I knew if it sounded too easy, you'd never go ahead with it. I discouraged you on purpose."

Like Chiang, May-ling failed to realize that she lived in a cocoon and it was to the advantage of the spinners to keep her there. "Got the photographs of your paintings back from Jo Lansing* a few days ago," Emma wrote six months later. "She had shown them to three experts, without identifying the artist, and they all agreed they were done by a person with real ability. They believed them to be copies of other paintings and recommended that the artist do more original work, to gain greater freedom. She herself, while no expert, was quite impressed, the same for me. . . . I so hope you have time to keep it up, for not only do you have real ability, but you get such satisfaction out of it."

Shortly after moving to Taiwan, May-ling had also invited five friends to help her start a prayer group like the one organized by her mother and carried on by Ai-ling after Madame Soong's death. "My friends were enthusiastic from the start," May-ling said. "In the beginning, a certain self-consciousness in praying aloud had to be overcome. . . . People who have known each other intimately can suddenly seem strangers in the presence of God." Each member took her turn leading the meeting, starting with a reading from the Scriptures, talking about herself in relation to the lesson, and going on to a general discussion.

---

* A woman at the Metropolitan Museum of Art whom May-ling had recommended as a source of experts in Chinese art.

By the time May-ling wrote about her group, it had expanded to forty women and had led her to a personal conversion. While reading one day about the crucifixion of Christ, she said that she had

> paused at a passage where the soldier used a spear to pierce His side, causing blood and water to flow from the wound. I had read that passage many times before, and it had never particularly moved me. This time, however, I wept. At last I felt that the suffering and pain of Jesus Christ were for me. I cried and cried, overcome with my own unworthiness. It was a peculiar sensation, at once great grief and great release . . . my tears were a torrent. I could not control myself. At the same time, my heart felt light and relieved, with a sense of atonement. . . . When I told of this to a few of our group, some instantly understood and recognized what I tried to convey.

Though May-ling's spiritual life was bringing her joy, her physical condition was giving her problems. Ever since her arrival in Taiwan, she had been suffering from her usual neurodermititis, which apparently became much worse in late 1951. To relieve the discomfort, her doctor prescribed a new drug.* "It was miraculous," she wrote Emma. "In two days my skin cleared completely, and I felt so well and energetic that I got more work done within a week than I had in the past three months. The only trouble was that I could not sleep more than two or three hours a night, for it was very stimulating. . . . It is such a powerful drug, however, that one cannot keep on it always." Six months later, however, she was still on the drug, which not only revved her up but made her "look awfully swollen and puffy."

In August of 1952, May-ling flew to San Francisco, where she stayed in a hospital for two months undergoing treatment. Told by the doctors that she should remain in the United States to recover, she took a United Airlines plane, in which a "special bed" had been built, to New York, where she moved into the Kung home on Long Island. In September, she received a cable from Chiang, inquiring about her health and saying he missed her.

"The weather is cold and no longer humid, and I think that this is the right weather for you to recuperate when you come back to Taiwan, which I hope will be soon." But May-ling stayed where she was, missing both Chiang's sixty-sixth birthday and their twenty-fifth wedding anniversary. "It is a great pity that we can't be together this year," he wired. ". . . I hope that we can be together every year from now on and never separate again."

---

* Adrenocorticotropic hormone (ACTH).

May-ling wanted to attend Eisenhower's inauguration in January, but there was no precedent for foreign heads of state (or their wives) appearing at what was considered a "purely domestic event," so she had to settle for tea at the White House in March. There, according to Wellington Koo, "Madame Chiang was able with her usual skill, she confidentially told me afterwards, to bring up a few serious questions of special interest to our country to the President's attention." The following month, against the advice of her doctors, she "suddenly" decided to fly home. The reason had to do with her friend K. C. Wu.

❦

Dr. K. C. Wu, the governor of Taiwan, was a liberal and reformer. He had a fine reputation in the United States, and *Time* had put him on its cover in the summer of 1950. Ever since then, Chiang had been trying to entice or coerce Wu into working with Ching-kuo. But in 1952, the governor took a tour of the provinces, urging local leaders not to "look up" to satisfy their superiors but to "look down" to serve their people. "When I returned to Taipei," Wu said, "I heard that my speeches had greatly displeased Chiang. Even while I was still on my tour he had chosen to show his displeasure by ordering the executions of almost eight to ten persons every day . . . on charges of being Communists or Communist-affiliated." These executions, he claimed, had resulted in the death of nearly a hundred people. A similar trip undertaken by Wu in November of 1952, shortly before elections, had resulted in the arrest of 998 people by various branches of Ching-kuo's secret police; when challenged, however, the police could produce evidence against only three or four of their victims.* The detainees, Wu explained, were "civilian leaders in their various localities. arrested in order to intimidate them to vote a certain way in the forthcoming elections"; thus, "all possible opposition to Kuomintang candidates had been . . . crushed." The final blow was the kidnapping of two city councillors. When Wu asked that the policeman responsible be dismissed, Chiang had him promoted instead.

Having discovered that he was being spied on, that his phones were tapped, and that his servants were reporting on him, Wu tried to resign, but his resignation was refused by Chiang, who claimed that the governor was "over-wrought" and gave him a month's sick leave. Wu took his wife up to their mountain home at Sun Moon Lake, saying that he would not return until his resignation was accepted. Since the governor was, in his own words,

---

* An additional eighteen had committed misdemeanors like getting into drunken brawls; Wu ordered these men sent to court to be tried and the rest set free.

"very popular with the Formosan people" and "strong in the American press," Chiang was determined to get him back.

As soon as Wu's resignation became known, May-ling flew home. "She never liked Chiang Ching-kuo," Wu said, "and she knew that if I were to go, it meant further strengthening of Ching-kuo's position." But Madame Chiang's proposed return had put Wu into a Chinese quandary: if he went to meet her, he would be denying his resignation; if he did not go, he would be committing a social gaffe. Since the Chiangs and the Wus were good social friends, Wu sent his wife, Edith, to the airport. Chiang was also there, and "he smiled and greeted her warmly in front of everybody."

"I came back because of K.C.," May-ling whispered to Wu's wife as soon as she saw her. "Will you please ask K.C. to come down from Sun Moon Lake right away. I am quite surprised that he did not come to see me here." When Wu's wife answered that she knew her husband would not return, May-ling said she would go to see him the following day. But Chiang refused to let her go. After a multiplicity of messages sent back and forth, Wu finally agreed to come down from the mountain to see May-ling. Although she insisted on taking him outside her home to talk, explaining that the house was bugged,* nothing was settled on either side.

On the way back up the mountain there was an attempt on Wu's life. His car had clearly been tampered with, and had he and his wife not changed their plans and stopped for lunch, giving the driver and a mechanic time to check what was wrong, they would all have been killed. Determined to find out if Chiang was part of the plot, Wu sent him a letter quoting the words of a famous minister about to be executed by his emperor on a false charge: "My crime is worthy of death, but my sovereign is always wise." Adding the question "Would Your Excellency have great mercy upon your faithful servant?" he requested an interview with the G-mo. "Chiang," he said with Chinese logic, "could react only in one of two ways. If he knew nothing about the attempt he would think that I had seriously misunderstood him and he would call me to see him. . . . If he had known of the attempt, he would know that I had guessed he was at the back of the whole thing, and he would not see me." Not surprisingly, Wu never received an answer to his note, and a week later he was dismissed from his position as governor.

Passport applications for high officials or politically "sensitive" persons had to be passed by Chiang Kai-shek, but after some difficulty, the Wus were given passports and permission to travel. It was said that Madame Chiang, hearing that another attempt would be made on Wu's life on his

---

* This was apparently done so that Chiang could hear what guests were saying among themselves before appearing at his parties.

way to the airport, convinced her husband that such a murder would have serious repercussions in Taiwan's relationship with the United States. Although Wu and his wife were allowed to leave, Chiang kept their teenage son in Taiwan as hostage. The Wus moved to Evanston, Illinois, and kept quiet for thirteen months. While there, they wrote May-ling three times, asking for help in getting a passport for their son. She had already replied twice that she could do nothing, when they received a third letter from her asking Wu to return to Taiwan to become secretary-general of Chiang's office.* When he refused, rumors were spread around Taiwan that Wu had embezzled public funds, absconded with a half-million dollars, and was living in luxury in the Waldorf Towers in New York City. No newspaper in Taiwan would carry his statement to the contrary, although Wu's father paid to have it run.

On February 7, 1954, Wu appeared in Chicago on a television program similar to *Meet the Press*. Pushed by reporters, he talked about the Taiwanese government's "use of Communist tactics in fighting communism." In retaliation, the president of the Legislative Yuan denounced him, and the National Assembly demanded his recall to Taiwan for disciplinary action. On March 15, *The New York Times* reported Wu's open break with Chiang and the subsequent attempt on his life. "But the greatest concern for me," Wu said, "was to get my younger son out of Formosa. Of course, now I could openly state that Chiang had been holding my son as a sort of hostage, and I wrote him a letter asking him to issue a passport to my son in thirty days. I said, 'If you still persist in refusal after thirty days I will be compelled to take other action." His son, whom Ching-kuo's Youth Corps had been trying to get to denounce his father, was finally allowed to join his parents in Illinois.

Once he was free to speak, Dr. Wu wrote a series of "open letters" to members of the National Assembly, warning them that reform was needed if the Taiwanese government were to survive. He wrote mainly about Chiang Ching-kuo's police, who "interfered with free elections . . . made numberless illegal arrests . . . tortured and . . . blackmailed . . . relying on their special backing . . . [they] . . . have no regard for law." The letters were duly suppressed, and Chiang answered Wu by accusing him of "treason," "dereliction of duty," and "corruption in office." Wu replied—from the safety of Illinois—that he would be happy to stand trial in an American or international court, but not in any court set up by the generalissimo.

---

* Chiang had recently fired his secretary-general in what was considered "a serious blow to 'liberalism' within the Chinese Government." (National Archives: RG 59, CDF (1950-1955) Box 4218, November 19 and 27, 1953.)

China's former ambassador to the United States, Dr. Hu Shih, also spoke out, explaining to a reporter from *The New York Times* that he felt he had a "moral obligation" to return to Taiwan to vote in the National Assembly: "I hope this new assembly will be the beginning of a new era. . . . 'Obey the leader' [Chiang Kai-shek] has become one of the basic slogans of the Kuomintang's anti-Communist . . . campaign. . . . Loyalty should be to the state and not to an individual. . . . I would like to see still more freedom of press and person in Taiwan."

52

He [Chiang] still ruled like a feudal chieftain, giving high positions to his relatives, his favorite generals, and his two sons. They could commit no wrong, and were never called to account. Corruption was widespread; the army ruled; the secret police were everywhere.

—ROBERT PAYNE

THERE WERE few men like K. C. Wu who refused to be silenced and who were lucky enough to escape from the clutches of Chiang and his police. When it came to matters of "face," the generalissimo never hesitated to persecute those who defied his will—always, of course, in the name of the honor of the state.

In the fall of 1951, a big corruption story had erupted on the pages of *The New York Times* and *The Washington Post* involving Chinese generals who resented the fact that military supplies purchased through Lend-Lease were being routed through the Chinese procurement office in Washington, thus limiting their opportunities for squeeze. Brought to light by Lieutenant General P. T. Mow, now chief of staff of the Chinese air force* and Mow's executive officer, Colonel Hsiang, the story started when Mow discovered a transfer of $430,000† from New York to Hong Kong, ordered by General Chou Chih-jo, the G-mo's chief of staff.‡ Mow told Walter Judd about the transfer, and Judd wrote Chiang to ask for an explanation. The G-mo promised to institute an inquiry, which he did not do. Instead, he set up an investigation of Mow, with whom he was furious for causing him to lose face with Judd. According to Hsiang, "the President's first thought was . . . to deny the case, but finally he decided to admit the truth after Madame Chiang and Mr.

---

* It will be remembered that Mow had been married to Chiang Kai-shek's first wife's sister.

† Equivalent to $3,563,000 today.

‡ Early in the war, Madame Chiang, Donald, and Chennault had all tried to have Chou, known for his "stupidity and inefficiency," removed, but the G-mo had always refused, since he believed Chou was loyal to him. (Cornell University, Division of Rare and Manuscript Collections, James M. McHugh papers, File C-105, "Changes in Chinese Airforce Administration, March 7, 1938.)

Kung convinced him that denying the case would not solve the problem, but would show . . . that he was untruthful and insincere." Chiang asked Mow to come to Taiwan to testify, but Mow wisely refused. In a lengthy letter to Wellington Koo, China's ambassador in Washington, Chiang explained that the money had been needed to move military factories from the mainland to Taiwan and that it was important to get Chinese funds out of the United States to prevent their being frozen. An obvious cover-up, the letter concluded with a paragraph in which the G-mo warned, "From now on, if any official of the Government stationed in a foreign country should attack the high officials in the Government irresponsibly, without first knowing all the actual facts, and thereby undermine the prestige of the Government he will be severely punished under law so that the honor of the nation may be preserved."

Meanwhile, Mow and Hsiang's inquiries into methods of procurement had uncovered the machinations of Commerce International Corporation; CIC was the designated contractor for the Board of Supplies of the Executive Yuan of the Taiwanese government, which was discovered to be in league with Chou. According to *The Washington Post*, CIC organized and paid the salaries of an entity called the American Technical and Military Advisory Group, based in Taiwan, headed and staffed by retired U.S. Admiral Charles M. Cooke, Jr. Ross Koen* tells us that "the real importance" of this group was its ability "to channel contracts for supplies directly to CIC and permit them to bypass official Chinese procurement offices abroad." As retired military men, Cooke's group was "in a position to apply pressure in Washington to grant more money to Chiang with which to pay the exorbitant prices charged by their employer." For this service, CIC received $750,000† a year.

As a typical example of malfeasance, Mow and Hsiang pointed to a cable from General Chou in May of 1950 telling them to negotiate with CIC officials in the United States for the purchase of "a large quantity of bombs located by CIC in Europe." But according to the *Post*, these bombs were surplus American property that had been sold to a private company in Italy under the proviso that they be used for civilian purposes only—i.e., the shells as scrap metal and the explosives processed into fertilizer. Hsiang calculated that the asking price was double that by which new bombs could

---

* The author of *The China Lobby in American Politics*. (See Laura Tyson Li, *Madame Chiang Kai-shek*, pp. 402–3, for how the Nationalist Government and the China Lobby pressured the U.S. government to ban the book, how the publisher "was forced" to destroy 4,000 copies, and how some of the remaining 800 books disappeared from library shelves.)

† Equivalent to $6,215,000 today.

be bought directly from the U.S. government. He took the case to the Senate Preparedness Subcommittee, which conducted an "exhaustive and expert" inquiry, during which the vice president of CIC tried to bribe him with close to $8,000 for each of twenty-five F-51 planes purchased through CIC for the Chinese air force. In another deal, Mow said, General Chou had tried to purchase some F-51 planes through CIC at $36,840 each, when they were available through the U.S. government for $16,000.

On November 14, 1951, Chiang's Nationalist government sued Mow and Hsiang in U.S. Federal Court, demanding the return of $7 million* in unused funds entrusted to them and all government records in their possession. The two men tried but failed to have the suit dismissed and, when they did not appear in court, lost the case by default. Mow escaped to Mexico, where he was arrested by the Mexican government at Chiang's request and held in prison for nearly three years before being freed on bond, despite the fact that a Mexican judge ruled that he was a political refugee entitled to asylum. Hsiang's wife, harrassed by process servers, and his two young sons, chased through the streets of Washington by "unidentified persons," managed to escape to Hong Kong and from there presumably to Communist China. Both Mow and Hsiang disappeared into thin air.

❦

UNABLE OR UNWILLING to see his own failings, Chiang was unlikely to change his ways or those of his underlings. After the move to Taiwan, his main object in life was to convince the world that he was still the legitimate head of all of China. "In the eyes of the uninvolved," Crozier writes, "Chiang's claim to sovereignty over the Chinese mainland was viewed as at best an absurdity and at worst an impertinence." In spite of the fact that members of the National Assembly were supposed to be elected every six years, most of its members had come to Taiwan from the mainland, and, "solemnly, year after year until death claimed them, the ageing legislators sat on, claiming to represent the interests of distant 'constituents' in the mainland provinces of China, with whom they had long since lost all contact." While the doddering delegates postured, local Taiwanese were reduced to minor positions in the government. As before, the KMT bureaucrats owed their high positions to Chiang, who saw to it that they were given large properties to make up for what they had lost on the mainland. And as before, they received very minimal compensation for their work and were expected to make up the difference in squeeze. "Corruption was so widespread," according to Payne, "that it affected all departments of government at all levels." It was, he tells us, "especially prevalent among policemen, tax officers and school administra-

---

* Equivalent to $58,000,000 today.

tors, who demanded the payment of bribes from the teachers before they were given positions."

There was an occasional attempt to paper over the squeeze. The mayor of Taipei, arrested for taking bribes from the bus administration, was shocked that he, a high official of the KMT, could be brought to court. He produced an account book that showed that he had never in his entire political life accepted a bribe and was acquitted, while his judges were given higher positions in the judiciary. His wife, convicted of embezzling $300,000, was given a deferred sentence.

This kind of pseudojustice demoralized the average islander, who, according to Payne, "learned to obey, pay bribes and live quietly and obscurely. The overhelming might of the regime, exercised through the army and the secret police, enforced obedience. The revolutionary Kuomintang had degenerated into a comparatively small body of men exercising the rights of prison wardens." To remain safe from Ching-kuo's police, the average citizen had to either support Chiang vociferously or become completely apolitical. As in all such regimes, the arts and sciences suffered.

The publicity surrounding Wu had been particularly bad for Ching-kuo, and "to remove him from the scene temporarily," approaches were made to the U.S. Department of Defense, which invited him to the United States. Li tells us that the trip was endorsed by both Defense and State, who let it be known that they hoped a sojourn in America would broaden the G-mo's son's "intellectual horizon—on which Soviet Russia looms so large." Traveling from coast to coast, Ching-kuo was feted with receptions and banquets, after which he usually went into the kitchen to meet the help. In Washington, he called on President Eisenhower and had "a friendly exchange" with Secretary of State John Foster Dulles. The secretary, explaining that he had "heard from some of our representatives that the General was a little rough in his methods," cautioned him on the necessity to preserve the human rights of prisoners—advice to which Ching-kuo "murmured an inaudible acknowledgment."

The break with the Wus had also affected May-ling, whose skin rash flared up again, and, accompanied by Jeanette Kung, a nurse, and two male attendants, she returned to the hospital in San Francisco. "I think the balmy California weather and the medical care will eventually affect a cure," she wrote Wellington Koo, adding that her doctors were "of the opinion that some form of allergy is the basis of my illness." After allergy tests and a month in the hospital, she left for New York for more treatment. Her friend Dorothy Thomas* visited her in the hospital there; to prevent anything

---

* The social secretary of the American Legation in Peking in the 1920s; married to James A. Thomas, head of the Far Eastern division of the British American Tobacco Company.

touching her skin, she lay under what Thomas described as "a bamboo sort of cage," over which the nurses put the sheets and blankets. Later, she asked Thomas to come visit her at the Kung home in Long Island: "I asked my daughter-in-law to come with me, and when we got there . . . I looked up and there was a screen on the second floor, and behind the screen there was something moving. And when we got into the living room, Anne, my daughter-in-law, said, 'What do you think that was?' I said, 'That was Madame Chiang. She was looking at us. That's what they always do. They always look at you first before they see you, you know. That's why they have so many screens.' "

Before leaving New York, May-ling had lunch with another friend and fellow writer, Grace Oursler. She had originally met the Ourslers* in Shanghai, where, Grace said, the two woman had formed what her husband, Fulton, called "friendship-at-first-sight." Madame had sent a long cable and subsequent letter when Fulton died, the sort of communication which, according to the widow, "sealed my knowedge of the depth of that friendship." But Grace had not heard from her friend for two and a half years when Madame's secretary suddenly called with an invitation to lunch in New York.

"I am very concerned," May-ling told Grace. "Certain spiritual questions torment me. I want you to try and remember anything Fulton ever said on the subjects. I feel certain if I could only sit and talk to him, I would find the answers. So often he gave me the thought I needed." The questions were, of course, unanswerable: "When was civilization going to find a new answer to war? . . . When would a good, fully dedicated Christian fight? . . . Can one condone wrong in others and to others and still be a good Christian? . . . Wasn't this a time for Believers to hold out a hand to those who had no Faith?" etc. These questions "haunted" Grace Oursler during their subsequent correspondence. People with whom she spoke about this, she said, "urged" her "to ask Madame Chiang to give the world a share in her spiritual battle." The ladies cabled back and forth until Grace, who had gone "to Hollywood on business," decided to keep on going across the Pacific to Taiwan.

She arrived in February of 1955, only to find May-ling "so exhausted as to be actually ill" from dealing with refugees from the Tachen Islands, recently evacuated by the Nationalists. Grace had arranged for her trip to be financed by an advance on an article on Madame's spiritual quest for *Good Housekeeping* magazine—a fact that "enormously disturbed" May-ling, who offered to refund the money. She told Oursler "that she thought I had come

---

* Fulton Oursler was the author of popular books on Christian themes; his wife, Grace, who had started her career by writing "racy" books under the pseudonym Dora Macy, had become a freelance journalist.

to her as a loving friend when she was in great distress. . . . She told me that she herself wanted nothing and would take nothing: she is exceedingly sensitive about past criticism on money matters, not only of herself but of the entire Chinese set-up."

"For eighteen days and nights we worked together on this piece," Oursler wrote in an introduction to the article. "Madame dictated, pouring out her heart as the words and memories tumbled from her lips." In writing about the finished product to Herbert Mays of *Good Housekeeping,* Oursler was highly enthusiastic: "I am in love with it and somehow feel that it and she were inspired."

But Grace was lonely in her admiration. Accompanied by a four-page, single-spaced commentary, the piece was turned down by *Good Housekeeping* as "much, much too long" with "too many arguments on behalf of Chiang and the Nationalists." Oursler then combined two of her own essays—one on the Madame, the other on Taiwan—with Madame's manuscript, but *The Saturday Evening Post* refused this version as well.

It was not until two months later, in June, that the Fleming H. Revell Company accepted the piece for publication, first as a condensation for *Reader's Digest,* then in book form, titled *The Sure Victory,* for Christmas. "There is no other periodical which I would prefer more than the 'Digest' for its publication," May-ling wired Grace, when she got the good news. This was followed by some bad news from the publisher: "Dear Grace: Enclosed is the introduction which you so graciously wrote for *Sure Victory.* . . . we regret exceedingly that Madame Chiang did not approve of its being included in the book."

❧

IN APRIL 1955, Chiang's faithful supporter, *Time* magazine, once again put him on its cover, calling him "Man of the Single Truth" and quoting from a fable of Archilochus: "The Fox knows many things, but the hedgehog knows one big thing." The interviewer who settled down on Chiang's "veranda, with its silvery curtains and pale green furnishings," described its owner as a man who imparts an air of "sureness. . . . For among the foxes of the world, Chiang Kai-shek long ago found the hedgehog's one big thing: the world's primary and implacable enemy was and is the Communist conspiracy directed from Moscow."

For some years the generalissimo had been working on his second book, *Soviet Russia in China,* which he completed in 1956, the year he turned seventy. Like his earlier effort, it is a compilation of Chiang's theories put into words by his secretaries. Unlike *China's Destiny,* it benefits from contributions from his wife, who shared his belief that the Russians had been the cause of all of China's ills. With her broader outlook on the world, however, May-ling had managed to tone down her husband's rhetoric, complaining to Emma Mills after it came out that the publishers had not sent her the galleys as requested and that it still "needed further editing."

The author's note at the beginning of *Soviet Russia in China* is dated December 1, 1956, the day of the Chiangs' twenty-ninth wedding anniversary: "In reviewing our past," Chiang wrote, "my wife and I share an acute consciousness of failure in not living up to the lofty ideals instilled in us by our mothers. . . . The double challenge of the mainland remaining unrecovered and our people therein crying out in vain for deliverance aggravates our sense of regret." In the text itself, Chiang blamed China's catastrophies on the Russian Communists working through their surrogates, Mao Tse-tung and Chou En-lai, going so far as to actually claim that it was the CCP that had caused the "hatred between landlords and tenants" on the mainland. He also accused the Communists of "precipitating a war with Japan" in order to gain time to overcome the Nationalists. Ignoring the fact that he himself had used the threat of a separate peace with the Japanese during World War II, Chiang blamed the Russians for spreading "rumors . . . to the effect that the Chinese Government was carrying on secret negotiations with Japan for cessation of hostilities" in order to get the United States to stop giving aid to the Nationalists. "This was Moscow's plot," Chiang said, "but few could see it at the time."

In reviewing the Korean War, Chiang also rode on moonbeams, claiming that "if . . . the Republic of China's troops had been used . . . it would have had a great political and psychological effect on the Chinese Communist troops in action, and the latter could have been crushed in Korea. If the troops I offered* could have pursued the enemy . . . they . . . would have fostered an anti-Communist revolutionary movement on the Chinese mainland. . . . I believe that the Western powers' objection to the dispatch of an expeditionary force to Korea by the Republic of China was the *greatest cause for the stalemate in the Korean War*" (the italics are Chiang's).

Perhaps the G-mo's most ludicrous claim, however, had to do with his fights with Stilwell, which he blamed on the American Communists who said that members of the CCP were merely "agrarian reformers." According to Chiang, "General Stilwell was one of those influenced by this propaganda. . . . I regret to say that he had no idea whatsoever of the Chinese Communists' schemes. . . . General Stilwell's subsequent dispute with me was created entirely by the Communists and their friends. . . . I should have

---

* It will be remembered that the generalissimo offered troops only after he was assured that they would be refused.

confided in him all the facts about Soviet Russia's intrigues and her real aims. . . . I regretted very much that I did not do this. . . . On this point it might be said that I made a mistake. To this day my heart still aches over this unfortunate affair."

What *Soviet Russia in China* makes abundantly clear is that, as one of Chiang's biographers put it, the generalissimo "understood the Russian Communists better than he understood the Chinese Communists," and it was this lack of comprehension, along with the widespread corruption of his own government, that had landed him where he was.

⚘

WHILE POLITICAL LIFE withered and died on Taiwan, the economy thrived. But, according to Crozier, the "prosperity, economic growth, [and] relative contentment" meant less to Chiang than word of international crises that might help him in his dream of reconquering the mainland, and bad news about the Communist government cheered the G-mo far more "than all the record-breaking statistics of Taiwan's booming economy." When the Communists sent seventy-odd vessels to bomb the island of Yikiangshan—a dot on the map north of the Tachen Islands—and annihilated 720 of the generalissimo's soldiers, Chiang's spirits rose at the prospect of U.S. military action and were just as quickly dashed when the crisis petered out. Left out of the Southeast Asia Defense Treaty, signed in Manila in September 1954, his ego was soothed by a visit from John Foster Dulles, who visited Taiwan after signing the treaty. Meanwhile, vast amounts of economic and military aid continued to flow to the government in exile from the United States.

Shortly after Dulles's visit, President Eisenhower sent the Chiang's friend Roy Howard of Scripps Howard Newspapers to see if the G-mo could be persuaded to give up the islands of Quemoy and Matsu, which he had long claimed as essential to the defense of Taiwan. The four of them, the Chiangs and the Howards, met at Sun Moon Lake. With May-ling translating, it quickly became clear that, as Howard put it, "Chiang intends to defend Quemoy and Matsu if he has to do it alone. His reason is that if he does not do so he is sunk anyway," i.e., defeat could be overcome, but such a retreat—read loss of face—would result in the "complete collapse" of the Taiwanese army.

The following year, at the end of May, May-ling decided to go back to the United States, the source from which more blessings should have been flowing. Planning "a triumphal return to the American spotlight," Madame did not listen to friends like journalist George Sokolsky, who, aware of her tendency to try to impress audiences with her erudition, sent her a copy of Lincoln's Gettysburg Address along with some advice: "If anything is being done here to keep Formosa before the American people, it must be done very quietly.... You can always do more for your country than anyone else as long as what you say is you, simple, sweet, to the heart." The advice of John Foster Dulles, who told her that she should speak whenever possible about "the evils of Communism," was more to her liking. "Now, Madame," he told her, "we in America are doing all that we can to fight Communism and to acquaint our people with the necessity of eradicating Communist aggression, but *you* should take every opportunity to speak on what Communism means."

According to an FBI office memo, Madame was "an extremely gracious and effective platform speaker," although in at least one instance—what the bureau called a "very brilliant performance" before the American Chemical Society—it was clear that "not all present were as strongly opposed to world communism as was Madame Chiang Kai-shek." In spite of early FBI reports of financial malfeasance on the part of members of the Soong family, Madame Chiang and FBI Director J. Edgar Hoover were becoming friendly acquaintances, exchanging articles and books based on their mutual hatred of communism, and in 1960, May-ling was added to the director's "Special Correspondents list."

During her stay in the United States, Madame met Roger Straus, head of the publishing house Farrar, Straus & Company,* and tried to sell him her husband's book. She was, according to Straus, "a particularly handsome woman ... obviously smart as hell ... brilliant ... well dressed and well jeweled, and had a great presence. She was very cool, very aloof, but I found her a most intriguing character ... she had an Oriental look, but she was very American in terms of business conversation and social conversation." Straus managed to convince himself that the generalissimo's book was a "historical document that should be published," primarily because Madame told him that she had "a lot of notes and journals" and was currently writing her own autobiography, which he "wanted very badly."†

When she wasn't speaking, writing, or selling, Madame spent time with Emma and pursued a new passion for antiquing. She browsed in the New York shops, where, according to DeLong, she spoke to the dealers in pidgin English so they would not know who she was. Her companion-secretary, Miss Garvey, would then go back and buy what she wanted. In one shop the dealer said that the lady who had been there looked a lot like

---

* Later Farrar, Straus & Giroux.

† Needless to say, there were probably no significant notes or journals (or at least none that this writer has been able to track down) and eventually no book by her.

Madame Chiang Kai-shek. "Many people think so," said Garvey, "but not if you saw them together. Besides, I believe Mme. Chiang speaks better English."

Most of the time, however, Madame Chiang spent her energies warning Americans about Communism. As if to prove her contention, in late August the mainlanders lobbed 50,000 shells in two hours at the island of Quemoy and continued their attack for five days. Chiang immediately called on the United States for food, ammunition, and other necessities, which were escorted in by the U.S. Seventh Fleet or airdropped there from planes. Ten days after the bombings, the Madame warned an audience in Chicago, "If this state of affairs is allowed to continue, and specifically the foreign policy pronouncements of the United States are made to look ridiculous in the eyes of the world, then Communist tyranny will overrun and overpower not only the non-Communist areas of Asia, but in time the Western Hemisphere as well."

A week later, on September 11, Eisenhower issued a statement saying that the bombings were "part of . . . an ambitious plan of armed conquest . . . [to] . . . liquidate all the free-world positions in the Western Pacific area and bring them under captive governments . . . hostile to the United States and the free world." Although Dulles had announced that the United States would be in favor of the Nationalists evacuating the offshore islands pursuant to a cease-fire, the matter was finally settled by a communiqué issued jointly by Chiang and Dulles saying that the United States believed that the Nationalist government was the "authentic spokesman for free China"—which, according to Crozier, "proved that Chiang Kai-shek and his regime . . . were safe but circumscribed." That was clearly not enough for Madame Chiang, who appeared on *Meet the Press* quoting a refugee from the mainland as saying that the people there were asking "Why doesn't the Republic of China use nuclear weapons on the mainland?" Pursuing this line of thought, she claimed that a Taiwanese invasion of mainland China is "growing nearer and nearer every day . . . because we are responding to the cries of suffering of tortured, oppressed people."

The editors of *The Philadelphia Inquirer* were outraged, responding in their lead editorial, "Mme. Chiang has no objections whatever to a nuclear war—to help Chiang keep his grip on two islets impossible to defend." Some days later, May-ling, who had taken to her bed with "inflammation of back and shoulder muscles from a draft in the TV studio," discussed the crisis on Quemoy with Emma. "The Nationalists' opportunity of counting on a comeback attempt over the situation is foolhardy," Emma told her. "The idea of America getting involved over the off-shore islands isn't popular." "I know it," May-ling confessed to her friend.

Nevertheless, she cabled to commend Ching-kuo for going to the front lines in Quemoy to talk to the soldiers. It was, she said, "very important for their morale. We are going through difficult times. . . . Don't let your father get overtired, and please pay special attention to the state of his health." Stepmother and stepson had grown closer over the past few years; Ching-kuo now addressed her as "Mother" and signed his cables "Son Ching-kuo." Four weeks later she wrote, "Today is your father's birthday. I cannot be there, and I hope you are with him and treating him well. I'm so tired after these months of meeting visitors and preparing speeches. I have a foot ache, and the doctor said that I need an operation. But I have received so many invitations for November, so I will wait until these are over. I will let you know when I am going into the hospital."

Claiming that Madame Chiang had "become one of the most sought-after speakers in the country," *Newsweek* noted, "Even her critics were coming to admire Mme. Chiang's eloquence, however fiery her arguments. And most Americans, whether they agreed with her or not, couldn't help liking the way the tiny, courageous woman threw her punches straight from the shoulder." Occasionally, however, May-ling's need to impress her audience interfered with her message. In addressing the American Bar Association in Los Angeles, she could not resist the temptation to insert references to the *Sachsenspiegel* (a law book from the German Middle Ages) and the *Schwaben-spiegel* (a legal code circa 1275 A.D.).

In June 1960, President Eisenhower paid a state visit to Taiwan, and Chiang took the opportunity to tell him that the time had come to establish guerrilla bases on the mainland—centers of resistance for which he needed planes and telecommunications equipment. On his return to Washington, Eisenhower, who had promised to take the G-mo's request under advisement, was told by the Pentagon that such an undertaking would "meet with almost certain defeat with undesirable consequences for both [Taiwan] and the United States." But, Eisenhower went ahead with the joint planning for a project that was never executed because he thought it would placate the generalissimo.

Two years later, a carefully orchestrated barrage of what the U.S. Embassy called a "crescendo of demands for counterattack" on the Chinese mainland resounded throughout the island. Six months earlier James McHugh had warned that "Chiang Kai-shek is in a Gotterdammerung mood," and in his New Year's speech of January 1, 1962, the G-mo appealed directly to the mainlanders, saying that "the time for collective action is here. Our armed forces have made adequate preparations for the counter-offensive and therefore are capable of moving into action at any time. Have no fear of lack or shortage of supplies or assistance. Both will be forthcoming once you take action." At the end of January, Chiang told a group of American newspaper editors that the Nationalists' return to the mainland was "fast approaching." A month later his vice president told the Legislative Yuan that "we must not wait idly for the Peiping regime to collapse. We must improve ourselves and destroy them with our own strength." These statements were accompanied by supportive editorials in the island's leading newspapers.

Although the Taiwanese took the campaign for the simple morale builder it was,* President John F. Kennedy, who was now in office and preferred ambiguity in the matter of Taiwan, was sufficiently alarmed to send Averell Harriman to secure the G-mo's promise that the Taiwanese government would consult with the United States and do nothing behind its back. Chiang, who informed Harriman that the Communist regime on the mainland was in a state of collapse, told the diplomat that he could assure Kennedy that any action taken would be "with full US knowledge" and that "nothing would be hidden."

Meanwhile, the G-mo did what he could to harass the Communists— gathering intelligence, sabotaging communications, and dropping guerrillas onto the mainland. Frogmen swam up the Min River to Fukien to blow up Communist ships and damage their harbors. Although Taiwan advertised the great achievements of these raids, they were rarely successful, and by the beginning of 1963, Chiang's government had to admit that 172 of its guerrillas had been killed. There was, however, one large group of guerrillas that did more than try to organize cells of resistance. In 1949, at the time that Communist troops were overrunning southern China, some 12,000 Nationalist soldiers had crossed the Chinese border into Burma. Four years later, in response to Burmese complaints and a U.N. resolution, Chiang agreed to remove his soldiers from foreign soil. Although close to seven thousand persons were brought to Taiwan—an evacuation paid for by the United States—it was noted that the new arrivals to the island were either very young or old. It seems that all the able-bodied young men had been left behind to tend the poppy fields and produce the opium that paid for military equipment. It was never established whether these men operated on their own or under the aegis of Chiang, although Crozier said that "the Nationalist government is involved in the opium traffic in the 'Golden Triangle' where Burma, Laos, and Thailand overlap." This state-

---

* About this time, T.V. wrote May-ling that, according to his sources, "W [Chiang] is talking blue streaks of invasion to keep up the spirits of his civilian and military." (HA: T. V. Soong papers, Box 63, Folder 33, T.V. Soong to Madame Chiang Kai-shek, April 27, 1963.)

ment, which appeared in one of two articles written for the London *Times* in 1973, would certainly go along with Chiang's old practice of funding his war against the Communists through the opium trade. It also underlines the fact that the generalissimo's objectives and methods were still those of a classic Chinese warlord.

53

We like to have a figure to center our interest and curiosity and adulation; something in the constitution of the American people lends itself to this setting up of an idol. Usually along with the hero-worship moves the undercurrent of criticism, a darker tide set in motion by jealousy and envy and malice.

—HELEN HULL

ALTHOUGH CHIANG and May-ling lost no opportunity to rail against the Communists, their presence on the mainland and in Russia served as a convenient excuse for the policy of political repression that continued to characterize the Chiang regime. In 1960, Lei Chen, a former Kuomintang official, poet, teacher, and editor of *Free China Fortnightly* who was sympathetic to the woes of native Formosans, tried to start a new party called the China Democratic Party. Lei apparently believed that his former connections with the KMT would keep him out of trouble, but his party lasted only the few days it took for him and his fellow members to be arrested. The order to imprison Lei came from the G-mo himself, acting in his capacity of head of the military. One of Lei's colleagues admitted that in 1953 he had attempted to win Lei over to the Communist cause, and, since Lei had not informed against the man, he too was treated like a Communist agent and interrogated for the better part of a month, while his writings, subjected to rigid examination, were naturally found to be subversive. When Chiang told some American journalists that Lei would be proven guilty of helping the Communists, he rendered the verdict with total confidence—in spite of the fact that Lei's trial was not scheduled to take place for three weeks. No lawyer dared represent Lei when he was brought to trial on charges of sedition and conspiracy to overthrow the government, charges that demanded the death penalty, but a kind judge sentenced him to only ten years' imprisonment. While there, he wrote a poem* of tragic resignation that resounded deeply with the Taiwanese and caused the magazine in which it appeared to be banned. Lei's wife, who had sneaked her husband's writing out of prison, was denied visiting rights, which were reinstated only after some traveling foreign dignitaries asked that she be allowed to see her husband once a month.

---

* See endnote.

A tragic corollary to the story of Lei Chen involves a young Taiwanese named Su Tung-chi, who signed a petition seeking mercy for Lei. A graduate of Meiji University in Tokyo, Su was thirty-nine years old with a wife and five young children. Security officers entered Su's home one morning at 2:00 A.M., took both adults away, and searched their home for "incriminating evidence," coming up with several old copies of Lei's *Free China Fortnightly*, and some copies of *Reader's Digest,* translated into Japanese.* Su was charged in a military court with plotting rebellion, sentenced, and presumably executed. His wife was given a life sentence. The rationale for cases like this and others was the imminent Communist threat to the island, but, according to a 1960 report by American intelligence, "The strength of the existing Communist undercover organization is . . . generally believed to be negligible."

A few years later, Professor Peng Ming-min, a former chairman of the Department of Political Science at National Taiwan University, and two of his former students were denounced by the printers they had hired to make 10,000 copies of antigovernment political tracts masquerading as examination papers. Sentenced to eight years in prison, Peng was pardoned six months later by Chiang under pressure from scholars around the world, including Henry Kissinger and John Fairbank. Peng later published an article asserting that the state of "national emergency" proclaimed during the Chinese Civil War in May 1949 had "suspended most of the guarantees and protections of individual rights and freedom written into the Chinese National Constitution" and had no basis in reality. "Clinging to the fiction that it is the sole legitimate government of all China, the Nationalist Government views the Communist victory in China as nothing but a 'state of Communist rebellion,'" he explained. Noting "the Government's tenacious refusal to accept reality," Peng called the emergency laws, still in effect twenty years after the Civil War, "grossly cynical devices to suspend the constitutional guarantees, deny political freedom and suppress the legitimate aspirations of the local population, all for the convenience of the authoritarian control of the regime." Among the most egregious provisions that Peng cited were statutes prohibiting public meetings, strikes, and demonstrations; the law that provided for offenders to be tried before military rather than civil courts; provisions calling for the death penalty for such crimes as circulating rumors, inciting riot, and disrupting the money market; and the payment of monetary rewards to "security agents, investigators, prosecutors and judges . . . in proportion to the severity of the sentence rendered."

While using the Communist bogey to clamp down on dissenters, Chiang

* The Japanese language was forbidden on Taiwan.

strengthened his efforts to maintain his government-in-exile as the legitimate representative of the Chinese in the United Nations. He was enabled to do this partly by latching onto the powerful position of the United States and partly by using Taiwan's technological superiority, a legacy from the Japanese, to help emerging African nations. He invited representatives from Africa to Taiwan to study new methods of agriculture and between 1960 and 1966 sent more than 630 experts to nineteen African countries to help them raise their rice yield. When the time came to vote for or against retaining Chiang's government as the representative of China at the United Nations, these countries felt obliged to support him.

In January 1964, however, General Charles de Gaulle announced that France would recognize the government of Communist China, and the next day, France and the USSR agreed to negotiate a five-year trade agreement. Infuriated, Madame allowed anger to override both her powers of reason and syntax, writing Clare Boothe Luce that the "French recognition of the Chinese Communists, opportunistic and unprincipled in its motives, was made among other reasons as part and parcel of a schema of defiance impregnated by an emotionalism of a special Gaulist brand of French grandeur bidding for hemispheric leadership." Within two weeks, Chiang broke off diplomatic relations with France. As he always did when he was in trouble, he sent May-ling to the United States. She left China in August of 1965 and, as before, stayed away for more than a year.

❦

WITH THE SILVER wings of a Nationalist air force officer pinned to her shoulder, Madame Chiang, according to *Newsweek*, "tiptoed gently down the gangway" at Travis Air Force Base in California. Inside the VIP guest lounge, Madame, "very much the same unruffled, stunningly attired, defeat-defying figure of decades ago," announced the theme of her trip: the return of the Nationalists to the mainland. After a rest at the St. Francis Hotel in San Francisco, she was driven to Chinatown, where "she appealed for support of the Formosa regime, whose popularity lately has been faltering among the American Chinese community." Then she was off to New York. Before leaving the airport she spoke to reporters, saying that she doubted that the Chinese Communists would deliberately get involved in a fight with the U.S. military. "I think Red China once considered the United States a paper tiger. But the fact that the United States has shown power has made them think twice. Now they think there is life in the paper tiger," she said, referring to the large numbers of troops the United States, now led by President Lyndon B. Johnson, was currently sending into Vietnam. The Nationalists, she asserted, were "very much concerned" about the Vietnam War. "What happens in Vietnam," she said "affects not only Southeast Asia, but Asia, Africa, Latin America and in time, the whole world."

There were ten cars in the motorcade that took Madame Chiang to T.V.'s apartment at 1133 Fifth Avenue.* For the first time, the G-mo's wife had eschewed the excuse of illness, and her trip to the U.S. was billed simply as a response to invitations from "many of her friends." Although she was now said to be sixty-seven years old and had had a gallstone removed the previous year, her voice, according to the reporter from *The New York Times*, was "cheery," her step was "sprightly," and she "demonstrated that she had lost none of her purposeful drive." Certainly, she wasted no time delivering her message, calling immediately on arrival for the destruction of atomic plants on mainland China. The fact that the People's Republic of China possessed the atom bomb "jeopardizes the position of every nation in the world," she said. "We should try to cut out the cancer before it permeates any further."

The article in the *Times* describing Madame's arrival was followed some days later by an irate letter to the editor from the president of United Formosans for Independence, complaining about May-ling's "warmongering statement." "The toll of American lives," he wrote, "would be hundreds of times greater than in Vietnam. Millions of Chinese people also would die. Is such human sacrifice worth making to satisfy the ambitions of a small band of Nationalist leaders? . . . The recovery of the Chinese mainland is a lost cause," he declared, calling for elections to form a new government representative of the inhabitants of the island. "The days of Chiang Kai-shek have been over for nearly twenty years."

An article on May-ling herself, entitled "Many-Sided Empress," also followed a few days after her arrival. Describing her as "dainty but formidable" and referring to her as "the charming eloquent courageous personification of 'Free China,' " the anonymous author of the piece did not hesitate to add that for May-ling's detractors, "she is the Dragon Lady, imperious and calculating. East and West are blended in her personality—or, more accurately, her personalities . . . she can be the poised Wellesley alumna, the haughty empress, the hard-boiled politician, the lady patriot, even the coquettish Georgia belle."

---

* When he first tried to buy this apartment, T.V. was turned down by the board of directors of the cooperative building for no apparent reason except the obvious one that he was Chinese. He then asked former Treasury Secretary Henry Morgenthau, Jr., to write a letter of recommendation to the board. Morgenthau complied with a letter, giving his "personal guarantee" that Mr. and Mrs. Soong would not open a Chinese laundry in the building. (Story from Henry Morgenthau, Jr.'s, son, Robert Morgenthau.)

Two days later, Madame Chiang could be seen riding "triumphantly" on Chinatown's Mott Street in a bubble-topped limousine, led by a marching band. In response to rumors of possible trouble, the FBI had alerted the New York Police Department, and what one reporter described as a "wedge of plainsclothesmen" from the department "hustled" Madame through the crowd to a basement auditorium at the Chinese Community Center.

Dressed in a beige silk suit with ankle-length skirt and long white gloves, she seemed smooth and unflappable—until she was told that there were conflicting versions of her age. "What does it matter whether I am 64 or 67* or something else?" she shot back. "You can tell the age of a person not by the calendar but by his or her purpose in life, character and willingness to be of service to the world."

Madame's own purpose came under scrutiny in the next article about her visit, as the press, which had grown more skeptical of her motives over the years, described her arrival in Washington, D.C., in a private railway car as the "once familiar figure . . . charmingly eloquent, politically forceful" woman on "a mission wrapped in feminine and perhaps diplomatic mystery." Her reception, the reporter wrote, "was a far cry from those of a decade and more ago when she swept into town as the courageous personification of 'free China.' " This time, she was met in the capital by 250 members of the Washington Chinese community, including Miss Chinatown of 1965, but the only American greeters of note were Mrs. Dean Rusk, wife of the secretary of state, and Lloyd Hand, chief of protocol. They left with her in a White House limousine and dropped her at the Shoreham Hotel, where she occupied the Presidential Suite.

No one seemed to be able to figure out why Madame Chiang had come to the nation's capital or whether she would be able to see President Johnson or Secretary of State Rusk, until one official at the Chinese Embassy leaked the fact that she was to have tea with Lady Bird and dinner with the Rusks. When asked by reporters about the purpose of her trip, she repeated "somewhat sharply" that she had been "invited here by many friends." Protestations to the contrary, it was clear that she had come on a mission. "The only surmise," said the reporter, "is that the Generalissimo is concerned that Nationalist Chinese interests are being neglected in the American preoccupation with Vietnam and has sent his wife to spread the message that Nationalist China and South Vietnam are both parts of the same struggle with Communist China."

Madame Chiang, still numbered in 1965 by the Gallup Poll as one of

---

* She was sixty-eight or, by Chinese reckoning (they consider a newborn already one year old), sixty-nine.

the "10 Most Admired Women in the World," gave eighteen major speeches in the United States in a little over a year. "It will be a test of her notable eloquence and charm," one *Times* reporter wrote, "for there may not be too attentive an audience for a voice of a past which many would just as soon remain forgotten." But May-ling had apparently not lost her appeal. President Johnson, who dropped in just to say hello while she was being entertained at a small tea party by the first lady, took her on a tour of the White House himself. The Johnsons welcomed her in spite of the fact that a few years earlier, when he was vice president, the Chiangs had been "very curt and cold" to both of them when they arrived in Taiwan, assuming they had been sent to "lecture them on the way they were doing things and cut back on . . . aid."

From Taiwan, the G-mo reinforced his wife's efforts. In an interview with Hanson Baldwin of *The New York Times,* Chiang declared that the Vietnam War was unwinnable in Vietnam "no matter how many troops" the United States sent in and that it "must be won elsewhere." Declaring that the South Vietnamese had "indicated" that they would be happy for help from Taiwan over and above the technical, agricultural, and economic assistance the island had been providing, Chiang claimed that they would never ask directly or officially, because they understood that U.S. policy opposed the use of Taiwanese troops in Vietnam. "There is very little our forces could do as long as you remain on the defensive," he told the American reporter, adding that 600,000 Taiwanese soldiers were keeping half a million Chinese Communist troops out of the Vietnam War on the mainland opposite the island.

Back in New York, May-ling once again made the mistake of relying on David Kung and his sister Jeanette for assistance in her mission. They even managed to alienate Elizabeth Luce Moore, turning down her invitation to Madame Chiang for a visit to the China Institute. "She [Moore] has now gone to Europe in a huff," Emma wrote in her journal, "as has her brother Henry Luce, & said that neither the China Institute or United Services to China would take part in a large joint Waldorf dinner being considered by the China organizations—and Moore controls both boards. Dr. George Armstrong, recently chosen ABMAC [American Bureau for Medical Aid to China] president, had written Mayling & received an unsatisfactory reply from David. A second letter hasn't been answered. Why did she hedge herself in with these two?" Whether it was the influence of the Kung siblings or her own actions, May-ling seems to have made quite a few enemies on this trip. The executive assistant of ABMAC complained to Emma that Madame Chiang was "doing more harm than good here. Soon stories will appear that she had better go home." Emma did not disagree, confiding to her journal that her friend "certainly is a spoiled brat in many ways, & inconsiderate in her demands, no realization of what it means to the other fellow. She feels free to call upon just about anybody, disregarding their assigned duties."

While in the United States, Chiang's wife paid a visit to her old alma mater, Wellesley College. Since plans had been made for three meals to be given there in her honor, a letter arrived informing the president of the college that Madame was "allergic to alcohol, all seafood, parsley, peaches, strawberries and all spices." She received a standing ovation before launching into her standard speech on "ambivalent thinking," which, she contended, aided the imperialistic ambitions of the Communists. Dubbed by *The Boston Globe* "a kind of Mother Courage of anti-communism," she was a recipient—along with General Omar Bradley, Walter Judd, Cardinal Mindszenty, and other sufficiently conservative figures—of the Order of Lafayette, an honor given by officers who had served in France at their annual dinner in New York. The awards were presented by Colonel Hamilton Fish, president of the order, for "distinguished leadership in combating communism."

In early March of 1966, the *Times* reported that Chiang Kai-shek was running unopposed for his fourth term as president of the Chinese Nationalist government. Claiming that he would prefer to retire but was "prepared to bear without complaint the burden of the heaviest duties and to face the severest trials and tribulations," the generalissimo made history, becoming the longest-ruling dictator of modern times, outlasting even Stalin by fifteen years. In spite of the fact that he was now in his early eighties, the subject of who would take over when he died was taboo. "No one dares mention the topic," said one young member of the KMT, ". . . no preparations have been made for a day which could be tomorrow." Moreover, elections continued to be rigged through pressure on opposition candidates, which forced them to withdraw; restrictions on campaign activities; and the stuffing of ballot boxes.

In April, Chiang issued a statement saying that capture of the mainland could be accomplished by the Nationalist Chinese if the United States would only give him the tools he needed to do the job. "We can return to the mainland with our own forces alone," Chiang told an AP reporter. "There is no need for American combat troops. We do not want to bring the United States into any war. On the mainland it is between us and the Chinese Communists. We have enough strength once we reach the mainland." Chiang's reasoning was based on his wishful thinking that the minute the Nationalist forces hit the beach, they would be greeted with cheers by their compatriots, disillusioned with the Communist regime. The fact that the United States was unwilling to lift the lid off Nationalist forces continued to rankle the G-mo. Both he and May-ling tried to explain that the United States was repeating in Vietnam the mistakes it had made during the Korean War, when it had refused to allow MacArthur to use Chinese troops or bomb the Chinese mainland. In June, Chiang even sent Ching-kuo to Washington to see Secretary of Defense Robert McNamara to promote his newest plan of capturing five southwestern provinces—a plan that, Ching-kuo confided to an acquaintance, he himself did not endorse.

At his inaugural, Chiang, borrowing General MacArthur's self-reverential characterization when he was fired by Truman, described himself as an old soldier "indifferent to name and position and oblivious to fame and slander. I have often lived in suffering, humiliation, danger, false accusations, enemy infiltration and subversion and narrow escapes from death," he said. "I have scored many successes but I have also met with many defeats. All these experiences of successes and failures and precarious living and narrow escapes have made me an undiscouraged old soldier."

This and various other announcements emanating from Taiwan reminded Americans of the continued presence of their long-term guest, Madame Chiang, who had not gone home, as they might have expected, to attend her husband's inauguration. Instead, she continued to do quite a bit of speechifying, traveling to the Midwest, where she spoke in Detroit, Grosse Pointe, Chicago, and Lincoln, Nebraska, on subjects dear to her heart: Peiping's desire to keep the United States involved in Vietnam so Washington would not focus on the Chinese Communists' attempts to take over the world; her objection to current liberal tendencies of the American government toward criminals, as exemplified in the Miranda decision;* and, of course, the necessity of keeping Red China out of the United Nations.

But political speeches, sentimental journeys, and extraneous awards did not seem enough of an excuse for such a lengthy sojourn. An article titled "Mystery Shrouds Mrs. Chiang Here" appeared in the Times in April of 1966, questioning the reason for her visit and reporting that she had just moved into a luxury apartment on the East River owned by her nephew and special assistant, Louis Kung. "Informed observers" commented that "Mrs. Chiang may be trying to persuade the Administration to support nationalist troop landings on the Chinese mainland as part of a general escalation of the war in South Vietnam."

Six months later, in October of 1966, Senator William Fulbright of Arkansas asked the State Department to advise the Senate of "the precise

---

* The Miranda decision declares that suspects cannot be interrogated before being informed of their rights.

status" of Madame's sojourn in the United States and explain "under what auspices she has come to seek to influence our foreign policy." The State Department replied that she was in the United States on a private visit. But Fulbright was not far off the mark. Before she left the country, the G-mo's wife wrote Secretary of State Dean Rusk a lengthy letter, saying that in spite of "certain elements in the American public" that were trying to get Communist China into the United Nations, she knew she could "take comfort in the knowledge that in the midst of certain muddy thinking and rash proposals, your wisdom and experience make you a tower of strength helping President Johnson to steer the United States China policy along the right course with calmness and vision."

The letter was dated October 23, 1966, the day she left the United States to go home.

54

Taiwan . . . is the unresolved last chapter of China's civil war, or a flagrant example of American interference in China's internal affairs.

—Joseph Lelyveld, 1975

Madame's visit to the United States was followed immediately by that of her stepson Ching-kuo. In June 1965, the U.S. aid program for Taiwan had come to an end, and the timing of both trips—she left Taipei in August—clearly had to do with the cessation of economic support. Since 1950, the United States had given the island over $1.4 billion, the largest sum of money it had bestowed per person on any country. By 1965, Taiwanese per capita income was the second highest in the world next to Japan's, and during that year alone, the United States also spent some $130 million in military purchases from the islanders.

By 1966, it had become clear that Ching-Kuo (called "the Prince" by the staff at the U.S. Embassy) was now the man to be reckoned with in Taiwan. Although the Americans continued to refuse his father's offer of Chinese troops for Vietnam, Ching-kuo, as the new Taiwanese minister of defense, had already established a Special Warfare Center in Indochina. The third largest foreign contingent on Vietnamese soil, it helped the government of General Nguyen Van Thieu and supported the air activities of the CIA. As Taylor put it, the generalissimo's son "had been the country's real CEO—except for the key areas of economic and financial affairs" for some time. Chiang Kai-shek, now seventy-eight, had begun to recede into the background. His eyesight was failing, and his staff, who read his papers for him, made it their business to protect him even more (if that were possible) from unpleasant facts. The G-mo loved, however, to talk about Vietnam: the problems, the military tactics employed, and most of all, the Communists' use of underground tunnels, which, he said, he himself had encountered during the Civil War.

After his new appointment, Ching-kuo had moved his family into a larger home, cut down on his drinking, and, some say, even stopped his affairs with other women. There was still nothing in his mode of living to suggest luxury or grandeur. The fruit in his home was almost always rotten, because Ching-kuo ate the old fruit first, leaving the fresh produce to spoil.

He had a cook who was forced to take a second part-time job because he received so little salary. A diabetic, Chiang's son ignored all the rules against eating sweets and getting checkups. To avoid the appearance of impropriety or profiteering from his position, he did not allow his sons to enter private business—an obvious reaction to the accusations that continued to dog his father's relatives by marriage.* At both Thanksgiving and Christmas May-ling continued to entertain the family, its offspring, and the Young Marshal with his longtime mistress, whom he had married after converting to Christianity.

Madame Chiang had never lost her fondness for children—nor her unhappiness at not having produced any of her own. "She was devastated," according to her nephew Leo Soong. "She said she had had some problem. She was always talking about a doctor in Nanking or Chungking who 'essentially sterilized her' in an operation. She loved children, and I know she wanted to have children." Faced with reality, however, May-ling managed to find solace in her nieces and nephews—whether it was the older Kung offspring, who provided her with assistance in daily life, or the younger children of her brother T.A., who spent summers with their aunt and to whom she wrote delightful letters, sprinkled with drawings substituted for words. "She was very playful, we had a very good time with her," Leo said.

Not all May-ling's family relationships were so easy. K. C. Wu claimed that Madame and her stepson Ching-kuo were "continually at loggerheads with each other." Dr. Wu said that Madame Chiang had always been "very nice to me and my wife personally. But I think the real reason that she supported me . . . was that she knew that I did not agree with Ching-kuo in the matter of political policies." In a letter to T.V., May-ling complained that on one of Ching-kuo's early trips to the United States, he had neglected to toast President Kennedy or even stand up to speak, thus preventing his host from offering any toasts and Dean Rusk from giving the speech he had prepared for the evening. "Such a breach of protocol is really unheard of," she claimed. Although Chiang Kai-shek had continued to try to bring his wife and son together, his efforts were offset by Jeanette Kung, who had enormous influ-

---

* Ching-kuo's eldest son worked at the Taiwan Power Company, his second son was interested in politics, and the youngest entered military school. His daughter married a man who had been divorced three times and was eighteen years her senior. Around 1941, Ching-kuo had started an affair with his secretary, and in May of 1942, she gave birth to twin sons. Six months or so later the children's mother died under highly mysterious circumstances, and the boys were raised by their grandmother. Since Chiang Kai-shek had proposed that the boys take their mother's name, few people outside the intimate family even knew of their existence until John Chang entered politics.

ence over Auntie May and never agreed with Ching-kuo about anything. A noticable improvement, however, had taken place in the stepmother-son relationship in 1949, when they were both worried about Chiang Kai-shek's surviving the victory of the Communists. At the time, May-ling was in the United States looking for support, and through frequent cables back and forth, some sort of understanding had been established between them.

Although Chiang's adopted son, Ching Wei-kuo, attended family functions with his second wife, he had virtually disappeared from the political scene. Wei-kuo's first wife had died after a miscarriage, and in 1957 he married Ellen Cui, who was half Chinese and half German. Named to the operations bureau in the Ministry of Defense, Wei-kuo worked there briefly before being sent to the United States to attend the U.S. Army Air Defense School. He was given little or no responsibility on his return, and his career came to a sudden, dramatic halt with the appointment of General Chao Chih-hua as his successor as commander of the 1st Armored Division. General Chao, a former prisoner of the Communists whose loyalty Wei-kuo had guaranteed, scuttled Wei-kuo's chances for military or political advancement by assembling the troops of the armored division and announcing that they were to drive their tanks to Taipei and take over the government. The G-mo, Chao claimed, was not working vigorously enough against the Chinese Communists. The soldiers—there were several thousand of them—were apparently shocked into inaction, but a senior political officer climbed up on the platform, grabbed hold of Chao, and threw him to the floor, thus ending his "two-minute coup." Chao's action led to nothing but the destruction of Wei-kuo's position with his stepfather and the hierarchy of the KMT.

Oddly enough, Wei-kuo had better rapport with the Taiwanese than Ching-kuo did, partially because he was "a conventional military officer," a joiner (the Elks, the Rotary Club, the Masons), and an "effective public speaker." Wei-kuo's wife also got along better with Madame Chiang than the wife of Ching-kuo. She liked fashion as much as May-ling, who was proud of her figure—"Look, Dr. Xiong," she told Chiang's personal physician, "I can wear my clothes from thirty years ago!"—and the two ladies continued to discuss clothing and hairstyles well after May-ling reached her seventies and eighties.

While Wei-kuo's political star eclipsed, Ching-kuo's rose. In the spring of 1965, President Johnson sent the first American fighting troops into combat in Vietnam.* While Madame Chiang was quoted praising the American president for taking "such a firm stand," and Chiang was insisting yet again that the time to attack the mainland was "now or never," Ching-kuo re-

---

* They had previously been identified as technical advisers.

mained attached to reality. "While the Nationalist Government must nour-
ish the hope of returning to the mainland in order to sustain morale on the
island of Taiwan," he said, "the key men of my generation realize that it may
be a long time before a non-Communist regime can be re-established in
Mainland China—perhaps not in their lifetimes . . . the young generation of
leaders . . . feel their primary aim . . . and strategy should be to maintain an
intimate and cooperative understanding with the United States and to support U.S. policy in East Asia."

On March 22, 1966, Seymour Topping of *The New York Times* wrote from
Taipei that Chiang had not only won a fourth term in office but had been
given the power to bypass the Legislative Yuan and rule by executive decree.
The rationale for this was that the generalissimo needed new powers to suppress "the Communist rebellion." Since these powers had been granted to
him nearly twenty years earlier, the real reason behind the vote was an at-
tempt to control the succession after his death. To guarantee Chiang's wishes,
C. K. Yen, the sixty-one-year-old premier, who had played a large role in
Taiwan's economic success, was elected vice president because Ching-kuo,
Chiang's chosen successor, was only fifty-six at the time, too young by Chinese standards to take over if his father died during his six-year term. C. K.
Yen notwithstanding, there were now just two men who counted in Taiwan:
Chiang Kai-shek, because he employed the actors, and Chiang Ching-kuo,
because he controlled the arm of the government that ferreted out and ne-
gated anyone whom the government even suspected of disagreeing with its
policy or methods.

The Chinese Nationalist government also began buying U.S. naval vessels and airplanes to increase its forces. Up until then, the Taiwanese navy
was estimated to be capable of transporting little more than one division
of soldiers across the strait, but with the new vessels it could get two battalions and an airborne regiment over the one hundred miles of ocean. Chiang
had convinced himself that a combination of the Cultural Revolution, which
started in April 1966, and the escalation of the Vietnam War (there were currently some 400,000 to 500,000 American troops on the ground) would
yield new opportunities for an assault, and he was currently spending
$2.00 on the Nationalist military for every $1.00 received from the United
States.

By late 1966, when May-ling returned to Taiwan from the United States,
the infamous Red Guards were on the rampage on the mainland. The horrors of the Cultural Revolution initially encouraged the G-mo, who announced that the Nationalist government would respond to a request for
assistance from mainlanders within six hours. There were reports that sister
Ching-ling's home had been vandalized by the Guards, who had also dese-

crated a shrine dedicated to Sun Yat-sen and the graves of the "bourgeois" Soong parents.* Up until this point, it seems, Ching-ling had been insulated from the common privations of life behind the Iron Curtain. With two security men detailed to her house at all times, she had been free to do her social and charity work and supervise the hospital in Shanghai named after her. Now the Red Guards entered her home and threatened to cut her hair down to the Communist-favored short bob. "If they cut my hair, I'll cut theirs off," she responded, referring to their heads. (She had promised her mother never to change her traditional style of a bun in the back.) In spite of this, May-ling's sister remained remarkably tolerant of the Cultural Revolution until the day Mao sent his wife, Chiang Ching, to explain it to her. The leader of the Gang of Four "took a didactic tone" with Ching-ling, "praised the Red Guards to the skies," and "turned sullen when Soong said there should be some check on their harming innocent people." Later, in writing to a friend, the Soong family Communist referred to Chiang Ching as "that shameless slut." Meanwhile, the Red Guards burned down the British Embassy in Peking and, claiming that Soviet "social imperialism" was as bad as "American imperialism," began to harass diplomats from Russia.

There was another aspect to this Sino-Soviet break, which had started some years earlier over border disputes and wound up in an all-out competition for the leadership of the Communist world. What worried the Taiwanese was an obvious and growing interest in Washington in establishing a relationship with Peking now that it was no longer allied to Moscow. The Senate Foreign Relations Committee had begun talking about "containment without isolation" for China, saying that the goal of the United States should be to include it in the community of nations. The CIA decreased the size of its Taiwanese station, cut back on its support of Ching-kuo's covert operations, and canceled several sorties aimed at the mainland. Even though the U-2 overflights continued, it was "apparent," according to one observer, that the Amerian and Taiwanese secret services "began to watch each other as much as they cooperated."

It fell to Madame Chiang to make one last-ditch effort to rope the Americans into supporting the Nationalists' plans for invading the mainland. Early in April, Senator Harry F. Byrd came to Taiwan and met with the G-mo, his wife, and his son. According to a report from the U.S. Embassy in

---

* Chou En-lai, who was not only Ching-ling's friend but realized her symbolic importance to the party, stepped in to stop the harassment, issuing an order that said, "It is absolutely forbidden to attack Comrade Soong Ching-ling." Moreover the Soong parents' graves were restored to her satisfaction and guards were sent to patrol the graveyard and her homes. (Jung Chang, *Mme. Sun Yat-sen*, pp. 124–25.)

Taipei, during their conversation Madame Chiang "made a major plea for U.S. supporting the GRC [Government of the Republic of China]'s return to the mainland. She said only U.S. logistic support was needed for the GRC to upset the Communist regime. She claimed that now is the moment to move. . . . She claimed that no American lives would be lost and only a moderate amount of logistic support was required since the populace on the mainland would turn on their Communist rulers when GRC support was at hand." But Senator Byrd "strongly discouraged" Madame, explaining that "the American people were not prepared for the risks of such an undertaking. He said that the American people already had in Vietnam a deeper involvement in combat than they had anticipated and that they would be unwilling to make additional large scale military commitments, which he was convinced would be required." In conclusion, he "complimented the Madame on her persuasive presentation," saying that the United States would certainly support its defense treaty commitments but no more.

Nevertheless, when former Vice President Nixon arrived in Taipei at the end of April 1967, he said he too got "something of a pitch concerning the mainland" from Chiang. The G-mo told Nixon he thought the United States "should carefully consider the case" for a Nationalist attack, to which Nixon replied that "it was unthinkable that the U.S. could underwrite" such a venture and that the United States "cannot possibly under present circumstances provide the needed support." The future president—he would be elected the following year—pointed to the danger of the United States becoming involved in a "long and inconclusive war on the mainland" that the American people would never support, adding that such actions "might cause Peiping and Moscow to close ranks" against Taiwan and the United States. Nixon said he found the G-mo "in a cordial and animated mood" when they met over a three-hour lunch, at which they were joined by Madame Chiang, who interpreted and "occasionally" participated in the discussion. "It would have been impossible to find a better interpreter than the Wellesley-educated Madame Chiang," Nixon commented. "In addition to her easy eloquence . . . she knew her husband's thinking so thoroughly that she could interpolate accurately when an expression or term in one language had no precisely corresponding form in the other. . . . I believe Madame's Chiang's intelligence, persuasiveness, and moral force could have made her an important leader in her own right."

When Nixon took office in January 1969, he was known as a supporter of the Nationalist government, as well as a personal friend of the Chiangs and Madame's nephew Louis Kung.* Nevertheless, the Chiangs were pain-

---

* Louis Kung had not only worked with the China Lobby to elect Nixon but had encouraged him when he was defeated for U.S. president and governor of California, mak-

fully aware that the new president of the United States had written an article two years earlier for *Foreign Affairs* magazine saying that other countries, especially the United States, must not allow mainland China to remain a pariah in the community of nations. According to Nixon, the time had come for the United States to look beyond the war in Vietnam. "Asia, not Europe or Latin America," he said, "will pose the greatest danger of a confrontation which could escalate into World War III. . . . we simply cannot afford to leave China forever outside the family of nations. . . . The world cannot be safe until China changes. Thus our aim . . . should be to induce change. . . . For the short run . . . this means a policy of firm restraint. . . . For the long run, it means pulling China back into the world community."

During his first year in office President Nixon outlined the Guam Doctrine (later called the Nixon Doctrine), in which it was stated that although the United States would continue to provide material and economic support to its friends and allies who were fighting the Communists, those friends and allies must assume the primary responsibility for their own defense. Shortly thereafter, he and his national security advisor, Henry Kissinger, began making small moves to ease tensions with the Chinese Communists, both for the reasons stated above and as one step toward ending the Vietnam War. By the end of the year, U.S. companies were allowed to trade "nonstrategic" goods with the People's Republic of China, and the U.S. Seventh Fleet was no longer patrolling the strait between Taiwan and the mainland.

Washington's new, conciliatory attitude toward Communist China and a noticable breach between the United States and its Chinese Nationalist allies—the slippage was widening by the month—resulted in an official trip made by Ching-kuo in the spring of 1970 to determine what Nixon was planning vis-à-vis Peking. Described by the U.S. Embassy in Taipei as "a rather enigmatic figure" with a "quick grasp of economic problems" and "a vague egalitarianism and populist concern for the common man," the G-mo's son, recently named deputy premier by his father and now de facto leader of the Taiwanese, arrived in Washington. Unlike his stepmother-in-law, Ching-kuo received royal treatment: a room at Blair House, the official White House guest residence; an hour and a half with Nixon in the Oval Office; a private half hour with Kissinger, who was said to have walked across Pennsylvania Avenue from the White House for that purpose; and meetings with the secretaries of state and defense. All these men assured Ching-kuo that their "exploratory" talks with the Chinese Communists would not affect U.S. friendship for Taiwan.

---

ing him, according to a letter from T.V. to May-ling at the time Nixon became president, "our most precious asset." (HA: T. V. Soong files, Box 63, Folder 33, draft of a letter, T.V. to Madame Chiang Kai-shek, March 22, 1969.)

But a few months later, in the fall of 1970, Washington proposed setting up a hotline with Peking, and for the first time President Nixon used the official name "People's Republic of China" in referring to the government on the mainland. Responding to U.S. overtures, Mao informed delegates to the Central Committee meeting of the PRC that China's most dangerous enemy was now the USSR and that his government and the United States had begun negotiations to reestablish relations between their two countries. Topping explained Peking's enthusiasm for rapprochement this way: "Since the mid-sixties the Chinese Communists had been plagued by a nightmare of encirclement by the Soviet Union, India, Japan and the United States. In the months before the Nixon visit, the anxieties in Peking sharpened, and there was more preoccupation with the dangers, real or imagined, of the encirclement and dismemberment of China than with the quarrel over Taiwan." Moreover, according to Chang and Halliday, Mao wanted an excuse "to relaunch himself on the international stage."

On April 6, 1971, in a happening that came to be known as Ping-Pong diplomacy, a young American Ping-Pong player walked over to speak with the Chinese team at a tournament in Japan. What was meant as an apolitical gesture of friendship was taken by the ever-subtle Chinese as an official indication of a desire for rapprochement. They reacted by inviting the American team to China, and four days later, nine players, two spouses, four officials, and ten reporters became the first Americans to officially set foot on the mainland since 1949. The trip included an exhibition match (the Americans lost), a visit to the Great Wall, a performance by the Canton Ballet, and a banquet in the Great Hall of the People, hosted by Premier Chou En-lai, who told his guests that they had "opened a new chapter in the relations of the American and Chinese people."

In spite of this warming trend, Richard Nixon and Henry Kissinger kept their ongoing negotiations with the Chinese Communists under wraps. The president, who had first visited Taipei in 1953 and established a rapport with the Chiangs, was still concerned about the effect of his future trip on them, and during the first week in July he sent Don Kendall, the chairman of Pepsi-Cola, to Taiwan with an oral message for the G-mo: "Whatever the future may hold, I'll never forget my old friend."* Days later, on July 9, 1971, Kissinger made his secret trip to Peking to confer with Chou, performing

---

* Nixon and Kendall had helped each other in the past as well. Kendall owed the fact that he had not been fired as president of the company to a photograph taken at the American Trade Exhibition in Moscow in 1959 (the scene of the famous Kitchen Debate) showing Nikita Khrushchev and Nixon both drinking Pepsi. Conversely, when Nixon's law firm won the Pepsi-Cola account, one of Nixon's biographers says that it

what one Nixon biographer called "a verbal conjuring trick of consummate skill." They agreed that the United States would acknowledge that Taiwan was a part of China and would begin to withdraw its military forces from Taiwan "as the tension in the area diminishes," i.e., as the Chinese reduced their support for the North Vietnamese. Kissinger offered to support Communist China's admission to the United Nations but said the United States would also support Taiwan's effort to keep its seat in the organization. Half an hour before Kissinger's secret departure from the mainland capital, Nixon went on the air to apprise the world of this astonishing rapprochement—news the Taiwanese Foreign Ministry received via the American ambassador. The next day the KMT and independent newspapers on the island complained that the Nationalists could no longer trust the United States, and the National Assembly accused President Nixon of "betrayal." According to the China News Service, "This country is angry and justifiably so. President Nixon has treated us shabbily without cause. He has been less than frank with an ally. He is consorting with the enemy at a time when our United Nations seat is seriously challenged."

On July 17, Chiang received a personal message from Nixon:

> I deeply regret that I was not able to inform you at an earlier date of the substance of my announcement of July 15. . . . I recognize that these actions are disturbing to the Republic of China. In seeking to reduce tensions in the world, however, I wish to assure you that the United States will maintain its ties of friendship with your country and will continue to honor its defense treaty commitment to the Republic of China. I am proud of my long personal association with you, and I know the American people will continue to cherish their friendship with the people of the Republic of China.

Years later, Kissinger echoed the sentiments of the president. "I felt sorry for what we had to do to them," he told the author, "but we had to do it." The month after Kissinger's trip, the U.S. proposal of dual representation for China in the United Nations elicited a sour response from Chiang Kai-shek, who claimed that he would rather be "a broken jade on the ground than a whole tile on the roof." As former supporters of Nationalist China "rushed to embrace Peking," Taiwan agreed to give up its seat on the Security Council in order to remain in the world body; this decision, Taylor said, came from Ching-kuo, since his father's health was growing steadily worse. On October

---

was "directly attributable" to their friendship and Nixon's help (probably through the Chiangs) in setting up Pepsi franchises on Taiwan. (Jonathan Aitken, *Nixon*, p. 310.)

25, 1971, the U.N. General Assembly voted to seat the PRC and to "expel the representatives of Chiang Kai-shek"—a development that May-ling blamed on Ching-kuo, apparently refusing to communicate with him for some time thereafter. Although the United States made a show of lobbying for Taiwan, it was noted that on the day of the General Assembly's vote, Kissinger was back in Peking making plans for Nixon's historic trip. Two weeks earlier, Nixon, who said that his "personal friendship" with the Chiangs made "the rapprochement with Peking . . . a profoundly wrenching personal experience for me," had sent California Governor Ronald Reagan to Taipei, ostensibly for the annual celebration of the Double Tenth, but in fact to inform the generalissimo of the president's plans to go to China himself.

Before Nixon traveled to China in February 1972, he sent another conciliatory message to Chiang Kai-shek, and Ching-kuo assured the U.S. ambassador in Taipei that his government would make no "unusual movements or actions" that might lead to an unfortunate incident. Although there was television coverage of Nixon's arrival in China, there was no broadcast of the first meeting between the U.S. president and Mao Tse-tung, hence no public airing of one of Mao and Chou's first exchanges with Nixon and Kissinger:

Chairman Mao:	Our common old friend, Generalissimo Chiang Kai-shek, doesn't approve of this. . . . He calls us Communist bandits. . . .
President Nixon:	Chiang Kai-shek calls the Chairman a bandit. What does the Chairman call Chiang Kai-shek?
Prime Minister Chou:	Generally speaking we call them Chiang Kai-shek's clique. In the newspapers sometimes we call him a bandit, we are also called bandits in turn. Anyway, we abuse each other.
Chairman Mao:	Actually, the history of our friendship with him is much longer than the history of your friendship with him.
President Nixon:	Yes, I know.

Taiwan was clearly on the minds of the participants, and both Nixon and Kissinger went to "some length" to reassure the Chinese that the United

States would not support any Nationalist movement toward independence. "I told the Prime Minister," Kissinger said, "that no American personnel . . . will give any encouragement or support in any way to the Taiwan Independence Movement. . . . What we cannot do is use our forces to suppress the movement on Taiwan if it develops without our support." President Nixon said much the same thing in a communiqué, issued albeit in private, that affirmed "the ultimate objective of the withdrawal of all U.S. forces and military installations from Taiwan." Communist China emerged from the talks, according to Topping, no longer menaced by both the United States and Russia, while the latter "had been nudged into a triangular relationship with China and the United States in which it would have to weigh new risk factors before making an overt move against either of the two other powers," an "inhibition" that was good for the United States as well.

After Nixon flew home from Shanghai, the assistant secretary of state for East Asian affairs and one of Kissinger's assistants flew to various Asian capitals in an attempt to relieve concerns other nations might have over the presidential visit. Among these was, of course, Taipei, where the envoys held a "long and cordial meeting" with Ching-kuo. He assured them that he was not "too disturbed" as long as the Mutual Security Treaty of 1954* remained in force and U.S. military aid continued. As one of the Americans put it, "Our relationship with them will continue because they have nowhere else to go." At eighty-four, Chiang Kai-shek was less forgiving. His inaugural address of May 1972 was a grim one, in which he complained of being confined to his island. "One step backward," he said, "would leave us no place for burial." It was for this reason, Chiang claimed, that he had "summoned the courage and determination to accept this office, despite my advanced age and the gravity of the duties and responsibilities."

⚊⚊

NOT LONG AFTER this, on May 26, 1972, Ching-kuo became premier. In an effort to forestall America's inevitable diplomatic switch from Taipei to Peking, Ching-kuo invited a number of VIPs and reporters to visit Taiwan, and he increased purchases of U.S. military equipment. Between 1971 and 1978, exports and imports between the United States and Taiwan zoomed— from $1.3 billion to $7.4 billion.† Stressing administrative reform on the island, he named native Taiwanese as governor of the island, vice premier,

---

* A pact signed by the United States and Taiwan in October 1954 after a crisis on Quemoy in which the United States committed to defending Taiwan providing that Chiang agreed not to attack the mainland.

† $1,300,000,000 = $6,900,000,000 in today's dollars, $7,400,000,000 = $24,430, 000,000.

interior minister, and minister of communications. At his first cabinet meeting, he set down Ten Rules of Reform, in which officials were no longer allowed to patronize "girlie restaurants" or give extravagant weddings and funerals. He cracked down on bribes and other abuses of office, and more than fifty government officials were arrested for smuggling.

While Ching-kuo was steering the Taiwanese government toward the left, Madame Chiang, whose husband was clearly dying, was forced to limit her political activities to local organizations like her Women's League. The absence of political work and power at such a pivotal time in the affairs of Taiwan and the Kuomintang must have been very hard on her.

55

❦

It was clear that—in death as in life—the Generalissimo's heart was not in Taiwan.

—JAY TAYLOR

ON AUGUST 15, 1967, May-ling's brother-in-law H. H. Kung died in New York at the age of eighty-six, and a memorial was held in Taipei at which Chiang Kai-shek gave the eulogy. Dedicated to resurrecting Kung's tarnished reputation at the expense of T. V. Soong, the G-mo attributed two of T.V.'s major accomplishments—"establishment of a uniform national currency" and "unification of the financial systems of the provinces"—to Kung. Claiming that Kung had "made a larger contribution to the fight against Japan than anyone else," Chiang blamed Kung's resignation on the Communists, who had "left no stone unturned in spreading rumors to dupe the people. . . . It was self-evident that Dr. Kung was a man of integrity," the G-mo continued, "not of corruption; and that he was competent, not incompetent. Once he was out of office, the nation's finances and economy fell apart and the Communist plot to overthrow the government succeeded in less than three years." According to *The New York Times,* however, the truth was the exact opposite: "When Mr. Kung left China in 1947 for retirement in the United States he left behind an economic disaster the Communists soon turned to account."

Less than two years later, at the end of February 1969, May-ling's youngest brother, T.A., chairman of the Bank of Canton, died of a brain hemorrhage in Hong Kong at the age of sixty-one. His body was returned to San Francisco, where a service for three hundred was held in Grace Cathedral. Among the mourners, the *San Francisco Chronicle* reported, was Madame Chiang, "in poor health and . . . emotionally upset . . . [who] required assistance" to enter the cathedral. All of the Soong sisters and brothers were in attendance except Ching-ling, who, the *Chronicle* assumed, "chose to remain in mainland China." The choice, however, had not been hers. T.A. had been Ching-ling's favorite brother, but she had to engage the help of Chou En-lai and his wife to even get permission to send a wire of condolence.

Six months later, Chiang and May-ling were riding in their limousine up to their mountain home when a jeep swerved over the dividing line of the road. The escort car preceding them stopped suddenly, and the limo plowed into it. Almost a year later, Madame's secretary informed Emma Mills that the Madame was "still unable to write or paint and cannot stand for any length of time on her left leg" since "the jolt to her head was so severe that it caused injury to the spinal cord with resultant pain in her right arm and hand and her left leg." Unlike her husband, May-ling spent some days in the hospital, complaining of whiplash and other spinal injuries, which did not seem to improve for over a month—or until President Nixon offered to send an American osteopathic specialist to Taiwan to consult with her doctors.

When she returned home, Madame Chiang hired a young nurse who had attended her several years earlier, brought in this time for night duty. It was a tough assignment, according to the nurse, due to "the constant massaging." And as soon as she had become accustomed to the work, Madame's niece "Jeanette Kung brought Madame Chiang and me a new 'weapon'—a new-style massage machine, shaped like a hand grenade. Jeanette Kung attached it to my hand and turned on the power. The machine was supposed to do the work, but it was very heavy and the strong vibrations bothered me. However, Madame Chiang liked it very much. From then on, it was necessary for me to use the machine, and my work became much harder."

Being a nurse, a maid, or even a woman in the Chiang home had never been particularly easy. The G-mo refused to deal with women telephone operators, going so far as to hang up the phone if a female voice answered. During the 1960s, when the miniskirt was in vogue, a young nurse arrived at the Chiang residence to take up her duties with Madame Chiang. Happening to go into his wife's room, Chiang frowned when he saw the young woman. The next day he pulled his wife aside: "Maybe you can find an opportunity to tell the new nurse not to wear those mini-skirts. They are too short. Her legs are exposed. Where are her manners?" For an elderly man with two ex-wives and many mistresses, Chiang's prudishness seems odd. He even objected to women wearing slacks, and it was not until after his death that May-ling listened to her doctors and wore them to keep warm.

In October of 1970, a year after the accident, May-ling wrote Emma to say she was "much better" but "still not fully recovered," and eighteen months after the collision, she was still referring to it: "I am not completely over the effects of the auto accident. . . . Better, yes, and doing some work, painting, and seeing guests, but not yet fully back on my usual routine. Recently I had a minor operation on my good foot as I had overstrained it in trying to compensate for the leg and foot which are not yet fully recovered."

Meanwhile Chiang, who had been thrown from the backseat of the limo into the front, had escaped serious injury, but his dental bridge had cut into his gums, and for some time thereafter he had difficulty speaking. He was also beginning to show more serious signs of decline—an enlarged prostate, hardening of the arteries, back trouble—and had been unable to stand for more than a few minutes during his most recent inauguration.

Physically debilitated, the G-mo remained his intractable self. Unwilling to give up "the reins of power," he had become "progressively isolated," according to H. K. Yang, Taiwan's vice foreign minister. He was, Yang said, "severely handcapped in making critical decisions by not having the frank, uninhibited thinking of his advisers," and even Chiang Ching-kuo would "not take a position until he knows what the President's inclination is." Yang also contended that Chiang was "adversely influenced by the alleged selfish, ultraconservatism of Madame Chiang," who was "interested in preserving a preeminent status for herself and not greatly concerned with the need for making difficult adaptations to the exigencies of the current critical situation."

In late April of 1971, May-ling lost her older brother T.V., who died at the age of seventy-seven at a dinner party in San Francisco. His body was returned to New York, where he had been living and where services were held at the Church of the Heavenly Rest. "Mrs. Chiang Kai-shek was to have been in New York today for the funeral of her brother, Dr. T. V. Soong," *The New York Times* reported. "She canceled her trip yesterday, after she was informed that the Communist Chinese might send her sister here too." According to Li, May-ling was "already airborne" when she had the plane turn around and go back to Taiwan; the government, according to Ching-kuo, worried that the Communists had plotted a "United Front trap," i.e., a metaphorical reconciliation between the two Chinas via the sisters.

Ching-ling, who was currently living in Peking, had been given a palace with many servants on the banks of the Imperial Lakes. Ignoring her early Methodist training, she apparently gave dancing parties and "would glide gracefully" by with Chou En-lai. "Mao did try," said one of Ching-ling's friends. "But from what I hear, wasn't very agile." Journalist Harrison Salisbury attended a dinner in her home in the summer of 1972, and he, like everyone else, was captivated by his hostess. "To dine with Mrs Sun," he said, "is to be in a presence. There is no other way to describe this vigorous woman who still flashes a smile that has something of a schoolgirl's grace in it and whose wit has not been dulled by the years." Nor had immersion in the proletarian culture of the Chinese Communists changed the standard of living that Ching-ling shared with her sisters. She began the evening by apologizing for the service—"my waiters have all gone off to the rural training schools for political reorientation and the new ones just aren't well trained"—and then begging her guests' indulgence for the cuisine: "The old cooks are dying, and the youngsters don't want to learn—they think it's menial."

In response to condolences on the death of T.V., May-ling wrote Emma that "the family deeply feels the loss, both of him and of my younger brother T.A., who died just two years previously—both so suddenly and unexpectedly—neither giving any sign or indication of sickness or discomfort before passing. Their sudden and unexpected deaths, coming so closely together, have of course made our loss the much harder to bear." Since this was the very least she could have said about her older brother, we have to assume that May-ling and T.V. were still on the outs at the time of his death and that she refused to admit, perhaps even to herself, what her brother had done for China.

William S. Youngman, onetime president of China Defense Supplies, later head of C. V. Starr,* was named trustee of T.V.'s estate and made up for his sister's lack of generosity in the eulogy he delivered at the funeral. Calling T.V. "one of the truly great leaders of the free world—and humanity," Youngman described Soong's "incredible performance" in convincing leaders of the most powerful nations . . . that China deserved its place among them. "No other man in the world could have argued that case so successfully," he claimed. History, Youngman added, would confirm the fact that Soong "above all was the one man who . . . was able to bring China into economic and political dialogue with the modern world. A true citizen of two worlds—he was an indispensable link between them."

According to one *Wall Street Journal* report, T.V. "had amassed over $70 million"† by 1943, twenty-eight years before his death. But the report

---

* C. V. Starr (named for Cornelius Vander Starr) was the parent organization of AIG Insurance, started in Shanghai in 1919, in which May-ling's family, according to one Chinese gentleman who knew them quite well, "had substantial investments." (Notes from a conversation between Lionel Tsao and Barbara Thompson Davis.)

† Worth $871,168,000 today. This estimate of T.V.'s worth was traced by the author to an "outside confidential source of unknown reliability," the wife of a "prominent Chinese official" who spoke to the FBI in 1942. The following year the Japanese propaganda machine operating out of Hong Kong began "making announcements over the radio to the effect that T. V. Soong has $70,000,000 in either the Chase National Bank or the City National Bank in New York City." But Francis Biddle, the U.S. attorney general, warned that "many of the charges made by the confidential informant about the Soong family are so patently false that they seem to be either enemy-inspired or put forth with extreme malice." (FBI files: Memorandum for Mr. J. Edgar Hoover re Soong Family from Lawrence M. C. Smith, Chief Special War Policies Unit, January 30, 1943, no. 65-31284-103; Memorandum, April 30, 1942, no. 31284-94; Memorandum for Mr. Lawrence M. C. Smith, February 24, 1943, no. 65-31284-79 (?); Memorandum for Mr. J. Edgar Hoover re

also cited his city of residence as San Francisco, so it is hard to credit.* Since his estate was recorded for the courts at something less than $10 million† before taxes, Li believes it was "virtually certain that he had kept substantial assets off shore, where they would be impossible to trace."

Ai-ling, who was in Taiwan at the time of T.V.'s death, remained for the summer with her sister and had an operation on her eye. "She was well on the road to recovery when suddenly she developed iritis [inflammation of the iris] in both eyes and had to remain several weeks in a dimly lit room," May-ling wrote Emma. "I could certainly sympathize with her, for I had had the same condition at the Cairo Conference." May-ling also told her friend that she needed a rest: "I have had one cold after another all summer and nerve pain in my leg is still there."

May-ling's complaints about her own health coincided with an embarrassing mishap with her husband. Chiang suffered from constipation, and to relieve this condition, a glycerin ball was often inserted in his anus. On this particular occasion, the G-mo's attendant, an unfortunate man named Chian, inserted two balls into what was later described as a muscle next to the anus—a mistake that caused excessive bleeding, necessitated surgery, and left Chiang confined to a painful month of recuperation during which he could neither sit nor stand. Chiang ordered Chian into prison, but Ching-kuo wanted to execute him in accordance with military law. The controversy was settled when a member of the household suggested that he be confined in the guardhouse of the presidential home so that he could not speak about the incident to anyone. Although Madame told Chian more than once, "You have destroyed the President's health. You are the devil," she agreed five years later, after Chiang's death and much "begging and pleading from all sides," to set Chian free.

Soong Family, March 25, 1943, no. 65-31284-101. Material furnished to author by Justice Department under Freedom of Information Act inquiry.)

* In 1985, Sterling Seagrave published. *The Soong Dynasty,* in which he cited the *Encyclopaedia Britannica*'s characterization of T.V. as "the richest man in the world." Youngman wrote Seagrave a letter saying that T.V. "brought little out of China after the War . . . died possessed of a very modest fortune which he honestly acquired mostly in the U.S.A. by sound investment and hard and able work." Youngman added, "You could have found the details if you had taken the trouble to look at the Surrogate records in New York after his death. With the able assistance of Sullivan and Cromwell I examined all his financial records and those of his banks and can say as certainly as anyone can that there were no undisclosed assets such as you suggest." (Wellesley Colledge Archives: William Sterling Youngman to Sterling Seagrave, March 18, 1985.)

† Equivalent to $53,148,000 today.

In July of 1972, Chiang Kai-shek suffered cardiac arrest, leaving him an invalid for the remainder of his life. Not wanting to move him to a hospital, May-ling had an emergency medical station set up in the Chung Hsing Hotel, where he lapsed into a coma and she, Jeanette Kung, and Ching-kuo all took rooms near him. According to a member of the household, Madame Chiang was "very calm" and directed the operation like "the commander on a battlefield." She ordered doctors and nurses from the veterans' hospital brought in to attend him at the hotel. All their days off and vacations were canceled, and no one either from the hospital or the hotel was allowed to contact members of their families; if their families inquired, they were told that their relatives had gone south on a business trip and would be back in a few days, leading the wives of various doctors to believe that their husbands had disappeared. Six months later Chiang came out of the coma but remained an invalid and was moved back and forth between the hospital and his home, where he stayed in bed or in a wheelchair and received visits from his son Ching-kuo in the mornings and evenings.

In spite of all May-ling's precautions and prevarications, stories about the G-mo's ill health began to circulate around the island. To prove that her husband was all right, Madame set up several phony photo opportunities— the generalissimo at home offering his youngest grandson and bride a traditional cup of tea during their wedding (Chiang had been far too ill to attend the ceremony); Chiang speaking with ten officials who visited him in the hospital during the Eleventh Congress of the KMT (his right arm had to be taped to the armrest of his chair, as he could not control the movements of his hand); and a family visit in which Chiang was photographed with his youngest great-grandson in his arms (the child was placed there just long enough to snap the picture).

It was during this difficult period that May-ling lost her favorite sister, Ai-ling. She had gone to New York in September of 1973 to see Ai-ling, who was seriously ill, but left four days before Ai-ling died. One of May-ling's friends said that neither she nor Ching-ling attended Ai-ling's funeral, since both were afraid of running into the other.

Among the younger members of the Soong and Chiang families, May-ling's favorite remained Jeanette Kung, H. H. and Ai-ling's daughter. Madame had asked Jeanette to come to Taiwan to run some charitable and non-charitable enterprises, including the Grand Hotel in Taipei, the Women's League, the orphanage schools like those she had established on the mainland, and a new center for children with polio. When it was decided to expand the hotel to accommodate the foreigners who were coming to Taiwan, Chiang himself had asked Jeanette to take charge of the project. "Under Miss Kung's management, the construction costs were all used for the building, and not one cent was put into private pockets," according to a member of the household. At the same time, however, most of the competent people on the project could not get along with Jeanette. It was the same story in the Chiang residence. She was "troublesome," and "a lot of people did not like her."

Madame Chiang had always felt guilty about Jeanette, because when she was a little girl with eczema, Madame had suggested that Ai-ling put her in boys' clothes—loose pants and long-sleeved shirts—to protect her skin, and from that time on, Jeanette had refused to dress like a girl. Whether it was or was not guilt that had originally created the relationship, May-ling and her niece were extremely close. When she was not living with her aunt, Jeanette had what Chiang's personal physician referred to as "two women who called themselves Miss Kung's wives." They were about Jeanette's age, and one had a husband and children.*

Jeanette often ran the Madame's homes for her. Although May-ling spoke in the Shanghai dialect to her husband and the household, she spoke English to Jeanette in order to keep the servants from understanding. Described by Chiang's doctor as "slim and short . . . not pretty and . . . overbearing," Jeanette made sure never to offend the G-mo or the Madame, but "as to the rest [of the household], she ordered them about in a very rude way." Very smart, Jeanette was May-ling's one-woman "FBI," reporting errors, scandals, and bribes back to the mistress of the house. This trait, however useful in a large Chinese household, apparently backfired when Chiang began to suffer from his heart condition. Jeanette, who was very interested in medicine, bought a lot of books on the subject, including some on diet and medicine, and began to harass the doctors, insisting that their methods

---

* One of Madame's personal attendants told the following story, which may or may not be true: "Of all the members of the 'first family,' Jeanette Kung was the most special. One summer day Soong May-ling asked me to go see her niece in the hotel in which the family was staying. 'I haven't seen Ling Wei [Jeanette] for a long time. Would you get her for me?' When I got to Jeanette's room, heavy fumes of wine were coming from her door. . . . I knocked on the door and told her who I was. She said, 'The door is open. You can come in.' Entering her room I was really shocked by the scene: Jeanette was wearing nothing more than a very thin man's waistcoat, and she was chatting and drinking with two doctors from Chiang Kai-shek's medical team. 'Madame asked me to come see what you are doing.' Jeanette remained perfectly calm and 'Please tell Madame I am chatting with my friends, but don't mention that I am drinking!' " When the attendant returned to Madame Chiang, she guessed immediately that her niece was drinking. "Soong May-ling apparently knows Jeanette like the back of her hand. Until today, the scene of her drinking with her friends in a man's waistcoat has stayed with me." (Zhu Zhong-sheng, "Madame Chiang Soong May-ling and Mr. Ching-kuo," thesis, 1999.)

and medications were wrong. Because of her position in the Chiang household, they were afraid of her, and it took some time before May-ling could
convince her niece to stop second-guessing the medical team in charge of
her husband.

The year before Chiang's death, May-ling engineered a minor triumph
when U.S. Ambassador Walter McConaughy, who had asked for and been
refused visits to the G-mo, requested an audience to say good-bye before
returning to the States. Madame was concerned about Taiwan's relationship with the United States, since mainland China was now in the United
Nations and Japan had just cut diplomatic ties with the island. She invited
the ambassador for dinner and had Chiang placed in his chair to greet
McConaughy. Although he wheezed and gasped for air, May-ling smoothed
things over, performing her usual job of interpretation during the visit.
Meanwhile, the doctors, who had warned her against removing the G-mo's
heart monitor for too long, waited anxiously with oxygen behind the dining
room doors.

During Chiang's last illness, May-ling assumed his role, along with her
own, of outraged spokesperson against the Communists. Four months after
he was taken ill, she spewed out her anger and frustration at the British in an
address to the Twenty-seventh World Congress of the Junior Chamber International in Taipei. Filled with arcane words she must have thought would
impress her youthful audience—supererogatory, correlational, fugacious,
quodlibet, troke—she contended that Great Britain's recognition of the Chinese Communist regime on the mainland reminded her of "the remarkable
similarity of a festival of complacency, lulled by auto-hypnosis, which pervaded the British leadership prior to World War I." She also offered the following sentence on the French: "I have made some mention of history to
show that although in her excitable Gallic affinity for bungling, half-efficient
and half-inefficient, committing cataclysmic blunders and undergoing many
terrible and dark hours, France, pitched against the proverbial methodic furor Teutonicus, was able to ultimately survive."

As the G-mo's wife grew more outspoken, she had also become more
unreadable, due to her insistent use of unusual words and long, convoluted
sentences. The best explanation this author can find for these self-defeating
literary tics is May-ling's awareness of her own intellect in a society in which
women's minds were not highly regarded and her understandable if unfortunate need to exhibit that intelligence to the world. This was certainly the
case with a long article written in the spring of 1975, entitled "We Do Beshrei
It." The title, she explained, came from Yiddish and meant "Don't talk about
it, don't tempt it and it will go away." Furious at the "much touted U.S.-
Soviet and the U.S.-Chinese Communist renewed effort at detente during

the latter part of 1974," she suggested looking at "some of the current endog-
enous [internal] socio-economic problems as well as some of the exogenous
[external] international political problems that beset and ineffectuate [not
in the dictionary] the United States." These were listed, in no particular order, as the inability of American children to read, the acceptance of obscen-
ity, widespread violence, the availability of drugs, welfare fraud, dreadful
nursing homes, dishonesty in government, permissiveness in raising children, strikes, long hair, economic depression, and an "energy crunch." She
complained that detente between the United States and the USSR and the
United States and the PRC had given the Chinese Communists time to
catch up in nuclear weaponry while "protecting them against the U.S.S.R."
Or, as she put it, "Chou [En-lai] has maneuvered the U.S. into being a policy bodyguard to give protection to him gratis while Chou the predator plots
future predations [robberies, plundering] with assurance and impunity . . .
he is far and away ahead of both superpowers in his subtle brilliant strategy."
But the Madame concluded, "I have faith that certain ineludible and fundamental principles are again emerging regnant and that self-interest, I repeat
self-interest, of the superpowers will insure wiser and thought-out decisions.
Fictive reality ensconced in transitory emotions and psychological com-
plexes seated in shallow arrogance and vanity, are in essence all exercises in
futility." (At this point, it must be admitted that this author was tempted to
try to read the article, printed in both languages, in Chinese.)

APRIL 5, 1975, was the last day for a devoted Chinese to engage in his annual
ritual of sweeping his ancestors' tombs. According to tradition, the Chinese
soul is divided into three parts: one part remains hovering in or around the
body, a second enters the holy tablets placed in the family ancestral hall,
while the third ascends to the spiritual realm, where it receives rewards or
punishments for its life on Earth. On this night ancestral ghosts rise, walk
around, and prepare to return to their places. It was a particularly clear night
when the doctor on duty called Chiang's physician to say that the generalissimo's heart had stopped. The physician rushed into Chiang's bedroom,
where he injected a stimulant into the patient's heart, which started beating
again.

May-ling came in and was seated at her husband's bedside when his
heart stopped for a second time. The doctor gave Chiang another injection
and was preparing to give him a third when May-ling said, "Just stop." It was
shortly before midnight, and a huge storm suddenly erupted over the island,
complete with thunder and lightning. According to Ching-kuo, "As Father
lay dying, the rain poured down and the wind howled as though the whole

universe were changing its coloration in order to mourn him." To which
Ching-kuo's biographer added, "Even Harvard-educated officials in the city
thought this was more than a coincidence."

In spite of the explosion of the elements, Chiang's death, according to
The New York Times, was "not expected to have any significant impact on the
politics of the Nationalist Chinese Government or on the political morale
of the people here." This the *Times* ascribed to the fact that Ching-kuo had
emerged "as a strong leader who has seemed to gain the confidence of most
of the population." *Newsweek* went further: "The fact of the matter is that
Chiang's death made very little political difference at all." Asked how he felt
about Ching-kuo succeeding his father, one member of the political section
of the U.S. Embassy in Taipei replied, "It was a very good feeling. A feeling
that here's a good pragmatic business-like Chinese who was going to take
over from the doddering old man."*

As was traditional, Ching-kuo and Wei-kuo wrapped their father's body
in a white cloth for burial. Chiang had left a political testament calling on
his supporters to continue to fight the Communists and regain the mainland. He also left a will asking that his body not be placed in the grand memorial that was to be built in his memory but kept in a mausoleum by the
Lake of Mercy in the mountains, so that his bones could be transported
home one day to the mainland.

Chiang's body lay in state during the week before the funeral, which followed eleven days after his death. The long delay was explained by the fact
that little had been done to prepare for the funeral beforehand, since such
preparations were considered to be in bad taste. The hiatus gave citizens
from around Taiwan time to view the open casket, and it was estimated that
one out of every six islanders came to Taipei to pay homage. The television
network, "closely supervised" by the government, showed officials, soldiers,
factory workers, children, businessmen, and housewives crying before altars
with pictures of Chiang draped in black.

A state funeral was held on April 16. More than three hundred foreign
dignitaries were in attendance. Members of the staff of the U.S. Embassy
had been carefully coached as to the proper behavior. "He [Chiang] had a
vast, very fancy state funeral which the entire diplomatic corps had to attend. We were taught how to go up by threes to the podium and bow from
the hips to his portrait in a gesture of sympathy or respect. The whole diplomatic corps was lined up and had to go through this: click, click, bend at the

---

* The same member of the staff repeated the most vivid—if callous—announcement of
Chiang's death: "We wanted to send a two-word telegram [to Washington]: 'Peanut
planted.' But we decided the Ambassador wouldn't appreciate this, even in jest."

hips, bend twice and move off." No VIPs came from any of the countries allied with China in World War II except Vice President Nelson Rockefeller, who attended with a six-person delegation named by President Gerald Ford.* According to Anna Chennault, it was she who "persuaded the vice-president to go," probably because Madame Chiang had been at her husband's rites. The service, according to the Taiwan Missionary Fellowship, was "very Christian," and Chiang's body was entombed with a Bible and a copy of the devotional classic *Streams in the Desert*. The service was televised for the islanders. The coffin was then put on a flatbed truck, covered in yellow and white flowers, and taken to its "temporary" resting place—which had been built into the side of the tree-covered mountain overlooking the lake.

A memorial service, attended by more than 1,100 people, was also held at the National Cathedral in Washington, D.C. Among the speakers were what the reporter for *The Washington Post* called "two of the most prominent anti-communists in the United States," the Reverend Billy Graham and retired Army General Albert C. Wedemeyer. Graham spoke of May-ling as "one of the world's most intelligent and beautiful women" and of Chiang himself as "a true believer" whose faith was "personal," "genuine," and "quiet." He claimed that it was "public knowledge among the leadership in Taiwan" that a few hours before he died, the generalissimo had "called together his wife, his son, and a five or six of the leading men of the Government . . . [and] spoke to them about his last wishes, ending with the phrase, 'These things and my Christian faith I have never departed from.'"† A more believable tribute came from General Wedemeyer, who said that during his two years as chief of staff to the generalissimo, his "respect and esteem" for Chiang "as a gentleman, as a patriot, and as a dedicated leader steadily grew." The service, which ended with the hymn "Onward, Christian Soldiers," was, according to the *Post* reporter, "studded with biblical references to steadfastness in the face of adversity."

---

* Nixon had resigned on August 9, 1974.

† There were several versions of the deathbed scene. One member of the household claimed that on the evening of his death, Chiang grabbed Ching-kuo's hand and told him that if he was obedient to his mother, May-ling, he, Chiang, could die in peace. According to a journalist, Chiang "was said to have called" May-ling and Ching-kuo to his bedside and asked them to join hands and promise that they would treat each other "like mother and son." But since Chiang was reportedly in a coma at the end of his life, and since the scene between father and son is not mentioned in Taylor's excellent biography of Ching-kuo, these stories, certainly Graham's rendition, most likely inaccurate. (Ling Pei-jun, United Press, on Zhu Zhong-sheng, "Madame Chiang Soong May-ling and Mr. Ching-kuo.")

While obituary writers around the world blamed Chiang for losing China, the residents of the island of Taiwan settled into official mourning. Movie theaters and other houses of entertainment closed down for a month; games like golf and billiards were forbidden; television stations were limited to black-and-white films on the G-mo's life or his funeral; and bars were closed, although it was said that some of their more enterprising employees stood outside these establishments in the street in order to lure customers inside.

"The President's departure from this world was very hard for me to quite accept as reality," May-ling wrote Emma a month later. ". . . It was actually the people's undescribably intense and inconcolable [sic] grief which forced me to regain something like routine life. Literally millions of them were out of their homes, many riding buses, bicycles, scooters, motorcycles and their own cars overnight from one end of the island to the other to pay their respects to the President, tearful, kneeling, wailing, prostrate, stricken respect. . . . Because of their sorrow, somehow my own sorrow became less important. My heart went out to them, to these generous, magnificent people whom I must serve as I have always served. . . . And on the whole route to Tsu Hou [Lake of Mercy] . . . over two million people were lined up solid, some places ten deep. . . . Emma, unless you have seen this with your own eyes, I cannot quite describe the feeling and ethos to you."

BUT MAY-LING'S WISHFUL descriptions of the grief of the Taiwanese will never compete with the scene that took place in the home of Mao Tse-tung, the man who had driven Chiang Kai-shek into his island exile. According to the most recent biography of Mao, the chairman took an entire day off to privately mourn the passing of his old enemy. It is said that he neither ate nor spoke during that day but listened to the same tape of stirring music over and over again, beating time on his bed and "wearing a solemn expression." The music had been composed for Mao to a twelfth-century poem, written to say good-bye to another rival "who bore an uncanny resemblance to Chiang" and had been exiled to a remote part of China. The poem read as follows:

> You and I are men of history
> No little men chattering about minor affairs!
> Go, let go, my honoured friend
> Do not look back.

Mao himself died seventeen months later.

PART NINE

1975–2003

56

The storm center of the world has gradually shifted to China. Whoever understands
that mighty empire socially, politically, economically and religiously, has a key to
politics for the next five hundred years.

—JOHN HAY, SECRETARY OF STATE, 1898–1905

IN SEPTEMBER 1975, five months after Chiang died, May-ling left for the
United States with more than a dozen personal aides and nurses. From then
on, except for specific occasions, she made her home in New York.

On leaving Taipei, she said that she had been sick for the past two years
but "was unable to attend to my own illness as the President was not well."
Diagnosed with breast cancer the year her husband died, she had already
undergone the first of two mastectomies in Taiwan. According to DeLong,
she "mustered strength to fly to New York for further medical care."

There were probably other reasons for her departure. It was said that
Madame Chiang and her supporters thought that she should be named president of the Kuomintang after the death of her husband but the idea was
vetoed by the old men of the party. Then she tried to put David Kung into
a top position. When that was rejected as well, the G-mo's widow realized
that she was politically superfluous and left the island. Chiang Ching-kuo
saw her off and supported her as she walked to the airplane.

In October she invited Emma out to the Kung estate—now owned by
the Kung children—on Long Island. "May-ling looks much the same,"
Emma wrote in her journal, "but has help on steps. Right arm pains her from
the breast removal as does her left leg, due to whip-lash [from the auto accident in 1969]. Has two Secret Service men, and brought over two of her
own, a trained nurse, amah, cook, etc." Shortly after this, May-ling became
ill—"very sick for three and a half months. Skin and nerve condition."

In spite of the fact that May-ling reported that she was suffering from
shingles, she returned to Taiwan in April 1976 for the first anniversary of
her husband's death. In June, she wrote Emma that she was "still having
pains. . . . Inflamed nerve roots have still not healed; they have been so
badly damaged. Portions of the skin on the outside are well, but there are
still angry-looking red patches and inflamed nerve ends that are causing me
intense pain—after six long months." It was almost a year later when she

wrote Walter Judd that she was "gradually recovering from the prolonged affliction" of herpes zoster (shingles) in which "the "pains and sufferings were indeed excruciating and almost unbearable at times." When she left the island at the end of four months, she claimed that she was now suffering from an ulcer and muscular pains from her old injury, and she apparently checked into Johns Hopkins Hospital in Baltimore before returning to Long Island.

Although May-ling and Wedemeyer seem to have been out of touch during this period, the general corresponded with her nephew and owner (or co-owner) of her New York apartment, David Kung. As they exchanged gifts and greetings, it became clear that David did not like being addressed as David Kung. "All those of my generation, viz. 76th generation,* all have their middle name ending with Ling," he informed Wedemeyer. "So a Chinese scholar would know which generation I belong to. All my father's generation end with Hsiang. . . . I am very proud of my Chinese name and ancestry. I need not embellish it with the name of a Jewish King. Besides, I do not think I am able to be as adulterous as he was and be contrite and repentant so many times! It would be too tiring although a lot more fun!"

A year later, a telegraphed invitation from Wedemeyer evoked this reponse from Madame's nephew: "I note it was addressed 'Care David L. K. K'ung.' For reasons I already explained to you in my letter of February 11, 1978, I am very proud of my Chinese name, K'ung Ling Kai or L. K. K'ung, and of my Chinese ancestry. I shall appreciate it if you will instruct your secretary to have the correction made in your address book. . . . I wish I had gone into the Army or Navy so that I could sign myself, as you have, with an appropriate title such as Colonel, General, Rear Admiral or Admiral, whatever."

May-ling lived with the Kungs in the United States—either in David's apartment in Manhattan or the Kung house in Lattingtown, Locust Valley, Long Island. Neighbors in the country claimed they never saw her, only the limousines going by, and, according to the mayor of Lattingtown, "She lived here for 30 years and nobody knew she was here until she left." Although she had her hair washed in the local beauty parlor, this was done on Sundays or holidays, when the village shopping center was closed. She was seen arriving in a "two-car entourage," and while she was inside, two Chinese bodyguards were observed to "pace nervously outside." There was a plainclothesman stationed at the door of the house, and her bodyguards continued to be supplied by the U.S. government. "I see her damn limousines go

---

* It will be remembered that David's father, H. H. Kung, was a direct descendant of Confucius in the seventy-fifth generation.

by every once in a while," said the editor of the local paper. "She must be going out of her mind, now that the United States has taken some sense and decided to recognize that there are 900 million people over there in China. . . . Personally, I don't care what she thinks. The only thing I want to write about her is her obituary. I think she's caused the world a lot of grief."

The apartment in the city was a duplex at 10 Gracie Square, one of the most elegant buildings in New York, looking out over the East River. Its eighteen rooms—seven family bedrooms and many servants' rooms—were furnished in the style of another era with wall-to-wall carpeting and lots of brocade. Red was the predominant color, and May-ling's bedroom, which featured a portrait of her, was decorated in red silk. There were beautiful jades and ivories, lovely paintings and Chinese cabinets in the public rooms, but the Western furniture that shared these large spaces was overgilded, over-carved, and overdone.

Madame Chiang, according to another tenant at 10 Gracie Square, was not much of a presence in the building, except when she came and went, "so erect that she looked like a young girl, even in her nineties." She had three small dogs—a Yorkshire terrier and two Bijons—that, in the words of one New York columnist, "were also getting old and wobbly along with their centenarian mistress." Since some members of her staff had not been willing to move to New York, her complement of aides had been somewhat re-duced. Nevertheless, she employed twenty-four servants (the author assumes that this was three shifts of eight people each), most of whom were housed in a lesser apartment building nearby. According to the same columnist, trouble arose at 10 Gracie when the Madame's neighbors became "aware of the pungent dishes and the smoked Peking duck being prepared." One neighbor confirmed that the duck was hung out of the kitchen window, and the stench of cooking oil lodged itself in the elevators. It was finally, how-ever, not the odors but cockroaches that led the other occupants of the building to complain. "Exterminators were dispatched," the columnist re-ported. "Then inspectors were dispatched to confirm mission accomplished. Looking into anybody's closet or cupboard can be an edifying or a fascinat-ing experience. Looking into those of the once-most-powerful woman in the world was even better than that. . . . Like one closet that was all Gold Bars. I'm talking Fort Knox, not Hershey's."

From her home in Manhattan, the G-mo's widow continued to keep up with world affairs through both American and Chinese newspapers. In 1979, she sent out appeals for the "boat people," going so far as to take out an ad in *The New York Times* denouncing Vietnam for expelling them and appeal-ing to "the countries commanding expansive territory" to take them in. She also continued to exchange the occasional letter with Emma Mills, writing in April 1980 that she had not been in touch because "after I recovered from the influenza virus I suffered an attack of cystitis and am still being treated for it. What with one thing and another I haven't been out of the apartment for over two months!"

The following year, on May 29, 1981, Ching-ling died in Beijing at the age of ninety. She had given her papers to her nephew David Kung just before he left the mainland. As he wrote a friend, "She did not want it to fall into the hands of the Communists. She even gave me a few pistols belonging to the President and said she did not want them to be used against 'you all.' True she did not agree with the Government, but she was not [a] Communist. I have always had the greatest respect for her integrity."

Ching-ling had written her last article three months before her death. As an outspoken critic of the Cultural Revolution, she called on the Chinese people "to build socialism . . . with democracy and legality, so that such abuses will never recur." A symbol of righteousness, she had been seated next to Mao in the Chinese delegation to the 1957 Moscow meeting of world Communist parties when he signed their declaration. It was said that Jawaharlal Nehru had photographs of two women in his room—one was Madame Nehru, the other, Sun Ching-ling.

Two weeks before her death, as her health began to fail, Sun's widow, according to *The Washington Post*'s Michael Weisskopf, was "named China's honorary head of state and given a dramatic deathbed induction into the Communist Party.* . . . Capitalizing on her tremendous popularity, China's ruling Communist Party . . . devoted extraordinary attention to her final days. . . . Leaders . . . lined up at her bedside. Newspapers extolled her. Medical bulletins were issued every day, a practice not even used when Chairman Mao Tse-tung was dying in 1976."

Madame Sun was given a state funeral, and the funeral committee wired condolences to her relatives and friends in the United States, Hong Kong, and Taiwan, offering to pay traveling expenses for any of them who wished to attend the services in the Great Hall of the People. Deng Xiao-ping gave the eulogy, in which he said that Madame Sun had harbored "deep concern for the future of Taiwan" and hoped that the two Chinese governments would hold reunification talks in the near future. Among those invited by the Communists was May-ling, who, even if she wanted to go, would not have been allowed to do so by the Taiwanese government.

---

* It will be remembered that she had applied for membership in the party years earlier but had been rejected. "You would play a greater role for the revolution if you stay outside the party for the time being," she was told at the time. ("Around the World: Widow of Sun Yat-sen Given Full Membership in Party," *The New York Times*, May 17, 1981.)

Ching-ling had apparently asked to see her little sister while she was alive. According to Anna Chennault, Ching-ling had even written a letter that she gave Anna to deliver personally to May-ling. But after reading the letter, May-ling made no effort to contact her sister, merely telling Anna, "I have got the letter." Ching-ling's body was cremated, and she was the only one of the Soong offspring in a position to have her ashes taken to Shanghai to be buried in the family plot beside their parents.

A few years later, May-ling received a letter from Chou En-lai's widow, Teng Ying-chao. Chou himself had died from bladder cancer less than a year after Chiang Kai-shek, and more than a million mourners had gathered to pay homage to him as his body was removed from the hospital. His efforts to mitigate some of the excesses of the Cultural Revolution and Mao's absence from his memorial had set off a spontaneous demonstration in Tiananmen Square—a protest against Mao's policies, brutally suppressed by the military. In spite of this, Chou's widow, Teng, an old revolutionary, had written May-ling a letter urging accommodation—another attempt to bring the Taiwanese back into the Chinese fold.

Teng's letter was never released for publication, but in February of 1984 the G-mo's widow composed an "Open Letter" in reply. Printed in *Asian Outlook*, it gave May-ling an opportunity to hold forth on several of her favorite subjects, all having to do with the cruelty and dishonesty of Communists, both Chinese and Russian. "A few years ago, during the reign of terror of the 'Gang of Four,' " May-ling wrote Teng, "you were put under physical pressure and mental agony that drove you to the brink of suicide. . . . It is distressing to ponder that even you with your long association in the innermost circle of the Communist Party came to near self-destruction." Moving on from there, May-ling explained that when her deceased brother-in-law Sun Yat-sen had tried to get help for his fledgling republic, the Russians had responded with "a paltry supply of Czarist vintage rifles, some machine guns and ammunition" and then taken advantage of "Dr. Sun's generosity of spirit . . . prevaricating and twisting the truth . . . [planting] Communist cells in our body politic." As for Teng herself, May-ling wrote, "the Communist Central Committee is putting you in an embarrassing and awkward position . . . it is resorting to the old refrain of united front, hoping to use deceit once more to bring about 'cooperation.' . . . Surely sanity demands—nay, commands—the recognition that the real China is now in Taiwan."

❦

BACK ON THE island, Ching-kuo had been named head of the Kuomintang in 1975 and president of the Chinese Republic in 1978. Although one of his first acts after his father's death had been to commute the sentences of 3,600 inmates, including some 200 political prisoners, his early years in office were known more for economic advances than any significant softening of the harsh laws espoused by his father. According to Lelyveld of *The New York Times,* writing in 1975 at the time of Chiang's death, Ching-kuo's earlier attempts at reform had not yet taken hold. "University teachers say that they have to be wary of informers in their classrooms; the mail of visiting scholars is opened and read. There are political prisoners—estimates run from 1,000 to 2,000—and occasionally stories of people being taken from their homes at night for lengthy, sometimes brutal interrogations under martial-law decrees that have been in force since the Nationalists got here. Elections are still rigged, and the press closely supervised."

On the economic front, however, Ching-kuo was highly successful in modernizing transportation and industry on the island, giving Taiwan a growth rate of 13 percent, a per capita income of $4,600, and the second largest foreign exchange reserve in the world. According to the *Los Angeles Times,* "by combining shrewd economic policy with shirtsleeve political tours of the countryside, where he slurps noodles with farmers and dances with aboriginal tribes, C.C.K. [Chiang Ching-kuo] has proved himself a far more popular and effective leader than his father ever was."

At the end of 1978 President Carter announced that the United States would no longer recognize the ROC as the legitimate government of China, that it would end all official contact with the KMT, and that it would withdraw its troops from Taiwan. Carter's declaration was so unexpected that the American ambassador had to wake Ching-kuo in the middle of the night to deliver the bad news. Along with the withdrawal of American support, Taiwan's president was also having problems with his health. He had begun to complain that his feet and legs were bothering him. By 1983, he could barely walk but refused to use a wheelchair. Having had one operation on his eyes in 1982, he was told he needed another, and after this second operation, his health began a steeper decline.

Realizing that he did not have very long to live, Ching-kuo began to prepare Vice President Lee Teng-hui to take over the presidency after his death. Although Wei-kuo's name came up as a possible successor—he was about to retire from the army—Ching-kuo offered him a couple of ambassadorial posts that would have kept him out of Taiwan. Wei-kuo declined, and they finally settled on secretary-general of the Taiwanese National Security Council, an appointment that gave him as much political clout as Ching-kuo thought he could handle.

In the spring of 1986, Ching-kuo was given a pacemaker to deal with cardiac arrhythmia, but he continued to complain of shortness of breath and began to use a wheelchair in public. With his time to liberalize the government clearly drawing to a close, he appointed a committee of twenty-four people to study three major areas in need of political reform: the end of martial law, the legalization of opposition parties, and the retirement of the ancient members of the assembly who were still hanging on to their mainland constituencies. Although he could have issued emergency edicts to cover these changes, Ching-kuo believed that they must be brought about in a constitutional manner. During a meeting that year with Katharine Graham, publisher of *The Washington Post,* he announced that his government was planning to "propose" the end of martial law on the island. When the task force charged with changing the National Security Act suggested continuing restrictions on freedom of speech, Ching-kuo refused. "That would simply be old wine in new bottles," he said.

❦

AWARE OF WHAT Ching-kuo's biographer called "the avalanche of reform that seemed about to tumble down" on the island, and sensing that authoritarianism might still have a chance, May-ling had arrived with an entourage in Taipei toward the end of October 1985. She was eighty-nine, and it was her first trip back to the island in nearly ten years, allegedly undertaken to celebrate the one hundredth anniversary of Chiang Kai-shek's birth* on October 31. At this point, the G-mo's widow still held two positions in the party: chair of the People's Central Advisory Commission and head of a special women's group. "She is well respected by the populace in general," said the secretary-general of the party, a close associate of Ching-kuo.

To honor the day, Chiang Kai-shek's widow visited his tomb and delivered a speech, explaining that although she now lived outside the country, she kept up with advancements on the island and hoped that the principles for which the Kuomintang stood would "shine over the mainland once again." In a written message released for the occasion, she blamed her physical condition for her long absence. "Incapacitated as I am by a fracture of the femur [upper leg bone], I have just now returned to be with my countrymen and family members to witness the progress and prosperity of Taiwan." It was noticed that although she sat through the proceedings in a wheelchair, she was able to stand at the podium to deliver her speech with no help.

Many Taiwanese understood that Madame's visit was an attempt to support the ultraconservative elements in the KMT, and they were not surprised when she sidestepped all questions about her plans to return to the States

---

* It was actually the ninety-ninth by Chinese reckoning and the ninety-eighth in the West.

and moved into the old presidential residence in suburban Taipei, entertaining officials from the government, the party, and the military. When Ching-kuo asked her to issue a statement supporting his political reforms, she said, "I am fully cognizant of a prolepsis* of malicious misreading of my thought given to you here"—a statement that even stumped the erudite editors of *The Economist* magazine, who commented that Madame Chiang's "language was so arcane that it baffled interpretation." This was followed by a speech given at a banquet of the American University Club and the American Chamber of Commerce entitled "And Shall It Be See Ye to It?" Using such words as "catenae" (connected series), "timeous" (early), "moloch" (an object of sacrifice), and "corban" (an offering to God), Madame railed at the ethics of the press, which she continued to accuse of underplaying the dangers of communism.

Once May-ling started writing, she seemed unable to stop, moving on in an article entitled "Modern China" to what she termed a "multi-layered" portrait of the United States. She defined what was good in America as the "Jeffersonian conception of democracy," which had succeeded in producing a nation whose citizens take political freedom as "their inherent right," and what was evil as America's "recognition of the Red Regime in mainland China." This led to enconiums for Eisenhower and Dulles and the information that "As I always pay attention to important publications, I get . . . volumes of documents of the U.S. State Department right after they are published." She lauded her husband's defense of Quemoy and Matsu and a secret wire from Eisenhower to Churchill warning him against trying to compel Chiang to give up the islands. She criticized the Japanese for not issuing an apology for their barbarity in World War II and advised them that their children would be better off knowing the truth. On and on she wrote, inserting the names of everyone from Karl Marx to former U.N. Ambassador Jeane Kirkpatrick and ending with a quote from William James: "The enemy of a state is not external, but comes from inside." This article, like most of her previous writings, was written to impress; unlike them, it lacked form and discipline. Explaining that these memories and pronouncements were like the pictures of a revolving kaleidoscope flashing through her mind, she jumped from theme to theme, unreliable assumption to ill-considered conclusion.

The observer has to feel somewhat sorry for Madame Chiang at this point in her life. Not only had she grown old and superfluous, but she had

---

* Prolepsis: a "false description of an event before the event has taken place . . . the anticipation of your opponent's argument." (William Safire, "On Language," *The New York Times Magazine,* January 18, 1987.)

suddenly come face-to-face with demonstrations on her home territory against her husband's legacy. She must have been appalled by electoral campaign banners reading "Oppose the Chiang Family" and "Oppose All Tyranny," to say nothing of cartoons of her stepson in the guise of a pig and written references labeling him "Piggy." The election of 1986, labeled by Taylor "the end of the imperial presidency on Taiwan," featured a bomb thrown into the courtyard of Kuomintang headquarters and a public burning of the KMT flag. Although Ching-kuo was urged to retaliate to these events by arresting key members of the new Democratic Progressive Party, which demanded self-determination for the Taiwanese, he simply ordered the release from jail of thirteen more political prisoners.*

As if this open rejection of everything she had fought for were not enough, May-ling's friend Emma Mills died while she was in Taiwan. Emma had broken her hip in 1984 in her apartment and had been unable to call for help. By the time her neighbors began to worry about her, it was too late. Suffering from days of dehydration resulting in severe senility, she was confined in a nursing home. May-ling had gone to Connecticut to see her before leaving for Taiwan, but Emma had been unresponsive.

Madame's stepson was also in bad physical condition. Nearly blind in his left eye and with very limited vision in his right, Ching-kuo tried to speed up reforms in the three areas he had targeted earlier. By the end of 1987, the Legislative Yuan had passed a new National Security Law: it lifted the emergency martial law that Chiang Kai-shek had put into effect nearly a half century before, and designated January 1, 1988, as the day for submitting applications to register new political parties. But, according to Taylor, "of all the changes on Taiwan itself that year, the most dramatic was the opening of legal travel to the mainland"—the removal of a thirty-eight-year-old ban that allowed tens of thousands of Taiwan's residents to apply for permits to visit their relatives.

The G-mo's widow gave Christmas Eve dinner for the family that year for the first time in more than a decade. During the evening Ching-kuo told a doctor friend that he was not feeling well. But the next day when the doctor called with a date for Ching-kuo's admission to the hospital, the president put off the appointment in order to appear at the December 25 Constitution Day Ceremony. Since the government had moved to Taiwan, it had become traditional for the president to deliver a major policy speech to the National Assembly at this event, although Chiang Kai-shek had not

---

* With all this ferment, the KMT still won almost 70 percent of the popular vote, 59 of 73 contested seats in the Legislative Yuan and 68 of 84 open seats in the National Assembly.

been able to make an appearance during the two years preceding his death. Ching-kuo was wheeled onstage, but someone else had to read the remarks he had prepared for the occasion. Undeterred by the poignancy of the situation, members of the Democratic Progressive Party in the audience waved placards calling for new parliamentary elections, while outside the hall hundreds of citizens chanted slogans demanding democracy.

On January 12, 1988, in the last of Ching-kuo's previously targeted reforms, the old men representing mainland constituencies were finally retired from parliament. But that morning Ching-kuo complained about not feeling well, and early in the afternoon he had a severe hemorrhage, went into shock, and died. Observing the usual outward forms, the Chinese Communist Party sent a wire of "deepest condolences" and "sincerest sympathy," declaring itself "shocked to learn that Kuomintang chairman Chiang Ching-kuo has passed away."

The following day, a group of four leaders of the KMT named Taiwanese Vice President Lee Teng-hui interim head of both the party and the government in spite of a letter objecting to the choice from Madame Chiang. "For Mei-ling and the Chiang Kai-shek old guard, the notion that a native Taiwanese would become both president and leader of the Party seemed the death-knell of the KMT's historic role," Taylor explained. According to the papers, Premier Yu and his assistants stayed up all night trying to figure out how to say that they could not comply with Madame's wishes without causing her to lose face. Two days later, Yu received a 3:00 A.M. phone call from one of Ching-kuo's sons, reiterating his stepmother's objection to the appointment. Nevertheless, on January 27, the Standing Committee voted unanimously to appoint Lee.

On January 29, 1988, Ching-kuo was buried in a "temporary resting place" near his father, awaiting the day when their remains could be sent to the mainland. Although May-ling remained in Taiwan, she rarely appeared in public after her failed attempts to reroute the Taiwanese government. Two weeks after Ching-kuo's death, the Young Marshal, now age ninety, was finally released from house arrest; he eventually moved to Hawaii and died at the age of one hundred.

❦

WHILE ON THE island, Madame received another visitor: the great opera star Beverly Sills. Ms. Sills had been approached by Ching-kuo's daughter-in-law Nancy, who had asked her to bring the opera—singers, musicians, stage-hands, and all—to Taiwan for the opening of their Performing Arts Center. Asked if she would like to meet Madame Chiang while she was there, Ms. Sills said that of course she would but assumed from the fact that Madame was eighty-nine, ailing, and seldom saw outsiders, she never would. Nevertheless, while she was helping the opera crew unload equipment on the docks, Ms. Sills's translator came over and told her that "Madame Chiang Kai-shek is prepared to receive you." Since she had dressed for the work in old slacks and sweater with a scarf on her head, Sills responded that she would like very much to go but had to go back to her hotel and change her clothes. "No, I don't think so," the interpreter replied.

"I got into a Cadillac limousine with a driver," Sills said, "and my sergeant major [the military man assigned to her while she was on the island], who sat up front, and my translator. We drove about twenty minutes and came to a huge enclosure; it looked like a steel wall and was covered with a jungle [of foliage]. I was taken out of this limousine and put into another one. Electric gates opened. We drove through the electric gates, which closed, drove another five minutes, and I was taken out of this limousine, put into *another* one, and finally brought up to a house which was so covered by leaves and foliage that I couldn't tell the size of it. But the doors were huge. Everybody was very polite, although nobody spoke English. When I asked the translator what was going on, she said, "When it's important, I'll start to translate."

Ushered into a room, Sills was "impressed by two things. Virtually everything in the entire room was done in lavender jade; every piece of jade in the room was lavender. . . . I also had the strange feeling that I was being watched . . . that they [the watchers] were behind the paintings on the walls. Finally a general or a colonel or some man with lots of decorations and a uniform took me down a long corridor. Sliding panels opened, and I was taken into a room that had to be a hundred feet long. It had all Chinese furniture, lots of books on one wall, and a huge fireplace—it was warm, but the fire was roaring—and in front of it sat the most exquisite creature I had ever seen. She was dressed top to bottom in black with a huge pearl [on her hand]. I couldn't take my eyes off her . . . she was less than five feet tall and was seated on one of those high chairs like the ones they use in doctors' offices. She had a cane and very white makeup. She had tiny hands, and the reason I noticed the pearl is because it was like a football on her. She was beautifully made up, she spoke wonderful English. I didn't notice any accent at all. . . . There was a tea set in front of her with a silver teapot with three-dimensional silver butterflies and little silver ferns all over it. 'I am so pleased you could come,' Madame Chiang said. 'Would you like some tea?' " There was a woman standing next to her who poured. When Sills commented on the teapot, Madame answered, "You should see the treasures that are still in China."

They discussed Ms. Sills's book *Bubbles*, and the Madame offered to show Sills her paintings. They got into a little cage elevator and went up to the library. "There were four watercolors on this wall, and she said to me, 'I painted these for the general.' I said, 'They're lovely' and asked what they represented, and she said, 'They are the four seasons.' " When Sills asked what the Chinese characters said, Madame replied, " 'Remember they were for the general,' then answered, 'I divided them up, and they say, 'Without you there would be no seasons.' At which point I said, 'They're lovely, and I think I have tired you out.' She answered, 'I've enjoyed it so much, and will you sign your book?' " Sills's book was on the table with a pen. "God knows what I wrote," said Sills. "I was so flustered. I was standing there in those dirty black pants. [She had taken off the scarf.] I didn't know if I should shake her hand, I really didn't know what the protocol was, so I looked at her and said, 'It has been such a great honor,' and she said 'You must never tell anybody about this visit. It must not be in the newspapers,' and I said, 'I would never do that.' Then I asked, 'May I shake your hand?' and she said, 'Please do,' and I shook this teeny, tiny hand and went out. The general was waiting at the bottom of the elevator. We got into the limo, and we only changed once . . . and I've never talked about it before, this little weird moment in time."

Nor, so far as we know, did Madame Chiang, who stayed in Taiwan until the fall of 1991, attending the Thirteenth Party Congress of the KMT in 1988. According to Susan Chira of *The New York Times,* "the former President's widow and symbol of the party's past emerged from seclusion to praise the party's 'glorious history' and recount her memories of the first national congress in 1924." She "sat straight in her chair as a party official read her speech" and "left to a standing ovation, waving a white handkerchief" at the 1,200 delegates. At the congress, John Chiang, one of Chingkuo's illegitimate twin sons, was elected to the post of deputy foreign minister.

Before leaving the island, Madame had her personal physician flown in from the States to remove an ovarian tumor, but she herself refused to leave, saying that she did not want to travel in a wheelchair and that she could not get the government to give her a private plane or her traveling expenses. She was still there to comment on the killings in Tiananmen Square of 1989, issuing a statement condemning "the bloody and satanic carnage of innocent human lives" and attacking the "dastardly communist poltroons" responsible for it at a ceremony in which she was awarded an honorary doctorate of law by Boston University.

By the time Madame Chiang decided to return to the States, the political trend in Taiwan had turned against her, so much so that there were demonstrations outside her residence. When she and her entourage finally flew back to New York in September of 1991, she was ninety-four years old. According to reports of the day, she left with more than ninety suitcases and boxes filled with books, clothes, paintings, delicate wood furniture, and antiques.

May-ling returned to the island only one more time, in 1994, to visit her niece Jeanette Kung, who was dying of cancer. She stayed for three or four days, and a week or so later, Jeanette died.

❦

The next Taiwanese election (in 2000) was a three-way race among Lien Chan, an immensely rich member of the KMT; Chen Shui-bian, a former mayor of Taipei, from the Democratic Progressive Party; and James Soong, an independent. Getting back at Soong for criticizing her during her 1988 attempt to influence the political situation, Madame took the unprecedented step of calling a press conference in New York and releasing a statement supporting Lien Chan in the election.* According to *The Christian Science Monitor,* the generalissimo's widow still had "a small but fiercely loyal group of followers," and her "endorsement could sway many party members who have defected to support Soong." But ending a half century in office, the Kuomintang lost the election, finishing a distant third to Chen Shui-bian of the DPP and the independent candidate, Soong. Ten days later, Madame Chiang turned 103 in her New York apartment, to which she had retreated a decade earlier, old and infirm but apparently still unwilling to allow the political life of Taiwan to go on without her.

---

* An odd circumstance in the election of 2000 concerns John Chang, one of Chiang Ching-kuo's illegitimate twin sons, who had risen in the KMT hierarchy to the positions of foreign minister (1996), vice premier (1997), and secretary-general of the presidential office (1999–2000). Chang had been considered a potential running mate for Lien in 2000 until a sex scandal having to do with a mistress scuttled his chances, and he removed himself from contention. He remains a member of the Legislative Yuan, where he serves as chairman of the Interior Affairs Committee. In 1991, Chang asked to be recognized as a member of the Chiang family but was refused; seven years later he asked if he might call on Madame Chiang in New York, but this request was also refused. Nevertheless, in 2005, he officially changed the spelling of his name to Chiang.

57

She is considered a historic figure but no longer a saint.
—TENG TIEN-TSE, SPOKESMAN FOR THE TAIPEI CITY GOVERNMENT, 1997

ALTHOUGH SHE kept the outward appearance of remaining in control, the problems of old age affected May-ling in the same ways they affect every other old woman. While still in Taipei, her servants noticed that she had begun to have difficulty putting on makeup. As one attendant put it:

> Most of the time she applied her eyebrow darkener and lipstick higher or lower than where it belonged. Her foundation would be thick on one side and thin on the other. If she stayed home, we would turn a blind eye to these flaws. When she had an appointment, guests, or a party, she would always ask us, 'Is my makeup okay?' and we would deal with what was wrong. For grand parties, we did her makeup ourselves. . . . When she was seeing close relations, she rarely put on makeup, although she wore it when Chiang Ching-kuo, Chiang Wei-kuo, or her grandchildren visited. Her skin remained in good condition, her cheekbones were high, and there were no freckles on her face. Fashion-wise, she was out-of date, as she spent most of her time in the residence. She knew this and always asked Mrs. Xiao [a friend of Jeanette Kung] or Madame Chiang Wei-kuo about what was in vogue.

In her nineties May-ling suffered from the typical arthritis of old age and was hard of hearing. But in the summer of 1995, when she was ninety-eight, she traveled to Washington, where, on a steamy July 26, she was the guest of honor at a reception held in the Caucus Room of the Russell Senate Office Building, hosted by Senators Paul Simon, son of Chinese missionaries, and Robert Dole. The walls had been decorated for the occasion with photographs of Madame taken with Churchill, Roosevelt, Truman, Eisenhower, and other leaders of her era. Waiters offered champagne to three hundred guests, among whom were Senators Jesse Helms, Strom Thurmond, and Alan Simpson; Caspar Weinberger and Tricia Nixon Cox were also there, along with a few veterans of the Flying Tigers. According to Francis X. Clines, writing in *The New York Times,* the reception had "a Norma Desmond aura of expectation about it, a celebrity from a silent era." Dressed in a red-and-black patterned silk cheongsam, jade earrings, and a shawl, the honoree was seated in a special chair behind a cordon of red velvet rope to give her two-minute speech. Explaining that she was in Washington to attend celebrations of the fiftieth anniversary of the end of World War II, she stated in a quiet but firm voice that China had been forced to defend itself "unaided and alone" from 1937 until 1941 but followed this up by thanking the American people from the bottom of her heart for the spiritual support and material aid after Pearl Harbor. It was noted that the G-mo's widow "came into the reception on her own two feet," although she was helped by a young member of her family. "She was alert and she was bright," commented Simpson. "She was clicking on all cylinders."

Senator Simon, speaking before the event, had attempted to overcome the inevitable objections: "We're trying to low-key the political side of this, so far with some success. . . . I'm not trying to rewrite history. . . . She is the only major figure left from World War II." Still, it was noted that there were no officials of the Clinton administration present, since the U.S. government was in the process of trying to convince Beijing that the United States recognized only one China. According to a spokesman for Senator Dole, the event should not be taken as a statement of American policy toward China and/or Taiwan, and in a television interview, Assistant Secretary of State Winston Lord* said that former President Bush and even President Reagan had not favored diplomatic relations with Taiwan.

Everyone was nervous because of the uproar raised by Beijing when President Lee Teng-hui of Taiwan had visited the United States during the previous month. But the reception proceeded without incident with several hundred Chinese standing outside waving the flag of the Republic of China and flowers sent by the president and premier of Taiwan on prominent display at the entrance to the Caucus Room. "Big-footed security personnel stood behind her, dour Taiwanese gentlemen with wires coming from their ears," said one reporter, adding that when Madame was ready, they were given a signal to escort her from the room. "The procession moved along in an ungainly way, and as the old dowager left the room she kept cocking her head back toward the crowd, giving everyone the same brittle smile, waving her last goodbyes again and again."

The following year Madame Chiang made another public appearance, this time at the preview of an exhibit of Chinese art treasures titled "Splendors of Imperial China: Treasures from the National Palace Museum, Taipei." The exhibit, which was shown at the Metropolitan Museum of Art in New York, included some 450 pieces of art, all of which Madame Chiang

---

* Later ambassador to the PRC.

managed to see during her visit. Although she toured the premises mostly by wheelchair, she did get up to walk around two of the galleries and was reported gazing "intently" at two items, one of which was a portrait of the first emperor of the Sung Dynasty (the dynasty from which Charlie Soong had taken his name) from the tenth century. At one point she turned to the photographers, who apparently found her far more interesting than the exhibition, informing them that she was "going to break your cameras."

Madame, who had been the guest of honor at a luncheon before the exhibit, had clearly not lost the ability to charm her hosts. Philippe de Montebello, director of the museum and her luncheon partner, was suitably noncommittal with the press: "She is clearly a grande dame and a calm and serene presence," he said. William Luers, President of the Museum, who described Madame as sitting quietly with her head down, reported that she suddenly came alive when it was her turn to speak, launching into a discussion of the history of Sino-American relations and the importance of this particular exhibit. She was, he said "stunning in the way she spoke. There wasn't a woman in the room who could have done what she did."

Although Madame Chiang was able to rouse herself for the occasional public appearance, by her late nineties she had started to withdraw. According to her friend Eleanor Lambert, "She's hardly able to walk anymore. She comes in and we have lunch, then we go back and sit down, and then her mind begins to wander and she repeats herself."

But the Madame always pulled herself together for her birthday celebration in March, when friends, relations, and guests from Taiwan—mostly ladies from the National Women's League dressed in celebratory red—gathered for a two-day event, which usually started with a party the night before at her niece Rosamonde's home and culminated in a "very crowded" dinner in Madame's own apartment at 10 Gracie Square. She was, in the words of one guest, "always beautifully dressed" when she came downstairs to make her appearance and had "all the children kiss her" before being escorted into the dining room. "Typically," according to her nephew Leo Soong, "there would be two or three children from the Hua Hsing Children's Home in Taipei* to sing and dance, along with the principal and some of the teachers. Mme. Chiang, of course, was always very fond of children as my brother and I knew from spending vacations with her in Taiwan when we were growing up."† When she left her guests to go upstairs, it was always with an "imperial wave" and "Good-bye, everyone!" in a "strong voice, not wimpy."

---

* Madame's orphanage school.

† T.A.'s boys had spent almost every summer with their aunt, beginning in the late 1950s.

Leo Soong visited his aunt twice a year for the last ten years of her life. Asked if she remained lucid, he replied that "she was lucid in her own way . . . episodically" as he put it, occasionally mistaking him for someone else. "So we had some slightly unusual conversations," he said, "but the personality was there, and within that construct she always had important points to make." According to Leo, she received a daily report from Taiwan, probably from a secretary who culled it from the newspapers, and her favorite magazine was *Guideposts,* a monthly interfaith publication founded by Norman Vincent Peale in 1945, featuring stories of religious inspiration.

When she was around ninety-nine, she told Leo, "You know, my sisters are dead, my brothers are dead. I don't know why God has left me." He was visiting her for a week, and "every day she would raise the same question. On the last day she kind of came to an answer: I think God has left me here so that I can bring those family members who don't know Christ to him." He said that she "was always concerned about her family" and talked about the fact that Ching-ling had not been allowed to go to Taiwan to see Leo's father, T. A. Soong. He felt that the sisters "missed each other and would have liked to see each other in the later years, but it was not possible. . . . 'if only my sister Ching-ling were still alive,' " he quoted her as saying.

In 1998, the Kung home in Lattingtown, a small community of large estates where Madame had lived on and off since her arrival in the United States, was sold to a developer for subdivision. Known as Hillcrest, the thirty-six-acre property and the home where she had her own "suite" was by that time owned in trust by seven descendants of H. H. and Ai-ling Kung. The sale of the property was noted by the odd reporter, but the sale of the contents of the house hit newspapers from the *Financial Times* to *USA Today* and was covered by ABC's *World News Tonight.* This was because of the crowds—more than ten thousand Chinese who came from as far away as Virginia, Massachusetts, and Ohio to walk up the 500-foot gravel driveway to gaze at, sit on, or consider bidding for the objects remaining in the house after the more valuable things had been removed by the family. Except for a pair of elaborate nineteenth-century French chandeliers ($62,500), a nineteenth-century British cathedral clock ($64,000), a brushwork scroll by Chiang Kai-shek ($21,000), and three of Madame's own paintings ($11,500),* most of the contents of the home were undistinguished. That, however, did not prevent former residents of Taiwan and even the mainland from coming to gawk. "For the overseas Chinese, she is *the* first lady," said a reporter for the *Chinese Daily News* in New York. "There is only one Madame."

---

* According to a Taipei-based paper, all of her paintings were purchased by one of her nieces.

On December 13, 1999, the Braswell Galleries, an auction house in Norwalk, Connecticut, opened the house to possible bidders at 9:00 A.M., but by 11:00, there was such a crush that the mayor of Lattingtown, the Nassau County police, and the local fire marshals ordered it closed, giving tickets to some of the people in line in order to prevent riots. Two dozen policemen had to be called in to stop the fights that broke out and to display a sign at the appropriate off-ramp of the expressway saying simply "GO BACK" in Chinese. According to one report, the lucky ones who had arrived early seated themselves on May-ling's bed, "touched her dresser" and "posed for photos before her photograph." Although the owner of the auction gallery obviously hoped that the frenzy of interest would carry over into the sale that took place the following weekend, adding a number of pots and pillows to the inventory, most of the items sold for approximately what they were worth—except for an ordinary bed of pale green wood with a flowered headboard from the master bedroom. Estimated to bring $300 to $500 but believed to have been slept in by Madame herself, it sold for $8,000.

Although the generalissimo's widow avoided the hoopla surrounding the sale of family possessions, she did manage to get herself to Flushing, Queens, on January 1, 2000, for the opening of an exhibit of Chinese paintings sponsored by *World Journal*, the largest Chinese-language newspaper in North America, at a gallery in their office. She arrived a little before 4:00 P.M. with her niece Rosamonde and was welcomed by a contingent of Taiwanese officials from Washington representing President Lee Teng-hui. Once the ribbon-cutting ceremony was over and the forty-odd guests had been placed in two lines, Madame, who had contributed ten paintings (five landscapes and five florals) to the exhibit, was wheeled down the aisle to greet them, followed by a retinue of seven to ten, all Chinese except for one stern-looking lady in a tweed suit, presumably her secretary-companion. Madame's attendants had made sure that her makeup had been carefully applied; she wore a long black coat with a fur collar, diamond earrings, a big diamond ring, and low-heeled black pumps. She looked well but stayed for only half an hour. Her niece explained to the representative of one local paper that "Madame has not given interviews for many years, but wanted to come to the art exhibit." She said that her aunt used a wheelchair because she had been in a car accident many years earlier, from which she had never really recovered. Otherwise she was in good health.

On the day the exhibit opened, it attracted around two thousand visitors, most of whom came to see May-ling's paintings, and before it closed, it had drawn a total of about thirteen thousand. One Chinese gentleman, a teacher from Brooklyn who dabbled in calligraphy, was surprised to find her work "very good" and, he believed, the work of a person at peace with herself. "When she painted these, she probably forgot about the world," he commented. For a young man from Long Island, they were the work of "someone who is trying to hold onto tradition."

Two months later, when May-ling's paintings were shown at the Asian Art Museum in San Francisco, along with calligraphy and paintings by five masters of the genre, she was called "quite a good painter," by Emily Sano, Director of the Museum, who expanded her assessment for the *San Francisco Chronicle:* "It takes a marvelous spirit to live through such tumultous periods and become a painter, to pick up the paintbrush and focus on this very aesthetic expression, appreciation of nature, culture in a really deep sense. It's truly admirable." But to journalist Ron Gluckman, Madame Chiang was nothing more than "an ambitious dabbler." He found her work "nondescript, without any memorable style" and noted that the sketch entitled *Lotus: A Gentleman among Flowers* was "a work that looks just like any of the silk paintings on sale outside temples and tourist traps across China." The intense interest shown that evening led Gluckman to the conclusion that Madame's "paintings were less works of art than an emotional link with history" for the viewers, many of whom, he said, "arrived in wheelchairs and leaning on walkers." Debilities aside, the evening, "drew a tux-and-gown-crowd," and it follows that many of the gowns were traditional cheongsams.

On March 25, 2002, Madame Chiang celebrated her 105th birthday at the usual party in her New York apartment. She wrote a purple brocade gown with jade jewelry. "She was in very good spirits," said the director general of the Taipei Economic and Cultural Office in New York. "She didn't say a word last year. I was told only now that last year, she didn't feel well—a fever. This year, she was marvelous."

The following year, however, she was unable to join her friends and family for the annual celebration. She had come down with pneumonia, for which she had been hospitalized, and had just returned to her apartment. A few months later, she is said to have caught cold, which apparently developed once again into "minor symptoms of pneumonia," and on October 23, 2003, Soong May-ling Chiang died "very peacefully" at 11:17 P.M. in her own bed. Her niece Rosamonde, her niece's husband, and an unidentified younger member of the family were with her. At the headquarters of the Nationalist Party in Taipei, it was announced that Madame Chiang, "beloved by the people of Taiwan, who bridged the turbulence of three centuries," had passed away during the night.

According to Susan Braddock, another resident of 10 Gracie Square who happened to arrive home at the time Madame's body was being removed, the scene was "very solemn, very beautiful, and dignified." An "honor guard of young Chinese" was standing in the driveway of the building, "protecting Madame Chiang all the way as her body was brought out wrapped in a tartan wool blanket" and put into a hearse. It was apparently not so peaceful on the street, however, where photographers were trying to get by the police, called in by the family to keep them from taking pictures.

Her body was taken to a nondenominational funeral chapel in Manhattan, where it was placed in a closed coffin, banked with flowers. Above the coffin was a huge painting of Madame as a younger woman. According to *The New York Times,* "those who came to pay their respects . . . were mostly . . . people whose lives she had intimately touched, like the orphans of Nanjing, children whose fathers died fighting the Japanese in World War II. Now well into their sixties and beyond, half a dozen waited their turn in line, bowed their heads several times to the dark bronze coffin, then bowed their heads to Madame Chiang's niece, nephew and other relatives." Later on, outside the building, they told the *Times* reporter

how Madame Chiang had set up a school for more than 300 of the dead soldiers' children in Nanjing and visited them regularly, taking them to church services and sometimes tucking them in at night. When the Communists sent her husband . . . and the Nationalists into exile on Taiwan in 1949, she moved the school there and kept in touch with many of the orphans for the rest of her life. "We called her Mama, and she always tells everybody, 'These are my kids,'" said Flora Lee, speaking for her husband, Gien-Feng Lee, 68, a retired businessman. . . . Another orphan, Dr. Howard Shiang, 65, a cardiac researcher . . . wept as he told how he had planned to show Madame Chiang a scientific paper he had delivered at a conference in Seattle, wanting her to be proud of him as a parent might, but then learned she had died."

It is said that Alden Whitman of *The New York Times,* a famous obituary writer who used to travel in search of the great and near great, had gone to Taipei to interview May-ling back in the summer of 1968. After he turned on his tape recorder, she told him that she really had not wanted to speak with him but had finally decided to do so out of kindness. Then, for the next fifteen minutes, she read him an article that she had written for the interview, lambasting the *Times* for ignoring the Communist infiltration of the labor unions, which, she claimed, had led to Chiang's loss of the mainland. After this, she spoke with Whitman for a few minutes, and he left. It was only later, when he tried to transcribe his tape, that he discovered there was nothing on it and that she must have unplugged it from the wall without his noticing.

Other obituary writers were mostly evenhanded, but even the most laudatory tempered their articles with references to money apparently siphoned off by the family. One former China correspondent, Seth Faison of *The New York Times*, who referred to Madame as "a dazzling and imperious politician" whose "skill ... alternately charming and vicious, made her a formidable presence," added that it "became clear in later years that the Chiang family had pocketed hundreds of millions of dollars of American aid intended for the war." Bart Barnes of *The Washington Post* put it this way: "Supporters of the Chiangs tended to see them as the embodiment of all that was good in China and as the leaders in a valiant struggle against the forces of evil. ... To their enemies, the Chiangs were the opportunistic overseers of a corrupt and decadent political apparatus that had little or no regard for human life or the well-being of China. Madame Chiang was the 'Dragon Lady,' imperious, hard-boiled and calculating."

According to the *China Times*, published in Taipei, it was Madame Chiang's ability to speak English and familiarity with Western culture that had breached the gulf between China and the West. "There is no doubt that no other first lady in the history of the modern world could be compared with our Madame Chiang with the exception of Eleanor Roosevelt. ... It was her efforts that changed the Big Three into the Big Four." *The Union*, the second largest newspaper in Taiwan, gave the Chiangs credit for hanging on to their island. "If they had decided to flee overseas," it said, "Taiwan would have fallen into the hands of the People's Republic of China."

From the mainland the Communists, who tend to be generous at the time of death, "offered deep condolences and extended sincere sympathy" to her relatives. Although they criticized the Madame for representing Chiang's regime, "which betrayed the will ... of our Chinese nation," she was, in the words of the chairman of the Chinese People's Political Consultative Conference, a "noted and influential person in the modern era of Chinese history, who had been dedicated to the Chinese people's War of Resistance Against Japanese Aggression, opposed to separating the nation, and hoped for the peaceful reunification across the Taiwan Straits." This set the tone for other mainland testimonials, which latched onto May-ling's efforts during World War II and her supposed belief in the peaceful unification of China. No one, of course, mentioned the fact that her blueprint for unification would have been at the opposite end of the political spectrum from the one proposed by the Communists.

Only one obituary* was downright nasty. An editorial from the *Taipei*

---

* At least that this author found.

Times,* entitled "So Long and Good Riddance," labeled Madame Chiang "perhaps the most evil woman to wield any kind of power" in the twentieth century; claimed that it was "Luce's power and T. V. Soong's bribery" that had "bought Congress in 1943"; stated that "Chiang and his cronies" had sold "most of the materiel that the US supplied" during World War II to the Japanese; and said that the Chiangs in Taiwan were guilty of "depriving Taiwanese of political power and suppressing dissent with great brutality." Although the last salvo was fair, the editorial was an obvious polemic based on exaggeration and rumor and motivated solely by political partisanship.

While the opposition ranted in Taiwan, Madame's body was interred in a family plot in Ferncliff Cemetery in upstate New York. Like her husband, she had wanted to be buried on the mainland, and they had both hoped to be moved there in the future. A representative of the Taiwanese government in New York said that only members of her family attended the interment. The president of Taiwan, Chen Shui-bian of the Democratic Progressive Party, whose election in 2000 had ended fifty years of Kuomintang rule, paid his respects to Madame during a two-day visit to New York. According to the press release, written before the event, President Chen was expected to bow before a portrait of Madame Chiang, then present a flag of Taiwan and a citation of her contributions to the nation to her family.

A memorial was held for Soong May-ling Chiang on November 5, 2003. In spite of the fact that she was a strong Methodist, the service took place at St. Bart's Episcopal Church on Park Avenue, considered one of the most elegant and chic houses of worship in the city of New York. More than seventy-five bouquets of white roses, lilies, hydrangeas, and scarlet orchids were placed at the bases of the pews, and a large picture of Madame was set on an easel in front of the congregation with huge white arrangements on either side and more white flowers on the floor. Almost everyone dressed in black, a nod to the traditional color of mourning in America.

The service itself, conducted in Chinese and English, was mostly a religious one with the singing of hymns and the recital or singing of psalms. The invocation was given by the rector of the church, and the message was delivered by the Reverend Lien Hwa Chow, who came from Taiwan for the service. A large program, written in English and Chinese, presented a picture of Madame Chiang on the cover and a lengthy biography of her inside. "The

---

* The *Taipei Times* is one of three English-language newspapers in Taiwan; it generally takes its editorial line from the Pan-Green Coalition, a political group including the Democratic Progressive Party (DPP), which favors a separatist identity from the mainland. It was formed in opposition to the Pan-Blue Coalition, built around the KMT and the Nationalist identity—hence the reviling of both Chiangs.

whole world is in mourning for this outstanding lady of modern China," it read. ". . . Madame Chiang's wisdom, determination and elegance will be remembered by all." Although remarks were given by two gentlemen from Taiwan and Senator Paul Simon, it was the Reverend Chow, the Chiangs' minister for forty years, who summed up the sentiments of the congregation with his words "We are all God's creatures, but May-ling Soong was God's masterpiece."

She would have loved that—along with all the photographers stationed on Park Avenue and the members of the congregation immortalizing their own attendance at the event by snapping pictures of one another up and down the aisles of the cathedral. She would doubtless have objected to such inappropriate behavior in a house of worship, but she would have loved it.

NOTES

Note: Full biographical details on books can be found in the bibliography.

FOREWORD

1 "When China . . . world": Chang with Halliday, *Mme Sun Yat-sen.* p. 29.

1 "for his . . . politics": Tuchman, p. 260.

1 "You never . . . Life": Ibid., p. 449.

CHAPTER ONE

5 "Along with . . . production": T. Christopher Jespersen, "Madame Chiang Kai-shek and the Face of Sino-American Relations: Personality and Gender Dynamics in Bilateral Diplomacy," in Samuel C. Chu, p. 121.

5 "go from . . . water": Burke, p. 7.

6 "one of . . . Atlantic": Ensign Arthur Tourtellot, "C. J. Soong and the U.S. Coast Guard," *The United States Naval Institute Proceedings,* 75, no. 552 (February 1949).

6 "probably the . . . Carolina": Eunson, p. 8.

7 "Send him . . . education": Webb, p. 123.

7 "not as . . . son": Ibid., p. 124.

7 "Dear Sir . . . Soon": Burke, pp. 7–9.

8 "At first . . . morning": John C. Orr, "Recollections of Charlie Soon," *World Outlook,* April 1938, p. 8.

9 "rather low . . . inches": Eunson, p. 10.

9 "too many . . . McTyeire": Clark, pp. 23–24.

10 "an empire . . . page": Burke, pp. 34–35 ff.

10 "He will . . . Chinaman": Burke pp. 34–35.

11 "One day . . . talk": Mike Bradshaw, Jr., "Chinese Lad Left Trinity College to Found Own Dynasty," *The News & Observer,* July 28, 1936.

13 "Brother Burke . . . think": Burke, pp. 30–31.

13 "because, as . . . pain!": Schaller, p. 19.

14 "the great . . . reckoning": Koo, *Hui-Lan Koo,* p. 257.

14 "Please enter . . . always": Burke, pp. 52–55.

15 "I could . . . month": "A Letter from Rev. Charley Soon," *Raleigh Christian Advocate,* October 19, 1892.

15 "more like . . . colleague": Lattimore, *China Memoirs,* p. 141.

17 "I must . . . me": Madame Chiang Kai-shek, "What Religion Means to Me," *World Outlook* (reprinted from *Forum*), May 1934, p. 8.

CHAPTER TWO

18 "The only . . . face": William Foreman, "America Online," Associated Press, APTV 10-24-03 0838EDT.

18 "tedious sermons . . . prayers": HA: George E. Sokolsky papers, Box 35, Folder 16, Madame Chiang Kai-shek, "The Main Attack."

18 "Why do . . . believe": Clark, p. 44.

18 "Why can't . . . May-ling": Hahn, *The Soong Sisters,* p. 42.

21 "No thank . . . plague": Burke, pp. 232–33.

22 "well-behaved . . . work": Clark, p. 47.

22 "Trying to . . . don't": Burke, p. 237.

22 "not fit . . . animal": Clark, p. 47.

22 "the Chinese . . . one": Burke, p. 241.

22 "immoral, degraded . . . race": Schaller, p. 20.

22 "Of course . . . charming": Burke, p. 242.

23 "Why, May-ling . . . it": Hahn, pp. 53–54.

23 "keeping up . . . mind": J. B. Powell, "Introduction," *The China Weekly Review,* vol. 14, no. 1, pp. 2–3.

23 "She was . . . piece": WCA: "Before Meeting Mme. Chiang Kai-shek," *Worcester Telegram,* March 7, 1943.

24 "I suppose . . . otherwise": WCA: "A Letter from Madame Chiang Kai-shek," *The Piedmont Announcements,* September 1938, p. 1.

24 "rather plain": WCA: "Mme. Chiang, as Wellesley Student, Never Went Out with American Boys," clipping from unknown newspaper, taken from a scrapbook collected by Betty S. Wheeler of Wellesley, March 8–31, 1943.

24 "Scarlett O'Hara accent": WCA: "The China Syndrome," *U.S. News & World Report,* April 22, 1991.

24 "she spoke . . . longer": WCA: "Mme. Chiang, as Wellesley Student, Never Went Out with American Boys," clipping from unknown newspaper, taken from a scrapbook collected by Betty S. Wheeler of Wellesley, March 8–31, 1943.

24 "She wrote . . . her": Ibid.

24 "She formed . . . direction": WCA: "Mme. Chiang Tells of her War Duties," *The New York Times,* July 10, 1938.

25 "There always . . . doorstep": WCA: Jean Harrington, "Madame Chiang Kai-shek (Mei-ling Soong), *The Wellesley Magazine* 22 no. 3 (February 1938), p. 185.

25 "My one . . . fat": WCA: Mary Patterson Routt, "College Girl," *Pasadena Star-News,* April 9, 1943.

25 "occasional . . . childlike vanity": DeLong, p. 25.

25 "But you . . . now!": WCA: Louise Leung, "China's First Lady Fulfills Promise to Old Classmates," unidentified newspaper clipping.

25 "As things . . . force": Ibid.

Chapter Three

27 "Great Within . . . it": Llewellyn, p. 201.

27 "a civilized . . . sword": Lattimore, *The Making of Modern China*, p. 80.

29 "will you . . . not?": Mitamura, p. 31.

30 "As we . . . death?": HA: Nym Wales papers, Box 30, Shao Yuan-chung, "Confucius and Present Day China," *The Peiping Chronicle*, August 30, 1934.

30 "family-minded . . . gentleman": Lin Yutang, "Some Hard Words about Confucius," *Harper's Monthly*, May 1935.

32 "compulsory": Epstein, *From Opium War to Liberation*, p. 4. (Note: Epstein takes this quote from *Chinese Repository*, vol. 5 (1837), quoted in S. Wells Williams, *The Middle Kingdom*, 1848.)

33 "They had . . . men": Tuchman, p. 33.

33 "for the . . . thought": Cantlie and Jones, pp. 16–17.

33 "even less . . . conscience?": Schaller, p. 12.

34 "The walls . . . pieces": Levy and Scott-Clark, pp. 98–99.

35 "Edicts are . . . enjoyment": Morrison, p. 48.

35 "no time . . . bible": Schaller, p. 11.

35 "up from . . . ago": Hugh Murray, "Swampland to Commercial Port," in Baker, p. 1.

36 "mud men": Pan Ling, p. 8.

36 "The Small Sword . . . apprehension": Chesneaux, p. 85.

36 "It is . . . can": Dong, p. 15.

37 "Philistines to . . . girth": Ibid., pp. 25–27.

37 "they begin . . . cigars!": Hauser, pp. 19–20.

38 "the biggest . . . clothing": Dong, p. 29.

Chapter Four

39 "I have . . . judgment": Paludan, p. 214.

39 "most lasting contribution": Ibid., p. 209.

39 "to bring . . . strength": Llewellyn, p. 182.

40 "When her . . . maidens": Dorn, *The Forbidden City*, p. 202.

40 "tried, just . . . star": Llewellyn, p. 183.

41 "a transparent . . . eggs": Levy and Scott-Clark, p. 143.

41 "naval construction": Elizabeth Luce Moore, "China's Soong," *Fortune*, June 1933.

41 "to soften . . . actors": Cameron, p. 12.

41 "the most . . . Our Hart": Seagrave, *Dragon Lady*, p. 146.

42 "always fooling . . . eunuchs": Ibid., p. 124.

43 "stood, towering . . . them": Spence, *The Gate of Heavenly Peace*, p. 31.

44 "painted, brocaded . . . eunuchs": Tuchman, p. 39.

44 "relegated to . . . life": Cantlie and Jones, *China*, p. 21.

Chapter Five

47 "China cannot . . . rebellion": "China in the United States," *The New York Times*, July 23, 1881.

47 "every reasonable persuasion": Sharman, p. 14.

47 "performed important . . . dexterity": Cantlie and Jones, p. 31.

48 "for reforming . . . army": Seagrave, *The Soong Dynasty,* p. 70.

48 "What China . . . you": Yu and Tang, p. 283.

50 "seems an . . . rebellion": Spence, *The Gate of Heavenly Peace,* p. 16.

50 "The vehicle . . . agitators": Cantlie and Jones, p. 41.

51 "While I . . . late": Sharman, pp. 47–48.

51 "Scotland Yard . . . with": Cantlie and Jones, pp. 43–44.

52 "the most . . . China": Sharman, p. 92.

52 "The five . . . career": Leonard Hsu, p. 55.

52 "After my . . . popular": Ibid., p. 59.

53 "If they . . . place": Sharman, p. 128.

53 "As soon . . . expectations": Leonard Hsu, p. 63.

53 "Wuchang occupied . . . revolutionists": Sharman, p. 128.

54 "Yes, for . . . meantime": Chang with Halliday, *Mme Sun Yat-sen,* p. 28.

54 "a good . . . due": Sharman, p. 138.

55 "to devote . . . undertaken": Cantlie and Jones, p. 252.

56 "have to . . . women": Cornell University Library, Division of Rare and Manuscript Collections, James M. McHugh papers, Box 13, Folder 5, no. 2770, draft for book, chapter 1, p. 15. (Note: This comes from an entry in McHugh's personal diary, dated November 24, 1937.)

56 "Ai-ling's Charlie . . . forever": Selle, pp. 139–40.

CHAPTER SIX

57 "For the . . . him": Chang with Halliday, *Mme Sun Yat-sen,* p. 31.

57 "upward mobility . . . group": Fairbank, *The Great Chinese Revolution,* p. 170 passim.

58 "The imperialist . . . privilege": Ibid., p. 173.

59 "punitive expedition": Sharman, p. 164.

60 "The Greatest . . . Waterloo": Ching-ling Soong, "The Greatest Event of the Twentieth Century," *The Wesleyan,* April 1912.

61 "They owned . . . before": George Sokolsky, "The Soongs of China," *The Atlantic Monthly,* February 1937, p. 186.

61 "You can't . . . revolution": Hahn, *The Soong Sisters,* p. 91.

61 "the Greatest . . . Aristocrat": Elizabeth Luce Moore, "China's Soong," *Fortune,* June 1933, p. 44.

61 "The Sage": Chang with Halliday, p. 80.

61 "intelligent, suave . . . shrewd": Moore, p. 44.

61 "This was . . . love!": Columbia University Library, COHO, H. H. Kung, "The Reminiscences of K'ung Hsiang-hsi," as told to Julie Lien-ying How, February 10–June 10, 1948, p. 41.

62 "perennial fixer": Moore, p. 46.

62 "I can . . . me": Epstein, *Woman in World History: Soong Ching Ling,* p. 35.

63 "Not our . . . today": Sharman, pp. 177–78.

64 "the bigger . . . prisoner": Bloodworth, p. 102.

64 "I didn't . . . divorce": Edgar Snow, *Journey to the Beginning,* p. 88.

65 "My mother . . . husband": Epstein, *Woman in World History,* p. 41.

65 "My father . . . me!": Edgar Snow, *Journey to the Beginning,* p. 89.

65 "Bill, he . . . friend": Burke, p. 265.

CHAPTER SEVEN

66 "The [Chinese] . . . teapot?": Mitamura, p. 82.
66 "Just think . . . immensely": Hahn, *The Soong Sisters,* p. 104.
66 "broke down . . . now": WCA: Emma DeLong Mills papers, MS to EM, July 3, 1917.
66 "I lost . . . all": Ibid., MS to EM, August 7, 1917.
67 "He is . . . rude": Ibid., MS to EM, December 15, 1917.
67 "a great . . . joke!": Ibid., MS to EM, August 7, 1917.
67 "shocked and . . . home": Ibid., MS to EM, September 6, 1917.
67 "With the . . . valuable": Ibid., MS to EM, September 13, 1917.
67 "We have . . . use": Ibid., MS to EM, August 7, 1917.
67 "We . . . enjoy . . . time": Ibid., MS to EM, September 28, 1917.
68 "furious. The . . . be!": Ibid., MS to EM, August 7, 1917.
68 "Two letters . . . be": Ibid., MS to EM, August 16, 1917.
69 "he always . . . it": Ibid., MS to EM, October 13, 1917.
69 "rather indifferent . . . Barbarian!": Ibid., MS to EM, August 16, 1917.
69 "busy & . . . day": Ibid., MS to EM, September 15, 1917.
69 "we actually . . . again!": Ibid., MS to EM, October 11, 1917.
70 "Sir": Ibid., MS to EM, September 28, 1917.
70 "Like your . . . China": WCA: May-ling Soong to Helen Esse, October 26, 1917.
70 "Fancy a . . . night": WCA: Mills papers, MS to EM, October 26, 1917.
70 "as though . . . off": Ibid., MS to EM, December 7, 1917.
71 "as abysmal . . . world": Dong, p. 155.
71 "for a song": Hauser, pp. 137–38.
71 "I . . . spent . . . machines": Madame Chiang, *Conversations with Mikhail Borodin,* p. 72.
71 "wards of . . . employ": Dong, p. 162.
71 "In the . . . vats": Madame Chiang, *Conversations with Mikhail Borodin,* p. 72.
72 "Women and . . . cauldron": Dong, p. 161.
72 "the richest . . . parents!": WCA: Dr. Hu Shih, "She Played a Part in Chinese Literature, Politics and War," *The Chinese Press,* March 26, 1943, p. 8.
73 "The woman . . . merit": Bloodworth, p. 73.
73 "Tomorrow you . . . you": Mah, p. 10.
73 "Being a . . . Hotel": May Tan, "Happiness in Different Worlds" (unpublished memoir).

CHAPTER EIGHT

75 "There is . . . stayed": Sheridan, *China in Disintegration,* p. 92.
75 "engaged in . . . impotency": Weale, p. 318.
75 "well-meaning but powerless": Schiffrin, p. 188.
76 "shaped like . . . head": Gunther, p. 274.
76 "the greatest . . . all": Koo, *Hui-Lan Koo,* p. 242.
77 "model governor": Gunther, p. 278.
77 "the physique of . . . tiger": Tuchman, p. 119.
77 "Three Things . . . Eighty-Six": Ibid., pp. 135–36.

78 "Pockmarked, syphilitic . . . affairs": WCA: Theodore White, "Chiang Kai-shek," *Life,* March 12, 1942.
78 "We stayed . . . disguised": Chang with Halliday, *Mme Sun Yat-sen,* p. 35.
78 "He spoke . . . goal": Snow, *Journey to the Beginning,* p. 92.
78 "You know . . . escape": Hahn, *The Soong Sisters,* p. 108.
80 "most important . . . on": Chang with Halliday, *Mme Sun Yat-sen,* p. 36.
81 "Several papers . . . fire": WCA: Emma DeLong Mills papers, MS to EM, June 5, 1919.
82 "Shanghai," she . . . Shanghai": Ibid., MS to EM, June 15, 1919.
83 "At 106 . . . Party": Baker, pp. 74–75.
84 "At present . . . away": Rand, p. 128.
84 "When the . . . me": Sharman, p. 227.

CHAPTER NINE
86 "[B]efore he . . . destiny": Pinchon P. Y. Loh, p. 62.
86 "In my . . . free": Hsiung, pp. 7–8.
87 "At play . . . personalities": Pinchon P. Y. Loh, p. 11.
87 "endured thirty-six . . . bitterness": Ibid., p. 7.
87 "frequently discriminated . . . origin": Ibid., pp. 17 ff.
87 "It will . . . fire": Crozier, pp. 34–35.
88 "endowed with . . . child": Pinchon P. Y. Loh, p. 8.
88 "He went . . . examination": Ibid., p. 15.
88 "She blamed . . . me": Ch'en Chieh-ju, pp. 54–55.
89 "Chiang Kai-shek . . . impression": Loh, p. 17.
90 "tiny portions . . . instructions": Crozier, pp. 38–40.
90 "More manipulative . . . unscrupulous": Dong, p. 90.
90 "a none . . . underworld": Edgar Snow, "China's Fighting Generalissimo," *Foreign Affairs,* 16, no. 4, July 1938, p. 613.
90 "to deliberate . . . depression": Pinchon P. Y. Loh, pp. 20–32.
91 "big and . . . stride": Koo, *Hui-Lan Koo,* p. 95.
92 "fiery, uncompromising . . . alienation": Pinchon P. Y. Loh, pp. 24–29.
92 "Alas!" he . . . did?": Dong, p. 92.
92 "into a . . . debauchery": Fenby, p. 43.
93 "the brains . . . him": Columbia University Library, COHO, interviews with George Sokolsky by C. Martin Wilbur, 1962, p. 29.
93 "one of . . . Movement": Pinchon P. Y. Loh, p. 24.
93 "a fabulous . . . town": Han Suyin, *A Mortal Flower,* p. 51.
93 "kingmaker by instinct": Dong, p. 92.
93 "The sudden . . . principles": Crozier, p. 51–52.
94 "become a . . . Kai-shek": Ch'en Chieh-ju, p. 27.
95 "About two . . . struggle": Chang with Halliday, *Mme Sun Yat-sen,* pp. 40–43.
97 "Small, slight . . . seen": DeLong, p. 52.
97 "pro-Russian and . . . foe": Ch'en Chieh-ju, pp. 111–12.
97 "come quickly": Pinchon P. Y. Loh, p. 83.
98 "What rubbish . . . here": Crozier, pp. 57–58.
98 "The need . . . behalf": Pinchon P. Y. Loh, pp. 83–89.

Chapter Ten

99 "Psychologically, all . . . Americans": George E. Sokolsky, "The Soongs of China," *The Atlantic Monthly,* February 1937, p. 185.

99 "Miss Soong . . . feet": Koo, *Hui-Lan Koo,* p. 261.

99 "When she . . . Shanghai": Franklin D. Roosevelt Library, Official File 200-3-N: President's Trip File: War Conference, November 11–December 17, 1943.

99 "The streets . . . others": Buck, p. 230.

100 "Don't send . . . home!" Hahn, *The Soong Sisters,* p. 75.

100 "a great . . . kindnesses": Webb, p. 235.

100 "become very . . . temper": WCA: Emma DeLong Mills papers, MS to EM, March 19, 1918.

100 "Mother says . . . swollen": Ibid., MS to EM, undated, received May 28, 1918.

101 "grand euphemism": Seagrave, *The Soong Dynasty,* p. 143.

101 "I took . . . maid": WCA: Mills papers, MS to EM, April 9, 1918.

101 "We certainly . . . constantly": Ibid., MS to EM, July 18, 1919.

101 "wrestling with . . . days!": Ibid., MS to EM, August 1, 1918.

102 "I wish . . . writing": Ibid., MS to EM, August 15, 1918.

102 "really a . . . house": Comment from the author's Chinese translator.

102 "The inside . . . us": WA: Mills papers, MS to EM, May 15, 1918.

103 "one that . . . luxury-loving": Dong, p. 98.

103 "the moonlight . . . Kingdom": Ibid., p. 97.

103 "The evidence . . . Road": J. O. P. Bland, "Shanghai Revisited," *National Review* (London), December 1920, p. 526.

103 "came to . . . convenience": Fairbank, *The Great Chinese Revolution,* pp. 177–79.

104 "Some were . . . sinister": Caldwell, p. 12.

104 "sinister aura . . . lord": Wakeman, *Policing Shanghai,* pp. 30–31.

105 "A carload . . . view!": Coble, p. 39.

106 "protect and . . . stocks": Y. C. Wang, "Du Yueh-Sheng (1888–1951): A Tentative Political Biography." *Journal of Asian Studies* 26, no. 3 (May 1967), p. 435.

106 "Imagine that . . . breast": Eastern Web Service, "Tales of Old Shanghai—Opium," www.talesofoldchina.com/shanghai/business/t-opium.htm.

107 "a gaunt . . . claws": Sues, pp. 89–90.

107 "an amazing . . . War": Columbia University Library, COHO: interviews with George Sokolsky by C. Martin Wilbur, 1962, p. 26.

Chapter Eleven

108 "If we . . . ago": Shi, *Soong May-Ling and China,* p. 95.

108 Mother said . . . undergoing": WCA: Emma DeLong Mills papers, MS to EM, September 20, 1918.

108 "I felt . . . pay": Ibid., MS to EM, September 21, 1918.

109 "a whopping . . . fun": Ibid., MS to EM, October 29, 1918.

109 "The streets . . . you?": Ibid., MS to EM, November 14, 1918.

110 "In former . . . sold": Cameron, pp. 66–67.

110 "I go . . . interviews": WCA: Mills papers, MS to EM, December 7, 1918.

111 "women lose . . . children?": Ibid., MS to EM, April 9, 1919.

111 "you are . . . well": Ibid., MS to EM, May 15, 1919.

111 "idea of . . . advice": Ibid., MS to EM, April 15, 1919.

111 "I am . . . around": Ibid., MS to EM, June 5, 1919.

111 "I think . . . are": Ibid., MS to EM, July 9, 1919.

112 "The town . . . something": Ibid., MS to EM, July 24, 1919.

113 "many hundreds . . . factories": Ibid., MS to EM, June 29, 1919.

113 "had the . . . honorable": Ibid., MS to EM, undated.

113 "all my . . . daughter": Ibid., MS to EM, August 18, 1919.

113 "a great . . . whole": Indiana University, Lilly Library, Manuscripts Department, Emily Hahn papers, response to questions, May-ling to Hahn, undated.

113 "Sometimes I . . . scatter-brain": WCA: Mills papers, MS to EM, September 29, 1919.

113 "ecstatic mood": Ibid., MS to EM, August 10, 1921.

114 "become so . . . engagements": "What to Do with Capote, Frost, and Kissinger?" *The Boston Globe*, December 31, 2005.

114 "terribly strict": WCA: Mills papers, MS to EM, March 21, 1920.

114 "I am . . . you!": Ibid., MS to EM, July 6, 1921.

114 "as irritable . . . dear": Ibid., MS to EM, February 11, 1920.

115 "he [T.V.] . . . it": George E. Sokolsky, "The Soongs of China," *The Atlantic Monthly*, February 1937, pp. 185–86.

115 "I had . . . off": WCA: Mills papers, MS to EM, February 11, 1920.

115 "a thing . . . family": Ibid., MS to EM, October 11, 1920.

115 "not nearly . . . callers": Ibid., MS to EM, April 21, 1921.

116 "I think . . . America": Ibid., MS to EM, April 28, 1921.

116 "literally dragged . . . all": Ibid., MS to EM, May 25, 1921.

117 "I know . . . flavor": Ibid., MS to EM, July 6, 1921.

119 "Of course . . . month": WCA: Mills papers, Emma Mills diary, January 26, 1922.

119 "she never . . . myself": DeLong, pp. 47–54.

120 "magnetic pull . . . inconsequential": Ibid., p. 64.

CHAPTER TWELVE

121 "We are . . . meat": Sun Yat-sen, *The Three Principles of the People*, p. 6.

121 "Dr. Sun . . . Russia": Spence, *The Search for Modern China*, p. 335.

122 "The real . . . Russia": Fletcher S. Brockman, "Foreign Control at Peking Means War, Says Sun Yat-sen," *The New York Times*, July 22, 1923.

122 "the European . . . wait": Ch'en Chieh-ju, pp. 131–35.

123 "The realization . . . begun": Jacobs, p. 8.

123 "No foreigner . . . action": Sokolsky, p. 35.

123 "He made . . . next": Chang with Halliday, *Mme Sun Yat-sen*, p. 38.

124 "You cannot . . . respected": Ch'en Chieh-ju, pp. 136–37.

125 "because we . . . Kuomintang": Chiang Kai-shek, *Soviet Russia in China*, p. 27.

126 "to proceed . . . man": Jacobs, pp. 132–33.

126 "The military . . . delay": Payne, p. 100.

126 "Because of . . . nucleus": Crozier, p. 71.

126 "You must . . . home": Ch'en Chieh-ju, p. 143.

127 "a very . . . commander": Ibid., p. 155.

127 "which seemed . . . mask": Tuchman, p. 117.

127 "Stop!" Chiang . . . death": Ch'en Chieh-ju, pp. 155–56.

127 "Each Sunday . . . forget": Han Suyin, *Destination Chungking*, p. 30.

128 "The aim . . . changed": Ch'en Chieh-ju, pp. 141–42.

128 "an intellectual . . . background": Kai-yu Hsu, p. 2.

129 "Kwangtung [Canton's . . . soon": Ibid., pp. 146–49.

130 "Protector of Canton": Fenby, p. 85.

130 "not sure": Ch'en Chieh-ju, p. 151.

131 "The doctor . . . afraid": DeLong, p. 68.

131 "We felt . . . sister": Soong Mei-ling to Liao Cheng-zhi, August 17, 1982, http://bbs
.chinanews.com.cn/thread-155863-1-1.html.

131 "one day . . . will": Columbia University Library, COHO, H. H. Kung, "The Reminiscences of K'ung Hsiang-hsi," as told to Julie Lien-ying How, February 10–June
10, 1948, p. 58.

131 "Revolutionary Saint": Elizabeth Luce Moore, "China's Soong," *Fortune*, June 1933,
p. 112.

132 "No one . . . Kuomintang": Sokolsky, p. 38.

132 "Sun Yat-sen . . . alive": Cornell University Library, Division of Rare and Manuscript Collections, James M. McHugh papers, Box 13, Folder 5, no. 2770, draft for
book, chapter 1, p. 11.

CHAPTER THIRTEEN

133 "If I . . . leadership": Ch'en Chieh-ju, p. 155.

133 "stood at . . . ladder": Ibid., p. 157.

133 "humbler of . . . hearts": Fenby, p. 80.

133 "brilliant and erratic": Payne, p. 105.

133 "dapper to . . . dandy": Ch'en Chieh-ju, p. 89.

133 "make Canton . . . revolution": Ibid., p. 148.

134 "The defeat . . . years!": Ibid., pp. 161–64.

135 "one could . . . other": "Canton Growing Redder," *The North-China Herald*, November 28, 1925.

135 called "incidents" . . . us": Crozier, pp. 78–79.

136 "imperious commands . . . ambition": Ch'en Chieh-ju, pp. 164–77.

136 "every move . . . self-aggrandizement": "Chiang Kai-shek of Canton," *The North-
China Herald*, July 10, 1926.

136 "The past . . . rendered": Ch'en Chieh-ju, p. 177.

137 "inspection": Ibid., p. 181.

137 "an enormous crowd": Chang with Halliday, *Mme Sun Yat-sen*, p. 51.

138 "Dearest Dada . . . be": WCA: Emma DeLong Mills papers, MS to EM, January 22,
1926.

138 "Madame Sun . . . there": HA: Chiang Kai-shek, diary, Box 4, January 17, 1926.

140 "Though these . . . inside": Hsiung, pp. 246–47.

140 "told to . . . hands": Ch'en Chieh-ju, p. 201.

141 "the purpose . . . people": Chiang, *Soviet Russia in China*, p. 43.

141 "a momentous . . . China": Madame Chiang Kai-shek, *Conversations with Mikhail
Borodin*, p. 1.

142 "We paid . . . rifles": Jacobs, p. 212.

142 "I expect . . . propaganda": Tuchman, p. 120.

142 "The revolutionary . . . independence": Payne, p. 117.

143 "he conquered . . . political": "The Army of the Republic of China," *Fortune*, September 1941, p. 47.

143 "China has . . . victories": Lewis P. Gannett, "New Strong Man Holds Half of China," *The New York Times*, November 14, 1926.

CHAPTER FOURTEEN

144 "General Chiang . . . army": *The North-China Herald*, 1926.

144 "Very soon . . . country": Payne, p. 117.

144 "the Chicago . . . China": Rand, p. 26.

145 "very conservative . . . penetrated": Ch'en Chieh-ju, p. 229.

145 "a morose nonentity": Han Suyin, *A Mortal Flower*, p. 73.

145 "mouthpiece": H. H. Brayton Barff, "Eugene Chen: China's Scorching Tongue," *The New York Times*, April 10, 1927.

145 "a small . . . gesture": Sheean, *Personal History*, p. 205.

145 "as if . . . carnival": Barff, "Eugene Chen."

146 "to a . . . movement": Jacobs, pp. 226–31.

147 "the divergencies . . . Kuomintang": Madame Chiang, *Conversations with Mikhail Borodin*, p. 5.

147 "outwardly congenial . . . thinking": Ibid., p. 65.

147 "undoubtedly the . . . abroad": FBI files, Madame Chiang Kai-shek, "Eroded Spirit and the Result of Fragmented Policy" (address given at Drake University), April 6, 1959, not numbered. Material furnished to the author by the Department of Justice in response to Freedom of Information Act inquiry.

147 "he kept . . . means": Madame Chiang, *Conversations with Mikhail Borodin*, p. 89.

147 "must find . . . America": Ibid., p. 24.

147 "As I . . . magnetism": Ibid., pp. 6–9.

148 "He was . . . dedication": Ibid., p. 68.

148 "delighted" servant . . . Mayling": Hahn, *Chiang Kai-shek*, p. 87.

149 "These people . . . China": Dong, pp. 175–76.

149 "The coolie . . . spoils": Sheean, p. 200.

150 "On March . . . Forces": Chiang, *Soviet Russia in China*, pp. 46–47.

150 "apparently a . . . suffered": Tuchman, p. 133.

151 "Nanking outrage . . . foreigners": *The North-China Herald*, April 23, 1927.

151 "a little . . . necessary": Columbia University Library, COHO, interviews with George Sokolsky by Professor C. Martin Wilbur, 1962, p. 4.

151 "The revolution . . . return": Tuchman, pp. 132–33.

151 "frantically sought . . . Kuomintang": Coble, p. 28.

151 "In late . . . force": Han Suyin, *A Mortal Flower*, p. 71. (Note: Du is spelled Dou in the original quote.)

152 "And so . . . left": Dong, p. 183.

152 "Simultaneously," *The* . . . roll": Isaacs, p. 175.

152 "fed alive . . . locomotives": Dong, p. 184.

152 "Her intestines . . . alive": Sheean, p. 227.

152 "many innocent . . . killed": Taylor, p. 42.

153 "beloved friend . . . power": Jacobs, p. 246.

153 "I, your . . . single-handed": Crozier, p. 94.

153 "the new . . . Yangtze": Clifford, p. 178.

154 "self-interest . . . drawn": Jacobs, p. 246.

154 "ally of . . . International": "Moscow's Idea of a Traitor," *North China Daily News*, April 23, 1927.

154 "The Revolution . . . Kai-shek!": Ch'en Chieh-ju, p. 223.

154 twelve "crimes" . . . Party": Crozier, p. 107.

154 "await orders . . . imperialists": Ch'en Chieh-ju, pp. 220–24.

155 "no rice . . . money": Han Suyin, *A Mortal Flower*, p. 74.

155 "Business men . . . boats": "The Kuomintang and Communism," *The North-China Herald*, April 23, 1927.

Chapter Fifteen

156 "Our only . . . sooner": Han Suyin, *A Mortal Flower*, p. 106.

156 "Down with . . . imperialism!": Jacobs, p. 263.

156 "pacify the . . . countryside": Rand, p. 49.

156 "the jewel . . . nation": Chang with Halliday, *Mme Sun Yat-sen*, p. 18.

156 "Mme. Sun . . . heroism": Sheean, pp. 208–9 ff.

157 "Like Sheean . . . history": Snow, *Journey to the Beginning*, pp. 82–83.

157 Sheng Hsuan-huai: It was said that Sheng, supposedly the richest man in China at the time, gave both his fourth son, Edward (known as "Number Four"), and Edward's schoolmate T. V. Soong $8,000 to invest, but T.V., who, the storyteller claimed, was "an inveterate and unsuccessful" speculator in his youth, lost his within a year. Another, similar story says that Sheng gave T.V. and his younger brother T.L. more than $700,000 to set them up in business but that they lost the money. It was also said that later on, when T.V. was minister of finance, he forced Edward Sheng to buy $5 million in Chinese government bonds, for which he gave Edward his personal receipt but never delivered the bonds. After many months, Edward went to Nanking and confronted T.V., calling him "a swindler and a damn crook." It was also reported that T.V., as finance minister, called old man Sheng a traitor and put a government ban on his estate, which meant that his properties could neither be sold nor mortgaged. It is impossible to gauge the accuracy of any of these stories beyond the obvious conclusion that there was a lot of bad blood between T.V. and the Shengs. (HA: Lauchlin Currie papers, Box 1, letter Lucius R. Holbrook, Jr., to Lauchlin Currie, April 16, 1943; Box 5, "FDR Memorandum, Note for personal files," March 17, 1943, and April 5, 1943.

158 "On the . . . workers": Yang, p. 10.

158 "persuasion and . . . meetings": Sheean, pp. 233–35 ff.

159 "How can . . . time": Wang, Jiang, and Rao, pp. 26–27, and Sheean, p. 235.

159 "happened to . . . shores": Sheean, pp. 235–36.

159 "The plight . . . execution": Frederick Moore, "Rich Chinese Flee Extortion or Death," *The New York Times*, May 3, 1927.

160 "a veritable . . . 'Communists'!": Coble, pp. 34–35. Note: All these examples of extortion come from Coble.

161 "left infantilism": Jacobs, p. 265.

161 "the mass . . . army": Isaacs, p. 251.

161 "the only . . . Kuomintang": Jacobs, p. 280.

161 "indecisive in . . . leap": Isaacs, p. 197.

161 "The area . . . price": Rand, p. 54.

162 "instruction and contemplation": Jacobs, p. 204.

162 "Moscow thought . . . Wuhan": Ibid., pp. 273–75.

163 "courage of . . . fellows": Isaacs, p. 198.

163 "commonplace": Jacobs, p. 282.

163 "Having achieved . . . events": "Galen Leaves Hankow," *The North-China Herald*, August 9, 1927.

163 "[A]ll revolutions . . . militarist": "Madame Sun's Withdrawal," *The Nation*, September 21, 1927.

164 "a certain . . . death": Sheean, p. 264.

164 "If you . . . anyway!": Randall Gould, "Madame Sun Yat-sen Keeps Faith," *The Nation*, January 22, 1930.

164 "I think . . . things": Rand, pp. 63–64.

164 "the worst . . . exiles": Chang with Halliday, *Mme Sun Yat-sen*, pp. 61–65.

165 "at a standstill": George E. Sokolsky, "Sudden Resignation of Chiang Kai-shek," *The North-China Herald*, August 20, 1927.

CHAPTER SIXTEEN

169 "By education . . . state": T. Christopher Jespersen, "Madame Chiang Kai-shek and the Face of Sino-American Relations: Personality and Gender Dynamics in Bilateral Diplomacy," in Samuel C. Chu, p. 125.

169 "Pardon me . . . party": Zhiang, pp. 28–30.

170 "a small . . . secretary": Leonard, p. 49.

170 "Do you . . . while": Hahn, *The Soong Sisters*, p. 119.

170 "She thought . . . declined": Snow, *Journey to the Beginning*, p. 85.

170 "Chiang's remarriage . . . circumstances": Crozier, p. 115.

171 "May-ling will . . . leave": HA: Chiang Kai-shek, diaries, Box 4, July 29, 1926.

171 "the divergences . . . policy": Madame Chiang, *Conversations with Mikhail Borodin*, p. 4.

171 "I missed . . . May-ling": *Chiang Kai-shek Diary*, ed. Wang Yu-gao and Wang Yu-zheng, with an introduction to this section (one of five) called "Stories of Love," by Chen Jin-jin, June 26, 1928, pp. 275–88.

171 "An invitation! . . . sister": Ch'en Chieh-ju, pp. 186–94.

172 "out of . . . you": Ibid., p. 216. Although Jennie Chiang places this letter after Chiang's meeting with Ai-ling, it probably predates their conference and may even predate May-ling's trip to Hankow (Wuhan) during the winter of 1926–1927.

173 "the subtle . . . Finance": Ibid., pp. 237–38.

174 "Do you . . . that": Chen Ting-yi, pp. 263–65.

176 "desperate . . . country!": Ch'en Chieh-ju, pp. 238–43.

176 "I telegraphed . . . away": HA: Chiang Kai-shek, diary, Box 5, March 21–June 25, 1927.

177 "He came . . . forever": Ch'en Chieh-ju, pp. 251–53.

177 "Mme. Chiang . . . dispatches": Ibid., pp. 255–56.

178 "Political enemies . . . wife": Henry F. Misselwitz, "Chiang Blames Foes for Talk of 'Wife,' " *The New York Times,* September 25, 1927.

178 "I am . . . world?": Crozier, p. 116.

179 "We love . . . you?": Chen Jin-jin, "Stories of Love," *A Study of Modern Chinese Women,* vol. 2, pages 275–88.

179 "to arrange . . . marriage": George E. Sokolsky, "Chiang Kai-shek's Visit to Shanghai," *The North-China Herald,* October 1, 1927.

179 "I got . . . trick" HA: Chiang Kai-shek, diary, Box 8, June 20, 1931.

179 "instructions from . . . outcast": Ch'en Chieh-ju, pp. 261–63.

181 "I reached . . . possible": HA: Chiang Kai-shek, diary, Box 5, October 3, 1927. (Note: The original translation reads, "I took the same car with T.V. . . .").

181 "At 1:30 . . . joy": Ibid., Box 5, November 10, 1927.

181 "that bluebeard": Chang with Halliday, *Mme Sun Yat-sen,* p. 66.

182 "Throughout Chinese . . . Mei-ling": "Marriage of Chiang Kai-shek and Soong Mei-ling," *Shanghai Star,* June 14, 2006, www.chinadaily.com.cn/star/2001/06/14/cu18-2 html.

182 "It was . . . simple": Hahn, *The Soong Sisters,* pp. 139–45.

182 "foreign atmosphere . . . concerned": "Chiang Weds Mme. Sun Yat-sen's Sister; 3,000 See Rites for Wellesley Girl Bride," *The New York Times,* December 2, 1927.

182 "The bride . . . vests": Hahn, *The Soong Sisters,* pp. 139–43.

182 "In the . . . married": HA: Chiang Kai-shek, diary, Box 5, December 1–2, 1927.

183 "When I . . . society": Li, pp. 80–81.

CHAPTER SEVENTEEN

184 "Subordination and . . . society": Thomas L. Kennedy, "Activism among Women of China's Traditional Elite," in Samuel C. Chu, p. 7.

184 "the most . . . would": HA: Chiang Kai-shek, diary, Box 5, December 24–29, 1927.

184 "not think . . . wife": DeLong, p. 77.

184 "her pain . . . described": HA: Chiang Kai-shek, diary, Box 6, August 25, 1928.

185 "believed that . . . anything": Oursler, pp. 350–52.

186 "to her . . . anxiety?": Sues, pp. 69–70.

187 "in face . . . uncertainty": "Chiang Kai-shek's Manifesto," *The North-China Herald,* January 14, 1928.

187 "She is . . . time": Chen Jin-jin, "Stories of Love," in *A Study of Modern Chinese Women,* vol. 2, pp. 275–88.

188 "This town . . . them": Tuchman, p. 111.

188 "During past . . . country": Tong, vol. 1, pp. 208–9.

188 "We are . . . finish": Fenby, p. 175.

188 "One may . . . it": "The Nationalist Budget," *The North-China Herald,* May 12, 1928.

188 "Soong replaced . . . regime": Parks Coble, "The Soong Family and Chinese Capitalists," in Samuel C. Chu, p. 73.

189 "easy and . . . uncomfortable": Indiana University, Lilly Library, Manuscripts Department, Emily Hahn papers, Madame Chiang Kai-shek, Answers to questions posed by Hahn, pp. 2–3 ff.

189 "There was . . . water": Cornell University Library, Division of Rare and Manuscript Collections, James M. McHugh papers, Box 13, Folder 4, no. 2770, draft for book, foreword, p. 4.

189 "It was . . . belong": Hahn, *The Soong Sisters*, p. 146.

190 "I see . . . are!": Academia Historica, Taipei, Chen Jin-jin, "Stories of Love," in *A Study of Modern Chinese Women*, vol. 2, pp. 275–88.

190 "I miss . . . can": Academia Historica, Taipei, CKS, wire to Madame, March 13, 1928, File 080200/628, Microfilm 0607.

190 "The streets . . . retching": Abend, pp. 80–81.

191 "efforts at . . . Japanese": Rodney Gilbert, "Events of Monday, May 7," *The North-China Herald*, May 12, 1928.

191 "malice and . . . Expedition": "Events of Sunday, May 6: General Chiang Kai-shek's Report," *The North-China Herald*, May 12, 1928.

191 "I just . . . affairs": Academia Historica, Taipei, Madame, wire to CKS, May 5, 1928, File 080200/627, Microfilm 0561.

191 "absolutely a rumor": Ibid., CKS, wire to Madame, undated, File 080200/628, Microfilm 0607.

191 "Please persuade . . . matters": Ibid., CKS, wire to Madame, May 21, 1928, File 080200/628, Microfilm 0607.

192 "she may . . . reunion!": Chen Jin-jin, "Stories of Love," *A Study of Modern Chinese Women*, vol. 2, pages 275–88.

192 "Please send . . . people": Academia Historica, Taipei, CKS, wire to Madame, June 3, 1930, File 080200/628, Microfilm 0607.

192 "Please buy . . . quick": Ibid., CKS, wire to Madame, June 3, 1930, File 080200/628, Microfilm 0607.

192 "uncrowned Emperor . . . faithless": Edgar Snow, "Son of the Grand Marshal," *New York Herald Tribune Magazine*, December 15, 1929.

193 "I know . . . Chinese": Payne, p. 142.

193 "I would . . . China": Zhengzhong, "An Interview with Tang De-gang about Chang Hsueh-liang's Oral History," *Wan Xiang*, vol. 3 (March 2002), pp. 2–3.

193 "an air . . . shoulders": Snow, "Son of the Grand Marshal."

194 "How do . . . ago": Zhengzhong, "An Interview with Tang De-gang about Chang Hsueh-liang's Oral History."

194 "glorious red": Koo, *Hui-Lan Koo*, p. 238.

194 "Thirty-year-old Chang . . . Manchuria": Ibid., pp. 244–45.

194 "stand the . . . weather": Chen Jin-jin, "Stories of Love," *A Study of Modern Chinese Women*, vol. 2, pages 275–88.

194 "When he . . . heresies": Payne, p. 143.

196 "She was . . . hand": Cornell University Library, Division of Rare and Manuscript Collections, James M. McHugh papers, Box 13, Folder 5, no. 2770, draft for book, chapter 1, pp. 3–4.

196 "ugly rumor . . . them": Ibid., p. 12.

CHAPTER EIGHTEEN

197 "Wherever she . . . became": Hahn, *The Soong Sisters,* p. 148.

197 "widespread heresies . . . Kai-shek": Han Suyin, *A Mortal Flower,* p. 107.

197 "The Fourth . . . China": Crozier, p. 122.

198 "One picked . . . quivering": Levy, *Two-Gun Cohen,* p. 3.

199 "within just . . . wife": HA: Chiang Kai-shek, diary, Box 6, December 1, 1928.

199 "arrogant and . . . dictatorship": Crozier, p. 130.

199 "I have . . . sleep": "Chiang Kai-shek Displeased," *The North-China Herald,* December 8, 1928.

200 "After the . . . danger": Tong, vol. 1, p. 243.

200 "The Northern . . . Kuomintang": Sheridan, p. 240.

200 "The Japanese . . . prefer?": "Self-Sacrifice of Samurai Contrasted with Greed of China's Militarists" (Chiang Kai-shek on How Japan Made Herself Mighty), *The North-China Herald,* January 5, 1929.

201 "At every . . . paid": Han Suyin, *A Mortal Flower,* pp. 97–99.

202 "the enormous . . . West": Ibid., p. 184.

202 "wizardry of . . . 1937": Parks Coble, "The Soong Family and Chinese Capitalists," in Samuel C. Chu, p. 73.

203 "the royal family": Hallett Abend, "Chiang's Royal Aims Are Laid to His Wife," *The New York Times,* December 9, 1928.

203 "Although we . . . country": www.trumanlibrary.org/oralhist/fetterfw.htm.

203 "unbelievably long . . . protection": Tong, vol. 1, pp. 268–78.

204 "enormous . . . China": Sheridan, *Chinese Warlord,* pp. 261–62.

206 "the luxury . . . circles": Koo, *Hui-Lan Koo,* p. 223.

206 "with reluctant feet": Tuchman, p. 184.

206 "Good Morning . . . Lampson": Hahn, *Chiang Kai-shek,* p. 138.

206 "The institution . . . mother-in-law": WCA: Henry Lieberman, "Madame Sun—China's 'Conscience,' " *The New York Times,* May 11, 1946.

206 "These children . . . doing": Hahn, *The Soong Sisters,* pp. 144–46.

207 "some very . . . silkworms": WCA: Madame Chiang Kai-shek, "A Letter from China," *The Wellesley Magazine,* December 11, 1930.

207 "the last . . . virtue": Sues, pp. 116–19.

208 "As she . . . earrings": WCA: Louisa Wilson, "Americans Should All Be Good According to China's First Lady," New York *Sun,* September 24, 1931.

208 "rather modest . . . cake?": Columbia University, Butler Library, Frank Rounds, "Interview 2 with Dr. Bluma Swerdloff," October 1, 1962, pp. 58–59.

CHAPTER NINETEEN

210 "He [Chiang . . . piety": White and Jacoby, p. 123.

210 "being built . . . Sun": Chang with Halliday, *Mme Sun Yat-sen,* p. 69.

210 "the life-like . . . body": Cornell University Library, Division of Rare and Manuscript Collections, James M. McHugh papers, Box 13, Folder 5, no. 2770, draft for book, chapter 1, p. 10.

211 "thin line . . . upwards": J. M. D. Hoste, "State Funeral of Dr. Sun Yat-sen," *The North-China Herald,* June 8, 1929.

211 "abundantly clear . . . party": Hahn, *The Soong Sisters*, p. 158.

212 "Chiang sanctified . . . capital": Levy, p. 172.

212 "raise arms . . . rebel": Crozier, p. 139.

212 "one of . . . warlords": Sheridan, p. 267.

212 "a year . . . Staff": Payne, p. 152.

213 "It is . . . country": HA: Walter H. Judd papers, Box 175, Folder 4, "Chiang Kai-shek Thunders against Party's Sins," *The Shanghai Times*, October 22, 1932.

213 "My wife . . . me": Chen Jin-jin, "Stories of Love," *A Study of Modern Chinese Women*, vol. 2, pages 275–88.

213 "The deeper . . . be": Ibid., March 15, 1931.

213 "I felt . . . painful": Ibid., August 6, 1934.

214 "Rev. Jing . . . Christianity": HA: Chiang Kai-shek, diary, Box 7, February 21, 1930.

214 "I feel . . . Christ": WCA: "Chinese Leader Now Christian," clipping from unidentified newspaper, October 23, 1930.

214 "startled all . . . Nanking": WCA: *St. Louis Post-Dispatch*, October 23, 1930.

214 "embraced the . . . political": WCA: M. B. Schnapper, "Wellesley Girl Credited with Converting Kai-shek," clipping from unidentified newspaper, undated.

215 "There's Methodism . . . madness": Burke, p. 347.

215 "not shy . . . status": Leong, p. 118.

215 "the greatest . . . people": WCA: "Madame Chiang's Vision of a Chinese Christian Church," speech given at Wuhan Missionary Prayer Meeting, April 16, 1938.

215 "religion was . . . yours": HA: George E. Sokolsky papers, Box 35, Folder 16, Madame Chiang Kai-shek, "The Main Attack."

216 "We Chinese . . . moment": Leo Soong, "Family Reminiscences," 2004.

216 "SHOTS FIRED . . . Nanking": "Canton Says Chiang Seeks War on Japan," *The New York Times*, July 23, 1931.

216 "foreign garb . . . detail": "Assassins Thwarted in Attempt on Finance Minister," *The North-China Herald*, July 23, 1931.

216 "The Mother . . . China": "The Mother-in-Law," *The North-China Herald*, July 28, 1931.

216 "Oh, my . . . yourselves": Academia Historica, Taipei, CKS, wire to Madame, July 26, 1931.

216 Led by . . . buried: The author is indebted for the description of Madame Soong's funeral to Fenby, pp. 199–200.

217 "First," she . . . God's": Madame Chiang Kai-shek, "What Religion Means to Me," *The World Outlook* (reprinted from *Forum*), May 1934, p. 9.

217 "seems to . . . utility": Eastman, *The Abortive Revolution*, pp. 32–40.

218 "In the . . . situation": Eastman, "Fascism in Kuomintang China: The Blue Shirts," *The China Quarterly*, no. 49 (January–March, 1972), p. 5.

218 "richly exposed . . . it": Eastman, *The Abortive Revolution*, pp. 39–40.

219 "Cold, hard . . . China": Caldwell, pp. 73–75.

219 "the establishment . . . revolution": Eastman, *The Abortive Revolution*, p. 43.

220 "one of . . . China": Eastman, "Fascism in Kuomintang China," pp. 1–2.

CHAPTER TWENTY

221 "It is . . . limitless": "Warns of Tokyo's Plans," *The New York Times,* December 31, 1935.
221 "gorging on . . . late": Han Suyin, *A Mortal Flower,* p. 166.
222 "In order . . . Mongolia": Payne, p. 153.
222 "The way . . . Europe": Crozier, p. 147.
223 "The military . . . power": Columbia University, RBML, William Henry Donald papers, W. H. Donald to Harold K. Hochschild, February 20, 1932.
223 "red-faced, serious . . . nose": Auden and Isherwood, p. 55.
223 "as influential . . . elsewhere": Cornell University Library, Division of Rare and Manuscript Collections, James M. McHugh papers, H. B. Elliston, "China's No. 1 White Boy," *The Saturday Evening Post,* March 19, 1938, p. 34.
223 "adamant nondrinker": Ibid., p. 31.
223 "Nationalusts": Selle, p. 252.
223 "There was . . . policy": Chang and Halliday, *Mao: The Unknown Story,* p. 103.
223 "To declare . . . resistance": Payne, p. 157.
224 "Little did . . . statesmen": Hsiung, p. 306.
224 "Everyone, peasants . . . ages!": Koo, *Hui-Lan Koo,* pp. 270–78.
224 "almost insane . . . frustration": Payne, p. 156.
225 "With a . . . him": "Adroit Chiang," *Time,* February 1, 1932.
225 "The coming . . . raiser": Payne, p. 158.
226 "extremely anxious . . . occupy": Sokolsky, pp. 254–55.
226 "It was . . . face": Lois Snow, *Edgar Snow's China,* p. 55–56.
228 "obey Generalissimo . . . rare": Selle, p. 281.
228 "Do you . . . China": Fenby, p. 222.
228 "ramshackle village . . . countrymen": Hallett Abend, "Truce Conference Is Opened in China," *The New York Times,* May 31, 1933.
228 "one of . . . train": Abend, pp. 204–5.
229 "Internal security . . . aggression": Payne, p. 159.
229 "What is . . . exam?": Academia Historica, Taipei, CKS, wire to Madame, January 8, 1933, File 080200/628, Microfilm 0607.
229 "It has . . . healed?": Ibid., CKS, wire to Madame, March 16, 1933.
229 "Shanghai is . . . me?": Ibid., CKS, wire to Madame, March 17, 1933.
229 "very powerful . . . poet!": WCA: Madame Chiang Kai-shek to Sophie Hart, January 17, 1934.

CHAPTER TWENTY-ONE

231 "The Kuomintang . . . repression": Han Suyin, *A Mortal Flower,* p. 369.
231 "Cultivate these . . . dying": Madame Chiang Kai-shek, *China Shall Rise Again,* p. 293.
231 "The struggle . . . effected": Hsiung, pp. 361–62 (appendix).
232 "in an . . . way": Payne, pp. 162–64.
232 "hosing urine . . . public": Cornell University Library, Division of Rare and Manuscript Collections, James M. McHugh papers, Box 13, Folder 5, no. 2770, draft for book, chapter 1, p. 6.

232 "If we . . . nation": Eastman, *The Abortive Revolution*, p. 68.

233 "Priggery and . . . interior": Auden and Isherwood, p. 66.

233 "Holding that . . . hair": HA: Nym Wales papers, Box 32, "Chiang Kai-shek to Forbid 'Permanents' as Bad for Health," *Peiping Chronicle*, January 18, 1935.

233 "All wedding . . . midnight": Ibid., Box 30, "Chinese Marriage Reform Association Adopts Regulations," *The China Weekly Review*, April 7, 1934.

233 "each and . . . fastened": "New Life Movement in Chungking," *The North-China Herald*, February 11, 1936.

234 the "stunned" . . . Plan": Sues, pp. 5–7.

234 "welcomed by . . . famishing": WCA: Madame Chiang Kai-shek, "China's Spiritual Mobilization," in *China at War*, undated (probably 1937–1938).

235 "It is . . . prestige": Library of Congress: Nelson T. Johnson papers, Box 54, NTJ. "The New Life Movement and its Significance," undated.

235 "In the . . . job": Crozier, pp. 152–53.

236 "Great Wall . . . tightened": Ibid., p. 159.

236 "the tactics . . . fish": Chang and Halliday, p. 125.

236 "best collaborator . . . Confucius": Meier-Welcker, pp. 651–52 ff.

237 "Go north . . . collaboration": Kai-yu Hsu, p. 111.

237 "we ourselves . . . Tse-tung": Han Suyin, *A Mortal Flower*, pp. 310–11.

238 "across the . . . rainstorm": Snow, *Red Star over China*, p. 180.

239 "Oh, it . . . wall": Crozier, p. 179.

239 "REVOLT HAS . . . worthless": Selle, pp. 285–96.

241 "One can . . . belts": "Pain in the Heart," *Time*, December 28, 1936.

241 "And here . . . north-west": Auden and Isherwood, p. 129.

242 "a tremendous . . . soldiers": Tong, vol. 2, p. 354.

242 "sense a . . . figure": Selle, p. 304.

243 "He has . . . wonderful": Tong, vol. 2, pp. 366–67.

243 "a tremendous . . . influence": Library of Congress: Nelson T. Johnson papers, Box 32, Clarence E. Gauss to NTJ, September 23, 1934.

243 "She is . . . admiration": Fenby, pp. 264–65.

243 "in an . . . man": Selle, pp. 304–6.

CHAPTER TWENTY-TWO

245 "Chiang was . . . match": Raymond Carroll, "The Last of the Big Four," *Newsweek*, April 14, 1975.

245 "not brilliant . . . frivolous": Taylor, pp. 12–13.

245 "good emotional relations": Wang Feng, p. 18.

245 "Ching-kuo is . . . mute": Taylor, pp. 14–17.

246 "the Red . . . Wall": Ibid., pp. 21–31.

246 "Chiang Kai-shek was . . . traitor!": "Father Flayed," *Time*, April 25, 1927.

246 "a long . . . career": Taylor, p. 37.

247 "very talented . . . plow": Ibid., pp. 55–61.

248 "When I . . . China": Ibid., pp. 63–70.

249 "tired because . . . us": Academia Historica, Taipei, Madame, wire to CKS, April 21, 1936.

249 "If you . . . Shanghai": Ibid., CKS, wire to Madame, May 3, 1936.

249 "Have you . . . much": Ibid., CKS, wire to Madame, August 28, 1936.

249 "I slept . . . therapy": Ibid., Madame, wire to CKS, September 23, 1936.

249 "The result . . . fever": Ibid., Madame, wire to CKS, October 26, 1936.

250 "How are . . . much": Ibid., CKS, wire to Madame, undated.

250 "October 31 is . . . therapy": Ibid., Madame, wire to CKS, October 28, 1936.

250 "touching telegram": Ibid., CKS, wire to Madame, undated.

250 "Now that . . . me": WCA: Katherine Woods, "A People and a Leader in Tribulation and Greatness," review of Sven Hedin, *Chiang Kai-shek, Marshal of China* by *The New York Times Book Review,* December 15, 1940.

250 "We should . . . traits": WCA: White, "Chiang Kai-shek," *Life,* March 2, 1942.

250 "My situation . . . ointment": Academia Historica, Taipei, Madame, wire to CKS, November 29, 1936.

250 "very worried": Ibid., CKS, wire to Madame, November 30, 1936.

251 "I got . . . survival": Ibid., Madame, wire to CKS, December 1, 1936.

251 "he found . . . property": Columbia University, RBML, William Henry Donald papers, W. H. Donald to Harold K. Hochschild, January 17, 1937.

252 "bull-necked, loudmouthed . . . dog": Leonard, p. 84.

252 "How can . . . Japanese?": www.sina.com.cn, October 28, 2001, Web site of Renmin, Hong Kong, edited by Wu-min.

CHAPTER TWENTY-THREE

253 "Chinese politics . . . picturesque": James M. Bertram, *First Act in China,* p. xi.

253 "I sent . . . you": Chiang, *A Fortnight in Sian,* pp. 58–64.

255 "Chiang's concept . . . Heaven": Edgar Snow, "China's Fighting Generalissimo," *Foreign Affairs* 16, no. 4 (July 1938).

255 "What do . . . all": Chiang, *A Fortnight in Sian,* pp. 64–80.

257 "I cursed . . . trouble": Columbia University, RBML, William Henry Donald papers, W. H. Donald to Harold K. Hochschild, January 17, 1937.

257 "learned the . . . live": Chiang, *A Fortnight in Sian,* p. 87.

257 "was quite . . . respect": Columbia University, RBML, William Henry Donald papers, W. H. Donald to Harold K. Hochschild, January 17, 1937.

257 "regard my . . . mother": HA: *Chiang Kai-shek Diary,* ed. Wang Yu-gao and Wang Yu-zheng.

257 "long wanted . . . so": Madame Chiang, Kai-shek, *Sian: A Coup d'Etat* p. 90.

257 "I was . . . us": www.sina.com.cn, October 28, 2001, Web site of Renmin, Hong Kong, edited by Wu-min.

258 "so acute . . . up": Chiang, *A Fortnight in Sian,* p. 96.

258 "I gathered . . . threat": HA: T. V. Soong papers, Box 60, Folder 3, T. V. Soong, "Notes on Sian," December 20, 1936.

258 "I met . . . leader": www.sina.com.cn, October 28, 2001, Web site of Renmin, Hong Kong, edited by Wu-min.

258 "He [Chiang] . . . him": HA: T. V. Soong papers, Box 60, Folder 3, T. V. Soong, "Notes on Sian," December 20, 1936.

258 "Should T.V. . . . wet": Chiang, *A Fortnight in Sian,* p. 97.

259 "There has . . . Generalissimo": Madame Chiang Kai-shek, *Sian: A Coup d'Etat,* p. 2.

259 "What Chang . . . disgrace": Snow, *Random Notes on Red China,* pp. 1–2.

259 "I was . . . peacefully": Cornell University Library, Division of Rare and Manuscript Collections, William Reginald Wheeler papers, no. 4284, June 1937.

259 "It was . . . ordered": Columbia University, RBML, William Henry Donald papers, W. H. Donald to Harold K. Hochschild, January 17, 1937.

259 "important functionaries . . . return": HA: T. V. Soong papers, Box 60, Folder 3, T. V. Soong, "Notes on Xian," December 23, 1936.

259 "regarded as . . . Sian": Madame Chiang Kai-shek, *Sian: A Coup d'Etat*, pp. 4–5 ff.

259 "had a . . . scrap": Cornell University Library, Division of Rare and Manuscript Collections, James M. McHugh papers, H. B. Elliston, "China's No. 1 White Boy," *The Saturday Evening Post*, March 19, 1938, p. 31.

259 "the Gissimo . . . mighty": Columbia University, RBML, William Henry Donald papers, W. H. Donald to Harold K. Hochschild, April 26, 1937.

260 "still furious . . . Chang Hsueh-liang": "The Longer Soong May-ling Lives, the Longer I Will Live," Zhengzhong, "An Interview with Tang De-gang about Chang Hsueh-liang's Oral History," *Wan Xiang*, 2002.

260 "wracked with . . . crucial": Wakeman, p. 234.

260 "anxious and apprehensive": Madame Chiang Kai-shek, *Sian: A Coup d'Etat*, p. 27.

260 "repeatedly asked . . . him": HA: T. V. Soong papers, Box 60, Folder 3, T. V. Soong, "Notes on Sian," December 20, 1936.

260 "that if . . . situation": Madame Chiang Kai-shek, *Sian: A Coup d'Etat*, pp. 27–29.

260 "I was . . . man": Chiang, *A Fortnight in Sian*, p. 101.

261 "My husband . . . heads": Madame Chiang Kai-shek, *Sian: A Coup d'Etat*, pp. 29–44.

262 "You started . . . heads": HA: T. V. Soong papers, Box 60, Folder 3, T. V. Soong, "Notes on Sian," December 24, 1936.

262 "if they . . . magnanimity": Madame Chiang Kai-shek, *Sian: A Coup d'Etat*, p. 44.

262 "According to . . . back": Wakeman, p. 234.

263 "they would . . . government": Snow, *Random Notes on Red China*, p. 2.

263 "In reality . . . settled": Madame Chiang Kai-shek, *Sian: A Coup d'Etat*, pp. 45–48.

263 "a long . . . subordinates": Chiang, *A Fortnight in Sian*, pp. 107–10.

263 "the first . . . misdeeds": Madame Chiang Kai-shek, *Sian: A Coup d'Etat*, p. 51.

264 "Flying Palace": Tuchman, p. 196, footnote.

264 "A true . . . it": "The Longer Soong May-ling Lives, the Longer I Will Live," Zhengzhong, "An Interview with Tang De-gang about Chang Hsueh-liang's Oral History," *Wan Xiang*, 2002.

264 "Are you . . . alone!": Leonard, pp. 105–8.

264 "erupted with . . . occasion": Crozier, p. 189.

CHAPTER TWENTY-FOUR

269 "Recent events . . . end": "Man and Wife of the Year," *Time*, January 3, 1938.

269 "unquestionably saved . . . life": H. B. Elliston, "China's No. 1 White Boy," *The Saturday Evening Post*, March 19, 1938, p. 31.

269 "with the . . . them": Columbia University, RBML, William Henry Donald papers, W. H. Donald to Harold K. Hochschild, January 17, 1937.

269 "the perpetual . . . himself": Payne, p. 219.

269 "pleaded with . . . leniently": Cornell University Library, Division of Rare and Manuscript Collections, H. H. Kung, June 1937.

269 "always found . . . live": "The Longer Soong May-ling Lives, the Longer I Will Live,"

Zhengzhong, "An Interview with Tang De-gang about Chang Hsueh-liang's Oral History," *Wan Xiang*, 2002.

270 "I think . . . right": www.sina.com.cn, October 28, 2001, Web site of Renmin, Hong Kong, edited by Wu-min.

270 "Communist plot . . . Communists": HA: Walter H. Judd papers, Box 175, Folder 3, "Young Marshal Reveals Truth of Sian Kidnap," November 25, 1974.

270 "perhaps the . . . set": "Pain in the Heart," *Time*, December 28, 1936.

270 "I never . . . accurate": Columbia University, RBML, William Henry Donald papers, W. H. Donald to Harold K. Hochschild, January 17, 1937.

271 "I trusted . . . me": Chiang, *A Fortnight in Sian*, p. 70.

271 "I sincerely . . . ease": Hsiung, p. 332.

271 "hard as . . . pallet": Farmer, p. 265.

271 "wrong policy . . . Party": www.chairmanmao.org/eng/wen/wen23.htm.

272 "Welcome, my . . . mother": "Man and Wife of the Year," *Time*, January 3, 1938.

272 "With a . . . heart": Crozier, pp. 194–95.

273 "seek peace . . . ourselves": Ibid., p. 197.

273 "to chastise . . . behavior": Payne, p. 226.

273 "anti-Japanese . . . us": Tuchman, pp. 210–16.

274 "divine mission": Ibid., p. 184.

274 "The Japanese . . . Asia": Ibid., p. 215.

274 "We Chinese . . . hearts": Chiang May-ling, "Appeal to Women of China," in *Madame Chiang's Messages in War and Peace* (Nanking, 1937).

274 "more likely . . . powers": Tuchman, p. 213.

275 "Hong Kong's . . . Shanghai!": Dong, p. 194.

275 "the glitter . . . royalty": Graham Earnshaw, www.talesofoldchina.com.

276 "any fighting . . . bystanders": Tuchman, pp. 213.

276 "with detachment . . . City": Han Suyin, *Destination Chungking*, p. 74.

276 "Under incessant . . . wife": Tuchman, pp. 213–14.

277 "Americans speak . . . woman": WCA: Anthony Billingham, "The Man and the Woman Whom China Obeys," *The New York Times Magazine*, November 7, 1937.

277 "wholesale slaughter . . . time": "Message to Women of the World, Madame Chiang on Present Fighting," *The North-China Herald*, September 8, 1937.

277 "the primary . . . there": Tuchman, pp. 219–23.

277 "Oh, she . . . Japanese": Selle, p. 340.

278 "How the . . . feet": Farmer, p. 42.

278 "For endless . . . refugees": Dong, p. 254.

278 "filth, disease . . . madness": "Death and Conquest," *Time*, January 3, 1938.

278 "bodies and bits": "Staff of the Hongkong and Shanghai Bank," in *Shanghai: Electric and Lurid City*, ed. Barbara Baker, p. 179.

278 "the worst . . . moment": Dong, p. 254.

278 "You can . . . everybody": Madame Chiang, "Broadcast to the People of America," in *Madame Chiang's Messages in War and Peace*, September 12, 1937.

280 "In this . . . smell": Auden and Isherwood, pp. 252–53.

CHAPTER TWENTY-FIVE

281 "One thing . . . husband": Edgar Snow, "China's Fighting Generalissimo," *Foreign Affairs* 16, no. 4 (July 1938), p. 623.

281 "A self-defeating . . . on": Tuchman, p. 212.

281 "Japan is . . . savages": Madame Chiang Kai-shek, "China Bewildered at World Silence," *The North-China Herald,* September 15, 1937.

281 "He looked . . . struggle": "Generalissimo on U.S. Attitude," *The North-China Herald,* September 29, 1937.

282 "The alarm . . . occurred": WCA: Emma DeLong Mills papers, Madame Chiang Kai-shek, "China Takes Her Stand," reprinted in *The Far Eastern Mirror* from *Forum,* December 1937.

283 "Aviation," according . . . Orient": Claire Lee Chennault, p. 35.

283 "My God . . . side": Alsop with Platt, *I've Seen the Best of It,* p. 174.

283 "the most . . . aviation": Leonard, pp. 175–76.

283 "bomber generals": Seagrave, *The Soong Dynasty,* p. 360.

284 "half-dozen rickety . . . uniform": Claire Lee Chennault, p. 36.

284 "peasant": Anna Chennault, "Memories of Madame Chiang Kai-shek," *Da Gong* (Hong Kong), November 2, 2003.

284 "General Scaroni . . . force": Claire Lee Chennault, pp. 37–38 ff.

285 "I reckon . . . Colonel": DeLong, p. 102

285 "Combat training . . . navigation": Claire Lee Chennault, pp. 39–40.

285 "a crackerjack . . . seat": Columbia University Libraries, Sebie Biggs Smith transcription of interview on cassette, p. 143.

285 "How many . . . Settlement": Claire Lee Chennault, pp. 41–45.

287 "in right . . . stunt": Leonard, p. 178.

287 "We love . . . us": "Adventures of a Flying Tiger," *Weekend Standard,* August 19, 2006, www.thestandard.com.hk/, accessed September 6, 2006.

288 "princess": Schaller, p. 62.

288 "suggested . . . squad": Claire Lee Chennault, p. 53.

288 "greatly disturbed . . . China": HA: Claire Chennault papers, Box 1, AUG, CC to Madame Chiang Kai-shek, November 27, 1941.

289 "Sir . . . gun?": Leonard, p. 179.

289 "It was . . . eyes": Claire Lee Chennault, p. 55.

289 "We got . . . replacements": Columbia University Libraries, Sebie Biggs Smith, transcription of interview on cassette, p. 73.

289 "I was . . . want": Leonard, pp. 131–32.

290 "Wing Commander . . . place": Library of Congress: Nelson T. Johnson papers, Box 32, Willys R. Peck to NTJ, "Memorandum of Conversation with Second Secretary J. Paxton Hall," May 24, 1937.

291 "gutted . . . abruptly": Li, pp. 143–44.

291 "completely by . . . crestfallen": Cornell University Library, Division of Rare and Manuscript Collections, James M. McHugh papers, no. 2770, "Memorandum for the Ambassador: Changes in the Chinese Airforce Administration," February 28, 1938.

291 "a sour . . . lot": Tuchman, p. 235.

291 was "misused" . . . disappeared": Davies, p. 249.

291 "Tell the . . . conclusion": Crozier, p. 206.

Chapter Twenty-six

292 "The morning . . . insincere": Grant, *Turbulent Era,* vol. 2, p. 1205, footnote.

292 "Either I . . . relentless": Iris Chang, pp. 68–72.

293 "Trust our . . . you": Ibid., p. 120.

294 "On Hsiakwan . . . executed": Ibid., pp. 47–48.

294 "pictures that . . . pictures": Farmer, p. 101.

295 "No matter . . . pig": Iris Chang, pp. 49–50.

295 "There were . . . eyes": Ibid., p. 119.

295 "massive outcry . . . things": Ibid., pp. 52–59.

296 "a splendid . . . brutes": Ibid., pp. 121–26.

296 "a good . . . since": Auden and Isherwood, pp. 49–50.

296 "She is . . . figure": Ibid., p. 65–69.

297 "Every Japanese . . . Pigs": Ibid., p. 54.

297 "My last . . . unanswered": DeLong, p. 107.

297 "Our national . . . war": WCA: Emma DeLong Mills papers, MS to EM, November 7, 1937.

298 "all evening": WCA: Mills papers, Emma Mills diary, 1937–1941.

298 "You should . . . me": WCA: Mills papers, EM to MS, November 16, 1937.

298 "very sketchy . . . house": Ibid., EM to MS, June 10, 1940.

299 "I am . . . at": HA: Hornbeck papers, Box 150, W. H. Donald to Stanley Hornbeck, January 23, 1939.

299 "filled with . . . power": Tuchman, p. 234.

299 "a beautifully . . . woman": Farmer, p. 146.

300 "After an . . . them": Freda Utley, *China at War,* pp. 197–98.

300 "the democratic . . . China": WCA: Mills papers, MS to EM, January 6, 1938.

301 "the motives . . . Japanese": Ibid., MS to EM, April 23, 1938.

301 "I visited . . . them": Ibid., MS to EM, April 26, 1938.

301 "to show . . . can't": "Mme. Chiang Kai-shek Sends Spoons to Wellesley '17," *The New York Times,* May 12, 1938.

301 "You are . . . more": WCA: Mills papers, MS to EM, April 26, 1938.

301 "I've sometimes . . . mind": Ibid., EM to MS, May 17, 1938.

301 "shone a . . . aspects": Ibid., EM to MS, June 21, 1938.

302 "After all . . . prominence!": Ibid., EM to MS, June 28, 1938.

302 "my views . . . penetrate": "Powers Aid Japan, Mme. Chiang Says," *The New York Times,* June 12, 1938.

302 "a crippled . . . Nations": "Mme. Chiang Flays Powers' 'Realism,' " *The New York Times,* June 13, 1938.

302 "a surcease . . . tortures": "Mme. Chiang Looks to a Greater China," *The New York Times,* June 14, 1938.

302 "They are . . . them": WCA: Mills papers, EM to MS, June 14, 1938.

302 "I quite . . . arguments": Ibid., MS to EM, June 28, 1938.

302 "the strangest . . . misplaced?": Farmer, pp. 172–73.

303 "of interest . . . conditions": WCA: Mills papers, MS to 1917 and other Wellesley Friends, September 26, 1938.

303 "I am . . . derriere": Ibid., MS to EM, September 26, 1938.

CHAPTER TWENTY-SEVEN

304 "The rest . . . happens": Laurence Greene, "China's Miracle-an-Hour Man," *New York Post,* March 18, 1943.

304 "There is . . . leaders": Cornell University Library, Division of Rare and Manuscript Collections, James M. McHugh papers, JMcH, "Strictly Confidential, Present Political Situation in China," September 14, 1938.

304 "bound by . . . devotion": Ibid.

304 "to build . . . everywhere": Selle, p. 339.

304 "probably the . . . Washington": WCA: "Mei-ling ('Beautiful Mood') Helps Her Husband Rule China," *Life,* August 16, 1937.

305 "innumerable": WCA: Helen L. Mansfield to Dorothy P. Howerth, September 4, 1937.

305 "The greatest . . . doctors!": WCA: Fulton Oursler, "China's Strong Woman Talks," *Liberty,* n.d. (probably 1937).

305 "The Person . . . politics": Zhang Ning-yi (translator), "Madame Chiang and Modern China," from the Russian Archives, Taipei Zhongzheng Cultural and Educational Association, 2002.

305 "Almond-Eyed Cleopatra . . . genius": WCA: Lady Grace Drummond-Hay, "Almond Eyed Cleopatra Is 'Power Behind Power' in War-Time China," *Cincinnati Times-Star,* April 29, 1938.

306 "Well, he's . . . he?": Henry Lieberman, "Madame Sun—China's 'Conscience,'" *The New York Times,* May 11, 1946.

306 "It is . . . defence": Library of Congress: Theodore Roosevelt, Jr., papers, Box 27, Donald to TR Jr., May 3, 1938.

306 "Our people . . . now": Ibid., TR Jr. to Donald, June 5, 1938.

307 "Since I . . . catastrophes": Ibid., Donald to TR Jr., December 30, 1938.

308 "There wasn't . . . painting": Fenby, p. 331.

308 "To the . . . democracy": WCA: Madame Chiang Kai-shek, "To the Fifteenth National Convention of the Y.W.C.A.," April 28, 1938.

308 "The <u>Panay</u> . . . 1940": WCA: Emma DeLong Mills papers, EM to MS, April 12, 1938.

309 "It will . . . worried": Ibid., EM to MS, November 11, 1938.

309 "Not atrocity . . . general": Ibid., EM to MS, May 9, 1938.

309 "prefer pictures . . . themselves": Ibid., EM to MS, June 28, 1938.

309 "too long . . . occupation?": Ibid., EM to MS, September 3, 1938.

309 "Through 1937 . . . China": "Man and Wife of the Year," *Time,* January 3, 1938.

309 "China has . . . history": Tuchman, p. 238.

310 "tearing his . . . late": Ibid., p. 236.

310 "anti-aircraft defence . . . farmers": Auden and Isherwood, p. 37.

311 "When I . . . Chungking": Library of Congress: Theodore Roosevelt, Jr., papers, Box 27, Donald to TR Jr., December 30, 1938.

311 "a staggering . . . equipment": Crozier, p. 208.

311 "We moved . . . back": Madame Chiang Kai-shek, *The Sure Victory,* p. 14.

312 "the great . . . Manchukuo": Crozier, pp. 210–12.

313 "position gave . . . Yuan": Ibid., p. 241.

313 "merely recognizing . . . army": Edgar Snow, "China's Fighting Generalissimo," *Foreign Affairs* 16, no. 4 (July 1938).

313 "themselves out . . . inefficiency": Cornell University Library, Division of Rare and Manuscript Collections, James M. McHugh papers, JMcH, "Strictly Confidential, Present Political Situation in China," September 14, 1938.

313 "that could . . . capital": Boorman, vol. 1, p. 205.

314 "bad temper . . . once": Ch'en Li-fu, p. 24.

314 "obsession about . . . squeeze": Beal, p. 252.

314 "Two silent . . . authority": White, "*Life* Looks at China," *Life*, May 1, 1944.

314 "one of . . . China": Edgar Snow, "China's Fighting Generalissimo."

314 "came to . . . inefficiency": Crozier, p. 242.

314 "Let us . . . Japanese": Payne, p. 260.

CHAPTER TWENTY-EIGHT

315 "Madame Kung . . . all": WCA: Pearl S. Buck, "The Sister 'Dictators': Behind the Chinese Dragon," scrapbook of items by or about Madame Chiang Kai-shek, collected by Hetty S. Wheeler (1935–1940), unidentified magazine, September 1937.

315 "The runway . . . airport": White, *In Search of History*, p. 69.

315 "Every drop . . . river": Library of Congress: Owen Lattimore papers, Box 28, Folder 16, Vincent Sheean, "A Day in Chungking: Lifting Mist Reveals a Patient China at Work," *The New York Herald Tribune*, November 8, 1941.

315 "the Heavenly-endowed province": Fenby, p. 334.

315 "Shanghai," according . . . place": WCA: Emma DeLong Mills papers, MS to EM, August 14, 1939.

316 "The city . . . barges": White, *In Search of History*, p. 71.

316 "no escape . . . turn": Camp, p. 99.

316 "numerous . . . large . . . ferocious": Farmer, p. 207.

316 "were woken . . . fright!": Hoo, p. 84.

317 "as if . . . Appalachia": White, *In Search of History*, p. 74.

317 "not a . . . house": Chen San-jing, "The Oral History of Doctor Xiong Wan," p. 64.

317 "a solemn . . . rigidity": Martha Gellhorn, "Her Day," *Collier's*, August 30, 1941.

317 "If I . . . here": "Chiang in Chungking," *The Honolulu Advertiser*, magazine section, May 14, 1939.

318 "grunt" the . . . "all": Fenby, p. 326.

318 "With the . . . Government": Cornell University Library, Division of Rare and Manuscript Collections, James M. McHugh papers, no. 2770, Box 13, Folder 4, draft for book, foreword, p. 2.

318 "perfect dears . . . circumstances": Fenby, p. 341.

319 "I just . . . city?": Ernest O. Hauser, "Old Chiang," *The Saturday Evening Post*, August 28, 1943.

319 "His niggardly . . . difficult": WCA: White, "Chiang Kai-shek," *Life*, March 2, 1942, p. 76.

319 "intense nervous . . . Madame": WCA: F. Tillman Durdin, "Worth Twenty Divisions," *The New York Times Magazine*, September 14, 1941.

319 "the work . . . him": Cornell University, Division of Rare and Manuscript Collec-

tions, James M. McHugh papers, JMcH, "Strictly Confidential, Present Political Situation in China," September 14, 1938.

320 "He was . . . despise": White, *In Search of History*, p. 77.

320 "slim, rather . . . grunt": Salter, p. 215.

320 "There were . . . ruler": Payne, pp. 237–38.

320 "few Chinese . . . him": Edgar Snow, "China's Fighting Generalissimo," *Foreign Affairs* 16, no. 4 (July 1938).

320 "I feel . . . counts": Cornell University Library, Division of Rare and Manuscript Collections, James M. McHugh papers, no. 2770, letter or note, Reel 1, 1941.

321 "the chief . . . again": Library of Congress, Clare Boothe Luce papers, Box 595, Folder 11, Theodore White, "Politics in China," June 1, 1940.

321 "A beautiful . . . queen": White, p. 143.

321 "a great . . . hair": WCA: Pearl S. Buck, "The Sister 'Dictators': Behind the Chinese Dragon," scrapbook of items by or about Madame Chiang Kai-shek, collected by Hetty S. Wheeler (1935–1940), unidentified magazine, September 1937.

321 "I was . . . anything": Chang with Halliday, pp. *Mme Sun Yat-sen*, 79–82.

322 "embraced all . . . Corinthians": Snow, *Journey to the Beginning*, p. 87.

323 "Among the . . . Chiang": Chang with Halliday, *Mme Sun Yat-sen*, pp. 92–93.

323 "devoted her . . . work": Cornell University Library, Division of Rare and Manuscript Collections, James M. McHugh papers, JMcH, "Strictly Confidential, Present Political Situation in China," September 14, 1938.

323 "chief interests . . . amassed": Snow, "China's Fighting Generalissimo," *Foreign Affairs* 16, no. 4 (July 1938).

323 "Though few . . . family": Edgar Snow, "China Has Three First Ladies," Toronto, *Canada Evening Star*, June 21, 1941.

323 "very bossy . . . stubborn": Author's conversation with Lily Yen Zee, Shanghai, March 25, 2003.

323 "To her . . . all": George Sokolsky, "The Soongs of China," *The Atlantic Monthly*, February 1937, p. 186.

324 "Less strikingly . . . richly": Mowrer, p. 80.

324 "90 percent . . . gossip": Tuchman, p. 412.

324 "amazed by . . . honesty": Lattimore, p. 142.

324 "purse-proud . . . Hong Kong": Sheean, *Between the Thunder and the Sun*, p. 370.

324 "had told . . . rest": Cornell University Library, Division of Rare and Manuscript Collections, James M. McHugh papers, JMcH, "Strictly Confidential, Present Political Situation in China," September 14, 1938.

324 "When will . . . possible": Academia Historica, Taipei, CKS, wire to Madame, undated (in answer to hers of March 22, 1939).

324 "The problem . . . me": Ibid., Madame, wire to CKS, April 3, 1939.

324 "I read . . . urgent": Ibid., CKS, wire to Madame, undated (answer to above).

324 "I am . . . okay": Ibid., Madame, wire to CKS, February 16, 1940.

324 "How do . . . there": Ibid., CKS, wire to Madame, February 17, 1940.

325 "much better . . . me": Ibid., Madame wire, to CKS, February 21, 1940.

325 "My sisters . . . Empire!": Chang with Halliday, *Mme Sun Yat-sen*, p. 94.

325 "avuncular shine . . . China": Gellhorn, pp. 56–58. On July 30, Hemingway sent a long letter about the animosity between the Nationalists and the Communists to Secretary of the Treasury Henry Morgenthau, saying that a "Mr. White" had asked

him to evaluate what he saw while in China. As it turned out—at least according to a Canadian journalist named Peter Moreira—the man was Harry Dexter White, a deputy at the Treasury Department and spy for the Russians, who forwarded Hemingway's analysis to someone who gave it to Soviet agents in New York. (Peter Moreira, "Ernest Hemingway, Secret Agent," *Toronto Star,* March 19, 2006.)

326 "who can . . . am": WCA: Martha Gellhorn, "Her Day," *Collier's,* August 30, 1941.

327 "an influence . . . overestimate": WCA: Pearl S. Buck, "The Sister 'Dictators': Behind the Chinese Dragon," scrapbook of items by or about Madame Chiang Kai-shek, collected by Hetty S. Wheeler (1935–1940), unidentified magazine, September 1937.

CHAPTER TWENTY-NINE

329 "[T]here has . . . later": HA: Kohlberg papers, Box 160, Vanya Oakes, "Heir to Chiang's Mantle," *Magazine Digest,* December 1945.

329 "a round . . . chins": White and Jacoby, p. 111.

329 "undoubtedly more . . . Soong": Coble, p. 162.

329 "basically anti-foreign": Cornell University Library, Division of Rare and Manuscript Collections, James M. McHugh Papers, JMcH, "Strictly Confidential, Present Political Situation in China," September 14, 1938.

329 "one great . . . Daddy": White and Jacoby, p. 112.

329 "in a . . . man": HA: Kohlberg papers, Vanya Oakes, Box 160, "Heir to Chiang's Mantle," *Magazine Digest,* December 1945.

329 "was sitting . . . him": Lattimore, *China Memoirs,* p. 79.

330 "a brilliant . . . intelligence": Columbia University Library, COHO: Dr. K. C. Wu, "Reminiscences for the Years 1946–53," as told to Professor Nathaniel Peffer and Professor C. Martin Wilbur, May 1961, revised and corrected November 1963, part D, vol. 2, no. 3, pp. 335–38.

330 "conceal his . . . Kung": Cornell University Library, Division of Rare and Manuscript Collections: James M. McHugh papers, JMcH, "Strictly Confidential, Present Political Situation in China," September 14, 1938.

330 "Mme. Kung . . . danced": Alsop with Platt, p. 220.

330 he is . . . reputation: One of these centered around stories about a man named Sonne, who represented a firm that had sold a mint in 1920 to the then Chinese government for a million dollars. The bill was unpaid, and by 1928, when the KMT was in power, mints could be purchased for only $250,000. Sonne, according to the story, "was prepared to accept almost any settlement," but T.V. "asked him to present the original bill for one million dollars, for which he handed him back $650,000." Sonne said he was "positive" that T.V. "pocketed the $350,000" and said that "Li Ming [another Chinese banker] could confirm this." This same Li Ming, who was chairman of the board of directors of the Bank of China, also confirmed that T.V.'s wife charged the Bank of China for her opera tickets. "Oh, yes," he said, "they charge most of their living expenses to T.V.'s expense account at the Bank of China." (HA: Lauchlin Currie papers, LC, "FDR Memorandum 1943, Not for the files," May 15, 1943.)

Another story was told by a man named Sutterle, an old resident of Shanghai: "Some years ago we worked up a plan to rehabilitate the China Merchants' Steam Navigation Company. . . . The plan was to buy new ships to replace the old, out-moded ones and to transfer the business management to the Dollar Steamship Company's Offices." But the planners "failed to consult T.V.," and the Chiang government appointed someone with veto power to sit on the company board. "Before the Government man would allow the contract to be signed, he insisted that we put up $700,000 in cash . . . as a token of good faith." The government man took the money and disappeared. Although the government later returned the money, in order "to save the Government and T.V.'s face," the chairman of the board, a gentleman named Marquis Li, "was tried, convicted by a Government packed Court and I believe died in jail." (HA: Roy Holbrooke to Lauchlin Currie, April 16, 1943.)

331 "lost no . . . domineering": Cornell University Library, Division of Rare and Manuscript Collections, James M. McHugh Papers, JMcH, "Strictly Confidential, Present Political Situation in China," September 14, 1938.

331 "I have . . . health": HA: Kohlberg papers, Box 160, Vanya Oakes, "Heir to Chiang's Mantle," *Magazine Digest,* December 1945.

331 "He refused . . . subscribes": Swanberg, p. 95.

332 "Being minister . . . dog": Coble, p. 130.

332 "engineered the ousting": Columbia University Library, COHO: Dr. K. C. Wu, "Reminiscences for the Years 1946–53," as told to Professor Nathaniel Peffer and Professor C. Martin Wilbur, May 1961, revised and corrected November 1963, part D, vol. 2, no. 3, p. 338.

332 "he who . . . Chiang": Hahn, *Chiang Kai-shek,* pp. 179–80.

332 even "suggested" . . . Chiang": Columbia University Library, COHO: interview with George Sokolsky by Prof. C. Martin Wilbur, 1962, p. 22.

332 "T. V. Soong . . . China": Sokolsky, "The Soongs of China," *The Atlantic Monthly,* February 1937, p. 187.

333 "I wanted . . . task": "Mr. T.V. Soong's Resignation," *The North-China Herald,* November 1, 1933.

333 "a willing . . . cashier": Cornell University Library, Division of Rare and Manuscript Collections, James M. McHugh Papers, JMcH, "Strictly Confidential, Present Political Situation in China," September 14, 1938.

333 "If I . . . again": Tuchman, p. 411.

333 "new shoes . . . fills": "Reflection," *The North-China Herald,* November 1, 1933.

334 "for the . . . health": Fenby, p. 238.

334 "This is . . . fight": Abend, p. 215.

334 "apparently had . . . banks": Coble, pp. 195–96.

335 "What is . . . before": Arnold, p. 413.

335 "There has . . . thousands": Crozier, p. 243.

336 "While it . . . it": http://jean-monnet.net/menu06/page1us.html.

336 "widely considered . . . organization": Cornell University Library, Division of Rare and Manuscript Collections, James M. McHugh papers, JMcH, "Present Political Situation in China," no. 1-38, January 20, 1938.

336 "a mixture . . . policy": Snow, *Journey to the Beginning,* p. 90.

336 "She is . . . known": Columbia University Library, COHO: Dr. K. C. Wu, "Reminiscences for the Years 1946–53," as told to Professor Nathaniel Peffer and Professor C. Martin Wilbur, May 1961, revised and corrected November 1963, category 5A, vol. 2, no. 3, 325.

336 "influential persons": Coble, p. 249.

336 "Madame Kung . . . useful": Columbia University Library, COHO: Dr. K. C. Wu, "Reminiscences for the Years 1946–53," as told to Professor Nathaniel Peffer and Professor C. Martin Wilbur, May 1961, revised and corrected November 1963, part D, vol. 2, no. 3, pp. 322–27.

336 "one of . . . moment": Coble, p. 207

337 "That evening . . . attendants": Leith-Ross, p. 208.

337 "specific proof . . . squeal": Cornell University Library, Division of Rare and Manuscript Collections, James M. McHugh Papers, JMcH, "Strictly Confidential, Present Political Situation in China," September 14, 1938.

337 "The protection . . . activity": Coble, "The Soong Family and Chinese Capitalists," in Samuel C. Chu, p. 77.

A report from the U.S. Treasury Department on a man named Martin Gold says that Gold, an employee of the William Hunt Company in Chungking, had been entrusted to negotiate for the company for contracts to print paper money for the Central Bank of China. Although there had been "considerable criticism of defective notes shipped by the Hunt Company" the first time around, Gold obtained a new contract for supplying 100-yuan banknotes. During the course of the negotiations, he sent a cable about the size and design of these notes to his office in Chungking, which ended "Present sent Rosamonde" (Rosamonde was the eldest of the Kung daughters). Ten days later, Hunt cabled Gold congratulations on obtaining the contract. In May 1942, Gold was in New York, where, according to the Office of Censorship, he purchased diamonds and other jewelry in the amount of $30,000 to be taken back to China for the account of Dzung Kying, payment to be made out of the Central Bank of China's account with the Chase Bank in New York, "by order of Rosamonde." It was also noted that, in fact, the name " 'Dzung Kying could be the Chinese counterpart . . . of David Kung [Rosamond's brother]." (HA: Lauchlin Currie papers, "Treasury Department," October 20, 1943.)

338 "modern Borgia": Cornell University Library, Division of Rare and Manuscript Collections, James M. McHugh papers, JMcH, "Strictly Confidential, Present Political Situation in China," September 14, 1938.

338 "go away . . . do": Ibid.

339 "Someone has . . . criticize!": Selle, pp. 348–49. (Note: Neither the university nor its president is identified by the author of the book.)

339 "the Chinese . . . conditions": Columbia University Library, RBML, William Henry Donald correspondence, Harold K. Hochschild to Earl Albert Selle, January 31, 1947.

339 "more and . . . am.": Selle, p. 349.

339 "Let's leave . . . needed": Wu Jing-ping, *Study of Historical Materials,* vol. 2.

339 "engaged a . . . war": Library of Congress, Clare Boothe Luce papers, Box 595, Folder 7, Ernest O. Hauser, "China's Soong," undated (1941).

340 "assumed the . . . position": Cornell University Library, Division of Rare and Manuscript Collections, James M. McHugh papers, JMcH, "Strictly Confidential, Present Political Situation in China," September 14, 1938.

340 "Hitler spoke . . . look": Columbia University Library, COHO, "The Reminiscences

of K'ung Hsiang-hsi, as told to Julie Lien-ying How, February 10 to June 10, 1948," pp. 121–22.

341 "I thought . . . Government": Ibid., p. 114.

341 "went to . . . desk": Salter, pp. 218–19.

341 "A royal . . . modesty": HA: Nym Wales papers, Box 32.0, Annie Lou Hardy, "Madame Kung's Georgia Visit," *The Shanghai Spectator,* October 20, 1932.

342 "controlled by . . . agreement": Columbia University Library, COHO: "The Reminiscences of K'ung Hsiang-hsi, as told to Julie Lien-ying How, February 10 to June 10, 1948," pp. 114–23.

342 "real nice . . . China": Blum, *Roosevelt and Morgenthau,* p. 218.

CHAPTER THIRTY

343 "The Japanese . . . blood-stream": HA: Walter H. Judd papers, Box 175, Folder 1, Alfred Kohlberg, "Portrait of Chiang."

343 "Millions have . . . income": Jonathan Marshall, "Opium and the Politics of Gangsterism in Nationalist China, 1927–1945," *The Bulletin of Concerned Asian Scholars,* July–September 1976, p. 20.

343 "in effect . . . soldiers": Columbia University Library, COHO, interviews with George Sokolsky, conducted by Professor C. Martin Wilbur, 1962, p. 39.

344 "Finance Minister . . . come": "Spring Comes to Chiang Kai-shek," *Time,* April 27, 1931.

344 "honorary advisers . . . vice": Marshall, p. 32.

346 "Inasmuch as . . . taxes": Ibid., p. 22.

346 "being over-zealous . . . gingerly": "The Opium Traffic on the Yangtze," *The North-China Herald,* April 8, 1930.

347 "the Chinese . . . benefitted": Marshall, p. 25.

347 "Du Yueh-sheng . . . Shanghai": Ibid., p. 38.

347 "It is . . . resistance": Madame Chiang, *China Shall Rise Again,* p. 10.

347 the "Seven Deadly . . . war": Ibid., p. 38.

347 "China was . . . fear": Radcliffe Institute, Harvard University, Schlesinger Library: Frances Gunther papers, William H. Chamberlin, review of *China Shall Rise Again,* unidentified source, January 1941.

348 "I have . . . day": WCA: Emma DeLong Mills papers, MC to EM, January 14, 1939.

348 "glad . . . you . . . frazzle": Ibid., MC to EM, June 17, 1939.

348 "almost non-existent . . . returns": Ibid., EM to MC, March 14, 1939.

348 "some way . . . work": Ibid., EM to MC, August 1, 1939.

348 "an assortment . . . highways": Ibid., MC to EM, November 10, 1939.

348 "difficult to . . . with": Ibid., MC to EM, November 1, 1939.

348 "It comes . . . Europeans": Ibid., EM to MC, December 18, 1939.

349 "It takes . . . blood": Taylor, p. 96.

349 "In some . . . bone": "Life in Occupied Kiangsu," *The North-China Herald,* February 28, 1940.

349 "make a . . . Japan": National Archives: RG 59, CDF (1940–1944), Box 5849, January 20, 1940.

349 "the most . . . traitor": Ibid., January 23, 1940.

349 "Japanese tool . . . meat": Library of Congress: Theodore Roosevelt, Jr., papers, Box 27, Donald to TR Jr., December 30, 1938–January 1, 1939.

350 a "godsend" . . . gather": "Japan-in-China," *Fortune*, September 1941.

350 "enjoyed H. H. Kung's . . . writers": Crozier, p. 219.

351 "during the . . . died": White and Jacoby, p. 210.

352 "buzzed with . . . ruthlessness": White and Jacoby, p. 76.

352 "The Sino-Japanese . . . party": Crozier, p. 237.

352 "The communists . . . out": Library of Congress: Clare Boothe Luce papers, Box 595, Folder 11, Theodore White, "Crisis in China," March 15, 1941.

353 "dispatches had . . . war": Snow, *Journey to the Beginning*, p. 236.

353 "Now . . . challenged": Crozier, pp. 236–40.

CHAPTER THIRTY-ONE

354 "The Japanese . . . might": Han Suyin, *Destination Chungking*, p. 218.

354 "resembled nothing . . . anthill": Payne, p. 239.

354 "The bombing . . . impossible": WCA: Emma DeLong Mills papers, MC to EM, May 10, 1939.

355 "The door . . . coolies": Farmer, pp. 233–34.

355 "Do what . . . bombs": WCA: Mills papers, MC to EM, May 10, 1939.

356 "Other generals . . . resting": Han Suyin, *Destination Chungking*, p. 225.

356 "obliged to . . . sores!": HA: T. V. Soong papers, Madame Chiang to T. V. Soong, Box 63, Folder 33, June 12, 1941.

356 "improved by . . . percent": WCA: Madame Chiang, "Hospitals on the Changsha Front," January 10, 1940.

356 "Friends of . . . Japan": WCA: Text of Broadcast by Madame Sun Yat-sen, Madame H. H. Kung, and Madame Chiang Kai-shek, from Chungking, China, 7:45 P.M., April 17, 1940, NBC National Hookup, reprinted in *China Monthly*, June 1940, pp. 7–8.

357 "told that . . . lawmakers": WCA: Mills papers, EM to MC, April 22, 1940.

357 "Society people . . . reprisals": Ibid., EM to MC, April 8, 1940.

357 "the spirit . . . lows": WCA: Theodore H. White, "Chiang Kai-shek," *Life*, March 2, 1942.

357 "the most . . . world": Chang and Halliday, *Mao*, p. 232.

357 "We have . . . fig-leaves!": WCA: Mills papers, MC to EM, June 16, 1940.

358 "scratched out . . . earth": "The Unbelievable Burma Road," *Fortune*, September 1941.

358 "an unbelievable . . . pieces": Library of Congress: Clare Boothe Luce papers, Box 595, Folder 11, Theodore White on smuggling, April 25, 1941.

359 "When I . . . again": White, "Chiang Kai-shek," *Life*, March 2, 1942.

360 "Both parties . . . war": WCA: Mills papers, EM to MC, July 22, 1940.

360 "stuck to . . . life": HA: Lauchlin Currie papers, John O'Donnell and Doris Fleeson, "Capitol Stuff," *Times Herald*, February 17, 1941.

360 "direct channel . . . trusted": Li, p. 163.

360 "a very . . . themselves": HA: Lauchlin Currie papers, Box 4, LC, "Report on Some Aspects of the Current Political, Economic and Military Situation in China," March 15, 1941, p. 2.

360 "many incompetent . . . influence": Ibid., Box 4, LC, Notes on Conference with Chou-en-lai at British Ambassador's Home, February 4, 1941.

360 "I got . . . whisper": Ibid., Box 4, LC, "Report on Some Aspects of the Current Political, Economic and Military Situation in China," March 15, 1941, p. 3.

360 "reached a . . . Communists": Ibid., pp. 8–9.

361 "I did . . . Finance": Ibid., p. 20.

361 "too long . . . accommodating": Ibid., Box 4, LC, "Points," undated.

361 "4 coolie-loads . . . presents": Ibid., Leonard Lyons, *The New York Times,* March 24, 1941.

361 "convinced that . . . essential": Ibid., Box 4, LC, "Report on Some Aspects of the Current Political, Economic and Military Situation in China," March 15, 1941, p. 32.

361 "quite neurotic . . . deficiencies": Ibid., Box 4, LC, "At Chiang's Week-end Cottage," February 16, 1941.

361 "carry the . . . back": Tuchman, pp. 275–80.

362 "the Morgan . . . China": "Pain in the Heart," *Time,* December 28, 1936.

362 "one of . . . relations": WCA: R. T. Elson, "China Pays in Blood," *Maclean's,* May 1, 1942.

362 "T.V.," she . . . time": Tuchman, p. 499.

362 "like asking . . . stars": Ibid., p. 278.

362 "It is . . . Atlantic": "The Time Is Now," *Fortune,* September 1941, p. 43.

362 "Early in . . . goods": Thomas G. Corcoran with Philip Kooper, "Rendezvous with Democracy," unpublished autobiography, chapter on Pacific wars, pp. 2–8.

363 "The British . . . hemline": Ibid., p. 13.

363 "actors, farmers . . . fictions": Ibid., p. 17.

363 "opened the . . . considerable": Tuchman, pp. 281–82.

364 "doing everything . . . Britain": Chuikov, pp. 80–81.

364 "a frank . . . President": HA: T. V. Soong papers, Box 36, Folder 5, Chiang Kai-shek, wire to T.V., April 19, 1941. (Note: The reason the author says the wire was at least partially if not wholly generated by May-ling is the choice of wording. "Heart to heart" is not a phrase that would have been used by Chiang or anyone else in his entourage except his wife.)

364 "would be . . . China": Franklin Delano Roosevelt, "We Choose Human Freedom," radio address delivered on May 27, 1941, available at www.usmm.org/fd/emergency .htm.

364 "The trouble . . . Kai-shek": Swanberg, p. 148.

365 "the greatest . . . centuries": Ibid., pp. 185–86.

365 "so much . . . fever": Library of Congress: Claire Boothe Luce papers, Box 101, Folder 5, Madame Chiang Kai-shek to CBL, August 15, 1941.

365 "The time . . . Europe": "The Time Is Now," *Fortune,* September 1941.

365 "the greatest . . . Manchuria": Tuchman, p. 289.

365 "I suppose . . . itself": Newman, p. 59.

366 "equal status . . . treatment": Tuchman, p. 289.

366 "He [Chiang] . . . Communists?": Crozier, p. 221.

366 "for the . . . insurrection": Davies, p. 216.

366 "not a . . . situation": Tuchman, pp. 283–84.

367 "To our . . . perfidy": Payne, p. 241.

CHAPTER THIRTY-TWO

368 "If you . . . allies": Mosley, p. 261.

368 "Kuomintang officials . . . you?": Han Suyin, *Birdless Summer*, p. 235–36.

368 "if there . . . available": Chang with Halliday, *Mme Sun Yat-sen*, pp. 98–99.

369 "Where is . . . answer": Lin Bo-wen, "Family Affairs in T. V. Soong's Documents," *Chinese News*, April 17, 2004.

369 "I would . . . me": HA: T. V. Soong papers, Box 63, Folder 14, Sun Ching-ling to T. V. Soong, January 12, 1942.

369 "large, well-fed": Alsop with Platt, p. 184.

369 "tough, grasping": Ted Herman, interviews with members of the Shanghai American School, Class of 1936, October 15, 2000.

369 "welcomed . . . by . . . clothing": Ching-ling to T.V., in Kuo and Wu, eds., *T. V. Soong: His Life and Times,* January 12, 1942, p. 58.

370 "If it . . . good": HA: T. V. Soong papers, Box 64, Folder 3, Madame Chiang Kai-shek to T. V. Soong, January 1, 1942.

370 "control priorities . . . silences": Tuchman, pp. 300–301.

371 "faith and . . . Empire": Davies, p. 224.

371 "The British . . . colonialism": White and Jacoby, p. 152.

372 "The G-mo's . . . forces": Tuchman, pp. 308–10.

373 "suits very . . . starves": Ibid., p. 25.

373 "the daily . . . man": Ibid., p. 91.

373 "determination and . . . town": Ibid., pp. 148–49.

374 "the Government . . . jelly": Ibid., p. 188.

374 to "continue . . . gained": Ibid., pp. 193–96.

374 "very charming . . . job": Ibid., pp. 244–45.

374 "the status . . . power": Ibid., p. 259.

375 "need not . . . East": HA: T. V. Soong papers, Box 61, Folder 1, TVS to John J. McCloy, January 6, 1942.

375 "I take . . . Generalissimo": Ibid., Box 61, Folder 1, TVS to Henry L. Stimson, January 23, 1942.

375 "Tell him . . . elements": Tuchman, pp. 320–22.

375 "a military . . . China": Theodore White, "Chiang Kai-shek," *Life*, March 2, 1942.

375 "rather than . . . Cape": Tuchman, pp. 316–31.

376 "too delicate . . . temperament": HA: Lauchlin Currie papers, Box 3, Folder "China Politics & Government," notes from Ambassador Gauss to LC, February 22, 1942.

376 "grave political . . . imperative": Crozier, pp. 230–31.

377 "like a . . . pan": Theodore White, "Chiang Kai-shek."

377 "It was . . . China": Georgetown University Library, Special Collections Division, Thomas Murray Wilson papers, Box 1, Folder 5.

377 "bubbly letters . . . crush": Li, p. 170.

377 "They will . . . conference?": Tuchman, pp. 331–32.

378 "quite failed . . . watching": Li, p. 174.

378 "He [Chiang] . . . better": Payne, p. 243.

378 "We shall . . . spirit": Li, p. 175.

378 "a cool reception": Hoo, p. 73.

378 "The time . . . eyes": WCA: Madame Chiang Kai-shek, radio broadcast, June 13, 1942.

378 "the superiority . . . Chinese": "First Lady of the East Speaks to the West," *The New York Times,* April 19, 1942.

378 "the exploitation . . . ours": WCA: Madame Chiang Kai-shek, "China Emergent," *The Atlantic Monthly,* May 1942.

378 "Madame Chiang's . . . Government": WCA: Letter to the Editor on "China Emergent," *The Atlantic Monthly,* July 1942.

379 "is the . . . produced": WCA: Clare Boothe Luce, "What One Woman Can Do," *The Atlanta Constitution,* July 26, 1942.

379 "outstanding achievement . . . cause": White, "Chiang Kai-shek."

379 "The gallant . . . statesmen": Crozier, p. 234.

379 "one of . . . tooth": Willkie, p. 117.

379 "oily and . . . relief": Tuchman, pp. 333–34.

379 "Chinese passengers . . . puking": Stilwell, p. 49.

380 "I'm a . . . pays": HA: Joseph Stilwell papers, Stilwell, "The Black Book," undated.

CHAPTER THIRTY-THREE

383 "Among the . . . woman": Caldwell, p. 112.

383 "It was . . . fantastic": Stilwell, pp. 50–51.

383 "No-one ever . . . Finance": Hoo, p. 78.

384 "The one . . . men": Tuchman, p. 340.

384 "probably responsible . . . Kai-shek": White and Jacoby, p. 105.

384 "Payrolls were . . . right": Ibid., p. 140.

384 "Chinese higher . . . ammunition": HA: Frank Dorn papers, Box 1, Folder 30, Frank Dorn, memo to The Commanding General, Headquarters USAF in CBI, "Will the Chinese Fight?" January 4, 1944.

384 "Chinese officers . . . whim": White and Jacoby, p. 140.

385 "They told . . . ATTACK": Stilwell, p. 53.

385 "If China . . . cut": HA: T. V. Soong papers, Box 61, Folder 1, T.V. Soong (?), "Notes on the Conversation between the Generalissimo and Stilwell."

385 "What a . . . troops": Stilwell, pp. 53–55.

385 "Ah, Your . . . work": Tuchman, pp. 345–46.

386 "We had . . . down": Stilwell, p. 63.

386 "keep it up": Tuchman, p. 349.

386 "Stubborn bugger . . . offensive": Stilwell, p. 64.

386 "fatally compromised . . . mysterious": Tuchman, pp. 351–52.

386 "The pusillanimous . . . off": Stilwell, pp. 76–83.

388 "We are . . . man!" Tuchman, p. 360.

388 "Before I . . . Burma": Stilwell, p. 80.

388 "Yep, yep . . . spoon": Tuchman, p. 360.

388 "When we . . . me": HA: Walter H. Judd papers, Box 175, Folder 2, Robert Eunson, "First Lady Hopes U.S. Will Continue Firm Vietnam Stand," March 19, 1965.

389 "acres of streets": Tuchman, p. 361.

389 "In all . . . Burma": HA: T. V. Soong papers, Box 62, Folder 2, Chiang Kai-shek, wire

to Franklin Delano Roosevelt, April 12, 1942. (Also in Chiang Kai-shek's letter to Churchill, Columbia University, Rare Book and Manuscript Library.)

389 "The Generalissimo . . . off": HA: Lauchlin Currie papers, Folder Chiang Kai-shek, Madame Chiang Kai-shek, "Anti-British Sentiment Expressed in Cables from Madame Chiang Kai-shek," April 12, 1942.

389 "complete absence . . . removed": Franklin D. Roosevelt Library: Harry Hopkins Collection, Box 152, Folder China, "Telegram from Generalissimo Chiang Kai-shek to the President", dated Chungking, April 13, 1942.

389 "could have . . . killed": Tuchman, pp. 365–73.

390 "responsibility for . . . officers": HA: Lauchlin Currie papers, Box 3, "Anti-British Sentiment Expressed in Cables from Madame Chiang Kai-shek," May 6, 1942.

390 "sole idea . . . deviation": Tuchman, p. 375.

390 "physically courageous . . . foolhardy": HA: Dorn papers, Box 4, Folder 15, Dorn, notes on Stilwell, undated.

391 "made fellow . . . Cheerio": Tuchman, pp. 376–78.

391 "when cornered . . . country": Crozier, p. 232.

391 "By the . . . life": Tuchman, pp. 379–82.

392 "stupid gutless . . . CKS": Ibid., p. 383.

392 "No doubt . . . undignified": Corcoran, p. 27.

392 "an exalted . . . be": Tuchman, p. 387.

392 "completely wiped . . . hell": Tuchman, pp. 384–85.

Chapter Thirty-four

394 "Chiang thought . . . him": White and Jacoby, p. 125.

394 "Suspicious, secretive . . . qualities": Davies, p. 262.

394 "Obstinate, pig-headed . . . him": HA: Joseph Stilwell papers, Stilwell, "The Black Book," pp. 6–8.

394 "a lily-livered . . . offense": Mosley, p. 301.

394 "Among a . . . offered": John Leighton Stuart, "How the Communists Got China," *U.S. News & World Report*, October 1, 1954, p. 47.

394 "They would . . . this": Schaller, p. 79.

395 "total collapse . . . crucial": Tuchman, p. 389.

395 "making headway . . . propaganda": HA: Lauchlin Currie papers, Box 1, Madame Chiang Kai-shek, cable to Lauchlin Currie, May 22, 1942.

395 "power-worshipping . . . enemy": Madame Chiang Kai-shek, "First Lady of the East Speaks to the West," *The New York Times*, April 19, 1942.

395 "no exploitation . . . state": Madame Chiang Kai-shek, "China Emergent," *The Atlantic Monthly*, May 1942.

396 "a pity . . . recommendations": HA: Lauchlin Currie papers, Box 3, Folder Madame Chiang Kai-shek, LC to Madame Chiang Kai-shek, May 26, 1942.

396 "to rough . . . program": T. Christopher Jespersen, "Madame Chiang Kai-shek and the Face of Sino-American Relations: Personality and Gender Dynamics in Bilateral Diplomacy" in Samuel C. Chu, p. 133.

396 "I told . . . more": Stilwell, pp. 113–14.

397 "to bring . . . him!": Tuchman, p. 392.

397 "jumped up . . . etc.": Stilwell, p. 115.

397 "supremely confident": Tuchman, p. 398.

397 "borne [the] . . . Yunnan": HA: Claire L. Chennault papers, Box 1, AVG, CLC, wire to General C. K. Chow, March 25, 1942. (Note: The original written in cablese, i.e., "Borne brunt in defense Rangoon comma Burma and Yunnan. Stop.")

397 "The five-hour . . . earth": "Adventures of a Flying Tiger," *Weekend Standard,* August 19, 2006, available at www.thestandard.com.hk/weekend_news_detail.asp?pp_cat=30&art_id=25355&sid=, accessed September 6, 2006.

397 "a bottleneck . . . you": Tuchman, pp. 394–95.

398 "We're going . . . are": Stilwell, pp. 120–21. (Note: Original reads "And we're going," etc.)

399 "and such . . . you": Tuchman, pp. 399–402.

400 "captivated" by . . . did": Davies, p. 212.

400 of "prestige" . . . all": HA: Lauchlin Currie papers, Box 4, "Memo for the Files," July 3, 1942.

401 positively "vitriolic" . . . him!": HA: Lauchlin Currie papers, Box 4, "Incidental Notes," September 3, 1942.

401 "the prior . . . Chungking": HA: Lauchlin Currie papers, LC, "Report on Visit to China," August 24, 1942, pp. 4–12.

401 "dealing with . . . East": Ibid., pp. 27–43.

401 "Gen. Chiang . . . power": HA: Lauchlin Currie papers, Box 63, Folder 16, Joseph Chiang, notes, February 27, 1943.

402 "all aid . . . know": Tuchman, pp. 409–10.

402 "Put 50 . . . fast": Ibid., pp. 418–19.

403 "poisonous paper work": Stilwell, p. 141.

403 "gleam of . . . fog": Tuchman, p. 422.

403 "now arrived . . . success": Stilwell, p. 140.

403 "the architectural . . . Empire": Tuchman, p. 423.

404 "accomplish the . . . outside": Ibid., p. 431.

404 "he took . . . salutary": HA: Lauchlin Currie papers, Box 5, LC, "Interview with General Marshall, December 5," December 5, 1942.

404 "If the . . . seas": Tuchman, p. 444.

Chapter Thirty-five

405 "One makes . . . these": Davies, p. 255.

405 "a great . . . charisma": Cowles, p. 65.

405 "the most . . . Bryan": Tuchman, p. 424.

405 "a dear . . . magnificently": Library of Congress: Clare Boothe Luce papers, Box 110, Folder 4, CBL to Madame Chiang Kai-shek, August 25, 1942.

405 "a magnificent . . . needs": Cowles, p. 86.

405 "Willkie arrives . . . doctrines": Stilwell, p. 156.

406 "quite carried . . . wisdom": Crozier, p. 253.

406 "incredibly muddy": Willkie, p. 112.

406 "fat bouquets . . . on": Peck, p. 429.

406 "Before we . . . will": Willkie, pp. 127–28.

407 "The school . . . passed": Peck, pp. 429–30.

407 "These orphaned . . . nations": WCA: "Willkie to 'Howl' for a Free World," *The New York Times,* October 4, 1942.

407 "Military China . . . river": Willkie, pp. 145–49.

409 "cold battlefields . . . benefit": Tuchman, p. 427.

409 "an unreal . . . dormant": Cowles, p. 87.

409 "Only a . . . great": WCA: "Willkie Conducts Talks with Chinese Leader," *The* (Herkimer, N.Y.) *Telegram,* October 5, 1942.

409 "I can . . . position": Willkie, pp. 133–34.

409 "Before the . . . Madame": Cowles, pp. 87–89.

410 "there was . . . love": Pearson, p. 388. (Note: These last two quotes come from Cowles via Drew Pearson, while the others are directly from Cowles.)

410 "Wendell, you're . . . attraction,": Cowles, p. 89.

411 "There is . . . Representative": HA: Lauchlin Currie papers, Box 1, John Paton Davies, Jr., to LC, October 6, 1942.

411 "Mike," he . . . week": Cowles, p. 89.

411 "neuralgia in . . . visitor": WCA: Wendell Willkie, "Wendell Willkie Calls on Madame Chiang Kai-shek," *Look,* December 29, 1942.

412 "jumped into . . . kiss": Pearson, p. 388.

412 "I have . . . you": HA: Lauchlin Currie papers, Box 3, Folder Madame Chiang Kai-shek, Eleanor Roosevelt to Madame Chiang Kai-shek, September 16, 1947.

413 "most anxious . . . else": Tully, p. 330.

413 "does not . . . unfeasible": Sherwood, pp. 660–61.

413 "still seemed . . . dead": Lattimore, *China Memoirs,* p. 168.

413 "so moved . . . friend": *Preliminary Compilation of Primary Historical Materials of the Republic of China,* ed. Qin Xiao-xian, p. 782, Madame Chiang, wire no. 3 to Chiang Kai-shek, November 28, 1942.

413 "She expressed . . . lot": Ibid., pp. 783–84, Madame Chiang, wire no. 4 to Chiang Kai-shek, December 4, 1942.

413 "highly nervous . . . her": Roosevelt, *This I Remember,* pp. 282–83.

414 "perfectly made . . . eyes": Harvard University, Radcliffe Institute, Schlesinger Library: Frances Gunther papers, notes, January 1943.

414 "brief note . . . implies": WCA: Emma DeLong Mills papers, EM to MC., November 29, 1942.

415 "Thinking over . . . possible": *Preliminary Compilation of Primary Historical Materials of the Republic of China,* ed. Qin Xiao-xian, p. 785, Madame Chiang, wire no. 5 to Chiang Kai-shek, December 24, 1942.

415 "Roosevelt has . . . goal": Ibid., p. 787, Madame Chiang, wire no. 7 to Chiang Kai-shek, January 1943.

416 "would naturally . . . command": University of Indiana, Lilly Library, Wendell Willkie papers, Wendell Willkie to Miss L. W. D'un, December 11, 1942.

416 "no organic . . . found": HA: T. V. Soong papers, Box 63, Folder 16, Drs. Robert F. Loeb and Dana W. Atchley to Chiang Kai-shek, May 2, 1943.

416 "on the . . . once": Thomas J. Watson, introduction to Thomas, *The First Lady of China,* 1943.

416 "She should . . . obligations": Roosevelt, *Autobiography,* p. 249.

416 "very favorably . . . him": HA: Lauchlin Currie papers, Box 3, LC, notes from January 27 and February 2, 1943.

416 Chiang's "progress . . . satisfactory": HA: Lauchlin Currie papers, Box 3, Dana W. Atchley, M.D., to Eleanor Roosevelt, January 20, 1943.

416 "As you . . . years": HA: T. V. Soong papers, Box 63, Folder 16, Robert F. Loeb to T. V. Soong, February 25, 1943.

CHAPTER THIRTY-SIX

417 "If the . . . eyelash": Frank McNaughton, "Mme. Chiang in the U.S. Capitol," *Life*, March 8, 1943.

417 "Chinese boy's . . . interesting-looking": WCA: Mary Hornaday, "New York Gives Big Welcome to China's Little Mme. Chiang," *The Christian Science Monitor*, March 2, 1943.

417 "too close": Tuchman, p. 449.

417 "What do . . . sophisticated": Perkins, p. 74.

418 "some of . . . her": HA: Lauchlin Currie papers, Box 63, Folder 16, Joseph Chiang, notes, February 27, 1943.

418 "If I . . . truth": Zhang Ning-yi (translator) "Madame Chiang and Modern China," from the Russian Archives, Taipei Zhongzheng Cultural and Educational Association, 2002.

418 "a very . . . you": Harry J. Thomas, "In the Nation's Capital" in *The First Lady of China: The Historic Visit of Mme. Chiang Kai-shek to the United States*.

419 "marked the . . . battle": Roosevelt, *My Day*, p. 283, February 19, 1943.

420 "aroused a . . . Atlantic": Tuchman, p. 446.

420 "A little . . . dramatic": Roosevelt, *My Day*, p. 283, February 10, 1943.

420 "She wore . . . praised": John Gittings, "Madame Chiang Kai-shek," available at www.guardian.co.uk/obituaries/story/0,3604,1070646,00.html.

420 "the chamber . . . applause": "In the Nation's Capital" in *The First Lady of China: The Historic Visit of Mme. Chiang Kai-shek to the United States*.

420 "I have . . . America": *Preliminary Compilation of Primary Historical Materials of the Republic of China*, ed. Qin Xiao-xian, p. 793, Madame Chiang Kai-shek, wire no. 17 to Chiang Kai-shek, February 16, 1943.

420 "modern science . . . handclapping": "In the Nation's Capital" in *The First Lady of China: The Historic Visit of Mme. Chiang Kai-shek to the United States*.

421 "Goddam it . . . tears": "Madame," *Time*, March 1, 1943, p. 23.

421 "There is . . . dives": Allene Talmey, "May Ling Soong Chiang," *Vogue*, April 1943.

421 "In just . . . graceful": WCA: Malvina Stephenson, "A Lady 'Worth 50 Divisions' Captures the U.S. Capital," unidentified newspaper clipping, February 28, 1943.

421 "tight-fitting . . . person": Shi Zhi-yu, "How the American Mass Media Reported Madame Chiang's Visit to the U.S.A."

422 "Mrs. Chiang . . . Nordics": WCA: "Mrs. Chiang Puzzles Newsmen with 'Gobineau' and 'Obtunded,' " *The New York Herald Tribune*, February 8, 1943.

422 "The extraordinary . . . us": "In the Nation's Capital" in *The First Lady of China: The Historic Visit of Mme. Chiang Kai-shek to the United States*.

422 "We welcome . . . citizenship": Leong, p. 150.

422 "There can . . . table": "China in War and Peace," *The New Republic*, March 1, 1943, p. 270.

422 "too proud . . . parable": WCA: Ann Cottrell, "Mrs. Luce Has Praise for Talk by Mrs. Chiang," unidentified newspaper clipping, February 18, 1943.

423 "It was . . . themselves": HA: T. V. Soong papers, Box 23, Folder 2, Raymond Clapper, "Clapper Recalls Visit to Mme. Chiang in Chungking," February 25, 1943.

424 "Joe Kennedy . . . delivery": Leong, p. 136.

424 "the wife . . . notices": WCA: "The Famous Woman Who Exceeds Her Advance Notices," unidentified newspaper clipping, August 22, 1942.

424 "five years . . . millions": WCA: Bob Considine, "Chiang, Trained in Jap Army, Knows Key to Victory over It," *The Atlanta Constitution,* July 8, 1942.

424 "Today unconquered . . . service": WCA: "Chiang Kai-shek," *Bridgeport Post,* September 6, 1942.

424 "Madame Chiang . . . woman": WCA: Clare Boothe Luce, "What One Woman Can Do," *The Atlanta Constitution,* July 26, 1942.

424 "one of . . . world": WCA: Elsa Maxwell, "The Wisdom of Life," St. Louis, Mo., *Star-Times,* December 12, 1942.

424 "will go . . . China": WCA: "Elsa Maxwell's Particles," Reading, Pa., *Times,* August 3, 1942.

424 "I saw . . . character?": Roosevelt, *Autobiography,* pp. 249–50.

425 "the impression . . . shoulders": Roosevelt, *This I Remember,* p. 285.

425 "Kung brats . . . circles": National Archives: RG 226, Entry 210, Box 401, File 11, June 14, 1943.

425 "was kept . . . Presence": Ibid., undated.

425 "an imperative . . . direction": Tully, pp. 331–32.

426 "talk beautifully . . . democracy": "Mrs. Chiang Chided by Mrs. Roosevelt," *The New York Times,* December 5, 1945.

426 "just crazy . . . country": Tuchman, p. 450–51.

426 "of all . . . alone?": Doris Fleeson, "Mme. Chiang Gave Roosevelts a Record Number of Headaches," *Buffalo Evening News,* December 14, 1945.

426 "Well," the . . . Washington": HA: T. V. Soong papers, Box 30, Folder 8, "Confidential Resume of Interchange Between the President and Congressman Walter H. Judd Concerning Madame Chiang Kai-shek."

427 "I have . . . sex": "In the Nation's Capital" in *The First Lady of China: The Historic Visit of Mme. Chiang Kai-shek to the United States.*

427 "Madame Chiang . . . U.S.": WCA: "Trials and Errors," *Fortune,* March 2, 1943, p. 62.

CHAPTER THIRTY-SEVEN

429 "David Selznick . . . seen": WCA: Hedda Hopper, "Looking at Hollywood," *The Atlanta Journal,* April 8, 1943.

429 "the need . . . state": WCA: Telegram, Drs. Robert F. Loeb and Dana W. Atchley to Consul General Yu, February 16, 1943.

429 "Few of . . . high-mindedness": "In the City of Skyscrapers" in *The First Lady of China: The Historic Visit of Mme. Chiang Kai-shek to the United States.*

430 "she was . . . had": Leong, p. 140.

430 "green": "In the City of Skyscrapers" in *The First Lady of China: The Historic Visit of Mme. Chiang Kai-shek to the United States.*

430 "more like . . . people": WCA: "We Must Try to Forgive," *Time,* March 14, 1943, p. 17.

430 "In these . . . forgive": "In the City of Skyscrapers" in *The First Lady of China: The Historic Visit of Mme. Chiang Kai-shek to the United States.*

431 "incomparable. I . . . health": HA: T. V. Soong papers, Box 63, Folder 16, Robert F. Loeb to Madame Chiang Kai-shek, March 4, 1943.

431 "the most . . . Kai-shek": WCA: Rev. George Harold Talbott, D.D., "Madame Chiang's Big Meeting," *Passaic Herald News,* March 13, 1943.

432 "turned very sour": HA: Lauchlin Currie papers, Box 5, "FDR Memorandum, Notes for the Files," April 5, 1943.

432 "a schedule . . . certain": HA: T. V. Soong, Box 63, Folder 16, Dr. Robert F. Loeb to L. K. Kung, with enclosure, March 4, 1943.

432 "In her . . . breeze": WCA: Mary Hornaday, "Toughest Reporter Is Slave to Mme. Chiang's Charms," Buffalo, N.Y., *News,* March 29, 1943.

433 "One morning . . . said": Cowles, p. 90.

434 "She had . . . Willkie": Author's interview with Eleanor Lambert, March 1998.

434 "cultivate an . . . campus": WCA: Letter to Madame Chiang Kai-shek (letter unsigned, but probably from Mildred McAfee, president of the college), April 20, 1942.

435 "It was . . . did": WCA: Letter from an unidentified classmate on the letterhead of the Pittsburgh Chapter, American Red Cross.

435 "She seemed . . . fortyish": WCA: Catherine Coyne, "Mme. Chiang Near Emotional Collapse," clipping from unidentified newspaper.

435 "Students, Faculty . . . hurts!')": Hull, p. 10.

435 "Strong emotions . . . return": "Alma Mater" in *The First Lady of China: The Historic Visit of Mme. Chiang Kai-shek to the United States.*

435 "Mme. Chiang . . . Teacher": "Mme. Chiang Stumps Even Her Teachers," *The Christian Science Monitor,* March 9, 1943.

436 "perfection at . . . using": WCA: Carl Sandburg, "Mei-ling, China's Great Gift to Us," clipping from an unidentified Chicago newspaper, March 1943.

437 "are so . . . people": "By the Golden Gate" in *The First Lady of China: The Historic Visit of Mme. Chiang Kai-shek to the United States.*

437 "Mme. Chiang . . . this": WCA: "Mme. Chiang Calls Country Realistic," *The New York Times,* March 27, 1943.

437 "The present . . . violence": "By the Golden Gate" in *The First Lady of China: The Historic Visit of Mme. Chiang Kai-shek to the United States.*

437 "Who is . . . eyes?": WCA: Dorothy Walker, "Mme. Chiang's Point of View Is American," San Francisco, Calif., *News,* March 25, 1943.

437 "Madame Chiang's . . . unity": Jespersen, "Madame Chiang Kai-shek and the Face of Sino-American Relations" in Samuel C. Chu, p. 137.

437 "for chosen . . . me": Lattimore, *China Memoirs,* pp. 168–69.

438 "the elite . . . ultra": Edwin Schallert, "Elite of Filmland Meet Mme. Chiang," *Los Angeles Times,* April 2, 1943.

438 "one of . . . tour": "Land of Sun and Flowers" in *The First Lady of China: The Historic Visit of Mme. Chiang Kai-shek to the United States.*

438 "overdetermined historical display": Leong, p. 141.

438 "reinforced by . . . bands": "Land of Sun and Flowers" in *The First Lady of China: The Historic Visit of Mme. Chiang Kai-shek to the United States.*

439 "China, a . . . guest": "China, a Symphonic Narrative," notes taken by the author from a film of the event.

439 "We were . . . war": Jespersen, p. 138.

439 "mischievous statements": Li, p. 227.

440 "a bigger . . . best?": DeLong, pp. 173–74.

440 "I tried . . . debts": Li, p. 227.

440 "My dear . . . lectures": Indiana University, Lilly Library, Wendell Willkie papers, Wendell Willkie to Madame, August 14, 1943.

440 "She strikes . . . ability": Kennedy, pp. 560–61.

441 "official shopper": National Archives: RG 226, Entry 201, Box 410, File 11, June 24, 1943.

441 "I hate . . . show": Ibid., June 25, 1943.

441 "a deep-seated . . . visit": Ibid., June 23, 1943.

CHAPTER THIRTY-EIGHT

443 "There is . . . friends": Tuchman, p. 81.

443 "The consensus . . . complete": Ibid., pp. 452–54.

443 "stupidity and . . . equanimity": White and Jacoby, pp. 174–76.

444 "dogs eating . . . darkness": HA: Lauchlin Currie papers, Box 5, Theodore White, Loyang Cable no. 114 to David Halburd, March 13, 1943.

444 "one of . . . frosting": White and Jacoby, p. 176.

444 "the matter . . . press": White, pp. 154–55.

445 "the greatest . . . powerful": White, "*Life* Looks at China," *Life*, May 1, 1944.

445 "to help . . . return": Payne, p. 251.

445 "revision": White, "*Life* Looks at China."

445 "chills and . . . statesman": Fairbank, *Chinabound*, pp. 252–53.

445 "with the . . . public": HA: Lauchlin Currie papers, Box 3, Folder Chiang Kai-shek, "Comments on 'China's Destiny' by Two American Observers in China," June 17, 1943.

446 "plan . . . campaigns": Arnold, pp. 407–22.

446 "Dear Joe . . . job": Tuchman, p. 457.

446 "brushed too . . . difference": Arnold, p. 427.

446 "poison pen style": HA: Roger J. Sandilands papers, John K. Fairbank to RJS, February 22, 1988.

446 "Alsop was . . . man": HA: Kohlberg papers, Box 5, Walter T. Ridder, "The Brothers Cassandra, Joseph and Stewart," *Reporter*, October 21, 1954.

447 "a cousin . . . Roosevelt": HA: T. V. Soong papers, Box 1, Schedule A.

447 "apocalypse in Asia" Almquist, p. 37.

447 "grandiose . . . air": Tuchman, pp. 458–59.

447 "the one . . . produced": Jack Belden, "Chennault Fights to Hold the China Front," *Life*, August 10, 1942.

447 "Churchill is . . . now": HA: T. V. Soong papers, Box 63, Folders 12 and 33, T. V. Soong to Madame Chiang Kai-shek, March 18, 1943.

448 "as a . . . her": Leong, pp. 146–47.

448 "with some . . . things": Davies, p. 267.

448 "responsible for . . . China": Tuchman, p. 475.

448 "In conversation . . . world": Franklin D. Roosevelt Library, FDR papers as President, Map Room File, Box 1, 1941–April 1945, Intelligence Report, May 21, 1943.

448 "on record . . . strategy": Wu and Kuo, p. 506, May 17, 1943.

448 "for many . . . G-mo": Tuchman, p. 474.

449 "To call . . . mistake": Franklin D. Roosevelt Library, FDR papers as President, Map Room File, Box 10, Folder Chiang Kai-shek, January 1943–Dec. 1943, Chief of Staff George Marshall to FDR, April 12, 1943.

449 "We hope . . . him": "Uncle Joe" *The New York Times,* April 30, 1943.

449 "cogent and . . . Chiang Kai-shek": Tuchman, pp. 470–72.

449 "The Madame . . . skirt": HA: Joseph Stilwell papers, Stilwell, "The Black Book," p. 13.

449 "He's a . . . me": Tuchman, p. 475.

450 "Sister [May-ling] . . . President": HA: T. V. Soong papers, Box 59, Folder 4, T. V. Soong to Chiang Kai-shek, April 16, 1943.

450 "against overwhelming . . . fight": HA: T. V. Soong papers, Box 61, Folder 5, Joseph W. Alsop, "Memorandum for Dr. Soong," undated.

450 "when Stilwell . . . time": HA: T. V. Soong papers, Box 60, Folder 6, T. V. Soong, wire to Chiang Kai-shek, June 1943.

450 "the Chinese . . . soldier": HA: Stanley Hornbeck papers, Box 103, NN, SH, "Memorandum of Conversation," September 28, 1943.

450 "bad or . . . China": HA: T. V. Soong papers, Box 61, Folder 1, T. V. Soong, "Memorandum on General Stillwell," August 20, 1943.

450 "It is . . . immediately": HA: T. V. Soong papers, Box 60, Folder 9, T. V. Soong, two wires to Chiang Kai-shek, September 1943 and undated.

450 "to persuade . . . me": Alsop with Platt, pp. 217–20.

451 "get acquainted . . . Stilwell": Tuchman, p. 477.

451 "full of bugs": Stilwell, p. 217.

452 "Uncle Chump . . . Jack": Swanberg, p. 2.

452 "The planes . . . infection": Author's interview with Sidney Lumet, May 2000.

452 "from medicine . . . 1944": Tuchman, p. 482.

452 "medieval cesspool": White and Jacoby, p. 160.

452 "Some of . . . price": HA: Claire L. Chennault papers, Box 1, Folder AVG, Major Lin Wen Kuei to CLC, December 6, 1941.

452 "had whorehouses . . . dirty": White, p. 146.

453 "Officers pimping . . . knew": Tuchman, p. 482.

453 "Chennault's whore-house . . . GCM": HA: Joseph Stilwell papers, Stilwell, "The Black Book," pp. 18–19.

453 "the longest . . . out": Tuchman, pp. 481–92.

CHAPTER THIRTY-NINE

454 "My Chinese . . . Li?": Caldwell, p. 61.

454 "a joyful . . . husband": WCA: "Madame Chiang in Chungking, Ill from Trip," unidentified newspaper clipping, July 4, 1943.

454 "The President . . . done": Franklin D. Roosevelt Library, Harry L. Hopkins papers, Box 135, Chiang Kai-shek, War Department, Correspondence, June 4–17, 1943.

454 "We thought . . . Burma": Hagley Museum and Library, Wilmington, Del.: Sonia Tomara, "Madame Chiang Nearly Fell into Japan's Hands," *The New York Herald Tribune,* July 11, 1943.

454 "was feeling . . . landed": WCA: "Madame Chiang in Chungking, Ill from Trip."

454 "The weather . . . trip": Drew Pearson, "Washington Merry-Go-Round," *The Washington Post,* September 6, 1943.

454 "weary and airsick": Hagley Museum and Library, Wilmington, Del.: Tomara, "Madame Chiang Nearly Fell into Japan's Hands."

454 "The generalissimo . . . met": Ibid.

455 "Where the . . . everybody?": Li, p. 236.

455 "Peanut was . . . Chinese": HA: Joseph Stilwell papers, Stilwell, "The Black Book," p. 30.

455 "When I . . . him": HA, Joseph Stilwell Papers, Stilwell to his wife, p. 215.

455 "Mme. present . . . crash": HA: Joseph Stilwell papers, Stilwell, "The Black Book," p. 30.

455 "M.L. looks . . . America": Epstein, pp. 418–19.

456 "washing China's . . . doghouse": Service, pp. 108–9.

456 "I'm always . . . need": Soong Ai-ling to Soong Ching-ling, "An Anthology of Soong Ching-ling's Correspondence, collected by the Memorial Museum of Soong Ching-ling's Former Residence in Shanghai," no. 50, June 15, 1947.

456 "I wonder . . . me": Ibid., no. 58, November 5, 1947.

457 "This [transfer] . . . planes": Green, p. 21.

457 "After a . . . through": Stilwell, p. 212.

457 "it would . . . rival": Tuchman, p. 487.

457 "in a . . . Excellency": HA: T. V. Soong, wires to Chiang Kai-shek, August 23, 1943, and August 25, 1943.

458 "bad leaks . . . information": HA: Lauchlin Currie papers, Box 5, LC to Harry Hopkins, June 15, 1943.

458 "The only . . . Japanese": Caldwell, p. 56.

458 "Only Donovan . . . up": Dunlop, pp. 426–27.

459 "manage": Wakeman, *Spymaster,* p. 325.

460 "the first . . . statement": Tuchman, p. 493.

460 "Too Much . . . enrichment": Hanson W. Baldwin, "Too Much Wishful Thinking About China," *Reader's Digest,* August 1943.

460 "The Great . . . China": Fussell, pp. 161–62.

460 "Our Distorted . . . chorus": Nathaniel Peffer, "Our Distorted View of China," *The New York Times Magazine,* November 7, 1943.

461 "Summoned to . . . somewhere": HA: Joseph Stilwell papers, Stilwell, "The Black Book," p. 57.

461 "lead China . . . place": Tuchman, p. 498.

461 "over the . . . government": HA: Lauchlin Currie papers, Box 5, "George Sokolsky on T. V. Soong," February 17, 1944.

461 "the same . . . dynasties": Tuchman, p. 499.

461 "Lunch & . . . me": HA: Joseph Stilwell papers, Stilwell, "The Black Book," pp. 60–64.

462 "haughty . . . up": Stilwell, pp. 228–29.

462 "Mme. Chiang . . . tour": National Archives: RG 226, Entry 210, Box 401, File 11, October 6, 1943.

463 "The G-mo . . . swat": HA: Joseph Stilwell papers, Stilwell, "The Black Book," pp. 69–75.

464 "a tremendous . . . else": Feis, pp. 78–79; "these ruthlessly self-centered women" comes from Alsop with Platt, p. 223.

464 "dramatic eclipse": Service, p. 78.

464 "there was . . . home": Stilwell, p. 235.
464 "secured the . . . State": HA: Memo Leo Soong to Dr. Elena Danielson, February 21, 2005.
464 "In the . . . well": HA: T. V. Soong papers, Box 63, Folder 17, T. V. Soong to Chiang Kai-shek, December 23, 1943. (Note: The author has changed some of the language in the translation.)
465 "Madame Chiang . . . me?": HA: T. V. Soong papers, Box 58, Folder 1, T.V. to Li Shi-zeng, June 17 (presumably 1944).
465 "Uncle Joe": HA: Joseph Stilwell papers, Stilwell, "The Black Book," p. 78.

CHAPTER FORTY
469 "What a . . . democrat": HA: Joseph Stilwell papers, Stilwell, "The Black Book," pp. 85–86.
469 "the climax . . . eyes": Crozier, p. 249.
469 "to put . . . powers": Stilwell, p. 237.
469 "there should . . . power": Franklin D. Roosevelt Library, FDR papers, Map Room File, Box 17, Folder 3, message from Churchill to Roosevelt, November 17, 1943.
469 "to keep . . . away": HA: Roger J. Sandilands Collection, John Fairbank to Sandilands, February 22, 1988.
470 "sadly distracted . . . personality": Churchill, pp. 289–90.
470 "You think . . . bite": HA: Walter H. Judd papers, Box 175, Folder 2, Robert Eunson, "First Lady Hopes U.S. Will Continue Firm Vietnam Stand," March 19, 1965.
470 "capriciousness": Davies, p. 278.
470 "the full . . . express": Tuchman, p. 516.
471 "driven absolutely mad": Davies, p. 278.
471 "Terrible performance . . . back": Stilwell, p. 245.
471 "the most . . . brain": Alanbrooke, pp. 477–80.
472 "well-guarded . . . end": Moran, pp. 139–40.
473 "childish": Davies, p. 278.
473 "we will . . . on": Mosley, p. 262.
473 "Now let . . . so": Stilwell, p. 255.
474 "The President . . . Asia": Tuchman, p. 518.
474 "be expelled . . . Japan": http://www.niraikanai.wwma.net/pages/archive/cairo.html.
474 "My dear . . . he?": Feis, p. 109.
475 "wife's support . . . much": Chiang Kai-shek Archive: Chen Jin-jin, "Stories of Love," in *Study of Modern Chinese Women*, ed. Wang Yu-gao and Wang Yu-zheng, vol. 2, pp. 275–88.
475 "poor leadership": Tuchman, p. 522.
475 "four hundred . . . pigtails": Davies, p. 280.
475 "Well, Joe . . . Ha!": Stilwell, pp. 251–52.
476 "lore of . . . do": Davies, p. 281.
476 " 'I take . . . truck": Stilwell, pp. 251–56.
476 "She realizes . . . 'noble' ": HA: Joseph Stilwell papers, Stilwell, "The Black Book," p. 95.
477 "denied the . . . inflation": Blum, *Roosevelt and Morgenthau*, p. 269.
477 "an elaborate . . . etc., etc.": HA: Roger J. Sandilands papers, John Fairbank to RS, February 22, 1988.

477 "went through . . . projects": Blum, *Roosevelt and Morgenthau*, pp. 463–76.
479 "large reserves . . . effort": Tuchman, p. 527.
479 "They [the . . . government": Blum, *Roosevelt and Morgenthau*, pp. 476–79.
480 "dignity of . . . doors": Kerr, pp. 158–61.
481 "outrageous," UNRAA . . . shirts": Library of Congress: Roy W. Howard papers, Box 235, Foreign File, Randall Gould to RH, November 25, 1948.

CHAPTER FORTY-ONE
482 "The manners . . . China": White and Jacoby, p. 256.
482 "a philanthropic . . . overtones": Caldwell, p. 19.
483 "shocked by . . . again": Dorn, pp. 116–22.
485 "propaganda blitz . . . demons": Fenby, p. 416.
486 "merciless military extortion": White and Jacoby, p. 178.
486 "peppery Cantonese": Ibid., p. 70.
486 "As far . . . doomed": Ibid., p. 187–88.
487 "hopelessly inadequate": Tuchman, p. 585.
487 "Over in . . . hope": Stilwell, pp. 306–7.
487 "the nation . . . people": "Sun for Enlightenment," *Time*, April 24, 1944.
487 "Perhaps nothing . . . personality": White, "*Life* Looks at China," *Life*, May 1, 1944.
488 *The Four* . . . approached": Diana Lary, "Creating the Role of the Leader's Consort: Madame Chiang Kai Shek," *Sino-American Relations*, March 2004.
488 "There are . . . small": White, "*Life* Looks at China."
489 "The Generalissimo . . . back": Wallace, pp. 349–50.
489 "launched forth . . . Communists": Feis, p. 147.
489 "case against . . . on": Wallace, p. 351.
489 "given every . . . regime": Tuchman, pp. 593–94.
490 "to comment . . . disease": Lattimore, *China Memoirs*, p. 186.
490 "painful maladies . . . strain": WCA: Emma DeLong Mills papers, MS to EM, April 6, 1944.
490 "Chinese Communists . . . Japan": Feis, p. 140.
490 "deteriorating at . . . Stilwell": Franklin D. Roosevelt Library, FDR papers, Map Room File, Box 10, FDR–Chiang Kai-shek, January 1944–December 1944, "Memorandum for the President from the U.S. Chiefs of Staff," July 4, 1944.
491 "drastic measures . . . stake": Ibid., "Message from the President to the Generalissimo," July 6, 1944.
491 "After the . . . tops": Tuchman, p. 541.
492 "a limey . . . King": Mosley, p. 301.
492 "The British . . . moon": Tuchman, p. 548.
492 "It takes . . . Japs": Stilwell, pp. 271–77.
492 "By provoking . . . own": Tuchman, pp. 551–58.
493 "We had . . . corpses": Stilwell, pp. 282–83.
493 "How was . . . pressure": Tuchman, pp. 561–68.
493 "brutally embarassing . . . airfield": Ibid., pp. 573–74.
494 "the only . . . years": White and Jacoby, p. 159.
494 "I consider . . . for": Tuchman, pp. 578–86.
494 "A corporal . . . enemy": H. R. Isaacs, "Kweilin Destruction," *CBI Roundup*, 1944.
495 "Thus in . . . China": White and Jacoby, p. 197.

CHAPTER FORTY-TWO

496 "It would . . . zero": Chang with Halliday, p. 99.

496 "try to . . . Americans": Princeton University, Seeley G. Mudd Library: John Foster Dulles Oral History Project, Transcript of a Recorded Interview with Walter H. Judd by Philip A. Crowl, Washington, D.C., December 11, 1965.

496 "There is . . . country": Ibid.

496 "T.V. says . . . bill": Stilwell, p. 331.

496 "a Chinese . . . CKS": Tuchman, p. 620.

497 "*I* would . . . orders": Ibid., p. 410.

497 "adopted the . . . delays": Ibid., pp. 629–30.

497 "must . . . be . . . responsibility": Feis, p. 189.

498 "the harshest . . . incandescent": White and Jacoby, pp. 220–21.

498 "the greatest . . . them": Fenby, pp. 428–29.

498 "cutting my . . . knife": Stilwell, p. 343.

498 "Thus," as . . . challenges": Schaller, p. 88.

498 "in accordance . . . procedure": Franklin D. Roosevelt Library, FDR papers, Map Room File, Box 10, FDR–Chiang Kai-shek, January 1944–December 1944, C.H. (Cordell Hull) to FDR, "Memorandum for the President," April 28, 1944.

498 "immense influence": National Archives: RG226, Entry A1-170, Box 401, November 21, 1944.

498 "must go": Tuchman, p. 636.

498 "on this . . . yield": HA: T. V. Soong papers, Box 36, T. V. Soong, wire to H. C. Chun, October 11, 1944.

499 "the situation . . . it": University of Oklahoma, Western History Collections, Patrick J. Hurley Collection, Box 90, Folder 5, Stilwell, telegram to Marshall, October 10, 1944.

499 "THE AX . . . late": Stilwell, p. 345.

499 "Stilwell has . . . Chiang Kai-shek": Feis, pp. 194–95.

499 "the pro-Chinese-Communist . . . Stilwell": HA: Alfred Kohlberg papers, Box 5, Joseph Alsop, "Budens and Morris," *The New York Herald Tribune*, September 4, 1951.

499 "Stilwell's dismissal . . . Ho": HA: Kohlberg papers, Box 5, Joseph Alsop, "The Foredoomed Mission of General Marshall," *The Saturday Evening Post*, January 21, 1950.

500 "pliant bad . . . worse": HA: Kohlberg papers, Box 5, Joseph Alsop, "Chiang Kai-shek, 1953," *The New York Herald Tribune*, October 30, 1953.

500 "very decent . . . developed": Tuchman, p. 643.

500 "the most . . . deepest": "Once China's Heroine, Soong Ching-ling" *The New York Times*, September 21, 1966.

500 "nonsense . . . qualities": "Roosevelt and China," *The New York Herald Tribune*, November 2, 1944.

501 "lushly reported . . . things": Fairbank, *Chinabound*, pp. 245–46.

502 "Chungking is . . . warlord": Service, pp. 93–96.

503 "on the . . . doctors": Seagrave, *The Soong Dynasty*, p. 413.

503 "On the . . . necessary": "Denials by Chiang at Party Related," *The New York Times*, December 1, 1944.

503 "In leading . . . convinced": Hahn, *Chiang Kai-shek*, pp. 292–93.

504 "Even during . . . request": White and Jacoby, p. 123.

504 "First Lady . . . ransom": Grace Davidson, "First Lady of China Too Chic," *Boston Post*, July 20, 1944.

504 "pale and listless": "Mme. Chiang Now in Brazil Reportedly for 'Rest Cure,' " *Boston Herald*, July 15, 1944.

504 "I haven't . . . illness?": Academia Historica, Taipei: CKS, wire to Madame, July 20, 1944.

505 "I have . . . here": WCA: Emma DeLong Mills papers, EM to MS, August 9, 1944.

505 "Mayling is . . . China": DeLong, p. 184.

505 "not supposed . . . humidity": HA: T. V. Soong papers, Box 58, Folder 1, Madame Chiang, telegram to T. V. Soong, August 15, 1944.

505 "physicians fear . . . recovery": "Madam Chiang Not Told of Wendell Willkie Death," *The New York Times*, October 9, 1944.

505 "conduct was outrageous": White and Jacoby, p. 112.

506 "bad odor . . . family": FBI files: American Embassy, Taipei, "Possible Return of Dr. H. H. Kung to China: Visit of Madame H. H. Kung," U.S. State Department, Foreign Service Despatch 793.00/1-2957, February 12, 1957. (Material furnished to the author by the Department of Justice in response to a Freedom of Information Act inquiry.)

506 "indifferent reception . . . intolerable": Bill Costello, "China's Richest Man, Irked at Poor Reception, Makes Sure That It Won't Happen Here Again," *The Washington Post*, July 2, 1944.

506 "suffering the . . . course": DeLong, pp. 184–85.

506 "Are you . . . again": Academia Historica, Taipei, CKS, wire to Madame, November 29, 1944.

507 "Your birthday . . . possible": Ibid., CKS, wire to Madame, March 19, 1945.

507 "How she . . . phrases": DeLong, p. 208.

507 "I'll be . . . accident": Ibid., p. 191.

507 "a chronic . . . shocked": HA: Frank Dorn papers, Box 4, Folder 10, Dorn handwritten notes, March 9, 1945.

508 "changed discord . . . cabal": "Madame Chiang Applauds Wedemeyer Book," *Taiwan Journal*, November 23, 1987.

508 "with lightly . . . resistance": WCA: United Press, "Mme Chiang Will Stay in U.S., Say Chinese," undated, source unknown.

508 "When could . . . China": Ibid.

Chapter Forty-three

509 "History is . . . miscalculations": Tuchman, p. 166.

509 "overbearing self-confidence": Lattimore, *China Memoirs*, p. 85.

509 "a preposterous . . . China": Davies, p. 342.

509 "Moose Dung . . . Shek": Fenby, p. 438.

509 "He works . . . mistakes": HA: Frank Dorn papers, Box 4, Folder 14, Dorn handwritten notes, "Situation (Sino-American) in China," undated.

510 "disaster": Service, p. 329.

510 "inept, incompetent . . . reactionary": Princeton University: Seeley G. Mudd Library:

The John Foster Dulles Oral History Project, Transcript of a Recorded Interview with Walter H. Judd by Philip A. Crowl, Washington, D.C., December 11, 1965.

510 "Hurleyed out . . . China": Schaller, p. 103.

510 "an island . . . army": White and Jacoby, pp. 249–52.

510 "exploded rather . . . expanded": Ibid., p. 199.

511 "almost to . . . them": Ibid., pp. 208–11.

511 "The Chinese . . . China": Feis, p. 160.

511 "among the . . . China": Schaller, p. 99.

511 "immediately . . . insist": Tuchman, p. 591–93.

512 "The Yenan . . . newspapers": Feis, p. 162.

512 "They are . . . determination": Service, pp. 194–95.

512 "if you . . . thoughts": Chang and Halliday, *Mao*, p. 256.

512 "big and . . . face": Davies, p. 346.

512 "playing a . . . become": HA: Dorn papers, Box 1, Folder 56, John Davies, "Comments on Current Crisis," December 5, 1944.

512 "The Communists . . . future": Ibid., Box 4, Folder 14, Dorn handwritten notes, "The Situation (Sino-American) in China," undated.

513 " 'Don't worry . . . settlement": Service, p. 331.

513 "An impressive . . . Kai-shek": White and Jacoby, p. 254.

513 "You have . . . requested": Service, p. 332.

514 "an extremely . . . reason": HA: Frank Dorn papers, Box 1, Folder 46, report from John Service for General Stilwell, "The Need for Greater Realism in Our Relations with Chiang Kai-shek," October 10, 1944.

514 "The Chinese . . . support": Feis, p. 263.

514 "to take . . . helpful": Ibid., p. 222.

514 "buffoon . . . 'negotiations' ": HA: Frank Dorn papers, Box 4, Folder 14, Dorn handwritten notes, "Situation (Sino-American) in China," undated.

515 "We must . . . negligible": Feis, pp. 235 (footnote 11)–237.

515 "It was . . . war": Ibid., pp. 243–50.

516 "It should . . . interests": U.S. Department of State, *United States Relations with China* (The White Paper), p. 115.

517 "The generalissimo . . . team": HA: Lauchlin Currie papers, Box 5, Harold R. Isaacs, "The Situation in China since Stilwell's Recall," December 22, 1944.

518 "If CKS . . . public": HA: Frank Dorn papers, Box 4, Folder 5, handwritten notes, March 8, 1945.

518 "Our dealings . . . Chiang": Service, pp. 161–64.

518 Although the . . . elsewhere: John Service, recalled from China at Hurley's behest, was later accused by McCarthy of Communist sympathies; although he was cleared of that charge by the Tydings Committee, he was fired by the State Department. He appealed his dimissal, won his case in the Supreme Court, and returned to State but left after realizing that he would no longer be given important assignments. He ended his career at the Center for Chinese Studies at the University of California at Berkeley.

John P. Davies left China in 1945 after Hurley accused him of being a Communist and threatened to ruin his career at the State Department. He subsequently served in Russia, Germany, and Peru. In spite of the fact that nine investigations from 1948 to 1954 failed to produce any evidence of disloyalty or Communist sympathies, he was dismissed in 1954 by Dulles, who claimed he had "demonstrated a lack of judgment, discretion and reliability." Davies was eventually exonerated of the charge but spent ten years outside the United States before returning home. Both Service and Davies had warned that the Communists would win the civil war, thus arousing Nationalist animosity.

John C. Vincent, who was head of the China desk and the Far Eastern Division at State from 1944 to 1949, was described by McCarthy "as (1) a big Communist tremendously important to Russia, as (2) a part of an espionage ring in the State Department, and (3) as one who should 'not only be discharged but should be immediately prosecuted.' " In spite of the fact that the Tydings Committee concluded that "the McCarthy charges are absurd," he was suspended by the State Department. Vincent was eventually cleared of disloyalty charges and allowed to retire. (Koen, pp. 216–223.)

CHAPTER FORTY-FOUR

519 "Has China . . . Yalta?": Furuya, p. 822.
519 "hard-boiled, shrewd . . . it": HA: Lauchlin Currie papers, Box 5, Harold R. Isaacs, "The Situation in China since Stilwell's Recall," December 22, 1944.
519 "the world's . . . prick": Schaller, p. 89.
519 "sententious" and . . . man": HA: Frank Dorn papers, Box 4, Folder 18, handwritten notes on Wedemeyer, undated.
519 "General Stilwell . . . <u>command</u>": HA: Albert C. Wedemeyer papers, Box 81, Folder 1, Claire L. Chennault to ACW, July 6, 1945.
520 "misapprehension or misinformation": Ibid., November 6, 1944.
520 "has been . . . character": Ibid., Box 82, File 23, ACW to George C. Marshall, December 10, 1944.
520 "In the . . . reorganizing": HA: Lauchlin Currie papers, Box 5, Harold Isaacs, "The Situation in China since Stilwell's Recall," December 22, 1944.
520 "The Chinese . . . effort": HA: Wedemeyer papers, Box 82, File 23, ACW to George C. Marshall, December 10, 1944.
521 "one of . . . US": HA: Lauchlin Currie papers, Box 5, Harold Isaacs, "The Situation in China since Stilwell's Recall," December 22, 1944.
521 "Elder sister . . . better": Lin Bo-wen, "Family Affairs in T. V. Soong's Documents," *Chinese News*, May 17, 2004.
522 "frequent and . . . Kai-shek": HA: Lauchlin Currie papers, Box 5, Harold R. Isaacs, "The Situation in China since Stilwell's Recall," December 22, 1944.
522 "many intricate . . . them": HA: Wedemeyer papers, Box 82, Folder 23, ACW to George C. Marshall, August 1, 1945.
522 "We are . . . aware": Lin Bo-wen, "Family Affairs in T. V. Soong's Documents," *Chinese News*, May 17, 2004.
522 "an ambitious . . . Soong": HA: Lauchlin Currie papers, Box 5, Harold R. Isaacs, "The Situation in China since Stilwell's Recall," December 22, 1944.
522 "Madame Kung . . . government": Ibid., "George Sokolsky on T. V. Soong," February 17, 1944.
523 "We have . . . road": Feis, p. 275.

523 "I wonder . . . that?": Tuchman, p. 652.

523 "the great . . . illusion": Feis, p. 284.

523 "Stalin agreed . . . conversation": U.S. Department of State, *United States Relations with China* (The White Paper), p. 96.

524 "our future . . . Communism": Feis, p. 291.

524 "It is . . . satisfactory": National Archives: Microfilm, RG59, CDF (1945–1949), LM-184, Roll 50, Frames 628-29, June 28, 1945.

524 "the impression . . . meaning": Feis, pp. 301–4.

525 "clearly indicated . . . disappointment": HA: Walter H. Judd papers, Box 165, Folder 20, Wedemeyer to WHJ, July 7, 1951.

526 "categorically": Feis, p. 319.

526 "I am . . . it" Ibid., p. 330.

527 "What do . . . Mao?" Crozier, p. 273.

527 "repeatedly urged . . . objectives": HA: Judd papers, Box 175, Folder 1, "Chiang Steals Some GOP Thunder," *The Washington Post*, February 25, 1953.

527 "looking somewhat . . . soon": Nancy MacLennan, "Mme. Chiang Opens Peace Campaign," *The New York Times*, August 15, 1945.

CHAPTER FORTY-FIVE

529 "Manchuria has . . . whereabouts": Davies, p. 25.

529 "false, vicious . . . propaganda": Neal Patterson, "Mme. Chiang Convalescing after 8 Months of Treatment," *Washington Times Herald*, June 19, 1945.

529 "a largely . . . airplane": Beal, p. 9.

530 "for three . . . savages": Cornell University Library, Division of Rare and Manuscript Collections, James M. McHugh papers, no. 2770, letter to his wife, Reel 1, June 30, 1946.

530 "one of . . . Manchuria": White and Jacoby, pp. 283–85.

531 "nation-wide counter-offensive": Mao, p. 289.

531 "Our troops . . . Communists": Feis, pp. 357–64.

532 "peace, democracy . . . strife": Crozier, p. 284.

533 "has become . . . place?": "Mr Hurley's China," *The New York Herald Tribune*, November 2, 1945.

533 "Ambassador Hurley's . . . center": Feis, p. 409.

533 "a considerable . . . China": U.S. Department of State, *United States Relations with China* (The White Paper), J. Patrick Hurley to President Harry S. Truman, appendix 50, p. 583.

533 "If we . . . guaranteed": Chang and Halliday, *Mao*, p. 295.

534 "guarantee": Hahn, *Chiang Kai-shek*, p. 332.

534 "general agreement": Crozier, p. 276.

535 "Chinese carpetbaggers": Cornell University Library, Division of Rare and Manuscript Collections, James M. McHugh papers, no. 2770, letter to his wife, Reel 1, June 30, 1946.

535 "Today there . . . can": Ibid., letter to his wife, Reel 1, July 26, 1946.

535 *"We've been* . . . arrest": Crozier, pp. 278–79.

535 "one of . . . politics": Salter, p. 212.

535 "often criticized . . . censure": Boorman, vol. 3, p. 153.

536 "many of . . . ministers": Crozier, pp. 301–2.

536 "unfavourable . . . unfavourable": HA: Arthur N. Young papers, Box 881, Arthur Young, "Short Notes on Current Articles," undated.

536 "a left-wing . . . ills": Henry Lieberman, "Madame Sun—China's 'Conscience,'" *The New York Times Magazine,* August 11, 1946.

537 "I have . . . it": WCA: Emma DeLong Mills papers, EM to MS, August 16, 1946.

537 "we should . . . cooperate": HA: Albert C. Wedemeyer papers, Box 83, Folder 7, ACW to T. V. Soong, August 10, 1946.

538 "I would . . . over": Beal, pp. 341–42.

CHAPTER FORTY-SIX

541 "He [Marshall] . . . in": Bland, p. 580.

541 "continued support . . . China": HA: T. V. Soong papers, Box 39, Folder 11, memorandum, November 10, 1945.

541 "a vigorous . . . solution": White and Jacoby, p. 293.

541 "We had . . . dollars": Feis, p. 423.

541 "renewed encounter . . . cheeks' ": Mosley, p. 372.

542 "very mediocre": Taylor, p. 138.

543 "the remotest chance": Mosley, p. 367.

543 "Inasmuch as . . . settlement": Keith E. Eiler, "Devotion and Dissent: Albert Wedemeyer, George Marshall, and China," in Bland, p. 99.

543 "special message . . . friendship": Li, p. 269.

543 "It is . . . world": Henry R. Lieberman, "Mme. Chiang Ends North China Visit," *The New York Times,* January 27, 1946.

543 "just about . . . perfect": Beal, p. 50.

544 "ran a . . . thinkers": White and Jacoby, pp. 294–96.

544 "their greedy . . . etc.": Mosley, pp. 377–78.

545 "closely . . . nation": HA: T. V. Soong papers, Box 37, Harry S. Truman, confidential letter to Chiang Kai-shek, August 12, 1946.

545 "it was . . . chat": Beal, pp. 100–102.

546 "the evil . . . China": HA: Stanley K. Hornbeck papers, Box 150, "A Man Named Donald," *The Washington Post,* February 23, 1945.

546 "Time and . . . grateful": Ibid., Dean Schedler and C. Yates McDaniel, "Donald, Long Hunted by Japs, Found with Rescued Internees," *The Evening Star,* February 24, 1945.

546 "One day . . . die": Selle, p. 367.

547 "Do you . . . fine": Columbia University Library, RBML, William Henry Donald correspondence, Ida du Marc to K. C. Li, November 12, 1946.

547 "land reformers . . . France": Crozier, p. 298.

548 "only thing . . . checkers": Beal, p. 177.

548 "the Kuomintang . . . settlement": HA: T. V. Soong papers, Box 61, Folder 11, Chou En-lai to George C. Marshall, September 30, 1946.

548 "The more . . . hopper": Cornell University Library, Division of Rare and Manuscript Collections, James M. McHugh papers, no. 2770, letter to his wife, Reel 1, July 31, 1946.

549 "a long . . . inch": Beal, p. 246.

549 "His old . . . ceiling": Cray, p. 582.

549 "terrible . . . him": Beal, pp. 246–47.

549 "The abstention . . . it": Ibid., pp. 279–92.

550 "It is . . . moved": Stuart, "How the Communists Got China" (condensation of book entitled *Fifty Years in China), U.S. News & World Report,* October 1, 1954, p. 45.

550 "very cold . . . mission": Columbia University Library: Frank Rounds, interview by Dr. Bluma Swerdloff, Interview 2, October 1, 1962, pp. 81–82.

551 "interested in . . . involved": Li, p. 279.

551 "Never," he . . . mission": William C. Bullitt, "A Report to the American People on China," *Life,* October 13, 1947.

CHAPTER FORTY-SEVEN

552 "Chiang stood . . . dissented": White and Jacoby, p. 288.

552 "support free . . . pressure": Crozier, p. 303.

552 "a howling . . . go": Frederick Gruin, "Week of the Winds," *Time,* March 10, 1947.

553 "Because of . . . state": HA: T. V. Soong papers, Box 63, Folder 5, T. V. Soong notes, undated.

553 "the Chinese . . . Communists": Crozier, p. 304.

553 "accusing the . . . supporting": Wedemeyer, pp. 382–91.

554 "he still . . . with": Crozier, p. 310.

554 "the odds . . . people": U.S. Department of State, *United States Relations with China* (The White Paper), pp. 380–84.

555 "rallied to . . . defence": Crozier, p. 311.

555 "achieved only . . . China": Koen, p. 32.

555 "clever and charming": Charles Wertenbaker, "The China Lobby: I. The Legacy of T. V. Soong," *Reporter,* April 15, 1952, p. 4.

555 "a Polish . . . watched": FBI files, Memorandum for Mr. Lawrence M. C. Smith, Chief, Special War Policies Unit, from John Edgar Hoover, Director, no. 65-31284-99, February 24, 1943. (Material obtained from the Department of Justice in response to Freedom of Information Act inquiry.)

555 "influential Americans . . . expedited": Charles Wertenbaker, "The China Lobby: I. The Legacy of T. V. Soong," *Reporter,* April 15, 1952, pp. 5–6.

555 "very bad": HA: Lauchlin Currie papers, Box 5, LC, "Memorandum for the President," June 27, 1942.

555 "Because the . . . munitions": Wertenbaker, "The China Lobby: I. The Legacy of T. V. Soong," *Reporter,* April 15, 1952, p. 6.

556 "under circumstances . . . duty": Wertenbaker, "The China Lobby: II The Pattern of Enrichment," *Reporter,* April 15, 1952, pp. 8–9.

557 "selfless, altogether . . . it": Wertenbaker, "The China Lobby: III. Voices in the Wilderness," April 15, 1952, p. 13.

557 "mild-mannered, unassuming . . . man": Keeley, p. 11.

557 "the handkerchief king": Ibid., p. 27. The figure of $1 million comes from Cabell Phillips, "Is There a China Lobby? Inquiry Raises Questions," *The New York Times,* April 30, 1950.

557 "Valenciennes" and "Cluny Venise": Wertenbaker, "The China Lobby: XI. The World of Alfred Kohlberg," *Reporter,* April 29, 1952, p. 20.

557 "secretly, behind . . . States": William C. Bullitt, "A Report to the American People on China," *Life*, October 13, 1947.

557 "were able . . . rate": Wertenbaker, "The China Lobby: III. The Pattern of Enrichment," April 15, 1952, p. 10.

558 "the fabric . . . currency": Eastman, p. 173.

558 "a disastrous . . . Generalissimo": National Archives: RG 59, Entry 339A, Box 13, TS—Chiang—1948, Philip D. Sprouse to W. Walton Butterworth, July 7, 1948.

558 "The Generalissimo . . . fit": National Archives: Microfilm, RG 59, CDF (1945–1949), LM 184, Roll 58, Frames 12–28, Roger D. Lapham, "The China Problem," July 13, 1949.

559 "Poorly fed . . . Communists": Schaller, p. 115.

559 "a stubborn . . . wrong": National Archives: Microfilm, RG 59, CDF (1945–1949), LM 184, Roll 58, Frames 12–28, Roger D. Lapham, "The China Problem," July 13, 1949.

559 "the economic . . . day": Eastman, pp. 173–75.

560 "the general-in-charge . . . Shanghai": Taylor, pp. 154–55.

560 "the nation's . . . entrepreneurs": Eastman, p. 180.

560 "substantial payment": Taylor, p. 161.

560 "For over . . . behaviour": Eastman, p. 188.

560 "The experience . . . poorer": Taylor, pp. 156–57.

561 "brothers . . . other": Taylor, p. 160.

561 "her favorite nephew": National Archives: Microfilm file 184, Roll 58, Frame 494, September 2, 1948.

561 "After [the] . . . Shanghai": U.S. Department of State, *United States Relations with China* (The White Paper), p. 880.

562 "The orderly . . . populace": "China," CIA Document no. RDP79-01082A0001 000020035-0, p. 8. (Material furnished to the author by the Central Intelligence Agency in response to Freedom of Information Act inquiry.)

562 "direct and . . . position": National Archives: RG 59, Entry 399A, Box 13, TS—Chiang—1948, CKS to Harry S. Truman, November 9, 1948.

562 "There is . . . forces": Ibid., File 306.0015, NSC 22/2, memo from the Joint Chiefs of Staff to the Secretary of State, December 16, 1943.

563 "Communists were . . . Yangtze": "China: You Shall Never Yield," *Time*, December 6, 1948.

563 "couldn't be . . . village": Library of Congress, Roy W. Howard papers, Box 235, Foreign File, Randall Gould to Roy Howard, November 25, 1948.

563 "quite dubious . . . arrangements": pp. 202–3.

563 "this task . . . her": Library of Congress, Roy W. Howard papers, Box 235, RH to W. C. Nyi, November 29, 1948.

563 "on what . . . position": CIA: MORI DocID 922062, December 10, 1948.

CHAPTER FORTY-EIGHT

564 "They wanted . . . are": Miller, p. 283.

564 "demands of . . . disasters": Crozier, p. 318.

564 "a frantic . . . line" Drew Pearson, "Merry-Go-Round," *The Washington Post*, December 2, 1948.

564 "Cash My-check": Interview: "William Kirby Discusses the Legacy of Madame Chiang Kai-shek," *All Things Considered* (NPR), October 24, 2003.

564 "She came . . . that": Miller, pp. 288–89.

564 "a change . . . it' ": Harold L. Ickes, "Time to Tell China of Changed Attitude of People in U.S.," Toledo, Ohio, *Blade,* December 10, 1948.

565 "Her traveling . . . wear": "Mme. Chiang's Wardrobe Contrasts with Early Luxury," *Rochester Times-Union,* December 4, 1948.

565 "official affairs . . . better": Academia Historica, Taipei: Madame, wire to CKS, December 20, 1948.

565 "TOP SECRET . . . laughter": Mosley, pp. 435–36.

566 "no battle . . . fight": Topping, p. 50.

566 "an unpredictable . . . Wellesley": HA: Walter H. Judd papers, Box 175, Folder 1, Edgar Ansel Mowrer, "Bearing Olive Branches to U.S.," December 1948.

566 "I hope . . . soon": Academia Historica, Taipei: CKS, wire to Madame, December 9, 1948.

566 "pressed . . . freedom": National Archives: RG 59, Entry 399A, Box 13, TS—Chiang—1948, CKS, message to Madame Chiang, December 27, 1948.

567 Most people . . . generosity: In June 1951, President Truman ordered an investigation into the China Lobby, and the resulting report, however inconclusive, states (among other things): "1. It is clear that a substantial amount of money . . . had been devoted in this country to a wide-spread publicity and propaganda campaign on behalf of Chiang Kai-shek and the Nationalist Government. 2. It is also apparent that there is a very close connection between many of the people prominently associated with this propaganda campaign and certain American politicians and public figures who are most active in the support of the Nationalist Government of China. 3. . . . There are some *indications* but no clear proof that direct financial transactions have taken place . . . between Chinese Nationalist sympathizers and American political personalities. . . . 5. There is available evidence of large-scale corruption and profiteering on the part of certain officials of the Chinese Nationalist Government during and immediately following the end of the war. . . . 6. . . . we have indications that there is a direct relationship between the money now being used for propaganda through graft and profiteering. . . . 7. Since the passing of money, if any, between Chinese persons or their agents and American politicians has been skillfully conducted in a very devious manner . . . such transactions cannot be successfully exposed without a thorough investigation . . . and even then probably could not be completely revealed unless credible informers be found." (Truman Library, James S. Lanigan to Theodore Tannenwald, Jr., "Memmorandum Re: China Lobby," October 9, 1951.

567 "urgently needs . . . aid": CIA: MORI DocID 922062, December 10, 1948.

567 "try my . . . this": Academia Historica, Taipei: Madame, wire to CKS, December 20, 1948.

567 "according to . . . Marshall": Ibid., Madame, wire to CKS, December 21, 1948.

568 "peace-making . . . Communists": Ibid., CKS, wire to Madame, December 23, 1948.

568 "having a . . . plans": Ibid., Madame, wire to CKS, December 23, 1948.

568 "I spoke . . . request": Ibid., Madame, wire to CKS, January 1, 1949.

568 "the year ... been": Columbia University Library, RBML, Madame Chiang Kai-shek, "New Year's Message," December 31, 1948 (also in "Madame Chiang Undismayed," *The New York Times,* January 1, 1949).

569 "one of ... history": Crozier, p. 320.

569 "two notorious incompetents": Topping, p. 44.

569 "I did ... criminals": Crozier, p. 324.

570 "decide to ... Communists": Academia Historica, Taipei, CKS, wire to Madame, January 17, 1949.

570 "to cease-fire ... safeguarded": Crozier, p. 325.

570 "She has ... questions": "Mme Chiang Is Silent," *The New York Times,* January 22, 1949.

570 "I could ... Heigh-ho": Dong, p. 290.

571 "Your father ... people": Academia Historica, Taipei, Madame Chiang, wire to Chiang Ching-kuo, January 21, 1949, File 080200/627, Microfilm 0561.

571 "The U.S. ... now?": Ibid., Madame, wire to CKS, January 27, 1949. (Note: Madame spells Li Tsung-jen as Li Zong-ren.)

571 "There is ... together": Ibid., Madame, wire to CKS, February 22, 1949.

572 "talk about everything": Ibid., CKS, wire to Madame, March 8, 1949.

572 "not anxious ... nation": Ibid., Madame Chiang, wire to Chiang Ching-kuo, February 15, 1949, File 0802006/26, Microfilm 0561.

572 "I have ... later": Ibid., Madame, wire to CKS, March 5, 1949, serial no. 871.

572 "close friends": Ibid., Madame, wire to CKS, April 13, 1949, serial no. A1036.

CHAPTER FORTY-NINE

573 "The Communists ... fed?": HA: Alfred Kohlberg papers, Box 5, Stewart Alsop, "China, a Summing Up—II," *The New York Herald Tribune,* July 8, 1949.

573 "In my ... demanding": Author's telephone conversation with Dr. Paul Marx, March 2, 2006.

574 "What attitude ... KMT": Crozier, p. 333.

574 "Farewell Leighton ... aggression": Philip West, "Liberal Persuasion and China: Soong Meiling and John Leighton Stuart," in Samuel C. Chu, p. 66.

574 "the thick ... city": HA: Kohlberg papers, Box 55, Stewart Alsop, "Going, Going," *The New York Herald Tribune,* May 13, 1949.

575 "Chiang Kai-shek's ... weapon": Dong, pp. 291–92.

575 "moral and ... itself": U.S. Department of State, *United States Relations With China* (The White Paper), p. 409.

575 "ashamed to ... city": Crozier, p. 341.

575 "CCP in ... back": Academia Historica, Taipei, Madame, wire to CKS, May 16, 1949.

575 "The foreign ... helpful": Ibid., Madame, wire to CKS, May 18, 1949.

575 "Please remember ... organization": Ibid., CKS, wire to Madame, May 20, 1949, serial no. 481.

576 "If communism ... defeatism": "Chiang Appeals for U.S. Aid; Sees New War if Reds Win," *The New York Times,* July 6, 1949.

576 "I'm so ... possible": Academia Historica, Taipei: Madame Chiang, wire to Chiang Ching-kuo, September 15, 1949, File 0802006/26, Microfilm no. 0561.

576 "You are . . . campaign": Ibid., Madame, wire to CKS, November 17, 1949.

576 "too many . . . Riverdale": DeLong, p. 201.

576 "These stocks . . . Housemother": WCA: Emma DeLong Mills papers, MSC to EM, August 9, 1949.

577 "Since I . . . aid": Academia Historica, Taipei, Madame, wire to CKS, January 10, 1949.

577 "strategy to . . . politicians": Philip Horton, "The Inner Circle," *Reporter,* April 29, 1952, p. 5.

577 "concern[ed] with . . . Hong Kong": FBI files: WFO 97-766, June 19, 1953, number illegible. (Material obtained through Department of Justice in response to Freedom of Information Act inquiry.)

578 "The persistent . . . mainland!": Swanberg, pp. 351–52.

578 "the most . . . disguises": Charles Wertenbaker, "The Smiling Counselor," *Reporter,* April 29, 1952, p. 8.

579 "helped materially": Cabell Phillips, "Is There a China Lobby? Inquiry Raises Question," *The New York Times,* April 30, 1950.

579 "subsidiary . . . China": Philip Horton, "Politics Is Politics, but Business Is Business," *Reporter,* April 29, 1952, p. 7.

579 "between one . . . million": Charles Wertenbaker, "The Ubiquitous Major," *Reporter,* April 15, 1952, p. 21.

579 "Privately held . . . million": "The White Paper," Annex 135, "Report to President Truman by Lieutenant General Albert C. Wedemeyer, U.S. Army, Part II—China," *Economic,* p. 770.

580 "the Major . . . larger": Wertenbaker, "The Ubiquitous Major."

580 "in the . . . millionaire": Harry Hurt III, "Mr. Kung's Secret Compound," *Texas Monthly,* December 1984, p. 118.

580 "the line . . . obligation": CIA-RDP79-01082A000100020035-0, p. 8, undated.

580 "could get . . . Communists": Charles Wertenbaker, "The Smiling Counselor," *Reporter,* April 29, 1952, p. 10.

581 "has been . . . sound": Harold Hinton, "White Paper Blunt," *The New York Times,* August 6, 1949.

581 "more the . . . weaknesses": Alden Whitman, "The Life of Chiang Kai-shek," *The New York Times,* April 6, 1975.

581 "We picked . . . horse": McCullough, p. 744.

581 "the Chinese . . . fruit": Chang and Halliday, *Mao,* p. 108.

582 "Meanwhile . . . responsibilities": Crozier, p. 344.

582 "could be . . . communists": FBI: Memorandum from R. D. Cotter to W. D. Sullivan, September 13, 1965, p. 3. (Material furnished to the author by the Department of Justice in response to Freedom of Information Act inquiry.)

582 "Our embassies . . . situation": Academia Historica, Taipei, Madame Chiang, wire to CKS, December 14, 1949.

CHAPTER FIFTY

587 "Taiwan became . . . America": Richard Chu, "Historical Relations," *Asian Affairs: An American Review,* Fall 1989, p. 107.

587 "one of . . . Orient": Kerr, p. 5.

587 "From the . . . mission": Parris H. Chang, "Beautiful Island," *The Wilson Quarterly*, Autumn 1979, pp. 61–63.

588 "rich, orderly . . . modernized": Kerr, p. 48.

588 "It is . . . island": Ibid., p. 73.

588 "brutal and insensitive": Crozier, p. 351.

588 "We think . . . eats": "Island Redoubt," *Time*, July 4, 1949.

588 "prominent Commissioner . . . specialist' ": Kerr, p. 115.

589 "multiplied fantastically . . . life": Ibid., pp. 162–79.

589 "marched into . . . truth": Ibid., pp. 216–17.

589 "Our fine . . . maladministration": Ibid., p. 250.

590 "committee for . . . life": Ibid., p. 266.

590 "We saw . . . castrated": Ibid., pp. 299–301.

590 "a whole . . . lost": Chang, "Beautiful Island," pp. 67–68.

590 "one of . . . China": Crozier, p. 242.

591 "entire shiploads . . . back": Kerr, pp. 366–70.

591 "not provide . . . Formosa": Ibid., p. 387.

591 "return to . . . protest": Madame Chiang Kai-shek, *The Sure Victory*, pp. 23–24.

592 "to my . . . demand": "The Text of Mme. Chiang's Farewell," *The New York Times*, January 9, 1950.

592 "tired and . . . airliner": "Mme. Chiang Kai-shek Starts for Formosa," *The New York Times*, January 11, 1950.

592 "a brief handclasp": "Mme. Chiang in Formosa," *The New York Times*, January 13, 1950.

593 "a strange room": Burton Crane, "Chiang Leads Spartan Life in His Formosa Retreat," *The New York Times*, February 12, 1950.

593 "Chiang and . . . other": Chen Jan-jing, *Oral History of Dr. Xiong Wan*, p. 64.

594 "because . . . improved": Crane, "Chiang Leads Spartan Life in His Formosa Retreat," *The New York Times*, February 12, 1950.

594 "Mme. Chiang . . . unnecessary": "Mme. Chiang Asks Advisers from U.S.," *The New York Times*, January 21, 1950.

594 "Mme. Chiang . . . paid": "Mme. Chiang Sifts Charge Wounded Men Are Unpaid," *The New York Times*, January 22, 1950.

595 "Golden Gate . . . Yes!": "Mme. Chiang Visits Island War Front," *The New York Times*, February 6, 1950.

595 "pretty well . . . city": Burton Crane, "American Opinion a Factor," *The New York Times*, March 9, 1950.

595 "not so . . . volunteer": Emily Hahn, "The Old Boys," *The New Yorker*, November 7, 1953, pp. 138–41.

596 "very tired . . . circles": WCA: Emma DeLong Mills papers, diary of trip to Taiwan, p. 29.

596 "When I . . . profession": WCA: Mills papers, "Report on Taiwan," pp. 9–10.

596 "land rent . . . class": Crozier, p. 352.

597 "policy of terror": Kerr, p. 394.

597 "the Gimo . . . students": Taylor, p. 192.

597 "often encouraged . . . country": Li, pp. 347–54.

CHAPTER FIFTY-ONE

599 "Even Chiang . . . found": Topping, p. 399.

599 "moral weaklings . . . us": "The Text of Mme. Chiang's Farewell," *The New York Times,* January 9, 1950.

599 "the Americans . . . mood": Crozier, p. 354.

599 "away from . . . alliance": James Chase, p. 224. (Note: Original says "weaning" instead of "wean.")

599 "I shouted . . . defense": Stuart, pp. 239–40.

600 "whether the . . . securities": HA: Alfred Kohlberg papers, Box 160, Constantine Brown, "Wealthy Chinese Could Aid Chiang," *New York Journal-American,* May 3, 1950.

600 "preferred and . . . pursued": FBI: J. Edgar Hoover, directive no. 62-31284-107, May 3, 1949. (Material furnished to the author by the Department of Justice in response to Freedom of Information Act inquiry.)

600 "the biggest . . . streak": Joseph Lelyveld, "A 1½-China Policy," *The New York Times,* April 6, 1975.

601 "they looked . . . moment": HA: Kohlberg papers, Box 28, "Chiang Kai-shek," *Time,* April 18, 1955.

601 "most anxious . . . us": Princeton University, Seeley G. Mudd Library: John Foster Dulles Oral History Project, Transcript of a Recorded Interview with W. Averell Harriman by Philip A. Crowl, Washington, D.C., August 16, 1966.

601 "chatty private . . . danger": Mosley, pp. 460–61.

602 "I know . . . like": Li, p. 330.

602 "The most . . . mainland" HA: Kohlberg papers, Box 28, "Chiang's Own Plan," *U.S. News & World Report,* December 15, 1950.

602 "Chinese Nationalists . . . Communists": Ibid., "What Shall We Do about China?" interview with Stanley K. Hornbeck, December 15, 1950.

603 "a cornucopia . . . training": Taylor, p. 206.

603 "I have . . . Beast?": WCA: Emma DeLong Mills papers, MSC to EM, January 26, 1951.

603 "If we . . . China": Crozier, p. 359.

604 "our government . . . not": Princeton University, Seeley G. Mudd Library: John Foster Dulles Oral History Project, Transcript of a Recorded Interview with Generalissimo and Madame Chiang Kai-shek, by Spencer Davis, Taipei, Taiwan, September 24, 1964.

604 "interminable truce negotiations": Crozier, pp. 359–60.

604 An astounding . . . painting": WCA: Mills papers, MC to EM, October 21, 1951.

605 "If you . . . purpose": Emily Hahn, "The Old Boys," *The New Yorker,* November 7, 1953, p. 142.

605 "Got the . . . it": WCA: Mills papers, EM to MC, April 8, 1952.

605 "My friends . . . convey": Madame Chiang Kai-shek, *The Sure Victory,* pp. 29–35.

606 "It was . . . always": WCA: Mills papers, MC to EM, December 5, 1951.

606 "look awfully . . . puffy": Ibid., MC to EM, June 10, 1952.

606 "special bed": FBI: Office Memorandum to Director, FBI from SAC, San Francisco, document no. 62-7149-36, October 17, 1952. (Material furnished to the

author by the Department of Justice in response to Freedom of Information Act inquiry.)

606 "The weather . . . soon": Academia Historica, Taipei, CKS, wire to Madame, September 10, 1952.

606 "It is . . . again": Ibid., CKS, wire to Madame, November 30, 1952.

607 "purely domestic event": Columbia University Library, RBML, Wellington Koo papers, "Conversations: 1953, Notes on the Question of Her Excellency Madame Chiang Kai-shek's Visit to Washington to Attend General Eisenhower's Inauguration as President of the United States," p. 4.

607 "Madame Chiang . . . attention": Ibid., Box 166, Folder L5, March 18, 1953.

607 "suddenly": Li, p. 352.

607 "look up . . . Communist-affiliated": Columbia University Library, COHO, Dr. K. C. Wu, "Reminiscences for the Years 1946–53," as told to Professor Nathaniel Peffer and Professor C. Martin Wilbur, May 1961, revised and corrected November 1963, part C, vol. 2, no. 3, pp. 219–20. (Note: Original says "looking" rather than "look.")

607 "civilian leaders . . . over-wrought": Ibid., pp. 226–31.

608 "very popular . . . here": Ibid., pp. 245–48.

608 "My crime . . . me": Ibid., p. 265.

608 "sensitive": National Archives: RG 59, CDF (1950–1954), Box 4218, March 30, 1954.

609 "use of . . . communism": "Wu's Talks in U.S. Scored in Taipei," *The New York Times*, February 28, 1954.

609 "But the . . . action": Columbia University Library, COHO, Dr. K. C. Wu, "Reminiscences for the Years 1946–53," as told to Professor Nathaniel Peffer and Professor C. Martin Wilbur, May 1961, revised and corrected November 1963, part C, vol. 2, no. 3, pp. 297–99.

609 "interfered with . . . law": Kerr, p. 481.

609 "treason . . . office": Ibid., p. 423.

610 "moral obligation . . . Taiwan": Henry R. Lieberman, "Hu Shih Explains Role in Formosa," *The New York Times*, February 24, 1954.

CHAPTER FIFTY-TWO

611 "He [Chiang] . . . everywhere": Payne, p. 315.

611 "the President's . . . insincere": HA: Walter H. Judd papers, Box 190, Folder 2, Colonel Hsiang to Walter Judd, May 2, 1951.

612 "From now . . . preserved": Ibid., Folder 1, Chiang Kai-shek to Ambassador Wellington Koo, May 23, 1951.

612 "the real . . . employer": Koen, pp. 50–51.

612 "a large . . . expert": HA: Judd papers, Box 190, Folder 1, Alfred Friendly, "Four Agencies Probe Acts of Chiang's U.S. Contractor," *The Washington Post*, September 9, 1951.

613 "unidentified persons": "Accused Aide's Kin Back in Red China," *The New York Times*, March 2, 1952.

613 "In the . . . contact": Crozier, p. 364.

613 "Corruption was . . . wardens": Payne, pp. 301–2.

614 "to remove . . . temporarily": Li, p. 356.

614 "intellectual horizon . . . acknowledgment": Taylor, pp. 219–20.

614 "I think . . . illness": Columbia University Library, RBML, Madame Chiang to Wellington Koo, May 28, 1954.

615 "a bamboo . . . screens' ": Columbia University Library: COHO, interview Dorothy Thomas, "Memoir," session 3, May 27, 1981, pp. 170–71.

615 "friendship-at-first-sight . . . lips": Georgetown University Library, Special Collections Division: Grace Perkins Oursler papers, Box 1, Folder 17, GPO, Introduction to "[The] Sure Victory."

616 "I am . . . inspired": Ibid., GPO to Herbert R. Mays, March 30, 1955.

616 "much, much . . . Nationalists": Ibid., Herbert R. Mays, "Comments on 'The Sure Victory,' " undated.

616 "There is . . . publication": Ibid., Madame Chiang to GPO, June 2, 1955.

616 "Dear Grace . . . book": Ibid., William R. Barbour, President, Fleming H. Revell Company, to GPO, August 25, 1955.

616 "Man of . . . Moscow": HA: Alfred Kohlberg papers, Box 28, "Chiang Kai-shek," *Time*, April 18, 1955.

617 "needed further editing": WCA: Emma DeLong Mills papers, MC to EM, July 28, 1957.

617 "In reviewing . . . regret": Chiang Kai-shek, *Soviet Russia in China*, author's note.

617 "hatred between . . . tenants": Ibid., p. 61.

617 "precipitating a . . . Japan": Ibid., p. 68.

617 "rumors to . . . hostilities": Ibid., p. 105.

617 "This was . . . time": Ibid., p. 112.

617 "if . . . the . . . *War*": Ibid., pp. 339–40.

617 "agrarian reformers . . . affair": Ibid., p. 118.

618 "understood the . . . Communists": Payne, p. 295.

618 "prosperity, economic . . . collapse": Crozier, pp. 362–66.

618 "a triumphal . . . spotlight": Li, p. 373.

618 "If anything . . . heart": HA: George E. Sokolsky papers, Box 35, Folder 16, George Sokolsky to Madame Chiang Kai-shek, May 12, 1958.

619 "the evils . . . means": Princeton University, Seeley G. Mudd Library, John Foster Dulles Oral History Project, Transcript of a Recorded Interview with Generalissimo and Madame Chiang Kai-shek, by Spencer Davis, Taipei, Taiwan, September 24, 1964.

619 "an extremely . . . Kai-shek": FBI Office Memorandum from A. H. Belmont to L. V. Boardman on Madame Chiang Kai-shek, no. 62-71649-40, July 17, 1958. (Material furnished to the author by the Department of Justice in response to Freedom of Information Act inquiry.)

619 "Special Correspondents list": FBI Office Memorandum from M. S. Jones to Mr. DeLoach on Madame Chiang Kai-shek, no. 622-71649-54, January 13, 1960. (Material furnished to the author by the Department of Justice in response to Freedom of Information Act inquiry.)

619 "a particularly . . . badly": Columbia University Library, COHO, Roger Straus, pp. 618–20.

620 "Many people . . . English": DeLong, p. 211.

620 "If this . . . well": Walter Lister, Jr., "Mme. Chiang Warns Loss of Quemoy," *The New York Herald Tribune*, September 4, 1958.

620 "part of . . . circumscribed": Crozier, pp. 368–69.

620 "Why doesn't . . . people": "Visitor from the East: 'Missimo' Speaks Out," *Newsweek*, October 6, 1958.

620 "Mme. Chiang . . . defend": WCA: Editorial: "The Arrogant Mme. Chiang," *The Philadelphia Inquirer*, September 23, 1958.

620 "inflammation of . . . it": DeLong, p. 212.

621 "very important . . . health": Academia Historica, Taipei, Madame Chiang, wire to Chiang Ching-kuo, October 8, 1958, file 080200/627, microfilm 0561.

621 "Today is . . . hospital": Ibid., Madame Chiang, wire to Chiang Ching-kuo, October 31, 1958, file 080200/627, microfilm 0561.

621 "become one . . . shoulder": "Visitor from the East: 'Missimo' Speaks Out," *Newsweek*, October 6, 1958.

621 "meet with . . . States": Taylor, p. 253.

621 "crescendo of . . . counterattack": National Archives and Records Administration (NARA) RG 59, CDF (1960–1963), CO154, Reel 5 (microfilm), March 25, 1962.

621 "Chiang Kai-shek . . . mood": Cornell University, Division of Rare and Manuscript Collections, James M. McHugh papers, JMcH to Hugh Barton, July 14, 1961.

621 "the time . . . action": Ibid., March 20, 1962.

622 "fast approaching . . . strength": Ibid., March 25, 1962.

622 "with full . . . hidden": Ibid., Reel 4, March 14, 1962.

622 "the Nationalist . . . overlap": Brian Crozier, "The Golden Triangle Loses Its Shine," *The Times* (London), September 28, 1973.

CHAPTER FIFTY-THREE

624 "We like . . . malice": Helen Hull, *Mayling Soong Chiang*, p. 21.

624 a poem:

Tolerate others, restrain yourself; freedom will be seen and democracy be
    practiced.
Accept criticism and correct mistakes, don't complain, don't blame, don't shirk.
Don't exaggerate, speak less and do more.
Don't speak against others, don't speak highly of yourself.
Let bygones be bygones, whatever will be will be.
Be faithful and diligent,
Tilling without harvesting.
Keep yourself straight, ignore others' talk.
Do whatever should be done, look upon death as going home.
These are the principles for one to live by, to deal with people or to rule a nation.
(Payne, p. 305.)

625 "incriminating evidence": Kerr, p. 449–50.

625 "The strength . . . negligible": "Taiwan, June 1960," FBI file MORI Doc ID: 10975,

Case No. 85-601, Document No. 14, from the Dwight D. Eisenhower Library. (Material furnished to the author by the Department of Justice in response to Freedom of Information Act inquiry.)

625 "national emergency . . . rendered": P'eng Ming-min, "Public Offences in Taiwan: Laws and Problems," *The China Quarterly*, July–September 1971, pp. 471–93.

626 "French recognition . . . leadership": Library of Congress, Clare Boothe Luce papers, Box 220, Folder 3, Madame Chiang Kai-shek to Clare Boothe Luce.

626 "tiptoed gently . . . community": "The Return of Missimo," *Newsweek*, November 6, 1965, pp. 22–23.

626 "I think . . . world": John Sibley, "Mrs. Chiang Kai-shek Urges Attack on Red China, *The New York Times*, August 30, 1965.

627 "many of . . . friends": "Mrs. Chiang Flying to U.S.," *The New York Times*, August 23, 1965.

627 "cheery . . . further": Sibley, "Mrs. Chiang Kai-shek Urges Attack on Red China."

627 "warmongering statement . . . years": I-te Chen, "Mrs. Chiang's Plea for Attack on China," *The New York Times*, September 7, 1965.

627 "Many-Sided Empress . . . belle": "Many-Sided Empress," *The New York Times*, September 4, 1965.

628 "triumphantly": John Sibley, "Chinatown Hails Mrs. Chiang's Visit," *The New York Times*, September 6, 1965.

628 "wedge of . . . hustled": Sibley, "Chinatown Hails Mrs. Chiang's Visit."

628 "What does . . . world": "Many-Sided Empress," *The New York Times*, September 4, 1965.

628 "once familiar . . . China": John W. Finney, "Out of the Past—Mrs. Chiang," *The New York Times*, September 12, 1965.

629 "10 Most . . . World": Bart Barnes, "Madame Chiang Kai-shek Dies, Chinese Chief's Powerful Widow," *The Washington Post*, October 25, 2003.

629 "It will . . . forgotten": Finney, "Out of the Past—Mrs. Chiang."

629 "very curt . . . aid": Columbia University Library, COHO, Washington Press Club Project, Sarah McClendon, pp. 92–93.

629 "no matter . . . defensive": Hanson W. Baldwin, "Chiang Says War in Vietnam Can't Be Won There," *The New York Times*, November 12, 1965.

629 "She [Moore] . . . duties": DeLong, p. 218.

630 "allergic to . . . spices": WCA: Letter Colonel H. L. Soong to Margaret Clapp, November 26, 1965.

630 "ambivalent thinking": "Mrs. Chiang at Wellesley," *The New York Times*, December 8, 1965.

630 "a kind . . . anti-communism": "The Wellesley Graduate Who Became Taiwan's First Lady," *The Week*, November 7, 2003.

630 "distinguished leadership . . . communism": "Lafayette Order to Give Awards Dec. 15 at Plaza," *The New York Times*, November 28, 1965.

630 "prepared to . . . tribulations": Payne, p. 319.

630 "No one . . . tomorrow": National Archives: RG 59, CDF (1967–1969), Box 1984, May 23, 1969.

630 "We can . . . mainland": Melvin Gurtov, "Recent Developments on Formosa," *The China Quarterly*, July–September 1967, p. 60.

631 "indifferent to . . . soldier": "Chiang, at 4th Inaugural, Says He Is Undiscouraged," *The New York Times*, May 21, 1966.

631 "Mystery Shrouds . . . Vietnam": Alfred Friendly, "Mystery Shrouds Mrs. Chiang Here," *The New York Times*, April 17, 1966.

631 "the precise . . . policy": "Data on Mrs. Chiang Asked," *The New York Times*, October 4, 1966.

632 "certain elements . . . vision": National Archives: RG 59, CDF (1967–1969), Box 1984, Madame Chiang to Secretary of State Dean Rusk, October 23, 1966. Two years later she wrote Rusk a very long letter congratulating him on his testimony before the Senate Foreign Relations Committee, detailing the illnesses "with accompanying fever" that had kept her from writing earlier, and saying that he had, with his testimony, "added one more friend who appreciates to the full your unwavering firmness and seemingly inexhaustible patience under trying exacerbations and unwarrantably deliberate goading thrown in from time to time with sardonic irrelevancies calculated to tire out and try the patience of a Job." The letter featured words such as "Bovean" and "sensorium" and included quotations from a nineteenth-century German Protestant jurist and a seventeenth-century French queen. (Ibid., July 22, 1968.)

CHAPTER FIFTY-FOUR

633 "Taiwan . . . is . . . affairs": Joseph Lelyveld, "A 1½-China Policy," *The New York Times*, April 6, 1975.

633 "had been . . . affairs": Taylor, p. 272.

634 "She was . . . her": Author's interview with Leo Soong, 2005.

634 "continually at . . . policies": Columbia University Library, COHO, Dr. K. C. Wu, "Reminiscences for the Years 1946–53," as told to Professor Nathaniel Peffer and Professor C. Martin Wilbur, May 1961, revised and corrected November 1963, part C, vol. 2, no. 3, pp. 319–20.

634 "Such a . . . of": HA: T. V. Soong files, Box 63, Folder 33. Madame to T. V. Soong, October 7, 1963.

635 "two-minute coup": Taylor, p. 271.

635 "a conventional . . . speaker": National Archives: RG59, CDF (1967–1969), Box 1984.

635 "Look, Dr. Xiong . . . ago!": Chen San-jing, *The Oral History of Dr. Xiong Wan*, p. 64.

635 "such a . . . stand": HA: Walter H. Judd papers, Box 175, Folder 2, Robert Eunson, "First Lady Hopes U.S. Will Continue Firm Vietnam Stand," March 19, 1965.

635 "now or . . . Asia": Taylor, pp. 273–74.

636 "the Communist rebellion": Seymour Topping, "Chiang Gets Fourth Term with Broader Powers," *The New York Times*, March 22, 1966.

637 "If they . . . slut": Epstein, pp. 558–59.

637 "apparent . . . cooperated": Taylor, p. 286.

638 "made a . . . presentation": National Archives: RG 59, CDF (1967–1969), Box 1984, April 5, 1967.

638 "something of . . . ranks": Library of Congress, Averell Harriman papers, Box 43,

Department of State airgram, "Former Vice President Nixon's Interview with President Chiang Kai-shek," April 28, 1967.

638 "in a . . . right": Nixon, p. 242.

639 "Asia, not . . . community": Richard M. Nixon, "Asia after Vietnam," *Foreign Affairs,* October 1967.

639 "a rather . . . man": National Archives: RG 59, SNF (1970–1973), Pol 15-1, Chinat, Box 2203, April 10, 1970.

640 "Since the . . . Taiwan": Topping, p. 414.

640 "to relaunch . . . stage": Chang and Halliday, *Mao,* p. 601.

640 "opened a . . . people": www.pbs.org/wgbh/amex/china/peopleevents/pande07.html.

640 " 'Whatever the . . . diminishes": Aitken, pp. 428–32.

641 "betrayal": Taylor, p. 304.

641 "This country . . . challenged": HA: Judd papers, Box 201, Folder 2, China Information Service, "News from China," July 16, 1971.

641 "I deeply . . . China": National Archives: RG 59, SNF (1970–1973), Pol 15-1, Chinat, Box 2203, July 17, 1971.

641 "I felt . . . it": author interview with Dr. Henry Kissinger, 2009.

641 "a broken . . . Kai-shek": Taylor, p. 305.

642 "personal friendship . . . me": Nixon, p. 242.

642 "unusual movements . . . actions": Taylor, p. 308.

642 "Chairman Mao . . . know": Steven E. Phillips, ed., *China, 1969–1972,* vol. 17 of *Foreign Relations of the United States,* ed. Edward C. Keefer (Washington, D.C.: U.S. Government Printing Office, 2006), pp. 678–79.

642 "some length": William Burr, "Nixon's Trip to China," p. 1, National Security Archive (www.nsarchiv/NSAEBB/NSAEBB106/index.htm).

643 "I told . . . support": Kissinger to Nixon and Chou En-lai, February 24, 1972, National Security Archive (www.nsarchiv/NSAEBB/NSAEBB106/press.htm).

643 "the ultimate . . . Taiwan": Taylor, p. 308.

643 "had been . . . inhibition": Topping, p. 421.

643 "long and . . . disturbed": Taylor, p. 308.

643 "Our relationship . . . go": Phillips, vol. 17, p. 858n4.

643 "One step . . . responsibilities": National Archives: RG 59, SNF (1970–1973), Pol 15-1, Chinat, Box 2203, April 20, 1972.

644 "girlie restaurants": Taylor, pp. 308–10.

CHAPTER FIFTY-FIVE

645 "It was . . . Taiwan": Taylor, p. 321.

645 "establishment of . . . years": HA: Albert C. Wedemeyer papers, Box 46, Folder 5, Chiang Kai-shek, "In Memoriam, Dr. H. H. Kung," September 2, 1967.

645 "When Mr. Kung . . . account": Oberlin College Archives, "H. H. Kung Dead, Chinese Leader," *The New York Times,* August 16, 1967.

645 "in poor . . . assistance": FBI files: Note to Director from SAC, San Francisco, no. 62-71649-105, March 17, 1969. (Material furnished to the author by the Department of Justice in response to Freedom of Information Act inquiry.)

645 "chose to . . . China": "300 at Services for T. A. Soong," *San Francisco Chronicle,* March 15, 1969.

646 "still unable . . . leg": WCA: Emma DeLong Mills papers, Pearl Chen to EM, October 23, 1969.

646 "the constant . . . harder": Wang Feng, p. 30. (Note: The nurse referred to Madame's niece as Jennifer rather than Jeanette Kung.)

646 "Maybe you . . . manners?": Ibid., pp. 49–50.

646 "much better . . . recovered": WCA: Mills papers, MC to EM, October 13, 1970.

646 "I am . . . recovered": Ibid., MC to EM, March 15, 1971.

647 "the reins . . . situation": National Archives: RG 59, SNF (1970–1973), Chinat, Box 2202, Conversation of Vice Foreign Minister H. K. Yang with Ambassador, March 24, 1972.

647 "Mrs. Chiang . . . too": Albin Krebs, "Sisters Not to Meet," *The New York Times,* May 1, 1971.

647 "already airborne . . . trap": Li, p. 405.

647 "would glide . . . agile": Chang with Halliday, *Mme Sun Yat-sen,* p. 119.

647 "To dine . . . menial": Harrison E. Salisbury, "Dinner with Mrs. Sun Yat-sen in Old Peking," *The New York Times,* June 3, 1972.

648 "the family . . . bear": WCA: Mills papers, MSC to EM, November 9, 1971.

648 "one of . . . them": HA: T. V. Soong papers, Box 64, Folder 64.

648 "had amassed . . . million": HA: T. V. Soong papers, Box 64, Folder 18, from "The Millennium," a *Wall Street Journal* report.

649 "virtually certain . . . trace": Li, p. 405.

649 "She was . . . there": WCA: Mills papers, MSC to EM, November 9, 1971.

649 "You have . . . sides": Wang Fong, *Forty Years in the Service of Chiang Kai-shek and His Son,* narrated by Wang Yuan, p. 190.

650 "very calm . . . battlefield": Ibid., pp. 208–10.

650 "Under Miss . . . way": Chen San-jing, *The Oral History of Doctor Xiong Wan,* pp. 153–66.

651 "FBI": Wang Feng, p. 60.

652 "the remarkable . . . survive": Madame Chiang Kai-shek, "Address to the 27th World Congress of the Junior Chamber International," Taipei, Taiwan, November 17, 1972.

652 "We Do . . . futility": Madame Chiang Kai-shek, "We Do Beschrei It," Spring 1975.

653 "Just stop": Taylor, p. 321.

653 "As Father . . . him": HA: Walter H. Judd papers, Box 174, Folder 7, Chiang Ching-kuo, "Thoughts of My Father at Plum Terrace," source unknown.

654 "Even Harvard-educated . . . coincidence": Taylor, p. 321.

654 "not expected . . . population": "Chiang Kai-shek Is Dead in Taipei at 87," *The New York Times,* April 6, 1975.

654 "The fact . . . all": "The Last of the Big Four," *Newsweek,* April 14, 1975.

654 "It was . . . man": Georgetown University Library, Special Collections Division, FAOHP (Foreign Affairs Oral History Project), Box 12, interview with Frank H. Burnet, February 22, 1990.

654 "closely supervised": "Funeral for Chiang to Reflect Varied Traditions," *The New York Times,* April 8, 1975.

654 "He [Chiang] . . . off": Georgetown University Library, Special Collections Division, FAOHP, Box 12, interview with Frank H. Burnet, February 22, 1990.

655 "persuaded the . . . go": Anna Chennault, "Memories of Soong May-ling," *Da Gong* (Hong Kong), November 2, 2003.

655 "very Christian": http://members.aol.com/WELSTA12/last.htm.

655 "two of . . . States": Jay Mathews, "Chiang Kai-shek Eulogized at Memorial Service Here," *The Washington Post,* April 17, 1975.

655 "one of . . . quiet": HA: Judd papers, Box 175, Folder 3, "Billy Graham's Tribute to Chiang Kai-shek," *Asian Outlook,* April 1975.

655 "public knowledge . . . from' ": HA: Judd papers, Box 175, Folder 2, Memorial Tributes to Chiang Kai-shek, April 16, 1975.

655 "respect and . . . grew": Ibid., General Albert C. Wedemeyer, "Chiang Kai-shek— Defender of Freedom," April 16, 1975.

655 "studded with . . . adversity": Mathews, "Chiang Kai-shek Eulogized at Memorial Service Here."

656 "The President's . . . you": WCA: Mills papers, MC to EM, May 13, 1975. (Note: Madame translates the name of the lake as "Lake of Kindness.")

656 "wearing a . . . *back*": Chang and Halliday, pp. 652–53.

CHAPTER FIFTY-SIX

659 "The storm . . . years": HA: Walter Judd papers, Box 174, Folder 2, Directors, American China Policy Association, Inc.: "Statement of American Policy re China," for Secretary of State George C. Marshall, January 23, 1947.

659 "was unable . . . well": HA: Judd papers, Box 175, Folder 3, "Madame Chiang Comes to U.S. for Medical Treatment," September 17, 1975.

659 "mustered strength . . . condition": DeLong, pp. 223–24.

659 "still having . . . months": WCA: Emma DeLong Mills papers, MSC to EM, June 15, 1976.

660 "gradually recovering . . . times": HA: Judd papers, Box 163, Folder 17, Madame Chiang to Walter Judd, March 4, 1977.

660 "All those . . . fun!": Ibid., David Kung to General Wedemeyer, February 11, 1978.

660 "I note . . . whatever": Ibid., David Kung to General Wedemeyer, April 12, 1979.

660 "She lived . . . left": James T. Madore and Tom Demoretcky, "Madame Chiang's LI Home Sold," *Newsday,* August 17, 1998.

660 "two-car entourage . . . outside": WCA: Charles T. Powers, "Once the 'Most Powerful Woman in the World,' Now a Recluse," *The Albany Times-Union,* February 18, 1979.

660 "I see . . . grief" WCA: Powers, "Once the 'Most Powerful Woman in the World,' Now a Recluse."

661 "so erect . . . nineties": Author's interview with Susan Braddock, November 27, 2006.

661 "were also . . . Hershey's": http://www.newyorksocialdiary.com/socialdiary/2003/socialdiary10_27_03.php.

661 "the countries . . . territory": "Ad by Mrs. Chiang Asks Aid for the 'Boat People,' " *The New York Times,* July 20, 1979.

662 "after I . . . months!": WCA: Mills papers, MC to EM, April 18, 1980.

662 "She did . . . integrity": David Kung, letter to Loh I-cheng, in Loh, p. 148.

662 "to build . . . recur": Chang with Halliday, *Mme Sun Yat-sen,* p. 132.

662 "named China's . . . 1976": Michael Weisskopf, "Soong Ching-ling, Widow of Sun Yat-sen, Dies in Peking at Age 90," *The Washington Post,* May 30, 1981.

662 "deep concern . . . Taiwan": James P. Sterba, "Soong Ching-ling Is Eulogized by Deng," *The New York Times,* June 4, 1981.

663 "I have . . . letter": Anna Chennault, "Memories of Soong May-ling," *Da Gong* (Hong Kong), November 2, 2003.

663 "Open Letter . . . Taiwan": Columbia University Library, Madame Chiang Kai-shek, "Text of an Open Letter to Teng Ying-chao," *Asian Outlook,* April 1984.

664 "University teachers . . . supervised": Joseph Lelyveld "A 1½-China policy," *The New York Times,* April 6, 1975.

664 "by combining . . . was": HA: Judd papers, Linda Mathews, "Chiang Outshines His Father as Taiwan Ruler," *Los Angeles Times,* November 21, 1977.

665 "propose . . . bottles": Taylor, pp. 408–9.

665 "the avalanche . . . down": Taylor, p. 409.

665 "She is . . . general": Jim Mann, "Mme. Chiang's Return to Taiwan Fuels Rumors of New Bid for Political Power," *Los Angeles Times,* November 1, 1986.

665 "shine over . . . Taiwan": Jim Mann, "Mme. Chiang's Return to Taiwan."

666 "I am . . . interpretation": William Safire, "On Language," *The New York Times Magazine,* January 18, 1987.

666 "multi-layered . . . inside": Madame Chiang, "A Review of My Opinions," *Modern China,* December 4, 1986.

667 "Oppose the . . . Taiwan": Taylor, p. 409.

667 "of all . . . mainland": Ibid., pp. 416–18.

668 "deepest condolences . . . away": Robert Delfs, "Kind Words from Zhao Cut No Ice in Taiwan," *Far Eastern Economic Review,* January 28, 1988, p. 20.

668 "For Mei-ling . . . role": Taylor, pp. 423–24.

669 "Madame Chiang . . . time": Author's interview with Beverly Sills, January 30, 2006.

670 "the former . . . handkerchief": Susan Chira, "Taiwan President Will Also Head Party," *The New York Times,* July 9, 1988.

670 "the bloody . . . poltroons": "Madame Chiang Condemns 'Satanic Carnage,' " *China Post,* June 13, 1989.

671 "a small . . . Soong": "Madame Chiang Backs Taiwan's Ruling Party Candidate," *The Christian Science Monitor,* April 6, 2000.

CHAPTER FIFTY-SEVEN

672 "She is . . . saint": WCA: Annie Huang, "Taiwanese Differ on Opinions of 100-Year-Old Madame Chiang," *Staten Island Advance,* March 17, 1997.

672 "Most of . . . vogue": Wang Feng, pp. 42–43.

672 "a Norma . . . era": Francis X. Clines, "Latest Taiwan Uproar Brings Back Old Hand," *The New York Times,* July 24, 1995.

673 "unaided and alone": Gene Kramer, "Short, Spectacular Appearance by 97-Year-Old Widow," Associated Press, July 27, 1995.

673 "came into . . . cylinders": Adam Platt, "The Final Bow," *The New Yorker,* August 14, 1995.

673 "We're trying . . . World War II": Clines, "Latest Taiwan Uproar."

673 "Big-footed security . . . again": Platt, "The Final Bow."

674 "intently . . . presence": "Chronicle," *The New York Times,* March 13, 1996.

674 "stunning in . . . did": Author's interview with William Luers, March 1, 2006.

674 "She's hardly . . . herself": Author's interview with Eleanor Lambert, 1998.

674 "very crowded": E-mail, Leo Soong to author, June 21, 2006.

674 "always beautifully . . . her": Author's interview with Shirley Young, 2000.

674 "Typically . . . up": E-mail, Leo Soong to author, June 21, 2006.

674 "imperial wave . . . wimpy": Author's interview with Shirley Young, 2000.

675 "she was . . . alive' ": Author's interview with Leo Soong, April 6, 2005.

675 "For the . . . photograph": Rich Hampson, "The Magic of Madame Chiang Going Strong," *USA Today,* January 29, 1999.

676 "Madame has . . . exhibit": "Madame Chiang's Art Exhibit," *World Journal,* January 2, 2000.

677 "very good . . . tradition": Chau Lam, "Chiang's Voice," *Newsday,* January 10, 2000.

677 "quite a . . . admirable": Jesse Hamlin, "Show Reveals Artistic Side of Madame Chiang," available at www.sfgate.com/cgi-bin/article.cgi?file-/chronicle/archive/2000/01/27/DD37626.DTL accessed February 2, 2009, accessed February 27, 2006.

677 "an ambitious . . . crowd": Ron Gluckman, "The Art of War," *Asia Week,* March 10, 2000.

677 "She was . . . marvelous": James Barron, "Over the Century Mark," *The New York Times,* March 27, 2002.

677 "minor symptoms . . . pneumonia": William Foreman, Associated Press Television News Library, APTV 10/24/03, Story 389856.

677 "very peacefully": www.com/2003/WORLD/asiapcf/east/10/24/obit.madame.chiang.ap.

677 "beloved by . . . centuries": William Foreman, AP, APTV 10/24/03 083BEDT.

678 "very solemn . . . blanket": Author's interview with Susan Braddock, 2005.

678 "those who . . . died": Joseph Berger, "An Epitaph for Madame Chiang Kai-shek: 'Mama,' " *The New York Times,* October 25, 2003.

679 "a dazzling . . . war": Seth Faison, "Madame Chiang, 105, Chinese Leader's Widow, Dies," *The New York Times,* October 24, 2003.

679 "Supporters of . . . calculating": Bart Barnes, "Madame Chiang Kai-shek Dies; Chinese Chief's Powerful Widow," *The Washington Post,* October 25, 2003.

679 "There is . . . Four": *China Times,* October 25, 2003.

679 "If they . . . China": "Looking at Madame Chiang Soong May-ling from a Taiwanese Perspective," *The Union,* November 6, 2003.

679 "offered deep . . . sympathy": *People's Daily,* October 25, 2003.

679 "which betrayed . . . nation": Obituary Madame Chiang Kai-shek, *People's Daily,* November 5, 2003.

679 "noted and . . . Straits": *People's Daily,* October 25, 2003.

680 "So Long . . . brutality": Editorial: "So Long and Good Riddance," *Taipei Times,* October 27, 2003.

681 "The whole . . . all": "The Life of Madame Chiang Kai-shek," Memorial Program, November 5, 2003.

681 "We are . . . masterpiece": Rev. Lien Hwa Chow, "Message," Memorial Service, November 5, 2003.

BIBLIOGRAPHY

BOOKS

Abend, Hallett. *My Life in China*, 1926–1941. New York: Harcourt, Brace and Company, 1943.

Aitken, Jonathan. *Nixon: A Life*. Washington, D.C.: Regnery Publishing Inc., 1998.

Alanbrooke, Field Marshal Lord. *War Diaries, 1939–1945*. Edited by Alex Danchev and Daniel Todman. Berkeley: University of California Press, 2001.

Almquist, Leann Grabavoy. *Joseph Alsop and American Foreign Policy: The Journalist as Advocate*. Lanham, Md.: University Press of America, 1993.

Alsop, Joseph W., with Adam Platt. *I've Seen the Best of It: Memoirs*. New York: W. W. Norton & Company, 1992.

Arnold, H. H. *Global Mission*. New York: Harper & Brothers, 1949.

Auden, W. H., and Christopher Isherwood. *Journey to a War*. New York: Random House, 1939.

Baker, Barbara, ed. *Shanghai: Electric and Lurid City*. Hong Kong: Oxford University Press, 1998.

Barnes, Joseph. *Willkie*. New York: Simon and Schuster, 1952.

Beal, John Robinson. *Marshall in China*. Toronto: Doubleday Canada, 1970.

Belden, Jack. *Still Time to Die*. New York: Harper & Brothers, 1943.

Bland, Larry I., ed. *George C. Marshall's Mediation Mission to China, December 1945–January 1947*. Lexington, VA. George C. Marshall Foundation, 1998.

Bloodworth, Dennis. *The Chinese Looking Glass*. New York: Farrar, Straus and Giroux, 1966.

Blum, John Morton, ed. *The Price of Vision: The Diary of Henry A. Wallace, 1942–1946*. Boston: Houghton Mifflin Company, 1973.

———. *Roosevelt and Morgenthau*. Boston: Houghton Mifflin Company, 1970.

Boorman, Howard L. *Biographical Dictionary of Republican China*. New York: Columbia University Press, 1967.

Booth, Martin. *Opium, A History*. New York: St. Martin's Griffin, 1996.

Buck, Pearl S. *My Several Worlds*. New York: John Day Company, 1954.

Burke, James. *My Father in China*. New York: Farrar & Rinehart, 1942.

Caldwell, Oliver J. *A Secret War, Americans in China, 1944–1945*. Carbondale and Edwardsville: Southern Illinois University Press, 1972.

Cameron, Nigel. *Old Peking Revisited*. Hong Kong: FormAsia Books Limited, 2004.

Camp, LaVonne Telshaw. *Lingering Fever: A World War II Nurse's Memoir*. Jefferson, N.C.: McFarland & Company, 1997.

Cantlie, James, and C. Sheridan Jones. *Sun Yat Sen and the Awakening of China*. New York: Fleming H. Revell Company, 1912.

Chang Chun-ming. *Chiang Kai-shek*. New York: St. John's University, 1981.

Chang Iris. *The Rape of Nanking*. New York: Basic Books, 1997.

Chang Jung. *Wild Swans*. New York: Anchor Books, Doubleday, 1991.

Chang Jung, and Jon Halliday. *Mao: The Unknown Story*. London: Jonathan Cape, 2005.

Chang Jung, with Jon Halliday. *Mme Sun Yat-sen*. Harmondsworth, UK: Penguin Books, 1986.

Chase, James. *Acheson*. New York: Simon & Schuster, 1998.

Ch'en Chieh-ju. *Chiang Kai-shek's Secret Past*. Boulder, Colo.: Westview Press, 1993.

Ch'en Li-fu. *The Storm Clouds Clear over China: The Memoir of Ch'ea Li-fu*. Stanford: Hoover Institution Press, 1994.

Chen San-jing. *The Oral History of Dr. Xiong Wan*. Recorded by Li Yu-qing. Beijing: Tuan-Jie Press, 2006.

Chen Ting-yi. *H. H. Kung*. Qingtao: Qingtao Press, 1998.

Chennault, Anna. *The Education of Anna*. New York: Times Books, 1980.

Chennault, Claire Lee. *Way of a Fighter*. New York: G. P. Putnam's Sons, 1949.

Chesneaux, Jean, ed. *Popular Movements and Secret Societies in China, 1840–1950*. Stanford, Calif.: Stanford University Press, 1972.

_____. *Secret Societies in China in the Nineteenth and Twentieth Centuries*. Ann Arbor: University of Michigan Press, 1971.

Chiang Kai-shek. *Diary, 1897–1943*. Edited by Wang Yu-gao and Wang Yu-zheng. Taipei: Academia Historica.

Chiang Kai-shek. *Soviet Russia in China: A Summig Up at Seventy*. New York: Farrar, Straus and Cudahy, 1957.

Chiang Kai-shek, Madame. *China Shall Rise Again*. New York: Harper & Brothers, 1940.

_____. Conversations with Mikhail Borodin. Taipei: World Anti-communist League, China Chapter, 1977.

_____. *Selected Speeches, 1958–1959*. Mount Vernon, N.Y.: Peter Pauper Press, 1959.

_____. *Sian: A Coup d'Etat*, and Chiang Kai-shek, *A Fortnight in Sian: Extracts from a Diary*. Shanghai: The China Publishing Company, 1937

_____. *The Sure Victory*. Westwood, N.J.: Fleming H. Revell Company, 1955.

_____. *This Is Our China*. New York: Harper & Brothers, 1940.

Chu, Samuel C., ed. *Madame Chiang Kaishek and Her China*. Norwalk, Conn.: EastBridge Signature Books, 2005.

Chu, Valentin. *The Yin-Yang Butterfly: Ancient Chinese Sexual Secrets for Western Lovers*. New York: G. P. Putnam's Sons, 1994.

Chuikov, Vasilii I. *Mission to China: Memoirs of a Soviet Military Adviser to Chiang Kaishek*. Norwalk, Conn.: Eastbridge, 2004.

Churchill, Winston S. *The Second World War*, vol. 5. London: Cassell & Co., 1952.

Clark, Elmer T. *The Chiangs of China*. New York: Abingdon-Cokesbury Press, 1943.

Clifford, Nicholas R. *Spoilt Children of Empire: Westerners in Shanghai and the Chinese Revolution of the 1920s*. Hanover, N.H.: Middlebury College Press, 1991.

Coble, Parks M., Jr. *The Shanghai Capitalists and the Nationalist Government, 1927–1937.* Cambridge, Mass.: Harvard University Press, 1986.

Collis, Maurice. *The Great Within.* London: Faber and Faber Limited, 1942.

Corcoran, Thomas G., with Philip Kooper. "Rendezvous with Democracy" (unpublished memoirs). Washington, D.C., 1980.

Cowles, Gardner. *Mike Looks Back.* New York: Gardner Cowles, 1985.

Cray, Ed. *General of the Army: George C. Marshall, Soldier and Statesman.* New York: Touchstone, 1990.

Crozier, Brian. *The Man Who Lost China: The First Full Biography of Chiang Kai-shek.* New York: Charles Scribner's Sons, 1976.

Cuthbertson, Ken. *Nobody Said Not to Go: The Life, Loves, and Adventures of Emily Hahn.* Boston: Faber and Faber, 1998.

Davies, John Paton, Jr. *Dragon by the Tail: American, British, Japanese, and Russian Encounters with China and One Another.* New York: W. W. Norton & Company, 1972.

DeLong, Thomas A. *Madame Chiang Kai-shek and Miss Emma Mills: China's First Lady and Her American Friend.* Jefferson, N.C.: McFarland & Company, 2007.

Der Ling, The Princess. *Two Years in the Forbidden City.* New York: Dodd, Mead and Company, 1929.

Dong, Stella. *Shanghai, 1842–1949.* New York: William Morrow, 2000.

Dorn, Frank. *The Forbidden City.* New York: Charles Scribner's Sons, 1970.

_____. *Walkout with Stilwell in Burma.* New York: Pyramid Books, 1973.

Drage, Charles. *The Life and Times of General Two-Gun Cohen.* New York: Funk & Wagnalls Company, 1954.

Dunlop, Richard. *Donovan: America's Master Spy.* Chicago: Raud McNally & Company, 1982.

Eastman, Lloyd E. *The Abortive Revolution: China Under Nationalist Rule.* Cambridge, Mass.: Harvard University Press, 1974.

_____. *Seeds of Destruction: Nationalist China in War and Revolution, 1937–1949.* Stanford, Calif.: Stanford University Press, 1984.

Epstein, Israel. *From Opium War to Liberation.* Peking: New World Press, 1956.

_____. *Woman in World History: Soong Ching Ling.* Beijing: New World Press, 1995.

Eunson, Roby. *The Soong Sisters.* New York: Franklin Watts, 1975.

Fairbank, John. *Chinabound: A Fifty-Year Memoir.* New York: Harper & Row, 1982.

_____. *The Great Chinese Revolution, 1800–1985.* New York: Harper & Row, 1986.

_____. *The United States and China.* Cambridge, Mass.: Harvard University Press, 1983.

Farmer, Rhodes. *Shanghai Harvest: A Diary of Three Years in the China War.* London: Museum Press, 1945.

Feis, Herbert. *The China Tangle: The American Effort in China from Pearl Harbor to the Marshall Mission.* Princeton: Princeton University Press, 1953.

Fenby, Jonathan. *Chiang Kai-shek: China's Generalissimo and The Nation He Lost.* New York: Carroll & Graf Publishers, 2004.

Fontenoy, Jean. *The Secret Shanghai.* New York: Grey-Hill Press, 1939.

Freedman, Russell. *Confucius: The Golden Rule.* New York: Scholastic Press, 2002.

Furuya, Keiji. *Chiang Kai-shek: His Life and Times.* New York: St. John's University, 1981.

Fussell, Paul. *Wartime.* New York: Oxford University Press, 1989.

Gellhorn, Martha. *Travels with Myself and Another: A Memoir.* New York: Dodd, Mead & Company, 1978.

Gillin, Donald G. *Falsifying China's History: The Case of Sterling Seagrave's "The Soong Dynasty."* Stanford, Calif.: Hoover Institution Monograph, Series 4, 1986.

Grant, Joseph C. *Turbulent Era.* Boston: Houghton Mifflin Company, 1952.

Greene, Felix. *A Curtain of Ignorance.* Garden City, N.Y.: Doubleday & Company, 1964.

Gronewold, Sue. *Beautiful Merchandise: Prostitution in China, 1860–1936.* New York: Institute for Research in History and the Haworth Press, 1982.

Gunther, John. *Inside Asia.* New York: Harper & Brothers, 1938.

Hahn, Emily. *Chiang Kai-shek: An Unauthorized Biography.* Garden City, N.Y.: Doubleday & Company, 1955.

———. *The Soong Sisters.* Garden City, N.Y.: Doubleday, Doran & Company, 1942.

Halberstam, David. *The Powers That Be.* New York: Alfred A. Knopf, 1979.

Han Suyin. *Birdless Summer.* New York: G. P. Putnam's Sons, 1968.

———. *Destination Chungking.* Boston: Little, Brown and Co., 1942.

———. *A Mortal Flower.* New York: G. P. Putnam's Sons, 1966.

Hauser, Ernest O. *Shanghai: City for Sale.* New York: Harcourt, Brace and Company, 1940.

Hoo, Mona Yuma-Nina. *Painting the Shadows: The Extraordinary Life of Victor Hoo.* London: Eldridge & Co., 1998.

Hooker, Mary. *Behind the Scenes in Peking.* Oxford: Oxford University Press, 1987.

Hsiung, S. I. *The Life of Chiang Kai-shek.* London: Peter Davies, 1948.

Hsu, Kai-yu. *Chou En-lai: China's Gray Eminence.* Garden City, N.Y.: Doubleday & Company, 1968.

Hsu, Leonard S. *Sun Yat-sen: His Political and Social Ideals.* Los Angeles; University of Southern California Press, 1933.

Hull, Helen. *Mayling Soong Chiang.* New York: Coward McCann, 1943.

Isaacs, Harold R. *The Tragedy of the Chinese Revolution.* Stanford: Stanford University Press, 1961.

Jacobs, Dan N. *Borodin: Stalin's Man in China.* Cambridge, Mass.: Harvard University Press, 1981.

Kahn, E. J., Jr., *The China Hands.* New York: Viking Press, 1975.

Keeley, Joseph. *The China Lobby Man: The Story of Alfred Kohlberg.* New Rochelle: Arlington House, 1969.

Kennedy, Joseph P. *Hostage to Fortune: The Letters of Joseph P. Kennedy.* Edited by Amanda Smith. New York: Viking, 2001.

Kerr, George H. *Formosa Betrayed.* Boston: Houghton Mifflin Company, 1965.

Koen, Ross Y. *The China Lobby in American Politics.* New York: Macmillan Company, 1960.

Koo, Madame Wellington. *Hui-Lan Koo* (her autobiography as told to Mary Van Rensselaer Thayer). New York: Dial Press, 1943.

Koo, Madame Wellington, with Isabella Javes. *No Feast Lasts Forever.* New York: Quadrangle: New York Times Book Co., 1975.

Kuo Tai-chun and Wu Jing-ping, ed. *T. V. Soong: His Life and Times.* Shanghai: Fudan University Press, 2008.

Lash, Joseph P. *Eleanor and Franklin: The Story of Their Relationship, Based on Eleanor Roosevelt's Private Papers.* New York: W. W. Norton & Company, 1971.

Lattimore, Owen. *China Memoirs.* Compiled by Fujiko Isono. Tokyo: University of Tokyo Press, 1990.

———. *The Situation in Asia.* Boston: Little, Brown and Company, 1949.

_____. *Solution in Asia.* Boston: Little, Brown and Company, 1949.

Lattimore, Owen, and Eleanor Lattimore. *The Making of Modern China,* New York: Franklin Watts, 1944.

Leith-Ross, Sir Frederick. *Money Talks: Fifty Years of International Finance.* London: Hutchinson & Co., 1968.

Leonard, Royal. *I Flew for China.* Garden City, N.Y.: Doubleday, Doran and Company, 1942.

Leong, Karen J. *The China Mystique: Pearl S. Buck, Anna May Wong, Mayling Soong, and the Transformation of American Orientalism.* Berkeley: University of California Press, 2005.

Levy, Adrian, and Cathy Scott-Clark. *The Stone of Heaven: Unearthing the Secret History of Imperial Green Jade.* Boston: Little, Brown and Company, 2001.

Levy, Daniel S. *Two-Gun Cohen.* New York: St. Martin's Press, 1997.

Levy, Howard S. *Chinese Footbinding.* New York: Bell Publishing Company, 1957.

Li, Laura Tyson. *Madame Chiang Kai-shek: China's Eternal First Lady.* New York: Atlantic Monthly Press, 2006.

Linebarger, Paul. *Sun Yat Sen and the Chinese Republic.* New York: Century Co., 1925.

Little, Mrs. Archibald. *Intimate China: The Chinese as I Have Seen Them.* London: Hutchinson & Co., 1899.

Llewellyn, Bernard. *China's Courts and Concubines.* London: Allen and Unwin, 1956.

Loh, I-cheng. *Memoir.* Taiwan: Bookzone Press, 2002.

Loh, Pinchon P. Y. *The Early Chiang Kai-shek: A Study of His Personality and Politics, 1887–1924.* New York: Columbia University Press, 1971.

Mah, Adeline Yeo. *Falling Leaves: The True Story of an Unwanted Chinese Daughter.* New York: Broadway Books, 1999.

Mao, Tse-tung. *Selected Works,* vol. 3. Peking: People's Publishing House, 1967.

McCullough, David. *Truman.* New York: Simon & Schuster, 1992.

McCunn, Ruthanne Lum. *An Illustrated History of the Chinese in America.* San Francisco: San Francisco Design Enterprises, 1979.

Meier-Welcker, Hans. *Seeckt.* Frankfurt: Bernard & Graefe, 1967.

Miller, Merle. *Plain Speaking: An Oral Biography of Harry S. Truman.* New York: Berkley Publishing Corporation, 1973.

Misselwitz, Henry Francis. *The Dragon Stirs: An Intimate Sketch-Book of China's Kuomintang Revolution, 1927–29.* New York: Harbinger House, 1941.

Mitamura, Taisuke. *Chinese Eunuchs: The Structure of Intimate Politics.* Rutland, Vt.: Charles E. Tuttle Company, 1970.

Moore, V. Elizabeth, M.B.E. *We Go to China with Lady Cripps.* London: P. J. Press, 1948.

Moran, Lord (Sir Charles Wilson). *Churchill.* Boston: Houghton Mifflin Company, 1966.

Morrison, George Ernest. *An Australian in China.* London: Horace Cox, 1895.

Mosley, Leonard. *Marshall, Hero for Our Times.* New York: Hearst Books, 1982.

Mowrer, Ernest Albert. *Mowrer in China.* Harmondsworth, UK: Penguin Books, 1938.

Newman, Robert P. *Owen Lattimore and the "Loss" of China.* Berkeley: University of California Press, 1992.

Nixon, Richard. *Leaders.* New York: Warner Books, 1982.

Oursler, Fulton. *Behold This Dreamer!* Boston: Little, Brown and Company, 1964.

Paludan, Ann. *Chronicle of the Chinese Emperors.* London: Thames and Hudson, 1998.

Pan, Ling. *In Search of Old Shanghai.* Hong Kong: Joint Publishing Co., 1983.

Payne, Robert. *Chiang Kai-shek.* New York: Weybright and Talley, 1969.

Pearson, Drew. *Diaries, 1949–1959.* Edited by Tyler Abell. New York: Holt, Rinehart and Winston, 1974.

Peck, Graham. *Two Kinds of Time.* Boston: Houghton Mifflin Company, 1950.

Perkins, Frances. *The Roosevelt I Knew.* New York, Viking Press, 1946.

Powell, John B. *My Twenty-Five Years in China.* New York: Macmillan Company, 1945.

Qin, Xiao-xian, ed. *Preliminary Compilation of Primary Historical Materials of the Republic of China.* Taipei: Party History Committee of the Central Committee of the KMT, 1981.

Rand, Peter. *China Hands.* New York: Simon & Schuster, 1995.

Roosevelt, Eleanor, *Autobiography.* New York: Harper & Brothers, 1937.

———. *My Day.* New York: Pharos Books, 1990.

———. *This I Remember.* New York: Harper & Brothers, 1949.

Salisbury, Harrison E. *China: 100 Years of Revolution.* New York: Holt, Rinehart and Winston, 1983.

Salter, Arthur. *Personality in Politics: Studies of Contemporary Statesmen.* London: Faber and Faber, 1947.

Sandilands, Roger J. *The Life and Political Economy of Lauchlin Currie.* Durham, N.C.: Duke University Press, 1990.

Schaller, Michael. *The United States and China in the Twentieth Century.* New York: Oxford University Press, 1979.

Schiffrin, Harold Z. *Sun Yat-sen, Reluctant Revolutionary.* Boston: Little, Brown and Company, 1980.

Seagrave, Sterling. *Dragon Lady: The Life and Legend of the Last Empress of China.* New York: Vintage Books, 1993.

———. *The Soong Dynasty.* New York: Harper & Row, 1986.

Selle, Earl Albert. *Donald of China.* New York: Harper & Brothers, 1948.

Sergeant, Harriet. *Shanghai.* New York: Crown Publishers, 1990.

Service, John S. *Lost Chance in China: The World War II Dispatches of John S. Service.* New York: Random House, 1974.

Sharman, Lynn. *Sun Yat-sen: His Life and Its Meaning.* Stanford: Stanford University Press, 1968.

Sheean, Vincent. *Between the Thunder and the Sun.* New York: Random House, 1943.

———. *Personal History.* Garden City, N.Y.: Doubleday, Doran & Company, 1936.

Sheridan, James E., *China in Disintegration.* New York: Free Press, 1975.

———. *Chinese Warlord.* Stanford: Stanford University Press, 1966.

Sherwood, Robert E. *Roosevelt and Hopkins: An Intimate History.* New York: Harper & Brothers, 1948.

Shi, Zhi-yu. "How the American Mass Media Reported Madame Chiang's Visit to the U.S.A. on February 20, 1943." *Modern China* (journal). Taipei: Kuomintang Press, 1996

———. *Soong May-ling and China.* Taipei: Shang Zhi Culture Press, 2001.

Snow, Edgar. *Journey to the Beginning.* New York: Vintage Books, 1972.

———. *Random Notes on Red China, 1936–1945.* Cambridge, Mass.: East Asian Research Center, Harvard University, 1974.

———. *Red Star over China.* New York: Grove Weidenfeld, 1973.

Snow, Lois Wheeler. *Edgar Snow's China.* New York: Vintage Books, 1983.

Sokolsky, George E. *The Tinder Box of Asia*. Garden City, N.Y.: Doubleday, Doran & Company, 1932.

Spence, Jonathan D. *The Gate of Heavenly Peace*. Harmondsworth, UK: Penguin Books, 1982.

_____. *The Search for Modern China*. New York: W. W. Norton & Co., 1990.

Stilwell, Joseph W. *The Stilwell Papers*. New York: William Sloane Associates, 1948.

Stuart, John Leighton. *Fifty Years in China*. New York: Random House, 1954.

Sues, Ilona Ralf. *Shark's Fins and Millet*. Garden City, N.Y.: Garden City Publishing Co., 1944.

Sun Yat-sen. *The Three Principles of the People*. Taipei: China Publishing Company, 1981.

Swanberg, W. A. *Luce and His Empire*. New York: Charles Scribner's Sons, 1972.

Tan, May. "Happiness in Different Worlds" (unpublished memoir).

Taylor, Jay. *The Generalissimo's Son: Chiang Ching-kuo and the Revolutions in China and Taiwan*. Cambridge, Mass.: Harvard University Press, 2000.

Thomas, Harry J. *The First Lady of China: The Historic Wartime Visit of Mme. Chiang Kai-shek to the United States in 1943*. Armonk, N.Y.: I.B.M., 1969.

Thomson, James C., Jr. *While China Faced West: American Reformers in Nationalist China, 1928–1937*. Cambridge, Mass.: Harvard University Press, 1980.

Tong, Hollington K. *Chiang Kai-shek*. Shanghai: China Publishing Company, 1937.

Topping, Seymour. *Journey Between Two Chinas*. New York: Harper & Row, 1972.

Tuchman, Barbara W. *Stilwell and the American Experience in China, 1911–45*. New York: Bantam Books, 1972.

Tully, Grace. *F.D.R., My Boss*. New York: Charles Scribner's Sons, 1949.

U.S. Department of Defense. *A Pocket Guide to Taiwan*. Washington, D.C., 1958.

U.S. Department of State. *China, 1969–1972*. Washington, D.C.: U.S. Government Printing Office, 2006.

_____. *United States Relations with China*. Washington, D.C.: Department of State Publications, 1949.

U.S. Special Service Division, U.S. Army. *A Pocket Guide to China*. Washington, D.C.: War and Navy Departments, 1942.

Utley, Freda. *China at War*. London: Faber and Faber Ltd., 1939.

van de Ven, Hans J. *War and Nationalism in China, 1925–1945*. London: Routledge-Curzon, 2003.

Wakeman, Frederic, Jr. *The Fall of Imperial China*. New York: Free Press, 1977.

_____. *Policing Shanghai, 1927–1937*. Berkeley: University of California Press, 1995.

_____. *Spymaster: Dai Li and the Chinese Secret Service*. Berkeley: University of California Press, 2003.

Wallace, Henry A. *The Price of Vision: The Diary of Henry A. Wallace, 1942–1946*. Edited by John Morton Blum. Boston: Houghton Mifflin Company, 1973.

Wang Feng. *Beauty and Sorrow: The Real Soong May-ling*. Beijing: Unity Press, 1998.

Wang Song, Jiang Shi-min, and Rao Fang-hu. *T. V. Soong*. Wuhan: Wuhan Chubanshe, 1993.

Wang Yuan (narrated by), Wang Feng (recorded by). *Forty-three Years in the Service of Chiang Kai-shek and His Son*. Beijing: Hua Wan Press, 2003.

Warner, Marina. *The Dragon Empress: Life and Times of T'zu-hsi, 1835–1908*. New York: Macmillan Company, 1972.

Weale, B. L. Putnam. *The Fight for the Republic in China*. New York: Dodd Mead and Company, 1917.

Webb, Mena. *Jule Carr: General Without an Army*. Chapel Hill: University of North Carolina Press, 1987.

Wedemeyer, Albert C. *Wedemeyer Reports!* New York: Devin-Adair Company, 1958.

White, Theodore H. *In Search of History*. New York: Harper & Row, 1978.

White, Theodore H., and Annalee Jacoby. *Thunder Out of China*. New York: Da Capo, 1980.

Willkie, Wendell. *One World*. New York: Simon and Schuster, 1943.

Worcester, G. R. G. *Sail and Sweep in China: The History and Development of the Chinese Junk as Illustrated by the Collection of Junk Models in the Science Museum*. London: Her Majesty's Stationery Office, 1966.

Wu Jingping. *Study of Historical Materials*. Shanghai: Shanghai Municipal Archives, 1994.

Wu Jingping, and Kuo Tai-chun, eds. *Select Telegrams Between Chiang Kai-shek and T. V. Soong (1940–43)*. Taiwan: Academia Historica (n.d.)

Wu, Sylvia. *Memories of Madame Sun*. Santa Monica, Calif.: Dennis-Landman, 1982.

Yang Jin. *T. V. Soong*. Hebei: People's Press, 1999.

Yu Xin-min and Tang Ji-Yuan. *The Founder of the Soong Family*. Ha'erbin: Bei Fang Wei Yi Press, 1986.

Zhang Ning-yi. "Madame Chiang and Modern China," trans. from the Russian. Archives. Taipei: Zhongzheng Cultural and Educational Association, 2002.

Zhiang Zi-ge. *Working at the Side of May-ling Soong*. Beijing: Tuan Jie, 2003.

Periodicals and Press Releases

The Albany Times-Union; All Things Considered (radio); *Asian Affairs: An Historical Review; Asian Outlook; Asia Week*; Associated Press; *The Atlanta Constitution; The Atlanta Journal; The Atlantic Monthly; Blade* (Toledo, Ohio); *Boston Herald; Boston Post; Bridgeport Post; Buffalo Evening News; Buffalo News; The Bulletin of Concerned Asian Scholars; Canada Evening Star; CBI Roundup; China Monthly; China Post; The China Quarterly; China Times; The China Weekly Review; Chinese News; The Chinese Press; The Christian Science Monitor; Cincinnati Times-Star; Collier's; Da Gong* (newspaper); *The Evening Star; Eastern Economic Review; The Far Eastern Mirror; Foreign Affairs; Fortune; Harper's Monthly; The Herkimer, N.Y. Telegram; The Honolulu Advertiser; Journal of Asian Studies; Liberty; Life; Look; Los Angeles Times; Maclean's; Magazine Digest; Modern China; The Nation; National Review* (London); *New York Herald Tribune; New York Herald-Tribune Magazine; The New Republic; News* (San Francisco, California); *Newsday; The News & Observer; Newsweek; New York Post; The New York Times; The New York Times Book Review; The New York Times Magazine; The New Yorker; New York Sun; The North-China Herald; North-China Daily News; The Outlook; Pasadena Star News; Passaic Herald News; The Peiping Chronicle; People's Daily* (Beijing); *The Philadelphia Inquirer; The Piedmont Announcements; Raleigh Christian Advocate; The Reader's Digest; Reporter; San Francisco Chronicle; The Saturday Evening Post; Shanghai Star; Shanghai Times; St. Louis Post Dispatch; Sino-American Relations; Star-Times* (St. Louis, Missouri); *A Study of Modern Chinese Women; Taipei Times; Taiwan Journal; Texas Monthly; Time; The Times* (London); *Times* (Reading, Pennsylvania); *Times-Union* (Rochester, New York); *Toronto Star; The Union* (Taiwan); *USA Today; U.S. News & World Report; United Press; United States Naval Institute Proceedings; Vogue; The Wall Street Journal; Wan Xiang* (magazine); *The Wash-*

ington Post; Washington Times Herald; The Week; Weekend Standard; The Wellesley Magazine; The Wesleyan; The Wilson Quarterly; Worchester Telegram; World Journal; World Outlook.

WEB SITES

www.talesofoldchina.com; www.chinadaily.com; www.trumanlibrary.org; www.sina.com
.cn; www.chairmanmao.org/eng/wen/wen23.htm; www.thestandard.com.hk/; www.jean-
monnet.net; www.usmm.org; www.guardian.co.uk; www.nl.newsbank.com; www.eisen
howermemorial.org; www.pbs.org; www.gwu.edu/~nsarchiv/; www.members.aol.com/
WELSTA12/last.htm; www.newyorksocialdiary.com; www.sfgate.com; www.cnn.com.

ARCHIVAL SOURCES

Academia Historica, Taipei
Chiang Kai-shek Diary
Telegrams between Chiang Ching-kuo and Soong May-ling: 1943–1965
Telegrams between Chiang Kai-shek and Soong May-ling: 1928–1955

Central Intelligence Agency, Documents Concerning
Madame Chiang Kai-shek
T. V. Soong
H. H. K'ung

Columbia University, Butler Library
Oral History Research Office (COHO)
Reminiscences of Sebie Biggs Smith
Reminiscences of H. H. Kung
Reminiscences of Frank Rounds
Reminiscences of George Sokolsky
Reminiscences of Roger W. Straus
Reminiscences of Dorothy Thomas
Reminiscences of Wu Kuo-chen (K.C. Wu)
Rare Book and Manuscript Library (RBML)
Harold K. Hochschild Papers
Helen Hull Papers
Wellington Koo Papers

Cornell University, Division of Rare and Manuscript Collections
James Marshall McHugh Papers
William Reginald Wheeler Papers

Duke University, Rare Book, Manuscript and Special Collections Library
James Gordon Hackett Papers
Charles Jones Soong Collection
James A. Thomas Papers
Basil Lee Whitener Papers

Federal Bureau of Investigation, Documents Concerning
Madame Chiang Kai-shek
Hsiang-hsi Kung (H. H. Kung)
Tse Ven Soong (T. V. Soong)

Georgetown University Library
Special Collections Division
Edwin W. Martin Papers
Grace Perkins Oursler Papers
Thomas M. Wilson Papers
Foreign Affairs Oral History Project (FAOHP)
Frank H. Burnet, interviewed by C. S. Kennedy
Leonard Ungar, interviewed by C. S. Kennedy

Hagley Museum and Library, Manuscripts and Archives Department
Daniel Rochford Papers

Harvard Law School Library
Joseph Keenan Papers

Herbert Hoover Presidential Library (HHPL)
George S. Drescher Logbooks
Madame Chiang Kai-shek in Post Presidential Individual Files

Hoover Institution on War, Revolution, and Peace (HA)
Chiang Kai-shek Diaries
Claire Lee Chennault Papers
Lauchlin Currie Papers
Frank Dorn Papers
Stanley K. Hornbeck Papers
Walter H. Judd Papers
Alfred Kohlberg Papers
Thomas Edward LaFarge Papers
Paul Linebarger Papers
Roger J. Sandilands Papers
George E. Sokolsky Papers
T. V. Soong Papers
Joseph W. Stilwell Papers
Nym Wales Papers
Albert C. Wedemeyer Papers
Arthur N. Young Papers

The University of Indiana, the Lilly Library, Manuscripts Department
Emily Hahn Papers
Wendell Willkie Papers

Library of Congress, Manuscript Division (LC)
Averell Harriman Papers
Roy W. Howard Papers
Nelson T. Johnson Papers
Owen Lattimore Papers
Clare Booth Luce Papers
Theodore Roosevelt, Jr., Papers

National Archives and Records Administration (NARA)

New York Public Library

Oberlin College Archives

The University of Oklahoma
Western History Collections
  Patrick J. Hurley Collection, China Papers

Paley Center for Media

Princeton University Library, Seeley G. Mudd Manuscript Library
Hamilton Fish Armstrong Papers
Allen Dulles Papers
James Forrestal Papers
George Kennan Papers
Arthur Krock Papers
Karl L. Rankin Papers
Whiting Willauer Papers
  The John Foster Dulles Oral History Collection:
Generalissimo and Madame Chiang Kai-shek
W. Averell Harriman
Walter H. Judd
Henry Luce
Richard M. Nixon
George K. C. Yeh

Radcliffe Institute for Advanced Study, The Arthur and Elizabeth Schesinger Library
Mary Dingman Papers
Frances Fineman Gunther Papers

Franklin D. Roosevelt Presidential Library and Museum
Harry Hopkins Papers
F.D.R. Papers
Eleanor Roosevelt Papers

Harry S. Truman Library
President's Secretary's Files
  Oral History Interviews:
Arthur Ringwalt

Wellesley College (WCA)
Emma DeLong Mills Papers
Class of 1917: Madame Chiang Kai-shek

Wesleyan College Archives
Soong Sisters Collection

ACKNOWLEDGMENTS

THE CHINESE, as I discovered early in this venture, are not prone to talk about themselves or anyone they know. Nonetheless, I am indebted to the following people who helped me—some with personal knowledge, some with books or articles of interest, and some with research. A few of them are no longer with us. Listed in alphabetical order, they are:

Marcia Allert, Anthony Appiah, Tom Blanton, Susan Braddock, Ralph Buutjens, Schuyler Chapin, Richard Cohen, Ann Coleman, David Patrick Columbia, Fleur Cowles, Jan Cowles, Ruda Dauphin, Robert Davis, Jimmy Davison, Richard Defendorf, Elizabeth Drew, Laurette Feng, David Fromkin, Frances Gabriel, Betsy Gotbaum, The Hon. Henry Grunwald, Richard Kent Heller, Ted Herman and members of the Class of 1936 of the Shanghai American School, Townsend Hoopes, David Kahn, Dr. Henry Kissinger, Mrs. Wellington Koo, William and Corinne Krisel, Ron Kwan, Eleanor Lambert, The Hon. Winston Lord and Betty Bao Lord, The Hon. William Luers, Sidney Lumet, Dr. Paul Marks, Boaz Mazor, Tex McCrary, Donald Newhouse, Kip Bleakley O'Neill, Desiree Quintero, Eleanor Randolph, William D. Sare, Arthur Schlesinger Jr., Beverly Sills, Bickley Simpson, Liz Smith, Leo and Shirley Soong, Phillips Talbot, May Tan, John Taylor, Daniel Teas, Deborah Toll, Bradford Trebach, Lionel Tsao, Robert Viau, Hugo Vickers, Shirley Young,

Most of all, I want to thank my beloved editor, Alice Mayhew, for her enthusiasm, expertise, and devotion; my big troubleshooter, Roger Labrie; my agent, Lynn Nesbit, who has put up with me for a long time; my wonderful assistant, Arlene Tucker; and my Chinese researcher and translator, without whom I could not have written this book. As always, there is my friend Barbara Davis, who travels with me to odd places, manages to read too many drafts of my work—and to whom I have dedicated this book.

INDEX

❧

Page numbers beginning with 683 refer to notes.

Stilwell, Joseph (*cont.*)
  and Chiang Kai-shek, 390, 391, 392*n*,
    394–95, 396–97, 401, 403, 404, 448,
    455, 460–65, 469, 491, 497–99, 521,
    617–18
  Chinese troops trained by, 402, 403
  closes brothels, 453
  considered for command of Chinese
    army, 490–91, 496, 497–99
  dismissal of, 463–64, 499, 501, 508–9,
    517*n*, 519, 522, 524
  escape from Burma, 390–92, 396, 450
  FDR's meeting on Burma with, 475–76
  personality of, 372–73
Stimson, Henry, xviii, 371, 372, 386, 404,
    479, 499
Stowe, Leland, 555–56
Stratemeyer, George E., 534
Straus, Roger, 619
Streams in the Desert, 655
Stuart, John Leighton, xviii, 394, 548, 550,
    551, 553, 568, 574, 590, 599–600
Sues, Ilona Ralf, 207–8
Sulzberger, Arthur, 307
Sumatra, 66
Summer Palace, 35
Sun, Annie, 63
Sun, Soong Ching-ling (Rosamonde), 19,
    54, 63–65, 78, 80, 116, 120, 123–24,
    145, 147, 158, 161, 163, 165, 213, 275,
    300, 322, 325, 330, 370, 411, 427*n*, 444,
    455–56, 500, 512, 536–37, 549, 581–82,
    645, 647–48, 650
  alternative government sought by,
    322–23
  in American radio broadcast, 356
  appearance, 321
  appendectomy, 249
  article on revolution, 60
  birth of, 16
  Chiang condemned and criticized by,
    163–64, 322, 323, 536
  Chiang's alleged proposal to, 170–71
  as Communist Party icon, 156–57
  at congress of KMT, 137, 138
  in Cultural Revolution, 636–37
  death of, 662–63
  education of, 23, 24, 60
  escape from Canton, 95–97
  escape from Hong Kong, 369

  at Mao's proclamation of Republic of
    China, 581–82
  marriage, 63–65, 66, 321
  in meeting with Feng, 162
  in negotiations over Ching-kuo, 247
  speech on women's rights by, 130
  at Sun's burial, 210–12
  at Sun's death, 131
  as Sun's secretary, 62, 63
Sun Chuan-fang, xviii, 77, 141, 149
Sun Fo, xviii, 145, 156, 161, 162, 211, 487,
    558, 574
Sung Chiao-jen, 58
Sung Dynasty, 15, 674
Sun Tzu, 89
Sun Yat-sen, xviii, 15, 16, 44, 47–56, 58,
    62, 63, 90, 93, 121, 126, 129, 130, 135,
    144, 148, 152, 157, 163–64, 169, 170,
    171, 172, 182, 183, 194, 196, 199, 223,
    256, 272, 318, 445, 487, 514, 558, 636,
    663
  and Ai-Ling, 56
  in Canton, 128–30
  and Hakka General, 95–98, 120, 125, 129
  illness and death, 130–32, 133, 136, 137,
    143, 158
  imprisonment in England, 51–52
  inauguration, 54, 150
  marriages, 56, 63–65, 66, 321
  public speaking, 123–24
  religion of, 47, 49, 51, 56, 65
  southern government set up by, 78, 80,
    84, 85, 115–16
  Soviet relations with, 84, 121, 122,
    123–25
  state burial, 204, 210–12
  and Shih-kai, Yuan, 54–55, 57, 58, 59, 62
Sun Yat-sen University, 246
Supreme National Defense Council, 513
Sutterle (businessman), 709–10
Su Tung-chi, 625
Swanberg, W. A., 578*n*
Sydney Daily Telegraph, 223

Tai Chi-tao, 95*n*
Tai Li, xviii, 219, 260, 262, 269, 368*n*, 380,
    458–59, 460, 482, 544
Taipan, 36–37
Taipei, 614
Taipei Economic and Cultural Office, 677

ABOUT THE AUTHOR

HANNAH PAKULA is the author of *The Last Romantic,* which Graham Greene called one of the three best books of the year, and *An Uncommon Woman,* which was a *Los Angeles Times* Book Award finalist. She lives in New York City.

The National Archives and Records Administration
Columbia University Rare Book and Manuscript Library
Library of Congress, Manuscript Division
Division of Rare and Manuscript Collections, Carl A. Kroch Library, Cornell University
Wellesley College Archives
Memorial Museum of Soon Ching-ling, Shanghai, China
The University of Oklahoma Western History Collections
The Lilly Library/University of Indiana

Winston Churchill, excerpt from letter to Franklin Delano Roosevelt
(November 17, 1943), Map Room File, Box 17, Folder 3. FDR Library.
Copyright © Winston S. Churchill. Reproduced with permission of Curtis Brown, Ltd.,
London on behalf of The Estate of Winston Churchill.

David Kung, excerpt from a letter to Albert C. Wedemeyer (February 11, 1978),
Box 46, Folder 6. Wedemeyer Papers, Hoover Institution on War, Revolution and Peace.
Reprinted with the permission of Gregory Kung.

Eleanor Roosevelt, excerpt from a letter to Madame Chiang Kai-shek
(September 16, 1947), Box 3, Folder Madame Chiang Kai-shek. Lauchlin Currie Papers,
Hoover Institution on War, Revolution and Peace. Reprinted with the permission
of Nancy Roosevelt Ireland, Trustee, Anna E. Roosevelt Trust.

George Sokolsky, excerpt from a letter to Madame Chiang Kai-shek (May 12, 1958),
Box 35, Folder 16. George Sokolsky Papers, Hoover Institution on War,
Revolution and Peace. Reprinted with the permission of George Sokolsky.

Charlie Jones Soon, letter to Dr. Young J. Allen and letter to his father (June 1881) from
James Burke, *My Father in China*. Reprinted with the permission of Curtis Brown, Ltd.

Soong May-ling (Madame Chiang Kai-shek), letter to Chiang Kai-shek
from Ch'en Chieh-ju, *Chiang Kai-shek's Secret Past: The Memoirs of His Second Wife*.
Reprinted with the permission of Westview Press/Perseus Books Group.

And a special thanks to Elizabeth Chiang for the Estate of Soong May-ling
(Madame Chiang Kai-shek) for permission to reprint the many previously
unpublished quotes by Soong May-ling.

ILLUSTRATION CREDITS

Picture Research by Jerry Marshall at pictureresearching.com

T.V. Soong: His Life and Times, by Wu Jingping and Tai-chun Kuo (Fudan University Press,
    2008): 1, 2, 3, 5, 52, 53
Courtesy of Archives and Special Collections/Willet Memorial Library/Wesleyan College:
    4, 15
Courtesy of Wellesley College Archives: 6, 22
Courtesy of Thomas A. DeLong: 7
© Three Lions/Hulton Archive/Getty Images: 8
Private Collection: 9
Photograph courtesy of the Peabody Essex Museum (NegA9940): 10
From J. J. Matignon, *Superstition, crime et miserie en Chine,* 1899: 11